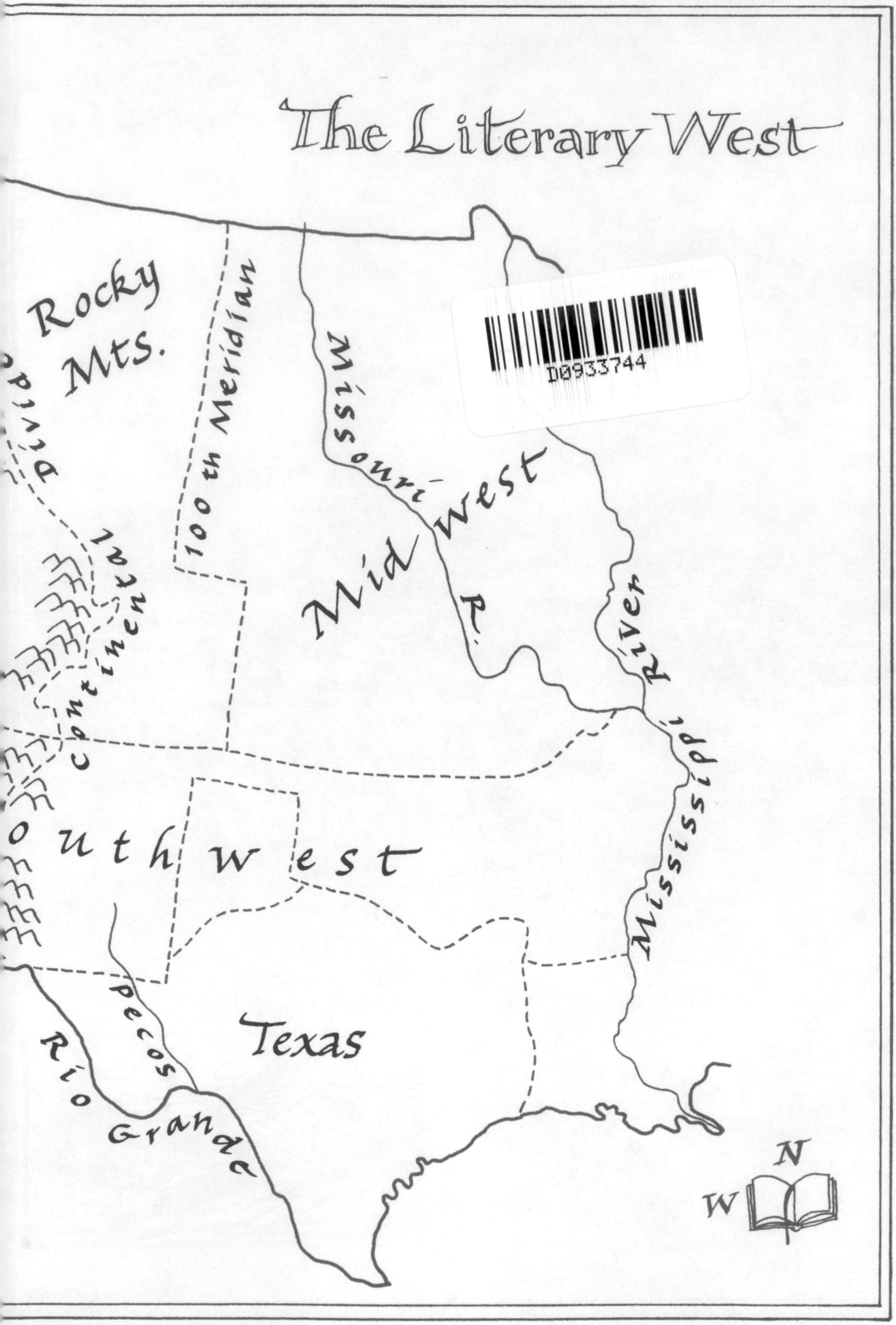

The Literary West

Rocky Mts.

Continental Divide

100th Meridian

Missouri R.

Mississippi River

Mid West

S o u t h w e s t

Texas

Pecos

Rio Grande

N
W

UPDATING THE LITERARY WEST

UPDATING
the
LITERARY
WEST

SPONSORED BY
The Western Literature Association

Texas Christian University Press
Fort Worth

Library of Congress Cataloging-in-Publication Data

Updating the literary West / sponsored by the Western Literature Association
        p.   cm.
    Includes bibliographical references and index.
    ISBN 0-87565-175-5
    1. American literature — West (U.S.) — History and criticism. 2. West (U.S.) — In
literature. I. Western Literature Association (U.S.)
PS 271.U64 1997
810.9'3278 — dc21

                                        97-9120
                                           CIP

Design by Whitehead and Whitehead of Austin, Texas.
Type composed at Texas Christian University Press in Goudy Old Style.
Printed and bound at BookCrafters, Chelsea, Michigan.

Contents

V

Section VII: The Popular West

Max Westbrook

Preface

A *Literary History of the American West* (1987) has become established as a basic reference for studies of western writing. The editors of that volume, however, hoped that the work of the seventy-one contributors would begin, rather than conclude, the exploration of the literary West. They felt strongly that they were dealing with a field remarkably varied, rewarding, relevant, and most of all, *alive*.

Shortly after publication of *LHAW*, it became clear that the emergence of new writers and the continued work of established writers and critics were creating the need for a supplementary volume. In a climate of nationwide canon examination, it also became evident that the western canon itself—the basis of *LHAW*—needed to be re-examined. A variety of cultural viewpoints, along with new tactics for literary study, promised fresh insights into the stories, poems, plays, and nonfiction prose of the American West. The list of new authors fast rising into prominence was extensive; long-recognized writers needed to be reread through new lenses; and the territory of literary criticism had opened up to the study of a wider, and constantly widening, range of subjects. In spite of its nearly fourteen hundred pages, *LHAW* had not covered, could not cover, all the substantive topics nor all the writers who deserved attention.

Following the model of *LHAW*, *Updating the Literary West* begins with a chronology to map the territories of concern and the major publications from 1980 through 1996. A section on "Counterviews, Challenges,

and the Canon" then identifies the newly developing literary and interdisciplinary criticism used throughout the following chapters.

Part Two, "Encountering the West," takes up some nineteenth-century writers whose output calls for more extended examination and features discussions of topics now available to the more inclusive critical
outlook of today. Part Three introduces readers to the "New Wests,"
that is, to recent literary activity across the West, region by region, and
again to the practical criticism basic to the study of contemporary western writing. Fundamental to the concept of "New Wests," and seen here,
are several versions of cultural and personal consciousness-raising that
influence how we read new writers and selected earlier writers whose
handling of multicultural and gender differences, for example, requires
further illumination.

The "New Wests" are treated first by subregions: The Far West,
California, the Southwest, Texas, the Midwest, and the Rocky Mountains. There follows "Popular West," representing a kind of coming of
age of western literary studies. When the Western Literature
Association was founded in 1966, the term "western" was assumed by
the general public to mean "pulp" or "genre western," and WLA members were at pains to focus on higher, more "serious" literature, in order
to establish their region's literary legitimacy. Now it is more widely felt
that the way is clear to take up popular western writing as another
revealing part of the American experience.

As with LHAW, *Updating the Literary West* has been produced by a
team effort, undertaken in grateful recognition of the region's literature
itself and of the women and men who write it. We expect that in another
couple of decades, the inherent dynamism of the West and its writers
will warrant further scholarly updating. Until then, may this volume be
used in the spirit of enterprise and appreciation with which it has been
written.

Acknowledgments

The editors thank the National Endowment for the Humanities for
the generous research grant that made this volume possible, and Arthur
Huseboe of Augustana College, Sioux Falls, South Dakota, who with his
staff at The Center for Western Studies secured the NEH grant.

Augustana College served as the business office for the project, as it had for *LHAW*, and again we are most grateful for this support.

At Utah State University, the final editing and compilation of this book were greatly facilitated by Kate Boyes, Betsy Ward, Angela Hill, Therese Anderson, and Chris Okelberry, computer wizards, and the writers and editors are much in their debt.

To these institutions and people, our profound thanks.

Dan Flores
with the Editors

Chronology, 1980-1996

In the ten years since the publication of *A Literary History of the American West*, western writing has developed a significantly larger presence in the national literary stream. A distinctive element in this larger presence is the creative nonfiction emphasizing place, natural environment, and personal reminiscence within that realm. The following chronology of events and texts reflect that presence.

1980:

Paul Brooks, *Speaking for Nature*
Frederick Turner, *Beyond Geography: The Western Spirit Against the Wilderness*
Alaska National Interest Land and Conservation Act becomes law
Ella Leffland, *Last Courtesies*
Maxine Hong Kingston, *China Men*
Elmer Kelton, *The Wolf and the Buffalo*
Katherine Anne Porter dies

1981:

Raymond Carver, *What We Talk About When We Talk About Love*
J.S. Holliday, *The World Rushed In*
William Saroyan dies

Larry McMurtry, "Ever a Bridegroom: Reflections on the Failure of Texas Literature," in *The Texas Observer*

1982:

Paul Shepard, *Nature and Madness*
Richard Rodriguez, *Hunger of Memory*
Kenneth Rexroth dies
David Arnason, *Fifty Stories and a Piece of Advice*
Richard Brautigan, *So the Wind Won't Blow It All Away*
Joan Givner, *Katherine Anne Porter: A Life*
William Kloefkorn, *Houses and Beyond*
Richard Hugo dies
Rolando Hinojosa, *Rites and Witnesses*

1983:

David Rains Wallace, *The Klamath Knot*
Dorothy Bryant, *A Day in San Francisco*
Gerald Haslam, *Hawk Flights: Visions of the West*
Margaret Laurence, *A Place to Stand On*
Joan Didion, *Salvador*
The Texas Literary Tradition, symposium held at the University of Texas at Austin; results published by James Ward Lee, et al., *The Texas Literary Tradition: Fiction, Folklore, History*
Robert Kroetsch, *Alibi*
Don Graham, *Cowboys and Cadillacs: How Hollywood Looks at Texas*

1984:

Audrey Thomas, *Intertidal Life*
George Bowering, *Kerrisdale Elegies*
Louise Erdrich, *Love Medicine*
Douglas Unger, *Leaving the Land*
R. G. Vliet dies

1985:

Fred Wah, *Waiting for Saskatchewan*, wins Governor-General's Award

Carole Gerson, ed., *Vancouver Short Stories*

Cormac McCarthy, *Blood Meridian*

Donald Worster, *Rivers of Empire: Water, Aridity, and the Growth of the American West*

Kevin Starr, *Inventing the Dream: California Through the Progressive Era*

Marc Reisner, *Cadillac Desert*

Frederick Turner, *Re-Discovering America: John Muir in His Time and Ours*

Bill Devall and George Sessions, *Deep Ecology: Living as if Nature Mattered*

Gretel Erhlich, *The Solace of Open Spaces*

Ursula LeGuin, *Always Coming Home*

Larry McMurtry, *Lonesome Dove*

R. G. Vliet, *Scorpio Rising*

Rolando Hinojosa, *Dear Rafe*

1986:

E. F. Dyck, ed., *Essays on Saskatchewan Writing*

Barry Lopez, *Arctic Dreams*

John McPhee, *Rising From the Plains*

James Welch, *Fools Crow*

Georgia O'Keeffe dies in Santa Fe

Everett Reuss, *A Vagabond for Beauty*

Larry McMurty's *Lonesome Dove* wins the Pulitzer Prize

Richard Brautigan dies

1987:

Last wild California condor is captured and taken to the San Diego Zoo for captive breeding

Frank and Deborah Popper's original "Buffalo Commons" article, calling Great Plains settlement "the longest running environmental miscalculation in American history," appears in *Planning*

George Bowering, *Caprice*

Margaret Laurence dies

Diane Bessai and Don Kerr, eds., *NeWest Plays by Women*

Dennis Cooley, *The Vernacular Muse*

Vera Norwood and Janice Monk, eds., *The Desert is No Lady*

Patricia Nelson Limerick, *Legacy of Conquest*

Wallace Stegner, *The American West As Living Space*
William Kittredge, *Owning It All*
Michael Dorris, *A Yellow Raft in Blue Water*

1988:

William Berry, *Dream of the Earth*

Ian Frazier, *The Great Plains*

Alston Chase, *Playing God in Yellowstone*

Stewart Udall, *The Quiet Crisis and the Next Generation*

William Kittredge and Annick Smith, eds., *The Last Best Place: A Montana Anthology*

Twenty-one years after the Alianza Courthouse Raid in New Mexico, Amador Flores is arrested for illegal occupation on the former Tierra Amarilla Grant

Daphne Marlatt, *Ana Historic*

Arnold R. Rojas dies

Charles Bukowski, *Beautiful & Other Long Poems*

Robert Duncan dies

Mary Austin, *Cactus Thorn* (previously unpublished)

Ronald E. McFarland and William Studebaker, *Idaho's Poetry: A Centennial Anthology*

1989:

Dave Foreman, *Confessions of an Eco-Warrior*

Roxanna Robinson, *Georgia O'Keeffe: A Life*

Exxon Valdez runs aground and spills eleven million barrels of oil in Prince William Sound, Alaska

Robert Kroetsch, *Completed Field Notes*

Edward Abbey dies at home and is buried by friends at an undisclosed location in the desert

John Haines, *The Stars, the Snow, the Fire*

Robert Laxalt, *The Basque Hotel*

Tomás Rivera, *The Harvest*

Amy Tan, *The Joy Luck Club*

N. Scott Momaday, *Ancient Child*

Molly Gloss, *Jump-Off Creek*

Margaret Laurence, *Dance on the Earth*

Shelby Hearon, *Owning Jolene*
William Goyen dies

1990:

Sky Lee, *Disappearing Moon Cafe*
Jeanne Perreault and Sylvia Vance, eds., *Writing the Circle: Native Women of Western Canada*
Thomas King, *Medicine River*
William DeBuys, *River of Traps*
Edward Abbey, *Hayduke Lives*
Kevin Costner's film, *Dances with Wolves*, based on Robert Blake's novel
Ted Turner buys the Flying D Ranch in Montana and begins stocking it with buffalo
Gary Snyder, *The Practice of the Wild*
Wallace Stegner, *The Collected Stories of Wallace Stegner*
Norman Maclean dies
Richard Ardinger and Ford Swetnam, *High Sky Over All: Idaho Fiction at the Centennial*
Américo Paredes, *George Washington Gomez*

1991:

Mary Clearman Blew, *All But the Waltz: Essays on a Montana Family*
Richard Nelson, *The Island Within*
William Least Heat Moon, *Prairyerth*
Leslie Marmon Silko, *Almanac of the Dead*
Gary Holthaus, et al., *A Society to Match the Scenery*
Robert Redford directs *The Milagro Beanfield War*, based on John Nichols' novel
Max Oelschlaeger, *The Idea of Wilderness: From Prehistory to the Age of Ecology*
Judith Minty, *Yellow Dog Journal* and *Dancing the Fault*
Geoff Sadler, ed., *Twentieth-Century Western Writers* (second edition)
Terry Tempest Williams, *Refuge: An Unnatural History of Family and Place*
A. B. Guthrie, Jr. dies
Sandra Cisneros, *Woman Hollering Creek and Other Stories*
Jack Schaefer dies

1992:

Jane Tompkins, *West of Everything: The Inner Life of Westerns*
James Galvin, *The Meadow*
Charles Bowden, *Desierto*
Wallace Stegner, *Where the Bluebird Sings to the Lemonade Springs*
Charles Wilkinson, *Crossing the Next Meridian*
William Kittredge, *Hole in the Sky*
Norman Maclean, *Young Men and Fire*
Annie Dillard, *The Living*
Texas' Palo Duro Canyon, spiritual home to southwestern artists Frank
    Reaugh, Alexander Hogue, and Georgia O'Keeffe, attracts devel-
    oper who wants to build an Old West "Disneyland"
Cormac McCarthy's *All the Pretty Horses* wins the National Book Award
Robert Kroetsch, *The Puppeteer*
Jack Hodgins, *Innocent Cities*
Louis Owens, *The Sharpest Sight*
E. A. Mares, *The Unicorn Poem & Flowers and Songs of Sorrow*
Clint Eastwood directs *The Unforgiven* from the Alan Le May novel
First captive-bred California condors released into the wild

1993:

Wallace Stegner dies
Robert Redford directs *A River Runs Through It* from Norman Maclean's
    novella
The Oregon Literature Series begins publication
Lee Maracle, *Ravensong*
Thomas King, *Green Grass, Running Water*
William Stafford dies
Gerald Haslam, *The Great Central Valley: California's Heartland*
Janet Campbell Hale, *Bloodlines: Odyssey of a Native Daughter*

1994:

Charles Bukowski dies
Len Engel, *The Big Empty*
Great Basin National Park in Nevada opens
Reed Noss and A. Y. Cooperider, *Saving Nature's Diversity*

Wes Jackson, *Becoming Native to This Place*
Cormac McCarthy, *The Crossing*
Ralph Ellison dies

1995:

Western Literature Association holds annual meeting in Vancouver, the
    first meeting outside the United States
Wayson Choy, *The Jade Peony*
Sinclar Ross dies
Jack Hodgins, *The Macken Charm*
Robert Kroetsch, *A Likely Story: The Writing Life*
After an absence of almost seventy years, wolves are returned to
    Yellowstone National Park
The United States Fish and Wildlife Service announces pending plan to
    return 100 Mexican wolves to the Southwest
The Fish and Wildlife Service begins public hearings on various plans to
    return grizzlies to the Selway-Bitterroot Wilderness, Idaho-Montana
Gary Snyder, *A Place in Space*
Theodore Rozsak, *The Voice of the Earth*
Alston Chase, *In A Dark Wood*
William Cronon, ed., *Uncommon Ground: Toward Reinventing Nature*
Gary Soto, *New and Selected Poems*
Californian Robert Hass becomes the first westerner appointed Poet
    Laureate of the United States
William Everson dies
Chitra Divakaruni, *Arranged Marriage*
Frank Waters dies

1996:

Russell Means, *Where White Men Fear to Tread*
David Long's *Blue Spruce* awarded Richard and Hinda Rosenthal
    Foundation Award in Literature from American Academy of Arts
    and Letters
Gary Snyder, *Mountains and Rivers without End*

Part One

Counterviews,
Challenges,
and the
Canon

SueEllen Campbell

"Connecting the Countrey": What's New in Western Lit Crit?

"The wind from S.W.," wrote William Clark, "the weather moderated a little, I engage my self in Connecting the Countrey from information. river rise a little." December 19, 1804, a Wednesday. A couple of weeks later, on Saturday, January 5: "I imploy my Self Drawing a Connection of the Countrey from what information I have recved—"

These resonant words spark my imagination and make me think— about finding one's way, about making maps, about reading, interpreting, and writing stories, about exploration and language, textuality and history, networks and topographies.

Every story, of course, is multiple, or can be told in many ways, read in many more. Every version is partial, shaped by the teller's partiality. And every one raises a boundless array of questions for the scholar and critic, whose choice is shaped by another multiplicity of factors, not least the historical moment and the state of the critic's discipline.

For instance: the journals of Lewis and Clark. After rereading them and talking about them with students in a graduate seminar—at the same time as I've been finishing the research for this chapter and thinking about what kinds of issues are current—I'd like to ask questions like these:

—The expedition party was multicultural; traveling along boundaries, crossing and recrossing them, they moved through multicultural spaces, a kaleidoscope of home and exotic, cooperation and conflict.

3

Where in the journals do these matters surface, and to what effect? How did they matter to what happened, to what was written? Where cultures intersect, what kinds of communication do and don't occur, what kinds of cultural exchange? What stories lie hidden in the margins, in the experience of Sacagawea, York, Charbonneau, the thousands of Mandans, Tetons, Arikaras, Shoshones, Yakimas, Tillamooks the explorers met? If we were to focus on the party's many translators, what would we see? How important was Sacagawea? Did only her cultures and languages and knowledge of the land matter, or was it also important that she was a woman, with a child? Can we even separate these things? The other women they met, those women who fed the Americans, traded with them, were sometimes the objects of trade: what are their stories? How do culture-specific concepts of sexuality and gender appear, intersect? The powerful metaphor of President Jefferson as the Father and the Native people as his children: do the implications of this go beyond the obvious? (Who is the Mother?) And the landscape: is it represented in gendered terms?

— Everywhere in the journals, the journey, I see textuality, language, discourse: the written texts themselves, multivocal; the twisted veins of intertextuality (other exploration accounts; paintings, poetry, philosophy; political documents; Jefferson's instructions; natural history records; countless others); the naming of places, the explorers' names carved on trees, another man's name tattooed on a woman's arm; the English words spoken by the coastal people — "musket," "knife," "damned rascal," "son of a bitch" — and the Americans' efforts to learn and record words in other languages; the sign language of the Plains; other nonverbal signs, which the Americans sometimes think they understand, bare feet and pipe-smoking, offers of food and women, the prairie set afire; natural signs — the color of water in the tributary, the tracks of deer and grizzlies; dozens of maps — verbal, in a body's gestures, on paper and animal skins, drawn on the ground, small piles of sand for mountains; and then, after the fact, all the edited versions, the selected editions, spelling and grammar corrected or not, certain subjects cut along with redundancy and irrelevancy and awkwardness and other kinds of noise (but what is noise? if we listen to it, what will we hear?); fictional versions, popular history, primary school textbooks, patriotic videotapes, versions beyond counting. Where might all these traces lead, what complexities might they uncover?

—How do the explorers find their way through unfamiliar space? Their path is never simple or direct: they follow tangents and tributaries, send hunters and scouts out in loops, split into smaller parties, take off on their own, trace the meandering paths of water, adapt themselves to geological and botanical contours. What sense of space do they have when they begin, when they finish? All the maps they use and create: what can we see here about geographies both abstract and concrete, about the travelers' interactions with the land? Through what lenses do they see this land—scientific, philosophical, aesthetic, economic, logistical—and where do these lenses blind them, sharpen their sight? Does anything connect their reading of the landscape with our reading of their text? What can they tell us that we have forgotten—about the European diseases that had traveled their route before them, about the intricate dependencies linking fires and prairies, communities of humans and animals and plants? In what ways do these journals complicate, even dissolve, our notion of "wilderness," press us to think critically about it, move towards some kind of reconception?

—The explorers' path lay through land that was not only culturally and ecologically but also politically and economically complex. How important to their success in negotiating this terrain was their considerable skill in improvisation? In diplomacy or moments of danger, in trade, in the need to find food? What kinds of things are exchanged along their route, by whom, for what purposes overt and covert, with what satisfactions on both sides, what trading of advantage? Those coins they hand out with Jefferson's picture: what kind of power might have resided in those representations, for the donors, for the recipients? Or the very popular blue beads? Or the many mutual displays of dancing? What sorts of relations are forged, and between whom, in these exchanges, and what identities—personal or collective—do they embody or enact? How many kinds of power are visible in these journals, not just the obvious ones (military connections, weaponry, the growing power of the American nation, the Indians' knowledge of the land), but the subtler exchanges that mark almost every day? What discourses of knowledge (science, diplomacy, trade, military discipline) come into play, and how? What larger national and international forces press upon them, and upon the people they meet, and how? What about the journals themselves, the cultural work they have done and continue to do, the ways they can be read as representing the history and character of the United States? And all the different ways these journals are in turn represented,

5

or, to put this question in a different framework, the ways they have been commodified and consumed?

My questions, of course, tell a story of their own. It's a story about my own journey through the territory I've called "What's New in Western Lit Crit?" my effort to combine "what information I have recved" into some kind of "Connection of the Countrey." It's thus also a story about the similar journeys of many other contemporary scholars and critics. And, since I've tried to illustrate some of the kinds of questions that these critics are asking right now, it's also a story about the emerging topography of the territory itself.

* * *

I'll attempt a nutshell summary, a quick, schematic map: What's new is a widespread critical rethinking of the traditional stories (histories, myths, texts, interpretive paradigms) of the American West, a rereading and retelling of these stories as complex, multivocal fragments of discourse thoroughly embedded in equally complex and intertwined social, cultural, political, economic, and ecological networks.

Why? There's no clear linear progression, no clear pattern of cause and effect. Instead, there's a loose and shifting field of contributing forces and interests and related bodies of work. Among these I'd want to mention (with an emphatic reminder that these lists are partial, the people I name only examples, signposts to vaster areas):

—The social upheaval in the U.S. during the sixties and seventies, including racial violence, the civil rights movement, the women's movement, the Vietnam War and protests against it, the Chicano movement, the Watergate scandal, the pressure on college campuses for "relevance," the environmental movement, and so on. Similar upheaval occurred elsewhere in the world as well, perhaps most importantly in the breaking apart of the old European colonial empires. One broad effect of all this was to train a generation of critics, to quote a then-popular bumper sticker, to "question authority."

—The tremendous changes in the larger field of literary criticism that have been wrought by recent critical theory, much of it of French origin, all those diverse but tangled ideas and tactics we sometimes lump together as "post-structuralist" or "post-modernist" theory: revisions of Freud (as in Jacques Lacan) and Marx (as in Louis Althusser, Raymond Williams, Fredric Jameson); linguistics based on Saussure and

6

Wittgenstein and subsequent theories of textuality in general; Derridean deconstructions of the transparency of language, the stability of binary oppositions, the yearning for an impossible Presence; the many feminisms; the philosophical and ethnographic decentering of European culture and the shift to post-colonial perspectives (Tzvetan Todorov, Edward Said, Gayatri Spivak, James Clifford); the insistent voices of members of marginalized groups of all kinds; the Foucauldian critiques of power, concepts, institutions, knowledge, discourse; the resulting new vision of the relationships between "literary" works and everything that surrounds them, history, politics, economics, popular culture (the "New Historicism," "Cultural Studies," "Cultural Poetics"); and more.

—Compelling and provocative work by scholars in such areas as American Studies (Annette Kolodny, Richard Slotkin, Walter Benn Michaels, Sacvan Berkovitch, Jane Tompkins), the New Western History (Patricia Limerick, Donald Worster, Richard White), environmental history and philosophy (including ecofeminism and deep ecology), ecology and other natural sciences, and geography. Everywhere around the field of western literature there is exciting new material to consider.

Navigating through this landscape can feel like trying to find a trail in a blizzard, thigh-deep in drifts, face blasted by wind-driven splinters of ice and snow. So much going on, so much to read, so much to learn.

* * *

So how does all this show up in the more innovative recent criticism of western American literature? Can we create any kind of theoretical order? I'll sketch another quick map. Let's think of two giant categories of questions, two subsets of a very broadly defined "post-structuralism." One we'll call "textuality." Here we'll put questions about the apparent but deceptive transparency of language and other kinds of representations: What's hidden by the surface meanings of texts? What if we focus on the margins or between the lines? What if we listen to the "noise," to the silences, or reverse "foreground" and "background"? The second we'll call "cultural historicism." Here we'll put questions about the relationships between literary texts and all the other things that surround them. What dynamics link literature with economics and politics? In what ways are different kinds of texts woven together? What cultural work does literature do? Into both categories we'll add such questions as

7

these: Which/whose texts have we read, and why, and through whose lenses? Which/whose have we ignored, and why? What texts should we read? What will a different set of texts do to our sense of the West, of western literature?

* * *

With these broad questions in mind, I'll turn to specific essays, books, and critics.

—The canon. It has exploded, partly with newly written material, partly with newly recovered older material, most notably to include the literature of western women and of the West's many cultures other than the European American.

Though there's lots of recent feminist work on western literature, surprisingly little of it is strongly influenced by contemporary theory. (The French, British, and post-colonial versions of feminism, for instance, remain nearly invisible.) Categories like "the frontier" are being reconsidered from the perspective of women; there's a general interest in the construction of subjectivity for characters, readers, and critics (for example, Roberta Rubenstein's *Boundaries of the Self* and Diane Freedman's *An Alchemy of Genres*); and many feminist critics are (consequently) moving across the boundary between impersonal and personal criticism, a move that can be seen elsewhere as well.

On the literatures of Native Americans and Chicanos, in contrast, post-structuralist and especially post-colonial critiques are thriving, moving into new territory with dizzying speed and sophistication. (This is where some of the most innovative feminist work appears as well.) A handful of names and short titles, again just as a signpost: the essay collections *Narrative Chance*, edited by Gerald Vizenor, and *Reconstructing a Chicano/a Literary Heritage*, edited by María Herrera-Sobek; Arnold Krupat's *Ethnocriticism* and *The Voice in the Margins*; David Murray's *Forked Tongues*; Louis Owens' *Other Destinies*; Rafael Pérez-Torres' *Movements in Chicano Poetry*; Ramón Saldívar's *Chicano Narrative*; José David Saldívar's *The Dialectics of Our America*; and Tey Diana Rebolledo's *Women Singing in the Snow*. Typically, these critics find that the literature they're interested in itself manifests many of the concerns of recent theory: a complex crossing of all kinds of boundaries (linguistic, cultural, geographical); a sense of subjectivities as contingent, multiple, contested, and culturally produced; an acute awareness of the importance of history; and so on. Thus, for instance, both in his fiction and in his criticism, Gerald Vizenor recognizes and plays with the post-modernity of Native American tricksters. And for Rafael Pérez-Torres, post-coloniality, post-modernity, and the production of identity are at once critical frameworks and central issues for contemporary Chicano/a poets. Students of all western literatures have a lot to learn from this body of criticism.

—Ecocriticism. Here, too, the canon has expanded to include literary nonfiction about nature and the environment, not all but much of which is western. And here, too, this expansion has included both newly written and newly recovered works, anthologies, regional collections, rereadings of older canonical works from new perspectives, scholarly and critical studies of individual writers and of the genre as a whole, and a growing number of books that blur the line between criticism and literature. There's a new journal devoted to this criticism, *ISLE*, and a new organization, ASLE (Interdisciplinary Studies in/Association for the Study of Literature and Environment), which grew to more than 600 members in its first three years.

As with western feminism, many ecocritics work largely with traditional theoretical assumptions and procedures — doing thematic studies, for instance, or considering what happens to canonical works when we focus on their treatment of the natural world, charting the generic characteristics of various forms of nature writing, offering unifying readings of major writers, and so forth. Indeed, it's not unusual to hear such statements as that through nature writing we can re-experience an unmediated contact or even unity with the real world — in what I'd call an expression of desire for a pre-structuralist (and pre-Freudian, pre-Nietzschean) Eden. Since many ecocritics are partly motivated by their own personal engagement with the natural world and their concern about environmental problems, the impulse towards a kind of simple and practical realism is strong.

Other ecocritics find themselves trying to negotiate a kind of middle ground between such theoretically problematic realism and the any-thing-goes-but-it's-all-just-language world of deconstruction. The natural world itself is not culturally constructed, they insist, but our perceptions and representations of it certainly are, and those perceptions and representations in turn materially alter the non-human world. Thus in "A Place for Stories: Nature, History, and Narrative," the historian William Cronon looks at the role of narrative in competing histories of the Dust Bowl; in *The Fall into Eden*, David Wyatt traces the historical links between topography and imagination in the literature of California; John P. O'Grady's *Pilgrims to the Wild* explores the shapes of desire in the wilderness travels and texts of five westerners; Bruce Greenfield's *Narrating Discoveries* develops a Foucauldian analysis of North American discovery narratives from Samuel Hearne to Thoreau (including a chapter on Lewis and Clark which helped spark my own questions); in an array of essays, Michael P. Cohen wonders about the post-modern implications of such things as mountain climbing along historic routes, indoor climbing gyms, cross-country ski training and racing, the idea of wilderness areas, the Bureau of Land Management's practice of "chaining" to clear land for grazing, and going for walks; and I have written about the implications of what wilderness travelers eat, the conceptual common ground of post-structuralist and biocentric theory, and the intersections between the personal and the culturally constructed in our experiences of wild places. One distinctive and especially intriguing characteristic of this emerging field, as some of these critics demonstrate, is its crossing of disciplinary boundaries—into environmental philosophy (including ecofeminism and deep ecology), natural history and the natural sciences, theoretical ecology, environmental history, and post-modern ethnography and geography. As newcomers to this territory, literary ecocritics have everything to gain from an acquaintance with the diverse, sophisticated, and eloquent work of historians like William Cronon, Richard White, Donald Worster, Alfred Crosby, and Carolyn Merchant, scientists like E. O. Wilson and Daniel Botkin, ecofeminists like Susan Griffin, ethnographers like James Clifford, ethnobotanists like Gary Paul Nabhan, and geographers like Yi-Fu Tuan, Carl Sauer, and Edward Soja. They exemplify an encouraging variety of ways to balance some kind of concrete engagement with the physical world with a subtle inquiry into the complexities of human culture, perception, and language.

Rebecca Solnit's *Savage Dreams: A Journey into the Hidden Wars of the American West* will serve as a brief example, though it's a difficult book to describe. Half about the Nevada nuclear test site and half about Yosemite National Park, the book deals with landscape aesthetics and wilderness preservation, anarchy and activism, nuclear science and anti-nuclear protest, literature and environmental history, the Shoshone people in Nevada and the Miwok people in Yosemite, country music, and lots of other things. As she notes in her acknowledgments, "Much of what I was interested in was the border territories between disci-plines" (xi). Or, as she explains in more detail and more metaphorically,

> There is a theory about lines of energy that traverse the earth, run-ning through sacred sites, called "ley lines...." I'm not sure about ley lines, but I believe in lines of convergence. These lines are no more visible in the landscape than ley lines, and I am not even proposing that they have any existence at all outside our imagina-tions—which are themselves crucial territories. These lines of convergence are the lines of biography and history and ecology that come together at a site, as the history of nuclear physics, the Arms Race, anti-Communism, civil disobedience, Native Ameri-can land-rights struggles, the environmental movement, and the mysticism and fanaticism deserts seem to inspire in Judeo-Christians all come together to make the Nevada Test Site, not as a piece of physical geography, but of cultural geography, not merely in the concrete, but in the abstract. Such places bring together his-tories which may seem unrelated—and when they come together it becomes possible to see new connections in our personal and public histories and stories, collisions even. A spiderweb of stories spreads out from any place, but it takes time to follow the strands. (23-24)

The task of ecocriticism, we might say, is to follow these strands.

—The western range. Remember the two big categories of post-structuralist theoretical premises and questions I described above? One is about textuality, the other about historicity and culture; one about language and discourse, the other about the inextricability of literature and everything else. In some pieces of writing, and at moments in oth-ers, these two categories can be distinguished. More often, these days, they too are thoroughly interwoven, as my final examples of what's new in western lit crit will suggest.

We make sense of the world around us, and of our relationships with it, by telling stories. The more complicated or troubling that world or those relationships seem, the more urgently we return to these stories, and the more we struggle to revise them. In the case of the West, of course, part of what is most troubling is its history of violent conquest, both of people and of land. Again and again in western literature, popular culture, and criticism, we see the struggle to understand and live with this history.

In "The New Historicism and the Old West," for instance, Forrest Robinson explores the western American version of "bad faith, the retreat from unbearable truth" and looks at texts (including *Shane*) that "negotiate a compromise between competing impulses to reveal and to conceal what is often glimpsed, but less frequently confronted, in received constructions of the real" (113). In essays like "The Solace of Animal Faces" and "'The Heart of the Wise Is in the House of Mourning,'" Stephen Tatum works with such diverse "texts" as the preserved body of Roy Rogers' horse Trigger, cowboy songs, and a cowboy hat with an attached shank of long hair to investigate similarly large issues: how we try to arrest modernization and mechanization partly through the commodification of cowboy culture, how we face the mystery of death, how we yearn for connection with the nonhuman, particularly animals.

Other critics are interested in the ways western culture constructs our sense of what it means to be American, or western, or, especially, male, questions also foregrounded by such recent texts as Cormac McCarthy's novels and Clint Eastwood's film *The Unforgiven*. Building on her work with nineteenth-century female domestic culture, Jane Tompkins sees in the western (both fiction and film) a determined and paradoxically alluring rewriting of American culture as masculine, anti-woman, anti-language, domineering, and violent. Lee Clark Mitchell also rereads classics like *The Virginian* and *Riders of the Purple Sage*, looking at issues of discursive control, gender construction, the eroticizing of landscapes, self-deconstructing narrative forms, and such historical forces as women's suffrage, the Social Purity movement, and the "white slavery" scare. To read Tompkins and Mitchell with or against each other is to recognize an enticing new territory of critical questions.

My two final examples deal in quite different ways with the problems of possession and self-possession. Opening with the feeble inscriptions on the land (houses, roads, plow lines) made by Willa Cather's pioneer characters, Howard Horwitz investigates the historical complexities of private property in *O Pioneers!* as they are tied to property law, gender, homesteading, aesthetics, and self-representation. And in one chapter of his book about the culture of working cowboys, Blake Allmendinger writes about branding as a surprisingly complex system of inscription that means very different things for cattle owners (for whom it marks possession of property) and cowboy workers (for whom it marks first their own dispossession and then later, through subversion and reappropriation, their religious and spiritual superiority).

As all westerners know, what it means to own something (or someone, even oneself) is as vexed, immediate, and practical a question now as it has always been. Perhaps the work of critics like these can help us to find our way through this question's tangled thickets.

* * *

Perhaps, in fact, I can generalize even further and say that all the critics I've mentioned and many more I haven't are themselves trying to find a path through the West — through complicated and often troubled thickets of race, ethnicity, gender, cultural and linguistic difference, and environmental behavior. Perhaps, like Lewis and Clark, we are all exploring what lies around us, trying to understand where we are, where we've been, and where we're going, asking questions of everyone we meet.[1]

On those cold winter days when William Clark engaged himself in "Connecting the Countrey from information," the Corps of Discovery had traveled only as far as what is now North Dakota. When he finished his map, he wrapped it carefully for its journey back to President Jefferson, and then he started again on his own long walk. There was a lot of country still ahead, and he wanted to see it.

Notes

1. My own guides to this critical territory have included Bill Ashline, Michael Cohen, Charles Crow, Cheryll Glotfelty, Melody Graulich, Alex Hunt, David Mogen, Mark Schlenz, Scott Slovic, Steve Tatum, and Rod Torrez.

Selected Bibliography

Allmendinger, Blake. *The Cowboy: Representations of Labor in an American Work Culture.* New York and Oxford: Oxford University Press, 1992.

Botkin, Daniel B. *Discordant Harmonies: A New Ecology for the Twenty-First Century.* New York and Oxford: Oxford University Press, 1990.

Buell, Lawrence. *The Environmental Imagination: Thoreau, Nature Writing, and the Formation of American Culture.* Cambridge, Massachusetts, and London: Harvard University Press, 1995.

Campbell, SueEllen. *Bringing the Mountain Home.* Tucson: University of Arizona Press, 1996.

———. "Feasting in the Wilderness: The Language of Food in American Wilderness Narratives." *American Literary History,* 6:1 (1994): 1-23.

———. "The Land and Language of Desire: Where Deep Ecology and Post-Structuralism Meet." *Western American Literature,* 24:3 (1989): 199-211.

Clifford, James and George E. Marcus, eds. *Writing Culture: The Poetics and Politics of Ethnography.* Berkeley: University of California Press, 1986.

Cohen, Michael P. "A Brittle Thesis: A Ghost Dance, A Flower Opening." In Oelschlaeger, Max, ed. *The Wilderness Condition: Essays on Environment and Civilization.* San Francisco: Sierra Club, 1992.

———. *A Garden of Bristlecone Pines.* Reno: University of Nevada Press, 1997.

———. "Literary Theory and Nature Writing." In Elder, John, ed. *American Nature Writers.* New York: Scribners, 1996.

———. *The Pathless Way: John Muir and American Wilderness.* Madison: University of Wisconsin Press, 1984.

———. "Postmodern Conditioning." *Terra Nova* (April 1996).

Cronon, William. *Changes in the Land: Indians, Colonists, and the Ecology of New England.* New York: Hill and Wang, 1983.

———. *Nature's Metropolis: Chicago and the Great West.* New York and London: W. W. Norton & Company, 1991.

———. "A Place for Stories: Nature, History, and Narrative." *The Journal of American History,* 78:4 (1992): 1347-1376.

Crosby, Alfred W. *Ecological Imperialism: The Biological Expansion of Europe, 900-1900.* Cambridge and New York: Cambridge University Press, 1986.

During, Simon, ed. *The Cultural Studies Reader.* New York and London: Routledge, 1993.

Eagleton, Terry. *Literary Theory: An Introduction.* Minneapolis: University of Minnesota Press, 1983.

Finch, Robert and John Elder, eds. *The Norton Book of Nature Writing.* New York: W. W. Norton, 1990.

Foucault, Michel. *The Foucault Reader.* Paul Rabinow, ed. New York: Pantheon, 1984.

Freedman, Diane P. *An Alchemy of Genres: Cross-Genre Writing by American Feminist Poet-Critics.* Charlottesville: University Press of Virginia, 1992.

Glotfelty, Cheryll and Harold Fromm, eds. *The Ecocriticism Reader: Landmarks in Literary Ecology.* Athens: University of Georgia Press, 1996.

Greenblatt, Stephen. *Marvelous Possessions: The Wonder of the New World.* Chicago: University of Chicago Press, 1991.

———. *Renaissance Self-Fashioning: From More to Shakespeare.* Chicago: University of Chicago Press, 1980.

Greenfield, Bruce. *Narrating Discovery: The Romantic Explorer in American Literature, 1790-1855.* New York: Columbia University Press, 1992.

Griffin, Susan. *Woman and Nature: The Roaring Inside Her.* New York: Harper & Row, 1978.

Halpern, Daniel, ed. *On Nature: Nature, Landscape, and Natural History.* San Francisco: Sierra Club Books, 1987.

Haraway, Donna. "The Promises of Monsters: A Regenerative Politics for Inappropriate/d Others." In *Cultural Studies.* Lawrence Grossberg, Cary Nelson, Paula A. Treichler, eds. New York and London: Routledge, 1992.

Herrera-Sobek, María, ed. *Reconstructing a Chicano/a Literary Heritage: Hispanic Colonial Literature of the Southwest.* Tucson: University of Arizona Press, 1993.

Horwitz, Howard. *By the Law of Nature: Form and Value in Nineteenth-Century America.* New York and Oxford: Oxford University Press, 1991.

Kolodny, Annette. *The Land Before Her: Fantasy and Experience on the American Frontiers, 1630-1860.* Chapel Hill: University of North Carolina Press, 1984.

Krupat, Arnold. *Ethnocriticism: Ethnography, History, Literature.* Berkeley: University of California Press, 1992.

———. *The Voice in the Margin: Native American Literature and the Canon.* Berkeley: University of California Press, 1989.

Lentricchia, Frank and Thomas McLaughlin, eds. *Critical Terms for Literary Study.* Chicago: University of Chicago Press, 1990.

Limerick, Patricia Nelson. *Legacy of Conquest: The Unbroken Past of the American West.* New York: Norton, 1987.

Lyon, Thomas J., ed. *This Incomperable Lande: A Book of American Nature Writing.* Boston: Houghton Mifflin, 1989.

Michaels, Walter Benn. *The Gold Standard and the Logic of Naturalism.* Berkeley and Los Angeles: University of California Press, 1987.

Mitchell, Lee Clark. "'When You Call Me That...': Tall Talk and Male Hegemony in *The Virginian.*" PMLA, 102 (1987): 66-76.

———. "White Slaves and Purple Sage: Plotting Sex in Zane Grey's West." *American Literary History* 6:2 (1994): 234-264.

Merchant, Carolyn. *The Death of Nature: Women, Ecology, and the Scientific Revolution.* New York: Harper & Row, 1980.

———, ed. *Key Concepts in Critical Theory: Ecology.* Atlantic Highlands, New Jersey: Humanities Press, 1994.

Murray, David. *Forked Tongues: Speech, Writing and Representation in North American Indian Texts.* Bloomington: Indiana University Press, 1991.

Nabhan, Gary Paul. *Gathering the Desert.* Tucson: University of Arizona Press, 1985.

Norwood, Vera. *Made from this Earth: American Women and Nature.* Chapel Hill and London: University of North Carolina Press, 1993.

O'Grady, John P. *Pilgrims to the Wild.* Salt Lake City: University of Utah Press, 1993.

Owens, Louis. *Other Destinies: Understanding the American Indian Novel.* Norman: University of Oklahoma Press, 1992.

Pérez-Torres, Rafael. *Movements in Chicano Poetry: Against Myths, Against Margins.* Cambridge: Cambridge University Press, 1995.

Rebolledo, Tey Diana. *Women Singing in the Snow: A Cultural Analysis of Chicana Literature.* Tucson: University of Arizona Press, 1995.

Robinson, Forrest G. "The New Historicism and the Old West." *Western American Literature,* 25:2 (1990): 103-123.

Rubenstein, Roberta. *Boundaries of the Self: Gender, Culture, Fiction.* Urbana and Chicago: University of Illinois Press, 1987.

Said, Edward W. *Orientalism.* New York: Pantheon, 1978.

Saldívar, José David. *The Dialectics of Our America: Genealogy, Cultural Critique, and Literary History.* Durham: Duke University Press, 1991.

Saldívar, Ramón. *Chicano Narrative: The Dialectics of Difference.* Madison: University of Wisconsin Press, 1990.

Slotkin, Richard. *The Fatal Environment: The Myth of the Frontier in the Age of Industrialization, 1800-1890.* New York: Atheneum, 1985.

———. *Regeneration Through Violence: The Mythology of the American Frontier.* Middletown, Connecticut: Wesleyan University, 1973.

Slovic, Scott. *Seeking Awareness in American Nature Writing.* Salt Lake City: University of Utah Press, 1992.

Soja, Edward W. *Postmodern Geographies: The Reassertion of Space in Critical Social Theory.* London: Verso, 1989.

Solnit, Rebecca. *Savage Dreams: A Journey into the Hidden Wars of the American West.* San Francisco: Sierra Club Books, 1994.

Spivak, Gayatri. *In Other Worlds.* New York: Routledge and Kegan Paul, 1987.

Tatum, Stephen. "'The Heart of the Wise Is in the House of Mourning.'" In *Eye on the Future: Popular Culture Scholarship into the Twenty-First Century.* Marilyn F. Motz, et. al., eds. Bowling Green, Ohio: Bowling Green State University Popular Press, 1994. Pp. 57-72.

———. "The Solace of Animal Faces." *Arizona Quarterly,* 50:4 (Winter 1994): 133-156.

Todorov, Tzvetan. *The Conquest of America.* Richard Howard, trans. New York: Harper & Row, 1984.

Tompkins, Jane. *The Cultural Work of American Fiction 1790-1860.* New York and Oxford: Oxford University Press, 1985.

———. *West of Everything: The Inner Life of Westerns.* New York and Oxford: Oxford University Press, 1992.

Veeser, H. Aram, ed. *The New Historicism Reader.* New York and London: Routledge, 1994.

Vizenor, Gerald, ed. *Narrative Chance: Postmodern Discourse on Native American Indian Literatures.* Albuquerque: University of New Mexico Press, 1989; rpt., Norman: University of Oklahoma Press, 1993.

White, Richard. *"It's Your Misfortune and None of My Own": A New History of the American West.* Norman: University of Oklahoma Press, 1991.

———. *The Roots of Dependency: Subsistence, Environment, and Social Change Among the Choctaws, Pawnees, and Navajos.* Lincoln: University of Nebraska Press, 1983.

Williams, Raymond. *Keywords: A Vocabulary of Culture and Society.* Rev. ed., New York and Oxford: Oxford University Press, 1983.

———. *Marxism and Literature.* New York and Oxford: Oxford University Press, 1977.

Wilson, Edward O. *The Diversity of Life.* New York and London: W. W. Norton & Company, 1992.

Worster, Donald. *Rivers of Empire: Water, Aridity and the Growth of the American West.* New York and Oxford: Oxford University Press, 1985.

———. *The Wealth of Nature: Environmental History and the Ecological Imagination.* New York and Oxford: Oxford University Press, 1993.

Wyatt, David. *The Fall into Eden: Landscape and Imagination in California.* New York and Cambridge: Cambridge University Press, 1986.

Krista Comer

Feminism, Women Writers and the New Western Regionalism: Revising Critical Paradigms

An unprecedented boom in western women's writing is afoot. Since the mid-1970s, both the big publishing houses and small presses have picked up scores of new writers, and, in the process, have created a new market of female readers. Mainstream media have followed this developing movement and have repeatedly run stories on what *Newsweek* called a "literary explosion."[1] Writers' festivals which headline new female stars like Pam Houston have sprung up in sexy western towns such as Steamboat Springs. And Leslie Silko, Sandra Cisneros, Louise Erdrich, and Maxine Hong Kingston have earned, between them, two MacArthurs, a National Book Award, and two National Book Critics Circle Awards. Taken together, all of these developments suggest a flourishing, and new, literary culture is sweeping the West. Women writers are in its forefront; indeed, their stories may come to define what's new in western literature today.

Now, as for criticism about this literature, that's a different story. There is very little of it. Indeed, many of the assumptions structuring the field of western criticism at the onset of the 1960s are problematic both for thinking about women writers and for representing what's different about the literary West after the 1960s. But the interest here is not to produce generational polemic rather, let us consider what it is we mean by "the West" and "western," because, increasingly, a variety of definitions compete for public consumption. The writers we defend or advance, and the ways we justify our literary programs, amount to our

17

contributions to current debates about the West, western history, and national history.

My claim, at its broadest, is that the new regionalism by women is decidedly feminist and that its feminism points out remarkable but often unobserved gaps in western literary criticism. This is not to say that writers agree about what constitutes "feminism" or female liberation. They do not. Competing strands of feminist thought at work in recent texts include: an exploration of female sexuality, an interest in working-class culture, a concern for environmental health, a conviction that the West was settled not by a heroic pioneer effort but by imperial conquest, and an intense preoccupation with racial identity and the history of race relations. Neither the themes nor the writers explored here by any means exhaust all the possibilities—many deserving writers are neglected.[2] However, a thematic approach offers a paradigm for conceptualizing the new female regionalism that addresses both the gender gap in western criticism and the tension between the Old and the New West. It also permits consideration of commonalities between writers who are usually considered separately.

First, a few definitions. The new western regionalism by women differs from the important body of literature written immediately before the 1970s by Jean Stafford, Hisaye Yamamoto, Jessamyn West, Mildred Walker, Fabiola Cabeza de Baca, Niña Otero-Warren, Dorothy Johnson, Edna Ferber, Lois Phillips Hudson, Hope Sykes, Joan Didion, Joanne Greenberg, Diane Wakoski, Tillie Olson and others. These writers' representations of the West unquestionably if indirectly, influence, current regionalists' narratives. However, the two groups belong to different historical moments and are motivated, finally, by different social and aesthetic phenomena.

The new regionalism is a literary movement inspired by unprecedented social, demographic and economic change in western states, the emergence of an alternative publishing industry headquartered in the West, the consolidation of the cultural wing of the civil rights, the women's and environmental movements, the grassroots anti-imperialist/anti-intervention activism of the 1970-80s, the New Western History, and finally, by feminist criticism of western literature itself.[3] Moreover, the new regionalism appears at roughly the same moment as American post-modernism, often as an implicit challenge to it.

Though the new regionalism by women is sometimes thought to have begun only in the mid-1980s, it originates earlier, in 1972-1974. Initially it comes out of literary magazines like *Third Woman* and *Sun Tracks*, founded by Chicanas and Native women as places to feature their own work — mainly poetry. The connection to the regional West is prominent throughout these magazines, though by no means do writers produce conventional western narratives; many do not even accept the legitimacy of the geopolitical boundaries which define today's western states. The commercial boom which followed in the 1980s consolidated the careers of many other writers, and it is in these later years that white women writers began to be highly visible.

Gender and Western Criticism

One of the most puzzling facts about the new regionalism by women — from a critical standpoint — is that critics don't write about it. Certainly one reads plenty about Silko, Kingston, Erdrich, or Cisneros, but analyses are framed through race or ethnicity, rather than through western regionality in any geographic/historic or imaginative sense. As far as the most popular of white women writers go, Barbara Kingsolver, Terry Tempest Williams, Mary Clearman Blew or Pam Houston, very few critical pieces had been published through the first half of 1997. Why? The Western Literature Association, certainly, doesn't suffer a lack of interested critics. And early feminist criticism, say by Annette Kolodny or Melody Graulich, was of a quality that seemed sure to promote a flurry of subsequent scholarship.

One obvious explanation is that the boom in western regionalism is so recent that western critics haven't yet caught up with the trend. Furthermore, the diverse literary histories that inform this body of texts — encompassing many races, languages, sub-regional histories, and formal styles — makes critical interpretation overwhelmingly complex. But the problem is deeper than the newness of this movement. The problem is conceptual. And the fact that women's narratives come out of an array of traditions, the regional often seeming the *least* important, compounds the critical challenge.

The absence of critical attention to female regionalism is both a product and symptom of a larger conceptual gap in western criticism which has rendered it unable to accommodate feminist aesthetics and consciousness. Western criticism is saddled with male-centered, white-centered and pre-contemporary aesthetic ideals which disable it on questions of gender and race and on the post-1960s period in which these issues predominate. A look at one of the finest thinkers on western regional culture, Wallace Stegner, provides a quick case study.

In the mid-1960s, Stegner's essays "History, Myth and the Western Writer" (1967) and "Born a Square" (1964) provided a critical blueprint for much later scholarship.[4] And that critical blueprint, to a surprising extent, remains intact. In a nutshell: Stegner read a range of western narratives written from 1880 to 1960 (by Vardis Fisher, Mary Austin, Conrad Richter, Willa Cather, O. E. Rölvaag, Walter Van Tilburg Clark, Frank Waters, Eugene Manlove Rhodes, and A.B. Guthrie). He broadly characterized them thus: they displayed a tendency toward realist narrative, a nostalgic tone, a belief in heroic virtue, a focus on the romantic frontier past rather than the urban present, a marked attention to western landscape, and a recurrent concern for gendered conflict, represented via what Stegner calls the "roving man" and "civilizing woman." Above all, Stegner believed, western narratives were hopeful. In them lived the founding promise of westward expansion: the West was America's "geography of hope," the place where American dreams came true. Stegner's West was a last stand of liberal humanism.

Despite some dissenters, including, in later essays, Stegner himself, the critical paradigm established in the 1960s remained the dominant trend in western criticism in the 1980s.[5] Though there are exceptions, most scholars persisted in defining the "authentic West" through antimodern rhetoric, continuing the notion that the West is "hope's native home."[6] And the majority of historical narratives about western literary history were drafted through white male writers.[7]

Of the last charge, Stegner himself was guilty. His thinking about gender was one major issue he did not significantly revise. Stegner took racial oppression seriously and reformulated western literary history to account for it. But he was impatient with the notion of women's oppression. He believed men and women were different — and they should be left to their separate and "natural" inclinations. Neither did he believe in "women's literature" *as a literature*. Two critical categories existed for him: region and race. Both shun the category "woman." In one of his last essays, "Coming of Age" (1992) Stegner implicitly figured Kingston as a "non-white," not a "woman" writer. Silko, too. Didion implicitly was a "western" writer, not a "white" or "woman" writer. Indeed, when questioned directly, Stegner said the notion of a female aesthetics made him "wince," and he called an attempt to theorize one "chasing moonbeams."[8]

Thus, though Stegner's West was certainly no "melodrama of beset manhood," neither was it a narrative which staged women's historical concerns at its center. For all its focus on gendered conflict and inclusion of white women writers, Stegner's early paradigm theorized western literature in terms of an implicit masculine norm. That norm permitted no space for thinking about misogyny, male privilege, a restrictive gendered division of labor, or the institutional structures (law, education, religion, family) that house and enforce gender difference.

Feminist criticism has taken up the field's slack by focusing on women writers and deconstructing the gendered bias of western literary traditions. Feminist critics have begun the task of conceptualizing pre-Civil War and modernist women's literature, especially as it relates to landscape representation. They also have recovered many single writers and evaluated the issues that drive their works. And yet, hampered by the anti-modern bent within western studies, the field as a whole lacks the sophistication of many other areas of feminist critical inquiry.

The initial edited volumes devoted to critical essays on women and western literature, *Women, Women Writers, and the West* (1979) and *Women and Western American Literature* (1982), both offered readings of short pieces by major and minor white women writers and demonstrated misogynist or marginalized female imagery in the established male greats of western writing. The balance of 1980s scholarship expanded and refined criticism about recognized white writers. Critics like Susan Rosowski, Lois Rudnick, Melody Graulich, Helen Stauffer, Charlotte Goodman, and others wrote biographies and essays on Gertrude Atherton, Willa Cather, Mabel Dodge Luhan, Mary Austin, Mari Sandoz, and Jean Stafford.

The major area of feminist critical accomplishment has been in the effort to theorize gender and landscape representation. Literary critic Annette Kolodny's *The Land Before Her* (1984) is the trend-setting work. Kolodny argues that unlike men, nineteenth-century white women writers figured western landscapes as domestic gardens.[9] In so doing, they subverted the gender politics inherent in the language of "virgin land," language which sanctioned Anglo men's right both to the land and, implicitly, to women's sexuality. Kolodny's book is ambitious and creative. It demonstrates the problems white women writers faced when they tried to mimic travel and exploration narratives — forms widely regarded as the precursors of the male western novel. Kolodny begins the task of writing white westering women's literary history. She shows that women's literature owes as much to the narrative strategies used in domestic fiction and captivity narratives, as it owes to travel narratives. Despite its age, Kolodny's book remains the most sustained conceptual work in the field.

The Desert Is No Lady (1987), edited by Vera Norwood and Janice Monk, takes the field in a promising direction. Via a study of the desert in twentieth-century women's writing and art, the book considers the role of racial difference in landscape perception, as well as adding a gendered analysis to the only theoretical work on space and region, that of perceptual geographers. Though some of Monk and Norwood's findings seem a bit well-worn (female representations of cyclicality vs. male linearity, creative process versus product, etc.), this book's focus on the difference that race makes in women's representations of gender is an important theoretical move. And the beginning conceptualization of pieces of modernist, contemporary, and southwestern female literary history is necessary and valuable. The book itself is a showpiece of southwestern women's painting, photography, and weaving.

Melody Graulich's "O Beautiful for Spacious Guys" (1989) anticipates theoretical changes within feminist discourse, especially deconstruction of the binaries "male" and "female" and the transition from women's to gender studies. Graulich agrees with other feminists that the male-biased frontier myth did not easily adapt itself to female experience or storytelling. Graulich's real interest, however, is to caution feminists not to sell short women's traditional values (the "warmth of the hearth") that are devalued within the western ideal. For it is in the reconciliation of the two binaries within both male *and* female writing—hearth and freedom—that "universal human dreams" (as Graulich puts it) are represented.

Finally, Jane Tompkins' *West of Everything: The Inner Life of Westerns* (1992) engages the masculinism of popular westerns. Tompkins reads the emergence of the genre western in the late 1800s as a male-gendered response to nineteenth-century female-gendered literary domesticity. Popular westerns provided a kind of cultural space, Tompkins suggests, in which the late nineteenth-century "crisis of masculinity" was negotiated.[10] The values of individualism, the cowboy's stiff upper lip and aggression—all found in popular westerns—contested the values of empathy and interdependent community represented in domestic fiction. The more aggressive "male" values emerged as victorious from the nineteenth-century cultural gender wars, Tompkins contends, and they then dominate twentieth-century popular representations of the West.

Despite its accomplishments, feminist scholarship is underdeveloped. Any number of writers and issues remain to be explored. Neither does a "big picture" yet exist for the modernist period, the contemporary period, the new regionalism, or the relationship of postmodernism to literary western writing. Above all, no matter the period under study, feminists need critical paradigms that take into account the simultaneous and complex workings of gender, race, region, class, nature and sexuality. This kind of analysis is implicit in the following consideration of the new regionalists' representations of the post-Vietnam West.

Theorizing Today's West

One of the hallmarks of the new female regionalism is a feminism that above all is revisionist. It critiques and remakes aspects of early contemporary feminist politics that writers find oppressive or limited. The revisionist impulse also motivates writers' interventions on any number of male-dominated representations of western culture. The writers examined here turn conventional western tropes — the West as land of fresh starts, western landscape as regenerative resource — toward feminist ends. They also use conventional feminist narratives — a focus on female-centered spirituality or sexuality — in distinctly western ways. In the process they remake both feminist and western discourse.

These texts, generally speaking, are not heroic, not rural, not nostalgic, not focused on the past, not told exclusively via realist narrative. Women writers do not hold up the West as a geography of national hope. They do not have the same faith in liberal humanist philosophy as did earlier generations of western intellectuals. Their representations of gendered relations are significantly more complicated than Stegner's "roving man" and "civilizing woman." Women characters take for themselves a large measure of the freedom white western men have historically enjoyed — sexual freedom, freedom of mobility, freedom from child rearing, freedom to challenge authority. At the same time they retain many of the values traditionally associated with female culture: ideals of family, community, interpersonal relations, and caring for the sick and dying. What emerges is a West in which the categories of "woman" and "West" are not mutually exclusive. And once the oppositional status of these categories is undone, a host of other western identities become apparent.

One of these new identities is the Indian *woman*. Leslie Silko's first collection of poetry, *Laguna Woman* (1974), demonstrates an early tendency in feminist narratives by western women: a focus on female sexuality.[11] Like the work of most Native women writers of the period, Silko's collection celebrates a long-standing Native tradition of respect between the sexes.[12] However, a considerable number of Native writers also speak about male violence against women and female underachievement.[13] *Laguna Woman* dialogues with these texts, as well as with white feminism's focus on reproductive freedom. It speaks, too, to the dominant trope of western landscape representation: nature as salve for the nation's ills. Silko challenges the very legitimacy of a nationalist claim upon western lands.

In direct conversation with the debates surrounding *Roe v. Wade* (1973), *Laguna Woman* opens with "Poem for Myself and Mei: Concerning Abortion, Chinle to Fort Defiance April 1973." En route to an abortion clinic on a spring morning bursting with sunshine and butterflies, the speaker in the poem discloses ambivalences about the ethics of abortion. Butterflies double as fetuses, the reader realizes, and like the poem's pebbles, fetuses are alive. They are life. And yet, in spite of a fetus' status as life, this poem is no condemnation of abortion.

The poem makes clear that the speaker's need to control her reproductive ability comes not out of a war between the sexes (as it did for many white feminists) but from a conflict between the pre- and the post-Columbian worlds. The speaker's ethical dilemma is different from that of white feminists, for it grows from her cosmological worldview. She faces no simple "choice." The fetus, like any pebble or wind or butterfly, is alive and is invested with a distinct spirit. But face the choice she will, for the sexual politics of this post-Columbian world necessitate she be able to control her reproductive ability. So, too, will she live with the compromised ethics that "choice" requires.

Silko again takes up sexual politics in two humorous poems about typical feminist frustrations, "Si'ahh Aash'" and "Mesita Men" (1972). Both affirm female desire and poke fun at the dominance of masculine sexuality in sexual discourses. "Mesita Men" is startling, unadorned. Its very brevity (twelve words) suggests the kind of sex Mesita men want: fast, without much fuss. The poem's speaker isn't interested. Implicitly, female desire isn't in a hurry. It's no fuss, to her, to take her time. "Si'ahh Aash'" shows more narrative cunning, for its name highlights the Laguna Pueblo word for a man who sleeps with women who have husbands. And yet finally, when reflecting upon the word *Si'ahh aash'*, one realizes it is not about male but about married women's sexuality. Apparently the sexual appetite of married women is hearty, and if their husbands fail to satisfy, they go elsewhere.

The ways Silko figures western landscape throughout this collection are familiar to those who know the literary West. The natural world motivates narrative; it evokes color, feeling, reverence, even plot development and resolution. What is unfamiliar is that the area west of the 98th meridian is not represented as "the American West." That West— permeated by frontier mythology, the landscape on which American character was formed—is nonexistent here. *Laguna Woman* narrates another topography, whose boundaries nullify the political logic underlying "the American West."[14] This representation of "western" lands does not conflate western regional with American national identity. In the process, Silko displaces one of the most treasured national myths: the West as America. Silko's landscapes return the land to the people from whom it was stolen.

Judith Freeman provides a good point of departure from Silko, for *The Chinchilla Farm* (1989) takes us out of the Southwest, away from standard symbols of western identity ("natural" landscapes and Indian mysticism), and locates us in the heart of the western anti-myth, Los Angeles.[15] Given the many western narratives Freeman deploys to get to Los Angeles, however, her California is not west of the West. California is the West. Like Silko, Freeman redefines western boundaries, and her's include one of America's most urban landscapes.

The Chinchilla Farm, an otherwise well-reviewed first novel, has been roundly criticized for its Pollyannish ending, whereby folk philosopher Verna Flake—a fallen Mormon, a woman who finds a better life in Los Angeles after her adulterous husband leaves her—marries rich and educated Vincent. Verna, Vincent and their new baby live happily ever after on the California beachfront. And Verna is able, she reveals on the last page, "to write this book." What kind of story is this, feminists might demand, whose "happy ever after" ending is defined so traditionally by marriage, child, and millionaire husband whose wealth facilitates wife's sudden literary career?

Freeman's ending clearly advocates a more relationally oriented and less professionally oriented feminism. Importantly, the reason she advocates this reorientation is not for love of women's culture (the backdrop for much relational feminism) but for love of working-class culture.

Jolene, the single self-proclaimed "radical" of the book, is the kind of upper-middle-class feminist Freeman critiques. For, would Jolene, busy artist that she is, assist someone like Inez, a battered woman, in her flight from her abusive husband? Or someone like Duluth, a homeless man who needs a second chance? No. It is Verna, out of a Mormon lend-a-helping-hand philosophy, who hauls Inez to Mexico, with Duluth in the back seat.

The ending is also conventionally western. Western horizons provide personal renewal, economic opportunity, a place where a practical woman can get ahead. Even as Freeman makes use of these familiar tropes, however, she critiques them. The final happy-ever-after scene suggests not only that ambition-driven feminism is elitist and hollow but that class relations in today's West are more stratified than ever. This is no land of economic opportunity. Only by marrying a rich husband will this working-class woman achieve class mobility. Moreover, only by breaking with an hostility in western narratives toward intellectualism and high culture might Freeman pose some of the philosophical queries she cares about. Namely, "How do you go on *without anything to connect you to it all?*" (198). To answer this question, she must break further with the western ideal. To the extent that Freeman opposes individualist conceptions of self and society, she revises that most hallowed western image, the self-reliant individual man. This book instead, as its title suggests (for chinchillas mate for life), gets at why and how people bond, what makes for lifelong commitment. The place where people stay together, where feminism puts people, not careers, first — that's the West, as Freeman would have it.

Class allegiances also play an important role in the ways that white women writers depict their love of western rural lands. In fact, among writers whose subject matter is the land itself, the issue of class divides one feminist camp from the another. In the first camp are writers who work the land (like many of the Rocky Mountain regionalists) — the ranchers or fifth or sixth-generation homesteaders whose hardscrabble lives keep them close to the economic edge.[16] The second camp are those who define themselves through ecofeminist thought and whose interest is not working but "protecting" the land.[17] Both camps advocate a more relational feminism like that of Judith Freeman. But if Freeman sees relationality tied up with working class values, those who work the land see it as a guard against rural female isolation. Ecofeminist relationality is different altogether, for it is tied up with a return to women's relationship with what they call Mother Earth. This return is usually infused with spiritual meaning of some kind and with female empowerment. A middle-class identity implicitly informs much of ecofeminist thought — Terry Tempest Williams' *Refuge* is a characteristic work.[18]

Williams brings an explicitly feminist outlook to the West's most developed literary tradition: the nature essay. As does most ecofeminism, *Refuge* links women's oppression with the exploitation of nature. The immediacy of this relationship is all the more apparent given that the women of Williams' family ("The Clan of One-Breasted Women") have contracted cancer from the fallout of nuclear tests conducted in the 1950s in Utah. Most of "the Clan" have died.

If, like most ecofeminists, Williams aligns "woman" with "nature" (a theoretical move that gives ecofeminism a bad name among most feminist thinkers), she does not align "woman" with "mother." Neither does she, as do many ecofeminists, connect female spirituality to paganism. Rather she liberates her Mormonism from its masculinist moorings, and feminizes it by adding "The Motherbody" as counterpoint to the Mormon Godhead. Finally, and most interestingly, Williams departs from the redemptive landscape narrated in most western nature essays. Landscapes are as social as kinship systems, and the meanings humans bring to them are just that: statements of human desire.

One of the book's recurrent female dilemmas is that of "selfishness," defined as a female life not dedicated to child rearing. Female "selfishness," the book argues, enables women to know their own minds and hearts. Women need solitude, quiet, a respite from the demands that silence their own voices. Williams' embrace of individual freedom as a path to female liberation reveals her sympathy with the middle-class values that dominate the feminist mainstream. However, here is also where she departs from it, for individual freedom is not enough. Williams' women need wilderness, too, for in it they find their ultimate mentor — one which teaches them to trust "female experience." Williams' experiences in the wild empower her to speak out against nuclear proliferation, and above all, to trust herself. This trust is apparently behind her decision to remain child free. As such she does not rewrite her own family genealogy through the "Earth Mother" symbols one often sees in ecofeminist thought, whereby women and mother (like woman and nature) are conflated. Williams' consistent focus on "family" thus does not reinvent the most traditional of family female roles: woman as mother.

In a departure from much nature writing, this text self-consciously figures nature as a symbolic (versus "natural") topography. Though often Williams writes nature through both aesthetic and spiritual narratives, she also writes nature as a social landscape, onto which humans narrate their need for hope and respite from life's griefs. This nature writer's landscapes offer stiff medicine: there is no protection, ultimately, against the agony of loss.

If Williams distances herself from redemptive landscapes, she does not distance herself from a reliance on "primitive peoples" as models for redemptive alternative cultures. Her Kenyan friend comes to be representative of "the African woman," whose connection to the land is ostensibly an ideal one. And Williams narrates her mystical re-connection with her deceased mother via the Mexican Day of the Dead ritual, not her own Mormonism. Williams' representations of racial others in reductive, monolithic or romantic terms raises serious questions about the role of primitivism and appropriation in ecofeminist thought. It exposes the degree to which ecofeminism is a white racial discourse. It also exposes the class bias that informs today's environmentalism: the notion that people can "get away from it all" into "other" cultures or recreational wilderness is one which depends upon significant disposable income and leisure time.[19]

The impulse to envision a female-centered history and spirituality is also shared by Chicana Gloria Anzaldúa (though without the primitivist overtones). To accomplish her goals, however, Anzaldúa faces a more complex nexus of problems than does Williams. Mestizas, like herself, Anzaldúa argues, live on the United States-Texas border, and that border remains *una herida abierta*, an open wound, where the "Third World grates against the first and bleeds."[20] Anzaldúa's discussion of female-centered lineages thus must digress significantly into Spanish and Anglo-American imperial conquest of Aztlán — the mythic pre-Columbian cultural homeland claimed by Chicanos/as, located in today's Southwest. Like many of the new regionalists, she describes a West still reeling from conquest.[21]

Anzaldúa's *Borderlands/Las Fronteras* has become a classic in Chicana studies, for it sets out a host of problems Chicanas face in American and Mexican American culture. In *Borderlands* Anzaldúa narrates a history of native peoples in the Southwest and Texas who are victimized by Spanish colonialism and American expansion; she also writes a history of female oppression from the post-Columbian period to the present.

She links both colonial legacies with contemporary gender roles which constrain Mexican American female opportunity, freedom, sexuality and spirituality. Anzaldúa puts imperialism center stage, and, as does Silko, reminds readers that "western space" is defined, by some western writers, in ways that dispute America's right to western lands. Unlike Silko, whose representations of white intrusion are often implied and subtle, Anzaldúa makes use of the "in your face" strategy of much gay liberation activism.

The "borderlands" Anzaldúa narrates are not just geographic but also sexual, linguistic, psychological, spiritual, and political. As a lesbian she is shunted to the borders of a homophobic and heterosexist society. As someone whose first language is Spanish, she lives on the linguistic border of an English-speaking society that considers Spanish a language to be unlearned. As an outsider in both U.S. and Mexican culture, an alien on either side of the border, Anzaldúa argues that the psychological health of new mestizas depends on their ability to live *sin fronteras*, to become a crossroads where multiple selves can coexist. Borderlands consciousness values racial cross-fertilization and cultural complexity. It refuses dualistic thinking. This is the consciousness necessary, Anzaldúa believes, for Americans to negotiate the twenty-first century.

Like Anzaldúa and many other western writers, Maxine Hong Kingston thinks of gender in racialized terms.[22] Like Anzaldúa, Kingston articulates racial identity by invoking and revising western regional history. And finally, like Anzaldúa, Kingston uses formal strategies which are distinctly postmodernist. Kingston's dazzling cultural literacy, however, reveals a class identity quite at odds with Anzaldúa's. Though they share similar politics — those which affirm diversity and interracial bonds in the twenty-first century — their audiences are significantly different. Kingston is interested in remaking western literature itself. In *Tripmaster Monkey*, Kingston rewrites not just Asian-American literary history but that of the nation, the American West, and especially that of California.[23]

Wittman Ah Sing, "our hero" we are told by the narrator with considerable irony, is a fifth-generation Chinese-American hippie whose name signifies his authenticity as an American subject by aligning him with quintessential democratic American poet Walt Whitman. In the book's opening pages the narrator drops a series of literary names (Hemingway, Acosta, the Beats, and Wittman's own) to indicate that this text is, in part, about American literature. The narrator goes on to list those writers whom protagonist Wittman would read to anyone interested in western American literature: Saroyan, Steinbeck, Kerouac, Twain, Robert Louis Stevenson, Muir, Stegner, John Fante, Carlos Bulosan, Gertrude Atherton, Jack London, Ambrose Bierce, and the diaries of internment camp victims. This list sets the stage for Kingston's own cultural interventions, and they are racial, regional and gendered.

Like her character Wittman Ah Sing, Kingston "want[s] to spoil all those stories coming out of and set in New England Back East" (34). The reason to do so is to "blacken and to yellow Bill, Brooke, and Annie" (34). That is, Kingston's case for the American-ness of Asian identity is explicitly linked to western regional history. She sees her own racialized tale as better located within a California literary tradition than one coming out of the Northeast. Indeed the play-within-the-novel, *Journey to the West* (a conglomeration of Chinese folk tales and legends), is staged as a western American cultural event, very much in the improvisational Beat tradition. Moreover, Wittman proclaims himself "an artist of all the Far Out West" (19), someone with "cowboy's eyes."

Kingston not only makes inroads into western American literature by adding Asian America to its cast of literary characters but also demonstrates the limits of that masculinist literature in its ability to represent women's wants, needs, and experiences. Though Wittman is the book's protagonist, he is not, interestingly, the book's dominant voice. That role is occupied by a mischievous feminist narrator who, through her depiction of and distance from Wittman, reveals the gender ideals that guide his sense of himself, his role in the world, and his understanding of women. What we learn is that Wittman, by and large, knows very little about women, nor does he listen to what women tell him about themselves.

Through Wittman, the narrator develops a broader critique of the masculine bias that informs contemporary definitions of Asian-American cultural identity. That identity, shaped in large part by the leadership of writer Frank Chin, is, in Kingston's opinion, fatally militaristic. Its racial separatism and essentialism also suits men, she argues, for through them, men control who women love, who women take as political allies. Kingston's cultural nationalism, in contrast to Frank Chin's, is explicitly anti-separatist, antiessentialist, interracial, and pacifist. She opens up her new vision of the twenty-first-century West to wonder: "Whatever there is when there isn't war has to be invented. What do people do in peace?" (306).

Conclusion

Though the new regionalism by women speaks to many old western themes, its overall representation of the West is radically different. Its narratives are not classically heroic, driven by dreams of individualist freedom. Writers care more about human community, and the places of women, men, and children in that community. Nostalgia for the nineteenth-century frontier has given way to a thorough reckoning with the consequences of an imperial past for present-day race relations. The legacy of western environmental exploitation is reckoned with, too. The formal vehicles women writers adopt are sometimes realistic, but often writers engage postmodernist formal strategies. Along with the dialogue with postmodernism comes a challenge to the liberal humanist thinking that underlies notions that the West is "hope's native home."

The new feminist regionalism intervenes upon and reconstitutes, then, the very terms through which the West will be hereafter defined. Instead of conflating the West with a monolithic (and white male-biased) conception of the nation, writers reconceive the various possible narratives of nation, at times destabilizing those narratives so fundamentally that the "center" of the nation can be located only at its borders.

If a good part of the current writerly impulse is to revise old paradigms, another is to appropriate those paradigms and redeploy them in new ways. Thus, finally, the West comes into contemporary discursive play in one of its oldest and most Eurocentric guises: as a topography of desire. And yet this time, it is *women's desires* that are being explored or represented via western stories. This author would argue that women's desires are considerably more humble than those conventionally imposed on western spaces. But, then again, the very act of affirming multiracial female desire at all — especially in a space devoted to Eurocentric and masculinist pleasure — is an act with consequences we might not yet foresee.

Notes

1. "Don't Fence Them Out," *Newsweek*, July 13, 1992, pp. 52-54. *Life, People,* and *Time* also ran stories.

2. For example, Marilynne Robinson, Alison Baker, Ruthanne Lum McCunn, Karen Joy Fowler, Karen Tei Yamashita, Fae Myenne Ng, Linda Hogan, Octavia Butler, Sherley Anne Williams, Amy Tan, and Susan Lowell.

3. On economic and social change see Patricia Nelson Limerick, "The Realization of the American West," paper presented at The New Regional Conference, University of Mississippi, 1993. Also see Richard Maxwell Brown, "The New Regionalism in America, 1970-81," *Regionalism and the Pacific Northwest*, William G. Robbins, et al., eds. (Corvallis: Oregon State University Press, 1983), pp. 37-96. On alternative publishing see Gerald Haslam, "Unknown Diversity: Small Presses and Little Magazines," J. Golden Taylor ed. *A Literary History of the American West* (Fort Worth: Texas Christian University Press, 1987). The other claims here are my own.

4. From *The Sound of Mountain Water* (New York: Doubleday, 1969).

5. For Stegner's dissent, see "Coming of Age: The End of the Beginning," *Where the Bluebird Sings to the Lemonade Springs: Living and Writing in the West* (New York: Random House, 1992); also see *The American West as Living Space* (Ann Arbor: University of Michigan Press, 1987).

6. Exceptions include Judy Nolte Temple, ed., *Open Spaces, City Places: Contemporary Writers on the Changing Southwest* (Tucson: University of Arizona Press, 1994); Judy Nolte Lensink, ed., *Old Southwest/New Southwest* (Tucson: Tucson Public Library, 1987); David Fine, ed., *Los Angeles in Fiction* (Albuquerque: University of New Mexico Press, 1984); Glen Love, *New Americans: The Westerner and the Modern Experience in the American Novel* (London: Association of University Presses, 1982); Michael Kowalewski, ed. *Reading the West: New Essays on the Literature of the American West* (New York: Cambridge University Press, 1996); Blake Allmendinger, *The Cowboy: Representations of Labor in an American Work Culture* (New York: Oxford University Press, 1992); Forrest G. Robinson, *Having It Both Ways: Self-Subversion in Western Popular Classics* (Albuquerque: University of New Mexico Press, 1993).

7. Examples of major works include Harold Peter Simonson, *Beyond the Frontier: Writers, Western Regionalism, and a Sense of Place* (Fort Worth: Texas Christian University Press, 1989); A. Carl Bredahl, Jr., *New Ground: Western American Narrative and the Literary Canon* (Chapel Hill: North Carolina University Press, 1989); Mark Siegel, "Contemporary Trends in Western American Fiction," *Literary History of the American West*, pp. 1182-1201; Martin Bucco, "Epilogue: The Development of Western Literary Criticism," *Literary History of the American West*, pp. 1283-1316; David Wyatt, *Fall Into Eden: Landscape and Imagination in California* (New York: Cambridge University Press, 1986); John Milton, *The Novel of the American West* (Lincoln: University of Nebraska Press, 1980); William T. Pilkington, *Critical Essays on the Western American Novel* (Boston: G. K. Hall, 1980). In two cases Mary Austin is written into western literary history but without much grappling with gendered issues.

8. Personal correspondence of September 25, 1992, and October 27, 1992.

9. See Mary Austin Holley, Eliza Farnham, Caroline Kirkland, Alice Cary, E.D.E.N. Southworth, Maria Susanna Cummins.

10. For one rendering of the "crisis of masculinity," see Gail Bederman, *Manliness and Civilization: A Cultural History of Gender and Race in the United States, 1880-1917* (Chicago: Chicago University Press, 1995).

11. This collection was published by Greenfield Review Press, Greenfield Center, New York. Female sexuality is a topic for other 1970s writers. See Ella Leffland, Dorothy Bryant, Joan Didion, Lorna Dee Cervantes, Wanda Coleman, Maxine Hong Kingston, Carolyn See. In the 1980s see Sandra Cisneros, Cherrie Moraga, Gloria Anzaldúa, Mary Helen Ponce, Denise Chavez, Pat Mora, Louise Erdrich, Janice Mirikitani, Cynthia Kodohata, Sallie Tisdale, Pam Houston, Kate Braverman, and Terry McMillan.

12. See Paula Gunn Allen, Janet Campbell Hale, Elizabeth Cook-Lynn, Opal Lee Popkes.

13. See Joy Harjo, Anita Endrezze-Danielson, Wendy Rose.

14. Other writers whose landscape representations destabilize conventional national definitions of the West include Ana Castillo, Gloria Anzaldúa, Wendy Rose, Mitsuye Yamada. The kind of theoretical and political move I suggest here is taken up regularly in post-colonial theory.

15. Originally published by Vintage Books, New York.

16. See Annick Smith, Mary Clearman Blew, Patricia Henley, Melanie Rae Thon and Kim Barnes. Teresa Jordan, Leslie Ryan and Cyra McFadden also narrate hardscrabble stories, though they are not tied directly to working the land. California "Oakie" and Fresno poets often articulate their relationships to the land in working-class terms too (i.e., Wilma Elizabeth McDaniel).

17. Barbara Kingsolver is the most prominent of these writers.

18. This book was published by Pantheon, New York, 1991.

19. For an incisive critique of the wilderness ideal and its problematic relationship to contemporary environmentalism, see William Cronon, "The Trouble with Wilderness, or, Getting Back to the Wrong Kind of Nature," *Uncommon Ground: Toward Reinventing Nature* (New York: Norton, 1995).

20. *Borderlands/Las Fronteras: The New Mestiza* (San Francisco: spinsters/aunt lute, 1987), p. 3.

21. This theme is most pronounced among Native American and Chicana writers. However other nonwhite writers make use of the conquest paradigm to discuss their own racial oppression (i.e. Mitsuye Yamada on Japanese internment). White women at times take it up, too. See Barbara Kingsolver, Jane Candia Coleman.

22. This is true for virtually all of the women-of-color writers mentioned throughout this essay. It is also true for some white women, especially Ella Leffland, Barbara Kingsolver and Judith Freeman.

23. Originally published in 1989 by Alfred Knopf, New York.

Selected Bibliography

Armitage, Susan, et al., eds. *Women in the West: A Guide to Manuscript Sources.* New York: Garland Publishing, 1991.

Bataille, Gretchen M. and Kathleen Mullen Sands. *American Indian Women: Telling Their Lives.* Lincoln: University of Nebraska Press, 1984.

Bederman, Gail. *Manliness and Civilization: A Cultural History of Gender and Race in the United States, 1880-1917.* Chicago: University of Chicago Press, 1995.

Blew, Mary Clearman and Kim Barnes, eds. *Circle of Women: An Anthology of Contemporary Western Women Writers.* New York: Penguin, 1994.

Brown, Richard Maxwell. "The New Regionalism in America, 1970-1981." In *Regionalism and the Pacific Northwest*, William G. Robbins, et al., eds. Corvallis: Oregon State University Press, 1983.

Cisneros, Sandra. "Cactus Flowers: In Search of Tejana Feminist Poetry." *Third Woman*, 3:1-2 (1986): 73-80.

Graulich, Melody. "Gettin' Hitched in the West." Paper presented at Western Literature: A Symposium, University of Wyoming, 1992.

———. "O Beautiful for Spacious Guys." *The Frontier Experience and the American*

Dream. David Mogen, et al., eds. College Station: Texas A&M University Press, 1989.

————. "The Guides To Conduct That A Tradition Offers: Wallace Stegner's *Angle of Repose*." *South Dakota Review*, 23:4 (Winter 1985): 87-106.

Johnson, Susan Lee. "'A Memory Sweet to Soldiers': The Significance of Gender in the History of the 'American West.'" *Western Historical Quarterly*, 24:4 (November 1993): 495-517.

Kolodny, Annette. *The Land Before Her: Fantasy and Experience of the American Frontiers, 1630-1860*. Chapel Hill: University of North Carolina Press, 1984.

Lee, L.L. and Merrill Lewis, eds. *Women, Women Writers, and the West*. New York: Troy Publishing Company, 1979.

Monk, Janice, ed. *Making Worlds: Metaphor and Materiality in the Production of Feminist Texts*. Tucson: Southwest Institute for Research on Women, University of Arizona, forthcoming.

Morin, Karen. "The Gender of Geography." *Postmodern Culture*, 5:2 (January 1995).

Morrissey, Katherine G. "Engendering the West." In *Under an Open Sky: Rethinking America's Western Past*. William Cronon, George Miles, and Jay Gitlin, eds. New York: W.W. Norton, 1992. Pp. 132-144.

Murphy, Patrick D. *Literature, Nature and Other: Ecofeminist Critiques*. Albany: State University of New York, 1995.

Norwood, Vera and Janice Monk, eds. *The Desert Is No Lady: Southwestern Landscapes in Women's Writing and Art*. New Haven: Yale University Press, 1987.

Rose, Gillian *Feminism and Geography: The Limits of Geographical Knowledge*. Oxford: Polity Press, 1993.

Saldívar, José David. *The Dialectics of Our America: Genealogy, Cultural Critique, and Literary History*. Durham: Duke University Press, 1991.

Schlissel, Lillian, Vicki L. Ruiz and Janice Monk, eds. *Western Women: Their Land, Their Lives*. Albuquerque: University of New Mexico Press, 1988.

Southwestern American Literature. Special Issue: The Southwest by Women (Summer 1995).

Stauffer, Helen Winter and Susan J. Rosowski, eds. *Women and Western American Literature*. Troy, New York: Whitson, 1982.

Tompkins, Jane. *West of Everything: The Inner Life of Westerns*. New York: Oxford University Press, 1992.

Vizenor, Gerald. *Narrative Chance: Postmodern Discourse on Native American Literatures*. Norman: University of Oklahoma Press, 1993.

Wong, Sau-ling Cynthia. *Reading Asian American Literature: From Necessity to Extravagance*. Princeton, New Jersey: Princeton University Press, 1993.

Yalom, Marilyn. *Women Writers of the West Coast*. Palo Alto: Stanford University Press, 1984.

Robert F. Gish

Reperceiving Ethnicity
in Western American Literature

The American West and its literatures, by their very nature, invite continuous reperception, ready always for redefinition and remapping. Such is the nature of a dreamed and realized, imagined and real place existing as it does in psyche and memory, in myth and in geography. The "West" has always meant different things, different places, different ideas to different peoples.

The "inside our culture" perceptions of ethnic artists and historians, by persons "of color," hold up a different mirror to what is seen in looking west and show us what reflections of expression and complexion linger on those who look. By adopting new metaphors of history and art as far from color-blind and ethnic lenses in art and history as alternative means for seeing who we are and what our cultural histories are, we are allowed a better sense of the "relativity of otherness."

Historical and literary truths then become significant not as absolutes but as relative to who is doing the telling, who is being told, who is selecting and ordering the stories and the histories. Ronald Takaki, in keeping with this pluralistic or multicultural perspective, questions the assimilations of the "melting pot" in favor of the distinctions of a "salad bowl," or a "different mirror," and reminds us that, "America does not belong to one race or one group...and Americans have been constantly redefining their national identity from the moment of first contact.... By sharing their stories, they invite us to see ourselves in a different mirror."[1]

The ethnic American West presents not only different muses and sources of inspiration but a myriad of "virtual" or approximated realities of place and race as both personal experience and the empathic or imagined perceptions and interpretations of it.

In this post-modern sense the wests of burgeoning virtual realities merge with ethnic realities. The American West thus becomes many American Wests. American Indians and minorities of various kinds give texture and plurality to monoculture, to the one-dimensionality of *the* American West, perceivable now as simultaneously Anglo Old West and Ethnic New West. The new history and the new ethnicity, the new politics of gender are predicated on reperceiving what the West once was thought to be. These transvaluations can now posit not just the Euro-American "winning of the West," but ethnic perceptions of the losing of the West as well.

Such shifts in historical and cultural perception have gained considerable momentum since A *Literary History of the American West* was published in 1987, the year, coincidentally, which saw the publication of such surprisingly popular, canon-war-inducing books as Alan Bloom's *The Closing of the American Mind* and E. D. Hirsch's Cultural Literacy. Now, as the update to the original *LHAW* is published, Hirsch has another book, *The Schools We Need: Why We Don't Have Them*, to add to the debate; and Lawrence W. Levine's *The Opening of the American Mind: Canons, Culture, and History* counters Bloom and extends the long-enduring culture wars of the 1990s.[2] So many new technological waves of knowing have swept over human society in the past decade that the alleged certainties and realities of Bloom and Hirsch and their allies in opposition to cultural pluralism and multiculturalism seem yearly less categorical, less secure.

Here at century's turning the information explosion blasts along with one new future-shockwave after another, causing futurists like Alvin Toffler and John Naisbitt, along with time travelers like Michael J. Fox, to look back to the future — old Wests become new. Western American literature and western American literary history, like American literature and American history at large, are now more interdisciplinary, more "transregional," and yes, more "virtual" than imagined ten years ago. Although resolution has not yet come and revolution is held off for the moment, backlash and incivility rear their ugly heads too often for any real social or civil comfort.

What is certain is that real and virtual Wests are countering and combining in fascinating ways with numerous ethnic Wests. The verdict is still out, long past the Civil War and during our own "civil wars," on whether ethnic nationalism, transnationalism or globalism will set the agenda for national interpretations of *e pluribus unum*, whether the United States is really one nation or many.

From a traditional point of view, the complexity of the current western literary scene is daunting. Twenty thousand years of oral literatures of indigenous peoples, widely unrecognized as "literature" for the past century, now are acknowledged alongside bilingual and electronic texts as demonstrating a level of literary history of profundity and significance.

The give-and-take of political correctness and of more encompassing culture wars and information wars has replaced the myths of Marshal Dillon and Dodge City, the scripts of cavalry-Indian conflicts, the skirmishes between ranchers and sodbusters. Those older notions of literary ethnicity as "other" and "exotic" to Anglos and those notions' attendant value systems are largely discussed now in terms of Euro-American hegemony, of cultural usurpation and appropriation.

The values of that hegemony, in ethnocentric assumptions used to identify, explain, and justify the American West (values oriented to Anglo demarcation points, to westering and to the ethnocentric notions of Manifest Destiny) are now undergoing such thorough revision as to be considered naïve by proponents of the "New History," the "New Literary History," the "New American Studies" and the "New Ethnicity." No longer does the emerging discipline of Ethnic Studies — united with Women's Studies and Environmental Studies in concerns about ethnicity, class, race, and the environment — still whine unheard in the academic wilderness.

New West issues of ethnicity, environmentalism and gender all invite reperceptions of old groups, old social and cultural dynamics. To think of the American West rather than American Wests, to accept a monocultural "place" as the exclusive domain of westering Anglo pioneers and settlers, of cowboys and ranchers, the groups that were thought to give sole essence and meaning to what they narrated and "staked out," is now more widely understood as reductive and distorted.

Both in history broadly construed and literary history more specifically interpreted, the role of minorities now works toward more relativistic understanding of the complexity of that idea known so generally but ethnocentrically as "the American West." "West of what?" comes the cry. West is "here and now" from indigenous perspectives. West is perhaps still west, although maybe urban and rural, from Anglo and African American perspectives. West, however, is east from Asian American perspectives. West is north from Mexican American perspectives. West is everywhere in the immediacy of the digitalized monitor. These new (but really old) multicultural and pluralistic perceptions of the American West view it as much more culturally laced and laminated, much more fluid and mutable, much less Euro-American than heretofore seen.

So the voices come, left, right, center, often in cacophony. Conservative voices still hold considerable sway, not only in national politics and in public and higher education but in the spectrum of views perceiving and reperceiving the West.

Legislative initiatives emanating largely from California, under the rubrics of "Proposition 187" and "Proposition 209" (the California Civil Rights Initiative) enter the fray with a new-old, almost mocking sneer, and seek to limit services to illegal immigrants, to redefine gender and ethnic preferences and affirmative action as reverse discrimination rather than remediation or reparation. Such "western" initiatives which promise soon to spread east prove anew that the conflicts about who shall lay power-wielding claim to America and the American West still exist and are building a new phase of national definition and debate about citizenship, civil rights, and ethnicity.

Well-intended western writers, long suffering from the eastern literary establishment's condescension and disparagement, cry out "Enough!" at new charges against politically incorrect western writings. Certain traditional western writers are moved to defend themselves, to answer back, to justify the older, more traditional assumptions of the western, by definitions of Anglo pioneer heroism.

Elmer Kelton, for example, among the much revered and canonized western novelists, insists that the "new historians" oftentimes either deliberately or unknowingly overlook positive elements in western history: "Where I find the most fault with many of today's revisionist writers [Kelton says] . . . is in their penchant for seeing our forebears' pioneering experience only in the darkest terms. Surely it must be possible to exalt the minority viewpoints of the Western experience without automatically condemning the white male pioneers to perdition. . . . They [new historians] classify our ancestors as greedy, racist villains . . . our white, Anglo-Saxon ancestors at least . . . with few if any redeeming qualities."[3]

Arguments also arise about the merits of literature by American Indians as opposed to literature about American Indians — or any other United States ethnic or racial group, for that matter. Western writers like Tony Hillerman are both championed and condemned for "cultural appropriation" or cultural "misappropriation," depending on varying audience responses from inside or outside ethnic perspectives.

On the eve of the twenty-first century, then, there are more Wests than the Anglo-Saxon pioneers could ever suspect in their fabled and journaled imagining. Fixed assumptions of a single Euro-American West are now infused with the "New History," "New American Studies," and new attitudes toward other cultures and other ethnicities. The literary history of American Wests is now rife with acknowledgment that American Indians, Mexican Americans, Asian Americans, African Americans and countless other ethnicities have earned a western place.

This explosion of ethnic, multicultural, and pluralistic literatures means that older notions of Anglo superiority must make serious accommodations. The culture wars both in academe and in United States society have replaced older "showdowns" as the central conflict in western American studies. Ethnic literature, American Indian literature, Chicano/Chicana literature, Asian American literature, African American literature now more than ever before extend the boundaries of the western American canon.

This compartmentalization of western American literature beyond the traditional geographical subregions should not be so much condemned as a hopeless balkanization of American culture as it should be understood. As Lawrence Levine asserts, the attempts of thirty years ago to reduce the American literary canon to "major" writers of America, or "masters" of American literature, and subsequently *Twelve American Writers* (1962) and then *Eight American Writers* (1963), were so increasingly exclusive as "anthologies" to ignore oral and folk literature, any and all black writers, and "[bypass] the entire southwestern United States as well as Native American and immigrant writers of any kind...."[4]

Philip Fisher traces the various transmutations and eclipses of regionalism in relation to myth, rhetoric and ethnicity in his attempts to describe the evolution of the New American Studies. And there is much to be drawn from his exposition for the understanding of both western American studies and western American literary history, just as there is in Philip Rahv's provocative dichotomy of thirty years ago whereby all American writers were divided into palefaces and redskins. More recently, Toni Morrison in her discussions of the Africanist presence in American literature makes a similar point about the transformation of race into image and metaphor: "It is no accident and no mistake that immigrant populations (and much immigrant literature) understood their 'Americanness' as an opposition to the resident black population. Race, in fact, now functions as a metaphor so necessary to the construction of Americanness that it rivals the old pseudo-scientific and class-informed racisms whose dynamics we are more used to deciphering."[5]

According to Fisher, the claim for pluralism in American culture is long-standing and resistant to myth or ideology. Where the quest for pluralism resides is in what Fisher calls the "episodes of regionalism" in American culture whereby ethnicity and place enrich each other. Historically, the nation oscillates between the notion of itself as a single unified order and as a number of weakly joined districts. At times this disunity is along geographical lines. Abraham Lincoln, says Fisher, reconciled some of this through his own self-made myth, as did railroads and the telegraph as conquerors of a place grown too large for the earlier Federalist unity of Washington and Jefferson. Similarly, an American way of life, "of Singer sewing machines, Coca-Cola, Remington rifles, and Ford Model Ts" has unified regions around mass-produced goods rather than the right to vote or property ownership.[6]

When regionalism became "ethnic" in the early twentieth century as a result of massive immigration, Fisher asserts that

> The local color was not that of climates and regions but of what are called metaphorically, hyphenated Americans: Jewish Americans, Italian Americans, Irish Americans, WASPS, and Chinese Americans, Poles, Swedes, and Russians. It was a regionalism of languages, folk customs, humor, music, and beliefs set over against the pull of what came to be called Americanization.[7]

The "regionalism" now holding sway in America, insists Fisher, is the regionalism of gender and race. However, says Fisher, this current regionalism of ethnicity must be seen as playing off "a central technological culture made up of the new media — television and film — but also against the older forces of education and mass representation."[8] The next phase of racial and ethnic regionalism, although Fisher does not explicitly advance it, is easy to surmise without too much extrapolation: virtual reality become virtual ethnicity.

In a knowledge-based, technocratic, electronic, worldwide web of satellite television transmission across the global village, "cultures" (and this is meant in the broadest sense of cohering, self-identified units) are no longer confined to the physical place of older identities. Old designations of East/West, North/South, rural/urban, sophisticated/countrified all reconstitute and realign themselves as readily as the Pentium or any other chip will allow. The transcendence of ethnicity is easily seen in countless startling new ways within the worlds of advertising, publicity, and commerce as "target audiences" are colored in.

More people in Chicago and New York, probably, subscribe to magazines like *Arizona Highways* and *New Mexico* than do residents of those states. And the exact real and virtual whereabouts of Texas and California — on television, in movies, and in national politics — becomes ever more blurred and equivocal. There are more cowboys in Ted Turner's television programming and more head of buffalo on the Turner/Fonda ranches than in the prototypic "real" West.

Television, movies, popculture in general have contributed greatly to the demise of the "real" and the rise of the "virtual" West. Computers and the new software and hardware of virtual reality promise to abolish the strictly Anglicized West — or laminate it with alternatives. In his discussions of the social, technological, and theoretical ramifications of the "electronic word," Richard Lanham is most instructive.

To reperceive ethnicity or the ethnicity of place in the context of the literary history of the American West, as part and parcel of a widening inclusion of perceptions, of voices and the expression of those voices, is not any different, really, than inviting a democratization of the West and the history of westering. Reperceiving western American literature in this way is analogous to Lanham's insistence that we are involved in a systemic change from specialized inquiry to general thinking.[9]

To follow Lanham's idealized "experimental humanism" model of curriculum change into the context of reperceiving the literary history of the American West is to see the rich, generalized spectrum, an interactive and comparative spectrum of ethnicity, class, gender, ecology, geology, geography, the arts, the sciences, the social sciences all interacting — at times hierarchical, at times not, but simultaneously democratic, dialectical, and dialogic.

Among literary critics, Gerald Graff advocates a reconciliation of opposites by means of the teaching of the processes of disagreement —

whether cultural or textual. His argument may be transferred to the reperceiving of the literary history of the American West.[10]

Western American historian Glenda Riley is only one of several new scholars who seek to broaden perspectives and approaches. Her advocacy of a more inclusive conceptualization of the American West involves a thoroughgoing reperception: "One [approach] is to rethink historical categories entirely, so that we teach and write about families, power relationships, violence, and perhaps global interactions.... Another possibility...is to study groups of people at their intersection with the intention of revealing and analyzing their various viewpoints."[11]

American Indian historian Alfonso Ortiz in "Indian/White Relations: A View from the Other Side of the 'Frontier,'" in addition to redefining "civilization," "savagism," "Manifest Destiny," and "wilderness," makes a forceful argument for not only reperceiving but renaming times and places and events in the American Wests from Indian points of view.

> The point to all of these objections to standard historical categories, of course, is that they are all self-serving, because what you get depends on who is in charge of defining these terms. As terms, they have always been defined by persons from the East, facing westward. And of course these people defining the terms have always put themselves on the civilized, Christian, and law-abiding side of the line. Indeed, when we contemplate how Indian people have been defined in American history, as uncouth, devil-worshipping savages who had no proper notions of law or government and who, moreover, kept putting themselves on the wrong side of the frontier, one has to wonder just how they managed to survive during the thousands of years before Europeans came over to rescue them from their miserable condition.[12]

Some of the essays found in this 1997 update are best read, then, in the vein of "Counterviews and Challenges" to more traditional, loosened but still ensconced perceptions of the West. Readers, regardless of ethnicity, must all attempt to provide answers for the now pervasive but still nagging question, "Whose West?" "Where West?" Now, in the past, and in the next century? Reperceptions of western literary history argue for a more fully and accurately perceived West—something from "the other side of the frontier," something bolder in both its real and virtual being and significance than the Anglo-European ethnocentric assumptions and definitions.

Notwithstanding the profound issues of the relativity of truth and the relativity of otherness, of virtual reality versus real reality, of the intersections of ethnicity with race and place, we know one thing for certain: there were and are many Wests and many stories and accounts of them. The whole story, the whole varied fabric depends on weaving together all the strands. Only then will the figure in the carpet come into focus.

Notes

1. Ronald Takaki, *A Different Mirror: A History of Multicultural America* (Boston: Little Brown, 1993), 17.

2. For a contextual discussion of the "catalyst" roles of Bloom and Hirsch in ensuing debates on multiculturalism, see Rick Simonson and Scott Walker, "Introduction," *The Graywolf Annual Five: Multi-cultural Literacy* (St. Paul: Graywolf Press, 1988), ix-xv. See also, E.D. Hirsch, *The Schools We Need: Why We Don't Have Them* (New York: Doubleday, 1996); Lawrence W. Levine, *The Opening of the American Mind: Canons, Culture, and History* (Boston: Beacon Press, 1996).

3. Elmer Kelton, "Politically Correct or Historically Correct?" *The Roundup Magazine*, 1 (September-October 1993): 5.

4. Levine, *The Opening of the American Mind*, p. 95. See also Gerald W. Haslam, *Many Californias: Literature from the Golden State* (Reno: University of Nevada Press, 1991), pp. 361-372, as exemplary of multicultural infusion.

5. See Philip Fisher, *The New American Studies* (Berkeley: University of California Press, 1991). See also Philip Fisher, "American Literary and Cultural Studies Since the Civil War," *Redrawing the Boundaries: The Transformation of English and American Literary Studies*, Stephen Greenblatt and Giles Gunn, eds. (New York: MLA, 1992), pp. 232-250. Also see Toni Morrison, *Playing in the Dark: Whiteness and the Literary Imagination* (New York: Vintage Books, 1993), p. 47. For Philip Rahv's essay, "Palefaces and Redskins," see *Image and Idea: Twenty Essays on Literary Themes* (New York: New Directions, 1957), pp. 1-7.

6. Philip Fisher, "American Literary and Cultural Studies Since the Civil War," 241.

7. Ibid.

8. Ibid., 242.

9. See Chapter Four in Richard Lanham's *The Electronic Word: Democracy, Technology, and the Arts* (Chicago: University of Chicago Press, 1993).

10. See Gerald Graff, *Professing Literature* (Chicago: University of Chicago Press, 1987). Also see Paul Berman, ed., *Debating P.C.* (New York: Dell, 1992), p. 26.

11. Glenda Riley, "Writing, Teaching and Recreating Western History Through Intersection and Viewpoints," *Pacific Historical Review*, 62 (August 1993): 340.

12. Alfonso Ortiz, "Indian/White Relations: A View from the Other Side of the 'Frontier,'" *Indians In American History*, Frederick W. Hoxie, ed. (Wheeling Illinois: Harlan Davidson, Inc., 1988), p. 8.

Kathleen A. Boardman

Western American Literature and The Canon

"From Western Lit to Westerns As Lit." Under this 1988 headline, *Wall Street Journal* writer David Brooks railed against the decline of western civilization and the university as we know it: trendy college courses and misguided scholarship, he said, were abandoning the great books of western civilization in favor of pop culture and trash fiction. The degeneration had progressed so far that well-known scholars were presiding over courses in cowboy lit. The short article took a superficial and conservative stance toward the canon controversy that has occupied academics and many members of the general public for some thirty years. But the headline caught on: a few years later, Richard Lanham, Gerald Graff, and other prominent scholars at a national conference on education and the canon also used "western lit or westerns as lit" to stand for an opposition between high culture and popular culture and between canonical and noncanonical writing (Lanham 34; Graff 51). In discussing the controversies of canon formation, these writers and speakers carefully considered the interests of women, diverse ethnic groups, and members of various social classes. Yet they did not examine "western lit or westerns as lit" because it never occurred to them that it might touch a nerve with anyone.

In the either-or world captured by this phrase, western American literature disappears. In this world, "western lit" is not Cather, Stegner, and Waters, nor is it Silko, Abbey, and Rivera. It's Virgil, Shakespeare, and Milton—or perhaps Hawthorne, Emerson, and Faulkner if the

44

American canon is to be the focus. At the other extreme, the western writer (someone who lives in or writes about the American West) collapses into the western writer (someone who writes cowboy stories). In the face of this dichotomy, readers and writers of western American literature can either dust off our "born to be misunderstood" placards or examine the ways we have participated — and do participate — in reconceptualizing literary canons. For example, we do not have to accept the either-or choices offered by the canon debate. We might point out that the "western lit/westerns-as-lit" dichotomy does not represent a choice between "high standards" and "anything goes." Rather, it represents no choice at all, for both so-called alternatives arise out of a traditional assumption that western culture has moved ever westward, pushing away at one frontier after another: that canonical works galvanize and perpetuate this movement and popular works exploit it.

Underrepresented in the traditional "closed" canon (shown in anthology contents, syllabi and curricula, and topics of scholarly articles), the American West has had mixed success in newer, expanded canons. In many anthologies and curricula, representation by western women and non-Anglo writers has improved somewhat, but often their western backgrounds and topics are ignored. This tells us that any reconceptualization of the canon must be accompanied by a continuing reimagining of the West. Traditionally the West has represented the frontier, the self-reliant white male hero, the myth of virgin land and the fresh start, the safety valve for illiterates and misfits, the last gasp of the American Dream and the backwater of the American mainstream; this shallow set of stories has made it difficult for many critics to visualize works of western American literature as part of either a traditional closed canon or a postmodern open canon. As a new, raw, uncultured area (its ancient peoples ignored) the West could not produce works that met the standards of the eastern literary establishment; as the master narrative of the final frontier (its many shifting boundaries and multiple dreams overlooked), western American literature represents something of an embarrassment to revisionist multiculturalists.

The recent national discussions of canon and canonicity represent a challenge for the study of western American literature; any attempt to define or make a space for the writing of the American West needs to take into account these broader issues. As western American writers, readers, and scholars respond to the American literary canon, what assumptions are we authorizing? What challenges do we face as scholarship and pedagogy lead to a canon of western American writing? What values underlie our choices of texts, approaches, and strategies for inclusion in a larger American canon? When we use canonicity as a way of legitimizing western American writing and our study of it, do we also risk essentializing a body of work or freezing a method of study? Do we need to choose between excellence and inclusiveness, coherence and diversity, aesthetic qualities and cultural context? Informal conversations with colleagues at conferences suggest our continuing ambivalence about canon: we express annoyance that the West is still underrepresented in the expanded canons and new anthologies but worry that whenever we make up a list of "best books to teach" or "must-reads" we are engaging in canonizing activity.

* * *

The *Wall Street Journal* article should remind us that "canon" is not the esoteric topic of a priestly class of English professors debating the contents of their scriptures. The canon controversy has continued for so long because it has practical consequences — in the classroom, in the curriculum, in the library, at the political rally, in the profession. What writings will be taught? Which will be readily available to readers? Which will become common topics of conversation and which will be forgotten? Who has the power to decide these things? Canon preservers have been as eager as canon revisers to direct their persuasive appeals to the general public. In fact, the discussions over the nature and contents of the literary canon, common on campuses since the sixties, sprang to life again in the eighties when E. D. Hirsch's *Cultural Literacy* appeared with its argument that "every American needs to know" a mainstream cultural canon. Even so-called "canon busters" — certain African-Americanists, feminists, and political Leftists who have been troubled by the hierarchy and exclusion that any canon represents — have not turned away from the discussion. To ignore canon issues means to abandon the field to others, for the requirements of syllabi, anthologies, and journals make some canonizing inevitable.

As Carey Kaplan and Ellen Cronan Rose have suggested, the most recent battle over canon has been primarily a contest for the attention of the common reader, and thus it is important for teaching. Gerald Graff agrees that students should be enabled to join in on the canon conflicts themselves, not just study the results:

> Urging us to cut out the nonsense and get back to "just" reading
> good books evades what is centrally at issue in the conflict over the
> canon: What does it mean to "read" a text? What does it mean to
> call a book "great"?...Reading always takes place in a context of
> interests, and those interests vary from reader to reader and culture
> to culture....No text, however eloquent, interprets and teaches
> itself. (59)

Jan Gorak remarks that canon has been viewed as a model and guide
for production of works of art (x); that is, writers as well as readers,
students, and teachers have a stake in the debates. Paul Lauter, long
an advocate of an inclusive canon, also points to political and professional implications: "Debating the canon turns out to be a symbolic
way of arguing a variety of other social and political issues — basically,
who has power and how it is exercised" because "defining what is 'central' and what is 'marginal,' a basic function of canonization, will itself
help decide who studies, who teaches, and who has power in determining priorities in American colleges" (*Canons and Contexts* ix, x).
More is at stake, though, than professional turf: when we talk about
canons, we are talking about the survival of knowledge. This may
sound like a conservative's argument, but it comes from Lauter. If we
agree, he says, that knowledge becomes accessible to us primarily
through narrative (that stories shape us), then we must be concerned
with "what of human knowledge a particular set of narratives — a
canon or a historical construct — encodes, makes accessible — or
obscures" ("Literatures of America" 51).

Although they differ deeply in their conceptions of society, educational institutions, and literary study, all but the most reactionary and
polemical debaters seem to agree that "the process of canon formation
and reformation is an organic and ongoing process" (Kaplan and Rose
xix). Certainly they disagree about the extent of this reformation.
Canon preservers generally admit that a few works may move in and out
of the canon, that worthy critics might disagree about some of the works
to be included, and that new works may be added from time to time. But
they don't want to change the basic standards for admission: canonical
works are classics that withstand the test of time. If in doubt, we should
opt for stability — to achieve some cultural common ground, to preserve
and encourage artistic quality, or to draw readers' attention to the best
that has been written. The canon serves as a measuring rod or standard,

as a map with the center clearly marked, or as a treasury that can be utilized by a community or an individual.

Canon revisers object to the elitism of "an ossified canon" (Kaplan and Rose xvii) of "timeless 'classics' that institutionalize the world they already control" (9). They insist that we continually examine not only the canon's contents but the cultural values and power structures on which that canon is based. Over the years, the scholarship of canon revisers has made available the work of "forgotten" writers, often minorities and women, who did not make it into the traditional canon because their strengths did not match the values of the canonizers. Focusing on culture — or context — revisers also cast a spotlight on uncanonized literary traditions and trace the popularity of works that have been neglected. The canon visualized by revisers is not a museum but a gallery, not a set of scriptures but a conversation. At its best, it is "the aesthetic and cultural embodiment of a given time continuously scrutinized" (Kaplan and Rose 4). Finally, those who see canons as "cultural capital" argue that both canon preservers and canon challengers miss the point of the debate: the literary syllabus constitutes "a kind of knowledge-capital whose possession can be displayed upon request and which thereby entitles its possessor to the cultural rewards of the well-educated person" (Guillory ix). Both open and closed canons function this way.

The expansion of the American canon has created anxiety as well as vitality. Right now, consensus and continuity are increasingly appealing, particularly for those who worry about fragmentation in literary scholarship. The new American literary histories of the eighties represent in part a response to these concerns. On the other hand, movements toward "reconciliation and consolidation" worry critics like Annette Kolodny, who says that "the zeal to assert common ground could have the impact of abbreviating the mapping of alternative landscapes" (294). Literary historian Emory Elliott notes a "dialogic opposition" between "the attempt to unify, to provide coherence, organization, and continuity" and "divergent or centrifugal impulses pulling away from the center toward plurality of method and diversity of authors and texts" (617). Even the *Heath Anthology of American Literature* (Lauter, ed.), describing itself as "an anthology of unprecedented richness, one which realizes the goal of an expanded American canon," assures readers that it offers both continuity and diversity in an "intermingling of unfamiliar and traditional literary voices."

Those of us interested in western American literature's canon must also deal with these contrary impulses toward common ground and alternative landscapes. Westerners have entered the discussions of a transforming canon from several different directions which can generally be divided into four approaches or stances toward canon; they overlap somewhat, but each identifies the literary American West differently and entails its own assumptions about what a canon represents. The tensions between continuity and diversity, definition and expansion, are reflected in these positions; so is the interplay between notions of western American canon and American literary canon. The marginalist and traditionalist stances emphasize coherence, identity, and continuity; the other two stances, here labeled difference and diversity, value multiplicity, inclusiveness, and defamiliarization. Traditionalist and difference stances are most interesting for their claims about the place of western American literature in an American canon, while marginalist and diversity approaches do more to conceptualize a western American canon. Although each of these stances presents its own difficulties, the interactions among these positions have enriched canon discussion in the American West.

Marginalists

The marginalist's or outsider's perspective—that eastern literary tastemakers and canonizers have misunderstood and unfairly excluded western American literature—has long been appealing to supporters of regional literatures. While resisting their placement at the edges of canon, marginalists also try to exploit the advantages of that position. In a recent critical essay, Glen Love hints at an outsiders' literary tradition when he refers to the "long line of western writers who saw their work ignored and devalued by metropolitan critics" (199). In a 1990 newspaper review, Wallace Stegner expresses delight in the quality of new western writing but disdain for the critical establishment: "So far, I can't think of a nationally influential critic who reads western writing in the spirit of those who wrote it, and judges them according to their intentions" (*Bluebird* 141). In his often-quoted manifesto that launched the first issue of *Western American Literature* in 1966, J. Golden Taylor proclaims that "the prevailing critical condescension toward Western literature is as notoriously uninformed and prejudiced as it is supercilious" (3).

The first step in informing the uninformed, according to Taylor, is to point out the difference between western American literature and the western. First exploited by easterners writing "westerns," the West has been dismissed, despite its "rich and diverse culture," as the home of horse opera. Taylor urges westerners to set aside defensiveness and get busy, for "if the genuinely good literature of our region is ever to be recognized and taken seriously at home or in the world at large, it must be read and critically assessed by knowledgeable scholars familiar with the world it represents" (3). Taylor's manifesto derives its energy from its insistence that ignorant eastern critics need to be shown something; but his emphasis is on what westerners should do for themselves. It is as important that the American West respect its literature as that the world respect it; the critical scholarship must be done by people who know the land, culture, and language represented in the writing.

While not questioning the universality of standards for goodness, Taylor suggests that the goodness of a piece of writing is not self-evident to everyone with literary taste or experience; it must be revealed in western writing by people who understand the western geographical and cultural context as well as literary standards. The marginalist position, with its proclamation that easterners set the standards and make the canonical choices, might conceivably have gone on to proclaim a contingency of values: your idea of what's good is just different from ours. But it does not. Marginalists resist not the traditional canonical standards but the application of them. Their vision is of a continuity broken through no fault of their own; their role is to insist on legitimacy and visibility for the literature they value. Thus, the marginalist seeks to legitimate western literature and its study by creating an outsiders' canon. In Stegner's words, "We'll have a solid western tradition sooner if we pay attention to its major achievements and bring them to general notice" (*Conversations* 143). "While appreciating a wide variety of world literatures," Taylor asserts, "we may with good-humored inflexibility insist upon the legitimacy of studying our own" (4).

Like most groups who have recently identified themselves as marginalized, western American marginalists are pulled in two directions: the conviction that their material ought to have wider recognition and pleasure in the sense of identity that outsider status confers. Adding to this ambivalence, western American canon building entails its own form of exclusion. Establishing a canon that provides western identity and visibility involves finding, or constructing, common and distinctive characteristics of western literary works: what's western about western literature, and which western American works are good enough to deserve stature? As a western American canon emerges from the work of scholars that Taylor, Stegner, and the Western Literature Association were calling for, how do we assure ourselves that it does not represent the same sorts of gaps and marginalizing processes that marginalists can so easily see in the American canon?

Western American Literature has nurtured a western American canon that has some stability and also some flexibility: it encloses its canonical works and authors, but the gate is not locked. A look at the tables of contents of the journal's thirty years shows us that Willa Cather is by far the most written-about author in that publication, with nearly forty articles and two special issues devoted to her works. Now firmly situated in an expanded American canon, Cather is also identified as a western regionalist, as a woman, and as an author who valued high art and western civilization. The next group, with between eight and fifteen articles devoted to each, includes Edward Abbey, Walter Van Tilburg Clark, Hamlin Garland, Robinson Jeffers, Jack London, Frank Norris, Gary Snyder, Wallace Stegner, and Mark Twain. The membership of this de facto canon is rounded out with the authors who are the subjects of four or more articles each: Mary Austin, Thomas Berger, James Fenimore Cooper, Stephen Crane, H. L. Davis, Thomas Hornsby Ferril, Vardis Fisher, A. B. Guthrie, Bret Harte, Ernest Hemingway, Washington Irving, Norman Maclean, Frederick Manfred, Larry McMurtry, John Neihardt, Mari Sandoz, Jack Schaefer, Jean Stafford, Frank Waters, and Owen Wister. Of course, a journal's table of contents is a product of negotiations between editors and contributors. This list does not show what sorts of manuscripts were submitted, nor can it report on gaps the editors would have liked to fill with articles that were never submitted, but it does give a general view of the authors whom scholars and editors thought were worthwhile over a thirty-year period.

Over a generation, preferences and visions change. Despite Taylor's initial squeamishness, there have been a number of articles exploring the formula western novel and western movies. Articles on nature and environmental writing, on critical approaches, and on "rediscovered" writers have become more frequent. While some concern has been expressed that the old standbys of the western American canon have lately been neglected as canon expansion has gotten underway even at the regional level, *Western American Literature* contents indicate that this is generally not the case. While no article devoted entirely to Vardis

Fisher has appeared since 1970, and nothing on Norris, Clark, or Sandoz since the mid-eighties, scholars published on Garland, Guthrie, Jeffers, London, Waters, and others in the late eighties and early nineties. Even Thomas Berger, who might understandably have been ignored by westerners in the past ten years, was discussed in two articles in 1988. During the same time period, the Boise State University Western Writers Series, under the editorship of James Maguire and Wayne Chatterton, has taken an inclusive approach with monographs on more than 120 western authors. James Work's recent anthology, *Prose and Poetry of the American West*, is necessarily more selective. The introduction uses marginalist rhetoric, but Work presents his choices as a personal canon, a "gallery" of literature *he* considers "of lasting interest and artistic value" (xii), and he acknowledges that readers may well have other favorites.

Noting that many marginalized literatures have lately become fashionable and that "marginalization is power," Ian Marshall has playfully suggested that western American literature's marginal position should draw the interest of mainstream scholars:

> Canons and aesthetic criteria and critical practices are being re-evaluated and to some extent replaced, so it has become commonplace to argue on behalf of an author or work or standard or practice precisely *because* it has been overlooked in some way.... We who argue that western literature deserves more attention have joined the academic chorus of marginalized voices, along with women, Chicanos, African-Americans, Native Americans, Canadians, and so on. (232-233)

But the opening of the American canon to marginalized literatures has not meant inclusion for many works of the marginalists' western American canon. The two-volume *HarperCollins' American Literature* (1994), which aims to cover every recognized classic and celebrate diversity, does have twenty westerners out of some 250 selections, but no western literary classics. This latest slighting may have occurred because many works of this marginalized canon are written by white men — mainstream writers from the point of view of most marginalized groups.

It's a bitter double-bind, but one that might have been predicted. Many who have argued that western American literature is neglected also agree that if it were seen truly, it would be part of the American canonical tradition — thus claiming both marginalization and continuity. Stegner, for example, declares, "You achieve stature only by being good enough to deserve it, by forcing even the contemptuous and indifferent to pay attention" (*Bluebird* 138). But other marginalized groups point out that they have been ignored because they don't fit the tradition at all, that their standards for "good enough" are not lower than the mainstream's but different. Those westerners who have traditionally been excluded because of race, class, sexual orientation, ethnicity, or gender do not see regional marginalization as their main problem. In fact, they draw attention to their own marginalization *within* western American literature. Elizabeth Cook-Lynn says that the literature traditionally defined as western "simply leaves Indians out of it as any kind of ongoing contributors":

> I don't read the literature of the "American West" either for pleasure or instruction. If I read it at all it is out of obligation, that is, as a scholar I *must* read certain texts, and the works of many writers and thinkers who influence our times. The difficulties which they present to me as a reader and as a writer are enormous. . . . The truth is I don't see many real Indians in the works of American Western fiction writers, even today. (Morris 35-36)

Although the claim of being unfairly neglected by the literary establishment still makes for a rousing polemic, it is no longer possible for western American literature to find an identity as alienated outsider and claim moral high ground as a victim of exclusion. As the spotlight falls upon marginalized groups and works, it has also become necessary to examine the marginalizing activities implicit within western American literature itself — and many marginalists have joined in this task. At the same time, our current confidence that western literature can be seen as a worthy and vital body of work with a literary tradition of its own owes a good deal to the marginalist position.

Traditionalists

The traditionalist position outlined here has nothing to do with reaffirming a closed canon or unchanging Great Tradition; most western traditionalists view canon as a dynamic process rather than an ossified list.

Like the marginalists, traditionalists are annoyed that "where literary achievement is concerned, writers in the West may be shunned as 'regionalists,' their very real experiences — in one culture, experiences from a living past that is several thousand years old — denied access to universality" (Blackburn 52). This "universality" is a key concern for traditionalists, who generally seem more active than marginalists in seeking connections between western American literature and the American canon. The key element of the traditionalist position is that continuity is the basis for canon: from this perspective, western American literature is an important part of *the* American literary tradition, whether it "extends," "transforms," or "critiques" it. Some traditionalists take a "great books" approach to canon; they do not seriously challenge either the criteria for judging those great books or the power implicit in canon-making. Others look at myth or big ideas as sources of coherence for canon: using such traditional concepts as "the frontier," traditionalists try to open them for dialogue with formerly excluded groups — but without giving up the unifying force that the concepts represent.

Alexander Blackburn provides an example of the first traditionalist position: he sees a western renaissance occurring along the same lines as the American Renaissance and the Southern Renaissance. While making few claims for the early writing of the West, he insists that many post-1930s works are mature and worthy of canon status:

> The distinguishing sign of the modern, serious, post-romantic West is precisely that recognition [that "we" lost the West], and an attempt to "win" the area truly — to be worthy of it. In other words, a certain tragic vision of history is necessary for literary maturity and is suggested when the writing, along with a revised awareness of history, evokes certain deeper, positive, and universal values. (60)

Blackburn's declaration of the West's literary coming-of-age follows the pattern established by earlier scholarly work on the Southern Renaissance. Tension, transformation, and a tragic sense are key characteristics of both the South's and the West's best work — in fact, of the best American work. Depth and universality are also important criteria. Blackburn's standards of literary maturity and quality fit those of aesthetic formalism, and in this passage he also identifies the frontier myth as the source of tragic vision that is necessary in good literary work. He does not examine those aesthetic criteria with western literature in mind, but he assures us that certain western writings meet the criteria. While refusing to name a western American canon, Blackburn outlines what should be covered in a book on the western renaissance: five major writers (Waters, Clark, Jeffers, Stegner, Abbey), or fifteen "masters," or a hundred masterful writers, or eleven classic works. These authors and works fit the literary tradition already embodied in a traditional American canon.

A second traditionalist position promises to provide coherence to efforts to open the canon, to help us see "an underlying unity in our diversity" (Mogen 29). David Mogen, Mark Busby, and Paul Bryant, in their collection *The Frontier Experience and the American Dream*, claim that "the frontier idea structures a Great Tradition in American literature" (8). A careful study of the many versions of and reactions to this "national frontier mythology" (Mogen 15) would do away with highbrow-lowbrow distinctions and allow for the integration of regional, ethnic, and women's writings into a distinctive, myth-based American literary canon. With a nod to the Turner thesis, the authors say that "the existence of a frontier of settlement, and of unsettled and even unknown lands beyond, has generated in the American literary imagination a set of images, attitudes, and assumptions that have shaped our literature into a peculiarly American mold" (3).

Mogen, Busby, and Bryant might be expected to embrace the American West as a rich site of dialogue on the frontier experience: western American literature, including writings by women and minorities who are critical of frontier attitudes, is crucial for an understanding of frontier myth. Yet the western American writing that enters Mogen's Great Tradition may have to accept relabeling as "frontier literature." Although Mogen notes that "existing anthologies do *not* adequately represent the best Western writing" (18), he takes a further step that may make some westerners uncomfortable. Because of the perennial difficulty in defining "the West," he proposes that we erase western literature's identity as the writing produced in a geographical region: "'the West' in American culture signifies a region located in history and in the imagination as well as in geography" (18), and every American region has had its own frontier. So western writing cannot expect to be included in the Great Tradition just because many people associate the frontier with the trans-Mississippi West. If it is included, it will be identified by the approach(es) it takes to the myth: the "West" of the imagination takes priority over the place we call the West.

This frontier approach to canon draws attention to a traditional American theme as a lightning rod for discussion among diverse groups, many of whom "enter the dialogue of American literature to portray the frontier experience from their perspective as threatening and exclusive" (Mogen 6). It promises canon expansion with no loss of coherence:

> Understanding the dialectical and dialogical nature of this literary tradition will help open up the literary canon, by revealing how different regions, ethnic groups, classes, and genders have adapted frontier archetypes and enriched the American Dream.... Their literature reveals that it too has been greatly affected by the same symbolic structures and images, though often in an inverted way. (5-6)

It sounds like a fascinating conversation, and indeed the oppositional nature of the dialogue leads to some absorbing essays in this collection. Mick McAllister, for example, explores the differences between the linearity of the mainstream "westering" narratives and the circularity of tribal stories about returning home. He complicates the comparison by pointing out that this is not an Indians-versus-Anglos distinction: many folktales of European origin also end with the adventurer's return home. Melody Graulich describes how women are outsiders to the frontier myth — both in being prevented from entering a "man's world" and in the trivialization of the domestic and other activities in which women regularly engaged.

Unfortunately, there is a problem with the frontier dialogue: the formerly excluded groups, although invited to participate all they want, are (or have been) constrained to discuss a topic chosen by someone else. Women and various ethnic groups are the "other," and their literature is characterized as an "inversion" of the dominant myth, or as a response to it. This amounts to "showing that America's cultural and ethnic minorities helped to shape the very literary and cultural canon that has effectively marginalized or excluded them... [thus] in effect rewriting the American literary tradition in a way that *reifies*, rather than reconstructs... the traditional literary canon" (Verhoeven xvi). So although the language is that of canon expansion and reconstruction, the project of *The Frontier Experience and the American Dream* is traditional.

This dilemma is typical of many canon-related projects which bring in outsiders but do not reconceptualize canon itself. Regardless of the amount of response and critical comment that is elicited by these sincere attempts at common ground, the experience of one powerful group of Americans sets the terms of the dialogue and shapes the terms of the canon. Mogen, Busby, and Bryant emphasize that they are not claiming the frontier myth as the "only significant context for an understanding of American literature" (5). But the insistence on a central theme, particularly when that theme is the traditional frontier or the flight into the wilderness, has a totalizing effect. We can see this in Mogen's language as he invites us to visualize "the shape of the overriding cultural mythology that incorporates our historical, regional, and personal mythologies" (29). In struggling toward the goal of continuity, traditionalists need to find a way to move beyond disclaimers ("there are other ways to do this"). One possibility might be to substitute a comparative approach for the "overriding cultural mythology" approach: perhaps the dialogue between peoples can begin at the level of myth encountering myth, or story overlapping story.

Difference and the Challengers

Like the traditionalists, the western American critics whom I call the challengers are primarily interested in the inclusion of western American literature in the American canon. Like the marginalists, the challengers point out distinctive qualities of western writing. But instead of insisting that it's just as good as canonized works, or that it continues the same myth or treats similar themes, challengers argue that the literature of the West arises from a different consciousness, or that it is expressed in different forms, or that it expresses uniquely western attitudes. Any canon, then, that does not substantially recognize western American works is unrepresentative: these literary works have perspectives that are indispensable for an expanding canon.

In *New Ground*, A. Carl Bredahl challenges the American canon: "I do not desire to see noncanonical works simply brought into the canon, an action that would only reinforce the power of those defining the canon," he says. "Rather, I would like to see the canon broken open by imaginations that violate the assumptions built into the whole idea of a canon" (ix). This is the rhetoric of the canon buster. But the argument Bredahl develops is that of a canon reviser. He asserts that the western

American literary imagination, arising from repeated encounters with western landscape, resists enclosure and values surface, and that these preferences place western works in direct opposition to the values currently expressed in the canon: enclosure and depth. While "works accepted into the traditional literary canon have in common a preoccupation with enclosure based upon discomfort with the openness of space" (147), says Bredahl, "what characterizes the noncanonical imagination is a rejection of eastern enclosures, both physical and mental, and a struggle to narrate the fascination with space and to thereby accept and draw upon the possibilities of wilderness" (156). This imagination is expressed not only in subject matter and attitude but in new forms, like the "divided narrative." Although a typical eastern response to these western narratives is that "something in the work does not come up to the expectations or standards of canonical narrative" (147), these so-called failures are really strengths by western standards.

Thus the West is not behind the East — still too romantic, still too realistic, still too optimistic. It's different from the East. The provinces are not "coming of age" — they represent a different imagination: "If we mistakenly assume that the traditional canon, as maintained in college reading lists and anthologies from the major eastern publishers, fully describes the American imagination, we miss a significant aspect of our culture" (48). This is a typical argument for inclusion. But Bredahl pushes further by asserting that the canon should break open for a body of work that will offer it a "healthy corrective." Because it respects surfaces "of land and of those whose lives are interdependent with it" (48), the western imagination is less susceptible than the traditionally canonical imagination to "postmodern despair" or "modern alienation" (147). It is also more likely to create a new story of new relationships between human beings and their "social and physical ecosystems" (147). Thus, by expanding to include western American literature, the canon can be not only more representative but also healthier, more constructive, and more responsive to environmental issues. Finally, Bredahl uses the arguments of difference to reconceptualize canon itself. The traditional canon is conceived as an enclosure, providing order and guidance but negating the imaginative demands of space. Bredahl asks us to conceive of a canon that offers disclosure rather than definition, possibility rather than protection, expansion rather than preservation.

The reconceptualization of canon that Bredahl calls for has been occurring for some time now, in the many theoretical and philosophical discussions accompanying the creation of new anthologies, literary histories, and curricula. Bredahl's version of the challenger's argument is that because literature has to do with imagination, form, and style, canon revisers must remember to consider differences at these levels, not just in the demographics of race, gender, and class. As Paul Lauter points out, when critics ask of an author's stories "questions drawn from other literary contexts" the author may be "portrayed as engaging despite her formal shortcomings, rather than seen as important because of her formal innovations" (*Redefining* 28). Bredahl asks us to ask the right questions about western American literature. Yet to make his argument, he has to bypass difference and multiplicity at the regional level and theorize one western imagination rather than many; he limits the definition of western American literature in order to make claims about a western imagination. California native Maxine Hong Kingston, with a postmodernist's attitude toward surfaces, might be annoyed to find she lacked a "western imagination." Although Bredahl's approach to canon focuses on the impact of land—physical surface—rather than myth, it still owes something to the idea of frontier which structures many traditional approaches. The western imagination, he says, is interested in "exploration of a continually opening frontier" rather than with "mapping out and taming the land" (156).

Bredahl's interest in land *as* land in the West echoes many recent attempts to define western American literature in terms of its difference from and necessity to the American canon. Of course, a sense of place is important in defining any regional literature simply because the literature is identified by place rather than something else, like ethnicity. The general argument is that because of the sparse population, dramatic land forms, extremes of climate and natural phenomena, and land-based economy of much of the West, nature plays a larger role in the literature of the West than it does in other literatures: western authors express a sense of place; they pay more attention to the particulars of natural setting; they are more nature-oriented and even environmentally aware. Tim Poland perceives that "in much western literature, the usual relationship between character and landscape is inverted. Rather than a landscape that exists as setting for human action and is imprinted with human qualities, the landscape in much western writing functions more like a character in itself and imprints on the human characters its own qualities" (197-198). This vision, argues Poland, is a healthy corrective to the anthropocentrism that generally dominates our consciousness

59

and interferes with our relationship to the world. Glen Love refers to "the literature of the American West, where nature continues to occupy a much larger place than it appears to in the eastern and urban imagination" (196) and argues that nature writing will one day be nationally important in both literary and political contexts.

Although valuable for identifying the uniqueness of western literature and for urging its admission to a more environmentally responsive American canon, this notion of difference requires some literary gerrymandering of the West. Despite occasional disclaimers, the West is identified as rural rather than partly urban. A number of readers have wondered at the lack of attention to urban lives in western American literature, given that most people in the West live in cities. But defining a rural West as "other" to the urban East has other consequences. For example, Blackburn asks why Raymond Carver, certainly a canonical modern author, is rarely identified as western. Blackburn detects anti-western conspiracy, but readers' failure to connect Carver with the West may also be due to his urban settings and subjects. In making ruralness an important ingredient of westernness, westerners may have accommodated rather than resisted eastern stereotypes, thus making certain western works invisible and excluding certain authors from westernness. At the same time, openness and attentiveness to the natural world may be neither solely western nor uniquely American. Challengers use western difference as a powerful argument to break open canonical enclosures, but they keep encountering the boundaries that they have drawn.

Diversity and the Networkers

While the challengers are interested in western literature's relationship to a larger canon, the diversity stance serves primarily as a perspective on western American literature, emphasizing pluralism and open-endedness. I use the label "networkers" for those who provide ways to theorize diversity in the western American canon. Generally they are less interested in defining what's western about western literature than in examining the webs of influence that pass through the literary West.

If the traditionalists and marginalists draw on the Turner thesis as a helpful paradigm for a western literary history, networkers share the New Western historians' vision. Patricia Limerick suggests that we see the West not as a process (as Turner did) but as a place, for "the West as place has a compensatory, down-to-earth clarity that the migratory, abstract frontier could never have" (26). In this version of the West, place is important not as landscape but as a literal "common ground": the West is not where we all escaped to the wilderness, but where we all met — American Indians, Hispanics, Asians, Europeans. Generally these were not happy meetings, and misunderstandings persist into the present:

> As Western dilemmas recur, we wish we knew more not only about the place but also about each other. It is a disturbing element of continuity in Western history that we have not ceased to be strangers. The problem of mistaken identity runs from past to present. (Limerick 349)

Looking again at the strong connection Lauter makes between canon and the survival of knowledge, we may conclude that these mistaken identities and our inadequate literary canons are interrelated. Mary Clearman Blew makes a more optimistic connection between a diverse western American literature and a New Western approach to history:

> The most important thing about the revisionist historiography is its willingness to listen to many voices and see the many different facets of the West. And one characteristic of contemporary writers in the West is their diversity. I can't think of any writer who claims that hers (or his) is *the* West. (Morris 30)

Instead of opposing diversity to continuity, Blew is proposing diversity *as* continuity.

To illustrate how this approach works, we can contrast the emphasis on the continuity of the frontier myth in *The Frontier Experience and the American Dream* with the variety of Teresa Jordan and James Hepworth's anthology *Stories That Shape Us: Contemporary Women Write about the West*. In the latter volume, the stories do not treat one overarching myth, nor are they chosen for a particular expression of westernness. Yet Hepworth and Jordan are not presenting "just stories" — an ethical principle informs the project. "Stories ease our passage from one way of seeing ourselves to another" (21), and if we tell the wrong stories, we can ruin our lives and other people's lives as well. Although no single set of principles informs our judgment of the stories, we know it's good to keep telling and listening to (or writing and reading) many stories from as wide a variety of storytellers as possible.

In her introduction, Jordan suggests that a grasp of multiplicity is a benefit of maturity. Drawing on the language of feminist and multiculturalist canon revisers, she discusses the importance of a new "lens" or way of seeing. "As a child," she says, "I thought that 'my' West was the only one that mattered." But growing up and attending college outside the West helped her "understand that the pioneer story...is a lens that filters out other stories." Once she realized this, "Stories that had been invisible before suddenly burst into view"(18). Using the example of Maxine Hong Kingston's autobiography of her California girlhood as a Chinese-American, Jordan shows how an emphasis on diversity changes the conception of "what's Western." Although it seemed at first that *The Woman Warrior* wasn't western enough to provide an excerpt for their volume, Jordan and Hepworth eventually realized that "Kingston's experience as a young girl shamed into silence by her fear of speaking English *is* a story of the 'real' West" (20-21).

If we apply new lenses to the concept of canon, networkers say, we see that many peoples of the West have their own canons. According to Leslie Marmon Silko,

> the ancient people perceived the world and themselves within the world as part of an ancient, continuous story composed of innumerable bundles of other stories.... The ancient Pueblo people sought a communal truth, not an absolute truth. For them this truth lived somewhere within the web of differing versions, disputes over minor points, and outright contradictions. (31-32)

Silko's version of a traditional canon of stories sounds somewhat like Mogen's approach to frontier experiences—offering both continuity and diversity. The challenge for networkers, however, is to overlay these bundles of stories from various cultures and generations in the West without relying on any one culture's "continuous story" to make sense of the whole. This sounds daunting—although it does call up a vision of hypertext as a metaphor for canon. More seriously, it suggests the kinds of expertise that a competent reader of western American literature might need. For example, Wayne Ude notes that Silko, James Welch, and N. Scott Momaday, "novelists who belong among the best the West, and the nation, have yet offered" (60), all work deliberately within both an American Indian tradition and the tradition of the American romance novel. Thus Taylor's "knowledgeable scholars familiar with the world" that western literature represents must now know more than one tradition.

Borderlines—not just "frontiers" but national borders, reservation boundaries, cultural boundaries—are drawn all over the West. Networkers try to make these borders visible, question them, perhaps cross or blur them. In literature, this applies to language borders, the borders between oral and written literatures, and canon borders:

> Our peoples and writers have been flowing back and forth over the space these [national] boundaries now delineate since before the colonial adventure began. These borders make little sense when one is studying the histories, say, of Native- or Hispanic- or African-American literature.... How does one categorize a work like Rudolfo Anaya's *Bless Me, Ultima*, which crosses so many of these linguistic and cultural divides? What "Americanist" pedagogy could do justice to the traditions, historical representations, and contexts of utterance in *Black Elk Speaks* or James Welch's *Fools Crow*? Can the borders between Native-, Hispanic-, and Anglo-American literature be drawn without recalling the political treacheries that imposed a series of violated borders upon indigenous peoples and settlers from Mexico? (Jay 9)

In Gregory Jay's vision, borderlines evoke not a frontier myth but a political and pedagogical challenge. Using canonical borders to evoke political borders may be the last word in contextualizing. It begs a comparison with Bredahl's more psychological approach to canonical "enclosures" as the expression of an eastern imagination. For networkers like Jay and Silko, borders that are set and violated are as bad as those that confine.

A common practice in the literary world—the interview with the practicing writer—provides another model for the networker's approach to canon. Even steadfast canon preservers agree that one mark of a canonical work is the influence it has had on other artists. If we could plot the interrelationships and influences between writers, we would be able to see the canonical works at the places where those lines of influence converged. The canonical works are those that writers have admired, discussed, imitated, and resisted. Gregory Morris, for example, asks contemporary western writers how they see themselves in relation to a western American literary tradition. Their responses suggest that, although a few name some early and mid-century western authors as forces to be reckoned with, their network of influence generally extends outside the West. So, while Bredahl explains that Ivan Doig "builds on the efforts of the westerners of the imagination who preceded him" (146), Doig says, "I'm interested in *writing*, not specifically in Western writing. I'm trying to see what the other literary rivers of the world look like" (Morris 77). Gretel Ehrlich says, "Except for Stegner and Guthrie and others, we're all pretty much contemporaries of each other" (97), and John Keeble agrees that "the West has a really shallow literary tradition. I mean the roots of it, the written language, don't go very far back. At least in the white tradition" (163). Tom McGuane defines western American tradition as something to resist: "not just the corny cowboys-and-Indians West, but the pompous or backward-looking or nativist West of Wallace Stegner, Vardis Fisher, and even A. B. Guthrie" (211). This version of a networker's western canon, then, would not go very deep, but it would cross the boundaries of the West.

Jay also suggests that we finesse the borders between literature and writing, between dead authors and living writers, between established and emerging writers, by teaching "American Writing" rather than "American Literature"—or "Western American Writing" rather than "Western American Literature." This approach makes "the test of time" less important than "the ongoing conversation." Most current approaches to canon use the trendy term "dialogue" to describe what they are doing. In most cases, though, the dialogue is a fairly lopsided conversation, where one party decides what the topic will be and the others chime in. Networkers go furthest to ensure that everyone has a chance at topic control.

The *Literary History of the American West* moves toward diversity and dialogue when it discusses authors under regional headings (gathered under the subtitle "Many Wests") and again in separate essays on various literatures: oral traditions, western American Indian writers, Mexican-American literature, Scandinavian immigrant literature, western women's writing, popular westerns. The recent proliferation of anthologies of western writing demonstrates not only the literary flowering of the West but also multiple ways of organizing that work: by newness of the authors (*New Writers of the Purple Sage*), by region (*The Last Best Place*), by gender (*She Won the West*), by ethnicity (*Neon Pow-wow*).

The influence of diversity can also be seen in this *Updating* volume, which examines literatures (children's literature, exploration narratives, diaries, expedition reports), groups (California women, miners), and critical approaches that address the new knowledge and multiple lenses that critics must now bring to western American literature.

Despite its advantages, the diversity approach has its limitations. Although aesthetic issues are not impossible to discuss, they are generally of secondary importance. The main problem, though, is the fragmentation that always threatens: it's difficult to keep a decentered approach to canon from flying apart. A healthy "pluralism," which, in Jay's words, "teaches respect for the diversity of America's 'common culture,'" can disintegrate into "particularism," which "advocates conflicting ethnocentrisms" (7). Perhaps because of this tension, some networkers' articles on reconceptualizing and teaching the American literary canon discuss open-endedness in astonishingly doctrinaire language. This has not occurred in western American approaches, perhaps because so far they have not had to deal heavily with the literary weight of the past. In fact, it's possible that a diversity approach works better for a canon that is more "horizontal" than "vertical," one that is not drawing upon centuries of written materials. If so, it is limited indeed, for the literary roots of the West are not necessarily shallow.

How can we envision a diverse western American canon that is not flying apart into chaos? Adopting an analogy by Limerick, we can compare a diverse canon, with its emphasis on networks and webs of influence, to a subway system:

> Every station in the system is a center of sorts — trains and passengers converge on it; in both departure and arrival, the station is the pivot. But get on a train, and you are soon (with any luck) at another station, equally a center and a pivot. Every station is at the center of a particular world, yet that does not leave the observer of the system conceptually muddled, unable to decide which station represents the true point of view from which the entire system should be viewed. On the contrary, the idea of the system as a whole makes it possible to think of all the stations at once — to pay attention to their differences while still recognizing their relatedness, and to imagine how the system looks from its different points of view. (291)

Where western American canon is concerned, some of those subway stops are outside the territorial borders — in Mexico, Canada, New York, in urban centers — and users of the system come from even further out. This metaphor takes into account the increasing globalization that has been occurring. As John Keeble says, "It's important that Western writers not become entrenched in their Westernness, because the world doesn't operate that way anymore. . . . The Alaskan fishery is controlled by the Japanese; you can't write poems about salmon without knowing that" (Morris 163). It's not necessary to choose between western region and global perspective; neither do we have to decide between coherence and diversity, for we can "pay attention to the parts, and pay attention to the whole" (Limerick 292).

* * *

In a 1990 article for the *Los Angeles Times*, Wallace Stegner said he was happy that a literary award was being given from Los Angeles. All writers — not just western American writers — are eligible for this award, but it is being judged and presented from the West Coast, and thus it may represent a more informed attitude toward the West, he said. Several people have expressed their wish for an American literature anthology published in California rather than New York or Boston — assuming that more western writers and a better understanding of the West might be included. Such a book is not forthcoming, but it is still interesting to speculate on the contents of a western American anthology of the American literary canon.

Several other canons appear to be forming, canons that cut through the American West and include substantial work by western writers. Collections of nature writing and environmental literature contain numerous representations of the West, as do most of the already canonized works of American Indian authors. These, too, are literatures that began by being marginalized, and it may be that their approaches to canon mirror some of the western approaches here described. It's possible that the label "regional," once the death knell for canonicity, has become less pejorative as the term "universal" has become suspect. The many regional anthologies within the West suggest this renewed interest, as do the critical studies of women regionalists. It may be that the reconceptualization of regions as part of a network, rather than as isolated enclosures, has revitalized regionalism.

In looking again at the dichotomy imposed upon us at the beginning —western lit versus westerns as lit — we may decide that we don't much care about it. We may agree with Gerald Graff that we don't have to choose between the classic and the pop, but that we can put them in dialogue with each other by "teaching the conflicts." We may decide we are interested in writing and its relationship to culture, and that westerns can be as fascinating a study as any other. Or we may still object to being identified with the western, not because the genre is subliterary and embarrassing but because it stamps one myth on our varied region(s). In canon discussions, western American literature must get out from under the western myth, which not only makes many stories invisible, as Jordan points out, but also flattens the whole literary experience of the West.

In examining canon debates, I have found many interesting discussions of the tension between continuity and diversity. But there seems to be little variety or depth in discussions about the relationships between culture (or context) and art. Jane Tompkins' well-known suggestion is that we should replace the question, "Is it any good?" with "the notion of literary texts as doing work, expressing and shaping the social context that produce them" (200). But if we take Tompkins' suggestion as a way to discuss the value of a piece of writing, then we need to figure out how to evaluate the work that text does in shaping context. As Jacqueline Bacon warns us, "If we do not highlight that many questions can be asked about a work's relevance, we risk replacing one idea of 'good' with another (equally contingent) one" (510). "Human beings can hardly refrain from judging the things they make," says John Guillory, who regrets that we are a long way from developing a "sociology of judgment" (xiv). But perhaps as readers of literature, we ought to be able to develop ways to discuss a text's capability to please (as well as to move and instruct) even though we are not yet able to account for each point in terms of its social context. There are many questions that can be asked about the goodness of a literary work, and students need to be able to ask them so that they can discover, confirm, and transform their own standards for excellence: what pleases them, what makes them uncomfortable, and why. Aesthetic issues are particularly important in western American literature, for even before the canon debate began, western writings were discussed — when they were discussed at all — primarily as historical or cultural documents, rarely as art.

As a western American teacher, I want students to have a chance to engage with western writing as readers *and* as writers. A lofty, distant, overly aestheticized canon — although it may be intellectually stimulating for many readers — can have a deadening effect on writers, who feel they can never enter such refined company. But an overly defined, overly limited canon, even if it's local and familiar, can also have a deadening effect because it doesn't offer enough possibilities. Various parts of the West appear to have developed a critical mass of contemporary writers who, with a polite nod or angry words for their literary forebears, draw their energy for writing from their own lives and from each other. In turn, they can be as helpful as a canonical tradition in inspiring newer writers. The discussion of canon is important for westerners because it represents a demand for timely attention for a wide variety of western American literatures. But a more important goal is the continued literary vitality of the American West. A healthy literature requires both a canon and a renaissance — that is, a literary tradition and a critical network of productive writers and attentive readers.

Selected Bibliography

Bacon, Jacqueline. "Impasse or Tension? Pedagogy and the Canon Controversy." *College English*, 55:5 (September 1993): 501-514.

Blackburn, Alexander. "A Western Renaissance." *Western American Literature*, 29:1 (May 1994): 51-62.

Bredahl, A. Carl, Jr. *New Ground: Western American Narrative and the Literary Canon*. Chapel Hill: University of North Carolina Press, 1989.

Brooks, David. "From Western Lit to Westerns as Lit." *Wall Street Journal*, February 2, 1988: 36.

Elliott, Emory. "New Literary History: Past and Present." *American Literature*, 57:4 (December 1985): 611-621.

Gorak, Jan. *The Making of the Modern Canon*. Atlantic Highlands, New Jersey: Athlone, 1991.

Graff, Gerald. "Teach the Conflicts." *South Atlantic Quarterly*, 89:1 (Winter 1990): 51-68.

Graulich, Melody. "'O Beautiful for Spacious Guys': An Essay on the 'Legitimate Inclinations of the Sexes.'" In *The Frontier Experience and the American Dream: Essays on American Literature*. David Mogen, Mark Busby, and Paul Bryant, eds. College Station: Texas A&M University Press, 1989. Pp. 186-204.

Guillory, John. *Cultural Capital: The Problem of Literary Canon Formation*. Chicago: University of Chicago Press, 1993.

Hirsch, E. D., Jr. *Cultural Literacy: What Every American Needs to Know*. Boston: Houghton Mifflin, 1987.

Jay, Gregory S. "The End of 'American' Literature: Toward a Multicultural Practice." In

The Canon in the Classroom: The Pedagogical Implications of Canon Revision in American Literature. John Alberti, ed. New York: Garland, 1995. Pp. 3-28.

Jordan, Teresa. Introduction. *The Stories That Shape Us: Contemporary Women Write about the West*. Teresa Jordan and James Hepworth, eds. New York: Norton, 1995.

Kaplan, Carey, and Ellen Cronan Rose. *The Canon and the Common Reader*. Knoxville: University of Tennessee Press, 1990.

Kolodny, Annette. "The Integrity of Memory: Creating a New Literary History of the United States." *American Literature*, 57:2 (May 1985): 291-307.

Lanham, Richard A. "The Extraordinary Convergence: Democracy, Technology, Theory, and the University Curriculum." *South Atlantic Quarterly*, 89:1 (Winter 1990): 27-50.

Lauter, Paul, et al., eds. *The Heath Anthology of American Literature*. Lexington, Massachusetts: D. C. Heath, 1990.

———. *Canons and Contexts*. New York: Oxford University Press, 1991.

———. "The Literatures of America: A Comparative Discipline." In *Redefining American Literary History*. A. LaVonne Brown Ruoff and Jerry W. Ward, Jr., eds. New York: MLA, 1990. Pp. 35-51.

Limerick, Patricia Nelson. *The Legacy of Conquest: The Unbroken Past of the American West*. New York: Norton, 1987.

Love, Glen. "Et in Arcadia Ego: Pastoral Theory Meets Ecocriticism." *Western American Literature*, 27:3 (November 1992): 195-208.

McAllister, Mick. "Homeward Bound: Wilderness and Frontier in American Indian Literature." In *The Frontier Experience and the American Dream: Essays on American Literature*. David Mogen, Mark Busby, and Paul Bryant, eds. College Station: Texas A&M University Press, 1989. Pp. 149-158.

McQuade, Donald and Robert Atwan, eds. *HarperCollins' American Literature* (2 vols.). New York: Harper, 1994.

Mogen, David, Mark Busby, and Paul Bryant, eds. *The Frontier Experience and the American Dream: Essays on American Literature*. College Station: Texas A&M University Press, 1989.

Morris, Gregory L. *Talking Up a Storm: Voices of the New West*. Lincoln: University of Nebraska Press, 1994.

Poland, Tim. "'A Relative to All That Is': The Eco-Hero in Western American Literature." *Western American Literature*, 26:3 (November 1991): 195-208.

Silko, Leslie Marmon. *Yellow Woman and a Beauty of the Spirit: Essays on Native American Life Today*. New York: Simon & Schuster, 1996.

Stegner, Wallace and Richard W. Etulain. "The American Literary West." *Conversations with Wallace Stegner on Western History and Literature*. rev. ed. Salt Lake City: University of Utah Press, 1993. Pp. 123-143.

Stegner, Wallace. *Where the Bluebird Sings to the Lemonade Springs: Living and Writing in the West*. New York: Random House, 1992.

Tompkins, Jane. *Sensational Designs: The Cultural Work of American Fiction, 1790-1860*. New York: Oxford University Press, 1985.

Ude, Wayne. "Forging an American Style: The Romance-Novel and Magical Realism as Response to the Frontier and Wilderness Experiences." In *The Frontier Experience and the American Dream: Essays on American Literature*. David Mogen, Mark Busby, and Paul Bryant, eds. College Station: Texas A&M University Press, 1989. Pp. 50-66.

Verhoeven, W. M., ed. *Rewriting the Dream: Reflections on the Changing American Literary Canon.* Amsterdam/Atlanta: Rodopi, 1992.

Work, James C., ed. *Prose and Poetry of the American West.* Lincoln: University of Nebraska Press, 1990.

Part Two

Encountering the West

James H. Maguire

Encountering the West

In *Basin and Range* (1981), *Rising from the Plains* (1986), and *Assembling California* (1993), John McPhee tells us how new theories such as the concept of plate tectonics have changed the way geologists look at the landforms of the American West. The Grand Tetons, the Great Plains, and the Grand Canyon appear to have changed little in the past half-century, but for geologists today, tectonic plate theory has radically changed the significance of these landscapes. Similarly, for the last several decades, books of the Old West have had much the same appearance as when they first came off the press, but new views of the West's history and new theoretical approaches to literature have, for many of us, changed their significance. New views and theories have combined with a flood of new research to alter how we see the literary record of encounters with the West.

Histories such as Patricia Limerick's *The Legacy of Conquest* (1987), Michael P. Malone and Richard W. Etulain's *The American West* (1989), and Richard White's *"It's Your Misfortune and None of My Own"* (1991) have given us new, sometimes revisionist, ways of looking at the western past. No longer is western history a virtually unblemished record of noble and heroic pioneers winning a new land; now more of the costs of conquest are counted, the voices of victims heard. Such revisionist views mesh with the approach taken by intellectual and cultural historians such as Richard Slotkin, whose *The Fatal Environment* (1985) and *Gunfighter Nation* (1990) extend the provocative study of the frontier begun in his *Regeneration Through Violence* (1973). Slotkin traces the evolution of the Puritan belief in "regeneration through violence" and charts its movement westward with the conestogas and with leaders like General George Armstrong Custer.

Revisionist historians have been joined by literary regionalists who have, in recent decades, made their claims for regionalism's significance more assertive and broader. Harold P. Simonson's *Beyond the Frontier* (1989), A. Carl Bredahl, Jr.'s *New Ground* (1989), and Frederick Turner's *The Spirit of Place* (1990) argue that regionalism cannot be ignored, since place is one of the forces that shapes mind. Of course, that shaping process is not news; but Simonson, Bredahl, and Turner give us new insights into the ways that place influences thought and feeling.

At the state level, studies such as David Wyatt's *The Fall into Eden* (1986), Kevin Starr's cultural histories of California, and Arthur R. Huseboe's *An Illustrated History of the Arts in South Dakota* (1989) have examined the role of place in shaping the literary traditions of individual western states. To measure the vitality of these traditions, examine the numerous state literature anthologies published in recent decades. Although some western states have had comprehensive collections at least since the 1930s, John R. Milton's *The Literature of South Dakota* (1976) provided a model for the many state anthologies issued in the 1980s and 1990s, including James H. Maguire's *The Literature of Idaho* (1986), William Kittredge, et al.'s *The Last Best Place* (Montana, 1988), Gerald Haslam's *Many Californias* (1992), the six-volume Oregon Literature Series (1993-95), and Thomas J. Lyon and Terry Tempest Williams' Utah anthology, *Great & Peculiar Beauty* (1995). These state studies and anthologies have not only shown the importance, in a local context, of the Old West's minor writers, they have also taken a critical approach that corrects some earlier assessments that read more like hagiography than analytical evaluation.

Numerous pages would be required just to list representatives of the following post-1980 publication types: anthologies of contemporary western literature; specialized collections devoted to western writing by women, American Indians, Chicanos, and other groups; anthologies limited to genres such as western poetry, drama, and nature writing; and anthologies focused on one period or event in western American history. (For authors, titles, and other information about such books, see the book review section of *Western American Literature*. The last issue of each volume of the journal includes an index to all reviews in that volume.) Like the state anthologies, these collections show that some writers who are neglected and forgotten at the national level attract interest and assume greater importance when the focus is more local or regional. And as James C. Work argues in the preface to his *Prose and Poetry of the American West* (1990), canons are no longer sacrosanct, and we should therefore pay at least some attention to writers and works earlier excluded.

How much attention? Wallace Stegner (who, before his death in 1993, was regarded by many as the dean of western literature) sometimes said we should focus more on the region's major authors and their masterpieces instead of resurrecting minor writers and their works. At other times, however, Stegner himself gave more than a helping hand in some of those resurrections, as when his Pulitzer Prize-winning novel *Angle of Repose* (1971) brought Mary Hallock Foote's writings renewed notice. Much more consistent than that summary makes them seem, Stegner's views are expressed in three notable volumes of his final decade: Richard W. Etulain, ed., *Conversations with Wallace Stegner* (1985; rev. ed., 1990); *The American West as Living Space* (1987); and *Where the Bluebird Sings to the Lemonade Springs* (1992). Stegner's essays serve as benchmarks for intelligent assessment of the West's literature.

Western American literature begins with its oral traditions—and many of those traditions continue today. Since the completion of *A Literary History of the American West*, new studies have added to our understanding of the Native American oral tradition. Among the new studies are Andrew O. Wiget's *Native American Literature* (1985), Karl Kroeber, et al.'s *Traditional American Indian Literatures* (1986), Brian Swann and Arnold Krupat's *Recovering the Word* (1987), A. LaVonne Brown Ruoff's *American Indian Literatures* (1990), Kenneth Lincoln's *Indi'n Humor* (1991), and David Murray's *Forked Tongues* (1991). Growing out of the oral tradition, Indian autobiographies constitute such a substantial and significant part of western literature that the editors of *Updating* have included in this section Mick McAllister's essay on the subject. Folklorists continue to study the West's other oral traditions, and they have given us books such as Jan Brunvand's *The Mexican Pet* (1986), *Curses, Broiled Again!* (1989), and *The Baby Train and Other Lusty Urban Legends* (1993), Barre Toelken's *Morning Dew and Roses* (1995), and Roger L. Welsch's *Catfish at the Pump* (1986) and *Touching the Fire* (1992).

Much of the West's written *donnée* consists of as-told-to accounts that began as parts of oral tradition. In recent decades, literary scholars have been inclined to regard as literature more of the oral traditions and their written offshoots, as well as journals and diaries. As a result, many anthologies of American literature now include excerpts from western exploration narratives written from the 1540s to the time of the Lewis and Clark expedition (curiously, few anthologies include anything from the Lewis and Clark journals, which are to the West what William Bradford's *Of Plymouth Plantation* is to New England). Although *A Literary History of the American West* mentions these early western accounts, it does not convey a sense of the size and range of this body of writing. Why such neglect? Probably because most of the early narratives consist of page after page of details drier than the deserts they describe, passages such as: "Went 10 leagues today. Hot again. Much wind and dust." More recently, however, studies such as Robert Thacker's *The Great Prairie Fact and Literary Imagination* (1989) and Erlinda Gonzalez-Berry, et al.'s *Pasó por Aquí* (1989) have found literary oases among the desiccated heaps of humdrum fact. In one of the chapters in this section of *Updating*, Donald A. Barclay and Peter Wild pinpoint these rediscovered oases and survey the considerable body of writing in which these passages are embedded.

The early exploration narratives reach their acme in *The Journals of the Lewis and Clark Expedition*. Under the editorship of Gary E. Moulton, the University of Nebraska Press has published a new and superb multivolume edition of the journals. This scholarly resource will perhaps inspire new analyses of the journals as literature, studies like John Seelye's "Beyond the Shining Mountains: The Lewis and Clark Expedition as an Enlightenment Epic" (*Virginia Quarterly Review*, 63 [Winter 1987]: 36-53).

After Lewis and Clark, although many narratives of the Old West continued to include elements of exploration, the emphasis shifted to adventure. Mountain men not only trapped beaver and explored almost every drainage in the West, they also fought Indians, wrestled grizzlies, hunted buffalo, and told some tales taller than the Rocky Mountains. The likes of Jim Beckwourth, Kit Carson, and Moses "Black" Harris even came up with a new lingo to describe their "mountain doin's," a patois that is the subject of Richard C. Poulsen's *The Mountain Man Vernacular* (1985). Also building upon earlier histories and biographies of mountain men by historians such as Dale L. Morgan and LeRoy R.

Hafen, Richard Batman gives us a detailed look at the life and times of one especially peripatetic trapper in *James Pattie's West* (1986).

Long before most mountain men had grown old or "gone under," the military, lawmen, and outlaws had arrived in the West and had engaged in exploits that added to the region's legends. As Michael Koury informs us in his chapter in *A Literary History of the American West*, so much has been written by and about the military in the Old West that just the books about Custer and the Battle of the Little Bighorn could fill a small library. Since Koury completed his chapter, additional Custer books have appeared, the most notable being Evan S. Connell's *Son of the Morning Star* (1984). Popular interest in the military of the Old West remains high, as evidenced by the success of both the book and movie versions of Michael Blake's *Dances with Wolves* (1988). Lawmen and outlaws continue to be popular subjects, too; and studies such as Stephen Tatum's *Inventing Billy the Kid* (1982) have given us new scholarly insights.

If libraries can be filled just with the Old West's exploration and adventure narratives and with accounts of the Army and of lawmen and outlaws, what more remains of the Old West's written *donnée*? Plenty. So much, in fact, that *Updating* includes the following new chapters: Kathleen A. Boardman's "Paper Trail: Diaries, Letters, and Reminiscences of the Overland Journey West"; Lawrence I. Berkove and Michael Kowalewski's "The Literature of the California and Nevada Mining Camps"; and Jan Roush's "Ranch-Life Narratives." Each of these chapters surveys another considerable body of writing; and the scholars assert that not only is the Old West's early writing important as the seedbed for many of the novels, short stories, poems, and plays of the twentieth-century West, but some of it is literature in its own right.

Whether raw material or literature, the narratives of the Old West provided a foundation for the region's literary genres. Here, too, new research and new literary theories have led, if not to wholesale reassessment, at least to a widespread feeling that the West's early literature *should* be reassessed. Hitherto neglected and "minor" writers have increasingly become the subjects of articles and of papers presented at meetings of the Western Literature Association. To give some idea of the case that might be made for renewed attention to dozens of nineteenth- and early-twentieth-century "minor" western writers, we include in this section Benjamin S. Lawson's "Joaquin Miller" and Lawrence I. Berkove's "Ambrose Bierce." So many women writers have been rediscovered that we also include Ida Rae Egli's "Early Western Literary

77

Women." We also found that by not including in *A Literary History of the American West* a chapter on children's literature, we had overlooked an important subject and neglected many worthy writers. To make up for that omission, this section of *Updating* includes Fred Erisman's essay on western children's literature.

In the Old West, some children read not only what adults said was acceptable for children, but also what was forbidden—namely, dime novels. Twentieth-century western children continued breaking the taboo by reading popular westerns by Zane Grey, Max Brand, Louis L'Amour, and their confederates. Because the popular western has had such a strong vogue since the 1860s, its history is important to an understanding of the more literary (or "elite") western American novel. That history is explored in detail in Christine Bold's *Selling the Wild West* (1987), which shows some of the relationships between changes in the publishing industry and alterations in the popular western. In *Having It Both Ways: Self-Subversion in Western Popular Classics* (1993), Forrest G. Robinson takes a New Historicist approach to explain how works such as Zane Grey's *Riders of the Purple Sage* (1912) feed our fantasies without upsetting our sense of values (until we see what's happening in the novels).

Almost as popular as the western, the short story has always been one of the West's strongest genres. Since 1985, the Twayne Studies in Short Fiction Series has included titles on western writers such as Raymond Carver, Willa Cather, William Saroyan, and John Steinbeck. In the other sections of *Updating*, you will find individual chapters on short story writers such as Carver. We also include, as an updating of the chapter on "world westerns," Geoff Sadler's essay on European popular westerns.

Of pre-1950 western poets discussed in *A Literary History of the American West*, Robinson Jeffers has received most of the recent attention, not only because of the celebration of the centennial of this major writer, but also because of the publication of Tim Hunt's four-volume edition of Jeffers' collected poetry. Published by Stanford University Press (1988-), Hunt's superb edition should reinvigorate Jeffers studies; and understanding Jeffers is vital to understanding western American poetry. Another pre-1950 western poet, John G. Neihardt, is one of the subjects of Helen Stauffer's essay in *Updating*. Neihardt and one of his contemporaries, Thomas Hornsby Ferril, have been discussed in numerous papers presented at recent meetings of the Western Literature

Association. Pre-1950 western women poets have received as much attention as have Neihardt and Ferril, as this list of recent studies shows: Dorothy Koert, *The Lyric Singer: A Biography of Ella Higginson* (1986); Nancy Kirkpatrick, ed., *Sharlot Herself: Selected Writings of Sharlot Hall* (1992); and Shelley Armitage, *Peggy Pond Church* (1993).

Book-length studies of two pre-1960 western American dramatists were also published after 1985: Phyllis Cole Braunlich's *Haunted by Home: The Life and Letters of Lynn Riggs* (1988); and Ralph F. Voss' *A Life of William Inge: The Strains of Triumph* (1989). Walter Meserve also includes some rediscovered dramas in his discussion of "The American West of the 1870s and 1880s as Viewed from the Stage" (*The Journal of American Drama and Theatre* 3:1 [Winter 1991]: 48-63). Three nineteenth-century dramas have been reprinted in *California Gold-Rush Plays* (1983), edited by Glenn Meredith Loney. Additional interest in early western drama is apparent not only in articles such as Rudolf Erben's "The Western Holdup Play: The Pilgrimage Continues" (*Western American Literature*, 23:4 [February 1989]: 311-322) and Helen Lojek's "Reading the Myth of the West" (*South Dakota Review*, 28 [Spring 1990]: 46-61), but also in lively presentations of early plays, staged by Phyllis Doughman's Readers' Theatre, at annual meetings of the Western Literature Association.

An even livelier interest has been shown in the West's nature writing. The signs of this increased interest include the founding of the Association for the Study of Literature and the Environment in 1992, a new quarterly (*Interdisciplinary Studies in Literature and Environment*), and an outpouring of books, articles, dissertations, and anthologies related to the subject. Thomas J. Lyon, whose chapter on nature writing appears in *A Literary History of the American West*, says that "Likely reasons for the new status of nature writing are not far to seek." He cites environmental decline and loss, particularly vivid in the American West because of the area's phenomenally rapid population growth and heavy exploitation of natural resources. A second reason, he says, "is the emergence of critical theories about literature which deconstruct the Cartesian, unitary self and the economic and political institutions that have furthered the self's ambitions in the world to the detriment of nature."

Selections of the best nature writing have been gathered in anthologies such as Lyon's *This Incomperable Lande* (1989), as well as in *The Norton Book of Nature Writing* (1990), *Being in the World* (1993), and

American Nature Writers (1996). Turn-of-the-century western nature writers John Muir, John C. Van Dyke, and Mary Austin are included in such collections, and their seminal importance to the genre is recognized along with Thoreau's. But much of the recent excitement generated by nature writing comes from the work of contemporary authors like Richard Nelson, David Quammen, Ann Zwinger, Gary Paul Nabhan, and Jack Turner. Muir, Van Dyke, and Austin continue to influence the western nature essayists of our day, who argue with great urgency against the West's overdevelopment, decrying in Turner's words, "our tendency to tolerate everything..." (*The Abstract Wild* [1996]). Pre-1950 nature writing began a tradition that western writer Barry Lopez says "will not only one day produce a major and lasting body of American literature, but...might also provide the foundation for a reorganization of American political thought."

If any writers are to change American political thinking, they will need a deep understanding of the popular electronic media, since movies and television pervasively exert their subtle force on the American psyche. Studies like Max Westbrook's "The Night John Wayne Danced with Shirley Temple" (*Western American Literature* 25 [August 1990]: 102-123) show how Hollywood conveys a worldview counter to the values of a democratic culture. In *West of Everything: The Inner Life of Westerns* (1992), Jane Tompkins, too, attacks the western fantasies that popular writers and movie moguls peddle to the public. Better informed and more insightful, Ann Putnam's "The Bearer of the Gaze in Ridley Scott's *Thelma and Louise*" (*Western American Literature* 27 [February 1993]: 291-302) serves as a model of film analysis that should be applied to the almost century-long succession of movies about the West.

More than a century has passed since Frederick Jackson Turner presented his "frontier thesis," which had a formative influence on western literary historiography. For at least half a century, Turner's views have been the subject of critical examination; and, as might have been expected, the 1993 observance of the centennial of Turner's thesis brought a spate of books and articles. Three other writers of that period who also had a strong influence on the region's literary historiography — Theodore Roosevelt, Owen Wister, and Frederic Remington — continued to attract scholarly attention, notably in a collection of articles, *Owen Wister's West* (1987), edited by Robert Murray Davis, and in Max Westbrook's "Bazarov, Prince Hal, and the Virginian" (*Western American*

Literature, 24 [August 1989]: 103-111), which shows what an anti-democratic elitist Wister's Virginian really is.

Brian Harding gives a similarly revolutionary critique of Henry Nash Smith's *Virgin Land* (1950). In "The Myth of the Myth of the Garden," Harding returns to some of the nineteenth-century sources Smith examined and comes to a different conclusion (*American Literary Landscapes: The Fiction and the Fact*, ed. Ian F. A. Bell and D. E. Adams [New York: St. Martin's Press, 1988], 44-60). Harding's point, as paraphrased by Fred Erisman (who wrote the chapter in *A Literary History of the American West* on early western literary scholars), is that "The Garden of the West...was in reality a truck garden rather than a subsistence plot."

Harding is not alone in his reexamination of *Virgin Land*, a book that more than any other forced a reluctant American academy to acknowledge that the study of western American literature is a worthwhile scholarly pursuit. Before his death, Smith himself offered a reassessment of his earlier landmark work. In "Symbol and Idea in *Virgin Land*" (*Ideology and Classic American Literature* [1986], Sacvan Bercovitch and Myra Jehlen, eds.), Smith explains why he did not use the term "ideology." He reaffirms his thesis, but he also points out some of the weaknesses in his development of it. His main regret seems to be that "*Virgin Land* suffers to some extent from [Frederick Jackson] Turner's tunnel vision" (28). What Smith means by "Turner's tunnel vision" is his "refusal to acknowledge the guilt intrinsic to the national errand into the wilderness" (28).

Will *Virgin Land* still be read a century from now? Will any books of the Old West survive a millennium? As Washington Irving so charmingly pointed out in "The Mutability of Literature" (*The Sketch Book*), only the greatest of books survive the passage of centuries. Since literature is a process, we can expect that the books of the Old West will in due course go the way of most writing. That is not to say that any of the West's early literature will continue to have precisely the same significance. As the Tetons to the geologist, the West's literary beginnings to the literary scholar will, in their significance, shift and alter with changing currents of thought.

Ida Rae Egli

Early Western Literary Women

The settling of the West from the Great Plains to the Pacific Coast was polychromatic, multiethnic, paradoxical and often life-threatening. From first settlement, women were a part of this challenging landscape "so varied that variety itself seems to have been its major characteristic" (Haslam 4). And almost from the outset they offered their writings to the pastiche that became the literary myth of the West. This huge new frontier offered them space in which to be imaginative. It was, as historian Ralph Henry Gabriel put it,

> a manifestation of that romantic spirit which stirred America... the same spirit which in other realms expressed itself in the transcendentalism of Emerson and in the architecture of the Greek Revival. For many Americans the migration...was a wistful search for a Never Never Land. (Royce ix)

After an initial spate of diaries and histories, and as early as 1851, serious writers such as Dame Shirley fictionalized California Gold Rush vignettes from lynchings to quiet, slice-of-life moments between mothers and children, offering varied literary images of the West from uniquely female points of view. And yet those women serious about their writing struggled. While they might receive some momentary reward for literary prose or poetry—some received even more—they generally realized that even in the liberal frontier West, it was "a man's world."

Any success they had was the gracious occasional gift of men like Bret Harte, who edited the *Overland Monthly* in San Francisco in the 1860s. This meant western women writers seldom saw themselves as "real writers" but more often as wives or working women who wrote as an avocation. Most had little opportunity and almost no encouragement. Often they were heckled by men and traditionalist women alike. This resistive milieu caused even the accomplished Jessie Benton Frémont, who supported Colonel John Frémont and her daughter the last two decades of their lives with her writing, to dub her work "harmless puddings."

Paradoxically, while there was an overwhelming national enthusiasm for western expansion and a desire for images of life in the West, there was, as the nineteenth century progressed, a widening chasm between East and West, cut by the literature each was producing. As Gerald Haslam puts it, "during the very period when the West seemed most remote and unreal, American writing [on the East coast] matured" (Haslam 3). Nearly all western writers encountered this chasm, but because the gender disparity was a major issue for nineteenth-century women writing in the West, they found the gap much harder to bridge than did their male counterparts. While editors in the East searched for "naturalistic" and "realistic" stories and novels and formed their literary taste according to a 200-year-old phallocentric literary tradition, writers in the West were overwhelmed by the romance and high adventure that characterized the broad and wide, rough and unsubtle frontier. Understandably, hungry western audiences were, in general, more appreciative of western writings and the literary efforts of women, especially during the gold rush in California when "freedom was in the very air . . . for the country offered a unique and seductive draught of liberty" (Levy 108); or, as one emigrant, Mary Jane Megquier, described the West's reception to women in 1849, "it is all the same whether you go to church or play monte, that is why I like [the West], you very well know that I am a worshipper at the shrine of liberty" (Levy 108). Still, after East met West with the transcontinental railway in 1869, most of those making the decisions about what was to be printed (and praised), even in the West, resided in New York City. There the immutable patriarchy shunned most work by women and saw western writers all too often as local colorists or mere regionalists.

Regional they were, certainly, writing in the flat Texas Panhandle or "Literary San Francisco" or the high Colorado Rockies, regions as diverse as anywhere in the world. But that their regionalism somehow made them mediocre was a misbegotten stereotype. Wallace Stegner commented on this stereotype by saying, "the moment we segregate a writer and put the tag 'Western' on him [or her] we have implicitly downgraded him [or her] into some secondary category" (Raskin 5). And until well into the second half of the twentieth century, this down-grading impaired the efforts of western women writers. Their perspective on the West, necessary to our full understanding of western settlement, was regularly overlooked. And because they sometimes chose subtle subject matter and projected a clearly female voice, a second erroneous stereotype — that women were essentially trivial — made people believe that women in the West didn't write anything important. But the truth is, they saw nature's grand and minute connecting fibers and heard the sound of broken hearts that accompanied western expansion. Now, at the end of the twentieth century western women's literature is finally being sorted out, reviewed, written about in doctoral theses, given in reprinted versions as Christmas gifts. The reevaluation of this body of work is being undertaken by "rebellious readers" reexamining women's manuscripts with open minds, questioning the stereotypes of the old patriarchal authority that in earlier decades rebuffed western women's literature, offhandedly calling it "romantic" and "gibberish." These revisionist critics are seeing afresh the women who walked from East to West, delivered babies in oxcarts, survived cholera epidemics, and worked alongside male counterparts as boardinghouse proprietors, stage coach drivers, nurses, and farmers. The new critics are cogent analysts of the woman's West, and their literary rediscoveries are refreshing now that the cowboy-and-Indian era has finally died.

But a lasting and devastating loss to world literature was caused by the failure of editors and publishers to solicit and produce manuscripts of women of color or non-Anglo background in the early West. Ironically, while eastern publishers promoted realism, naturalism, and regionalism as progressive literary genres, they wouldn't print the real desecration wrought upon native peoples by Manifest Destiny enthusiasts. In the continuing research of the 1990s, some surviving fragments of manuscripts by non-Anglo, western women writers are being unearthed. The Held Poage Research Library in Ukiah, California, for instance, held safely buried for decades the story of a sixteen-year-old Lassik girl whose village was attacked in 1862 by California troopers under the command of a Colonel Lipitt. All the men in the village were killed, including her father, brothers, and her grandfather, then chief of the Lassik nation. She and other women and children were sold into slavery. Her oral narrative, transcribed by a local botanist, gave voice to Lucy Young's story (Ttcetsa, her Lassik name). Notable in Lucy's story is her authentic native voice, her pathos and suffering, and her untrammeled passion for life amid surrender.

> White people come find us. Want take us all to Fort
> Seward. We all scared to dead. Inyan boy tell us:
> "Don't fraid, won't kill you."
> Tookted us to Fort Seward, had Inyan women
> there, all man killed. (Young 52)

Also, published in 1995 as the result of a doctoral dissertation is a biography on Sui Sin Far (Edith Maud Eaton), who wrote both in Los Angeles and Washington state describing the Chinatowns of the West (*Sui Sin Sar/Edith Maud Eaton: a Literary Biography* by Annette White-Parks), to be accompanied by a reprinting of the author's turn-of-the-century collection called *Mrs. Spring Fragrance and Other Writings* (edited by Amy Ling and Annette White-Parks). There are far too few of these nineteenth-century ethnic women's transcripts in print, even though more are being published almost monthly. In all western states, and in California in particular, at the height of the westering movement Euro-American women made up less than sixty percent of the female population. Women came to the West from as far away as China, Chile, Ireland, and Panama, and in even larger numbers from bordering Mexico. But the largest group of non-white women by far was those indigenous to the West. Tribal peoples, speaking more than fifty dialects in California alone, suffered up to ninety percent casualties from disease, encroaching settlers, and state and federal troops. The deep-seated racism and discrimination faced by these women in the settling West explain their lost literary voices.

Nowhere in the nineteenth-century West was there more opportunity for women than in California just after the Gold Rush of 1848 and statehood in 1850, when for upward of two decades local writers, among them several women, generated a writing style and body of literature seemingly wrapped in the golden glow of a sunset at the "Gate" itself. Some of these women were known as members of the Sagebrush School; others freelanced up and down the coast. But they all saw the West through matrifocal eyes and were, to some readers, less asynchronous with the natural rhythms of the powerful frontier than their male counterparts.

Walt Whitman understood these natural rhythms and regularly espoused the view that in expanse there is possibility and opportunity for renewed artistic freedom, so he advised young writers, among them Adah Menken and Ada Clare, budding feminist poets he felt "born too early," to move West. "'I chant the new empire, grander than before' he sang," suggesting writers and artists could give not only inspiring expression to the notions of Manifest Destiny and freedom but also a new gender-neutral connotation to the term "brotherhood" (Ferlinghetti 14). Both ardent young writers, Menken and Clare were polished academics guided by Whitman; they had idled away evening hours together at Pfaff's Tavern on lower Broadway in New York City. All were frustrated with the tightening conventionality imposed by New York publishers and literary critics.

Clare and Menken hit San Francisco in 1863, Adah Menken to write Whitmanesque poetry for the *Golden Era* and to stamp her sleek physical impression on San Franciscans by riding a fiery horse across the local stage wearing little more than a transparent body stocking in an adaptation of Lord Byron's *Mazeppa*. Ada Clare wrote a column for the *Golden Era* which should have left no doubt in readers' minds that women could think and write as well as men. She described Californians as a "people without any remembered past, save as it may sometimes come to themselves and their neighbors in a confused sense of having been born in some other place at some vaguely remote period" (Clare 304). She was witty, funny, intelligent, and gutsy. An evocative and controversial writer, she aroused the envy of several male journalists, who were losing readership. One in particular began an attack on her, espousing the still socially sanctioned notion that women should not write for the public, to which in her column of April 3, 1864, she responded in parody: "There is something effeminate in the literary or artist man, that our sex repudiates. We do not want man to be too highly educated, we want him sweet, gentle, and incontestably stupid" (Clare 306).

Clare, Adah Menken, and other women like poet Ina Coolbrith and short story writers Josephine Clifford and Frances Fuller Victor joined forces in San Francisco with male writers. They collaborated to fulfill to some degree Walt Whitman's fantasy: a new literary genre specific to the unpredictable and natural West. Representatives of the local male literati were Mark Twain, Bret Harte, Joaquin Miller, Charles

Warren Stoddard, Ambrose Bierce, and others crossing paths at the office of the *Overland Monthly*. Meeting socially as a writer's collective, these men and women dubbed themselves the Sagebrush Group, and perhaps this term to some degree described their writing. Blown by the winds of adventure and the gold rush, being "of the landscape," thriving in an atmosphere free of convention and narrow circumspection, they dared to strive for the truth they had found on the Pacific Coast. The writing each did was unique, as individualized as Twain's "The Celebrated Jumping Frog of Calaveras County," Bret Harte's "The Luck of Roaring Camp," Adah Menken's "Resurgam," a frankly stark free-verse poem about love and abandonment, or Ina Coolbrith's later-to-be-discovered autobiographical poem "Mother's Grief," exposing the pain of the high infant morality rate. What makes their writing "Sagebrush" literature, or to coin a more accurate term, Sagebrush Realism, is its emphasis on a stark, candid realism amid a western mythology, somewhat archetypal characters, and a hyperbole popular with local readers. This literature reflects the complex but fresh landscape that produced it.

Also, unlike oligarchic editors and critics who held tight control over writers and printed matter on the East Coast, San Francisco editors and writers were much more responsive to a primary source: California readers. These California readers were voracious for printed matter, both in the cities (California housed more college graduates per capita in the 1860s than any other state in the union) and in the mining camps and outlying regions, and they were especially receptive to women. In part this was because women were outnumbered in many frontier California settings (in the early years often twelve to one, later in the 1860s probably four to one) and because the mercurial and transitory Pacific lifestyle caused readers to seek solace and comfort, or shared pain, in the printed word. Also, the proceeds of the gold rush, $80,000,000 in 1850 alone, afforded Californians the "luxury" of printed matter. The popularity of women writers soared, sold periodicals, and brought the distaff voice to lonely women in Sonoma and Monterey Counties, to men in mining camps around Sonora and Oroville, to urban readers up and down the state eager for a "culture."

Among the women successful in California during the Sagebrush period (approximately 1855-1870) besides Ina Coolbrith, Ada Clare, and Adah Menken, were Dame Shirley (Louisa Amelia Knapp Smith Clapp), Josephine Clifford, Jessie Benton Frémont, Georgiana Kirby, Frances

Fuller Victor, Helen McCowen Carpenter, Ella Sterling (Clark) Cummins Mighels, and to varying degrees at different times, several others.

Frances Fuller Victor was perhaps the most consummate professional, writing fiction, nonfiction, and poetry with a commanding and cogent feminist bias. She made her living working for Hubert Howe Bancroft, researching and writing four volumes of the *Bancroft Histories* while producing her own stories, novels, biographies and poetry as well. Perhaps her best work is in *The New Penelope and Other Stories and Poems,* a collection of neoclassic poetry and Sagebrush tales that challenge in quality much writing by men in the genre. Included too is her revisionist novella *The New Penelope,* a western parody of Odysseus' Penelope from the point of view of an Oregon boardinghouse matron held hostage by a husband whom she found to be a bigamist even before the marriage could be consummated. There is a Kate Chopin pitch to this tale, though tuned by the Sagebrush muse, exposing both the stifling protective attitudes toward women on the frontier and the hypocritical social standards, aimed at controlling women, which crept in with settlement. In 1873, literary historian and writer Ella Sterling Cummins enhanced Victor's reputation by describing her work as "bright and readable, as ... some of the strongest work ... yet attempted by any woman writer ... of substantial quality" (Cummins 23, 159).

Coming to California earlier than Victor, at mid-century, when the landscape was even more unpredictable and lawless, other women like Sarah Royce and Dame Shirley had initiated a female literary tradition. Capturing beautifully the distaff version of wagon travel west, Sarah Royce in 1849 wrote a log, which she later used as a basis for her memoir, *A Frontier Lady* (1932). Royce came from Iowa overland by oxen and prairie wagon with her husband to search for gold. Spiritual, projecting incredible images of events and passing terrains, Royce's voice speaks in the ear of her reader rather like the "good mother" goddess of western frontiering and California pioneer life. Dame Shirley landed in mining camps Rich Bar and Indian Bar outside Marysville, California, in the summer of 1851, one of never more than five women in each of these camps. Her husband was a young physician who had come to the West to achieve fame. She immediately realized the writing potential there and set about drafting to her sister Molly in Massachusetts twenty-three letters, later to be published as *The Shirley Letters* in *The Pioneer,* a San Francisco daily, in 1854 and 1855. Immediately received with vociferous enthusiasm, her weekly letters drew wide acclaim, so much so that Bret

Harte borrowed extensively from them to create his own mining stories. Moreover, she was among the first to exhibit the regional Sagebrush style, her characters somehow mythical, archetypal, yet colorfully California gold rush real. But fame did not save her shaky marriage, and once away from the mines and settled again in San Francisco as a school teacher, alone with a "normal" life, she lost the muse that had spoken to her so eloquently at Rich and Indian Bars.

These women and others paved the way for women writers, including the articulate young woman who joined Ina Coolbrith and Bret Harte at the *Overland* office as the new secretary. Moving west from Washington, D.C., the wife of a U.S. Army lieutenant, Josephine Clifford was first published while living in the Southwest. Erudite, with a style rich in illuminating detail, Clifford soon produced stories that emphasized the cultural clashes and strained relationships unavoidable in California and in the Southwest. She was regularly published within the state, and her anthology *Overland Tales* came out in 1877, to be followed by a novel, *The Woman Who Lost Him*. She then married Santa Cruz rancher and environmentalist Jackson McCrackin and turned to saving the old-growth redwoods and local flora and fauna. After her husband's death she established the Santa Cruz *Sentinel* and, though almost blind, wrote until well into her eighties, her writing always sensitive and affecting.

Two other women who achieved flickering literary fame during this era are Jessie Benton Frémont, wife of Colonel John C. Frémont, and Georgiana Kirby, a Massachusetts school teacher and Brooke Farm resident befriended by Margaret Fuller and Nathaniel Hawthorne. Transplanted in California several miles outside the Santa Cruz mission, Kirby wrote there for several decades beginning in 1852. She sometimes penned Socratic dialogues in a journalistic format, sometimes wrote fiction. Her writing evoked the day-to-day ebb and flow of the frontier—of anticipating childbirth alone on a new homestead, of the disparate needs of men and women in an uncompromising countryside. She describes too the stifled creative mind that atrophies in prolonged seclusion. And her short stories have an unsentimental "realness" to them. Her style evidences the influence of both Fuller and Hawthorne—although her plots and settings are western. The "two wives" story, for instance (one wife in California, another east of the Rockies, a common occurrence in the West), is dramatized in Kirby's "A Tale of the Redwoods."

The pampered and academically impressive daughter of Senator Thomas Hart Benton of Missouri, Jessie Benton Frémont led a unique life in relative luxury near what is now Yosemite National Park at the Mariposa Ranch, purchased for $3,000 by Colonel Frémont after a topographical survey excursion to the West in the 1840s. Home on "Las Mariposas" was a crude log house, but it was furnished with marble-topped tables, Persian rugs, and servants. While living in California on and off between 1848 and 1860, on the seventy square miles of original Mexican land grant, she wrote colorful tales of life around Yosemite, of native peoples pushed onto unproductive lands, of wilderness being "tamed" all around her — tales of anxious miners and settlers trying to scurry for a living within what she considered her own Bear Valley. She juxtaposed claim jumps with her search for a "washer-woman" and angry she-bears protecting cubs with local native peoples trying to survive. Her animated tales are good examples of Sagebrush realism; but overall one can feel that Frémont was to some degree holding back, perhaps bypassing professional notice so as not to outdo her increasingly recalcitrant and inept husband, later a failed Civil War general. John Frémont drew up to $39,000 per month from his Mariposa properties through much of the 1860s, yet he had fallen into humiliation and bankruptcy by the early 1880s. Perhaps the story she should have told is that one. But one can see, as her biographer Pamela Herr did, that arriving in California afraid, homesick, and physically frail, Jessie Frémont "not only survived but emerged far stronger" (Herr 305). She enjoyed a healing at Las Mariposas, and her stories are representative of the wellness many women spoke of as a response to the California landscape.

A much different life fell to Ina Coolbrith. She was perhaps California's best early woman writer and was named California's first poet laureate at an elaborate formal ceremony on June 30, 1915, at the Panama Pacific International Exposition in San Francisco. A poet of exactness, in her later lyrics she freely delves into the extremes of female midlife consciousness: "As grows the rose / The thistle grows" (Coolbrith "Rose"). Coolbrith ripened early in the 1860s and molded the standard for California poetry but was, at the height of her poetic powers, knocked from prominence and respect by tragedies in her extended family and by the untimely death of California's budding literary tradition.

Once the Transcontinental Railway connected East to West at Promontory, Utah, on May 10, 1869, it wasn't long before the Sagebrush group was exposed to a chilling challenge. The literary community that might have fictionalized the changing face of California life was overwhelmed by a flood of eastern publications now easily transported and marketed, and more importantly, by traditional publishing politics that also came west and with few exceptions excluded women from publishing opportunities. Unable to compete, many local writers of both genders either left the West or found other occupations. Ina Coolbrith became Oakland Public Library's most notable librarian, inspirant to Jack London and Isadora Duncan. After twenty years' service she was dismissed for publicly commenting on the rather shabby upkeep of the library building. She wrote until her death in 1928, maintaining a keen sensitivity for nuance and an eye for the outcast and forgotten, the shards of life and death:

> What use the questioning? this thing we are:
> A breath called life, housed for a little space
> In how infinitesimal a star,
> Men vanished, leaving neither sound nor trace.
> (*Wings of Sunset* 201)

Comparable to Coolbrith as social critic, but with a rare endorsement by both eastern and western literary establishments, Helen Hunt Jackson earned and has sustained an enduring reputation among women writers of the early West. Her novel *Ramona* (1884), the first of three books aimed at Indian reform, presents the story of an illegitimate, half-Indian, half-Scottish girl, orphaned early but raised on a Spanish *rancheria* under the reprimanding eye of one Señora Moreno. Ramona falls in love with an Indian ranch hand, Alessandro, but is forbidden by Senora Moreno to marry him, so they run away together at a time when Californians accepted neither Indians nor those with Ramona's adopted Spanish background. The anguish that befalls the young couple is that which befalls the innocent and pure of heart when thrust into a world of greed, hate, and lawlessness. The story reveals what destroyed California's hope for a utopian society: the immigrating Anglo's forceful and insensitive drive to own; the heartbreaking losses dealt the conquered Spanish order, and the alien land, food, and way of life forced on native peoples (encouraged by California's Indian extermination laws of the 1860s). Critics have occasionally attacked Jackson for being sentimental, but *Ramona* seems no more inclined toward sentimental romanticism than Nathaniel Hawthorne's *The Scarlet Letter*, no more socially censorious than the later political novels of Theodore Dreiser and Sinclair Lewis. Like these other works, *Ramona* addresses serious social issues apparent in the nineteenth-century West. Admired now are Jackson's clearly universal themes like youthful, optimistic love turned to madness; the frailty of life in the face of unyielding elements; and the recurring injustice of ethnic displacement. From her home in Colorado, Jackson also wrote a fiction series on the Southwest and poetry as well.

Also of solid reputation, and a primary example of the western novelist and short fiction writer, is Mary Hallock Foote (1847-1938), who wrote twelve novels and four collections of short fiction, and sketched pen-and-ink and watercolor illustrations of several western states during her fifty-year residence there. Her last novel, *The Ground-Swell* (1919), is generally considered her best work, but her sensitivity to western women's issues is also visible in many shorter pieces. School teacher Frances Newell, in the story "In Exile" (from *No Rooms of Their Own*), characterizes a common frustration experienced by western women — that life in new western towns and cities seemed sad and forlorn at first, starkly unadorned when contrasted with "cultured" eastern settings, Victorian architecture and richly productive gardens. Schoolmistress Newell wonders "if a girl born and brought up among the hills of Connecticut, could have the seeds of ennui subtly distributed through her frame, to reach a sudden development in the heat of a California summer?" She longs for "the rains to begin, that in their violence and the sound of the wind she might gain a sense of life in action by which to eke out her dull and expressionless days" (235). In what seems at first a rather traditional romantic closure, Newell joins forces with a local mining engineer (ringingly autobiographical for Foote) and together they light a fire in the hearth of the stark log house he has recently constructed.

But a "rebellious" reader will see more, an emotional diffidence common in the West, perceptively reflected in some women's literature of that period. As the narrative concludes, the young engineer questions Miss Newell: "You said to-day that you were, happy, because in fancy you were at home. Is that the only happiness possible to you here?" Frances Newell replies, "I am quite contented here.... I am getting acclimated." He continues with candor. "I wish you had as little as I have, outside of this room where we stand together." And almost under her breath she replies, "I don't know that I have anything" (254). Then, when the couple lights the fire, Foote makes it clear they have the whole western frontier and the rest of their lives together, to somehow bridge the vast loneliness and transmute frontier brutality. A consummate danger lies just beyond the cabin, but human warmth and hope are within. What creeps through the chinks of the narrative is that there are few social safeguards, almost unlimited potential for future prosperity or agonizing calamity, and a daily need for human interaction, approbation, and love — a need acute amid the acidic social fiber of the West. This romance, Foote tells us, is not Charlotte Bronte's Gothic romance with an effusive Rochester, nor an Edith Wharton New York parlor romance, nor the Puritan romance defined by Hawthorne in *The Scarlet Letter,* but a necessitous and distanced romance set in unimaginably wide western spaces.

Compared to California's gold rush, vigilantism, and Bear Flag Revolt, mid-century in the Northwest was less dramatic. There were ghastly battles between native peoples and settling intruders, and later in the century, farther east, there were disgraceful episodes like the Battle of the Little Bighorn and Wounded Knee. But even with this chaos, the Northwest and Midwest followed a more predictable frontiering pattern. Women writing there often mirrored the pioneer experience: some worshiping the bounty of the land and the grace of the plentiful rain; others espousing the unpredictability of both nature and man.

Women who wrote in the Rocky Mountain states generally recorded a coarser existence than those in the rich valleys, whether they stayed to help populate the states they came to, or moved on, as did Isabella L. Bird, an aristocratic English horsewoman. Sometimes alone and sometimes with a guide, Bird rode up, over, and around many of the Rocky Mountains after first perusing the grandeurs of Lake Tahoe and Donner Lake. With a guide known as Rocky Mountain Jim, she scaled Longs Peak in the late fall of 1873 after having worked for weeks with a family of homesteaders completely worn out by challenges faced on their Colorado ranch. All this she narrates in clear English prose in *A Lady's Life in the Rocky Mountains.* Her portraits of the country — dense forests; the occasional grizzly and brown bear crossing her path; the quiet and absolute civility of untouched nature; the immigrants, Indians, and animals who called the mountains home — capture the sense of a changing but masterful landscape. The power of it all is seen as she reaches Denver:

> The windy cold became intense, and for the next eleven miles I
> rode a race with the coming storm. At the top of every prairie roll
> I expected to see Denver, but it was not till nearly five that from a

considerable height I looked down upon the great "City of the Plains," the metropolis of the Territories. There the great braggart city lay spread out, brown and treeless upon the brown and treeless plain, which seemed to nourish nothing but wormwood and the Spanish bayonet. The shallow Platte, shriveled into a narrow stream with a shingly bed six times too large for it, fringed by shriveled cotton-wood, wound along by Denver, and two miles up its course I saw a great sandstorm, which in a few minutes covered the city, blotting it out with a dense brown cloud. (Bird 137)

There were, of course, other women writing in the intermountain West at the time, hundreds in fact, but of writers of literary pieces there are few. One strong voice is that of Sarah Winnemucca (Hopkins), a Northern Paiute educated by mission nuns. She spent her adult life working as an emissary between her native nation and the U.S. government and its Bureau of Indian Affairs. Her book, *Life Among the Piutes* (1883), is almost too vivid in its portrayal of the brutal treatment of Paiutes around Winnemucca, Nevada, especially by the pillaging Bureau of Indian Affairs agents. Winnemucca's book is written in a functional style with minimal artistry, but it is riveting nonetheless because of its compelling narrative voice and historical reverberation.

Among others writing locally in the Northwest was Abigail Scott Duniway, whose *Path Breaking: An Autobiographical History of the Equal Suffrage Movement in Pacific Coast States* (1914) is set in Portland and chronicles the suffrage movement during the last quarter of the nineteenth century, juxtaposing it to some degree with the historic events that held most of the national focus. And Maria Ward's *Female Life Among the Mormons: The Thrilling Narrative of Many Years' Personal Experience with Brigham Young and His Followers* (1890) is a muckraking and uncomfortable Great Basin account of the lives of women in the early Mormon community, of early leaders Joseph Smith and Brigham Young, and of their responses to the women around them. This book reads rather like *People* magazine, scandalous sometimes, overreaching at others, but is seldom dull. The tabloid tone causes one to question the motives of the author, and sometimes it is monotonous and predictable; but it is also illuminating in plot and history.

One among many books by Marah Ellis Ryan, A *Chance Child: Comrades, Hendrex and Margotte, and Persephone: Being Four Tales* (1896) collects tales written in and about the West with others written about the Civil War or set against eastern landscapes. Often stereotyped and predictable, the stories nonetheless project a cultured character. And her last production, *Told in the Hills* (1905), offers images of the Pacific Northwest and the romantic Kootenai spring. This is light reading. Ryan never reaches far beneath the surface of her characters, but throughout her work there are soaring descriptions of the Northwest's natural grandeur.

In *The Grains* (1854), Margaret Jewett Bailey writes an account not only of her trip around the Horn to arrive at the Oregon Methodist Mission in September of 1837, but also of her rather battering relationship over two decades with her country-doctor husband. Insight into the mission practice in the Northwest and into the lack of legal and social protection for women on the early frontier makes this book interesting, but it is not the work of a woman dedicated to the art of writing — it jerks, starts, and wanes for pages.

In the Southwest, a land unparalleled for stark natural beauty, one of soft deserts, mountain-rimmed arroyos, and sheer cliffs, agriculture was not just a matter of dropping seeds into rich valley soil. One wouldn't predict a colony of women writers there, but as early as 1833 settling women were writing histories and fiction throughout the region, beginning with Mary Holly's *Texas* (1833). An epistolary travel and pioneering log, it was intended to entice emigrants to settle in the Lone Star State — but the narrative lags and is rather clumsy (Major 10).

In 1846, Susan Shelby Magoffin, the first woman to travel the Santa Fe Trail full circle, seemed historically always to be in the right place at the right time as she wrote *Down the Santa Fe Trail and into Mexico: 1846-1847* (1926). Hardly deprived of luxury, with a lady-in-waiting and two boy servants provided by her wealthy Santa Fe trader husband, Susan had the time and money Virginia Woolf alluded to in 1928 as criteria for women to write. And although she never achieved beautiful expression, she did have a sensitive eye for significant detail in the midst of the U.S. war with Mexico. Her narrative is historically accurate and buoyant although it loses some of its perk as she rounds Santa Fe. And unfortunately the trip seems to have ruined her health. Although she did return to Kentucky and bear three children, she died in 1855, still in her twenties.

Behind Susan Magoffin came a trail of women who in various shades of emotive historicism record early settlement: army encampments, Indian wars, and the failing possibilities for Native Americans. Susan

Wallace, in *The Land of the Pueblos* (1889), writes a colored but also colorful account of Southwest history methodically researched and narrated by a seasoned storyteller. Occasionally Wallace lapses into Victorian judgments about the "aborigines," but she is a disciplined formalist and observer. Martha Summerhayes began *Vanished Arizona* (1908) in 1874 as she walked behind her husband through a sequence of southwestern and western command post assignments. The manuscript contains no real surprises although it offers abundant surface detail, good action, and a nineteenth-century lady's voice that encourages easy reading if not a transcendence of everyday thought. Somewhat more accomplished are the novels written by women in and around Texas: Augusta J. Evans (Wilson), *Inez, a Tale of the Alamo* (1855), a historical romance; Amelia Barr, *Remember the Alamo* (1888); Mollie E. Moore Davis *In War-Times at La Rose Blanche* (1888), a tender, slightly southern-flavored opuscule precise in its dialect, humor and human pathos, and *Under the Man-Fig* (1895), an even better volume through which one can almost see native bluebonnets swaying in a Columbia, Texas, wind. A charming book to sink into on quiet evenings, Davis' novel lays out a unique and believable image of southwestern elegance (Major 82). Finally an unhesitatingly worthy novel, Marah Ellis Ryan's *The Flute of the Gods* (1909) is a well-researched historical fiction, one of the first to admiringly portray the Southwest's native cultures. Set in a sixteenth-century Hopi village, the narrative moves like a cool spring stream through native legend about the "White Seekers of Treasure" and the conflict that would scar all Southwest life.

One other author needs to be mentioned here. Mary Austin in 1903 published *The Land of Little Rain*, a beautifully written collection of remembrances of turn-of-the-century Southwest. She went on later to publish much more about the land of violet deserts that fascinated her.

These early western manuscripts by women have been for 150 years bruised by a crushing landslide of eastern literary tradition and negative stereotypes—and only in the last three decades have selected pieces been rescued by defiant revisionist scholars. Whether another Kate Chopin, Zora Neale Hurston or Katherine Anne Porter will be anthologized to represent women's experiences in the nineteenth-century West is open to debate. Perhaps early western women writers will rise from obscurity to rekindle the memory of the nineteenth-century woman's West. "The critical task" of "finding forms that are open-ended and that convey the largeness and expansiveness" of the West is still at hand

(Raskin 7). But we can assume that in the next decades revisionists will force a radical reevaluation of the contributions made by nineteenth-century western women.

Of importance now to the literary history of the West is the fact that from as early as 1850 in California with the Sagebrush writers, and occasionally throughout the century in other regions of the West, women developed a compelling body of literature. To pass judgment on western American literature without reading the best of what has been written by women is like watching Mark Twain's Calaveras County frog with one leg, hopping in circles and beating down a worn path.

Now Isabelle Allende in San Francisco writes rich portraits of "American" women in magical realism (a stylistic cousin to Sagebrush realism); and Alice Walker, Maxine Hong Kingston, Joan Didion, Louise Erdrich, and Elizabeth Heron redraw the lives of other women and men in all phases of our history. They bring into focus a century-old chasm in women's literary history. We can begin to fill that gap by the reprinting of works like Frances Fuller Victor's *New Penelope,* Ina Coolbrith's *Songs from the Golden Gate,* and Josephine Clifford's *Overland Tales.* Certainly, we each have a stake in the woman's voice of the Old West.

Selected Bibliography

Austin, Mary. *Land of Little Rain.* Boston: Houghton, 1903.

Bailey, Margaret Jewett. *The Grains, or Passages in the Life of Ruth Rover, with Occasional Pictures of Oregon, Natural and Moral.* Corvallis: Oregon State University Press, 1854.

Barr, Amelia. *Remember the Alamo.* New York: Dodd, 1888.

Bird, Isabella L. *A Lady's Life in the Rocky Mountains.* Norman: University of Oklahoma Press, 1960.

Clappe, Louise A.K.S. (Dame Shirley). *The Shirley Letters.* Layton, Utah: Peregrine Smith, 1983.

Clare, Ada. "The Man's Sphere and Influence." In *No Rooms of their Own: Women Writers of Early California,* Ida Egli, ed. San Francisco: Heyday Books, 1992.

Clifford, Josephine. *Overland Tales.* San Francisco: Bancroft, 1877.

Coolbrith, Ina. "Rose and Thistle." In *Ina Coolbrith: Librarian and Laureate of California.* By Josephine Dewitt Rhodehamel and Raymund Francis Wood, eds. Provo: Brigham Young University Press, 1973.

———. "The Unsolvable." In *Wings of Sunset.* New York: Houghton Mifflin, 1929.

———. *Songs from the Golden Gate.* New York: Houghton, Mifflin, 1895.

Duniway, Abigail Scott. *Path Breaking: An Autobiographical History of the Equal Suffrage Movement in the Pacific Coast States.* Portland: James Kerns & Abott, 1914.

Egli, Ida Rae. *No Rooms of Their Own: Women Writers of Early California.* San Francisco: Heyday Books, 1992.

Far, Sui Sin. *Mrs. Spring Fragrance and Other Writings*. Amy Ling and Annette White-Parks, eds. Champagne: University of Illinois Press, 1995.

Ferlinghetti, Lawrence, and Nancy J. Peters. *Literary San Francisco*. San Francisco: City Lights Books and Harper and Row, 1980.

Foote, Mary Hallock. "In Exile." In *No Rooms of Their Own: Women Writers of Early California*. Ida Rae Egli, ed. San Francisco: Heyday Books, 1992.

———. *The Ground-Swell*. Boston and New York: Houghton Mifflin, 1919.

Haslam, Gerald W. Introduction. *Western Writing*. Albuquerque: University of New Mexico Press, 1974.

Herr, Pamela. *Jessie Benton Frémont*. Norman: University of Oklahoma Press, 1988.

Holly, Mary Austin. *Texas*. Baltimore: Armstrong and Plaskitt, 1833.

Hopkins, Sarah Winnemucca. *Life Among the Piutes: Their Wrongs and Claims*. 1883; rpt. Bishop, California: Chalfant Press, 1969.

Jackson, Helen Hunt. *Ramona*. 1884; rpt. New York: Penguin Books, 1988.

Levy, Jo Ann. *They Saw the Elephant: Women in the California Gold Rush*. Hamden, Connecticut: Archon Books, 1990.

Magoffin, Susan Shelby. *Down the Santa Fe Trail and Into Mexico*. New Haven: Yale University Press, 1926.

Major, Mabel, and T.M. Pearce. *Southwest Heritage: A Literary History with Bibliographies*. Albuquerque: University of New Mexico Press, 1972.

Mighels, Ella S.C. *Story of the Files*. San Francisco, California: World's Fair Commission of California, 1893.

Moore, Mollie E. *In War Times at La Rose Blanche*. Boston: Houghton, 1888.

———. *Under the Man-fig*. Boston: Houghton, 1895.

Nin, Anais. "Gender and Creativity." In *The Norton Anthology of Literature by Women*. Sandra Gilbert and Susan Gubar, eds. New York: Norton, 1985.

Raskin, Jonah. *James D. Houston*. Boise: Boise State University Western Writers Series, 1991.

Rhodehamel, Josephine DeWitt and Raymund Francis Wood. *Ina Coolbrith: Librarian and Laureate of California*. Salt Lake City: Bringham Young University Press, 1973.

Royce, Sarah. *A Frontier Lady*. Lincoln: University of Nebraska Press, 1932.

Ryan, Marah Ellis. *A Chance Child: Comrades, Hendrex and Margotte, and Persephone: Being Four Tales*. New York: Rand McNally, 1896.

———. *The Flute of the Gods*. New York: Stokes, 1909.

———. *Told in the Hills*. New York: Rand McNally, 1905.

Summerhayes, Martha. *Vanished Arizona*. Philadelphia: Lippincott, 1908.

Victor, Frances Fuller. *The New Penelope and Other Stories and Poems*. San Francisco: A. L. Bancroft & Co., 1877.

Wallace, Susan. *The Land of the Pueblos*. New York: John B. Alden, 1888.

Ward, Maria. *Female Life among The Mormons: A Thrilling Narrative of Many Years' Personal Experiences with Brigham Young and His Followers*. Philadelphia: The Keystone Publishing Co., 1890.

White-Parks, Annette. *Sui Sin Far/Edith Maud Eaton: A Literary Biography*. Champagne: University of Illinois Press, 1995.

Wilson, Augusta Evans. *Inez, A Tale of the Alamo*. New York: Harper, 1855.

Young, Lucy. "Out of the Past: Lucy's Story." In *No Rooms of Their Own: Women Writers of Early California*. Ida Rae Egli, ed. Berkeley: Heyday Books, 1992.

Lawrence I. Berkove
and Michael Kowalewski

The Literature of the Mining Camps

For the world as well as America, the thrilling news that gold and silver were to be had for the taking in the West fired the imagination. The West's already mythic aura brightened anew. The demand for writing about the West grew more insistent, and the literature of the mining camps was an on-the-ground response to this market. Men and women with impressive and varied verbal talents were among those who immigrated to the West, and in the relatively few years of the heyday of prospecting and the beginning of industrial mining they created a regional literature of surprising range and power.

Subsequent generations of writers have used the Old West as a fictile era, to be shaped retrospectively by the issues of later days. Some great authors have used its settings and situations to create memorable works of art, and the continuous outpouring of new literature about the Old West has absorbed the attention of contemporary readers at the expense of the semi-forgotten original writers of the mining camps. The wheel is turning, however, and there are now signs of a revival of interest in their work. One of the reasons for this revival is historical; mining camp literature is authentic because its authors had firsthand knowledge of what they wrote about. Whoever is seriously interested in the time and place they depicted must read them. But another reason is aesthetic; they were good writers and much of what they wrote still reads well and has intrinsic appeal. The foundation they established for western literature remains an enduring and attractive part of the structure.

Mining Camp Authors: California

In May of 1848, Sam Brannan, who helped finance the general store at Sutter's Fort in Sacramento, noticed that some of the workers there were beginning to pay for their purchases in gold. He went out to the Coloma sawmill to verify the fact that James Marshall had indeed discovered gold in a diversion ditch at the mill some four months earlier. He immediately journeyed to San Francisco, where, as legend has it, he wandered the streets waving a quinine bottle full of glittering dust, shouting: "Gold! Gold, from the American River."

The effect was electric. A human avalanche of prospectors, speculators, doctors, lawyers, sailors, shopkeepers, gamblers, actors, former slaves, artists, and writers poured into California to try their hand at placer mining in the foothills of the Sierra Nevada (and later in the northern coastal mountains and the southern Cascades). California was the first region of the United States to undertake precious-metal mining on a large scale, and between 1848 and 1852 some $200 million in gold was taken from the placer mines. But it was not simply a new extractive industry that made the Gold Rush a historical phenomenon. It was the carnivalesque atmosphere of swagger and possibility, expectation and boomtown optimism that sent fortune-seekers from China, England, Sweden, France, Germany, Australia, Hawaii, South America, and the eastern United States scurrying to "see the Elephant" in California.

The boom-and-bust mentality of the Gold Rush helped energize an art and literature that tended to stress the novel and the picturesque. Franklin Walker has pointed out that the emphasis was on lawlessness rather than law; gambling rather than the slow accrual of a fortune; the prostitute with a heart of gold rather than the pioneer mother; the abandoned orphan rather than the extended family with solicitous relatives in China, Mexico, or New Jersey (Walker 1). The trials of the patiently grubbing, homesick "honest miner" did not captivate writers' imaginations. As Joseph Henry Jackson puts it, "a hero hip deep in an icy mountain torrent is a chilly hero at best; there is . . . little greatness in subsisting on moldy pork and soggy biscuit in order to get rich. A dyspeptic shaking with ague is not the stuff of which legends are built" (Ridge xix-xx).

The jostle of competitive publishing venues open to writers on the California frontier also undoubtedly contributed to the sensationalistic or melodramatic cast of much gold-rush writing. As early as 1850, some fifty printers worked in San Francisco, and the city boasted that by the mid-fifties it published more newspapers than London (many in languages other than English). Writers could see print quickly in reputable journals like the *Pioneer*, the *Golden Era* and, after 1868, the *Overland Monthly*, as well as in ephemeral local publications with names like *Hombre*, *Satan's Bassoon*, or the *Wine, Women, and Song Journal*.

In fiction, the one notable work inspired by the mining camps was John Rollin Ridge's sensationalist romance, *The Life and Adventures of Joaquín Murieta, the Celebrated California Bandit* (1854). The first novel published by an American Indian (Ridge was half Cherokee), *Joaquín Murieta* is primarily remembered for establishing Murieta's image as a folk hero, a Mexican miner driven to become an outlaw because he is unjustly persecuted by gold-hungry Anglos motivated by "the prejudice of color, [and] the antipathy of races, which are always stronger and bitterer with the ignorant and the unlettered" (Ridge 9-10).

Ridge evoked the uneasy, often violent interracial relations of miners on a polyglot frontier. The tensions were not only between whites and non-whites but among minority groups as well. The California Indians are treated as subhuman by Murieta's gang and Chinese miners are repeatedly brutalized by the Mexican desperadoes: 150 Chinese at one point are left scattered "along the highways like so many sheep with their throats cut by the wolves" (Ridge 97). The daring and bloodthirsty exploits of Murieta and his gang take place in a romantic landscape of secluded arroyos and dusty canyons. As we can see in his description of Calaveras County, for instance, Ridge portrayed the gold mines as rough but bustling communities where nature, as a panoramic sweep, matched the larger-than-life human spectacle of the camps:

> Its mountains were veined with gold — the beds of its clear and far-rushing streams concealed the yellow grains in abundance — and the large quartz-leads, like the golden tree of the Hesperides, spread their fruitful branches abroad through the hills.... The busy wheels of the sawmills with their glittering teeth rived the mighty pines, which stood like green and spiral towers, one above another, from base to summit of the majestic peaks. Long tunnels, dimly lighted with swinging lamps or flickering candles, searched far into the bowels of the earth for her hidden secrets. (82-83)

The classical allusion to the Hesperides adds a flicker of mythological glamour that helps transform a workaday setting into a landscape of adventure full of soaring forests and subterranean secrets.

Gold-rush drama embodied the love of melodrama and action displayed in *Joaquín Murieta*. One of the first eyewitness dramas about the Gold Rush was David G. "Doc" Robinson's *Seeing the Elephant* in the early 1850s. The manuscript of this and other plays by Robinson have been lost, but contemporary accounts of the play indicate that it dealt with gullible miners who head west with overblown hopes of striking it rich, only to encounter bad weather, hunger, and bandits.

Amongst the popular melodramas and farces of the day like *Bombastes Furioso* (many of them given unisex performances in the predominantly male camps) were Warren Baer's musical satire, *The Duke of Sacramento* (1856), Alonzo Delano's sentimental melodrama, *A Live Woman in the Mines; or, Pike County Ahead* (1857), Charles E. B. Howe's romantic melodrama, *Joaquin Murieta de Castillo, the Celebrated California Bandit* (1858), and Joseph Nunes' *Fast Folks; or the Early Days of California* (1858). These were followed by later reminiscent plays about the mines like Bret Harte's *Two Men of Sandy Bar* (1876), Bartley Campbell's *My Partner* (1879), and Joaquin Miller's *The Danites in the Sierras* (1877) and *'49: The Gold-Seeker of the Sierras* (1884).

Often more historical curiosities than fully realized dramatic works, many of these plays nevertheless have a kind of rough-and-ready impudence that can still beguile. Delano's *A Live Woman in the Mines*, for instance, features characters with names like Sluice Box and High Betty Martin — who wears men's clothes and carries a gun: "a specimen of a back-woods western Amazonian," Delano notes, "who is indomitably persevering and brave under difficulties, but withal with woman's feelings when difficulty is over" (66). The play is insensitive in its portrayal of California Indians, but it still manages to include fresh portraits of the miners yearning for feminine company or news from home. The characters speak a wild and woolly western vernacular that is indebted to the Southwest humorists, as when an express rider recounts his latest journey:

Run the gauntlet between a pack of cayotes [sic], three grizzlies, and a whole tribe of Digger Indians — killed two horses and jumped a ledge a hundred feet — hung myself by the heels in the bushes — turned forty somersets down a canyon — slept three nights on a snow bank — froze three legs stiff, had 'em amputated and climbed the hill next morning on crutches, and have brought lots of letters for the boys.... Please take the bags, and give me a glass of brandy and water without any water in it. (Loney 90)

Not only does Delano's farce focus upon the excitement caused by the arrival of a woman in the mines, it also comically presents the miners' starvation. When the food runs out, the men dine on rats and boots. They also tie the last piece of pork on a string; each man swallows the pork, then pulls it out and passes it on.

Whatever attention is due gold-rush poetry, fiction, and drama, the true imaginative wealth of the era resides in its nonfiction. No other aspect of the American frontier witnessed such an outpouring of letters, journals, diaries, and personal narratives, much of it still uncatalogued, let alone read and interpreted. There are more written documents about the California Gold Rush than about any other nineteenth-century historical event except the Civil War. Yet despite the human drama and the historical importance of the period, the literature of the California mining camps remains largely neglected. It has been read primarily by historians who have emphasized its documentary value rather than its imaginative and aesthetic complexity.

This neglect of contemporary accounts stemmed in part from the fact that writers in the late 1860s and 1870s, particularly Bret Harte, quickly transformed the Gold Rush into mythic history. As Kevin Starr puts it, "Harte depicted the Gold Rush as quaint comedy and sentimental melodrama, already possessing the charm of antiquity. As pseudo-history, as an uproarious and Dickensian saga, Harte's Gold Rush gave Californians a stabilizing sense of time past" (49). Harte's image of the stout-hearted, red-shirted 49er went through further permutations, becoming, when drained of his melancholy and unruliness, the entrepreneuring pioneer of the California boosters. However useful such reimaginations of the mining camps may have been for later popular historians and chambers of commerce, they tended to obscure the actual accomplishments of mining camp literature.

The literary neglect of gold-rush writing, while undeserved, is not entirely surprising. Letters and diary entries often consisted of simple, unrefined, sometimes ungrammatical prose that addressed practical matters such as the price of meals or hardware, mining techniques, and claim disputes. Yet in the best works, this very emphasis on the demands of everyday life — on the mud, heat, and fleas in the camps — contributes to the rough-hewn piquancy of these memoirs.

The best mining camp narratives blend satire and affection in unanticipated ways. This is certainly the case in what Wallace Stegner rightly calls the "finest of all Gold Rush books" (Harte viii): *The Shirley Letters*, a group of twenty-three letters written by Louise Amelia Knapp Smith Clappe (1819-1906) to her stay-at-home sister in Massachusetts. Published serially in 1854 and 1855 in the *Pioneer* under the *nom de plume* "Dame Shirley," Clappe's letters from two crude camps high in the upper canyons of the Feather River displayed both a belletristic verve and a clear-eyed but warmly tolerant view of the rowdy masculinity of the mines. "How would you like to winter in such an abode?" Clappe asked her sister in an early letter:

> in a place where there are no newspapers, no churches, lectures, concerts or theaters; no fresh books, no shopping, calling nor gossiping little tea-drinkings; no parties, no balls, no picnics, no *tableaux*, no charades, no latest fashions, no daily mail, (we have an express once a month,) no promenades, no rides nor drives; no vegetables but potatoes and onions, no milk, no eggs, no *nothing*.

Yet just when Clappe makes this social milieu sound irredeemably crude and dispiriting, she adds a characteristic twist: "I expect to be very happy here. This strange, odd life fascinates me" (54).

In her last letter, Clappe states that she has moved from being a "feeble and half-dying invalid" to a "perfectly healthy" woman who will miss the mines: "I *like* this wild and barbarous life; I leave it with regret" (198). A parallel process is at work in Alfred T. Jackson's *The Diary of a Forty-Niner* (1906), a little-known but remarkable journal. Very little is known about Jackson; in fact his authorship of the book cannot be authoritatively confirmed. Originally from Connecticut, Jackson spent just over two years, from 1850 to 1852, on Rock Creek near Nevada City. His diary details his life with his friend and mentor, "Pard," and his romance with his French sweetheart, Marie. In disarmingly simple but responsive prose, Jackson chronicles his own transformation of character. He moves from being a timid, morally censorious greenhorn, homesick — "way off here out of the world" (3) — for the safety of the New England countryside, to being a more adventuresome and broad-minded Californian, at home in the stimulating environment of the foothill mines. Though headed out of the mines at the end of the book, Jackson is unwilling to return to Connecticut to "vegetate" on a farm. He has discovered the pleasures of good friendship and reading Byron's poetry out loud. At their farewell dinner in a Nevada City hotel with "a couple of baskets" of champagne, Marie expresses the crowd's general sentiments when she exclaims, "Oh! zey are ze good boys, and in our hearts we will nevair, no nevair, forget zem" (183).

A number of other gold-rush narratives are worthy of note. Many are by Americans: Bayard Taylor's *Eldorado, or Adventures in the Path of Empire* (1850); Walter Colton's *Three Years in California* (1850); Edward Gould Buffum's *Six Months in the Gold Mines* (1850); Leonard Kip's *California Sketches With Recollections of the Gold Mines* (1850); Alonzo Delano's *Life on the Plains and Among the Diggins* (1854), which was later supplemented by a collection of thirty-six letters to newspapers in *Alonzo Delano's California Correspondence* (1952); Eliza Farnham's *California In-Doors and Out* (1856); Mrs. D. B. Bates' *Incidents on Land and Water, or Four Years on the Pacific Coast* (1858); J. Ross Browne's *Crusoe's Island . . . with Sketches of Adventures in California and Washoe* (1864); Franklin A. Buck's *A Yankee Trader in the Gold Rush: The Letters of Franklin A. Buck* (1930); Sarah Royce's later reminiscences in *A Frontier Lady: Recollections of the Gold Rush and Early California* (1932); J. Goldsborough Bruff's journals and drawings in *Gold Rush* (1949); and Mary Jane Megquier's letters from 1849 to 1856, collected in *Apron Full of Gold* (1949). Others are by Europeans: the English sportsman Frank Marryat's *Mountains and Molehills or Recollections of a Burnt Journal* (1855); the Scottish artist and writer J. D. Borthwick's *Three Years in California* (1857); and the Belgian landscape gardener Jean-Nicolas Perlot's account of his experiences in the southern mines, collected in *Gold Seeker* (1985).

Realistic prose accounts of the Gold Rush were often less well-known in California than the work of frontier humorists like Alonzo Delano (1802?-1874) and George Horatio Derby (1823-1861). Delano published *Life on the Plains* and other works under his legal name in the East, but he presented himself as the long-nosed character Old Block in San Francisco. He wrote popular whimsical sketches, or "whittlings from his penknife," of western types like the miner and the gambler for San Francisco's *Pacific News*. These articles were collected in two books: *Pen Knife Sketches, or Chips from the Old Block* in 1853 and *Old Block's Sketch Book, or Tales of California Life* in 1856. Delano was a productive author who never considered writing his exclusive occupation. He moved to

Grass Valley later in his life, opened a bank, invested in quartz mines, and was an enthusiastic Grass Valley promoter.

George Horatio Derby was a caricaturist and U.S. Army topographical engineer assigned to California in the early 1850s after service in the Mexican War. He wrote under the pseudonyms John Phoenix and John P. Squibob and became famous as a wag and practical joker. His letters, squibs, and burlesques appeared in various California papers. His most notorious escapade occurred in 1853 when he was left in charge of editing the San Diego *Herald* while its editor, a friend of Derby's, was away. Derby changed the political alliance of the paper from Democratic to Whig and turned the weekly into a comic journal complete with mock advertisements and mock editorials. The audacity of the stunt gained statewide attention; it was the comic culmination of Derby's previous satires on phrenologists, land speculators, pompous politicians, and pretentious literary reviewers. His occasional prose was collected in two volumes, the popular *Phoenixiana; or Sketches and Burlesques* (1855), which went through some twenty-six printings, and the posthumous *Squibob Papers* (1865).

Derby, Delano, Ridge, and Clappe, were the first writers to help lodge the California Gold Rush in the American imagination. They form a lively and still unappreciated pool of literary talent that anticipated the work of those writers — including Twain, Harte, Joaquin Miller, Ambrose Bierce, Ina Coolbrith, and Prentice Mulford — who reached maturity in the 1860s, 1870s, and 1880s and whose work in California would end up overshadowing their own.

Mining Camp Authors: Nevada

Mining developed in Nevada after the California Gold Rush begun in 1849 began to dwindle. The high period of the California prospectors — small-time placer miners who staked small claims and sought with pick and pan to locate gold deposits that would make them rich or at least well off — lasted little more than a decade. Very quickly, companies formed that bought up claims and consolidated them into larger operations that could introduce the efficiencies and economies of industrial mining. Once this development got underway, a backward wave of prospectors moved eastward across the Sierra Nevadas to prospect the less populous and more arid eastern slope. Gold was found in Nevada as early as 1850, but not until 1859 was the Comstock Lode, the incredibly rich concentration of silver and gold ores, discovered. From then until about 1880 were the peak years of mining in Nevada, and the mineral wealth of the state attracted not only prospectors, engineers, lawyers, and financiers, but also men of outstanding literary talent.

They were early called "Sagebrushers" after the hardy shrub that dominated most of the state. Most of them began in California, received formative influence in Nevada, and then spread out again to California and other parts of the West, publishing their writings in regional as well as Nevada newspapers and magazines. All began as journalists, but quickly branched out into specialties such as fiction, humor, verse, history, and even drama. Until very recently, the Sagebrush School was almost totally neglected, and still is insufficiently researched. Its life, though brief, was brilliant. It produced one world-famous author, at least one of national significance, a number of very competent ones, and a body of writing that, in representing the values and traditions of the Old West, gave American literature an invaluable legacy.

Mark Twain is the most famous alumnus of the Sagebrush School. His stay in Nevada was brief but critical. Between August 1861 and May 1864, Twain's career was launched and shaped. He began work on the *Virginia City Territorial Enterprise*, one of the great newspapers of the West, early in 1862. Also members of its staff during his tenure on the paper were Dan De Quille, Joseph T. Goodman, Rollin M. Daggett, Alf Doten, Denis McCarthy, James W. E. Townsend, and Steve Gillis. It would be hard to imagine a more talented, spirited, and fearless group of journalists than these men, and their influence on Twain was profound and long-lasting. With their tutelage and encouragement, he quickly became an adept in the traditions of western humor, especially the refined art of poker-faced hoaxing. He learned broader values than had been taught him back in Missouri and he also learned to infuse them into his writing. His early sketches, "Petrified Man," "A Bloody Massacre Near Carson," and "Washoe — 'Information Wanted,'" exemplify the edged humor he perfected; they were funny but they each attacked a target of deceit or ineptitude. After Twain moved to California in 1864, he continued to contribute to the *Enterprise* humorous pieces touched with ethical sarcasm which exposed the brutality and venality of the San Francisco police, and other scandals.

Dan De Quille (the pen name of William Wright, 1829-1898) was, next to Twain, the most famous Nevada author. De Quille's reputation as a journalist and humorist was already extensive in 1861, when he joined the *Territorial Enterprise* as its editor in charge of mining and local news. De Quille maintained two careers: as a working journalist and as a literary figure. The first secured his livelihood; the second his fame. De Quille's former reputation largely rested on his *The Big Bonanza* (1876), the classic contemporary biography of the Comstock Lode. Since the 1980s, however, many of De Quille's stories have been collected and either republished or published for the first time from manuscripts, and it is now possible to appreciate a much fuller spectrum of his art.

De Quille was a master of the art of the hoax, and no discussion of this distinctively American form can be complete without attention to his contributions. Some of his hoaxes consisted of broad and obvious humor, as when he engaged his roommate Mark Twain in mock duels of calumny in the columns of the *Enterprise*, where each would enormously but hilariously magnify into miracles of disaster minor injuries the other sustained. Some of his hoaxes rank with the best ever devised and are American classics. He wrote, for example, a tongue-in-cheek account of the death of an inventor of "solar armor," a sort of diving suit cooled by a portable air-conditioner. The man died while testing out the suit on a walk across Death Valley in the summer not because the suit failed but because he could not turn off the machine; he froze to death. The story was reported in *Scientific American* and in the *London Telegraph*. The editor of the latter paper expressed a desire for more information, so De Quille obliged by inventing a sequel. Three years after Twain wrote his notorious hoax, "Petrified Man," De Quille quietly published "A Silver Man," reworking the same impossible situation but with a great deal more plausible detail to give it credibility. He was successful in rehoaxing the same audience that had fallen for Twain's hoax. Each of his hoaxes had some key that was a giveaway to an alert reader, something impossible or tainted by ascription to an unreliable source. As late as 1894, De Quille published his last major hoax, a fascinating "news story" about a "lost island" in the Aleutians that supposedly abounded in fur-bearing animals. Its unreliability as fact, however, is signalled at the end by its being linked to Jim Townsend, one of the Comstock's most famous and accomplished liars.

De Quille was a naturally gifted storyteller, and he published a number of fine tales that show psychological sensitivity or ethical purpose. Among the best of his short stories are "The Fighting Horse of the Stanislaus," "The Eagles' Nest," "A Strange Monomania," and "An Indian Story of the Sierra Madres." Each of these stories is highly enter-

taining, and each has subtle depths. De Quille also wrote several striking novellas: *The Gnomes of the Dead Rivers* (1880), *The Sorceress of Attu*
(1894), and *Dives and Lazarus* and *Pahnenit, Prince of the Land of Lakes*,
both composed in the mid-1890s. (Only *Gnomes* was published in his
lifetime.) These narratives are exceptional in their antimaterialistic
bent, their spirituality, and their remorse at the terrible damage caused
by exploitation of the pristine American wilderness and the aboriginal
cultures that lived in it. De Quille, therefore, holds many surprises for
students of the Old West not familiar with him.

Joseph Thompson Goodman (1838-1917) is certainly one of the most
colorful and impressive figures of the Nevada scene. Talented, versatile,
fearless, and high-minded, Goodman quickly turned the *Territorial
Enterprise* from the near-defunct weekly which he bought in 1861 into a
prosperous and vital daily, read widely in the United States and in all the
world's financial centers. Part of Goodman's success, of course, was
related to the growing importance of the Comstock's mines; investors
around the world were eager for reliable information about production
and prospects. But also important were his imagination and enterprise,
and his seeking out the best talents available, paying them generously,
and encouraging them to do their best work. Dan De Quille's mining
reports were trusted by everyone as being both accurate and honest, and
the *Enterprise* early established its lead in this critical area, but
Goodman also published feature articles and stories by De Quille and
Twain and sponsored a bold editorial policy that exposed corruption and
cruelty.

Goodman was able to do this because the *Enterprise* was probably the
only fully independent newspaper in Nevada; all the others were dependent either on government or mining company patronage, and were
hence obliged to be circumspect. Goodman, however, felt himself
beholden to no one, and did not hesitate to speak plainly and forcefully
on all issues he thought important. His editorial campaigns, therefore,
make fascinating reading.

Goodman also had a good deal of literary talent. In 1870, while on a
tour of Europe, he sent back a series of memorable travel letters that
were published in the paper and have been collected and reprinted. He
maintained a friendly but serious rivalry with Rollin Mallory Daggett in
the field of poetry. Neither man produced any great poetry, but
Goodman did compose some memorable verse. He also wrote some
plays, at least one of which, *The Psychoscope* (1871) has survived and has

been reprinted. It was written in collaboration with Daggett and, in addition to its early use of detective and science-fiction motifs, is remarkable for incorporating scenes of audacious realism more than one generation ahead of any other American play. Later in life, Goodman wrote memoirs, which have been collected and reprinted, and short stories, at least one of which is notable, "The Trumpet Comes to Pickeye!" It is a witty satire on a pusillanimous editor who quickly learns what ethical compromises he must make to publish a successful newspaper, and is in the same tradition as Twain's "Journalism in Tennessee."

Rollin Mallory Daggett (1831-1901), one of Goodman's editors, earned the reputation of being a fluent but pugnacious writer. He helped coach Mark Twain on how to write the letters challenging another editor to a duel that obliged Twain to leave Nevada precipitously, one step ahead of the law. Before coming to Nevada, Daggett in 1852 was one of two founders of *The Golden Era*, one of the first literary journals on the West Coast. Apart from his editorial duties, Daggett wrote a good deal of verse, much admired by his contemporaries, and he collaborated with Goodman on *The Psychoscope*. Though both men were reputedly offered $10,000 for the rights to the play by a director who wished to tone down its realistic scenes, they refused on principle.

In the latter part of his career, Daggett became a congressman from Nevada (1879-1881) and minister to Hawaii (1882-1885). He returned to his interest in literature in 1882, when he published *Braxton's Bar*, a novel about gold mining. In conjunction with Hawaii's King Kalakaua, he published *The Legends and Myths of Hawaii* (1888). In the last decade of his life, he wrote memoirs and fiction for various periodicals. One of his stories, "My French Friend" (1895), may be a precursor of Willa Cather's "Paul's Case."

Samuel Post Davis (1850-1918) was best known as an editor of the *Carson Morning Appeal*, but the verse, short stories, and humorous sketches he wrote and published in such periodicals as *The Argonaut* and the *Overland Monthly* were well received in their day and still make good reading. His main collection of fiction, *Short Stories* (1886), includes such favorites as "A Christmas Carol," "The Mystery of the Savage Sump," and "A Typographical Howitzer," the last two of which include Joe Goodman and Mark Twain as characters. He continued to write fiction, publishing much of it in the *San Francisco Examiner*, and although the rest of it remains, at present, uncollected, some individual works, such as "My Friend, the Editor," achieved a fame of their own. Towards the end of his career, Davis wrote some memoirs and his two-volume *The History of Nevada* (1913). These books, along with their predecessor, Myron Angel's *History of Nevada* (1881), are standard reference works.

A unique Sagebrusher was James William Emery Townsend (1838-1900), the original of Bret Harte's "Truthful James." "Truthful" was used ironically, as Townsend, more commonly known as "Lying Jim," was one of the most talented and notorious liars of the Comstock, no small accomplishment. He was famous for his ability to spin elaborate and elegant yarns at a moment's notice. Twain mentions him in *Roughing It* as being hoaxed by an even greater lie than he could compose, but this was early in his career. In later life he participated in one of the most creative scams in Comstock history when he singlehandedly printed a regular newspaper in a deserted mining town, peopling it with imaginary citizens and reporting in detail about them and fictional mining operations, so that foreign investors could be inveigled into buying stock in nonexistent companies. Some of his journalism has been collected, but more needs to be known about Townsend and his literary prevarications.

Charles Carroll "Judge" Goodwin (1838-1917) was a miner, rancher, and judge before he became an editor of the *Territorial Enterprise* from 1876 to 1880, when it was controlled by the financier William Sharon. He moved to Salt Lake City, where he became editor and proprietor of the *Salt Lake City Daily Tribune*, one of the eminent newspapers of the West. Goodwin was fearless in upholding his principles, but they included opposing the Mormon Church, defending the cause of silver, banning the immigration of Orientals, and supporting the captains of industry and finance who dominated the West. Apart from his editorials, Goodwin's literary contributions are restricted but notable. His best fictional accomplishment is "Sister Celeste" (1885), a lovely and moving short story. He later incorporated it into a novel, *The Comstock Club* (1891), a romanticized and historically interesting reflection of Comstock attitudes and values. His memoir, *As I Remember Them* (1913), consists of brief, openly partisan and questionably accurate vignettes of eminent personalities of the West.

The main legacy of James W. Gally (1828-1891) is fiction. He lived in Nevada little more than ten years but began his literary career there. Under the pen name of "Singleline" he contributed to the *Territorial Enterprise*. In 1875 he moved to California and there contributed fiction to a variety of West Coast periodicals. Two of his most popular works were anthologized in the volume *Sand, and Big Jack Small* (1880), but more of his fiction remains to be collected, and all of it remains to be studied.

Whoever wishes to know about the Comstock must make the acquaintance of Alfred R. Doten (1829-1903). He was a well-known and respected journalist before he eventually became editor of the *Gold Hill Daily News*. His journalism, however, is not nearly as important as his journals, which he kept on an almost daily basis from 1849 to just before his death. Doten was the Pepys of the Comstock, and his journals, collected and edited by Walter Van Tilburg Clark, are incomparably valuable for their inside views of life on the Comstock and for their accounts of its notable personalities and events. Doten also published some memoirs and fiction, both of which are collected in the third volume.

The main distinction of Fred H. Hart (?-1897) derives from his editorship of the *Reese River Reveille* from 1875 to 1878. As a regular feature of that newspaper, he began to compose and print whimsical accounts of what he called "the Sazerac Lying Club." Following the decorum earlier represented by Dickens in his adventures of the Pickwick Club, the members of the Sazerac told "stretchers" and tall tales. The popularity of this feature led to their collection, in 1878, in *The Sazerac Lying Club: A Nevada Book*. The book was very popular and quickly ran into several editions.

J. Ross Browne (1821-1875), although strictly speaking not a Sagebrusher, deserves mention with them because he published one of the first memorable accounts of Comstock life in "A Peep at Washoe," in the *Harper's Monthly* issues of December, 1860, and January and February, 1861. The series consisted of description, anecdote, opinion, and many touches of local color. More than straight travel writing, it was well known to Comstockers (De Quille took sharp issue with it on the basis of its accuracy) and was a forerunner of Twain's *Roughing It* in layout as well as subject matter.

The Sagebrush School thus came into existence around 1860 and lasted until the death of its last members, around the second decade of the twentieth century. In addition to those writers listed above, Ella Sterling Cummins would add a few more: Harry R. Mighels, John Franklin Swift, Joseph Wasson, and Arthur McEwen. What made them all Sagebrushers was their intense love of the way of life that they tasted for several decades, the years when the Old West hit its peak. Their writing is usually characterized by literary talent, at the very least, and

often it is excellent. It is inexplicable that the literature that was produced by these writers has been so long neglected, as it is not only quintessentially western but also of a quality and spirit that frequently lift it
above writing that receives more attention.

* * *

A literary fascination with the western mining frontier has persisted
since its heyday in the mid- to late-nineteenth century. Other nineteenth-century nonfictional accounts like Mary Hallock Foote's *A
Victorian Gentlewoman in the Far West* (published in 1972) or Joaquin
Miller's *Life Amongst the Modocs: Unwritten History* (1873) offer vivid
records of life in western mining communities. The same is true of fiction, in works like Foote's novel *The Led-Horse Claim: A Romance of a
Mining Camp* (1883), Frank Norris' *McTeague* (1899), and stories by
Ambrose Bierce ("The Haunted Valley," "The Famous Gilson Bequest,"
and "The Night-Doings at 'Deadman's'") and Jack London ("All Gold
Canyon").

The transitory boomtown conditions of gold and silver rushes, as
Rodman Paul notes, "led to an extraordinary carelessness with human
lives and natural resources. Men, minerals, the soil, trees, and the rivers
and creeks were all spent in profligate fashion, with no regard for efficient utilization or the future" (446). Today many corporate mining ven-
tures are associated not with local color but with hazardous chemicals,
toxic waste, and the disruption of indigenous communities.
Nevertheless, twentieth-century writers have expressed a continuing
interest in mining-camp life. Nonfiction accounts include everything
from Mary Austin's whimsical sketch of the "pocket hunter" in *The Land
of Little Rain* (1903) to the work of later writers — like Maxine Hong
Kingston in *China Men* (1980) — who have helped re-envision the participation of non-Anglo miners in the camps. Modern fiction features
stories by William Sydney Porter such as "The Ransom of Mack";
Stewart Edward White's fiction about mining life (both his 1902 novel,
The Claim-Jumpers and stories like "The Prospector"); Dashiell
Hammett's first novel, *Red Harvest* (1929); John Weld's 1941 novel, *The
Pardners*; Robert Lewis Taylor's *The Travels of Jamie McPheeters* (1958),
a picaresque tale about the adventures of a teenage boy and his father
en route to California from Louisville in 1849, which won the Pulitzer
Prize in 1959; Wallace Stegner's fictional account of Mary Hallock

Foote in *Angle of Repose* (1971); David Wagoner's comic western about Colorado mining camps, *The Road to Many a Wonder* (1974) and *Tracker* (1975); and Ruthanne Lum McCunn's "biographical novel," *Thousand Pieces of Gold* (1981), about a Chinese-American pioneer woman. Together with the excellent collection of writings about Butte, Montana, anthologized in *The Last Best Place*, these works attest to an unflagging interest in the complex mixture of history, culture, geology, and greed that has made western mining an irresistible literary subject for a century and a half.

Primary Bibliography

Bierce, Ambrose. *The Complete Short Stories of Ambrose Bierce*. Ernest Jerome Hopkins, ed. Lincoln: University of Nebraska Press, 1984.

Buffum, Edward Gould. *Six Months in the Gold Mines*. In *From Mexican Days to the Gold Rush: Memoirs of James Wilson Marshall and Edward Gould Buffum, Who Grew Up with California*. Doyce B. Nunis, Jr., ed. 1850; rpt., Chicago: The Lakeside Press, 1993.

Clappe, Louise A. K. S. *The Shirley Letters*. 1854-55; rpt., Salt Lake City: Peregrine Smith, 1985.

Daggett, R. M. and J. T. Goodman. *The Psychoscope: A Sensational Drama in Five Acts*. Lawrence I. Berkove, ed. 1871; rpt., Reno: Great Basin Press, 1997.

Delano, Alonzo. *Life on the Plains and Among the Diggings*. 1854; rpt., Ann Arbor: University Microfilms, Inc., 1966.

De Quille, Dan. *The Big Bonanza*. Intro. Oscar Lewis. 1876; rpt., New York: Crowell, 1969.

———. *Dives and Lazarus*. Lawrence I. Berkove, ed. Ann Arbor: Ardis, 1988.

———. *The Fighting Horse of the Stanislaus*. Lawrence I. Berkove, ed. Iowa City: University of Iowa Press, 1990.

———. *The Gnomes of the Dead Rivers*. Lawrence I. Berkove, ed. 1880; rpt., Sparks, Nevada: Falcon Hill Press, 1990.

———. *The Sorceress of Attu*. Lawrence I. Berkove, ed. 1894; rpt., Dearborn: University of Michigan-Dearborn, 1994.

Derby, George Horatio. *Squibob: An Early California Humorist*. Richard Derby Reynolds, ed. San Francisco: Squibob Press, 1990.

Doten, Alfred. *The Journals of Alfred Doten, 1849-1903*. 3 vols. Walter Van Tilburg Clark, ed. Reno: University of Nevada Press, 1984.

Emrich, Duncan, ed. *Comstock Bonanza*. New York: Vanguard, 1950.

Farnham, Eliza W. *California, In-Doors and Out; or, How we Farm, Mine, and Live Generally in the Golden State*. 1856; rpt., Nieuwkoop, The Netherlands: B. DeGraaf, 1972.

Goodman, Joe. *Heroes, Badmen and Honest Miners*. Phillip I. Earl, ed. Reno: Great Basin Press, 1977.

Harte, Bret. *The Outcasts of Poker Flats and Other Stories*. Wallace Stegner, intro. New York: New American Library, 1961.

Jackson, Alfred T. *Diary of a Forty-Niner*. Chauncey L. Canfield, ed. 1906; rpt., New York: Turtle Point Press, 1992.

Loney, Glenn, ed. *California Gold-Rush Plays*. New York: Performing Arts Journal Publications, 1983. (Includes Alonzo Delano, *A Live Woman in the Mines, or Pike County Ahead* [1857]; Bret Harte, *Two Men of Sandy Bar* [1876]; and Charles E. B. Howe, *Joaquin Murieta de Castillo, The Celebrated California Bandit* [1858].)

Marryat, Frank. *Mountains and Molehills; or Recollections of a Burnt Journal*. 1855; rpt., Philadelphia: J. B. Lippincott Company, 1962.

Megquier, Mary Jane. *Apron Full of Gold: The Letters of Mary Jane Megquier from San Francisco, 1849-1856*. San Marino, California: The Huntington Library, 1949.

Miller, Joaquin. *'49: The Gold-Seeker of the Sierras*. New York: Funk and Wagnalls, 1884.

———. *The Danites in the Sierras*. Chicago: Jansen, McClurg, 1881.

Perlot, Jean-Nicolas. *Gold Seeker: Adventures of a Belgian Argonaut During the Gold Rush Years*. Helen Harding Bretnor, trans. New Haven: Yale University Press, 1985.

Ridge, John Rollin. *The Life and Adventures of Joaquín Murieta, the Celebrated California Bandit*. Joseph Henry Jackson, intro. 1854; rpt., Norman: University of Oklahoma Press, 1986.

Roeder, Richard B., ed. "Writings About Butte." In *The Last Best Place: A Montana Anthology*. William Kittredge and Annick Smith, eds. Seattle: University of Washington Press, 1988. Pp. 447-514.

Royce, Sarah. *A Frontier Lady: Recollections of the Gold Rush and Early California*. 1932; rpt., Lincoln: University of Nebraska Press, 1977.

Taylor, Bayard. *Eldorado, or Adventures in the Path of Empire*. 1850; rpt., Lincoln: University of Nebraska Press, 1988.

Taylor, Robert Lewis. *The Travels of Jamie McPheeters*. Garden City, New York: Doubleday, 1958.

Weld, John. *The Pardners: A Novel of the California Gold Rush*. New York: Charles Scribner's Sons, 1941.

Secondary Bibliography

Angel, Myron. *History of Nevada*. 1881; rpt., Berkeley: Howell-North, 1958.

Berkove, Lawrence I. *Ethical Records of Twain and His Circle of Sagebrush Journalists*. Elmira, New York: Elmira College Center for Mark Twain Studies, 1994. (Quarry Farm Papers 5.)

———. "Rollin Mallory Daggett's 'My French Friend': A Precursor of 'Paul's Case'?" *Willa Cather Pioneer Memorial Newsletter*, 38:2 (Spring 1994): 31-34.

Berson, Misha. *The San Francisco Stage, Part I: From Gold Rush to Golden Spike, 1849-1869*. San Francisco: San Francisco Performing Arts Library & Museum Journal, 1989.

Cummings, Ella Sterling. *Story of the Files: A Review of Californian Writers and Literature*. 1893; rpt., San Leandro, California: Yosemite Publications, 1982.

Davis, Samuel Post. *History of Nevada*. 1913; rpt., Las Vegas: Nevada Publications, n.d.

Dwyer, Richard and Richard Lingenfelter, eds. *Lying on the Eastern Slope: James Townsend's Comic Journalism on the Mining Frontier*. Miami: Florida International University Press, 1984.

Holliday, J. S. *The World Rushed In: The California Gold Rush Experience*. New York: Simon & Schuster, 1981.

Jackson, Joseph Henry. *Anybody's Gold: The Story of California's Mining Towns*. New

York: D. Appleton-Century, 1941.

Kowalewski, Michael. "Imagining the California Gold Rush: The Visual and Verbal Legacy." *California History*, 71:2 (Spring 1992): 61-73.

Levy, Jo Ann. *They Saw the Elephant: Women in the California Gold Rush*. Norman: University of Oklahoma Press, 1992.

Mason, Jeffrey D. "*My Partner* (1879) and the West." In *Melodrama and the Myth of America*. Bloomington: Indiana University Press, 1993. Pp. 127-154.

Paul, Rodman W. *California Gold: The Beginning of Mining in the Far West*. Cambridge: Harvard University Press, 1947.

————. "Gold and Silver Rushes." In *The Reader's Encyclopedia of the American West*. Howard R. Lamar, ed. New York: Harper & Row, 1977. Pp. 445-451.

————. *Mining Frontiers of the Far West, 1848-1880*. 1963; rpt., Albuquerque: University of New Mexico Press, 1974.

Starr, Kevin. *Americans and the California Dream, 1850-1915*. New York: Oxford University Press, 1973.

Walker, Franklin. *San Francisco's Literary Frontier*. 1939; rpt., New York: Alfred A. Knopf, 1943.

Fred Erisman

Children's Literature In and Of the West

Only recently has the American West begun to fare well at the hands of writers for the young. To be sure, the region has since the mid-nineteenth century been a regular and reliable subject and setting for stories of exploration and adventure, but the treatment accorded it has rarely risen above the stereotypically formulaic. And therein lies much of the significance of western writing for children. As it preserves the formulas and the stereotypes, it shapes them into a newly mythic vision of the West. And, as it melds the formulas and the familiar with a greater regional reality, western writing for the young truly offers a sense of "growing up with the country" that provides new perspectives on the nation's sense of itself.

The evolution of western writing for the young falls readily into three major periods. The first, the pre-western era prior to 1890, builds upon a generalized consciousness of the larger region, for the most part unshaped by any specific articulation of a pervasive mythic vision. The works of this era are content merely to describe, focusing upon the picturesque elements — landscape, population, or action — of the region. The authors, predominantly eastern, work from a largely second-hand, often superficial notion of the region and present it in conventionalized ways. The second, the classical western era (1890–1940), reflects a more coherent national perception of the West, as authors begin to draw parallels between the region and the nation. Works in this period probe more deeply, echoing the growing national consciousness of the region, considering the diverse materials that make up the West, and integrating them as functioning parts of the story at hand. Significantly, they also begin to crystallize a mythic vision of the region as a place of natural splendor, individual affirmation, and democratic opportunity, free of the artificial constraints of the older, established societies of the East. These romantic attributes are accentuated in the later years of the period by a growing awareness that the "West" they describe is inexorably disappearing, if not already vanished. First-hand accounts of landscape, flora, and fauna begin to appear, leading next to stories drawing upon the environment and peoples of the West, frequently written by authors, female as well as male, who are themselves citizens of the region.

The final period, the post-western era (1940–the present), acknowledges the continuing vitality of the western myth, but tempers it with an increasing awareness of the social, economic, and cultural realities shaping western life. "The West" becomes an organic part of the story, as authors isolate or abstract elements from the larger scene and go on to consider their implications. The three eras together document the extent to which western works for the young increasingly speak to issues of national identity and social cohesion, demonstrating that such juvenile literature works as a social and intellectual influence of note.

The origins of a distinctively "western" literature for children lie, in great part, in an article in *The Atlantic Monthly* of December, 1865. There, in "Books for Our Children," Samuel Osgood calls for the creation of an *American* literature for children — a literature that, by drawing upon uniquely American materials and values, will equip young Americans for the new world emerging in the post-Civil War era. Like the emerging "local color" writing for adults, Osgood asserts, such a literature will help to heal the wounds of the war just ended, will encourage among the young a sense of national purpose and destiny, and will instill a genuinely democratic tendency to judge others by their character and achievements rather than by their circumstances.

Osgood's essay reflects the pre-western era's attitudes toward the child and child-rearing. Children must be guided, to be sure, presented with examples of the very best in moral and factual knowledge, but they remain distinctive entities with needs and interests peculiarly their own. The literature provided them must address those interests as well as those of the larger nation. The essay reflects as well the emerging movement toward literary realism, which holds that American literature must deal with life as it is empirically observed. And, in its emphasis upon the unity present within American diversity, it reflects the divisiveness of the war just ended and the first stirrings of the unifying movement toward local color and, later, literary regionalism.

Although, as Osgood makes clear, the time was ripe for the appearance of western writings for children, the machinery of children's publishing was still firmly situated in the East. Despite the appearance of publishers in Chicago, St. Louis, and San Francisco, the production of children's books between 1865 and 1890 was dominated by houses situated in New York and Boston. Among the New York publishers were Harper and Brothers, G. P. Putnam's Sons, and Charles Scribner and Sons, whose children's lists included such authors as Charles C. Coffin, Mary Mapes Dodge, Martha Finley, and Horace E. Scudder. Boston publishers noteworthy for children's publishing included Lee and Shepard, D. Lothrop and Co., and Roberts Brothers, publishers of Louisa May Alcott, Thomas Bailey Aldrich, Lucretia P. Hale, and Oliver Optic. Their eastern origins and traditions notwithstanding, though, publishers were receptive to new approaches; western materials and authors, when they began to appear, found relatively ready acceptance.

Children's publishing prior to 1890 is bolstered by the burgeoning of magazines for the young. Among the earliest of these is the Boston-based *The Youth's Companion*, established in 1827 as an overtly religious journal, which after the Civil War evolved into a general-interest periodical. Harriet Beecher Stowe and Hezekiah Butterworth were contributors, as were, later, C.A. Stephens, Henry Ward Beecher, Rebecca Harding Davis, William Dean Howells, and others. Rivaling the *Companion* was *St. Nicholas*, published in New York by Scribner's (later The Century Co.). Begun in 1873 and edited by Mary Mapes Dodge, it included western authors and subjects from the outset, quickly becoming the premier American children's magazine. Early contributors were Noah Brooks, Mary Hallock Foote, and Helen Hunt Jackson; later ones included L. Frank Baum, Jack London, Theodore Roosevelt, Mark Twain, and Kate Douglas Wiggin. It was followed in 1879 by *Harper's Young People,* edited by Kirk Munroe, which during its twenty-year lifetime published Dan Beard, Theodore Roosevelt, Edward Everett Hale, Robert E. Peary, and Buffalo Bill Cody.

Led by *St. Nicholas*, the three magazines entertained their young readers yet presented them with factual knowledge of the United States, its social and political institutions, its peoples, and its place in the larger world. This knowledge was accompanied by an emphasis upon integrity, duty, and conscientiousness — generalized and unifying virtues as applicable in the post-Civil War world as in the pre-war years. Though based in the East, these magazines quickly developed a national reader-ship among the young. Accompanying young readers westward as the population moved, they became a powerful agency in the assimilation of the West into the larger nation, and they provided early outlets for some of the best writers of and about the West.

Shaping the early outlook of the pre-western era is the dime novel, which burst upon the literary scene in 1860. Inexpensively priced and widely disseminated, the dime novel was directed toward the growing adult reading public; however, younger readers soon appropriated it, to the dismay of their elders, and it quickly became a staple for children. Beadle and Adams, a New York firm and the first and most prominent of the dime-novel publishers, recognized the appeal their product held for young readers and soon began publishing works merchandised directly to that audience. Beadle's Boys' Books of Romance and Adventure was inaugurated in 1874 and was followed in 1881 by Beadle's Boys' Library of Sport, Story and Adventure.

From the outset, the dime novel draws upon western — or, at least, frontier — materials. The first such work, Ann S. Stephens' *Malaeska, the Indian Wife of the White Hunter* (1860), although set in Colonial-era New York, establishes Indians and Indian conflict as a staple. Edward Ellis' *Bill Biddon, Trapper; or, Life in the North-west* (1860) extends the setting through Nebraska to the upper reaches of the Yellowstone, while Ann S. Stephens' *Sybil Chase; or, The Valley Ranche. A Tale of California Life* (1861) takes its materials from the life of a gambler in California. The boys' books quickly followed suit. Among the earliest of the Books of Romance and Adventure series are J. Stanley Henderson's *Prairie Chick; or, The Quaker among the Red-Skins* and C.L. Edwards' *Silver Tongue, the Dacotah Queen; or, Pat among the Red-skins* (both 1874). The first volume of the Boy's Library of Sport, Story and Adventure is Prentiss Ingraham's *Adventures of Buffalo Bill from Boyhood to Manhood. Deeds of Daring and Romantic Incidents in the Life of Wm. F. Cody, the Monarch of Bordermen* (1881), one of countless volumes to sing the praises of Buffalo Bill.

Other adventure stories available to young readers did little to cor-rect the dime novels' melodramatic vision of western existence. The Irish-born Mayne Reid drew upon his experiences as a veteran of the

Mexican War and his time as Indian fighter and hunter to produce *The Rifle Rangers* (1850) and *The Scalp Hunters* (1851), both set in Mexico, and *The Boy Hunters* (1852), the tale of a quest after a white buffalo, originating in Louisiana. Even more popular were the writings of "Harry Castlemon" (Charles Austin Fosdick), which include *Frank on the Prairie* (1868), the three-volume Rocky Mountain Series of 1871-72, the three-volume Boy Trapper Series of 1878-79, and, late in his career, the three-volume Pony Express Series (1898-1900).

Although the dime novel portrayal of the West left a lasting mark, other works strove to temper the melodrama with a more balanced vision of the emerging region. In addition to such titles as Francis Parkman's "Adventures of Pierre Radisson" (1889), *Youth's Companion* carried "R.E."'s "Perils of Western Travellers" (1840), dealing with Indians along the upper Mississippi, and the anonymous "Lady Miners in California" (1850). The McGuffey Readers (1837 ff) advanced the notions of Manifest Destiny (Thomas Smith Grimke's "Duty of the American Orator") and western identity (Daniel Drake's "The Patriotism of Western Literature"), both in the Fourth Reader, but also offered a view of the Indian as something other than an indigenous peril. Charles Sprague in "Prospects of the Cherokees" (Fifth Reader) protested inhumane treatment of the Indian and went on in "North American Indians" (Sixth Reader) to paint the Indian as a noble savage on the brink of extinction.

The influence exerted by these works is apparent from the echoes of them that appear in other children's books of the period, for here one finds implicit reinforcement of the West's being a region of adventure, violence, and savagery. Mark Twain, for example, in *The Adventures of Tom Sawyer* (1876), establishes that Tom is an avid reader of dime novels. When Tom and his friends run away to live as pirates on a Mississippi River island, they vary their adventure with an interlude of playing Indians (perhaps of eastern tribes, since they pillage English settlements). The West appears even in such quintessentially New England-rooted works as Louisa May Alcott's *An Old-Fashioned Girl* (1870), *Little Men* (1871), and *Jo's Boys* (1886). In the first of these books, the son of a failed Boston businessman turns away from his New England origins to find identity and self-confidence in the West. In the latter two, Dan, a decent if disruptive denizen of Plumfield School, reveals an empathy for the natural world and goes West to find his fortune. He serves prison time for killing a man in a mining-town brawl, and dies heroically defending the Indian peoples he has befriended and come to respect. All three works paint the region as one of manly freedom and opportunity, but the latter two imply that sensitive easterners may have difficulty surviving if they cannot accept the region's unique demands.

Only in the historical novels does a genuinely alternative vision appear. In these works, authors strive to give a reasonably accurate picture of the land and the kind of life that is lived in it; though they aim, certainly, at telling an absorbing story, they are also concerned with sketching a more realistic picture of the West. Thus, in *The Boy Emigrants* (1877; serialized in *St. Nicholas*), Noah Brooks presents a strikingly non-melodramatic account of the rigors of the westward movement. In *Juan and Juanita* (1888; serialized in *St. Nicholas* with illustrations by Frederic Remington), Frances Courtenay Baylor offers an adventuresome yet authentic picture of Anglo, Mexican, and Indian life in the American Southwest. And, though *The Hoosier Schoolboy* (1883; also serialized in *St. Nicholas*) looks back to the region of the old Northwest Territory, Edward Eggleston uses the landscape and general frontier environment to enhance his account of life in a rural school.

Throughout these writings one can see the evolving picture of the West available to American youth. For the most part, works emphasize the melodramatic aspects of the region, using the hazards of the West, whether from the landscape or from its peoples, to make it a place of peril and adventure. The majority of readers neither expected nor demanded anything more of the accounts. In its openness, its wildness, and its freedom, the children's literary West offered a dramatic contrast to life in the more settled regions, and the thrills it provided became commonplace. Only late in the period do writers begin to treat the region as something more than a stage setting, preparing the way for the second major era in the presentation of the West.

The classical western era, the fifty years from 1890 to 1940, is in many ways the Golden Age of western children's literature. The older views persist, to be sure, but the fully developed western myth begins to exert its influence. Works written late in the period not surprisingly show the influence of the cinematic West, and "the West" itself expands to incorporate the Midwest, the Great Plains, and the Mountain West. In this period children's works begin to evince a sense of the West as a distinctive place, and to reveal their authors' growing awareness that the region's diverse components have a direct effect upon life and, therefore, upon the stories that might be told.

Adventure stories, a staple of western juvenile writing, not surprisingly show the least development; for the most part, they cling to the patterns and images created a generation earlier. Thus, for example, the numerous publications of the Stratemeyer Syndicate, established by Edward Stratemeyer, offer a West reminiscent of that of the dime novel. Stratemeyer's own *Three Young Ranchmen; or, Daring Adventures in the Great West* (1901; by "Captain Ralph Bonehill") is blood-and-thunder adventure set in the mining West. "Victor Appleton's" *Tom Swift Among the Diamond Makers* (1911) uses the Rockies as a setting for its mixture of science fiction and adventure, while the five volumes of The Saddle Boys series (1913-1915), by "Captain James Carson," take the young heroes from adventures in the Rockies through a sojourn in the Grand Canyon to rustlers and a roundup in the Southwest.

Adventure writers other than Stratemeyer and his stable found the West equally attractive. Although E. J. Craine quickly moves the action of the eight-volume Airplane Boys series (1930-32) from Texas to Canada and then on to Central and South America, her two teenaged heroes are sons of Texas ranchers, and much of the novelty of the early volumes comes from the boys' efforts to incorporate airplanes into ranch operations. Perhaps the most telling evidence of the persistence of the adventurous West, however, occurs in three works set not in the West but in the urban Midwest. Penrod Schofield, hero of *Penrod* (1914), *Penrod and Sam* (1916), and *Penrod Jashber* (1929), by Booth Tarkington, lives a conventionally placid middle-class existence in a small midwestern city of the pre-World War I twentieth century. One of the running jokes of the three books is the continuing saga of "Harold Ramorez, the Road-Agent," Penrod's intermittent effort at the dime novel. Although Penrod is a comfortable denizen of a post-Turnerian America, the myth of the West retains its magic; when the pressures of school, parents, and conventional civilization become too oppressive, he turns to the *persona* of "Harold Ramorez" and loses himself in sketching melodramatic adventures in the mountains and along the trail.

The stereotypical adventure tales notwithstanding, the West in this period takes on new subtleties. The English-born Ernest Thompson Seton uses his boyhood experiences in Canada and, later, the western United States, to good effect in a series of books emphasizing the redemptive qualities of the natural world and its wildlife. *Wild Animals I*

Have Known (1898), although scrupulously accurate in its physical and behavioral portrayal of the grizzly bear, the wolf, the rabbit, and other creatures, works within the tradition of the animal story, attributing human thoughts and emotions to animals in order to make a social point. The later *Two Little Savages* (1903) goes still further, incorporating an enormous amount of Indian lore into its account of how a summer of camping and woodcraft leads an urban boy to greater maturity and insight.

Even more unconventional is *The Wonderful Wizard of Oz* (1900), by L. Frank Baum, for its "West" is the economically battered Midwest of the later Populist era. The book is shaped by Baum's experiences in Dakota Territory, where the Depression of 1893 wiped out his hopes of making a fortune, and the drought-ridden Kansas farm where the story begins is a far cry from the fertile West of American myth. Dorothy Gale's escape to Oz only adds to the impact, for the Wizard himself proves to be a pitchman from Omaha, and Dorothy's three companions, the Scarecrow, the Tin Woodman, and the Cowardly Lion, are tantalizingly reminiscent of some of the most prominent national and regional political figures of the time. Fantasy it is and fantasy it remains, but *The Wonderful Wizard of Oz* would be a far lesser book without its western components.

The expanding view of the West in the classical period extends to factual works, as well. Historical and biographical accounts burgeon, giving young Americans new perspectives on the West, its environment, and its peoples. William Dean Howells relates his Ohio boyhood in *A Boy's Town* (1890; serialized in *Harper's Young People*) and *My Year in a Log Cabin* (1893; abridged in *Youth's Companion* in 1887), while Hamlin Garland offers the story of his early days in the upper Midwest in *Boy Life on the Prairie* (1899). The same year sees *The Court of Boyville*, by the Kansas-born William Allen White, short stories describing boyhood life within the settled confines of a small town. Childhood of a different sort appears in Charles Eastman's *An Indian Boyhood* (1902), in which Eastman, a Dartmouth-educated Sioux physician, looks back to his youth on the Plains. William O. Stoddard, author of more than seventy boys' books, offers an early account of Plains Indian life in *Little Smoke; A Tale of the Sioux* (1891). For his part, Emerson Hough offers a corrective to stereotypical portrayals of western life in *The Story of the Cowboy* (1897), and extends "the West" to Alaska with his Young Alaskans series (1908 ff).

Other facets of Native American life and lore appear in James Willard Schultz's *With the Indians in the Rockies* (1911) and *Sinopah, the Indian Boy* (1913), while George Bird Grinnell draws upon his work as naturalist and ethnologist for *Wolf Hunters* (1914) and the several "Jack Danvers" stories. *The Trail Book* (1918) and *Children Sing in the Far West* (1928), by Mary Austin, collect stories and songs from the West's native peoples. Stewart Edward White returns to an older "West" with *The Magic Forest* (1903), a mystical account of a boy's encounter with Ojibway life and lore, and *Daniel Boone, Wilderness Scout* (1922), one of the first substantial biographies of the legendary frontiersman. Finally, Will James, in the Newbery-Prize-winning *Smoky the Cowhorse* (1926), blends an authentic picture of cowboy life with the traditional genre of the animal story to bring new vigor to familiar materials. These accounts, and others like them, supply new perspectives and new images to balance the stereotypes. Though certainly not lacking in incident and excitement, they give a new authenticity to the portrayal of the region.

By far the greatest advance, however, comes in the appearance of family stories firmly rooted in the West. In their portrayals of daily life in areas newly settled, they work to amend the stereotypes and add new detail to the developing vision of the West. Among the earliest of these is *A Summer in a Cañon* (1889), by Kate Douglas Wiggin, which uses a camping trip in California to suggest the distinctiveness of the countryside and the state's ethnic diversity. Carol Ryrie Brink's *Caddie Woodlawn* (1935), which, like *Smoky*, won a Newbery Prize, is set in rural Wisconsin of the Civil War era. Its heroine, the tomboy Caddie, gains credibility through her naturalness and through Brink's matter-of-fact treatment of midwestern life. Brink's presentation strips that life of melodrama, offering instead a convincingly human picture of what western existence must actually have been.

"Westering," as a term and as a concept, appears explicitly in *The Red Pony* (1937), by John Steinbeck, a work that, although not initially written for children, features a youthful protagonist and has found its way into the juvenile canon. The physical West is present in the day-to-day efforts of young Jody Tiflin's parents to scrape a living from their small ranch, but the region is also present as an idea. Jody's grandfather is an old wagon boss, and his incessantly repeated tales of the westward movement capture the boy's imagination, giving the lad at last a sense of the epic, national sweep that westering constituted. In its combination of the details of western place, the inevitable clashes of family life, and the underlying sense of a national myth, *The Red Pony* speaks to the growing-up of a country as well as of a boy.

The most distinguished of the family stories, however, are the eight Little House books of Laura Ingalls Wilder. Drawing upon Wilder's own childhood, the first volumes, *Little House in the Big Woods* (1932), *Little House on the Prairie* (1935), and *On the Banks of Plum Creek* (1937), relate the life of the Ingalls family from 1872 to 1879, as they roam from the Big Woods of Wisconsin to a farm in Minnesota. Later titles, beginning with *By the Shores of Silver Lake* (1939) and *The Long Winter* (1940), take the family still farther west to Dakota Territory, where in 1880 they at last settle permanently. Laura finds work as a teacher and in 1885 marries another homesteader, becoming herself a part of the region. Although the books are novels and cannot be relied upon as a factual account of Wilder's life (Wilder's daughter, Rose Wilder Lane, substantially reshaped the stories to emphasize their "American" qualities), they nonetheless stand as a compelling gloss to the larger story of "growing up with the country" and an enduring evocation of the epic sweep of western life.

The enduring power of that life becomes clear in the Post-Western years following 1940. Ushered in by the Second World War and complicated in later years by the Cold War, the Korean conflict, and the Vietnam experience, the period is characterized by a growing American consciousness of the larger world. Emerging from World War II as the first of the world superpowers, the nation is compelled to reevaluate its role in world affairs, and the insularity of the pre-war years necessarily begins to fade. This reevaluation is paralleled by a new seriousness in children's literature, reflected in greater emphasis on social, economic, and environmental issues and the ways they affect the life of the region. The West, not surprisingly, lends itself to these concerns, and the works that emerge after 1940 suggest the degree to which the region has become assimilated into the larger national culture.

The appeal of adventure stories continues into the post-war years, but three substantial works by Jack Schaefer illustrate how an old form can be transformed by new approaches. *Shane* (1949), an adult work quickly appropriated by younger readers, gains in power from its point of view. Long after the events he relates take place, Bob Starrett tells of the coming of a mysterious stranger to his family's Wyoming ranch, and the personal, family, and community tensions that result. While the book can be read with pleasure as a straightforward action story, Bob's dual point of view (that of youngster on the scene *and* of adult looking back to a momentous childhood experience) gives *Shane* a level of human poignancy rarely found in juvenile *or* adult writing.

First Blood (1953) continues Schaefer's interest in the maturing process, as the adolescent Jess Harker slowly comes to realize the responsibilities of adulthood. Jess' growth to greater maturity is strengthened by Schaefer's linking it with the day-to-day routine of the stage line that employs him and with the misguided individualism of Race Crim, the flamboyant gunman he so admires. *Mavericks* (1967) looks at the issues from the other side, in the reminiscences of Old Jake Hanlon. Jake has done it all and seen it all, savoring every moment of his life, but only as an old man does he come to understand that he has been an active player in the destruction of all that he has loved. His is a simple story that echoes long afterward in the mind, and it takes western adventure for the young into areas unthinkable a generation before.

Another area of western juvenile writing that surpasses its origins is the historical story, as modern writers consciously strive to emphasize the history and peoples of the American West. Some deal with Hispanic culture; Joseph Krumgold's *And Now Miguel* (1953; Newbery Prize) sets a story of growing up against the backdrop of the Sangre de Cristo Mountains, while Jack Schaefer's *Old Ramon* (1960) builds upon the evolving relationship of an old sheepherder, a boy, and a dog. Others, such as Laurence Yep's *Dragonwings* (1975), take up Asian culture; Yep's picture of a Chinese family in the San Francisco of the early twentieth century does a great deal to correct pervasive stereotypes. Still others, by far the largest group, deal with American Indian cultures. These include Laura Armer's picture of a Navajo boyhood, *Waterless Mountain* (1931); Scott O'Dell's Newbery-winning *Island of the Blue Dolphins* (1960), with its account of Karana, an Indian girl stranded on a California island for eighteen years; Mari Sandoz's *The Story Catcher* (1965), the story of a Sioux boy's yearning to become a warrior; and mystery writer Tony Hillerman's *The Boy Who Made Dragonfly* (1972), a retelling of a Zuñi legend.

History of another sort informs the Orphan Train Quartet by Joan Lowery Nixon. Comprising *A Family Apart* (1987), *Caught in the Act* (1988), *In the Face of Danger* (1988), and *A Place to Belong* (1989), the quartet builds upon one of the oddest and most poignant episodes in western American history. In 1854, Charles Loring Brace's Children's Aid Society initiated the effort to ship impoverished youngsters from the slums of the city to the West, where they might be adopted to grow up in healthier and more sustaining surroundings. Called "placing out," the undertaking operated until 1929, reflecting the degree to which the West seemed in the public mind to offer a solution to the problems of the urbanized East. Nixon's books capture both the drama of the undertaking and the enduring dream that, in the West, life will be better.

Embracing, as they do, the family story as well as the historical story, Nixon's Orphan Train stories attest to the continuing vitality of the family in the West. In the evolution of the family story, moreover, one finds the clearest evidence of how the West and its issues are assimilated into larger concerns. Thus, for example, Mary O'Hara's Goose Bar Ranch trilogy (*My Friend Flicka* [1941], *Thunderhead* [1943], and *Green Grass of Wyoming* [1946]) tells a straightforward story of the personal and economic trials facing the McLaughlin family over seven years on their Wyoming ranch prior to World War II. Behind the McLaughlins' immediate story, however, is a larger, more haunting one, a story of the West itself. They have come west in search of the American Dream, only to find themselves not in the land of the limitless frontier, but rather in a region that the frontier has long since passed by. Using much the same materials as *The Red Pony*, but extending its theme of westering still further, O'Hara's trilogy is one of the first modern stories to look searchingly at the closing of the frontier as it affects life in the middle and later twentieth century, and her account anticipates much of the frustration and uncertainty of the later decades of the century.

Just as evocative, in its own way, is Patricia Maclachlan's *Sarah, Plain and Tall* (1985). The Sarah of the title is an eastern spinster, well set in the ways of her New England fishing village. She decides to come west as a mail-order bride, however, joining the household of a widower who has decided his children need a female presence. Set in the farming West rather than the ranching or mining West, the book dramatizes the motifs of growth, adaptation, and synthesis that the best of western literature contains. Sarah must adapt to a life far from the rhythms, sounds, and smells of her coastal village; her farmer husband must adapt to the presence of a second strong-minded adult; the children must deal with the subtle changes worked in their father as well as with the new ideas and insights Sarah brings. With its quiet emphasis upon the importance of integrity and resilience, *Sarah, Plain and Tall* makes of familiar materials a richly sustaining story of how the blending of West and East creates a synthesis that surpasses either.

What the future holds for juvenile writing in and of the West is uncertain, but the general outlook is hopeful. Many authors, like their adult-oriented counterparts, inevitably follow market trends and social fads; the growing prominence given to ethnic and revisionist stories as the decade of the nineties draws to a close shows how much writing for the young reflects the willingness of authors and publishers to ride the crest of whatever wave seems likely to sell books. At the same time, however, a modest but consistent nucleus of writers puts story first and message second. Their works are likely to endure, and their works reflect the true significance of juvenile literature as a genre.

The West is as much an idea as it is a region. In many respects, the West of the mind, whether that of an adult or a child, is the creation of generations of writers whose works have shaped national consciousness of the region and have defined its attributes in the national mind. And here the juvenile works make perhaps their greatest contribution. Their West is communicated to the young, who, as they mature, test the vision against the reality. Sometimes there is conflict, but sometimes there is reinforcement, and out of the process emerges a steadily evolving, steadily maturing vision of the West and its potential. As young readers grow to adulthood, they carry with them an awareness of a region richly complex and steadily progressive, a synthesis of myth and reality, stereotype and actuality, that equips them to deal responsibly with the region's issues and circumstances. In their adult enterprises, these young readers will further shape the region; their reading, through the years, will be one of the elements that has made them what they are and what the region becomes. It will be the vindication of Osgood's call for an *American* literature for children, and is no small achievement for a body of literature all too often ignored.

Selected Bibliography

Atkins, Annette. "The Child's West: A Review Essay." *New Mexico Historical Review*, 65 (October 1990): 477-90. Essay-review dealing with Elliott West's study of western childhood (q.v., below) and other related works.

Baum, L. Frank. *The Wonderful Wizard of Oz*. Michael Patrick Hearne, ed. 1900; rpt., New York: Schocken, 1983. A complete text of *The Wizard* supplemented by reviews and critical articles.

Bingham, Jane M., ed. *Writers for Children*. New York: Scribner, 1988. Concise bio-bibliographies of major authors, American and world, including many with western ties.

Cameron, Eleanor. *The Green and Burning Tree*. Boston: Little, Brown, 1969. Helpful ruminations on "the compelling power of place" and other attributes of children's literature.

Clark, Beverly Lyon. "American Children's Literature: Background and Bibliography." *American Studies International*, 30:1 (April 1992): 4-40. A comprehensive overview of basic secondary works.

Commager, Henry Steele, ed. *The St. Nicholas Anthology*. New York: Random, 1948. A thoughtful sampling from the most noteworthy of American children's periodicals.

Donelson, Kenneth L. "Some Adolescent Novels About the West: An Annotated Bibliography." *Elementary English*, 49 (May 1972): 735-739. Fifty-five titles covering forty years of publishing. Few will agree with all of Donelson's selections.

Erisman, Fred. "American Regional Juvenile Literature, 1870-1910: An Annotated Bibliography." *American Literary Realism*, 6:2 (Spring 1973): 109-122. Selective listings of primary and secondary sources, with brief commentary.

————." 'Growing Up With the Country' in Young Adult Fiction." *Roundup Quarterly*, 4:2 (1991 N.S.): 5-14. A thematic reading of selected works for or about children in the West.

————. *Laura Ingalls Wilder*. Boise: Boise State University Western Writers Series, 1994. The author of the "Little House" books examined as a western writer.

————. "Regionalism in American Children's Literature." In *Society & Children's Literature*, James H. Fraser, ed. Boston: Godine, 1978. Pp. 53-75. How children's literature has dealt with the various American regions.

Holt, Marilyn Irvin. *The Orphan Trains: Placing Out in America*. Lincoln: University of Nebraska Press, 1992. A comprehensive account of the "placing out" episode.

Holtz, William. *The Ghost in the Little House: A Life of Rose Wilder Lane*. Columbia: University of Missouri Press, 1993. Rose Wilder Lane's role in shaping the "Little House" books.

Johannsen, Albert. *The House of Beadle and Adams*. 2 vols. Norman: University of Oklahoma Press, 1950. The standard history of the dime novel.

Johnson, Deidre. *Edward Stratemeyer and the Stratemeyer Syndicate*. New York: Twayne (TUSAS 627), 1993. An authoritative account of Stratemeyer's work and influence.

Kelly, R. Gordon, ed. *Children's Periodicals of the United States*. Westport, Connecticut: Greenwood, 1984. A comprehensive critical guide to American children's magazines.

————. *Mother Was A Lady*. Westport, Connecticut: Greenwood, 1974. Changes in nineteenth-century American social thought as manifested in juvenile literature.

Lindberg, Stanley W., ed. *The Annotated McGuffey*. New York: Van Nostrand, 1976. Representative selections, with commentary, from the entire McGuffey series.

MacLeod, Anne Scott. *American Childhood: Essays in Children's Literature of the Nineteenth and Twentieth Centuries*. Athens: University of Georgia Press, 1994. Particularly helpful on how children are treated in the literature of their times.

[Osgood, Samuel]. "Books for Our Children." *The Atlantic Monthly*, 16 (December 1865): 724-735. Where it all begins.

Smith, Henry Nash. *Virgin Land: The American West as Symbol and Myth*. Cambridge: Harvard University Press, 1950. How dime novels, among other works, affected Americans' vision of the West.

Tebbel, John. *A History of Book Publishing in the United States*. 4 vols. New York: Bowker, 1972-1981. The evolution of American publishing houses and their philosophies.

Thompson, Lowell, et al., eds. *Youth's Companion*. Boston: Houghton Mifflin, 1954. Representative selections from the other great nineteenth-century periodical for children.

West, Elliott. *Growing Up with the Country: Childhood on the Far Western Frontier*. Albuquerque: University of New Mexico Press, 1989. An insightful overview of child life in the frontier West.

Mick McAllister

Native Sources:
American Indian Autobiography

If we come to American Indian autobiography hoping for a direct experience of American Indian life with as little mediation as possible, we are as likely to find it as we are to find unpolluted water or food without chemical additives; our success is based in part on our definitions, our tolerances, and our tastes. The autobiography has an inherent close focus that at once provides a wealth of personalized detail and, at the same time, runs contrary to the very idea of cultural generalization. To illustrate, imagine attempting, as rare historians have brilliantly done, to capture the spirit of a time and place like New England of the 1830s in three or four exemplary lives. Or imagine choosing a single contemporary personal memoir to represent "Americans in the last half of the twentieth century." The diversity of American Indian experience and values across the dimensions of time, location, and cultures must, as we learn more about it, overwhelm the thinking generalizer.

The history of American Indian autobiography has as its unifying thread the desire to preserve, define, or create that direct experience. This desire to have autobiography serve as a cultural record sparked anthropologists' great interest in "life stories" from the twenties through the sixties. However, much of the anthropological collecting was tainted by a kind of naïveté about the effect of the collector on what was collected. As physicists Werner Heisenberg and Erwin Schrödinger discovered about observations of physical matter, the subject could not be "observed" without the observation affecting his or her life. If the life were written from translated field notes, then the editorial work of the anthropologist almost inevitably shaped the content and presentation. Even if it were based upon the subject's own journals and transcript of her own words, it would, like Don Talayesva's in *Sun Chief*, be modified by the editorial process and, almost inevitably, revised and augmented as a result of the anthropologist's expectations, consciously or not.

The best-known instance of collector intervention is the controversial relationship of John G. Neihardt to *Black Elk Speaks*. Since Robert Sayre and Sally McCluskey first brought the question forward, there has been a broad spectrum of scholarly response to the realization that Neihardt did considerably more than "collect" this life. Raymond de Mallie and others have brought from their study of the relationship between *Black Elk Speaks* and Neihardt's field notes a new understanding of the nature of the interaction between collector and subject. Scholars like David Brumble have posited in light of this problem that an American Indian autobiography is by its nature a bicultural document. Just as the reader brings cultural preconceptions to the finished document, the intervening collector/editor adjusts the literary artifact to accord with cultural and personal notions of what is interesting, what important, what inconsequential.

Aside from the pictographic biographical materials studied by Hertha Wong, all American Indian autobiographical materials come into being through non-Indian agencies, often for non-Indian reasons. The ego as the neurotic post-Renaissance man conceives it is a peculiarly western idea. For a member of a traditional Indian culture, only very limited autobiographical information is likely to be significant. Within these cultures, a Plains Indian man might tell "coup stories" in the interest of personal advancement, children might be told stories from the lives of exemplary men and women as part of their education (with an emphasis on same-sex exemplars), individuals with shamanistic powers might preface the use of those powers with a life story to validate those powers. Often the narrator might arrange for an audience of validators — members of the tribe familiar with the speaker's exploits and willing to vouch for the accuracy of the account.

The earliest self-expressing American Indian autobiographies — those of William Apes, Peter Jones, George Copway — often were confessional, stories of fallen savagery redeemed by Christian conversion, less validation of traditional culture than repudiation of it. While early published writers often had as their goal the education of white

America, the very education that prepared the writers distanced them from the culture they chose to defend. The anthropological life story in vogue in the first half of the twentieth century often was not written for self-expression, self-examination, vindication, or validation. It was, instead, "coerced," written for hire and detailed according to the interests of the employer, sometimes even shaped in defiance of the subject's desires. Anthropologist Leo Simmons tricked Don Talayesva into writing about secret Hopi ceremonies for *Sun Chief*. Ruth Underhill demanded that her Papago subject give her childhood stories over the woman's firm objections.

When the recording of a life story is voluntary, then one must examine the volunteer's motives. If we read *Crashing Thunder* as a record of traditional Winnebago life, we must keep in mind that the subject is a member of the Peyote religion. In fact, neither he nor the Winnebago traditionals who were his contemporaries would regard him as a "traditional" Indian at all, any more than a small farming community like Valhalla, North Dakota, would consider their Unitarian high school science teacher an example of their traditional values. Similarly, the autobiographies of literate, white-educated Indians such as Charles Eastman, Luther Standing Bear, and Don Talayesva cannot be read as unmediated records of traditional life: the reader must constantly keep in mind that the subject is distanced from that life by the very disjunction that prepared him to write about it.

When we come to American Indian autobiography, we may think we will learn what it means to be Indian. This is likely to be a self-delusion, however, and it is certainly misguided. The culture is more likely to be presented in an unmediated form by the unexceptional person writing unselfconsciously than by the individual interested in telling her story: One thinks of Samuel Pepys' journal or the interviews collected by Studs Terkel on various subjects. The closer a document gets to the reality of "being Indian," the less interesting we are likely to find its contents. Such "pure" anthropological tracts as the "Life Story" of the Navajo hand-trembler Gregorio quickly illustrate this. He grew up, tended sheep, got married, learned hand-trembling — a life's work, no less but no more. It is as mundane, after all, as the monotonous records of the rare mountain man who took the time to keep a journal of his daily rounds in the icy streams of the Rockies, the struggling farmer detailing the expense of turning grassland to cornfield, or the Valhalla librarian ruminating on the town's "cultural poverty."

The day-to-day realities of Indian life are no more savage, brutal, and mean than those of white people of the same time, place, and economic circumstance. Given the pluralism of Indian culture and the ambiguous relationship of subject to culture present in any autobiography, we must constantly be on guard against hasty generalization. Even if *Black Elk Speaks* were precisely what it is taken for by the naïve reader — the literal translation of a traditional Indian's autobiographical monologues — it would still be unwise to generalize about Plains Indians or even the Lakota based upon Black Elk's words. He was, after all, an exceptional man, his personality extraordinarily religious, even in the context of a religious culture, and his life by no estimation average or typical.

The unsophisticated reader takes from the stories of people raised in the traditions of the tribe a value rather like that of processed meat: there is nutrition in it, tainted with preservatives and foreign flavorings. We may or may not know they are there, we may or may not tolerate them, we each have our own mental fulcrum the nurture and pollutant must balance on. The most significant differences between, say, *Pretty-shield: Medicine Woman of the Crow* and Dorothy Johnson's excellent novel *Buffalo Woman* or Colin Stuart's *Walks Far Woman* are extra-literary, not the presence of an illusion but the nature of that illusion. For Johnson, the impelling, seed event is an act of the imagination; for Frank Linderman and Pretty-shield, it is the proximity of two living minds in conversation. The result, in terms of accuracy of representation, is in fact quite similar. For some readers, such books as Charles Eastman's, Luther Standing Bear's, or *Black Elk Speaks* have the same value as first-person fictions. They read for information, and the illusion of the narrative voice is no more than a flavoring, artificial or not. For others, the personal voice is a critical part of the experience; if these are not Luther Standing Bear's words, then the book is essentially a lie. Such absolutism betrays ingenuousness about the process of creating books and the relationship of voice, document, fiction, and writer.

Maxwell Perkins rewrote Thomas Wolfe. We don't like to say it so baldly, but it remains true that Wolfe's books were extensively revised before publication. What is more, the voice of *Look Homeward, Angel* is a fictive voice reshaping autobiography to the not altogether unselfish purposes of the writer. Wolfe tells us the "truth" about his life in thinly disguised fiction which his editor then polishes into a publishable manuscript. The difference between this process and the creation of an American Indian autobiography is one of degree rather than kind. For all the protests that the work is fiction, Wolfe's novels, like such notorious brothers and sisters as Karl Shapiro's *Edsel* and Jack Kerouac's *Dharma Bums*, are savored for their "truth": the veiled portraits and hints behind the fictions. In the first-person autobiography, the confusion of author, subject, and editor is pervasive, even in recent American Indian texts. For example, *Fools Crow*, the first-person narrative of Frank Fools Crow, a contemporary ceremonial chief of the Sioux, includes, according to a final note, "photos by the author." The photos are by Thomas E. Mails, the editor.

For many readers, the American Indian and the horse tribes of the Plains were one and the same thing. At most, some understanding that there were settled peoples in the Southwest might complicate that understanding. The popular nonfiction view of the Indian focused, prior to the American Indian literary renaissance of the 1960s, on these people. The story collections and narratives of George Bird Grinnell, James Willard Schultz, and George E. Hyde, like the life stories transcribed and published by Frank Linderman, offer accurate and readable views of traditional Plains Indian life. For a full discussion of these documents, Lynn Woods O'Brien's *Plains Indian Autobiographies*, a pamphlet of the Boise State University Western Writers Series, is the place to begin. Buried in the pile of popular books by Grinnell, Schultz, and Hyde, prior to its rediscovery in the early 1960s, is the astonishing *Black Elk Speaks*.

Peter Nabokov's revision of the narrative of the Crow warrior Two Leggings may be the most self-aware of these works. Nabokov took a manuscript deposited at the Museum of the American Indian by anthropologist William Wildschut and revised it extensively. Nabokov records in his notes and commentary a description of the process of revision, going so far as to offer some samples of original and revised text. With no first-hand acquaintance with the long-dead subject, who was born around 1850 and died in 1923, forty years before Nabokov first saw the manuscript, he researched the Crow warrior's life in collateral documents as well. The result is a first-person narrative with all the appearance of authenticity. Its value, as Nabokov and his reviewers pointed out, was that Two Leggings was not a great chief but a common man, a good but undistinguished warrior, a representative of his tribe and way of life. These large claims may seem a bit naïve, but the meat of *Two Leggings* is worth tasting.

With the possible exception of *Two Leggings*, the closest the reader will come to an autobiographical narrative of an unacculturated Indian in these works is the paired set of life stories by Frank Linderman, *Plenty-coups* and *Pretty-shield*. Like John G. Neihardt, Linderman interviewed his subjects at length and then created from the interviews a narrative account of the lives, respectively, of an important Crow chief and a woman of some standing in the same tribe. Both were born near the middle of the nineteenth century, and both were living essentially (but by no means absolutely) unacculturated lives. In both books, Linderman is a first-person presence, asking his questions through an interpreter, recording visual cues and relying on his own knowledge of sign language to verify the verbal interpretation, addressing the reader directly. As his preface to *Pretty-shield* attests, he was very aware of the potential for distortion in the process that created the book. Speaking little or no English, Pretty-shield could only have verified the work (as she apparently did with a touching method preserved in the Bison Book facsimile editions) if it were "read" to her in a reverse of that complex process. Linderman does not approach his subjects with the agenda of the anthropologist but with the casual, respectful attention of a younger person eager to hear the life of an elder. He asks at one point if Plenty Coups regards himself as a full-blood Crow, given the fact that his grandfather was Shoshone; and Plenty Coups' reply — that he is full-blood because the man's wife was Crow — does not lead to a discussion of Crow kinship rules, which were obvious to Plenty Coups and possibly unknown to Linderman.

Another similarly authentic work of the period is the narrative of the Nez Perce warrior Yellow Wolf, recorded by Lucullus McWhorter and published by Caxton Printers in 1940. Like Pretty-shield and Plenty Coups, Yellow Wolf was unwilling to tell of his life after the reservation, because "nothing happened." Like many anthropological collectors, McWhorter is frustrated by Yellow Wolf's unwillingness to discuss his childhood for the same reason. Like Linderman, McWhorter makes a honest attempt to allow his subject to tell his story, his way. The result is a book the reader can come to with greater understanding of the subject's culture and values than the collector had, and still enjoy and learn from.

Other books and narratives are worth looking at, but they are all ultimately unsatisfying. *The Warrior Who Killed Custer: The Personal Narrative of Chief Joseph White Bull*, translated and edited by James H. Howard, exists in a more readable form as Stanley Vestal's retelling in *Warpath*. White Bull created his manuscript as a work for hire; the manuscript itself is more interesting than the story it tells. White Bull began with a coup résumé, what he considered to be meant by "a life." Like Pretty-shield, Plenty Coups, and even, interestingly enough, Black Elk, White Bull identifies his life with what others would call his *way* of life. His life is the record of his notable deeds before he became a reservation Indian; it ends with his acceptance of the reservation. Urged to supplement his narrative, he strives to put his accomplishments as a "civilized man" into the perspective of a count, and his supplement is a list of deeds accomplished on the reservation. He is unwilling to describe his childhood not from cultural reticence but because "nothing happened." The white reader/editor disagrees.

Perhaps nothing more immediately reveals the meddling hand of the editor in an American Indian life than the subject's expressions of concern with self-understanding. This is not to say that traditional American Indian people progressed through their lives unconcerned with personal faults, ignorant of the merit of the examined life. It is rather that a traditional Indian would not embark upon his or her autobiography as a journey of self-discovery. It is a paradox: the loss of "self" was an effect of cultural pollution, the result of becoming an "individual." Indian people knew who they were, most of the time. Setting aside for the moment the Senecan tradition of public confession, a person who chose to tell her own story did it because her story had value beyond her own experience of it. When a man told his story, he already knew how it would come out. Self-examination was, like other intimate bodily functions, a private activity.

It was an unfortunate circumstance that Freudian psychology and Boasian anthropology were roughly contemporaneous. As a result, many autobiographical accounts of the time show an atypical concern with childhood and the "shaping experience," the biographical "cause" of character. The American Indian individual filled with self-doubt took those doubts to peers and elders, to clan meetings and society members. A boy found out who he was through culturally determined behavior like fasting, traveling, dreaming. Similarly, a girl's identity was defined by patterns and discoveries revealed to her by her family and community. The very notion raises the hackles of the feminist or the libertarian. A girl was "told" who to be; a boy "conformed" to his community's notions of self. The dilemma of understanding without judging, viewing the other culture without shading its values with our own, may be insoluble. When we approve the Plains cultures that tolerated the homosexual orientation of the "berdache" and disapprove the other Indian cultures for which certain "abnormal" behavior was de facto proof of witchery and punished with summary (and often horrifyingly brutal) execution, we are imposing our cultural values in both cases.

Whether Don Talayesva wrote about sex and self-doubt because he was an aberrant Hopi or because those subjects were selected for him by the white collector who paid him by the page, the fact remains that while *Sun Chief* may be in many ways an accurate account of Hopi life, it is not a representative life, not representative of the traditional primitive society from which the subject came, possibly not even representative of the state of that society at the time it was written. Don Talayesva is no more the Hopi Everyman than James Joyce, writing in Switzerland, is the "conscience" of the Irish "race." That said, *Sun Chief* is a remarkable document, the life story of a man who accepted acculturation, tried it, and then rejected it. Don Talayesva was, like many of his American Indian contemporaries, kidnapped by the American government and carried off to boarding school in an attempt to surgically excise his tribal roots. After a life-threatening illness, he decided that his identity required the adoption of traditional Hopi culture and, like the fictional hero of many works about the contemporary Indian, his story is the attempt to recapture and assimilate that disappearing past. Like so many works of American Indian autobiography, his narrative can be valued for the authenticity of the voice and the wealth of detail, while we keep in mind that the voice is filtered through an invisible but pervasive and sometimes distorting veil.

We are left, at last, with the documents, not the lives. Perhaps nothing illustrates this dilemma and the frustration it creates more than the handling of secret religious information in *Sun Chief*. Talayesva preferred not to provide such information; but under pressure from Leo Simmons, he agreed to discuss anything that was already revealed in other published documents, and then he learned to his horror just how many secrets had been betrayed in the existing anthropological literature. Given that context, we cannot tell what of the information Talayesva reports about ceremonies was volunteered, what coerced, and what, conceivably, interjected for the sake of "completeness" by his anthropologist editor. We have a record of Talayesva's own encounter with the worst of the brigand-anthropologists, H. R. Voth, and his desire to "kick him off the mesa" (no merely metaphorical threat, as anyone who has seen the cliffs of Oraibi can attest).

What shows through the dense layers of the narrative and gives value to the document is the authentic foundation of character and values. For Talayesva, witchery is a given of life, and we see that clearly, whether we find in his fears of the worldwide conspiracy of witches an untainted affinity with the supernatural or a preliterate echo of right-wing paranoia over the Trilateral Commission. A good deal of what is commonplace for him is disturbingly or pleasantly alien for the non-Hopi reader, and a larger proportion of that alien quality is the commonplace of traditional Hopi life of his time.

Don Talayesva grows an ego under the nurturing attention of Leo Simmons and other anthropologists. He imagines himself ending his days surrounded by children who will gather to hear the story of his life. He has learned self-importance; he has come to adopt the non-Hopi notion that his life is uniquely significant. By becoming an autobiographer, he has given up some essential part of his character as a Hopi. Ironically, the anthropologist who collected his life found Don Talayesva appealing because he had chosen to "be Hopi." Like the butterfly collector with his chloroform and pins, Leo Simmons killed with his attention the very thing he valued in Don Talayesva. By encouraging self-examination, by giving Talayesva the Euro-American idea that self-absorption is the best mode of self-knowledge, by distorting his subject's sense of what mattered, Simmons became the snake in the Hopi garden and the undoing of Don Talayesva's rebirth as a Hopi. Talayesva learned to value self for its own sake; he learned to be not-Hopi.

Self-expression is not a concept alien to Indian cultures; and self-worth, in the context of the community, is affirmed. It is not the concept but the mode that distinguishes American Indian attitudes from those of post-Renaissance Euro-Americans. A few historically important American Indian personages chose to tell their lives, to record them for literate people. Luther Standing Bear, an acculturated Sioux from the turn of the century, was one. His books, like those of Charles A. Eastman, straddle two cultures. Raised in a traditional manner, Standing Bear assimilated, moved to Los Angeles, and became a prominent advocate of Indian rights. His books describe the traditional life of the Sioux, not from within, but from the distance of someone who chose another life. Standing Bear understands that the appeal of his life is cultural rather than personal; it is not mere happenstance that one volume of his "autobiography" is entitled *My People the Sioux*. His story differs from the accounts by Two Leggings, Plenty Coups, Wooden Leg, and other tellers of their life stories in that he writes from the perspective of his Los Angeles home at once inside the world of his own life via memory but, in all other ways, outside as a result of his life choices. Like Sarah Winnemucca, Luther Standing Bear is secure in a sense of self. As with both Winnemucca and Charles Eastman, his literary purpose is not self-examination. His is a record of a time gone and the defense of a defeated and embattled people.

If Luther Standing Bear stepped outside his traditional culture to observe and record it, Sarah Winnemucca moved with ease between her two worlds, her life a challenge to the notion that the worlds were intrinsically disjunct. She would have been a significant historical figure even if she had not written her autobiography. Self-taught as a speaker and writer, she took up the cause of justice for Indians, particularly the Paiutes, and quickly became well regarded as a lecturer on Indian subjects. Accounts of her lectures make it clear that she was an effective speaker, her English solid and educated. Her letters show a writer's grasp of language. That she should have written her autobiography was a natural extension of her professional life. Lacking a manuscript, we cannot determine to what degree her work was shaped and revised to suit the reading audience. What emerges from the narrative is an intelligent persona, committed to her political cause but not especially concerned with either her own identity or the Platonic idea of "Indianness." Sarah Winnemucca grew up in the center of a culture rapidly evolving from something almost unimaginably primitive (on the "ladder" of cultural evolution, the hunter/gatherer societies of people such as the Paiutes are placed close to the bottom) to a new thing accommodating to the juggernaut of Euro-American technology. She was, certainly, a witness to some of the most savage racial exploitation in the history of white/Indian relations, behavior justified in the white mind by the perception that the Indians of Nevada were scarcely human. She consciously became living proof of the error of that racist view, but she also, like her contemporary Charles Eastman, came to accept and appreciate the value of the oppressing culture. For Sarah Winnemucca, the San Francisco parlor and the Nevada desert were not lifestyles to choose between but places to be. Her absorption into both the life of the Paiutes and the life of the white people she spoke to in defense of her Indian relatives was not, for her, the problem of her identity but the identity itself.

Charles Eastman, like Sarah Winnemucca, Quanah Parker, and Luther Standing Bear, created for himself an identity shaped by both his cultures. The essential question of his life is not What shall I be: White or Indian? but What shall I do, being who I am? Raised as a tribal Sioux child, Eastman moved from his own Indian boyhood to the boarding school, Dartmouth College, and a career as a doctor, lecturer, and writer. He married a white woman, a teacher and writer herself, and he devoted his life to what his contemporaries would have called "the betterment of his race." He was, in the glib political labelling of our time, an "apple," the Indian equivalent of an "Uncle Tom." He held views the politically correct do not consider goodthinkful: that the attempt to preserve the Indian "way of life" did a material disservice to his people, that the end of that way of life was inevitable and the survival of Indian people depended upon adopting "civilization." He was influenced greatly by the two great racist dogmas of nineteenth-century liberal intellectuals: social Darwinism and cultural evolution (both now the stamping ground, in Orwellian irony, of the reactionary Right).

And yet his books celebrate the essential goodness and humanity of the life he grew from. If he sees the traditional Indian way of life as "childish" and "savage," to be loved, accepted, and left behind with the inevitability of any maturing growth, that view is the prerogative of someone who lived the savage life, and a view as valid, however politically objectionable, as the romantic endorsement of that life by the late-twentieth-century intellectual looking back fondly upon an imagined paradise of unschooled ecologists, models of political toleration idylling in greener grass. It was Charles Eastman who tended the living at the Wounded Knee killing ground on a raw, shameful winter day in 1890, and his objections to the white exploitation of the reservation system at Pine Ridge cost him his job. When he told the story in *From the Deep Woods to Civilization* thirty years later, he indicted the ethical and moral poverty of white America with anger no less vehement for its coolness. It is not white culture that Eastman endorses, but the idea of civilization. Charles A. Eastman and Nicholas Black Elk were contemporaries; Eastman was roughly ten years older than Black Elk. Considering that Eastman quite probably wrote his autobiography and Black Elk's was shaped in its most specific detail by one of the last great American Romantics, a poet whose notions of the Indian were more indebted to Rousseau than to Sitting Bull, it is a sad irony that it is *Black Elk Speaks*, that masterpiece of impersonation, rather than Eastman's books with their unwelcome truths, that became the quintessential American Indian autobiography.

Black Elk Speaks is the only logical stopping place in a discussion of American Indian autobiography. It is a book that defies literary discourse, best summed up in a comment Black Elk himself made regarding an element of Sioux theology: Whether it happened so or not, you know it is true. The truth of *Black Elk Speaks* is not the voice, which is multiple removes from the larynx of the ancient holy man whose story is somewhere in the book. It is not a literary truth; Neihardt, a minor anachronism of a poet, did not make this book, which rises like an oak from the weedy thicket of his romantic novels and epic poems. It is as if Anthony Trollope had incidentally written *The Heart of Darkness* or Edgar Allan Poe "Dover Beach." The artifact of the book begs to be explained in supernatural terms.

It is also unique in comparison to the spate of life stories from the period, unique and yet the epitome of the genre. Like Plenty Coups, Yellow Wolf, and White Bull, Black Elk assembled witnesses to attest to the accuracy of his story. Like Frank Linderman, Neihardt created the illusion of the first-person voice, so that we forget that the voice — unlike Eastman's, Winnemucca's, or Luther Standing Bear's — is itself a fiction. Like Eastman and Winnemucca, Black Elk chose to tell his story from a sense of duty. He was, like Copway, Apes, and Paul Radin's various Peyote religion Winnebagos, a fallen soul at once confessing and redeeming himself. Although emphatically a traditional Lakota, whose circumstances kept him from the experience of Carlisle boarding school and forced acculturation, he chose to leave the reservation for a while, to see for himself the nature of white society. He didn't reach Dartmouth or the literary parlors of San Francisco, but he had been to see the elephant, going with Buffalo Bill to London.

Black Elk Speaks is all at once an accurate if highly personal record of the evanescent Plains Indian horse cultures, a firsthand account of the end of that period and the white injustice that terminated it, the story of a person caught between two conflicting worlds, and a religious and philosophical document as uniquely American and significant, in its way, as The Book of Mormon. Recent scholarship has emphasized the complex person behind the romanticized religious figure Neihardt and Black Elk created together. Such studies are the greasy mechanics' view of the humming engine of myth. Ultimately, it does matter whether Black Elk renounced traditional Lakota medicine to save his Catholic soul, it does matter whether the Great Vision was Black Elk's or "Flaming Rainbow's," it does matter whether Black Elk's theology is

Lakota or not, whether he really faced Custer's troops on a hot June day in Montana.

And, ultimately, it does not. The salient truth of autobiography is, ultimately, that very little can be known. Mark Twain and Orson Scott Card couple public orthodoxy with a pen at the service of different Gods. Ben Franklin creates his historic self through the extended fiction of his autobiography. We lose track, as we age, of that distinction, so crucial to the young, between what we did and what we wish we had done. Respect for the integrity of the fact demands that we try to determine "whether it happened so or not"; still, the real merit of a life lies not in its telling but in its effects. By that measure, measured by the American Indian pride that Black Elk's story inspired, by the renaissance of respect for Indian values and the rebirth of understanding of our place in the web of life the book sponsored and nurtured, we can see, surely, that it is true.

Bibliography

The core secondary source for current theory is David Brumble's excellent *American Indian Autobiography*, supplemented with his extensive bibliography. Also provocative and useful is Hertha Wong's *Sending My Heart Back Across the Years*. Wong extends "autobiography" to include non-verbal records like winter counts, and she thus provides good analysis of visual art as well as verbal. The student of American Indian autobiography cannot ignore the work of Arnold Krupat, particularly his discussion of the subject in *For Those Who Come After*.

Primary sources for the student of American Indian autobiography represent a massive body of material that continues to grow. The as-told-to autobiography and the nonliterary memoir continue to be popular forms of American Indian autobiography, as witness recent collaborations with Thomas Mails and Richard Erdoes and books such as Joseph Medicine Crow's *From the Heart of Crow Country* and Joseph Iron Eye Dudley's *Chouteau Creek*. In addition to these traditional narratives, American Indian writers such as Scott Momaday, Leslie Silko, and Ray Young Bear offer by the example of their memoirs new ways of looking at autobiographical writing.

Primary Sources

Citing primary sources for American Indian autobiographies is rife with complications. At what point does a work cross the border between autobiography and fiction, vague as a forest at twilight? Neihardt's *When the Tree Flowered* is fiction; *Black Elk Speaks* is not. Some might even argue that assertion; other distinctions are even less certain. How much farther would one have to go than Peter Nabokov's revisions of *Two Leggings* to arrive at fiction?

Once a work is selected, does one cite it according to the subject's name, and if so, which name and which spelling? Note, for instance, that Sarah Winnemucca Hopkins is listed below as "Winnemucca, Sarah (Hopkins)"; this is to place her conveniently in the alphabetical list. Some common names, such as "Sam Whitewolf," are in fact pseudonyms, and some subjects have been published under a variety of names and pseudonyms. Often, the book is better known by the collaborator's name than by the subject's. For example, the name "Sam Blowsnake" may mean nothing to a researcher looking for "Paul Radin's" *The Autobiography of a Winnebago Indian* and *Crashing Thunder*, and it would be convenient but tasteless to place both books on the list under the familiar name of the collector, as would be the case with Ruth Underhill's *Papago Woman* or the Crow autobiographies collected by Frank Linderman.

Even titles are less straightforward than one might hope. Linderman's books offer a case in point. The title page of the 1972 Bison Books facsimile reprint of *Pretty-shield* mentions that it was originally published as *Red Mother*. And *Plenty-coups, Chief of the Crows* (1962 Bison facsimile title page) was variously published and reprinted as *American: The Life Story of a Great Indian, Plenty-coups, Chief of the Crows,* and *American: Plenty Coups, Last of the Crows.*

Finally, there is the problem of collection date, original publication date, and the publication date of the edition currently best known. It was the reprint of *Black Elk Speaks* that initiated the discovery of this classic work, nearly thirty years after it was originally published. That interest, synergistic with other events of the American Indian literary renaissance of the 1960s, led to the rediscovery and printing of a wealth of manuscripts and obscure published papers, many of them part of the traditional corpus in spite of their eventual publication dates, such as Peter Nabokov's *Two Leggings*. In despair, I have cited the work by the common form of the subject's name (or pseudonym) and a convenient publication (often a Bison Books reprint, from the University of Nebraska). When there is a significant lapse between the given publication date and the original printing (or the date of the manuscript's creation), I have given the original date after the title of the book. Finally, if the collector/editor/amanuensis is as well known as the subject and even, in many cases, likely to be given as the "author" in the library citation, I have included that person's name in brackets. I have also taken the liberty of not citing full titles when it seemed unnecessary. The full title of William Apes' autobiography is a good example of what I have attempted to avoid: *A Son of the Forest. The Experience of William Apes, A Native of the Forest. Comprising a Notice of the Pequod Tribe of Indians. Written by Himself.*

The following is no more than a brief overview listing key works. For an exhaustive bibliography of American Indian autobiographies, including more contemporary works and items incidentally embedded in larger works and anthropological papers, see H. David Brumble's *An Annotated Bibliography of American Indian and Eskimo Autobiographies* (Lincoln: University of Nebraska Press, 1981). Brumble cites individual personal narratives in such varied locations as the stories collected and retold by nineteenth-century writers like George Bird Grinnnell and James Willard Schultz. He also includes, with explanations, well-known hoaxes and falsifications like *The Memoirs of Chief Red Fox*. In the interest of space, I have omitted such works and writers from the list below, regardless of their popularity. Were it not ethically repugnant to augment the publicity of these self-serving fictioneers (and their sibling flutists, jewelers, Christmas card artists, sorcerers, and shamans), some of whom have had enormous and continued success with their impersonations, an entire article could be written on the fake American Indian, his self-creation and, the illusion completed, his "autobiography."

Apes, William. *A Son of the Forest.* New York: author, 1829.

Black Elk. *Black Elk Speaks.* 1932. Lincoln: University of Nebraska Press, 1979. [John G. Neihardt].

Blowsnake, Sam. *The Autobiography of a Winnebago Indian.* New York: Dover, 1963 [1920]. [Paul Radin].

———. *Crashing Thunder.* 1926. Lincoln: University of Nebraska Press, 1983. [Paul Radin].

Bonnin, Gertrude. *American Indian Stories.* 1921. Lincoln: University of Nebraska Press,

1985. A Sioux woman, member of the "Red Progressive" group, writing autobiographical stories under the name "Zitkala-Sa."

Campbell, Maria. *Halfbreed*. Toronto: McClelland and Stewart, 1973. Canadian Métis woman.

Chona, Maria. "The Autobiography of a Papago Woman." In *Papago Woman*. 1936. New York: Holt, Rinehart, and Winston, 1979. [Ruth Underhill].

Copway, George. *Life, History, and Travels of Kah-ge-ga-gah-bowh*. Albany: Weed and Parsons, 1847.

Crow Dog, Mary. *Lakota Woman*. New York: Harper and Row, 1990. [Richard Erdoes].

Dudley, Joseph Iron Eye. *Chouteau Creek*. Lincoln: University of Nebraska Press, 1992. Contemporary Yankton Sioux memoir.

Eastman, Charles Alexander. *Indian Boyhood*. Boston: Little, Brown, and Co., 1902.

———. *From Deep Woods to Civilization*. Lincoln: University of Nebraska Press, 1977 [1916].

Fools Crow, Frank. *Fools Crow*. New York: Doubleday and Co., 1979. [Thomas E. Mails].

Gregorio. "The Life Story" in Leighton, Alexander and Dorothea, *Gregorio, The Hand-Trembler. Papers of the Peabody Museum of American Archaeology and Ethnology*, 40:1 (1949): 45-81.

Jones, Rev. Peter. *Life and Journals of Kah-ke-wa-quo-na-by: (Rev. Peter Jones), Wesleyan Missionary*. Toronto: Anton Green, 1860.

Lame Deer, John Fire. *Lame Deer, Seeker of Visions*. New York: Simon and Schuster, 1972. [Richard Erdoes].

Left Handed. *Son of Old Man Hat. A Navaho Autobiography*. 1938. Lincoln: University of Nebraska Press, 1967. [Walter Dyk].

Mathews, John Joseph. *Talking to the Moon*. Chicago: University of Chicago Press, 1945. Personal memoir of an Osage writer.

Mitchell, Emerson Blackhorse. *Miracle Hill*. Norman: University of Oklahoma Press, 1967. Third-person autobiography of a Navaho boy enrolled at the American Indian Art Institute under T. D. Allen.

Mountain Wolf Woman. *Mountain Wolf Woman, Sister of Crashing Thunder*. Ann Arbor: University of Michigan Press, 1961. [Nancy Oestreich Lurie].

Nowell, Charles. *Smoke from their Fires*. 1941. Hamden, Connecticut: Archon, 1968. [Clelland S. Ford].

Qoyawayma, Polingaysi. *No Turning Back*. Albuquerque: University of New Mexico Press, 1964. Third-person narrative of a Hopi woman who became a school teacher.

Parker, Ely S. "Writings of General Parker: Extracts from His Letters, and an Autobiographical Memoir of Historical Interest." *Publications of the Buffalo Historical Society*, 8 (1905): 520-536.

Plenty-coups. *Plenty-coups, Chief of the Crows*. 1930. Lincoln: University of Nebraska Press, 1962. [Frank B. Linderman].

Pretty-shield. *Pretty-shield, Medicine Woman of the Crows*. 1932. Lincoln: University of Nebraska Press, 1974. [Frank B. Linderman].

Savala, Refugio. *The Autobiography of a Yaqui Poet*. Tucson: University of Arizona Press, 1980. [Kathleen Sands].

Sekaquaptewa, Helen. *Me and Mine*. Tucson: University of Arizona Press, 1969. Autobiography of a Hopi Mormon. [Louise Udall].

Standing Bear, Luther. *My Indian Boyhood*. New York: Houghton Mifflin, 1931.

———. *My People the Sioux*. Lincoln: University of Nebraska Press, 1975 [1928].

Sundance, Robert. *Sundance*. La Canada, California: Chaco Press, 1994.

Talayesva, Don. *Sun Chief*. New Haven: Yale University Press, 1942. [Leo W. Simmons].

Two Leggings. *Two Leggings: The Making of a Crow Warrior*. New York: Crowell, 1967. [Peter Nabokov].

White Bull, Chief Joseph. *The Warrior Who Killed Custer: The Personal Narrative of Chief Joseph White Bull*. James H. Howard, trans. and ed. Lincoln: University of Nebraska Press, 1968.

White Calf. *Piegan: A Look from Within at the Life, Times, and Legacy of an American Indian*. Garden City: Doubleday, 1962.

Whitewolf, Jim. *Jim Whitewolf: The Story of a Kiowa-Apache Indian*. New York: Dover, 1969.

Winnemucca, Sarah [Hopkins]. *Life Among the Piutes*. 1883; rpt., Reno: University of Nevada Press, 1994.

Wooden Leg. *Wooden Leg: A Warrior Who Fought Custer*. 1931; rpt., Lincoln: University of Nebraska, 1962. [Thomas B. Marquis].

Yellow Wolf. *Yellow Wolf: His Own Story*. Caldwell, Idaho: Caxton, 1940. [Lucullus V. McWhorter].

Secondary Sources

Bataille, Gretchen, and Kathleen Sands. *American Indian Women: Telling Their Lives*. Lincoln: University of Nebraska Press, 1984. Critical study of women's autobiographies, including Maria Chona, Mountain Wolf Woman, and Maria Campbell.

Brumble, H. David. *American Indian Autobiography*. Berkeley: University of California Press, 1988. Traces his subject from the preliterate models of autobiography to the use of personal narrative in such contemporary writers as Scott Momaday.

———. *An Annotated Bibliography of American Indian and Eskimo Autobiographies*. Lincoln: University of Nebraska Press, 1981. Thorough but in need of an update.

Canfield, Gae Whitney. *Sarah Winnemucca of the Northern Paiutes*. Norman: University of Oklahoma Press, 1983. A recent biography.

Castro, Michael. *Interpreting the Indian: Twentieth-Century Poets and the Native American*. Albuquerque: University of New Mexico Press, 1983. Good discussion of *Black Elk Speaks*.

Copeland, Marion W. *Charles Alexander Eastman (Ohiyesa)*. Boise: Boise State University Western Writers Series, 1978.

DeMallie, Raymond. *The Sixth Grandfather: Black Elk's Teachings Given to John G. Neihardt*. Lincoln: University of Nebraska Press, 1984. The transcripts from which Neihardt created *Black Elk Speaks*, with extensive notes and introduction.

Eastman, Elaine Goodale. *Sister to the Sioux: The Memoirs of Elaine Goodale Eastman, 1885-1891*. Kay Graber, ed. Lincoln: University of Nebraska Press, 1978. Wife of Charles A. Eastman, Carlisle Indian School teacher, poet.

Hertzberg, Hazel. *The Search for an American Indian Identity: Modern Pan-Indian Movements*. Syracuse: Syracuse University Press, 1959. Discussion of "Red Progressives" Gertrude Bonnin, Carlos Montezuma, Charles A. Eastman, and the La Flesche family.

Krupat, Arnold. *For Those Who Come After: A Study of American Indian Autobiography*. Berkeley: University of California Press, 1985.

La Flesche, Francis. *The Middle Five*. Boston: Small, Maynard, 1900. An account of the Indian boarding school system by an Omaha intellectual from the turn of the century, member of the distinguished La Flesche family. La Flesche was, like Ella Deloria and others, educated as a writer, teacher, and anthropologist. He used his skills to preserve the stories, songs, and cultural values of the Omaha people, focusing on tribal rather than personal history.

Liberty, Margot. *American Indian Intellectuals*. St. Paul: West Publishing Co., 1978. Pieces on important American Indian figures such as Charles A. Eastman, Francis La Flesche, John Joseph Mathews, and Sarah Winnemucca.

McCluskey, Sally. "Black Elk Speaks, and So Does John Neihardt." *Western American Literature*, 6 (1972): 231-242. One of the first essays to look closely at the relationship of Neihardt to the text.

Neihardt, Hilda. *Black Elk and Flaming Rainbow*. Lincoln: University of Nebraska Press, 1995. Neihardt's daughter remembers her father's relationship with Black Elk.

O'Brien, Lynn Woods. *Plains Indian Autobiographies*. Boise: Boise State University Western Writers Series, 1978. Brief but excellent overview of the subject; O'Brien advances the idea of preliterate autobiography.

Peterson, Eric. "An Indian, An American: Ethnicity, Assimilation, and Balance in Charles A. Eastman's *From the Deep Woods to Civilization*." *Studies in American Indian Literature*, 4 (1992): 145-160. Discusses traditional oral stylistics in Eastman's book.

Powers, William. "When Black Elk Speaks, Everybody Listens." In *Religion in Native North America*. Christopher Vecsey, ed. Moscow: University of Idaho Press, 1990. A scholar of Lakota religion on Black Elk's "orthodoxy" as an Oglala holy man.

Rice, Julian. *Black Elk's Story: Discerning Its Lakota Purpose*. Albuquerque: University of New Mexico Press, 1991.

Sayre, Robert F. "Vision and Experience in *Black Elk Speaks*." *College English*, 32 (1971): 509-535.

Smith, William F. "American Indian Autobiographies." *American Indian Quarterly*, 2 (1975): 237-45.

Steltenkamp, Michael F. *Black Elk: Holy Man of the Ogallala*. Norman: University of Oklahoma Press, 1993. A biography of Nicholas Black Elk.

Swann, Brian. *I Tell You Now: Autobiographical Essays by Native American Writers*. Lincoln: University of Nebraska Press, 1987. Brief essays by dozens of contemporary Indian writers and artists.

Theisz, R. D. "The Critical Collaboration: An Approach to the Study of Native American Bi-autobiography." *American Indian Culture and Research*, 5 (1981): 65-80.

Vestal, Stanley. *Warpath: The True Story of the Fighting Sioux Told in a Biography of Chief White Bull*. Boston: Houghton Mifflin, 1934.

Wilson, Raymond. *Ohiyesa: Charles Eastman, Santee Sioux*. Urbana: University of Illinois Press, 1983.

Wong, Hertha Dawn. *Sending My Heart Back Across the Years*. New York: Oxford University Press, 1992. Thorough discussion of nonliterary autobiographical documents, such as pictographic records. Excellent comparison of Black Elk and Charles Eastman.

Donald A. Barclay and Peter Wild

Pre-Lewis and Clark Exploration Narratives of Western North America

ontemporary writings about the West as a dreamland, a place of hopes (or failed hopes), about the interplay of natives and invaders, or about the spiritual balm of nature's beauty have predecessors in the works of the earliest explorers. In this sense, there's a followable line from Spanish explorer Pedro de Castañeda—who not only celebrated the pristine beauty of the West but also waxed nostalgic over the region as a land of lost youth and lost opportunity—to the similar attitudes of modern-day westerners like Wallace Stegner and Edward Abbey. What Robert Thacker says about the American prairie holding sway over writers may well apply: The landscape has "...dictated its terms..." generating a similar cluster of responses over the centuries (143). To ignore the relationship, as through the years men struggled with fantasy and reality to come to terms with a myth-shrouded wilderness kingdom, is to miss a huge portion of the background behind the West's literary heritage.

The background goes deeper than many have supposed. The journey of Lewis and Clark (1804-1806), the first crossing of the continent by United States citizens, for example, is so famous as to overshadow its predecessors. Pre-Lewis and Clark exploration narratives of the American West? Except for the widely acknowledged contributions of the Spanish far to the south, the question may seem silly; few but specialists in the field know that any exist. The fact is, however, that for years before Lewis and Clark arrived at the mouth of the Columbia River, adventurers from England, France, Russia, Spain, and the American Colonies had been probing the West by land and from the sea. A surprising number left not only accounts of the journeys but responses that shed light on the development of western American literature. The writings were, in fact, early documents in that canon.

As to public recognition, some of the host of Spanish conquistadors making sallies into the American West have fared rather well. Schoolchildren are familiar with the trek that took Coronado arcing far north from Mexico to the plains of Kansas in pursuit of the tantalizing Seven Cities of Gold. Perhaps such men are better known than their northern counterparts because they were exotic Catholics traveling through the American Southwest, a land whose giant cactuses, desert spaces, and Indian cultures lend the region an aura of romance in the minds of many Americans.

Yet whether named John R. Jewitt or Juan Bautista de Anza, whether Peter Pond or Gaspar Perez de Villagrá, almost all of the explorers, from north or south, famous or forgotten, suffer a similar fate. Their works rarely are accorded the status of literature.

This is not without some good reasons. As William T. Pilkington points out, historical documents chronicling everyday experience can be downright tedious. They often fall far short of literature, that is, works of the imagination manipulated for artistic effect (1-2). But an absolute distinction between the two categories is not always clear. Some early accounts, such as Cabeza de Vaca's *Relación*, employ a considerable range of literary craft throughout. Others, such as Jonathan Carver's *Travels*, only occasionally shine forth as literature. Carver's book is a mostly plodding, if historically valuable, record of journeys in the upper Mississippi region, typical in its style of many early accounts. But every once in a while Carver's stodgy prose leaps beyond itself into transcendental realms. Paddling his canoe across a placid lake, for example, Carver pauses to marvel at the clarity of the water beneath him. Moved by the sight of the rocky bottom, he feels suspended in an otherworldly ether (132-133).

The first words written about the American West were Spanish words. In fact, all of the earliest western writers — including the important figures of Cabeza de Vaca, The Gentleman of Elvas, Fray Marcos de Niza, and Pedro de Castañeda — entered the West in the service of Spain. Besides serving the same government, these early western writers also served the same fabulous vision of the West, one based on expectations of cities as filled with gold and souls as the fabulous treasure cities of Mexico and Peru. Because all of these European-born writers failed to realize their fabulous expectations, their narratives attempt to come to terms with the failure of the real West to live up to the imagined West, thereby establishing a theme that remains a vital part of western American literature.

Cabeza de Vaca (c. 1490-c. 1557) was the first to write about the West, and under his pen the West becomes an edenic land of vast, untapped resources and peaceful natives eager for Christianization. Indeed, the farther west Cabeza de Vaca traveled, the better the land becomes. This improvement in the land closely parallels the writer's own psychological transformation from a proud conquistador — originally lusting for gold but eventually left half-dead and destitute on the Texas coast — to a peace-loving faith healer adored by the native throngs for whom he becomes an eloquent advocate.

Fray Marcos de Niza (c. 1495-1558), who hopefully projected a fabulous El Dorado where there was in truth only a small adobe farming settlement, was the most blatantly deceptive of the four earliest western writers. Fray Marcos' fairy tale so played into the fabulous desires of the time that it almost single-handedly inspired the large and costly Coronado expedition. What Coronado and his men actually found was so different from what de Niza had described, however, that the unfabulous reality of it nearly inspired the padre's death at the hands of the disgruntled conquistadors. More honest in his account is The Gentleman of Elvas (fl. 1538-1557), who describes the de Soto expedition's foray into, and retreat from, a harsh western landscape. Since Elvas measures riches only in conquistador terms — cities, gold, and easily plundered supplies of food — the West is to him a desert wasteland, the last in a long line of disappointing locales in the unexplored North.

Because it was written many years after the events it describes, Pedro de Castañeda's (d. c. 1565) narrative of Coronado's 1540 expedition is perhaps most poignantly aware of "the difference between the report which told about vast treasures, and the places where nothing like this was either found or known" (Castañeda 343). Castañeda came to see the West as a treasure house of natural resources rather than as the location of some undiscovered El Dorado, thus aligning his view with that of Cabeza de Vaca. Through their revised vision of the West, both writers set the stage for the more rational, though still dream shaded, pursuits of the next wave of Spanish explorers who would push north from the settlements of Mexico into the unknown.

Throughout and beyond the period of Spanish exploration, the North remained the land of the unknown. And the idea of venturing northward had for the Spanish and their descendants much of the same psychological and political weight as the idea of venturing west had, and still has, in the United States. One of the first to attempt to settle the far North was Gaspar Castaño de Sosa (d. c. 1596), who in 1590 led some 200 pioneers out of Mexico with the intention of illegally settling what is now New Mexico. Unlike the *entradas* of the earlier conquistadors, the goal of Castaño's expedition was not to loot a ready-made fortune from the natives but to establish mines and farms. After much struggle against rough country, Indians, and each other, Castaño and company failed in their pursuit. But the account of their expedition survives to tell an archetypal pioneering tale that will seem familiar to anyone who has read a nineteenth-century pioneer diary or seen a covered-wagon Western. Similarly, Hernán Gallegos' (fl. 1581-1589) account of the 1591 Chamuscado-Rodriguez Expedition will seem familiar to fans of frontier literature. Gallegos, one of a handful of soldiers escorting the first group of missionaries to the northern pueblos, comes off as a rawhide-tough frontiersman as he and his companions outfight, outbluff, and outwit the "barbarians" the padres hope to Christianize.

It fell to Juan de Oñate (c. 1549-1624) to lead in 1598 the first successful European attempt to settle the northern lands that are now New Mexico, but Oñate's own narratives have little to do with the details of settlement. Instead, they show a leader who is in many ways a throwback to earlier conquistadors as he ranges northwards in hopes of finding the rumored treasure city of Quivira, fights the natives at every turn, and vastly overstates the wealth of the land. Besides Oñate's own narratives, his expedition generated at least two other accounts of literary interest. One is Vicente de Saldívar Mendoza's (fl. 1590-1600) telling of a failed attempt to domesticate buffalo, a tale that points the way to later western stories detailing similar failed encounters between the European mind set and western nature. The other important literary document to come out of Oñate's exploration is Gaspar Pérez de Villagrá's (c. 1555-1620) *Historia de la Nueva México*, a verse history published in 1610 that lays claim to being the first American epic.

The next major account of northward exploration, that of Diego Vargas (1643-1704), brings Spanish exploration to the brink of the eighteenth century and the Age of Enlightenment. Throughout the eighteenth century, Spanish explorations ceased to be general wanderings and became missions with specific purposes: to subdue rebels, to fend off potential foreign invasions, to find a better route between two known points. And though the purposefulness of these later explorations may make the accounts of them seem more rational to the modern mind — to seem less the stuff of myth and literature than the accounts of the earlier expeditions — the later explorations still traversed unknown country and still kindled literary wonderings about what the existence of all this vast, harsh country might mean.

In 1688 Vargas went into New Mexico with the pragmatic purpose of retaking it from the rebellious Pueblo Indians who had driven out the Spanish in 1680. Vargas' account of his successful expedition is, however, less an example of pragmatic reporting than of the autobiographical bragging by which many historical figures of the West transformed themselves into legendary figures. Vargas' heroic qualities are even more inflated in *Mercurio Volante*, a highly fictionalized version of his exploits. The author of *Mercurio Volante*, Carlos de Sigüenza y Góngora (1645-1700), comes off as something of a Hispanic Ned Buntline through his florid description of events he did not witness.

The 1719-1720 campaign of Antonio de Valverde (1671-c. 1726) into Colorado was inspired by the eighteenth-century geopolitics that had Madrid fearing a French invasion of the Spanish New World possessions. Valverde tells of a campaign against an imaginary French and Indian army, and taken as a whole his diary spins a suspenseful tale of pursuit and retreat through the unknown lands of eastern Colorado.

Besides exploring the North by land, the Spanish also explored from ships that sailed along the Pacific Coast. The narrative of Miguel Costanso (fl. 1764-1811) tells of a disastrous 1769 voyage by sea to San Diego, during which the ship's company is left stranded and has to be rescued in classic western fashion by a cavalry troop riding overland from Mexico.

Ships supplied the missions and settlements in Alta California, but the colonial authorities also wanted the assurance of overland supply routes from Mexico. To establish such a route Juan Bautista de Anza (1735-1788) led two round trips from northern Mexico to California, the first in 1774 and a second in 1776. Several accounts of these expeditions exist, including Anza's own informative but highly bureaucratic one. More literary is the narrative of Anza's second trip written by

Father Pedro Font (1738-1782). Font, frequently in conflict with Anza and other authorities, humanizes the expedition by pulling away the wooden mask of stoic heroism and single-mindedness that so often covers the faces of early explorers.

Because Anza's route was difficult and dangerous, the Dominguez-Escalante expedition left Santa Fe, New Mexico, in 1776 in search of a better path to California. Dominguez-Escalante did not find a better route but did encounter some of the roughest and most spectacular country in the Southwest—including the Grand Canyon of the Colorado River. Fray Silvestre Vélez de Escalante's (c. 1750-1780) narrative of his travels has been described by Bernard DeVoto as "the most serene document in the annals of American exploration" (292), and its serenity is indeed a contrast to the complaining found in Font's narrative.

The last major pre-Lewis and Clark Spanish exploration narrative was that of Pedro Vial (1746?-1814). Vial led several explorations to find better trade routes between Santa Fe and other points. In 1792 he led an expedition from Santa Fe to St. Louis, during which he spent six weeks as a captive of the Kansas Indians. Vial was frequently a terse diarist, but his detailed account of his captivity qualifies as a fine example of the Indian captivity narrative.

Long before the Pilgrims established their colony in New England, Sir Francis Drake (1541?-1596) was leaving his mark on what would become known as the American West. Curiously, it would be a mark of tolerance toward another culture by a man charged by the Queen of England to wreak havoc on Spain's trade routes. According to Francis Fletcher's *The World Encompassed by Sir Francis Drake*, in 1579 the scourge of the Spanish Empire fled the hornet's nest stirred up along the western coast of South America by sailing north far into unknown waters. Landing in the region of San Francisco Bay for repairs before sailing westward around the world to England, Drake made friends with the coastal Indians, dealing honestly with people of "a tractable, free, and louing [sic] nature..." (131). The unusual harmony begun by Drake turned sour as other explorers encountered Indians. Both the conflict and the lost opportunity would become major themes haunting western American literature.

Years later and farther yet to the north, tensions between a hesitant sea captain and his naturalist/doctor produced an unusual exploration account. In 1742, trying to determine where rumored North America actually lay, Vitus Bering, a Dane in the service of the Russian Empire, caught a glimpse of Alaska through the fog, then lost heart at the bad weather and sailed for home. Georg Wilhelm Steller (1709-1746), a scientist of the German Enlightenment eager to go ashore, scoffed at the timorous Bering and griping to his *Journal* wrote a personal complaint laced with sarcasm, irony, vivid imagery, and the psychological insights of a novel.

Earlier, thousands of miles away on the eastern seaboard, French colonists spreading into the Canadian wilderness after furs left writings that preview adventure tales typical of the American West. When young Pierre Esprit Radisson (1636?-1710) was out hunting, Iroquois Indians pounced on the teenager and carried him off for ghoulish tortures with other white prisoners. Escaping and undiscouraged, Radisson became a pathfinder to the west and north. His *Explorations* offers a swashbuckling story of conniving and picturesque adventures played out from 1652 to the close of Radisson's life against the backdrop of magnificent nature.

Amid such literary excitement, veracity hardly was the issue as the West became for many explorer/writers a fantastic place, a stage for sociopathic liars creating their own heroic identities and anticipating Mark Twain's Duke and Dauphin. Chief among them was a vainglorious priest. In *A New Discovery*, missionary Father Louis Hennepin (1640?-1705?) abandoned reality, claiming among other improbable bouts of derring-do to have beaten La Salle to the mouth of the Mississippi River. Yet Hennepin nonetheless became a wildly popular writer through his bright lies.

Not all frontiersmen were entertaining scalawags. Yet even as sober a man as Pierre Gaultier de La Vérendrye (1685-1749) saw wavering shapes as he peered across the northern Plains. The last of the great French explorers, in 1739 La Vérendrye pieced together the geography of the Missouri River, the key to the West. For all that, as his *Journals* reflect, confusion plagued even this earnest and skeptical man. Through the Indians the trader heard of Spanish colonies somewhere off to the southwest, of glowing mountains, of troves of silver, and tribes of dwarves. Part of the problem lay with the nature of his information, often scrambled as it passed through several Indian languages. Part, too, lay with the Indians themselves, who delighted in spinning tales to hoodwink white men. In either case, the West continued to grow into a domain largely of the imagination, a region glittering with possibilities but showing few clear lines between fact and fiction.

Nevertheless, science and the growing rationality of the European

Enlightenment slowly began to modify the fanciful impulse. The shift had both practical and personal elements behind it. A highly risky and physically dangerous business, the fur trade of North America was becoming ever more organized and competitive as it expanded westward through the forests and out into the spaces beyond. For their own financial survival, traders vying with one another realized the advantages of understanding both the native peoples who supplied them with pelts and the geography that lay ahead. The traders knew about the Pacific Ocean from sea captains who were beginning to touch shore and exchange goods with the Indians. No one had yet traversed the continent, however, and the possibility of cutting costs by establishing an overland route and opening trading posts on the western coast became an ever more tantalizing lure, a lure uppermost in the minds of Lewis and Clark. Financial gain aside, some men also traveled for the pure adventure of it, for the old human excitement of seeing what was "on the other side of the mountain." As can be imagined, the circumstances tempted a variety of sinewy, single-minded, and sometimes violent figures into the unknown.

Among the British and predominately Scottish explorers gradually taking over the fur trade from the earlier French was Alexander Henry (? - 1814). His journals condemn the liquor used to part Indians from their furs as "the root of all evil" (209), but to Henry it apparently was a necessary evil for commerce. In near clinical fashion, his prose sets down the minutiae of wilderness life, dutifully recording from 1799 to 1814 a ghastly array of mutilations and tortures by Indians whose society is falling apart around them. Henry's writing is all the more powerful because it combines the accuracy of a Samuel Pepys with the detachment of an Émile Zola.

Illustrating dual truths — that similar conditions can produce radically different literary results and that scientists can possess enviable literary grace — David Thompson (1770-1857) stands in marked contrast to Henry. An excellent cartographer who mapped huge areas of the northern Rockies and the Pacific Northwest, Thompson also mapped the human heart. His journals, covering his experiences from 1784 to 1812, show Thompson a tolerant man revealing his Indian companions with the humor, charming eye for detail, and psychological insights that might be the envy of a modern novelist.

In the meantime, on the other side of the unknown, the growing trade by sea with the coastal Indians was producing its own brand of early literature. Two of the works are unique for quite separate reasons. The first author, Frances Hornby Barkley (1769-1845), wrote an account of her life at sea during a voyage in 1786 to 1787 with her captain husband, a man who plied the Pacific Coast and engaged in a certain amount of skullduggery to outwit the competition. Mrs. Barkley's diaries are one of the extremely rare examples of women writing before Lewis and Clark's exploration narratives.

The devotee of hair-raising travel thrills could hardly ask for a more adrenaline-washed story than the narrative of John R. Jewitt (1783-1821). Seized in 1803 during a takeover of his vessel by Indians, the sailor writes a complex captive's tale of horrors, scheming, and salacious encounters. This is blended with a nice sense for creating dramatic tension, albeit such language as "six naked savages, standing in a circle around me ... with their daggers uplifted in their hands, prepared to strike" (12) abounds, together with severed heads. The fact that a later hand likely doctored Jewitt's earlier and plainer account for artistic effect illustrates the avid use of western materials for eastern audiences. A comparison of the fairly rude original with its sophisticated though horror-strewn successor shows the adaptation process at work.

It's unfortunate that many people in the United States do not know about Scottish-born Alexander Mackenzie (1764?-1820). Of far more historical than literary importance, Mackenzie crossed Canada in 1793, completing the first transcontinental trek to the Pacific, and his resulting book spurred President Jefferson to organize the expedition of Lewis and Clark. Making no pretense of being a litterateur, Mackenzie nonetheless manipulates his words toward an overall design. Hoping to gain credibility with his cautious government and move it to establish trading posts on the Pacific, Mackenzie lets the drama of his crossing emerge from a reserved and factual recitation of his trials — trials indeed dramatic enough in themselves when plainly stated.

The mysterious loner and the romantic dreamer play large roles in the literature of the frontier. Acting the first part was a man from Connecticut, Peter Pond (1740-1807). Between 1775 and 1788, while ranging far ahead of other explorers, energetic Pond penetrated Canada clear to Alberta, setting up his trading business there and inspiring Alexander Mackenzie to try for the Pacific. Pond's observations have the charms of realism lightened by Yankee humor, yet standing behind them is a shadowy figure, a violent man quick to murder for slight offense. As is true of many frontier figures, Pond continues to be a mystery. His shabby but intriguing reputation may be the concoction of Canadian traders disdainful of Americans and envious of Pond's successes.

Of a different sort entirely was Pond's contemporary, John Ledyard (1751-1789), a wilderness Don Quixote so quirky that Thomas Jefferson quipped that the young man "has too much imagination..." (160). Having failed at both the fur trade and in his airy scheme to walk across Siberia, the mercurial idealist on a voyage to the Pacific Northwest with Captain James Cook in 1778 nonetheless attempted to see the world through Indian eyes and expressed a childish faith in nature's goodness. These two literary traits were unusual for his time.

Like faint, ancient trails buried under six-lane freeways, so exist the early narratives of the American West. With the wealth of western literature produced in the last two hundred years — novels, films, nature writing, poems — we have largely lost sight of how the earliest attempts to write about the West pointed the way for what came later. And with so much new, imaginative western writing vying for our attention, few of us have time or inclination to sift through the old narratives, many so far out of print as to be lost to all but the dedicated scholar. This is unfortunate, for there is beauty, brilliance, and drama to be found in the writing of those who saw a West that no writer before them had seen and that no one, writer or illiterate, will ever see again. As the bicentennial anniversary of the Lewis and Clark expedition is marked, we can only hope that the narratives of western exploration which preceded Lewis and Clark's journals will come into the light and receive the full attention they deserve.

Selected Bibliography

Primary Sources

Barkley, Frances Hornby. "The Mystery of Mrs. Barkley's Diary: Notes on the Voyage of the *Imperial Eagle*, 1786-87." W. Kaye Lamb, ed. *British Columbia Historical Quarterly*, 6 (January 1942): 31-75.

Cabeza de Vaca, Álvar Núñez. *The Account: Álvar Núñez Cabeza de Vaca's Relación*. Martin A. Favata and José B. Fernández, trans. Houston: Arte Público Press, 1993.

Carver, Jonathan. *Travels through the Interior Parts of North America, in the Years 1766, 1767, and 1768*. 1778; rpt., Minneapolis: Ross and Haines, 1956.

Castañeda, Pedro de. "The Narrative of the Expedition of Coronado, by Pedro de

Castañeda." 1596. Frederick W. Hodge, ed. In *Spanish Explorers in the Southern United States, 1528-1543*. Herbert Eugene Bolton, ed. New York: Scribner's, 1907. Pp. 275-387.

Castaño de Sosa, Gaspar. "Castaño de Sosa's 'Memoria.'" In *The Rediscovery of New Mexico, 1580-1594*. 1864-1884. George P. Hammond and Agapito Rey, ed. and trans. Albuquerque: University of New Mexico Press, 1966.

Costanso, Miguel. *The Costanso Narrative of the Portola Expedition: First Chronicle of the Spanish Conquest of Alta California*. 1770. Ray Brandes, ed. and trans; rpt., Newhall: Hogarth, 1970.

Fletcher, Francis. *The World Encompassed by Sir Francis Drake*. 1628. W.S. Vaux, ed; rpt., London: Hakluyt Society, 1854.

Font, Pedro. *Font's Complete Diary of the Second Anza Expedition*. Vol. 4 of *Anza's California Expeditions*. Herbert E. Bolton, ed. Berkeley: University of California Press, 1930.

Gallegos, Hernán. *The Gallegos Relations of the Rodriguez Expedition to New Mexico*. George P. Hammond and Agapito Rey, ed. and trans. Santa Fe: El Palacio Press, 1927.

Gentleman of Elvas. "The Narrative of the Expedition of Hernando de Soto by the Gentleman of Elvas." 1557. Theodore H. Lewis, ed. In *Spanish Explorers in the Southern United States, 1528-1543*. Herbert Eugene Bolton, ed. New York: Scribner's, 1907. Pp. 129-272.

Hennepin, Louis. *A New Discovery of a Vast Country in America*. 1698. 2 vols. Reuben Gold Thwaites, ed; rpt., Chicago: A. C. McClurg, 1903.

Henry, Alexander. *New Light on the Early History of the Greater Northwest: The Manuscript Journals of Alexander Henry and of David Thompson*. 3 vols. Elliott Coues, ed. New York: Harper, 1897.

Jewitt, John R. *Narrative of the Adventures and Sufferings of John R. Jewitt While Held as a Captive of the Nootka Indians of Vancouver Island, 1803 to 1805*. 1815. Robert F. Heizer, ed; rpt., Ramona: Ballena Press, 1975.

La Vérendrye, Pierre Gaultier de Varennes de, et al. *Journals and Letters of Pierre Gaultier de Varennes de La Vérendrye and His Sons*. Lawrence J. Burpee, ed. Toronto: Champlain Society, 1927.

Ledyard, John. *John Ledyard's Journal of Captain Cook's Last Voyage*. 1783. James Kenneth Munford, ed; rpt., Corvallis: Oregon State University Press, 1963.

Mackenzie, Alexander. *The Journals and Letters of Sir Alexander Mackenzie*. 1801. W. Kaye Lamb, ed; rpt., Cambridge: Cambridge University Press, 1970.

Mendoza, Vicente de Saldívar. *Spanish Exploration in the Southwest, 1542-1706*. Herbert Eugene Bolton, ed. New York: Scribner's, 1930.

Niza, Marcos de. *Discovery of the Seven Cities of Cibola*. 1864-1884. Percy M. Baldwin, ed. and trans; rpt., Albuquerque: El Palacio Press [1926].

Oñate, Juan de. *Spanish Exploration in the Southwest, 1542-1706*. Herbert Eugene Bolton, ed. New York: Scribners, 1930.

Pond, Peter. *Five Fur Traders of the Northwest*. Charles M. Gates, ed. 1933; rpt., St. Paul: Minnesota Historical Society, 1965. Pp. 11-59.

Radisson, Pierre Esprit. *The Explorations of Pierre Esprit Radisson*. 1885. Arthur T. Adams, ed; rpt., Minneapolis: Ross and Haines, 1961.

Sigüenza y Góngora, Don Carlos de. *The Mercurio Volante of Don Carlos de Sigüenza y Góngora: An Account of the First Expedition of Don Diego de Vargas into New Mexico in 1692*. Irving Albert Leonard, ed. and trans. Los Angeles: The Quivira Society, 1932.

Steller, Georg Wilhelm. *Journal of a Voyage with Bering: 1741-1742.* 1781, 1793. O.W. Frost, ed. Stanford: Stanford University Press, 1988.

Thompson, David. *Travels in Western North America, 1784-1812.* 1962. Victor G. Hopwood, ed; rpt., Toronto: Macmillan, 1971.

Valverde, Antonio de. *After Coronado: Spanish Exploration Northeast of New Mexico, 1696-1727: Documents from the Archives of Spain, Mexico, and New Mexico.* 1719. Alfred Barnaby Thomas, ed; rpt., Norman: University of Oklahoma Press, 1935.

Vargas, Diego. *First Expedition of Vargas into New Mexico, 1692.* J. Manuel Espinosa, ed. and trans. Albuquerque: University of New Mexico Press, 1940.

Vélez de Escalante, Silvestre. *The Dominguez-Escalante Journal: Their Expedition through Colorado, Utah, Arizona, and New Mexico in 1776.* Ted J. Wamer, ed. Fray Angelico Chavez, trans. Provo: Brigham Young University Press, 1976.

Vial, Pedro. *Pedro Vial and the Roads to Santa Fe.* Noel M. Loomis and Abraham P. Nasatir, eds. Norman: University of Oklahoma Press, 1967.

Villagrá, Gaspar Pérez de. *Historia de la Nueva México, 1610: A Critical and Annotated Spanish/English Edition.* 1610. Miguel Encinas, Alfred Rodriguez, and Joseph P. Sanchez, eds. and trans; rpt., Albuquerque: University of New Mexico Press, 1992.

Secondary Sources

Barclay, Donald A., James H. Maguire, and Peter Wild, eds. *Into the Wilderness Dream: An Anthology of Pre-Lewis-and-Clark Western Exploration Narratives.* Salt Lake City: University of Utah Press, 1994.

Bolton, Herbert Eugene, ed. *Spanish Exploration in the Southwest, 1542-1706.* New York: Scribner's, 1930.

Burpee, Lawrence J. *The Search for the Western Sea: The Story of the Exploration of North-Western America.* 2 vols. 1907; rpt., New York: Macmillan, 1936..

DeVoto, Bernard. *The Course of Empire.* 1952; rpt., Lincoln: University of Nebraska Press, 1983.

Jefferson, Thomas. *The Papers of Thomas Jefferson.* 24 vols. (Vol. 12.) Julian P. Boyd, ed. Princeton: Princeton University Press, 1955.

Morison, Samuel Eliot. *The Great Explorers: The European Discovery of America.* New York: Oxford University Press, 1978.

Pilkington, William T. *Imagining Texas: The Literature of the Lone Star State.* Boston: American Press, 1981.

Thacker, Robert. *The Great Prairie Fact and Literary Imagination.* Albuquerque: University of New Mexico Press, 1989.

Thrapp, Dan L. *Encyclopedia of Frontier Biography.* 3 vols. Glendale: Arthur H. Clark, 1988.

Jan Roush

Ranch-Life Narratives and Poems

UPI Dateline: Clarendon, Texas, December 31, 1989: A man believed to have been the oldest working cowboy in Texas died the way he wanted, stretched out in the prairie grass with his boots on, his friends said.

Thomas Everett Blasingame, 91, was found lying on his back Wednesday by fellow cowhands at the JA Cattle Company ranch near Clarendon in the Texas Panhandle. His saddled horse was standing nearby.

"If he had written it down on paper, he wouldn't have changed a word," said Buster McLaury, the cattle foreman on the ranch.

About 400 people attended the graveside services Saturday at the JA Cattle Company cemetery near Clarendon. The last burial in the cemetery had been in 1899.

Johnny Farrar, the ranch's business manager, said Blasingame was riding a young horse he was training just before his death.

"He must have known he was in trouble, dismounted and just laid down and died," Farrar said.

Blasingame's son, Thomas E. Blasingame, Jr. of Hereford, said the cowboy was laid to rest during a traditional "cowboy funeral," with the hearse accompanied to the graveyard by Blasingame's riderless horse and cowboys on horseback.

Blasingame was born Feb. 2, 1898.

"[He] had chosen to be a cowboy when he was a little kid," said [his son]. "The reason he lived so long was because he did what he did for his entire life."

Ranch-life narratives have documented the culture for over 130 years since herding cattle became an economic way of life in the American West. In spite of numerous accounts of Gabriel's trumpet sounding the demise of this life, such narratives still are being written, almost in defiance of the doomsayers. Thomas Blasingame's obituary is mute testimony that such a way of life continues today relatively unchanged. Its details starkly capture how one group of people has had so much influence on the characterization of the American West. What is puzzling is why a relatively minor group in the overall colonization of a young country has had such an impact. Even more puzzling is why they are defined, and define themselves, in terms of a lifestyle that requires so much sacrifice of the very things an increasingly urbanized society values: leisure time, material wealth, an easier way of life.

Seldom in the history of the United States has one era captured the interest and romantic fancy of the populace as did the last quarter of the nineteenth century played out on the vast stage of the American West. Its cast of thousands easily rivaled the great biblical epics Cecil B. DeMille produced in the 1950s, especially if one takes into account the huge herds of cattle that roamed the plains and built the empires of colorful cattle barons from Texas to Montana. But it is the keeper of these cattle, that unique breed of man called the cowboy — and by extension the men and women who comprise the ranching community today — who so caught the imagination of the American public, as well as an international audience in countries as diverse as Germany, Japan, and Australia. The character of the American cowboy is as well-known abroad as that of local folk heroes.

So thoroughly did the cowboy capture the imagination that he rapidly took on mythic proportions, spawning the wide range of qualities and ideals so vividly portrayed in ranch-life narratives. Long hours in the saddle, the tedium of trailing cattle across rough terrain, the onerous task of tending them in all climatic conditions have provided the very means by which the myth of the cowboy, indeed the entire ranching community, has emerged. Over the years the ordinary cowboy has become the more-than-ordinary man who employs a certain reckless daring, an attentiveness to duty in the face of adversity, and an implacable belief in honor among men. He exemplifies strong individualism and a sense of freedom in a struggle against nature, against the encroachment of technology, against organized social institutions.

In the early accounts from the end of the nineteenth century, the cowboy took on these mythic proportions initially with little recognition of that fact. He was just doing his job. And indeed no job would seem to be removed further from the qualities normally associated with myth. The cowboy was first of all a hired hand. The work he was required to do was dirty, bone-wrenching, and tedious, all for minimal pay. At $35 a month, the average cowboy was not going to become an entrepreneur; indeed, he was hard-pressed to keep himself clothed and equipped with the necessities the job demanded. In spite of these realities, he emerged from the open range era a mythical figure with a code all his own.

As cowboys became more conscious of their status, they felt that being a good hand involved more than just skillfully handling cows; somehow the job also had to further that mythological goal. Through narrative, cowboys have typically done just that.[1] In song, verse and prose they have attempted to share with each other, and anyone else who cared to listen, what it is like to cowboy, to *be* a cowboy — in a sense to preserve their mythical place in America. Under certain conditions, narrative becomes the articulation of a way of life for an entire group or occupation, rendered the more powerful by insiders who are speaking (primarily to each other) for that group. Montana rancher and cowboy poet Wally McRae has noted that such chronicles are "a way of explaining our life to ourselves.... Traditions tend to slip away from us if we don't remind ourselves of those traditions. One of the ways you can remember is to put them into poetry or song."[2]

Occupational groups have always expressed such shared values and attitudes in many narrative forms, not only in prose as diverse as jokes, anecdotes, and legends but also in poetry and song. The feelings thus articulated provide a means of both understanding and sympathizing with such groups. In his essay, "The Deeper Necessity: Folklore and the Humanities," folklorist William A. Wilson says that "behind each expression lies the human urge, the deeper necessity, to communicate significant experience and emotion and to influence the surrounding world through the artistic, and therefore powerful, use of language" (156-157). It is this deeper necessity that has inspired ranch-life narratives since cowboys first started driving cattle to market after the Civil War.

Hundreds of titles reflecting various aspects of ranch life have been published since the 1860s with more appearing every year. More than 300 volumes comprise the L. J. and Mary C. Skaggs Cowboy Poetry Library, housed in the Fife Folklore Archives at Utah State University.

The collection travels each year to Elko, Nevada, for the Cowboy Poetry Gathering. At the Gathering, ranch people from all over the West browse through the volumes while seeking full text to supplement half-remembered lines of poems they have learned, read narratives that were written over a century ago or just last year, and add their own volumes of self-published accounts to the collection for others to see the next year.

In this wealth of tales, two areas are proliferating. The first includes early historical accounts that have languished undiscovered in attics or dusty archive boxes in libraries and museums around the West and are just now coming to light as more scholars express an interest in reconstructing the history of the West. The second represents contemporary ranchwomen's narratives, an especially fast-growing area as more and more women are taking an increasingly active role in that reconstruction of western history.

On one level, ranch-life narratives have changed very little over the years. In spite of technological advances and changes in business economics, ranching is much the same today as it was in the 1880s. Cowboys still work long hours tending stock for little pay. Gone are the huge roundups and the trail drives that brought herds numbering in the tens of thousands to distant markets, but feeding, doctoring, cutting and branding have changed little since the days of such immense spreads as the King, Matador, or XIT ranches. Hence the chronicles demonstrate a remarkable consistency, reflecting in part the nature of the work (in spite of two existing traditions of working cattle — buckarooing or cowboying — overall there are just so many ways to ready livestock for market) and in part the mythologizing impetus that embodies the ranching community's pride in its cultural traditions. On another level, however, one can see a change in the attitude or stance members of this community have taken over the years.

Accounts reflecting the history of ranching can be divided roughly into three periods defined by this change: (1) the era of the open range beginning in the 1860s and continuing until the late 1880s or early 1890s when certain catastrophic events combined to bring an end to it; (2) the era immediately following when ranchers retooled their thinking and methodology to establish new techniques more in accordance with a controlled, fenced-in range, ending roughly with the Taylor Grazing Act of 1934; and (3) the current period beginning after World War II and continuing today, when an increasing environmental awareness applied its own pressures on traditional ranch life.

The earliest accounts concentrate on collecting a herd of cattle and establishing a ranch, founding a business. This was the era right after the Civil War when the country was trying to recuperate from the economic and physical devastation of the land. The West became a place for healing, a place to begin again where no one cared about anyone's past and circumstances were equal to all. With perseverance and hard work, one could build a cattle empire and many did. "Among the Cowboys," an 1881 article from *Lippincott's Magazine*, describes the genesis and immensity of the large ranches, chronicling the rags-to-riches theme of such men as Richard King and R.E. Stafford (Bradford 565-571). Having lived with ranchmen for eighteen months, Louis Bradford ably portrays firsthand what it took to build huge herds and trail them to market; he notes that the first trail drive to Kansas took place in 1860 with 25,000 cattle and describes in vivid detail one of the largest drives ever undertaken when in 1874 "half a million beeves were driven through":

> The trail was beaten into a broad path a mile wide and extending fifteen hundred miles in length. For miles and miles the string of lowing herds stretched along, while the keen riders darted hither and thither, keeping them well on the trail. At night the voices of the men singing to their sleeping cattle could be heard all along the line, while the long string of camp-fires [threw] their lurid glare against the black vault overhead.... (569)

These early narratives, most frequently written from the viewpoint of the cowboy himself rather than that of the cattle baron, focus on rounding up cattle and taking them to market. As such, they are directly connected with the land. Generally, the cowboy reacts to the land rather than initiating action upon it: something happens, a storm causing cattle to stampede, for example, or a major blizzard that causes the cattle to drift and freeze; the people involved then simply pick up the pieces and go on. There is almost a fatalistic notion that they cannot change the forces of nature but rather are victims of its whims—an attitude that spawned the first call of doom for the open range.[3] This way of life was brought to a close by such devastating natural events as the crippling blizzards of the late 1880s but more insidiously by such man-made events as the introduction of barbed wire that effectively fenced off huge sections of open range where cattle had once grazed unchecked with no consideration given to the long-term impact on the environment.

Primarily masculine in orientation—these are, after all, *cowboy* accounts—such narratives often have a picaresque quality, a glorified on-the-road adventurousness that often combines with a *bildungsroman* approach to shape the protagonist's character. One of the earliest and best narratives, Baylis John Fletcher's *Up the Trail in '79* (1966), fits nicely into this category. Fletcher, a young cowboy, vividly describes a trail drive of 2,000 cattle north to Kansas and on to Wyoming. Though he did not write the account until about thirty years after the events, it still resonates with authentic details and observations, from gathering the herd to delivering them at the railroad station.

Other narratives include such trail adventures as part of larger descriptions of the open-range ranching life. Brief discussions of Andy Adams' *The Log of a Cowboy* (1903), Teddy Blue Abbott's *We Pointed Them North* (1939), and Charles Siringo's *A Texas Cowboy* (1885) were all included in the original volume of the *Literary History of the American West* as excellent examples of early cowboy life, even though Adams' narrative is a fictive composite of many such experiences, as is J. Frank Dobie's embellishment of John Young's simple narrative in *A Vaquero of the Brush Country* (1929). All of these include descriptions of real events by actual participants, and all are held in great respect as authentic accounts of what early ranching life was like.

Some of these narratives were not immediately published, instead lying in library archives or family trunks. *Up the Trail in '79* is such an example; so, too, is Reuben Mullins' narrative, *Pulling Leather*. This volume, covering the pivotal years of 1884-1889 on the Wyoming range, is a good example of how such accounts finally come to light after more than a half-century of obscurity, for Mullins wrote his saga in the 1930s and it lay undiscovered until published in 1988. Like Fletcher's account, it is a literate recording of one cowboy's actual experiences on the open range just at the close of the era. It differs, however, in the philosophical commentary that runs counterpoint to the narrative itself, for Mullins' primary objective was to counter the romanticizing of the cowboy found in fiction and in film. What he wanted to do, he said, was "give a comprehensive routine of cowboy life and work, just as it was conducted through all its diversified ramifications, which were manifold" (xii).

Spanning the years from 1879 to 1936, Will Barnes' *Apaches & Longhorns* (1941) provides a transition from the first era of ranch-life narratives into the second. The book is particularly prophetic, for it is more than a cowboy's or rancher's view of the range; it also includes Barnes' experiences as a soldier on the early frontier, as well as his later years with the U. S. Forest Service. The multiple perspective records more starkly than any others the changes that brought the open-range era to an end and presaged the shape of the second period. Barnes chronicles how first the Arizona range and then that of northern New Mexico were overstocked, forcing Barnes to sell out in the early 1900s. Based on his experiences as a former cattleman and then grazing inspector, Barnes' observations in the mid-1930s concerning grazing permits and the role stockmen would have to take conveyed a prescient warning to the ranching industry:

> Today, I think it can be said without fear of contradiction that the majority of permittees using the grazing-lands of our National Forests will admit the value of the plans in use for handling their livestock, and will admit, also, that the cattle industry must be secondary to the primary purpose for which the Forests were created — the production of timber and the protection of the great watersheds of the West. I can see how, at this very day, certain matters are coming to the front which, if not met by the stockmen in a wise and constructive spirit, may possibly imperil their continued use of the ranges. (206)

That enlightened attitude, a result of culminating forces on ranch life during its first two eras, survives today.

Chronicles from the 1890s through the Depression were still most often written from the viewpoint of the cowboy himself, but now — after the introduction of barbed wire forced them to become attached to a fenced-in environment — a ranch-bound one. Cowboys' lives continued to be arduous and fraught with dangers, but it was a different kind of peril. Instead of the catastrophes portrayed in early "up the trail" narratives or cowboy songs like "Little Joe the Wrangler," the dangers now lay closer to home. Narratives during this era portray the daily hazards of working cattle: being thrown from half-broken broncos or gored by wild-eyed steers, for instance, or losing a thumb to a misplaced dally. They also portray the risks inherent in the increasingly complex ranching business, brought about not only by climate but by increasing governmental controls, culminating in the Taylor Grazing Act of 1934 that Will Barnes prophesized in *Apaches & Longhorns*. Nor was the Taylor

Act the only major legislation that dramatically changed range life; the same period also saw the introduction of both the federal income tax and the inheritance tax.

It is this domesticated, regulated lifestyle that is reflected in volumes from the second period. Although there are some notable prose accounts like Spike Van Cleve's *Forty Years' Gatherin's* (1977), Jack Thorpe's *Tales of the Chuckwagon* (1926), Jo Mora's *Trail Dust and Saddle Leather* (1946), and Will James' *Lone Cowboy* (1942), many of the best accounts of this way of life are found in poetry. During this era not only were earlier cowboy poems and songs first collected, but new verses were created — verses that today remain the foundation on which the ranching community defines itself to outsiders. Of the former category, two collections remain especially valuable: Jack Thorpe's *Songs of the Cowboys*, first published in 1908, and John Lomax's *Cowboy Songs*, released in 1911. Of these two, it is Thorpe's that is more valuable as an accurate documentation of cowboy life because Thorpe faithfully recorded the songs as he heard them on his 1,500-mile horseback odyssey in 1889 and 1890, while Lomax fused many versions of a song into one in an attempt to reach a popular audience (Lomax xxiii). Lomax's collection contains more songs overall (112, including two fragments). Thorpe's original collection of twenty-three songs, however, was later expanded to 101 for the 1921 edition; more importantly, it not only includes notes on where he collected these songs but also gives credit to authorship if known.

In his essay "Banjo in the Cow Camps," Thorpe outlines his odyssey and discusses the criteria he used in collecting, noting that he was "mainly interested in songs that had all the elements of the range — the cow range, and its special codes and points of view.... Things that cowboys liked, things they hated, incidents of the here and reflections on the hereafter — these were the chief themes of their songs" (Thorpe 60). These same themes echo in the newly written poetry from this second period of ranch-life narratives.

Noted folklorists Austin and Alta Fife, keen observers of western life, have said that such folk literature of the cowboy simultaneously conveys "extremely universal [yet] extremely simple and communicable" (Fife, 1964, 22) themes. The many collections of verse published during this era bear this thesis out, for they convey most frequently the everyday life of the ranching community, often in the face of governmental intervention; here, too, are the first nostalgic recordings of a way of life that is no more.

A few of these cowboy poets are especially effective in portraying universal themes and are the ones most recited by today's ranchers as representative of their culture. Among the best collections are S. Omar Barker's three volumes: *Rawhide Rhymes* (1968), *Songs of the Saddlemen* (1954), and *Buckaroo Ballads* (1928); Badger Clark's *Sun & Saddle Leather* (1915); Curley Fletcher's *Songs of the Sage* (1986); and Bruce Kiskaddon's *Rhymes of the Range* (1947) and *Western Poems* (1935).

Of these, the poems of Kiskaddon are pre-eminent in reflecting the everyday ranching lifestyle because of their breadth. Whether discussing the discomfort of wearing wet boots or musing over what happens after shipping cattle in the fall, Kiskaddon's poems stand the test of the dictum by which ranching people judge what is real among all the "wannabes": "We'll just know."[4] Though his best-known poems were not written until some twenty years after he quit cowboying and was working as a bellhop in a downtown Los Angeles hotel, Kiskaddon was able to convey succinctly and compellingly the essence of the ranchman's life. Today, his works are recited more often than those of any other ranch-life poet.

Individual poems from two other collections, William Lawrence Chittenden's *Ranch Verses* (1897) and Henry Herbert Knibbs' *Songs of the Lost Frontier* (1930) are sometimes still recited, but as a whole these two collections are more literary, conveying little of the total cowboy experience. In addition, there are single poems by cowboy poets that have achieved the status of classics. D.J. O'Malley's "When the Work's All Done This Fall," which chronicles the everyday danger of herding cattle as it describes the death of a cowboy caught in a cattle stampede who "won't see his mother when the work's all done this fall," comes to mind, as does Gail Gardner's "The Sierry Pete's," later popularized under the title "Tying a Knot in the Devil's Tail," which humorously plays out the age-old Faustian theme of encountering the devil and winning, cowboy-style.

Authorship of some of the best-known poems remains in dispute today. "Little Joe the Wrangler," attributed to Thorpe, or "The Strawberry Roan," now thought to have been written by Curley Fletcher, are debated. Even the origin of "The Sierry Pete's" was once in question in spite of Gardner's possessing proof that he had penned the lines while traveling east across Kansas during World War I on his way to join the aviation section of the Army Signal Corps.[5] Disputes about authorship arose because such narratives so effectively caught the core of the ranching experience that they quickly entered oral tradition and remain an integral part of it today. For those interested in the often strange evolution of such works, John I. White effectively traces their origins in *Git Along Little Dogies* (1975), relying on personal correspondence with many of the authors as well as on years of research.

Immediately following World War II not many new accounts were on the market, but the last few decades have seen a proliferation of materials, especially with the advent of the Cowboy Poetry Gatherings held yearly since 1985 at Elko, Nevada. During this time the ranching community realized that what it thought was a little-known tradition of writing and reciting cowboy poetry was instead widely shared throughout the West.[6] The idea of regional folklorists who had been doing fieldwork with various individual cowboy poets throughout a seventeen-state area of the West, the first Gathering in Elko brought together between fifty and sixty poets to perform before a relatively small crowd of about 500. Since then, the Gathering has grown yearly with hundreds of poets performing before crowds of thousands who strain the capacity of Elko at the end of every January.

The interest fueled by international coverage has increased the production of such ranch-life narratives; more importantly, it has fostered an awareness among the ranch people that what they do is of enduring interest to the world and has given them an arena for promoting their culture. At a time when perceived pressures brought about by environmentalist groups have made the ranchers feel that they are an endangered species, this forum allows them to respond to such criticisms and to defend their way of life. Hence many new accounts have been written in the past decade that attempt not only to convey the ongoing traditions of range life but also to chronicle changes in the tradition that will allow ranching to survive as a way of life.

Of the many poets who are writing today, two stand out: Waddie Mitchell and Baxter Black, both of whom write new poems as well as recite the classics. In addition to these men are others, almost as well-known, such as Wallace McRae, who documents the continuing stress brought by struggles over land use. His poetry, chronicling the struggles of securing the family ranch against mining and other land use concerns, strikes a responsive chord throughout the community.

It is the struggle over land use that has fostered the greatest change in attitude during this third era of ranch-life narratives. The most significant examples of this change lie in the narratives of contemporary ranchwomen, which most clearly reflect a conciliatory stance toward the land. This new voice expresses another view of the forces that have shaped the land and the people who inhabit it. Without repudiating the mythic strains that for over a century have created a strong, masculine image of the West, this feminine voice expands the image in original, sometimes startling ways.

These new stories are of stewardship and respect for both the land and the people within it, delighting in its diversity; through a variety of lenses, they attend to the details of living, of sharing, of communing with one's environment in ways not attended to before. These tales neglect none of the characteristics found in accounts of the earlier eras: stories of self-reliance and resourcefulness, rugged individualism, stoicism, tenacity and courage. Nor are they gentler in their telling. However, since they are being told with broader characterization, presenting both male and female accounts, they resonate with greater impact.

Very few women's accounts during the first two eras of ranch-life narratives achieved much attention. Only recently, with this new stance toward the environment, have such early accounts as Nannie T. Alderson's *A Bride Goes West* (1942), Agnes Morley Cleaveland's *No Life for a Lady* (1941), and Elinore Pruitt Stewart's *Letters of a Woman Homesteader* (1914) received the attention they deserve for accurately recording a woman's viewpoint of the range during the latter part of the nineteenth and early part of the twentieth centuries. This enriched outlook continues with examples from the second era — works not published until well after World War II. Alice Marriott's *Hell on Horses and Women* (1953) is the first collection by or about ranch women for the period. In it, Marriott incorporates selections from fifty-two interviews with ranching women whose accounts cover experiences from 1895 to the 1950s, though most are concentrated in the post-war era. Two very different yet representative accounts (each written from different perspectives of time and space while sharing a timelessness) are Pearl Baker's *Robbers Roost Recollections* (1976) and Jo Jeffers' *Ranch Wife* (1964). Baker chronicles a life of being born into a ranching family around the turn of the century in the harsh, unpopulated terrain of southeastern Utah, and Jeffers describes marrying into an Arizona ranching family during the 1950s after growing up in a small midwestern town and being educated at Stanford and the University of Nottingham, England. Underlying all of these narratives is an awareness of the land, of the necessity of safeguarding this resource.

Nowhere is this awareness quite so evident, however, as in the last two decades of contemporary western women's writings, for it is here that one finds a heightened sense of responsibility, of accountability for one's actions. Teresa Jordan notes in her introduction to *Graining the Mare* (1994), the first collection of ranch women's poetry, that when she was preparing the bibliography for *Cowgirls* (1982), her oral history of women cowboys, she found fewer than three dozen first-person narratives by women in ranch culture over an eighty-year span (1). Thanks to a rewriting of the West that attempts to make all voices heard, women are now more amply represented. Mixing forms like poetry, the personal essay, and oral history to express such topics as stewardship of the land beyond the immediate needs of caring for families, contemporary ranchwomen are making certain that their experiences, too, join those that have long defined the West. Expanding on the theme of stewardship expressed over a half-century ago by Will Barnes, ranchwomen like Teresa Jordan, Linda Hasselstrom, Mary Clearman Blew, Judy Blunt, and Page Lambert join together to provide a broader perspective of what the West was — and what they hope it will become.

It is this conciliatory stance reflective of the third era of narratives that may ultimately decide whether there will be a fourth — or any future — era. In a modern West fraught with acrimonious debates over the environment, the ranching community frequently finds its lifestyle threatened. Though assured of its status in the history of the West, the ranching community is painfully aware that for its way of life to continue it must connect not only to the past but also to the future. Linda Hasselstrom alludes to that connection in her introduction to *Land Circle* (1991) when she says that "[m]ost of us who ranch today realize that while we may operate in physical isolation on the arid plains, alone in our hardships, our solitude is only the appearance. In reality, the cash in our pockets and the cows in our pastures are connected by invisible umbilical cords to cows and businesses all over the world" (xiv). With such awareness, then, perhaps ranch narratives will continue to portray the life that has been so much a part of the history of the American West.

Notes

1. Hal Cannon, personal interview, Salt Lake City, Utah, December 27, 1985. Cannon, the director of the Western Folklife Center now located in Elko, Nevada, is known throughout the ranching community as the creative force behind the Cowboy Poetry Gathering.

2. Wallace McRae, quoted in "When the Work's All Done This Fall: Songs, Stories, and Poems from Montana Cattle Camps and Cow Trails," produced by the Montana Folklife Project as text accompanying the Montana Cowboy Poetry Collection, Skaggs Cowboy Poetry Library, Fife Folklore Archive, Utah State University Merrill Library Special Collections.

3. Joseph Nimmo, Jr., in "The American Cowboy" (*Harper's New Monthly Magazine* [November 1886]) notes that "[t]he journey from southern Texas to Montana requires from four to six months. Herds are also driven from Oregon and Washington Territory to Wyoming and eastern Montana. It is impossible for one who has not had actual experience in 'riding on trail' to imagine the difficulties involved in driving a large herd of wild cattle over mountain ranges, across desert lands where in some cases food and water are not found for many miles, and where streams must be crossed which are liable to dangerous freshets.

"A large part of the northern ranges is embraced in the area [termed] 'the birthplace of the tornado.' Thunder and lightning are here frequent, and they are especially terrifying to range cattle. The most thrilling incident in the life of the cow-boy occurs on the occasion of a thunder-storm at night."

4. Mike Korn, Montana folklorist, notes this essential feature in his definition of cowboy poetry: "The verse reflects an intimate knowledge of that way of life and of the community from which it maintains itself in tradition. . . . Cowboy poetry may or may not in fact be anonymous in authorship, but [it] must have qualities, content and style which permit it to be accepted into the repertoire of the cultural community as a reflection of that community's aesthetic in style, form and content." His definition is what all "real" cowboy poetry is judged by in today's ranching community. See Mike Korn, "A Definition of Cowboy Poetry," *Cowboy Poetry from Utah: An Anthology*, Carol Edison, ed. (Salt Lake City: Utah Folklife Center, 1985), p. 14.

5. Gail Gardner, personal interview, Prescott, Arizona, December 12, 1986.

6. In his foreword to *Cowboy Love Poetry*, compiled and edited by Paddy Calistro, Jack Lamb, and Jean Penn, Waddie Mitchell states: "Not too many years ago, before 'Cowboy Poetry' was discovered by folklorists like Hal Cannon who recognized its worth, we cowboy poets had very little to do. We just wrote our little ditties for the cowboys, ranchers and country folk of the inner circle of our lifestyle.

"In the past decade, though, that has changed. Cowboy poetry is finding its own way into the publishing and entertainment arena. The interest has been phenomenal" (ix).

Selected Bibliography

Abbott, E. C. ("Teddy Blue") and Helena Huntington Smith. *We Pointed Them North*. Norman, Oklahoma: University of Oklahoma Press, 1954.

Adams, Andy. *The Log of a Cowboy: A Narrative of the Old Trail Days*. Boston and New York: Houghton Mifflin, 1931.

Alderson, Nannie and Helena Huntington Smith. *A Bride Goes West*. Lincoln, Nebraska: University of Nebraska Press, 1942.

Baker, Pearl. *Robbers Roost Recollections*. Logan: Utah State University Press, 1976.

Barker, S. Omar. *Buckaroo Ballads*. Santa Fe: Santa Fe New Mexican Publishing, 1928.

———. *Rawhide Rhymes*. Garden City: Doubleday, 1968.

———. *Songs of the Saddlemen*. Denver: Sage Books, 1954.

Barnes, Will C. *Apaches & Longhorns: The Reminiscences of Will C. Barnes*. Frank C.

Lockwood, ed. Los Angeles: The Ward Ritchie Press, 1941; rpt., Tucson: University of Arizona Press, 1982.

Bradford, Louis C. "Among the Cowboys," *Lippincott's Magazine* (June 1881): 565-571.

Cannon, Hal, ed. *Cowboy Poetry: A Gathering.* Salt Lake City: Gibbs Smith, 1985.

———, ed. *New Cowboy Poetry: A Contemporary Gathering.* Salt Lake City: Gibbs Smith, 1990.

Chittenden, William Lawrence. *Ranch Verses.* New York: G. P. Putnam's Sons, 1897.

Clark, Badger. *Sun and Saddle Leather.* Boston: Gorham Press, 1915.

Cleaveland, Agnes Morley. *No Life for a Lady.* Boston: Houghton Mifflin, 1941.

Dobie, J. Frank. *A Vaquero of the Brush Country.* Austin: University of Texas Press, 1929.

Fife, Austin. "Tying Knots in the Devil's Tail, and Other Cowboy Songs." *The Western Folklore Conference: Selected Papers.* Austin Fife and J. Golden Taylor, eds. Logan: Utah State University Press Monograph Series. 11:3 (June, 1964): 22.

Fife, Austin and Alta Fife, eds. *Ballads of the Great West.* Palo Alto, California: American West Publishing, 1970.

———. *Heaven on Horseback: Revivalist Songs and Verse in the Cowboy Idiom.* Logan: Utah State University Press, Western Texts Society Series, June, 1970.

———. Intro. *Songs of the Cowboys* by N. Howard "Jack" Thorpe. New York: Clarkson N. Potter, 1966. P. 6. This essay is chapter one of Thorpe's autobiography, *Pardner of the Wind.*

Fletcher, Baylis John. *Up the Trail in '79.* Norman: University of Oklahoma Press, 1966.

Fletcher, Curley. *Songs of the Sage.* Salt Lake City: Peregrine Smith Books, 1986.

Hasselstrom, Linda. *Going Over East: Reflections of a Woman Rancher.* Golden, Colorado: Fulcrum, 1987.

———. *Land Circle.* Golden, Colorado: Fulcrum, 1991.

———. *Windbreak: A Woman Rancher on the Northern Plains.* Berkeley: Barn Owl Books, 1987.

James, Will. *Lone Cowboy: My Life Story.* New York: Charles Scribner's Sons, 1942.

Jeffers, Jo. *Ranch Wife.* Tucson: University of Arizona Press, 1964.

Jordan, Teresa. *Cowgirls.* New York: Doubleday, 1982.

———, ed. *Graining the Mare: The Poetry of Ranch Women.* Salt Lake City: Gibbs Smith, 1994.

———. *Riding the White Horse Home.* New York: Vintage Books, 1994.

Kiskaddon, Bruce. *Rhymes of the Ranges and Other Poems.* By the author, 1947.

———. *Western Poems.* Los Angeles: Western Livestock Journal, 1935.

Knibbs, Henry Herbert. *Songs of the Lost Frontier.* Boston: Houghton Mifflin, 1930.

Lanning, Jim and Judy Lanning, eds. *Texas Cowboys: Memories of the Early Days.* College Station: Texas A&M University Press, 1984.

Lomax, John A. *Cowboy Songs and Other Frontier Ballads.* New York: Sturgis & Walton, 1911.

———. *Songs of the Cattle Trail and Cow Camp.* New York: Macmillan, 1927.

Marriott, Alice. *Hell on Horses & Women.* Norman: University of Oklahoma Press, 1953.

Mora, Jo. *Californios: The Saga of the Hard-riding Vaqueros, America's First Cowboys.* Garden City: Doubleday, 1949.

———. *Trail Dust and Saddle Leather.* New York: Charles Scribner's Sons, 1946.

Mullins, Reuben B. *Pulling Leather: Being the Early Recollections of a Cowboy on the Wyoming Range, 1884-1889.* Jan Roush and Lawrence Clayton, eds. Glendo, Wyoming: High Plains Press, 1988.

Roach, Joyce Gibson. *The Cowgirls.* Denton: University of North Texas Press, 1990.

Thorpe, N. Howard ("Jack"). *Songs of the Cowboys*. Variants, Commentary, Notes and Lexicon by Austin and Alta Fife. New York: Clarkson N. Potter, 1966.

————. *Pardner of the Wind*. Lincoln: University of Nebraska Press, 1941.

————. *Tales of the Chuckwagon*. Privately printed, 1926.

Siringo, Charles A. *A Texas Cowboy*. Lincoln: University of Nebraska Press, 1950.

Stewart, Elinore Pruitt. *Letters of a Woman Homesteader*. Boston: Houghton Mifflin, 1914.

Van Cleve, Spike. *40 Years' Gatherin's*. Kansas City: The Lowell Press, 1977.

Wellman, Paul I. *The Trampling Herd*. New York: Carrick & Evans, 1939.

Westermeier, Clifford P., ed. *Trailing the Cowboy*. Caldwell, Idaho: Caxton Printers, 1955.

White, John I. *Git Along Little Dogies: Songs and Songmakers of the American West*. Urbana: University of Illinois Press, 1975.

Wilson, William A. "The Deeper Necessity: Folklore and the Humanities," *Journal of American Folklore*, 101:400 (April-June, 1988): 156-157.

Kathleen A. Boardman

Paper Trail: Diaries, Letters and Reminiscences of the Overland Journey West

In 1864, not far from the Black Hills, a small wagon train was ambushed by a band of Oglala. Soon the men of the party were dead or had fled, and the surviving women and children were prisoners. Among them was Fanny Kelly, who stoically accepted separation and loss yet could not conceal her terror. To comfort her, one of the Indians gave her some books and letters he had salvaged from the burning wagons. Quickly concealing these in her clothing, she began to devise the first of many plans for escape. Wherever she traveled with her captors, she surreptitiously dropped a crumpled fragment of a letter, hoping that her people would be able to follow the trail, find her, and rescue her. This plan turned out to be futile. Yet Fanny Kelly's paper trail can serve as an emblem for the writing of many other emigrants who hoped their readers would be able to "follow" their long journey west.

During the middle decades of the nineteenth century, some 2,000 emigrants wrote their way across half a continent. They used their diaries and letters, and later their reminiscences, to mark the trail, to say, "I was here," and, "I hope you can follow me." Many of the diaries marked the trail by faithfully recording landmarks and daily mileages. Some diarists saw themselves as providing a guide for emigrants who would come later. Some wanted to leave their own mark, under the impulse that caused thousands to carve initials on Chimney Rock and Independence Rock along the California-Oregon Trail. Many writers struggled to describe sights and feelings that, they feared, their loved ones who had not made the journey would be unable to comprehend. Some wrote to make their experiences comprehensible to themselves.

Like Fanny Kelly's trail of letter scraps, emigrants' writings are also often fragmented, misleading, or cryptic. Diarists wrote under difficult physical conditions. Letter writers tried to spare the feelings of those back home by minimizing illnesses, danger, or fear. Writers of reminiscences had to deal with memory lapses, confusion about places and events, and the need to spin an exciting tale for the grandchildren. Other constraints were not quite so obvious. Social codes prevented many emigrants from writing about everything they had experienced. Some writers candidly admitted their omissions: "I have left out all such parts as should not be 'Recollected,'" writes one forty-niner, "for there has many scenes taken place & been exhibited on the 'Plaines' that should sleep in their silent and dreary wilds & never be spoken or read of by civilized men" (Heckman 16). Women generally observed codes of modesty that prevented the mention of such topics as pregnancy, childbirth, and spousal abuse; many men and women believed complaint was a sign of weakness. Many emigrants, or their children, recopied diaries, editing and censoring as they went along. Because many reminiscences were dictated, additional gaps and changes occurred in the narratives.

Finally, the amateur writers of the westward movement faced a problem that also plagues professionals: how to describe the unfamiliar in familiar terms. On the face of it, the journey and the new life in the West provided a gold mine of impressions, a fertile field for anecdote. As one bibliographer says, "Even the most impoverished imagination was supplied with an endless variety of subject matter to choose from: the trail, wagon problems, landmarks, stifling dust, mosquitoes, wild buffalo, the endless line of graves and dead animals, and the debilitating consequences of the journey itself" (Mintz xiv). Certainly, many travelers took the opportunity to follow their own interests: some described geologic features, some the plant life, some the clouds and weather patterns, some the Indians' appearance and behavior. (One gourmet faithfully described each new food he encountered: prairie dog, antelope, badger, buffalo, snake.) At the end of the journey there was still plenty of potential subject matter in the challenge and culture shock of the new life in the West. But, as Stephen Fender points out, emigrants who made the overland journey after the mid-1840s found themselves in an environment that was both "underplotted" and "overplotted": it was utterly alien, with few recognizable natural features and even fewer "marks" of civilization, yet it had already been described many times in explorers' accounts and emigrant guidebooks. Therefore, most diarists and writers of reminiscences turned to familiar models to help them describe the unfamiliar. Like Fanny Kelly, they marked their own trail with bits of phrases and descriptions that had already been written by other people. Often even these seemed inadequate, and many diarists and autobiographers expressed frustration with their inability to describe adequately their experiences and observations. Still these "strangers in a strange land" (as many called themselves) persevered with their writing. The sheer numbers of these firsthand accounts and the articulateness of many of them make it possible for latecomers to follow a paper trail West. Because many emigrants also wrote explicitly about their efforts to make their experiences understandable, it is also possible to glimpse the writing practices and language choices of the people who kept these accounts.

* * *

In the early 1840s, the first parties of American emigrants took their wagons along trails explored by trappers and fur companies, intending to settle permanently in the West. In 1840, Joel Walker's family and several missionary couples, under American Fur Company auspices, followed the Snake River to Oregon. The next year, the Bidwell-Bartleson party, guided by mountain man Thomas Fitzpatrick, followed the Platte River across the Great Plains, then the Sweetwater to South Pass, then on to Soda Springs, where some wagons continued on to Oregon, and the rest turned toward the Humboldt River, the Sierra Nevada, and California. Like the traders, army officers, and missionaries who had preceded them, and like hundreds of settlers who followed a few years later, Walker and Bidwell left written records. Although Walker's recollections are brief, Bidwell's diary is detailed and absorbing, designed to be read by emigrants who would follow him to California. Overland travel increased quickly: Oregon migration peaked in the mid-forties, and the first Mormon emigrants reached the Great Salt Lake in 1847. Diaries became more numerous. Travelers now could use books by Bidwell, John C. Frémont, Joel Palmer, Edwin Bryant, Lansford Hastings and others as guides to routes through the plains, mountains, and deserts. They also used these books, along with newspaper articles and the Bible, as models for writing.

The pace of westward migration and journal keeping changed drastically when hundreds of thousands of forty-niners thundered across the plains and mountains, more than doubling the emigration figures of all previous years. These travelers were not typical of their predecessors or successors. Most were men traveling without families; many were urban folk; some were very well educated. Comparatively few planned to settle permanently in the West: they intended to "make their pile," "see the elephant," and go home. Forty-niners believed they were involved in a remarkable historical event. Many also viewed the trip as a holiday adventure, and their diaries served as their vacation snapshots. At least one of every ten overland travelers in 1849 left a written record.

After 1849, the ratio of diary keepers to travelers declined although four times as many overlanders rolled westward during the 1850s as during the 1840s. In some ways overland travel during the fifties and sixties was more dangerous than in the earlier years. Certainly the journeys were worth recording, yet general interest in writing and reading about them faded. Perhaps it was difficult to think of something new to say. Still it was fairly common for emigrants to keep records for themselves and their families. Many came from the upper Midwest and out of a family tradition of moving on west to new land. With each move, friends and family members were left behind, so writing represented a way to maintain connections that would otherwise have been severed. Mormon emigrants, including those in the handcart companies of the late fifties, also continued to write a great many diaries.

Overland emigrants followed the heavily used California and Oregon Trails (which carried an estimated ninety percent of overland travelers), the Mormon Trail north of the Platte River, and later the Pikes Peak Trail to the Colorado gold rush, and the Bozeman Trail to the mines of Montana and Idaho. The Santa Fe Trail was primarily a commercial route throughout its sixty-year existence, and comparatively few traders were moved to keep diaries of their routine journeys; but some gold-seekers and settlers used this and other southwestern trails to reach California, and they left records of their trip. People who traveled west by sea also kept diaries; and if they had fewer adventures to record, they also had the leisure to write lengthy letters home. Once at their destination, many emigrants ceased writing while others, who had not thought or cared to keep diaries of their journey, became persistent letter writers. Years later, urged on by advancing age, curious children, and enthusiastic pioneer societies, many recorded their reminiscences.

By the time the railroad spanned the continent, between 350,000 and 500,000 Americans had made the overland emigration; hundreds of thousands more traveled by sea, some more than once. Bibliographer Merrill J. Mattes estimates that the years up to 1866 produced more than 2,000 central overland narratives: one recordkeeper for every 250 travelers. It is remarkable that so many people of all ages chose to leave written records. Whatever their individual motives for writing, most of the diarists and autobiographers seemed to have a sense of history and a conviction that others would be interested in what they had to say.

They were right. In the past century and a half, their firsthand accounts have been used and perused by many individuals and groups for a wide variety of purposes. Family and friends provided the original audiences for many of the diaries. Family members also instigated and facilitated the writing of reminiscences. Often a son, daughter, or other close relative took notes as an aging emigrant dictated his or her story. Personal interest and family pride motivated these early readers; typically, trail records and letters were treasured within a family for several generations, included in family histories, and given to libraries. Peering through the trail accounts of relatives, descendants teased out family traditions and traits, as this typescript introduction to a goldseeker's diary suggests: "Tradition has it that Grandfather Hunt came back poorer than he went. But he 'saw the Elephant'. And his descendants can point to him as a worthy exponent of that well-known Hunt determination to 'go places and see things'" (Hunt 1).

Pioneer societies, which sprang up shortly after the first wave of emigrants arrived at their western destinations, played a large role in preserving journals, collecting stories from old-timers, and celebrating heritage. Generally they preserved and encouraged firsthand accounts as pieces of heroic epic and as tools to "teach our children to glorify the heroes of the past" (Eastham 9). Exclusive and occasionally pretentious, pioneer societies saw trail accounts as precious and unique. As an Oregon Pioneer Association official asked rhetorically, "Where else in the history of man, civilized or not, do you read the story of a 2,500-mile march through hostile country, over unexplored desert and mountain?" (Eastham 9). At the same time, society members recognized that exaggeration and truth-bending might occur in their epic stories. One of them joked, "Every genuine old pioneer is in honor bound to have had the hardest time on the plains of any other person living or dead" (Unruh 2).

Historians and history buffs, particularly in the first half of the twentieth century, generally shared in the celebratory mood, even as they used the firsthand accounts primarily as sources of information about trails, travelers, and events. Early historians of the West like Hubert Howe Bancroft encouraged emigrants to record their reminiscences as part of a larger historical project, the amassing of information about events and travelers. Dale L. Morgan has noted that the journals are important for the historian in several ways: as records of the journey; as records of journeys in particular years; as expressions of the values of the emigrants and their communities; and as accounts of interaction with the natural environment. Early histories have in common the technique of "quoting at length from various diarists" (Unruh 16), and scholars like Morgan and Kenneth Holmes have edited extensive collections of firsthand accounts. Analytical, critical and interpretive histories also draw heavily on the diaries and reminiscences. Some prominent examples include George Stewart's *The California Trail* and John Unruh's *The Plains Across*. J. S. Holliday's *The World Rushed In* is constructed around the Gold Rush diary of William Swain, while JoAnn Levy's more recent *They Saw the Elephant* focuses on women forty-niners. Sesquicentennials of important trail years have spurred the writing of new histories that draw heavily on trail diaries, including Lloyd W. Coffman's account of the Oregon migration of 1843 and Thomas A. Rumer's study of the 1844 wagon trains.

One self-proclaimed "maverick historian," Merrill J. Mattes, writes that his "fifty-year romance" with the Oregon-California Trail began when he saw its landmarks and wagon ruts. Overland diaries have been important sources for the individuals and trail societies who retrace, mark, and maintain parts of the overland trails. Diaries provide information about route, descriptions of natural features, and historical background that enriches the modern journey along the trail. Irene Paden's *Wake of the Prairie Schooner* has been a model of the travelogue-history that makes generous use of emigrant accounts of the Oregon-California Trail.

Novelists, too, have dipped into the diaries and reminiscences for material. James Michener reports that he consulted three dozen diaries as he wrote *Centennial* and adds that diary entries are interesting for their own sake, with much that is "new or sardonic or instructive." Michener notes one diarist, John Edwin Banks, whose brief account "contains material for several novels": large wagon companies fall apart;

a murderer is condemned to hang; a boy is run over by a wagon; a man is shot by his wife and her lover (Mattes x). Louis L'Amour, A. B. Guthrie, and Emerson Hough have written novels based on firsthand accounts, and, more recently, Molly Gloss has incorporated fictionalized diaries into The Jump-off Creek. In her acknowledgments Gloss writes, "I am greatly indebted to many published and unpublished diaries, letters and journals of women who settled the West. I hope their strong, honest voices can be heard in this book."

Social and cultural critics like John Mack Faragher and Lillian Schlissel look to the firsthand accounts for evidence about family patterns, work, gender roles, attitudes about class and race, and social practices. For them, the gender and social backgrounds of diarists are as important as what the diarists encountered on the journey. Women's accounts, generally less interesting to pioneer societies and other boosters because of their lack of epic content, have provided useful insights into issues on which most men were silent: the upheaval caused by leaving home; the everyday duties of emigrant women and men; the special problems of child care on the trail; the new pressures placed on family life in the West. According to Schlissel, diaries show that emigration "dis-assembled" families. The "extended" family was overextended in space, and frontier settlers were only "fragments of families" who "yearned to connect with those who had been left behind" (Schissel, 1989, xv). Such a reading of the emigrants' records sees them not as heroic histories of a single migration and a simple life on the frontier — but rather as accounts of lives marked by abrupt transitions.

* * *

Now that the westward movement has been meticulously documented and repeatedly described, thanks largely to the material provided in firsthand accounts, it is also possible to focus not only on what the writers said, but on how they said it and why. How did the emigrants use writing, and what did they think it was supposed to accomplish? What were they aiming to communicate, and what kinds of questions were they confronting and ignoring in their writing? What challenges did the difficult, unfamiliar environment and their own uncertainty present to them as writers? Rhetorical critics like Stephen Fender investigate the language the emigrants used to describe what they were seeing and doing — scientific language, romantic description, religious rhetoric, and the clichés of boosterism. Such readings focus on the discourses that shaped emigrants' attitudes and writing practices. How did emigrant writers deal with 1) the aims and circumstances of their writing; 2) loneliness, fear, and disaster; 3) description of sublime or bizarre surroundings; 4) radical changes in themselves and their circumstances?

To a certain extent, diaries, letters, and reminiscences differ in form, audience, purpose, and perspective. But they also overlap considerably. Most overlanders did not distinguish between "diary" and "journal," but they believed that these forms obligated them to try to write every day. Diaries occasionally doubled as extended letters to loved ones or first drafts of books. Some diaries were used as notes for letters or reminiscences and then destroyed. Often, letters were also the first reminiscences, summarizing highlights of the journey soon after the writers had arrived at their destinations. Like diaries, letters provided fairly immediate accounts of new living environments and changed social codes. Writers of reminiscences, which generally appeared in the late nineteenth and early twentieth centuries, had the advantage of time and perspective. They could shape entertaining tales. They could look back with some humor or amazement at their earlier selves — as Catherine Haun does in a passage that recalls the elaborate clothes she packed for the trip West: "With this marvelous costume I had hoped to 'astonish the natives' when I should make my first appearance upon the golden streets of the mining town in which we might locate" (Schlissel, 1992, 168). Yet writers of reminiscences, particularly those who rely solely on memory, often become confused about everyday details or neglect them altogether.

Many diaries are logs, with brief notations of date, miles traveled, rivers forded, landmarks, weather conditions, availability of grass and water, condition of stock, illnesses and accidents, prices of supplies, and unusual events. Although the average log-keeper had no official function in the wagon company, his diary provided a personal record of progress, notes for later reminiscences, and a way to apply structure to bewildering experiences. Many diarists kept track of the graves seen along the trail each day and some even copied the words from each marker. Patty Sessions, midwife and 1847 Mormon emigrant, kept a list of all the babies she delivered on the trail. Keturah Belknap listed every item her family packed. Patrick Breen, stranded in the Sierra with the Donner Party in 1846, began a terse daily record of snowfall, dwindling supplies, illnesses, and deaths, interspersed with brief supplications to

God. Keeping track on the trail became a crucial activity for each log-keeper.

Writers of more elaborate diaries generally discussed their purposes for writing and the difficult conditions they faced as writers. Elizabeth Dixon Smith, bound for Oregon in 1847 with her husband and eight children, introduces her diary, recopied as a letter to her women friends in Indiana: "Dear Friends by your request I have endevered to keep a record of our journey from the States to Oregon though it is poorly done owing to me having a young babe and besides a large family to doo for and worst of all my e[d]ucation is very limited" (Holmes, I, 116). At intervals throughout the trip she interweaves the themes of the journey's hardship and her difficulty with writing. In July she expresses frustration: "I could have writen a great deal more if I had had the opertunity some times I would not get the chance to write for 2 or 3 dayes and then would have to rise in the night when my babe and all hands was a sleep light a candle and write" (126-127). In November, with her husband ill after several disastrous river fordings, she sounds desperate: "I have not told half we suffered. I am inadiquate to the task" (143). California-bound Cephas Arms was more confident of his writing ability but just as eager that the folks back home should know how difficult it was for him to keep writing. He concludes his diary with this note: "You will find many errors. I have written as usual on my knees, up in my wagon, and by candle light.... More than that ox-teams are not very literary" (Arms 119). What Smith says about her abilities as a diarist might be emblematic for the way emigrants viewed their entire journey in retrospect: unequal to a task, they did it anyway. Arms adds another facet. Instead of criticizing emigrants' writing, readers should be impressed that it was done at all.

John H. Benson (1849) and William Kilgore (1850) both left their immediate families behind when they made their journeys to California. They envisioned their diaries as extended letters home. Kilgore wrote so that his family would know about his experiences; Benson promised his wife to write something every day. The Benson family had already relocated twice, carrying their household goods by wagon, so she was "familiar with camp life, and qualified to read between the lines of such a record" (2). In his entries, Benson strives to be an engaging storyteller, and he seems to be on the lookout for anecdotes about women. In the migration of 1849, famous for its maleness, he finds stories to tell his wife of physically courageous women: one hunts buffalo with a pistol on horseback ("some who had not seen her start thought her horse was run-ning away with her"); another breaks up a fight between two male strangers. Kilgore's account is more everyday. His diary lists all his sup-plies and faithfully records the miles traveled each day; his other recur-ring concerns include the weather, route and road conditions, game, wood, prices of supplies, illness, and kinds of people encountered along the way. His diary must have been helpful a few years later when Kilgore brought his whole family West. Kilgore writes that he sometimes used his saddle as a desk, that he once wrote in a cave, and that he occa-sionally found a moment to write while waiting to ford a dangerous river. These difficulties were noted and appreciated by the families. In his preface to the typescript of his father's diary, Benson's son expresses his amazement at his father's ability to keep his commitment: "My interest (which may be largely filial) is not more in the record itself, than it is in the fact that (amid all the vicissitudes of the road) he kept it for the 142 days of the journey, without a single skip" (3).

Henry Austin's service to his wagon company as a physician in 1849 excused him from other duties so that he had time to "journalize." He saw himself as something of a tourist and travel writer. In his diary, Austin seems to enjoy portraying *himself* within his unusual surround-ings. May 27: "writing this in the sick waggin." June 7: "While the repairs [of an axel brace] were going on I set down upon a stump in the middle of the road and rote my journal." On July 26, Austin climbed to the top of Independence Rock and sat there writing his journal. On August 18, he tried a word painting of a sublime landscape, not neglect-ing to describe himself describing it:

> We have just passed over a considerable mountain the view of the surrounding country from which is of the grandest character moun-tain after mountain in rapid succession peak after peak towering almost into the clouds to the west of where I am now sitting is a lofty range of gloomy looking mountains shrouded in mist. The wagons are ahead plowing up the dust and winding their way up hills and through vallies in the moust circuitous manner. I am sit-ting on a stone by the road side writing my journal a gentle breeze is blowing the sun shining brilliantly lofty mountains surround me on every side. (63)

Many nineteenth-century trail diarists continued in the tradition of the Puritan journal-keepers, viewing their diaries as tools of self-examination and self-improvement. Mollie Dorsey Sanford, who emigrated first to Nebraska and then, in 1857, to Pikes Peak during the Colorado gold rush, suggests that self-improvement is a good motive for diary keeping:

> I have thought for years that I would keep a Journal. I know it is a source of improvement and pleasure, and have only postponed it, because I have thought my life too monotonous to prove interesting. In going to a new country, where new scenes and new associations will come into my life, there *may* be *some* experiences worth recording. At least the employment will divert my mind in many a lonely hour. (1)

Sanford also hints at another reason for diary keeping — loneliness. Her journal is to be "a confidant or bosom friend, now that I am to leave so many near and dear" (1). Her diary was not a letter; it was written for herself. But it was a substitute for conversations with friends. (Much later, Sanford edited her diary.)

One traveler who had publication in mind from the outset was John Bidwell. Shortly after arriving in California, he sent a diary manuscript to a publisher in Missouri who was "aware that a great many persons ... [were] anxious to get *correct information*, relative to Oregon and California" (ix) and hurried to market an edition in 1842. In his account, Bidwell provides information about route, equipment, vegetation, streams, game, and good camping places, but his journal is also rich with descriptions and anecdotes that would have interested even the stay-at-homes. He tells of passing "rusty mountaineers" who "looked as though they never had seen, razor, water, soap, or brush" (4). He describes herds of buffalo on the banks of the Platte, "completely clouded by these huge animals, grazing in the valley and on the hills — ruminating upon the margin of the river, or crowding down its banks for water" (6). He expresses concern about the buffalo's extinction after seeing "the immense quantity of Buffalo bones, which are every where strewed with great profusion," and he empathizes with the Indians "who behold with indignation the shameful and outrageous prodigality of the whites, who slaughter thousands" (5-6). He explains that his party cooked fresh meat in a hot spring: "perfectly done in 10 minutes — this is no fish story!" (21). He complains about the company's leadership, tells about being betrayed by a guide, bitterly criticizes the California missions, and extols the healthful climate of the West. He tells about climbing a mountain for fun while waiting for the party to get ready to move. He narrates his ordeal in the Sierra, where he "could see no prospect of a termination to the mts. mts. mountains!" and became so hungry that he ate half-raw mule meat. In short, Bidwell writes well enough to guarantee the sale of his book and provide a model for future diaries.

David Carnes also thought of himself as a guidebook writer, but, traveling in 1849, he was already too late. Carnes' journal, labeled as "Intended for Revision and Correction," was written originally in pencil. Writing in pen *over* the penciled version, Carnes made spelling corrections and minor revisions. Apparently he had read a number of guidebooks before he made his own entries, for on several dates he noted important features of the trail that had been neglected by his predecessors. In his June 3 entry, for example, Carnes describes a little ravine with trees and a fine spring "not noted by any of the guides." On August 15 he writes, "I have not seen any discription of these springs & must have been passed by unnoticed by all former travelers." By Carnes' time, most routes west had been fairly well established with most of the stops and landmarks along the way. Like many modern scholars, Carnes had to stretch to find territory neglected by his predecessors. Despite the care he lavished upon it, his diary never became a book.

A recurring problem for most emigrant writers was how to deal—in writing—with fear, loneliness, danger, and other low points of the journey. Despite the general opinion that it was best not to mention such things, a surprising number of diaries and reminiscences detail some struggle with fear and loss. Expressions of such emotions were somewhat justified if they were part of a larger story—the pilgrim's testimonial of perseverance, faithfulness, and Providence. Thus, most emigrants who describe their homesickness, their fear of Indians and disease, or their dread of being lost in the wilderness, go on to explain how they overcame or controlled these feelings, or how God provided a solution. Their stories serve as a latter-day pilgrims' progress, an encouragement to others, and a way for emigrant writers to come to terms with their fears.

Although they were not the only emigrants to feel homesick, women generally were readier to reveal such feelings in their reminiscences. Catherine Haun tells of waking up homesick near the frontier and bursting into tears at the beauty of the farm country in the morning sunlight.

Just then, she recalls, she saw a flock of wild geese that "seemed to encourage me to 'take to the woods'":

> Thus construing their senseless clatter I paused in my grief to recall the intense cold of the previous winter and the reputed perpetual sunshine and wealth of the promised land. Then wiping away my tears, lest they betray me to my husband, I prepared to continue my trip. I have often thought that had I confided in him he would cer-tainly have turned back, for he, as well as the other men of the party, was disheartened and was struggling not to betray it. (Schlissel, 1992, 169)

After wryly noting that she had heard the message she wanted to hear, Haun offers several remedies for homesickness and asserts that her feel-ings are neither unique nor limited to women.

Upon finding herself for the first time without shelter on the treeless prairie, forty-niner Sarah Royce felt acute distress, which she describes vividly in her memoir:

> It was a chilling prospect, and there was a terrible shrinking from it in my heart; but I kept it all to myself and we were soon busy making things as comfortable as we could for the night.... At first the oppressive sense of homelessness, and an instinct of watchful-ness, kept me awake.... However, quiet sleep came at last, and in the morning, there was a mildly exultant feeling which comes from having kept silent through a cowardly fit, and finding the fit gone off. (4-5)

Like Haun, Royce can look back over the years to describe feelings that she kept hidden at the time; also like Haun, she emphasizes that she took immediate steps to combat these feelings with useful activity and a good night's sleep.

Typical of many diarists, John Benson hints at his homesickness by describing others and by saying "we" whenever he discusses loneliness. Early in his journey of 1849, he notes the many travelers he passes on their way home — particularly the ones who admit they are homesick. Later he mentions "thoughts of home (on which we do not dare to dwell too much for fear of that dread distemper homesickness)" (49). During that same summer, Adonijah Welch, a former lawyer and school principal, wrote a letter to his hometown newspaper describing homesickness as an "attachment to localities" that could spring up overnight:

> We started early. As I looked back from the head of our long line, to the spot which had just been the scene of bustle and activity, but now so silent and lonely, I could but indulge in feelings of sadness. We naturally love the place we have once called home; but attach-ment to localities, as in the case of the "*voyageur*," must soon be sundered.
>
> Saturday evening our white-topped wagons rolled in, and formed the corral on that beautiful spot. Then the hum of busy life commenced. The ringing of the axe — the crack of the rifle — the hissing of the frying-pan, and the loud call of the sergeant of the guard mingled together. Then we ate with a relish, our rude fare — we laughed and joked merrily, and talked of past scenes, pleasant to the memory, and future prospects high with hope. A few hours of sound and refreshing sleep, and the horn sounded, the cattle were yoked, the tents struck, the word was given to "roll on," and we left our brief home forever. (21-22)

Whether he is sublimating homesickness or writing instant nostalgia, Welch in this letter shares with outsiders his affection for the "beautiful spot" and teaches that overland travel requires not one departure but many. While Haun and Royce write about hiding their homesickness, Benson and Welch gain comfort from a shared sense of sadness.

Vigorous activity and a positive attitude, however, were not sufficient remedies for other trials of the overland journey: deadly illness, acci-dent, Indian attack, and starvation. Cholera, which plagued travelers of 1849 and 1850, was terrifying because it struck suddenly and killed quickly. After burials of several company members early in his journey, John Benson writes, "They had all died of cholera in less than twenty hours from the time they were taken. One who has not felt it, cannot know what it means to meet face to face with sickness & death under such conditions" (11). Diaries indicate that some travelers took unusual steps to distance themselves from the peril of cholera: one group threw out all its beans; one family added hot pepper sauce to their drinking water. A diarist from Ohio assured himself that the disease attacked mainly Missourians, who had "peculiar habits" (Taylor 137). But most travelers understood that they, too, might feel a stomach cramp one morning and be dead by nightfall. This knowledge aroused empathy as well as dread. In 1853, Amelia Stewart Knight wrote about a trailside funeral: "With sadness and pity I passed those who perhaps a few days before had been well and happy as ourselves" (Schlissel, 1992, 204). Knight's passage echoes a familiar religious warning: health and good fortune are fragile and impermanent, not to be depended on.

Death appeared in a variety of forms and was duly recorded by the diarists: drownings, poisonings, gunshots, other accidents with wagons and animals. Most stories of these tragedies were told by onlookers — or at even greater distance, by the recorders of grave markers. William Kilgore was fascinated by the bruiseless body of a drowned man and the desperate grief of another drowned man's wife: "She Beged them for Gods Sake to let her go and Drown with him" (48). An anonymous diarist narrated a shooting accident with typical terseness. Two hunting parties had gone out separately, and "one of the men that was ahead said we would scare the other Boys and have some fun so down we went on all fours Bang went a rifle down went one of our men they suposeing us to be Wolves he died in about twenty minutes so much for fun on the Plains" (*Diary of an Unknown Scout* 4).

Henry Austin, one of the diarists who kept track of every grave he saw, found a note on a fresh grave informing him that the dead man had eaten a poisonous root. Austin reports, "In a broken tin cup on the grave was a paper on which was written the following: He was in such pain that he tore this cup down with his teeth" (92). Such messages, carefully recorded even by men who had chosen to travel alone, indicate emigrants' concerns about human connections. If leaving a family behind was sad, the thought of losing a family member, particularly a provider, in an alien land was horrifying, "truly appalling" (Taylor 133). Worse yet would be to disappear without a word. Emigrants were compulsive message-leavers: one traveler wrote that along the trail "every bone or horn ... is endorsed with numerous individuals' and companies' names.... Papers are stuck up on sticks, recording unfortunate circumstances, encounters with Indians, and cautionary advice" (Buffum, in Holliday 132). If nothing could provide sure protection against disaster in the wilderness, perhaps it was still possible to be saved from obliteration through writing. Diarists who recorded signs and grave markers increased this possibility.

As frightening as illness or accident, and certainly more fascinating, were the Indians. In the early years of emigration, fears of Indian depredations proved largely unfounded, even as more travelers became aware of the magnitude of the differences between peoples. Emigrants wrote humorously but nervously about these discoveries. Mary Jones recalls one night in 1846 on the Platte when "the guard fired off his gun and hollered 'Indians' and every man was up and to his gun. It was a false alarm. It was only a dog that stuck his head above the bank" (3). Henry Austin was present when guards mistook a blanket over a saddle for an Indian and fired at it. Josiah Gregg, regular traveler on the Santa Fe Trail, describes a "camp of false alarms," where some false reports of Indian attacks, combined with the untimely howl of a hungry wolf, emptied a camp. John Bidwell describes the agitation of "the green ones" in his party as they were visited by forty Cheyenne: "When I asked [a young emigrant] how many indians there were? he answered with a trembling voice, half scared out of his wits, there lots, gaubs, fields and swarms of them!!!" (4-5). David Carnes, passing a deserted Pawnee village, dryly notes: "The government has caused them to evacuate this town. . . . The inhabitance have been removed to insure protection to the hardy pioneer" (21). John Benson comments with exasperation on the rumors and unnecessary fears that followed him all the way to California: "I have traveled about 4 and a half months & probably over 2000 miles, most of the way in what was supposed to be a hostile Indian country. Rumors [of] depredation were afloat much of the time, but I have not seen a single hostile Indian. All I have met were extremely friendly" (67-68).

As Indians accumulated reasons to be hostile to whites, later travelers had better reasons to fear violence. On her way to California in 1862, Jane Gould Tourtillot not only heard rumors of Indian attack but saw the dead and wounded from a wagon train six miles ahead that had been plundered by Indians. "It is not an enviable situation to be placed in," she says in her diary, "not to know at night when you go to bed, whether you will all be alive in the morning or not" (Schlissel, 1992, 226). On the Gila Trail in 1851, Olive Oatman was taken prisoner when most of her family was killed by Apaches. Her account of the years that followed suggests a trancelike state but also describes a discipline and resignation that echoes Sarah Royce's remedy for homesickness: "At times the past with all its checkered scenes would roll up before me," she reports, "but all of it that was the most deeply engraven upon my mind, was that which I would be the soonest to forget if I could. Time seemed to take a more rapid flight; I hardly could wake up to the reality of so long a captivity" (168).

Another observer who described the westward movement in her reminiscences was Sarah Winnemucca of the Northern Paiutes. Like the whites, the Paiutes suffered from foolish early fears and later well-founded desperation. Sarah Winnemucca recalls the day that mothers buried their children to hide them from the emigrants because they had heard rumors of white cannibalism in the Sierra: "Our mothers told us that the whites were killing everybody and eating them. So we were all afraid of them. Every dust that we could see blowing in the valleys we would say it was the white people" (11). Although the rumors of cannibalism proved exaggerated, Sarah Winnemucca and her family learned over the next few years what they did need to fear, and her account covers them all: destruction of winter supplies; rape of unprotected women; unjust imprisonment; murder; child stealing; and theft of land and property.

If it was difficult to express fear and loss in acceptable ways, it was even harder for emigrants to describe the unfamiliar lands through which they were passing. While the average traveler could choose to remain silent about suffering, most felt compelled to comment on the natural environment. Many gave up after a brief struggle. The landscape was bizarre and tedious, sublime and uncomfortable, endless and changing, monumental and insubstantial. Diaries and reminiscences abound with comments about the inexpressibility of the landscape, as the writer's own sense of inadequacy blends with common nineteenth-century motifs: the inability of humans to describe inexpressible handiwork of God; and the man of action's inability to write poetically. Calvin Taylor's diary emphasizes his awareness of a literary tradition of indescribability and religious awe: "It has in truth been said, no language can describe the beauty of these western prairies and no painter can sketch them, so vast, so boundless, a fit emblem of the mighty ocean" (127-128). Approaching the Platte a few weeks later, he writes, "The mind becomes confused and bewildered, lost as it were, in immensity. It is in situations like this that man knows and feels his own insignificance and dependence, that in comparison man, with all his boasted skill and knowledge is but a mere worm, grovelling in the dust of God's footstool" (134). Unable or unwilling to capture the scene in his own words, he turns to language that has already been certified. Many diarists and letter-writers deferred to "abler pens" when they found themselves in difficulty over the sublime. Many hoped that someday an artist would come to paint the scene. Some turned to scientific language and tried to estimate heights, depths, and distances. Some echoed sermons or romantic literature. James Bennett, a former printer, hit upon the expedient of copying passages from his guidebook into his diary. Upon arriving at Solitary Tower and Chimney Rock, he quoted extensively from Joel Palmer's *Journal of Travels over the Rocky Mountains*, not neglecting to give credit to "Mr. Palmer" (36-37).

Some emigrants take up the "indescribability" motif but with a difference: some things are impossible to communicate because of shortcomings in the intended audience. Non-emigrant readers cannot possibly understand such strange surroundings and experiences. Amelia Stewart Knight declares, "It would be useless for me with my pencil to describe the awful road we have just passed over. let fancy picture a train of wagons and cattle passing through a crooked chimney and we have Big Laurel Hill" (Schlissel, 1992, 215). Elizabeth Dixon Smith writes to her friends, "You in the states know nothing about dust it will fly so that you can hardly see the horns of your tongue yoke it often seems that the cattle must die for the want of breath and then in our waggons such a specticle beds cloths vituals and children all completely covered" (Holmes, I, 131).

If everyday annoyances would be impossible for the uninitiated to understand, then they could not begin to comprehend the more profound experiences. Sarah Royce almost died on the desert. Then she saw a burning bush and knew that God would take care of her. In her reminiscences, she resigns herself to reader skepticism and lack of understanding: "Only a woman who has been alone upon a desert with her helpless child can have any adequate idea of my experience," she declares (45). Forty years after spending the winter of 1844 stranded alone in the Sierra, Moses Schallenberger recounts the day when his two stronger companions decided to try to reach the lowlands: "The feeling of loneliness that came over me as the two men turned away I cannot express" (Stewart, 1953, 74). But then he goes on to tell about his solitary months in the snow: "It was difficult for me to decide which I liked best, crow or coyote" (76). These emigrants tell their readers that understanding will be impossible, that any attempt to communicate such things will be futile; then they try to describe them anyway.

For those who press on with their descriptions, a common technique is to compare the unfamiliar with the familiar: a mountain road with a crooked chimney. Perhaps expressing a longing for the illusion of civilization, many emigrants compare rock formations with city silhouettes. The reading backgrounds of some diarists give their comparisons a strange twist: the scenes they use for comparison are familiar to them from books, not from experience. Herman Hunt says of the prairie near the Platte, for example, "It reminds me of pictures I have seen of the Parks of England" (3). John Benson writes, "I have never seen such beautiful scenery as the bluffs present. They have the appearance of an oriental city with mosques and mansions in every shape and size" (20). Henry Austin describes some rocks that are "undoubtedly of volcanic origin presenting every imaginable form and verity of size and reminding one of coral grottos the founts of faries genie and giants" (70).

However, James Clyman, seasoned mountain man and early settler, draws on everyday experience in 1844 for earthy comparisons. To Clyman, Chimney Rock from a distance "looked like an old dry stub not larger in appearance than your finger," but as he approached, it "changed its appearance & Shewed like a large conicle fort with a Tremendeous large & high flag staff & top taken off with out towers & verious fictures of defence" (96). Clyman could also reach beyond the everyday without resorting to clichés. Headed for Oregon, he describes a day in "the most Barren Sterril region we have yet passed nothing to disturb the monotony of the Eternal Sage plain which is covered with broken cynders much resembling Junks of pot mettal & Now & then a cliff of Black burned rock which looks like Distruction brooding over dispair" (115-116).

Elizabeth Smith draws on her readers' own everyday experiences to bring her descriptions home. "Still we have sage to cook with I do not know which best it or buffalo dung jest step out and pull a lot of sage out of your garden and build a fire in the wind and bake boil and fry by it and then you will guess how we have to doo" (Holmes, I, 127). Like many women diarists, Smith turns away from the literary landscape and the epic description in favor of ordinary details:

> all the herbs in this region is prickry and briery the sage dredful on ones clothes it grows from 1 to 6 feet high has a stalk like our tame sage or sedge the leaves are smaller and very narrow it has a sage taste though it is very biter. besides we travle through a shrub called greece wood jenerly not so large as the sage it is very thorny we have to use it sometimes to burn. then there is the prickly pair it is any and every where lookout for bare feet. (Holmes, I, 124)

Why were so many emigrant writers convinced that their audiences would have no idea what they were saying? Perhaps they were thinking of their own naïveté and inexperience before beginning the journey. Particularly in memoirs, they express amusement or amazement at their own ignorance when they started out. Margaret Ann Frink (1850) writes, "We knew nothing of frontier life, nor how to prepare for it" (59-60). Sarah Royce recalls, "We began our journey...guided only by the light of Fremont's *travels*, and the suggestions, often conflicting, of the many who, like ourselves, utter strangers to camping life, were setting out for the 'Golden Gate'" (3). Hermann B. Scharmann (1849) writes more negatively of this ignorance: "This overland journey is one of the most unfortunate undertakings to which a man may allow himself to be lured, because he cannot possibly have any conception before starting, of this kind of traveling" (13). James Clyman is troubled by all the emigrants he meets on the trail as he makes a trip east in 1846. It is strange, he writes in his diary, "that so many of all kinds and classes of People should sell out comfortable homes in Missouri and Elsewhare pack up and start across such an emmence Barren waste to settle in some new Place of which they have at most so uncertain information but this is the character of my countrymen" (260). Clyman decides that the unknown and the unknowable must be precisely what people are after: "all ages and all sects are found to undertake this long tedious and even danger-ous Journy for some unknown object never to be realized even by those the most fortunate and why because the human mind can never be sat-isfied never at rest allways on the strech for something new some strange novelty" (265). While he may have been describing himself more than others, Clyman here suggests a motive for all the comments in hundreds of diaries about indescribable landscapes and inexpressible hardships and the impossibility of communicating the experience to the uniniti-ated. Certainly, writers expressed frustration with their limitations as describers; they echoed motifs of earlier landscape writings; they thought about their former ignorance. But they also certified that they had at least glimpsed the "unknown object," and that they, like Clyman, had seen "something new some strange novelty."

The last difficult task faced by most emigrant diarists was taking stock. How had they changed? Had the trip been worth it? What would they now have to get used to? What surprises or disillusionments had met them at their destination? Writers of reminiscences were most apt to end triumphantly, like Catherine Haun, who says, "Upon the whole I enjoyed the trip, spite of its hardships and dangers and the fear and dread that hung as a pall over every hour.... I like every other pioneer, love to live over again, in memory those romantic months, and revisit, in fancy, the scenes of the journey" (Schlissel, 1992, 185). Diary and letter writers, still in the midst of taking stock, were more ambivalent. They had begun to recognize that both they and their circumstances had changed and that these changes had cost something. Disillusionment pervades this short passage, written by John Benson shortly after he reached the Sacramento "diggins." "Most of the emigrants I talked with seemed to be rather down hearted & uncertain as to their movements. One fellow told me he was lying over to try & figure out why he came. I told him I felt like joining him, but didn't feel like lying over for so long a time" (70). Benson ends his diary shortly after this entry, without saying whether he overcame his disorientation.

In his diary Richard May seems thrilled with the changes in himself —he is healthier, stronger, and leaner (having lost more than fifty pounds due to abstemious living); he has become an expert oxen driver. He writes like a booster of the simple life of the western "mountaineers," who tell him "there is more real pleasure in one year in the mountains than a whole lifetime in a dense and settled country" (29). Yet his mind is not settled on this point. As he reflects on the entire journey, he is not certain that he has made a good trade by exchanging his life in the Midwest for the opportunities of California: "We periled everything but honor to reach this golden land. Our lives and property has been suspended on the most trivial casualty.... But in this country...to have a social conversation is a great rarity. Politics and religion are lost in the rage of gain" (57). James Hutchings, too, celebrates his sense of achievement but modifies it with a sense of loss. After crossing the Forty Mile Desert, he writes, "I have today walked more than fifty miles, twenty-six yesterday, twenty-five the day before, forty the day previously — making one hundred forty-one miles in four days, and owing to traveling at night, standing guard, and other duties, have slept but five and three-quarters hours in the four days. I get very tough, but am much worn down, and am three years older in looks" (176). Emigrants frequently mentioned that they would be unrecognizable to friends back home. Adonijah Welch, secure in his education and social class, refers to "amusing changes in our personal appearance" (88). But another traveler ends his journal with these emphatic words: "*We all look dirty and sun burnt and realy feel ashamed of our appearances*" (Brown 79).

Emigrants like these were struggling with their new ability to see themselves as others saw them, and not necessarily liking what they saw. For example, men who traveled alone not only had to learn quickly how to do their own cooking, washing, and mending, but also had to adjust to the *idea* of themselves doing this "women's work." This struggle appeared in many diaries, and it was often the first in a series of experiences that caused emigrants to see themselves from inside and outside, and to compare what they had been with what they had become. Calvin Taylor writes about performing "operations of a domestic nature such as cooking, washing clothes, etc., in which we cannot boast of any great proficiency...in the performance of which could we be seen many a laugh might be indulged in at our expense" (131). Seeing himself and his companions from "outside" led Taylor to comment on differences in custom: "It is amusing to see men collecting it [buffalo chips] by the arm load & bag full...and to see us preparing our meals with it would doubtless shock the nerves of the delicate & refined votaries of fashion. So much has habit & custom to do with our likes & dislikes" (140). In a similar vein, John Benson comments on the Plains Indians: "They seem to be possessed of the necessities of life, and to be contented and happy, and I could not help wondering what they really thought of us bull whackers, with our assumption of superiority (going somewhere) at the rate of a few miles a day. We would not trade places with them for anything in the world and they would not trade with us" (16). These men, at least, tried to overcome their discomfort with a dose of cultural relativism.

Cultural relativism suited Mary Jane Megquier, self-proclaimed "worshipper at the shrine of liberty" (43), who expresses in letters her delight in the new, free life in San Francisco yet still sees herself through the eyes of the people back home. To her daughter she writes, "I suppose you will have a good laugh to see your Mother tripping the light fantastic toe" (54). Her letter to her mother is more defensive: "I suppose you will think it very strange when I tell you I have not attended church for one year not even heard a prayer but I cannot see but every thing goes on as well as when I was at home" (56). Megquier's letters express her willingness to see herself as others see her and to face the difference between what she was back home and what she is now. Still she does not seem at ease, despite her references to "circumstances." "Among the many that have died in this country not one that I have heard of has expressed the least anxiety about the future which plainly shows to me that it is the circumstances that surround them that causes so much anxiety as to what will become of them after death" (43), and "I dislike very much to hear that this one is not respectable, or that one when perhaps if we would look about us with the eyes of others we should find something equally wrong" (56). Having endured separation and the difficulties of travel (Megquier went by sea and through Panama), she still had to come to terms with "home."

After her experiences on the overland trail, Sarah Royce became a devout Christian. Ironically, she arrived in California just as ethical values were up for grabs. Unlike Megquier, Royce believed that people from the "States" who arrived in the West were not so much freed from constraint as deprived of traditional support. She writes, "It was very common to hear people who had started on [a] downward moral grade, deprecating the very acts they were committing, or the practices they were countenancing; and concluding their weak lament by saying 'But *here* in California we *have* to do such things'" (109-110). Sarah Royce's memoir is an account of her struggle against circumstances.

Less successful than Royce in contending with circumstances in the West was Abigail Malick, Oregon emigrant. The new land rewarded her labor, but the frontier destroyed her family: one son drowned, one son disappeared in the gold fields, one daughter died in childbirth, another daughter became mentally ill, a third daughter ran off to join a theater company, and her youngest son became a gambler and ne'er-do-well. Abigail Malick's letters to her eldest daughter in Illinois express her unhappiness and her desire to sell her property and go east: "I Am Tierd of Being here and Haveing So Mutch Trouble About Every Thing About this Land.... Some Times I Think I Sirtenly Will get Insane" (Schlissel, 1989, 76). But she never left her Oregon farm. Apparently she never resolved her ambivalence. Or perhaps, knowing how much the farm had cost, she could never sell it for what it was worth. Like many emigrants, Abigail Malick widened the gap between expectation and reality by writing about it.

* * *

In 1859, Lovina Walker Weeks left Michigan with her husband and two young daughters to travel to California in a wagon train led by her brother, who had made the trip before. In spite of chronic illness, she kept a brief but regular diary. Seventy years later, her younger daughter, Florence Weeks Blacow, added her own reminiscences to a new typescript of her mother's journal. The resulting counterpoint of diary and reminiscence interweaves Lovina's paper trail with Florence's memories of the trail she experienced "from a little girl's point of view" (6). Lovina's entries mention landmarks, graves, meal preparations, and nights spent holding tent poles in violent storms; Florence's entries dwell on horses, buffalo and a horned toad her uncle showed her. When Lovina describes "beautiful country," Florence responds that she has no memory at all of scenery. Lovina mentions crossing a stream; Florence describes playing in it. Lovina does not describe the family's departure from home, but Florence gives details and adds, "how plainly I remember it" (1). Lovina logs the days when she was ill; Florence recalls her anxiety that her mother would die. Lovina does not mention Indians. Florence tells how a traveler almost set off a battle by shooting a dog, and how her mother made biscuits for the Indians when the trouble was over. Lovina notes that the company has lightened the wagons again. Florence recalls her favorite little wooden chair, sitting alone by the side of the trail.

On the page, as on the journey, Florence follows in her mother's footsteps, partly defining them, partly obliterating them. She builds her own story out of bits and pieces of her mother's diary; she fills in some of her mother's silences; she adjusts her mother's diary to her own experience of the trail, admitting that some of her mother's statements are a mystery to her. The Weeks-Blacow account reminds us that the act of writing a simple log is an entry into a discourse that carries the writer along. As readers, we enter this stream as well by constructing a story of emigration out of the accumulated choices and perceptions of individual writers, who are in turn shaped by circumstance. The gaps between this mother's diaries and daughter's reminiscences suggest the wide open spaces that remain between accounts of the westward movement.

Selected Bibliography

Bibliographies

Heckman, Marlin. *Overland on the California Trail, 1846-1859: A Bibliography of Manuscript and Printed Travel Narratives*. Glendale, California: A. H. Clark, 1984.
Mattes, Merrill J. *Platte River Road Narratives: A Descriptive Bibliography of Travel Over the Great Central Overland Route to Oregon, California, Utah, Colorado, Montana, and Other Western States and Territories, 1812-1866*. Urbana: University of Illinois Press, 1988.
Mintz, Lannon W. *The Trail: A Bibliography of the Travelers on the Overland Trail to*

California, Oregon, Salt Lake City, and Montana During the Years 1841-1864.
Albuquerque: University of New Mexico Press, 1987.

Commentaries and Collections on Overland Travel to the Pacific

Coffman, Lloyd W. *Blazing a Wagon Trail to Oregon: A Weekly Chronicle of the Great Migration of 1843.* Enterprise, Oregon: Echo Books, 1993.

Faragher, John Mack. *Women and Men on the Overland Trail.* New Haven: Yale University Press, 1979.

Fender, Stephen. *Plotting the Golden West: American Literature and the Rhetoric of the California Trail.* New York: Cambridge University Press, 1981.

Hafen, Leroy R. and Ann W. Hafen, eds. *Handcarts to Zion: The Story of a Unique Western Migration 1856-1860.* Glendale, California: A. H. Clark, 1960.

Hill, William. *The Santa Fe Trail: Yesterday and Today.* Caldwell, Idaho: Caxton, 1992.

Holliday, J. S. *The World Rushed In.* New York: Simon & Schuster, 1981.

Holmes, Kenneth. *Covered Wagon Women: Diaries and Letters from the Western Trails, 1840-1890.* 10 vols. Glendale, California: A. H. Clark, 1983.

Levy, JoAnn. *They Saw the Elephant: Women in the California Gold Rush.* Norman: University of Oklahoma Press, 1992.

Morgan, Dale L., ed. *Overland in 1846: Diaries and Letters of the California-Oregon Trail.* 2 vols. Georgetown, California: Talisman Press, 1963.

Paden, Irene D. *The Wake of the Prairie Schooner.* New York: Macmillan, 1943.

Rumer, Thomas A. *The Wagon Trains of '44: A Comparative View of the Individual Caravans in the Emigration of 1844 to Oregon.* Spokane: A. H. Clark, 1990.

Schlissel, Lillian. *Women's Diaries of the Westward Journey.* New York: Schocken, 1992.

Schlissel, Lillian, Byrd Gibbons, and Elizabeth Hampsten. *Far from Home: Families of the Westward Journey.* New York: Schocken, 1989.

Stewart, George. *The California Trail.* New York: McGraw-Hill, 1962.

———. *The Opening of the California Trail.* Berkeley: University of California Press, 1953.

Unruh, John D. *The Plains Across.* Urbana: University of Illinois Press, 1979.

Diaries, Letters, Reminiscences and Other Works Cited

Arms, Cephas. *The Long Road to California: The Journal of Cephas Arms, Supplemented by Letters by Traveling Companions on the Overland Trail in 1849.* Mt. Pleasant, Michigan: John Cumming, 1985.

Austin, Henry. "1849 Diary of Henry Austin." Ts. Bancroft Library, Berkeley, California.

Belknap, Keturah. "Memorandum." Rpt. in Kenneth L. Holmes, ed. *Covered Wagon Women: Diaries & Letters from the Western Trails, 1840-1890.* Vol. I. Glendale, California: A.H. Clark, 1983. Pp.194-231.

Bennett, James. *Overland Journey to California: Journal of James Bennett Whose Party Left New Harmony in 1850 and Crossed the Plains and Mountains until the Golden West Was Reached.* Fairfield, Washington: Galleon Press, 1987.

Benson, John H. "Forty Niner John H. Benson: From St. Joseph to Sacramento." E. A. Benson, ed. Ts. MS 0713. Nebraska State Historical Society, Lincoln.

Bidwell, John. *A Journey to California with Observations about the Country, Climate and the Route to This Country: A Day-by-Day Record of the Journey from May 18, 1841, to November 6, 1841.* San Francisco: John Henry Nash, 1937.

Brown, William Richard. *An Authentic Wagon Train Journal of 1853 from Indiana to*

California. Barbara Wills, ed. Mokelumne Hill, California: Horseshoe Printing, 1985.

Carnes, David. "Journal of a Trip across the Plains in the Year 1849. (Intended for Revision and Correction)." Ms. Bancroft Library, Berkeley, California.

Chiles, Col. J. B. "A Visit to California in Early Times by Col. J. B. Chiles." 1878. Copy of ms., Bancroft Library, Berkeley, California.

Clyman, James. *Journal of a Mountain Man*. Linda M. Hasselstrom, ed. Missoula: Mountain Press, 1984.

"Diary of an Unknown Scout." ("McGuirk Diary"). 1854. Ts. NC 306. Special Collections. University of Nevada, Reno. (Ms. Bancroft Library, Berkeley, California.)

Eastham, E. L. "The Occasional Address." *Transactions of the Thirteenth Annual Re-Union of the Oregon Pioneer Association for 1882*. Salem, 1886. Pp. 7-11.

Frink, Margaret A. *Journal of the Adventures of a Party of California Gold-Seekers*. Rpt. in Holmes, *Covered Wagon Women*, Vol. II.

Gloss, Molly. *The Jump-Off Creek*. Boston: Houghton Mifflin, 1989.

Hopkins, Sarah Winnemucca. *Life among the Piutes: Their Wrongs and Claims*. New York: G. P. Putnam, 1883. Facsimilie rpt. Reno: University of Nevada Press, 1994.

Hunt, Herman. "Diary of Herman Hunt from April 2, 1850, to March 25, 1851." Ts 82-49. Special Collections. University of Nevada, Reno.

Hutchings, James Mason. *Seeking the Elephant, 1849: James Mason Hutchings' Journal of his Overland Trek to California, Including his Voyage to America, 1848, and Letters from the Mother Lode*. Shirley Sargent, ed. Glendale, California: A. H. Clark, 1980.

Jones, Mary A. (Smith). "Recollections of Mary A. Jones, Alamo, Contra Costa Co., Calif. (Compiled When She Was Past Her Eightieth Year. Courtesy of Mrs. J. C. James, Alamo.)" Ts. Bancroft Library, Berkeley, California.

Kelly, Fanny. *Ho for Idaho!* Rpt. in *Captured by the Indians: 15 Firsthand Accounts, 1750-1870*. Frederick Drimmer, ed. New York: Dover, 1961. Pp. 330-369.

Kilgore, William H. *The Kilgore Journal of an Overland Journey to California in the Year 1850*. Joyce Rockwood Muench, ed. New York: Hastings House, 1949.

Lindsey, Tipton. "The Plains and Deserts of North America: A Journal of a Trip to California (Overland) 1849." Ts. California State Library, Sacramento. Quoted in Heckman, *Overland on the California Trail, 1846-1859*.

May, Richard M. *A Sketch of a Migrating Family to California in 1848*. Fairfield, Washington: Galleon Press, 1991.

Megquier, Mary Jane. *Apron Full of Gold: The Letters of Mary Jane Megquier from San Francisco 1849-1856*. 2nd ed. Polly Welts Kaufman, ed. Albuquerque: University of New Mexico Press, 1994.

Oatman, Lorenzo D. and Olive A. Oatman. *The Captivity of the Oatman Girls among the Apache and Mohave Indians*. San Francisco: Grabhorn Press, 1935; rpt., New York: Dover, 1994.

Palmer, Joel. *Journal of Travels over the Rocky Mountains*. Cincinnati: J. A. & U. P. James, 1847. Facsimilie rpt. Ann Arbor: University Microfilms, 1966.

Royce, Sarah. *A Frontier Lady: Recollections of the Gold Rush and Early California*. New Haven: Yale University Press, 1932.

Sanford, Mollie Dorsey. *Mollie: The Journal of Mollie Dorsey Sanford in Nebraska and Colorado Territories 1857-1866*. Lincoln: University of Nebraska Press, 1959.

Scharmann, Hermann B. *Scharmann's Journey to California, from the Pages of a Pioneer's Diary*. Margaret Hoff Zimmerman and Eric W. Zimmerman, trans.; rpt., New York: Books for Libraries, 1959.

Sessions, Patty. "The Diary of Patty Sessions, 1847." Rpt. in Holmes, *Covered Wagon Women*, Vol. 1. Pp. 165-186.

Smith [Geer], Elizabeth Dixon. "Diary." Rpt. in Holmes, Vol. 1. Pp. 116-148.

Taylor, Calvin. "Overland to the Gold Fields of California in 1850: The Journal of Calvin Taylor of Cincinnati." Burton J. Williams, ed. *Nebraska History* 50 (Summer 1969): 125-149.

Weeks, Lovina Walker. "Diary of Lovina Walker Weeks of Her Trip Across the Plains, with Notes by Her Daughter Florence Weeks Blacow." Ts. 92-45. Special Collections, University of Nevada-Reno.

Welch, Adonijah. Letters dated June 4, 1849 and August 30, 1849. Published in Hillsdale (Michigan) *Whig Standard*. December 11, 1849 and January 29, 1850. Rpt. in Arms, Cephas. *The Long Road to California*. Mt. Pleasant, Michigan: John Cumming, 1985. Pp. 21-22, 88.

Benjamin S. Lawson

Joaquin Miller

The fame and influence of Joaquin Miller, his poetry and prose, appear to remain phenomena of the late nineteenth and early twentieth centuries. But the characteristics of Miller and his work which made for his great contemporary popularity have found a more than temporary new significance in critical schemes which redefine the relevance of those same traits. Miller has not changed, but our assessment of his accomplishment has. A diachronic interest and approach finds him still ensconced as a major figure in the post-Civil War West of the Pacific slope and San Francisco, an actual as well as literary frontiersman. The outline of his career has been several times documented by scholars: his childhood immigration to the West via the Oregon Trail; personal and professional struggles in Oregon and California; his lives as wild westerner and the man who lived among the Modocs; his failure among the literati of the Barbary Coast and his conquest of London; his celebrity as man and writer from 1870 until after 1890. If we cannot quite recapture the tone of a time that could find Miller's verse aesthetically satisfying and truly original, we do find Miller notable as purveyor of a myth of the West, a writer once considered by many a major poet but now appropriated by popular culture, a man much concerned not only about the western land but also its peoples. Our emphasis on place and cultural studies rather than elitist and narrowly defined art has refigured the image of Joaquin Miller.

If hypercritical readers find Miller inadequate and derivative, trite and simplistic, as a "serious" writer, they must still take seriously his impact on the culture of his time. He appeared at just the propitious moment in American history when the Far West was being settled, when literary images of the region of necessity could not be held to the measure of realism. In a period lacking thorough knowledge about the actual West, the region could become to eastern and European eyes just what writers like Miller wanted to make it. And Miller made it a grand and exotic land, a land of adventure and romance. Even his migrations enacted the dynamics of meaningful cultural myths. Not born in the Far West, Miller trekked to a territory which could therefore be to him not only a place but a time, his own and a collective future. The West in anticipation becomes possibility and opportunity, malleable in the imagination because never present, never here or now, always a space of dreams and the sunny golden lands Miller envisioned and later commemorated in verse and prose. During his early days in Oregon and California Miller was only sporadically contented or successful in journalism and the law as well as in activities more befitting the pioneering westerner: mining, Pony-Express riding, living among Native Americans, possibly horse stealing. His marriage to author Theresa Dyer ended in 1869 and his writing met an indifferent reception in San Francisco. His turn to the East and Europe reminds us that the arbiters of taste, even for western writers, belonged to a traditional cultural establishment, and it was in England that Miller became not only the "Poet of the Sierras" but also the "Byron of Oregon." Having cashed in his western literary treasures for the coin of the realm of literary fame and respectability, Miller continued to affect the ways of the authentic and colorful westerner, playing up to outsiders' images when he returned to New York and Washington, D.C. By the late 1880s he had long been certified as a western author and came full circle by settling in the Oakland hills, briefly pushing on to the further frontier of Alaska and the Yukon.

Miller's materials were regional and his audiences encouraged him in his depicting an intriguing and exotic West. Regardless of his subjects, however, his verse was generally in the vaguely wandering yet predictable and sentimental sing-song register of an exhausted British romanticism. In fact, Miller wrote that romance was inherent to poetry, that some soulful subjects seem profaned by prose. His mellow measures made the poetry readily understood by an appreciative public, but his subject matter was what really made his name. The early *Songs of the Sierras* (1871) was an instant and immense success and set the tone for the many volumes which followed and were less popular only because the appeal of novelty began to fade: "songs" of "sunlands," "Italy," "far-away lands," "Mexican seas," "the soul." Miller created myths of the West and of the westerner as man and writer. The poems from *Songs of the Sierras* most pertinent in this image making include "Arizonian," "Californian," "The Last Taschastas," "The Tale of the Tall Alcalde," and "Kit Carson's Ride." (One poem again points up the characteristic division in Miller between content and style and turns east in its homage to "Burns and Byron.") Miller's lack of realism made his portraits of a region and its people seem only more appealing. He poetically evokes plain, prairie, canyon and mountain in quaint old diction, meter, and rhymes. Although he celebrates "the mighty men of 'Forty-nine,'" his sympathies also clearly lie with dispossessed Native Americans or with the Mexican-Americans from whom he annexed his pen name. Miscegenation becomes emblem of adopting and adapting western lands, since Miller helped to fix the tradition of depicting Native Americans as ancestrally and mysteriously allied with the very landscape. Heroes' pursuit of various "brown maidens" may alienate them from other white characters, but it furnished fantasies of assimilation and vicarious thrills for nineteenth-century readers: they could indulge the feeling that even Anglo-Americans could experience dangerous, possibly transforming, adventures and at the same time eventually find homes amid an otherwise inhuman and alien vastness. Miller domesticated his lush landscapes with unconventional marriages made conventional by old-fashioned chivalry.

Miller continued to mine the West in prose fiction, the personal essay, the autobiography, and drama as well as poetry. His lesser-known works dealt with Europe and the American East, with soulful longing and with a never-satisfied search for ideal Beauty. Of note for its images and popularity during the crucial early period of Miller's career is the autobiography, *Life Amongst the Modocs* (1873). Here his concern for Native Americans takes a turn to polemics a decade before Helen Hunt Jackson's Euro-American appropriations *A Century of Dishonor* or *Ramona*. His Indian daughter Cali-Shasta is mourned as "the last of the children of Shasta"; "Shadows of Shasta" figures as the first chapter's somber and alliterative title and as the title of the 1881 fictionalized version of Miller's protest. The melodramatic action-packed novel *First Fam'lies of the Sierras* (1876) — retitled *The Danites in the Sierras* (1881) as a play — shows Miller obviously in the fashionable mode of Bret

Harte's "The Luck of Roaring Camp," and its diatribe against the Mormons for their polygamy and putative slyness and violence sounds another significant note in western literature. Images of Miller and images created by Miller continued current in collected editions of his poems published in 1910 and 1923, and in further editions of his auto-biographical writings, like *Overland in a Covered Wagon*, issued as late as 1930.

Joaquin Miller both enacted and celebrated the western movement and perceived what should perhaps not be celebrated. His avenue to fame exhibits again the paradox of the regional writer's having to seek acceptance and an audience outside an area rich in substance but poor in number or formal sophistication of readers and cultural institutions like publishing. But if Miller the man sometimes was a "splendid poseur," his works were not a calculated selling-out to non-westerners' expectations, for he genuinely believed in the higher reality of romance. In the end, Miller created a western myth that was also a myth of all America. Decades after his death he remained a mainstay in American classrooms by way of the poem "Columbus," in which a determined "Sail on!" becomes the answer to every challenge; he thereby reminds us that America was and is the West as a land of the future in which failure is impossible because the future never arrives. Power fantasy prevails even when we are "empty, idle, hungered, waiting / For some hero" ("At Our Golden Gate"). Yet the West could also represent the end rather than eternal beginnings. The stunning sunlit "Sierras from the Sea" stand "as lone as God," "serene and satisfied" above human strife as one looks eastward from the appropriately named Pacific. Miller's journey to the sunset was a "pilgrimage" engaging "thousands and hundreds of thousands who peopled the ultimate west" (*Overland in a Covered Wagon*). The Shasta which Miller described as a monolith nearly sacred to him and the Modocs cast very long shadows indeed.

Selected Bibliography

Primary Sources

First Fam'lies of the Sierras. London: G. Routledge, 1875.

Joaquin Miller's Poems. 6 vols. San Francisco: The Whittaker and Ray Company, 1909-1910.

Life Amongst the Modocs. London: Richard Bentley and Son, 1873.

Memorie and Rime. New York: Funk and Wagnalls, 1884.

Overland in a Covered Wagon: An Autobiography. Sidney G. Firman, ed. New York and London: D. Appleton, 1930.

The Poetical Works of Joaquin Miller. Stuart Sherman, ed. New York: G. P. Putnam, 1923.

Shadows of Shasta. Chicago: Jansen, McClurg, 1881.

The Ship in the Desert. Boston: Roberts Brothers, 1875.

Songs of the Sierras. London: Longman, Green, Reader, and Dyer, 1871; and Boston: Roberts Brothers, 1871.

Songs of the Sun-lands. Boston: Roberts Brothers, 1873.

Secondary Sources

Frost, O. W. *Joaquin Miller*. New Haven: Twayne, 1967.

Lawson, Benjamin S. *Joaquin Miller*. Boise: Boise State University Western Writers Series, 1980.

Marberry, M. Marion. *Splendid Poseur: Joaquin Miller — American Poet*. New York: Thomas Y. Crowell, 1953.

Peterson, Martin S. *Joaquin Miller: Literary Frontiersman*. Palo Alto: Stanford University Press, 1937.

Walker, Franklin. *San Francisco's Literary Frontier*. New York: Knopf, 1939.

White, Bruce A. "The Liberal Stances of Joaquin Miller." *Rendezvous*, 19 (Fall 1983): 86-94.

Lawrence I. Berkove

Ambrose Bierce

Ambrose Bierce arrived in the West in 1866. Except for his three-year sojourn in London between 1872 and 1875, the West was his home until 1899. Along with Mark Twain and Bret Harte, Bierce has generally been acknowledged to be one of the region's three greatest nineteenth-century authors. The West provided Bierce with the basic material for his journalism, it was the focus of a number of his short stories, and it helped shape the way he thought and wrote.

Probably the most obvious influence the West had on Bierce was the model of the unrestrained and forceful editorial style then so common in western newspapers. Mark Twain parodied that style in "Journalism in Tennessee" (1869) which, despite its misleading title, was a thinly disguised reflection of journalism in the Comstock where editors enjoyed great latitude in subject matter and style provided only that they were willing to back up what they said with fists or guns. Bierce had a deep love of honesty and plain speaking and a correspondingly deep hatred of scoundrels, bigots, and chicanery, and he was willing to risk combat. But Bierce was reputed to be a crack shot, and no one ever tested his reputation. Where other western writers derided their opponents with vituperation, Bierce cultivated what has been called "beautiful abuse," a style of insult whose wit and elegance compelled admiration even as it stung. An "antepostmortem" epitaph for one of his enemies reads, for example, "Here lies Frank Pixley, as usual." This cannot be improved upon for brevity and pith. Bierce thus refined the western confrontational style into a form of art.

It is not sufficiently appreciated that Bierce was a working journalist for most of his life in the West. He was one of the first writers William Randolph Hearst hired in 1887 for his newspaper, the *San Francisco Examiner*. Bierce wrote a regular column for the paper until he left San Francisco for Washington, D.C., in 1899. Before the *Examiner*, Bierce had worked as a writer or editor for several distinguished western publications, the *San Francisco News-Letter and California Advertiser*, the *Argonaut*, and the *Wasp*. On all of them, he earned the reputation of having a scathing wit and being fearlessly outspoken.

For each of these periodicals Bierce wrote a column of commentary on current affairs, usually local news. Describing himself in his third person persona of "the Town Crier" Bierce in 1872 summed up both his credo and his subject matter: "The only talents he [the Town Crier] has are a knack at hating hypocrisy, cant, and all sham, and a trick of expressing his hatred. What wider field than San Francisco does God's green earth present?" Bierce rejected the notion that satire "should cut, not mangle" and disagreed with W. D. Howells's advice that good satire should be subtle. "Let us mangle!" he cried, and deliberately turned away from the neat model of Horace to the examples of "that coarse Juvenal, and that horrid Swift." As Bierce saw it, vice existed not abstractly, but in particular individuals and deeds, so his attacks were, even for the West, unusually personal and biting. One of his targets unintentionally complimented Bierce's skill at satire when he described Bierce as "the man with the burning pen."

Bierce has been often dismissed as a crank and a curmudgeon. While it is true that he was contentious and sometimes over-extended his area of expertise, it is also true that he usually chose his targets carefully and was often the main or the most effective opponent of corrupt or overbearing power figures in San Francisco and California. Along with Twain and Harte, he was a formidable opponent of bigotry, and a champion of such minorities as Chinese, Mormons, and Jews.

On a larger scale, Bierce was in the forefront of the journalistic attacks on the railroad monopolies that had so profound an impact on the development of the West, yet he also opposed the populist sentiment that was directed against the railroads because he saw no gain to the republic in replacing the tyranny of the few with the tyranny of the many. He was also a forerunner of investigative journalism. He was the first writer to expose the Bancroft history "factory" in California when he reported that most of the impressive tomes published over the signature of Hubert Howe Bancroft were, in fact, ghostwritten. Bierce's extended campaign in 1896 of blistering revelations about the financial machinations of Collis P. Huntington was a main cause of the defeat of the $130,000,000 Funding Bill scam. And though Hearst, Bierce's employer, helped promote the Spanish-American War in 1898, Bierce opposed it at the outset and remained a critic of military tactics during the war and political policy afterward. Thus, while he was largely regarded as a maverick in his own time, many of the positions and values Bierce upheld or pioneered as a western journalist are now considered to be nationally normative or even advanced.

The West played a largely underestimated role in Bierce's development as a short story writer. A significant number of his tales from his early, middle, and late periods have western settings. His first important short story was "The Haunted Valley," published in the *Overland Monthly* in 1871 under the editorship of Bret Harte. It is about the socially doomed love affair of an American prospector and a Chinese woman. This interesting tale, besides being notable for Bierce's atypical use of dialect, embodies a criticism of social (especially racial) injustice, and is a forerunner of his later stories. It is also an early example of how Bierce had successfully worked out how to handle irony and emotion in his fiction and how he began to develop his most characteristic theme, the tragic limitation of reason. "The Stranger" (1909), a haunting story about the victims of an Apache massacre, was Bierce's last tale. It is a somber conclusion to his literary career and also a serious reflection on the long war that in his time was summed up in the title of Theodore Roosevelt's popular book, *The Winning of the West*. The story characteristically expressed Bierce's dissent from a national cliché.

Bierce had had a hand in the "winning of the West." He first came to the West with an 1866-1867 military expedition charged with inspecting military posts in the Dakotas and Montana. Upon completion of the tour of inspection, Bierce settled in San Francisco. He recalled, in one of his later newspaper articles, witnessing an Indian attack in which "frontiersmen" distinguished themselves by their ineptness and cowardice in battle. In 1880 Bierce left San Francisco for a job as the supervisor of a gold mining company in the Black Hills. It lasted only three months, but they were eventful. They supplied Bierce with a good deal of experience with highwaymen and with commercial and judicial corruption. These experiences, in addition to the frequent encounters he had in San Francisco with hypocrisy, cant, and sham, helped shape his philosophy.

Bierce called himself a cynic, but he meant it in the original sense of the term, one who served truth by testing all claims to virtue by examination for selfish motives. As with Mark Twain, Bierce's experience in the West taught him to be skeptical of human nature and human enterprise. Again like Twain, Bierce became a master of the distinctively western art of the hoax and was especially sensitive to the tendency of the mind to be deceived and even to deceive itself. Bierce participated in some playful hoaxes, such as *The Dance of Death* (1877), a pseudonymous diatribe against dancing; a journalistic conspiracy in 1899 to pass off a poem by Herman Scheffauer as a work of Poe's; and his own story, "The Death of Halpin Frayser" (1899).

On a deeper level, Bierce so internalized the art of the hoax that it became a characteristic of his style, even for stories not western in setting. "The Famous Gilson Bequest" (1878), which shows some obvious influence of Bret Harte, may also in its plot of how a will hoaxed an entire community into revealing its corruption bear some comparison to Twain's later masterpiece, "The Man Who Corrupted Hadleyburg" (1899). "The Man and the Snake" (1890) is an ironic but searching study of how the mind can deceive itself. The outstanding legacy of the influence of the western hoax in Bierce's fiction, however, may be in his greatest short story, "An Occurrence at Owl Creek Bridge" (1890). In it, Peyton Farquhar's mind succeeds in hoaxing him—and practically every reader of the story. Like his more famous contemporary Twain, Bierce assimilated the West and transformed its lessons into great literature.

Selected Bibliography

Primary Sources

Bierce, Ambrose. *The Collected Works of Ambrose Bierce.* 12 vols. New York and Washington: Neale, 1909-1912.

———. *Skepticism and Dissent: Selected Journalism, 1898-1901.* Lawrence I. Berkove, ed. Ann Arbor: UMI Research Press, 1986.

Secondary Sources

Berkove, Lawrence I. "Ambrose Bierce's Concern with Mind and Man." Dissertation, University of Pennsylvania, 1962.

———. "'Hades in Trouble': A Rediscovered Story by Ambrose Bierce." *American Literary Realism,* 25:2 (Winter 1993): 67-84.

Davidson, Cathy N., ed. *Critical Essays on Ambrose Bierce.* Boston: G.K. Hall, 1982.

Fatout, Paul. *Ambrose Bierce and the Black Hills.* Norman: University of Oklahoma Press 1956.

Francendese, Janet. "Ambrose Bierce as Journalist." Dissertation, New York University, 1977.

Grenander, M. E. *Ambrose Bierce.* New York: Twayne, 1971.

McWilliams, Carey. *Ambrose Bierce: A Biography.* New York: A. & C. Boni, 1929; rpt., n.p.: Archon, 1967.

Part Three

New Wests: 1980 and Beyond

Susan J. Rosowski

New Wests

"New Wests" represents not settled territory but explorations and surveys of evolving literary landscapes. In describing their work, contributors to "New Wests" employ language of discovery and metaphors of mapping; implicitly, they challenge their readers to respond in kind, so that they too become engaged in the ongoing process of mapping and remapping.

As a representation of materials selected and organized at a particular time and in a particular context, a map is best read comparatively, alongside earlier maps purportedly representing the same subject. The most cursory reading of *Updating the Literary West* alongside its predecessor, *A Literary History of the American West*, reveals that changes since 1987 have been dramatic and far reaching. California, formerly included in the section "Far West," now has a section for itself, as does Texas, formerly treated within the "Southwest." "The Great Plains" is now the preferred name for what was then called the "Midwest," and the term "Heartland" now refers to Central California as well as to Kansas and Nebraska. Demographic changes appear in reconfigurations of race, ethnicity, and gender. Ethnic writers, discussed in a section of their own ten years ago, are now integrated throughout as both the subjects of essays and the scholars writing those essays. Women writers were represented in only sixty-five of the 1,323 pages of *LHAW* and by only eleven of its seventy-one contributors. In *Updating*, significant new attention has been given to women writers of the West past and present; thirty-four of the ninety-six editors and scholars involved in the project are women.

Understanding that mapping is an ongoing process is nothing new for scholars of the literary West. In the past as now, "West" is a term of orientation that involves positioning oneself *vis-a-vis* a subject. Traditionally scholars have asked how *does* one determine "West" when writing of a frontier that moved, and what *is* one's relationship to place when complicated by a Jeffersonian grid of ownership applied over the natural contours of the land? A decade ago editors of A *Literary History of the American West* acknowledged the semantic dilemma of referring to a singular "West" when in fact they were dealing with many Wests. They responded by titling their core section "Settled In: Many Wests," which they divided into four subsections, each focusing on one of the West's sub-regions because "Each sub-region has its own distinctive landscape and history" (Maguire 323). Within each sub-region, separate essays focused upon individual writers.

The map today isn't nearly so neat. Outside of page limitations, no restrictions were made upon editors of each of its seven sections: no common definitions were legislated, and no standardized taxonomies were imposed. What resulted reflects each editorial team's sense of how best to represent writing in their area. Two sections are identified by the name of a state ("California" and "Texas"); two by direction (the "Far West" and the "Southwest"); two by geography and ecology ("Rocky Mountains" and "Great Plains"); and one by literary characteristics (the "Popular West"). Within each section, editors have organized their materials by principles appropriate to those materials: names of states and of individual writers comprise some chapter headings, while genres and ideas comprise others.

Questions that ensue are those of literary studies — and our culture — today. Glen Love acknowledges that without California "any generalizations about the Far West may seem open to question," and Tom Pilkington admits that "eliminating Texas creates a huge hole in the map of the [Southwest], leaving an oddly shaped — even gerrymandered — district." Do the designations "Far West" and "Southwest" remain useful, given the fact that their most populous states think of themselves as countries in themselves? What does one learn from such a map, gerrymandered and filled with holes as it is?

By one reading, California now sets the magnetic field. "Today more publishing writers live in California...than the remainder of the West combined," Gerald Haslam writes; its great Central Valley is "the richest farming region in the *history* of the world"; and it comprises "the mainland's first state with a non-white majority." As if in confirmation of California's effect beyond its borders, the reader of essays about other regions will find the ex-Californian backtracking through the Rocky Mountains, in-migrating to the Far West, and setting up shop in the Southwest.

Within individual sections of "New Wests," the relationship of demography to place helps to explain emphases distinctive to a region. The Pacific Northwest, where in-migration is most dramatically felt upon a fragile ecology, is providing leadership in ecoliterary criticism; and in writing of the Great Plains, where population is flat or declining, scholars give the most attention to retrieval of lost and restitution of neglected writers. It is significant, perhaps, that the call for theory figures most strongly in the "Popular West," the single section unattached to a specific region and place.

What is clear is that the essays comprising "New Wests" represent not a settled territory, but the search for points of orientation by which inhabitants of a region might identify themselves. Having explained the shift from "Midwest" to "Great Plains" as the preferred term for her section, Diane Quantic looks to ecology and geography to explain its literary focus "on the land's transformation from wilderness space to usable place," the pioneer story replayed with variations on irony and nostalgia. Greg Morris looks to geography to explain that "the vast Rocky Mountain landscape seems to embrace and to accommodate" "its complex weave of political, cultural, and economic contrasts," and Glen Love writes of the Far West that "Geographically, it is also worth noting that all of these Far West regions covered here, excepting Nevada, border on the Pacific Ocean." As for Nevada — that single state that contradicts defining the Far West by its Pacific Ocean border, Ann Ronald writes, "I can't impose a Nevada-ness on a collection of diverse authors who have nothing in common other than the fact that they live in a very large state. There is no central figure, no central theme....I'm totally unable to think of much beyond a stark terrain that a few of the writers mention on occasion" (Ann Ronald to author, December 26, 1995).

Rather than seeking a definition of "West," readers might more productively trace its permutations through the essays comprising this volume. When bordered by the Pacific Ocean, "West" means not opportunity but instead the limitations imposed by the natural frontier of the

Pacific Ocean. As "West" has folded back upon itself, the Rocky Mountains have inherited the western myth as a "contemporary Paradise Besieged." And in popular culture where "West" refers to neither direction nor to location but rather to an idea that has been commodified and made portable, interpreting its significance involves tracing it linguistically within hemispheric and global contexts of export and import.

While "West" remains the lingua franca whose meaning is determined in context, other terms have all but disappeared. As the moving point of confrontation between civilization and wilderness, the frontier has left the literary West only to resurface in academic discourse. The MLA-sponsored volume, *Redrawing the Boundaries: The Transformation of English and American Literary Studies* (1992) illustrates my point. After describing the rapid changes in the profession of literary studies, editors Stephen Greenblatt and Giles Gunn propose redrawing its boundaries by two contrasting definitions of frontier: a frontier representing a notion of limit, such as those that devolve from "impassable rivers or mountains," versus a frontier conceived "as the zone between antagonists" negotiated by appropriation, confrontation, and ambition. It is the second notion that Greenblatt and Gunn propose for literary studies, specifying that "what is meant here by *frontier* is not a fixed line but the furthest point to which you can push your forces, extend your influence" (5-8). Insert "civilization versus wilderness" and this frontier between antagonists sounds unnervingly like the old one of confrontation and conflict resulting in conquest or defeat.

Had Greenblatt and Gunn looked to the new Wests represented in this volume, they would have found that the notion of a shared life in place is what scholars are advocating as the necessary alternative to the territorial antagonisms of the past. Glen Love acknowledges the Pacific Ocean as the natural boundary by which older western myths and movements "have been brought up short by the realization that there is no longer an absolute 'away.'" Given such a limit, "We are faced, in Robert Frost's terms, with what to make of a diminished thing. As William Kittredge says, 'There is no more running away to territory. This is it, for most of us. We have no choice but to live in community.'"

"If we're lucky we may discover a story that teaches us to abhor our old romance with conquest and possession," writes Kittredge. In looking for that instruction, scholars of new Wests turn to the communities being created by the novelists, poets, and essayists who are the subjects of their essays. "Every group that comes to think of itself as a unified people *must* generate a mythology that supplies national or group identity," writes Pilkington from the Southwest, who then refers to a Texas myth which he explains not ideologically but by the decentralized, regional, alternative publishing outlets of institutes, presses, workshops, journals and anthologies. "What has in fact emerged among these writers is a sense of regional writerly community," Morris writes of the Rocky Mountain section; "[D]espite the terrific artistic and geographic distances among them, these writers have still enjoyed a reasonable coherence of vision and spirit." In explanation Morris turns, as did Pilkington, not to a particular ideology but instead to the means by which writers are brought together: university writing programs and presses, literary magazines and journals, writers' workshops, state arts councils and the Western States Arts Federation. Those programs, along with anthologies, form "created communities" that "are excellent starting points for any reader interested in discovering the best new voices speaking from" a region.

Institutes, presses, and anthologies all — like *Updating the Literary West* itself — inevitably invite questions about what voices are included, by what criteria were they selected, and by whom. Discussed theoretically in a separate section, issues of canonicity are played out here in "New Wests." And again, reading *Updating the Literary West* alongside its predecessor is useful. Max Westbrook introduced *A Literary History of the American West* with "conceptual questions about the project itself" that have to do with acknowledging difference: "The history of the American West has been defined by groups conscious of their own history but too often unaware or unappreciative of any other history. Anglo pioneers, for example, tended to think of themselves as moving into a new world...and yet up ahead were unknown millions of indigenous citizens, many with an oral tradition of power and sophistication.... Likewise, the oversimplification of 'red' versus 'American' ignores long-established Hispanic civilization in the Southwest and in California, the influence of French trappers and missionaries, Scandinavian developments in north-central America, German communities established in Texas and throughout the West, and the stories of blacks, Asians, and literally dozens of other ethnic groups" (xvii).

Whereas a premise of *A Literary History of the American West* was the need to heighten awareness of others' history, the premise of "New Wests" is the need to live within multiple contexts; and whereas the premise of *LHAW* was to rectify oversimplified oppositions, that of "New Wests" is to work together. Points of reference are, increasingly, inside and outside, rather than self and other. "The literary landscape and roster in this state look different from within than from without," Haslam says of California; making the same point from another perspective, Christine Bold argues for resituating definitions of the popular West within a hemispheric context and addressing its terms of identity formation that tend to privilege a dominant culture over minority interests. As if in counterpoint, Gerald Haslam describes "the real (thus non-stereotypical) California" by listing its leading writers and then noting "nary a paleface in the group." Like other terms in "New Wests," *minority* must be defined in context.

The basic shift is paradigmatic, however. Whereas writing of the Old West proceeded from assumptions of opposition — West versus East, settlement versus wilderness, civilization versus savagery — writing of the New Wests proceeds from assumptions of both: inside *and* outside, the individual *in* community. Once the modernist's lament that the center cannot hold has given way to an acknowledgement of multiple centers, the aim is no longer to resolve difference but instead to find points of convergence.

For those points of convergence, scholars of "New Wests" look to imaginative literature with respect and to the land with humility. In the following essays, writers describe differences and commonalities with a quite remarkable absence of rancor, hostility, aggression, and appropriation. Their common premise is that the subject is more important than the critic. This is a collection designed not to theoretize the West or problematize texts; instead, it is to invite readers to explore a field and to participate in the communities that comprise it. This is a politics of mapping that invites readers to become citizens.

Works Cited

Unless otherwise noted, all quotations are from essays included in "New Wests."

Greenblatt, Stephen, and Giles Gunn, eds. "Introduction." *Redrawing the Boundaries: The Transformation of English and American Literary Studies.* New York: Modern Language Association, 1992.

Maguire, James H. "Introduction." "Part Two: Settled In: Many Wests." *A Literary History of the American West.* J. Golden Taylor, et al., eds. Fort Worth: TCU Press, 1987. Pp. 319-325.

Taylor, J. Golden, et al., eds. *A Literary History of the American West.* Fort Worth: TCU Press, 1987.

Westbrook, Max. "Preface." *A Literary History of the American West.* J. Golden Taylor, et al., eds. Fort Worth: TCU Press, 1987. Pp. xv-xx.

I
The Far West

Glen A. Love

The Far West

We thank the goodness and the grace
That brought us to this lovely place;
And now with all our hearts we pray
That other folks will stay away.
(Pease 161)

These lines, reputedly the common prayer of the summer residents of Maine coastal retreat Mount Desert at the turn of the last century, may suggest a modern-day confluence for the five states — Washington, Oregon, Nevada, Alaska, and Hawaii — covered in this section of *Updating the Literary West*. Of course, without the inclusion of California, whose multiplicity and population of thirty million have accorded it a section of its own in this volume, any generalizations about the Far West may seem open to question. On the other hand, California, as the nation's most populous state, may today represent to its less "developed" neighbors the sort of crowded and frenetic place which was the urban East a hundred years ago, and for which Frederick Jackson Turner's West, and even the fashionable Maine summer colonies like Mount Desert, were seen as safety valves. As the California dream fades, its residents move in increasing numbers to Oregon, Washington, and Nevada, and even to far-off Alaska and Hawaii, where the less recently arrived join with the settled residents in decrying the hordes of newcomers. Going way back, such must have been the lament of the original human inhabitants of these western regions, when threatened with displacement by more powerful tribes, and later by white European encroachment.

Aggressive in-migration, and attendant problems of growth, change, and alteration (for the worse) of the natural landscape, are, of course, very real and serious problems of the far-western states. The apprehension may be seen behind two common tendencies of their recent literature, the first of which is the increasing presence of environmental and nature writing, which in the great American pastoral tradition stands in opposition to the forces of industrialization and spreading urbanism. The second tendency might be described as the search for personal roots, particularly in historical and ethnic heritages threatened with obliteration in the mass commercial culture. But the search is closely related to what poet Richard Hugo called that "obsessive quality of emotional ownership" which defines the regional sensibility (37).

In both cases we see the artistic and aesthetic grounding of the local, the specific, and the personal struggling to assert itself against a creeping homogenization, a vast network of interchangeable urban experiences. More and more, far western writers seem to assert the particular and the unique and the natural in the face of an assault of photocopied shopping centers, ubiquitous freeways, mind-numbing TV, and consumer zombiism. What comes through in many of these writers is an attempt to fashion alternatives less destructive and wasteful of both the human spirit and the natural world.

This increasing attention to the local, the personal, and the regional (or "bioregional," as it is likely to be called today) seems not just geographically, but also politically and technologically, motivated. Geographically, in the sense that the older myths and actualities of westering and movement have been brought up short by the realization that there is no longer an absolute "away." We are faced, in Robert Frost's terms, with what to make of a diminished thing. As William Kittredge says, "There is no more running away to territory. This is it, for most of us. We have no choice but to live in community. If we're lucky we may discover a story that teaches us to abhor our old romance with conquest and possession" (68). Geographically, it is also worth noting that all of these Far West regions covered here, excepting Nevada, border on the Pacific Ocean. "I live at the dawn of the century of the Pacific," writes Tim Egan, one of the Northwest's liveliest new interpreters. Now, instead of looking eastward to Europe, all eyes look to the Pacific. As

Egan points out, "Since 1980, more immigrants have arrived on the West Coast, most of them from Asia, than came to the United States at any other time after the last great European wave in the early twentieth century. A similar immigration trend has hit British Columbia, where a third of all Vancouver citizens trace their ancestry to China" (252).

The mention of British Columbia reminds us that the forty-ninth parallel is an imaginary line across a single, unified landscape, a political border, not a bioregional one. So there are strong reasons for including that far western portion of Canada in our thinking about the Far West, and Laurence Ricou, of the University of British Columbia, argues persuasively for border-crossing thinking in the later pages of this section.

Politically, the Far West's assertion of the local seems to arise from a lessening of national confidence and faith, occasioned by the Vietnam debacles of the 1960s and by a series of horrifying assassinations and political crimes and excesses, climaxing in the resignation of President Richard Nixon from office in 1974. Inhabitants of the Far West seem to behave like those of other regions in giving more attention to local issues, over which they may feel they can exercise more control. Whether this is an abdication of national allegiance or a healthy reassertion of Josiah Royce's notion of wholesome provincialism is open to debate. But no one can doubt that most of us live the greater part of our lives as provincials — that is, as citizens of a specific place — and that it is better to be educated than ignorant about one's home place.

Technology has also contributed to the literary claiming or reclaiming of the provinces of the Far West. Modern inventions, noted Lewis Mumford many years ago, allow for a resurgence of regionalism by making the region independent of the metropolis. Writers no longer need to serve their apprenticeships in Greenwich Village or Paris. In the age of the computer and the internet, the hinterlands no longer wait to be instructed by edicts from the cultural capitals. Indeed there are no more cultural capitals, insofar as literature is concerned. The notion of a center of literary authority, such as New York was in the first two-thirds of this century, is no longer viable when, say, Missoula, Montana, emerges as the place where the action is, and when publishers, presses, journals, workshops, and writers' groups may flourish anywhere.

Along with these more immediate causes for the resurgence of the literary region, there is the inevitable, longer historical process by which, over the last century and a half, immigrants to the Far West have come to regard themselves as belonging to this place. Of course, the native peoples whom the first settlers encountered when they arrived in the Pacific Northwest, or Nevada, or Alaska, or Hawaii, had lived in these places for thousands of years and had evolved a rich tradition of oral literature. But more recent written literature had to evolve through a process similar to that described by historian Louis Hartz in analyzing the growth of the cultures of ex-colonial "new" societies. That process moved through three stages, from the imitative, to the aggressively regional, to the confident and widely participatory. Applying the Hartz model to the far western states addressed here (which began as far-flung "colonies" of the East), we may see them as somewhere near the end of the process, still often strongly asserting their regionality, but also possessed of a new level of confidence that one associates with the more cosmopolitan tastes and instincts of a maturing aesthetic. While many far western writers, like the aggressive regionalists of the 1920s and '30s such as H. L. Davis and James Stevens, may insist upon the artistic potential of their literary territory, they are no longer victims of the cultural cringe which for so many years has left them having to justify themselves — always unsuccessfully — before the dismissive judgments of the East. Contemporary far western writers, place-centered yet also participants in the international and multicultural currents, reflect a new sense of assurance. No longer having to defend their place and origins as legitimate literary material, they simply go their own way with confidence. Without that confidence, as Wallace Stegner reminded us, a region's books cannot be great.

Keeping these background considerations in mind, one can look more closely at the contemporary literature of the Far West. The newfound sense, even in the most sophisticated of today's writers, of a fresh assertion of the importance of place and natural environment is strongly in evidence. One thinks of Annie Dillard's remarkable first novel, *The Living* (1992), set in northwest Washington state, as well as her essays and memoirs from her years spent in Bellingham. Nature writing figures prominently in other recent works from Washington. The state's southwest corner, a place of heavily cut-over forest lands, gains literary and ecological distinction in Robert Pyle's *Wintergreen* (1986), while Bruce Brown marks the demise of the homing salmon in *Mountain in the Clouds* (1982), and the fate of the old-growth forests is memorably recorded in a number of recent works of natural history. Brenda Peterson unites people with nature in her widely admired *Living by Water* (1990), while fellow Seattleite Jonathan Raban brings a new sense of the Northwest metropolis to his *Hunting Mister Heartbreak* (1990).

From Oregon in recent years have come a number of important place-centered books, including David Rains Wallace's *The Klamath Knot* (1983), Kim Stafford's *Having Everything Right* (1986), George Venn's *Marking the Magic Circle* (1987), William Kittredge's *Owning It All* (1987), and John Daniel's *The Trail Home* (1992), and Chris Anderson's *Edge Effects: Notes from an Oregon Forest* (1993). In addition have come place-derivative works such as Ursula K. Le Guin's *Searoad: Chronicles of Klatsand* (1991), allusive to Oregon's north coast, and a number of the pieces in her *Going Out with Peacocks, and Other Poems* (1994). Her poetry has recently documented the Portland neighborhood where she lives and is paired with photographs by Roger Dorband in *Blue Moon over Thurman Street* (1993). Oregon has been gifted with the works of a number of poets led by the example of William Stafford. Stafford's passing (he died in 1993) marks the loss of a major figure in the poetry and presence of the West.

Other notable place-defined works of the Northwest include octogenarian author Clyde Rice's remarkable autobiographical works, beginning with *A Heaven in the Eye* (1984), and Molly Gloss' *The Jump-Off Creek* (1989). Shannon Applegate unites place and tradition in her moving family history, *Skookum* (1988). The works of central Oregon writer and rancher Dayton O. Hyde, especially *Don Coyote* (1986), bring a new ecological voice to the business of ranching. Seattleite Tim Egan's *The Good Rain* (1990) and Portlander Sallie Tisdale's *Stepping Westward* (1991), a pair of beautifully crafted personal overviews of the Pacific Northwest, pull the region together as a distinctive place, threatened and yet hopeful. Several recent anthologies contribute to our understanding of the Northwest and its writers, including Nicholas O'Connell's *At the Field's End: Interviews with Twenty Pacific Northwest Writers* (1987), Lex Runciman and Steven Sher's *Northwest Variety* (1987), Bruce Barcott's *Northwest Passages* (1994), and Mayumi Tsutakawa's handsomely illustrated *Edge Walking on the Western Rim* (1994).

From Nevada, Joanne de Longchamps' *The Schoolhouse Poems* (1975), Stephen Trimble's *The Sagebrush Ocean* (1989), and Ann Ronald's *Earthtones* (1995) deepen our sense of the high desert. Alaska's place-centered writers include Richard Nelson, whose *The Island Within* (1989) is a profound study of the linkages between place, animals, and humans; and distinguished Alaskan poet John Haines, whose two books of essays, *Living Off the Country* (1981) and *The Stars, the Snow, the Fire* (1989), are nature writing worthy of the best of his poems. Further examples of memorable Alaskan place-centered prose are included in John Murray's *A Republic of Rivers* (1990). Of course, one cannot omit Oregonian Barry Lopez's masterful Alaska nature writing in *Arctic Dreams* (1986), winner of the National Book Award for nonfiction. British Columbia's distinguished naturalist and fly-fishing writer Roderick Haig-Brown is brought back to deserved attention with the recent reissue of two of his novels, *Timber* (1942) and *On the Highest Hill* (1949), both in the Oregon State University Press' Northwest Reprint Series. Judging from the number and quality of these and other works of natural and spatial consciousness, we must think in terms of place and environment, as well as ethnicity and gender, as we participate in the remaking of the American literary canon.

On the topics of ethnicity and gender, the Far West gives evidence of full participation in the national literary re-evaluation. One example is the resurgence of the presence of indigenous peoples in the literature of this region. Following years of displacement, contemporary writers from such backgrounds seek to reclaim a heritage which had all but disappeared. Notable examples might include works by Native Hawaiians, such as John Dominis Holt's *Waimea Summer* (1976) and Haunani-Kay Trask's *Light in the Crevice Never Seen* (1994). From Alaska, the collection *Raven Tells Stories* (1991), edited by Joseph Bruchac and James Ruppert, offers the work of a number of Native Alaskan writers, while Washington's Sherman Alexie has won a wide following with his recent books, beginning with *The Business of Fancydancing* (1992). Louis Owens' *Wolfsong* (1991) is a notable addition to the genre, as are the novels of native Oregonian Craig Lesley, *Winterkill* (1984), *River Song* (1989), and *The Sky Fisherman* (1995), and Lesley's anthology of Indian voices, *Talking Leaves* (1991).

The continuing process of immigration has contributed much to the enrichment of far western literature, as is evidenced especially in the many important works by Asian-American writers. In the Northwest, building upon the pioneering work of Monica Sone's *Nisei Daughter* (1953) and John Okada's *No-No Boy* (1957), one notes such recent works as Ken Mochizuki's *Baseball Saved Us* (1993) and Lawson Inada's *Legends from Camp: Poems* (1992). From Hawaii Milton Murayama's *All I Asking for Is My Body* (1975), Cathy Song's *Picture Bride* (1983), and

Garrett Hongo's *Yellow Light* (1982) and *Volcano* (1995) are representative of Asian-American writers addressing the conflict of warring values. Still other ethnic themes are evident in such contemporary writers as African-American Seattleites Colleen J. McElroy (*What Madness Brought Me Here*, 1990) and Charlotte Watson Sherman (*Killing Color*, 1992), and in the Basque heritage of Nevadan Monique Urza's *Deep Blue Memory* (1993).

Finally, a widely praised six-volume anthology, the Oregon Literature Series, under the general editorship of George Venn, demonstrates how all of the diverse themes and approaches mentioned above can be found in the literature of a single state. The series, published in the early 1990s by Oregon State University Press, includes a historical range of Oregon texts in six volumes: *The World Begins Here* (fiction); *Many Faces* (autobiography); *Varieties of Hope* (prose); *From Here We Speak* (poetry); *The Stories We Tell* (folk literature); and *Talking on Paper* (letters and diaries). These books are seen as a national model by John Frohnmayer, chair of the National Endowment for the Arts. They suggest in another format the newly informed attention to place in the study of literature which marks so much of the emerging writing of the Far West.

Works Cited

Egan, Tim. *The Good Rain*. New York: Alfred A. Knopf, 1990.

Hartz, Louis. *The Founding of New Societies* New York: Harcourt Brace, 1964.

Hugo, Richard. "Problems with Landscapes in Early Stafford Poems." *Kansas Quarterly*, 2 (Spring 1970): 37.

Kittredge, William. *Owning It All*. St. Paul, Minnesota: Graywolf Press, 1987.

Pease, Otis A. "Comment by Otis A. Pease." In Gastil, Raymond D. "The Pacific Northwest as a Cultural Region: A Symposium," *Pacific Northwest Quarterly*, 64:4 (October 1973): 147-162.

Bruce Barcott

Washington

Washington novelists took off in so many directions in the 1980s that it's difficult to find any commonality other than the use of the long-form story in the English language. Tom Robbins, the region's most popular writer throughout the 1970s and 1980s, created novels filled with whimsical countercultural characters and convoluted, almost absurd, plots. Like Betty MacDonald in *The Egg and I* (1945), Robbins derived a stream of eccentric characters and hilarious situations from the unending dreariness of the northwestern rain. In *Another Roadside Attraction*, Robbins' 1971 debut, the body of Christ ends up in the hands of a band of hippie misfits living in a converted hotdog stand in the Skagit Valley. In subsequent works, like *Even Cowgirls Get the Blues* (1976), *Still Life with Woodpecker* (1980), and *Half Asleep in Frog Pajamas* (1994), Robbins turned out pun-filled sentences that twisted and tumbled like gymnasts on the mat. He delighted his fans even as he enraged many critics, who found little rhyme or reason to his stories. Robbins didn't mind; the whole point of his work was to add to the cosmic laughter of the world, not to probe its tragedy. "There's a level on which life might be perceived as a joke, on which it literally is a joke, and this bothers a lot of people," he once said. "The trickster's function" — that is, Robbins the writer's — "is to break taboos, create mischief, stir things up: In the end, the trickster gives people what they really want, some sort of freedom" (Egan, "Creating Perfect Sentences" 4B).

232

Raymond Carver went in another direction, creating solemn, realistic short stories about hard times, failing marriages, and working-class frustration. If Robbins' characters loved to laugh with life, Carver's people were those upon whom life had played particularly cruel jokes. He wrote about Americans trapped by bad times, liquid habits, and shameful acts. Marriages crumbled before the reader's eyes; infidelity, alcoholism, and bankruptcy hung around his characters like bad colds. With his collections *Will You Please Be Quiet, Please?* (1976), *What We Talk About When We Talk About Love* (1981), *Cathedral* (1983), and *Where I'm Calling From* (1988), Carver sparked a renaissance in the American short story and gave legitimacy to the spare style of writing known as minimalism. His literary and personal partnership with poet Tess Gallagher in Port Angeles proved fruitful for both. Gallagher, one of the Northwest's premiere poets whose best work can be found in the 1987 collection *Amplitude: New and Selected Poems*, encouraged Carver to take up poetry, and Carver encouraged Gallagher to write short stories, which she did in the book, *The Lover of Horses* (1986).

Between the extremes of Robbins and Carver were novelists who made varied use of the Northwest. Ursula Hegi's *The Salt Dancers* (1995) employed a Spokane background and a first-person narrator to explore child abuse in a parent-daughter relationship. John Keeble wove two of Washington's most enduring practices and problems — smuggling and white-Asian relations — into his 1980 novel, *Yellowfish*, about a man hired to smuggle four Chinese immigrants from Vancouver, British Columbia, to San Francisco via Reno. Keeble proved to be another writer unable to resist the rich anecdotal trove of Northwest history; the novel is peppered with historical detail laid out by the smuggler, who also happens to be an amateur historian. A few years later Keeble explored more contemporary issues of American foreign policy and political repression, but to lesser literary effect, in the novel *Broken Ground* (1987).

Ethnic relations also figure prominently in more recent books. In his 1994 novel, *Snow Falling on Cedars*, David Guterson uses the trial of an Asian American man accused of murdering a white fisherman to examine tensions between European American and Asian American immigrants and residents around Puget Sound during and after World War II. In Guterson's story, set in 1954 on an island in the San Juans, the residual anger and prejudice of the war surface in the heat of the trial: "This island's full of strong feelings," the accused, Kabuo Miyomoto, tells his lawyer, "people who don't speak their minds but hate on the inside all the same.... [N]ow there's a fisherman everybody liked well enough who's dead and drowned in his net. They're going to figure it makes sense a Jap killed him. They're going to want to see me hang no matter what the truth is" (294). The forced relocation of Japanese Americans during the war had been explored during the 1950s, most notably by Monica Sone in her poignant 1953 memoir, *Nisei Daughter*, and by John Okada in his 1957 novel, *No-No Boy*. But Guterson's novel is emblematic of the re-examination of the camps that has taken place fifty years after Executive Order 9066, in museum exhibits, the visual arts (see especially the paintings of Roger Shimomura), and even in children's literature in the form of Ken Mochizuki's 1993 book, *Baseball Saved Us*.

One of the strongest voices to emerge in Washington during the 1990s has been that of Sherman Alexie, a Spokane/Coeur d'Alene Indian who first won attention for his 1992 collection of poems and stories, *The Business of Fancydancing*. In that and the subsequent story collection, *The Lone Ranger and Tonto Fistfight in Heaven* (1993), and the novels *Reservation Blues* (1995) and *Indian Killer* (1996), Alexie wrote about life on an eastern Washington reservation with a stark realism, a biting, sometimes bitter wit, and a deep underlying sense of connection to his family and his tribe. He wrote about all-Indian six-foot-and-under basketball tournaments, about sneaking alcohol into high school dances, about a champion fancydancer who filled his friends' wallets, stomachs, and coolers. By the mid-1990s, Alexie had become one of Washington's better-known literary figures, and his dramatic, sometimes confrontational, public readings never failed to draw a crowd.

Annie Dillard, best known for her extraordinary personal narrative, *Pilgrim at Tinker Creek* (1974), moved to Bellingham in 1974 to become a writer-in-residence at Western Washington University. She returned east five years later, but continued to draw upon the Pacific Northwest as a spiritual and creative source. *Holy the Firm*, her 1977 rumination on time, reality, and the will of God, was set near Puget Sound, and many of the essays in her 1982 collection, *Teaching a Stone to Talk*, and her 1989 memoir, *The Writing Life*, resulted from her encounters with the people and the natural world of the Northwest. In 1992 Dillard completed her long-awaited first novel, an ambitious project again centered around Bellingham. In the 1930s and 1940s, Archie Binns (*You Rolling River*, *The Land is Bright*), Nard Jones (*Wheat Women*, *Swift Flows the River*), and Allis McKay (*They Came to a River*) had turned Washington's pioneer past into historical novels that hit all the familiar keys: eastern bride struggles in wild Northwest, Oregon Trail pioneers suffer but persevere, missionaries do God's rough work, Indians massacre young boy's family, etc. With *The Living* (1992), Annie Dillard breathed new life into the historical novel. Throwing out the old White Settlers Tame the Wilderness model, Dillard populated her novel with white, Native American, and Asian characters who led fairly despairing and wholly unheroic lives in the dark forests and unrelenting wetness of early Bellingham. "I wanted to write about itty-bitty people in a great big landscape, the way Turgenev does," she once said about the novel (Cantwell 40).

Seattle became something of a literary magnet in the 1980s, attracting writers from all over America and abroad. Novelists Mark Helprin, Michael Chabon, and Pete Dexter all spent productive years writing in the comparative solitude of the Pacific Northwest, although the region had little or no effect on their work. The Northwest has influenced the work of two writers from England, however, both of whom moved to Washington in the late 1980s: Denise Levertov and Jonathan Raban. The damp climate and gray mood of the region can be seen in some of Levertov's poems in her 1992 book, *Evening Train*. These lines are from "Settling" in that collection:

> Now I am given
> a taste of the grey foretold by all and sundry,
> a grey both heavy and chill. I've boasted I would not care,
> I'm London-born. And I won't. I'll dig in,
> into my days, having come here to live, not to visit.
> Grey is the price
> of neighboring with eagles, of knowing
> a mountain's vast presence, seen or unseen.

Raban came to research Seattle's late-1980s immigration boom for his 1990 book, *Hunting Mister Heartbreak*, and unexpectedly became part of it himself. "By the end of the 1980s, Seattle had taken on the dangerous luster of a promised city," Raban wrote. "The rumor had gone out that if you had failed in Detroit you might yet succeed in Seattle — and that if you'd succeeded in Seoul, you could succeed even better in Seattle" (242). In the Seattle chapters of *Heartbreak*, Raban took the pulse of this city of immigrants, flush with the success of Boeing, the software industry, and some new quality known as "liveability" that the rest of the nation craved. He found Seattle proud, a little smug, but nervous about losing some of its character amid the sudden growth and adulation. Five years into his Northwest residency Raban completed *Bad Land*, a historical rumination on the settlement of the West that focused on the homesteaders of eastern Montana who went bust in the dry years of the 1920s and 1930s and moved still farther west to Seattle and other coastal cities, where they stayed for good and became the parents and grandparents of Raban's neighbors and acquaintances. The deeper story, Raban wrote, was how the failed promise of homesteading had scorched the soul of the rural West.

Tobias Wolff left Washington in his teens, but continues to return to it in his writing. *This Boy's Life*, his remarkable 1989 memoir of growing up in the tiny logging and factory town of Concrete, Washington, provided a startlingly clear picture of a young boy struggling to find his way between an abusive stepfather, a depressing town, and a possible escape that seems just out of reach. The Northwest often turns up as a setting or in a character's background in Wolff's fiction, as in the short story collection *In the Garden of the North American Martyrs* (1981) and the short novel *The Barracks Thief* (1984).

The personal and historical essay remains a strong genre in Washington letters. Murray Morgan has been turning out highly literate historical essays since the 1950s: *Skid Road* (1951), *The Last Wilderness* (1955), *Puget's Sound* (1979). And more recently Timothy Egan, the Northwest correspondent for *The New York Times*, has taken up Morgan's mantle, relaying his impressions of the region back East and unearthing some of Washington's hidden history. His 1990 book, *The Good Rain*, was a mix of memoir, history, and reportage that touched upon everything from volcanoes to salmon to anti-communism in eastern Washington. Two years later he wrote *Breaking Blue*. It is a story about a Spokane murder solved after fifty years, and is marked by Egan's ability to bring the desperate atmosphere of the 1930s Depression to life. And he continues to search the Northwest for stories. "[E]verything Theodore Winthrop reveled in," he wrote at the end of *The Good Rain*, "the glaciers, the virgin forests, the green islands, the plump rivers, the fir-mantled volcanoes, the empty range of the high desert, Grandpa's trout streams, and the alpenglow, are here—a land that has yet to give up all its secrets" (254).

Selected Bibliography

Primary Sources

Alexie, Sherman. *The Business of Fancydancing: Stories and Poems.* Brooklyn: Hanging Loose Press, 1992.

———. *Indian Killer.* New York: Group West, 1996.

———. *The Lone Ranger and Tonto Fistfight in Heaven.* New York: Atlantic Monthly Press, 1993.

———. *Reservation Blues.* New York: Atlantic Monthly Press, 1995.

Binns, Archie. *The Land is Bright.* New York: Scribner's, 1939.

———. *You Rolling River.* New York: Scribner's, 1947.

Carver, Raymond. *Cathedral.* New York: Knopf, 1983.

———. *What We Talk About When We Talk About Love.* New York: Knopf, 1981.

———. *Where I'm Calling From.* New York: Atlantic Monthly Press, 1988.

———. *Will You Please Be Quiet, Please?* New York: McGraw-Hill, 1976.

Dillard, Annie. *The Living.* New York: HarperCollins, 1992.

———. *Teaching a Stone to Talk.* New York: Harper & Row, 1982.

———. *The Writing Life.* New York: Harper & Row, 1989.

Egan, Timothy. *Breaking Blue.* New York: Knopf, 1992.

———. *The Good Rain.* New York: Knopf, 1990.

Gallagher, Tess. *Amplitude: New and Selected Poems.* St. Paul: Graywolf, 1987.

Guterson, David. *Snow Falling on Cedars.* San Diego: Harcourt Brace, 1994.

Hegi, Ursula. *The Salt Dancers.* New York: Simon & Schuster, 1995.

Jones, Nard. *Swift Flows the River.* New York: Dodd, Mead, 1940.

———. *Wheat Women.* New York: Duffield & Green, 1933.

Keeble, John. *Broken Ground.* New York: Harper & Row, 1987.

———. *Yellowfish.* New York: Harper & Row, 1980.

Levertov, Denise. *Evening Train.* New York: New Directions, 1992.

MacDonald, Betty. *The Egg and I.* Philadelphia: Lippincott, 1945.

McKay, Allis. *They Came to a River.* New York: Macmillan, 1941.

Mochizuki, Ken. *Baseball Saved Us.* New York: Lee & Low, 1993.

Morgan, Murray. *The Last Wilderness.* New York: Viking, 1955.

———. *Puget's Sound: A Narrative of Early Tacoma and the Southern Sound.* Seattle: University of Washington Press, 1979.

———. *Skid Road: An Informal Portrait of Seattle.* New York: Viking, 1951.

Okada, John. *No-No Boy, A Novel.* Tokyo; Rutland, Vermont: Tuttle, 1957; rpt., Seattle: Combined Asian American Resources Project, 1976.

Raban, Jonathan. *Bad Land.* New York: Pantheon, 1996.

———. *Hunting Mister Heartbreak.* London: Collins Harvill, 1990; rpt., New York: Burlingame, 1991.

———. "The Next Last Frontier: A Newcomer's Journey through the Pacific Northwest." *Harper's Magazine,* 287 (August 1993): 30-48.

Robbins, Tom. *Another Roadside Attraction.* Garden City: Doubleday, 1971.

———. *Even Cowgirls Get the Blues.* Boston: Houghton Mifflin, 1976.

———. *Half Asleep in Frog Pajamas.* New York: Bantam, 1994.

———. *Still Life with Woodpecker.* New York: Bantam, 1980.

Sone, Monica. *Nisei Daughter.* Boston: Little, Brown, 1953.

Wolff, Tobias. *The Barracks Thief.* New York: Ecco Press, 1984.

————. *In the Garden of the North American Martyrs: A Collection of Short Stories.* New York: Ecco, 1981.

————. *This Boy's Life: A Memoir.* New York: Atlantic Monthly Press, 1989.

Secondary Sources

Barcott, Bruce. "City of Writers." *Seattle Weekly,* May 1, 1991, 38-47. Article on influx of writers to Seattle.

————. "Tobias Wolff Comes Home Again." *Seattle Weekly,* December 7, 1994, 43-45. Interview with Wolff.

————. "Why We Keep Talking About Raymond Carver." *Seattle Weekly,* October 20, 1994, 20-28. Article on Carver's literary legacy.

————, ed. *Northwest Passages: A Literary Anthology of the Pacific Northwest from Coyote Tales to Roadside Attractions.* Seattle: Sasquatch, 1994. Historical Northwest literary anthology.

Cantwell, Mary. "A Pilgrim's Progress." *New York Times Magazine,* April 26, 1992, 34-36, 40, 42. Profile of Annie Dillard.

Egan, Timothy. "Creating Perfect Sentences in an Imperfect Universe: In the Creative Process with Tom Robbins." *New York Times,* December 30, 1993, B1, 4. Interview with Robbins.

Ives, Rich, ed. *From Timberline to Tidepool: Contemporary Fiction from the Northwest.* Seattle: Owl Creek Press, 1986. Collection of contemporary northwest fiction.

————. *The Truth About the Territory: Contemporary Nonfiction from the Northwest.* Seattle: Owl Creek Press, 1987. Collection of contemporary northwest nonfiction.

O'Connell, Nicholas. *At the Field's End: Interviews with Twenty Pacific Northwest Writers.* Seattle: Madrona, 1987. Northwest author interviews.

Walkinshaw, Jean, producer. *To Write and Keep Kind.* Seattle: KCTS, 1992. Fifty-eight-minute documentary on Raymond Carver.

Michael Powell

Oregon

As the homing salmon swimming in that turbid water searched for swirls of Clackamas nectar, so I too loved the river of my childhood.

—Clyde Rice, *Nordi's Gift* (89-90)

"The fish are more than money," one tribal elder confides to Danny Kachiah, hero of Craig Lesley's *Winterkill* (1984; 29) and *River Song* (1989). It is 1957, and the U. S. Army Corps of Engineers is about to close the floodgates on The Dalles Dam, to drown the millennial Indian fishing grounds at Celilo Falls on the mighty "Oregon," the Columbia River—America's most powerful and the world's most dammed. "An' no white power company's got the right to swagger out here wavin' greenbacks in poor folks' faces!" frets Gus Orviston's mother in David James Duncan's *The River Why* (1983). "Nobody's got the right to wreck a way of life!" (137).

In the June 1953 issue of *Holiday* magazine, H. L. Davis wrote "Probably it is as well" to put an end to the Indians' "unsanitary" habitation at Celilo Falls, saying, "It can't be good for human beings to live as anachronisms" (115). Now, however, there is a powerful undercurrent in Oregon literature, an undammed narrative stream that roars over these falls. As Oregon naturalist Joseph Cone observes, "For longer than anyone knew, Celilo Falls had been a thriving gathering point for Indians, a place of abundance" (*A Common Fate* 143).

In Oregon, certainly, whose prevailing metaphor is wetness, there is no currency like that of a river. But the point Lesley's elder Celilo makes is essentially one of style. Danny now dedicates himself to preserving the too few precious traditions he has learned from his Nez Perce father, hoping to pass them on to his own less interested son. We are constantly reminded, by Lesley and other Oregon writers, of the importance of "right telling." In *The River Why,* a chapter titled "The River Writes," Duncan tempers the enormity of Celilo Falls' pending inundation when his hero meets a Warm Springs Indian, the wise Thomas Bigeater. "This is not forever," Bigeater gestures, preferring a more magnanimous view. "Dams break. Rivers never do" (136).

In "Appreciating Oregon" (*Legends from Camp,* 1992), Lawson Inada's poet asks us to imagine the difficulty of driving from San Francisco to Seattle if, instead of Oregon, there were only a gigantic "Bay of Oregon," whose bountiful shore must be skirted at great length (96). Notwithstanding its immense public grandeur, however — its vast tracts of forest, mountains, desert, and dunes; its much-journeyed glaciers, lakes, rivers, and ocean — Oregon seems to have blossomed in literature as a very private landscape, often revealing, as in Clyde Rice's Clackamas sentiment, the "nectar" of a severely tested childhood. For contemporary Oregon, the mythic salmon have come to symbolize not only the tragic drama of diminishing returns, but the recuperative vigor of far-traveled memory, masterfully "reeled in" through a narrative stream that leaps with life hoping to "spawn."

Historically, literature has ascribed to Oregon the ambivalence of being both romantic and remote. American romantics saw Oregon's unsung "ample geography" (Emerson's term ["The Poet," 1844]) as a facile image of distant grandeur, unknown and uncontested. As Max Westbrook notes in his preface to *A Literary History of the American West* (1987), "Oregon Territory loomed in the national psyche as the ultimate in newness" (xviii). But if, to Joaquin Miller, no other state could boast Oregon's "rush of waters, the misty tang of mold and somber wood" (*The Oregonian,* October 21, 1907, 8), to H. L. Davis, concluding his large color spread in *Holiday,* Oregon was little more than a "place where stories begin that end somewhere else" (121). (For a fuller examination of this divided affection, sampling from Malamud to Least Heat Moon, see Powell, "Somewhere Else.")

Written on the banks of the Snake River in 1961, Richard Brautigan's *Trout Fishing in America* (1967), though hardly the rod-and-reel treatise one might expect from its title, nevertheless belongs properly to a strong line of Northwest fishing narratives that boasts, in addition to Norman Maclean's *A River Runs through It* (1976), Duncan's *The River Why* and Ted Leeson's *The Habit of Rivers* (1994). Brautigan's is, of course, a satire: "USED TROUT STREAM FOR SALE. / MUST BE SEEN TO BE APPRECIATED" (104). But whereas Maclean's narrative reaches back to a time and a river whose fishing seemed untroubled by industrial encroachment, Duncan's and Leeson's, though fervent in their love of angling, are as merciless as Brautigan's in their vitriol against the damming of Oregon's precious waterways. Oregon, sneers Leeson, "is 'the Beaver State,' an unwitting reference to the eagerness of its public officials and private utilities to throw up a dam at the first sniff of moving water" (43).

Portland-born Clyde Rice is the octogenarian author of "autobiographical" *A Heaven in the Eye* (1984), its sequel, *Nordi's Gift* (1990), and a spur, *Night Freight* (1987). Focusing narratives on Oregon as a place with a beginning *and* an end, he and The Dalles-born Craig Lesley have both earned national acclaim. Rice, born in 1903, sends his namesake south to San Francisco as a young man, then brings him and his family back to Oregon on a long Joad-like trip during the Depression. Rice writes naturalistic recollection ("I welcomed adversity as a way of life" [*Nordi's Gift* 74]) with a youthful vigor and a memory that is as shocking in its detail as it is in its reach over time. The same power is nurtured by Lesley's pen, using in his first two novels a Native American point of view to fashion close-up recollections of Columbia River fishing tradition. "Take a good look," Danny Kachiah's too-mortal father tells him the day the floodgates close below Celilo Falls (*Winterkill* 30). In Lesley's third novel, *The Sky Fisherman* (1995), sixteen-year-old Culver Martin, the narrator, wishes to undrown his father from a "Lost River" in post-1957 Oregon, beside the spirited getaway town of "Gateway." The "Sky Fisherman," it turns out, is a transcendent constellation: "Indian legends," Culver says, "claim the stars are campfires at the centers of villages. Around these campfires storytellers gather" (304). But this particular casting seems almost comic, if not naturalistic, for the long line of deaths its young angler reels in over so short a time: "It was," he confesses, "a weird summer" (171).

In "After Celilo" (1991), Shoshone-Bannock writer Ed Edmo gives a firsthand account of his childhood displacement from Celilo Village. Like Duncan's Thomas Bigeater, Edmo is determined and succinct, the depth of his poetic still water more than evident in the selection that comprises *These Few Words of Mine* (1985). In "Celilo Blues," Edmo's poet points a finger, as Kesey's "Chief" Bromden had, at the government's drowning out the voice of the Indian. Edmo characterizes the U.S. agents as "deafened / ears that are paid / not to hear," so that, salt in the wound, "again / we drowned" (13). (Early in 1957 at the University of Oregon, telling his professor "it hasn't all happened yet" [7], Ken Kesey wrote a brief television drama called "Sunset at Celilo," whose proprietary cause would drive the narrator of *One Flew over the Cuckoo's Nest* five years later [University of Oregon Special Collections: Ax279, Box 15, Folder 4].)

Wade Curran, in Robin Cody's *Ricochet River* (1992), recalls, as Duncan's Gus Orviston does, a childhood field trip to see Celilo Falls. Watching the "Rickety wooden platforms" from which the Indians fish, he discovers how "The best of the salmon leapers moved quickly and got through," an idea reinforced by his dam-dynamiting Indian friend, Jesse Howl. Curran is encouraged by the salmon's homing instinct, "imprinting," and presses his own narrative return to "Celilo Falls for a view of the whole scheme, now defunct, of people-before-dams" (49). In his later travelogue, *Voyage of a Summer Sun* (1995), Cody returns to Celilo Village, "the hub of Northwest civilization for thousands of years," as he eloquently canoes "the legendary River Oregon, the river of large poetry, of coffee-table photo books, of raw, unfinished beauty" (245, 262). Perhaps the finest of these "photo books" is *Bridge of the Gods* (1980) by Chuck Williams, a Cascade Indian who tells us that "Evil spirits, sometimes in the form of monsters, hid at such places as Celilo Falls and the Great Cascades to eat canoeists who thought portaging unnecessary" (26)!

Molly Gloss' *The Jump-Off Creek* (1989) is set not far away in the Blue Mountains of 1890s northeastern Oregon, a "heel-sucking" place where there are three seasons, "Winter, Thaw, and August," and the only dams are on farms the fish can still reach (73, 125). The strength of this diary-interspersed novel is its unexceptional depiction of an exceptional woman. "I've never once gone anywhere alone but berry picking or fishing and that within a loud yell of a man," cowboying Lydia Sanderson is told by the first woman she meets at her new "jumping-off" point, "so I daresay I wouldn't be bored with hearing how your life has been different from that" (78).

Ken Kesey has returned to the novel with *Sailor Song* (1992) and, with

Ken Babbs, *Last Go Round* (1994), as well as *Caverns* (1990), the multi-authored product of a writing class he taught at the University of Oregon in 1987 and 1988. *Sailor Song* is a mock epic on the last comic edge of ecological survival during the "near future." The setting is Alaska, near waters whose "shining stars" are the Pacific salmon; but the novel is fragrant with images of Kesey's home state, the sun setting "the way it often does at the end of the dreariest Oregon days, to tantalize you" (529, 222).

Last Go Round is the hospital bedside recollection of a nonagenarian "buckaroo" from the very first Pendleton Round Up held in 1911. The original competitors, who would become collaborators, were a black, an Indian, and a white, the official winner, who now sits in the Pendleton hospital he once swore he would never return to. He delivers his second-person monologue, his ultimate "go round," to an unspeaking youngster from Watts, another ambiguous "winner," who may or may not want to regain consciousness of the long-standing racial quagmire this novel portrays in Oregon.

Richard Brautigan's *Revenge of the Lawn: Stories, 1962-1970* (1971) and *The Hawkline Monster: A Gothic Western* (1974) both drew significantly on Oregon settings. But his best novel, the last published before his death in 1984, is the cinematographic *So the Wind Won't Blow It All Away* (1982), a wet, rainy, and forlorn projection of its hero's orphan-like childhood "at the head of a wagon train of baby buggies crossing the Great Plains going West in the pioneer days to homestead Oregon" (12).

John Haislip (*Not Every Year*, 1971) celebrates his home on the Oregon coast in *Seal Rock* (1986), where he finds Russians out fishing on "*my* horizon." "Then why take my fish," he asks, "out of a bay that's been / winding down for years?" (24-25). And in *Ruined Cities* (1987), Portland poet Vern Rutsala asserts artistic possession of a perfectible landscape. "We invented these trees and mountains," he writes in "Wilderness." "With our pens we drew / the creeks and nudged bear and deer from deep shadows. / None of this was here before we came" (54).

William Stafford, long popularly regarded as Oregon's poet laureate, died in August of 1993. In "Report from an Unappointed Committee," Stafford contrasts nature with "a sculptor named Ugly...making / a strange opposite that is not beauty," then enumerates indifferent cosmic energies he sees at work. "In the backcountry a random raindrop / has broken a dam," he confides. "And a new river is out feeling for a valley / somewhere under our world" (*An Oregon Message*, 1987, 135). *Oregon English Journal* dedicated the whole of its Spring 1994 issue to Stafford, gathering works of his own, a bibliography, and tributes by many who knew him, including "My Father's Place" by his son, Kim R. Stafford, who continues to write rich evocations of Oregon.

Native Americanist Jarold Ramsey pointed in 1977 to what he saw as "a certain natural wholeness of parts," an implicit sense of "home," that local peoples have long felt for the lay of the land that is Oregon (*Coyote Was Going There* xx). Ramsey's *Reading the Fire* (1983) enlarges that notion of ancient "Oregon" narrative, of its place in the foreground to "American Literature" (194). In *Don Coyote* (1986), Dayton O. Hyde (*Yamsi*, 1971) nurses his "solitary inclination" and his coyotes on a ranch east of Crater Lake, where he envisions "private land coming to the fore as the wildlife refuges of the future" (191). In *Hole in the Sky* (1992), an expansive William Kittredge remembers growing up nearby: "in the one-room Adel schoolhouse, I used to write Warner Valley, Lake County, Oregon, USA, World, Universe — wondering where it ended" (29). Oceanward, in *The Klamath Knot* (1983), David Rains Wallace probes the convoluted geology, the "paradoxical" landscape, of Oregon's southwest corner. Just to the north, Shannon Applegate (*Skookum*, 1988) dramatizes the arrival of her prominent pioneer family through the Willamette Valley, including the loss overboard of several during their descent of the Columbia rapids in 1843. Completing a circuit of her own in *Stepping Westward* (1991), Portlander Sallie Tisdale mocks "Mr. Columbia River's" glib commercial justification of the dams. "Celilo Falls, once a layered white cascade of foam and salmon, is drowned today," she laments. "It is a quick tourist hop off the road, a mild ache of wishing in the sepia photographs and neat scripted explanation" (7).

But Columbia River Indians, perched on their precarious scaffoldings over Celilo Falls, have returned to fish in the steady current of recent Oregon writing. Many more of us, perhaps, than would otherwise ever have traveled there are now reading vivid reconstructions of Celilo fishing scenes ("they smoked their pipes upside down," recalls Danny Kachiah, "to keep the tobacco dry" [*River Song* 43]). Cruising high above the Columbia Gorge in an "iron bird," Ed Edmo's poet puts his "few words" to unequivocal purpose: "we speak in whispers / we plan assault / on the invaders," he writes, looking down to where his forebears had once guided "cavalry / in circles / of doom." A stewardess offers him another cup of coffee. I agree, he says, closing the last poem of *These Few Words of Mine*, and "nodding pick up / my weapon / my pen" — to etch, we must hope, a salmon-rich right telling that will yield a real return (24).

Selected Bibliography

Brautigan, Richard. *So the Wind Won't Blow It All Away*. New York: Delacorte Press, 1982.

Cody, Robin. *Ricochet River*. New York: Knopf, 1992.

Cone, Joseph. *A Common Fate: Endangered Salmon and the People of the Pacific Northwest*. New York: Henry Holt, 1995.

———. *Voyage of a Summer Sun: Canoeing the Columbia River*. New York: Knopf, 1995.

Davis, H. L. "Oregon." *Holiday*, 13 (June 1953): 34-37, 108, 110, 112-113, 115-118, 120-121.

Duncan, David James. *The River Why*. San Francisco: Sierra Club Books, 1983.

Edmo, Ed. "After Celilo." In *Talking Leaves: Contemporary Native American Short Stories*. Craig Lesley, ed. New York: Dell, 1991. Pp. 70-73.

———. *These Few Words of Mine*. Marvin, South Dakota: Blue Cloud Quarterly Press, 1985.

Gloss, Molly. *The Jump-Off Creek*. Boston: Houghton Mifflin, 1989.

Inada, Lawson Fusao. *Legends from Camp: Poems*. Minneapolis: Coffee House Press, 1992.

Kesey, Ken. *Sailor Song*. New York: Viking, 1992.

Kesey, Ken and Ken Babbs. *Last Go Round*. New York: Viking, 1994.

Kittredge, William. *Hole in the Sky: A Memoir*. New York: Knopf, 1992.

Leeson, Ted. *The Habit of Rivers; Reflections on Trout Streams and Fly Fishing*. New York: Lyons and Burford, 1994.

Lesley, Craig. "The Catch." In *The Interior Country: Stories of the Modern West*. Alexander Blackburn, ed. Athens, Ohio: Swallow Press/Ohio University Press, 1987. Pp. 49-59.

———. *River Song*. Boston: Houghton Mifflin, 1989.

———. *The Sky Fisherman*. Boston: Houghton Mifflin, 1995.

———. *Winterkill*. Boston: Houghton Mifflin, 1984.

Powell, Michael. "Somewhere Else: Ambivalent Images of Oregon in American Postwar Narrative." *The Pacific Northwest Forum*, 3 (Fall 1990): 54-61.

Rice, Clyde. *A Heaven in the Eye*. Portland: Breitenbush Books, 1984.

———. "Leaving the Fold: A Boyhood in Oregon." In *Growing Up Western*. Clarus Backes, ed. New York: Knopf, 1989. Pp. 125-152.

———. *Night Freight*. Portland: Breitenbush Books, 1987.

———. *Nordi's Gift*. Portland: Breitenbush Books, 1990.

Stafford, William. *An Oregon Message*. New York: Harper & Row, 1987.

Wallace, David Rains. *The Klamath Knot: Explorations of Myth and Evolution*. San Francisco: Sierra Club Books, 1983.

Williams, Chuck. *Bridge of the Gods, Mountains of Fire; A Return to the Columbia Gorge*. New York: Friends of the Earth, 1980.

Ann Ronald

Nevada

W hen thinking of Nevada literature, most readers recall *The Ox-Bow Incident* (1940) and Walter Van Tilburg Clark. Certainly Clark can be called the touchstone by which western Nevada literature currently is measured, but more and more writers now make their homes in the Silver State, now write about its spaces, now boast talent and craftsmanship and artistic accomplishment. A stroll through the new Nevada Writers Hall of Fame in the Library of the University of Nevada, Reno, introduces the range of recent Nevada literary achievements.

If Walter Van Tilburg Clark is the patriarch of Nevada letters, Robert Laxalt is the man who inherited the master's mantle. Next to Clark, Laxalt's reputation looms largest; indeed, Clark and Laxalt were the first two inductees in the Nevada Writers Hall of Fame in 1991. Author of twelve books, Bob Laxalt is best known for his depictions of Basque immigrants and their families. Beginning with *Sweet Promised Land* (1957), a nostalgic memoir of his sheepherder father, and *A Man in the Wheatfield* (1964), selected by the American Library Association as one of six distinguished novels published that year (an honor shared with Saul Bellow and Ernest Hemingway), Laxalt draws a portrait of rural Nevada and of those who settled there:

> These were the men of leather and bronze who had been rich as barons one day and broke and working for wages the next, who had

ridden big and powerful horses, and who had met in the lonely desert and talked a while, hunkering over a sagebrush fire and a blackened coffeepot, and, even though they had battled with life, they had learned to accept it, because they had learned first to bow their heads to the winter blizzards and the desert sun. And my father was one of them. (*Sweet Promised Land* 3)

Laxalt's prose, as sparse as the landscape and as angular as his characters' lives, well captures the high desert terrain described in a book he wrote in 1977 for the Norton States and Nation Series, *Nevada: A Bicentennial History*. His recent trilogy — *The Basque Hotel* (1989), *Child of the Holy Ghost* (1992), and *The Governor's Mansion* (1994) — further dramatizes the state's complexities and fictionalizes more of the Laxalt family history. The three novels emphasize the stoicism of hard-working Basque immigrants, the struggles of first-generation sons as they both embrace and distance themselves from their heritage, and the difficult successes of those young men after they reach maturity.

Two more longtime Nevada residents — and two more relatively unknown authors — joined the university library's Writers Hall of Fame the year after Robert Laxalt's induction. Joanne de Longchamps, a poet and artist who moved to the state after her marriage in 1941, published her first book, *And Ever Venus*, in 1944. During the next four decades, while she studied off and on with Walter Clark, six more collections appeared and individual poems found their way into such places as *Prairie Schooner*, *The New York Times*, and *American Scholar*. The best of her often uneven work has been revived in a recent anthology, *Torn by Light* (1993), selected and edited by Shaun T. Griffin.

Most critics agree that a slender 1975 volume, *The Schoolhouse Poems*, contains her finest pieces. Not only do the poems reveal a mastery of her craft, but the subject matter shows her ability to blend the personal with the natural world, her deepening sensitivity to her surroundings, her struggles with the tragedies of her own life. One poem, "Late Letter to Walter Clark," marks de Longchamps' respect for a mentor and friend, but also exposes her fascination with death and the grave.

> Those who met in a snowhill
> for the opening and closing
> of cold earth given you,
> spoke of deep grayness — then

of stasis mercifully broken;
the sun rayed out in a skyspace,
catching a sudden spiral
and wheeling wings granted
the healing movement of birds. (*Torn by Light* 101)

Because the land is so bare, de Longchamps once remarked of her adopted state, "You learn to live with the absolute elements." Through her poetry, she sought to reconcile such barren elements with a life beyond despair.

A native Nevada author, Sessions S. "Buck" Wheeler, joined the Writers Hall of Fame at the same time Joanne de Longchamps was honored posthumously. In contrast with the often unhappy poet, Wheeler felt very much at home in the desert landscape and wrote several books that attempt to define what makes Nevada geographically unique. A far more eclectic group next entered the Hall. Since moving to Reno in 1956, Virginia Coffman has penned more than forty historical thrillers and countless other romantic paperbacks published under a variety of pseudonyms. Hart Wegner, in contrast, has published short stories in serious literary journals on both sides of the Atlantic; a 1988 collection, *Houses of Ivory*, received widespread critical acclaim. Charleton Laird, an English professor whose texts once were synonymous with freshman English and also the author of two westerns set in the nineteenth century, was honored, too. Wilbur Shepperson, a University of Nevada, Reno, historian who wrote a number of scholarly books, was inducted the following year.

After that, the Writers Hall of Fame committee turned back to poetry. First they chose A. Wilber Stevens, founding editor of *Interim*, author of *The World Is Going to End Up in Burma* (1988), of *From the Still Empty Grave* (1995), and of numerous poems published in journals like *Poetry Northwest* and *The Literary Review*. The committee chose another southern Nevada poet the following year. Stephen Shu-Ning Liu, born in China near the Yangtze River, was the first Nevada writer to receive a National Endowment for the Arts Fellowship in Creative Writing. Next the committee honored Kirk Robertson, author of *Driving to Vegas* (1989) and *Just Past Labor Day* (1996) and editor of the rural Duck Down Press. This three-year recognition of Nevada poetic achievements well demonstrates the vibrancy of the 1990s Nevada poetry community. A 1991 anthology of Nevada poets, edited by Shaun T. Griffin, showcases that energy. *Desert Wood*'s two hundred and fifty pages reveal the artistic talents of forty-nine different writers. While serious poets like Gary Short, Gailmarie Pahmeier, and William Wilborn form the back-bone of Griffin's collection, non-Nevadans are probably more aware of the connections between Nevada and cowboy poetry. The best verses from the Cowboy Poetry Gathering held in Elko every January are avail-able in Hal Cannon's anthologies.

When making his editorial decisions for *Desert Wood*, Griffin con-fronted the dilemma faced by those who select authors for inclusion in the Nevada Writers Hall of Fame. What, exactly, is a Nevada writer? Obviously Bob Laxalt is a Nevada writer; so, too, is Joanne de Longchamps. But Stephen Liu? Virginia Coffman? How to compare Reno's Emma Sepulveda-Pulvirenti, a bilingual Spanish poet born in Argentina, with nila northSun, a Shoshone Chippewa born in Schurz, Nevada? How to judge novelists like Bernard Schopen or Catherine Dain—two talented writers whose formula fiction is firmly grounded in northern Nevada terrain—with David Eddings, a Carson City resident whose best-selling science-fiction novels take place in worlds quite for-eign to Nevada soil? And how to correctly categorize Hunter Thompson's 1971 aberration, *Fear and Loathing in Las Vegas* or John Gregory Dunne's *Vegas: A Memoir of a Dark Season* (1974)? Such ques-tions must puzzle anyone who attempts to break the boundaries of regional writing.

Over the years, the Nevada Writers Hall of Fame selection commit-tee has answered these questions by embracing anyone with a Nevada connection. Thus their awards to Liu and Coffman; thus a list of nomi-nees that includes not only literary figures but also scholars, journalists, and even cowboy poets. Perhaps such all-encompassing enthusiasm for any sort of Nevada writing indicates the very youthfulness of Nevada lit-erary activity. With a history little more than a century old and with few more than a million residents today, the Silver State has yet to produce a long list of major writers. On the other hand, more and more Nevada authors are publishing more and more polished literary works.

Frank Bergon's *Shoshone Mike* (1987) recounts vigilante actions that match *The Ox-Bow Incident* in cowardice and complexity. Monique Urza's *Deep Blue Memory* (1993) uncovers another Laxalt layer of Nevada's Basque heritage. Teresa Jordan, now an Elko resident who recalls a Wyoming heritage in *Riding the White Horse Home* (1993), won a recent fellowship in creative writing awarded by the Nevada State

Council on the Arts. The list continues. Ann Herbert Scott's *Someday Rider* (1989) was a runner-up for the children's award from the National Cowboy Hall of Fame in 1989. Gary Short's *Flying Over Sonny Liston* won the 1996 Western States Book Award for Poetry. Douglas Unger, currently teaching at UNLV, published an outstanding midwestern novel, *Leaving the Land*, in 1984. *Kinsella's Man* (1994), written by Californian Richard Stookey but set in eastern Nevada, is an equally sensitive fictional assessment of change. Meanwhile, essayists Stephen Trimble and Ann Ronald draw from the texture of the landscape to portray what makes the high desert unique. A collection of short stories by David Kranes, *Low Tide in the Desert* (1996), unearths another literary setting.

Literary activity thrives in Nevada today, in part because of the proactive publishing program of the University of Nevada Press. But Nevada is no different from the rest of the West, where regional writing is fast becoming national literature. While the 1987 *A Literary History of the American West* assessed the contributions of novelist Walter Van Tilburg Clark, it mentioned no other Nevada writers. This update not only corrects the notion that no one else writes in the Silver State but posits that before long the Nevada Writers Hall of Fame will expand to a second wall in the university library. The names of the winners will be more familiar, too.

Selected Bibliography

Bergon, Frank. *Shoshone Mike.* New York: Viking, 1987.

———. *The Temptations of St. Ed and Brother S.* Reno: University of Nevada Press, 1993.

———. *Wild Game.* Reno: University of Nevada Press, 1995.

Cannon, Hal, ed. *Cowboy Poetry: A Gathering.* Salt Lake City: G. M. Smith, 1985.

———. *New Cowboy Poetry: A Contemporary Gathering.* Layton, Utah: Peregrine Smith Books, 1990.

de Longchamps, Joanne. *Torn by Light: Selected Poems.* Shaun T. Griffin, ed. Reno: University of Nevada Press, 1993.

Dunne, John Gregory. *Vegas: A Memoir of a Dark Season.* New York: Random House, 1974.

Fox, William L. *Geograph.* Reno: Rainshadow Edition, 1994.

Fox, William L., ed. *Tumblewords: Writers Reading the West.* Reno: University of Nevada Press, 1995.

Griffin, Shaun T,. ed. *Desert Wood.* Reno: University of Nevada Press, 1991.

Jordan, Teresa. *Riding the White Horse Home.* New York: Pantheon Books, 1993.

Kranes, David. *Keno Runner: A Dark Romance.* Reno: University of Nevada Press, 1995.

———. *Low Tide in the Desert.* Reno: University of Nevada Press, 1996.

Laxalt, Robert. *The Basque Hotel.* Reno: University of Nevada Press, 1989.

————. *Child of the Holy Ghost*. Reno: University of Nevada Press, 1992.

————. *The Governor's Mansion*. Reno: University of Nevada Press, 1994.

————. *A Man in the Wheatfield*. New York: Harper & Row, 1964.

————. *Nevada: A Bicentennial History*. New York: Norton, 1977.

————. *Sweet Promised Land*. New York: Harper, 1957.

Liu, Stephen Shu-ning. *Dream Journeys to China*. Beijing: New World Press, 1982.

Pahmeier, Gailmarie. *With Respect for Distance*. Reno: Rainshadow Editions, 1992.

Robertson, Kirk. *Just Past Labor Day: Selected and New Poems, 1969-1996*. Reno: University of Nevada Press, 1996.

Ronald, Ann. *Earthtones: A Nevada Album*. Photographs by Stephen Trimble. Reno: University of Nevada Press, 1995.

Scott, Ann Herbert. *Someday Rider*. New York: Clarion Books, 1989.

Short, Gary. *Flying Over Sonny Liston*. Reno: University of Nevada Press, 1996.

Stevens, A. Wilbur. *From the Still Empty Grave*. Reno: University of Nevada Press, 1995.

Stookey, Richard. *Kinsella's Man*. Reno: University of Nevada Press, 1994.

Thompson, Hunter. *Fear and Loathing in Las Vegas*. New York: Random House, 1971.

Trimble, Stephen. *The Sagebrush Ocean*. Reno: University of Nevada Press, 1989.

Tronnes, Mike, ed. *Literary Las Vegas*. New York: Henry Holt, 1995.

Unger, Douglas. *Leaving the Land*. New York: Harper & Row, 1984.

Urza, Monique. *The Deep Blue Memory*. Reno: University of Nevada Press, 1993.

Wegner, Hart. *Houses of Ivory*. New York: Soho, 1988.

Wheeler, Sessions S. *Paiute*. Reno: University of Nevada Press, 1986.

Wilborn, William. *Rooms/Poems*. Omaha, Nebraska: Cummington Press, 1991.

Eric Heyne

Alaska

Alaska is an American colony, and the literature of Alaska has reflected that colonization. The most famous "Alaskan" writers either visited briefly (Jack London traveled down the Yukon River en route from the Klondike) or were never actually in Alaska (Robert Service lived in and wrote about Canada). The list of contemporary outsiders who have mined Alaska for setting and characters includes Norman Mailer (*Why Are We in Vietnam?* 1967), John McPhee (*Coming into the Country*, 1977), Joe McGinniss (*Going to Extremes*, 1980), John Hawkes (*Adventures in the Alaskan Skin Trade*, 1985), Martin Cruz Smith (*Polar Star*, 1989), Barry Lopez (*Arctic Dreams*, 1986), Barbara Quick (*Northern Edge*, 1990), Ken Kesey (*Sailor Song*, 1992), and James Michener (*Alaska*, 1988). Granted, some of these writers put in their time in the state and produced books with genuine insight into Alaska. Lopez, for instance, is a frequent visitor and collaborator with Alaskan artists. McPhee's book is the best single introduction to Alaska. Nevertheless, Alaskans feel that they have been misrepresented as often as fairly portrayed and that their beauties of landscape and quirks of character have been carted south like timber or gold.

As long as the state's population was so small (less than half a million people) and transient, the odds were against any body of significant writing arising within Alaska. Since the Alaska pipeline's completion the population has stabilized somewhat, however, and more than fifteen years of oil money have helped build writing programs in Fairbanks and

Anchorage (many of the writers mentioned in this essay either taught in or graduated from those programs), and have funded a network of support for Native artists so that the indigenous population (which was always relatively stable) could begin publishing its writers. Today it is possible to talk about a body of literature that is genuinely *of* Alaska, not just about it.

The best-known Alaskan poet, John Haines, is discussed separately in this section. John Morgan is a meditative poet who walks, bicycles, and just plain sits his way through the long day that is an Alaskan year, pondering history, suffering, love of wife and child and stranger. His lyrics of thirty or forty lines build slowly, often beginning from landscape and ending deep in the human heart. Thirty-five years in Alaska have given Tom Sexton's poetry range and ease, a powerful feeling of being at home, complicated by an equally profound sense of loss and the passage of time. Peggy Shumaker has a gift for imagining the feelings of others, including people from many cultures, and an equal talent for honest self-revelation. Her deeply sensual poetry discloses how much the heart lives on the skin and the tongue, in the eyes and ears, out on the edge. From his home in Unalaska, Jerah Chadwick writes with enormous sympathy and vision about the history and culture of the Aleutians. Sheila Nickerson has published fiction and nonfiction as well as several books of poetry; many of her poems are about the ways we weave our civilized lives against a wild backdrop. Ann Fox Chandonnet's poetry moves quietly back and forth between white and Native experience, revealing what is universally human. Nora Marks Dauenhauer writes plays, stories and poems incorporating Tlingit language and beliefs. She has collaborated with her husband, Richard Dauenhauer, also a poet, on many works of oral history, bilingual education, and linguistics. Tlingit history and art also inform the work of Robert Davis, whose poems convey the tragedy of white conquest within a broad historical context that transcends self-pity. Dozens of Inupiat, Yupik, Aleut, Athabaskan, Tlingit, Haida, and Tsimshian poets are in print, their work often accompanying other expressions of art such as dance, carving, weaving, fiddling, and painting, in a broad movement giving voice to the varieties of Alaska Native experience. The collection *Raven Tells Stories* (1991), edited by Joseph Bruchac and James Ruppert, includes many of the best of these newly heard voices.

Popular or genre literature is well represented by Alaskan writers. The state's enormously varied terrain, from coastal fishing villages to interior mountain ranges and modern western cityscapes, and its strong, living Native American cultures provide compelling backgrounds for science fiction, fantasy, detective novels, and children's fiction. Michael Armstrong, David Marusek, George Guthridge, and Terry Boren are among the state's best science-fiction writers, Elizabeth Scarborough is internationally known for both science fiction and fantasy, and Elyse Guttenberg has published fantasy and historical novels with accurate and beautiful northern settings. Dana Stabenow recently published the fifth of her Kate Shugak detective novels, and Sue Henry's *Murder on the Iditarod Trail* was published in 1991. Richard Parry's *Ice Warrior* (1991) is an espionage tech-thriller a la Tom Clancy. Among Alaskan children's writers the best known is Nancy White Carlstrom, but there are many others working with Alaskan animals and Native traditions and themes.

Mainstream fiction by Alaskans is rarer than poetry or genre fiction. Perhaps this is because of competition from celebrity outsiders (Mailer, Hawkes, et al.), or because the exotic aspects of setting always threaten to overwhelm character and voice. Velma Wallis' *Two Old Women* (1993), a small book retelling an Athabascan legend, became a surprise best-seller. Although it stirred some controversy among those who felt Wallis made use of a story that was community property and showed Athabascan culture in a negative light, the book has been generally well received among Alaskans and outsiders alike. It will be interesting to see how her 1996 *Bird Girl and the Man Who Followed the Sun* is received. Nancy Lord's two collections of stories are mostly about women who struggle to balance the beauty, isolation, and danger of life on "the last frontier." Jean Anderson is a versatile and surprising writer who includes within one story collection a wide range of experiences, styles, and tones.

Much of the best contemporary Alaskan writing is creative nonfiction, including a blend of personal experience and nature writing. Richard Nelson's *The Island Within* (1989) may be the best book ever written about Alaska. Nelson is an anthropologist now writing full-time from his home in Sitka. Infused with a spirituality learned from Inupiat and Athabascan teachers, and deeply informed by his own intimacy with the natural world, Nelson's writing rivals that of William Least Heat Moon, Barry Lopez, and Annie Dillard. Among the best up-and-coming writers of Alaskan nonfiction are Natalie Kusz, John Hildebrand, Nick Jans, Sherry Simpson, and Carolyn Kremers.

Selected Bibliography

Anderson, Jean. *In Extremis and Other Alaskan Stories*. Kaneohe, Hawaii: Plover Press, 1989.

Armstrong, Michael. *Agviq: The Whale*. New York: Warner Books, 1990.

Bruchac, Joseph and James Ruppert, eds. *Raven Tells Stories: An Anthology of Alaskan Native Writing*. Greenfield Center, New York: Greenfield Review Press, 1991.

Carlstrom, Nancy White. *Northern Lullaby*. New York: Philomel Books, 1992.

Chadwick, Jerah. *Absence Wild: Aleutian Poems*. Seattle: Jugum Press, 1984.

Chandonnet, Ann Fox. *Canoeing in the Rain: Poems for My Aleut-Athabascan Son*. Forest Grove, Oregon: Mr. Cogito Press, 1990.

Dauenhauer, Nora Marks. *The Droning Shaman: Poems*. Haines, Alaska: Black Current Press, 1988.

Dauenhauer, Richard. *Frames of Reference: Poems*. Haines, Alaska: Black Current Press, 1987.

Davis, Robert. *Soul Catcher*. Sitka, Alaska: Raven's Bones Press, 1986.

Gutheridge, George, and Janet Berliner. *Child of the Light*. Clarkston, Georgia: White Wolf Publishing, 1995.

Guttenberg, Elyse. *Summer Light*. New York: HarperCollins, 1995.

Henry, Sue. *Murder on the Iditarod Trail*. New York: Atlantic Monthly Press, 1991.

Heyne, Eric and Anne Tayler, eds. Special literary issue, *The Northern Review*, 10 (Summer 1993).

Hildebrand, John. *Reading the River: A Voyage Down the Yukon*. Boston: Houghton Mifflin, 1988.

Jans, Nick. *The Last Light Breaking: Living Among Alaska's Inupiat Eskimos*. Anchorage: Alaska Northwest Books, 1993.

Kremers, Carolyn. *Place of the Pretend People*. Anchorage: Alaska Northwest Books, 1996.

Kusz, Natalie. *Road Song: A Memoir*. New York: Farrar, Straus & Giroux, 1990.

Lord, Nancy. *Survival: Stories*. Minneapolis: Coffee House Press, 1991.

Mergler, Wayne, ed. *The Last New Land: Stories of Alaska Past and Present*. Anchorage: Alaska Northwest Books, 1996.

Morgan, John. *Walking Past Midnight*. Tuscaloosa: University of Alabama Press, 1989.

Murray, John, ed. *A Republic of Rivers: Three Centuries of Nature Writing from Alaska and the Yukon*. New York: Oxford University Press, 1990.

Nelson, Richard. *The Island Within*. San Francisco: North Point Press, 1989.

Nickerson, Sheila. *On Why the Quiltmaker Became a Dragon*. Fairbanks, Alaska: Vanessapress, 1985.

Parry, Richard. *Ice Warrior*. New York: Pocket Books, 1991.

Scarborough, Elizabeth. *The Goldcamp Vampire*. New York: Bantam, 1987.

Sexton, Tom. *The Bend Toward Asia*. Anchorage: Salmon Run Press, 1993.

Shumaker, Peggy. *Wings Moist from the Other World*. Pittsburgh: University of Pittsburgh Press, 1994.

Simpson, Sherry. *Alaska's Ocean Highways*. Fairbanks: Epicenter Press, 1995.

Stabenow, Dana. *Play With Fire*. New York: Berkley, 1995.

Wallis, Velma. *Two Old Women: An Alaska Legend of Betrayal, Courage, and Survival*. Fairbanks: Epicenter Press, 1993.

Seri I. Luangphinith and Russell H. Shitabata

Hawaii

Hawaii has been the site of many racial and cultural intersections; thus, its literary traditions reflect heterogeneity. Until the arrival of the missionaries in 1820, Hawaii's literary tradition consisted of the *mele* ("song"), the *oli* ("chant"), and the *hula* ("dance"). The combination of the three symbolized for Native Hawaiians the narrative links between gods and men, teachers and students, past generations and present descendants.

The establishment of the Protestant church in Hawaii, however, prompted the abandonment of the *ai kapu*, or ancient legal system, and the condemnation of pagan ways, traditional song and dance as well. By 1900, Hawaiian "antiquities" became a subject for study by individuals concerned with the lack of Native interest in Hawaiian folklore due to earlier Christian mandates. Scholars such as Charles Reed, Samuel Castle, and Sanford B. Dole (also plantation owners) documented the evolution of the Hawaiian people. In part, this project was fueled by the sentiment that only educated minds outside the native culture could appreciate the true value of Hawaiian lore.

While Native Hawaiian narratives became relegated to the annals of the Hawaiian Historical Society and the Bishop Museum, the Islands were not devoid of literary craft. In fact, colonization of the Pacific prompted the fascination of many mainland writers with the lands of savage beauty and idyllic innocence. James A. Michener locates in the South Pacific a symbolic landscape where a "vast and heaving waste of

256

water imprisons the imagination of anyone who has traveled widely upon it" (*The Spell of the Pacific* vii). Anthologies such as A. Grove Day and Carl Stroven's *A Hawaiian Reader* (1959) and *The Spell of Hawaii* (1968), and W. Storrs Lee's *Hawaii: A Literary Chronicle* (1967) offer a range of writers who fell under the exotic, hypnotic allure of Hawaii, among them Robert Louis Stevenson, Jack London, Mark Twain, C. W. Stoddard, and Herman Melville.

The ancient arts were never completely silenced, however, despite the efforts of clergymen and misguided anthropologists. During King David Kalakaua's reign (1874-1891), Native Hawaiian arts were revived under a cultural renaissance that prompted the resurgence of traditional Hawaiian crafts and sciences. This heightening of cultural awareness survives among Native Hawaiians, many of whom look to the old ways for material and inspiration. Joseph P. Balaz's Native Hawaiian anthology, *Ho'omanoa* (1989), looks at a number of artists who utilize a genre reminiscent of traditional Hawaiian oral narratives. Mahealani Ing writes:

> Blood and sinew
> Sensate with the drumming of pahu
> Clash of ka la'au....
> Voices rise out of shadows
> And intone an ancient cadence:
>> E Laka e
>> Pupu weuweu
>> E Laka e
>> 'Ano'i Aloha e....
> (16)

By blending Hawaiian and English, traditional chant and western poetry, Ing produces a discourse between two contentious cultures. Despite the anger that arises from the recognition that this "hula show" is the "resort manager's grand idea / Of Christmas in Hawai'i" (15) the chant also speaks of "aloha," which can simultaneously mean salutations, love, kindness, grace, and charity. Among other Hawaiians included in *Ho'omanoa* are Dana Naone Hall, Joseph P. Balaz, and Michael McPherson.

In addition, writers such as John Dominis Holt and Haunani-Kay Trask have embraced canonized forms such as the short story, the novel, political tracts, and post-colonial poetics as means of cultural expression and grievance. Holt's work, which includes *Hanai: A Poem for Queen Liliuokalani* (1986) and *Waimea Summer* (1976), addresses the problem of growing up *hapa-haole* (half-Caucasian) in the Islands, of finding a stable identity in a post-contact, multi-ethnic Hawaii. In *Hanai*, Holt witnesses the overthrow of Queen Liliuokalani and hears his white predecessors speaking of half-breeds. The poet must confront his dual heritage, which makes him colonizer and colonized at the same time: he can neither bear the white man's burden nor adopt the role of the exploited Hawaiian. Instead, the poet envisions the *makaainana*, which includes both the *ulu* grower (Hawaiian) and the stevedore (Anglo-American), who must join forces if they are to survive and depose the colonization brought about by big business.

Haunani-Kay Trask's newest title, *Light in the Crevice Never Seen* (1994), is hailed as the first Native Hawaiian work published on the mainland. Her poetry is a collection of mythological references, vivid imagery and powerful cries of remonstration aimed at an audience unaware of the trials of the indigenous population. She writes of: "Trying to find you / Between Japanese / Tourists and haole honeymooners / Dragging your skirts / And dying lei / Like silent chains" (54). For Trask, ignorance fuels participation in industries like tourism, which not only enslaves the exoticized culture, but innocent vacationers as well. She goes on to declare that the mainstream way of viewing "aloha," of trying to be "Hawaiian at heart," is nothing short of cultural theft and degradation based upon maintaining foreign supremacy.

Colonization and development also included other ethnic experiences. By the early 1900s, many Japanese, Chinese, Filipino, Portuguese, and Korean nationals were brought to Hawaii as plantation laborers. Conflicts between the values of first-generation immigrants and their children have proven to be fertile literary ground. Milton Murayama's *All I Asking for Is My Body* (1975), for example, presents a coming-of-age story set on a Hawaiian sugarcane plantation of the 1930s and the struggles between familial obligations and individual desires.

While many of Eric Chock's poems in *Last Days Here* (1990) deal with the result of Hawaii's development ("Poem for George Helm: Aloha Week 1980" and "Home Free," for instance), others reflect on the painful route through plantation life. In "Pulling Weeds," the speaker considers how the childhood chore of weeding is part of his heritage, a lesson from the canefields that his father has passed down. By contrast,

"Manoa Cemetery" is a remembrance for the speaker's late grandfather who was born in Hanalei, and "Hanapepe Bon Dance" questions what has been lost between the generations since the red dirt of plantation life was left behind.

Current literature exploring Hawaii's plantation history can be read as elegiac, calling into the present a life that is no longer there, but the resonance of which nonetheless lingers. Garrett Kaoru Hongo's poems from *Yellow Light* (1982) certainly bear out such a reading. "Roots" and "C & H Sugar Strike" reflect first-generation laborers and their failure to find representation in the records of legitimate history, while "Kubota" offers a vignette of a plantation life vital in its lyricism, but tragic in its growing absence from memory.

In a different vein of writing, Lois-Ann Yamanaka's *Saturday Night at the Pahala Theater* (1993) explores the definition of feminine body and identity in the interstices of local Hawaiian culture. In Yamanaka's poetic storytelling, gendered boundaries inscribe themselves on the female narrator physically and psychologically. For a young woman coming of age, the broad mix of cultures prescribes a problematic definition of femininity and sexuality, rather than a diverse and open-ended one. A similar poetic effort can be found in *Picture Bride* (1983), by Korean poet Cathy Song. Her poem, "Youngest Daughter," considers how female bodies are marked by the crossings of plantation life and a life of cultural responsibility. In "Wailua," Song also articulates ways in which individuals can positively reclaim past experiences through acts of private tenderness.

Cultural negotiations can be employed as a loose frame for considering Hawaii's literature. Even the writing of this essay has proven to be a negotiation of success and failure: success in terms of making Hawaii's literary history more available for scholarly debate, and failure through limiting the range of that history because of a necessarily selective presentation.

Selected Bibliography

Primary Sources

Balaz, Joseph P., ed. *Ho'omanoa: An Anthology of Contemporary Hawaiian Literature.* Honolulu: Ku Pa'a, 1989.

Beckwith, Martha W., ed. and trans. *The Kumulipo: A Hawaiian Creation Chant.* Chicago: University of Chicago Press, 1951.

Carroll, Dennis, ed. *Kumu Kahua Plays*. Honolulu: University of Hawaii Press, 1983.

Chock, Eric. *Last Days Here*. Honolulu: Bamboo Ridge Press, 1990.

Chock, Eric and Darrell H. Y. Lum, eds. *Pake: Writings by Chinese in Hawaii*. Honolulu: Bamboo Ridge Press, 1989.

Day, A. Grove. *Books about Hawaii: Fifty Basic Authors*. Honolulu: University Press of Hawaii, 1977.

Day, A. Grove and Carl Stroven, eds. *A Hawaiian Reader*. New York: Appleton-Century-Crofts, 1959.

———. *The Spell of Hawaii*. New York: Meredith, 1968.

———. *The Spell of the Pacific; An Anthology of Its Literature*. James A. Michener, intro. New York: Macmillan, 1949.

Holt, John Dominis. *Hanai: A Poem for Queen Liliuokalani*. Honolulu: Topgallant, 1986.

———. *Waimea Summer: A Novel*. Honolulu: Topgallant, 1976.

Hongo, Garrett Kaoru. *The River of Heaven: Poems*. New York: Knopf, 1988.

———. *Volcano: A Memoir of Hawai'i*. New York: Knopf, 1995.

———. *Yellow Light*. Middletown, Connecticut: Wesleyan University Press, 1982.

———, ed. *The Open Boat: Poems from Asian America*. New York: Doubleday, 1993.

Iida, Deborah. *Middle Son*. Chapel Hill: Algonquin Books of Chapel Hill, 1996.

Ing, Mahealani. "Calvary at 'Anaeho'omalu." In *Ho'omanoa*. Joseph P. Balaz, ed. Honolulu: Ku Pa'a, 1989.

Kono, Juliet S. *Hilo Rains*. Honolulu: Bamboo Ridge Press, 1988.

Kono, Juliet S. and Cathy Song, eds. *Sister Stew: Fiction and Poetry by Women*. Honolulu: Bamboo Ridge Press, 1991.

Lee, W. Storrs, ed. *Hawaii: A Literary Chronicle*. New York: Funk and Wagnalls, 1967.

Lum, Darrell H. Y. *Little Bit Like You*. Honolulu: Kumu Kahua, 1991.

———. *Pass On, No Pass Back!* Honolulu: Bamboo Ridge Press, 1990.

Lum, Wing Tek. *Expounding the Doubtful Points*. Honolulu: Bamboo Ridge Press, 1987.

Murayama, Milton. *All I Asking for Is My Body*. San Francisco: Supa Press, 1975.

Nunes, Susan. *A Small Obligation and Other Stories of Hilo*. Honolulu: Bamboo Ridge Press, 1982.

Pak, Gary. *The Watcher of Waipuna*. Honolulu: Bamboo Ridge Press, 1992.

Song, Cathy. *Picture Bride*. New Haven: Yale University Press, 1983.

Trask, Haunani-Kay. *Light in the Crevice Never Seen*. Corvallis, Oregon: Calyx Books, 1994.

Tyau, Kathleen. *A Little Too Much is Enough*. New York: W.W. Norton, 1996.

Yamanaka, Lois-Ann. *Saturday Night at the Pahala Theater*. Honolulu: Bamboo Ridge Press, 1993.

———. *Wild Meat and the Bully Burgers*. New York: Farrar, Straus & Giroux, 1996.

Secondary Sources

Daws, Gavan. *Shoal of Time: A History of the Hawaiian Islands*. Honolulu: University Press of Hawaii; rpt. New York: Macmillan, 1968. Daws discusses the history of the fiftieth state with reference to socio-economic developments, mainly plantation and multinational business interests.

Dougherty, Michael. *To Steal a Kingdom: Probing Hawaiian History*. Waimanalo: Island Style Press, 1992. Explores events leading to the overthrow of the Hawaiian monarchy.

Hawaiian Historical Society. *Annual Report*. Honolulu: The Society, 1892. Early publication addressing Hawaiian culture from an anthropological perspective.

Malo, David. *Hawaiian Antiquities*. Nathaniel B. Emerson, trans. Honolulu: Hawaiian Gazette, 1903. Malo is among the earliest Native Hawaiian scholars to pursue the preservation and the analysis of Hawaiian culture (including language).

Sumida, Stephen H. *And the View from the Shore: Literary Traditions of Hawai'i*. Seattle: University of Washington Press, 1991. A comprehensive study of the history of Hawaiian literature.

Laurie Ricou

The Pacific Northwest as a Cross-Border Region

The idea of a Pacific Northwest region shared by two countries (however diverse its constituent communities) has a considerable history. Native American peoples in what is now British Columbia, Washington, and Oregon shared and share language groups, art forms, and economic and political cultures (Ricou *passim*). Captain George Vancouver's (1757-1798) enthusiasm for honoring crew members, friends, and prominent associates wrote a British imperial accent into the regional toponymy on both sides of the eventual boundary. The prolonged search for an international boundary in the Pacific Northwest also seems to reinforce the notion of a north Pacific region divided by an arbitrary political line. Whereas the forty-ninth parallel divided the Prairie provinces from the midwestern states on October 20, 1818, a border was not legally established between what became British Columbia and the United States until 1846 (and, in the Georgia Basin, not until 1871). In the crucially formative intervening years, the principle of a "free and open" territory was in force (Deutsch 64).

Naming this region, with its permeable and meandering boundary (at least in the Straits of Georgia and Juan de Fuca) is problematic. As one border-crossing short story notes whimsically, the political boundary destabilizes the most familiar name: "Hadn't they found, whenever they approached the border driving north, that the shell of velvet sky over the Pacific Northwest suddenly cracked and left them pinched into the southwest corner of something else?" (Debarros 8). For Gary Snyder, the "natural" definition of place is the "Ish nation . . . the drainage of all of Puget sound and the Straits of Georgia." This concept, he insists, provides

> a starter in learning where you are. For example, it's a great help in realizing where you are to know that the border between Canada and the United States is illusory. . . . It comes down to the nitty-gritty when you get into water quality control, air pollution control questions, or salmon runs. (O'Connell 317-318)

A more formally political version of the Ish nation emerged in the late 1980s with the increasing currency of the term "Cascadia" to identify "an imaginary country . . . that eschews national and state boundaries but respects the natural integrity and socio-cultural history that have united the region for centuries" (Quigley 3).

Evidently, if the term is connected to this region at least, *western* literature cannot reasonably be confined just to the United States or to Canada. And, cautioned by Snyder, literary critics cannot be satisfied with neatly limited national contrasts, or with the confines of a single discipline. One starting point would be the associations clustered about the words First Nations, ecology, island, edge, and Pacific. Northwest writers seem to find in these insistently linked and interdependent motifs their motivating questions about methods, about form and language: what semantic fields, what patterns of syntax, what lines of narrative, what procedures of translation lie within them? Consider, for example, the challenges and possibilities in writing toward "the timescape of the first peoples" (Doig 222). That Ivan Doig, Seattle-based novelist, can be added to the long list of writers who record an encounter with the cultures of the Native peoples interests only a statistician, but to find that Bill Reid, Vancouver-based Haida artist, defines an aesthetic to shape Doig's own syntax awakens the literary imagination:

> Scenes of this winter and of Swan's own western-edged seasons do flow together, in the way that beings mingle in one of those magical carvings of the Haidas. ("They weren't bound by the silly feeling that it's impossible for two figures to occupy the same space at the same time.") (Doig 241)

Many Indians appear in Oregon novelist H. L. Davis' *Honey in the*

Horn (1935), but this fact becomes relevant to literary method when "the Indian boy['s]" account of his people's creation myth serves as a guide to Clay's practical actions and his ethics, and the narrator's vernacular recounting of the story attempts to answer to the substance and language of some Native myth: "They [the people] were nothing but loose toots of vapor that went rocking around in mid-air, getting all mixed up with one another and wishing, without knowing exactly why, that they could get sorted out again" (49). To trace the parallels between Doig and Davis and, for example, the Indians wisecracking about fictional theory in George Bowering's *Burning Water* (1980) or *Caprice* (1987) seems much more informative than to differentiate them along national lines. *Slash* (1985), a polemical *bildungsroman* by First Nations writer Jeannette Armstrong, originating in the Okanagan community of British Columbia, must necessarily incorporate the events and politics of the American Indian Movement in the 1960s. Northwest writing seems first to require remembering, respecting and reinventing a different sense of time.

A trope figuring ecology is intimately connected to a search for native forms. The Pacific rain forest contains the greatest density of living matter on the planet (Griffith 49). Such an intricate tangle of growth is an overt object lesson in ecological interdependencies. In rhetorical terms, the ecological theme manifests itself in paragraph-long lists of plants, in an animistic running together of nouns. In what might be called a floritopography, H. L. Davis, for example, marks almost every change of setting by a trio, or quartet, of names of plants (and relatively seldom by a place name): "Flem Simmons' land-holding was a half-mile-square homestead claim astraddle of a creek bottom full of devil's-club stalks and skunk cabbage and wild-currant bushes and alder saplings" (139).

Davis' technique expresses a sensitivity to micro-climates and local ecologies, which accords with the frequent trope of the Pacific Northwest as multiple islands. Certainly, thousands of literal islands form the coastal geography—to connect just a few of them, British Columbia operates the largest public ferry system in the world. The whole West Coast cordillera, from Coast Range and Cascades to Rocky Mountains, appears to create a series of islands. Cole Harris notes that distances and "rugged terrain" (leading to difficulties in transportation) have led to "striking specialization" of land use in British Columbia. The pattern of settlement is of isolated one-industry towns based on extraction of resources from the earth (Harris 3-39). Geography dictates economic structure and demographic patterns: it confines communities to narrow, inaccessible valleys, which become cultural and psychological islands.

Perhaps as a consequence, writers frequently look to economic patterns for both general literary form and metaphorical possibilities. The life cycle of the salmon figures both movement of people and outlook on life in Hubert Evans' *Mist on the River* (1954). The patterns of loggers' storytelling in Martin Grainger's *Woodsmen of the West* (1908) dictate chapter divisions and propose the pragmatic necessity of gossip. Occupational sub-dialects flourish, many with a richly distinctive vocabulary and syntax. The haywire speech of the logger becomes literary language in Ken Kesey's *Sometimes a Great Notion* (1964) or in Peter Trower's poems.

When Northwesterners are not islanded in a single-industry town, confined by mountains or water, they tend to look toward the Orient, across the Pacific: at the end of the land, thoughts reach toward the next human community to the west. The metonymy Pacific Slope/Asian culture is rooted in history, both in the anthropologists' speculation that the First Peoples migrated across a land bridge linking Asia and North America, and in the humble legend of the voyage of Hwui Shan and a party of Buddhist monks in the fifth century A.D. The idea of an Asian heritage and inspiration often appears closely interconnected to Native American ethnopoetics and to concepts of Ecotopia, the powerful myth most extensively developed by Joel Garreau in his *The Nine Nations of North America* (1981). As Kenneth Rexroth points out in a survey of the influence of Chinese and Japanese models on modern poetry, Gary Snyder is a leader in urging "an ecological aesthetic, a blending of American Indian and Far Eastern philosophies of cooperation with, rather than conquest of, nature" ("The Influence" 273). Moreover, where form is concerned, Rexroth observes a suggestive resemblance between the patterns of gaps in Indian songs (as translated) — "'abstract' vocables and a few meaningful syllables" — and the ideographic method (271).

Other formal models include the extreme conciseness of the *haiku* and *utaniki* as they appear in the work of Fred Wah. Another is the importance of the alogical riddling of the *koan* to the poetry of Phyllis Webb. In the visual arts, the connections are more overt: the popularity of landscape prints by Takao Tanabe, Peter and Trudl Markgraf, and especially Toni Onley, show the appeal of blurred outlines and thin washes bleeding into one another. In the most familiar iconography, the shapes recede vaguely in the mist:

Many who live in the Northwest may not know Picasso from Andy Warhol, but are learned in the nuances of color and texture in nature: the color of pebbles, mustard green kelp, pine cones, and fir branches, silvered dead trees, plumed ferns, sea moss, scallop shells, gulls' wings — all these tones of white, gray, green, and brown. (Griffith 58)

One of the Northwest's most important Abstractionists, Mark Tobey, studied Chinese calligraphy in order to incorporate a different brush stroke and visual texture in his work. Morris Graves' evocative "white writing" developed from his admiration for Japanese art. Tobey, not entirely incidentally, traveled to Victoria in 1928 where he ran classes in Emily Carr's school and contributed his influence to her shift from representational to more abstract forms (Bellerby n.p.).

These are but a hint of the structures of comparison which seem essential to Canadian-American literary comparisons in the 1990s. The bio-region will provide a framework. Within it, we will recognize crossings, like those of the rivers, the birds, the pre-contact First Peoples and the polluted air, which are unaware of borders. They will provide the contexts and background to govern discriminations. They are a way of organizing one's thinking, but should not be an excuse for closing the mind — as many places exist as there are imaginations to word them.

Works Cited

Bellerby, Greg L. "Foreword," *Mark Tobey*. Victoria, British Columbia: Art Gallery of Greater Victoria, 1983, n.p.

Davis, H. L. *Honey in the Horn*. 1935; rpt., New York: Avon, 1962, p. 49.

DeBarros, Paul. "In a Draw." In *Roothog: Contemporary B. C. Writing*, John Dudley Harris, ed. Prince George, British Columbia: Repository Press, 1981, p. 8.

Deutsch, Herman J. "The Evolution of the International Boundary in the Inland Empire of the Pacific Northwest," *Pacific Northwest Quarterly*, 51:2 (1960): 64.

Doig, Ivan. *Winter Brothers: A Season at the Edge of America*. New York: Harcourt Brace Jovanovich, 1980, p. 222.

Garreau, Joel. *The Nine Nations of North America*. Boston: Houghton Mifflin, 1981.

Griffith, Thomas. "The Pacific Northwest," *The Atlantic Monthly* 237 (April 1976): 49, 58.

Harris, Cole. "Moving Amid the Mountains, 1870-1930," *B.C. Studies* 58 (Summer 1983): 3-39.

O'Connell, Nicholas, ed. *At the Field's End: Interviews with Twenty Pacific Northwest Writers*. Seattle: Madrona, 1987. Pp. 317-318.

Quigley, Eileen V. "Cascadia," *The New Pacific: A Journal of the Pacific Northwest and Western Canada* 4 (Fall 1990): 3.

Rexroth, Kenneth. "The Influence of Classical Japanese Poetry on Modern American Poetry." In *World Outside the Window: The Selected Essays of Kenneth Rexroth*. Bradford Morrow, ed. New York: New Directions, 1987. Pp. 271-273.

Ricou, Laurie. "Crossing Borders in the Literature of the Pacific Northwest." In *Borderlands*, Robert Lecker, ed. Toronto: ECW Press, 1991. Pp. 286-308

———. "Two Nations Own These Islands: Border and Region in Pacific-Northwest Writing." In *Context North America: Canadian/U.S. Literary Relations*, Camille R. La Bossière, ed. Ottawa: University of Ottawa Press, 1994. Pp. 49-62

———. "Children of a Common Mother: Of Boundary Markers and Open Gates," *Zeitschrift des Gesellschaft fur Kanada-Studien*, 11 Jahrgang/Nr. 1 & 2, Band 19120 (1990): 151-162.

Selected Secondary Sources

Bingham, Edwin R., and Glen A. Love, eds. *Northwest Perspectives: Essays on the Culture of the Pacific Northwest*. Seattle: University of Washington Press, 1978. The first collective scholarly attempt to define the literary region. Includes a still-useful annotated bibliography.

Harrison, Richard, ed. *Crossing Frontiers: Papers in American and Canadian Western Literature*. Edmonton: University of Alberta Press, 1979. A print record of a conference, held in Banff in 1978, that has had the greatest impact on comparative studies of the two western literatures. Emphasis is almost entirely on the Prairies and Great Plains.

Lecker, Robert, ed. *Borderlands: Essays in Canadian-American Relations*. Toronto: ECW Press, 1991. Fourteen multidisciplinary essays deriving from the *Borderlands* project, including three primarily on literature.

Lipset, Seymour. *Continental Divide: The Values and Institutions of the United States and Canada*. Toronto and Washington, D.C.: Canadian-American Committee, 1989; rpt. New York: Routledge, 1990. The most convenient source for compact summary of received opinion on the binaries which differentiate the two national cultures.

Ross, Morton L. "The Northern Boundary." In *A Literary History of the American West*. Sponsored by The Western Literature Association. Fort Worth: TCU Press, 1987. Pp. 1000-1013. A concise introduction to western Canadian literature and its border-crossing dimensions.

Gary Williams

Raymond Carver

Raymond Carver's work, which began to reach a national audience when Martha Foley included "Will You Please Be Quiet, Please?" in *The Best American Short Stories* 1967, was the product of a shy, sometimes self-destructive sensibility that drew its vision from the lives of the working poor among whom Carver grew up — and whose mode of perceiving he never fully left behind, despite the comfort and acclaim he enjoyed in the last decade of his life.

Although Carver was born in Clatskanie, Oregon, on May 25, 1938, his parents were southern transplants from Arkansas in the mid-1930s. In 1941 the family settled in Yakima, Washington, where Carver's father was employed as a saw filer in the lumber mill and his mother (sporadically) as a retail clerk or waitress. Carver and his younger brother spent much of their time outdoors, fishing and hunting. "We were a poor family," Carver told interviewers in 1984; "we didn't have much of anything in the way of material goods, or spiritual goods or values either" (Gentry and Stull 114). Married at eighteen, the father of two children by the time he was twenty, and for many years trapped in "some crap job or other" while he and his first wife Maryann struggled to go to school, Carver was an unlikely prospect for escape from this economic terrain but for his determination to be a writer.

His essay on John Gardner, reprinted in *Fires* (1983), records how Carver, while a student at Chico State, was helped to take the first meaningful steps toward realizing his goal. Gardner's willingness to offer line-by-line criticism and his prompting of Carver to read Hemingway, Faulkner, and Chekhov made Carver feel "the luckiest of men" and "wild with discovery." Carver's first published work appeared in student literary magazines, and "The Furious Seasons" was listed among the year's distinctive stories in *The Best American Short Stories 1964*.

Life after graduation, however—despite a year in the Iowa Writers' Workshop, where his work was more or less ignored—Carver later characterized as "ravenous." Driven to write and yet kept from it by the "ferocious" demands of parenting and the need to bring in money, he concluded that "if I wanted to write anything, and finish it, and if ever I wanted to take satisfaction out of finished work, I was going to have to stick to stories and poems" (*Fires* 34). The work accumulated very slowly. By 1968, despite some significant recognition, Carver had given himself fully over to the alcoholism that would nearly kill him before he was able to control it. Saddled with a seemingly perennial "wagonload of frustration," he later told Mona Simpson, he "more or less gave up, threw in the towel, and took to full-time drinking as a serious pursuit" (*Conversations* 37).

A great many of Carver's stories and poems offer a view of life as experienced through an alcohol-induced haze; he is, in fact, one of the finest chroniclers of lives wrecked by booze. There is sometimes a certain despairing humor in these portraits, but beneath it always is the feeling that real ugliness can erupt suddenly, without provocation, as it does in the stories "Tell the Women We're Going," "A Serious Talk," "One More Thing," "The Bridle," "Vitamins," and such poems as "Union Street: San Francisco, Summer 1975" and "From the East, Light." In 1971 Gordon Lish published "Neighbors" in *Esquire*; "Fat" appeared in *Harper's Bazaar*; and in a certain respect, as Carver later observed of the period of his ascension to national prominence, "things had never seemed better." In 1976 Lish collected some of Carver's stories and gave them to McGraw-Hill, which published them as *Will You Please Be Quiet, Please?* The following year, the book received a National Book Award nomination, and Carver's stature was secured. Yet the five or six years preceding his repudiation of alcohol on June 2, 1977, also provided some of the grimmest episodes in his life, interludes that even a decade later he would discuss only obliquely.

Will You Please Be Quiet, Please? is Carver's most eclectic collection of fiction, the stories reflecting changes in style and subject matter over a fifteen-year span. They are peopled with Carver's trademark characters

—waitresses, a mailman, a vacuum-cleaner salesman, mill workers, a mechanic, collectors of unemployment, folks Tess Gallagher described as "largely forgotten at the heart of the country" (Adelman and Gallagher 16). It is worth noting, however, that the population of Carver country includes professional people as well—such as Arnold Breit in "Are You a Doctor?"; Myers, the writer of "Put Yourself in My Shoes"; the student who reads Rilke to his attention-starved wife in "The Student's Wife"; Harry in "How About This?"; and Marian and Ralph Wyman of the title story, teachers whose relationship began in a Chaucer class.

Most of the stories conclude with an implication that things will be worse hereafter. Moments of heightened awareness seem unlikely to lead to a deeper grasp of meaning in these depressive, elliptic narratives, and thus Carver has come to be known as the purveyor of "low-rent tragedies" (Dickstein 509). Yet the possibility of positive change is also a note sounded occasionally in these early stories. The waitress who narrates "Fat" seems to take on emotional substance and to become dissatisfied with the insensitivity of those she lives among after her encounter with a customer with a gargantuan appetite who refers to himself as "we." And at the conclusion of the title story, Ralph Wyman—"marveling at the impossible changes he felt moving over him"—appears able to relinquish the jealousy and feelings of inferiority that earlier prevent him from understanding his wife's sensual nature.

Life in the blue-collar stratum, rather than in a particular part of the country, is the geography of these fictions: Carver never viewed himself as a regionalist. "People talk about the stories having a specific locale in the Northwest...yet I don't see them having such a specific place," he noted in 1988. "Most of the stories, it seems to me, could take place anywhere. So I suppose it's an emotional landscape I'm most interested in" (Gentry and Stull 247).

In November 1977, estranged from Maryann and his children and still very fragile after five months off alcohol, Carver met the poet Tess Gallagher at a writers' conference, and with her support he began to reassemble his life. There had been little new work for several years, but gradually, as his strength returned, he wrote the stories collected in *What We Talk About When We Talk About Love* (1981), bringing further acclaim but also the dubious distinction of recognition as the country's chief practitioner of "minimalist fiction," as reviewers began to call it. Carver referred to the collection as "a much more self-conscious book in the sense of how intentional every move was," attributing this impulse particularly to the advice of Gordon Lish. In the essay "On Writing" in *Fires*, Carver also acknowledged the tension-producing value of "the things that are left out, that are implied, the landscape just under the smooth (but sometimes broken and unsettled) surface of things" (26).

What We Talk About is Carver's most violence-riddled work, an assembly of dark narratives in which murder, suicide, sudden death, domestic mayhem, and mute but volatile fury are the rule rather than the exception. Yet in an influential review of the volume in *Atlantic Monthly* (June, 1981, 96-98) James Atlas, while praising the "bleak power" afforded by Carver's masterly narrative sense and "willfully simple style," objected finally to the "lackluster manner and eschewal of feeling." "One is left," he complained, "with a hunger for richness, texture, excess." This theme was taken up by a number of other commentators during the 1980s. This "new" Carver was chided for a perceived inclination to revere the banal and to relinquish moral authority. By the time such discussion reached its apex, however, Carver had already written the story "Cathedral" — "totally different in conception and execution," he told Mona Simpson, "from any stories that [had] come before" (Gentry and Stull 44).

This most-anthologized story, with its splendid climactic moment of sympathetic identification between an inclined-toward-jealousy redneck and a blind male friend of his wife's, is the clearest illustration of differences in tone and thematic emphasis that characterize several stories in the 1983 collection *Cathedral*. Similar moments occur in "A Small, Good Thing," "Where I'm Calling From," "Fever," and "Feathers," exemplifying Carver's own sense that in these narratives he was "breaking out of something [he] had put [him]self into, both personally and aesthetically." This leaven sharply distinguished the collection from its immediate predecessor and — taken together with a similar expansive spirit evident in the stories in *Fires* — led several critics to argue a "development" in Carver's career toward, in the words of one, "the expansive, digressive, more redemptive...Chekovian" stories of the last five years (Banks 101).

In 1983 Carver won the Mildred and Harold Strauss Living Award, which afforded him time to complete four more books — three poetry collections and *Where I'm Calling From* (1988), a compendium of seven new stories and those he wished to preserve (or revise) from earlier books. In this body of work, particularly in the poems, Carver seemed to embrace a directness of expression in which the line between life and artifice dwindled to invisibility; they are works that offer, in Greg Kuzma's memorable phrase about *Ultramarine* (1986), "experience delivered smoldering like new-born calves" (355). Their intensity surely derived in part from presentiment that little time remained.

During his last months, Carver worked with Gallagher to complete the final book, and in these labors were concentrated the affection, mutual admiration, and passionately supportive energy that had characterized their relationship for the previous eleven years. Gallagher's account of putting together *A New Path to the Waterfall* (1989) is the most intimate view available of the fuels by which Carver's imagination was fired and of the particularity of their collaborative zest. It also highlights an influence that became increasingly important to Carver — that of Chekhov, passages from whose stories, rendered as Carver-like poems, weave through the book, and whose death was the inspiration for Carver's last story, "Errand." Raymond Carver died on August 2, 1988.

In 1987 Carver wrote that "the resurgence of interest in the short story has done nothing less than revitalize the national literature" (*Michigan Quarterly Review*, 26 [1987]: 711). His major role in that revitalization was recognized in his last year in his being named to the American Academy and Institute of Arts and Letters. "Every great or even every very good writer makes the world over according to his own specifications," Carver wrote in 1981 (*Fires* 23). Though his humility prevented him from saying so, that is precisely what Carver did, crafting a clear and startling vision of people and circumstances that the rest of us had somehow overlooked. The best analogue for Carver's work may be Walker Evans' photographs in *Let Us Now Praise Famous Men* (1941) —not James Agee's gorgeous and pain-filled narrative (though the gorgeousness and pain are there in Carver's stories, too), but those stark, uncaptioned pictures. Who that looked carefully at them would ever see the same again?

Selected Bibliography

Primary Sources

Cathedral. New York: Knopf, 1983.
Fires. Santa Barbara: Capra, 1983; New York: Vintage, 1984.
Furious Seasons and Other Stories. Santa Barbara: Capra, 1977.
A New Path to the Waterfall. New York: Atlantic Monthly, 1989.
No Heroics, Please: Uncollected Writings. New York: Vintage, 1991.
Ultramarine. New York: Random House, 1986.

What We Talk About When We Talk About Love. New York: Knopf, 1981.
Where I'm Calling From: New and Selected Stories. New York: Atlantic Monthly, 1988.
Where Water Comes Together with Other Water. New York: Random House, 1985.
Will You Please Be Quiet, Please? New York: McGraw-Hill, 1976.

Secondary Sources

Adelman, Bob and Tess Gallagher. *Carver Country: The World of Raymond Carver.* New York: Scribner's, 1990. Carver's personal and published writing, interspersed with photographs of the people and places he wrote about. Insightful introduction by Gallagher.

Banks, Russell. "Raymond Carver: Our Stephen Crane." *The Atlantic,* 268 (August 1991): 99-103. Part review of Sam Halpert's first version of his oral biography, part retrospective.

Dickstein, Morris. "The Pursuit for the Ordinary." *Partisan Review,* 58:3 (1991): 506-513. Good insights into Carver's appeal, connection to his time, place among other writers.

Facknitz, Mark A. R. "'The Calm,' 'A Small, Good Thing,' and 'Cathedral': Raymond Carver and the Recovery of Human Worth." *Studies in Short Fiction,* 23:3 (1986): 287-296.

Gentry, Marshall Bruce, and William Stull, eds. *Conversations with Raymond Carver.* Jackson: University Press of Mississippi, 1990. A collection of the important interviews Carver gave. Contains a detailed chronology, including publication dates, prize dates. Previously published interviews augmented with new material from tapes. Excellent introduction by editors.

Halpert, Sam, ed. *Raymond Carver: An Oral Biography.* Iowa City: University of Iowa Press, 1995. Recollections of Carver gathered through interviews with a number of people close to him, including his first wife Maryann Burk. (Expanded edition of the first published in 1991 by Peregrine Smith Press of Layton, Utah.)

Meyer, Adam. *Raymond Carver.* New York: Twayne, 1995. The first book-length biography.

Kuzma, Greg. "Poems That Almost Stop the Heart." *Michigan Quarterly Review,* 27 (Spring 1988): 355.

Nesset, Kirk. *The Stories of Raymond Carver: A Critical Study.* Columbus: Ohio State University Press, 1995. Perceptive reading of each volume and of the shape of the whole career.

Shute, Kathleen Westfall. "Finding the Words: The Struggle for Salvation in the Fiction of Raymond Carver." *The Hollins Critic,* 24:5 (1987): 1-10.

Stull, William L., and Maureen P. Carroll, eds. *Remembering Ray: A Composite Biography of Raymond Carver.* Santa Barbara: Capra Press, 1993. Reminiscences, many published elsewhere, of Carver by the famous and obscure (his Port Angeles typist). Useful collection.

Stull, William L. "Beyond Hopelessville: Another Side of Raymond Carver." *Philological Quarterly,* 64:1 (1985): 1-15.

Kevin Bezner

John Haines

John Haines was born in Norfolk, Virginia, in 1924, but his family moved frequently because his father was a naval officer. Like many of the men of his generation, he joined the service in 1943. He followed his father into the U.S. Navy and saw action during World War II in the south-central Pacific and with the Atlantic fleet. After leaving the Navy in 1946, he attended the National Art School in Washington. He stayed until 1947 when he left for Alaska to homestead some seventy miles outside of Fairbanks.

By 1948, Haines was back in Washington, where he studied art at American University and worked as a statistical draftsman for the Navy Department. From 1950 to 1952, he attended the Hans Hofmann School of Fine Arts in New York City. Haines failed to earn a college degree, which separates him from the major members of his generation, including Robert Bly, Robert Creeley, Donald Hall, Donald Justice, and Richard Wilbur.

Haines returned to Alaska in 1954, committed himself to poetry, and spent the next fifteen years there, the bulk of the more than twenty-five years he has spent in Alaska. Perhaps no other poet of his generation has spent as much time alone. In 1965, he was awarded a Guggenheim Foundation Fellowship in poetry. The next year, when he was forty-two, his first collection of poems, *Winter News* (1966), was published.

In *Winter News*, Haines writes of his experiences in the Alaskan landscape in a simple, unadorned language reminiscent of Bly's *Silence in the*

Snowy Fields (1962), a debt Haines now downplays. Most critics note his attention to the landscape. Some, like Martin McGovern in his entry on Haines in *Contemporary Poetry,* have compared him to Thoreau. But while the landscape is apparent, it is so in ways most would not generally expect, as in the title poem:

> They say the wells
> are freezing
> at Northway where
> the cold begins.
>
> Oil tins bang
> as evening comes on,
> and clouds of
> steaming breath drift
> in the street.
>
> Men go out to feed
> the stiffening dogs,
>
> the voice of the snowman
> calls the white-
> haired children home.

There is often a dark, pervasive sense of blood and death, perhaps one reason why the critic Richard Tillinghast suggested a comparison between Haines and Robert Frost in his review of the book. The poems also look inward, more so than most critics have noticed. Many seem written by a man attempting to define his relationship to this world. Often, the poems are hesitant and so reveal a writer still learning to make his way as a poet, a concern noted by Peter Wild. A surreal quality pervades the poems.

Haines has stated that his second full-length collection, *The Stone Harp* (1971), represents a sharp departure from *Winter News,* a perception a number of critics accept. *The Stone Harp,* however, continues Haines' charting of the interior landscape even as he looks out upon the world. Many of the poems do look away from Alaska, although the title poem, which borrows an image used more effectively by Thoreau, is directly concerned with Alaska and so frames both the first section of the book, "In Nature," and the book itself. The Vietnam War intrudes in poems such as "War and Peace in the Pasture" and "Lies," an angry depiction of President Lyndon Johnson.

The true breakthrough in Haines' career came with the publication of a memoir, *The Stars, the Snow, the Fire* (1989), which examines his years in Alaska. The book documents both the life Haines had as a hunter and trapper and his loneliness in isolation. This book was followed by *New Poems: 1980-1988* (1990), which won the Western Arts Federation Award, the Lenore Marshall/*The Nation* Award, and the Poets Prize (shared with Mark Jarman). The book contains six sequences, including the powerful "In the Forest Without Leaves" and "Meditation on a Skull Carved in Crystal," which show evidence of Haines' earlier style but contain, as well, greater complexity both in theme and language. Here Haines also explores his sense of artists such as Edward Hopper and Pablo Picasso. His vision seems darker than in the past and more obsessed with his own personal death and the death of our species. Haines' collected poetry, *The Owl in the Mask of the Dreamer*, was published in 1993.

Most who know the work of Haines recognize his importance as both the last of a particular type, the man who leaves the East to start life anew in the open spaces of the West, and as a significant poet of a landscape and its influence on the mind of one man. While Haines has not had the influence of Bly or Snyder, or reception by a general or academic audience, he remains one of the quintessential writers of the West, and one whose finest poems stand beside the best of his generation, regardless of region.

Selected Bibliography

Primary Sources

Cicada. Middletown: Wesleyan University Press, 1977.

Fables and Distances: New and Selected Essays. St. Paul: Graywolf, 1996.

Living Off the Country: Essays on Poetry and Place. Ann Arbor: University of Michigan Press, 1981.

New Poems: 1980-1988. Brownsville, Oregon: Story Line, 1990.

News from the Glacier: Selected Poems, 1969-1980. Middletown: Wesleyan University Press, 1982.

The Owl in the Mask of the Dreamer. St. Paul: Graywolf, 1993.

The Stars, the Snow, the Fire. St. Paul: Graywolf, 1989.

The Stone Harp. Middletown: Wesleyan University Press, 1971.
Winter News. Middletown: Wesleyan University Press, 1966.

Secondary Sources

Bezner, Kevin and Kevin Walzer, eds. *The Wilderness of Vision: On the Poetry of John Haines*. Brownsville, Oregon: Story Line Press, 1996. The first comprehensive look at Haines' career, this book includes essays written for it and reprints of reviews and earlier essays.

Bezner, Kevin. Interview. *Green Mountains Review* 6 (Summer-Fall 1993): 9-15. Focuses on *New Poems*, but discusses Haines' background in art, his connection to the poetry of Yeats, and his emphasis on death.

Carruth, Hayden. Review of *The Stone Harp*. *Hudson Review*, 24 (Summer 1971): 320-327.

McGovern, Martin. "John Haines." *Contemporary Poetry*. Tracy Cevalier, ed. Chicago: St. James Press, 1991. Pp. 370-372.

Perkins, David. *A History of Modern Poetry: Modernism and After*. Cambridge: Harvard University Press, 1987. Sees Haines' work as emerging out of his solitary life in Alaska and connects him to the primal. An especially important source for comprehending Haines' place among the poets of his generation.

Tillinghast, Richard. Review of *Winter News*. *Poetry*, 109 (November 1966): 121-122.

Wild, Peter. *John Haines*. Boise: Boise State University Western Writers Series, 1985. A fine introduction to Haines' work. Wild argues convincingly for a connection between the early poetry of Haines and Bly, and also provides important details about Haines' relationship with his father.

Heinz Tschachler

Ursula K. Le Guin

In Ursula Le Guin's work western themes and ideas have unfolded over many years and many different worlds, primarily those of Earthsea, the Hainish planets, Orsinia, and the West Coast of the United States. Central to an understanding of Le Guin is the degree to which her worlds are different from our consensus reality. Critic Elizabeth Cummins has used a fictional spectrum, at one end of which are placed the fantasy works of Earthsea, that describe what "could not have happened." On the other end there are the science-fiction works set on the Hainish planets describing what "has not happened." Midway between the science-fiction end and the center of the spectrum is the world of Orsinia, a landlocked country in east central Europe, which is accounted for through scientific knowledge while it fantastically coexists in time and space with empirical reality. Finally, there is the world of the American West Coast, situated near the center of the spectrum. For Le Guin, the West Coast has ordinarily been the locale for speculative stories about America's future.

Paradoxically, the Orsinian world, although chronologically antedating Le Guin's other worlds, is the least well-known in her works. Not only was her first published story, "An die Musik," about Orsinia, but by the time of her first science-fiction publication in 1962 she had already written four novels (all of them unpublished) and a poem about Orsinia. Indeed, Orsinia is her country: the word Orsinia and Le Guin's first name, Ursula, share the same linguistic root. As James Bittner explains, "orsino, Italian for 'bearish,' and Ursula come from the Latin ursa." If Le Guin named her country after herself, she also claimed that inventing Orsinia was "a technique of distancing." Seen from a distance are characters who choose to stay, even though they are overburdened by history, often oppressed, and who thus reconcile their desire for freedom or development with the impossibility of "going west."

Perhaps it is not surprising that *Orsinian Tales* (1976), although nominated for the National Book Award in 1977, has had comparatively little critical attention. The stories lack the vast expanses of the magic of Earthsea or of the interstellar space of the Hainish world. Their plots do not so much change the course of history as they seem confined to exploring how individuals reconcile their desire for freedom or spirituality with the facts of the bleak world they inhabit. But the similarities and parallels between Orsinia and Hain are too obvious to be overlooked: in the Hainish novels — to date Le Guin has published six, from *Rocannon's World* (1966) through *The Left Hand of Darkness* (1969) to *The Dispossessed* (1974) — the microcosmic drama of *Orsinian Tales* unfolds on a macrocosmic scale. If the Orsinians' loyalty grows out of their inhabiting an oppressed and cramped world, the commitment shown by the Hainish people is necessitated by the sheer immensity and diversity of the interstellar expanses. This brings to the foreground the centrality to the national consciousness of the idea of going west. "He was a frontiersman," Shevek the protagonist of *The Dispossessed* realizes, "one of a breed who had denied their history [and thus] had been wrong, wrong in their desperate courage, to deny their history, to forego the possibility of return" (72).

With the world of the West Coast, Le Guin confronts the myth of the frontier with the most urgent dilemma. Those who — like Le Guin herself — live at the western edge of the U.S.A., may like the Anarresti "have cut themselves off"; yet for them there is no "new frontier over the next horizon." Consequently, they may wait for the end, or they can accept that they "make justice here, or nowhere." This is not an option that everyone is prepared to take, though. Thus in "The Ones Who Walked Away from Omelas," a story collected in *The Wind's Twelve Quarters* (1975), Le Guin imaginatively reconstructs the frontier myth: sympathy is not necessarily with the ones who walk away in protest, even though they apparently have every reason to do so, as the prosperity of their city depends on the suffering of a child. The very ignorance of the narrator, who purports that she "cannot describe [the walkers' destination] at all. It is possible that it does not exist," is a reminder that simply to pull up one's stakes and move on is not what responsible people do (259).

Le Guin's imaginative explorations of the frontier myth reach a new pitch of intensity both in the novel *The Lathe of Heaven* (1971) and in the novella "The New Atlantis" (1975). In both works, Le Guin has depicted natural and human home-world catastrophes. With nowhere to go, the characters in these works experience their own homeland becoming a strange land.

Home, Le Guin said in an interview given to promote *Always Coming Home* (1985), is the Napa Valley of Northern California. This has made the Kesh, the imaginary future people, "my people, and this place I'm writing about is my home" (McCaffery and Gregory 67). More than a reference to a geographic area, "home" is another word for community. This idea cannot be separated from a long tradition of anti-modernist sentiment, from German romantic sociology to the structuralist anthropology of Claude Lévi-Strauss, which Le Guin draws upon in her more recent essays. But as early as 1977 she asserted that "Community is the best we can hope for, and community for most people means touches: the touch of your hand against the other's hand, the job done together, the sledge hauled together, the dance danced together, the child conceived together."

Always Coming Home is Le Guin's longest and most ambitious work of fiction to date. It presents, in the form of an ethnograph, cultures that "might be going to have lived a long, long time from now in Northern California" ("A First Note" n.p.). Yet, as Kenneth M. Roemer has pointed out, despite Le Guin's popularity and reputation there were difficulties getting the book published and keeping it in print. Objections were raised, for instance, against the accompanying tape and the use of illustrations; nor did the integration of many different genres and different narrative voices go down well. The most contentious points, however, turned out to be Le Guin's all-out attack on the Judeo-Christian tradition, and her position of radical multiculturalism.

Significantly, the Kesh dance the "World Dance," which, we learn from a kind of appendix, "celebrated human participation in the making and unmaking, the renewal and continuity of the world." As befits a true community, the Kesh have replaced warfare and destructive personal relationships with childbirth and mothering. In their daily interactions with one another and their environment, they are a participatory society, very far removed from the one we know and that is apparently about to destroy itself. Like all of Le Guin's science-fiction novels, *Always Coming Home* is also a thought experiment, a heuristic device. Under its terms, we are asked to recognize parallels between Le Guin's Condor and the Indo-Germanic tribe of the Aryans who, around 2000 B.C., invaded the Indus valley and drove out the original inhabitants; by extension, we are asked to imagine a future archaeologist unearthing our own civilization. If, with *Always Coming Home*, Le Guin has embraced apocalypse, the novel, like any apocalypse, is at the same time a tale of adaptation and survival.

Following the development of Le Guin's thought and art, one notices a continuous expansion of the boundaries of literature. Thus, her work testifies not only to the centrality of western themes and ideas, but also to an evolution within western American literature, from a more literal concern with values and conditions inherent in exploration and colonization, to a reworking of these in new and surprising ways. As a result, there is a noticeable shift from implied universality to validation by subcultural groups, including women. Through her art, Le Guin has become part of the general movement of postmodernism as a cultural revitalization; its participants, by warring against the standards of the dominant culture, have sought not so much political power as legitimation for their particular social conventions and cultural productions. In this war, the idea of community has achieved importance as a means for making human society possible outside the structured sociopolitical system. This means, finally, that Le Guin's concept of a solidarity of women is "fragile but real" for the very reason that it is itself bound up with a society of atomized individuals who contradict its own design of a community.

Selected Bibliography

Primary Sources

Always Coming Home. New York: Harper & Row, 1985.
Buffalo Gals and Other Animal Presences. Santa Barbara: Capra Press, 1987.
Dancing at the Edge of the World. New York: Grove, 1989.
The Dispossessed: An Ambiguous Utopia. New York: Harper & Row, 1974.
The Farthest Shore. New York: Atheneum, 1972.
A Fisherman of the Inland Sea. New York: HarperCollins, 1994.

Four Ways to Forgiveness. New York: HarperPrism, 1995.

The Language of the Night: Essays on Fantasy and Science Fiction. Susan Wood, ed. New York: Putnam's, 1979.

The Lathe of Heaven. New York: Scribner's, 1971.

The Left Hand of Darkness. New York: Ace, 1969.

"The New Atlantis." *The New Atlantis and Other Novellas of Science Fiction.* Robert Silverberg, ed. New York: Hawthorn Books, 1975; rpt. as *The Compass Rose: Short Stories.* New York: Harper & Row, 1982.

Orsinian Tales. New York: Harper & Row, 1976.

Rocannon's World. New York: Harper, 1966.

Searoad: Chronicles of Klatsand. New York: HarperCollins, 1991.

Tehanu: The Last Book of Earthsea. New York: Atheneum, 1990.

The Tombs of Atuan. New York: Atheneum, 1971.

Unlocking the Air and Other Stories. New York: HarperCollins, 1996.

The Wind's Twelve Quarters. New York: Harper & Row, 1975.

A Wizard of Earthsea. Berkeley: Parnassus, 1968.

Secondary Sources

Bittner, James W. *Approaches to the Fiction of Ursula K. Le Guin.* Ann Arbor: UMI Research Press, 1984. Close reading of her pre-1979 works in terms of the romantic quest.

Cummins, Elizabeth. *Understanding Ursula K. Le Guin.* Columbia: University of South Carolina Press, 1990. Definitive and wonderfully perceptive. With comprehensive annotated bibliographies.

Haraway, Donna. "A Manifesto for Cyborgs: Science, Technology, and Socialist Feminism in the 1980s." *Socialist Review* (Berkeley, California), 15:2 (1985): 65-107. On the political potential of cultural post-modernism.

McCaffery, Larry, and Sinda Gregory. "An Interview with Ursula Le Guin." *Missouri Review*, 7:2 (1984): 64-85.

Roemer, Kenneth M. "The Talking Porcupine Liberates Utopia: Le Guin's 'Omelas' as Pretext to the Dance." *Utopian Studies*, 2:1-2 (1991): 6-18. Perceptive discussion of an often neglected and misunderstood story.

Slusser, George E. *Between Worlds: The Literary Dilemma of Ursula K. Le Guin.* San Bernardino, California: Borgo Press, 1993. On the contradictions in her work.

Cheryll Glotfelty

Barry Holstun Lopez

"Listen. Pay attention. Do your research. Try to learn. Don't presume. And always imagine that there's more there than you could possibly understand or sense" (O'Connell 16). This advice that Barry Lopez offers to writing students illuminates his own method and epitomizes the tone of deep respect and the presence of abiding mystery that characterize his work. "My passion is language and landscape," explains this pre-eminent nature writer, "and those two are inseparable for me" (Lueders 32). Through metaphors drawn from natural history and anthropology, Lopez's work espouses an unwavering set of values, among them courtesy, tolerance, dignity, wonder, reciprocity, responsibility, and community.

Lopez was born in 1945 in New York State, but grew up in the San Fernando Valley of California, where his affinity for the American West took hold. He received an A.B. and an M.A.T. from the University of Notre Dame, and did graduate work in folklore and journalism at the University of Oregon. Since 1970 he has been a full-time writer, living with his wife Sandra in the woods along the McKenzie River in Oregon. He has published in a wide variety of genres, among which fiction, natural history, and essays predominate.

Fiction

In *Giving Birth to Thunder, Sleeping with His Daughter: Coyote Builds*

283

North America (1977), dedicated to the Native peoples of North America, Lopez retells sixty-eight Coyote stories from nearly as many tribes. Lopez's engaging adaptations of these stories avoid the turgid prose of direct translation, present the full range of trickster tales, including the lewd and cannibalistic ones, and portray both the hero *and* trickster sides of Coyote, so that modern readers are both entertained and educated in American Indian traditions.

Desert Notes: Reflections in the Eye of a Raven (1976), the first collection of Lopez's own stories, is also the first book of a trilogy that includes *River Notes: The Dance of Herons* (1979) and *Field Notes: The Grace Note of the Canyon Wren* (1994). Each book consists of assorted stories told from different points of view, unified by their focus on place, by their inconclusiveness, and by their deliberate strangeness. The short pieces in *Desert Notes* could be described as invocations of desertness or as experiments in ways of seeing the desert. But despite one's striving to see the desert, questions remain, metaphors take you only so far, mystery endures.

River Notes, like *Desert Notes*, is saturated with a sense of place, this time a river's edge. *River Notes*, however, conveys a stronger sense of an unfolding narrative than does *Desert Notes*. Many of the stories are told by a man who has been depressed and lonely for a long time, who is separated from his wife, and who hopes to learn from the river how to be healed. The narrator makes several vain attempts to know the river, including hiring scientists to take precise measurements of flow, depth, and shore profile. Finally, during a drought year, acting upon a vivid dream, the narrator transfers a large fish from a shrinking pool to what remains of the river. This selfless, redemptive gesture opens the way for Blue Heron to speak to the man and teach him to dance. Rain follows. As in *Desert Notes*, Lopez's primary concern in *River Notes* is to discover respectful ways to enter into an intimate relationship with nature.

The final book of the trilogy, *Field Notes*, is a collection of twelve stories united not by a common landscape or a central character but by the context of modernity and the longing to connect. Whether or not they travel, the characters are journeyers: they are seeking intimacy and an understanding of their relationship to another person, to the past, to a place, to animals, to a moral life. Although the three books of the *Notes* trilogy are structurally dissimilar, thematically they share patterns of desire: to recover lost intimacy, to know a place without violating it, to see without gawking.

Winter Count (1981), a collection of nine short stories, represents Lopez's fiction at its best—spare, elegant, and resonant with mystery. Like the Mona Lisa's smile, there is a certain something animating these stories that remains elusive. In "Restoration," the narrator befriends a man who is restoring a collection of natural history books found in a nineteenth-century French mansion in North Dakota; while the restorationist loses himself in his craft, six antelope suddenly appear outside, then, as suddenly, vanish. All the stories explore dimensions of the poetic view, suggesting that both art and nature are replete with meanings that reason alone cannot fathom.

Lopez once remarked that he likes to keep trying different kinds of writing to avoid falling into the habit of imitating himself (O'Connell 13). *Crow and Weasel* (1990) is a fable, set in mythic time, about a journey that young Crow and Weasel take to visit lands farther north than their people's stories go. After exchanging stories with the Inuit people of the Arctic tundra, Crow and Weasel return to their home country, having survived many challenges and become mature men in the process. Weasel's closing words express a conception of wealth evident throughout Lopez's work: "It is good to be alive. To have friends, to have a family, to have children, to live in a particular place. These relationships are sacred" (63).

Natural History

In contrast to his fiction, which is elliptical and pared down, Lopez's natural history writing is accessible and amply developed. Like his fiction, Lopez's natural history explores facets of humanity's relationship with landscape, broadly construed to include animals, soils, and plant life. Lopez's natural-history titles have earned him the reputation of being one of America's finest contemporary writers. *Of Wolves and Men* (1978) won the John Burroughs Medal for distinguished natural history (see *A Literary History* 1252-1253), and *Arctic Dreams: Imagination and Desire in a Northern Landscape* (1986) received the National Book Award for general nonfiction. These books are notable for their eloquent blend of scientific information, history, Native American viewpoints, and personal experience.

The monumental *Arctic Dreams* stands as Barry Lopez's most renowned work to date, a philosophical inquiry into "the influence of the Arctic landscape on the human imagination" and the role of desire in our conduct with the landscape. Lopez is stirred by the "fundamental strangeness" of the Arctic, which serves to expose a traveler's prejudices and shake one out of complacency. What disturbs Lopez most is evidence everywhere of rapid change in the North—economic transformation, social dislocation, technological development, ecological damage.

After presenting a geographic and seasonal profile of the Arctic, focusing specifically on the quality of light there, Lopez develops chapters on muskoxen, polar bears, narwhals, and birds, followed by studies of ice types, mental maps, and Arctic explorers. As in *Of Wolves and Men*, he views animals from many angles, stopping often to ponder the ethics and significance of hunting. Throughout the book, contrasts are drawn between the Eskimo view and the western view of explorers, whalers, corporations, and scientists. *Arctic Dreams* manages without condescension to capture the exoticism of a foreign place in a way that simultaneously awakens our sense of wonder and arouses our concern over the loss of ancient relationships with the land.

Essays

An overview of Lopez's repertoire would be incomplete without mention of his many essays, which have appeared widely in periodicals such as *Harper's*, *North American Review* (for both of which he has been a contributing editor), *Orion*, *Antaeus*, *Wilderness*, *Country Journal*, *National Geographic*, and many others. A selection of fourteen of these pieces, slightly revised, is collected in *Crossing Open Ground* (1988). In most of these essays Lopez writes in a personal voice, describing places, experiences, and people, and the thoughts they have triggered. A majority of the essays are occasioned by a visit to a natural area—a desert in Southern California, a forest of the Pacific Northwest, a river in Alaska, the Kaibab Plateau of northern Arizona—sometimes solo, but usually accompanied by a friend or a guide. The trips generate reflections on the relationship of people and landscape.

Lopez's published lecture, *The Rediscovery of North America* (1990), sketches out a narrative also implicit in *Crossing Open Ground*: in the past, Native peoples lived in harmony with the land, inseparable from nature, in an intricate tapestry of relationships. The European conquest of America, however, has bequeathed a legacy of separation from the land, ruthless violence, and unrestrained greed—imperialist comportment the consequences of which are environmentally and culturally cat-astrophic. We must find a way to reorient our values and to rediscover this place as home. By protecting our remaining natural areas, studying the plant and animal communities that live there, respecting diversity, and learning from the wisdom of indigenous people, we can begin to reintegrate ourselves with the fabric of life. All of Lopez's writing embraces these concerns and offers the hope that, with courage and commitment, it will be possible for us to reach a new state of harmony with the landscape.

Selected Bibliography

Primary Sources

Arctic Dreams: Imagination and Desire in a Northern Landscape. New York: Scribner's, 1986.

Crossing Open Ground. New York: Scribner's, 1988.

Crow and Weasel. Tom Pohrt, illus. San Francisco: North Point Press, 1990.

Desert Notes: Reflections in the Eye of a Raven. Kansas City, Kansas: Sheed, Andrews & McMeel, 1976.

Field Notes: The Grace Note of the Canyon Wren. New York: Knopf, 1994.

Giving Birth to Thunder, Sleeping with His Daughter: Coyote Builds North America. Kansas City, Kansas: Sheed, Andrews and McMeel, 1977.

Of Wolves and Men. New York: Scribner's, 1978.

The Rediscovery of North America. Lexington: University Press of Kentucky, 1990.

River Notes: The Dance of Herons. Kansas City, Kansas: Andrews & McMeel, 1979.

Winter Count. New York: Scribner's, 1981.

Secondary Sources

Paul, Sherman. "Making the Turn: Rereading Barry Lopez." In *For Love of the World: Essays on Nature Writers.* Iowa City: University of Iowa Press, 1992. Pp. 67-107. A reflective ramble through Lopez's oeuvre, characterizing him as a moralist who embodies Aldo Leopold's "land ethic."

Rueckert, William H. "Barry Lopez and the Search for a Dignified and Honorable Relation with Nature." *North Dakota Quarterly,* 59 (Spring 1991): 279-304. Maintains that *River Notes* best exemplifies the importance of imagination in Lopez's writing and that all of Lopez's works urge us to reformulate our relation-ship to nature.

Slovic, Scott. *Barry Lopez.* New York: Twayne, forthcoming. The most complete biogra-phy to date of Lopez, along with a thoughtful study of his work in the context of American nature writing. Discusses Lopez's creative work by employing Lopez's own theories of narrative, with attention given to the role of stories in culture.

————. "'A More Particularized Understanding': Seeking Qualitative Awareness in Barry Lopez's *Arctic Dreams*." In *Seeking Awareness in American Nature Writing*. Salt Lake City: University of Utah Press, 1992. Pp. 137-166. Argues that Lopez supplements "mathematical knowledge" with primary personal experience in order to overcome estrangement and achieve full appreciation of the Arctic.

Spurlock, Duane. "An Introduction to the Writings of Barry Lopez: Seeing with New Eyes." M.A. Thesis. University of Kentucky, 1987. An excellent annotated bibliography of works written by and about Barry Lopez.

Wild, Peter. *Barry Lopez*. Boise: Boise State University Western Writers Series, 1984. A critical evaluation of Lopez's writing from his first magazine articles through *Winter Count* (1981), arguing that *Of Wolves and Men* (1978) is "mature, controlled, and inspired," in contrast to an earlier period of "jejune romanticism."

Interviews

Aton, Jim. "An Interview with Barry Lopez." *Western American Literature*, 21 (May 1986): 3-17.

Bonetti, Kay. "An Interview with Barry Lopez." *Missouri Review*, 11:3 (1988): 57-77.

Lueders, Edward. "Ecology and the Human Imagination: Barry Lopez and Edward O. Wilson." In *Writing Natural History: Dialogues with Authors*. Edward Lueders, ed. Salt Lake City: University of Utah Press, 1989. Pp. 7-35.

O'Connell, Nicholas. "Barry Lopez." In *At the Field's End: Interviews with Twenty Pacific Northwest Writers*. Seattle: Madrona, 1987. Pp. 3-18.

Laurie Ricou

David Wagoner

lthough David Wagoner, who was born in 1926 in Ohio and raised in Whiting, Indiana, began teaching at the University of Washington in 1954, the *Seattle Post-Intelligencer* reported at the end of 1959 that none of his writing had "been influenced by the Northwest" (Farrell). The publication of "A Guide to Dungeness Spit" in 1962 signaled his establishing imaginative control over a new and ancient place, his emergence as the Pacific Northwest's Robert Frost, his recognizing the guide book as a poetic model.

At poetry readings, Wagoner insists that it is "possible to be more than one poet at a time" (Wagoner Papers, Box 16, Folder 256); through more than a dozen books of poetry he has succeeded at the high modernist exercise in metaphysical wit, the insouciant *jeu d'esprit*, the cautious love lyric, the angry polemic, and the compressed narrative. The most overtly different Wagoner is the poet who re-imagines, in English, the metaphor and myth of North Coast Native peoples in *Who Shall Be the Sun?* (1978). There he writes his way into the Pacific Northwest through the oldest stories of its animals and trees, speaking in a voice, according to Wagoner, "evidently removed from [his own]," "the voice, perhaps, of the wise old grandfather I never had" (Interview with author).

Yet this inclination to the measured and oblique voice of the tribal elder may suggest how Midwest accent shapes Northwest regionalist, blending the flatlands deliberateness of an early poem, such as "Words Above a Narrow Entrance" (1963), with the exaggerated puzzlement of

"The Death of Paul Bunyan" (1976), and the homage to incidental generosity in "A Woman Feeding Gulls" (1983). Wagoner once tried to
describe his own poetic "signature":

Wind, bird, and tree
Water, grass, and light:
In half of what I write
Roughly or smoothly
Year by impatient year,
The same six words recur.
(*Collected Poems* 53)

Following this playful lead would suggest that Wagoner is a monosyl-
labic noun-obsessed poet, inclining to the generalized image (bird)
rather than the particular (*e.g.*, grebe), and focusing on the intricate
intertwining of the non-human, animate world. This anti-manifesto
implies other defining features: that David Wagoner is always the critic
(lyric is invariably fused with essay); that, as he sets (in stanza two) an
imagined cat near bird and tree, the voice is never far from irony; and
that the poet's stance before the natural world works toward total
acceptance. "Instead," he writes, shifting from fantasy to metaphor at
the beginning of the final stanza, "*I take what is*" (*Collected Poems* 53
[emphasis added]).

The developing poetics of acceptance in "The Words" signals one of
several ways in which David Wagoner may be classified among the *new*
regionalists. That is, like such writers as Ivan Doig or the Canadian poet
Robert Bringhurst, he is less interested in *describing* than in *listening* and
telling, in accord with ecology, "meaning the *imaginative* perception,
underscored by calamity, that our personal, familial, socio-economic,
spiritual, and environmental obligations are precariously, that is to say
organically, interrelated" (Ramsey 319). As Kim Stafford urges: "A place
is a story happening many times" (11). Wagoner's own recognition of
place as dynamic (both in time and space) marks him as a quiet advocate for a regionalism defined not by homogeneous landform but by culture. *Accuracy* of description, and *authenticity* are no longer trusted; language is inevitably slippery. Place is understood through styles and
narratives—not mapped in two dimensions by survey lines, but absorbed
through local knowledge and discovered within the layering of stories
told in place.

Hence, Wagoner looks for relational ways of interpreting landscape:

> Stand still. The trees ahead and bushes beside you
> Are not lost. Wherever you are is called Here,
> And you must treat it as a powerful stranger,
> Must ask permission to know it and be known.
> The forest breathes. Listen. It answers,
> I have made this place around you.
> ("Lost," *Collected Poems* 182)

For David Wagoner the poet, place is detected by waiting on the stories of the trees and birds, of the wind and water and light. But he is also a more active, more expansive storyteller, as his eight novels show. They are versions, albeit muted, of the best of the American tall-tale tradition, filled with the bemused subterfuge of an enthusiastic amateur magician.

The Road to Many a Wonder (1974) might be Wagoner's typical novel. It's a picaresque, on–the–road story of Ike Bender, a young man who at age twenty leaves an abusive father and the tyranny of "dirt farming" for the dream of Pikes Peak and a rush of gold. As with Twain and Dickens, a sentimental story line is given sustained interest by an ear for the inventive nuance of the vernacular. Ike and his wife Millicent are wise enough in the ways of Thoreau to manage to have someone else work and manage their gold mine while they retreat to focus on the wonders of nature. Ultimately, the novel, like "Lost," advocates standing still, paying attention, letting the light and water speak:

> ...I'd catch myself breathing and waking up for the sheer wonder of something most folks wouldn't of noticed, including me back before Dogtown—the shape the current makes turning aside at the head of an island;...the way the rain turns all colors falling through sunshine;...and on and on like that, forever if you've got a mind to. (134)

Several of Wagoner's novels, such as *Rock* (1958) and *The Escape Artist* (1965), might be described as tales of midwestern urban drift. The more successful novels, like *Road to Many a Wonder*, depend on a first-person narrator, whose naive yet savvy voice retells the history of westward migration. As in *Tracker* (1975), the reader's pleasure derives more from the slang of the narrator than from the suspense of the chase. In such novels as *Whole Hog* (1976) the appeal lies in trying "to keep up with the way [the characters] might be thinking," especially where the effort is "too much like trying to follow a horse whose feet never touched anything" (*Tracker* 3). Wagoner's novels push regionalism toward the post-modern — but they never quite get there. In the post-modern spirit, they are profoundly respectful of the local, yet continuously ironic, self-conscious, and self-critical; they frequently turn parodic, but will not abandon their grounding in realism. Since *The Hanging Garden* (1980), Wagoner has not published a novel. The novel, he once told an interviewer, "was a lark at first": "I would say my interest in poetry would exclude writing any more novels" (Farrell 3).

Unlike the tall-tale adventuring of the largely midwestern novels, humility in the presence of the powers of nature finds more congenial expression in the undecidable lyric. Inspired by the visionary Roethke, and inflected by the calm of Richard Hugo, Wagoner's is a listening and speaking poetry, whose bias against the writerly (paradoxical as it is) is prompted primarily by a growing appreciation for a radically alternative connection to the living world, especially as discovered in Native American cultures. Talking, because it necessitates listening, is a better means to understanding nature than the fixity and labelling of print. Wagoner presents the case in "Talking to the Forest" (*Collected Poems* 77). The first draft began with a seven-line rhetorical question, mulling "What can we give instead of old commands...?" In the second draft, the passage became stanza two, and is subsequently deleted entirely: thus, Wagoner turns the emphasis from the poet's own *angst* toward an opening where the reader/listener apparently drops in in *mid-conversation*: "We'll notice first they've quit turning their ears...." The intensely word-conscious regional poet is always looking for the "speech [which is] in our mouths this moment, waiting" (Wagoner Papers, Box 5, Folder 175).

Affiliation with a new regionalism implies, especially, ecological sensitivity. Standing still and listening usually leads to an acknowledgment that "The forest knows / where you are" ("Lost"), but frequently also to social criticism, especially of the logging industry, as in "Elegy for a Forest Clear-cut by the Weyerhaeuser Company" (*Collected Poems* 228). In his notes toward the poem, "For the Straightening of the Sammamish River" (another elegy with social commentary), are these fragments: "of time and the river. believing a river is only the water in it ... a river is only the water and not the way it goes. not where it goes..." (Wagoner Papers, Box 3, Folder 63). Description of the river from a particular vantage point is less crucial than imagining all the other places and things the river touches, and the wholeness in *the utter meaninglessness* of its path.

Typically Wagoner's Northwest poems meander. Their emphasis is on where each poem goes. "The Spawning Ground" (1963) is a good case in point. Place, in this poem, is found not in topography or on a map, but in an intricate conjunction of animate and inanimate detail which fuses the "foam" and "stones" of a shallow river, the female and male salmon themselves, the "ripe spawn" and the "gull and crow, blue heron and osprey," which appear at the end of the poem to signal the next phase in the web of ecological interdependence (*Nesting Ground* 24). The poet–naturalist looks for a bioregional pattern of necessary connection among specific flora and fauna and habitat.

Yet Wagoner knows that ecology often hugs sentimentality. Hence his best bioregional poems are also ironized by his discoveries within the descriptive language itself, so that instead of looking for pictorial realism, the poem is listening to how its own language might suggest a transactional, mobile connection to place. The new regionalism fears provincialism. Any possibility of sentiment or rhapsody must be curbed and tempered. In Wagoner's poetry — as in his best novels — the trace of *feeling* for place is restrained and interrogated by language play, by a taste for the irony discovered in language. "Reading the Landscape," which at once teases literary illusion ("the sweet nothings/of casual ... speech"), honors tall-tale euphemism ("on the seat/Of kings, the gluteus maximus"), and puns its way through oral tags ("exercise your freedom of chance"), nonetheless ends with something akin to reverence: "keeping a constant Here beside you/As faithfully as your death" (*In Broken Country* 101-102). Not only because he looks to share misunderstandings, but because, in Wagoner's poetry, verbal play is almost always qualified by something best described as prayer — a tone, or a silence (an end of words, a shutting up) which speaks of humility in contact with a nurturing and confusing power. Like Willy Grier, the tree nurse in Wagoner's novel *Money, Money, Money* (1955), "he like[s] slow things" (*Money* 214), and he slows down to pay them attention.

Selected Bibliography

Primary Sources

In Broken Country. Boston: Atlantic/Little, Brown, 1979.

Collected Poems (1956-1976). Bloomington: Indiana University Press, 1976.
Dry Sun, Dry Wind. Bloomington: Indiana University Press, 1953.
The Escape Artist. New York: Farrar, Straus & Giroux, 1965; London: Gollancz, 1965.
First Light. Boston: Atlantic/Little, Brown, 1983.
Money, Money, Money. New York: Harcourt Brace, 1955.
The Nesting Ground. Bloomington: Indiana University Press, 1963.
A Place to Stand. Bloomington: Indiana University Press, 1958.
The Road to Many a Wonder. New York: Farrar, Straus & Giroux, 1974.
Riverbed. Bloomington: Indiana University Press, 1972.
Staying Alive. Bloomington: Indiana University Press, 1966.
Tracker. Boston: Atlantic/Little, Brown, 1975.
Who Shall Be the Sun? Bloomington: Indiana University Press, 1978.
The David Wagoner Papers, Washington University, St. Louis, Missouri.

Secondary Sources

Cording, Robert K. "David Wagoner." In *Dictionary of Literary Biography*, Vol. 5: *American Poets Since WWII*, Part 2. Donald J. Greiner, ed. Detroit: Gale Research, 1980. Pp. 348-355. The most useful compact overview of Wagoner's work.

Farrell, Barry. "Northwest Novelists Win Recognition as Four UW Professors Score Top Successes," *Seattle Post-Intelligencer* (December 27, 1959), Pictorial Review 3.

McFarland, Ronald E. "David Wagoner's Comic Westerns." *Critique: Studies in Modern Fiction,* 28 (Fall 1986): 5-18. A useful definition of Wagoner's non-violent ethical message against the formula-western. Focuses on the novels from 1970 to 1976.

Peters, Robert. "Thirteen Ways of Looking at David Wagoner's New Poems." *Western Humanities Review,* 35 (Autumn 1981): 267-272. A slightly acerbic yet appreciative review of Wagoner's *Landfall* (1981), summarizing him as the essential middle-class, middle-age poet. Unusual in its length, it perhaps best summarizes the scholarly community's rationale for not paying attention to Wagoner.

Pinsker, Sanford. *Three Pacific Northwest Poets: William Stafford, Richard Hugo, and David Wagoner.* Boston: Twayne, 1987. A sensitive survey of Wagoner's poetry, incorporating a suggestive context of influences and analogues. Pinsker emphasizes Wagoner's dramatic monologues and his use of the "instructional mode."

Ramsey, Jarold. "'The Hunter Who Had an Elk for a Guardian Spirit,' and the Ecological Imagination." In *Smoothing the Ground: Essays on Native American Oral Literature.* Brian Swann, ed. Berkeley: University of California Press, 1983. P. 319.

Ricou, Laurie, Personal Interview, Seattle, January 16, 1990.

Stafford, Kim R. "There Are No Names But Stories," In *Places & Stories.* Pittsburgh: Carnegie-Mellon University Press, 1987.

II
California

Gerald Haslam

California

California entered the European mind with the publication of *Las Sergas de Esplandian* by Garci Rodriguez Ordonez de Montalvo in 1512: "Know ye that on the right hand of the Indies there is an island called California, very near the Terrestrial Paradise..." (*California Heritage* 48). It has rarely been viewed as conventional or common since, for it remains as much state of mind as state of the union.

By the turn of the twentieth century, Theodore Roosevelt observed, "When I am in California, I am not in the west, I am west of the west," and it was clear that this state remained misunderstood (*West of the West* xi). The terms of that confusion remain rooted in an inability to see past California's stereotype. Like many outsiders, Roosevelt failed to recognize that there were—and are—many Californias. At the very time he saw what he sought, vaqueros and cowboys herded cattle over much of the state's open territory; America's last "wild Indian," Ishi, struggled to survive in foothills east of the Sacramento Valley, which itself burgeoned with yeomen farmers; miners still haunted the state's deserts and foothills, and loggers were stripping vast forest to the north. Those sections were the West, period. In large measure, they still are, as the books of Hector Lee, Arnold R. Rojas, Theodora Kroeber, Frederick Faust, and Robert Easton illustrate.

Those who think California is "West Coast, not West" simply don't know what they're talking about; they are responding to illusion not reality. Geographically and culturally, the West Coast extends no deeper inland than the Coast Ranges—still largely unsettled—while the remainder of California includes a plethora of mountains, a vast valley, dense woodlands, and deserts edging it to the east. It is an expansive, varied domain with far more rural or unsettled land than urban sprawl. Still, the California of illusion seems to dominate the visions of outsiders —and some insiders, too. In the south at the time Roosevelt spoke, a great real-estate boom, wedded to an increasingly romanticized version of the mission past, was churning, and it attracted a largely conservative, WASP population. Hollywood would soon begin its move from sleepy village to motion-picture capital, producing a society that was indeed west of the West—west, perhaps, of anything. In fact, the very word "West" in that context took on new and bizarre connotations. Yet those places and events represent only one sub-region of this diverse province.

Today more publishing writers live in California than any other state —more than the remainder of the West combined if recent surveys are accurate. The San Francisco Bay Area and the greater Los Angeles region host the second- and third-largest collections of authors of any cities nationally (only New York City has more). Those two urban areas also harbor the bulk of the state's population. They also host two of the nation's largest clusters of alternative publishers and literary magazines, what editor Michael Anania has called "the fecund churning ground of our literary culture."

California not only boasts the nation's most geographically diverse terrain but also enjoys America's most ethnically diverse population. It is also quickly becoming—perhaps has already become—the mainland's first state with a non-white majority. That's not surprising, really, since this is where the United States has finally become one of the Americas, where Asia's eastern thrust meets Latin America's northern push, where more different languages are spoken than any other western locale, and where the concept of West continues to demonstrate its dynamism. Perhaps the most revealing fact is that Los Angeles now houses the world's second-largest urban Mexican population (only Mexico City tops it). Little wonder then that California has produced both the first major novel by a Mexican American author, Jose Antonio Villarreal's *Pocho* (1959), and the first one about a Mexican American character, John Rollin Ridge's *Life and Adventures of Joaquin Murieta, the Celebrated California Bandit* (1854), which is also the initial novel by a Native American.

Various parts of the state developed uniquely: San Francisco, for instance, in the late 1850s was a thriving heterogeneous city, while Los Angeles was a dusty Hispanic pueblo, and the Great Central Valley was little more than a wilderness. Five "geo-literary" affinity zones have developed: the Greater Bay Area, the Heartland, Wilderness California, Southern California, and Fantasy California.

The San Francisco Bay Area during the Gold Rush, for instance, developed a rough-hewn imitation of an eastern seaport, attracting to the region during the late 1840s and 1850s such estimable authors (along with their signal noms de plume) as Alonzo Delano (Old Block), George Horatio Derby (John Phoenix), Louisa Smith Clapp (Dame Shirley), and John Rollin Ridge (Yellow Bird). The following decade — San Francisco was by 1860 the fourteenth-largest city in the Union — saw the development of a national literary reputation by writers operating in the area, especially the Golden Gate Trinity (Bret Harte, Ina Coolbrith, and Charles Warren Stoddard, the three editors of the *Overland Monthly*, plus their partner Sam Clemens), a high point in western American letters. What was most important, perhaps, is that artists of the time reflected a distinctness still associated with the region; they believed themselves to be liberated from the East and from the Puritan past.

The Bohemian Club was founded in 1872, and originally at least it actually included bohemian artists. Avant garde movements have, in fact, continued to flourish on the North Coast. Late in the last century, for example, creative people began gathering at Carmel. Some, like Joaquin Miller, were links to the past; most, however, bespoke a new generation's dynamism: Jack London, Lincoln Steffens, Mary Austin, George Sterling, Nora May French, Stoddard, and a host of lesser-known authors.

By the early twentieth century, then, this had become one of America's most productive, most interesting literary regions. The North Coast's bohemians — up to and including Jack Kerouac, Allen Ginsberg, Gary Snyder and the rest of the Beats, Ken Kesey and his Merry Pranksters, Richard Brautigan and the Hippies, Jim Dodge (perhaps even Thomas Pynchon) and the North Coasters — have been everything from space cadets to geniuses.

The region is now a favorite settling spot for gifted, non-native writers — most of whom do not write about California. Al Young, Dorothy Allison, Gerald Rosen, Alice Walker, Herbert Gold, Ethan Canin,

Morton Marcus, David Bromige, Tillie Olsen, Maya Angelou, and Alice Adams, among many others, reside or have resided in Northern California. This area also features a trendy mixture of urban sophistication, "political correctness," neo-savagery, and ecological concern in the midst of environmental despoilment. Gary Snyder captures those qualities in "Marin-An"

> . . . the twang
> of a pygmy nuthatch high in a pine —
> from behind the cypress windrow
> the mare moves up, grazing.
> a soft continuous roar
> comes out of the far valley
> of six lane Highway — thousands
> and thousands of cars
> driving men to work.
> (*Many Californias* 180)

The state's rural heartland — principally but not exclusively the Great Central Valley — has attracted an ethnically and socially diverse series of migrants to labor in its fields. This region has typified the real California Dream, because people go there not for leisure, but for work — often toil — and the opportunities that follow from it. It has attracted the tough, the determined, and quite possibly the desperate.

This arena of the West has required no "New Historians" to reveal the dark side of frontier experience, for it has produced a literature that acknowledges the failures and the suffering, as well as the triumphs, inherent in the opening of the West. Since the emergence of three heartland natives, William Saroyan, William Everson, and John Steinbeck in the 1930s, this section has produced a steady stream of innovative, often brutally honest, writers. Saroyan exposed one of the region's three great concerns: the immigrant experience and its commonality for folks of all colors. Everson's mystical relationship with nature in his poems reintroduced a sacred apprehension of the land, the second major subject. Steinbeck combined both those elements, plus a social dimension that included questions of class and economic inequity, the third recurring regional thread.

Much writing from the heartland is rooted in the soil, the physical reality from which so many people wrest their livings. Harsh rural realities have shaped much of this literature, limiting illusion without harming expression. Oklahoma-born, Fresno-raised DeWayne Rail writes in "Pickers,"

> Scattered out like a handful of seeds across
> The field, backs humped to the wind,
> Faces like clumps of dirt in the white rows,
> Their hands keep on eating cotton.
> The long sacks fill and puff up tight,
> Like dreams of money they're going to make....
> (*California Heartland* 124)

A list of recent writers from this realm makes it clear that the heartland is now producing an extraordinary native-born crop, arguably the state's strongest: Richard Rodriguez, Gary Soto, Joan Didion, Luis Valdez, Maxine Hong Kingston, David St. John, Frank Bidart, Leonard Gardner, Joyce Carol Thomas, Larry Levis, David Mas Masumoto, Art Cuelho, Luis Omar Salinas, Sherley Anne Williams, as well as the Fresno poets, that creative cluster stimulated by Philip Levine. The list could be much longer. Only Didion and Bidart are not the products of working-class backgrounds; the writing of the rest has been tempered by the sometimes hardscrabble lives they have lived.

Because the heartland, with its farms and ranches, retains so much open space, it is often associated with wilderness California, but that is a mistake. The open fields of the Salinas or Central or Imperial valleys are in their own ways as developed as downtown Sacramento — exploited by corporate agribusiness. California is actually a mountain state slashed by that Great Valley and bordered by deserts; life in its undeveloped areas produces unique visions.

Outsiders don't always understand the dimensions of the Golden State's undeveloped regions, or the richness of its flora and fauna. Much land remains open: the Mojave and Colorado deserts; a remarkable and varied coastline; Bigfoot country northwest; northeast is a volcanic moonscape. California is, moreover, spined by those mountains: the Sierra Nevada, the Cascades, the Coast Ranges, the Tehachapis. All these places have inspired writers.

Look, for example, at the literary reclamation of the desert. Those barren lands had once been crossed by pioneers too intent on survival to notice the beauty surrounding them. By the turn of the century, however, those arid lands could be studied and sometimes romanticized. It was one of those interesting cases where changing circumstances allowed people to re-envision an area. John C. Van Dyke's *The Desert* was in 1901 the first in a series of books that changed the way those ostensible wastelands were viewed. J. Smeaton Chase, Charles Fletcher Lummis, and George Wharton James also contributed important work, but the finest of all American desert books, the most mystical and eloquent, remains Mary Hunter Austin's *The Land of Little Rain*, published two years after Van Dyke's volume.

California's mountains and forests boast as distinguished a cadre of authors as do its deserts. The master here, of course, is John Muir. His work ranged from romantic to scientific. In books such as *The Mountains of California* (1894) or *My First Summer in the Sierra* (1911), his prose soared toward poetry. Clarence King's *Mountaineering In the Sierra Nevada* (1872) actually paved the way for Muir, just as King climbed there before the Scotsman. Less rhapsodic but no less interesting than Muir's writing, and certainly pithy enough to merit attention, is William Henry Brewer's *Up and Down California, 1860-1864* (1930). When Brewer wrote his notes during the Civil War nearly all the state was still wilderness.

Sometimes ignored when considering wilderness California is its impact on poets and novelists, yet it has inspired some of the state's finest literature. For instance, much of Robinson Jeffers' remarkable poetry demonstrates the symbolic power of California's coastline and hills. After a circling vulture had examined his supine body many years ago on the central coast, Jeffers wrote:

> ... How beautiful he looked, veering
> away in the sea-light over the precipice. I tell you
>   solemnly
> I was sorry to have disappointed him. To be eaten
> By that beak and become part of him, to share those
>   wings and those eyes —
> a sublime end of one's body, what an enskyment;
>   what a life after death.
> (*Many Californias* 133)

George R. Stewart wrote of Sierra forests when he produced two of his most memorable novels, *Storm* and *Fire*, and one of Walter Van Tilburg Clark's strongest and most magical novels, *The Track of the Cat*, is set in eastern Sierra cattle country. David Rains Wallace's *The Klamath Knot* is a contemporary treasure. Gary Snyder has set much of his recent poetry in the Sierra Nevada. Jaime DeAngulo wrote compellingly of Big Sur. Ardis Walker explored the Kern Plateau in much of his poetry.

In the 1970s, a talented, long-term transplant to Southern California, only a few miles from the Kern Plateau, Gerald Locklin, captured some of the area's ironies in "Happy Hour":

> ...my students scorn the seaport village
> as a capitalistic scheme, which it is,
> and as an apotheosis of plastic,
> which of course it is...
>
> but was there any chance it would remain
> a stolid carapace for indigent fisherman,
> or that small businesses would lease space for arts
> and crafts authentic as the vanished sea bass?
>
> i wishy-washy will make the best of things:
> tanguery martinis, yachts beyond my means,
> and women that may not be.
> i will be happy at the happy hour.
> (*Many Californias* 250)

Stereotypes to the contrary, the vast majority of people who live in the tropic southland do indeed go to work and earn their livings like everyone else. They do so in a region clouded by myth. It is now a desert-turned-metropolis, largely as a result of water piped from else-where — a classic western American pattern — and it seems to be a pro-totype for other desert cites: Phoenix, Las Vegas, Albuquerque, El Paso, and the rest.

Few today would suspect that the area south of the Tehachapi Mountains was called "the cow counties" even late in the nineteenth century. Little touched by the Gold Rush, it remained largely Spanish-speaking through the 1860s. It also harbored a strong movement to split the state to avoid dominance by the economically and culturally advanced north. "At that time," Lawrence Clark Powell observes in *California Classics*, "Los Angeles was the toughest town in the West, a cesspool of frontier scum" (283).

While not a literary enclave like San Francisco, the region did produce an interesting body of writing in the nineteenth century. Most intriguing are Richard Henry Dana's early glimpses of Spanish California in *Two Years Before the Mast* (1840), a book that views the area as the first American settlers did, from the sea; William Manley's *Death Valley in '49* (1894), which describes a tortuous overland approach; a candid view of life in the 1850s is found in *The Reminiscences of a Ranger* by Horace Bell, who was described by a contemporary as "blackmailer, murderer, thief, house-burner, snake-hunter, and defamer of the dead" (*California Classics* 289).

The pivotal work in Southern California's literary history is, of course, Helen Hunt Jackson's *Ramona*, published in 1884. Intended to expose the plight of Mission Indians, the book ironically became the major factor in the creation of a romanticized mission past. Judging by the number of people who today claim their grandparents knew Ramona —or *were* Ramona—this appears to be an instance of fiction filling a historical vacuum, sucked into reality by promoters.

Before long Southern California hosted a considerable middle-class, middle-western, white, Protestant society—complete with annual Iowa picnics or Oklahoma picnics; that group, the white Protestants, brought the erstwhile Catholic missions back to life and encouraged the romantic version of the Hispanic past that still endures, what historian Carey McWilliams designated as "the myth of the mission past" (McWilliams, interview, March 8, 1980).

One reason southern California seems bizarre is that its nonconformists stand in high relief in such a conservative social setting. But that seemingly conventional, old-line WASP society has by no means been barren. Early in this century it produced, for example, what Kevin Starr has aptly labeled the "literary Pasadenans"—Lawrence Clark Powell, M. F. K. Fisher, Hildergarde Flanner, Ward Ritchie, and even nourished the young Robinson Jeffers—a remarkable fluorescence indeed.

In the 1930s, a unique literary response to a changing world emerged in the southland; crime and detective novels became a major mode of examining the effects of urbanization, industrialization and frustration. James M. Cain, Raymond Chandler, Dashiell Hammett and, later, Ross Macdonald produced novels significant enough to force serious critical attention as well as a new sense of the price exacted by obdurate urban reality. As Chandler himself explained, his stories were set in "a world gone wrong where the law was something to manipulate for profit and power" (*West Coast Fiction* xviii). With writers like James Ellroy, Sue Grafton and Walter Mosley now carrying the torch, crime and detective fiction remains one of the state's most vital literary flames.

Today, SoCal (as many call it) is a cultural hodgepodge — wild, woolly, unpredictable, and exciting. It is fitting, then, that Charles Bukowski was until his recent death probably the region's best-known contemporary writer. But there are plenty of others: Locklin, Carolyn See, Ron Koertge, Wanda Coleman, Hisaye Yamamoto, Kate Braverman, Rafael Zepeda, Christopher Buckley, Laurel Anne Bogan, Mike Davis, Mitsuye Yamada, Frank Chin, and Alurista, among many, many others.

In the midst of negative cliches and justifiable complaints about over-population, swishy trendiness and environmental problems, it is easy to forget that SoCal is one of the world's most exciting cultural centers — it doesn't follow trends, it sets them. Its huge and varied media complex sometimes obscures the equally huge and varied literary output of the area. While the quality of its air may be poor, the caliber and assortment of art in the greater-L.A. area is very high indeed.

That region's boundary with Fantasy California is Hollywood, the land of dreams. As literary historian Franklin Walker points out, although the 2,000-plus novels about the movie industry vary greatly, "nearly all agree that the life in the movie colony is artificial, the art meretricious, and the industry the graveyard of talent" (*A Literary History of Southern California* 259). Many writers of great talent have written those books: Harry Leon Wilson, Horace McCoy, Budd Schulberg, F. Scott Fitzgerald, and Norman Mailer among others.

In a 1945 movie, Robert Paige and Deanna Durbin sang,

> Ca-li-for-ni-ay!
> ...The climate is better
> The ocean is wetter
> The mountains are higher
> The deserts are drier
> The hills have more splendor
> The girls have more gender
> Ca-li-for-ni-ay!

This was an updated version of Rodriguez Ordonez de Montalvo's island called California inhabited only by black women whose "arms are all gold, as is the harness of the wild beasts which, after taming, they ride" (*California Heritage* 49). Fantasy California endures; it is the aspect of the state that remains least dynamic, thus least changed.

Fostered by unrealistic expectations, disappointment has been a common response to California. Even those who find what they expect may want more, or less, or something different. A distinguished transplant, novelist Herbert Gold, has written,

> Elsewhere, there is struggle for existence; we have heard of this in California. Here, for the massive middle class, the struggle sometimes comes down to a courageous battle against boredom and bland, and this is why love and marriage seem to have replaced the frontier for exploration; they have become the moral equivalent of war in a state where all the marriages end in divorce. (*Unknown California* 3-4)

Gold's observations are typical of the exaggeration the state stimulates, but tell a cotton-picker in Corcoran, a logger in Scotia, an oil worker in Taft, or perhaps a struggling Viet family in a crowded Westminster apartment that "boredom and bland" are their toughest problems. No, with this generalization, Gold has written about Fantasy California because he is using a caricature of the state to discuss a general, modern malaise.

For many Fantasy California seems to be the only one, a land of sun-bleached blondes with straightened teeth, hurrying on roller blades to hot tubs after working in their marijuana fields or, in the last century, a place where gold nuggets could be scooped up by the shovelful and fruit burgeoned year-round.

Fantasy California has produced an intriguing body of literature in all of the physical regions. To this richly imaginative realm can be assigned books as diverse as Evelyn Waugh's *The Loved One* (set in the Southland), Ernest Callenbach's *Ecotopia* (Wilderness California), Robert Roper's *Royo County* (Heartland) and Cyra McFadden's *The Serial* (Bay Area).

The apotheosis of Fantasy California's literature is Nathanael West's *The Day of the Locust*, published in 1939. As Powell explains, West wrote the novel "to formalize a tragic view of life. He perceived Hollywood and its product as the pure epitome of all that is wrong with life in the

United States." *The Day of the Locust* is not a book about a real California; it is a book about Nathanael West's response to Hollywood and to a world gone mad. A hint of his attitude may be gleaned from a letter he wrote to Josephine Herbst in 1933 shortly after he had become a screenwriter in tinseltown: "This place is Asbury Park, New Jersey....In other words, phooey on Cal. Another thing, this stuff about easy work is all wrong. My hours are from ten in the morning to six at night with a full day on Saturdays. There's no fooling here" (*California Classics* 351).

West produced a novel that typifies Fantasy Cal, a dark mirror limning the gap between expectation and reality. It is the area's greatest work because it combines those very elements with West's unique talent and sensitivity, extrapolating to national and international dimensions toward a powerful surreal vision, all in the guise of a California. As West and others demonstrate, artists can find in the Golden State's variety and complexity vehicles for writing about virtually anything — real or imagined.

Today, in the real, non-stereotypical California, cultural dynamism has become the principal theme. As a result, various reviewers and critics have, over the past five years, suggested that (among others, of course) Richard Rodriguez or Ronald Takaki may be California's leading writer of nonfiction, that Maxine Hong Kingston or Amy Tan may be its leading novelist, that Luis Valdez or Philip Kan Gotanda may be its leading playwright, that Gary Soto or Wanda Coleman may be its leading poet, that Hisaye Yamamoto or Jess Mowry may be its leading writer of short fiction — nary a paleface in the group. Moreover, Rodriguez, Hong Kingston, Valdez, Gotanda, and Soto are products of the agricultural Great Central Valley, not the state's traditional literary centers.

Of course, California also boasts plenty of distinguished white writers. A list of them might include best nonfiction writer, Joan Didion or Kevin Starr; best novelist, Gina Berriault or James D. Houston; best playwright, Suzanne Lummis or Michael Lynch; best poet, Diane Wakoski or Robert Hass; best short-fiction writer, Molly Giles or Ernest J. Finney. This arbitrary roster could of course be much longer, but the major point is that California's rich cultural mix allows two such lists to be assembled at all. In this state only the most obtuse believes America is merely a European creation. Of course, because of increasing ethnic and racial blending — producing solid writers such as Greg Sarris and Louis Owens — categories like "white" and "non-white" are themselves becoming anachronisms.

Any survey of post-World War II California writing suggests an important social message—more women, more non-whites, more working-class people are represented in the literature. That reflects changes in this state's society over the past 150 years or so. No matter what is said by romanticists yearning for the "halcyon days of the dons" or the "rollicking Gold Rush," California's society is more democratic, less class-and-race bound than before, and so is its literature.

Non-whites and women were, of course, important to California society from the start, but social customs and barriers prevented anything like representative exposure in the arts. For instance, despite the fact that a Japanese-born writer like Yone Noguchi was a stalwart in Bay Area bohemian movements at the turn of the century, a far more important historical reality was the pervasiveness in this state of "Yellow Peril" laws that subjected Asian emigrants to systematic and unrelenting discrimination.

In the last twenty-five years, however, authors as diverse as Gus Lee, Jeanne Wakatsuki Houston, Nellie Wong, Frank Chin, Amy Tan, Mitsuye Yamada, Genny Lim, Marilyn Chin, Jeff Tagami, Gotanda, Masumoto, Takaki, Yamamoto and Hong Kingston have created an Asian-American literary fluorescence. Unfortunately, bigotry still thrives, now more likely directed toward Southeast Asians—the most recent migrant group is usually targeted—but the road to literary achievement is no longer totally blocked. *Passages*, a revealing anthology of writing from Hmong, Lao, Cambodian and Vietnamese migrants, has been edited by Katsuyo K. Howard.

Writers out of the mainstream have found support and publication in the churning alternative press movement in California. Thanks to the emergence of small literary publishers and literary magazines, California produces, among other things, more poetry than any other state; there are literally thousands of new titles each year. A glance at Len Fulton's *The International Directory of Little Magazines and Small Presses* (published in Paradise, California, by the way) provides a sense of how rich and busy the alternative publishing scene on the Pacific coast is— everything from Noel Young's Capra Press or Malcolm Margolin's Heyday Books, to Marvin Malone's *Wormwood Review* or Glenna Luschei's *Cafe Solo*. James Sallis has observed that, "with current monolithic publishing trends," alternative outlets "may *be* our literature, what is left of it" (*A Literary History of the American West* 1023).

The California literary landscape and roster looks different from within than from without. Joan Didion, for instance — the gifted writer who seems to be the East's California expert — appears to be ignorant of and unsympathetic toward the vast working and middle classes. Novelist Diane Johnson, on the other hand, seems to have a hand on that dominant social pulse. Many significant writers are published locally, and with a population of over thirty million, California offers a considerable audience. Some writers are highly regarded but are not well known nationally, and vice versa. With so many authors, the state also hosts its share (and then some) of literary poseurs, many of whom are better at generating publicity than at producing memorable books. The career of one alternative-press favorite, Wilma Elizabeth McDaniel, offers a strong antidote for such phonies.

Born in 1918, this daughter of Oklahoma sharecroppers is a Dust Bowl migrant with only a high school education. She did not publish a book until she was fifty-five. McDaniel has no affiliation in the writing or university worlds; she has no agent. Moreover, Wilma does no public readings. She lives in rural Tulare far from poetry circles or even book reviewers. Nevertheless, the hardy McDaniel has become one of the Golden State's literary treasures, "absolutely unique and utterly irreplaceable," according to novelist James D. Houston (interview, April 7, 1994).

She accomplished that by writing with a vision unlike any other in the West's literary history — straightforward, lyrical, often funny, and always telling:

> Monday used to be
> the day after Sunday
> it meant washday to most women
> on Persimmon Road
> but seance to Ardella Pitts
> who always hung her dead husband up
>   with wooden pins
> beside a yellow trousseau gown
> and allowed the wind to whip him with daffodil might
> while she washed his shirts
> and put away each week
> until a man in overalls
>   who had no right
> broke Ardella's Contact with the

          great beyond
by installing a dryer
now we never see Mr. Pitts
and Ardella moans
that he doesn't love her any longer
("Clothes Dryer" in *California Heartland* 163-164)

McDaniel sees the wonder and the pain in poor peoples' lives, and she elevates them to their rightful place in the human scheme. "Just ordinary is so much of our lives," she explains. "I love the ordinary."

McDaniel's foil might be Kate Braverman, a gifted writer far better known outside the state. A generation younger (born in 1950), and as urban as McDaniel is rural, Kate grew up in relative affluence, the daughter of a show-biz attorney, and seemed to internalize Southern California's glitz early on. After graduating from UCLA, she found quick publication when her first novel *Lithium for Medea* was released. She quickly became a high-profile figure in the southland's literary scene, especially as a performance poet, even participating in those strange, noisy exercises called "poetry slams."

Braverman's verse and prose alike are noted for rich language and dense imagery:

How many women lay in darkness
in Tangier or Los Angeles.
Mexico City or Paris
considering their marriages
with the dresser mirror thus
and the fading roses
in a blue vase thus.
Through half-drawn blinds
street sounds rise
like a smoke that chokes

No vocabulary can define this poison
The man across the alley coughing
The student downstairs singing opera.
The couple fighting in Spanish
This is a death by implication....
("10 PM" in *Many Californias* 299)

As McDaniel writes in the main of the lives of small-town, impecunious characters, so Braverman writes of urban lives, of privileged lives, and often of lives assailed by drugs and madness and insecurity — assailed, as it were, by affluence and ennui. McDaniel's characters specialize in survival; they are tougher. Braverman's characters often manage that, too, but they are more given to self-indulgence and sweeps of depression. Both writers find ample material in California, with Kate enjoying far more publicity. What is most striking, though, is that these two talented women — so different yet so representative — are concurrent voices of this complicated culture.

Contrary to stereotypes, life for the overwhelming majority of citizens in most of the locales of California remains ordinary — dramatic but unspectacular. Has California become so independent a province that it can cultivate its own tradition without the endorsement of outside critics? Yes. Where then is the real California? It is out there where Californians — including authors — really live, a collection of distinct regions, of unique histories, and of varied people gathered under one name: we call all of it California, but it has no homogeneous geographic or cultural core. To paraphrase poet Gary Snyder, the state is a fiction but the regions are real. Actual people live in particular places — in Huron or Susanville, in Watts or Hayfork, in Bishop or El Sobrante — no one lives in the mythical golden state...except in their fantasies. That variety of places and that richness of people are the sources of the state's continuing literary prosperity.

Bibliography

General

Barrish, Bill. *Big Dreams*. New York: Vintage Books, 1994.

Bean, Walton and James J. Rawls. *California: An Interpretive History*. 6th ed. New York: McGraw-Hill, 1993.

Fradkin, Philip. *The Seven States of California*. New York: Henry Holt and Company, 1995.

Haslam, Gerald W. *The Other California: The Great Central Valley in Life and Letters*. Santa Barbara: Capra Press, 1990.

Haslam, Gerald W. (With photographers Stephen Johnson and Robert Dawson). *The Great Central Valley: California's Heartland*. Berkeley: University of California Press, 1993.

Houston, James, D. *Californians: In Search of the Golden State*. New York: Alfred A. Knopf, 1982.

McWilliams, Carey. *California: The Great Exception*. Salt Lake City: Peregrine-Smith, 1976.

Rice, Richard, William A. Bullough and Richard J. Orsi. *The Elusive Eden* (2nd ed.). New York: McGraw-Hill, 1996.

Starr, Kevin. *Americans and The California Dream, 1850-1915*. New York: Oxford University Press, 1973.

———. *Material Dreams: Southern California Through the 1920s*. New York: Oxford University Press, 1990.

Literary Studies

Fine, David, ed. *Los Angeles in Fiction*. Albuquerque: University of New Mexico Press, 1984.

Fine, David and Paul Skenazy, eds. *San Francisco in Fiction*. Albuquerque: University of New Mexico Press, 1995.

Houston, James D. "Imagining California." *San Francisco Focus* (May 1996): 78-82, 124.

Lyon, Thomas J., et al. *A Literary History of the American West*. Fort Worth: Texas Christian University Press, 1987.

Powell, Lawrence Clark. *California Classics*. Los Angeles: The Ward Ritchie Press, 1971.

Walker, Franklin. *A Literary History of Southern California*. Berkeley: University of California Press, 1950.

———. *San Francisco's Literary Frontier*. Seattle: University of Washington Press, 1939.

Wyatt, David. *The Fall Into Eden*. Cambridge: Cambridge University Press, 1986.

Anthologies

Caughey, John and Laree Caughey, eds. *California Heritage*. Los Angeles: The Ward Ritchie Press, 1962.

Egli, Ida Rae, ed. *No Rooms of Their Own*. Berkeley: Heyday Books, 1992.

Eisen, Jonathon and David Fine, eds. *Unknown California*. New York: Collier Books, 1985.

Haslam, Alexandra R. and Gerald W. Haslam, eds. *Where Coyotes Howl and Wind Blows Free*. Reno: University of Nevada Press, 1995.

Haslam, Gerald W., ed. *Many Californias: Literature from the Golden State*. Reno: University of Nevada Press, 1993.

Haslam, Gerald W. and James D. Houston, eds. *California Heartland: Writing from the Great Valley*. Santa Barbara: Capra Press, 1978.

Howard, Katsuyo K., ed. *Passages*. Fresno: Fresno State University, 1990.

Michaels, Leonard, David Reid and Raquel Scheer, eds. *West of the West*. San Francisco: North Point Press, 1989.

Peattie, Roderick, ed. *The Pacific Coast Ranges*. New York: Vanguard Press, 1946.

Soto, Gary, ed. *California Childhood*. Berkeley: Creative Arts Books, 1988.

Watts, Jane, ed. *Valley Light*. Bakersfield: Poet & Printer Press, 1979.

Yogi, Stan, ed. *Highway 99: A Literary Journey*. Berkeley: Heyday Books, 1996.

John P. O'Grady

Gary Snyder

Gary Snyder's oeuvre—from *Riprap* to *Mountains and Rivers Without End*—represents one of the great American spiritual autobiographies, *in process.* "Process" is the key word, since the work is ongoing, both literally and in a philosophical sense. Snyder's words are rooted in the physical fact of the American West, most espe-cially in the delectable mountains of the Pacific Slope. "Those unearthly glowing floating snowy summits," he says of the Cascade vol-canoes, "are a promise to the spirit" (*Practice of the Wild* 117). Snyder's is a composite sensibility, emerging from a diverse array of sources—the science of ecology, Buddhism, anthropology, philosophical anar-chism, and a profound sensitivity to language. The vision that unfolds is fluid: Life, like the world in which it takes place and between which there is no real separation, is not static but perpetually ongoing. Although Snyder is best known as a poet—coming of age during the San Francisco Renaissance of the mid-1950s—he has published no fewer than half a dozen prose volumes, including the most recent *A Place in Space* (1995). His influence as poet is perhaps exceeded only by his influence on environmental politics (an inspiration to at least two generations of activists), though Snyder himself would resist such arbitrary distinctions in the way he lives his life. He refers to it all as "the real work."

Years ago, Snyder's mentor and friend Kenneth Rexroth identified John Bunyan's *The Pilgrim's Progress* as one of the "best manuals for camping and woodcraft that will ever be written." In making this unlikely suggestion of Puritan allegory for a how-to manual on camping, Rexroth was calling attention to the spiritual preparation necessary for the contemporary individual to confront the "wild"; backpacking is both a form of spiritual practice and a metaphor for life. In this sense, today's pilgrim to the back country profits by packing along any of Snyder's books, but in the interest of economy might choose *No Nature: New and Selected Poems* (1992), which provides a generous survey of what the author feels is his most representative poetry.

Indeed, in surveying the real work of this life as it emerges in the published writings and interviews, one encounters the story of a spiritual quester whose journey begins along the western edge of North America, stretches across the Pacific for an extended sojourn in Asia, and then returns to the American West where the bindle-stiff is transformed into bio-regionalist, one who settles down on the west slope of the Sierra Nevada into a life that is a "reinhabitory process," aiming to turn the rootlessness of contemporary American culture inside out.

For all the spiritual affinities between Gary Snyder and Bunyan's Christian, however, there are profound differences, not the least of which is that, because of their theology, Puritans were apt at times drastically to undervalue — even dismiss — the material world. Because they believed that their true home was in Heaven, that their time here on earth was but a test of their spiritual mettle, the Puritans fell into a sort of dual consciousness, a mode of being that, from a Mahayana Buddhist perspective, is predicated upon a false dichotomy. One of the legacies of this Puritan split in American consciousness is the smorgasbord of dualisms that has long characterized the culture, which include such "contraries" as sacred/profane, civilization/wilderness, and culture/nature, just to name a few. Both by temperament and experience, Snyder chooses the middle way between these antinomies, proceeding as the eminently practical American poetic pragmatist, as can be seen in a recent poem, "How Poetry Comes to Me":

> It comes blundering over the
> Boulders at night, it stays
> Frightened outside the
> Range of my campfire
> I go to meet it at the
> Edge of the light

By meeting poetry at the threshold of ordinary consciousness, Snyder as poet is indeed a sort of pilgrim, journeying to a "far strange place" that he—and his readers—might be transformed. In this sense, rather than in the tradition of John Bunyan, Snyder's work ought to be situated in the Buddhist literature of pilgrimage, which, unlike the Puritan writings obsessed with "salvation," is all about transformation. This Buddhist literature of pilgrimage includes such texts as the final book of *The Flower Ornament Sutra* and the work of the great Japanese poet Basho, especially his travel sketches written in the *haibun* style.

Snyder was born in San Francisco on May 8, 1930, and spent his earliest years on a stump farm just north of Seattle, where not only did he encounter the vast forests of the Pacific Northwest but also the profound changes being wrought upon those forests by human beings. "When I was young, I had an immediate, intuitive, deep sympathy with the natural world which was not taught to me by anyone. In that sense, nature is my 'guru' and life is my sadhana" (*The Real Work* 92). By referring to life as his *sadhana* Snyder is using a Sanskrit term from the Vajrayana branch of Buddhism for a particular type of meditation practice best understood as a process of identification of a certain energy principle or pattern. From an early age, he recognized that there was no separation between one's actions in the world and one's actions in the mind: "There's not much wilderness left to destroy and the nature in the mind is being logged and burned off" (*Controversy of Poets* 551).

Because he "found very little in the civilized human realm" that interested him when he was growing up, Snyder was drawn to the wilderness of the Cascade range and to the study of Native American histories and cultures, beginning with the Salish of his boyhood home and eventually expanding his interest to include indigenous peoples worldwide. During his high school years in Portland, he began to climb mountains and spent many after-school hours in the library of the Mazamas, a local mountaineering club he had joined. In fact, Snyder's first publication, a somewhat satirical account of climbing Mount Hood, appeared in the 1946 *Mazama* annual.

Perhaps the most significant of Snyder's formative years were those he spent at Reed College, where he graduated in 1951. During that time he befriended fellow poets Philip Whalen and Lew Welch. Then, after a brief stint in graduate school in the Midwest, Snyder enrolled at the University of California to study Asian languages. It was during these years—the mid-fifties—that his career as a poet was launched. In addition to the inspiration he had derived from his experiences as a Forest Service lookout in the North Cascades and as a member of the trail crew in Yosemite National Park, Snyder's development as a poet received direction from the visionary company he was keeping. He was then living in the Bay Area at a time when a critical mass of creativity was building that would come to be known as the San Francisco Renaissance. Snyder suddenly found himself amid a dynamic cabal of poets that included Rexroth, Whalen, Allen Ginsberg, Michael McClure, Robert Creeley, and Jack Kerouac.

Right at the height of these poetic activities, however, in May 1956, Snyder departed for Japan to study Zen Buddhism, thus beginning an extended sojourn in Asia punctuated by occasional visits back to the West Coast. In 1967 he married Masa Uehara, and in the following year they moved permanently to California with their infant son, Kai. In 1969, their second son, Gen, was born. In 1971, Snyder and his family moved to San Juan Ridge in the foothills of the Sierra Nevada and built a home amid the mixed conifer forests above the South Fork of the Yuba River. For nearly a quarter century—which has brought many changes in his life, including appointment to the faculty at the University of California, Davis, divorce from Masa, and marriage to Carole Koda— San Juan Ridge has been the center of Snyder's poetic universe. "Crackly grass and Blue oak, the special smells of pungent sticky flowers, give way, climbing, through Digger pine and into Black oak and Ponderosa pine; sweet birch, manzanita, kitkitdizze. This is our home country. We dig wells and wonder where the water table comes from" (*Turtle Island* 111).

In addition to enjoying a large and enthusiastic popular audience, Snyder's work has received generous attention from literary critics, most of whom rightly focus on his profound social and ecological vision, his Buddhism, his interest in indigenous peoples and their cultures, his place in literary history, and his poetics. Surprisingly few, however, seem interested in what is surely one of Snyder's most important projects as poet, activist, and inhabitant of the American West: the reactualization of the physical world in human consciousness. David Robertson, in placing Snyder on the main axis of Northern California nature poetry, has described this tradition as the practice of "mattering," which is the repeated "accessing of the thing that is at one and the same time both spirit and matter" ("Real Matter, Spiritual Mountain" 210). Americans, for the most part, do not regard the land upon which they live as venerable, something worthy of reverence or respect. We talk of "sacred space," fully unaware of the problems inherent with such a world view that insists upon demarcating perception into the categories of sacred and profane. This attitude does in fact seem a legacy of the Puritan dual consciousness, compounded by the Cartesian split of Enlightenment thinking. Americans have their "national parks," which they treat as sacred places (and surely, to judge by visitation numbers one could say such places are "worshipped," even if in a rather debased form). Yet the compensatory principle of double consciousness is operative: For every national park we have a dozen sites on the EPA's Superfund clean-up list, we have urban "development" ceaselessly debasing "unprotected" agricultural and wild lands, we have smog drifting into the very national parks and wilderness areas we have declared sacrosanct, and so we have lost the view. While thousands of bureaucrats, corporate executives, and environmental activists struggle — each in their various ways — to solve the environmental problem, Snyder's work points us toward the heart of the problem, which is one of consciousness. In the "Economy" chapter of *Walden* Thoreau writes: "There are a thousand hacking at the branches of evil to one who is striking at the root." Thoreau's words serve as a gloss to Snyder's radicalism.

That we might better grasp this aspect of Snyder's poetics, let's return to the Vajrayana Buddhist practice of using the *sadhana* — meditation involving a particular type of liturgical text that describes in detail the various "deities" encountered in the process of spiritual realization. The deity that resides at the center of any given text needs to be understood not as an external being to be worshipped but as a principle of energy to be actualized. In some of the Vajrayana traditions, the landscape itself becomes the *sadhana* or mandala. And it is in this context that Snyder's work offers its greatest riches. "The childhood landscape is learned on foot," he writes in *The Practice of the Wild* "and a map is inscribed in the mind-trails and pathways and groves — the mean dog, the cranky old man's house, the pasture with a bull in it — going out wider and farther. All of us carry within a picture of the terrain that was learned roughly between the ages of six and nine" (26). We must, Snyder says, revisualize that childhood terrain, a first step toward re-actualizing all terrain.

In the "Introductory Note" to *Turtle Island* Snyder writes: "The poems speak of place, and the energy-pathways that sustain life." The land itself is a *sadhana*, each poem is a *sadhana*, and indeed ecology itself becomes a *sadhana*. The difference between Snyder (and indeed the reader of poetry) and the scientist is that the latter in studying the principles of nature insists always upon a clear distinction between subject (the consciousness of the scientist) and the object (the world), whereas the former recognizes no such distinction. Science seeks knowledge of the physical world, whereas meditative practice seeks knowledge of the mind that includes the physical world. Both are styles of consciousness. Poetry, too, is a style of consciousness, a meditative consciousness—one that Snyder plies to great advantage.

Unlike many who now utter the word ecology in various loose senses, Snyder's usage always honors its litter-mate economy—both words whelped from the Greek *oikos* meaning "house." In this sense, Snyder steps into the same territory opened by *Walden* in Thoreau's long introductory chapter, "Economy." Evidence of Snyder's affinity here can be seen in his 1969 prose volume *Earth House Hold* but even more compellingly in his recent selected poems, whose very title—*No Nature*—reminds us that, from a proper perspective, all arbitrary distinctions dissolve. "There is no single or set 'nature,'" he writes in the preface, "either as 'the natural world' or 'the nature of things.'" The final poem in the collection, "Ripples on the Surface," weds the shared lineage of the words ecology and economy to the Mahayana Buddhist understanding of *shunyata*, which translates roughly as "emptiness."

> The vast wild
>   the house, alone.
> The little house in the wild,
>   the wild in the house.
> Both forgotten.
>   No nature
> Both together, one big empty house.

Shunyata is the realization that all things are devoid of essence, but one must be careful not to confuse this with nihilism; *shunyata* does not mean that things are without reality or do not exist, but rather that— lacking self-nature—they are nothing more than mere appearances. The effect of the experience of this knowledge on the individual is an awakened sense of ethical obligation to the world. Thus Snyder's work —in the center of the Mahayana tradition now transplanted to the American West—always redirects our attention back to our individual practices in everyday life, where "life continues in the kitchen / Where we still laugh and cook, / Watching snow" (*No Nature* 380).

Selected Bibliography

Primary Sources

Axe Handles. San Francisco: North Point Press, 1983.
The Back Country. New York: New Directions, 1968.
Earth House Hold. New York: New Directions, 1969.
He Who Hunted Birds in His Father's Village. Bolinas, California: Gray Fox Press, 1979.
Left Out in the Rain: New Poems 1947-1985. San Francisco: North Point Press, 1986.
Mountains and Rivers Without End. Washington, D.C.: Counterpoint Press, 1996.
Myths and Texts. New York: Totem Press/Corinth Books, 1960; New York: New Directions, 1978.
No Nature: New and Selected Poems. New York: Pantheon, 1992.
The Old Ways: Six Essays. San Francisco: City Lights Books, 1977.
Passage Through India. San Francisco: Gray Fox Press, 1983.
A Place in Space. Washington, D.C.: Counterpoint Press, 1995.
The Practice of the Wild. San Francisco: North Point Press, 1990.
Regarding Wave. New York: New Directions, 1970.
Riprap & Cold Mountain Poems. San Francisco: Four Seasons Foundation, 1965; San Francisco: North Point Press, 1990.
Six Sections from Mountains & Rivers without End. San Francisco: Four Seasons Foundation, 1965.
Turtle Island. New York: New Directions, 1974.

Secondary Sources

Bly, Robert. "The Work of Gary Snyder." *The Sixties*, 6 (Spring 1962): 25-42.
Halper, Jon. *Gary Snyder: Dimensions of Life*. San Francisco: Sierra Club Books, 1991.
Lyon, Tom. "Gary Snyder, A Western Poet." *Western American Literature*, 3 (Fall 1968): 207-216.
Martin, Julia. "Practicing Emptiness: Gary Snyder's Playful Ecological Work." *Western American Literature*, 27 (May 1992): 3-19.
McLeod, Dan. "Gary Snyder." In *The Beats: Literary Bohemians in Postwar America* Part 2. *Dictionary of Literary Biography*. Vol. 16. Ann Charters, ed. Detroit: Gale, 1983. Pp. 486-500.
Molesworth, Charles. *Gary Snyder's Vision: Poetry and the Real Work*. Columbia: University of Missouri Press, 1983.
Murphy, Patrick D., ed. *Critical Essays on Gary Snyder*. Boston: G.K. Hall, 1990.
Norton, Judy. "The Importance of Nothing: Absence and Its Origins in the Poetry of Gary Snyder." *Contemporary Literature*, 28 (Spring 1987): 41-66.
Rexroth, Kenneth. "Smoky The Bear Bodhisattva." In *With Eye and Ear*. New York: Herder and Herder, 1970. Pp. 212-217.
Robertson, David. "Gary Snyder Riprapping in Yosemite, 1955." *American Poetry*, 2:1 (1984): 52-59.

———. "Real Matter, Spiritual Mountain: Gary Snyder and Jack Kerouac on Mt. Tamalpais." *Western American Literature,* 27 (November 1992): 209-226.

Shaffer, Eric Paul. "Inhabitation in the Poetry of Robinson Jeffers, Gary Snyder, and Lew Welch." *Robinson Jeffers Newsletter,* 78 (October 1990): 28-40.

Steuding, Bob. *Gary Snyder.* Boston: Twayne, 1976.

Whalen-Bridge, John. "Snyder's Poetic of Right Speech." *Sagetrieb,* 9 (Spring-Fall 1990): 201-214.

Yamazato, Katsunori. "Seeking a Fulcrum: Gary Snyder and Japan (1956-1975)." Doctoral dissertation, University of California, Davis, 1987.

John P. O'Grady

Kenneth Rexroth

Poet, painter, essayist, mountain climber, translator, philosophical anarchist, cultural critic, raconteur extraordinaire, autodidact, and literary curmudgeon, Kenneth Rexroth (1905-1982) is one of the West Coast's most significant writers. He is certainly its greatest religious poet. Indeed, the best of Rexroth's poems actually were written in monasteries, hermitages, or the wild mountains of the Pacific Slope. The sensibility that emerges in his poetry is eclectic and wide ranging, drawing with ease from the mystical traditions in Christianity, Judaism, ancient Greece, Taoism, and Buddhism. "Poetry is vision, the pure act of sensual contemplation" (*Bird in the Bush* 189). Kenneth Rexroth was an intellectual and poetic shaman.

Important as mystical experience may have been to him, Rexroth's work has a useful beauty. He cherished the poem's ability to communicate directly all manner of experience. "A love poem is an act of communication of love, like a kiss. The poem of contempt and satire is like a punch in the nose" (*Bird in the Bush* 12). Unlike the High Modernists, led by Ezra Pound, T. S. Eliot and poet-proponents of the New Criticism such as John Crowe Ransom, Rexroth embraced an aesthetic of clarity while rejecting technical emphases on form and rhetorical ingenuity. In the "Art of Literature" entry he originally wrote for the fifteenth edition of the *Encyclopedia Britannica*, Rexroth recorded: "Form simply refers to organization, and critics who attack form do not seem always to remember that a writer organizes more than words. He organizes experience.

Thus, his organization stretches far back in his mental process. Form is the other face of content, the outward, visible sign of inner spiritual reality" (*World Outside the Window* 290).

At the core of all this is yet another distinguishing feature of his poetry: a compelling moral vision. In one of his most important essays, "Unacknowledged Legislators and *Art Pour Art*," he presents the centerpiece of his poetics: "Poetry increases and guides our awareness to immediate experience. It organizes sensibility so that it is not wasted" (*Bird in the Bush* 6). Martin Buber's *I-Thou*, says Rexroth, was "one of the determinative books of my life" (*Bird in the Bush* 107). A reader can spot this at once in Rexroth's personal, pragmatic, and experiential approach to writing poetry. "The arts presume to speak directly from person to person, each polarity, the person at each end of the communication fully realized" (12). His poetry demonstrates a social awareness and engagement that made him an anathema to those readers (such as the New Critics) who insisted that art must stand autonomously or it cannot be considered art. Wrote William Carlos Williams in a review of *In Defense of the Earth* and *One Hundred Poems from the Chinese*: "Rexroth is a moralist with his hand at the trigger ready to fire at the turn of an hair" (Williams 182).

By all accounts Rexroth had a brilliant mind and a photographic memory. A high school dropout, he spent the last of his many creative years as a professor of poetry at the University of California, Santa Barbara. Despite this intellectual brilliance, he pursued in both his life and work a non-intellectualized individualism, a California literary tradition already well established by writers like Jack London, Frank Norris, Mary Austin, and Robinson Jeffers. "This is San Francisco speaking," he writes of Norris' *McTeague* but just as well could have been referring to his own work, "a city mercifully spared the westward radiation of the great light from Plymouth Rock" (*With Eye and Ear* 32). Rexroth cultivated a profound antipathy to Calvinism and the New England literary tradition (probably a reaction to the New Critics, who in the course of Rexroth's lifetime succeeded in canonizing writers such as Emerson, Thoreau, Hawthorne, and Melville), and he turned instead to Europe and especially Asia for his literary inspiration, citing the classical Chinese poet Tu Fu as "the major influence" on his work: "In some ways he is a better poet than either Shakespeare or Homer. At least he is more natural and intimate" (*Autobiographical Novel* 319). Rexroth in fact became one of the most important translators of Chinese and

Japanese poetry into English. His deep and abiding interest in Buddhism rippled down in the form of influence upon younger generations of West Coast writers, most significant among them Gary Snyder.

In his day, Rexroth enjoyed a substantial literary reputation, especially in the Bay Area, where during the fifties and into the sixties he gave a weekly Sunday evening radio broadcast on literary and cultural matters that made him if not a purveyor of taste certainly one of the liveliest and best-known figures in the region. He was also known to a national audience through his regular contributions to *The Nation* and other widely circulated magazines but he never gained acceptance among the New York literary establishment, most likely because of his relentless attacks on them in his literary journalism. He loathed the New Critics, who in those days dominated American colleges and universities, and ridiculed to no end the "professor-poets." Perhaps Rexroth's most egregious violation of American writing-industry decorum was to thumb his nose at the New York literary establishment and instead make California his lifelong home, pledging his allegiance to its mountains and waters rather than to the vanity of publishers, editors, and reviewers who make and break literary reputations at Manhattan cocktail parties. No wonder Morgan Gibson in 1967 called him "America's greatest underground poet." The same might still be said.

In surveying today's anthologies, one quickly realizes that Rexroth's work has yet to surface in the academic canon. In a significant way, this critical neglect is one result of the posturing Rexroth engaged in from the start of his literary career. In a lecture delivered in November 1936 to the Conference of Western Writers in San Francisco, he took up the cudgels he never laid down: "I believe that to a certain extent always, but in modern times especially, the poet, by the very nature of his art, has been an enemy of society, that is, of the privileged and the powerful. He has sometimes been an ally of the unprivileged and weak, where such groups were articulate and organized, otherwise he has waged an individual and unaided war" (*World Outside The Window* 1).

Ironically enough, for all his blustering against the New England Transcendentalists, Rexroth very much seems a latter-day Emerson or, especially, Thoreau, staking out the high moral and spiritual ground on the western edge of North America. Whereas his reputation in the academy may have suffered for his bilious hauteur, his poetry did not — and his readers became the beneficiaries of his courage. His influence on fellow writers has been immense, the short list including Snyder, Lawrence

Ferlinghetti, and Allen Ginsberg, all of whom do appear in the anthologies. Rexroth was at the center of the literary historical moment known as The San Francisco Renaissance. Much to his chagrin, he also acquired the moniker of "father of the Beat Generation," largely due to his having served as master of ceremonies at the famous Six Gallery poetry reading in San Francisco in October of 1955, and he was an early defender of and publicist for younger writers, including Jack Kerouac.

The details of Rexroth's life are abundant, colorful, and often contradictory. He loved to tell stories and embellish upon the facts, including those of his life, a tendency that forced his publisher to insist Rexroth title his autobiography *An Autobiographical Novel*. Midwesterner by birth and rearing, he did not embark upon a life in the West until advised by an unlikely spiritual benefactor, the anarchist Alexander Berkman, whom Rexroth had encountered in one of the Lost Generation cafes in Paris. "Go West," Berkman counseled the twenty-year-old aspiring artist. "There is more for you in the Far West than there is here. You can probably become famous here but you'll just be another one" (342). As if to repay the debt, Rexroth years later wrote an introduction to a new edition of Berkman's *Prison Memoirs of an Anarchist*. In 1927 Rexroth and his first wife, the painter Andree Dutcher, did indeed go West, settling in San Francisco. Although she died of epilepsy in 1940, he spent the next four decades in the City by the Bay, then moved south to Santa Barbara, where he was on the university faculty until his death in 1982.

Although Berkman might have been responsible for pointing Rexroth toward the West, it was the beauty of its mountains that held the poet in thrall for the rest of his life. He had an awakening to his life's purpose as he gazed upon the slopes of Glacier Peak, one of Washington's most prominent volcanoes: "To the southwest the great mountain rose up covered with walls of ice. There was no one near me for many miles in any direction. I realized then with complete certainty that this was the place for me. This was the kind of life I liked best. I resolved to live it as much as I could from then on. By and large I've kept that resolve and from that day much of my time and for some years most of my time was spent in the Western mountains" (282). During the thirties, Rexroth wrote a manuscript he called "Camping in the Western Mountains," one of the most eccentric books in all mountaineering literature. Part how-to manual, part anarchist philosophy, and part cranky opinion, the manuscript was never published, yet it stands as a record of the profound influence the western landscape played in Rexroth's creative life. "The mountains and glaciers, the forests and streams of America are a heritage shared equally by all the people, and they are not simply 'recreation areas,' but training grounds for group living and group sharing.... Each group that hikes or rides along the trail by day contented and alert, and makes camp at night 'decently and in good order' is a sort of test tube or kindergarten of the good life. So don't forget, when it's your turn to wash the dishes, the centuries are watching you."

Rexroth spent a great deal of his time in the outdoors. During his younger days in the summers, he would head to the backcountry of the Sierra Nevada for two months at a stretch, sometimes with companions and sometimes alone, adrift among the unpeopled ranges of the Kaweahs and the Great Western Divide, Clarence King country. He would often ascend those high and difficult mountains, but not as a mere "peak bagger"; mountaineering was for Rexroth—as it was for Petrarch, John Bunyan's Christian, and René Daumal—a form of spiritual practice. A reader encounters this in a poem like "Climbing Milestone Mountain, August 22, 1937," which fuses mountaineering, contemplation, and politics into a beautiful, accessible whole. The best of his mountain poems, though, are those that conjoin spiritual and erotic rapture to yield exquisite passion—"Incarnation" being representative, a poem that concludes in lines best described as Tantric in their revelatory power:

> Your thigh's exact curve, the fine gauze
> Slipping through my hands, and you
> Tense on the verge of abandon;
> Your breasts' very touch and smell;
> The sweet secret odor of sex.
> Forever the thought of you,
> And the splendor of the iris,
> The crinkled iris petal,
> The gold hairs powdered with pollen,
> And the obscure cantata
> Of the tangled water, and the
> Burning, impassive snow peaks,
> Are knotted together here.
> This moment of fact and vision
> Seizes immortality,
> Becomes the person of this place.
> The responsibility

Of love realized and beauty
Seen burns in a burning angel
Real beyond flower or stone.
(*Collected Shorter Poems* 162)

As counterpoise to this eroticism are the numerous poems of "withdrawal" that seem to come out of a monastic tradition of verse. During the thirties and forties Rexroth maintained a hermitage (actually an old sheepherder's shack) deep in one of the aromatic redwood and laurel canyons just north of San Francisco, and here he composed some of his finest work, including "The Signature of All Things," "Hojoki" (Japanese for "Account of My Hut," the title of a famous work in the Buddhist literature by Kamo no Chomei), and "Time Spirals." In his last years — during which he wrote the poems most clearly influenced by Buddhism — he remarked that he had lost interest in politics entirely, and now was "only interested in mystical experience."

Rexroth's experiences in the natural world had a profound effect on his sensibility as a poet, instilling in him an awareness of the immanence that put him at odds with the majority of his contemporaries. Whereas most modernist and post-modernist poetry seems preoccupied with directing attention to the poem itself, Rexroth's is a poetry of transmission. "A poem," he explained in a 1968 interview, "is an efficient vehicle for focusing attention, for giving direct experience" (Pondrom 320). This pragmatic approach to the poem invites comparison to the old Zen metaphor of the finger pointing to the moon: one would certainly be foolish to confuse the finger for the moon. A poetry — or a criticism — too caught up in its own language does indeed confuse the finger for the moon; it erects its own prison. Rexroth's nature poetry is among the best in American literature, and indeed provides a spiritual anodyne to the bleak vision of a critically acclaimed poet such as Robert Frost.

Central to Rexroth's poetics is his notion of "sacramental relationship." For him, poetry is a form of deep interpersonal communication. In this sense, poetry actually takes its place among those rituals that serve to establish and maintain community. Rather than privilege poetry as a "special" or "superior" activity, Rexroth restores it to its original religious context where it once again may be put to use. His radical practice reminds us that the origin of our word "poetry" is to be found in the ancient Greek verb *poein*, "to make." Thus poetry, like religion, is not something you believe but something you do. "In the arts — and ideally in much other communication — the relationship is not only active, it is the highest form of activity" (*Bird in the Bush* 13). Perhaps Rexroth's most considerable achievement was his effort to reinvigorate his culture's understanding of the poem, aligning it with other rites of passage, since all "the fundamental activities and relationships of life — birth, death, sexual intercourse, eating, drinking, choosing a vocation, adolescence, mortal illness — life at its important moments is ennobled by the ceremonious introduction of transcendence; the universe is focused on the event in a Mass or ceremony that is itself a kind of dance and work of art. This is the significance of religion" (*Autobiographical Novel* 252).

Selected Bibliography

Primary Sources

The Alternative Society: Essays from the Other World. New York: Herder and Herder, 1970.
American Poetry in the Twentieth Century. New York: Herder and Herder, 1971.
An Autobiographical Novel. New York: Doubleday, 1966.
Beyond the Mountains. New York: New Directions, 1951.
Bird in the Bush. New York: New Directions, 1959.
The Burning Heart: Women Poets of Japan. With Ikuko Atsumi. New York: Seabury, 1977.
"Camping in the Western Mountains." Unpublished ms. c. 1936. Special Collections, Doheny Library, University of Southern California.
Classics Revisited. Chicago: Quadrangle Books, 1968.
The Collected Longer Poems. New York: New Directions, 1968.
The Collected Shorter Poems. New York: New Directions, 1966.
Communalism: From its Origins to the Twentieth Century. New York: Seabury, 1974.
The Elastic Retort: Essays in Literature and Ideas. New York: Seabury, 1973.
Li Ch'ing Chou: Complete Poems. With Ling Chung. New York: New Directions, 1979.
Love in the Turning Year: One Hundred More Poems from the Chinese. New York: New Directions, 1970.
The Morning Star. New York: New Directions, 1979.
One Hundred More Poems from the Japanese. New York: New Directions, 1974.
One Hundred Poems from the Chinese. New York: New Directions, 1956.
One Hundred Poems from the Japanese. New York: New Directions, 1955.
The Orchid Boat: Women Poets of China. With Ling Chung. New York: Herder and Herder, McGraw-Hill, 1972.
Pierre Reverdy: Selected Poems. New York: New Directions, 1969.
Poems from the Greek Anthology. Ann Arbor: University of Michigan Press, 1962.
Selected Poems. Bradford Morrow, ed and introduction. New York: New Directions, 1984.
Thirty Spanish Poems of Love and Exile. San Francisco: City Lights, 1956.
With Eye and Ear. New York: Herder and Herder, 1970.

World Outside the Window: The Selected Essays of Kenneth Rexroth. Edited with a preface by Bradford Morrow. New York: New Directions, 1987.

Secondary Sources

Bartlett, Lee. *Kenneth Rexroth.* Boise: Boise State University Western Writers Series, 1988.

————. *Kenneth Rexroth and James Laughlin: Selected Letters.* New York: Norton, 1991.

Gardner, Geoffrey, ed. *For Rexroth.* New York: The Ark, 1980.

Gibson, Morgan. *Revolutionary Rexroth: Poet of East-West Wisdom.* Hamden, Connecticut: Archon Books, 1986.

Gutierrez, Donald. "Natural Supernaturalism: The Nature Poetry of Kenneth Rexroth." *Literary Review,* 26 (Spring 1983): 405-422.

Hamalian, Linda. *A Life of Kenneth Rexroth.* New York: Norton, 1991.

Hass, Robert. *Twentieth Century Pleasures: Prose on Poetry.* New York: Ecco Press, 1984. Pp. 223-234.

Hatlen, Burton and Carroll F. Terrell, eds. *Sagetrieb: Special Issue Kenneth Rexroth,* 2 (Winter 1983).

Knabb, Ken. *The Relevance of Rexroth.* Berkeley: Bureau of Public Secrets, 1990.

Lipton, Lawrence. "The Poetry of Kenneth Rexroth." *Poetry,* 40:3 (June 1957): 168-180.

Meltzer, David. "Kenneth Rexroth." In *The San Francisco Poets.* New York: Ballantine, 1971. Pp. 9-55. (Interview.)

Parkinson, Thomas. "Kenneth Rexroth, Poet." *Ohio Review* (Winter 1976): 54-67.

Pondrom, Cyrena N. "Interview with Kenneth Rexroth." *Contemporary Literature,* 10 (Summer 1969): 313-330.

Richards, Janet. *Common Soldiers.* San Francisco: Archer, 1979.

Robertson, David. "Kenneth Rexroth in Devil's Gulch." *American Poetry,* 8 (1990): 116-127.

Williams, William Carlos. "Two New Books by Kenneth Rexroth." *Poetry,* 90 (June 1957): 180-190.

Gerald Haslam

Robert Hass

When Californian Robert Hass was appointed Poet Laureate of the United States in 1995, many expressed surprise, not because he was not an accomplished artist, but because he was a westerner. "Can you believe it," critic Marek Breiger told this author, "they actually named a good *poet*, and from out here!" As the first westerner to be so honored, Hass' appointment symbolically celebrated verse from his region at a time when it seemed to be burgeoning; his selection was certainly no mere token for he does indeed bring strong literary credentials to the job.

How accomplished is he? After calling the Berkeley resident "one of our best..." Charles Molesworthy in a 1979 number of *Ontario Review* went on to assert, "he is that extremely rare person: a poet of fullness" (100). As such, the Laureate is an especially fitting representative of California, a state crammed with writers, transplants as well as natives.

Following the release of Hass's second volume of poetry, critic Robert Miklitsch wrote in *The Hollins Critic*, "Let me be blunt: the recent publication of Robert Hass' *Praise* marks the emergence of a major American poet" (2). Nothing has happened since to damage that assertion.

The Californian's powers of observation are distinct, just as his language is at once unlikely, appropriate, and unembellished. In *Field Guide*, for instance, he notes a scene in Marin County:

> ...Low tide: slimed rocks
> mottled brown and thick with kelp
> like the huge backs of ancient tortoises
> merged with the grey stone
> of the breakwater, sliding off
> to antediluvian depths.
> The old story: here filthy life begins....
> ("On the Coast Near Sausalito" 3)

Such passages led poet Stanley Kunitz to observe,

> Reading a poem by Robert Hass is like stepping into the ocean
> when the temperature of the water is not much different from that
> of the air. You scarcely know, until you feel the undertow tug at
> you, that you have entered into another element. Suddenly the
> deep is there, with its teeming life. (xi)

This poet, moreover, has also become a distinguished critic — his *Twentieth Century Pleasures: Prose on Poetry* (1984) won the National Book Critics Circle Award for criticism. That group's citation praised Hass, noting that he

> brings a poet's sensibility to powerful readings of Lowell, Rilke, and
> other central figures of our century, combining deep learning with
> passionate conviction. The criticism, like Hass' poetry, is robust,
> engaging, and utterly lucid. ("Robert Hass" 145)

His essays "are marked by a unified sensibility: a devotion to poetry and an abiding faith in poetry's importance to self-knowledge, to existence" ("Robert Hass" 145).

Born in San Francisco in 1941 to a businessman and a housewife, Hass graduated from Marin Catholic High School across the Golden Gate in Kentfield. He took his B.A. from St. Mary's College, a small, highly regarded Christian-Brothers' institution over the bay in then-bucolic Moraga.

While still a student, the poet's deep interests in the natural world and in spirituality were in evidence. During that period, too, the late 1950s and early 1960s, the Bay Area hosted an especially exciting literary scene, with the Beats — Kenneth Rexroth, Jack Kerouac, Allen

Ginsberg, Lawrence Ferlinghetti, Gary Snyder, et al.—dominating. "These were my models," Hass has revealed, noting also "the juxtaposition between experimental and cosmopolitan poetry" to be found in the area then. None of that was lost on the sensitive, talented young man.

The influence of Rexroth and Snyder can especially be seen in the Asian delicacy with which Hass is able to celebrate what might otherwise be mundane experiences. His West Coast upbringing seems to have alerted him to the often-ignored fact that America is not merely a European creation, and Asian influences are evident, especially in his undiluted observations of nature. Buddhism and Taoism—and, perhaps, his exposure to Catholicism—have also contributed to what critics have referred to as the "spiritual tone" of many of Hass' poems, especially those that evoke the momentous potential of apparently commonplace experiences. In 1995 the poet told interviewer Elizabeth Farnsworth on PBS's *McNeil-Lehrer News Hour*, "I feel strongly missionary about people having some relationship to art or some relationship to spiritual practice in their lives.... It seems to me that so much in our life conspires against us being conscious and alive in our lives while we're in them."

After finishing at St. Mary's in 1963, the young poet was a Woodrow Wilson Fellow during the 1963-64 academic year, and a Danforth Fellow from 1963 to 1967, while studying at Stanford University—with another of his major influences, Yvor Winters, among others—completing an M.A. (1965) and a Ph.D. (1971). All his considerable formal education, then, was accomplished in the Bay Area or in its nearby, surprisingly fecund countryside.

Perhaps as a result, in the contentious, freewheeling world of American poetry, he has been sniffed at as an "academic poet," and "one of the insiders." In California his background has been contrasted with that of such accomplished "outsiders" as Charles Bukowski and Wilma Elizabeth McDaniel. Hass is inarguably and without apology a product of higher education. "I think very much the influence for me in poetry is poetry," he says.

> Specifically Wordsworth and Pound and through them Snyder and Whitman and others.... I guess there is not one model. What I seem to return to most is Pound in the late *Cantos*, and Wordsworth's blank verse." ("Robert Hass" 145)

Of the poet's techniques, Ira Sadoff has observed that Hass

works well with the long, expansive line. He uses rhetorical repetition, the qualifying clause.... His diction is straightforward and
relaxed; he mixes the colloquial with the slightly formal without
breaking down the creditability of voice. And he is able to make
internal associative leaps.... (135)

All those skills were evident in *Field Guide*, his first collection of
poems. It won the 1973 Yale Younger Poets Award and was published in
that series. It revealed the emergence of a potentially major poet voice.
"*Field Guide* is an impressive first collection," wrote Linda W. Wagner,
"whether one is looking for a poet who develops a new track or one who
proves his skill along older routes.... Hass appears to do both" (89). The
young poet, with his love of the incantatory power of names, also
seemed to have been swayed by Walt Whitman:

> Chants, recitations:
> Olema
> Tamalpais Mariposa
> Mendocino Sausalito San Rafael
> Emigrant Gap
> Donner Pass
>
> Of all the laws
> that bind us to the past
> the names of things are
> stubbornest.
> ("Maps" 9)

Also, Hass' emphasis on the concrete suggested that William Carlos
Williams was another source of stimulation —

> On the oak table
> filets of sole
> stewing in the juice of tangerines,
> slices of green pepper
> on a bone-white dish...
> ("Song" 21)

In *Field Guide*, the poet also described a "furious dun-/ colored mal-

lard" that "skims across the edges of the marsh/ where the dead bass sur-
face/ and their flaccid bellies bob. . . ." Unburdened by regional illusions,
Hass wrote of a real West, full of adept observations, deep understand-
ings, and economical language. Of Kit Carson entering a Klamath village in northern California, he wrote:

> Carson found ten wagonloads
> of fresh-caught salmon, silver,
> in the sun. The flat eyes stared.
> Gills sucked the thin annulling air.
> They flopped and shivered,
> ten wagonloads. Kit Carson
> burned the village to the ground. . . .
> ("Palo Alto: The Marshes" 26)

Neither Indian nor fish would fare well at the hands of Manifest
Destiny.

The publication of *Praise* in 1979 confirmed the importance of the
young Californian, even to those, such as Sadoff, who had earlier
expressed concerns, however minor, about *Field Guide*:

> My reservations about this earlier book stemmed from some sense
> of chilliness that seemed to pervade a number of poems, as if the
> poems were wrought by an intellect distant from its subject matter.
> I have no such problems with *Praise.* . . . In fact, *Praise* contains four
> or five of the most moving poems I've read in years, and marks
> Hass's arrival as an important, even pivotal, young poet. . . . [It]
> might even be the strongest collection of poems to come out in the
> late seventies (133).

The deftness and directness of the poet's language in *Praise* produced
images that evoke reality without standing in its way.

> What I want happens
> not when the deer freezes in the shade
> and looks at you and you hold very still
> and meet her gaze but in the moment after
> when she flicks her ear & starts to feed again —
> ("Santa Lucia" 24)

The poet explained to interviewer Farnsworth that it wasn't "the big dramatic moments" he sought to emphasize, but "the ordinary ones." Hass' sensibility has remained distinctly western, and more: it is distinctly human, distinctly *existent*. He was aware of himself as a creature in the midst of an environment. Kunitz observes of Hass that "Natural universe and moral universe coincide for him, centered in a nexus of personal affections, his stay against what he describes as "'the wilderness of history and political violence'" (*Field Guide* xii). Also hailed for good reason in *Praise* was the poet's continuing economy of images and language.

With the essays in his next book, *Twentieth Century Pleasures: Prose on Poetry* (1984), Hass explored the interrelationship of images and existence that he, as a poet, so adroitly employs. "It seems to me," he suggests,

> that we all live our lives in the light of primary acts of imagination, images and sets of images that get us up in the morning and move us about our days....I do not think anybody can live without one, for very long, without suffering intensely from deadness and futility. And I think that, for most of us, those images are not only essential but dangerous because no one of them feels like the whole truth and they do not last. Either they die of themselves, dry up, are shed; or, if we are lucky, they are invisibly transformed into the next needful thing; or we act on them in a way that exposes both them and us. (*Twentieth Century Pleasures* 345)

The momentum of Hass' career continued with the publication of *Human Wishes* in 1989. Again, the poet accomplished a Basho-like merging of the ordinary and the extraordinary. He was by then so well established a figure on the American poetry scene that, within that always contentious domain, critical lines about his work had formed. Poet Gary Soto told this author simply, "He's just a fine poet. Period. And this book shows why."

Writing in *Choice*, however, another poet, Peter Wild, after acknowledging that "many readers will instantly perceive their own daily sentiments in *Human Wishes*," proceeded to fault Hass: "The poet dwells perhaps overmuch on passing moods, mistaking them for larger, more challenging issues" (Wild 3735).

It is perhaps inevitable that so personal and sensitive a writer as Hass would occasionally trouble critics such as Wild. As Soto says (with a grin), "We're all navel-gazers." But that same sensitivity can also produce lines startling in their beauty and in their sense of the personal —

> And to emerge, where the juniper
> is simply juniper and there is the smell
> of new shingle, a power saw outside
> and inside a woman in the bath
> a scent of lemon and a drift of song....
> ("Transparent Garments," *Praise* 15)

Perhaps an occasional lapse into the "pathetic" (to use Wild's word) is the price for enjoying Hass' far more numerous original and fruitful passages. If so, it is a bargain indeed, for so many of Hass' passages are both beautiful and complex; they are the product of not only intellectual churning but also a keen ear for and interest in "language as it's spoken." How can one not admire an artist who so clearly sees poetic possibilities?

> I told a friend I was going to try to write something about prosody and he said, "Oh great." The two-beat phrase is a very American form of terminal irony. A guy in a bar in Charlottesville turned to me once and said, loudly but confidentially, "Ahmo find me a woman and fuck her twenty ways till Sunday." That's also a characteristic rhythm: ahmo FIND ME a WOman/ and fuck her TWENty WAYS till Sunday. Three beats and then a more emphatic four. A woman down the bar doubled the two-beat put-down. She said "Good luck, asshole." Rhythms and rhythmic play make texture in our lives.... (*Twentieth Century Pleasures* 107)

Walt Whitman would have loved it.

Robert Hass has found poetry in language and in ordinary events; more importantly, he has found in poetry an important way of being human. As a result, he succeeds in showing his readers "the absolute value of being." As the poet himself told Farnsworth, "The trick is to see the world the way that we see it when it's heightened by crisis, without wishing on ourselves a crisis in order to see it."

Selected Bibliography

Primary Sources

Field Guide. New Haven: Yale University Press, 1973.
Human Wishes. New York: Ecco Press, 1989.
Misery and Splendor. Berkeley: Black Oak Books, 1989.
Praise. New York: Ecco Press, 1979.
Sun Under Wood: New Poems. Hopewell, New Jersey, 1996.
Twentieth Century Pleasures. New York: Ecco Press, 1984.

Secondary Sources

Boruch, Marianne. Review of *Twentieth Century Pleasures: Prose on Poetry*. *The Georgia Review*, 39:1 (Spring 1985), 205-207.

Breiger, Marek. Conversation with Gerald Haslam, June 1, 1995.

Davis, Dick. "Arguing in Unknown Quantities." *The Times Literary Supplement*, 4276 (March 15, 1985): 293-294.

Davison, Peter. "The Great Predicament of Poetry." *The Atlantic Monthly*, 243:6 (June 1976), 93-94, 96.

Eshleman, Clayton. "A Poet in Praise of Other Poets." *Los Angeles Times Book Review*, November 18, 1984, 8.

Farnsworth, Elizabeth. "Interview with Robert Hass." *McNeil-Lehrer News Hour*, Public Broadcasting System, August 1995.

"Hass, Robert 1941- ." *Contemporary Literary Criticism*, Vol. 18. Detroit: Gale Publishing Company, 1981. Pp. 208-213.

Hirsch, Edward. "Praise." *Poetry*, 165:6 (March 1985): 345-348.

Kunitz, Stanley. "Foreword." In *Field Notes* by Robert Hass (New Haven: Yale University Press, 1973).

Libby, Anthony. "Criticism in the First Person." *The New York Times Book Review*, March 3, 1985, p. 37.

Miklitsch, Robert. "'Praise,' The Poetry of Robert Hass." *The Hollins Critic*, 18:1 (February, 1980): 2-13.

Molesworthy, Charles. "Some Recent American Poetry." *The Ontario Review*, 11 (Fall-Winter 1979-80), 91-102.

"Robert Hass: *Twentieth Century Pleasures: Prose on Poetry*," *Contemporary Literary Criticism*, Vol. 39. Detroit: Gale Publishing Company, 1984. Pp. 145-150.

Sadoff, Ira. "Robert Hass's 'Praise'." *Chicago Review*, 31:3 (Winter 1980): 133-136.

Soto, Gary. Conversation with Gerald Haslam, April 7, 1995.

Wagner, Linda W. "Four Young Poets." *The Ontario Review*, 1 (Fall 1974): 89-97.

Waters, Michael. "Salad Days." *Southwest Review*, 60:3 (Summer 1975): 307-311.

Wild, Peter. Review of *Human Wishes*. *Choice*, 27:1 (March 1990): 3735.

Wood, Susan. "Discovering New Voices: 'Praise'." *Book World* (*The Washington Post*), August 8, 1979, p. 8.

Robert Brophy

William Everson

W illiam Everson lived the first three decades of his life in the San Joaquin Valley. Born in Sacramento on September 10, 1912, Everson spent his youth in Selma, fifteen miles south of Fresno, where his father was a printer and town bandmaster. There he grew from the soil, amidst crops, orchards, and grapevines, with the Coast Range to the west and the Sierra in the distance to the east.

A high-school teacher is said to have introduced him to writing poetry. But he attributed his strong vocational urge to a book by Robinson Jeffers that he took from a library shelf while attending Fresno State College. In this first phase of poetic growth he wrote as a farmer and laborer, in love with the earth and its diurnal and seasonal rhythms. By 1939 when he was twenty-seven he had two volumes of poetry published, *These Are the Ravens* and *San Joaquin*, both favorably received.

By then he had married his high-school sweetheart, Edwa Poulson, and bought a farm to grow muscat grapes. His poems image morning fogs, vine pruning, storms, plowing, harvests. Underlying them is a remoteness from people, often a world itself dark, a nature sometimes threatening.

As he grew into maturity, forces beyond the fecund earth and returning seasons began to weigh heavily on his psyche. War clouds filled eastern skies. The youth had by then moved beyond his mother's Christian Science and his father's agnosticism, finding a Jeffers-inspired pantheism in a god brimming in nature. But the divinity he sensed and celebrated in life, the beauty and wholeness, was proving fragile in the van of World War II. The fratricide in Europe seemed to recapitulate all human violence, some of which he recognized in himself and his Norwegian heritage. He resolved "not to wantonly ever take life ... /And seek to atone in my own soul/What was poured from my past" ("The Vow," *The Residual Years*, 119).

His poetry of this time — ironic meditations on nationalism, violence, and senseless loss — is to be found in the turbulent and powerful *The Masculine Dead* (1942). A conscientious objector, in 1943 he was summarily assigned a three-year stint in Oregon detention camps, not to be released till almost a year past the war's end. At Angels Camp, in Waldport on the Oregon coast northwest of Eugene, he joined a group of protesting artists, writers, and musicians, helping to write and print volume after volume of their poetry on the camp's crude mimeograph. From this period (1943 to 1946) came his *X War Elegies*, *Waldport Poems*, *The Residual Years*, and *Poems: MCMXLII*.

By war's end, confirmed in his vocation as poet and printer, he found the conflict had been personally devastating. By the day of his release, July 23, 1946, he had lost his wife to a friend and his farm to a marriage settlement. Uprooted and at loose ends, he journeyed to the San Francisco Bay Area. On an earlier furlough there he had met Kenneth Rexroth and bought for himself a Washington hand-printing press to be kept in storage. He moved to the East Bay, setting up his Equinox press behind a house on Ashbury Street near the Oakland-Berkeley border.

By 1948 Rexroth, then a strongly supportive friend and mentor, had not only brought Everson to the attention of publisher James Laughlin but helped him edit *The Residual Years* for a new printing by New Directions. From the book's critical notice and with the help of a perceptive and enthusiastic letter from fellow poet Robert Duncan, Everson was able to apply for and win a Guggenheim Fellowship.

At this time he was blessed by the friendship and love of Mary Fabilli, a graphic artist of the Berkeley area. Just when the buoyancy of his pantheism had been scuttled by his shattered marriage, Mary and her Catholicism offered him a personal, caring God who brought good from fracturing. At Christmas Midnight Mass, 1948, he experienced a mystical transfiguration centered on the creche and began instructions in the faith followed by baptism in the spring.

But the Church had strictures against union of the divorced; the marriage could not be blessed. Upon parting from Mary, Everson moved to the Maurin Catholic Worker House on Oakland's skid row, attracted by foundress Dorothy Day's pacifism and social vision to minister to the down-and-out. Here he again set up his press, christening it "Seraphim," and printing "Triptych for the Living," a three-part poem celebrating his conversion. At this time he also composed perhaps his most famous poem, "Canticle of the Waterbirds," invoking a nature which now bespoke a god both immanent and transcendent.

The Maurin House proved a brief waystation in his journey. At thirty-nine, seeking a life that integrated both his poet/printer vocation and his new-won attraction to contemplation, he discovered the Dominicans, a Catholic religious order also called the Order of Preachers. At St. Albert's House of Formation in Oakland and later at Kentwood in Marin County, he would spend the ensuing eighteen years in a rigorous daily routine of Mass, the Divine Office, private prayer, and manual labor mainly as a donatus, a lay brother without public vows.

For Everson, these were creative years. Now named Brother Antoninus, he again set up his press and, snatching time between manual assignments, undertook a printing of the new Latinate translation of the biblical Psalter, a work of self-exacting perfectionism and monumental beauty for which he quickly became famous. In 1954 for a short time he pursued priestly studies but soon realized that this was not his vocation. And in 1955, under the inspiration of a fellow Dominican, Victor White, he began what was for him a momentous, in-depth study first of Freud and then Jung, seeking a way of understanding the thrust of his own unintegrated psyche, especially his suppressed eroticism, and how it fit into God's plan.

Much has been written about the interrelation between the "Beat Poetry" movement and the "San Francisco Renaissance": both claimed the City by the Bay as home and included interlocking players. Rexroth, Duncan, Everson, and Jack Spicer, among others, were considered "Renaissance"; Allen Ginsberg, Lawrence Ferlinghetti, Jack Kerouac, Gary Snyder, and William Burroughs were "Beats." Renaissance came first, from the mid-1940s forward, the Beats following in the mid-fifties. The sobriquet "Beat" was tarred pejoratively, meaning scraggly, laid-back, dropped-out, counter-cultural, drug-fogged. Everson belonged to the Renaissance but was popularly identified with the Beats, especially by *Time* and *Life* magazines naming him the "Beat Friar."

Rexroth in San Francisco and Duncan in Berkeley hosted readings and workshops from the early fifties. In 1956 Rexroth's apartment was the scene of extraordinary readings arranged for *Life* magazine coverage, with Antoninus invited. The fall 1957 issue of *Evergreen Review*, co-edited by Rexroth and devoted to the San Francisco Renaissance, featured Antoninus along with Duncan and Ginsberg, who presented his notorious poem "Howl." Antoninus notes in the afterword of the delayed 1974 publication of his poem "River-Root" that his own highly sensual, nature-immersed, and erotic narrative of married love was composed in direct response to "Howl," "trying to redeem the libidinous Beat energies from the insane horror of Ginsberg's poem — to canonize them" (Bartlett, 1979, 171). This juxtaposition with Ginsberg may have been formative in enlarging Everson's own eroticism in subsequent poetry.

In fall 1955, a significant turning point, Antoninus gave his first public readings as a Dominican, initially at San Francisco State College, and then at St. Mary's College, Moraga, both to packed houses. For him it was the discovery of new powers. After St. Mary's, he noted in his journal:

> It confirmed my impression after the San Francisco State reading that this was my vocation in the Church. People will not read my poems, but when I read to them I can spellbind. Everything engages, all my faculties converge here, and I become for this brief time transcendently myself.... The ideational heart of the poem burns with an inexplicable revelation. It is this realization of my poems as vehicles for establishing contact between God and other souls that gives me the understanding of their prophetic character and led me back to writing again." (Bartlett, 1979, 170)

When in 1959 Antoninus was invited to read at the Universities of Detroit and Chicago, this charismatic communication intensified. But the triumph, though it was to preface the strategy of all Antoninus' future readings, had an untoward result. It and the consequent article in *Time* brought the "Beat Friar" to the attention of the archbishop of San Francisco, who ordered a stop to his readings in a religious habit, objecting to his lecturing as though he were a cleric and to his having been a pacifist.

After the archbishop's death in 1960, Antoninus — having shown his mettle by more than a year's obedient silence — was freed by his provincial to follow his platform readings and given release time to write. It was at this juncture, too, that the poet was brought under the influence of a person who first came to him for spiritual advice, Rose Tannlund, a woman moderately well off, socially adept and active in San Francisco, and a veteran of extended Jungian analysis. From the ensuing intense spiritual and emotional relationship came what was Antoninus' most extended erotic sequence, highlighting the theme of struggle for the reconciliation of the masculine and feminine within the self; it is amazing that his superiors in 1967 gave their imprimatur to *The Rose of Solitude*. In the meantime he had been presenting the poem as work-in-progress with riveting effect in successive readings.

In 1962 Everson/Antoninus' mentor Robinson Jeffers died. Though they had never met, the event struck hard. Jeffers had brought Antoninus to see nature as revelation, had imbued landscape with divinity, had shown the poet's celebration to be an act which made mankind somehow more worthy of the thunderous theophany that was the cosmos. Antoninus wrote that Jeffers "made me a religious man, gave me the dignity of faith in life and in God" (Bartlett, 1979, 191). At the San Francisco Museum of Art in June, Antoninus read his tribute to Jeffers, "The Poet is Dead," one of the great elegies of the century. The sophisticated audience was spellbound.

In September 1964, while still working on "The Rose of Solitude" and on a Jungian prose study seeking meaning for the nation after John Kennedy's death, Antoninus took his first vows as a Dominican. And it was at this point that into his life came the fourth and final key woman of his adulthood, Susanna Rickson, a student at San Francisco State College. As was the case with Rose, Susanna approached him as a counselor. Through four years, they grew in intimacy. As with each of his other loves, there came a poem: "Tendril in the Mesh." He named her "Persephone, the goddess of rebirth and all beginnings," and pictured himself as Pluto, Lord of the Underworld. She was twenty years old; he fifty-seven.

In fall 1968, Antoninus launched another acclaimed reading tour, this time of Europe. He returned to ask Susanna to be his wife and, at a reading at the University of California's Davis campus, announced publicly his intent to leave the Dominicans and marry. Reading "Tendril in the Mesh" (inspired by her), he concluded the evening by dramatically stripping off his Dominican robes. The transition from religious life to secular after eighteen years of mostly cloistered, contemplative living could not have been more monumental and, indeed, more traumatic. The couple lived at Marin County's Stinson Beach until there came an invitation that would usher in the final chapter of Everson's life.

Kresge College of the University of California, Santa Cruz, had been given a Washington handpress and had announced an opening for a printer and lecturer in poetry. The pastoral landscape of California, which had always been a touchstone for Antoninus, once more enveloped William Everson. From the soil and seasons of Selma he had evolved to confront the maternal Pacific and its dramatic coastal headlands; the couple found their home in a rustic former ranger's cabin a few miles north of Santa Cruz along Highway One. At the university he immersed himself in work with students, inaugurating Lime Kiln Press. His year-long lectureship, comprised of meditations on the archetypal bard's vocation, was titled "Birth of A Poet."

More than ever he became immersed in the primitive nature around him — primeval redwood forests, denizened by deer, cougars, and coyotes and streams accessed by sacrificial salmon. Whereas in religious life he had worn austere robes, tunic and scapula, with hair mostly cropped, he now donned buckskin and a bear-claw necklace with Whitmanesque flowing hair and beard. Poetry continued to come. In *Man Fate* he attempted "to work out the implications of his institutional break." Later poems began to reflect more fully his new terrain, centered upon his home, "Kingfisher Flat." His Lime Kiln Press turned out a succession of beautiful student-apprenticed, handcrafted works, most notably the nationally honored *Granite and Cypress*, a grouping of Jeffers' stonemason poems which so closely linked that poet day by day to the power and endurance of earth.

In spring 1977 Everson was diagnosed as having Parkinson's disease, a neurological disorder that would gradually and insidiously rob him of all but his unquenchable spirit. For seventeen years he battled it daily, still giving readings, but less and less able to evoke his inimitable congress with the audience. He could no longer work the handpress and had to resign his lectureship. Yet he continued to write, collecting his Dominican verse into the Shelley Award-winning *Veritable Years* (1978) and publishing *The Masks of Drought*, eighteen narrative poems from the California rainless seasons of 1976-1977. In these and following years he edited three key Jeffers poetic works, finished *The Excesses of God: Robinson Jeffers as a Religious Figure*, gathered a new anthology of selected poems, *The Blood of the Poet*, and launched into a long autobiographical poem, *Dust Shall Be the Serpent's Food*, of which he finished two cantos before his death. Work accomplished, his spirit passed quietly June 2, 1994, from his home at Kingfisher Flat.

Everson's own titles capture his life. Among them *The Crooked Lines of God*, his first collection of Catholic poems, encapsulates the axiom that "God writes straight with crooked lines." *Hazards of Holiness* reflects the cost to him of integrity and perdurance. In the subtitle of his 1957-1976 poem "River-Root," Everson had focused on a little-used word, "syzygy" (taken from the Greek denoting union, paired, yoked together) to express his poetic and life thrust. How perfect to describe his life mode. Relentlessly he sought syzygy within his psyche and with the world and with his Creator.

Discovery of God through violence was a theme of Jeffers, his mentor, but Everson stepped significantly beyond. Jeffers dealt with the external world, the cosmos self-immolating; Everson dealt with immolation within. The Passion of Christ was what he saw enacted, enfleshed everywhere in the natural world ("In All These Acts") but especially within the human soul.

Stylistically his poems are typically long stanza sequences of spirit-in-flesh discovery. His vocabulary is rich, staccato, and halfway eccentric: words like "purl, glyph, spilth, flensed, spunk, col, cob, spang, rouse, stave, lorn" will all engage in one poem. (Such unusual word choice is also exhibited in his most renowned prose book, *Archetype West* [1976].) Almost exclusively his subject matter is confessional, often dialogic with the divine. Through his "erotic mysticism" he sought a reconciliation of body-soul dichotomies, using sexual coition not only as metaphor, as so many mystics had before him, but as a point of discovery and congress with God. He leaned upon the mystery of "Incarnation," the insight that God is truly enfleshed, to be discovered in sexuality and not in its denial. He was ever searching out "archetype," the final archetype being God. William Everson was a poet of faith pursuing a world-reconciling Christ, of hope carrying him through many an upheaval and dark night, and of love found in and through psychic and mystic wholeness. Sacrament was his vision: the world as holy and overshadowingly beautiful. His was an indomitable spirit.

Selected Bibliography

Primary Sources

Poetry
The Blood of the Poet: Selected Poems. Seattle: Broken Moon Press, 1993.
The Blowing of the Seed. New Haven: William Wenning, 1966.

The Crooked Lines of God. Detroit: University of Detroit Press, 1959.

The Engendering Flood: Book One of Dust Shall Be the Serpent's Food. Santa Rosa: Black Sparrow Press, 1990.

The Hazards of Holiness. Garden City: Doubleday, 1962.

In the Fictive Wish. Berkeley: Oyez, 1967.

Man Fate: The Swan Song of Brother Antoninus. New York: New Directions, 1974.

The Masculine Dead. Prairie City: James A. Decker, 1942.

The Masks of Drought. Santa Barbara: Black Sparrow Press, 1980.

The Poet Is Dead. San Francisco: Auerhahn Press, 1964.

A Privacy of Speech. Berkeley: Equinox Press, 1948.

The Residual Years. Waldport: Untide Press, 1944; New York: New Directions, 1948, 1968.

River-Root. Berkeley: Oyez, 1976.

The Rose of Solitude. Garden City: Doubleday, 1967.

San Joaquin. Los Angeles: Ward Ritchie Press, 1939.

The Single Source. Berkeley: Oyez, 1966.

The Springing of the Blade. Reno: Black Rock Press, 1968.

Tendril in the Mesh. N.p.: Cayucos Books, 1973.

X War Elegies. Waldport: Untide Press, 1943.

These Are the Ravens. San Leandro: Greater West Publishing, 1935.

Triptych for the Living. Berkeley: Seraphim Press, 1951.

The Veritable Years. Santa Barbara: Black Sparrow Press, 1978.

The Waldport Poems. Waldport: Untide Press, 1944.

War Elegies. Waldport: Untide Press, 1944.

Prose

Archetype West: The Pacific Coast as a Literary Region. Berkeley: Oyez, 1976.

Birth of a Poet: The Santa Cruz Meditations. Lee Bartlett, ed. Santa Rosa: Black Sparrow, 1982.

Earth Poetry: Selected Essays and Interviews. Lee Bartlett, ed. Berkeley: Oyez, 1980.

The Excesses of God: Robinson Jeffers as a Religious Figure. Stanford: Stanford University Press, 1988.

On Writing the Waterbirds and Other Presentations: Collected Forewords and Afterwords. Lee Bartlett, ed. Metuchen: Scarecrow Press, 1983.

Prodigious Trust. Santa Rosa: Black Sparrow Press, 1996.

Robinson Jeffers: Fragments of an Older Fury. Berkeley: Oyez, 1968.

Take Hold upon the Future: Letters on Writers and Writing, 1938-1946 (William Everson with Lawrence Clark Powell). William R. Eshelman, ed. Metuchen: Scarecrow, 1994.

Secondary Sources

Allen, Donald. *The New American Poetry, 1945-60*. New York: Grove Press, 1960.

Allen, Donald and Warren Tallman. *The Poetics of the New American Poetry*. New York: Grove Press, 1973.

Bartlett, Lee. *The Beats: Essays in Criticism*. Jefferson: McFarland, 1981.

———. *Benchmark & Blaze: The Emergence of William Everson*. Metuchen: Scarecrow Press, 1979.

———. "Creating the Autochthon: Kenneth Rexroth, William Everson, and *The Residual Years*." *Sagetrieb*, 2:3 (1983): 57-69.

———. "Crooked Lines: William Everson and C.G. Jung." *Centennial Review*, 7:4 (1983): 288-303.

————. *William Everson*. Boise: Boise State University Western Writers Series, 1985.

————. *William Everson: The Life of Brother Antoninus*. New York: New Directions, 1988.

Brophy, Robert, ed. *William Everson: Remembrances and Tributes*. Long Beach: Robinson Jeffers Newsletter, 1995.

Campo, Allan, David A. Carpenter and Bill Hotchkiss. *William Everson: Poet from the San Joaquin*. Newcastle: Blue Oak Press, 1978.

Carpenter, David A. *Rages of Excess: The Life and Poetry of William Everson*. Bristol, Indiana: Wyndham Hall Press, 1987.

Cavanaugh, Brendon, O.P., Alfred Camillius Murphy, O.P., and Albert Deshner, O.P. "Brother Antoninus: A Symposium." *Dominicana*, 68 (1963): 33-53.

Charters, Samuel. *Some Poems/Poets: Studies in American Underground Poetry Since 1945*. Berkeley: Oyez, 1971.

Davidson, Michael. *The San Francisco Renaissance*. New York: Cambridge University Press, 1989.

Fass, Ekbert. *Towards a New American Poetics: Essays & Interviews*. Santa Barbara: Black Sparrow Press, 1978.

Gelpi, Albert. "Everson/Antoninus: Contending with the Shadow." Afterword. In *The Veritable Years*. Santa Barbara: Black Sparrow Press, 1978.

————. "After the Sign of Woman." Afterword. In *The Blood of the Poet*. Seattle: Broken Moon Press, 1993.

Hotchkiss, Bill, ed. *Perspectives on William Everson*. Grants Pass: Castle Peak Editions, 1991.

Kherdian, David. *Six Poets of the San Francisco Renaissance: Portraits and Checklists*. Fresno: Gilgia Press, 1967.

Lacey, Paul. *The Inner War: Forms and Themes in Recent American Poetry*. Philadelphia: Fortress Press, 1972.

Melzer, David. *Golden Gate: Interviews with 5 San Francisco Poets*. Berkeley: Wingbow Press, 1976.

Parkinson, Thomas. *Poets, Poems, Movements*. Ann Arbor: UMI Research Press, 1987.

Perkins, David. *A History of Modern Poetry: Modernism and After*. Cambridge: Harvard University Press, 1987.

Powell, James A. "William Everson (Brother Antoninus)." In *The Beats: Literary Bohemians in Postwar America*. Ann Charters, ed. Detroit: Gale, 1983.

Rexroth, Kenneth. *American Poetry in the Twentieth Century*. New York: Herder and Herder, 1971.

————. "The Residual Years: An Introduction." In William Everson's *The Residual Years*. New York: New Directions, 1968.

Rosenthal, M.L. *The New Poets: American and British Poetry since World War II*. New York: Oxford University Press, 1967.

Stafford, William E. *The Achievement of Brother Antoninus*. Glenview: Scott, Foresman, 1967.

Wakoski, Diane. "Neglected Poets 2: William Everson and Bad Taste." *American Poetry*, 2:1 (1984): 36-43.

Krista Comer

Joan Didion

J oan Didion occupies an anomalous position in western literary history. In both fiction and nonfiction, Didion has written widely about the West — especially California. And yet, because her essays, in particular, have captured a national audience, Didion maintains an indisputably national reputation. Her political analysis of the 1992 Democratic National Convention, which led the front page of the *New York Review of Books*, illustrates her status as national cultural commentator. Moreover her books on non-western topics (*Salvador*, *Miami*, *A Book of Common Prayer*, *Democracy: A Novel*, *After Henry*), establish Didion as a writer whose literary interests extend beyond regional boundaries. But Didion's best work remains that which is centered around California, and it is this body of writing that is most relevant to western narrative traditions.

Didion calls herself California's "native daughter," for she is great-great-great-granddaughter of a pioneer family who came west on a wagon train to the Sacramento Valley in 1846. Didion was born in that same valley in 1934, where she lived (except during the war years) until she entered the University of California at Berkeley in 1953. In 1956 she graduated from Berkeley. Having won *Vogue* magazine's prestigious Prix de Paris award, Didion moved to New York City, where she would live for the next eight years while working as a writer at *Vogue*, *National Review* and *Mademoiselle*. There she published her first novel *Run River* (1963). In 1964, after a seven-year acquaintance, she married the writer

John Gregory Dunne. They returned to California to make a home in Los Angeles, and in 1966 adopted an infant daughter, Quintana Roo Dunne.

Over the next twenty-five years, Didion published essays in a variety of places including *Holiday*, *Saturday Evening Post*, *New York Times Magazine*, *American Scholar*, *New York Review of Books*, and *New York Times Book Review*. She wrote a regular movie column for *Vogue*, and, with John Dunne, co-wrote several motion picture screenplays, including *The Panic in Needle Park* (1971), *Play It As It Lays* (1972), *A Star Is Born* (1976) and *True Confessions* (1980). With Dunne she also co-authored the "Points West" column in *Saturday Evening Post* (1967-1969), and "The Coast" column in *Esquire* (1976-1977). Her collected essays — her true claim to fame — appeared as *Slouching Towards Bethlehem* (1968) and *The White Album* (1979). She also produced three novels, the critically praised *Play It As It Lays* (1970), *A Book of Common Prayer* (1977), and *Democracy* (1984), as well as two books of political journalism, *Salvador* (1983) and *Miami* (1987). In 1994, in a tribute to her longtime editor, the late Henry Robbins, Didion published the essay collection *After Henry*. Most recently, *The Last Thing He Wanted* appeared (1996).

Many critics of western literature write about Didion's claim upon California, her affinity for pioneer history, her dialogue with the West as both American Dream and Tragedy. She is famous for her signature sensibility: a perfect ear, an eye for detail, a dire wit, and an understated delivery. Hers is a style of extreme economy. She writes about a world of old families, finer dress shops and restaurants, the best schools. Even the criminals she interviews are celebrities. She is the consummate insider, a registered Republican, impeccably connected, unapologetically elitist. The sensitivity to gender relations that Didion's female protagonists dramatize, however, presents critics with more of a problem, for Didion is no feminist. She disdains the category "woman writer." In more than one essay she ridicules the women's movement. All of these factors make Didion a problematic candidate for feminist endorsement.

And yet her California fiction is devoted not just to the cultural changes taking place in post-war California, but to the effect of those changes on California's women. The plot of Didion's first novel, *Run River* (1963), set in Sacramento, revolves around protagonist Lily Knight McClellan and the unfolding drama of her husband Everett, who in the first paragraph murders Lily's lover and, in the last two pages, kills

347

himself as solution to the family's problems. Giving the novel much of its moral tension is Didion's representation of nineteenth-century pioneer ancestors — hard workers with a sense of what they wanted — juxtaposed against a representation of the pioneers' contemporary Sacramento descendants, the aimless generation of 1938 to 1959, landed gentry whose lives, in spite of wealth and position, are undone by their own flaws. The moral tension thickens as Didion shows that, in an era noted for its rigidly defined gender roles and endless popular representations of the ideal woman, Lily Knight McClellan is entirely unsure of what she is supposed to be or do or want. The contemporary generation's "aimlessness" is lived out, that is, in very gendered ways.

Lily commits a woman's most unpardonable sins: she emasculates her husband through rampant infidelity, musters little interest in her children and none in her community. That is, she fails to meet the litmus tests of successful upper-class white femininity in the fifties. Lily is not a comforting refuge from the world, not an angel in the home, not a moral guide. She is nothing women are supposed to be. Like many educated women of the 1950s, something indefinable (that "problem with no name" that Friedan writes about in the same year *Run River* is published) contributes to Lily's uneasiness.

Lily tries to do the "right" things, write thank you notes in the appropriate amount of time, go to the right department stores. She wonders,

> [What it is] that young wives and mothers did. For a starter, they did not sit around by themselves on the Capitol steps smoking cigarettes in the rain [as does Lily]; she was sure of that. If they found themselves downtown after an appointment in the Medico-Dental Building they would have swatches to match, War Bonds to purchase, friends to meet for lunch. (71)

But Lily does not like the company of women, and she has no swatches to match. Further, she is in the Medico-Dental Building for scandalous reasons. As the supreme example of changing times, Lily clandestinely aborts a child she carries which is not her husband's. And this abortion, named only once and even then, vaguely, haunts the remaining narrative.

Abortion is, again, a pivotal issue in Didion's second novel, *Play It As It Lays* (1970). This book, a National Book Award nominee, depicts the fast-paced world of Hollywood of the late 1960s, a world where social malaise, sexual experimentation, drugs, and upper-class malice abound. In the tradition of literary noir, the philosophic dilemma of the book is the protagonist Maria Wyeth's confrontation with "nothingness." This confrontation with "nothingness," however, owes a debt not just to noir or Camus, but also to contemporary debates about women's reproductive freedom — which would culminate in three years in *Roe vs. Wade*. Maria's belief that "nothing applies" is due in large part to the devastation that follows her half-coerced abortion. Through Maria Wyeth, Didion makes clear that her brand of literary noir is inseparable from the gender politics of the sexual revolution.

Didion's noir also focuses on the gendered logics which structure the power relations of Hollywood as a workplace. Maria, female actress and model, is a commodity consumed by male directors, producers, and aspiring filmmakers. Her body is the collateral traded in exchange for Producer BZ's investment in her director/husband Carter's film. And Director Carter, not Maria, is the owner of this collateral. Maria sees no financial gain from its sale. Indeed, as soon as she separates from her director/husband, her body's value depreciates and she has trouble finding work, though Carter's new actress/girlfriend has a sudden wealth of acting options.

Didion has something to say, too, about the gender politics of filmic representation. Protagonist Maria is least satisfied with her husband's documentary film about her, entitled "Maria," one that ostensibly captures the "real" her as she goes about her daily business in New York City. Of the two films she has made, this one is honored by the film industry, given awards at film festivals and emulated by young filmmakers who want to "use" Maria in their own films. In a chilling contrast, Didion portrays Maria as less of an object and more of a subject in the role she plays in her *second* film: victim of a gang rape. The suggestion that a woman actress is more "herself" as rape victim than as the protagonist in a masculine narrative demonstrates Didion's (however complex) feminist leanings. The politics of gender, in Didion's final analysis, are stacked in favor of the men who control the means of representation.

In her focus on female sexuality, Didion anticipates feminist fiction of the 1970s by a decade. And in keeping with the anti-hero trend among many male western writers of the early 1960s, Didion creates the even newer and more rare anti-heroines. But critics should not read Didion primarily as a feminist. Her use of female protagonists serves a larger

349

project in which a concern for women is not central. Rather, via female characters, Didion makes a broader, sweeping statement about the decline and fall of western civilization and the western American Dream, the search for contemporary meaning, and post-modern decadence. This project finds very explicit articulation when women are no longer at the center of the narrative, as Didion's essays demonstrate. Didion's most representative voice emerges here, one targeted at a national audience and infused with a sense of regional pathos.

Didion's first collection, *Slouching Towards Bethlehem* (1968), is now regarded as a modern classic. The title essay, a report on San Francisco's Haight-Ashbury at the height of the counter-cultural movement in 1967, chronicles the notion that American culture is falling apart. As Didion puts it (quoting Yeats), "the center cannot hold." But all of the essays, in one way or another, reflect cultural disorder and the process of social revolution—western style. Though the book is often read as a *national* symbol that the center of American society was not holding, its gift is its representation of the specifically western regional brand of social chaos.

Where else in America can you get a Vegas wedding twenty-four hours a day? Or cameo portraits of John Wayne at his most manly, Joan Baez at her most airy, and the Reagans in a gubernatorial mansion modeled after the most suburban of California ranch tract homes? The focus on water, that precious resource in a region defined by its aridity, and Didion's love for Hoover Dam, again are topics that make sense only in a western context. But critics usually make this local picture into a sign for the nation, and western topics are then writ large upon a national narrative. After the 1960s, especially, California becomes a symbol for the national and the specificity of many of these tales as *western tales* is lost.

Didion frames her second essay collection, *The White Album*, in similarly regional terms, though again it is read by critics for the light it shines on national experience. The collection tells a series of primarily California stories—about the Manson cult member and convicted murderer Linda Kasabian, Huey Newton in the Alameda County Jail, about L.A. rock-'n'-roll eccentrics and Port Hueneme evangelists—which disturb Didion because they are stories "without a narrative." The mid-section, "The Woman's Movement," is Didion's most direct critique of 1970s feminism. In these vignettes lies a larger truth about life in postmodern California: language no longer holds the center of culture together. Didion has lost faith in "the narrative and the narrative's intelligibility." In this sequel to *Slouching Towards Bethlehem*, Didion doubts the premises of all the stories she has ever told herself. This is a fitting ending, for Didion remains ever the skeptic.

Selected Bibliography

Primary Sources

After Henry. New York: Simon & Schuster, 1992.
A Book of Common Prayer. New York: Simon & Schuster, 1977; Penguin, 1977.
Democracy. A Novel. New York: Simon & Schuster, 1984.
Miami. New York: Simon & Schuster, 1987.
The Last Thing He Wanted. New York: Knopf, 1996.
Play It As It Lays. New York: Farrar, Straus & Giroux, 1970; Penguin, 1970.
Run River. New York: Obolensky, 1963; Penguin, 1963.
Salvador. New York: Simon & Schuster, 1983.
Slouching Towards Bethlehem. New York: Farrar, Straus & Giroux, 1968.
Telling Stories. Berkeley: Bancroft Library, 1978.
White Album. New York: Simon & Schuster, 1979.

Secondary Sources

Davis, Mike. *City of Quartz: Excavating the Future in Los Angeles*. (Chapter 1). New York: Verso, 1990.
Felton, Sharon, ed. *The Critical Response to Joan Didion*. Westport, Connecticut: Greenwood Press, 1994.
Friedman, Ellen G., ed. *Joan Didion: Essays and Conversations*. Princeton: Ontario Review Press, 1984.
Henderson, Katherine U. *Joan Didion*. New York: Frederick Ungar, 1981.
———. "A Bibliography of Writings by and about Joan Didion." In *American Women Writing Fiction: Memory, Identity, Family and Space*. Mickey Pearlman, ed. Lexington: University Press of Kentucky, 1989.
Kuehl, Linda. "Joan Didion." In *Writers at Work: The Paris Review Interviews*, George Plimpton, ed. New York: Viking, 1981. Pp. 339-357.
Loris, Michelle Corbone. *Innocence, Loss and Recovery in the Art of Joan Didion*. New York: Peter Lang, 1989.
Stout, Janis P. *Strategies of Reticence: Silence and Meaning in the Works of Jane Austen, Willa Cather, Katherine Anne Porter and Joan Didion*. Charlottesville: University Press of Virginia, 1990.
Winchell, Mark Royden. *Joan Didion*. Boston: Twayne Publishers, 1980.
———. "Fantasy Seen: Hollywood Fiction since West." In *Los Angeles in Fiction: A Collection of Original Essays*, David Fine, ed. Albuquerque: University of New Mexico Press, 1984. Pp. 147-168.

Gerald Locklin

Charles Bukowski

Like Thomas Wolfe and Jack Kerouac, Charles Bukowski is one of those writers about whom it is almost impossible to construct an illuminating biography since his "Henry Chinaski" novels — *Ham on Rye, Factotum, Post Office, Women,* and *Hollywood* — and some of his poems and stories constitute a virtual life in themselves. There are also apparently few living witnesses to contradict or ratify his own versions of his childhood and early manhood. He had great hopes for the biography *Hank* by his onetime friend Neeli Cherkovski, but expressed disappointment with the final product. Still, the broad outlines of his life are common knowledge to his millions of readers and scores of disciples here and abroad. He was the subject of numerous interviews, videos, and journalistic articles, especially upon the occasion of the film *Barfly*, for which he had written a loosely autobiographical screenplay.

He was born Henry Charles Bukowski on August 16, 1920, in Andernach, Germany, and brought to America at the age of two. His father would today be termed abusive, a Prussian perfectionist who would take the razor strop to his son for missing a blade of grass when mowing the lawn. His mother's compliant mantra became "Henry, your father is always right." At school the unloved child had few friends and learned early on how to defend himself. At the onset of adolescence, he was afflicted by a massive attack of acne and boils that left him physically and psychologically scarred, confined him for weeks at a time to his home, and postponed sexual contact into his "barfly" years. He did, however, encounter the occasional English teacher who recognized his alienated genius and stirred his literary ambitions. He attended Los Angeles City College but did not graduate. In his early twenties he published in *Story* magazine and in Caresse Crosby's *Portfolio*. To his relief, he was declared psychologically unfit for World War II. He had discovered alcohol as a teenager, an event that he felt saved him from suicide, and he now accelerated into a ten-year binge which included jobs in the fields, a slaughterhouse, a dog-biscuit factory, gas stations, and as a shipping clerk, stock clerk, guard, and go-fer. He bussed around the county, staying alone or with women from the bars, in cheap rooms from which he was regularly evicted for drunken rages. He gathered rejection slips, listened to radio symphonies, and became disgusted with the writings of most of his famous contemporaries.

In his mid-thirties he almost hemorrhaged to death in the charity ward of Los Angeles County General Hospital. On his release he began writing poetry and was married for two and a half years to a Texas millionaire editor of a poetry magazine. Under the influence of Hemingway, Saroyan, Hamsun, Céline, Kafka, Artaud, and Fante, he stepped up his literary production while settling into an eleven-year stint as a postal worker.

He achieved his counter-culture fame in the 1960s, writing for underground newspapers such as L.A.'s *Open City* and *Free Press*. Here he elaborated the persona of Henry Chinaski in his *Notes of a Dirty Old Man*. He was becoming a small-press legend through limited editions of his poetry such as *Hearse, Loujon 7, Poets,* and *Midwest,* and he was prominently featured in classic little magazines such as Marvin Malone's *Wormwood Review* and Douglas Blazek's *Ole!*. His tenure with John Martin's Black Sparrow Press, founded explicitly to establish his work, began in 1968 with *At Terror Street and Agony Way,* followed in 1969 by *The Days Run Away Like Wild Horses Over the Hills.* But it was his novels and short stories that catapulted him to European fame, and it was revenues from them, along with sales to the movies and a rent subsidy from Black Sparrow, that allowed him to become one of the few poets in America to subsist on literary earnings alone. Martin rescued Bukowski from the post office at a time when, for apparently psychosomatic reasons, he could no longer lift his arms to stuff boxes. The publisher convinced him, counter to his preference for churning out poems, to produce at last the novel that his fans had been eagerly awaiting, *Post Office.* Nevertheless, Bukowski's poems opened new avenues for American poets in terms of accessibility, the vernacular, humor, the L.A.

urban landscape, the struggles of the working (and unemployed) class, the bar life, gender wars, and, most importantly, the rejection of the authority of the academic and literary (largely eastern) establishments. But his greatest popularity and most enduring achievements will almost certainly prove to reside in his novels. With the advocacy of the German translator Carl Weissner and the photographer Michael Montfort, this unlikeliest of careers was launched.

It is difficult to illustrate Bukowski's craft with excerpts because his poems are seldom short, and the best — "Fire Station," for instance — are often the longest. While others debated how best to restore narrative and dramatic structures to verse, Bukowski just sat down and did it. He had the sense of timing and construction (and the voice) of a W.C. Fields, which is one reason why his readings, some of which were recorded, drew throngs until he deliberately priced himself out of the market. To quote a line here and there makes about as much sense as telling a punchline without a buildup. But in the serio-comic "Yeah, man?" (from *Dangling in the Tournefortia*), the white protagonist pulls a knife on a Latino whose car is blocking his. Later the Anglo returns to find his apartment in a shambles:

> and then he looked
> in the toilet
> and down in the bowl
> was a freshly cut
> cat's tail
> furry and still
> bleeding
> in the water
> Larry hit the lever
> to flush it away
> and got an
> empty click
> lifted the lid
> looked inside
> and all the toilet parts
> were gone.

After a couple of hits of the beer he has brought back with him, Larry decides

that it was about time
he moved
further west.
(64-65)

This is not simply a nightmare tale of one man's misguided race relations; it is the demographic and demonological saga of white flight.
Bukowski may or may not be characterized as a revolutionary, but his
work is undeniably of political significance. He was a chronicler of the
symptomatic phenomena of our times. He was, to paraphrase George
Orwell's comment on Henry Miller, the proletarian given a voice. He is
probably the most gifted poet ever to speak from the infrared extreme of
the socio-economic spectrum.

Bukowski's idiom is the product of a movement at least as old as
Wordsworth's preface to the second edition of the *Lyrical Ballads*. In
America it weaves its way through Whitman, Robinson, Frost, Masters,
Lindsay, W.C. Williams, Oppen, Reznikov, Rakosi, Ginsberg, O'Hara,
and Edward Field, to become the dominant mode of poets today, especially in Southern California, as evidenced in anthologies such as *Many
Californias, A New Geography of Poets*, and *Stand-Up Poetry*. A poem of
moderate length that exemplifies Bukowski's unblinkingly Darwinian
view of life (one that avoids the indulgence of exclusively one- or two-
word lines that afflicts some later poems) is "the mockingbird":

the mockingbird had been following the cat
all summer
mocking mocking mocking
teasing and cocksure;
the cat crouched under rockers on porches
tail flashing
and said something angry to the mockingbird
which I didn't understand.
yesterday the cat walked calmly up the driveway
with the mockingbird alive in its mouth,
wings fanned, beautiful wings fanned and flapping,
feathers parted like a woman's legs,
and the bird was no longer mocking,
it was asking, it was praying
but the cat

striding down through centuries
would not listen.

I saw it crawl under a yellow car
with the bird
to bargain it to another place
summer was over.
(*Run with the Hunted* 387)

Bukowski not only liked both mockingbirds and cats — he was both.

It is hard to understand why some readers find Bukowski depressing. Is he not a veritable paladin of survival? If he came through, who can't? He is best when he is being funny and dirty and unsparing. He was one of our few naturalists to possess a sense of style and a sense of humor. He seems less authentic when waxing pseudopoetic or pseudophilosophical. He drank a bit, and he could be unfair, both in person and in print, at certain stages of the bottle. But in his finest moments there is a purity in his refusal to glorify or sentimentalize humanity or the human condition. Did Herman Melville, Mark Twain, or Nathanael West do those things?

He was not, however, without compassion, and he was capable of penning touching tributes to his dead former lover Jane, his wife Linda Lee, and his daughter Marina, to whom he was much more the devoted, responsible, and protective father than could have been generally known.

While Bukowski's novels (with the exception of *Pulp*) are almost strictly autobiographical, his short stories often veer into dream, nightmare, sexual fantasy, the cautionary tale, the tall tale, and recastings of archetypal narratives. He had to take his inspirations where he could find them because he wrote stories almost exclusively for paychecks, to deadlines, sometimes at the rate of a story per week. The generally high quality of these efforts is, therefore, more remarkable than the inevitable lapses. Two of his finest achievements are "There's No Business," about the demise of a Vegas lounge comedian, and "Bring Me Your Love," in which a man protests extravagantly to the woman he is visiting in a mental hospital that he does not have another woman waiting back at the motel—although we learn that in fact he does. Among the stories that illustrate his usually unremarked imaginative range are "Six-inch Man," "Fooling Marie," "Less Delicate Than the Locust," "Dr. Nazi," "No Way to Paradise," "Maja Thurup," and "Son of Satan."

Bukowski's preoccupation with the racetrack is legendary (Glover 32-33). Playing the horses provided him with a place to get away from his creative labors, his women, and his fans, to relax, to clear his mind, while renewing his acquaintance with that run of humanity alongside which he was no longer employed. Since he had come to hate bars, the track also provided a substitute for those venues of human interaction. As he took pride in his handicapping, he could feel alternately at one with and superior to the crowd. Each race provided a unique plot, though steeped in tradition, ritual, and legendry.

One of his strongest selections of poems was a book-issue of *The Wormwood Review* — *Horses Don't Bet on People & Neither Do I*. His phrasings are particularly meticulous here, and his subjects of a mature breadth: how to deal with juvenile delinquents, the tribulations of getting the locks changed on one's house, and the predictable advice given by a talk-show psychologist to a cuckolded husband. "*Kenyon Review, After the Sandstorm*" is a measured self-assessment of his place in our literature:

> coming off that park bench after that all-night
> sandstorm in El Paso
> and walking into the library
> I felt fairly safe even though I had less than
> two dollars
> was alone in the world
> and was 40 pounds overweight.
> it still felt normal and almost pleasant to
> open that copy of the Kenyon Review
> 1940
> and marvel at the most brilliant way these
> professors used the language to criticize each
> other for the way they criticized literature.
> I even felt that they were humorous about it,
> but not quite: the bitterness was rancid and
> red steel hot, but at the same time I felt the
> leisurely and safe places that language had
> evolved from: places and cultures centuries
> soft and institutionalized.
> I knew I would never be able to write
> in that manner, yet I almost wanted to be

one of them or any of them: being guarded,
fierce and witty, having fun
in that way

what I did know was that overeffusive language
properly used
could be bright and beautiful.
I also sensed that there might be
something else.
(*Wormwood Review,* 95 [1984] 121)

Selected Bibliography

Primary Sources (All published by Black Sparrow Press, Santa Rosa, California, unless otherwise noted.)

At Terror Street and Agony Way. 1968.
"Barfly" (screenplay). 1987.
Betting on the Muse: Poems and Stories. 1996.
Burning in Water Drowning in Flame: Selected Poems 1955-1973. 1974.
Dangling in the Tournefortia. 1981.
The Days Run Away Like Wild Horses Over the Hills. 1969.
Erections, Ejaculations, Exhibitions and General Tales of Ordinary Madness. San Francisco: City Lights Books, 1975.
Factotum. 1975.
Ham on Rye. 1982.
Hollywood. 1989.
Hot Water Music. 1983.
The Last Night of the Earth Poems. 1992.
Living on Luck: Selected Letters, 1960s-1970s. Vol. 2, 1995.
Love Is a Dog from Hell: Poems 1974-1977. 1977.
Mockingbird Wish Me Luck. 1972.
Notes of a Dirty Old Man. San Francisco: City Lights Books, 1969.
Play the Piano Drunk Like a Percussion Instrument Until the Fingers Begin to Bleed a Bit. 1979.
Post Office. 1971.
Pulp. 1994.
The Roominghouse Madrigals. 1988.
Run With the Hunted: A Charles Bukowski Reader. John Martin, ed. New York: HarperCollins, 1993.
Screams from the Balcony: Selected Letters 1960-1970. 1993. (The first in a series.)
Septuagenarian Stew: Stories & Poems. 1990.
Shakespeare Never Did This. San Francisco: City Lights Books, 1979.
Sometimes You Get So Alone That It Just Makes Sense. 1986.

South of No North: Stories of the Buried Life. 1973.
War All the Time: Poems 1981-1984. 1984.
Women. 1978.

Bukowski's work has been featured in hundreds of periodicals, but most regularly in the *Wormwood Review,* edited by Marvin Malone formerly of Stockton, California (now deceased). Bukowski's compositions have appeared in nearly every issue of the 143 released, several of them single-author back issues.

Secondary Sources

Sure, The Charles Bukowski Newsletter, Edward L. Smith, ed., began publication at Homeland, California, in May, 1991. Its tenth issue appeared in 1994 from Ojai, California.

Cherkovski, Neeli. *Hank: The Life of Charles Bukowski.* New York: Random House, 1991.

Ciotti, Paul. "Bukowski." *Los Angeles Times Magazine,* March 22, 1987, 18.

Esterly, Glen. "Buk: The Pock-marked Poetry of Charles Bukowski: Notes of a Dirty Old Mankind." *Rolling Stone,* June 17, 1976, 28-34.

Fogel, Al. "I Collect Charles Bukowski." In *Under the Influence: A Collection of Works by Charles Bukowski.* Sudbury, Massachusetts: Water Row Press, 1984.

Fox, Hugh. *Charles Bukowski: A Critical and Bibliographical Study.* Somerville, Massachusetts: Abyss, 1969, 1971.

Glover, David. "A Day at the Races: Gambling and Luck in Bukowski's Fiction," *Review of Contemporary Fiction,* 5 (1985): 32-33.

Harrison, Russell. *Against the American Dream: Essays on Charles Bukowski.* Santa Rosa: Black Sparrow Press, 1994.

Locklin, Gerald. *Charles Bukowski: A Sure Bet.* Sudbury, Massachusetts: Water Row Press, 1996.

Smith, Julian. "Charles Bukowski and the Avant-Garde." *The Review of Contemporary Fiction,* 5 (1985): 56-59.

———. "The Poetry of Charles Bukowski." Unpublished doctoral thesis, University of Hull, England, 1989.

"Special Charles Bukowski Issue." *Second Coming,* Vol. 2, Number. 3, 1974.

Charles L. Crow

Maxine Hong Kingston

axine Hong Kingston, born in Stockton, California in 1940, defines her heritage as "Very West Coast... Central Valley, as distinguished from San Francisco... Stockton, Sacramento, Fresno, all of the Valley in the North — Steinbeck's land" (Kingston and Islas 16). The westernness of Kingston has been underappreciated, but she may be read as a defining example of a "New West" writer. Thus, though indebted to her mainstream predecessors (like Steinbeck), she consciously reinterprets the West and works against its dominant stereotypes. Her founding myth is not the "westering" of European Americans, but the legend of Gold Mountain, built of the stories that Chinese told each other about America, especially the West (Lim and Ling 4). Her career thus far has been based on two tightly interrelated projects: "claiming America," that is, recovering the repressed stories of her people as an essential part of American history and of the West they pioneered (Kingston and Pfaff 1); and exploring the growth of the Chinese American artist who will tell these stories.

Kingston's three major books to date — *The Woman Warrior: Memoirs of a Girlhood Among Ghosts* (1977), *China Men* (1980), and *Tripmaster Monkey: His Fake Book* (1989) — have brought her honors and a wide audience and a somewhat uneasy role as the preeminent Chinese American author.[1] *The Woman Warrior* won a National Book Critics Circle Award and now has the status of a canonized text, frequently taught in college classrooms and excerpted in anthologies. A handbook on teaching *The Woman Warrior* has been issued by the Modern Language Association. Kingston has been declared a "Living National Treasure" in Hawaii, where she lived for many years. This eminence, though, has brought certain liabilities. Initial responses from mainstream critics, while usually favorable, often expressed latent cultural bias, historical ignorance, or condescending "orientalism"; at the same time, some other Chinese American authors, most notably Frank Chin, objected to her presentation of traditional Chinese culture and accused her of pandering to stereotypes in the minds of white readers.[2] This critical discourse is essential background for her *Künstlerroman* — *Tripmaster Monkey*.

The Woman Warrior and *China Men* were originally a single work, separated at a late stage of composition (Kingston and Pfaff 25). Though there are some stylistic differences, they employ essentially the same narrative voice. Both books challenge the reader with apparent genre-jumping: are we reading a novel, history, or autobiography? (The question of category was troubling to Kingston's publisher, A. A. Knopf, and to merchants when *The Woman Warrior* appeared. How was the book to be marketed, and where was it to be shelved?) Kingston mixes apparent literal autobiography with Chinese legend, presented as if equally real. Episodes of family history are undercut with reminders of how little the narrator could have known about the facts. Alternate versions of the same event are offered — a technique especially visible in *China Men*.

Now, more than twenty years after *The Woman Warrior*'s publication, and after schooling by Kingston and other post-modern writers, the question of which box to put the book in should seem naive to the educated audience. Even at first reading, however, most thoughtful readers understood its major themes. From its brilliant first sentence, Kingston constructs a struggle over voice: "'You must not tell anyone,' my mother said, 'what I am about to tell you.'" The child Maxine cannot speak above a whisper at public school; she covers paper with black crayon, scores zero on her IQ test. She struggles to find her own identity, or voice, as she negotiates the Chinese and American elements of her heritage. Though much of her struggle is, ultimately, with patriarchy, Kingston places in the foreground her relationship with her mother, Brave Orchid — a woman who is earthy, comic, wise, bossy, comforting, maddening, and a marvelous literary creation. Maxine eventually is able to defy her mother, to be the writer who tells the forbidden story of the "no-name woman" which begins the book. But the end of the book is reconciliation, not defiance. The last sequence of *The Woman Warrior* is an adaptation of the story of Ts'ai Yen, a Chinese woman who was captured by barbarians and eventually repatriated to become a celebrated poet. It is created jointly by the now-mature Kingston and her mother: "The beginning is hers, the ending, mine" (206). As opposed to the dominant European and American model of the artist as a loner and exile, Kingston celebrates community and collaboration as markers of the successful artist.

As a child, Kingston often hid in a basement, playing a game she invented and called "Talking Men." Once she retreated to this secret place while an angry uncle stamped about the house, bellowing her name (*China Men* 180-182).[3] Similarly, throughout *China Men*, Kingston explores her subject in her own imaginative way, showing some resistance and occasional hostility to the men she describes, even as she had once defied her ex-river pirate uncle — the biggest man she ever knew. *China Men* begins, in fact, with a cruel (and funny) fable of a Chinese warrior who was captured in the "Land of Women" and, with bound feet, forced to assume the role of a servant girl. Gender-reversal tales occur at several points in the book, and the narrative voice is distinctly female (the voice of *The Woman Warrior*), often nagging and correcting her male characters. Nevertheless, *China Men* is a usually sympathetic re-creation of the lives and voices of men who were pioneering Americans, who helped build the West (and Hawaii). Among them are her great-grandfather, grandfather, and father.

She tells her stories of family pioneers in defiance of the willed ignorance of other Americans, who learn nothing in school of minority history and persistently view Chinese Americans as foreign or exotic, as "sojourners." In the face of this ignorance, Kingston writes her chapter "The Laws," in which she risks breaking the continuity of the book, and, for seven and a half pages, simply recites the facts of institutionalized racism against Chinese in America. While acknowledging that this load of dismal history "affects the shape of the book," and might appear clumsy, Kingston considered the writing of it an essential act of liberation for herself and for Chinese American writers who would follow. The author having said it, her successors need not, since other Americans now have no excuse for cultural blindness toward Chinese America.

In claiming America for her ancestors, Kingston recovers the silenced voices of men who were also her predecessors as an artist. Nineteenth-century immigrants detained at Angel Island covered their barracks walls with poems. Her great-grandfather in Hawaii, Bak Goong, forbidden to speak while working, organizes a "shout party," digs a hole in the ground and invites his fellow workers to shout their messages and grievances into the earth. This communal act is improvised yet based on a Chinese legend. "We can make up customs," Bak Goong asserts, "because we're the founding fathers of this place" (118). A similar episode uniting Chinese tradition and American experience occurs when Maxine's grandfather, Ah Goong, after terrible hardships following the "Driving Out" of railroad workers, reaches Sacramento and is delighted to discover a performance of a Chinese opera. Usually dramatizing episodes of the "little tradition" of folk or non-academic literature, Chinese opera was a popular, not an elite form. The opera Grandfather saw presented the famous "Oath of the Peach Orchard," an event from the *Romance of Three Kingdoms*. In a complicated passage, Kingston celebrates this moment of Chinese popular art in America and conflates grandfather Ah Goong, in the audience, with Guan Goong, one of the three heroes of the *Romance of Three Kingdoms*, who was later deified in the Chinese pantheon: "Guan Goong, the God of War, also God of War and Literature, had come to America—Guan Goong, Grandfather Guan, our own ancestor of writers and fighters, of actors and gamblers, and avenging executioners who mete out justice. Our own kin. Not a distant ancestor but grandfather" (149-150).[4] Claiming America also means for Kingston claiming Chinese culture as a legitimate source for the Chinese American artist, which can be modified to fit the experience of Gold Mountain.

With *China Men* Kingston had told all of the stories based on her childhood she wished to tell. Her next book would be fiction, which—somewhat surprisingly, considering the strong fictional elements in her first two books—she considered a different imaginative activity. Nonetheless, *Tripmaster Monkey* is not a new departure in theme: it continues her "claiming America" project, and is, more explicitly, about the role of the Chinese American artist.

Tripmaster Monkey is a self-aware, metafictional novel, which on one level recreates the controversies over Kingston's first two books. Thus Frank Chin called *The Woman Warrior* a "fake book" because of its improvisations upon Chinese myth. Kingston retorts by subtitling her novel *His Fake Book* and giving it a hero who is a young aspiring Chinese American poet and playwright in the Bay Area of the 1960s. (There was only one such person, Frank Chin.[5]) It is not surprising, then, that

Kingston finds her punningly named protagonist, Wittman Ah Sing, "a nasty person," though entertaining (Kingston and Thompson 8). As a Chinese American artist, however, Wittman faces the same challenges as Kingston, struggling with oppressive stereotypes and drawing upon a hybrid literary heritage.[6]

Early in *Tripmaster Monkey*, Wittman stands at San Francisco's Coit Tower and recites Walt Whitman's poem "Facing West From California's Shores" (162). This is a defining moment in the novel. Wittman obviously is named after Walt Whitman, and, as a young American poet, lays claim to the Camden bard's heritage. Yet Whitman's poem celebrates the western migration of Europeans across North America as the essential American experience, an experience not shared by Asian Americans. When Wittman faces Asia, the "house of maternity," he imagines something quite different. Throughout *Tripmaster Monkey* there are passages like this, Kingston reminding us that minority and majority audiences inevitably respond differently to the same work.[7]

Wittman's quest—the plot of the novel—is to create a sprawling many-night epic play about Chinese American experience, which blends popular traditional Chinese novels (primarily *The Tale of Monkey*, *Romance of the Three Kingdoms*, and *The Water Margin*), and their opera adaptations, with mainstream U.S. literature, television and movies.[8] Thus Kingston again confronts the issue which had drawn criticism before.

Wittman's play is produced in his family's clan association building in Chinatown, with virtually every character of the novel taking roles. It is a community event, thus stressing Kingston's belief in the collaborative creation of art (as in the ending of *The Woman Warrior*). Most of the tensions of the novel—personal and aesthetic—are resolved in the play. Yet newspaper reviewers of the play's first night are imperceptive, even if complimentary, using words like "exotic" in praising it. Wittman has not entirely succeeded in "claiming America," in educating the white public to see Chinese Americans as being as American as they are, and their heritage now as part of America's heritage. In other words, Wittman's reviewers repeat the mistakes of reviewers of *The Woman Warrior*. For this reason Kingston ends the book with Wittman addressing the audience on closing night, lecturing them on the dangers of cultural stereotypes. It is a long passage, corresponding to "The Laws" in *China Men*; as with it, Kingston risks distorting her work, but takes the risk as something necessary for future Chinese American literature.

At mid-career, Maxine Hong Kingston is one of the best known of California's writers. Her books have engendered a rich critical discussion, particularly in narrative theory, and in scholarship from feminist and ethnic studies perspectives; and it might be argued that the discussion has helped shape and define the emerging field of Asian American studies. Several younger Chinese American women writers who have emerged in the years since *The Woman Warrior* must be indebted to the example of Kingston; more difficult to assess, but real, is Kingston's impact upon writers of other ethnicities, and the public's awareness of post-modern literary aesthetics. And as a writer who has helped to redefine the West as a multicultural and multilingual frontier,[9] Kingston has been an explorer in the tradition of her pioneering American ancestors.

Notes

1. Kingston has also published a volume of travel sketches, *Hawai'i One Summer* (1987), collected from pieces which earlier appeared in the *New York Times*. A major work in progress reportedly was destroyed when her home burned in the Oakland fire of October 1991.

2. See Kim 173, Cheung 102-04, and Lee 52-55 for discussions of Chin's objections.

3. Images of attics, basements, and tunnels appear often in *The Woman Warrior* and *China Men* and seem linked with memory and imagination. See also the last paragraph of *Tripmaster Monkey*.

4. More commonly Kuan Kung or Kuan Yu. Kingston is romanizing her own dialect of Cantonese.

5. The joke is complex. Wittman identifies himself with the Monkey King, trickster hero of *Journey to the West*, and takes the part of Monkey in the play he writes and produces. By fusing Chin and Wittman, Kingston makes Chin participate in a project he would have despised — adapting traditional Chinese culture for American audiences — and makes a monkey of him. Kingston doubtless knows the legend that the author of the Chinese novel *The Golden Lotus* had a poisoned copy of the book delivered to his rival.

6. Kingston had originally set the action in 1963, giving Wittman her own Berkeley graduation date of 1962. As the novel evolved, she chose to place the action in a generalized, slightly anachronistic 1960s in order to avoid specific events of 1963 such as the Kennedy assassination. See Kingston and Thompson 2.

7. See, for example, Wittman's angry response to the racial subtext of the movie *West Side Story* (70-72).

8. In English translations, *The Tale of Monkey* is also known as *Journey to the West*; *The Water Margin* is variously titled *The Water Verge* and *All Men Are Brothers*.

9. These terms draw on Annette Kolodny's essay "Letting Go Our Grand Obsessions."

Selected Bibliography

Primary Sources

China Men. New York: Alfred A. Knopf, 1980.
Tripmaster Monkey: His Fake Book. New York: Alfred A. Knopf, 1984.
The Woman Warrior: Memoirs of a Girlhood Among Ghosts. New York: Alfred A. Knopf, 1977.

Secondary Sources

Cheung, King-Kok. *Articulate Silences: Hisaye Yamamoto, Maxine Hong Kingston, Joy Koawa.* Ithaca: Cornell University Press, 1994.

———, and Stan Yogi. *Asian American Literature: An Annotated Bibliography.* New York: The Modern Language Association of America, 1988.

Heizer, Robert F. and Alan F. Almquist. *The Other Californians: Prejudice and Discrimination Under Spain, Mexico, and the United States to 1920.* Berkeley: University of California Press, 1971.

Kim, Elaine H. *Asian American Literature: An Introduction to the Writings and Their Social Context.* Philadelphia: Temple University Press, 1982.

Kingston, Maxine Hong with Timothy Pfaff. "Talk With Mrs. Kingston." *New York Times Book Review,* June 18, 1980, 1, 25-26.

———. "Cultural Misreadings by American Reviewers." In *Asian and Western Writers in Dialogue: New Cultural Identities,* Guy Amirthanayangam, ed. London: Macmillan, 1982, 55-56.

Kingston, Maxine Hong. *Hawai'i One Summer.* San Francisco: Meadow Press, 1987.

——— with Arturo Islas. "Maxine Hong Kingston." In *Women Writers of the West Coast: Speaking of their Lives and Careers.* Marilyn Yalom, ed. Santa Barbara: Capra, 1983.

——— with Phyllis Hoge Thompson. "This Is the Story I Heard: A Conversation with Maxine Hong Kingston and Earll Kingston." *Biography,* 6 (Winter 1983): 1-12.

Kolodny, Annette. "Letting Go Our Grand Obsessions: Notes Toward a New Literary History of the American Frontiers." *American Literature,* 64 (1992): 1-18.

Lee, Robert G. "*The Woman Warrior* as an Intervention in Asian American Historiography." In Lim, *Approaches to Teaching Kingston's* The Woman Warrior, pp. 52-63.

Lim, Shirley Geok-lin, ed. *Approaches to Teaching Kingston's* The Woman Warrior. New York: The Modern Language Association of America, 1991.

Lim, Shirley Geok-lin and Amy Ling. *Reading the Literatures of Asian America.* Philadelphia: Temple University Press, 1992. (Introduction.)

Smith, Sidonie. *A Poetics of Women's Autobiography: Marginality and the Fictions of Self-Representation.* Bloomington: Indiana University Press, 1987.

TuSmith, Bonnie. *All My Relatives: Community in Contemporary Ethnic American Literatures.* Ann Arbor: University of Michigan Press, 1993.

Takaki, Ronald. *Strangers from a Different Shore: A History of Asian Americans.* Boston: Little, Brown, 1989.

Joanne Allred

Diane Wakoski

Diane Wakoski was born in California in 1937. "The poems in her published books give all the important information about her life," reads the note about the author on the cover of *The Magellanic Clouds* (Black Sparrow Press, 1970). In fact, the puzzle pieces of biographical information scattered through Wakoski's early poems reveal little more than an orange tree or two, the backs of several men walking away and, at the center of the jigsaw, the face of a lonely, unloved child just coming into focus.

> When I was five years old, we lived on the
> edge of Orange County, in an orange grove,
> in a small two room house with a sagging
> screened porch...
> My father was never home. I was a
> child with a father who was a sailor...
> ("Smudging" 1970)

> I was a quiet child,
> afraid of walking into a store alone,
> afraid of my mother's bad breath,
> and afraid of my father's occasional visits home,
> knowing he would leave again;
> afraid of not having any money,

afraid of my clumsy body
that I knew
no one would ever love...
("Thanking My Mother For Piano Lessons," 1970)

Diane Wakoski's poetry results from her determination to follow the exhortation of the oracle at Delphi: *know thyself*. "The artist is the man looking at himself in the mirror. That narcissistic, constant search for self-knowledge," Wakoski said in a 1974 interview with Alan Goya. "And finally, in order really to get the ultimate self-knowledge, bursting, breaking through the mirror in this act that looks like it will shatter the self and only result in bloody damage. On the other side, where he can look out at the world, that is when he comes to art" (*Toward a New Poetry* 250). Indeed, some of her poems employ this sort of shattering force, leaving shards of self scattered far and wide. But after thirty-four large and slim collections of poetry, the puzzle of Wakoski's life now forms a fairly comprehensible picture.

According to the narrating persona Wakoski has invented to tell the stories in her poems, a painful childhood evolved into a troubled adolescence as the bookish, plain Diane, in a doomed effort to pass as a "California Girl," tried to emulate the manners and appearance the stereotype embodies: "Shall I/ tell you about the California Girl/ who was...always the last girl chosen on any team...I certainly knew that it didn't take brains/ or anything interesting/ to be a cheerleader./ But they were always on the edge of my mind/...this is what California is about. This is what American culture is about" ("California Girl," 1990). "Blue Suede Shoes," the opening segment of *Jason the Sailor* (1993), places Diane in The Home for Unwed Mothers: "1956. Pasadena, California.. .Most of us there are teenagers." The title poem of *Medea the Sorceress* (1991) fills out details of the episode:

She is told by the Social Worker that she has
FAILED because
    she still loves
    she doesn't regret doing anything for love,
    she doesn't believe she is bad
    she doesn't regret giving up her child
    she believes her life will go on, the same as it has always
       gone on

she won't talk about her mistakes.

> ... as if she were Medea, when the letters came
> talking casually about his dates with other girls, unpregnant girls,
> she decided that she would have no choice. She
> would kill him, and her children, and like the Sorceress
> leave for another world, in her chariot drawn by dragons.
> She gave up her baby. No regrets. Only the weak have regrets.
> She went to Berkeley, and she told him
> to go away ... She flew in her chariot
> with all her dragonlady power to Berkeley,
> then New York, then the Midwest, and finally to this Cafe
> where she sits telling the tale, not of the tribe,
> but of herself, and in spite of what others say, she knows
> that the song this Silvery Moon Questing lady of Dragonlight
>   sings,
> is the tale for at least half
> of the tribe.
> ("Medea the Sorceress" 1990)

This central poem provides an abridged index of the themes which drive Wakoski's poetry: 1) myth may be used as a template to make comprehensible the outlines of individual experience; 2) threads of betrayal are invisibly woven into the delicate, but opaque, fabric of romantic love; 3) following one's heart is never to be regretted, even when it results in symbolic murder; 4) the holy quest for love, "the song this Silvery Moon Questing Lady of Dragonlight sings," is at base the search for self-love, for identity, a quest given every human as birthright.

All poets face the dilemma of how much of one's life is appropriate subject matter for poems. The more or less disapproving posture assumed by much critical commentary on *confessional* poetry, a term ambiguously applied to various sorts of autobiographical writing, implies that publicly probing too far into the personal is somehow sordid and disgusting, exploitative in the way of tabloids. The particulars of individuality — unless they are the star-points of a mythic, heroic life — risk leading away from universality and into the dim and irrelevant underworld of self-absorption. The closing lines of "Medea" insist that "in spite of what others say," the story the poet tells of herself is "the tale for at least/ half the tribe."

Wakoski has bristled at being called a "Female Poet," hearing in the term a dismissive labeling of her work; still, the half of the tribe she refers to in these lines is plainly women. Although she has refused to identify herself as feminist (and she is surely correct in this discernment), the concerns of much of Wakoski's work are distinct to her gender. A poem that could only have been written by a woman, "I Have Had to Learn to Live With My Face" (*The Motorcycle Betrayal Poems* 1971), confronts the cultural and self-imposed pressure to meet a prescribed standard of physical beauty.

> . . . my face
> I have hated for so many years;
> my face
> I have made an angry contract to live with
> though no one could love it;
> my face that I wish you would bruise and batter
> and destroy, napalm it, throw acid on it,
> so that I might have another
> or be rid of it at last. . .

The self-hate in these violent lines verges on masochism, but the poem also voices a fierce desire to replace the hateful, ugly self-image with one more beautiful. The face as trope for self-image is appropriate because it can only be seen by reflection; and the mirror Narcissus-Diane leans toward most often to take her own measure is the reflecting pool of male assessment. Physical beauty, a recurrent theme for Wakoski, becomes metaphor for beauty that goes beyond the physical — she yearns to be beautiful to an adoring and faithful man, one who recognizes inner beauty. Wakoski has called this her "penis envy," which is not a want to possess a penis, but the desire to possess the bearer of one, or more pointedly, a desire to possess the power confirmed upon its bearer, which includes the image of self that has been assigned the bearer to mirror back. "I have always felt that I had to be with a man in order to be complete, and much as I might admire women who can be alone, some part of me thinks they are failures" (*Medea*).

As might be expected when identity is projected onto "the other" (a historically female propensity), Wakoski's attitudes about women are ambivalent at best. In "Fear of Women" (*Jason the Sailor* 1993), the narrator, Diane, reveals that "my fear of women has never made it possible/

for me to even want/ a woman as a friend." In the same poem she speculates that her mother (whom she identifies with the Medusa) was a closet lesbian and that her intuitive revulsion as a child compelled her own needy heterosexuality. For a woman, fear of women is fear of the self. One who perceives self-worth only in how she is valued by men is powerless, her self-esteem wholly dependent upon her ability to attract and hold a man. A woman who needs no man, whose snake power resides in her own head rather than being borrowed, is a Medusa.

The titles of some earlier collections — *Waiting for the King of Spain* (1976), *The Motorcycle Betrayal Poems* (1971), and *Dancing on the Grave of a Son of a Bitch* (1973) — suggest that the quest for "the right" man (mirror) is one that has long haunted Wakoski's work. "I have always idealized men, male culture, and anything that shows men loving and caring for women because this was left out of my childhood. The result is... that I wanted a man or men to love me" (*Jason the Sailor* 26). By at last fastening her search metaphorically to the Jason story, an allusion to her father's profession in the merchant marine, Wakoski recognizes, as Sylvia Plath did in her poem, "Daddy" (*Ariel* 1962), that her search for male validation is rooted in the residual need to be loved by an idealized, absent (and therefore unpleaseable) father.

Plath saw the force that craving male approval exerts as Hitlerian and her poetic solution to end the tyranny, whose realization fuels "Daddy," is to drive a stake through the vampire's fat black heart, a determination akin in spirit to Medea's murderous response to betrayal. Plath literally killed *herself* rather than the tyrannical expectation; but such expectation, once made conscious, becomes self-imposed. Faced with a similar betrayal of an abandoning father and unfaithful husband, Wakoski's answer has been to press on in the quest, resurrecting a Jason over and over in an attempt to alternately win his love and emotionally kill him again. Her determination to continue the search, even if doomed, is a life-sustaining choice, for the love sought is actually love of the self. In *Greed, Part 9*, a long poem addressed to Plath after her suicide, Wakoski says, "Here is our problem, Sylvia:/ how to feel enough anger to survive and yet not to spoil one's ability to love....I wont wont wont/ die/and let the world off easy./ Love is fighting the battle,/ even when you think you might lose./ I will go on,/ for love is the water that cannot be used up..." (*The Collected Greed* 113, 118).

If redemption from the school called "Confessional" is necessary for the salvation of autobiographical poets, what saves Wakoski is her veiling the drama of individual life in scarves of mythic metaphor, where Medea is able to "kill her children" and fly away in her dragon chariot to the cool emotional distance "silvery dragonlight" allows. When Medea flees, taking back the life she has given away (her children's lives), she is grief-stricken but whole, a sorceress whose regained power resides within. It is wholeness that Wakoski is after in identifying herself with Medea, for in the realm of archetype the dichotomies between personal and universal, between the self and the projected self, between real experience and the imaginary can be healed.

The persona who narrates Diane's story is variously invented: "I will call myself Diane, the Moon, The Lady of Light [reflected light], and in one of the many simultaneous worlds I'll occupy I'll tell the real story of my life, the deep reality" (*Jason the Sailor* 32). In "Creating a Personal Mythology," a 1974 lecture, Wakoski explained that she invented a mythic Diane for the poems, a Cinderella figure who was beautiful but covered with ashes, always waiting for the prince to come along and pick her out for her small foot. The invented Diane allows Wakoski to transcend the literal and individual: "...it is not autobiography you are writing, but your life you are *using* in order to write about life as other people experience it too.... Your father is not *your* father but an archetypal one.... The poet, then, is a person willing to see his life as more than itself and his autobiographical technique, ironically, should leave autobiography behind."

Given the facts of her poetic career, Cinderella was the appropriate metaphoric figure. Wakoski began writing poems at age seven. In high school she wrote sonnets and at Berkeley in the fifties she took writing courses with Tom Parkinson and Josephine Miles and was influenced by San Francisco poetry renaissance luminaries Robert Duncan and Kenneth Rexroth. After earning her degree in English, Wakoski moved to New York City where she taught in a high school plagued with the ills of urban life. She began publishing poems with her first collection, *Coins & Coffins*, appearing in 1962 when she was just twenty-five. Once launched, Wakoski's writing career rocketed, with four books being published in the next five years; *Inside the Blood Factory* (1968) drew wide attention to the young emerging poet. She started leading writing workshops in 1971 and a year later Wakoski began a regular column for *American Poetry Review* called "The Craft of Plumbers, Carpenters and Mechanics" that ran from November 1972 through April 1974. In 1976

Wakoski was offered a position at Michigan State University in East Lansing, where she remains Poet-in-Residence.

Toward a New Poetry (1980) brings together several installments of Wakoski's *American Poetry Review* column, along with critical essays and interviews from the seventies, and offers unique insight into her writing. From the vantage of seeing where her ideas about poetry have led, it's clear that Wakoski was defining guidelines her work has followed for two subsequent decades. Even the manner in which her poems have most changed, from their early associative surrealistic dazzle to the later prose-like narratives grounded in the actual and earthly, is forecast. "I discourage people from writing poetry which is too literal or too autobiographical when they are beginning because I think you should save that great material to work up to. For me the discovery of surrealism was a wonderful relief.... It allowed me to invent a life for myself" (Interview by Claire Healy 1974 [*Toward a New Poetry* 224]).

Wakoski's early poem "Apparitions Are Not Singular Occurrences" (1961) gives the flavor of how the mundane is vitalized and dramatized through surrealism:

> When I rode the zebra past your door,
> wearing nothing but my diamonds, I expected to hear bells
> and see your face behind the thin curtains.
> But instead I saw you, a bird, wearing the mask of a bird,
> and Death drinking cocktails with you.
> (*Discrepancies and Apparitions*)

Surrealism allowed Wakoski to tell the truth: "Poetry is the art of saying what you mean but disguising it," she once remarked, echoing Dickinson's adage. It provided her a means to write about experience without getting bogged down in the pain and ugliness of her literal life, past and present, while allowing the images to convey its often dark emotional reality:

> If I could sing one last song
> with water bubbling through my lips
> I would sing with my throat torn open.
> the blue jugular spouting that black shadow pulse,
> and on my lips
> I would balance volcanic rock

emptied out of my veins. At last
my children strained out
of my body. At last my blood
solidified and tumbling into ocean.
("Blue Monday," 1964 [*Inside the Blood Factory*])

One difficulty of relying on surrealism to convey real but disguised information is that, disconnected from a plot, a string of images may seem melodramatic, begging the reader's emotional response in a way unearned by the context of the poem. Occasionally in Wakoski's early poems the images make no visual sense and so seem self-indulgent or specious. Consider, for instance, these lines from "Rescue Poem" (*Inside the Blood Factory* 1964):

Black camels walk around
and through our eyes
stamping on the city streets.
We thread needles with our thin bones
and sew streets together
trying to hold them in finger pockets.

Whatever its limitations, surrealism gave Wakoski a way to begin what she conceives of as the project of poetry: "The role of the artist is to focus on the conflict between the desire for beauty and the natural ugliness the world imposes on us, to create beautiful artifacts that in some way give other people a sense of beauty, other than just the physical beauty of the world" (Healy interview, *Toward a New Poetry* 225).

Emerald Ice, Selected Poems 1962-1987 places early and late poems under one cover, documenting how Wakoski's art has matured. While early work implies that the fantasy world is the more vital one, the later poems draw images from the actual world, creating beauty by entering the physical more completely rather than escaping into dream-like imagination. This excerpt from "Braised Leeks & Fromboise" (*Emerald Ice*, 1985), where everyday garbage is transformed into something almost visionary, provides a case in point:

The ocean
this morning
has tossed someone's garbage

over its surface,
half oranges
that make my mouth pucker for
fresh Juice,
lettuce leaves
looking fragile, decorative, like scarves
for the white curling locks
of old water.
It is not hard
to think of women
coming up out of the dense green,
fully formed but not
of flesh, of some tissue, floating
goddess-like
and pale.

In her essay "Form Is An Extension of Content," Wakoski asserts that twentieth-century poetry can no longer be thought of in terms of form, "as if form were some pitcher we pour our contents into; as if there were a poem without a whole body of poetry around it; as if form were something physical instead of something conceptual" (*Toward a New Poetry* 100). Wakoski's poems are usually narrative, written almost exclusively in open forms: line breaks, indentation, and occasionally stanzas are the principal shaping devices, with the content—the primary images and ideas—determining any formal dictates. Recently the prose poem and simple prose narrative have become increasingly important in her work.

Wakoski has characterized her organizational strategy as development by digression. This approach is at the heart of the *Greed* poems. Each of the thirteen parts—published first as individual long-poems, now accessible under one cover in *The Collected Greed*—is an extended meditation whose title, in the nature of Francis Bacon's essays, introduces some facet of greed: "Self-Righteousness"; "Jealousy, A Confessional"; "The Shark—Parents & Children"; "Of Accord & Principle." Unlike Bacon, whose treatises defined abstractions with an authority like Aristotle's and an objectivity like God's, Wakoski's contemplations are autobiographical, sometimes surrealistic, self-interrogating, wandering, and often inconclusive. Her method of development is digressional rather than linear, employing various structures which may include verse, diary entries, image lists, letters to others, newspaper excerpts, and personal

375

narrative segments. The organizational effect is more like collage than a coherent representational composition.

A similar digressive, multiple-text structure characterizes Wakoski's most recent books: *Medea the Sorceress; Jason the Sailor;* and *The Emerald City of Las Vegas,* which together form a trilogy, *The Archeology of Movies and Books.* Published over a five-year span, the trilogy is in many ways a capstone to Wakoski's poetic work. Explicitly autobiographical, the poems probe almost psychoanalytically her Southern California roots and the experiences that shaped her assumptions about the world. Again myth provides the lens which focuses events — classical Greek, as reflected in the first two titles, and contemporary American, as implied by the third. The poems are punctuated by prose commentaries (often on the poems themselves) in the form of letters addressed to close male friends, as if the poet is speaking casually over coffee to someone she's sure is listening. The trilogy quotes long passages from other texts, most extensively Nick Herbert's *Quantum Reality: Beyond the New Physics.* The theories of quantum physics offer a fresh template for Wakoski to make sense of her life: the key ideas — that there exist parallel and simultaneous realities; that the past can be altered; that the act of perception influences outcomes at subatomic levels — provide yet another mythology for transforming the ugly into the beautiful without sacrificing truth.

The movies — that most pervasive (and most Californian) definer of contemporary America — embody for Wakoski a demonstration of multiple realities; film serves as metaphor for her own reflections cast upon the silver screen of memory, each scene shot in multiple "takes," with the poet-director at last in control of outcome. The tone of these volumes is philosophically chatty; what the narratives lack in intensity they gain in breadth, with individual pieces, like musical digressions, playing variations on a theme. Although wide ranging, the subject matter is, at heart, the same straw Wakoski has been spinning to gold since she began writing. Ultimately, the process itself becomes the quest:

I never forget fleeing
from California and the West
beyond snake worship
to the magic language of riddles
and spells. . .

I tell you though, no
sorcery will save you from
the major rules...

The rules
are about the patterns, the stories,
completing the cycles or rhythms.

Following this road
    in America, which is empty of everything
    but my car and hawks
    on the fence posts, is the quest.
("Medea's Chariot," *Jason the Sailor*)

Selected Bibliography

Primary Sources

Poems
Cap of Darkness. Santa Barbara: Black Sparrow Press, 1980.
Coins & Coffins. New York: Hawk's Well Press, 1962.
The Collected Greed, Parts 1-13. Santa Barbara: Black Sparrow Press, 1984.
Dancing on the Grave of a Son of a Bitch. Los Angeles: Black Sparrow Press, 1973.
Discrepancies and Apparitions. New York: Doubleday, 1966.
The Emerald City of Las Vegas. Santa Rosa: Black Sparrow Press, 1995.
Emerald Ice: Selected Poems 1962-1987. Santa Rosa: Black Sparrow Press, 1988.
The George Washington Poems. New York: Riverrun Press, 1967.
Inside the Blood Factory. New York: Doubleday, 1968.
Jason the Sailor. Santa Rosa: Black Sparrow Press, 1993.
The Magellanic Clouds. Los Angeles: Black Sparrow Press, 1970.
The Magician's Feastletters. Santa Barbara: Black Sparrow Press, 1982.
The Man Who Shook Hands. New York: Doubleday, 1978.
Medea the Sorceress. Santa Ana: Black Sparrow Press, 1991.
The Motorcycle Betrayal Poems. New York: Simon & Schuster, 1971.
The Rings of Saturn. Santa Rosa: Black Sparrow Press, 1986.
Smudging. Los Angeles: Black Sparrow Press, 1972.
Virtuoso Literature for Two and Four Hands. New York: Doubleday, 1975.
Waiting for the King of Spain. Santa Barbara: Black Sparrow Press, 1976.

Essays and Criticism
"The Birth of the San Francisco Renaissance: Something Now Called the Whitman Tradition." *The Literary Review*, 32:1 (Fall 1988): 36-41.
"Color Is a Poet's Tool." In *Poets' Perspectives: Reading, Writing, Teaching Poetry*. Sally Jacobsen, ed. Portsmouth, New Hampshire: Boynton/Cook, 1992.
Creating a Personal Mythology. Los Angeles: Black Sparrow Press, 1972.

"Ear & Eye: A Manifesto." *The Ohio Review*, 38 (1987): 14-19.

"Stalking the Barbaric Yawp." *Georgia Review,* 43:4 (Winter 1989), 804-815.

Toward a New Poetry. Ann Arbor: University of Michigan Press, 1980.

Secondary Sources

Bartlett, Lee. "Diane Wakoski." In *Talking Poetry: Conversations in the Workshop with Contemporary Poets.* Albuquerque: University of New Mexico Press, 1987.

Jaidka, Manju. "Sentimental Violence: A Note on Diane Wakoski and Sylvia Plath." *Notes on Contemporary Literature,* 14:5 (Fall 1984): 2.

Martin, Taffy Wynne. "Diane Wakoski's Personal Mythology: Dionysian Music, Created Presence." *Boundary 2: A Journal of Postmodern Literature & Culture,* 10:3 (Spring 1982): 155-172.

Ostriker, Alicia. "In Mind: The Divided Self in Women's Poetry." *Tendril,* 18 (1984): 111-138.

———. "What Are Patterns For? Anger and Polarization in Women's Poetry." *Feminist Studies,* 10:3 (Fall 1984): 485-503.

Plath, Sylvia. *Ariel.* New York: Harper and Row, 1962. P. 49.

Wagner, Linda. "Wakoski's Early Poems: Moving Past Confession." In *Still the Flame Holds: Essays on Women Poets and Writers.* Sheila Roberts, ed. San Bernardino: Borgo, 1993.

Jaime Herrera

Luis Miguel Valdez

Luis Miguel Valdez is considered by many to be the patriarchal figure in Chicano theatre history. His body of work — from the very
first *actos* to his most recent film work — gives evidence to the
contribution he has made to Chicano theatre.

Valdez was born in 1940, the second of ten children born to migrant
workers in California. Although his studies were frequently interrupted
by the family's constant relocation, Valdez showed an interest in theatre
at an early age. In a 1993 interview with Bettina Gray, Valdez explained
the impact that an art instructor had on his artistic ambitions. The
instructor took Valdez's brown paper lunch bag and converted it into a
papier-mâché mask in the image of a monkey. In that revealing moment,
Luis saw the transformation of the utilitarian to the artistic. Captivated
by the transformation, he decided to take part in the school Christmas
play. Unfortunately, his family moved before he could play the part of
that same monkey, but since then he knew that he would become a playwright. At the age of twelve he was holding puppet performances for his
friends and neighbors and eventually he followed his calling, enrolling in
college and receiving his degree in English from San Jose State College
in 1964.

It was during his university career that Valdez formally developed his
training in the theatre. In 1961 he won a regional play-writing contest
with a work titled *The Theft*. That success encouraged him to write his
first full-length play, *The Shrunken Head of Pancho Villa* (1963) which

was performed by the drama department at San Jose State College. After receiving his degree, he joined Ron Davis' San Francisco Mime Troupe, which based much of its work on the Italian *comedia dell'arte* and "agit-prop" theatre. According to Jorge Huerta, this experience greatly influenced Valdez: "His experiences with this company of actors . . . were very important in the formation of his own technique of staging and playwriting in the years to follow" (397). Yolanda Broyles-González also traces the evolution of Valdez's aesthetic to the Mexican popular performance tradition and places special emphasis on this tradition as a precursor to the growth of Chicano theatre:

> A more far-reaching model for constructing our understanding of El Teatro Campesino and of the Chicana/o theatre movement is one that seeks out a commonality of origin within the Mexican popular performance tradition. Only these common older roots can account for the notable homogeneity of a Chicana/o theatre movement that exploded onto the American scene from the *physical memory* of a dormant tradition. (*El Teatro* 4)

Scholars disagree as to the exact impact that all of these traditions had on Valdez, but taken in their entirety, Valdez's early experiences in theatre did influence and prepare him for the next step in his growth as a playwright. According to Nicolás Kanellos: "These lessons in presentational (rather than representational) theatre . . . served Valdez well in his next adventure, that of creating a grass roots theatre for Mexican farmworkers" (*Dictionary* 283). Valdez's upbringing in a family of migrant workers, his university training, his experience with the San Francisco Mime Troupe and the political situation in 1965 in Delano, California, all combined to help Valdez start El Teatro Campesino (the Farmworkers' Theater) and to further delineate his ideology as a Chicano playwright.

In 1965 Valdez traveled to Delano to help César Chávez organize farmworkers. With the support and advice of Chávez, Valdez spoke with the agricultural laborers. Using their experiences, his own experience and training, and farm laborers as actors, Valdez staged the first *actos* of what would eventually evolve into El Teatro Campesino. The *acto*, according to Valdez, was crucial in the beginning and in the growth of El Teatro Campesino: "Nothing represents the work of El Teatro Campesino (and other teatros Chicanos) better than the *acto*" (11). Kanellos defines the *acto* as a "short, flexible dramatic sketch that communicates directly through the language and culture of working class Chicanos in order to present a clear and concise social or political message" (*Dictionary* 283). Valdez's concept of the *acto's* function is directly linked to his activism and desire for the play to engage both the actors and the audience. In *Early Works* he emphasizes the five-fold role of the *acto*:

> Actos: Inspire the audience to social action. Illuminate specific points about social problems. Satirize the opposition. Show or hint at a solution. Express what people are feeling. (12)

In addition, Valdez explains the communal nature of the *acto*:

> ...the major emphasis in the acto is the social vision, as opposed to the individual artist or playwright's vision. Actos are not written; they are created collectively, through improvisation by a group. (12-13)

Initially, the Teatro joined with the newly formed United Farmworkers of America to fight for the rights of migrant workers by performing *actos*, primarily to audiences consisting of those same migrant workers. Valdez, however, felt that the Teatro needed to reach a wider audience; under his direction, the group took to traveling to different parts of California. For the next fifteen years, El Teatro traveled extensively and staged many different productions.

In 1966 and 1967, El Teatro toured the United States, including a performance in Washington, D.C., before the Senate Subcommittee on Migratory Labor. In 1967 El Teatro moved from Delano to Del Rey, California, and there established El Centro Campesino Cultural. In the same year, according to Kanellos,

> El Teatro Campesino began ... to achieve a national reputation for expanding audiences for theatre as well as for innovation and political comment.... During these and the next few years, through El Teatro Campesino, Valdez was to engage in a historical and thematic exploration of his people's culture, first dealing with contemporary issues, but then exploring theatrical forms that throughout history have appealed to grassroots Mexican audiences. (*Dictionary* 284)

In 1969, El Teatro appeared at the World Theater Festival in France. Also in that year, El Teatro relocated to Fresno, California. Valdez co-chaired a new Raza Studies Program at Fresno State College, where he taught the first Chicano Theater workshop, which in turn allowed for the first influx of student performers into El Teatro. By 1970, El Teatro had grown enough so that one group toured the midwestern and eastern United States and the rest of the ensemble attended United Farmworker rallies in California. By that year, Kanellos notes,

> El Teatro Campesino had pioneered and developed what would come to be known as teatro chicano, a style of agit-prop that incorporated the spirit and presentational style of *comedia dell'arte* with the humor, character types, folk and popular culture of the Mexican, especially as articulated earlier in the century by Mexican vaudeville companies that toured the Southwest in tent theatres. (*Mexican American Theater* 9)

In this same year Valdez also taught a Teatro workshop at U.C. Berkeley.

In 1971, with the publication of *Actos* by Luis Valdez for El Teatro Campesino, Valdez defined his ideology vis-a-vis the Chicano, including an emphasis on Aztlán as the mythic homeland of all Chicanos; an emphasis on nationalism and national theatre based on an Amerindian past; the emphasis on self-funding for all Chicano theatre groups in order to keep their political and social aims free from outside interests, including that of "Uncle Sam"; and the emphasis on El Teatro's loyalty —always—to the Chicano people or la Raza (*Luis Valdez* 6-10). Also in that year, El Teatro relocated to its present home, San Juan Bautista, California, and tours included one to Mexico and one throughout the southwestern United States.

For the following years, El Teatro and Valdez continued to thrive. El Teatro kept traveling, putting on performances throughout the United States, Mexico, and Europe. Valdez's *Zoot Suit* was performed in 1978 at the Mark Taper Forum in Los Angeles and had a brief Broadway run, where it was poorly received by the critics. Eventually, *Zoot Suit* was made into a film and released in 1981.

The year 1980 also marked an important change in El Teatro's organization. Broyles-González notes,

> Following *Zoot Suit*, El Teatro Campesino ceases to exist as a col-

lective ensemble and is transformed into a production company. . . .
The process of radical transformation includes installation of an
administrative apparatus (filled by persons not formerly associated
with the company) and a slowdown in artistic production. (*El Teatro*
245)

Nevertheless, Valdez and El Teatro continued to produce new works.
In 1982, *Corridos!*, based on Mexican popular ballads, was produced and
performed at different venues in California, including San Francisco's
Marine Memorial Theater in 1983 and Variety Arts Theater in Los
Angeles in 1984. It was filmed as a PBS production in 1987. The year
1987 also saw the release of Valdez's film *La Bamba*.

Throughout his career, Valdez has continued to seek a theatrical form
that best represents his artistic and social vision. He and El Teatro
developed the "corrido," which, according to Kanellos, ". . . breaks new
ground in exploring the poetic, symbolic, and psychosexual content of
popular Mexican ballads" (*Dictionary* 289). Valdez also developed the
mito, based on "Amerindian dance drama" (*Dictionary* 282). Also important in Valdez's theory of aesthetics has been his use of the Theater of
the Sphere. For Valdez, the emphasis of the Theater of the Sphere is on
Mayan and Aztec spirituality. In "Pensamientos Serpentinos," he urges
Chicanos: "We must all become NEO-MAYAS/Porque los Mayas/ really
had it together" (*Luis Valdez* 173). According to Broyles-González,
Valdez's Theatre of the Sphere ". . . constitute[s] a sustained effort to
build on the American roots (or at times fragments) of a Chicana/o 'cultural way of being' through recourse to that native ancestral culture" (*El
Teatro* 121).

During his long and successful artistic career as a playwright, actor,
director, and filmmaker, Valdez has sought to refine his aesthetics of
Chicano theatre and to define fully his own ideology as a Chicano,
though not without criticism. One area in which Valdez and his work
has been criticized is in its depiction of women and the role that Valdez
has played as patriarch of Chicano theatre. Broyles-González bemoans
the fact that although El Teatro Campesino should represent a communal vision, it has too often been seen as the work of one individual:

The history of the company has been constructed as the history of
the life and times of Luis Valdez. As such, El Teatro Campesino history has been shaped into a male-dominated hierarchical structure

that replicates oppressive dominant tendencies within society. (*El Teatro* xiii)

Furthermore, Broyles-González explains, the role of women — both onstage and offstage — was reduced to a stereotypical, minimal role controlled primarily by Luis Valdez, the "symbolic father or person in charge" (*Chicana Voices* 167). Thus, according to Broyles-González, the social vision of El Teatro is Valdez's individual and masculine vision.

Notwithstanding the criticism, there can be no denial of the impact that Valdez has had on Chicano theatre. Kanellos defends Valdez's place in Chicano theatre history:

> ...none can deny the importance of [Valdez's] role as an artistic leader, an innovator, and an energetic and tireless explorer of his people's art and culture; he is one of the very few artists who has been able to change the way his people are perceived. (*Dictionary* 291)

Selected Bibliography

Primary Sources

Plays
For a complete list of plays, see Yolanda Broyles-González, *El Teatro Campesino: Theater in the Chicano Movement* and Nicolás Kanellos, "Luis Miguel Valdez," *Dictionary of Literary Biography*.

Books
Actos. Fresno, California: Cucaracha, 1971.
Aztlán: An Anthology of Mexican American Literature, edited by Valdez and Stan Steiner. New York: Knopf, 1972.
The Shrunken Head of Pancho Villa. San Juan Bautista, California: Cucaracha, 1974.
Luis Valdez — Early Works: Actos, Bernabé and Pensamiento Serpentino. Houston: Arte Público, 1990.
Zoot Suit and Other Plays. Houston: Arte Público, 1992.

Motion Pictures
La Bamba, screenplay and direction by Valdez. Hollywood: Universal Pictures, 1987.
I am Joaquín, screenplay by Valdez. El Centro Campesino Cultural, 1969.
Los Vendidos, screenplay by Valdez, 1972.
Zoot Suit, screenplay and direction by Valdez. Hollywood: Universal Pictures, 1982.

Television
El Corrido. Corporation for Public Broadcasting, 1976.
Corridos! Tales of Passion and Revolution. Corporation for Public Broadcasting, 1987.
Los vendidos. Corporation for Public Broadcasting, 1972.

Secondary Sources

Broyles-González, Yolanda. *El Teatro Campesino: Theater in the Chicano Movement.* Austin: University of Texas Press, 1994.

———. "Women in El Teatro Campesino: ¿Apoco estaba molacha la Virgen de Guadalupe?" In *Chicana Voices: Intersections of Class, Race, and Gender.* Teresa Córdoba, et al., eds. Austin: Center for Mexican American Studies, 1986.

Gray, Bettina. "Bettina Gray Speaks with Luis Valdez." Films for the Humanities and Sciences, 1993.

Huerta, Jorge. "Luis Valdez." In *Chicano Literature: A Reference Guide.* Julio A. Martínez and Francisco A. Lomelí, eds. Westport, Connecticut: Greenwood, 1985.

Kanellos, Nicolás. "Luis Miguel Valdez." In *Dictionary of Literary Biography*, Vol. 122 (Chicano Writers, second series). Detroit: Gale Research, 1992.

———. *Mexican American Theatre: Legacy and Reality.* Pittsburgh: Latin American Literary Review, 1987.

Martínez, Julio A. and Francisco A. Lomelí, eds. *Chicano Literature: A Reference Guide.* Westport, Connecticut: Greenwood, 1985.

Joanne Greenberg

Dorothy Bryant

Writers pay a heavy price for being venturesome. Readers reach for the book that suits a mood, the academics want to categorize and explicate, and for both of these pursuits it is the consistent writer who has the advantage. Hawthorne is easier to categorize than Melville, Hemingway than Steinbeck, and this consistency gets public acceptance and critical praise more readily. But venturesome writers are often among the best.

Although they may reflect one another, no two pieces of Dorothy (Calvetti) Bryant's work are alike. Her range encompasses a cast of characters and variety of forms, and her situations are varied beyond the scope of most writers. A solid formula writer can find a style and subject that works, and enjoy a long, often lucrative, career so long as public taste doesn't change too much, but a venturesome writer may lose as many readers as she gains since readers will seldom try a writer again when a work has not fulfilled the readers' expectations.

In 1972, Lippincott brought out Bryant's first book, *Ella Price's Journal*, to solid praise from the *New York Times* and the *Saturday Review* ("a first rate work"). Ella Price, thirty-five, married and a mother, enters college as one of the new breed of nontraditional students, and finds herself awakened to intellectual pleasure and to the confusion of that pleasure with her sexual need and the sexual need of her professor. This is a theme that has been done before, but too often with leering condescension or *faux naif* ingenuousness. What is different in Bryant's treat-

386

ment is its edge, its fairness. Ella is no child, her professor a phony but not an evil one. The book is informed with a wry wisdom and permeated with what would become hallmarks of Bryant's work, honesty and balance, a refusal to settle for cheap shots or easy villains.

The Kin of Ata came next and was Bryant's most popular book. Random House published it and it picked up what was almost a cult following, finding a place with the specialized population of readers of fantasy. The book was Bryant's realization of the 1960s wish for social harmony. Once again, the theme was not new. One thinks of *Lost Horizon* or *Islandia*, or even *Brigadoon*, but greed and envy don't disappear in Bryant's communal dwellers, and it takes a huge expense of energy to blend personal autonomy with almost familial closeness. The community must deal with all the human problems of love and sexual jealousy, problems most Utopians assume will melt away.

The Kin of Ata did well and Random House might have looked forward to a dozen sequels and a solid career producing fantasy fiction. Such careers have been more possible since science fiction's emergence as a popular genre. Random House was to be disappointed.

Bryant's next book was *Miss Giardino*, a deep look into the life of a spinster school teacher, a woman whose love of learning and language surmounted her years of work with poor and exhausted students in an uncaring school environment. Anna Giardino wakes up in a hospital after a mugging attack near her school. Doctors and police ask her what happened but she is unable to remember. In her attempts to do so, we move into her life and experience the immigrant days of turn-of-the-century San Francisco. By the time we learn who the attacker was, we have covered a magnificent life of quiet and dogged heroism, and have seen and understood a world that will never appreciate or even recognize Anna's life.

Bryant had begun to stretch; her confidence was growing and she had let herself explore. In *Miss Giardino* the result of this exploration was a more daring and unconventional form than her previous work, but her strengths as a writer were even more in evidence. *Miss Giardino*, however, was not a reprise of *The Kin of Ata*. Random House cut Bryant loose.

The book was quiet and without romanticism so it was difficult for Bryant to get it placed. She decided to publish it independently. As her own publisher, she could get high quality printing for a modest sum, oversee the entire production, and above all, keep herself in print until word of mouth built circulation in a way most publishers cannot afford to do. Her two previous books had generated enough interest to guarantee at least a modest return for her efforts and an increasing reputation in San Francisco where she lives and where her readers and supporters assure her books will be given space in the stores. Wider readership has come. *Miss Giardino* was the first of the Ata Books, brought out by Bryant as her own publisher.

With no one to object to her virtuosity, Bryant began producing a remarkable array of exceptional novels. *Miss Giardino* in 1978, *The Garden of Eros* in 1979; a nonfiction handbook, *Writing a Novel*, in 1980; *Prisoners,* a novel, also in 1980; and *Killing Wonder* in 1981. In each, she opened outward in form, trying more, daring more without losing her basic strengths. The diary form in *Ella Price* widened in the first half of *Prisoners* to a series of letters between convict Gary Wilson and educated and idealistic Sally Morgan, a political activist who is convinced of the redemptive power of decency and compassion. Sally begins a correspondence with Gary, whose self-taught style ("my books, my writing, my thinking have taken my supine brain and uplifted it out of the decay of despare [sic]") is ludicrous but also moving. Gary needs a friend. Gary needs help. Gary's needs begin to fill Sally's days. Sally herself is foundering in a dozen causes which seem marginal or hopeless, small glories, hard mercies, and also foundering in truths about her own life she doesn't wish to face. Gary's cause at least seems one that is direct and unalloyed. Sally can serve. And she might just might save him.

But Gary is not simply a young man who has lost his way. His need is a black hole and his rage waits in it to demolish any kindness offered. In her honesty and wisdom, Bryant doesn't portray Gary as evil, either, only as deeply flawed, unable to open to simple gratitude, to accept or give ordinary affection, unable to have the confidence that builds work day by day into a book, a job, a life. By the end of *Prisoners*, the reader knows once more how many kinds of prisons there may be and how many kinds of prisoners.

Killing Wonder is a mystery novel, and in trying to find out who killed the celebrated novelist India Wonder, Bryant has some wicked fun about the envy and aspiration that bedevil the lives of novelists, some not as successful as their friends, none as successful as they wish to be. Again Bryant widens and deepens the "six characters in the room" form of so many detective stories. The motives she gives her characters provide insight into the lives of writers, their needs, jealousies, and the deep pleasure some of them find in the work itself, however poorly compensated.

With two exceptions, there is a constant presence in Bryant's work. It is her love for and knowledge of her home city, San Francisco, a city she has seen change from a clump of neighborhoods into a complex and cosmopolitan megalopolis, and she has studied the city through the years of these changes. In the 1960s she was politically active there in work for racial and religious equality and in the anti-war movement. In the years following, she also gave support to her gay son and his friends in their struggle for legal rights and against the violence done to them by gangs and by the police. But as the liberation movements of the late sixties went on, Bryant began to have questions about the trade-offs that sixties idealism was imposing on the world it had helped to create. The sexual liberation of the sixties had amplified some features of the gay lifestyle that she watched with mounting anxiety. Syphilis and gonorrhea were readily curable with antibiotics, the gay publications stated, and the social stigma of those diseases had almost disappeared. Those in the straight world who pointed to the dangers of casual sex were waved away as religious zealots.

When she was planning *A Day in San Francisco*, no one yet knew what the alarming increase of previously rare conditions such as pneumocystis pneumonia and Kaposi's sarcoma meant, but Bryant was becoming increasingly disturbed by what she was seeing in the young gay community — multiple bouts of VD treated ever less successfully with the antibiotics on which everyone was relying too heavily, new symptoms, new diseases, and the loveless, seemingly joyless coupling in bathhouses and men's rooms.

A Day in San Francisco takes place during the single day of the Gay Freedom parade in June 1980, and looks into the same-sex scene, its personal, political, and social world. Like all fine novels, its specific context goes far beyond its setting.

In subject and in form, the novel is unconventional. We read pages from a gay publication complete with ads and interviews. There's a speech given by the female protagonist, Clara Lontana, an essay and a medical brochure, all worked into the fiction of the revelatory day. The effect is a layered picture of the radical wing of the homosexual world as a complete subculture, closed to outsiders, its imperatives isolating it not only from the larger culture but also from parents and relatives no matter how loving or caring they are. It was a cry from the heart of such a loving parent, a cry muted of necessity and not well received by its hearers. It is a moving and absolutely honest book. *Kirkus Review* called it "a painful, probing novel of uncommon power."

Perhaps Bryant's readership was more political than literary, but judgment was rendered on the novel and the wider world took up that judgment. For years, Bryant's subsequent work was informally but effectively blacklisted. Her books were denied space in some bookstores and many reviewers refused to read her subsequent work because they had marked her as a homophobe.

Other writers have been hampered by a "betrayed" segment of their readership. George Orwell's *Homage to Catalonia* and Jack London's *John Barleycorn* are examples. Both were honest works and disappointing to readers conditioned to expect something else. In Orwell's case, his leftist readers wanted partisanship instead of honesty; in London's, his macho "nature red in fang and claw" readers didn't want to know about his alcoholism, however honestly it was portrayed. All three writers broke new ground; all three were castigated by a readership that prided itself on its free thinking. All suffered the anger that a conscious dissenter suffers at the hands of the faithful.

Orwell turned to fiction; London caved in. Bryant went on. Her subsequent books improved in depth and complexity. If sorrow deepens people, Bryant used her sorrow well, but *A Day in San Francisco* still touches and moves the reader and, a decade later, has gained additional poignancy as a vivid picture of radical gay life before AIDS, seen not by its apologists but by a loving outsider.

In 1986, *Madame Psyche* appeared, representing a further opening for Bryant. Her other novels had spanned periods no longer than six months. This novel covered the long lifetime of its main character, Mei Li Murrow. It was a bigger book, richer and denser, but with all of Bryant's gifts intact, passion and balance and a sense of reality that compels belief. The work is fiction but it seems to be the autobiography of a woman who lives life deeply and whose troubled course makes plain the huge gulf between spiritualism and spirituality.

Mei Li is the half-Chinese daughter of a virtual slave, of whom there were surprisingly many and of all races in the late 1800s. She grows up as a performing medium under the ambitious dictatorship of her half-sister and soon graduates from the crude table-rapping and gauze-on-a-stick manifestations to more sophisticated falsehood. In this she begins to learn what truth is and how to practice it in her relationships with people. Her half-sister and others want her to stay mired in the lie, but after a crisis Mei Li breaks free and goes on to build a life that is as interesting as it is worthwhile. Her final years are spent in a spiritual quest of the most exacting kind in, of all places, the Napa State Hospital. Bryant's understanding of that hospital's environment is the best I have ever read anywhere. As a milieu for spiritual growth, she makes it completely and unromantically believable.

The Test, released in 1991, is a novella of exceptional strength and it illustrates Bryant's philosophy on publishing. In spite of the advertising budgets and marketing resources of large publishing houses a short print run from a small press like Ata can be a self-fulfilling prophesy during a book's brief life. Bryant's strategy worked. *The Test* would probably not have been published in an economy favoring big books — the novella is a modest 146 pages — but it is the equal of other now celebrated classics: Janet Lewis' *The Wife of Martin Guerre* and Flannery O'Connor's *The Violent Bear It Away*.

Pat (one of the characters) is one of the "children," trying to look after a sometimes senile, sometimes merely recalcitrant father. Dad shouldn't be driving. He forgets where he is going, refuses to maintain his truck, and is nearly blind. He has failed his driving test and his license has been suspended, but his license and truck represent his manhood and independence. *The Test* takes the reader through the day Mr. Sancavei appeals his failed test. In the hours before the final appeal, Pat's calls and visit sum up the three-generation history of her family in America, its small triumphs, its man-woman wrangles, its compromises, and the difficult, knotted ways the family learns to survive.

The work is a triumph of precisely visualized family life and there isn't an extra or faulty word or unauthentic emotion in it. Its denouement is also perfect and perfectly realized.

In the early 1990s, Bryant decided to try her hand at writing plays. *Dear Master* and *Tea with Mrs. Hardy* were performed in Chicago, Santa Fe, Minneapolis and various places in California. The former won two awards. In yet another expansion, Bryant explored a long-time interest in Giuseppe Garibaldi, the Italian liberator and his lover and later wife, Anita. The novel *Anita, Anita* is a story of great dramatic reach and depth, because Garibaldi is one of the few "liberators" whose luster is untarnished by messianic pretensions and cruel zealotry.

The landscape of commercial fiction has gotten rockier and style is often substituted for substance. Many writers make careers out of being fashionably original on government and semi-governmental grants, a kind of "decorator/garret" situation. Bryant's independence, while difficult, has proved itself as earnest of true independence and this is reflected in the integrity and depth of her statement as well as its virtuosity and scope.

Selected Bibliography

Primary Sources

Fiction

Anita, Anita. Berkeley: Ata Books, 1993.

Confessions of Madame Psyche. Berkeley: Ata Books, 1986; London: Women's Press, 1988.

A Day in San Francisco, Berkeley: Ata Books, 1982.

Ella Price's Journal. New York: Lippincott, 1972; New York: Signet, 1973; Berkeley: Ata Books, 1982.

The Garden of Eros. Berkeley: Ata Books, 1979.

Killing Wonder. Berkeley: Ata Books, 1981; London: Women's Press, 1986.

The Kin of Ata Are Waiting. New York: Random House, 1976.

Miss Giardino. Berkeley: Ata Books, 1978.

Prisoners. Berkeley: Ata Books, 1980.

The Test. Berkeley: Ata Books, 1991.

Nonfiction

Writing A Novel. Berkeley: Ata Books, 1979.

Plays

Dear Master. First production, 1991.

Tea with Mrs. Hardy. First production, 1992.

Secondary Sources

"Author Dorothy Bryant: A Former Teacher Now Writes for Real Audiences" (an interview). *California English* (March-April 1988): 1417.

Berson, Misha. "A Love Letter to Flaubert and Sand." *San Francisco Chronicle-Datebook*, September 1, 1991, 39-40.

Darlington, Sandy. "For Novelist, Attention Is Great, But Not Always Easy." *The Montclarion*, March 2, 1983, 5.

Friedman, Mickey. "A Word-of-mouth Best Seller." *San Francisco Examiner*, April 2, 1978, 1C.

Gatlin, Rochelle. "Breaking an Unsound Barrier: Two Women Speak to Us All—Tillie Olsen and Dorothy Bryant." *San Francisco Bay Guardian*, October 5, 1978, 14.

Greenberg, Joanne. "Prophetic 'Day' in Life of a Writer." *Washington Times*, June 12, 1994, B7.

Holt, Patricia. "*PW* Interview: Dorothy Bryant." *Publishers Weekly,* September 5, 1980, 14.

———. "Berkeley Writer Tackles a Tough Contemporary Issue." *San Francisco Chronicle,* January 3, 1992, 23.

LaPaglia, Nancy. *Storytellers: The Image of the Two-Year College in American Fiction and in Women's Journals.* Dekalb: LEPS Press (Northern Illinois University), 1994. Pp. 29, 38-39 41-42, 101-102.

Maglin, Nan Bauer. "The Demoralization Paper." *College English,* 44:6 (October 1982): 575-582.

Shaw, Mary. "The View From Just Outside." *Washington Blade,* May 13, 1983, 23-24.

Stein, Ruthe. "Diary of an Older Student." *San Francisco Chronicle,* January 18, 1973, 3C.

Marek Breiger

Richard Rodriguez

I have become notorious among certain leaders of America's ethnic left. I am considered a dupe, an ass, the fool — Tom Brown, the brown Uncle Tom, interpreting the writing on the wall to a bunch of cigar smoking pharaohs. . . .

You who read this act of contrition should know that by writing I seek a kind of forgiveness — not yours. The forgiveness, rather, of those many persons whose absence from higher education permitted me to be classed a minority student. I wish they would read this. I doubt they ever will. . . .

— Richard Rodriguez, *Hunger of Memory*

Richard Rodriguez is an essayist in the American tradition of Frederick Douglass, Henry David Thoreau and Ralph Waldo Emerson. His style is lyrical, distinctive and intellectual. He makes use of private experience to make a social argument. Yet Rodriguez has been slandered by a radical academic community that has turned its back on the tenets of traditional liberalism. Like Shelby Steele, and in the giant footsteps of Ralph Ellison, Rodriguez is an ethnic writer who addresses universal American issues. He has used his ethnic background, both Spanish and Native American, to find links to a broader American community. To dismiss his essays, so well written, so deeply considered, so filled with personal struggle and pain, is to disgrace the idea of academia itself.

Rodriguez has been misunderstood on three major issues — affirmative action, bilingual education, and cultural diversity and cultural pride.

While Rodriguez supports affirmative action, he does not support entitlements based solely on race. He opposes bilingual education, not because he is ashamed of his heritage — Rodriguez himself is bilingual — but because he believes that bilingual education keeps immigrant children from mastering English and becoming American citizens in the fullest public sense. On issues relating to cultural diversity, Rodriguez opposes the cheerleading that has become endemic to women's, ethnic, and gay studies. But, in his own writing, Rodriguez has honored the culture and life of his Mexican father.

Rodriguez expressed his feelings about affirmative action in a series of essays that predated, and were later included in and revised for, *Hunger of Memory*. In "None of This Is Fair," Rodriguez traces his concern about the misuse of affirmative action through an anecdote from his own life. Born in 1944, Rodriguez became a "scholarship boy" before the days of affirmative action. His road was difficult and the price paid for academic success was high. As a child of Mexican immigrants, the boy entered Sacramento's Catholic schools not knowing fifty words of English. Spanish was the language of home, of family, of family protection and love. When the teacher, a nun, asked Rodriguez's parents to speak only English at home, his parents complied. They were willing to sacrifice for their children's success. And Rodriguez owes his success, as he makes clear, to his mother and father, as well as the Irish teaching nuns and brothers and his liberal Protestant and liberal Jewish university professors. Rodriguez's doctorate is due to his own hard work and to others' help as well. He is modest about his own accomplishments but he also argues what we know in our hearts — that successful individuals have had many people help them on their way. Rodriguez has made the point, too (on National Public Radio), that his experience is not unique; we all depend upon help from those outside of our own ethnic and religious group — a fact that very often goes unnoted and unnoticed.

"None of This Is Fair" opens in 1974, when Rodriguez must choose where he will begin his teaching career. He wants no special privilege based on race. It is a point of honor. He is who he is, at great cost and pain and pride — to his parents and himself. He wants no racial entitlement.

As a Ph.D. in Renaissance Literature, Rodriguez is besieged with job offers, even from universities where he has not applied, schools that seem to prize him not for his scholarship but for his surname. At one point, Rodriguez is challenged by a friend and colleague, a fellow teaching assistant:

> It's just not right, Richard. None of this is fair. You've done some good work, but so have I. I'll bet our records are just about equal. But when we look for jobs this year, it's a different story.... You're a Chicano and I am a Jew. That's — the only real difference between us.... (*The Complete Writer's Workout Book* 310)

Already ambivalent about affirmative action entitlement, Rodriguez reconsiders his academic career. He decides to reject all offers — to stand alone — to make it or not make it as a writer.

It would be a mistake to read Rodriguez's argument as an argument against affirmative action. The essay does not conclude with his rejection of academia. The essay concludes with a meditation upon those in our society who have been truly excluded. Rodriguez's writing is both poetic and compassionate. He argues against our hypocrisy. How easy it is to give a racial entitlement, a quota. How difficult it would be to help the devastated among our people, who, writes Rodriguez, "...do not ever imagine themselves going to college...white, black, brown — Always poor. Silent...."

He continues:

> the debate drones on and surrounds them in stillness. They are distant, faraway figures like boys I have seen peering down from freeway overpasses in some other part of town.... (*The Complete Writer's Workout Book* 311)

Bilingual education may have been started with noble motives, but it is Rodriguez's belief, and not his alone, that bilingual education has been a failure. Rodriguez knows what his family sacrificed by giving up Spanish; he knows, too, what he and his brothers and sisters gained through mastery of English — full entry into American society. He writes in "Aria: Bilingual Childhood":

Without question, it would have pleased me to have heard my

teachers address me in Spanish when I entered the classroom. I would have felt less afraid. I would have imagined my instructors were somehow related to me.... But I would have delayed — postponed for how long? — learning the great lesson of school: that I had a public identity...." (*The American Scholar* 30; later revised for inclusion in *Hunger of Memory*)

For Rodriguez, public identity is essential to becoming fully oneself, to becoming an individual, to having a personal voice and choice over one's life. Rodriguez does not minimize the loss of family intimacy when English replaced Spanish at home, but he later realizes that language, once mastered, can be both public and private. Love can be expressed in Spanish or English.

Intimacy thus continued at home; intimacy was not stilled by English.... I sensed the deep truth about language and intimacy.... Intimacy is not created by a particular language; it is created by intimates.... ("Aria" 39)

It cannot be known with certainty whether Rodriguez is wrong or right, or wrong and right about bilingual education. Unlike many of his detractors, Richard is fluent in both Spanish and English. Surely, his arguments should meet with honest debate, not with angry dismissal.

The last charge against Rodriguez — that he has turned his back on his culture and his family — is hard to understand at all. Both *Hunger of Memory* and *Days of Obligation* are absorbed with the relationship of Rodriguez and his mother and father. The author's parents are described with affection, sadness, love, and respect. The distance that Richard Rodriguez records — between immigrant parents and first-generation American children — has been written about by writers as culturally diverse as Alfred Kazin, Irving Howe, Amy Tan, Jean Wakutsuki Houston, Jose Antonio Villareal and William Saroyan. Like those other writers, Rodriguez does not celebrate distance but mourns it. That he accepts responsibility for the loss of intimate family love is an act of honesty, not of betrayal. In *Days of Obligation*, Rodriguez pays homage to his father's moral strength and dignity. He believes that what his father stands for — the way of old Mexico, a way of bravery and quiet dignity when facing life and death — is what we in California need now, at this time:

his smile was loving. But his smile claimed knowledge. My father knew what most of the world knows by now — that tragedy wins — that talent is mockery. In the face of such knowledge, my father was mild and manly. If there is trouble you want my father around ... for my father is holding up the world, such as it is.... (*Days of Obligation* 219)

Let this be stated clearly; Rodriguez is not a conservative. He is for affirmative action based not on race, but upon economic deprivation. He is for, as those who listen to Rodriguez's essays on the *News Hour with Tom Lehrer* know, almost unlimited immigration. He believes immigrants are the heart and soul of California's future. He has become, as evidenced by the writing in *Days of Obligation*, a student of Mexican culture and history.

Days of Obligation, less controversial than *Hunger of Memory*, is equally powerful. Its ten essays are chapters of a work that is contemporary, grounded in the facts of daily life, yet transcendent, far deeper than the concerns of daily journalism. All of the essays are worth reading, but two, "Late Victorians" and "Asians," are of particular importance. In "Late Victorians" Rodriguez writes about the AIDS epidemic — not to make a special plea for homosexual rights — but to pay his respects to others' bravery and selflessness. Writing as a gay man in San Francisco, the author finds the links that join humans, gay and straight, to each other as they try to ease the suffering around them:

And if gays took care of their own, they were not alone. AIDS was a disease of the entire city. Nor were Charity and Mercy only male, only gay. Others came. There were nurses and nuns and the couple from next door, co-workers, strangers, teenagers, corporations, pensioners. A community was forming over the city....

And the saints of this city have names listed in the phone book. ... (*Days of Obligation* 45)

For himself, Rodriguez is not claiming any special goodness. He writes with humility as an honest witness, allowing readers to see individuals — who have shown courage and sacrifice — in the face of tragic loss and pain.

"Asians" continues Rodriguez's argument, first introduced in *Hunger of Memory*. That argument, it becomes clear, is not so much a statement against bilingualism or multi-culturalism but one for a common American culture. In fact, Rodriguez is a true multi-culturalist. He argues for inclusion, for a dynamic, open American society. He writes to show that we are all, as Americans, connected with and dependent upon each other. He asserts:

> To argue for a common culture is not to propose an exclusionary or static culture. The classroom is always adding to the common text, because America is a dynamic society. Susan B. Anthony, Martin Luther King, Jr., are inducted into the textbook much as they are canonized by the U.S. Postal Service, not as figures of diversity, but as persons who implicate our entire society. (*Days of Obligation* 170)

Rodriguez opposes sentimentalizing American history or literature. A common culture, for Rodriguez, would not be uncritical. Yet he argues against the slogans of the "politically correct."

> Gay studies, women's studies, ethnic studies — the new curriculum ensures that education will be flattering. But I submit that America is not a tale for sentimentalists. . . .
>
> If I am a newcomer to your country, why teach me about my ancestors? I need to know about seventeenth-century Puritans in order to make sense of the rebellion I notice everywhere in the American city. . . .
>
> Once you toss out Benjamin Franklin and Andrew Jackson, you toss out Navajos. You toss out immigrant women who worked the sweatshops of the Lower East Side. Once you toss out Thomas Jefferson, you toss out black history. . . . (*Days of Obligation* 169-170)

Richard Rodriguez is an idealist. He writes as one who believes we have a future in the United States as one people. He writes for a humane common culture. He believes, as did Martin Luther King, Jr., that we Americans, of all races, ethnicities, and religions, can, one day, act as brothers and sisters. He believes in a nation where, as he remembers, ". . . My Mexican father was never so American as when he wished his children might cultivate Chinese friends. . . ." (*Days of Obligation* 171)

Selected Bibliography

Primary Sources

"Aria: A Memoir of a Bilingual Childhood," *The American Scholar* (Winter 1980-1981): 25-42.

Days of Obligation. New York: Viking, 1992.

Hunger of Memory. New York: Bantam Books, 1982.

"None of This Is Fair." In *The Complete Writer's Workout Book*, Carolyn Fitzpatrick and Marybeth Rusic, eds. Lexington, Massachusetts: D.C. Heath, 1988. Pp. 308-311.

Secondary Sources

Dobie, Kathy, "An American Son." *Vogue*, 213:12 (December 1992): 144-145.

Haslam, Gerald. "Writer on the Edge of Mexico." *This World*, December 12, 1987, 9-11, 23.

Jones, Malcolm Jr. "From Missions to Mestizos." *Newsweek*, December 14, 1992, 80-81.

Kirp, David L. "Beyond Assimilation." *New York Times Book Review*, November 22, 1992, 42.

Krasny, Michael and Ariel Sabar. "What Is Community?" *Mother Jones* (May-June 1994): 22.

Lacayo, Richard. "States on the Border." *Time*, January 25, 1993, 69-70.

Perera, Victor. "Labyrinth of Solitude." *Nation*, January 18, 1993, 63-65.

Portes, Alejandro. "The Longest Migration." *New Republic*, April 26, 1993, 38-41.

Shorris, E. "In Search of the Latino Writer." *New York Times Book Review*, July 25, 1990, 1-4.

Stavans, Ilan. "The Journey of Richard Rodriguez." *Commonweal*, March 26, 1993, 20-22.

"Voices of Our Times: Twentieth Century Prose." *English Journal*, 82:7 (November 1993): 145-147.

Wolfe, Manfred. "Two Cultures." *American Scholar* (Winter, 1994): 145-147.

Michael Kowalewski

James D. Houston

James D. Houston has spent most of his life on or near the coast of Northern California. He looks upon the valleys, shorebreaks, and coastal ranges from Eureka to Point Conception as his natural habitat. His parents came west from Texas in the thirties, "among the many thousands on the road in search of better luck, better weather, better jobs" (*Contemporary Authors* 155). The family moved first to San Francisco, where Houston was born in 1933, and then south to the Santa Clara Valley, where he finished high school and later attended San Jose State University, earning his B.A. in 1956. That same year he married a Japanese-American classmate, Jeanne Wakatsuki. He completed an M.A. in English at Stanford in the early sixties and was a Stegner fellow there in 1966. In 1962 he settled into a roomy Victorian home in Santa Cruz, where he has lived for a third of a century. During that time he has written a dozen works of fiction and nonfiction that include familiar western subjects (ranchers, country-western singers, barroom brawls, tales of ancestral pioneers) as well as more contemporary characters: dope dealers, Vietnam veterans, New Age barbers, poncho-clad hikers, the Dalai Lama.

Houston has repeatedly emphasized the importance of "a sense of place" to his writing: "By *place* I don't mean simply names and points of interest as identified on a map ... [but] the relationship between a locale and the lives lived there, the relationship between terrain and the feelings it can call out of us, the way a certain place can provide us with grounding, location, meaning, can bear upon the dreams we dream, can sometimes shape our view of history" (*The True Subject* 92). Writers who care about such matters do not simply write *about* a particular place, he contends, they write *from* it, exploring all the ways local ecology, topography, and climate bear upon meaning, history, culture, and dreams.

Houston emphasizes a sense of place about a state many associate with placelessness, with mobility, faddishness, and unchecked growth, not with "grounding, location, [and] meaning." Rooting oneself in a rootless culture, his work suggests, is not an easy task. It involves a continual balancing act that can be precarious and disorienting. As one of his characters puts it, "He has found life in his region like trying to grow a garden in the middle of a three-ring circus, with a family of trapeze artists swinging wildly above and prepared at any moment to commit suicide by plunging headfirst into his tomato vines. The odd thing is, [he] still believes it is possible to do this and not go insane" (*Continental Drift* 10).

The West Coast for Houston is "a region of abundance, excess, and high energy" with "the kind of uncontainable variety that resists all patterns" (*West Coast Fiction* ix-x). He focuses on California's biotic and geographical diversity and its role as a cultural crossroads, an intersection "where more and more histories meet, overlap, converge, [and] collide." He sees the state not only as the goal of westering Americans from the East, but as part of the Pacific Rim, "an enormous wheel, a mandala of interconnected places" ("Cross Currents" 54). The cross-cultural hybridization of multiple cultures in California — in the intermingling of Asian, Polynesian, and Anglo cultures, for instance — can be felt, he says, "in a thousand ways — in the markets, in the restaurants, on the roads, and in the martial arts academies, on the all-Asian TV channels where newscasters speak Mandarin, on the all-Hawaiian music show via FM radio out of Salinas every Sunday afternoon" ("Cross Currents" 54).

This rich mix of traditions and folkways has helped foster Houston's fascination with the unlikely, the improbable, and the unexpected. His best writing is energized by the incongruities and the inspired improbabilities of life along the Pacific Coast. "California is still the state where anything seems possible," he says, "still the place where people bring dreams they aren't allowed to have any place else and act them out in a way that brings out a certain kind of bizarre behavior" (Holt interview 6). "Bizarre behavior," of course, encompasses creativity and innovation as well as social fragmentation and the lunatic fringe. Houston's work explores all these elements of West Coast life.

His first western novel, *Gig* (1969), which won the Joseph Henry Jackson award for fiction, chronicles the events of a single Saturday night at a coastal piano bar called the Seacliff. The novel is narrated by the piano player, Roy Ambrose, "a jack-of-all-styles, [and] master of some," who offers a wry but uncynical view of the Seacliff's customers, who arrive in "sparkling Pontiacs and Lincolns" (27, 95). Attuned to every nuance of his customers' nostalgia, disaffection, and erotic forwardness, Ambrose watches as couples bait each other, celebrate their anniversaries, or send off a friend, amidst serapes and maracas, to Guadalajara. Music has an important place in Houston's life and *Gig* is laced with the lyrics of old favorites by Fats Waller, Cole Porter, and George Gershwin. The novel offers the first in-depth example of Houston's authority in writing about music and popular lyrics (see *The Men in My Life* 31-38).

The owner of the bar is Jack, a well-tanned, cardigan-clad smoothie with an insidious talent for taunting others. He runs afoul of Bo, an eccentric drop-out with an attention-getting beard. The inventor of a new instrument called the Reality Harp, Bo is fond of marijuana, wears buckskins and a string tie, and responds to Jack's provocations by publicly denouncing "the whole, fat, complacent, blindfolded herd of American middle-class morons" (91). Houston often lets characters voice this kind of sudden social indictment without either dismissing or endorsing it. Bo withdraws and a disgruntled but obliging Ambrose stays on to finish out the evening and continue his anatomy of human nature in this Saturday night tidepool.

Houston's next novel, *A Native Son of the Golden West* (1971), delves into the surfing culture of Hawaii (a topic which Houston, a surfer himself, had previously explored in *Surfing: The Sport of Hawaiian Kings* [1966], which he co-authored with Ben R. Finney). Twenty-two-year-old Hooper Dunlap, the novel's protagonist, quits college because "The goals are too precise. Too attainable. They scare him. He yearns for something improbable he can take real pride in, such as he has seen in the eyes of hitchhikers, and believers in Atlantis, and certain professors around UCLA with no known application for their research" (unpaginated prologue). Following a line of vagrant forebearers stretching back to eighteenth-century Scotland, Hooper's personal odyssey involves him with a fellow Southern Californian, Jonas Vandermeer, a beautiful Polynesian dancer named Nona (with whom Hooper has a son), and Jackson Broome, a gruff, ratty globetrotter who runs a Waikiki rooming house. Hooper is dead by the end of the book, but he lives on in the free-wheeling spirit of his son, who also personifies the novel's title.

The Charlie Bates stories — which appeared first in *The Adventures of Charlie Bates* (1973) and then, with revisions, in *Gasoline* (1980) — are full of improbable plot twists and a quirky sense of humor reminiscent of Tom Robbins and Terry Southern. Disaffected from his workaday life, Bates is a thirty-something Everyman who alternately loathes and revels in the automotive technology upon which he depends. In one story he cruises the streets during the Oil Crisis in search of gas:

> Charlie . . . has forgotten why he needs it. He is like the diver who has stayed below too long, kicking for the surface with that urgency near panic. The diver doesn't think about what he uses air for. He only knows his lungs cry out for lots of it and soon. So it is with Charlie and his car. The tank is almost empty. Far to the left his needle flutters over the lonesome letter E. (105)

The stories use erotic picaresque to satirize California's car culture. Bates drives a variety of vehicles: a red-white-and-blue VW bus, a used Volvo, and, in a story entitled "An Occurrence at Norman's Burger Castle," a kind of Day-Glo bulldozer meant to impress a wait-ress who goes out nightly with the driver of the most impressive vehi-cle. Bates' mishaps and adventures on congested freeways and in tun-nels and parking decks present a vision of technological overkill, as in the colossal traffic jam that gridlocks all of Southern California for several days in "Gas Mask." Bates' comic haplessness and his sexual escapades, however, usually manage to create a sense of wacky holiday affirmation.

Houston's next two novels, *Continental Drift* (1978) and *Love Life* (1985), focus on various members of the Doyle family, who live in the Santa Cruz Mountains. In *Continental Drift*, the head of the family is Montrose Doyle, a war veteran and a philosophical columnist for a local paper who likes yoga and Jack Daniels and who muses on the presence of the San Andreas fault — "a six-hundred-mile incision some careless surgeon stitched up across the surface of the earth" (3) — which runs through a portion of his ranch. Like many of Houston's characters, Monty is subject to premonitions, forebodings, hunches, and a rogue sense of serendipity as he struggles to unravel the mystery of a series of murders that have traumatized the area's residents.

The San Andreas fault is a trope of instability and the Doyle family attempts to hold itself together amidst a volatile mix of psychological and geological forces. The novel's atmosphere is thick with paranoia, jittery nerves, and a sense of impending doom. The narrative is also richly furnished with entertaining family vignettes and a tactile evocation of the central coast. The novel ends on a cleansing, reconciliatory note, with a family pilgrimage to a mountain hot spring.

Love Life is set some ten years after *Continental Drift* and is narrated by Holly Doyle, the wife of one of Monty's sons, Grover. The novel charts the uncertainties and anguish of a marital crisis sparked by Grover's infidelity. Holly impulsively departs for New York City for an adulterous fling of her own. When she returns, a fierce Pacific storm traps and isolates the family — as Houston has noted is common in Robinson Jeffers' narratives about Big Sur (*Reading the West* 231-250) — when they most desire to be apart. The demands of the storm (downed electric lines, mudslides, flood-swollen creeks) bring about a rapprochement and help Holly and Grover begin to rehabilitate their damaged marriage.

Houston's reputation as an incisive commentator on California culture rests solidly on his nonfiction as well as his fiction. He has edited two important collections of regional writing, *California Heartland: Writing from the Great Central Valley* (1978, co-edited with Gerald Haslam) and *West Coast Fiction: Modern Writing from California, Oregon and Washington* (1979), which includes an excellent discussion of western regional identity in its introduction. Houston has also written a number of book-length nonfictional works: most notably, *Farewell to Manzanar* (1973), which he co-authored with his wife, *Californians: Searching for the Golden State* (1982), and *The Men in My Life* (1987).

Farewell to Manzanar tells the story of Jeanne Wakatsuki's experience as a young child in a World War II internment camp for 10,000 Japanese Americans in the high desert of the Owens Valley. The Houstons evoke the fears, anxieties, and hardships of the evacuation and camp life without resorting to bitterness or invective. They do not neglect the guard towers, the barbed wire, and the humiliation of no privacy and loyalty oaths. But they also describe the mini-universe that evolved in the middle of nowhere: a world of glee clubs, softball leagues, bobby soxers, and a band called the Jive Bombers who would play any song except "Don't

Fence Me In." *Farewell to Manzanar* is Houston's most well-known work. It has sold over half a million copies and been used for years as a text-book in California schools. The screenplay for a television movie adapted from the book (by the Houstons and producer-director John Korty) was nominated for an Emmy in 1976.

Californians presents a series of personal profiles of everyone from fifth-generation Californians to recent arrivals in the state. Houston presents the views of winegrowers, psychics, environmental activists, and women ranchers in addition to more well-known personalities such as computer whiz Steve Jobs, Chicano playwright Luis Valdez, and L.A. Mayor Tom Bradley. A reflective personal narrative as well as a series of interviews, *Californians* offers not only a perceptive understanding of the history, ecology, and texture of everyday life in California, but Houston's most explicit attempt to make his peace with what he calls the "contra-diction and paradox, the intertwining yins and yangs" of his native land (282).

The Men in My Life contains a dozen introspective essays or "recol-lections of kinship," as Houston calls them, about his male relatives, friends, and acquaintances over the years. He addresses subjects as diverse as football, military service, and kung fu instructors. But the emotional heart of the book is Houston's wistful tribute to his father, in particular his belated recognition that his father's "Okie music," which he scorned as a young man, was capable of arousing "a calling in the blood." Houston finds himself "wishing to hell I had been born ten years before World War One," so he could have traveled East Texas with his father when he was twenty-four years old "and a singing fool" (34, 35, 38).

Houston's writing has, on occasion, been accused of being sentimen-tal or overly optimistic. He himself has aptly countered this charge by correcting the notion that a writer must condescend to his characters or his subject in order to be taken seriously. "I don't think it's a sign of low intelligence to have respect for the people you choose to write about," he says. "Every piece of writing that I've ever been moved by, the bot-tom line is affirmation. That's what I care about" (Schaefer interview). Houston continues to be one of California's preeminent contemporary writers. His work displays a complex generosity of spirit, a sanity and candor and clarity of recognition that serve both him and his characters well as they search for equilibrium and a sense of balance in a region of the West most famous for disrupting both.

Selected Bibliography

Primary Sources

Fiction
The Adventures of Charlie Bates. Santa Barbara: Capra, 1973.
Between Battles. New York: Dial, 1968.
Continental Drift. New York: Knopf, 1978; rpt., New York: McGraw-Hill, 1987.
Gasoline. Santa Barbara: Capra, 1980.
Gig. New York: Dial, 1969; rpt., Berkeley: Creative Arts Book Co., 1988.
Love Life. New York: Knopf, 1985.
A Native Son of the Golden West. New York: Dial, 1971.

Nonfiction
California Heartland: Writing from the Great Central Valley. Co-edited with Gerald Haslam. Santa Barbara: Capra Press, 1978.
Californians: Searching for the Golden State. New York: Knopf, 1982; rpt., Santa Cruz, California: Otter B. Books, 1992.
"'The Circle almost Circled': Some Notes on California's Fiction." In *Reading the West: New Essays on the Literature of the American West.* Michael Kowalewski, ed. New York: Cambridge University Press, 1996.
"Cross Currents: A Meditation on Tassajara's Hot Springs," *San Francisco Focus* (May 1995).
Farewell to Manzanar. With Jeanne Wakatsuki Houston. Boston: Houghton Mifflin, 1973.
The Men in My Life and Other More or Less True Recollections of Kinship. Berkeley: Creative Arts Book Company, 1987; rpt., St. Paul, Minnesota: Graywolf Press, 1994.
One Can Think about Life after the Fish Is in the Canoe. Santa Barbara: Capra, 1985.
Open Field. Co-authored with John Brodie. Boston: Houghton Mifflin, 1974.
Surfing: The Sport of Hawaiian Kings. Co-authored with Ben R. Finney. Rutland and Tokyo: Tuttle, 1966.
Three Songs for My Father. Santa Barbara: Capra, 1974.
"Words and Music." In *Contemporary Authors Autobiography Series*, Vol. 16. Detroit: Gale Research, 1992.
West Coast Fiction: Modern Writing from California, Oregon and Washington. James D. Houston, ed. New York: Bantam, 1979.
"A Writer's Sense of Place." In *The True Subject: Writers on Life and Craft.* Kurt Brown, ed. St. Paul, Minnesota: Graywolf Press, 1993.

Secondary Sources

Cheuse, Alan. "Double Wonder: The Novelistic Achievement of James D. Houston." In *San Francisco in Fiction: Essays in a Regional Literature.* David Fine and Paul Skenazy, eds. Albuquerque: University of New Mexico Press, 1995. Pp. 144-159.
Holt, Patricia. "James D. Houston: An Interview." *Publishers Weekly*, September 4, 1978, 6.
Raskin, Jonah. *James D. Houston.* Boise: Boise State University Western Writers Series, 1991.
Schaefer, Jay. "An Interview with James Houston," *San Francisco Review of Books* (March-April 1983): 9.

Gerald Locklin

Gerald Haslam

Gerald Haslam was born in 1937 in Bakersfield, California, and grew up in its roughneck suburb, Oildale. Half a century later he is considered to be the preeminent chronicler, in fiction and essays, of California's Great Central Valley. His assured status as a western writer, his secure reputation as one of America's leading regionalists, should not, however, obscure the larger horizons of his work. His regionalism is, like that of Mark Twain, William Faulkner, and John Steinbeck, the matrix of a universal accessibility and applicability, a matter of enduring literary value, and it awaits its rightful place in the canon currently under reconsideration.

Haslam emerged from the world of which he writes. From the age of thirteen he worked in the oil fields and packing sheds, acquiring a store of materials that would later prove invaluable. As a result of the classic status so quickly accorded his first collection of stories, *Okies* (1973), he came to be identified as an offspring of that migration. In fact, though, neither of his parents was from Oklahoma, but in his own words "everyone from Oildale was called an Okie" and most of his friends were from migrant families. His father was from Texas and young Haslam counted Merle Haggard among his classmates. Haslam has also established an archive on the Okie migration, but his ancestry is a mix of Irish, Spanish, Portuguese, Danish, German, Welsh, and Sephardic, with a trace of Indian. His mother imparted a distinct Hispanic influence and a spirit of tolerance. His father, a two-time honorable mention football

All-America at UCLA who regretted his own decision not to graduate, promoted educational goals in his son's life.

Haslam responded by flunking out of Sacramento State College after five semesters of sports, girls, the class presidency, and beer. He gained a few months of ranching experience in Utah and, drafted in 1958, lucked into writing features for military publications. He returned to Oildale in 1960, improved his grades, married his wife Jan, with whom he would have five children, and saved enough from oil work to enroll at San Francisco State. His M.A. thesis, "The Language of the Oil Fields" (1965 and published under the same title in 1972), would prove of great significance to his fiction. Haslam earned a doctorate from Union Graduate School in 1980. He has taught at Sonoma State University since 1967, specializing in linguistics, regional and ethnic literature.

A list of his favorite books tells a great deal about the themes and techniques of his own work. From Mildred Hahn's *The Hawk's Done Gone*, Steinbeck's *The Long Valley*, and William Saroyan's *My Name is Aram* we infer his sense of place and of the vernacular. *The Good Soldier Schweik* by Jaroslav Hascek and Dalton Trumbo's *Johnny Got His Gun* imply his social realism and liberal democratic values. James Baldwin's *Nobody Knows My Name* suggests his penchant for the personal essay, the autobiographical basis of much of his fiction, and the range of his sympathies. The presence of Wallace Stegner's *All the Little Live Things* pays homage to the writer who most conspicuously lifted western writing from the popular realm to that of art and extended its settings into the present.

Also listed are *The Collected Stories of Flannery O'Connor* and *The Complete Stories of Ernest Hemingway*. Among the elements in the Georgia writer's fiction that were bound to appeal to Haslam in his formative years were the sympathetic use of rural characters, the dialectal dialogue, the concern for the plight of blacks, and, less obviously, a religious transcendence of both secular and narrowly defined regional values. In the first story of *Okies*, "The Doll," a middle-aged, middle-class woman who sins mainly in her prideful sense of superiority to her neighbors, is offered the sort of strange opportunity at redemption that we associate with O'Connor. Two rugged "boys" from the Okie camp beside the Kern River come to her door asking to "mow your lawn or anythang" (1). Overcoming her initial revulsion, she allows them first a drink from her hose, then coffee, and finally yardwork, lemonade, and sandwiches.

She basks in her newfound liberalism, but nausea replaces sanctity when the retarded one, refused the use of her bathroom, wets himself. Her physical purgation may, as in O'Connor's "Displaced Person," constitute the first step in a purgatorial process.

"Sally Let Her Bangs Hang Down" from the same collection expresses Haslam's respect for religion when it functions not as a repressive force but rather satisfies profound social or psychological needs. A man finds acceptance of his wife's promiscuous past through Jesus' forgiveness of Mary Magdalene. The couple abandon honky-tonk ballads for gospel music and experience an ironic material reward with their Nashville hit, "What a Friend We Have in Jesus." Significantly, a current project of Haslam's (with Richard Chon and daughter Alexandra Haslam) is *West Coast Country: A Music and Its People in California*.

O'Connor would surely agree with the title of "His Ways Are Mysterious," the lead story in *Snapshots* (1985). Yet Haslam here goes her one better, achieving a critique of religious fanaticism without sacrificing the theme of spiritual awakening through the agency of the vulgar and the obsessed, as a self-appointed "Prophet," both fool and hypocrite, is brought low by his doppelganger. Echoes of Poe, Dickens, Dostoyevsky, Sartre, and De Sica mingle with O'Connor's in "Vengeance," wherein a boy with communicative disorders proves to be dumb as a fox in his relentless pursuit of a bicycle thief.

Haslam found in Hemingway's work not only a reinforcement of his preference for tight, direct syntax, with few convolutions, but also a personal code involving loyalty to friends, responsibility for family, a masculine commitment to honor (compare "Before Dishonor" in *Okies*), and a Catholicism that has quietly persisted into his mature years. He is less willing than O'Connor to subordinate social justice to the perspective of eternity. On the other hand, he shares with Hemingway a pre-Christian sense of the sanctity of the natural world, its rhythms and man's corresponding rituals, its formative and restorative powers, and an inevitable environmental concern. In relation to nature, both Hemingway and Haslam, though more the empiricists, are in a line of descent from Emerson and Thoreau, and both were influenced by contact with Native American notions of animism and harmony. And Hemingway was one of the many masters from whom he learned to reproduce the spoken word in dialogue and in first-person narrative.

Obviously aware of Hemingway's masterpiece of reconciliation "Fathers and Sons," and of that story's roots in Turgenev's novel and indeed in literature back through Shakespeare to Aeschylus, Sophocles, Homer, and the Bible, and also a male unashamed of that fact, Haslam has frequently examined the grandfather-father-son continuum. In "Crossing the Valley," a father fails to obstruct his siblings and in-laws from legally divesting the grandfather of his store. The old man has been a source of oral history for the grandson, and in his dotage he relives the past. The country value of independence without alienation shines forth in the harmony of the passing generations.

In one of his most admired stories, "That Constant Coyote," a man dying of cancer goes on a last camping trip with his wife to the grave that has for three generations been the spiritual center of the family ranch. In a sleep-like state induced by painkillers and alcohol, he is visited by his father and grandfather who prepare him for death: "You've done a good job and you're leaving good stock in that boy of yours and his kids...we're with you in this. Play out your hand" (*That Constant Coyote* 5-6). In its magical realism the story acknowledges another of the author's favorites, *The Collected Stories of Jorge Luis Borges*, representative of the contemporary flowering of Latin American fiction.

Haslam has noted his awareness of surrogate fathers, including uncles, who taught him self-reliance and who appear under various fictional names. "Someone Else's Life" is one of the finest fishing stories since "Big Two-Hearted River" and like *Shane* is narrated from a boy's point of view. The foreman for the always busy and criticizing father "taught me far more than how to catch fish...he had shown me how the wilderness, the privacy of the canyon could strip...layer after layer of civilized complexity from us" (*That Constant Coyote* 102). When the role model kills himself, the narrator, like Nick Adams, seeks therapy in the snowy woods.

Women in the families of Haslam's fiction also play an important role. One need only look to the wise grandmother of "The Horned Toad" or to the virtual absence of a father from Haslam's longest work, the novella *Masks*, or to an exclusively female story such as "A Prison of Words" to establish the sympathetic prominence of women in Haslam's work. But there is surely nothing gender-biased in the suggestion that the highest achievement of the majority of men might consist in their becoming good fathers. Thus, the Chinese laborer of "Sojourner" travels to the Sacramento Valley with the dream of bettering the economic conditions of his family. In "Compañeros," a father is powerless when his son is beaten by police. A surrogate father in "Ace Low" tries to horrify his youthful admirers out of following in his gambler's path, while the Indian father of "Medicine" practices homeopathic magic to save his last son from a corrupt shaman. "Uncle" Fate Newby, a three-hundred-pound "rasslin' champeen," exemplifies racial respect and goodwill in "Sweet Reason." In "The Horned Toad," a treatment of family burial responsibilities, the father voices the working-class ethic: "When you're family, you take care of your own." Uncle Fud Murray and Jake Garcia of "The Last Roundup" usher the youthful narrator through the rite of passage of a wet T-shirt contest at which he learns that you can look like a clown if you know you're a man, and that, in the world of men, the accurate placing of a beer bottle upside a head is still, regrettably, an occasional prerequisite to survival. The father of "Dust" must adopt an Indian method of slaughtering jackrabbits to save his family from starvation. An ex-slave is the protagonist of "The Killing Pen," and the relocation of a family is the theme of "Home to America." Thief begets thief in "Vengeance." Uncle Arlo Epps of "Upstream" provides an object lesson in manhood by literally swimming, like a salmon, up and over a waterfall to freedom from a nagging wife. But the many properly functioning families to be found in the "Other California" of Haslam's work stand in happy contrast to the degenerate or dysfunctional families that are a staple of urban California fiction and film.

From his own books, Haslam has identified a favorite that is not fiction, although it might qualify for that post-modernist genre, the "non-fiction novel." *Coming of Age in California* is a series of personal essays charting his lifelong engagement with the family, friends, and culture of his origins. "Bloodrites" analyzes the role of football as rite of passage:

> For an only child like me, raised by a mother who hated and sought to suppress male urges, the masculine rituals of controlled violence offered what I believe was a biologically necessary outlet for at least one of testosterone's urges. Everything from the smell of the training rooms to running the gauntlet in practice or going nose-to-nose in the pit, everything from the ceremonial taping of ankles and wrists to the prayer before a game conspired to move an apprentice warrior away from one world toward another where deep biological impulses could be channeled, validated, released. (58-59)

That "male bonding" has become a cliché does not vitiate the truth that football can teach respect for others and oneself based on meritorious performance and the overcoming of fear: "Like life itself, football is tough and you learn to take it or else" (58).

In "Pop," it is only when he is already a father himself that his father kisses him, choking out the words, "I should've done that when you were little" (6). And in his father's senility, the child becomes the parent, changing the father's diapers.

In a later signature story, "Condor Dreams," the author remains faithful to both the socioeconomic history and the poetry of the valley. A man striving to retain at least his original eighty of the 1,300 acres about to be foreclosed comes to accept the inherited faith of an old farmworker that we exist only in the dreams of an archetypal, not-yet-extinct condor:

> A startled moment later, he hovered above a great gray organism that sent misty tendrils into nearby canyons and arroyos, that moved within itself and stretched as far north into the great valley as his vision could reach.... The land too was breathing, he suddenly realized, its colors as iridescent as sunlight on the wings of condors. (*Condor Dreams* 8)

But readers should not allow the beauty, truth, and goodness of Haslam's work to obscure another of its most notable accomplishments: humor. Haslam can be one of the funniest of our writers, in the tradition of rural, dialectical comedy. It is in his "Tejon Club" series (*The Great Tejon Club Jubilee*) of practical jokes, double-crosses, and triple-paybacks that his gift is given freewheeling rein. Big Dunc, Bob Don, Wylie Hillis, and the other boys of "The Great New-Age Caper" debate the constitutional right to bear arms, and put to rout a new breed of fakir:

> Well, he hadn't bagged nothin' but a six-pack at Woody's Liquors in years.... Anyways, Big Dunc not only couldn't walk up an anthill without needin' oxygen, but he couldn't shoot worth a shit either, so I said, "I been out to the target range with you a time or two, Dunc, and the perfect place to be is in front a the target. You couldn't hit a elephant with birdshot." (173-174)

Haslam's work has from the start been characterized by that same diversity that marks the Central Valley itself, with a special empathy for victims of persecution such as the American Indians, the Chinese, the

Okies, and the Latino farmworkers. In recent years he has expanded his range to include the Armenian community of Fresno, crime in Sacramento, the relocation of the Japanese-Americans, the Vietnam veterans, soil and water pollution, and the monopolization of agriculture by conglomerates. His *The Great Central Valley: California's Heartland*, with photographs by Robert Dawson and Stephen Johnson, won awards from the American Association for State and Local History, the Commonwealth Club, and the Bay Area Book Reviewers Association. His multicultural anthology, *Many Californias*, which won the 1993 Benjamin Franklin Award, is a popular text in California studies. He has written regular columns for *California English* and the *San Francisco Chronicle's* Sunday magazine, *This World*. To his earlier anthologies, *Forgotten Pages of American Literature*, *Western Writing*, *Afro-American Oral Literature*, and *California Heartland* (with James D. Houston), he recently added with his co-editor daughter Alexandra, *Where Coyotes Howl and Wind Blows Free: Growing Up in the West*. A booklet on Lawrence Clark Powell joins those he earlier wrote on William Eastlake and Jack Schaefer. He recently co-scripted a film based on his tale of black cowboys, "Rider," and is working on others. *The Miyazaki Family: Missing in Action*, a short film based on Haslam's story "Missing in Action" (from *That Constant Coyote*), won a 1995 Golden Eagle Award from CINE.

Social, linguistic, and magical realism; narrative craft and humor, a celebration of the new diversity and of the best of traditional values; a sense of place, of family, of friendship; a renewal of the spirit of his great American literary avatars — these combine to place Haslam's work in the first rank of contemporary American writing.

Selected Bibliography

Primary Sources

Fiction
Condor Dreams and Other Fictions. Reno: University of Nevada Press, 1994.
That Constant Coyote: California Stories. Reno: University of Nevada Press, 1990.
The Great Tejon Club Jubilee. Walnut Creek, California: Devil Mountain Books, 1995.
Hawk Flights: Visions of the West. Big Timber, Montana: Seven Buffaloes Press, 1983.
The Man Who Cultivated Fire and Other Stories. Santa Barbara: Capra Press, 1987.
Masks: A Novel. Penngrove, California: Old Adobe Press, 1976.
Okies. Selected Stories. Santa Barbara and Salt Lake City: Peregrine Smith, Inc., 1975.

Snapshots: Glimpses of the Other California. Walnut Creek, California: Devil Mountain
    Books, 1985.
The Wages of Sin. Fallon, Nevada: Duck Down Press/Windriver Books, 1980.

Nonfiction
Coming of Age in California: Personal Essays. Walnut Creek, California: Devil Mountain
    Books, 1990.
The Great Central Valley: California's Heartland, with photographers Robert Dawson and
    Stephen Johnson. Berkeley and Los Angeles: University of California Press, 1993.
The Language of the Oil Fields. Penngrove, California: Old Adobe Press, 1972.
Many Californias: Literature from the Golden State. Reno: University of Nevada Press,
    1992.
The Other California: The Great Central Valley in Life and Letters. Santa Barbara: Capra
    Press, 1990; second edition, Reno: University of Nevada Press, 1994.
Voices of a Place: Social and Literary Essays from the Other California. Walnut Creek,
    California: Devil Mountain Books, 1987.

Secondary Sources

Bondavalli, Simona. "Continental Drift: La narrativa regionalenella California contem-
    poranea." Graduate Thesis, Univervita degli Sudi di Bologna, Italy, 1995.
Breiger, Marek. "Haslam's Oildale, Our California." *California English* (September-
    October 1992): 22-23.
Collins, Richard. "Three by Gerald Haslam." *The Redneck Review of Literature* (Spring
    1991): 13.
Doreen, Dianna. "Gerald Haslam." *The Poetry Center & American Poetry Archive News,*
    12 (1996): 7.
Dunbar-Ortiz, Roxanne. "One or Two Things I Know about Us: 'Okies' in American
    Culture." *Radical History Review* (Spring 1994): 4-34.
Dunn, Geoffrey, "Central Valley Boys." *San Francisco Review of Books,* 16:1 (Summer
    1991): 3-4.
Fine, David. "Pulse of the Heartland." *Westways* (August 1991): 66-67.
Haslam, Gerald. "Confessions of a Regional Writer." *California English* (January-February
    1984): 16-17.
    ———. "Who Cares What Happens In The Sticks? A Personal Approach to California's
    Regional Writing." *California English* (March-April 1987): 8-11.
    ———. "Life On (and Off) the Mid-List." *Poets & Writers* (July-August 1987): 1, 4-5.
Houston, James D. "Gerald Haslam's *The Other California.*" *California History* (Fall
    1993): 250-255.
LaPolla, Franco. "Cantori Del West: Penna & Colt." *Cultura e Spettacolo,* 14 (giugno
    1988), n.p.
Locklin, Gerald. "The Emergence of Gerald Haslam." *Small Press Review* (April 1989): 7.
    ———. *Gerald Haslam.* Boise: Boise State University Western Writers Series, 1987.
Locklin, Gerald and Charles Stetler. "Interview with Gerald Haslam." *Home Planet
    News,* 4:3 (Fall 1983): 19.
Maloney, Mary Grace. "Central Valley Mythology: The Works of Gerald Haslam,"
    Honors Humanities Thesis, Stanford University, 1985.
Peck, David. "Gerald Haslam, the Heartland's Voice." *The Californians* (January-
    February 1988): 48-49.

Penna, Christina. "Heartland." *California English* (March-April 1987): 12-14.

Ronald, Ann. "Foreword." *That Constant Coyote*. Reno: University of Nevada Press, 1990. Pp. xi-xxvi.

————. "Gerald Haslam and Ann Ronald: A Conversation." *Western American Literature* (Summer 1966): 115-137.

Siegel, Mark. "Present Trends: Fiction." In *A Literary History of the American West*. Fort Worth: Texas Christian University Press, 1987. Pp. 1185-1188.

Speer, Laurel. "Harry and Gerry." *Small Press Review* (June 1988): 5.

Weber, Mark. "Gerald Haslam." *Lawn Furniture: Guerrilla Poetics Publication* (Summer 1989): 2-3.

Weeks, Jonina. "A Contemporary Western Writer, Gerald Haslam: His Means to a New West and the World." Master's Thesis, Sonoma State University, 1988.

Wylder, Delbert. "Recent Western Fiction." *Journal of the West*, (January 1980): 62-70.

Elizabeth Renfro

Ella Leffland

Ella Leffland, writer and painter, believes that "probably everyone who turns to writing or painting or anything like that has a dollop of the outsider." For Leffland herself, this development of the artist-as-outsider perspective may be traced to her childhood in Martinez, California. Born in 1931 to Danish immigrants who referred to Denmark as "home," Leffland says she "thought we were on a vacation here for years!" This led to her feeling what she has described as "either a double sense of belonging or no sense of belonging," a theme she often returns to in her fiction: "I think coming from a family that was different and had a different attitude toward things had a bearing on the people I [write] about" (Ross 291-292).

This feeling was intensified during World War II, which Leffland describes as "the central experience of my childhood" (Bolle 68). Leffland's adolescence was filled with horror stories from Danish relatives about bombings and Nazi domination. At home, Martinez's location in the San Francisco Bay area made it an important shipyard site for the American war effort. The nervous citizens prepared constantly for anticipated Japanese bombing raids, and Leffland witnessed acts of "patriotic" terrorism against second- and third-generation Japanese American and Italian American families she had known all her life.

Critics agree that loneliness or isolation of the individual is a recurrent theme in Leffland's work. As John Romano puts it, in particular reference to *Last Courtesies* (1980), a collection of short stories, "at the center... is most often a character who is profoundly alone, suffers, and cannot make himself or herself understood" (3). Leffland's characters are isolated in a matrix of the competing demands of their own needs and values, and the desires and value systems of others — lovers, friends, family, community, country.

Critics disagree, however, in their readings of these characters. Romano calls Leffland's authorial presence "distinctly caring," adding that "her imagination is always bound up with sympathy." He argues that in *Last Courtesies*, "the principal business of these stories is bestowing sympathy" (3). Yet another critic, Stephen Goodwin, states that the stories leave the reader feeling the "dread power of nightmares," as the characters, while "sympathetic... are treated with a detachment that is the only bulwark against disgust" (5). Keith Monley wrote (prior to the release of *The Knight, Death and the Devil* in 1990) that while "Leffland's novels are, one and all, tales of redemption," this is "hardly the case in her short stories. It could even be argued that in *Last Courtesies*... the protagonist's 'obsession' proves terminal, but in any case the protagonist is certainly not redeemed" (492).

Much of Leffland's fiction seems to reflect what might be called "Western Gothic," a post-World War II West Coast version of Southern Gothic. Leffland's characters are, as is true in Southern Gothic fiction, strongly molded by and reflective of the setting in which they live. The mood, tone, personality, even values and moral codes of the characters are part and parcel of the mood, tone and character of their land and geographical setting, especially the land in which they spent their childhoods. Barren plains of Modoc County, backwoods country in Napa, icy and isolated Danish farms, Germany through its entire history — all define, reflect, create the characters reared there.

As in Southern Gothic fiction, many of Leffland's characters are aberrant or grotesque in some way, though often in more subtle ways than, for example, Carson McCullers' dwarf (*Ballad of the Sad Cafe*) or Flannery O'Connor's criminal Misfit ("A Good Man Is Hard to Find"). The behavior of Leffland's characters is often bizarre, at least in terms of expected or sanctioned behaviors, yet, fitting with the Southern Gothic tradition, entirely believable and appropriate (and therein lies some of the nightmare) and fitting with the tenor of the novel or short story, which is a blend of realism and "the supernatural" (Prescott 89a).

Some of the minor but equally bizarre (and often unappealing) characters in Leffland's novels also serve functions similar to the functions of O'Connor's and McCullers' secondary characters: They are unlikely agents of grace, catalysts to bring the vulnerable (often not entirely appealing themselves) protagonists to insight (if not redemption). While Leffland does not work with the Catholic themes predominant in O'Connor's stories, grace in Leffland's fiction is similarly tied to awareness and acceptance of an existing moral order — though this awareness and acceptance does not necessarily bring with it comfort, happiness, or even lessening of pain.

The importance Leffland places on exploration of the psychological and especially moral dimensions of character is another trait that parallels her work with that of the Southern Gothic authors. Like these writers, Leffland explores alienation both from and within moral order, as well as exploring — but not doubting the ultimate existence of — that moral order itself. Arguing against presenting characters who are abnormal ("which is fine") but who exist in a "void," she insists, as does O'Connor, on the existence of a moral framework: "I've always believed that characters are not interesting unless they have a place in a moral world, even if it's a place in conflict within that world" (Ross 292).

The protagonist of Leffland's first published novel, *Mrs. Munck* (1970), is struggling to enact her own version of justice based on her experience of a world that pretends to embrace but actually acts outside of a moral framework. At the novel's beginning, Rose Munck, a forty-three-year-old widow, is nervously and excitedly preparing for the arrival of her former husband's wheelchair-bound Uncle Patrick Leary, for whom she's offered to care. Already we are aware of a tension and a sense of being just outside "normal" in this woman who describes herself as having "always looked like a widow during [her] marriage" (3), and who today dresses herself in "a dress [she] seldom wore, full-sleeved, white, almost virginal" (8).

After Leary, protesting, has been "deposited" by his son at Rose's home in Port Carquinez and the two are alone, he tries to rise from the sofa, but falls to the floor. Rose simply looks at him, tells him that he'll have to try to get himself back to the sofa, and leaves him. Later that night, the old man tries to take a butcher knife to Rose. "Now we understand each other," they each say (16). Throughout this first-person novel, such scenes of cruelty and nightmarish emotion are presented clearly, matter-of-factly, and with a detachment that is chilling.

After the prologue, the novel moves into flashback, and readers learn what has taught Rose her emotional and moral distance. Hers has been a life of missing and missed human attachments. As an unloved only child growing up on a barren farm in northeastern California, young Rose watches her mother devote herself to pleasing a man "whose sun-slit eyes searched only for refuge, even in me, even in a scrap of a child" (20). When Rose rejects her mother's attempt to make Rose's "entire personality...a dowry, as hers had been" (18), her mother insists that "'it's them [men, husbands] that does the things that count, and it's us that's gotta make it easier for them'" (26).

Yet Rose, even as a child, knows there is something complex going on between her parents, something ugly and deep. One time, Rose sees her mother watch her husband's retreat with "a look of unspeakable contempt" (30). At this point, Rose "knew [her mother] would outlast Pa and that she knew this, and that somewhere down deep inside her ... [her mother] was very glad. Yet Rose realizes that "[her mother] would never admit hatred to me; she would not even admit it to herself. She was a lie" (30).

At sixteen, Rose escapes to San Francisco with dreams of "writing poems of grave beauty" (30) and saving money to travel the world. In her boardinghouse she meets several young men, also fledgling writers. When one of them tells her she should stop taking herself so seriously because she's "complete as [she is]...the light-bearer for man" (56), Rose has a moment of awakening:

> Everything fell into place. An almost rapturous fury took me. "I see it! I see why I've felt so at odds with myself...all dimmed and cramped up, as though I were stuffed into a box. It's that you won't see me, you twist me into something for your own use.... It's like a rape!...I'm a dumbbell! A lousy dumbbell! All this time you've been raping me and I've been feeling guilty, as though I didn't measure up, as though something was wrong with me...." (56)

When Rose is ill, her boss, Mr. Leary, unexpectedly comes by to visit her. Rose, "allow[s] [herself] the luxury of feeling watched over" and enjoys "the knowledge that he was actually watching me as I closed my eyes—as though I could be so interesting, so important" (61-62). When his visit culminates with forced sex, Rose vows to "never get close to a man again" (66). Yet when Mr. Leary returns the next evening and speaks admiringly of her books and writing, she lets him stay. Later, she looks in the mirror and sees "the face of someone I had cheated and humiliated and who reacted to my abuse with obscenely eager compliance" (76-77). After the affair ends in disaster, with the death of their baby during a violent brawl between Rose and Leary, Rose marries Leary's timid and ever-faithful nephew, Harley, and they move eventually to the cottage in Port Carquinez.

This is only the first third of the novel. The rest of the book develops the battle of wills between two scarred and crippled (Leary physically, Rose emotionally) people. While Leary himself increasingly draws strength from their confrontations and taunts Rose with her failed life and childlessness, Rose begins to question the satisfaction revenge can bring her. She finally realizes that she needn't accept the "predestined bond" that each man in her life has decreed between them, each bond "yet another compromise, another exile" (312).

Leffland's second novel, *Love Out of Season* (1974), was not as great a critical success as *Mrs. Munck*, though it too garnered a Commonwealth Club of California award, as well as a California Literature Medal Award. The novel is the story of Johanna Kaulbach, a young San Francisco painter, who falls completely under the spell of a "predestined bond" of passion for Morris Levinsky, a man equally drawn to her, but selfish, dishonest, and unable to return her love. Johanna, unlike Rose Munck, is well educated and a dedicated artist. From the beginning, she is aware that "she had not wanted to go with [Morris], but she had felt empty of will" (4).

When she decides to give in to the attraction, she discovers "that was the last decision I was capable of.... There's no more choice, only a drive, something that keeps going on. I have to have him" (153). Throughout the three years of their on-and-off relationship, Johanna increasingly surrenders her will and artistic self to this passion and denies to herself Morris' lies and infidelities, all the while knowing full well that she is losing her integrity: "'What I feel is that he's inside me, from head to foot,'" she tells a friend. "'If you peeled my skin away you'd find Morrie's body inside, like the yolk of an egg. It's as though I'm thinking with his brain and feeling with his heart'" (169).

When Johanna eventually frees herself, she does begin to paint again and takes a new lover. She explains to a friend, however, that she cannot marry her new lover, for there's no "X quality" there; that passion and attachment "only happens once. It burns itself out" (322).

There is a question here of love and morality: Does great passion (the "X quality," the "predestined bond") by its very consuming nature create its own morality? Does it preclude morality because it is inherently destructive? Is a passionate attachment—whether "pure" to art or secular to the flesh—always doomed (predestined) to be destructive? Is great passionate love of person, art, or ideal always consuming, ultimately annihilating the individual? Are we all doomed to this? *Love* implies the answer in the affirmative when, on the novel's last page, Johanna rides a bus away from Morris for the final time. The last sentence describes the motion of the bus as it pulls away: "[T]he bus... swung around a corner, heaving the crowd first to one side and then to the other, as a collective cry went up" (373).

This novel is complicated—as is *Mrs. Munck*—by the development of the secondary characters. Morris, Conrad, and several other characters appear as unique individuals with their own experiences and needs, all of which result in inevitable competing needs and inabilities to understand another person truly and to meet that other person fully.

As in Leffland's other novels, bizarre characters abound in *Love Out of Season*. One prime example is Josh, the young, wealthy owner of the gallery where Johanna occasionally works. He thrives on Johanna's rudeness: Having "sucked on her hatred for him, he burned with it, he was heavy and real with it, and when he walked his feet would ring solidly on the ground" (295). Such extreme characters all illustrate versions of human connection, none healthily functional, some grotesquely aberrant.

In her third novel, the highly praised *Rumors of Peace* (1979), Leffland softens both her approach and her views of human possibility. A heavily autobiographical *Bildungsroman*, the story is set in Mendoza (Martinez), California, during World War II. Suse Hansen, whom Leffland has said is about "95% [like me]" (Ross 292), is the youngest child of hardworking Danish immigrant parents, living in a stable, secure neighborhood in which "everyone was the same, neither rich nor poor" (5). Leffland uses the character of Suse to "[bring] to life [her] concern with the nature of moral growth.... [Leffland] is concerned not so much with the war itself as its effects, its implications for people far removed from the fighting" (Osborne 4).

The war has a devastating impact on Suse's life, shattering her sense of security and filling her with a dread certainty that her town will be bombed by the Japanese. This knowledge leaves her feeling utterly isolated from other children and even from the adults in her life: "I knew absolutely that I was ... alone in my understanding of what was going to happen" (16). From her fear and hatred for the "enemy," however, Suse draws an ugly strength. During an air raid drill, she has a revelation:

> I lay in a knotted ball, so terrified I couldn't breathe. Then suddenly a powerful, boiling sensation flooded through me. I hated them. My eyes flared with a picture of Japs lying headless, burned, trampled down like beetles or lice or rotten vegetation. I hated them. Forever, with my whole being, I hated them.
>
> I felt a long, quaking breath released and lay still. I was still frightened, but differently now. As though with control. And I no longer felt ashamed. (22)

Suse does, however, have moments when her detachment and control are shaken, as when school friends and their families are forced into internment camps. Her control is further shaken as she tries to negotiate the common adolescent hazards and concerns of love, acceptance, and life's purpose. When Suse realizes that hate alone won't answer the feelings and questions she has, won't make moral sense of the war, she throws herself into the study of history, looking for answers. A crush on a Jewish refugee, Egon, leads her to research what it means to be a Jew. All of this takes Suse "into the enigmatic heart of human nature" (Ross 289).

At the novel's close, Suse is still looking to her books and heroes for answers and wisdom, protesting to Egon that "'[t]here's nothing to depend on'" (387), and still wanting "everything, peace, glory, love, life ever-lasting..." (389). She is also, however, a person forever changed by the war, old beyond her years and aware that she must live in "a world full of moral questions" (Ross [paraphrasing Osborne] 289).

In her 1990 novel, *The Knight, Death and the Devil*, Leffland again explores the effects of the war, especially its effects on love and morality. This time, however, she moves from outsiders to the ultimate insider, recreating the life story of Luftwaffe chief Hermann Göring. The title is taken from a Dürer print, *Ritter, Tod und Teufel*, that Göring carried with him all his adult life. In this 700-page book, readers again have a story grounded in Leffland's recurrent theme of the interactive, definitional quality of person and place.

In her "Author's Note," Leffland describes the book as "a historical biographical novel." She states that she was "as scrupulous as humanly possible in adhering to the facts, in staying within the evidence" (7). To achieve this, Leffland has re-created "historically or biographically authenticated scenes... [interweaving them] with the fictional private scenes... so closely that it would be difficult to separate them into the two threads of fact and fiction; for the factual has gone through the creative imaginative process, while the fictional has been built out of facts" (8). Leffland frames Hermann Göring's life within the history of Germany itself. The book's early chapters present a history of the land and people from medieval times, illustrating a national psyche that could result in such offspring as Göring and the feeling that Germans were "God's chosen."

In structure the massive work is a pastiche: the narrative is primarily in the third person, sometimes limited omniscient, sometimes non-omniscient, moving from person to person for focus, so that the reader gets perspectives (some personal, some impersonal) from the knight himself, as well as other characters—even Hitler. Also interwoven are excerpts from various characters' journals and letters. In describing this approach, Leffland states, "I tried as much as possible to leave out the narrative voice.... And to speak through the points of view of the characters" (Bolle 68).

In her treatment of Göring, the self-identified "knight," Leffland strives to recreate the man's complexity, making him more than isolated, disembodied evil, showing him as "representing the human situation" (Bolle 68). While the book is very disturbing, most critics have agreed with Thomas Kenally's assessment that it is "rich and satisfying.... Among other things, [Leffland] gives us a credible sense of why Nazism inflamed so many imaginations. We feel with Göring and others the drag of that dark seduction.... [T]he connection between Hitler, the hard-nosed plebe, and Hermann the knight is consistently ambiguous and always fascinating.... She goes a large distance in giving us the resonance of the Göring life" (8).

It is a resonance that leaves us haunted with Leffland's recurrent question: Does great passion—for person, place, or ideal—always put the individual in annihilating conflict with the larger moral order?

Selected Bibliography

Primary Sources

The Knight, Death and the Devil. New York: Penguin Books, 1991. First published by William Morrow & Company, 1990.

Last Courtesies and Other Stories. St. Paul, Minnesota: Graywolf Press, 1985. First published by Harper & Row, 1979.

Love Out of Season. New York: HarperCollins, 1985. First published by Atheneum, 1974.

Mrs. Munck. St. Paul, Minnesota: Graywolf, 1985. First published by Houghton Mifflin, 1970.

Rumors of Peace. New York: HarperCollins, 1985. First published by Harper & Row, 1979.

Secondary Sources

Bolle, Sonja. "Ella Leffland." *Publishers Weekly*, February 2 1990, 68.

Goodwin, Stephen. "Symbols, Spiels, and Strangeness." *Washington Post*, October 19, 1980, "Book World," 4-5.

Kenally, Thomas. "The Fuhrer's Right-Hand Man." *New York Times*, February 11, 1990, sec. 7, 8.

Monley, Keith. "The Good, the Bad, and the Ugly: Reflections on Recent Short Fiction." *New England Review*, 11:3 (1980): 483-494.

Osborne, Linda. "Growing Up Under Fire." *Washington Post*, July 29, 1979, "Book World," 1, 4.

Prescott, Peter S. "A Short Story Bonanza." *Newsweek*, November 3, 1980, 89a.

Romano, John. "Tales of Sympathy." *The New York Times Book Review*, October 5, 1980, 3, 33.

Ross, Jean W. *Contemporary Authors*, Vol. 35 (Interview in New Revision Series). Detroit: Gale Research Inc., 1992. Pp. 288-293.

Robin Ganz

Gary Soto

In the early 1950s Fresno, California, was an arid and grimy city of 91,000 inhabitants. Many were caught in an economic chokehold that relegated them to a lifetime of punishing labor in the cotton field, the orchard and vineyard or the small factory. African American, "Okie," Chicano and Asian American families populated Fresno's blue-collar neighborhoods and by this time the racism of the thirties and forties had given way to a kind of mutual acceptance, born of the daily necessity of working together and by their shared "culture of poverty." Every weekday residents of Fresno's barrios and other inner-city neighborhoods would pile aboard trucks and buses that transported them to the lush and fertile farmland of the San Joaquin Valley that surrounds the city.

Against this backdrop of agricultural plenty and urban indigence, Gary Soto was born on Fresno's Braly Street on April 12, 1952. Frank Soto, Gary's paternal grandfather, had emigrated from Mexico to Fresno as a young man to escape the economic and political instability of pre-revolution Mexico. It was in Fresno that he met his future wife Paolo who sold ice cream cones on the street to support herself and her child; she'd married as a teenager in Mexico and had her first baby there before emigrating to Fresno after the Mexican Revolution. Gary's grandparents met, fell in love, married and worked in the fields, as did their children. Manuel Soto, their third son, was a charming and intelligent boy with elegant good looks and glimmering brown eyes. He and Angie Trevino, Gary's mother, met in 1947 at Edison High School. Like so many other young men and women

426

from Fresno's working class neighborhoods, neither Angie nor Manuel finished high school. They married at eighteen and soon began having children. Gary's older brother Rick was born on June 28, 1950, Gary's birth followed two years later, and his sister Debra was born on March 6, 1953.

One August day when Gary was five years old, Manuel Soto went to work at the construction site where he was then employed. A co-worker and family friend climbed a ladder with a tray of nails on his shoulder, lost his balance and fell on top of Manuel, breaking his neck. Gary's father died two days later; he was twenty-seven years old. In a narrative recollection entitled "This Man," Soto speculates that their neighbor "must have felt guilt and shame" because he turned his back on the Sotos after the accident. Here Soto imagines what could have taken place five doors down the street:

> [S]tarting off to the store, [he] thinks of Manuel, our father, maybe sees his face whole, maybe sees his face twisted and on the ground, the blood already drying. . . . But how much? How much of our father was on his mind? Did the kids in the street distract him, the neighbors on porches, a barking dog? Did he sing inside his head, worry about bills maybe think of work? . . . He bought his butter, went home to eat with his children, who after the accident never came over to play with us. . . . We lived poor years because our father died. We suffered quietly and hurt even today. Shouldn't this mean something to him? (*Lesser Evils* 82-83)

Within the Soto family an imperturbable silence and secrecy surrounded the dead father, compounding the pain of those who mourned him. Soto writes that

> [s]omething happened in our family without us becoming aware, a quiet between mother and children settled on us like dust. We went to school, ate, watched television that wasn't funny, and because mother never said anything, father . . . became that name we never said in our house. His grave was something we saw in photographs; his remembrance those clothes hanging in the back of the closet. (*Lesser Evils* 83)

For Soto the task of resurrecting his father's spirit on the printed page is a compelling one, made more difficult by his family's continuing taciturnity. Yet for the reader who accompanies Soto on his poetic journey, fresh meanings reveal themselves with each new work. Decades pass and father is still that name never spoken within the family but it is also the name that recurs more and more frequently in the heart and poetry of his son. In "Another Time" from the 1990 collection *Who Will Know Us?* Soto writes:

> ... Like father,
> whom we miss and don't know,
> Who would have saved us
> From those terrible years
> If that day at work he got up
> Hurt but alive. He fell
> From that ladder with an upturned palm,
> With the eyes of watery light.
> We went on with sorrow that found no tree
> To cry from. I can't go to his grave.
> I know this. I can't find my place
> Or wake up and say, Let him walk,
> Let him round the house but not come in.
> Even the sun with so much to give must fall.
> (97-98)

A year later in "Fall and Spring," from his collection of poems entitled *Home Course in Religion*, Soto uses a conversation with Scott, his boyhood best friend, to diffuse the layers of time and silence that conceal the events surrounding Manuel Soto's death.

> ... About then I began saying things like,
> Scott, I think I lived before. Or, Scotty,
> I have feelings around my eyes like I'm Chinese.
> He let me say these things and still be his friend. He told me
> That his father was dead. I ran sand through my fingers.
> I told him that when my father died
> My uncle heard gravel crunch in the path
> That ran along our house, and rock was one of
> The things God told us to look out for.

It may be that Gary Soto has only begun to write about the mystery and opacity of this profoundly important element of his experience and that we can expect to see the character and essence of Manuel Soto reanimated in his future work. Soto continues to honor his father in a fascinating pattern of discovery throughout his poetry and prose; each time he invokes his father in his writing, Soto beams new light on their unique relationship and on the damage that enforced silence inflicts on those who grieve the death of their beloved. With the apparent wealth of emotional territory that he has yet to explore, Soto may develop into a novel the theme of a child's early loss of a parent and the silence that often follows it.

Soto began to write at the age of twenty. A student at California State University at Fresno, Soto "lucked into" poet Philip Levine's creative writing class. He describes his chance meeting with Levine — and his first glimpse into his future as a writer — as pure kismet. When asked what would have happened if he hadn't ventured into Levine's class, Soto answered that he'd be mowing lawns in Fresno. Soto is an engaging conversationalist with a penchant for wry observations; his account of his own experiences is often peppered with jokes. Asked if he is serious, he assures listeners that he is.

Soto's discovery of his poetic voice coincided with a recognition of his own alienation: he realized that he was estranged not only from the culture of his heritage, but also from the Anglo world which simultaneously beckoned to him and rejected him. He experienced the epiphany of his otherness when he came upon a poem called "Unwanted" by Edward Field. Reading it, Soto saw his own aloneness described; additionally, the poem presented him with the first suggestion that he too was capable of satisfying himself and affecting others with the power of his words. What's more, in Field's poem Soto discerned that a sense of alienation was not unique to him but rather, "it was a *human* pain."

In 1974 Gary Soto graduated magna cum laude from California State University, Fresno. The next year he married Carolyn Oda, also a Fresno native, whom he'd met when he was twenty after she moved into the house next door to the apartment that Gary shared with his brother Rick. The brothers were "college poor," living on the food that Gary could take from their mother's refrigerator when Rick "called her into the backyard about a missing sock from his laundry — a ploy from the start." One day, walking home from the store, Soto saw Carolyn cracking walnuts on her front porch. During the next few weeks Gary artfully plotted, contriving numerous excuses to walk past her house, sometimes resorting to a low crouch behind a hedge until Carolyn appeared to water her geranium or sweep off her porch. So began the romance that is the mainstay of Soto's emotional life.

Ever since Gary could remember, his grandmother told him to marry

> a good Mexican girl — "no Okies, hijo...." For her, everyone who wasn't Mexican, black or Asian were Okies. The French were Okies, the Italians in suits were Okies. When I asked about Jews, whom I had read about, she asked for a picture. I rode home on my bicycle and returned with a calendar depicting the important races of the world. "Pues, si, son Okies tambien!" she said, nodding her head. She waved the calendar away and went to the living room where she lectured me on the virtues of the Mexican girl. (*Faces* 9)

But Gary fell in love with a Japanese American girl and their romance created a furor in his family. Gary's own fears were assuaged when he'd met Carolyn's parents, Japanese American farmers who had been imprisoned in internment camps during World War II. On his terrifying first visit with them, he was relieved to discover that "these people are just like Mexicans...poor people" (*Faces* 13). Now he had only to reassure his family. Soto writes about their anxious response to the news of his engagement to Carolyn

> who worried my mother, who had my grandmother asking once again to see the calender of the Important Races of the World. I told her I had thrown it away years before. I took a much-glanced-at snapshot from my wallet. We looked at it together, in silence. Then Grandma reclined in her chair, lit a cigarette, and said, "Es pretty." She blew and asked with all her worry pushed up to her forehead: "Chinese?" (*Faces* 11)

Five years after the marriage Carolyn gave birth to their daughter Mariko. Fatherhood stimulated Soto's imagination in a variety of ways. Often Mariko or some aspect of their relationship is the subject of a narrative recollection, or as in the instance he writes about in "Listening Up," Soto appropriates the wisdom of her childish "turns of language" for his own use. He writes:

> One summer I heard our three-year-old daughter Mariko say,

"The days are filled with air," and heard my writer self say, "That's mine. I said that. . . ."

Little philosopher, sophist, wise-guy in a little girl's dress — she spoke a beautifully true line that suggests that the business of living (jobs, friends, love, failed love, and so on) is only air, and maybe not even blue air at that. All is transparent as air — a breeze here a strong gust there, and people and days pass from our lives. . . . I took my daughter's line and made a poem from it. (*Faces* 33-35)

In his mid-forties, his daughter Mariko off to college, Gary Soto continues to chart new literary territory, blazing untraveled paths. One of our nation's most prolific and versatile writers, Soto has in the last decade increased his audience with the publication of two children's picture books, two short story collections, four novels and three poetry collections for young readers, as well as three novels. His recently published novel, *Jesse*, chronicles the adventures of two brothers as they make the difficult transition from post-adolescence to early adulthood. By turns hilarious and thrilling, it is one of Soto's most satisfying revelations about a Catholic's relationship with God. *Buried Onions*, released in early 1997, is Soto's most recent work of prose.

Currently at work on a libretto entitled *Nerd-landia*, comissioned by the Los Angeles Opera for a 1998 production, Soto divides his time between writing and producing. Soto is a community activist who founds and supports many educational and cultural programs for Chicano/a youth. Every summer, interested young people from two small towns near Fresno take part in the Coalinga and Huron House Program, for example; they live in a Berkeley fraternity or sorority house and take accelerated high school courses at the university. Soto and others comprise the program's board of directors. Many high school drama students participate in a production of Soto's latest one-act play entitled *Novio Boy*. Introduced to Soto's work in their English classes, other students from all over the country have the opportunity to meet the author when he visits their school for a talk and a reading.

Soto renews his literary spirit and engages a growing readership as he turns his attention from the short story to the essay, from novel to film and drama, and from poetry to prose and then back again. His readers have come to expect a fresh approach with each work as it appears. In this way, Soto constantly updates his concerns and charges them with an ongoing urgency. In the twenty-second year of his career, the persistent themes of Soto's work — poverty, racism and alienation — appear in his work freshly minted with all the gleam of newly polished gold and silver. With the 1995 publication of *New and Selected Poems* — which was nominated for the National Book Award — Soto captures the attention of an ever expanding readership. Soto encourages talented, young emerging writers as he traverses the nation spreading news of their stories — some angry and bitter, all demanding to be heard. At the same time Soto ameliorates some of the pain of his people with his boundless energy; wherever he goes he excites in his audience the promise of a dream deferred — a nationwide Chicano/a community.

Although, at present, Mexican America's literary movement lacks a geographical meeting place, its center resides in the soul of its writers. Along with other members of the Chicano/a literati Soto creates a forum and a focus for their most urgent concerns: the future of a critical discourse, how to make the transition from small ethnic presses into the mainstream, and reaching a more encompassing readership. In the hearts and minds of his colleagues and his readers of all colors, Soto is an ally, an antidote to loneliness and the embodiment of a new era for American multi-ethnic literatures. Soto's voice is the sound of many voices speaking — over the kitchen table, out on the street, in classrooms everywhere — across the borderlands and through the years.

Selected Bibliography

Poetry
Black Hair. Pittsburgh: University of Pittsburgh Press, 1985.
Canto Familiar/Familiar Song. New York: Harcourt Brace Jovanovich, 1995.
The Elements of San Joaquin. Pittsburgh: University of Pittsburgh Press, 1977.
A Fire in My Hands. New York: Scholastic, Inc., 1990.
Home Course in Religion. San Francisco: Chronicle Books, 1991.
Neighborhood Odes. New York: Harcourt, Brace, Jovanovich, 1992.
New and Selected Poems. San Francisco: Chronicle Books, 1995.
The Tale of Sunlight. Pittsburgh: University of Pittsburgh Press, 1978.
Where Sparrows Work Hard. Pittsburgh: University of Pittsburgh Press, 1981.
Who Will Know Us? San Francisco: Chronicle Books, 1990.

Prose
Baseball in April. New York: Harcourt Brace Jovanovich, 1990.
Buried Onions. San Diego: Harcourt Brace, 1997.
Crazy Weekend. New York: Scholastic, Inc., 1995.
Jesse. New York: Harcourt Brace Jovanovich, 1994.
Lesser Evils. Houston: Arte Público Press, 1988.

Living Up the Street. New York: Dell (paperback reissue), 1992.
Local News. New York: Harcourt Brace Jovanovich, 1993.
Pacific Crossing. New York: Harcourt Brace Jovanovich, 1992.
Small Faces. New York: Dell (paperback reissue), 1993.
A Summer Life. New York: Dell (paperback reissue), 1991.
Taking Sides. New York: Harcourt Brace Jovanovich, 1991.

Picture Books
Chato's Kitchen. New York: G. P. Putnam's Sons, 1995.
Old Man and His Door. New York: G. P. Putnam's Sons, 1996.
Too Many Tamales. New York: G. P. Putnam's Sons, 1993.

Anthologies
California Childhood. Berkeley: Creative Arts Book Co., 1988.
Pieces of the Heart: Recent Chicano Fiction. San Francisco: Chronicle Books, 1993.

Secondary Sources

Buckley, Christopher. "Keeping in Touch." *Abraxis* (1978): 16-17.
Cheuse, Alan. "The Voice of the Chicano." *The New York Times Book Review*, October 11, 1981, 15, 36-37.
D'Evelyn, Tom. "Soto's Poetry: Unpretentious Language of the Heart." *Christian Science Monitor*, March 6, 1985, 19-20.
Dunn, Geoffrey. "Central Valley Boys." *San Francisco Review of Books*, 16:1 (Summer 1991): 3-4.
Fields, Alicia. "Small But Telling Moments." *Bloomsbury Review* (January-February 1987): 10.
Klawans, Stuart. "The Small Time." *The Nation*, June 4, 1988, 798-799.
Paredes, Raymund. "Review Essay: Recent Chicano Writing." *Rocky Mountain Review of Language and Literature*, 41:1-2 (1987): 124-128.

David Fine

The Hollywood Novel

oward the end of Nathanael West's *The Day of the Locust* (1939) Tod Hackett, artist-turned-set designer, stands on a sound stage where the film *Waterloo* is being shot. He watches in horror as the extras playing Napoleon's troops storm the unfinished wood and canvas set of Mt. Saint Jean. The hill collapses under their collective weight, dropping the troops to the floor beneath, sending dozens to the hospital. The scene not only foreshadows the novel's apocalyptic ending — a movie premiere riot in front of "Khan's Persian Palace" — but in a bizarre way recapitulates Napoleon's own miscalculation at Waterloo. History and fiction converge in a way wholly unintended by the moviemakers, and the consequence of taking the facade for the reality, the prop for what it represents, is graphically realized. This kind of confusion lies at the center not only of West's novel but the greater number of novels that have taken Hollywood — the place and the industry — as their subject. From the pioneering novels of Harry Leon Wilson (*Merton of the Movies,* 1922) and the Graham brothers (*Queer People,* 1930), through the pivotal 1930s, and up to the present time, novels about Hollywood have turned on a narrative disjunction between reel and real life, local daydreaming and national realities.

The starting point for any discussion of the Hollywood novel is the fact that with the conspicuous exception of the Hollywood-raised Budd Schulberg, its chief creators were outsiders, writers drawn to the film capital in the years following the invention of the sound movies. The

434

Vitaphone created a demand for dialogue — writers who could write it as well as actors who could speak it. And the writers, seduced by Hollywood dreams of steady work and high salaries, poured into the film capital.

One of the early writers who came was Horace McCoy, a newspaper-man from Dallas who arrived in 1931 and whose hard-boiled fiction was soon to brand him with James M. Cain and Raymond Chandler as part of the California tough-guy, boys-in-the-back-room school. McCoy published in the thirties a pair of caustic novels, *They Shoot Horses, Don't They?* (1935) and *I Should Have Stayed Home* (1938), that establish the Hollywood metaphor and map the disjunctive zone of illusion and reality, promise and betrayal. The setting of the first is not Hollywood the town, nor the industry, but a dance marathon contest held in a hall perched at the end of the Santa Monica pier, the contestants a group of desperate Hollywood dream-seekers hoping not only to win prize money but to be discovered by a talent scout.

The marathon is an elaborate deception. On one level it is pure theater — a staged spectacle engineered by its gangster-promoters to draw crowds of thrill seekers — almost a parody of the Hollywood dream factory. On another it is a metaphor for the end of the line and the end of the dream. Dance, traditionally a celebration of life, becomes a rite of death, a *danse macabre* enacted at ocean's edge, the very edge of the continent. There are no celebrants, no winners, no Hollywood contracts, only an abrupt and crashing halt after thirty-seven days, 879 hours of circular movement that is tortuous, exhausting, and ultimately futile. When, at the end, McCoy's lead performers, Robert Syverton and Gloria Beatty, emerge from the dancehall onto the pier, Gloria urges her partner to "pinch-hit for God" and put a bullet in her head. He obliges; after all, they shoot horses, don't they?

I Should Have Stayed Home (1938) is an even blunter account of Hollywood betrayal. The leads again are a pair of young Hollywood dream-seekers, but it is a third character, Dorothy Trotter, who takes on Gloria's nihilistic role, hanging herself in prison when her dream runs out. A news photographer wants a picture of the death instrument, and one of the characters places a fan magazine in the dead girl's hand: the Hollywood publicity network with its small-town-girl-makes-good message is the real death instrument. Set against this lurid melodrama is a cast of minor characters who are an agglomeration of recognizable movieland types, each a consummate and compulsive role player — the homosexual actor, the lesbian screen goddess, the rich nymphomaniac widow, the hard-drinking cynical screenwriter, the tyrannical producer. The most interesting of the characters is a screenwriter named Heinrich who can't find work until he discovers he can attract attention by continually playing the clown at Hollywood parties, jumping into swimming pools fully clothed, swinging from trees, dancing on tables. "So now I'm getting two grand a week," he boasts.

Both novels reveal features that became in the years ahead pervasive in Hollywood fiction: a near-constant display of theatrics and masquerading reaching the point of an almost pathological failure to distinguish living and acting; a sexless, joyless sexuality, commodified and packaged, like the movies themselves, as voyeurism and fetishism; and a downward spiraling of characters, drawn to the Hollywood flame, toward exhaustion and collapse. *I Should Have Stayed Home*, set entirely in Hollywood, is the weaker of the pair, though, a rambling work that moves between sensationalism and farce and lacks the symbolic compression provided by the dance marathon in the earlier work.

West's Hollywood novel, published a year after *I Should Have Stayed Home*, finds its symbolic center on the studio back lot itself—the "dream dump" with its extravagant, exotic facades—and on the surrounding Hollywood landscape, both built and human. Hollywood, the neighborhood, appears as a vast annex to the studio lot, a giant spillover of sets and props. On and off the lot, the line between reality and illusion, living and performing, has all but disappeared. In a dense pattern of imagery linking exotic architectural facades, bizarre costuming, and absurd role-playing, West has given us the blackest of comedies about a place that has become, with the coming of the movies, the epicenter of an entire culture cheated and robbed by the puerile fantasies of the dream factory. *The Day of the Locust* is not only the severest indictment we have of the Hollywood dream, but the most far-reaching in its implications for American culture. More relentlessly than any other Hollywood novel, West's short book, hardly more than a novella, pursued the limits of the metaphor, traced the connections between studio-produced and national fantasies.

Fantasy assumes architectural form in the novel. The built landscape, projection of the collective dream of abrogating, denying past time by domesticating and commercializing it, is an outcropping of derivative styles drawn from all of history and geography. In the opening chapter Hackett walks home at dusk through a canyon lined with houses of every imaginable design, and the Yale-trained artist derisively concludes that only dynamite would be of any use against the Mexican, Samoan, Mediterranean, Egyptian, Japanese, Swiss, and Tudor designs that crowd the canyon. Each of the major characters lives behind a facade. Hackett's apartment building is a plain stucco box, its front overlaid with Moorish-Turkish garnish; screenwriter Claude Estee lives in a Mississippi-style plantation house, Homer Simpson in an "Irish" cottage complete with fake thatched roof.[1]

Such masquerades are the externalizations, the spatial projections, of the compulsive role-playing of the characters. Would-be starlet Faye Greener lives each day as if she were in a costumed movie. Her father, an ex-slapstick "fall guy," suffers, or feigns, a heart attack, plays it to its dramatic hilt, then dies. Claude Estee saunters back and forth on his plantation veranda, calls to his "black varmint" for a mint julep and gets the scotch and soda he really wants from his Chinese servant. Living and performing have become one and the same. Masquerade is the only reality West's characters know. In such a place even the natural world is pictured in terms of the unnatural, the man-made, the movie-made. The edges of trees at dusk are "a violet piping, like a Neon tube." The sky appears as a "blue serge sky" in which the moon pokes through "like an enormous bone button." What such images suggest is the sense of an organic world that has been corrupted and preempted by the materialistic and inorganic, a world from which we stand twice removed. It is the landscape of cinema, produced by technical skill, by well-placed props and effective lighting. And as such it defines the place where living and acting are indistinguishable.

And while the performers play out their roles, the "cheated" — all those tired, sexually titillated and frustrated midwesterners, for whom oranges and sunshine can no longer be enough — stare with resentment and burn with rage until their anger flares into collective violence in the final riot scene, actualizing the painting Hackett has been working on, "The Burning of Los Angeles." The extras, the cast of thousands, the bit players without speaking parts, become in West's final reel, the lead performers and tear the Hollywood props down. It is one of the most devastating endings in American fiction.

This same kind of masquerading recurs in the novels of West's Hollywood contemporaries, Aldous Huxley, F. Scott Fitzgerald, and Budd Schulberg. Huxley's *After Many a Summer Dies the Swan*, published in 1939, outstrips even West's contemporaneous novel in its use of architectural masquerades as metaphor for Hollywood illusion and confusion. The most extravagant of the structures is a castle, perched on top of the Hollywood Hills and owned by a decaying old millionaire, Jo Stoyte, who is dedicated to the proposition of living forever. Gothic with a vengeance, the castle presents the illusion that time can be held at bay. Stoyte also owns the exotic cemetery, "Beverly Pantheon," another emblem of the Hollywood version of immortality. Anticipating here his countryman Evelyn Waugh's fixation on cemeteries and the death industry in *The Loved One* (1948), Huxley renders the Hollywood cemetery (modeled by both writers on Forest Lawn) as a tribute not to the victory of heaven over earth, but the very opposite: the triumph of "the well-fed body, forever youthful, immortally athletic, indefatigably sexy." (12) This is the promise of Hollywood: the denial of age and mortality, the suspension of time and history. The grounds of the cemetery contain not only such Greco-Roman masquerades as the "Pantheon," but a collection of nude "Greek" statues, "all exuberantly nubile." The vast playground is dedicated to a heaven which promises everlasting sex, tennis, and swimming.

Near the beginning of his Hollywood novel *The Last Tycoon* Fitzgerald presents a scene that offers a similar prospect, here a case of mistaken identity that launches the plot and evokes the illusion of the suspension of time, history, and mortality. Producer Monroe Stahr, surveying the flood damage on the studio lot following an earthquake, encounters the illusion of his dead wife floating on the severed plaster head of the goddess Siva. For Stahr it is the illusion not that one can live forever, but that one can, Gatsby-like, recapture the past, become again, for a time, what one once was.

This studio mirage aside, Fitzgerald made little use of Hollywood's built landscape in the novel (surprising, perhaps, given the preoccupation with architectural masquerades in *The Great Gatsby*). In part this was because Fitzgerald chose a narrator, Cecilia Brady, who unlike either Nick Carraway, West's Tod Hackett, or Huxley's British narrator Jeremy Pordage, is an insider, daughter of a studio head (Valentino, she tells us, had come to her fifth birthday party). It is also because Fitzgerald's subject is not Hollywood the place, but Hollywood the industry, the making of movies at a particular time in their history. "My father," Cecilia writes, "was in the picture business the way another man might be in cotton and steel, and I took it tranquilly" (3).

Cecilia's patched-together story of the fall of producer Monroe Stahr (MGM's "boy wonder" Irving Thalberg) is the nostalgic story of the end of the line for the powerful, individualistic American moviemaker, the man who has served both art and commerce. Stahr, benevolent despot of the studio, is dragged down by forces that are both personal and industrial. Worn out by his futile love affair with the woman he took for his wife, and trapped between capitalistic studio power (eastern money interests and their studio allies) and the rise of a collectivized work force (the founding of a writers' guild), Stahr sinks downward toward total exhaustion.

The fall of a Monroe Stahr portends the rise of a Sammy Glick, the Hollywood tycoon as wheeler-dealer. In this sense Budd Schulberg in *What Makes Sammy Run?* (1941) takes over in his first novel where Fitzgerald ends in his last.[2] The benevolent despot of the studio, the man who was willing to make a good movie even when it didn't repay its budget, surrenders to the slick operator, the Hollywood hustler, whose rise to studio head comes about through a combination of plagiarism, deception, and sheer *chutzpa*. Schulberg, who grew up in Hollywood, the son of Paramount head B.P. Schulberg, tells the story, with a mixture of awe and contempt, from the point of view of Al Manheim, a New York newspaper columnist who comes to Hollywood as screenwriter. Instead of the outsider (Fitzgerald) telling his story from the perspective of an insider (Cecilia), we have in Schulberg the insider choosing an outsider as narrator.

The perspective allows Schulberg to expose Hollywood—and Glick, as its success model—as corrupt parody of the American Dream, an industry that celebrates and rewards image over substance, the self-constructed image of a Glick above real ability and talent. The barbarians have taken over the palace, and there is little place left for the honest craftsman. Sammy is what Hollywood has become. Manheim spends much of his narrative trying to answer the question posed by the novel's title. Sammy, he discovers, is running from the poverty of his East European immigrant Jewish childhood; history, personal and cultural, is simply a hurdle to jump. Schulberg, who was attacked (as Philip Roth was later) for his portrait of the unsavory Jew, manages to deflect some of the criticism by putting three other Jews in the novel, all sympathetic figures: Manheim, the novel's liberal, moral register; Julian Blumberg, the ghostwriter whose brains Sammy ruthlessly exploits; and the producer Sidney Fineman whom Sammy replaces as head of World Wide Pictures. Fineman is a Stahr-like figure, a man who wanted to make good pictures but is thoroughly worn down by his rivals. Sammy's rise is both made possible by, and measured against, the fall of Fineman and the victimization of Blumberg. Still another character who represents the defeat of energy and ability in Hollywood is Henry Powell Turner, a Pulitzer Prize-winning writer, reduced in Hollywood to an alcoholic hack.

Both *The Last Tycoon* and *What Makes Sammy Run?* offer the fable of Hollywood in decline from its Golden Age. A fall, though, assumes a previous height, and one has to ask whether, in Hollywood's history, there ever was such a time. Moviemaking has always been a commercial venture, and if real geniuses, real artists, did come along — a Griffith, a Chaplin, a Keaton, even a Thalberg — they were never part of the original thinking. Writing at the end of the Depression decade, Fitzgerald and Schulberg imposed their own, and the culture's, anxieties on Hollywood. Hollywood is both metaphor and scapegoat.

In the years after the war, as the studio system began its long unraveling and as independent productions were on the rise, Hollywood became in fiction, as in fact, less and less a geographic place. Hollywood was everywhere, everywhere that movies were made and moviemakers congregated. Peter Viertel's *White Hunter, Black Heart* (1953), an acidic *roman a clef* about John Huston and the making of *The African Queen*, was set on that continent; Norman Mailer's portrait of the movie colony, *The Deer Park* (1955) was set closer to home in a Southern California resort called Desert D'Or, a thinly disguised Palm Springs. And Rudolph Wurlitzer's *Slow Fade* (1984) takes place all over North America — Mexico and New Mexico, New York and Newfoundland — with a subplot in India.

Displaced, the Hollywood novel continued to reveal the same confusion between reality and masquerade. The built landscape in Mailer's novel is, like West's Hollywood, pure deception; everything is disguised to look like something else. Bars, where most of the action takes place, look like jungles, grottoes, or theater lobbies. With their false ceilings, irregular shapes, and garish colors, they distort the sense of both space and time.[3] Sergius O'Shaughnessy, the narrator, says of one bar, "Drinking in that atmosphere, I never knew whether it was night or day, and I think that kind of uncertainty got into everybody's conversation" (3). The movie people in the novel exhibit the same kind of confusion. Lulu Myers, the star of Supreme Pictures, is another version of the madonna/whore/love goddess blend, a Faye Greener who has made it big. Lulu, who has a penchant for making love while she speaks on the telephone, is engaged to leading man Teddy Pope, a closeted homosexual — a match urged by Herman Teppis, the tyrannical studio head, for its star-appeal publicity value. In a scene that recalls Cecilia Brady in *The Last Tycoon* coming upon a naked secretary tumbling out of her father's executive closet, Teppis lectures Lulu on purity, then has a prostitute delivered to his office.

In Wurlitzer's novel, *Slow Fade*, the movie/life confusion is set up in the beginning when rock band promoter A.D. Ballou wanders on horseback onto a movie set in the New Mexico desert and is struck by an Apache arrow. Ballou is then hired by the film's aging, grizzly director Wesley Hardin (a blend of John Huston and Howard Hawks) to co-write with Hardin's son Walker a script about his (Wesley's) daughter's disappearance in India — an attempt not to make a movie at all, but to find out what happened to the daughter and what has made Walker nearly catatonic. The novel intercuts sections of that emerging script with the story of Hardin's failed heroic and manic attempt to make one last western. The clear, precise imagery of the script is set sharply against the confused narrative of the fall of a once-powerful director, a narrative that itself becomes a movie when Ballou rolls the camera on Hardin's real-life collapse.

Slow Fade is another in the line of stories about the fall of a powerful moviemaker, but with a difference. Hardin is a director, not a producer or studio mogul. The old studio system that West, Fitzgerald, and Schulberg wrote about is gone, and with it, both the old antagonism between writer and producer, craftsman and mogul, and the place called Hollywood itself, the neon and nutburger zone that externalized a state of mind. Hollywood has become the world and the world Hollywood. What remains is the metaphor, which has been the most real, the most substantial thing about Hollywood since the beginning.

Notes

1. The modernist architect Richard Neutra wrote in 1941, "Motion pictures have undoubtedly confused architectural tastes," and went on to cite such structures in 1930s L.A. as "Half-timber English peasant cottages, French provincial and 'mission-bell'-type adobes, Arabian minarets, Georgian mansions on 50-by-120-foot lots, with 'Mexican Ranchos' adjoining on lots of the same size" ("Homes and Housing," in George W. Robbins and Leon D. Tilton, eds., *Los Angeles: Preface to a Master Plan* [Los Angeles: Pacific Southwest Academy, 1941, p. 196]). Whether motion pictures influenced the architectural landscape or vice versa is debatable. The fact that so many of the architects worked as set designers in the studios argues a reciprocal relationship.

2. Schulberg worked with Fitzgerald on a film about the Dartmouth Winter Carnival, which Schulberg later wrote about in a novel, *The Disenchanted* (1950). Both worked on their Hollywood novels at the same time. Fitzgerald's, uncompleted at his death in December 1940, was brought out by Edmund Wilson the next year.

3. This kind of spatial/temporal confusion is a recurring motif in Los Angeles fiction. See, for instance, Allison Lurie's *The Nowhere City* and Joan Didion's *Play It As It Lays*.

Selected Bibliography

Fiction

Fenton, Frank. *A Place in the Sun*. New York: Random House, 1942.

Fitzgerald, F. Scott. *The Last Tycoon*. New York: Charles Scribner's Sons, 1941.

Graham, Carroll and Garrett Graham. *Queer People*. 1930; rpt., Carbondale: Southern Illinois University Press, 1976.

Huxley, Aldous. *After Many a Summer Dies the Swan*. New York: Harper & Row, 1939.

Mailer, Norman. *The Deer Park*. New York: G.P. Putnam's Sons, 1955.

McCoy, Horace. *They Shoot Horses, Don't They?* New York: Simon & Schuster, 1935.

———. *I Should Have Stayed Home*. New York: A. A. Knopf, 1938.

O'Hara, John. *Hope of Heaven*. New York: Faber and Faber, 1938.

Schulberg, Budd. *What Makes Sammy Run?* New York: Random House, 1941.

———. *The Disenchanted*. New York: Random House, 1950.

Viertel, Peter. *White Hunter, Black Heart*. New York: Doubleday, 1953.

Waugh, Evelyn. *The Loved One*. Boston: Little, Brown, 1948.

West, Nathanael. *The Day of the Locust*. 1939; rpt., New York: New American Library, 1983.

Wilson, Harry Leon. *Merton of the Movies*. New York: Grossett and Dunlap, 1922.

Wurlitzer, Rudolph. *Slow Fade*. New York: A. A. Knopf, 1984.

Secondary Sources

Dardis, Tom. *Some Time in the Sun*. New York: Charles Scribner's Sons, 1976.

Fine, David. "Landscape of Fantasy: Nathanael West and L.A. Architecture of the Thirties." *Itinerary*, 7 (1978): 49-62.

———, ed. *Los Angeles in Fiction: A Collection of Original Critical Essays*. Albuquerque: University of New Mexico Press, 1984. See especially, David Fine, "Beginning in the Thirties: the L.A. Fiction of James M. Cain and Horace McCoy," 43-66; Gerald Locklin, "The Day of the Painter; the Death of the Cock," 67-84; Mark Royden Winchell, "Fantasy Seen: Hollywood Fiction Since West," 147-168; and Walter Wells, "Aldous Huxley and Evelyn Waugh in Hollywood," 169-188.

Fox, Terry Curtis. "The Hollywood Novel." *Film Comment*, April 1985, 7-12.

Galloway, David. "Nathanael West's 'Dream Dump.'" *Critique*, 6 (Winter 1963-1964): 46-64.

See, Carolyn. "The Hollywood Novel: The American Dream Cheat." In *Tough Guy Writers of the Thirties*, David Madden, ed. Carbondale: Southern Illinois University Press, 1968.

———. *The Hollywood Novel: A Partial Bibliography*. Boston: Faxan, 1966.

Spatz, Jonas. *Hollywood Fiction: Some Versions of the American Myth*. The Hague: Mouton, 1969.

Ward, J. A. "The Hollywood Metaphor: The Marx Brothers, S. J. Perlman, and

Nathanael West." In *S. J. Perlman: Critical Essays*, Stephen Gale, ed.. New York: Garland, 1992.

Wells, Walter. *Tycoons and Locusts: A Regional Look at Hollywood Fiction in the 1930s*. Carbondale: Southern Illinois University Press, 1973.

Widmer, Kingsley. "The Hollywood Image," *Coastlines*, 6 (Fall 1961): 17-27.

———. "The Last Masquerade: The Day of the Locust." In *Nathanael West: The Cheaters and the Cheated*, David Madden, ed. Deland, Florida: Everett/Edwards, 1973.

Paul Skenazy

The California Detective Novel

California detective fiction has many antecedents but no direct precedents. It began in the 1920s in popular magazines and, in the hands of Dashiell Hammett and Raymond Chandler, soon became synonymous with the so-called hardboiled or tough guy school of detective writing. Their notable successors, like Kenneth Millar (who wrote under the pseudonym Ross Macdonald), James Ellroy, Joseph Hansen, Sue Grafton and Walter Mosley, have since modified the form, but the generic iconography of these works, and their intimate links to the California landscape, have remained consistent.

In 1923, Samuel Dashiell Hammett (1894-1961) published his first short story about a nameless San Francisco detective who was an operative of the Continental Detective Agency in *Black Mask*, one of the most famous of what were called "pulps" because they were printed on cheap wood pulp—the cheapest that could hold print—and sold for anywhere from a dime to a quarter to a mass market of readers eager for tales of romance and adventure. Hammett was only one of many writers at the time who were recasting the English detective tradition into American vernacular and altering what was until then a staid and formal puzzle-solving form into a vehicle for the exploration of contemporary urban life.

Black Mask stories featured a new kind of sleuth: a man as eager to use a gun or fists as his brains, fast-talking and sharp-tongued, unemotional to the point of woodenness, and indifferent to the codes of law, morality, and domestic ethics that had dominated English detective fic-

tion to that time. These men were loners: isolates living in small apart-
ments, and almost always self-employed "private eyes." (The term comes
from the logo of the Pinkerton Detective Agency, which featured a large
open eye and the slogan, "We never sleep.") Narrated in the first person,
these tales recounted violent events in a slang that was considered
rough and racy, and seemed to echo the language of 1920s city streets.
As Raymond Chandler suggested in his introduction to *The Simple Art
of Murder* their power came from the "smell of fear which these stories
managed to generate":

> Most of the plots were rather ordinary and most of the characters
> rather primitive types of people...[who] lived in a world gone
> wrong....The law was something to be manipulated for profit and
> power. The streets were dark with something more than night....
> The...demand was for constant action; if you stopped to think
> you were lost. When in doubt have a man come through a door
> with a gun in his hand. This could get to be pretty silly, but some-
> how it didn't seem to matter.

The hardboiled detective story emerged just as the nation itself was
becoming urbanized; the 1920 census was the first in which more
Americans lived in cities than in the countryside. It was also a time when
the Puritan codes that had long ruled public life in America had become
law—the Eighteenth Amendment, for example, banned the sale of
liquor from 1920 to 1933—yet paradoxically those laws were losing force
among the masses of young men and women moving to the cities. World
War I had just ended, providing license for a decade of political oppression alongside immense prosperity, the acceptance of a gangster community in league with authorities to supply liquor, and a populace whose
spendthrift amorality masked a pervasive disillusionment.

Because of Hammett's talents and his location in San Francisco the
hardboiled genre soon became associated with the West Coast. That
association was strengthened over the next decade as more writers created stories and novels: Erle Stanley Gardner, Paul Cain (Peter Ruric),
Raoul Whitfield, Horace McCoy, and, slightly later, Raymond Chandler.
It is hard to say what beyond chance produced this congregation of talent in California at this moment. Certainly the lure of film writing had
something to do with it, and most of the writers besides Hammett
located their work in the Los Angeles area. But circumstance enforced

form to remarkable advantage in the 1920s and 1930s, until the tough-guy genre became a stock-in-trade of California storytelling. For readers, the fantasy vision of Los Angeles as a lush Garden of Eden promising perpetual fulfillment and San Francisco's reputation as an open and corrupt town long since established in gold rush days, encouraged an exoticism that filtered into many of these early tales.

The hardboiled detective novel was a hybrid form; it borrowed motifs from both the tradition of the western and from the naturalistic work of writers like Theodore Dreiser and Frank Norris at the turn of the century. John Cawelti and others have demonstrated the parallels between the tough guy and the classic western hero—the individualistic and idiosyncratic point of view, the pragmatic ethics, bachelorhood and a lack of personal ties, a suspicion of high culture and formal language, the mixture of protective zeal and angry suspicion in relation to women. But this heroism was tested and revised by urban circumstances that echo naturalism's focus on the city as a moral wasteland. The open landscapes (and sense of potential) of the western have been replaced by cities in decay, and frontier hardihood has given way to stories of blackmail and deception.

Though Hammett is justly famous for the way he established his settings by reference to San Francisco streets, the small towns dotting the coastline, and the winds, rains and fog so characteristic of the area, California was not yet a conditioning agent in his early stories and most of the characters seem relatively indifferent to the terrain. Hammett himself shifted the location of his fiction frequently in his brief writing career (he published little of significance after 1934), so much of it was not about California; whatever the setting, he focused his tales less on region than on the links between the underworld of crime and civic authority.

Still, his "Continental Op" stories and two novels, *The Dain Curse* (1929) and *The Maltese Falcon* (1930), were so dense with local reference that scholars have located the street corners, bars and apartment houses he referred to. More important than this use of locale, however, was the framework Hammett employed in the two novels, each of which involved the transplantation of European legend into California. In *The Dain Curse*, that legend was a family mythology of evil which made the young Gabrielle Leggett—heir to the Dane "curse"—feel herself doomed to destroy all those around her. She retreats from this fate into addiction and religious fanaticism. The obsession with blood, drugs, and spiritualism is emblematic of the haunting power of this irrational European legacy that she overcomes only with the help of the Op, who reveals the immediate circumstances behind a series of murders that surround her. The Victorian mansions of San Francisco provide a perfect gothic setting for the dark, brooding history that has been imported to California, leaving events in a deceptive fog that becomes the hallmark climate throughout the saga.

The fog as a suggestive trope for the uncertainty of one's moral and ethical perceptions is even more beautifully conceived in *The Maltese Falcon*, arguably Hammett's greatest creation. From the introduction of the detective, Sam Spade, in the very first paragraph of the novel as someone who "looked rather pleasantly like a blond satan," Hammett establishes a San Francisco in which deception controls names, identities, and most particularly the fate of a "glorious golden falcon encrusted from head to foot with the finest jewels," originally a gift to the Emperor Charles from the Knights of Rhodes in the sixteenth century (Chapters 1, 13). In his essay "The Writer as Detective Hero," Ross Macdonald suggests that the falcon represents "a lost tradition, the great cultures of the Mediterranean past."

Hammett keeps the significance of the falcon uncertain while insisting on its fetishistic hold on the imagination. The statue that is finally unveiled in the last pages is a fake, a lead imitation; whether an original actually exists remains unclear. The legend itself thus might be historically false, but the obsession isn't. In this way the falcon becomes a brilliant device for revealing characters whose lives take on clarity and meaning from the quest. It is Spade's job to maintain his skepticism in the face of the falcon's value.

Hammett established the basic structures of the hardboiled novel — the serial detective, the focus on blackmail, the concentration on warfare within families, the revelations about political corruption. The moral geography of the landscape in Hammett's fiction became more explicit in the work of Raymond Chandler and Ross Macdonald: the pervasive fog and rains a sign of disillusion and ambiguity; California an outpost at the edge of the new world and a proving ground for the faiths of the old. Hammett's books revealed the fragility of all institutional links and assurances, from family to friendship, love to religion. As Raymond Chandler noted in his essay "The Simple Art of Murder":

Hammett wrote ... for people with a sharp aggressive attitude to life. They were not afraid of the seamy side of things; they lived there. Violence did not dismay them; it was right down their street. Hammett gave murder back to the kind of people who commit it for reasons, not just to provide a corpse; and with the means at hand. . . . He put these people down on paper as they were, and he made them talk and think in the language they customarily used for these purposes.

Perhaps most important was Hammett's contribution to the image of the detective as a morally ambiguous hero. In the introduction to the Modern Library edition of *The Maltese Falcon*, Hammett once described Spade as "a hard and shifty fellow, able to take care of himself in any situation, able to get the best of anybody he comes in contact with" (viii-ix). In his ethics, the detective courted nihilism, but he maintained himself through the ceremonies and securities provided by detection as a profession. He was a middleman, a messenger and guide able to enter the homes of the wealthy and talk the talk of the poor, at home with the tactics of the police and the greed of the gangster. But he remained a contradictory and solitary man. Single, poor, disengaged, lonely but proud of, or in, his isolation, he had few outward loyalties. After he rescued Gabrielle Leggett in *The Dain Curse*, her infatuation with the Op gave way to a recognition that he was a "monster. A nice one, an especially nice one to have around when you're in trouble, but a monster just the same" (Chapter 22).

Along with this, the detective was, indeed, a "private eye" — a man able to see through the world's self-deceptions. As the moral center of these fictions, the detective echoed the transcendental "eye/I" of Emerson: the individual attuned to the emblematic significance of life's "clues." This private moral perception allowed the detective to resist the prescriptions and codes of others and instead reconstitute the world in his own terms. Thus, perhaps foremost, the detective was a storyteller, someone who deconstructs the stories of others and then rebuilds them, rearranging the seemingly random events that have occurred during the novel into a coherent or at least cohesive and corrective narrative that recapitulates what happens in a more plausible way.

* * *

Though Erle Stanley Gardner and others had been contributing stories to *Black Mask* from the 1920s on, the detective and crime tales only became a staple of the Los Angeles area in the 1930s, and reflected a Depression world, where Hollywood glamour and wealth appeared alongside poverty, and the enormous growth of Los Angeles created a complex landscape of a centerless city encroaching on the vast surrounding mountains, arid land and orchards. In the years between 1920 and 1960, while the population of San Francisco increased by about thirty percent, Los Angeles changed from a city of almost 570,000 to one of nearly two and a half million residents—nearly a 500 percent increase. (In the 1920s alone, the population of Los Angeles increased by more than 100,000 people a year.)

This meant that Los Angeles was a city with a past swamped by recent growth, with citizens whose sensibilities were nurtured elsewhere (primarily in the Midwest). The migrants were a group seeking a new beginning at continent's end, attracted by a combination of setting and weather, mystique and the promise of jobs.

The most famous of the Los Angeles thrillers concern this newly arrived population. James M. Cain's *The Postman Always Rings Twice* (1934), for example, takes advantage of the geographic and psychological freedom of car and highway in everything from the setting at a gas station to the violence that occurs along deserted mountain and coastal roads. It is a fierce little saga of two down-and-out drifters whose passion for each other reawakens their passion for life. That new life is bought, however, through another man's death, and this paradox dooms their ambitions as it liberates their desires.

Cain's novel set the stage for a tradition of stories that suggested California's seductive capacity to undermine the conventional social compacts of marriage and family in the name of feeling. Cain's own *Double Indemnity* (1936), the *noir* movement in film, and the detective tales of writers like Raymond Chandler (1888-1959) and Ross Macdonald (1915-1983) are examples. Like Hammett, Chandler and Macdonald were California migrants: Hammett was from Baltimore; Chandler, though born in Chicago, was raised in England; Macdonald, born in San Jose, California, moved to Canada as a child and only returned after World War II.

Chandler and Macdonald modified their own experiences to create a mythology of migratory culture in the period from 1930 to 1970. Their characters come to California from the Midwest. What they leave behind, however—a murky event, a crime, a submerged memory—

relentlessly stalks them. Their new lives erupt when these sinful or illegal, unlawful or just shameful past moments threaten to emerge, linking who they are pretending to be to who they once were.

Chandler's and Macdonald's mysteries, then, were always double stories in which two places and two times converged. California became the field on which the past asserted its claims in the present. The people who imagined California as a panacea were forced to recognize their criminal history as their own in the form of blackmail, the enactment of earlier crimes, or other historical visitations. The detective functioned as an intermediary, even medium, who joined past to present.

Hired to rescue his clients, the detective's deeper, more essential job was to discover the ties binding one life and place to others — time represented by geography. Los Angeles was portrayed as an atomized world filled with permanent transients. Neighbors knew each other only to peek or gossip. Respectability had replaced morality, envy substituted for desire. Blackmail (getting the lowdown on someone else) was the new form of intimacy. The detective's job was to penetrate the social fragmentation and reveal the interconnections of personal fear and public violence and greed. The detective proved a singular figure, able to face up to the truths he discovered and force others to do the same.

* * *

With his bicultural early life as a poor American child educated in England where he was dependent upon his well-to-do British relatives, Raymond Chandler's (1888-1959) was a sensibility divided between two centuries and nurtured by two worlds. It was that paradoxical position, both within and outside of the Southern California he chronicled, devoted to American slang and educated in Edwardian usage, that gives the peculiar feel to his writing. His ambition to "raise" the detective form and to see himself as an artist, along with his deep loyalty to the often graceless world of Los Angeles, make for a complex and shifting series of re-creations of Southern California. Detective Philip Marlowe's sometimes tender, sometimes acerbic, always watchful voice proves a perfect vehicle for Chandler's own mixtures of pride and contempt for Los Angeles and for the combination of metaphoric abandon and realistic density that is Chandler's trademark.

The central problem in a Chandler story, as in all mysteries, is that nothing is as it seems. But Chandler's bravura is to add a compensatory pleasure: nothing is ever just what it seems but always suggests some-thing more, something else. Even as Chandler presents the stark, demeaning aspects of his time, he frames his accounts by invoking the chivalric traditions of the past and playfully over-asserts his scenes with extravagant similes. His books bear sorrowful titles like *Farewell, My Lovely* (1940) and *The Long Goodbye* (1953), and feature characters with names like Grayle, Quest, and Knightly. The opening of Chandler's first novel, *The Big Sleep* (1939), sets the stage for this romantic fanfare, as we meet Marlowe below a stained-glass panel in which a "knight in dark armor" struggles in vain to rescue a lady tied to a tree. Later in the story, Marlowe looks at the chess board in his apartment and compares the rules that govern the game with the more human, less functional, laws governing his own moves: "Knights had no meaning in this game. It wasn't a game for knights" (Chapters 1, 24).

This grafting of old traditions to new circumstances is echoed by Chandler's plots, which are constructed as quests: an aging patriarch seeks a missing man who once kept him company; an ex-convict searches for his true love though he hasn't seen her for years; a woman arrives in town to find her sister. These quests, however, replace medieval fulfillment with contemporary perversity: the woman wants to profit from her sibling's fame; the true love is the one who turned her lover over to the police; the missing man was shot by the patriarch's daughter. In the process of discovering these truths, Marlowe unveils a Los Angeles where glamour preys on social inequities, police depart-ments cater to the monied, and the aristocratic families of the commu-nity have decayed into flamboyant clans greedy for power and addicted to gambling and dope. Marlowe's voice turns melancholy as he contem-plates the fate of his hometown in *The Little Sister* (1949): "I used to like this town. . . . Los Angeles was just a big dry sunny place with ugly homes and no style, but goodhearted and peaceful." Now, he says, what once might have become "the Athens of America" resembles "a neon-lighted slum . . . a big hardboiled city with no more personality than a paper cup" (Chapter 26).

Chandler's chronicles of this transformation are fragmentary but definitive. His skill is in the individual scene; even his best works like *The Big Sleep* and *Farewell, My Lovely* never achieve the pacing or formal narrative solidity of *The Maltese Falcon*. But his novels possess a literary density absent from Hammett. Prone to splenetic fits on the one hand and sentimentality on the other, at his best Chandler had a feel for loneliness and a flair for language that he expended for the lowliest and most troubled of his creations. Spotlighting dank rooms and dead-end lives, Chandler took full advantage of the detective story's insistent focus on the seemingly mundane and overlooked to call our attention to the unobserved oddities and casual interactions of the culture.

And he did so through Marlowe, a self-proclaimed "shop-soiled Galahad." In his dissertation on the hardboiled detective tradition, Robert Parker noticed that in California detective fiction, "the crime is the occasion of the story, but the subject of the story is not the detection, but the detective" (8). In "The Simple Art of Murder," Chandler made rather heady claims for his detective as a redemptive agent in a dangerous world: "down these mean streets a man must go who is not himself mean, who is neither tarnished nor afraid." Marlowe struggles to achieve this level of heroism—what in *The High Window* he calls "the justice we dream of but don't find" (Chapter 32); in the process, he becomes a modern incarnation of male principles stymied by his own ideals as much as the scene around him, able to report it all in the most expansive of contemporary California dialects.

* * *

Ross Macdonald saw himself as the inheritor of this distinct and distinctly California tradition. He borrowed his hero's name (Lew Archer) from a Hammett novel, and his own early writing style from Chandler. He moved Archer about 120 miles up the coast from Los Angeles to a small, wealthy town he called Santa Teresa (modeled after Santa Barbara). From his first novel published in 1944 until *The Blue Hammer*, which appeared in 1976, his books and essays bear the suggestive richness (and at times marring self-consciousness) of his own struggles to reclaim California as a homeland and to integrate the multiple dimensions of his background. Macdonald admits that popular fiction affords him "a mask for autobiography." Each of the eighteen novels in his Lew Archer series (begun with *The Moving Target*, 1949) presents a narrative reenactment of the past—frequently a moment associated with the first years of World War II—as a way to chronicle the woes of the late 1940s, 1950s, and 1960s.

Macdonald's distinction was to court a middle ground of craft: more carefully constructed and balanced narratives than Chandler's if less fierce and intense in their verbal range; a more sentimental attachment of detective and world than Hammett. Issues of political corruption that preoccupy Hammett and Chandler gradually give way to a growing interest in adolescent culture in books like *The Zebra-Striped Hearse* (1962). Chandler's focus on the decayed stature of wealthy aristocratic families becomes in Macdonald a psychoanalytic analysis of the nuclear family. Divorced, educated, remorseful, Archer increasingly becomes a surrogate parent, even amateur therapist, to a wayward and maimed adolescent, and his first-person narrative role shifts from cultural guide to function as what Macdonald calls the "mind" of the novel. Perhaps most important, Macdonald extended the form's attention to the land-scape as a moral register of human foible. The tension of constructed world and wild terrain that one saw as early as James M. Cain is trans-formed in Macdonald into a complex exploration of how legacies of per-sonal deceit and denial parallel and encourage environmental misuse. In an early novel exploring family legacies, for example, Macdonald images the past as a skeleton buried beneath the floorboards of a house; in *The Underground Man* (1971), the metaphor of a hidden former life has been expanded into an emblem of the human abuse of nature — a car buried in a forest clearing is uncovered amid a destructive fire which wipes out immense swatches of the wilderness.

* * *

The alternative voices that have emerged since 1970 have all taken their cue from Hammett, Chandler and Macdonald, as well as some of the more subversive and brooding thriller writers who focused on the mind and heart of the criminal and outcast. In James Ellroy's (1948-) "L. A. Quartet" (*The Blue Dahlia, The Big Nowhere, L.A. Confidential, White Jazz*) there is often little to distinguish hero and villain. Ellroy's trademark is a story told by a raging chorus of voices at an unremitting pace. Mind and heart are gone, idea has been converted to action, dia-logue substitutes for description and thought. The interchanges emerge in a clipped shorthand echo of street slang. It's difficult to find prose that's harder, scenes seedier, people more desperate or a city more per-vasively on the make than in the "L. A. Quartet," which makes the clas-sic Southern California writers like Chandler and Macdonald look like Pollyannas. The only discernible note of warmth is an infrequent but unmistakable nostalgia for a tattered ideal that mixes with the gritty vio-lence, the fractured bits of conversation, and the mock news headlines that litter Ellroy's pages. History in these works is less remembered than viscerally represented in a cacophony of desperation. But it is through such intensity that Ellroy has provided glimpses into the dark side of L.A. in the late 1940s and 1950s.

Most of the California mysteries of recent years have been more overt than Ellroy in their homage to the Hammett tradition, maintaining the urban focus, the explorations of social inequity, the tension of institution and individual, and the role of the detective as a mediator and social conscience able to cross cultural boundaries, enact his private code of humane justice, and provide a narrative that will reconstitute a sense of time and order. The best of these works have subverted such presumptions as they have confirmed the resilience of the form itself. With the introduction of detective characters from previously disenfranchised groups in the U.S., the male posturing and muscle-flexing, and the homophobia and misogyny, so frequent in both Hammett and Chandler, have been mocked and undermined. The earliest of these challenges was made by Joseph Hansen (1923-) in his Dave Brandstetter series about a gay insurance investigator, which began with *Fadeout* (1970). As Hansen noted in his essay "Matters Grave and Gay," "homosexuality serves mystery writers as shorthand for all that is repulsive in human form" (117-118); it took two years for Hansen to interest a publisher in his work, a decade more before the books gained broad readership in paperback. Other gay and lesbian detectives now ply the PI trade, including Michael Nava's Henry Rios (*How Town* [1990], *The Hidden Law* [1992]), a criminal lawyer based in Los Angeles whose cases take him across the state while he struggles to maintain links with his HIV-positive lover.

Among women writers, the most popular and consistently interesting has been Sue Grafton (1946-), known for her alphabet series (*A Is for Alibi*, *B Is for Burglar*, and so on) about Kinsey Millhone. Though Grafton admits that she "chose the classic private eye genre because I like playing hardball with the boys," and Millhone has had her shootouts and fistfights over the years, the emphasis in these books is on location, character, and social mores. *A Is for Alibi* (1982) sets the retrospective tone in the opening paragraph: "My name is Kinsey Millhone. I'm a private investigator, licensed by the state of California.... The day before yesterday I killed someone and the fact weighs heavily on my mind.... Aside from the hazards of my profession, my life has always been ordinary, uneventful, and good. Killing someone feels odd to me and I haven't quite sorted it through" (Chapter 1). Events haunt Millhone as they don't seem to haunt her male predecessors, and the recounting is shaded by this tone of self-scrutiny.

Millhone is a straightforward, wise-cracking twice-divorced woman in her thirties (she is aging slowly, about a year every two or three novels) who prefers wine to hard liquor, friendships to one-night love affairs. She maintains a strong local identification with her neighborhood world, runs every morning, lives in a converted garage behind the house of a retired baker, takes her food and drink business to Rosie's bar down the street. She willingly admits to "the latent felon in me," and quickly becomes implicated in the cases she solves — frequently crimes committed years before. Her attempts to piece together a narrative out of the scraps of truth embedded in the lies invariably lead to some invasion of her own world: her home is destroyed, her car wrecked, she discovers unknown relatives.

Kinsey Millhone legitimizes herself by pointing to her investigator's license. Ezekial "Easy" Rawlins, the African American hero of Walter Mosley's (1952-) series on South Central Los Angeles, doesn't have a license and wouldn't qualify for one. A professional without portfolio, Rawlins' legitimacy is his status in the neighborhood as a black homeowner and working stiff. In *White Butterfly* (1992), he describes himself as "a confidential agent who represented people when the law broke down." His career begins haphazardly in the first pages of Mosley's first novel, *Devil in a Blue Dress* (1990), which reads like a recapitulation of the opening of Chandler's *Farewell, My Lovely* fifty years before. A white man enters a bar frequented only by blacks. But this time, instead of viewing the scene through Marlowe, we see the white invasion through Rawlins' black sensibility as he sits over a drink, out of work, short on money, and ready for whatever comes along.

Mosley both confirms the traditional form of the hardboiled novel and reverses its valence. Like Chandler and Macdonald, Mosley's hero guides us through distinct and mutually exclusive worlds. South Central is like a foreign country, an internal colony of white America, complete with its own language, codes of conduct, and frontier. Easy is hired by whites to ferret out information closed to them by race. But what he discovers and how he uses his knowledge are always colored by his sympathies with the blacks who are his neighbors and friends.

The reader is never far from the pressures of power wielded with vain, unquestioning confidence by a white world that hasn't yet learned to doubt its privileged superiority: a bi-racial woman is dangerous to her lover because of his political ambitions; the deaths of three black women are ignored until the white daughter of a prominent citizen dies in similar circumstances; a family can't admit a longstanding affair between a rich white man and his black servant. Easy is caught in the middle, anxious to help others while struggling to protect what little he has.

Like those of his predecessors, Mosley's novels are stories of two times and places; as Mosley himself puts it in an interview with Jean Nathan: "The books are about black migration from the Deep South to Los Angeles and this blue-collar existentialist hero moving through time from the middle of the century to the present." Mosley reconstructs the consequences of those migrations: the achievements of so many blacks and the disintegration of a whole way of life as the initial dreams of a better time wane. As he reveals these lives in *Black Betty*: "There was no logic to the layout of the city. And there were more people every day. Sharecroppers and starlets, migrant Mexicans and insurance salesmen, come to pick over the money tree for a few years before they went back home. But they never went home. The money slipped through their fingers and the easy life weighed them down" (Chapter 4).

It is Mosley's ambition to suggest the forgotten historical legacy of these unrecognized lives. Each novel drops us back into a lost time — 1948 in *Blue Dress*, 1953 in *Red Death* (1991), 1956 in *White Butterfly*, 1961 in *Black Betty* (1994), 1963 in *A Little Yellow Dog*. It is like a high-speed slide show of African American life. We watch the neighborhoods change, watch the kids grow older, watch the racism remain — upfront, overt, unapologetic. Easy serves as historian and citizen, his accounts of others emblematic samplings of the cultural tale, his own life no less representative. He ages from book to book; by *Black Betty* he is a man of forty. He worries about his mortgage, gets in trouble with the IRS, saves money, buys property, marries. He adopts two children, fathers one, watches as his wife leaves him. He coexists with a neighborhood of cronies: his violent but loyal buddy Mouse; Quentin Naylor, the black cop with his polite speech patterns trying to make things work from the inside; the conniving Mofass, who runs Easy's businesses. Easy's role as detective fades imperceptibly into his role as an adoptive father. As he nurtures his abused and silent child, Jesus, back to health and voice, he also gives expression to the silenced culture.

Conscious of his own role from the first, Easy takes comfort in his position; as he describes it in *Devil in a Blue Dress*: "Behind my friendly talk, I was working to find something. Nobody knew what I was up to, and that made me sort of invisible; people thought that they saw me but what they really saw was an illusion of me, something that wasn't real" (128). Invoking the ghost of Ralph Ellison's *Invisible Man*, Mosley points out how detection, like race, can create a shifty security in the blind assumptions of others and creates one more spin on the ghostly spirit of the mysterious detective.

* * *

Asked in an interview with Jim Impoco why he thinks Los Angeles has become such a significant location for detective fiction, Walter Mosley suggested that it was because "it's impossible to know L.A. It's an extremely diffuse and diverse city.... It's a place of hiding. To be able to know a place, it has to at least in some ways want to be known. And L.A. just doesn't want to be known. L.A. is a big secret, which is why it's so good for the genre. "The California detective story has helped expose, if never quite reveal, the hidden life of Los Angeles and, by extension, the Pacific coast—a place people come to, Mosley goes on to say, "with the hope of building not only a new life but a new self." The form has been flexible enough to incorporate a range of voices and faces yet preserve its essential thrust, in which the vernacular uncovering of a world of secrets provides what Ross Macdonald calls a "passport to democracy and freedom."

Dealing in their different ways with issues of displacement, greed, and disillusionment, these writers have reinvented the genre as they have shaped their talents to its requirements. The tough-guy tale that began as popular fiction has now, with the publication of Raymond Chandler's work as part of the Library of America, entered the literary pantheon. Hardboiled California has become a staple of the imagination. However provisional we find the solutions, the pleasures of detection are renewed with each new variation of our regional fantasies.

Selected Bibliography

Bruccoli, Matthew J., and Richard Layman, eds. *Hardboiled Mystery Writers: Raymond Chandler, Dashiell Hammett, Ross Macdonald*. (Dictionary of Literary Biography Documentary Series, Vol. 6). Detroit: Gale, 1989. Biographical documents.

Cawelti, John. *Adventure, Mystery, Romance: Formula Stories as Art and Popular Culture.* Chicago: University of Chicago Press, 1976.

Fine, David, ed. *Los Angeles in Fiction*, Rev. ed. Albuquerque: University of New Mexico Press, 1995. Includes essays on Chandler, Macdonald, James M. Cain, Horace McCoy, and Walter Mosley.

Hamilton, Cynthia S. *Western and Hard-boiled Detective Fiction in America: From High Noon to Midnight.* Iowa City: University of Iowa Press, 1987.

Klein, Kathleen Gregory. *The Woman Detective: Gender and Genre.* Urbana: University of Illinois Press, 1988.

Knight, Stephen. *Form and Ideology in Crime Fiction.* Bloomington: Indiana University Press, 1981.

Macdonald, Ross. *On Crime Writing.* Santa Barbara, California: Capra Press, 1973. Includes the essays "The Writer as Detective Hero" and "Writing *The Galton Case.*"

Madden, David, ed. *Tough Guy Writers of the Thirties.* Carbondale: Southern Illinois University Press, 1968.

Mandel, Ernest. *Delightful Murder: A Social History of the Crime Story.* London: Pluto, 1984.

Margolies, Edward. *Which Way Did He Go?: The Private Eye in Dashiell Hammett, Raymond Chandler, Chester Himes, and Ross Macdonald.* New York: Holmes and Meier, 1982.

Marling, William. *The American Roman Noir: Hammett, Cain, and Chandler.* Athens: University of Georgia Press, 1995.

Parker, Robert B. "The Violent Hero, Wilderness Heritage and Urban Reality: A Study of the Private Eye in the Novels of Dashiell Hammett, Raymond Chandler and Ross Macdonald." Dissertation, Boston University, 1970.

Porter, Dennis. *The Pursuit of Crime: Art and Ideology in Crime Fiction.* New Haven: Yale University Press, 1981.

Roberts, Thomas J. *An Aesthetics of Junk Fiction.* Athens: University of Georgia Press, 1990.

Ruehlmann, William. *Saint with a Gun: The Unlawful American Private Eye.* New York: New York University Press, 1974.

Ruhm, Herbert, ed. *The Hard-Boiled Detective: Stories from Black Mask Magazine, 1920-1951.* New York: Vintage, 1977.

Skenazy, Paul. *The New Wild West: The Urban Mysteries of Dashiell Hammett and Raymond Chandler.* Boise: Boise State University Western Writers Series, 1982.

Raymond Chandler

Chandler, Raymond. 2 vols. Vol. 1: *Stories and Early Novels.* Vol. 2: *Later Novels and Other Writings.* Frank MacShane, ed. New York: The Library of America, 1995.

Chandler, Raymond. *Selected Letters.* Frank MacShane, ed. New York: Columbia University Press, 1981.

Chandler, Raymond. *The Simple Art of Murder.* Boston: Houghton Mifflin, 1950. This collection of Chandler's early stories was divided into two volumes when it was reprinted in paperback: *Trouble Is My Business* (New York: Ballantine, 1972), which includes the "Introduction" and "The Simple Art of Murder."

Durham, Philip. *Down These Mean Streets a Man Must Go: Raymond Chandler's Knight.* Chapel Hill: University of North Carolina Press, 1963.

Gardner, Dorothy and Katherine Sorley Walker, eds. *Raymond Chandler Speaking*. Boston: Houghton Mifflin, 1962; rpt., Berkeley: University of California Press, 1997.

MacShane, Frank. *The Life of Raymond Chandler*. New York: Dutton, 1976.

Marling, William. *Raymond Chandler*. Boston: Twayne, 1986.

Speir, Jerry. *Raymond Chandler*. New York: Ungar, 1981.

Wolfe, Peter. *Something More Than Night: The Case of Raymond Chandler*. Bowling Green, Ohio: Bowling Green University Popular Press, 1985.

Sue Grafton

Johnson, Patricia E. "Sex and Betrayal in the Detective Fiction of Sue Grafton and Sara Paretsky," *Journal of Popular Culture* (Spring, 1994): 97-106.

Dashiell Hammett

Dooley, Dennis. *Dashiell Hammett*. New York: Ungar, 1984.

Fine, David, and Paul Skenazy, eds. *San Francisco in Fiction: Essays in a Regional Literature*. Albuquerque: University of New Mexico Press, 1995.

Gregory, Sinda. *Private Investigations: The Novels of Dashiell Hammett*. Carbondale: Southern Illinois University Press, 1985.

Hammett, Dashiell. "Introduction." In *The Maltese Falcon*. New York: Modern Library, 1934.

Hansen, Joseph. "Matters Grave and Gay." In *Colloquium on Crime*. Robin W. Winks, ed. New York: Scribners, 1986. Pp. 111-126.

Johnson, Diane. *Dashiell Hammett: A Life*. New York: Random House, 1983.

Layman, Richard. *Shadow Man: The Life of Dashiell Hammett*. New York: Harcourt, Brace, 1981.

Marling, William. *Dashiell Hammett*. Boston: Twayne, 1983.

Nolan, William F. *Hammett: A Life at the Edge*. New York: Congdon & Weed, 1983.

Symons, Julian. *Dashiell Hammett*. San Diego: Harcourt Brace, 1985.

Wolfe, Peter. *Beams Falling: The Art of Dashiell Hammett*. Bowling Green, Ohio: Bowling Green University Popular Press, 1980.

Ross Macdonald (Kenneth Millar)

Bruccoli, Matthew Joseph. *Ross Macdonald*. San Diego: Harcourt Brace, 1984.

Milton, John R., ed. "Ross Macdonald." *South Dakota Review* (Spring 1986). Issue devoted to articles and memoirs on Macdonald.

Schopen, Bernard A. *Ross Macdonald*. Boston: Twayne, 1990.

Speir, Jerry. *Ross Macdonald*. New York: Ungar, 1978.

Walter Mosley

George, Lynell. "Walter Mosley's Street Scenes." *Los Angeles Times Magazine*, May 22, 1994, 14-17, 34-35.

Impoco, Jim. "On LA's Mean Streets." *U.S. News & World Report*, 119:8 (August 21, 1995): 55. (Interview with Walter Mosley.)

Mason, Theodore O., Jr., "Walter Mosley's Easy Rawlins: The Detective and Afro-American Fiction." *Kenyon Review* (Fall 1992): 173-183.

Mosley, Walter. "The World of Easy Rawlins," *Los Angeles Times Book Review*, July 14, 1991, 9.

Nathan, Jean. "Easy Writer," *Esquire* (June 1994): 42.

III
The Southwest

Tom Pilkington

The Southwest

What is the Southwest? No two definitions of the region, seemingly, are identical. For Lawrence Clark Powell, in *Books West Southwest*, the Southwest is "the semi-arid land from the Pecos of New Mexico-Texas to the Salinas of California, including deserts, mountains and river valleys, cities and seacoast" (ix). For Mabel Major and T. M. Pearce, in *Southwest Heritage: A Literary History*, the center of gravity shifts considerably eastward; the Southwest, they say, consists of the states of Arkansas, Oklahoma, Texas, New Mexico, and Arizona. Some commentators resort to fanciful methods of map-making. Erna Fergusson, in *Our Southwest*, still a good general introduction to the region, claims the heart of the Southwest lies in a triangle, formed by drawing a line from Fort Worth to Los Angeles to San Antonio, then back to Fort Worth.

Under the circumstances, the only sensible approach is the expansive one advocated by J. Frank Dobie. "The principal areas of the Southwest," he wrote in *Guide to Life and Literature of the Southwest*, "are Arizona, New Mexico, most of Texas, some of Oklahoma, and anything else north, south, east or west that anybody wants to bring in.... Life is fluid, and definitions that would apprehend it must also be" (14). In that spirit, the editors of this supplement have revised the borders of the region. *A Literary History of the American West* proceeds from the assumption that the Southwest comprises the states of Texas,

Oklahoma, New Mexico, and Arizona. In the present volume, Texas is treated as a separate regional entity.

Admittedly, eliminating Texas creates a huge hole in the map of the region, leaving an oddly shaped — even gerrymandered — district stretching from western Arkansas to the California border. Cultural and social homogeneity is hard to find. What can Fort Smith, Arkansas, and Yuma, Arizona, have in common? Not much, except that each has a turbulent frontier history — Yuma with its territorial prison; Fort Smith as the home of Isaac Parker, the infamous hanging judge, and Belle Starr, queen of the outlaws. Historically, Fort Smith is clearly a western town. The problem arises in selecting a sub-region in which to include it. The Southwest seems to make the most sense.

Since the introduction to the Southwest section in *LHAW* was written a decade and a half ago, little has changed — except for the acceleration of change. The region is still a paradox, a land both old and new. One critic speaks of the Southwest as "a unique bitemporal region containing within its boundaries both Indian hogans and urban highrises" (Temple xi). Such extremes cannot but engender a divided culture. On the one hand, environmentalists struggle to preserve the remains of a despoiled wilderness and a demoralized native culture. On the other, developers attempt to expand the boom, to squeeze as many dollars as possible from desert and plain being transmuted into suburb and city.

The developers are winning the battle, of course, and one has the feeling that a transformation of monumental proportions is occurring while nobody notices, not even the region's writers. Certainly, there is an occasional *Milagro Beanfield War* (John Nichols 1974) that makes comic capital from the conflict of tradition and "progress," and now and then someone dissects a modern southwestern city with anger and eloquence, as does Leslie Silko in *Almanac of the Dead: A Novel* (1991). Moreover, a large band of so-called "nature writers," tracing their ancestry back to John C. Van Dyke, Joseph Wood Krutch, and Edward Abbey, reside in the region. Charles Bowden, for example — in *Blue Desert* (1986) and *Frog Mountain Blues* (1987) — and Ann Zwinger — in *Run, River, Run* (1975) and *Desert Country Near the Sea* (1984) — scrutinize the natural order in a desert environment and champion the conservationist cause. But mostly the destruction of the wilderness and the urbanization of the Southwest are subjects that have remained unreported — or, at least, under-reported — in the region's literature. The fire and daring of an Edward Abbey are sorely missed in the Southwest.

Even without Texas, the Southwest has a tradition of spawning talented writers, both immigrant and homegrown. The tradition continues apace. In recent years, fifth-generation Arizona cattleman J. P. S. Brown — in such works as *Jim Kane* (1970), *Pocket Money* (1972), and *Native Born* (1993) — has published a series of excellent westerns. Elizabeth Tallent, in *In Constant Flight* (1983), *Museum Pieces* (1985) and other fiction, peers beneath the glitz of contemporary Santa Fe and, in so doing, has attracted the attention of reviewers on both coasts. Terry McMillan, in her best-selling *Waiting to Exhale* (1992), depicts middle-class African American life in modern-day Phoenix. Linda Hogan, in *Mean Spirit* (1990), has written one of the most talked-about southwestern novels in many years, a work that inspired entire sessions at a recent meeting of the Modern Language Association. Douglas Jones, of Fayetteville, Arkansas, in *The Court Martial of George Armstrong Custer* (1976), *Arrest Sitting Bull* (1977), *Roman* (1986), and many other novels, has crafted superior historical fiction about the West's frontier past.

However, the writers discussed in this section's subsequent chapters are, in this editor's estimation, the most worthy recent southwestern authors. The brief chapter on Edward Abbey is an update to material included in *LHAW*, critiquing the Abbey canon to and beyond his death in 1989. The chapters on Leslie Silko, Rudolfo Anaya, and N. Scott Momaday are also, in a sense, updates; Silko, Anaya, and Momaday, though not the subjects of separate chapters in *LHAW*, were prominently mentioned in that volume. The remaining chapters are given over to writers who were either completely overlooked or barely mentioned in *LHAW*.

Charles Portis, though often considered a southern writer since he hails from Arkansas, is the author of one of the century's classic western novels: *True Grit* (1968), a story best known, unfortunately, by its inferior celluloid version. If he had written nothing else, Portis would deserve attention as an important western writer. The late Ralph Ellison also produced a classic: *Invisible Man* (1952), one of the most distinguished of twentieth-century American novels. Though set in the South and in New York City, *Invisible Man*, as Ellison himself said on many occasions, was profoundly shaped by the author's Oklahoma boyhood and adolescence.

A native of New England and a Tennesseean by upbringing, Cormac McCarthy had already established himself as a leading American literary figure when he moved to El Paso, Texas, in the mid-1970s. McCarthy is treated here as a southwestern rather than a Texas writer since his western fiction — *Blood Meridian* (1985), *All the Pretty Horses* (1992), and *The Crossing* (1994) — roams across the entire Southwest from Texas to California, with lengthy side trips into northern Mexico. Sam Shepard is one of the most popular of recent American playwrights. Since much of his drama is set in the Southwest, Shepard has been designated a southwestern writer, though not a native of the region.

Another immigrant who has made literary hay in the Southwest is John Nichols, for more than two decades a resident of Taos, New Mexico. Using Chamisaville, a thinly disguised Taos, as setting, Nichols' northern New Mexico trilogy — especially *The Milagro Beanfield War* — has reached a large national audience. Simon Ortiz is one of the most talented of contemporary Native American writers. His poetry and fiction deserve more critical attention than they have thus far received, and the chapter that follows is intended as a start to redressing the neglect.

Probably the most striking success story that any southwestern writer has enjoyed in the last decade or so is that of Tony Hillerman. Hillerman's mystery novels, featuring Navajo detectives as protagonists, have become a national craze. Reviewers and literary critics have noted that, in addition to constructing ingenious plots, Hillerman also happens to be an excellent prose stylist. Barbara Kingsolver is yet another southerner who has made her way to the Southwest. A resident of Tucson, Kingsolver, in *The Bean Trees* (1988), *Pigs in Heaven* (1993), and other books, has melded southwestern elements with materials inherited from her southern past to create a unique literary blend.

For over a century, the Southwest has provided refuge and inspiration for artists in a variety of media. One happy by-product of the region's exploding population is that more and more writers appear to be attracted to the area. The majority of these writers, it is hoped, will examine the realities of life in the modern Southwest, rather than fall victim, as so many have in the past, to the bewitching romance of a colorful history and an awe-inspiring landscape.

Selected Bibliography

Balassi, William, John F. Crawford and Annie O. Eysturoy, eds. *This Is About Vision:*

Interviews with Southwestern Writers. Albuquerque: University of New Mexico Press, 1990.

Dobie, J. Frank. *Guide to Life and Literature of the Southwest*, revised edition. Dallas: Southern Methodist University Press, 1952.

Fergusson, Erna. *Our Southwest*. New York: Alfred A. Knopf, 1940.

Francaviglia, Richard, ed. *Essays on the Changing Images of the Southwest*. College Station: Texas A&M University Press, 1994.

Lensink, Judy Nolte, ed. *Old Southwest/New Southwest: Essays on a Region and Its Literature*. Tucson: Tucson Public Library, 1987.

Lewis, Tom. *Storied New Mexico: An Annotated Bibliography of Novels with New Mexico Settings*. Albuquerque: University of New Mexico Press, 1991.

Major, Mabel and T. M. Pearce, eds. *Southwest Heritage: A Literary History*, 3rd edition. Albuquerque: University of New Mexico Press, 1972.

Martin, Russell, ed. *New Writers of the Purple Sage: An Anthology of Contemporary Western Writers*. New York: Penguin, 1992.

Morris, Mary Lee. *Southwestern Fiction 1960-1980: A Classified Bibliography*. Albuquerque: University of New Mexico Press, 1986.

Powell, Lawrence Clark. *Books West Southwest*. Los Angeles: Ward Ritchie Press, 1957.

Temple, Judy Nolte, ed. *Open Spaces, City Places: Contemporary Writers on the Changing Southwest*. Tucson: University of Arizona Press, 1994.

Jan Roush

Tony Hillerman

For over two decades Tony Hillerman has written fast-paced, tightly plotted mysteries about crime on the reservations of the Southwest along with a variety of nonfictional works that also focus on this region. Together, fiction and nonfiction reveal his fascination with the bleak, sparse landscape of his adopted home and his deep admiration for the Navajo culture; pervading all is the notion of *hozho*, the central concept of the Navajo belief system that stresses being in harmony with one's environment.

Using desolate backdrops of sand-swept, sparsely populated land on which to weave stories of murder and intrigue, Hillerman fuses the elements of the traditional western with those of modern detective fiction to create a new genre: anthropological mystery. Though his authorial trademark is to fill each book with vivid anthropological detail, Hillerman nevertheless insists that what he is writing is, after all, entertainment. "My readers," he says, "are buying a mystery, not a tome of anthropology. . . . The name of the game is telling stories; no educational digressions allowed" (*Talking Mysteries* 39).

Entertainment it may be, but over the years he has honed his craft into art. Through the creation of his two main protagonists, Navajo detectives Joe Leaphorn and Jim Chee, along with their female counterparts and a host of memorable minor characters, all operating in a landscape imbued with *hozho*, Hillerman is able to entertain readers without sacrificing a realistic vision of Navajo life, in all its depth and complex-

468

ity. That he is successful is evident in his acceptance by Navajo, as well as Anglo, readers. In *Talking Mysteries*, he tells the story of discussing the works of Native American novelists like Leslie Silko, James Welch, and N. Scott Momaday with a Navajo librarian. "They are artists," he said. "I am a storyteller." And the librarian replied: "Yes. We read them and their books are beautiful. We say, 'Yes, this is us. This is reality.' But it leaves us sad, with no hope. We read of Jim Chee and Joe Leaphorn, and Old Man Tso and Margaret Cigaret, and the Tsossies and Begays and again we say, 'Yes, this is us. But now we win.' Like the stories our grandmother used to tell us, they make us feel good about being Navajos" (43).

Hillerman traces his fascination with the Southwest and its clash of cultures to a chance encounter with the Navajos before he even began his career as a writer. During a sixty-day convalescent furlough after being wounded in World War II, Hillerman was driving a truckload of pipe from Oklahoma City to the Navajo Reservation when about twenty Navajos on horseback crossed the road in front of him on their way to conduct an Enemy Way ritual to cleanse a just-returned serviceman like himself. Obtaining permission to attend the ceremony, he was struck by the concept of cleansing the man from exposure to foreign cultures and restoring him to harmony with his own environment. That scene, which had etched itself in his memory, twenty years later became the catalyst for Hillerman's first book, *The Blessing Way*.

The first three of Hillerman's mysteries set on the 25,000-square-mile Navajo Reservation, *The Blessing Way* (1970), *Dance Hall of the Dead* (1973), and *Listening Woman* (1978), focus on Joe Leaphorn, the older yet surprisingly modern Navajo. The second three — *People of Darkness* (1980), *The Dark Wind* (1982), and *The Ghostway* (1984) — focus on Jim Chee, the younger yet more traditional detective, who aspires to be a *yataali*, a Navajo singer, along with his job as a Navajo tribal policeman. Then beginning with *Skinwalkers* (1986) and continuing through *A Thief of Time* (1988), *Talking God* (1989), *Coyote Waits* (1990), and *Sacred Clowns* (1993), Hillerman brings the two protagonists together.

In his first novel, *The Blessing Way*, Hillerman establishes the milieu that he refines in each succeeding novel. Once he was committed to writing a novel, Hillerman deliberately chose the mystery format because he felt that its 80,000 words would be much easier to write than The Great American Novel at about 250,000 words. Even so, the novel took Hillerman three years to complete. Finally, tired of the entire project, he tacked on a final chapter and sent it off to an agent who had handled some of his nonfiction.

In its original version, although Leaphorn appeared, the major character was an anthropologist, Bergen McKee. But even the relatively brief appearance of Leaphorn with his emphasis on Navajo culture was too much for the agent. Her advice: abandon the project all together or else get rid of the Indian stuff. Fortunately for his fans, Hillerman ignored her advice and sent the manuscript off again, this time to an editor whose advice was to delineate Leaphorn more fully and write a better last chapter; then they would publish it. Hillerman followed this advice and the book was released, receiving enthusiastic reviews about Leaphorn and an honorable mention for Best First Mystery Novel.

In the second novel of the series, *Dance Hall of the Dead*, Leaphorn takes center stage. Not only does his character become more complex, but so, too, does the description of the world in which he operates. This is a world that requires balance and harmony with one's environment, a theme Hillerman continues to refine in the last novel in which Leaphorn appears alone, *Listening Woman*.

At this stage in his writing, Hillerman felt that he could not make the skeptical, sophisticated Leaphorn work with the concept he had for his next novel. He needed instead a protagonist who could still express surprise and curiosity about the Anglo world, someone who was much closer to the traditional Navajo ways; he found him in Jim Chee.

Jim Chee enters Hillerman's novels as a much more fully developed character than Leaphorn had been, an indication of Hillerman's maturation as a novelist. By imbuing Chee with the internal tension of trying to decide between becoming a *yataali*, a traditional Navajo singer whose job it is to restore *hozho* to The People's lives, or an FBI agent whose responsibility is to bring harmony to an essentially Anglo world, Hillerman is able to portray more sharply the external tensions between life on the reservation and the surrounding modern world. He continues to play with these tensions in *The Dark Wind* and *The Ghostway*, the next two novels that feature Chee as the sole protagonist. Then, again, his writing takes a leap forward.

Skinwalkers (1986) is generally considered Hillerman's breakthrough book. This is the novel that won the Spur Award from Western Writers of America. Hillerman's earlier works had already received awards from Mystery Writers of America, and he had an established, appreciative audience there. *Skinwalkers*, which brings Leaphorn and Chee together for the first time, allowed Hillerman to take his writing in a new direction while expanding his audience. With Leaphorn and Chee appearing as dual protagonists in the same book, Hillerman was able simultaneously to develop his characterization more fully and refine his major underlying theme of life, landscape, and the clash of cultures.

Once Hillerman has Leaphorn and Chee appear together, their differing world views gradually merge, moving closer together to bring each more in balance with the Navajo view of harmony with one's environment. To achieve this harmony within his protagonists, Hillerman depends increasingly on fuller characterization, with a resultant slowing of the action. The plots are still complex and finely woven, but they seem slower because of the thicker textualization of the characters, both major and minor.

Almost as important as the protagonists are the female counterparts that Hillerman creates to complement them. Following the paired relationships through the entire series gives the clearest indication of this development in Hillerman's writing. For instance, in the first three novels, Leaphorn remains a fairly flat character; though he has a wife, Emma, she remains a shadowy presence, known only to readers through one brief mention in *The Blessing Way*. Because Chee initially appears as a more fully developed character, Hillerman creates a female counterpart for him immediately: Mary Landon, the blonde, blue-eyed *biligaani* schoolteacher, whom Hillerman uses during all three Chee books to highlight Chee's internal tension as he vacillates between two worlds. That all changes in *Skinwalkers*. By the end of this book, Leaphorn has taken on much more dimension, in large part because Hillerman has also developed Emma's character as a foil for Leaphorn. The same is true of Chee. Because of the inherent problems in his relationship with Mary Landon, however, the conflict that defines his character is more clearly portrayed.

Each succeeding novel since *Skinwalkers* has continued to deepen the characterization of Leaphorn and Chee through their relationships with each other and with their potential mates. I say "potential" because in *Thief of Time* (1988), which follows *Skinwalkers*, readers discover that Emma has died; having Leaphorn a widower allows Hillerman to incorporate a vulnerability and poignancy into his character. The next three novels, *Talking God* (1989), *Coyote Waits* (1990), and *Sacred Clowns* (1993), continue to play on that vulnerability as Leaphorn moves through a gradual healing process into the tentative beginnings of a new relationship.

Where Leaphorn's development reflects a more mature, mellowing process that is almost bittersweet when seen through his relationships with women, Chee's progress, by contrast, is more volatile though it, too, ultimately reflects a mellowing and a movement toward a balanced center. Hillerman achieves this by replacing the sharp contrast between the Anglo world represented by Mary Landon with a more similar yet more modern world view of Janet Pete, a Navajo lawyer who grew up away from the reservation. Nowhere is this mellowing more evident than in *Sacred Clowns*. Here there is an increased use of humor, allowing for a lighter touch with less emphasis on the supernatural. Overall, this novel is more reflective, containing more personal, more romantic scenes. That is not to say, however, that the dramatic descriptions of landscape, the punch of a well-thought-out plot are missing. They are not; they have merely been enhanced.

Two of Hillerman's novels lie outside the oeuvre that has made his name a household word and garnered him numerous awards from such diverse groups as Mystery Writers of America, Western Writers of America, the Department of the Interior, the American Anthropological Association, and the Navajo Nation.

Hillerman's second novel, *Fly on the Wall* (1971), was originally intended to be a novel of character rather than action and to an extent it succeeds in that endeavor largely because it is about a life Hillerman was totally comfortable with, that of a journalist. It is the only one of Hillerman's novels written from a single viewpoint, that of an introspective (hence the title) political reporter, John Cotton, who discovers the highway construction scam on which the plot turns. Though he concedes he has ambiguous feelings about this book since it fell short of what he had intended, Hillerman still counts it among his favorites. The other anomaly among his novels is *The Boy Who Made Dragonfly* (1972), a retelling of a thirteenth-century Zuni myth that Hillerman likens to a Native American equivalent of a Bible story, teaching both history and morality to twentieth-century readers; it is significant in that it addresses the notion that every person is an integral part of a greater system, both the immediate community as well as the larger environment. These same concerns underlie the Navajo sense of *hozho* that lies at the heart of the eleven-book Leaphorn/Chee series.

Hillerman's nonfiction has not received the same critical attention as has his fiction, partially because much of it is scattered among various periodicals — both regional magazines like the *New Mexico Quarterly*,

New Mexico Magazine, and *Arizona Highways* as well as national publications such as *Reader's Digest, The Writer, Audubon, Elle,* and *The New York Times Book Review*—or in other book collections. However, his eight nonfiction books clearly illustrate the same themes of the impact of landscape and the profound admiration for the Navajos who inhabit it that are highlighted in his fiction. Throughout his prolific writing career, Hillerman continues to alternate between the reality of nonfiction and the flexibility of fiction, playing off the possibilities of each medium; yet all of his works are unified by these themes. In his nonfiction, however, landscape remains at the center while the characters themselves take center stage in the novels, especially the later ones.

Has Hillerman, then, succeeded in his aim of having readers develop an awareness of, and respect for, the Navajo culture? I think so. At the same time, his efforts place him firmly within the canon of western American literature for nowhere else in contemporary literature can readers find such a consistent and clearly delineated rendering of the nature of the Southwest and some of its oldest inhabitants in their struggle to obtain *hozho*.

Selected Bibliography

Primary Sources

Hillerman, Tony, ed. *The Best of the West: An Anthology of Classic Writing from the American West*. New York: HarperCollins, 1991.

Hillerman, Tony. *The Blessing Way*. New York: Avon, 1970.

———. *The Boy Who Made Dragonfly*. New York: Harper & Row, 1972.

———. *Coyote Waits*. New York: Harper & Row, 1990.

———. *Dance Hall of the Dead*. New York: Harper & Row, 1973.

———. *The Dark Wind*. New York: Harper & Row, 1982.

———. *The Fallen Man*. New York: HarperCollins, 1996.

———. *Finding Moon*. New York: HarperCollins, 1995.

———. *The Fly on the Wall*. New York: Harper & Row, 1971.

———. *The Ghostway*. New York: Harper & Row, 1984.

———. *The Great Taos Bank Robbery and Other Indian Country Affairs*. Albuquerque: University of New Mexico Press, 1973.

———. *Hillerman Country*. Photography by Barney Hillerman. New York: HarperCollins, 1991.

———. *Indian Country: America's Sacred Land*. Photography by Bela Kalman. Flagstaff: Northland Press, 1987.

———. *Listening Woman*. New York: Harper & Row, 1978.

———. *New Mexico*. Photography by David Muench. Portland: Charles H. Belding, 1974.

————. *People of Darkness*. New York: Harper & Row, 1980.

————. *Rio Grande*. Photography by Robert Reynolds. Portland: Graphic Arts Center Publishing, 1975.

————. *Sacred Clowns*. New York: Harper & Row, 1993.

————. *Skinwalkers*. New York: Harper & Row, 1986.

————. *The Spell of New Mexico*. Albuquerque: University of New Mexico Press, 1976.

————. *Talking God*. New York: Harper & Row, 1989.

Hillerman, Tony and Ernie Bulow. *Talking Mysteries*. Albuquerque: University of New Mexico Press, 1991.

————. *A Thief of Time*. New York: Harper & Row, 1988.

Secondary Sources

Erisman, Fred. *Tony Hillerman*. Boise: Boise State University Western Writers Series, 1989.

Greenberg, Martin, ed. *The Tony Hillerman Companion: A Comprehensive Guide to His Life and Work*. New York: HarperCollins, 1994.

Hieb, Louis A. *Tony Hillerman: From The Blessing Way to Talking God, A Bibliography*. Tucson: Press of the Gigantic Hound, 1990.

Winks, Robin, ed. *Colloquium on Crime: Eleven Renowned Mystery Writers Discuss Their Work*. New York: Charles Scribner's Sons, 1986.

Stephen Tatum

Cormac McCarthy

Before moving from Knoxville, Tennessee, to El Paso, Texas, in 1976, Cormac McCarthy (1933-) was a critically acclaimed but little-read author of three novels about the rural South. In 1979, after publishing his fourth novel, *Suttree*, which had been written over a period of nearly two decades, McCarthy began working solely on his first novel about the southwestern borderlands, focusing on historical events surrounding a band of adventurers who traversed the U.S.-Mexican border in the late 1840s and 1850s in search of Indian scalps to sell for bounty. "I've always been interested in the Southwest," he has said in the only interview he has granted. "There isn't a place in the world you can go where they don't know about cowboys and Indians and the myth of the West."[1]

With the 1985 publication of *Blood Meridian or The Evening Redness in the West*, and the subsequent publication of *All the Pretty Horses* (1992) and *The Crossing* (1994), the first two volumes of "The Border Trilogy," McCarthy has produced a stunningly brilliant and disturbing fictional portrait of borderland history between the late 1840s and the late 1940s, one that both revises the prevailing myths of the American West and challenges several of the reigning ontological and epistemological concepts of the West. His work has garnered several prestigious awards, including a MacArthur Fellowship. While none of his novels prior to *All the Pretty Horses* had sold more than 5,000 hardcover copies, both *All the Pretty Horses* and *The Crossing* were bestsellers, and the former was also given the National Book Award and the National Book Critics Circle Award. Such commercial and critical successes of late, as well as the notoriety that will follow from the impending film production of *All the Pretty Horses* and the eventual publication of the final volume in the border trilogy, have served or will serve to revise the previous labels he has worn as "the best unknown novelist in America" or the "best-kept secret in American letters."[2]

McCarthy's novels about the southwestern borderlands are distinctive in the canon of western American literature, let alone American literature, for the fresh way his characters introduce, as they gather at waterholes and campfires and around tables in kitchens and taverns during breaks in their migrations, compelling and complex narratives on the nature of being in the world. Taken together, his novels thematically forward a vision of the absolute fortuitousness of life, the frightfully ephemeral character of everything in the world, whose soil Billy Parham in *The Crossing* and John Grady Cole in *All the Pretty Horses* at times hold onto "as if to slow the world that was rushing away and seemed to care nothing for the old or the young or rich or poor or dark or pale or he or she" (301), and the irredeemably violent and tragic nature of experience. What counts in McCarthy's fiction is the necessity of confronting the *real*, which is to say the world as it is, as it presents itself rudely and mysteriously and contingently to human consciousness. As Judge Holden argues in *Blood Meridian*, verbal and photographic representations of experience foster lies and illusions, divorce us from the necessary, hard truths provided by a God who "speaks in stones and trees, the bones of things" (116). In McCarthy's work, the "things" of this world are viewed as being sufficient materially unto themselves and, simultaneously, repositories of profound mysteries.[3] Thus ideas or concepts or even place names devised by humans to supplement the world's supposed "lack" are superfluous, signs of a flawed human arrogance. And what any reader familiar with these novels quickly recognizes is how their fresh and compelling power flows largely from the nuanced way McCarthy integrates luminous, finely honed prose descriptions of stones, trees, bones, birds, waterways, and other "things" of the southwestern landscape into his larger narrations about his various characters' linear movements.[4] The result is a body of work whose remarkable power validates the links various critics have drawn between his novels and those of Melville and Faulkner.

In the second section of *The Crossing*, an older man — who lives alone with cats in a ruined adobe church in the village of Huisiachepic in northern Mexico — fixes breakfast for a young American cowboy named Billy Parham, who has entered the village after a solitary mountain sojourn following his doomed effort to return a pregnant wolf he had trapped to her home range. While Parham eats, the man tells him a lengthy story about how his own "seeking evidence for the hand of God in the world" (142) had led him to this isolated place and, as a result, into an intimate acquaintance with the travails of another man who had lost his parents during the Mexican-American War and, later, his son during a terrible earthquake. As Parham listens to the lengthy narration of compelling events and the knotty philosophical and theological issues they entail, he is told that the "truth" of this particular place was inseparable from the *corridos* or tales circulating about this particular long-suffering man, "And like all corridos it ultimately told one story only, for there is only one to tell" (143). Indeed, as the old man tells Parham near the end of his story, any narrator has as his task not that of choosing "his tale from among the many that are possible.... The case is rather to make many of the one" (155).

In his three novels published so far about the Southwest, one can track differences and new developments. *Blood Meridian*, for instance, contains far more violence and a wider range of diction, less dialogue and romance than the border trilogy. Nevertheless, due to the similarities provided by these novels' thematic concerns, their emphasis on the landscape as a figure for such concerns, and their investment in linear plots of adventure, it is fair to say that McCarthy himself provides several variations on the one tale. That tale centers on a youthful protagonist who understands, either instinctively or by force of circumstances, that (to quote from *All the Pretty Horses*) "there was something missing for the world to be right or he right in it..." (23). Whether named "the kid" (*Blood Meridian*), John Grady Cole (*All the Pretty Horses*), or Billy Parham (*The Crossing*), this protagonist undertakes adventures, hoping to find a place where, in critic Vereen Bell's words "it is possible to be one with the earth and to live in genuine human communion."[5] McCarthy metaphorically renders such wanderings after resonance with the natural and human world as a search for stolen horses or for a missing brother, or a journey on horseback in the company of a wolf. Main characters in *All the Pretty Horses* and *The Crossing* initially imagine Mexico exempt from the inexorable modernizing process, and the scalphunters in *Blood Meridian* think it only blank cartographic space open for violent conquest and exploitation. But in the course of their wanderings, which occasion various border crossings, these characters discover that there is no "outside of" or exemption from history. This realization occurs because the events and the individuals whose stories they encounter along the way — as well as the sonorous place names and the inscriptions on the landscape written by the fences, mines, waterholes, campsites, villages, and the roads or paths that loom up before their eyes — both evidence and enact the wheeling changes and the bloody ruptures of human history.

Even if history ultimately cannot be reversed or transcended — even if a John Grady Cole cannot, in the end, relive the ranching pastoral his grandfather knew in Texas by working with horses and cattle on an isolated, sprawling Mexican ranch; even if a Billy Parham cannot safely return the shewolf to the Mexican mountain wilderness and recover his childhood vision of wolves dancing in the snow under the moonlight — McCarthy's novels also dramatize how the truths of history that can't be escaped are both elusive and contingent. As several different storytellers in McCarthy's novels argue — due to the erosion of human memories in time, the fact that there is no human observer who is not simultaneously an invested participant in events, and because of the inherent gap between verbal representations and the world they seek to map — the past regularly invoked to explain the present and to justify future acts turns out to be "always this argument between counterclaimants" (*The Crossing* 411). Thus, the possibility of someone having a full knowledge of the past (and an ability to assess appropriately the authority of such knowledge) seems as likely an occurrence as Orpheus rescuing Eurydice. Indeed, uncertainty about the truths of the past — imaged in the border trilogy by characters searching for the *facturas* establishing ownership of horses or arguing about the sequence of events that has caused a wolf to appear before them — propels the narrative trajectory of McCarthy's novels forward.

As the burgeoning portraits of human and natural artifacts compiled by the Judge in *Blood Meridian* and as the opera glasses deployed by a prima donna to create an ocular ground containing the countryside and the departing forms of the Parham brothers on horseback in *The Crossing* suggest, humans in McCarthy's novels strive rationally to order the world with their actions and beliefs, their languages, genealogies, maps, and nomenclatures — and their rituals involving blood and sacrifices. But as the Judge tells Captain Glanton's men during a fireside colloquy in *Blood Meridian*, "existence has its own order and that no man's mind can compass, that mind itself being but a fact among others" (245). If humans could see it right, according to the Judge, they would see it "for what it is, a hat trick in a medicine show, a fevered dream, a trance bepopulate with chimeras having neither analogue nor precedent, an itinerant carnival, a migratory tentshow whose ultimate destination after many a pitch in many a mudded field is unspeakable and calamitous beyond reckoning" (245).[6]

Although humans devise and rely on philosophies which mediate the raw experience of the world, the problem, as Billy Parham is told by an old Mexican whom he consults about the right scent for trapping wolves, is that "Between their acts and ceremonies lies the world and in this world the storms blow and the trees twist in the wind and all the animals that God has made go to and fro yet this world men do not see" (46). However much his principal characters search for a certain ground or foundation, desire for their wishes and the things the world provides at hand to be in agreement (as they are said to be for horses and wolves prior to the advent of humans in their lives), McCarthy portrays them essentially occupying and repeatedly traversing a liminal world "between."[7] In his recent fictions this world "between" typically appears as a high desert floor containing *playas* and cracked earth and ringed by mountains, whose rocky outcroppings yet disclose a narrow pass leading over a divide and down into a verdant valley bisected by rivers and oak or cottonwood groves.

McCarthy fashions this evocative topography into a felt "world" said to be both lying in wait and not truly seen by humans as a result of death's presence. Death is manifest not only in his novels' recurrent, graphic depictions of violent death (which have led some reviewers to compare his work with that of filmmaker Sam Peckinpah) but also, for instance, in the novels' recurrent symbolic motif of a blood-red sun setting in the west, its fading light highlighting not only the reefs of clouds overhead but also the human forms and the tracks left by riders who pass or who have passed before its slanting light. From the perspective that all histories and remembrances are incomplete, McCarthy's novels, like the *corrido* described by a Yaqui Indian ranch foreman in *The Crossing*, demonstrate their fundamental allegiance not "to the truths of history but to the truths of men. . . . It [the *corrido*] believes that where two men meet one of two things can occur and nothing else. In the one case a lie is born and in the other death" (386). "That sounds like death is the truth," responds Billy Parham, and the affirmative response he receives to this remark underlies the conviction he hears earlier in the novel that "the wolf is a being of great order and that it knows what men do not: that there is no order in the world save that which death has put there" (45).

It is an implacable, ruthlessly determining world, to be sure, as scene after scene in McCarthy's novels dramatize. It can be said his work thematically furthers the tradition of American literary naturalism descending (to select western American exemplars) from Frank Norris down to James Ellroy. But the further point must be made that a world imagined to be "ruthless in selecting" and "lying in wait" is also, as McCarthy's participial grammar suggests, a *performative* world, a world in creation as well as having been created, a transient world in which, according to the Judge in *Blood Meridian*, "anything is possible." This world of possibility exists amidst the constraints posed by death's chancy presence, the limits posed by a landscape's matrix of elements, and the governance established by the human evolutionary heritage of the blood and instincts. This nevertheless "open" world is beautifully rendered through one of McCarthy's trademark syntactical strategies: his serial presentation of sentence fragments introduced by the subjunctive expression "as if," each fragment provisionally venturing a different interpretation of whatever action inaugurated the sequence. In McCarthy's lyrical choreography, uprooted humans and animals surely encounter the truth that calamitous death occurs frequently and without warning or logic, and that, as the Judge says, the world is ultimately "beyond reckoning."

But another truth, according to the *corridos*, is that "lies" are born. In McCarthy's southwestern novels "lies" connotes both the legendary songs sung in the wake of a Boyd Parham's ill-fated romance and resistance to the countryside's *patrons*, and, more abstractly, various human self-delusions involving what we might call existential "bad faith"—such as the denial that the destination of all voyages is the "unspeakable" one of death; and the refusal to see how the natural world which exists "between" human acts and ceremonies establishes an absolutely democratic, and hence ecological, order in which, regardless of human intentions and desires, "the right and godmade sun" rises every day "for all and without distinctions" (*The Crossing* 425). Still another possible connotation of "lies" brings us to one of the distinctive aspects of McCarthy's fiction: the narratives told by his successive narrator-characters in the novels about the swelling mysteries regarding who we are and how we should be in the world. In McCarthy's novels "All is telling" (155), as a character says in *The Crossing*, and the accumulating stories told about southwestern borderland history between the late 1840s and the late 1940s function, again like the *corridos*, in two ways: they disrupt the myths of mastery forwarded by the histories and theologies of those with power; they work to prevent the sum of some people's lives from being "lost to all history and all remembrance" (*Pretty Horses* 5).

Storytelling in McCarthy's novels, however, unlike the *corridos* represented as providing the "truths of men," strenuously displays a *dialectical* rather than a binary either-or logic: that is, "lies" or stories wittingly or unwittingly are shown to produce human deaths; human deaths inevitably spawn the "lies" or stories, which, as McCarthy typically presents them in indirect discourse form, have as their significant burden from the beginning a Nietzschean interest in gauging just how much truth a human spirit will dare, much less will endure, in the making of a difficult living in the world.[8] In the stories told to and about John Grady Cole, Billy and Boyd Parham, and the assorted cast of adventurers led by John Glanton and Judge Holden in *Blood Meridian*, we come to know that what one dares to risk in order for the world to be right or for one to be right in it, for however brief a time, discloses what one values at bottom; coming into contact with what one values is coterminous with discovering the true grounds of one's being, however benighted that being might be. Yet as McCarthy's dialectical logic would have it, a man's constantly becoming or coming into something *real* as a result of his immersion in the human history of blood and greed leads to his chastening: thus his spirit's "noon of expression" or "peak of achievement" should be seen as a "meridian" which is "at once his darkening and the evening of his day" (*Blood Meridian* 146-147).

What may not be so obvious but is nevertheless crucial to understanding McCarthy's fiction is that, as a character says in *The Crossing*,

> "Things separate from their stories have no meaning. They are only shapes. Of a certain size and color. A certain weight. When their meaning has become lost to us they no longer have even a name. The story on the other hand can never be lost from its place in the world for it is that place" (142-143).

Just as the above remarks about the importance of "telling" in his novels have implied, the explicit equation here of "story" and "place" — an equation structurally speaking analogous to the Judge's equation of God's spoken words and the material things of his creation — reminds us that McCarthy's borderland is a topography scrupulously constructed through verbal performances in stories and songs. Moreover, the assertion that "things separate from their stories have no meaning" reminds us that in McCarthy's work the space of representation carved out by stories about "the bones of things" and their encounters with humans is precisely the place where things are located, is the *exact* location of the real.[9] McCarthy's fiction, in its relentless preoccupation with the question of being, significantly advances the notion of being-in-the-world as a being that is completely present at every moment in its own appearing. What appears before humans in plain sight is not opposed to and does not veil profundity and reality, in other words, but rather evidences the very profundity of reality. This is why the prima donna in *The Crossing* tells Billy Parham that "The shape of the road is the road. There is not some other road that wears that shape but only the one" (230); and why he says, not improbably, near the end of the novel that "whether a man's life was writ in a book someplace or whether it took its form day by day was one and the same for it had but one reality and that was the living of it" (379-380).

Such quotations allow us to understand the accuracy of Steven Shaviro's assertion, in his reading of *Blood Meridian*, that McCarthy's epistemology is a "radical" one intent on subverting "all dualisms of subject and object, inside and outside, will and representation or being and interpretation."[10] As a result of this resistance to the traditional philosophical oppositions of surface/depth, appearance/reality, and copy/model, his fiction implicitly and explicitly critiques not only those characters who "believe that people can be improved in character by reason" (*Pretty Horses* 146), but also those characters who nostalgically engage in metaphysical speculations in search of a supposedly more profound reality lurking behind, beneath, or above the surface appearances of a world. The Judge declares, for example, to his auditors around a campfire that "Your heart's desire is to be told some mystery. The mystery is that there is no mystery" (*Blood Meridian* 252). The dense matrix created by the interactions of humans, animals, and the landscape does not lead to some higher truth beyond or external to the here and now, because in McCarthy's fiction the "seams" or the principle of "joinery" that holds creation together has been and always is hidden from us (*The*

Crossing 143). The characters and the stories they tell trace and retrace lines across the landscape's surface, these crossings seemingly impelled by a life force McCarthy usually identifies simply as "blood." But the true ground sought after in whatever manifest form remains elusive, both everywhere and nowhere, out of reach from where anyone is, impossible to hold even when it is in one's grasp — as John Grady Cole discovers in the wake of his moonlight swim with Alejandra; as Billy discovers when he holds the head of the dead wolf or the bones of his brother in his hands.[11]

Here we should consider the importance of the open gravesite in McCarthy's fiction, particularly the initial burial site in Mexico of Boyd Parham's bones, as a figure for a landscape where surface and depth bleed together and become indistinguishable and whose contours are overdetermined by an absent and, finally, unattainable presence.

* * *

Whereas some western American writers dramatize how dwelling in the world in a certain way can eventually bring us into coincidence with the center of our beings and hence into coincidence with the external world, for McCarthy the things, animals, and people lit by the sun and backlit by the moon are ultimately signs of non-presence. As the endings of his novels indicate — John Grady Cole alone on horseback passing before a setting sun; Billy Parham this time holding his face in his hands and weeping while he sits on an empty road as the sun rises — for McCarthy the trajectory of human affairs courses towards isolation and exile, not towards reconciliation and the forging of a community. As an old mozo tells John Grady Cole at the end of his discourse on the souls of horses, "among men there was no such communion as among horses and the notion that men can be understood at all was probably an illusion" (*Pretty Horses* 111). Given this fundamental estrangement between humans, given the world's indifference to providing ontological certainties, and given the catalogue of brutalities and atrocities McCarthy's novels graphically present, his work offers the most powerful and yet troubling reading experience in the canon of western American literature. At the same time, readers must recognize the sustained imaginative power, understated humor, and sheer lyrical quality of his prose, they must also consider whether his frank recognition of the brutal nature of the real monotonously promotes a bleakly pessimistic outlook, whether it is possible for extended scenes of loss and suffering to be transformed into an affirmative experience instead of narrowly and obsessively making, as one reviewer has negatively remarked, "enduring at whatever physical or spiritual cost an end in itself."[12]

Certainly reviewers and critics commenting on McCarthy's work have already begun to introduce these (and other) concerns. For his part, McCarthy in an interview has stated that the "good" writers — he includes Melville, Dostoyevsky, and Faulkner in this group — "must deal with issues of life and death," and that there's "no such thing as life without bloodshed. I think the notion that the species can be improved in some way, that everyone could live in harmony is a really dangerous idea. Those who are afflicted with this notion are the first ones to give up their souls, their freedom. Your desire that it be that way will enslave you and make your life vacuous."[13] Such notions as he describes here are afflictions that cause pain and suffering in that they foster an evasion of the brutality and the chanciness of the real. In this light one virtue of McCarthy's fiction, then, is its medicinal cleansing away of the illusory truths spawned to veil how reality offers humans no solace and guarantees no progress. In this regard his novels' representations of violence and stories told by characters about bloodshed and sacrifices in Mexican history offer a kind of homeopathic magic, in the same way that, according to the mozo who fought against Huerta, "men believe the cure for war is war as the curandero prescribes the serpent's flesh for its bite" (*Pretty Horses* 111).

In *The Crossing* an old Indian man tells Billy Parham that he must stop his wanderings and make himself a place in the world, for while the world "seemed a place which contained men it was in reality a place contained within them and therefore to know it one must look there and come to know those hearts and to do this one must live with men and not simply pass among them" (134). Billy's own heart is said to have an irregular beat by the doctors who examine him when he tries to enlist in the army, and this "flaw" only magnifies the point that even the heart's regular rhythm, its systole and diastole, displays a cleft in the center of being, just as the paths and roads McCarthy's characters travel divide and edge the earth, measure and name it "because the way was lost to us already" (*The Crossing* 387).[14] Yet even if there is no communion among men as there is among horses and even if their hearts finally cannot be understood, the paths and roads in McCarthy's fiction do bring singular mortal selves into the presence of others in alamedas and courtyards. In the border trilogy's public spaces the limits to communion posed by the characters' separate bodies and separate histories paradoxically provide the possibility of community, defined as a sense of shared purpose realized through the emergent communications among beings whose lives are always poised at the cusp of death and nothingness.[15]

Regardless of their specific histories, what McCarthy's narrators essentially communicate as they exchange stories is not despair about the absence of stability and security but rather the special savor of existence as it passes and changes, as it fluctuates and escapes closure. For McCarthy, both being in and witnessing the here and now lead to understanding how the things of the world are not only perishable but renewable, and this realization can foster the primitive pleasure associated with belonging unconditionally to the world as it is. Thus John Grady Cole, riding in the back of a flatbed truck taking *campesinos* to work after his harrowing experience in a Mexican prison, understands that "after and for a long time to come he'd have reason to evoke the recollection of those smiles and to reflect upon the good will which provoked them for it had power to protect and to confer honor and to strengthen resolve and it had power to heal men and to bring them to safety long after all other resources were exhausted" (*Pretty Horses* 219). A smile radiating spontaneous goodwill; an old Mexican woman, "her sons long dead in that blood and violence which her prayers and prostrations seemed powerless to appease" (*The Crossing* 390), nevertheless constantly on her knees in prayer; meals offered generously to travelers along the way no matter how humble the fare; wolves dancing in the snow; nesting cranes looking up to watch lovers meeting in a lake; a gypsy stopping to doctor a horse stabbed in the chest; the principled loyalty of John Grady Cole and Lacey Rawlins — these and other moments in McCarthy's fiction illustrate how experiences of suffering and loss are at times irradiated with numinous value and how in his fiction an immersion in the tragic does not, finally, mutilate the idea of life.

Notes

1. Richard B. Woodward, "Cormac McCarthy's Venomous Fiction," *New York Times Magazine* April 19, 1992, 36.

2. Phrases from reviews published in the *New York Times* and in *Newsweek* as quoted in Tom Pilkington, "Fate and Free Will on the American Frontier: Cormac McCarthy's Western Fiction," *Western American Literature*, 27 (February 1993): 311.

3. See Vereen Bell, *The Achievement of Cormac McCarthy* (Baton Rouge: Louisiana State University Press, 1988), p. 3.

4. The notable specificity of McCarthy's landscape descriptions follows from his philosophy of not writing about places — in this context, the borderlands including Arizona, New Mexico, Texas, Chihuahua, Sonora, and Coahuila — he has not personally visited. See Woodward, "Cormac McCarthy's Venomous Fiction," p. 28. Even so, the rhetorical registers of his style as the descriptions oscillate between the particulars of the scene and the geological or astrological features hovering on the horizon — these shifts in vision intensified by his sparse punctuation and his preference for stringing clauses together via the coordinate conjunction "and" — force us to recognize how the landscape is fashioned into a unique topographic world.

5. Vereen Bell, "'Between the Wish and the Thing the World Lies Waiting,'" *Southern Review*, 28 (Autumn 1992): 926.

6. Though the Judge is an absolutely unique character in McCarthy's fiction, reminding some critics of Melville's Ahab, his view of existence is echoed by the duenna Alfonsa in *All the Pretty Horses* when she relates her own, her family's, and Mexico's history to John Grady Cole: "For me the world has always been more of a puppet show. But when one looks behind the curtain and traces the strings upward he finds they terminate in the hands of yet other puppets, themselves with their own strings which trace upward in turn, and so on. In my own life I saw these strings whose origins were endless enact the deaths of great men in violence and madness" (231).

7. As the duenna Alfonsa, who intercedes in the love affair between John Grady Cole and her niece, tells him in *All the Pretty Horses*, "the world is quite ruthless in selecting between the dream and the reality, even where we will not. Between the wish and the thing the world lies waiting" (238).

8. These aphorisms from Nietzsche's *Ecce Homo* are pertinent to understanding McCarthy's fiction: "One can almost classify human beings according to how profoundly they suffer" (Aphorism 270); "How much truth does a spirit endure, how much truth does it dare? More and more that became for me the real measure of value" (Third aphorism of the "Foreword"). Quoted in Clement Rosset, *Joyful Cruelty: Toward a Philosophy of the Real*, David F. Bell, ed. and trans. (New York: Oxford University Press, 1993), p. 31.

9. The phrasing here, and the interpretation advanced in this paragraph, are indebted to Rosset, *Joyful Cruelty*, p. 44.

10. Steven Shaviro, "'The Very Life of Darkness': A Reading of *Blood Meridian*," *Southern Quarterly*, 30 (Summer 1992): 115.

11. "He took up her stiff head out of the leaves and held it or he reached to hold what cannot be held, what already ran among the mountains at once terrible and of a great beauty, like flowers that feed on flesh. What blood and bone are made of but can themselves not make on any altar nor by any wound of war. What we may well believe has power to cut and shape and hollow out the dark form of the world surely if wind can, if rain can, but which cannot be held never be held and is no flower but is swift and a huntress and the wind itself is in terror of it and the world cannot lose it" (*The Crossing* 127).

12. Walter Sullivan, review of *Blood Meridian*, *Sewanee Review*, 93 (Fall 1985): 653.

13. Woodward, "Cormac McCarthy's Venomous Fiction," p. 36.

14. With regard to the prevalence of the image of the heart in the novels, we should consider what John Grady Cole thinks about the sum of his experiences in Mexico: "He thought that in the beauty of the world were hid a secret, he thought the world's heart

beat at some terrible cost and that the world's pain and its beauty moved in a relationship of diverging equity and that in this headlong deficit the blood of multitudes might
ultimately be exacted for the vision of a single flower" (*Pretty Horses* 282). The interpretation here of McCarthy's topography and the themes they figure is generally
indebted to J. Hillis Miller's reading of Heidegger's topographic images of the cleft, the
bridge, and the encircling ring. See his *Topographies* (Stanford: Stanford University
Press, 1995), pp. 51-56.

15. The distinction between "communion" and "community" is drawn from Jean-Luc
Nancy, *The Inoperative Community* (Minneapolis: University of Minnesota Press, 1991),
pp. 26-28.

Selected Bibliography

Primary Sources

Fiction
All the Pretty Horses. New York: Knopf, 1992.
Blood Meridian or The Evening Redness in the West. New York: Random House, 1985.
Child of God. New York: Random House, 1974.
The Crossing. New York: Knopf, 1994.
The Orchard Keeper. New York: Random House, 1965.
Outer Dark. New York: Random House, 1968.
Suttree. New York: Random House, 1979.

Drama
The Stonemason. Hopewell, New Jersey: Ecco Press, 1994.

Secondary Sources

Bell, Vereen M. *The Achievement of Cormac McCarthy*. Baton Rouge: Louisiana State
University Press, 1988. First book-length study of McCarthy situates his "anti-
metaphysical bias" within the southern literary tradition.
———. "'Between the Wish and the Thing the World Lies Waiting.'" *Southern Review*,
28 (Autumn 1992): 920-927. Lucid essay-review of *All the Pretty Horses* concludes
that McCarthy's overall project is "to continue to believe in a numinous value at
the heart of existence while remaining wholly without reassurance about this project from the realities of political life" (926).
Cheuse, Alan. "A Note on Landscape in *All the Pretty Horses*." *Southern Quarterly*, 30
(Summer 1992): 146-148. Notes how McCarthy's skies and landscapes exist in
dialectical relation with the main characters' psyches.
Daugherty, Leo. "Gravers False and True: *Blood Meridian* as Gnostic Tragedy." *Southern
Quarterly*, 30 (Summer 1992): 130-139. Connects McCarthy's presentation of the
borderlands' murderous history with gnostic thought, concluding that his combi-
nation of "tragic enchantment" and "unrepressed gaiety" makes him "our finest
living tragedian" (139).
Luce, Dianne C. "Cormac McCarthy: A Bibliography." *Southern Quarterly*, 30 (Summer
1992): 143-151. Checklist of publications by and about McCarthy through *Blood
Meridian*.

Miller, J. Hillis. *Topographics*. Stanford: Stanford University Press, 1995.

Nancy, Jean-Luc. *The Inoperative Community*. Minneapolis: University of Minnesota Press, 1991.

Pilkington, Tom. "Fate and Free Will on the American Frontier: Cormac McCarthy's Western Fiction." *Western American Literature*, 27 (February 1993): 311-322. Surveys McCarthy's exploration of the theme of modified predestination in the western novels and links his thematic emphases with western writers R.G. Vliet and Edward Abbey.

Rosset, Clement. *Joyful Cruelty: Toward a Philosophy of the Real*. David F. Bell, ed. and trans. New York: Oxford University Press, 1993.

Sepich, John Emil. "'What Kind of Indians Was Them?' Some Historical Sources in Cormac McCarthy's *Blood Meridian*." *Southern Quarterly*, 30 (Summer 1992): 93-110. Examines historical sources for *Blood Meridian* and how McCarthy translates them into his unique fiction.

Shaviro, Steven. "'The Very Life of Darkness': A Reading of *Blood Meridian*." *Southern Quarterly*, 30 (Summer 1992): 111-121. Nuanced reading of McCarthy's "erotics of landscape" links the actions of Glanton's men to Bataille's concept of "nonproductive expenditure."

Sullivan, Walter. Review of *Blood Meridian*. *Sewanee Review*, 93 (Fall 1985): 653.

Woodward, Richard B. "Cormac McCarthy's Venomous Fiction." *New York Times Magazine* (April 19, 1992): 36.

Russell Burrows

John Nichols

John Nichols is best known for two comic novels, *The Sterile Cuckoo* (1965) and *The Milagro Beanfield War* (1974). But over the years he has worked in many roles: as a journalist and photojournalist, as a speech writer and political pamphleteer, as a screenwriter, even as a cartoonist. Always a colorful personality, he started out as a sixties-era Minute Man in opposition to the war in Vietnam. In recent years, he has adopted New Mexico as his home, where he has defended both the Bill of Rights and the ecological movement with a Latin flourish — "Hasta la victoria siempre" (*Last Beautiful Days of Autumn* 158).

His readers respond to him with every bit of the passion he pours into his lines. Many delight in his exuberant humor. Others hate his populist funny bone. Critics have panned his books, while political enemies have attacked him in public and cussed him over the phone. Yet all have had opportunity to know his views. Not only have his two popular novels been made into hit movies — Paramount brought out *Cuckoo*; Robert Redford and Moctesuma Esparza produced *Milagro* — but Nichols' other books have been making their separate ways: a series of four New Mexico-based novels, six New Mexico-based memoirs, two romantic novels, a Vietnam novel, a coming-of-age novel, and a hefty string of polemical magazine pieces and other occasional skirmishes.

The venerable Granville Hicks, writing as a critic for *The Saturday Review*, once despaired of Nichols' second novel, *The Wizard of Loneliness*, pronouncing it "a bit on the corny side" (30). Shot through

Hicks' condescension was a plaintive note, asking who was this young Nichols to indulge himself so blithely? What could come of so much silliness? Was he "trying to fabricate a best-seller?"

The critic's misfortune was to have landed on what has turned out to be Nichols' least characteristic story. A more patient look would have suggested that John Nichols was rapidly acquiring the social conscience by which he would make himself known. This began when, as a college student, he traveled to Guatemala and had his illusions shattered "about America, the Big Benign Superpower." The targets for his ridicule were, of course, the Vietnam hawks and the preppie colleges where they sent their sons. At the same time, he would not spare the drop-out, burn-out hippies. Since moving to the West and beginning to work as a screen-writer, he has respected neither the glitz of the movie industry nor the pretense of the artists' quarter in Taos. In all, Nichols has broken spears against the Forest Service, the Bureau of Land Management, the Interstate Streams Commission, Taos' real estate developers, and the region's molybdenum mines. He has even made time for so little as the Llano Quemado Dump outside of Taos, where illegal trash fires foul skies that should be diamond-bright.

Born in 1940 in Berkeley, California, Nichols was the child of an unlikely union: his father became a professor and curator for the Museum of Natural History in New York; his mother had been a society woman and a debutante. She died when Nichols was two, leaving the home somewhat unstable.

An adventure of his teenage years forged his love of the West. This began with an essay contest, "What Democracy Means to Me," which he won. The prize would have taken him to a student conference in New Mexico. But this vanished when word came that his school in Washington, D.C., had not paid its membership fees to the association that had run the contest. So his father, remembering his connections to a biological research station in Arizona, offered the possibility of a sum-mer job there. It was more than acceptable, and the boy dried his tears.

The western outing was that proverbial slipping of the parental noose. Nichols made good on his holiday in every way open to him: collecting animals for the museum, building with adobe, learning to swear in Spanish, outfitting himself with a cowboy hat and boots, fighting range fires with a government crew, and flirting with the girls at a Mexican brothel.

Returning to the East, he hacked his way through a prep school, escaped to Europe for a year to work on a novel, and got married. Times were tumultuous with the assassinations of Martin Luther King and Robert Kennedy, the Tet Offensive, and the rioting at the Democratic Convention in Chicago. But his personal fortunes were glowing. He was only twenty-five when *The Sterile Cuckoo* appeared, and he was twenty-nine when Paramount used his alma mater, Hamilton College, as the setting for the movie starring Liza Minnelli.

But it was shortly thereafter that he decided to ditch the New York rat race and move to the Southwest. He had not forgotten his madcap summer in Arizona. He packed up his Volkswagen bus, intent on clearing his head in the pure air of Taos. He was going to take a crack at writing the great American novel.

That would demand he rethink the comedy Granville Hicks had lambasted. *Cuckoo* and *Wizard* are both of a piece, insofar as they are set in an I-like-Ike America where youthful insouciance gives way to mild psychic distress. The "cuckoo," Pookie Adams, has her problems, to be sure. But she does not seem to be the danger to herself nor to her boyfriend, Jerry Payne, that many reviewers believed they saw. The story is a romance, and too much has been made of Pookie's and Jerry's suicide pact, which lacks a certain authenticity. Nor can the horseplay of the earlier chapters be accepted as a meaningful rendition of student life. The story is a comedy based on a narrow slice of that life.

The "wizard," Wendall Oler, is likewise a comic figure. He is a runt and a bookworm, whose troubles are more entertaining than instructive. In fact, all of the characters in these two early novels seem put together in such a way as to have given Nichols the boldest puppets with which to pull one gag after another.

But as he felt the political storm darkening, so did he darken his writing. In his own words, he began to suffer "a powerful fatigue," the oxymoron perhaps evoking his feelings of being torn between writing novels and actually going out on the streets to agitate for reform. Caught in this wartime "funk," he endured nine lean years before breaking free with what many regard as a cult classic, *The Milagro Beanfield War*. He had managed to succeed with *Milagro*—at least in part—by taking himself sternly in hand and yelling, "Nichols, lighten up!"[1]

There followed in rapid order the New Mexican trilogy: *The Magic Journey* (1978), *A Ghost in the Music* (1979), and *The Nirvana Blues* (1981). These still have a generous measure of Nichols' love of adolescent highjinks and of wordplay. But there is an added dimension to the humor. This answers to the greater necessity of Nichols' maturing social consciousness.

His humor, in this sense, is not so much a property grafted to the writing, but is the actual quality from which the writing comes. In other words, Nichols became an *interested* novelist, one willing to take sides.

We must understand, however, that the divisions do not cleave neatly along the established lines of the liberal/conservative split. Nichols has said, "On first arriving in Taos, I had an automatic sympathy for anyone rebelling against straight society. My experience in Taos changed all that. I quickly learned that rebellion without a political understanding and motivation is no rebellion at all" (*Mountains* 112).

In fact, Nichols had been charmed by the dream of New Mexico on its license plate logo, "Land of Enchantment." But the travel-poster version of the state lasted only until he moved in and found himself caught in conflicts wholly unexpected. He had come with half-formed suspicions, Marxist in their origin and hippie in their aspect, of the evils of private property. And yet, the traditional landholding of *old* New Mexico made perfect sense. It respected the natural limitations of the arid mountain landscape. As a way of understanding these patterns of land ownership, Nichols began to write about them.

Much of the success of *The Milagro Beanfield War* may well have come from the fact that Nichols worked without many preconceived notions. He drew his materials to himself *ad hoc*. The muckraking newspaper to which he had started contributing, *The New Mexico Review*, gradually suggested itself as the model for *Milagro's* newspaper, *The Voice of the People*. Nichols' fellow journalists, Ed Schwartz, Em Hall, and Jim Bensfield, seemed to offer themselves for the composite sketch of *Milagro's* crusading journalist, Charley Bloom.

Likewise, Nichols returned to an expose he had done on Joe Cisneros, a molybdenum miner unjustly fired for labor activism, and found the outline for *Milagro's* protagonist, Joe Mondragon. On a different front, Nichols' work with Andres Martinez, leader of the Tres Rios Association, taught him the water politics that fuels *Milagro's* central conflict. This becomes explosive, of course, when Joe Mondragon "illegally" cuts a ditch bank and turns the irrigation back onto his family's idle beanfield.

Nichols happened to find the material for *Milagro's* setting in Costilla, which had been reduced to a virtual ghost town when the natives there lost their water rights to aggressive real estate developers. Even Nichols' seemingly inconsequential meetings began to make their way into his novel. He had once offered a ride to an old-timer, one of the *viejitos*, who was going into Santa Fe for a political rally. This man's family stories helped Nichols create *Milagro's* Amarante Cordova, the mysterious old figure emblematic of Chicano spirit. Finally, Nichols found much of the *Milagro's* comedy in the confrontative political theater of Luis Valdez's Teatro Campesino.

Having succeeded so well with *Milagro*, Nichols found that one story wasn't nearly enough. He had to keep developing the Southwest's ethnic and economic strife. But rather than set another story in Milagro, he put Chamisaville on his canvas, the "insane asylum" for *The Magic Journey, A Ghost in the Music,* and *The Nirvana Blues.*

The twin themes running through these novels are fleecing the fleeceless peon and toughing it out on a tough land. Hucksters begin to make fortunes in Chamisaville when a smuggler's dynamite truck blows up and uncovers a hot spring. The humble accept this as a miracle, while other schemers begin work on The Holy Chapel of the Dynamite Virgin, complete with gift shop. The action in *The Magic Journey* centers on the redoubtable April McQueen, who forsakes her heritage to stir up Chicano resistance to those trying to exploit the town. Playing opposite her are Bart Darling, a film producer in *A Ghost in the Music,* and Joe Miniver, a drug dealer in *The Nirvana Blues,* both of whom represent the scum of our culture.

The criticism of these novels suggests Nichols suffered the same sort of falling off after *Milagro* that he went through after *Cuckoo*. He seemed bound to do comedy but had not found that essential spark of a good story. The plots in the trilogy have accordingly been episodic, or worse, baggy. They have felt forced, sometimes full to bursting, as Nichols, himself, has admitted:

> My stories often sprint away from their original intentions like delinquent children, gallumph blindly into all sort of unforeseen pitfalls, and finally with luck, stagger to the finish line as total strangers to the original schemes that launched them. (*Nirvana* vii)

Having laid this kind of track, it is not at all surprising that Nichols would try to break with humor in his next novel, *American Blood* (1987). This is his long-deferred Vietnam story that he had to set aside when, too angry to write anything coherent, he turned instead toward *Milagro.*

493

This sixth novel is not set in Vietnam; instead, the story follows those who brought the violence of the war home with them. The country as Nichols depicts it is unquestionably an empire. But it is one that has kept committing the greatest crimes of imperialism. It is thus shot through with lurid colors, appalling dangers, and profound tragedies. The story does admit of some relief, however, for the surviving characters, Mike and Janine, who find strength in clinging to one another.

American Blood remains Nichols' one attempt to work in dramatic realism. The novel will not provoke so little as a rueful snicker, though there is a measure of resolution in the conclusion. But be warned: it is a grim business getting there. Line for line there is probably more hard profanity and graphic sadism in *American Blood* than in any other domestic publication of recent years. Yet little of the violence can be called gratuitous, not by Nichols' creative lights, nor certainly by the social record of those who still carry with them the burdens of that war.

Nichols' two most recent novels, *An Elegy for September* (1992) and *Conjugal Bliss* (1994), resemble nothing so much as his first one, *Cuckoo*. The similarity is between the ribald good humor that discounts any possibility of lasting romance. *Cuckoo* was a young man's wistful view of lost love, while *Elegy* and *Conjugal* are more jaded. The leading men of these two stories are passing through what has come to stand as the modernist insignia: the midlife crisis. Although both of them are writers, they haven't the insights that would enable them to manage their lives. The "blissful" Roger of *Conjugal* is aware of this ironic failing of the know-nothing writer: "I am a professional..." he says:

> I know all the tricks to make literary drama serve inter-active functions. My books sell pretty well. People write me letters. They are touched and intrigued and excited by my prose. Some of them even consider me wise. (158-159)

That is, wise toward all but the women in his own life. He gets entangled in a draining marriage with Zelda. Emotionally, she is much younger than her years. Likewise, the anonymous fool in *Elegy* indulges himself in an affair with a youngster who had written a passionate fan letter. She is young enough to be his daughter. The action is fast, the sexuality — well, furious. These stories parody the sexual revolution, the aftermath of which seems still to reverberate in Nichols' life. These books amuse.

But both suggest that he indulged himself, as do his characters, in easy pieces.

Finally, there is Nichols' nonfiction, which extols life in New Mexico. He has six books: *If Mountains Die* (1979), *The Last Beautiful Days of Autumn* (1982), *On the Mesa* (1986), *A Fragile Beauty* (1987), *The Sky's the Limit: A Defense of the Earth* (1990), and *Keep It Simple* (1992). In these, he reveals himself as a lover of fly fishing the Rio Grande and of fulminating social and economic revolution. Nichols has complemented these books with his photography. Many of his shots are excellent in the way they evoke New Mexico's harsh beauty. The work in these six books is purely celebratory of the rich conflicts of living on a borderland of cultures.

At last report, Nichols was living well in Taos. He continues to enjoy much of what brought him to New Mexico. Despite allergies and heart trouble, he gathers piñon for his stove and clears ditches to his garden. These are big parts of the "subsistence hustle" by which he augments the living he earns from writing. Still the spiritual seeker, he has a medicine bundle that he carries with him when he must leave Taos to confer over movie scripts. He has two children, both of whom are nearly grown. He has married for a second time.

As for future work, a good bet is that he will keep mining the rich cultural and economic conflicts of the Southwest.

Note

1. In an interview in the *Bloomsbury Review*, Nichols accounted for the change of attitude he forced on himself: "When I wrote *Milagro*, I decided I needed to try and survive as a writer and I figured that if I wanted to get my polemics out I'd have to find another way of doing it. I was just being hard-assed, you know, writing books that were up-against-the-wall-honky-mother-fucker-black-power's-gonna-get-your-mama. So I bent over backwards to be humorous and it worked. It was a lot of fun." See John Sullivan's "The Scribe of Taos: An Interview with John Nichols" in the *Bloomsbury Review* (September-October 1981): 15-17.

Selected Bibliography

Primary Sources

American Blood. New York: H. Holt, 1987.
Conjugal Bliss: A Comedy of Marital Arts. New York: H. Holt, 1994.

"Conscience and Community." In *Heaven Is Under Our Feet: A Book for Walden Woods.*
Don Henley and Dave Marsh, eds. New York: Berkley, 1991.
Elegy for September. New York: H. Holt, 1992.
A Fragile Beauty: John Nichols' Milagro Country. Salt Lake City, Utah: Gibbs M. Smith,
1987.
A Ghost in the Music. New York: H. Holt, 1979.
If Mountains Die: A New Mexico Memoir. William Davis, photographer. New York: Knopf,
1979.
Keep It Simple: A Defense of the Earth. New York: Norton, 1992.
The Last Beautiful Days of Autumn. New York: Holt, 1982.
The Magic Journey. New York: Holt, 1978.
The Milagro Beanfield War. New York: Ballantine, 1974.
The Nirvana Blues. New York: Ballantine, 1981.
On the Mesa. Salt Lake City, Utah: Gibbs M. Smith, 1986.
The Sky's the Limit: A Defense of the Earth. New York: Norton, 1990.
The Sterile Cuckoo. New York: Avon, 1965.
The Wizard of Loneliness. New York: Putnam, 1966.

Secondary Sources

Hicks, Granville. "Labor Leader's Love Lost." Review of *The Wizard of Loneliness.*
Saturday Review, 26 (February 1966): 29-30.
Rawlings, Don. Review of *The Last Beautiful Days of Autumn. Western American
Literature,* 18 (May 1983): 54-56.
Sullivan, John. "The Scribe of Taos: An Interview with John Nichols." *Bloomsbury
Review* (September-October 1981): 15-17.
Wild, Peter. *John Nichols.* Boise: Boise State University Western Writers Series, 1986.

Bob J. Frye

Charles Portis

R eaders of Charles Portis need to pack their bags, for he invariably
takes them on the road in a quest for goals as various as $70, the
killer of Mattie Ross' father, a Ford Torino, the spread of
Gnomonic truth from Atlantis, and, in *Gringos*, peace of mind for the
good-natured narrator. Yet all of these quests are shaped and informed
by Portis' comic vision expressed in a wry, laconic, typically deadpan
style. His picaresque novels range widely in settings — from France to
British Honduras, from Fort Smith, Arkansas, and Gary, Indiana, to the
Indian Territory, Texas, and Mexico — as his comic amblers meander
about, looking for some justice, roots, and dignity. Ray Midge's observation in *The Dog of the South* characterizes Portis' typical plot: "A lot of
people leave Arkansas and most of them come back sooner or later.
They can't quite achieve escape velocity" (245).

Charles McColl Portis was born in El Dorado, Arkansas, on
December 28, 1933, the son of Presbyterian parents. Graduating from
Hamburg High School in 1951, Portis served in the United States
Marine Corps from 1952 to 1955. Following his discharge, he attended
the University of Arkansas, where he earned a B.A. degree in journalism
in 1958. After working as a reporter for the *Commercial Appeal* in
Memphis, Tennessee, in 1958 and the *Arkansas Gazette* at Little Rock in
1959-1960, Portis joined the *New York Herald Tribune* as a feature writer
in 1960. He then became the bureau chief in London for the *Herald
Tribune* but resigned abruptly in 1964.

Following his return to Arkansas in 1964, Portis became a freelance writer. In 1966 he published an article, "That New Sound from Nashville," in the *Saturday Evening Post*, where later that year his first novel, *Norwood*, appeared serially (entitled *Traveling Light*) before its book publication. John Idol notes that, although *Norwood* sold fairly well, *True Grit*, serialized in May 1968 in the *Saturday Evening Post* before its June publication, sold more than 60,000 hardbound copies, stayed on the best-seller list twenty-one weeks, and sold more than 1,500,000 copies in paperback. Paramount paid Portis $300,000 for the film rights to *True Grit*, in which John Wayne played Rooster Cogburn to earn his only Academy Award.

Portis did not publish another novel for ten years, although his deadpan comic bent is evident in his short spoof of advice columns, "Your Action Line," which appeared in 1977 in the *New Yorker*. In 1979 his novel *The Dog of the South* received mixed reviews, yet it appeared in paperback in 1985, the same year Portis' *Masters of Atlantis* came out to limited sales. His most recent novel, *Gringos* (1991), has garnered good reviews and reveals the maturation of his novelistic art since *True Grit*.

Focusing on *True Grit*, academic critics have largely ignored Portis' other four novels, except for two notable overviews of Portis' career, one by Michael Connaughton (1980) and another by John Idol (1993). Connaughton is particularly thoughtful in providing a regional perspective on Portis' work: "His fiction explores the clash between the temperaments and values of the old and new South and between traditional Southern traits such as independence and gentility and the untamed, willful quality of the Southwest" (264). Idol, meanwhile, discerns eight major themes in Portis' fiction: restlessness, spiritual dry rot, revenge, fairness, love, language, social criticism, and grit (361-364). A concise examination of his novels in chronological order helps reveal the development of his comic vision.

In *Norwood*, Portis' first novel, Norwood Pratt's father, an alcoholic auto mechanic, dies and the young Marine receives a hardship discharge to return from Camp Pendleton to Ralph, Texas, to take care of his sister, Vernell. Norwood misses his father's funeral but his friend Clyde reports that "the funeral home had scrubbed Mr. Pratt down with Boraxo and...he had never seen him looking so clean and radiant" (12). With Vernell employed and married, restless Norwood, "tard" of his service-station job, decides to recover a $70 debt from a Marine buddy, Joe William, now in New York City. Guitar slung over his back, he begins his foolish quest, naively agreeing to drive sleazy Grady Fring the Kredit King's "hot" car to New York for resale. Arriving only to find that Joe William has returned to Arkansas, Norwood heads home on a bus where he meets jilted Rita Lee, whose life goal is "to live in a trailer and play records all night" (170). En route he also meets midget Edmund B. Ratner, rescues "Joann the Wonder Hen" near an arcade, returns to Arkansas to collect his loan only to lend money immediately to Ratner, next punches out Grady, seeking justice, and brings his Rita Lee home to Ralph. *Norwood* draws on the picaresque tradition, reveals Portis' never-patronizing interest in the realistic and grotesque, and focuses on a quest for fairness by a good-natured but flawed innocent.

The author's comic inventiveness, combined with the formulaic western described by John Cawelti and others, resulted in *True Grit* (1968), Portis' best-known work, which three reviewers immediately called "a Western with a difference," "surely some kind of classic," and "the best smart-aleck kid performance since Huck Finn stepped off his raft" (Weeks 119, Blackburn 92, Sokolov 82). Stressing the theme of justice, the novel's opening and closing sentences include the word *avenge* with the latter illustrating Mattie Ross' unadorned style: "This ends my true account of how I avenged Frank Ross's blood over in the Choctaw Nation when snow was on the ground" (215).

True Grit is the story of Mattie's experiences as a fourteen-year-old Arkansas girl in the 1870s enlisting a drinking, gambling, greedy "one-eyed fat man" (192), Deputy Marshal Rooster Cogburn, to help her capture and punish Tom Chaney, her father's killer. They are joined in the Indian Territory search by Texas Ranger LaBoeuf, trailing Chaney for the reward offered by the Waco family of a murdered Texas senator. There is palpable tension between the plain narrative style of Mattie, now in her sixties — "Here is what happened" appears four times in the novel — and the melodramatic, almost mythic accomplishments of the unlikely western hero, Rooster Cogburn. In one comic scene Cogburn finishes a bottle, tosses it into the air and fires many times before finally hitting it on the ground. Embarrassed, he pulls a corn dodger out of his sack, flings it into the air, and misses again. After he and two other inept shooters waste sixty corn dodgers, Mattie observes: "Shooting cornbread out here on this prairie is not taking us anywhere" (164).

Although C. L. Sonnichsen in *From Hopalong to Hud* (1978) briefly notes that *True Grit* follows the trail of Robert Kreps' *The Hour of the Gun* and other similar spoofs, Michael Cleary cogently argues that

Portis' novel is much more than a mere parody of the traditional western. In 1982 he acknowledged Portis' craft of overlaying realism on "the romantic world of the west," revealing the characters' harsh lives: "Rooster has lost an eye, is wounded in the shoulder, has shotgun pellets embedded in his face; Mattie has an arm amputated; outlaws have their fingers chopped off and part of their lips shot away" (610). Then in his excellent *North Dakota Quarterly* article, Cleary underlines the truth of Tom Pilkington's observation in "The Comic Novel in the Southwest" that since "the Southwestern novel is no longer a stranger to the comic spirit," it appears "well on its way to attaining maturity" (93). Cleary shows how Portis skillfully prepares the reader for the final gun battle between Cogburn and the Lucky Ned Pepper gang so that "the enduring image is that of a resolute hero whose weapons find their marks with unerring accuracy" (84). Cleary contends that Portis' "portrayal of Rooster Cogburn and Mattie Ross as somehow comic and realistic and mythic is a commendable achievement" and concludes that "*True Grit* does not mock the familiar Western myth so much as it creates new variations and suggests other possibilities for Western writers" (85).

The Dog of the South (1979) and *Masters of Atlantis* (1985) can fruitfully be read as humorous preparations for Portis' *Gringos* (1991), an artful, more complex comic novel with effective satire.

Narrator Raymond Midge begins *The Dog of the South* plainly: "My wife Norma had run off with Guy Dupree and I was waiting around for the credit card billings to come in so I could see where they had gone" (3). His quest is for his Ford Torino they took — and for Norma, too. Tracing them from Little Rock through Texas and Mexico to British Honduras, good-natured but indecisive Raymond, twenty-six, encounters wacky characters, including Dr. Reo Symes, owner of a broken-down white bus with "The Dog of the South" painted on its side. After losing his medical license, strange Symes sold hi-lo shag carpet remnants, wide shoes by mail, hail-damaged pears, and "vibrating jowl straps door to door" (76). The sick doctor joins Ray to go to Belize, where Dupree's father owns a farm (near Mayan ruins, a focus of *Gringos*) and where Symes' mother runs Unity Tabernacle, primarily showing cartoons to would-be converts. Portis treats comically the questionable missionary work in Belize as he crowds his novel with zany characters and gentle satiric observations on religion, physicians, and politics. After a hurricane, Ray Midge returns with Norma to Little Rock, only to see the restless would-be airline stewardess leave, alone, for Memphis. Goodhearted, meandering Ray has been to Belize and back, but still the amiable ambler has no Torino, no Norma, no hopeful future.

In *Masters of Atlantis* a con man in France in 1917 provides American doughboy Lamar Jimmerson an "ancient" manuscript, *Codex Pappus*, which he claims contains Gnomonism, arcane knowledge from Atlantis. Jimmerson enlists effete Englishman Sydney Hen to spread Gnomonism in Europe and Asia while he returns to America and establishes a massive temple in Burnette, Indiana, "the most fashionable suburb of Gary" (21). After liar, draft-dodger, and Dr. Symes-like schemer, Austin Popper, joins the Gnomon Society and uses mass-market techniques to attract more members to it, a Hen-Jimmerson schism develops, the Gnomon centers drop to only one in La Coma, Texas, and the temple moves there into a trailer.

Portis' comic inventiveness pervades this satiric account of secretive true believers. Grotesque characters—Ed from Nebraska, "discharged from the army for attempting to chloroform women on a government reservation" (160); former Rosicrucian Maurice from Chicago, paranoid about aluminum cookware; crippled Fanny, Miss Hine, promoter of "Constantine Anos, unfortunate name" (170-171)—populate this strange, eventful history. Like Henry Fielding, Laurence Sterne, and Jonathan Swift, Portis employs artful humor, providing Swiftian echoes with the alchemical project of Romanian Professor Cezar Golescu to extract gold from bagweed. Like Swift, Portis attacks lawyers when Jimmerson gets booked to give a speech on Gnomonism at a lawyers' retreat where attorneys attend seminars on "Systematic Estate Looting and No One the Wiser" and "Making the Worse Cause Appear the Better," the latter a witty turn on a passage in the fourth voyage of Swift's *Gulliver's Travels*. As in his earlier novels, Portis comically utilizes malapropisms and ironic juxtapositions ("chicken livers, fudge" 67), but his satire is sharper than in previous novels as he ridicules the questioning of Popper by a Texas Senate committee investigating "various cults...preying on the senile, the college students, and other...weak-headed elements..." (195). Portis' social criticism is becoming more incisive.

In *Gringos*, Portis combines the lively plot of *True Grit* with the more direct satire of *Masters of Atlantis* and the generous, good-natured narrators of *Norwood* and *The Dog of the South*. Arklatex native Jimmy Burns is now doing odd hauling jobs out of Mérida in the Yucatan between Christmas and the New Year. An article followed by a mysterious letter signed "El Mago," published in the UFO newsletter *Gamma Bulletin,* has lured a strange variety of gringos on New Year's quests to the City of Dawn, a ruin on the Guatemalan border. There gather "real hippies, false hippies, pyramid power people, various cranks and mystics, hollow earth people, flower children and . . . Rudy Kurle, with his space invader theories" (33). Jimmy's serious confrontation with the thieving biker Big Dan and his Jumping Jacks, a hippie gang including a young female runaway; his search for lost UFO enthusiast Kurle, working on a book on space dwarfs; and his taking of supplies to a legitimate archaeological dig at Ektún all combine into a complicated quest. Still other zany Portis characters live in and around Mérida, including Minim, who "was in the Bowling Hall of Fame . . . and [a] sports poet" (72), an "ethnomusicologist" grant recipient spending most hours at Shep's In-Between Club, and, at Fausto's hotel, dying Frau Kobold, longtime widow of a pioneer photographer of Mayan ruins and the secret author of the "El Mago" UFO letter.

Unlike the early Portis novels (except *True Grit*) with their thin, picaresque plots, *Gringos* has an intertwined plot with some subtle connections, more fully drawn main characters who develop relationships, and more complicated quests climaxed by a violent clash between capable but modest Jimmy, helped by his friend Refugio, and grotesque Big Dan and his skinheads. Building on the amusing one-liners which appear in his earlier fiction, Portis' humor and satire take a sober coloring from the backdrop of several deaths during the narrative. Unpretentiously but surely Portis shoots folly as it flies. That Jimmy and Rudy's sister, Louise, marry, settle down in Mérida, and seem to have fulfilled that most important quest — peace of mind — appears evident as they conclude: "After all, we weren't genuine drifters, not by nature" (268). *Gringos* clearly reveals the author's maturing art.

Portis' fiction originates from a region centered in Little Rock. Yet his comic inventiveness, quirky but controlled, reveals humans as being, as Alexander Pope puts it, "the glory, jest, and riddle of the world" all at once, especially in *True Grit* and *Gringos,* raising his novels above mere provincialism. Mattie Ross is a new creation in American fiction, and Jimmy Burns, though a lesser character, is at once self-effacing and quietly heroic, commonsensical and a source of strong affirmation in a wacky world. In a 1983 interview in the *Texas Humanist,* William A. Owens, a writer of the Texas frontier, observes: "The only reason for regionalism is to make it an opening onto the universal." At his best, Charles Portis does just that. Going on the road with him in his fiction is delightfully engaging — and genuinely enlightening.

Selected Bibliography

Primary Sources

The Dog of the South. New York: Alfred A. Knopf, 1979.

Gringos. New York: Simon & Schuster, 1991.

Masters of Atlantis. New York: Alfred A. Knopf, 1985.

Norwood. New York: Simon & Schuster, 1966.

"That New Sound from Nashville." *Saturday Evening Post,* 239 (February 12, 1966): 30-35, 38-39.

"Traveling Light." *Saturday Evening Post,* 239 (June 18, 1966): 54-77; 239 (July 2, 1966): 48-75.

"True Grit." *Saturday Evening Post,* 241 (May 18, 1968): 68-85; 241 (June 1, 1968): 46-61; 241 (June 15, 1968): 44-57.

True Grit. New York: Simon & Schuster, 1968.

"Your Action Line." *New Yorker,* December 12, 1977: 42-43.

Secondary Sources

Blackburn, Sara. "Book Marks." *The Nation* (August 5, 1968): 91-92.

Cleary, Michael. "Charles (McColl) Portis." *Twentieth-Century Western Writers.* James Vinson, ed. Detroit: Gale, 1982. Pp. 609-610.

———. "*True Grit*: Parody, Formula, Myth." *North Dakota Quarterly,* 54 (Winter 1986): 72-86.

Connaughton, Michael E. "Charles Portis." *Dictionary of Literary Biography: American Novelists Since World War II.* 2nd ser. Vol. 6. James E. Kibler, Jr., ed. Detroit: Gale, 1980. Pp. 264-268.

Ditsky, John. "True 'Grit' and 'True Grit.'" *Ariel,* 4 (April 1973): 18-31.

Idol, John L., Jr. "Charles [McColl] Portis (1933-)." *Contemporary Fiction Writers of the South: A Bio-Bibliographical Sourcebook.* Joseph M. Flora and Robert Bain, eds. Westport, Connecticut: Greenwood Press, 1993. Pp. 360-370.

———. "Charles Portis 1933." *Beacham's Popular Fiction in America.* Vol 3. Washington, D.C.: Beacham, 1986. Pp. 1111-1117.

Pilkington, William T. "The Comic Novel in the Southwest." *My Blood's Country: Studies in Southwestern Literature.* Fort Worth: Texas Christian University Press, 1973. Pp. 81-93.

Sokolov, Raymond A. "The Young Novelists." *Newsweek,* July 22, 1968: 80, 82.

Shuman, R. Baird. "Portis' *True Grit*: Adventure Story or *Entwicklungsroman?*" *English Journal,* 59 (March 1970): 367-370.

Weeks, Edward. "The Peripatetic Reviewer." *The Atlantic* (June 1968): 116-119.

Charlotte M. Wright

Barbara Kingsolver

Raised in rural Kentucky and educated at De Pauw University in Indiana, Barbara Kingsolver made what she intended to be a short trip to Tucson in 1979 at the age of twenty-two. When she published her first novel, *The Bean Trees*, in 1988, she was still living there. Since then, she has produced a nonfiction work (*Holding the Line: Women in the Great Arizona Mine Strike of 1983* [1989]), a collection of short stories (*Homeland* [1989]), two more novels (*Animal Dreams* [1990] and *Pigs in Heaven* [1993]), a book of poems (*Another America* [1992]), a book of essays, (*High Tide in Tucson* [1995]), and various nonfiction pieces in magazines such as *Smithsonian*, *Natural History*, and *Architectural Digest*. She has become one of the Southwest's most popular writers, "the only writer who has been nominated four years in succession for the American Booksellers Association's Abby Award, which honors books that independent bookstore owners most enjoyed reading and recommending to customers" (*Current Biography Yearbook* 304). Altogether, her books have sold more than a million copies. Her writing awards include two American Library Association Notable Book awards, a PEN West fiction prize, an Edward Abbey Ecofiction Award, a Western Heritage (Wrangler) Award from the National Cowboy Hall of Fame, and the *Los Angeles Times* Book Award for Fiction.

A few critics and reviewers have alleged that her work is overly sentimental, that her characters are too wholesome, and that she is often *too* "politically correct." Rhoda Koenig of *New York* magazine complains that the tone of *Pigs in Heaven* is "a cute, dreamy mindlessness that sub-verts the issues of conflict and choice it propounds," and that a "sticky cloud of niceness soon envelopes all but one of the main characters and most of the minor ones, too" (99). R. Z. Sheppard's review in *Time* also finds the characters too "winsome," with too high a "sweetheart quo-tient" (65). Jack Butler in *The New York Times Book Review* considers Taylor Greer, main character of *The Bean Trees*, "too perfect, too right" in her confrontations against "prejudice, trauma, self-abnegation, chau-vinism." He claims that the author is for and against all the right causes, but because of this, the book's "reality suffers" (15).

Most reviewers, however, have nothing but praise for Kingsolver. Diane Manuel in *The Christian Science Monitor* calls Taylor Greer "a character to believe in and laugh with and admire...an independent and irreverent 80s heroine" (20). In the *Los Angeles Times Book Review*, Merrill Joan Gerber praises Kingsolver's abilities in *Pigs in Heaven*: "she's compassionate, she's smart, she can get into the skin of everyone from the airhead baby-sitter to the handicapped air-traffic control worker" (12). Wendy Smith in *The Washington Post Book World* argues that "those who see political correctness lurking behind every bush will doubtless be irritated by Kingsolver's careful, warmhearted denouement....But within the context of her sensitive story...her conclusion is both dra-matically and emotionally satisfying" (3). *Cosmopolitan's* Louise Bernikow has kudos for *Pigs in Heaven*: "This profound, funny, big-hearted novel, in which people actually find love and kinship in surpris-ing places, is also heavenly—managing to make you feel good without glossing over life's hardships. A rare feat and a triumph" (32).

Both her novels and her stories tend to feature a female as narrator and central character, although she does use shifting points of view, par-ticularly in *Animal Dreams*, to illuminate the thoughts and activities of other key characters, including males, most of whom are also well drawn and likable. All of Kingsolver's characters, of either gender, come from middle America and are either Anglo, Native American, or Chicano. She has said that she feels it is "important to illuminate the lives of peo-ple who haven't been considered glorious or noteworthy" (*Current Biography Yearbook* 304). Perhaps influenced by growing up in an area where, in her own words, people "depended heavily upon their neigh-bors to get through life..." (quoted in *Current Biography Yearbook*), her thematic content often deals with the necessity of cooperation, commu-nication, and community. Yet reading Kingsolver's work one seldom feels it is too didactic, too obvious in its "politically correct" message; one reason may be her propensity for humor, a factor which no doubt contributes to the popularity of her books.

The book that started it all, *The Bean Trees*, is an intriguing blend of southern and western elements. Jack Butler in *The New York Times Book Review* calls it "the Southern novel taken west" (15). It begins with a southern feel, the main character Taylor Greer talking about mud-bottomed ponds, tobacco farmers, boiled greens and eggs for dinner. It quickly turns into an on-the-road novel when Taylor buys a Volkswagen and leaves her small-town Kentucky life behind, heading into the sunset with no clear destination: "I promised myself...I would drive west until my car stopped running, and there I would stay" (12). But she is frightened by the sight of the Great Plains and turns south at Wichita, Kansas, thinking she can go around them. Her car gives out in central Oklahoma, where a mechanic overcharges her to repair it. She stops at a bar before moving on again and there, in the parking lot, a Native American woman deposits an obviously traumatized three-year-old child in her car, begging her to keep it, for its own safety. Taylor names the little girl "Turtle," for the way she clings to her, and continues her westward journey. The two find their way to Tucson, where Taylor meets another southerner-gone-west, Lou Ann Ruiz, a single mother who eventually becomes her roommate. Taylor soon becomes involved with the Sanctuary movement, through which she meets Esperanza and Estevan, two educated and sophisticated political refugees who eventually help her legally adopt Turtle.

There is a refreshing anti-mythic quality to *The Bean Trees*. For one thing, although the West becomes home to her, Taylor does not indulge in the usual paeans to the beauty of western landscape when describing it. When she crosses into Arizona at sunup, she describes the clouds as "pink and fat and hilarious-looking, like the hippo ballerinas in a Disney movie." The road takes Taylor and Turtle through "a kind of forest, except that in place of trees there were all these puffy-looking rocks shaped like roundish animals and roundish people. Rocks stacked on top of one another like piles of copulating potato bugs. Wherever the sun hit them, they turned pink. The whole scene looked too goofy to be real" (35). Other anti-mythic elements relate to Taylor's westward journey. While it is true that she sets out on her journey in order to escape the confines and restrictions of her hometown (a "safety net" theme), at the same time she is *not* rejecting society in favor of a carefree Kerouacian lifestyle, free of familial or social responsibilities. Taylor is looking for a home, for herself and her daughter; she is trying to find a community where she feels at home, rather than getting away from people altogether.

Kingsolver's second book, *Holding the Line: Women in the Great Arizona Mine Strike of 1983*, is nonfiction, but it, too, critiques aspects of the western myth—in this case, the myth that the West is a land of freedom and equal opportunity. Based on interviews she conducted with (mostly Mexican-American) women who took their husbands' places on the picket line when an injunction was placed on the men, *Holding the Line* documents the presence of discrimination in the West as blatant as anything in the South. In her feminist/Marxist approach to this story, Kingsolver reveals the underbelly of the American dream of freedom and civil liberty—at least for the working classes. In style, the book reads remarkably like a novel. Stanley S. Phipps, reviewing it for *Labor History*, applauds the author's "skill as a story teller," "excellent use of her oral interviews," and "thought provoking insights" (516).

Readers of her *Homeland and Other Stories*, published the same year as *Holding the Line*, will find a few characters and events that remind them of the nonfiction book. Vicki Morales, the central character in the powerful story "Why I Am a Danger to the Public," seems to be an amalgamation of the traits of several of the women Kingsolver met during her long months investigating the Arizona strike. By way of explanation (and incidentally providing insight into her creative process), Kingsolver says:

> That story was a collection of things that didn't quite happen but could have, and I sort of wish had. When you write nonfiction, often you'll interview someone and you'll think, if only she had said this, or, if only that had happened, it would be a much better story. But you can't make those changes, because you're honest, you have to say what really happened. So I collected all those what-ifs and turned them into this short story that was fictional but very much grounded in the truth of that strike. (Ross 288–289)

Another evocative story in the collection is "Rose-Johnny," about a child's fascination with, and eventual acceptance of, the androgynous town character whom everyone else ridicules and shuns. This story, like many in Kingsolver's oeuvre, is told from a child's point of view—a stylistic feature previously more akin to southern literature than to western literature, although that seems to be changing recently. All of the stories in *Homeland*, according to the author, "are about people who are finding a home, a place for themselves" (Ross 288), so the collection is a logical extension of Kingsolver's thematic explorations begun in *The Bean Trees*.

Set three years after *Bean Trees'* final scenes, *Pigs in Heaven*, its sequel, is also very much about home places. In this one, Taylor and Turtle are once again on the road, and once more without a definite destination in mind—only this time they are fleeing a specific danger—Annawake Fourkiller, a Native American attorney for the Cherokee tribe who is determined to deliver Turtle back into the arms of her tribal community. While they are on their own, Taylor and Turtle learn how difficult it is to survive without a network of family and friends. As *Newsweek* critic Laura Shapiro pointed out, Kingsolver challenges herself in this book "by pitting its cultural correctness against the boundless love between a mother and child. For all its political dimensions, this is no polemic but a complex drama in which heroes and villains play each other's parts— and learn from them" (61). This blending of hero/villain is another of Kingsolver's attempts to de-mythologize the West by refusing to indulge in the "good-guy/bad-guy" duality.

In addition to their roles as individuals on opposite sides of a volatile issue, Annawake and Taylor also function as symbols of the contemporary Native American and Anglo world views, especially those concerning the rights of the individual as opposed to the rights of the community. This dichotomy, central to *Pigs in Heaven*, shows up many places in the novel but is best encapsulated in an exchange between Annawake and Jax, Taylor's boyfriend. After hearing Annawake's story about why the constellation that Anglos call "the Pleaides" is called by the Cherokees "the Six Pigs in Heaven," Jax says, "So that's your guiding myth. Do right by your people or you'll be a pig in heaven." Annawake thinks this over and answers: "Yes. I had a hundred and one childhood myths, and they all added up more or less to 'Do right by your people....' What are yours?" Jax responds that he learned "the usual American thing"—that is, "if you're industrious and have clean thoughts you will grow up to be vice president of Motorola," which Annawake interprets as "Do right by yourself." Her disapproval of that world view is evident in her next words: "Your culture is one long advertisement for how to treat yourself to the life you really deserve. Whether you actually deserve it or not" (88).

This disdain for contemporary Anglo-American culture is also prominent in *Animal Dreams*, Kingsolver's novel which has — undeservedly — received less critical attention than the others. (An important exception is a *Washington Post Book World* review by Ursula Le Guin, who says the novel "belongs to a new fiction of relationship, aesthetically rich and of great political and spiritual significance and power.... This is a sweet book, full of bitter pain; a beautiful weaving of the light and the dark.") The narrator, Codi Noline, returns to her hometown after an absence of fourteen years. A rootless person in the midst of the firmly rooted, Codi's only grounding is the occasional letter she gets from her political-activist sister in South America. Her father, the town doctor who is now in the first stages of Alzheimer's disease, only serves to remind her of a miserable childhood spent feeling like a square peg in a round hole. Codi's life begins to turn around when she becomes reacquainted with Loyd — a Native American whom she had dated once in high school — and when she becomes involved in helping save the town's water supply from blatant polluting by a mining company.

With its ecological, ecofeminist message and activist central characters (both Codi and her sister Hallie), *Animal Dreams* owes much to *Holding the Line*. It is also, in some ways, a romance, because Loyd and Codi fall in love and, at the end, both sacrifice to be able to remain together. Yet there is more. The difficult but ultimately successful romance between the spiritual Loyd and the scientific Codi can of course be seen as representative of the necessity for Anglo and Native American to overcome their differences and join forces in order to assure their mutual survival.

Like her fiction, Kingsolver's poetry strives to represent a variety of experience, and it does so in a way that is accessible and self-revealing. "To me," she has said, "writing is writing. The word count will be different, but the process is the same" (Ross 289). Janet Bowdan finds in her *Southwestern American Literature* article that it is Kingsolver's poems specifically that "become and traverse borders — where she enables boundaries to be places of connection as well as of division" (1). Because of this, the poems in *Another America* are quite political in the sense that, as Bowdan says, "they attempt to reach people who can bring about change" (4). In Kingsolver's world, that is not the politicians but instead those who are underrepresented by the politicians in the current social situation — women, Native Americans, Chicanos. Her message, as usual, is that those who band together and form communities are the most likely to survive.

Kingsolver's writings, although they all develop thematically along similar lines, are by no means simplistic. There are no easy answers for the world's problems; there are lots of complex questions. But an individual — even a "rootless" one — can make a difference. She told Amy Pence in a *Poets & Writers Magazine* interview: "All my life I've been someone who just stands on the street corner and yells about things that are wrong" (18). Obviously, her writing is one way she "yells," and she feels she can make a difference. And an individual who has been fortunate enough to live in a community that becomes a home place is in an even better position to bring about changes. "Most of my life is about connectedness, and it's about community. I want people to believe that kind of stuff is worthy of literature" (20). In addition, she told a *Contemporary Authors* interviewer: "I feel strongly about social justice, ultimately whatever I write will contain my passions" (286). She continued: "One can write for the sake of writing, or one can write because one feels an urgent nugget of truth that must be hurled at the public at large. I'm of the second school of thought" (287). She sees the latter as a necessary role for the artist, and one that is too easily ignored in this country:

> People in the United States are not thinking of the arts as vital, whereas the poets of Latin America are like the Bruce Springsteens of that culture. They are revered because they are the questioning voices. People see them as a safety valve, like the miner's canary, voices that are the warning that goes off before the poison gas comes in and kills us all. Poets and artists are their nation's social critics, and they function that way. (Pence 18–19)

The literary territory Barbara Kingsolver continues to mine — in her fiction, her nonfiction, and her poetry — is a multicultural, political, and passionate place. Those few critics bothered by her characters' innate "goodness" or her overtly political messages are outnumbered by those who recognize Kingsolver as an important new voice in southwestern American literature.

Selected Bibliography

Primary Sources

The Bean Trees. New York: Harper & Row, 1988; rpt., New York: HarperPerennial, 1992.

Holding the Line: Women in the Great Arizona Mine Strike of 1983. New York: ILR
    Press/New York State School of Industrial and Labor Relations, 1989.
Homeland and Other Stories. New York: Harper, 1989.
Animal Dreams. New York: HarperCollins, 1990; rpt., New York: HarperPerennial, 1991.
Another America. Seattle: Seal Press, 1992.
Pigs in Heaven. New York: HarperCollins, 1993.
High Tide in Tucson. New York: HarperCollins, 1995.

Secondary Sources

Bernikow, Louise. Review of *Pigs in Heaven. Cosmopolitan* (June 1993): 32.
Bowdan, Janet. "Replacing Ceremony: The Poetics of Barbara Kingsolver." *Southwestern
    American Literature,* 20:2 (Spring 1995): 13-19.
Butler, Jack. "She Hung the Moon and Plugged in All the Stars." *The New York Times
    Book Review* (April 10, 1988): 15.
Current Biography Yearbook. New York: H. W. Wilson, 1994.
Gerber, Merrill Joan. "Those Ideas in the Air." *Los Angeles Times Book Review* (October
    31, 1993): 10, 12.
Koenig, Rhoda. "Portrait of the Artists' Friend." *New York* (June 14, 1993): 99-100.
Le Guin, Ursula K. Review of *Animal Dreams. Washington Post Book World* (September 2,
    1990): 1.
Manuel, Diane. "A Roundup of First Novels about Coming of Age." *The Christian Science
    Monitor* (April 22, 1988): 20.
Neill, Michael. "La Pasionaria: Barbara Kingsolver writes about a West where women are
    women and none of the heroes are cowboys." *People Weekly* (October 11, 1993):
    109.
Pence, Amy. Interview with Barbara Kingsolver. *Poets & Writers Magazine* (July-August
    1993): 14-21.
Phipps, Stanley S. Review of *Holding the Line. Labor History,* 31 (Fall 1990): 515-516.
Randall, Margaret. "Human Comedy." *The Women's Review of Books,* 5 (May 1988): 1, 3.
Ross, Jean W. Interview with Barbara Kingsolver. *Contemporary Authors,* 134 (1992):
    286-290.
Shapiro, Laura. "A Novel Full of Miracles." *Newsweek* (July 12, 1993): 61.
Sheppard, R. Z. Review of *Pigs in Heaven. Time* (August 30, 1993): 65.
Smith, Wendy. "The Mother and the Tribe." *Washington Post Book World* (June 13, 1993):
    3.

Mark Busby

Sam Shepard

An Ed Fisher cartoon in the January 6, 1986, *New Yorker* indicates how extensive playwright Sam Shepard's popularity had become by that date. Pedestrians walking along a New York street pass under a marquee with a notice proclaiming, "NOW PLAYING, THE SAM SHEPARD TO BEAT ALL THE OTHER SAM SHEPARDS AROUND TOWN." Shepard was featured on the covers of the November 11, 1985, issue of *Newsweek* and the November 1988 *Esquire*, and the March 1993 issue of *Modern Drama* was devoted to Shepard. Richard Gilman declared, "Not many critics would dispute the proposition that Sam Shepard is our most interesting and exciting playwright." Although Shepard's face and name became better known in the 1990s (primarily because of his work in film), since 1986 he has presented only two new full-length plays, *States of Shock* (1991) and *Sympatico* (1994), both of which received mixed reviews. Still, he remains one of America's most important playwrights. *The Modern Language Association International Bibliography* listed almost 200 entries for Shepard by the end of 1994, more than for Ralph Ellison, Larry McMurtry, and many of the major figures of western American literature. For the 1996-97 season the Signature Theater Company devoted an entire season to Shepard's work, including a brief new play, *When the World Was Green (A Chef's Fable)* cowritten with longtime collaborator Joseph Chaikin.

Throughout his plays Shepard demonstrates a concern that plagues American writers who mine the mythic lode. "It's one thing to have a dream," Shepard once said. "It's another thing to be killed by it" (Kroll

71). This curious paradox of American life makes Sam Shepard's plays riveting and helps account for his appeal. His work demonstrates over and over again the two sides of the American myth: the hope and promise of the dream of regeneration on the American frontier and the recognition that the dream has often been violent and destructive, that it appears as a "lie in the mind" continuing to entrap and destroy.

Samuel Shepard Rogers, III, was born in Fort Sheridan, Illinois, on November 5, 1943, but grew up in Duarte, California, where he was influenced by life close to the earth. His family owned an avocado ranch, and "Steve" (as he was called growing up), who once had the Grand Champion yearling ram at the Los Angeles County Fair, planned to be a veterinarian. He actually attended Mount Saint Antonio Junior College and majored in agricultural science. Instead, though, Shepard headed east in 1963 and transformed himself from Steve Rogers into Sam Shepard. First he became a waiter at the Village Gate, a popular jazz club, where he met Ralph Cook, the founder of off-off-Broadway's Theater Genesis. Cook encouraged Shepard to write, and Shepard's two one-act plays, *Cowboys* and *The Rock Garden*, were presented by Theater Genesis in 1964. Since that time Shepard has written over forty plays, five filmscripts, including Michelangelo Antonioni's *Zabriskie Point* (1970) and Wim Wenders' *Paris, Texas* (1984), and two collections of stories; directed two films based on his scripts, *Far North* (1991) and *Silent Tongue* (1993); appeared in over twenty movies including *Days of Heaven* (1978), *Resurrection, Raggedy Man* (1981), *Frances* (1982), *The Right Stuff* (1983), *Fool for Love* (1985), *Baby Boom* (1987), *Crimes of the Heart* (1987), *Thunderheart* (1992) and *Streets of Laredo* (1995); and has won more than ten Obie awards and a Pulitzer for *Buried Child* (1978).

Shepard's vitality as a playwright stems from his mythic imagination and concern with the loss of heroic ideals and coherent values the American West formerly represented. Often in dazzling, absurdist fashion, he presents a world that has fallen or is falling away from something valuable. His plays emphasize the fragmentation of a world searching for characters who can continue to embody positive mythic values in new ways. Legendary western figures such as Pecos Bill, Mickey Free, Paul Bunyan, and Jesse James appear in Shepard's plays; other characters are recognizable western types: the title characters in his first play *Cowboys* (1964) and its revision *Cowboys #2* (1967), the Morphan brothers in *The Unseen Hand* (1969), the old prospector in *Operation Sidewinder* (1970), Slim in *Cowboy Mouth* (1971), Hoss in *The Tooth of Crime*

(1972), Cody in *Geography of a Horse Dreamer* (1972), the cowboy side of Niles in *Suicide in B* (1976), and Lee in *True West* (1980).

When he was asked by a *Theatre Quarterly* interviewer in 1974 why he used cowboys, Shepard replied: "Cowboys are really interesting to me — these guys, most of them really young, about sixteen or seventeen, who decided they didn't want to have anything to do with the East Coast, with that way of life, and took on this immense country, and didn't have any real rules" (Marranca 190). In fact, throughout Shepard's work the mythic West of cowboys — the wide open landscape offering unlimited freedom and potential for individual self-fulfillment — enters and provides the conflict. Many of Shepard's characters wish to re-embody the cowboy figure, but the fragmented world in which they live offers little possibility of satisfaction. The cowboy is out of place in this world; those who wish to adhere to his image are limited by their attempts. A changed world requires new images, but the chaos of contemporary life provides no coherent ones to supersede the cowboy. Shepard explained to interviewer Carol Rosen: "Myth served as a story in which people should connect themselves in time to the past. And thereby connect themselves to the present and the future. Because they were hooked up with the lineage of myth. It was so powerful and so strong that it acted as a thread in culture. And that's been destroyed" (5).

In *Cowboys #2*, Stu and Chet, reminiscent of Samuel Beckett's Didi and Gogo in *Waiting for Godot*, act out a stereotyped Indian fight. As the play ends, with horse sounds clashing against car horns in the background, two suited men begin to read the play's script over again in monotone. Here, Shepard emphasizes the way that old images become crutches to support the contemporary world. In each reembodiment, however, the gap between the original and the copy grows wider, implying that the old images need to be transformed rather than imitated. In *Cowboy Mouth*, Cavale has kidnapped Slim, planning to make him a rock-and-roll star. What the world needs, she exclaims, is a "saint . . . a rock-and-roll Jesus with a cowboy mouth" (*Mad Dog* 100). Slim provides no redemption, but Mickey Free in *Operation Sidewinder* is able to transmute the Air Force computer made in the form of a gigantic sidewinder rattlesnake — representing the industrial, violent world — into an Indian god that provides the way to an apocalyptic redemption.

Even if the old images have to be changed, their positive value needs to be recognized and retained. In *Suicide in B*, Niles, the musician who is to kill various aspects of his former self to begin anew, praises the cow-

boy: "He discovered a whole way of life. He ate rattlesnakes for breakfast. Chicago wouldn't even exist if it wasn't for him. He drove cattle
right to Chicago's front door. Towns sprang up wherever he stopped to
wet his whistle. Crime flourished all around him. The law was a joke to
him" (143). In his confusion, though, Niles cannot distinguish between
freedom and anarchy. In Shepard's plays, *something* of the old should be
retained; the exact characteristics of this something, though, are murky.

Niles' emphasis on taking new forms may have presaged Shepard's
own changes. Toward the end of the 1970s Shepard began appearing in
films, some with Jessica Lange, his companion since 1982. His plays written during that time — *Curse of the Starving Class* (1978), *Buried Child*
(1978), and *True West* (1980) — are much more realistic than his earlier
work. More accessible and less irreverent, they nonetheless confront similar themes. What is the effect of the past, these plays seem to ask, especially its ties to the family? The mythic West calls for independent isolation, but the family, often in strangling, debilitating ways, remains
connected to the present, as Austin in *True West* discovers. How does one
establish his own identity with past images looming so large in the mind's
eye? The old West, the "looks within" place, is dead, Austin says in *True
West*: "There's no such thing as the West anymore. It's a dead issue!"
(35). What will replace it is ambiguous, but as the fertile field behind the
house in *Buried Child* suggests, possibility and opportunity still exist: they
simply must be perceived through the fog of the present.

One of the most compelling aspects of Shepard's plays derives from
his continuing use of important aspects of the gothic as he examines various aspects of the American frontier myth. Gothic images of dark, mysterious forces originally captured the American imagination as the early
settlers contemplated the frightening wilderness and its principal inhabitant, the American Indian. Shepard's plays include most of the elements of frontier gothic: Indians, captured women, strong hints of evil,
mystery, a conflict between the old and the new, incest, doubling, decaying houses, and, most importantly, a confrontation in the American
West that leads to a transformation of consciousness. Most of the plays
abound with magic and mystery and demonstrate how Shepard has
taken aspects of frontier gothic and fused them into an American drama
that frightens and delights. Perhaps the most significant element
Shepard employs is the emphasis on a changed consciousness resulting
from violence in the wilderness. As Richard Slotkin notes, central to
American mythology is violent change: "The first colonists saw in

America an opportunity to regenerate their fortunes, their spirits, and the power of their church and nation; but the means to that regeneration ultimately became the means of violence, and the myth of regeneration through violence became the structuring metaphor of the American experience" (*Regeneration Through Violence* 5). It is this "fusion of the traditional gothic theme of psychic disintegration with the larger theme of metamorphosis, or regeneration in the wilderness," that David Mogen points to as the distinctive aspect of frontier gothic. "As a result," Mogen continues, "the most gruesome horrors in American gothic are often emblems...of new forms of consciousness emerging from the wilderness experience" (345).

Of all Shepard's plays, one of the most representative is *The Tooth of Crime*, set in a mythic space where rock-and-roll stars control territory like old gunfighters. The reigning hero, Hoss, is being challenged by a "Gypsy Killer," Crow. The duel takes on the flavor of an old-fashioned fight between the established gunfighter and the young challenger, but it involves verbal performance. When the referee calls Crow a winner by T.K.O., Hoss responds with a "true gesture that won't never cheat on itself 'cause it's the last of its kind" (111) — suicide. The old world represented by Hoss is a kaleidoscope of past pop culture images: cowboy, outlaw, rock star, gangster, sci-fi hero. His replacement is an imitation of an imitation. Hoss is more sympathetic than Crow, suggesting that as this violent cycle continues, each succeeding change lacks the authenticity of the original.

Similar elements appear in *Operation Sidewinder* (1970) and *Buried Child* (1978). In the former, Shepard draws from and revises the frontier gothic by merging Native American and European images in a ceremonial apocalypse that suggests the beginning of a new chance for the American dream to be achieved through a new consciousness. *Buried Child* also uses gothic elements to examine the confrontation between past and present, old and new, but here Shepard incorporates more of the standard elements of gothic — a rambling old house, long-dead mysteries that unfold, and seemingly supernatural events — along with frontier imagery, incest, and doubling.

When Shepard returned to the stage after a five-year hiatus with *States of Shock* in 1991, the work reflected his interest in continuing themes and a return to his earlier, less realistic style. Presented during the Gulf War, *States of Shock* is set in a diner where a character called the Colonel brings Stubbs, a young disabled veteran of an unnamed war, for an outing from the hospital. The Colonel attempts to get Stubbs to recall the details of his wounding and the death of the Colonel's son, who supposedly was killed by the same artillery shell that wounded Stubbs. Before the play ends, Stubbs indicates that he was wounded by friendly fire and that perhaps the Colonel was involved in his wounding and is actually his father who has betrayed him. *States of Shock* again emphasizes the fragmentation and falling away from early values, paradoxically caused by the violence engendered by older American myths. At one point, the Colonel breaks into a Shepard monologue, the Shepard aria, and merges the old and new:

> Even in the midst of the most horrible devastation. Under the most terrible kind of duress. Torture. Barbarism of all sorts. Starvation. Chemical warfare. Public hangings.... Amputation of private organs. Decapitation. Disembowelment. Dismemberment. Disinterment. Eradication of wildlife. You name it. We can't forget that we were generated from the bravest stock. The Pioneer. The Mountain Man. The Plainsman. The Texas Ranger. The Lone Ranger. My son.... We have a legacy to continue, Stubbs. (24)

While *States of Shock* recalls Shepard's earlier, elliptical and absurdist style, his newest play, *Sympatico*, reflects the theme and style of the more realistic *True West*. Opening off Broadway in November 1994 with Shepard directing, *Sympatico* concerns two old friends, Carter and Vinnie, who fifteen years before had used Vinnie's then-wife Rosie to blackmail a horseracing official named Ames. Rosie and Carter had then run off together and become wealthy and successful. In the intervening time Vinnie had used the photographs of Rosie and Ames (now Simms) to extort money from Carter. As the play begins, Carter has returned to their hometown of Cucamonga, California, to get Vinnie to give him the photographs after Vinnie again asked for support.

Like *True West*, *Sympatico* highlights the connections between two dissimilar characters by dramatizing how each becomes transformed into the other as the play develops. In *True West* the two brothers, Austin and Lee, represent two sides of the American present: one sophisticated, cultured, ambitious, and successful; the other alienated and outcast, raw, wild, violent. As both plays unfold, the two characters exchange places and reveal that each is the double of the other. Shepard's plays emphasize that, despite the American belief in starting anew, the past is never over but continues to intrude into the present. The mythic American icon of *Sympatico* concerns horses, now reduced to the materialistic, debased sport of racing, and Shepard uses the interconnected blood of thoroughbreds to suggest the interrelationships that tie things together in paradoxically powerful and debilitating ways.

Shepard's plays achieve their appeal by concentrating on contemporary American characters who reenact the continuing American theme of regeneration through violence in settings fraught with images drawn from frontier gothic. He dramatizes a world caught between the past and the future, where America's violent frontier past lies like a stinger in the back of our minds, beckoning us back and keeping us from entering the future. Although he has finally slowed the phenomenal output that characterized his earlier period as a writer and although his newest plays lack the sweep of his best work, Sam Shepard continues to track the heart of true western American experience, mapping a metaphysical world that reveals in glimpses the hopes, dreams, and betrayals of American mythology.

Selected Bibliography

Primary Sources

Buried Child; Seduced; Suicide in B. New York: Urizen Books, 1979. (Contains all three plays.)

Cruising Paradise. New York: Alfred A. Knopf, 1996.

Fool For Love and Other Plays. New York: Bantam Books, 1984.

Four Two-Act Plays. New York: Urizen Books, 1980.

Hawk Moon: Short Stories, Poems, Monologues. New York: Performing Arts Journal Publications, 1981.

A Lie in the Mind. New York: New American Library, 1987.

Mad Dog Blues & Other Plays. New York: Winter House, 1972. (Includes *Mad Dog Blues, Cowboy Mouth, The Rock Garden, Cowboys #2.*)

Seven Plays. New York: Bantam Books, 1981.

States of Shock; Far North; Silent Tongue. New York: Vintage, 1993.

The Unseen Hand and Other Plays. New York: Bantam Books, 1986.

When the World Was Green (A Chef's Fable). Unpublished, premiered at the Hasty Pudding Theatre, Cambridge, Massachusetts, spring 1997.

Secondary Sources

Allen, Jennifer. "The Man on the High Horse," *Esquire* (November 1988): 141-151.

Busby, Mark. "Sam Shepard and Frontier Gothic." In *Frontier Gothic: Terror and Wonder at the Frontier in American Literature*. David Mogen, Scott P. Sanders and Joanne B. Karpinski, eds. Rutherford, New Jersey: Fairleigh Dickinson University Press, 1993. Pp. 84-93.

Chubb, Kenneth, and the editors of *Theatre Quarterly*. "Metaphors, Mad Dogs, and Old Time Cowboys." *Theatre Quarterly*, 4:15 (1974): 3-16. (Reprinted in *American Dreams: The Imagination of Sam Shepard, Bonnie* Marranca, ed. New York: Performing Arts Journal Publication, 1981. Pp. 187-209.)

DeRose, David J. *Sam Shepard*. New York: Twayne/Macmillan, 1992.

Hart, Lynda. *Sam Shepard's Metaphorical Stages*. New York: Greenwood Press, 1987.

Howard, Patricia, ed. "Special Issue: Sam Shepard and Contemporary American Drama." *Modern Drama*, 36:1 (March 1993): 1-166.

King, Kimball, ed. *Sam Shepard: A Casebook*. New York: Garland, 1988.

Kroll, Jack, Constance Guthrie, and Janet Huck. "Who's That Tall Dark Stranger?" *Newsweek*, November 11, 1985: 71.

Marranca, Bonnie, ed. *American Dreams: The Imagination of Sam Shepard*. New York: Performing Arts Journal Publication, 1981.

Mogen, David. "Frontier Myth and American Gothic." *Genre*, 14 (1981): 329-346.

Mottram, Ron. *Inner Landscapes: The Theater of Sam Shepard*. Columbia: University of Missouri Press, 1984.

Rosen, Carol. "'Emotional Territory': An Interview with Sam Shepard." *Modern Drama*, 36:1 (March 1993): 1-11.

Patraka, Vivian M. and Mark Siegel. *Sam Shepard*. Boise: Boise State University Western Writers Series, 1985.

Slotkin, Richard. *The Fatal Environment: The Myth of the Frontier in the Age of Industrialization, 1800-1890*. New York: Atheneum, 1985.

———. *Regeneration Through Violence: The Mythology of the American Frontier, 1600-1860*. Middletown, Connecticut: Wesleyan University Press, 1983.

Mark Busby

Ralph Ellison

Ralph Ellison's death on April 16, 1994, marked the end of a remarkable career and the beginning of another phase in American literary history. At his death Ellison had come to be recognized as one of the world's most distinguished men of letters primarily on the strength of a single novel, *Invisible Man* (1952), a work of singular importance to western American literature. Ellison often recalled Heraclitus' axiom that "geography is fate" and also noted that "where Frederick Jackson Turner's theory of the frontier has been so influential in shaping our conception of American history, very little attention has been given to the role played by geography in shaping the fate of Afro-Americans" (*Going to the Territory* 198). Ellison's geographical fate is manifest in his varied geographical experiences—from Oklahoma to Alabama to New York.

Geography influences his writing so thoroughly that the symbolic values of the three primary locations where he spent his life provide in microcosm a metaphor that permeates his work: thesis/antithesis=synthesis. His southwestern background provided him with freedom and possibility; the South offered restriction and limitation; the North allowed a mature synthesis. Writing requires constant interaction with the shadow of the past—with one's geography and history—to produce the synthesis of art, which, Ellison emphasizes, imagination offers: "As I say, imagination itself is *integrative*, a matter of making symbolic wholes out of parts" (*Territory* 198).

Ralph Waldo Ellison was born in Oklahoma City on March 1, 1914, the son of Lewis Alfred and Ida Millsap Ellison. All four of his grandparents had been slaves. His mother grew up on a White Oak, Georgia, plantation, and his father, from Abbeville, South Carolina, became a soldier and served in Cuba, the Philippines, and China. Lewis Ellison became a construction foreman, which eventually brought his family to Oklahoma.

The Ellisons and other African Americans who left the South for the Oklahoma frontier wanted better conditions for their children. Once settled, they fought hard to keep segregationist laws, like those in Texas, out of the Oklahoma constitution. Oklahoma, unlike Texas and Arkansas, had no tradition of slavery. Added to this history was a sense of connection between Native Americans, who constituted a significant proportion of Oklahoma's population, and African Americans. In Oklahoma, Ellison noted, "the atmosphere...there was a sense that you had to determine your own fate, and that you had a chance to do it" (West 12), that the world was possibility.

In fact, Ellison and his boyhood friends acted out positive aspects of the American frontier belief in a free and open territory that was later contradicted by his oppressive experience—a conflict central to Ellison's imaginative attempts to confront the reality of a seemingly free world that actually provides restraints: "One thing is certain, ours was a chaotic community, still characterized by frontier attitudes...which [encourage] the individual's imagination—up to the moment 'reality' closes in upon him—to range widely and, sometimes, even to soar" (*Shadow and Act* xiii). He refers to himself and his friends growing up in Oklahoma as "frontiersmen" who looked to a variety of heroic models: "gamblers and scholars, jazz musicians and scientists, Negro cowboys and soldiers from the Spanish-American and First World Wars, movie stars and stunt men, figures from the Italian Renaissance and literature..." (*Shadow and Act* xv-xvi). In fact, he says, he and his friends thought of themselves as "Renaissance Men," noting that "it was no more incongruous...for young Negro Oklahomans to project themselves as Renaissance Men than for white Mississippians to see themselves as ancient Greeks or noblemen out of Sir Walter Scott" (*Shadow and Act* xvii). These young, black frontiersmen thought that they "were supposed to be whoever [they] would and could be and do anything and everything which other boys did, and do it better" (*Shadow and Act* xvii).

For Ellison the frontier also represents the border area, the demarcating point where various forces come together in an integrative whole. Thus, amalgamation, assimilation, and cultural syncretism characterize his work. The American frontier looks both ways — west toward freedom and chaos, east toward restriction and tradition. Just as the southwestern jazz musician learned to improvise against and within the tradition, so Ellison's archetypal artist strives to achieve freedom within restriction, or to use an oxymoronic phrase — restricted freedom. Ordered chaos, visible darkness, traditional individuality, antagonistic cooperation — all characterize Ralph Ellison's complex world view drawn from experience on the frontier where cultural mixture flourished.

Ellison carried his southwestern knowledge of language and possibility when he left the territory for Tuskegee Institute in Alabama in 1933, where he discovered the restrictions and limitations of the Deep South. Then, with the great migration, Ellison went north to Harlem in 1936 and learned he had to chart new territory in the New York wilderness where freedom merged with chaos.

Ellison planned initially to become a musician, but fate led him to a friendship with Richard Wright, to writing book reviews and short stories, to working for the Federal Writers' Project, and to literature as a craft and discipline. Avoiding a Jim Crow army in World War II, Ellison shipped out as a cook with the Merchant Marine and continued to write. Depressed and sick after an especially difficult mission taking war supplies across the North Atlantic during the Battle of the Bulge, he came back to the states to recover and to write. Setting up in a friend's barn in Vermont, he suddenly typed: "I am an invisible man." He started to destroy the page, but when he reread it, he began to wonder what kind of voice would speak such words and set off down the path of writing what has become a twentieth-century American classic and probably the most important post-1950 American novel, *Invisible Man*. Selected by critics as "the most distinguished single work" published since World War II, in a *Book Week* poll in 1965 and another by *Wilson Quarterly* in 1978, *Invisible Man* returned to the forefront of American critical thought as the century drew to a close.

Despite the fact that most of *Invisible Man* is set in Harlem, the narrative relies on frontier imagery associated with the duality between freedom and restriction. It is an American bildungsroman in which the narrator moves from a frontier belief in freedom, simplicity, possibility, and harmony to a confrontation with the reality of restriction. The awareness that results emphasizes the "personal moral responsibility for democracy," which Ellison states is the significance of his fiction.

Invisible Man received the Russwurm Award, the Certificate of Award from the *Chicago Defender*, and the National Book Award. Additionally, Ellison won a Rockefeller Foundation Award, the American Medal of Freedom, the Chevalier de l'Ordre des Artes et Lettres from France, the Langston Hughes medallion for contribution in arts and letters from City College in New York, and the National Medal of Arts. His numerous public appointments include the vice presidency of the PEN America and the National Institute of Arts and Letters, trusteeship of the Citizens' Committee for Public Television and the John F. Kennedy Center in Cambridge, and membership in the National Council on the Arts and the Carnegie Commission on Educational Television. He lectured and taught widely, most notably as the Albert Schweitzer Professor of Humanities at New York University.

From 1960 until his death he published eight excerpts of a work-in-progress, *And Hickman Arrives*. These eight stories total almost 150 pages of prose in print, and Ellison's friends who saw the manuscript of the second novel suggest that it was over twenty inches thick. Disturbing historical events interrupted his progress, particularly political assassinations similar to one portrayed in the novel—an attempted assassination of a famous racist senator who as a boy of indeterminate race had grown up with an African American itinerant preacher. Also a fire in his home in the Berkshires in 1967 destroyed 368 manuscript pages. The published excerpts reveal a complex, carefully crafted work concerned with themes of interest to Ellison throughout his career: the spiral of history as the past boomerangs into the present, identity, resurrection, showmanship, amalgamation, and the positive and negative transformative power of language and narrative. Ellison began transcribing the novel on a word processor in the mid-1980s, and he left it almost complete. John Callahan, an English professor at Lewis and Clark College, was selected by Ellison's wife, Fanny, to assemble the second novel. Its publication will mark another milestone in a distinguished career. In 1996 Callahan edited *Flying Home and Other Stories*, which included several of Ellison's Oklahoma stories.

Besides his fiction, Ellison had an established reputation as an essayist. In 1964 he published *Shadow and Act*, a collection of essays, reviews, and interviews dating from 1942. They are important for revealing Ellison's background, particularly the effect of his Oklahoma past, his interest in music, and his knowledge of classic American literature. A second essay collection, *Going to the Territory* (1986), was published in 1986 and includes Ellison's essays written between 1964 and 1985, as well as some essays left out of *Shadow and Act*. *The Collected Essays of Ralph Ellison* was published in 1995. As an essayist, Ellison relies on his personal experiences to present his continuing concerns: a regard for history and the past, abhorrence of racial stereotyping, identity, the power of art to transform, the richness of African American culture, and amalgamation.

Ralph Ellison charted new frontiers in American literature in language that forces chaos to reveal its truth, and his posthumously published work will no doubt blaze new trails.

Selected Bibliography

Primary Sources

Fiction

"Afternoon." In *American Writing*. Otto Storm, et al., eds. Prairie City, Illinois: J. A. Decker, 1940. Pp. 28-37.

"And Hickman Arrives." *Noble Savage*, 1 (1960): 5-49. Reprinted in *Black Writers of America*. Richard Barksdale and Keneth Kinnamon, eds. New York: Macmillan, 1972. Pp. 693-712.

"Backwacking: A Plea to the Senator." *Massachusetts Review*, 18 (Autumn 1977): 411-416. Reprinted in *Chant of Saints*. Michael S. Harper and Robert B. Stepto, eds. Urbana: University of Illinois Press, 1979. Pp. 445-446.

"The Birthmark." *New Masses*, 37 (July 2, 1940): 16-17.

"Boy on a Train." *The New Yorker* (April 29-May 6, 1996): 110-113.

"Cadillac Flambe." *American Review*, 16 (February 1973): 249-269.

The Collected Essays of Ralph Ellison. John Callahan, ed. New York: Modern Library, 1995.

"A Coupla Scalped Indians." *New World Writing*, 9 (1956): 225-236.

"Did You Ever Dream Lucky?" *New World Writing*, 5 (April 1954): 134-145.

"Flying Home." *Cross Section*. Edwin Seaver, ed. New York: Fischer, 1944. Pp. 469-85. (Reprinted in *Dark Symphony: Negro Literature in America*. James A. Emanuel and Theodore L. Gross, eds. Toronto: Free Press, 1968. Pp. 254-274.)

Flying Home and Other Stories. John Callahan, ed. New York: Random House, 1996.

"I Did Not Learn Their Names." *The New Yorker* (April 29-May 6, 1996): 113-115.

"In a Strange Country." *Tomorrow*, 3 (July 1944): 41-44.

"Invisible Man." *Horizon*, 23 (October 1947): 104-107.

"Invisible Man: Prologue to a Novel." *Partisan Review*, 19 (January-February 1952): 31-40.

Invisible Man. New York: Random House, 1952. (Reprinted, 30th anniversary edition, New York: Random House, 1982.)

"It Always Breaks Out." *Partisan Review,* 30 (Spring 1963): 113-28.

"Juneteenth." *Quarterly Review of Literature,* 14 (1965): 262-276.

"King of the Bingo Game." *Tomorrow,* 4 (November 1944): 29-33. Reprinted in Emanuel and Gross, *Dark Symphony: Negro Literature in America.* Pp. 271-279.

"Mr. Toussan." *New Masses,* November 4, 1941, 19-20.

"Night-Talk." *Quarterly Review of Literature,* 16 (1969): 317-29.

"Out of the Hospital and Under the Bar." In *Soon, One Morning.* Herbert Hill, ed. New York: Knopf, 1963. Pp. 242-290.

"The Roof, the Steeple and the People." *Quarterly Review of Literature,* 10 (November 1960): 115-128.

"Slick Gonna Learn." *Direction* (September 1939): 10-11, 14, 16.

"A Song of Innocence." *Iowa Review,* 1 (Spring 1970): 30-40.

"That I Had the Wings." *Common Ground,* 3 (Summer 1943): 30-37.

Collected Nonfiction

Going to the Territory. New York: Random House, 1986.

Shadow and Act. New York: Vintage Books, 1953, 1964.

Secondary Sources

Bibliography

Covo, Jacqueline. *The Blinking Eye: Ralph Waldo Ellison.* Metuchen, New Jersey.: Scarecrow Press, 1974.

Collections

Benston, Kimberly W., ed. *Speaking For You: The Vision of Ralph Ellison.* Washington, D.C.: Howard University Press, 1987.

Bloom, Harold, ed. *Ralph Ellison.* New York: Chelsea House Publishers, 1986.

Gottesman, Ronald, ed. *The Merrill Studies in Invisible Man.* Columbus: Merrill, 1971.

Hersey, John, ed. *Ralph Ellison: A Collection of Critical Essays.* Englewood Cliffs, New Jersey: Prentice-Hall, 1970.

O'Meally, Robert G., ed. *New Essays on Invisible Man.* New York: Cambridge University Press, 1988.

Parr, Susan Resneck and Pancho Savery, eds. *Approaches to Teaching Ellison's Invisible Man.* New York: Modern Language Association, 1989.

Reilly, John M. ed. *Twentieth Century Interpretations of Invisible Man.* Englewood Cliffs, New Jersey: Prentice-Hall, 1970.

Trimmer, Joseph, ed. *A Casebook on Ralph Ellison's Invisible Man.* New York: Thomas Y. Crowell, 1972.

Journal Special Issues

Carleton Miscellany, 18 (1980).

CLA [College Language Association] Journal, 13 (March 1970).

Delta (Montpellier, France), 18 (1984).

Books

Baker, Houston A., Jr. *Blues, Ideology, and Afro-American Literature: A Vernacular Theory.* Chicago: University of Chicago Press, 1984.

Bone, Robert. *The Negro Novel in America*, rev. ed. New Haven: Yale University Press, 1965.

Byerman, Keith. *Fingering the Jagged Grain: Tradition and Form in Recent Black Fiction.* Athens: University of Georgia Press, 1985.

Busby, Mark. *Ralph Ellison*. New York: Twayne/Macmillan, 1991.

Callahan, John F. *In the African-American Grain*. Urbana: University of Illinois Press, 1988.

Cooke, Michael G. *Afro-American Literature in the Twentieth Century: The Achievement of Intimacy*. New Haven: Yale University Press, 1984.

Dietze, Rudolf F. *Ralph Ellison: The Genesis of an Artist*. Nuremberg: Verlag Hans Carl, 1982.

Dixon, Melvin. *Ride Out the Wilderness*. Urbana: University of Illinois Press, 1987.

Emanuel, James A. and Theodore L. Gross, eds. *Dark Symphony: Negro Literature in America*. Toronto: Free Press, 1968.

Gates, Henry Louis, Jr. *Figures in Black*. New York: Oxford, 1987.

————. *The Signifying Monkey*. New York: Oxford University Press, 1988.

Gray, Valerie Bonita. *Invisible Man's Literary Heritage: Benito Cereno and Moby Dick*. Amsterdam: Editions Rodopi, N.V., 1978.

Harper, Michael S. and Robert B. Stepto, eds. *Chant of Saints*. Urbana: University of Illinois Press, 1979.

Klein, Marcus. *After Alienation*. Chicago: University of Chicago Press, 1964.

Lewicki, Zbigniew. *The Bang and the Whimper: Apocalypse and Entropy in American Literature*. Westport, Connecticut: Greenwood Press, 1984.

Lewis, R. W. B. *Trials of the Word*. New Haven: Yale University Press, 1965.

List, Robert N. *Dedalus in Harlem: The Joyce-Ellison Connection*. Washington: University Press of America, 1982.

McSweeney, Kerry. *Invisible Man: A Student's Companion to the Novel*. Boston: Twayne, 1988.

Nadel, Alan. *Invisible Criticism: Ralph Ellison and the American Canon*. Iowa City: University of Iowa Press, 1988.

O'Brien, John. *Interviews with Black Writers*. New York: Liveright, 1973.

O'Meally, Robert G. *Ralph Ellison: The Craft of Fiction*. Cambridge: Harvard University Press, 1980.

Petesch, Donald A. *A Spy in the Enemy's Country*. Iowa City: University of Iowa Press, 1989.

Smith, Valerie. *Self-Discovery and Authority in Afro-American Literature*. Cambridge: Harvard University Press, 1987.

Stepto, Robert. *From Behind the Veil*. Urbana: University of Illinois Press, 1979.

Tanner, Tony. *City of Words*. New York: Harper & Row, 1971.

West, Hollie. "Growing Up Black in Frontier Oklahoma...From an Ellison Perspective." In *Speaking For You*. Kimberly Benston, ed. Washington: Howard University Press, 1987.

Paul M. Hadella

Leslie Marmon Silko

In 1985, four years into working on the novel *Almanac of the Dead*, Leslie Marmon Silko, celebrated Native American author of *Ceremony* (1977) and *Storyteller* (1981), reflected on her motives as a writer by stating: "I'm really aware of saying things so you don't offend someone, so you can keep their interest, so you can keep talking to them" (Coltelli 147). To anyone who has read *Almanac of the Dead*, these comments will seem incongruous with the novel's barely contained outrage. Reviewers have called the novel "wild, jarring, graphic," "raging," "vengeful," and "highly political."[1]

Indeed, Silko's comments from 1985 seem to apply to an earlier version of herself, not to the angry author of *Almanac of the Dead*. In Tayo, the traumatized war veteran in *Ceremony*, Silko created a memorable character who is both achingly "real" and resonantly emblematic of all Native Americans who have been left spiritually wounded by their participation in the white man's world. But it is upon Tayo's healing, which requires that he realize his connection with the land and come to terms with his mixed-blood heritage, that Silko places her emphasis, not upon denouncing "the white man." Likewise the modern and traditional stories in *Storyteller*, while often addressing racial prejudice and hatred, are more noteworthy for what they say about the Pueblo Indian sense of community and about the spiritual tie that exists between Pueblo people and the land of the Southwest. Nothing in Silko's earlier work foreshadows the vicious tone, much less the epic scope, of *Almanac of the Dead*.

Almanac sprawls over 700 pages, gazes into the lives of a few dozen characters, and encompasses the entire North American continent. It took Silko ten years to write the novel, which appeared in bookstores in November of 1991, on the eve of the controversial Columbus Quincentennial. To round out the commemoration of the Quincentennial, many publishers courted Native American reactions, suggesting that Americans were prepared for a certain amount of soul-searching.[2] But was America prepared for *Almanac of the Dead*? Its formidable size is just the first challenge that this novel presents to readers. More to the point, the cast of unredeemable characters that Silko parades across the pages — drug dealers, hired killers, unscrupulous land developers, sexual deviants, pornographers, human butchers — is unsavory to say the least.

In an era of political correctness, marked by an institutionalized hypersensitivity to offense taken by certain groups, Silko goes against the tide and indicts women, gays, and the disabled as accomplices in the network of evil that Euro-American culture has spread throughout the New World. Furthermore, in showing unchecked greed and exploitation to be symptomatic of a spiritually degenerate society, Silko provides a Native American perspective on a theme that has played an important role in defining western American literature. *Almanac of the Dead*, that is, could be seen as following a clear line of precedent established by such western American writers as Frank Norris and John Steinbeck — both outspoken critics, on an epic scale, of the social conditions that engender class conflict.

In Silko's mind, Tucson, the setting for much of *Almanac*, becomes a metaphor for everything that is wrong with white society. The city has long been a mecca for exploitative trade and commerce. Home to whorehouses and gambling halls in the 1880s, its opportunistic residents then "got rich off the Indian wars" by peddling bootleg whiskey (168). Today, because of its proximity to the Mexican border, it is home to any number of people profiting from international drug and arms trafficking.

Exploitation of the land, meanwhile, is foremost on the mind of Leah Blue, the wife of a semi-retired Mafia kingpin. Disdain for those who would abuse the land, a major theme in contemporary western American literature, takes on a certain vehemence with Silko, due, no doubt, to her Pueblo upbringing and to her feelings about the open-pit uranium mine that the United States government authorized on Laguna land in 1949. The mine, symbolic of humanity's willingness to wound the earth in order to carry out its own destructive purposes, appears in *Ceremony* as well as in *Almanac of the Dead*.[3]

For Leah Blue, the land around Tucson means just one thing: profit. Her dream is to transform parts of arid Tucson into a "city for the twenty-first century" called Venice, Arizona, complete with canals and gondolas. Obtaining the water rights for her dream city is no problem; Leah merely buys off the judge presiding over her claim. Typical of Silko's attitude toward those in white society responsible for enforcing law and order, the corrupt magistrate, Judge Arne, is last seen in the novel enjoying sex with his beloved basset hounds.

The preceding paragraphs of summary merely scratch the surface of this huge novel, yet they do bring into focus Silko's belief that we are living in the reign of Death-Eye Dog, a period foretold in ancient prophecies of widespread evil and perversion: "During the epoch of Death-Eye Dog human beings, especially the alien invaders, would become obsessed with hungers and impulses commonly seen in wild dogs" (251). But there is hope for the continent's indigenous people, according to Silko, for the prophecies also tell of a time when all things European will disappear, leaving the land in the hands of its original, respectful caretakers. In *Almanac of the Dead*, the dispossessed (mainly Indians, but also bands of homeless men of other races meeting in the arroyos of Tucson) are preparing, or have already begun, to wage war against their oppressors. From Alaska to Arizona and the Mexican state of Chiapas, their goal is the same: to take back the land that has been stolen from them.

An exception to the defiant Indians who are the norm in *Almanac of the Dead* is Sterling, from Silko's own Laguna Pueblo, who is no subversive. He is simply a man who is deeply saddened for having failed in his duty to keep a Hollywood movie crew away from sacred sites on the reservation. Sterling is punished by being banished from the pueblo. Over the years, the people of Laguna have suffered from a number of foreign intrusions that have never been vindicated. Sterling serves as a convenient scapegoat. "There were hundreds of years of blame that needed to be taken by somebody," writes Silko, "blame for other similar losses" (34). The tribal council, with its swift and harsh brand of justice, may seem fanatical. But when Sterling arrives in Tucson, a forlorn exile, he will encounter a world where lawlessness prevails. So which is better,

Silko seems to be asking: arch-conservative law, that, in truth, has the welfare of the entire community as its basis, or no law at all?

If the answer to this question is obvious to Silko, she seems far less certain about the ultimate effectiveness of armed revolution. It is true that the Euro-American culture depicted in *Almanac of the Dead* is diseased beyond healing and that the prospect of unseating its reign through violent overthrow seems to appeal to Silko on an emotional level. Yet her ambivalence towards violence as a solution surfaces, for example, in her undercutting of certain leaders of the revolution. Sterling returns home in the closing pages of the novel, having survived his collision with a destructive, spiritually bankrupt culture. In the sum total of many such individual triumphs, perhaps, lies the true course of revolution.

By all accounts, Silko's ten-year effort to complete the novel was a harrowing and consuming process. In 1988, while deep into her work on *Almanac of the Dead*, Silko described the book "as a voracious feeder" upon her psyche that "literally impose[d] itself upon" her (Coltelli 137). Silko's friend, the poet Joy Harjo, says in a review of *Almanac*: "I was truly worried for her life when she ventured into the Mayan calendar of the days searching out the stories that would form her novel. I knew she was risking her life..." (Harjo 210). The fruit of Silko's dark labor was a novel that stands as one of the strongest critiques of human cruelty and social injustice ever written in this country.

Notes

1. As of this writing, no in-depth criticism on *Almanac of the Dead* exists, though many reviews appeared just after the novel's publication. The reviews referred to here appeared in the *New York Times Book Review*, December 22, 1991: 6; *Time*, December 9, 1991: 86; and the *Utne Reader*, May 1992: 117.

2. A list of significant Native American texts published in 1992 to commemorate the Quincentennial would include not only *Almanac of the Dead* but *The Business of Fancydancing* by Sherman Alexie, *The Crown of Columbus* by Michael Dorris and Louise Erdrich, *Among the Dog Eaters* by Adrian C. Louis, *The Heirs of Columbus* by Gerald Vizenor, and *Talking Indian* by Anna Lee Walters. In monetary terms, Dorris and Erdrich's *The Crown of Columbus*, a best-seller, was the most successful of these.

Silko's low opinion of Erdrich's writing is a matter of public record. See Leslie Marmon Silko, "Here's an Odd Artifact for the Fairy-Tale Shelf," review of *The Beet Queen*, by Louise Erdrich, *Impact/Albuquerque Journal*, October 8, 1986: 10-11. This review was later reprinted in *Studies in American Indian Literature*, 10 (1986): 177-184.

Susan Perez Castillo examines Silko's review of *The Beet Queen* in "Postmodernism, Native American Literature and the Real: The Silko-Erdrich Controversy," *Massachusetts Review,* 32.2 (Summer 1991): 285-294.

3. For her autobiographical perspective on the Jackpile uranium mine of Laguna Pueblo see Silko's "The Fourth World," *Artforum,* 27 (Summer 1989): 124-127.

Selected Bibliography

Primary Sources

Almanac of the Dead. New York: Simon & Schuster, 1991.
Ceremony. New York: Viking, 1977.
"The Fourth World." *Artforum,* 27 (Summer 1989): 124-127.
"Here's an Odd Artifact for the Fairy-Tale Shelf." *Impact/Albuquerque Journal,* October 8, 1986: 10-11. Review of *The Beet Queen,* by Louise Erdrich. Reprinted in *Studies in American Indian Literature,* 10 (1986): 177-184.
Laguna Woman. Greenfield Center, New York: Greenfield Review Press, 1974.
Storyteller. New York: Seaver Books, 1981.

Secondary Sources

Coltelli, Laura. *Winged Words: American Indian Writers Speak.* Lincoln: University of Nebraska Press, 1990.
Harjo, Joy. "The World is Round: Some Notes on Leslie Silko's *Almanac of the Dead.*" *Blue Mesa Review,* 4 (Spring 1992): 207-210.
Krupat, Arnold. "Dialogic in Silko's *Storyteller.*" In *Narrative Chance: Postmodern Discourse on Native American Indian Literatures.* Gerald Vizenor, ed. Albuquerque: University of New Mexico Press, 1989. Pp. 55-68.
Owens, Louis. "'The Very Essence of Our Lives': Leslie Silko's Webs of Identity." In *Other Destinies: Understanding the American Indian Novel.* Norman: University of Oklahoma Press, 1992. Pp. 167-191. A close, insightful reading of *Ceremony,* focusing on Silko's "attempt to find a particular strength within what has almost universally been treated as the 'tragic' fact of mixed-blood existence."
Ronnow, Gretchen. "Tayo, Death, and Desire: A Lacanian Reading of *Ceremony.*" In *Narrative Chance: Postmodern Discourse on Native American Indian Literatures.* Gerald Vizenor, ed. Albuquerque: University of New Mexico Press, 1989. Pp. 69-90.
Seyersted, Per. *Leslie Marmon Silko.* Boise: Boise State University Western Writers Series, 1980. The earliest in-depth look at Silko's work and still a valuable resource.
Simard, Rodney, ed. *Studies in American Indian Literatures,* 5:2 (Spring 1993). An entire issue devoted to Silko's *Storyteller.*

Robert F. Gish

Rudolfo A. Anaya

Rudolfo A. Anaya has come as close to canonization in the mainstream of American authors as any Chicano/a or regional writer. He is widely anthologized, and recent mass paperback reissues and translations of his novels promise him an even wider readership.

As contradictory, divisive, and exclusionary as the present-day culture and regional wars may seem, Anaya has, over the past two decades, reached something of the status of Chicano *abuelo, cacique, or adelantero* —the equivalent of a Chicano William Dean Howells or J. Frank Dobie. Anaya, like those more traditional luminaries of U.S. and southwestern literary history, has served a key role as a mentor in assisting other Chicano/a writers, other sons and daughters of the great American Southwest.

Anaya's role as exemplar with universal appeal has not been an easy one in the face of leftist, nationalistic allegations that he has either refused or neglected to infuse direct doses of propaganda into his writings. Thus he poses a fascinating case study of the issues —both real and problematic—of the relationships between propaganda and art, aesthetics and politics.

Anaya is decidedly a Chicano author. More than a Latino author, a Hispanic author, a Mexican-American author, Anaya is first and foremost a Chicano. He has Indian and Mexican blood ties. He speaks on

behalf of the downtrodden, the poor, the deprived, the people of the bar-
rio, *la raza*, those working-class individuals who, like Anaya and his own
parents scraping out a living by farming in eastern New Mexico in the
1940s, share kinship and heartfelt affinity with the land, with the rivers
and mesas, the mountains and plains, *valle y llano* of the Southwest. It is
a West of mind, spirit, and myth which Chicanos regard as *Aztlán*, their
lost but reclaimed homeland which transcends geographic borders
between the United States and Mexico and extends far and away into
the *carne y hueso*, the blood and bone and psyche of *la familia, la gente*,
and their cause.

All of Anaya's novels are unified by the values of place as well as by
a certain interconnected, reflexive allusiveness of plot and character.
Well past mid-phase as a writer, he continues to produce works that present a panorama of place in a southwestern saga.

Anaya's first novel, *Bless Me, Ultima* (1972), came out of an apprenticeship of much labor and love — or as he avows, one writes "until
totally screwed and the hemorrhoids kick in — *hasta que te lleva la madre,
y las almorranas*." That love and labor, that devotion to the writer's craft
and the people's cause have provided him with his great theme and have
continued through two other novels, *Heart of Aztlán* (1976) and *Tortuga*
(1979), which present a kind of New Mexico or Aztlán trilogy unlikely
to be surpassed for its accuracy of twentieth-century Chicano ambience,
spirit of place, and overall cultural authenticity.

His most recent novel at the time of this writing, *Alburquerque*
(1992), confirms Anaya's continuing reverence for myths and tradi-
tions, his dedication to the Mexican American people and to the land.
It is more culmination than coincidence that the two heroes of
Alburquerque, Ben Chavez and his estranged but reclaimed son, Abrán
Gonzalez, are, as writer and boxer respectively, both fighters for the
primacy and sanctity of people and place, preservers of that northern
New Mexico city, that "*pueblo de Aztlán*" of Anaya's own home,
Albuquerque.

Anaya's volume of short stories, *The Silence of the Llano* (1982), also
perpetuates that same allegiance to the lives and landscapes of contemporary New Mexico, the larger southwestern U.S., and the ghost echoes
of *Nueva Granada*, and behind that, of the mythic ancestral and indigenous Aztec/Nahuatl center and home, *Aztlán*. The collection is a stunning array of stories dealing with the *llano estacado*, Anaya's boyhood
home, narratives infused with what, as a special rendering of the tech-

niques and sensibilities of "magical realism," can perhaps best be termed "Southwest mysticism."

These same echoes or laminations of cultures and racial/ethnic memories, combined with the yet-to-be-discovered future and restored in a spiritually imbued, numinous and enchanting nodality of place, are carried out in more explicit recountings of Chicano heritage and myth in two retold narratives. *The Legend of La Llorona* (1984) is an account of the ubiquitous, seductive, ever-searching, weeping woman so frequently (and so fearfully) encountered in Anaya's fiction and in Chicano culture, here dramatized as Malinche, the mistress of Cortez. *Lord of the Dawn: The Legend of Quetzalcoatl* (1987) is a casting of the at-once prophetic and apocalyptic myth of the plumed serpent and its role in the colonization of Mexico by Hernán Cortez and in the exodus from and promised return to Aztlán.

In *A Chicano in China* (1986), an account in diary or travelogue form of a trip Anaya and his wife took to China in 1984, Anaya achieves a unique and provocative thematic and structural fusion of the ancient and the modern — ancestral gleanings which jump continents and generations and do indeed merge East and West, ancient and modern. Much the same can be said for Anaya's explorations as a playwright in such productions as *Who Killed Don Jose?* (1987), and other dramas staged by Chicano/a theater groups in Albuquerque, Denver, and other regional cities.

In his numerous essays — for example, "The Writer's Landscape: Epiphany in Landscape" (1977), "One Million Volumes" (1982), and "An American Chicano in King Arthur's Court" (1990) — Anaya hits again and again on the crucial significance and efficacy of words and language (Spanish, English, and Spanglish) and the role of the writer as cultural creator, preserver, and conduit for the music and message of the earth, the land.

Through his own aesthetic and his own redemptive version of the Chicano protests and manifestoes of the 1960s, Rudolfo A. Anaya leads his readers, Chicano and non-Chicano alike, back to old, earth-felt, heart-felt beginnings. He explores how language reaffirms our humanity; how our human destiny is inextricably linked to *la tierra*, the sacred earth, a place never fully comprehended in its wondrous, limitless locale, and only nominally known as West, which blesses us with her goodness if we are only willing to realize it; how myth and story afford not only our identity but our hoped-for salvation beyond race, beyond place.

Selected Bibliography

Primary Sources

Books

Alburquerque. Albuquerque: University of New Mexico Press, 1992

Bless Me, Ultima. Berkeley, California: Quinto Sol Publications, 1972.

A Chicano in China. Albuquerque: University of New Mexico Press, 1986.

The Farolitos of Christmas. New York: Hyperion Books for Children, 1995.

Heart of Aztlán. Berkeley, California: Justa Publications, 1976; rpt., Albuquerque: University of New Mexico Press, 1988.

The Legend of La Llorona. Berkeley, California: Tonatiuh-Quinto Sol Publications, 1984, 1991.

Lord of the Dawn: The Legend of Quetzalcoatl. Albuquerque: University of New Mexico Press, 1987.

The Silence of the Llano. Berkeley, California: TQS Publications, 1982.

Tortuga. Albuquerque: University of New Mexico Press, 1979.

Zia Summer. New York: Warner Books, 1995.

Plays/Dramas

Who Killed Don Jose? In *New Mexico Plays*. Albuquerque: University of New Mexico Press, 1989, Pp. 197-231; rpt., *Anaya Reader*. New York: Warner Books, 1995.

Selected Essays

"An American Chicano in King Arthur's Court." In *The Frontier Experience and the American Dream: Essays on American Literature*. David Mogen, Mark Busby and Paul Bryant, eds. College Station: Texas A&M University Press, 1989. Pp. 180-185.

"One Million Volumes." In *The Magic of Words*. Albuquerque: University of New Mexico Press, 1982. Pp. 9-20.

"The Writer's Landscape: Epiphany in Landscape," *Latin American Literary Review*, 5:10 (Spring-Summer 1977): 99-100.

Secondary Sources

Dasenbrock, Reed Way. "Forms of Biculturalism in Southwestern Literature: The Work of Rudolfo Anaya and Leslie Marmon Silko." *Genre*, 21 (Fall 1988): 307-319.

Gish, Robert F. "Curanderismo and Witchery in the Fiction of Rudolfo A. Anaya: The Novel as Magic." *New Mexico Humanities Review*, 2 (Summer 1979): 5-13.

———. "Magic Realism and the Wailing Woman: La Llorona in Contemporary Mexican-American Literature." *Cross Timbers Review*, 2:1 (May 1985): 18-38.

Gonzalez, Ray. "Songlines of the Southwest: An Interview with Rudolfo A. Anaya." *The Bloomsbury Review*, 13 (September-October 1993): 3, 18.

Lamadrid, Enrique. "The Dynamics of Myth in the Creative Vision of Rudolfo Anaya." In *Paso Por Aqui: Critical Essays on the New Mexican Literary Tradition, 1542-1988*. Albuquerque: University of New Mexico Press, 1989. Pp. 243-254.

Lattin, Vernon E. "The Horror of Darkness: Meaning and Structure in Anaya's *Bless Me, Ultima*." *Revista Chicano-Requena*, 6 (Spring 1978): 51-57.

Martin-Rodriguez, Manuel M. "El tema de la culpa en cuatro novelistas chicanos." *Hispanic Journal*, 10 (Fall 1988): 133-142.

Mitchell, Carol. "Rudolfo Anaya's *Bless Me, Ultima*: Folk Culture in Literature." *Critique*, 22 (1980): 55-64.

Reed, Ishmael. "An Interview with Rudolfo Anaya." *San Francisco Review of Books*, 4 (June 1978): 9-11, 34.

Sanders, Scott P. "Southwestern Gothic: Alienation, Integration, and Rebirth in the Works of Richard Shelton, Rudolfo Anaya, and Leslie Silko." *Weber Studies*, 4 (Fall 1980): 36-53.

Waggoner, Amy. "Tony's Dreams—An Important Dimension in *Bless Me, Ultima*." *Southwestern American Literature*, 4 (1974): 74-79.

Robert F. Gish

N. Scott Momaday

When N. Scott Momaday edited *The Complete Poems of Frederick Tuckerman* in 1965, the relative academic obscurity, if not quaintness, of both Tuckerman and his Kiowa editor seemed secure. With the publication by the University of California – Santa Barbara of a limited edition of Kiowa folktales under the title, *The Journey of Tai-me*, two years later, Momaday became considerably less obscure, albeit primarily in academic awareness, and was nudged toward some wider career, some greater popular destiny as an author.

Then came *The Way to Rainy Mountain* (1969), an autobiographical triptych of the author's pilgrimage back to Oklahoma and the land of his parents, grandparents, and ancestors. The lyrical travel narrative joined with Momaday's prior interest in the Kiowa sun deity, Tai-me, to make a personal journey structured, layered, and laminated over and alongside larger myth and history. The result is a poetic and anthropological version of the journeys of the Kiowa people at large and Momaday's father's Wyoming and Oklahoma Indian heritage in particular.

When *House Made of Dawn* was published in 1968, something worthy of great merit came on the scene: merit and significance for the author and for the reading public. The Pulitzer Prize was only part of the greatness of *House*, for that award soon faded into the annals of formal recognition and fame. The real achievement of the book was in Momaday's artistry, for he fashioned something seldom found in the career of any writer and never before, at least in fictional form, by an American Indian.

It was a momentous book, both in itself and in what it signified and what it sparked: a renaissance of American Indian writing that would arc backward to certain earlier nineteenth- and twentieth-century traditions of the "Indian novel" and back even further to the impulses of 20,000 years of enduring indigenous oral telling. This renaissance would, though embracing Anglo-European, modern traditions of the novel, resurrect and redirect discoveries and rediscoveries of what by now extends to a second and third generation of American Indian artists who owe some part — large or small — of their vision and their voice to Momaday.

Momaday (always allusive to his previous-but-always-accumulating aggregate of past writings), building on the poetic sensibilities of Tuckerman and of his Stanford mentor, Yvor Winters, published two volumes of poetry, *Angle of Geese and Other Poems* (1974), a slim but powerful collection (allusive in its way to *House*), and *The Gourd Dancer* (1976), a book that, along with collecting previous poems in tandem with several new ones, confirmed as well Momaday's burgeoning abilities as a visual artist and illustrator.

Like most Americans, and in keeping with one of the dominant themes in all his writings, Momaday seeks to know, acknowledge and accept the converging lines of a mixed ancestry — Kiowa on his father's side, European (French) immigrant and Cherokee on his mother's side. In *The Names* (1976), as in his previous works, Momaday juxtaposes myth, exposition, photography, and various narrative forms to underscore the complexity of such familial and artistic convergences. In the naming is the knowing. And in the writing is the discovery of that knowing.

In recent writings, especially his second novel, *The Ancient Child* (1989), Momaday returns again to the rewriting, the reconsidering, the reworking of many of his earlier forms and themes wherein the child is father to the man. It is at once new and strange yet within Momaday's familiar fusion of paradoxical ideas and forms. The difference is that here the legend of Billy the Kid and of what is usually thought of as the outlaw "Old West" — the Anglo-American West — counterbalances Indian myth and the natural-supernaturalism of an estranged American Indian painter (an obvious artistic analogue to Momaday) named Locke Setman. The protagonist's quest (like Momaday's) is the search for father and family. In the finding of the mysterious, vivacious, and wise time-traveler and Navajo-Kiowa medicine woman, Grey, the novel merges and melds across time, outside of time, with the bear boy of Kiowa myth so familiar in *Rainy Mountain* — a myth which ultimately subsumes Set as central character and Momaday as ventriloquist novelist. Anglo West and Indian West prove as inextricable in story as in history.

The Billy the Kid portions of the novel work as a transitional entryway for Grey as archetypal seductress, ever alluring to both Billy and Set. Similarly, the Billy legend provides a mirrored variant of that other ancient child — the bear boy. It is between the boy of outlaw legend and the bear boy of Indian myth that Set seeks to "set" his own real yet iconographic self.

The bear boy/outlaw boy legends and myths are present, told and told once more, seemingly always inviting such culmination, such fusion of character and plot, in nearly everything Momaday has written. In *Child* the horizontal and vertical, synchronic and diachronic leaps and laminations so characteristic of Momaday's technique reach out to masterful if not always wholly successful strivings of narrative innovation.

So too with Momaday's most recent work, *In the Presence of the Sun: Stories and Poems* (1992), wherein the author combines, collects and appropriates — through stories about Kiowa shields and their imaged and real presence, and again, as in *Child* — the enigma of that ancient, murdering, alluring child, William Bonney. Here too are familiar reiterations of the grand American Indian/Anglo-American western story Momaday tells most satisfactorily and completely in *House*. Its retelling here proves that in the glorious byways of art, if there is but one story to tell, its telling proves infinite.

Ever in art, always in words, Momaday stresses *place*. He reminds us that "there is something about the establishment of place and the recognition of place that belongs in the realm of language"; that "where words touch the land, there is place" ("Language and Landscape" 1). To read Momaday, to know his word way is, then, to know place, to know West, and to know the greatness of place as word, word as West.

Selected Bibliography

Primary Sources

The Ancient Child. New York: Doubleday, 1989.
Angle of Geese and Other Poems. Boston: D. R. Godine, 1974.

The Gourd Dancer. New York: Harper and Row, 1976.
House Made of Dawn. New York: Harper and Row, 1968.
In the Presence of the Sun: Stories and Poems. New York: St. Martin's Press, 1992.
The Journey of Tai-me. Santa Barbara: University of California, 1967.
"Language and Landscape." *Humanities,* 15 (Summer 1993).
The Names. New York: Harper and Row, 1976.
Owl in the Cedar Tree. Flagstaff, Arizona: Northland Press, 1975.
The Way to Rainy Mountain. Albuquerque: University of New Mexico Press, 1969.

Secondary Sources

Kroeber, Karl. "Technology and Tribal Narrative." In *Narrative Chance: Postmodern Discourse on Native American Indian Literatures.* Gerald Vizenor, ed. Albuquerque: University of New Mexico Press, 1989. Pp. 17-37.

Lincoln, Kenneth. "Tai-me to Rainy Mountain: The Makings of American Indian Literature." *American Indian Quarterly,* 10 (Spring 1986): 101-117.

Manly, Kathleen E. B. "Decreasing the Distance: Contemporary Native American Texts, Hypertext, and the Concept of Audience." *Southern Folklore,* 51:2 (1994): 121-135.

Meredith, Howard. "N. Scott Momaday: A Man of Words." *World Literature Today,* 64 (Summer 1990): 405-407.

Nelson, Robert M. "Snake and Eagle: Abel's Disease and the Landscape of *House Made of Dawn.*" *Studies in American Indian Literature,* 1 (Fall 1989): 1-20.

Roemer, Kenneth M. *Approaches to Teaching Momaday's* The Way to Rainy Mountain. New York: Modern Language Association, 1988.

Scarberry-Garcia, Susan. *Landmarks of Healing: A Study of* House Made of Dawn. Albuquerque: University of New Mexico Press, 1990.

Taylor, Paul Beekman. "Repetition as Cure in Native American Story: Silko's *Ceremony* and Momaday's *The Ancient Child.*" *Swiss Papers in English Language and Literature,* Series Number 7 (1994): 221-242.

Waniek, Marilyn Nelson. "The Power of Language in N. Scott Momaday's *House Made of Dawn.*" *Minority Voices,* 4 (Spring 1980): 23-28.

Ann Ronald

Edward Abbey

Dick Kirkpatrick calls it "the greening of Edward Abbey." This phenomenon, rooted in the 1968 publication of *Desert Solitaire* and blossoming with the 1975 appearance of *The Monkey Wrench Gang*, has grown virulent since the author's death. Edward Abbey, the man, in many ways now looms larger than Edward Abbey, the author. Ed would have hated such reversals but, ironically, his own prose helped create the inversion. Abbey's nonfiction books recount numerous personal adventures and only thinly disguise a narrative voice. The penultimate fiction that Abbey called his "masterpiece," *The Fool's Progress* (1988), further confuses the distance between the author and his fictional persona.

Subtitled "An Honest Novel," *The Fool's Progress* traces the life and times of Henry Holyoak Lightcap, an eastern hillbilly turned western gadfly. While certain differences are obvious, the thrust of the tale is remarkably similar to Abbey's own lifetime adventures. The structure of *The Fool's Progress* belies its autobiographical story line, however, for this crafted novel finely balances the present and the past. The present leads Henry from Tucson to the Allegheny mountains—a madcap drive through New Mexico, across the Missouri and the Mississippi rivers, then up into the coal country of the Appalachian hills. In alternating chapters the narrator reconstructs Lightcap's past—juxtaposing foibles with triumphs, adventures with imaginings, reality with dreams. The narrative also slips back and forth between first person and third.

"Henry indulges himself in a favored fantasy," starts a paragraph on the second page; "I shall live the clean hard cold rigors of an ascetic philosopher," reads the very next sentence. If a reader believes *The Fool's Progress* is more autobiography than fiction, the author doesn't help, though his overall plan was something rather more profound.

Almost immediately after Abbey's death in 1989, a tiny book of epithets and aphorisms added to a growing autobiographical mystique. *A Voice Crying in the Wilderness (Vox Clamantis in Deserto)* (1989) offers notes from a secret journal, outrageous one-liners that range from religion to music to sports, from government to science to nature, from books to love to horses. David Petersen's lengthier selections from Abbey's journals, *Confessions of a Barbarian* (1994), carry an egocentric mystique still further. "Everything in the universe converges upon me," a young Abbey reveals in the first entry. Trusting the "confessions" as a rounded picture of Abbey's authorial consciousness is a mistake, however, since Petersen prints selections from notebooks containing four times as many words. Subjective, too, are the poems Petersen chose for *Earth Apples* (1994). Like the *Confessions*, the *Earth Apples* pieces — which sound more like prose than poetry — come from the notebooks and reveal more about states of mind than artistry.

Others are jumping on the "greening" bandwagon, too. James Hepworth and Gregory McNamee's likable *Resist Much, Obey Little* (1989) contains essays and observations more amusing than evaluative. The biography by James Bishop, Jr., *Epitaph for a Desert Anarchist: The Life and Legacy of Edward Abbey* (1994), outlines a journalist's overview of Abbey's life and a largely derivative reading of his prose. A one-hour documentary, *Edward Abbey: A Voice in the Wilderness* (1994), featuring interviews with sixteen close friends and family members and containing original clips and vintage photographs of Abbey himself, reveals even more about the writer's personality, explains even less about his literary accomplishments.

Somewhere in the greening, Abbey's books are getting lost. Perhaps that's just as well. His last novel, *Hayduke Lives!* (1990), a hastily written, unrevised fiction, brings the Monkey Wrench Gang back together in yet another encounter with Bishop Love and his megamachinery. While fun for Abbey aficionados to read, the book is too full of undisciplined effusions and sexual enthusiasms to hold interest for most readers.

On the other hand, his later nonfiction boasts as much control as his earlier prose. *One Life at a Time, Please* (1988) collects twenty-one lively essays, including the infamous Montana lecture, "Free Speech: The Cowboy and his Cow," where Abbey takes on the code of the cowboy West, the so-called "natural nobleman," and the western myth of "sacred cows." Such an essay is Abbey at his argumentative best, asking complicated rhetorical questions and displaying few rhetorical excesses. Another fine essay in *One Life at a Time, Please* states Abbey's artistic code directly: "the writer worthy of his calling must be more than an entertainer: he must be a seer, a prophet, the defender of life, freedom, openness, and always—*always!* [italics Abbey's]—a critic of society" ("A Writer's Credo" 174). That he generally lived up to his own creed is a measure of Abbey's worth as a major twentieth-century western writer. That his readers can mistake his personality for his achievements is an unfortunate analogue to what he actually accomplished.

By most criteria, Edward Abbey has had a profound impact on late-twentieth-century western American literature, most specifically on its newly reborn genre, "the personal nature essay," and on its new-found analytical alliance, "ecocriticism." With the 1968 publication of *Desert Solitaire*, Abbey reintroduced a way of blending the human voice with the extra-human natural world. Some would say he moved Thoreau into the modern age, but Abbey disagreed. "Read my books," he countered, "and you'll discover that only about ten percent of my words are concerned with conservation issues. The rest is play. Entertainment." A reader can never be sure. Abbey's later prose took seriously the writer's obligations as "prophet" and "defender of life." His last original collection of essays includes, for example, a staunch argument for monkey-wrench tactics. "Eco-defense means fighting back. Eco-defense means sabotage. Eco-defense is risky but sporting; unauthorized but fun; illegal but ethically imperative" ("Eco-Defense" 31). *Hayduke Lives!* may be the "play," the "entertainment" to which Abbey alluded in his self-assessment, but the "critic of society" defines the rules of the game.

Remembered by some for his moral message and by others for his irascible personality, Edward Abbey can be praised for his wisdom and wit. What brings the author of *Desert Solitaire* to the first rank of contemporary writers, however, is craftsmanship. A powerful arrangement of metaphor, image, and sign punctuates his best fiction, defines his best essays. "Good writing consists of having something interesting to say and saying it well," he wrote in late 1983. "Message and technique, content and form—neither alone is sufficient; both are essential." Both are wedded in those paragraphs that best bring to life a perfect Abbey world.

The odor of crushed sage in the hand. The fragrance of burning juniper. A mountain lion crouched on a canyon ledge. The word *canyon* itself. One black vulture soaring in lazy circles above the burning hills and ice-cream-tinted folds of the Painted Desert. Red mountains like mangled iron rising beyond dunes of golden sand. Stone ruins nestled in an alcove of a cliff. The cry of the coyote — first one, then a second, then a chorus as a full moon the color of a blood orange sinks beyond the skyline.

Not the greening of Edward Abbey, not even the black vulture, but the golden sand of his ideas, the blood orange of his prose are what future generations of readers finally must admire most.

Selected Bibliography

Primary Sources since 1984

The Best of Edward Abbey. San Francisco: Sierra Club Books, 1984.

Confessions of a Barbarian. Santa Barbara: Capra Press, 1986.

Confessions of a Barbarian: Selections from the Journals of Edward Abbey, 1951-1989. Edited and with an introduction by David Petersen. Boston: Little, Brown, 1994.

Earth Apples: The Poetry of Edward Abbey. David Petersen, ed. New York: St. Martin's Press, 1994.

The Fool's Progress: An Honest Novel. New York: Henry Holt, 1988.

Hayduke Lives! Boston: Little, Brown, 1990.

One Life at a Time, Please. New York: Henry Holt, 1988.

The Serpents of Paradise: A Reader. New York: Henry Holt, 1995.

A Voice Crying in the Wilderness (Vox Clamantis in Deserto). New York: St. Martin's Press, 1989.

Other Abbey Materials

Edward Abbey: An Interview at Pack Creek Ranch. Santa Fe: Vinegar Tom Press, 1991.

Edward Abbey: A Voice in the Wilderness (one hour VHS documentary). South Burlington, Vermont: Eric Temple Productions, 1993.

Freedom and Wilderness (two cassette recordings). Minocque, Wisconsin: NorthWord Press, 1987.

Resist Much, Obey Little: The Writer as Social Critic (one cassette recording). San Francisco: New Dimensions Foundation, 1989.

Wilderness Journal (one hour VHS documentary). Los Angeles: Stephen Fisher Productions, 1984.

Secondary Sources

Berger, Y. "The 'Burial of Edward Abbey' with Introduction and Annotations by Gregory McNamee." *Journal of the Southwest*, 35 (Fall 1993): 357-362.

Bishop, James, Jr. *Epitaph for a Desert Anarchist: The Life and Legacy of Edward Abbey.* New York: Atheneum, 1994.

Bryant, Paul T. "Echoes, Allusions, and Reality in *Hayduke Lives!*" *Western American Literature*, 25 (February 1991): 311-322.

———. "Edward Abbey and Environmental Quixoticism." *Western American Literature*, 24 (May 1989): 37-43.

Buell, Lawrence. *The Environmental Imagination.* Cambridge: Harvard University Press, 1995.

Cahalan, James M. "Edward Abbey, Appalachian Easterner." *Western American Literature*, 31 (November 1996): 233-253.

Davis, Carl. "Thoughts on a Vulture: Edward Abbey, 1927-1989." *Arts and Letters: A Liberal Arts Forum*, 15 (Fall 1989): 15-23.

Dixon, Terrell. "Abbey's Biocentric Epiphany: *Desert Solitaire* and the Teaching of Environmental Literature." *CEA Critic*, 54 (Fall 1991): 35-42.

Dougherty, Jay. "'Once-More, and Once-Again': Edward Abbey's Cyclical View of Past and Present in *Good News.*" *Studies in Contemporary Fiction*, 29 (Summer 1988): 223-232.

Gamble, David E. "Into the Maze with Edward Abbey." *South Dakota Review*, 26 (Spring 1988): 66-77.

Gesteland, B. J. "Edward Abbey, the Female Reader and the Feminist Critic." *Western American Literature*, 28 (November 1993): 233-234.

Greiner, Patricia. "Radical Environmentalism in Recent Literature Concerning the American West." *Rendezvous*, 19 (Fall 1983): 8-15.

Hepworth, James. "Edward Abbey, 1927-1989." *Western American Literature*, 24 (Summer 1989): 151-152.

Hepworth, James and Gregory McNamee, eds. *Resist Much, Obey Little.* Tucson: Harbinger, 1989; rpt., *Resist Much, Obey Little: Remembering Ed Abbey.* San Francisco: Sierra Club Books, 1996.

Jimerson, Kay. "Edward Abbey." *This Is About Vision: Interviews with Southwestern Writers*, William Balassi, John F. Crawford and Annie O. Eysturoy, eds. Albuquerque: University of New Mexico Press, 1990. Pp. 52-57.

Killingsworth, M. Jimmie. "Realism, Human Action, and Instrumental Discourse." *Journal of Advanced Composition*, 12 (Winter 1992): 171-200.

McClintock, J. I. "Edward Abbey's 'Antidotes to Despair.'" *Studies in Contemporary Fiction*, 31 (Fall 1989): 41-54.

———. *Nature's Kindred Spirits.* Madison: University of Wisconsin Press, 1994.

Mathe, Sylvie. "Desir du Desert: Hommage au Grande Desert Americain." *Revue Francaise d'Etudes Americaines*, 16 (November 1991): 423-436.

Murray, John A. "The Hill Beyond the City: Elements of the Jeremiaid in Edward Abbey's *Down the River with Henry David Thoreau.*" *Western American Literature*, 22 (February 1988): 301-306.

Ronald, Ann. "A Clean Hard Edge Divides (A Farewell to Ed Abbey)." *Redneck Review of Literature*, 16 (Spring 1989): 1-6.

Scheese, Don. "*Desert Solitaire*: Counter-Friction to the Machine in the Garden." *North Dakota Quarterly*, 59 (Spring 1991): 211-227.

Slovic, Scott. "Aestheticism and Awareness: The Psychology of Edward Abbey's *The Monkey Wrench Gang*." *CEA Critic,* 55 (Spring-Summer 1993): 54-68.

———. *Seeking Awareness in American Native Writing.* Salt Lake City: University of Utah Press, 1992.

Tatum, Stephen. "Closing and Opening Western American Fiction: The Reader in *The Brave Cowboy*." *Western American Literature,* 19 (Fall 1984): 187-203.

Western American Literature, 28 (May 1993). Edward Abbey Special Issue. Includes Paul T. Bryant, "The Structure and Unity of *Desert Solitaire*," 3-19; David Copland Morris, "Celebration and Irony: The Polyphonic Voice of Edward Abbey's *Desert Solitaire*," 21-32; David Petersen, "Cactus Ed's Moveable Feast: A Preview of *Confessions of a Barbarian: Pages from the Journals of Edward Abbey*," 33-42; Jack Loeffler, "Edward Abbey, Anarchism and the Environment," 43-49.

Wild, Peter. "Edward Abbey: The Middle-Class Maverick." *New Mexico Humanities Review,* 6 (Summer 1983): 15-23.

Marie-Madeleine Schein

Simon J. Ortiz

imon Ortiz is one of today's most respected Native American writers. Although he also writes short stories and children's literature, Ortiz is best known for his poetry, and his choice of subject for his poems is "his" Native America, the land he lives on, loves, respects, and jealously protects. His work, reflecting meticulous observations of a personal environment, constitutes a collage of "postcards from Native America," a journey across the regions he has traveled through. Most poems describe the Southwest, but a few take the readers to other states like Florida and the Dakotas. Throughout this journey across America, Ortiz points out many of the most outrageous violations of the land by Euro-Americans in the name of expansion, emphasizes the necessity of always cultivating the bond between Man and Nature, and celebrates the survival and the continuance of the Native American culture. Andrew Wiget notes:

> Anglo and Indian have been exposed to the power of Euro-American culture to alienate, dislocate and remap. Against such debilitating forces, Ortiz feels keenly the need to reaffirm the historical bond between people and the land. (16)

A biting sense of survival humor in most of his poems informs such reaffirmation and serves to undercut many of his revelations about the abuses perpetrated against his Native America and its native people.

Simon Joseph Ortiz was born on May 27, 1941, at the Acoma Pueblo, near Albuquerque, New Mexico. After finishing high school, he worked for a year in the uranium mines and processing plants of the Grants-Ambrosia Lake area. He then enlisted in the army and, in 1966 at the end of his service, he enrolled at the University of New Mexico. He later attended the University of Iowa, where he received an M.F.A. in 1969. He has taught creative writing and American Indian literature at San Diego State University, the University of New Mexico, and Sinte Gleska College in Rosebud, South Dakota. Today Ortiz lives in Tuscon, Arizona.

Ortiz' major works include several collections of poetry: *Going for the Rain* (1976), *A Good Journey* (1977), *Fight Back: For the Sake of the People, for the Sake of the Land* (1980), *Woven Stone* (1992), which includes poetry from previous anthologies as well as new poems, and *After and Before the Lightning* (1994). Ortiz has also authored two collections of short stories: *Howbah Indians* (1978) and *Fightin': New and Collected Stories* (1983).

His awards include a Discovery Award from the National Endowment for the Arts in 1969, an NEA Fellowship in 1981, the Pushcart Prize for Poetry, and a Lifetime Achievement Award for literature from the Returning the Gift Foundation and Native Writers Circle of the Americas in 1993.

What concerns Ortiz most are the changes that took place in America in the name of progress and expansion, changes that have betrayed the connection that Native Americans believe exists between human beings and the surrounding natural and animal world. He writes, "Everything that is around you is part of you" (*Woven Stone* 471). His latest collection of poems, *After and Before the Lightning*, continues to illustrate his love of his Native America by celebrating the beauty of the surrounding landscape — here the Rosebud Sioux Indian Reservation in South Dakota where he taught for a winter. In many of these poems, he expresses his bitterness and fear about excessive and irrational land appropriation by Euro-Americans. William Oandassan explains how Ortiz's attitude is determined by the sense of urgency he feels when he observes that the gap between land and people is widening:

> Ortiz' revulsion from urban life is best understood as an attempt to maintain identity in an antagonistic environment. The conservation of identity is especially crucial when one's sense of self is culturally founded on the land of one's birth. (35)

548

Predictably, then, Ortiz considers every infringement on this sacred bond between land and people as an attack on his personal chance at survival. The poem "Grand Canyon Christmas Eve 1969" illustrates his resentment of Euro-American encroachment upon the land. The poem describes a visit to the Grand Canyon that is suddenly disturbed by the message on a U.S. Forest Service sign:

> KAIBAB NATIONAL FOREST
> CAMP ONLY IN CAMPING AREA
> NO WOOD GATHERING
> GO AROUND OTHER SIDE OF ENCLOSED AREA
> &
> DEPOSIT 85 CENTS FOR WOOD

The message reminds the narrator that ancestral grounds have become the property of the U.S. government and triggers an outraged reaction:

> This is ridiculous.
> You gotta to be kidding.
> Dammit, my grandfathers
> ran this place
> with bears and wolves.
> And I got some firewood
> anyway from the forest,
> mumbling, Sue me.
> (*Woven Stone* 187-188)

The defiant spirit of this reaction is humorous, but the humor reveals more than it entertains, pointing to the tragedy and the absurdity of the situation presented in the poem.

Ortiz is also relentless in his criticism of the modernization of the Albuquerque area, which disturbed the traditional way of life of the Native Americans who live there. His views are made particularly clear in the poem "The State's claim that it seeks in no way to deprive Indians of their rightful share of water, but only to define that share, falls on deaf ears" (*Woven Stone* 254). The poem describes the changes occasioned by the arrival of the railroad, electricity, gas, highways, cable television, and phone, insisting that although land developers look upon progress as a necessity, Native Americans who lived in that region felt progress to be debilitating to them.

Several poems from *Fight Back: For the Sake of the People, for the Sake of the Land* reveal another environmental concern: the mining of uranium in New Mexico. Ortiz is particularly sensitive to the exploitation of Indian workers who supplied hard labor at low wages. Ortiz is also aware of the potential for severe medical conditions that resulted from exposure to the uranium. The poem "It Was that Indian" reflects the curse of the discovery of uranium near Grants, New Mexico, by an Indian named Martinez and presents two conflicting events: the initial positive publicity caused by the discovery of uranium, and later, the concern about the side effects to humans resulting from its extraction. The blame for the latter is placed on the Indian who discovered it, who no longer receives praise but derision.

Although many of Ortiz' poems focus on the unpleasant realities for today's Native American, many more celebrate the survival and the continuance of Native Americans and rebel against the perception of them by Anglos as vanishing Americans. All the poems in this category present an ironic duality of point of view and offer Ortiz many opportunities to use survival humor. On the one hand, the poems reveal that Euro-Americans have only a vague notion of the existence of Native Americans today; on the other hand, the poems attempt to counteract this lack of knowledge by emphasizing the presence of Native Americans throughout this country.

The best example of the syndrome of the Indian as an object of curiosity is the poem "A New Story," in which a Colorado woman calls a veterans hospital wanting to hire an Indian as an extra for a Frontier Day parade. She wants "a real Indian on a float/ not just a paper mache dummy/ but a real Indian with feathers and paint" (*Woven Stone* 364).

Ortiz also stresses survival and continuance in other poems that retell traditional tales about Coyote, the famous trickster character of the Southwest. In her article "*Canis Latrans latrans* in the Poetry of Simon Ortiz," Patricia Clark Smith underlines the importance of Coyote's main characteristics: he is arrogant, daring, and determined. She writes, "Coyote always gets up and brushes himself off and trots away within the narrative itself, perhaps not quite as new, but alive, in motion, surviving" (3). Coyote's innate ability to survive his adventures serves as a model for today's Native Americans. Often Ortiz' Coyote poems emphasize Coyote's alienation from the other animals and the fact that he is often rejected by them. Ortiz speaks of Coyote's hardships, of his constant scheming and bragging, but he makes clear that Coyote, like Native Americans, has always found a way to survive. Smith points out the essence of Ortiz' Coyote poems:

> Throughout the body of Ortiz's work the emphasis is unremittingly on Coyote's survival. The old stories Ortiz chooses to retell, and the new situations he records or invents, all make Coyote's continuance far more prominent than his foolhardiness. (3)

Ortiz presents the somber realities of his Native America through an acute, bittersweet, disturbing, and piquant sense of humor. Through comments and images presented from the point of view of a Native American, Ortiz is able to take stock of a land in which Native Americans and non-Natives must cohabit. He concludes that what he calls his Native America has survived and will continue to do so. Rather than seeking to divide, Ortiz strives to unify; when he laughs at the abuses he observes, it is with the hope that the wrongs can be corrected. William Oandassan praises Ortiz' intentions and notes:

> In a world where the rational mind has polluted the air, health, and water with its technology, an early people's awareness of their dependent relationship to the earth for their survival has much to teach modern people about living in harmony with the landscape. (27)

Ortiz' peculiar humor, a type of coping mechanism, sensitizes the non-Native audience to the Native American wish for continuance and survival of their people and their "Native America."

Selected Bibliography

Primary Sources

Poetry

After and Before the Lightning. Tucson: University of Arizona Press, 1994.

Fight Back: For the Sake of the People, for the Sake of the Land. Albuquerque: University of New Mexico, 1980.

From Sand Creek. New York: Thunder's Mouth Press, 1981.

Going for the Rain. New York: Harper & Row, 1976.

A Good Journey. Berkeley: Turtle Island, 1977.
Woven Stone. Tucson: University of Arizona Press, 1992.

Short Story Collections
Fightin': New and Collected Short Stories. New York: Thunder's Mouth Press, 1983.
Howbah Indians. Tucson: Blue Moon, 1978.

Children's Books
The People Shall Continue, with Sharol Graves. San Francisco: Children's Book Press, 1978, 1988.
Blue and Red. Acoma, New Mexico: Pueblo of Acoma, 1982.

Critical Studies
Song, Poetry, Language: Expression and Perception. Tsaile, Arizona: Navaho Community College Press, 1978.
A Poem Is A Journey. Bourbonnais, Illinois: Pternandon, 1981.
Earth Power Coming: Short Stories in Native American Literature, Ortiz, Simon, ed. Tsaile, Arizona: Navajo Community College Press, 1983.

Interviews
Bruchac, Joseph. *Survival This Way: Interviews with American Indian Poets.* Tucson: University of Arizona Press, 1987. Pp. 214-229.
Coltelli, Laura. *Winged Words: American Indian Writers Speak.* Lincoln: University of Nebraska Press, 1990. Pp. 103-119.

Secondary Sources

Evers, Larry. "The Killing of a New Mexican State Trooper: Ways of Telling an Historical Event," *Wicazo Sa Review,* 1:1 (1985): 17-25.
Gingerich, Willard. "The Old Voices of Acoma: Simon Ortiz's Mythic Indigenism," *Southwest Review,* 64 (Winter 1979): 19-30.
Lincoln, Kenneth. "The Now Day Indi'ns." In *Native American Renaissance.* Kenneth Lincoln, ed. Berkeley: University of California Press, 1983. Pp. 183-220.
Manley, Katherine. "An Interview with Simon Ortiz," *Journal of the Southwest,* 31:3 (1989): 362-377.
Oandassan, William. "Simon Ortiz: The Poet and His Landscape," *Studies in American Indian Literature* 2:1 (1987): 26-37.
SAIL (Studies in American Indian Literature), 8:3-4 (1984). Special issue on Simon Ortiz.
Schein, Marie. "Simon Ortiz." In *Dictionary of Literary Biography,* Vol. 120 (1991).
Smith, Patricia Clark. "Canis Latrans Latrans in the Poetry of Simon Ortiz," *Minority Voices,* 3 (Fall 1979): 1-18.
Wiget, Andrew. *Simon Ortiz.* Boise: Boise State University Western Writers Series, 1986.

IV
Texas

Tom Pilkington

Texas

In most literary histories, bibliographies, and anthologies having to do with American regional literature, Texas is considered part of the Southwest. Indeed, *A Literary History of the American West* includes Texas in its section on the Southwest. However, in recent years it has become plain that Texas—like California in the Far West—is so large and diverse a slice of real estate that it demands separate treatment as a region in its own right. Larry McMurtry supplies a clue to the chronology of this change in thinking. In his 1968 essay collection, *In a Narrow Grave: Essays on Texas*, McMurtry has a piece called "Southwestern Literature?" (emphasis on the question mark). Most of the writers he discusses are Texans, but as his title suggests, he considers Texas writing within a larger regional context. His famous (or infamous) 1981 broadside, "Ever a Bridegroom: Reflections on the Failure of Texas Literature," obviously narrows the focus; by that time, he had come to believe there was a body of writing, "failed" though it is, that may be designated "Texas literature."

In defining a region such as the Southwest, the commentator looks for similarities—geographical, historical, and cultural—that bind together the people of the area. The irony is that, on the surface, few such similarities appear to exist in the geo-political entity we call Texas. While we can look on a map and see clearly drawn boundaries, there is more topographical, cultural, and ethnic diversity within those borders than in most nations of the world. What does El Paso, with an annual rainfall of seven inches, have in common with Beaumont, sloshing through an average of seventy inches of rainfall a year? How can the rancher in the Trans-Pecos, whose work is done at an altitude of over a mile, relate to the rice farmer near the Gulf of Mexico, whose work is performed in the murky air of sea level?

The answer to the riddle, of course, is what has been labeled the "Texas myth," or "the Texas mystique." Every group that comes to think of itself as a unified people must generate a mythology that supplies national or group identity. Before America could be "invented," to use Garry Wills' phrase, a battery of such myths had to be commonly accepted and believed. Consider the myth of "the American dream," or the myth of America as a "melting pot." No other state of the Union has spawned as extravagant and full-blown a mythology as Texas. The result has been that, until very recently anyway, almost all people who live in the state, no matter how different the circumstances of their lives and environments, have thought of themselves as Texans. As Stephen Brook writes :

> The puzzle of Texas is that it is simultaneously diverse and unified. Climatically, topographically, economically, the east has no con-nection to the west; yet the Texans' sense of themselves, their cul-tural identity...links the rancher from San Angelo with the timber merchant from Nacogdoches like mountaineers at different heights yet on the same rope. (*Honkytonk Gelato* [1985])

Most Texans, then, consider themselves citizens of a separate and dis-tinct entity — of their own country, as it were. Texas is, to adopt a phrase apparently coined in 1915 by Zane Grey in his popular novel *The Lone Star Ranger*, "a world in itself." (Many a writer since, including George Sessions Perry in his 1942 volume *Texas: A World in Itself*, has perpetu-ated the cliché.) As historian T. R. Fehrenbach asserts, Texas is a "nation-state," and it boasts of its own music, food, clothing, and, most grandiose of all, a "Texas lifestyle." Thus the idea of a "Texas literature" should hardly come as a shock.

As early as 1936, this idea began to take shape. It was in that year, during the celebration of the state's centennial, that the Texas Institute of Letters was founded. The TIL was conceived of as a select body charged with fostering in Texas the creative act of writing and the crit-ical appreciation of that writing. Today the TIL sponsors annual ceremonies in which a number of cash awards, in a variety of categories, are bestowed on the best Texas books of the year. It works in a number of other ways to create cohesiveness — or clubbiness, depending on one's point of view — in the state's writing community. To some, however, a state's having its own institute of letters is absurd — European-sounding rather than American — and down through the years there have been those who have chided both the theory and practice of the organization. But the TIL, reflecting no doubt an irrepressible strain of chauvinism, continues to grow and flourish.

The driving force in the creation of the TIL was J. Frank Dobie. By the 1930s Dobie was, as James Ward Lee has observed, the "arbiter" of literary taste in Texas (*Range Wars* 123-136). I know several people, all native Texans, who own near-complete sets of Dobie's books (which, incidentally, are kept in print by the University of Texas Press). The books sit on shelves beside volumes by Louis L'Amour and Stephen King. My friends read Louis L'Amour and Stephen King; they do not, for the most part, read Dobie. Nonetheless Dobie is revered, if unread, by many Texans. He taught Texans how to succeed at the culture game. By "succeed" I mean "make money." It is often forgotten that by the late 1920s Dobie had attracted a large national reading audience and was making considerably more money selling articles to the *Saturday Evening Post* and other mass-circulation periodicals than from teaching at the University of Texas at Austin.

More important, he gave Texans in the 1920s and 1930s a literary and cultural identity. His folklore-collecting forays through Texas, the Southwest, and Mexico provided fodder for his explorations of southwestern culture in the popular media. The force of Dobie's personality awakened many Texans — and southwesterners — to the literary possibilities of the songs and tales that sprang from their colorful folk tradition. People across the country responded to the power of his rendition of southwestern folklore by dubbing him the Carl Sandburg of the Southwest. Thus, to this day, many Texans see Dobie as a natural resource, as important on the cultural level as cattle, cotton, and oil are — or were — on the economic level.

I prefer to think of Dobie as the father of Texas literature, a man who established a strong literary impulse in a place where none had previously existed. But if Dobie is the father, the matriarch of Texas letters is Katherine Anne Porter. The pair — born within two years of each other — are almost exact contemporaries. Porter's attitude toward Texas was

557

ambivalent. (The title of a recent collection of biographical and critical essays — *Katherine Anne Porter and Texas: An Uneasy Relationship* — gives some sense of her feelings.) By 1919, at age twenty-nine, she had abandoned the state for good. She lived in Mexico, Europe, Bermuda, Louisiana, and for the last several decades of her life, near Washington, D.C.

One of the more scandalous chapters in the checkered history of the Texas Institute of Letters occurred in 1939, when the group gave its annual award to Dobie's *Apache Gold and Yaqui Silver* rather than to Porter's masterful *Pale Horse, Pale Rider*, a gathering of three of her short novels. Porter was justifiably enraged. No discerning reader today would hesitate a millisecond in denouncing the choice. The decision clearly gave the appearance that the TIL was rewarding a good old local boy and snubbing an uppity woman who had left Texas two decades earlier. The episode served to estrange Porter even further from her native state and from its official literary spokesmen.

Still, Porter was always anxious about how her fellow Texans would judge her. She told an interviewer in the 1950s, "I am the first and only serious writer that Texas has produced." And later, in 1975, she would assert, "I happen to be the first native of Texas in its whole history to be a professional writer."[1] I believe Porter's significance to Texas literature lies in the fact that she supplied an alternate paradigm for budding Texas writers to follow. Dobie's paradigm was to stay home and till one's own literary and cultural soil; Porter's was the opposite, to decamp early and become a voluntary exile, and in the process to aim for higher stakes.[2]

Porter's claim to have been the first "professional writer" to emerge from Texas is not supported by the facts; Dobie earned far more money directly from his writings than Porter earned from hers. Actually Porter made her living more from her reputation among intellectuals than from her works themselves. She threw in with the so-called New Criticism and befriended such powerful New Critics as Robert Penn Warren and Cleanth Brooks, who found her symbol-laden tales and burnished prose style congenial to their mode of literary criticism. The result for Porter, from the 1930s on, was a steady string of lectures, foundation grants, and temporary appointments to teach in universities. In the end, Porter, despite her minuscule output (one medium-sized volume of *Collected Stories* and one novel), had her revenge. By the time of her death in 1980, her stories were routinely included in anthologies of American literature, introducing her name and her writings to new generations of readers, while nobody outside Texas — and fewer and fewer inside Texas — had ever heard of J. Frank Dobie.

Subsequent Texas writers have in general followed the Dobie paradigm or the Porter paradigm, though many interesting variations on the basic patterns have ensued. John Graves, for example, though living in New York City and Spain for about a decade in the late 1940s and early 1950s, has remained, for the most part, a Dobie-style homebody. Certainly he labors within the pastoral tradition established by Dobie — and by Dobie's friends, naturalist Roy Bedichek and historian Walter Prescott Webb. Graves sits on his four hundred acres of "hard scrabble" southwest of Fort Worth, meditating on the mysteries and intricacies of the natural order and of humanity's place in that order. However, his parsimonious output as a writer — two major books — resembles Porter's much more than Dobie's production.

On the other side of the coin is Graves' contemporary, William Goyen. Goyen remained in Texas long enough to take a degree at Rice University in Houston, but, following military service in World War II, he was an expatriate for the remainder of his life, living in New Mexico, New York City, Europe, and Los Angeles. Interestingly, though, he continued obsessively to write about Texas — in the novel *The House of Breath* (1950) and in many other novels and stories. Despite a residual bitterness because of the narrowness of his upbringing, he sometimes expressed, in his correspondence, love for the Texas land and culture. Like Porter's, Goyen's ambitions were high, and during his lifetime he built a modestly impressive international reputation; the gothic, surreal quality of his vision garnered considerable interest in his work in France and Germany.

The Texas writer who appears to have been most successful at surpassing his "parental" forebears, Dobie and Porter, has been Larry McMurtry, certainly at the moment Texas' best-known living literary figure. Beginning in the mid-1980s, with the enormous popularity of his epic *Lonesome Dove*, McMurtry (or McMurtry's agent, Irving "Swifty" Lazar) negotiated lucrative contracts with book clubs and publishers, screenwriting deals, and movie and TV adaptations of several of his tales. He has made more money, in real dollars, than J. Frank Dobie ever dreamed of making. Moreover, McMurtry has charmed the pants off the New York literary establishment even more successfully than did Katherine Anne Porter. In early 1986 *Lonesome Dove* won a Pulitzer Prize in fiction (the only other Texas writer to win a Pulitzer in fiction was Porter in 1966 for her *Collected Stories*). His books were subsequently reviewed in the *New York Review of Books*, the high church of American intellectuals. In the early 1990s, McMurtry served a two-year term as president of American PEN. He succeeded Susan Sontag in that post; before Sontag, Norman Mailer had been president. The ranch boy from Archer City, Texas, obviously has come a long way in the literary world.

While certain patterns in Texas writing, then, continue to play themselves out, social and demographic trends of recent decades have begun to muddy the waters somewhat. For one thing, Texas is now predominantly an urban state (with a population of more than eighty percent urban-dwellers, according to one recent analysis), while Texas literature —at least "classic" Texas literature—remains rural and largely anti-urban in orientation. A few of the state's most accomplished literary works have attempted to deal with urban experience. Billy Lee Brammer's *The Gay Place* (1961), for example, memorably evokes Austin in the late 1950s, and Edwin "Bud" Shrake's unjustly neglected novel *Strange Peaches* (1973) savagely skewers Dallas at the time of the Kennedy assassination. David L. Lindsey's series of mystery novels beginning in the early 1980s convincingly depicts the teeming, polyglot life of modern Houston. Otherwise, the complexity of the urban environment, it is fair to say, is a subject that only recently has begun to attract the attention of Texas writers.

Another trend that has had a radical impact on the literary scene in Texas is accelerating immigration into the state. Traditionally, as mentioned, outgoing traffic (especially among writers) has been heavy, as Texas artists and intellectuals have sought more salubrious intellectual climates in which to live and work. Lately, the incoming traffic has been just as heavy—or heavier. Inevitably, therefore, the question arises: how does one define the term "Texas writer"?

Dobie, Webb, and Bedichek—once worshipped as "The Holy Trinity of Texas Letters"—were clearly Texas writers; they were born and bred in Texas, and they proudly proclaimed their Texan-ness wherever two or three were gathered together to listen. Among today's authors, no one would dispute the fact that John Graves and Elmer Kelton and Benjamin Capps are Texas writers. On the flip side of the question, however, can authors such as Max Apple and Beverly Lowry and Laura Furman and Shelby Hearon, who grew up in other regions but have spent much time in Texas of late, be labeled Texas writers? Can James Michener, who lives in Austin and wrote *Texas* (1985) — which he modestly termed a "block-buster novel" about the state — be called, with any justice, a Texas writer?

A measured definition of the Texas writer must emanate from sources other than these pages. What cannot be denied is that the inexorable homogenization of American — and Texan — society makes it more and more difficult to say who is and who is not a Texas writer. Certainly migration, and the immigrant who is the human figure in the phenomenon of migration, is as much a part of the Texas myth as it is of the larger American myth. Migrant writers, like migrant executives of high-tech electronics industries, must be granted the right of citizenship.

A freshet of immigrant writers, then, as well as the large number of scribbling natives have combined to make for a lively and flourishing contemporary literary scene in Texas. Donald Barthelme — himself a notable writer from Texas, though he did not write about the state — said, not long before his death in 1989: "taking the thing state by state, there are more good writers in Texas than anywhere in the country save New York and California" (172). The chapters that follow focus on a handful of those "good writers" who were more or less ignored in *LHAW*. An exception is the brief piece on Larry McMurtry, which is an update on the *LHAW* chapter on McMurtry. The chapters on Rolando Hinojosa and Américo Paredes are partial exceptions; Hinojosa and Paredes were not given separate billing in *LHAW*, but they were prominently mentioned in that volume. Otherwise, the essays introduce the writers — Dorothy Scarborough, John Graves, R. G. Vliet, Elmer Kelton, Horton Foote, Walter McDonald, Sarah Bird, and others — who have been largely responsible for the richness and variety of literature in Texas in the twentieth century.

Notes

1. These quotations, as well as details of the preceding incident, are taken from Joan Givner, "Problems of Personal Identity in Texas' 'First Writer,'" in *Katherine Anne Porter and Texas: An Uneasy Relationship*. Clinton Machann and William Bedford Clark eds. (College Station: Texas A&M University Press, 1990), 41-57.

2. An early, and often unacknowledged, pioneer of the second paradigm was Dorothy Scarborough (see chapter to follow). Scarborough was twelve years older than Porter and in the mid-1920s had already established herself as a writer at a time when Porter was still struggling for acceptance. Scarborough was, however, first and foremost an academic, and she certainly never enjoyed as much purely literary success as did Porter.

Selected Bibliography

Barthelme, Donald. "Terms of Estrangement." *Texas Monthly*, 14 (January 1986): 172-174.

Bennett, Patrick. *Talking with Texas Writers: Twelve Interviews*. College Station: Texas A&M University Press, 1980.

Clifford, Craig Edward. *In the Deep Heart's Core: Reflections on Life, Letters, and Texas*. College Station: Texas A&M University Press, 1985.

Clifford, Craig, and Tom Pilkington, eds. *Range Wars: Heated Debates, Sober Reflections, and Other Assessments of Texas Writing*. Dallas: Southern Methodist University Press, 1989. (Reprints Larry McMurtry's "Ever a Bridegroom: Reflections on the Failure of Texas Literature," which originally appeared in the October 23, 1981, issue of *The Texas Observer*.)

Givner, Joan. "Problems of Personal Identity in Texas' 'First Writer.'" In *Katherine Anne Porter and Texas: An Uneasy Relationship*. Clinton Machann and William Bedford Clark, eds. College Station: Texas A&M University Press, 1990. Pp. 41-57.

Graham, Don. *Texas: A Literary Portrait*. San Antonio: Corona Publishing, 1985.

Graham, Don, James W. Lee and William T. Pilkington, eds. *The Texas Literary Tradition: Fiction, Folklore, History*. Austin: College of Liberal Arts of the University of Texas and the Texas State Historical Association, 1983.

Greene, A. C. *The Fifty Best Books on Texas*. Dallas: Pressworks, 1982.

Lee, James Ward. *Classics of Texas Fiction*. Dallas: E-Heart, 1987.

Pilkington, William T. *Imagining Texas: The Literature of the Lone Star State*. Boston: American, 1981.

William B. Martin

R. G. Vliet

When R. G. Vliet died of cancer on May 11, 1984, the career of one of the Southwest's most talented and original writers came to an end. During his publishing life of effectively twenty years, he had written three volumes of poetry, several short stories, three novels, and several plays. He received his B.A. and M.Ed. degrees from Southwest Texas State College (now University), taught school for two years in Texas, studied at the Yale School of Drama, and operated a Vermont family farmstead for over a decade. Through the years he accumulated numerous prizes and awards — among them Ford, Rockefeller, and National Endowment for the Arts Foundation fellowships and Texas Institute of Letters Awards for both poetry and fiction.

Although he is best known as a novelist, his poetry and his dramas were central to his career at different times, and he made a serious impact as a critic.

In spite of having lived most of his writing life in Pennsylvania, Mexico, and New England, Vliet is unquestionably a southwestern writer in that his major works are all deeply rooted in a Texas landscape that he made very much his own — the harsh area of scrub cedar, cut by clear, rocky streams and punished by extremes of intemperate weather that is located on or near the Edwards Plateau in Southwest Texas.

Alto Springs, his fictional version of Rock Springs, the county seat of Edwards County, functioned in his works much as Jefferson did in William Faulkner's fiction or Harrison in Horton Foote's plays.

Vliet took himself seriously as a poet and considered his first novel, *Rockspring* (1974), to be a temporary aberration instead of the new career direction it proved to be. He published three anthologies of poetry: *Events and Celebrations* (1966), *The Man With the Black Mouth* (1970), and *Water and Stone* (1980), as well as a separate illustrated edition of *Clem Maverick: The Life and Death of a Country Music Singer* (1983). His approach to nature, the subject of most of his short lyrics, is an interesting mixture of the Wordsworthian observer's, the scholar's, and the practical farmsteader's. Sensitive and charming though these works can be, they suffer, in my opinion, by comparison to Vliet's three long and more consciously artistic productions: "Water and Stone," "Passage," and "Clem Maverick," which have received less favor than they deserve, probably because of the whiff of the library they carry and their demand for fresh responses.

"Water and Stone," is constructed loosely in the form of a Noh play which could actually be produced as a one-acter. To a non-specialist its most recognizably oriental touches are flowering redbud branches waved by the chorus, musical interludes scored for flute and oboe, and a screen behind the bare platform stage "with a rock painted on it and streamers of white water." The form reminds us that Vliet seldom saw Texas scenery directly, but rather allusively, from a literary perspective, and that he was always a man of the theater, conscious of the power of sound and scene.

The poem tells the tale of eleven-year-old Len Benbow who, while fishing in the Nueces, is unable to save his younger brother from drowning. He bitterly accuses two picnicking couples who saw but failed to render aid. On their ritual return twenty years later they explain their dereliction and detail the forms of suffering their guilt has compelled. The choral interludes establish a sense of life composed of elemental forces and of the blossoming spring — when the drowning occurred — as delusive promise.

"Passage" is a major, 440-line poem made up of ten sections, each ranging from seventeen to eighty-seven lines of free verse, four of which are separately titled. It represents, certainly, the most sustained lyric work Vliet has done and the most directly autobiographical. Beginning with Section VI, it powerfully confronts the subject of death by cancer which was so much a part of his life from 1970 till its end in 1984.

> Now, after surgeon's knives, cobalt's
> basilisk stare, the destroyed blood

I dream of running...

In running, first as a child to evade the ridicule of bullies and then com-petitively in school and college, Vliet found a freedom which he likened to flight and which he imagined as an alternative to the immobility imposed by illness.

> I have come too close to the sun
> of disease! I want
> the joy of running, the quick foot.
> blood taste in my mouth: resurrection's
> hot flowers!

Clem Maverick is a tour de force of twenty stanzas mostly in the form of monologues by family members and associates of the now dead Clem being interviewed by an unnamed, unobtrusive narrator. The character of Clem is the product of Vliet's research into country music figures and is a synthesis of several well-known country and western stars. The tone ranges from broad satire in the first and last stanzas to moving expres-sions of deep feeling. Vliet takes the risk in this poem that the tawdri-ness of his subject matter will not compromise the artistry of the work, but discriminating readers can find in this poem as human a depiction of the quandary and the pain and the functioning of the performer-artist in America as they are likely to encounter.

Rockspring was Vliet's first novel or, more accurately, novella. Its intense lyricism and simple story line combine to make it very appealing. As Tom Pilkington explained in his afterword to the 1992 edition, it is an example of the captivity narrative which dealt with the special prob-lems of a white girl abducted by Indians (or Mexicans) — not only her terror of defilement by the darker "other" but her dubious position in Anglo society if she was fortunate enough to be rescued.

It is also a tale of a young girl's transition into womanhood under especially trying conditions. The action begins with Jensie, the protago-nist, tentatively exploring her new consciousness of her sexuality by committing her body to the sensuous currents of the Nueces River and ends six months later on the brink of her ambiguous return to her fam-ily, pregnant by one of her captors and mourning the murder of her teen-aged Mexican lover by a "red-haired, red-faced" neighbor, probably a surrogate for her father.

Once during her period of captivity she effected a brief escape, only to return after confirming Lear's discovery that life on a blasted heath during a storm, whether in Gloucestershire or on the Edwards Plateau, is unendurable alone and unprotected and that human society, any human society, is preferable.

Upon her return home she is far from being the innocent child stolen away earlier. Not only is she now emotionally a woman — one who has suffered and learned and acted — but she has become a Mexican! By sharing the life of the bandits she has seen her skin darken and her clothes and diet change. Their language has become hers and her name, in that new country, is no longer Jensie but *La Grullita* (the little white crane). Her father's neighbor only recognizes her by her white-blonde hair.

Critically, one has to acknowledge that *Rockspring* is a work of romantic excess, but its exuberance, its accurate evocation of setting and time, and its echoes of other star-crossed lovers make it hugely appealing. Also, it demonstrates authorial skills that Vliet was to utilize more fully in later works and expresses ideas that constitute intellectual and moral strengths in his major novels — that the violence of Texans is a natural response to their history in bleak and elemental surroundings, that man (woman, too) is always alone in nature, that racial differences are superficial.

Solitudes, Vliet's first major novel, exists in two forms: *Solitudes* was published in 1977 by Harcourt Brace Jovanovich and *Soledad*, closer to his original intention, was published posthumously in 1986 by the Texas Christian University Press with additions of an epilogue, an explanatory introduction by Vliet's widow, Ann, and an afterword by Tom Pilkington. As in all of Vliet's long narratives, the plot impetus is an act of violence, in this case the murder by a red-haired drifter, Claiborne (Clabe) Arnett or Sanderlin, of a distinguished Mexican rancher, don Alvaro de Reyes, after he takes refuge from a storm in a canyon where a band of rustlers is holding stolen cattle. It is followed by Clabe's long, arduous journey in search of the subject of a photograph carried by the murdered man, who proves to be the fascinating Soledad Kincaid, don Alvaro's granddaughter. After he locates her, there is confrontation, then sex, and finally separation — Soledad, in retreat to Mexico and what comfort her religion could provide; Clabe, with a new acceptance of himself and his place in life, off to homestead in Oklahoma.

The novel is compelling but also demanding and frustrating to most readers. It introduces many elements that are common to western novels but uses them for unexpected purposes. While a conventional western might explore the external effects of a murder — is the killer brought to justice? is revenge exacted? — Clabe in *Soledad* is both seeking an answer to why he killed don Alvaro and discovering the mysterious bond between his victim and himself. As he moves through the natural landscape, he also makes a parallel journey through an inner terrain seeking answers fundamental to his own existence. When C. L. Sonnichsen reviewed *Solitudes* he said, "There is no doubt that Vliet has a special talent for writing, but he is talking to [writing for] people who have a talent for reading"(*El Paso Times Sunday Magazine*, August 14, 1977, 19).

Certainly *Soledad* is not a conventional western. Ann Vliet, in an interview, said that her husband wasn't trying to write westerns at all and that he started *Soledad* as a western only, in his own words, "so he could kick it [the form] in the ass ... so that he could knock it to pieces" (quoted in Wright 29). He subverted the western by contradicting the stereotype of the "worthless Meskin," by making don Alvaro a distinguished, educated pillar of society and his Anglo killer an illiterate drifter and further by introducing forthright treatments of sex into a form that had long been the preserve of prudery and bashful cowboys. In *Soledad* there is comic sex (Clabe and Johnnie Lee Chant in Chapter 3), desperate, driven sex (Clabe and Soledad in Chapter 17), and even more contrary to the fresh-air wholesomeness of westerns, latent incest between don Alvaro and Soledad.

However, such rude handling of tradition was far from being an exclusive end for Vliet. His serious purpose was to discover and project truths that derived from the particular places and times he chose to deal with. One of the most powerful of these in *Soledad* is the declining influence of Hispanic landowners and their displacement by the more numerous and more aggressive Anglo settlers.

Scorpio Rising (1985), finished with desperate effort only a few days before Vliet's death, is a fitting culmination of his body of fiction. In it Vliet was more successful than earlier in keeping his passionate vision and his intense, poetic language sufficiently yoked to the service of his themes.

Strong connections are drawn between Vliet's experience of localized violence in the area of Rock Springs, Texas, encountered through formal and informal histories and his residence there; his understanding of the function of violence within the frame of Greek drama; and his personal sense that "the shockwaves of an old violence in a Texas town don't go away until the story's been told over and over. And maybe not then" (50). This theme of violence and its ramifications in *Scorpio* is initiated by the 1904 murder of a young rancher, Carson Gilstrap, a week before his wedding day. The murder is planned by his selfish, headstrong fiancée of seventeen, Victoria Ann Castleberry, and executed by Junior Luckett, an ugly, hunchbacked clerk in her father's store, so enamored of her that he placed no limits on his willing service. It expands to include the lynching of a suspected Mexican ranch hand, the revenge murder of Luckett by Gilstrap's brothers and the decline of Victoria Ann and her adoring father.

At the beginning of the novel in 1976, the poisonous influence of this chain of events is still felt. Rudy Castleberry, Victoria Ann's grandson and narrator of Part I of *Scorpio*, is himself an ugly hunchback living a life of pain and humiliation in virtual exile.

The treatment of the crime is an excellent example of Vliet's method of imposing a consciously literary form onto indigenous events. In this case the murder plot derives from Thomas Middleton and William Rowley's seventeenth-century play, *The Changeling*. Beatrice and DeFlores, the murderers, become Victoria Ann and Luckett. The victim, Tomaso de Piracquo, becomes Victoria Ann's betrothed, and Alsemero, Beatrice's new love, becomes Earl St. Clair, the man Victoria Ann killed for.

A second theme deals with the cruelty of love and the thoughtless tyranny of the beautiful over the ugly. Not only is this developed once, when Victoria Ann in 1904 uses Junior Luckett, whom she has reviled, as her instrument of murder, but the action is replicated in the 1976 scenes set in Massachusetts as the hunchbacked Rudy is used by the beautiful ex-hippie Lita as entertainer, confessor, and babysitter without any consideration of him as a man with his own desires. As Rudy muses, "It struck me . . . that most women, even the nicest ones, think ugly men, all on account of their ugliness are pure eunuchs. Or ghosts. They don't *see* you" (70).

The third theme is anchored in the ignorance and narrow piety of frontier Texas. Victoria Ann had no standard for selecting a husband to meet her needs since she had never been allowed to know she had any. Based on her father's standards of economics and prestige, she accepted Gilstrap's proposal. Then, with her longings stirred for a more glamorous life by romantic novels, she desired St. Clair. Ironically it was forced sex, demanded by Junior Luckett as payment for his murderous act, that introduced Victoria Ann to her sexuality and made her an enthusiastic and aggressive sexual partner. When she and Luckett are exposed to their avengers in coitus, their compound guilt is revealed but also their fulfillment.

A formal feature of the novel that has attracted controversy is the time warp that Rudy Castleberry steps into as he exits an Amtrak train in 1976 and finds himself in his grandfather's Houston, Texas, of 1902. Readers can explain it with varying degrees of satisfaction as a dream or as a hallucination brought on by one or another psychic trigger, but Vliet obviously did not want it to be "explained." He had earlier expressed little confidence in the realistic style and uses this jump-cut to make the point that resonant events of the past influence the present in multifarious ways, some of which will frustrate the philosophies of modern Horatios.

In spite of Vliet's efforts as a playwright over more than twenty years, he wrote only one play, *The Regions of Noon*, that he considered worth preserving. Even it is a minor accomplishment relative to his significant achievements in poetry and fiction, but his dramatic sensibility contributed to the quality of both of them. Among his notes in the Vliet Archive of the Southwestern Writers Collection at Southwest Texas State University are plans to recast one of his early plays as a novel.

R. G. Vliet was an original writer who was at the same time driven and complex, and one whose virtues are inextricably linked to his difficulties. His body of work, cut short as it was, is impressive and deserves a wider public and closer reading than it has so far received.

Selected Bibliography

Gish, Robert. "R. G. Vliet's Lonesome Cowboys: Language and Lyricism in the Contemporary Western Novel." *Southwestern American Literature*, 9:1 (1983): 5-21.

Martin, William B. "R. G. Vliet." In *Texas Plays*. Dallas: Southern Methodist University Press, 1990. Pp. 223-227.

Pilkington, Tom. Afterword. *Rockspring*. By R. G. Vliet. Dallas: Southern Methodist University Press, 1992. Pp. 121-129.

———. Afterword. *Soledad*. By R. G. Vliet. Fort Worth: Texas Christian University Press, 1986. Pp. 265-269.

———. "The Significance of the Frontier in Texas Literature." *The Texas Literary*

Tradition: Fiction, Folklore, History. Don Graham, James W. Lee and William T. Pilkington, eds. Austin: University of Texas, 1983. Pp. 94-107.

Vliet, Ann. Introduction. *Soledad*. By R.G. Vliet. Fort Worth: Texas Christian University Press, 1986. Pp. xi-xvi.

Vliet, R. G. *Clem Maverick: The Life and Death of a Country Music Singer*. Bryan, Texas: Shearer, 1983.

————. *Events and Celebrations*. New York: Viking, 1966.

————. "The Frontier of the Imagination." In *The Texas Literary Tradition: Fiction, Folklore, History*. Don Graham, James W. Lee and William T. Pilkington, eds. Austin: University of Texas, 1983. Pp. 108-112.

————. *The Man With the Black Mouth*. Santa Cruz: Kayak, 1970.

————. "The Nature and Education of a Poet." *Southwest Review*, 69:1 (1984): 49-54.

————. "On a Literature of the Southwest: An Address." *The Texas Observer*, April 28, 1978, 19.

————. "The Regions of Noon." In *Texas Plays*. William B. Martin, ed. Dallas: Southern Methodist University Press, 1990. Pp. 229-266.

————. *Rockspring*. New York: Viking, 1974; rpt., Dallas: Southern Methodist University Press, 1992.

————. *Scorpio Rising*. New York: Random House, 1985.

————. *Soledad, or Solitudes*. Revised edition with introduction by Ann Vliet and afterword by Tom Pilkington. Fort Worth: Texas Christian University Press, 1986.

————. *Solitudes*. New York: Harcourt, 1977.

————. "The Southwest as Cradle of the Poet." In *The American Southwest: Cradle of Literary Art*. Robert W. Walts, ed. San Marcos: Southwest Texas State University, 1981.

————. *Water and Stone*. New York: Random House, 1980.

Wright, Kay Hetherly. "R. G. Vliet's *Soledad*: Rewriting the Southwest." *Southwestern American Literature*, 18:1 (1992): 13-30.

Craig Clifford

John Graves

> How should one write, what words should one select, what forms and structures and organization, if one is pursuing understanding? (Which is to say, if one is, in that sense, a philosopher?) Sometimes this is taken to be a trivial and uninteresting question. I shall claim that it is not. Style itself makes its claims, expresses its own sense of what matters. Literary form is not separable from philosophical content, but is, itself, a part of content — an integral part, then, of the search for and the statement of truth.
>
> —Martha Nussbaum, *Love's Knowledge*

John Graves once described Caroline Gordon's novel *Aleck Maury, Sportsman* with the following enigma: "It never goes anywhere, but it's a wonderful book." Friends of mine have tried to teach John Graves' *Goodbye to a River* (1960) to urbanites of the fast-lane 1990s, and, although a handful of students are deeply moved, many complain that the book moves too slowly, that nothing ever happens, that there's no point to it. Even an English professor I know, who has lived for many years in an easy-paced small West Texas town, once criticized Graves' writing with the following pronouncement: "Come on, man, this is the twentieth century."

As fate had it, John Graves was born in the twentieth century, in 1920 in Fort Worth, Texas. In his words, he was one of those "born English majors." After receiving his B.A. from Rice University in

1942, during which time he discovered he wanted to be a writer, he put in three years with the U.S. Marines during World War II. He completed a master's degree in English at Columbia University in 1948 so that he could fall back on teaching if he couldn't make enough money writing.

In the last analysis, though, my English professor friend was not entirely wrong. In many ways, John Graves is a man of the nineteenth century—or the early twentieth century—from a time when great American writers lived in Paris and in Spain and wrote for *Harper's* and the *Atlantic Monthly* and *The New Yorker*. From a time when sentences were carefully crafted, Hemingway's short ones just as much as Faulkner's interminable ones; when "open punctuation" was nothing but a typesetter's fantasy.

To be sure, Graves' writing is writing for slow readers, for readers who wish to wander, without certainty or clearly identified goals, but with the assurance that they are traveling with a craftsman skilled in storytelling and ruminating and wordsmithing. The proper contrast is the fast writing of the slick-covered monthlies and colorized newspapers of the waning years of the twentieth century. The great irony—and it's not the only contradiction this man embodies—is that early in his career Graves developed a knack for slick-magazine writing. While studying at Columbia, he published his first short story in *The New Yorker*—"far too auspicious a beginning," he once commented in an interview. Back in New York in the early fifties, Graves developed a knack for writing commercial fiction: "I must have done a dozen or so in all, and maybe seven of those really crummy slick things got published. Scared me, and I quit" (Bennett 67).

But he certainly didn't abandon "commercial" writing. While living for three years in Spain, he wrote travel pieces for *Holiday*. He wrote for Stewart Udall, when Udall was secretary of the interior in the middle sixties. He contributed a considerable body of writing to *Texas Monthly* for several decades, some of it light and quaint and some of it deceptively and quietly thoughtful (although it is worth noting that the frequency of his contributions to *Texas Monthly* declined as the frequency of perfume ads soaked in the product increased).

Actually, though, Graves writes—even at his slickest—very much in the older sense, the original sense, of the essay—in the sense of the French *essayer*, to "attempt." When Montaigne designated his meandering personal and philosophical reflections *Essais*, he meant to indicate the tentative trial-and-error nature of his thought. "If my mind could gain a firm footing," he says, "I would not make attempts (*je ne m'es-saierais pas*), I would make decisions; but it is always in apprenticeship and on trial" (314-315). For that reason, he seems to wander, sometimes aimlessly; but, in fact, it is a controlled wandering. "I love the poetic gait, by leaps and gambols.... It is the inattentive reader who loses my subject, not I..." (372-373). In a fine essay on the essay, Joseph Epstein says, "The essay is—or should be—ruminative" (400). It is a chewing and a rechewing of the matter. Epstein himself doesn't take this claim seriously enough, for he also claims that the essay is ultimately a "modest" literary form. The belief that the essay is a modest literary form—Epstein calls it "piece work"—is a longstanding literary prejudice which has haunted John Graves for the entirety of his career.

Every critical discussion of Graves' writing, this one not excluded, finally turns to the question: will he ever put forward the Great Texas Novel (*pace* Larry McMurtry)? Novelist Beverly Lowry's remark about the possibility of a John Graves novel was: "I want it. I want to be able to have it, to read it" (Holley 44). His mastery of words and characters and tone evokes the question. In fact, Larry McMurtry says that *Goodbye to a River* "represents not so much an abandonment of fiction as a form of accommodation with it. Though based on a real trip, it is essentially an imaginary voyage whose affinities stretch back to *Gulliver* and beyond" (30).

Graves himself keeps the question alive, having admitted in an interview: "I think you can do more with fiction; the greatest potential is there, but something about me and long fiction has not so far been compatible" (Bennett 67). (As for short fiction, "The Last Running," a short story originally published in the *Atlantic Monthly* and later in book form, is no more or less a work of fiction than *Goodbye to a River*.) Norman Maclean sidestepped the issue by calling *A River Runs Through It* a work of fiction, even though it is probably less fictionalized than Graves' river book. Perhaps Graves should have done the same.

Over the years Graves has talked about a novel stored away in a trunk, finished but never published—and another one unfinished but abandoned. In fact, in 1975 he deposited a novel manuscript at the Humanities Research Center at the University of Texas with the instructions that it remain under lock and key for fifty years. (In 1985 he agreed to move the unveiling up to five years after his death.) Off and on, Graves has hinted at a "turn" in his writing, something involving the Gulf Coast and fishing... fiction, perhaps?

If John Graves publishes a novel, I'll read it. But, in the end, it is just as silly to respond to Graves' fictionalized essays by asking why he hasn't written a conventional novel as it would be to complain that Frank O'Connor should have written novels instead of short stories or Robert Frost novels instead of poems. Leaving psychological speculation to the armchair psychologists, it must be said that John Graves is one of the most accomplished practitioners of ruminative essay writing in the English language. In an overview of Graves' work which appeared in *The Texas Humanist* in 1984, Joe Holley compares Graves to his fellow Texas wordsmiths in this way: "He's certainly not the best known, nor with three books in the past twenty-five years, is he the most prolific. For sheer force and eloquence of prose, however, John Graves may be the master" (42).

Counting a short story published in book form, *The Last Running*; a magazine article published in book form, *Blue and Some Other Dogs*; a contribution to a book for the Sierra Club; text for a couple of collections of photographs; and a few other odds and ends, the number of books might be stretched to half a dozen or so. Add to this list *A John Graves Reader*, an anthology of Graves' writing from over the years, some of it previously published and some not, published by the University of Texas Press in the fall of 1996. But, as Graves himself admits, only two of these offerings count as full-fledged organically conceived books: *Goodbye to a River* and *Hard Scrabble: Observations on a Patch of Land* (1974). The third of his book-length works, *From a Limestone Ledge* (1980), is a collection of *Texas Monthly* pieces, displaying the distinctive Graves voice and style but largely reiterating the themes of the first two books. In the second book, *Hard Scrabble*, Graves recounts his attempt to restore four hundred acres of worn-out land near Glen Rose, Texas, where he has pretty much resided since 1960. The themes of that book are similar to the first, but the structure is less artistically satisfying. In the end, Graves has written but one masterpiece, his first book, *Goodbye to a River*.

Fellow writers cajole Graves to write more; and he is quick to comment on his own sparse output. In *The Perfect Sonya* Beverly Lowry's frustration shows up in a character who is unmistakably based on John Graves. Will Hand is obligatorily haunted, not just by an unfulfilled desire to write fiction, but by his inability to write more. The heroine of the novel puts her finger on the reason:

"A masterpiece."

"A what?"

"You feel the need to write a masterpiece."

A wave of dust blew against the windows. Will sulked.

"If not a masterpiece then why bother. If not that then nothing, right? It's a trap...." (233)

For John Graves, a limited literary output is not a trap, but an accomplishment. It's certainly no more of a trap than the mechanical-x-number-of-pages-a-day approach that characterizes the careers of many writers. *Ad hominem* seems unavoidable here: how many of his well-meaning compatriots have written one masterpiece that will stand the test of time? One can imagine that fifty or one hundred years from now — assuming that there are still books at all — thoughtful readers will pick up *Goodbye to a River* and find it rewarding, compelling, distinctive, beautiful. When it has been grouped with other works of "Texas literature," it has sometimes been denied the proper yardstick; for the merits of this book require comparison with the great tradition of the American and English-language essay which informs its every syllable. For artistry — and for substance — I can think of no book written by a Texan, and few written by Americans, that surpasses John Graves' *Goodbye to a River*.

The book began — the contradiction again — as a work underwritten by *Sports Illustrated*. It is based on a three-week canoe trip that Graves took on a stretch of the Brazos River west of Fort Worth in anticipation of the transformation of the river that a series of proposed dams and reservoirs would bring about. Not sporty enough, the magazine piece ended up in *Holiday*. But the materials and the inspiration demanded a book-length meandering. Graves wraps a story about a canoe trip down the Brazos River around a boatload of human and natural history, a subtle echoing of timeless literary traditions, and soul-stirring meandering ruminations about all of those things a person thinks about in the resonant silence of solitude.

The force of personality — strong but ironic, unmistakable but self-effacing — comes through in his writing. But if the force of personality invites comparison with J. Frank Dobie, it is a J. Frank Dobie who, at his best, can write like a Faulkner. A contradiction of backwoods crotchetiness and literary highmindedness, of sinewy substance and artistic style. And like the Carolyn Gordon novel Graves so admires, even his book about a journey down a river, in a certain sense, doesn't go anywhere. Graves' essays take Montaigne's "poetic gait," his "leaps and gambols," to

a sublime extreme. They seem slow, seem to have no point, because...
they have no point. They are *about* something, about important things—
about self-understanding and the power of places, about things Texan and
things human. But they do not simply make a point, they do not offer
commentary; rather, they take us on a journey of reflection and discovery,
or, better, through the process of trying to discover. "He is popularly
thought to be a kind of country explainer," McMurtry wrote in 1981,
"when in fact he seems more interested in increasing our store of mysteries than our store of knowledge" (29-30).

There is no point for the reader to agree or disagree with, no argument to analyze, no conclusion to accept or reject; a reader who takes
the work seriously must think and reflect and ponder right along with
the author—must *undergo* something. The reader may go looking for
the definitive statement about the Brazos River, about environmental
protection, about being a Texan or being rooted anywhere—but will
come away with an irreducible, but truthful, sense of ambivalence
deeply felt and deeply thought, with a reverence for the tragedy and
comedy of things human.

In that sense, Graves is not the nature writer he's often considered to
be, but someone who reflects on the entanglements of things human and
things natural. He's no Roy Bedichek, no Annie Dillard, no Aldo
Leopold. In a sense, he's less of a naturalist than Thoreau, although he's
often dubbed the Texas Thoreau. Neither is John Graves an environmental activist. In fact, Larry McMurtry characterized Graves' approach
in just this one word: he *considers* things. Indeed, in spite of his work for
Stewart Udall and for the Sierra Club and a continuing temptation and
repeated invitations to become more of an environmental activist, by
and large Graves has clung stubbornly, and wisely from an artistic standpoint, to ruminative, inconclusive considerations of human relations
with nature. A number of contrasts come to mind. He shares Edward
Abbey's ironic playfulness, but not his activism. He shares Wendell
Berry's love of the land, but not his purity. Somehow, west of the
Mississippi the spirit of Mark Twain seems to work against any aspirations to purity....

I was initially attracted to Graves because of the ideas, the ruminative
quality of his essays—and, yes, because he writes about my homeland—
but my wife, Mallory Young, a word connoisseur from day one, convinced me that Graves is at least as much a word person as an idea person (Young 3). Graves considers, observes, ruminates, ponders; but

there is a quality in the words that carries the weight of all the considering and ruminating. In a short piece for a collection called *Growing Up in Texas*, Graves remarks: "So despite all the hodgepodge reading I did, I had an early chance to see that good books were sense and language woven together, and that the weaving mattered greatly" (Dobie 70).

Looking more closely at what makes John Graves' prose so attractive, I see that the trial-and-error process of working out the thoughts and the stories, the ambivalence, the meandering and questioning, filter right down to the very words and sounds and commas. It is not just a matter of taking the reader through the process of discovery, through the process of ruminating; it is a matter of taking the reader, with great skill and artistry, through the process of finding the right words. Paradoxically, Graves gives us the perfect words to convey the sense of looking for the perfect words—groping around in earthy native Texas tones or reaching to John Milton for an elevated ring. The proliferation of ellipsis dots, the generous use of commas, the starting and stopping and starting over again of Graves' sentences, give us a sense of the uncertain struggle for just the right sound, just the right word, to make the thing that the words are about step out into the open and show itself. Paradoxically, the starting and the stopping and the commas and ellipsis dots he pulls off with perfect clarity.

In *Talking with Texas Writers* Graves talks about a sense of rhythm:

> You come to know that such a rhythm and word pattern and so on fits the feeling that you are after at a certain point. It becomes sacred, and you don't dare tamper with it. It's got to be a feeling; it can't be a knowledge. I write and rewrite along. I can have gone over something ten times, and a certain sentence will bother me every time I go through, and I stop and look at it, and can't see anything wrong with it. Perfectly all right. I say baloney and go on. In the end just some little rhythmic thing, maybe a word of three syllables where there ought to be two or something like that. It doesn't have anything to do with meaning; it has to do with rhythm. (Bennett 77)

Norman Maclean tells a story about a New York editor rejecting *A River Runs Through It* because it had trees in it. Graves has certainly dealt with the prejudice against settings west of the Hudson River; but the quintessential editor story for Graves involves a young copy editor at Knopf who changed all of the idiosyncratic commas and ellipsis dots in *Good-bye to a River*, as he puts it, because she thought "she was helping out that poor old illiterate down in Texas" (Bennett 76). Knopf ended up footing the bill for changing the galley proofs back to the original "leaps and gambols" — to that piece of wandering but seamless perfection that has to do with a feel for rhythm — and, if I may differ, with the meaning that that rhythm conveys. It is a rhythm of writing and of life that causes John Graves to say, at the end of the river trip:

> Full of driftingness and sloth, I let it carry me along, dallying, stopping for explorations and to lie in the sun, making no speed at all. I had a feeling that I could go on forever, if there were only river enough and time. But there weren't. (*Goodbye* 289)

That rhythm, of writing and of life, still causes some readers — even in the twentieth century — to make the same remark about *Goodbye to a River*.

Selected Bibliography

Primary Sources

Blue and Some Other Dogs. Austin: Encino Press, 1981.
From a Limestone Ledge: Some Essays and Other Ruminations about Country Life in Texas. New York: Knopf, 1980.
Goodbye to a River. New York: Knopf, 1960.
Hard Scrabble: Observations on a Patch of Land. New York: Knopf, 1974.
A John Graves Reader. Austin: The University of Texas Press, 1996.
Landscapes of Texas: Photographs from the Texas Highways Magazine. Introduction by John Graves; preface by Frank T. Lively, Bob Parvin, and Tommie Pinkard. College Station: Texas A&M University Press, 1980.
The Last Running: A Story. Austin: Encino Press, 1974.
Texas Heartland: A Hill Country Year. With Jim Bones. College Station: Texas A&M University Press, 1975.
The Water Hustlers. Section on Texas. With Robert H. Boyle (New York) and T. H. Watkins (California). San Francisco, New York: Sierra Club Books, 1971.

Secondary Sources

Bennett, Patrick. "John Graves: A Hard Scrabble World." In *Talking with Texas Writers: Twelve Interviews*. College Station: Texas A&M University Press, 1980. Pp. 63-88.
Busby, Mark. "John Graves." In *American Nature Writers*. John Elder, ed. New York: Scribner's, 1996.

Dobie, Bertha McKee, et al. *Growing Up in Texas: Recollections of Childhood*. Austin: Encino Press, 1972.

Epstein, Joseph. "Piece Work: Writing the Essay." In *Plausible Prejudices: Essays on American Writing*. New York: W. W. Norton & Co., 1985.

Grover, Dorys Crow. *John Graves*. Boise: Boise State University Western Writers Series, 1989.

Holley, Joe. "John Graves: A Master of Details and Ruminations." *The Texas Humanist*, 6 (March-April 1984): 40–44.

Lopate, Phillip. "The Essay Lives — in Disguise." *New York Times Book Review* (November 18, 1984): 1, 47-49.

Lowry, Beverly. *The Perfect Sonya*. New York: Viking, 1987.

McMurtry, Larry. "Ever a Bridegroom: Reflections on the Failure of Texas Literature." In *Range Wars: Heated Debates, Sober Reflections, and Other Assessments of Texas Writing*. Craig Clifford and Tom Pilkington, eds. Dallas: Southern Methodist University Press, 1989. 13-41. Originally published in the *Texas Observer*, 23 (October 1981).

Montaigne, Michel Eyquem de. *Essays and Selected Writings: A Bilingual Edition*. Donald M. Frame, ed. and trans. New York: St Martin's Press, 1963.

Young, Mallory. "On Reading John Graves, Slowly." *Texas Books in Review*, 6 (1984): 3-5.

Kenneth Davis

Elmer Kelton

Winner of six Spur Awards from Western Writers of America, San Angelo novelist Elmer Kelton has done much in his forty-one books to keep alive the image of the American cowboy as well as other popular figures including cavalrymen, pioneering ranchers who established and maintained large operations, and small ranchers and farmers whose efforts were also key factors in the building of the American West.

Son of a ranch manager and his wife who for a time taught school, Kelton is a university-trained writer whose degree from the University of Texas was in journalism with a minor in English. His career as a writer of western fiction began with the acceptance of a story in *Ranch Romances*. He earned his living for more than forty years, however, as an agricultural journalist and retired after many years as associate editor of *The Livestock Weekly*, a respected trade journal.

Kelton's childhood on a large ranch near Crane, Texas, where he heard the cowhands tell stories as they sat on the porch after supper, was a major influence on the content and style of his fiction. During a childhood bout with a lung disorder, Kelton became an avid reader, especially of books concerning the West and its history. Reading about the West became a lifelong habit, as did watching western movies.

Kelton's university training was interrupted by service in the U.S. Army during World War II, but when he returned, he finished his studies and accepted a job as an agricultural journalist in San Angelo, Texas,

580

where he and his wife continue to live. As a journalist, he came in contact with many westerners who later became sources for his most dramatic characterizations. His work in journalism also influenced his prose style: spare, efficient, and full of carefully chosen details which help create verisimilitude and give the reader an accurate vision of the West. He is a meticulous researcher who frequently uses major library holdings in the Barker Collection at the University of Texas, or in the Southwest Collection at Texas Tech University. Many of his characters—such as Charlie Flagg in *The Time It Never Rained* (1973), Wes Hendrix in *The Man Who Rode Midnight* (1987), and Hewey Calloway in *The Good Old Boys* (1978)—are so real to readers that many times Kelton is asked if this or that individual—usually the questioner's father or grandfather—served as the model.

Kelton's fiction is of two sorts: the shorter, simpler novels, which were written early in his career, and the longer, more complex ones, which tend to explore the consequences of the western myth. Of the forty-one novels he has written, thirty-one can be classified as shorter, or even genre fiction, although they, too, exemplify the careful craftsmanship which has won Kelton many awards.

The shorter novels, most of which were written between 1955 and 1971, earned Kelton a strong following among fans of action fiction about Texas. With *The Day the Cowboys Quit* (1971), winner of the Western Writers of America Spur Award as Best Western Novel of the year, his fiction began a movement toward the longer, more literary works which in time would earn five more Spur Awards and numerous other recognitions. In these novels, Kelton's overriding theory about what makes good fiction is clear: it must have carefully presented, believable conflicts, including man against time, man against nature, man against other men, and man against himself.

Kelton agrees with readers who say *The Time It Never Rained* (1973) is his best work. Written and rewritten over a ten-year period following the severe drought of the 1950s, it clearly illuminates Kelton's belief in the basic elements of conflict. The unlikely hero, Charlie Flagg, must do battle with nature, his fellow citizens of Rio Seco, with the federal government, and with himself, as he is caught up in all-but-overwhelming forces of change. Flagg is a traditional everyman figure who embodies many of the qualities long associated with westerners. But in dealing with the devastation of long years of drought, with bureaucratic tyrants, with neighbors and erstwhile friends who lose patience with his stubbornness, and with racial prejudice directed against his longtime employees and friends, he does not emerge victorious in the usual ways of the western hero. Instead, in experiencing nearly total physical defeat, he gains spiritual strength almost in the manner of a Shakespearean tragic protagonist.

In *The Time It Never Rained* and in the remaining longer novels, Kelton's dedication to depicting the West realistically is clear. A Kelton hero does not vanquish his enemies, win the hand of the heroine, or find serenity in general. More often than not, he must stoically accept what his sometimes harsh, unforgiving environment metes out. Most of Kelton's characters simply endure, rather than triumph. Yet the novels are not bleak; in fact, there is much humor in them. *The Time It Never Rained*, for instance, presents a grandly comic coyote hunt to relieve momentarily the novel's somber themes. (Even this comic relief serves, however, to complement Kelton's characterization of Charlie Flagg. For just as the coyote escapes the collective determination of dozens of foes, so does Charlie emerge as survivor.) *The Good Old Boys* is perhaps Kelton's most comic novel. Throughout, it uses folk speech for humorous effect, and there are many funny scenes, including hero Hewey Calloway's roping of a small automobile. Yet *The Good Old Boys* also exhibits the same elements of conflict found throughout the rest of Kelton's fiction. Hewey is the good old boy caught in conflicts with changing times, with himself and others, and with nature. His strong determination to be independent, to be true to himself, gives way temporarily as he stays a season to help work his brother's family farm. He is attracted for a time to a schoolteacher who eventually recognizes that Hewey's nature precludes his ever settling down. Unlike his nephew, who embraces the coming age of mechanization, Hewey clings to the old ways. The old ways do not win in *The Good Old Boys*, but in an effort to soften the coming inevitable changes, Kelton lets Hewey, ever the free if irresponsible spirit, ride away to seek out what is beyond the next hill.

A major contribution Kelton makes to the body of writings about Texas and the American West is his insistence on historical accuracy, balance, and realism. Whether he is writing about a tough-spirited individual who founded a major ranch (*Stand Proud*, 1984), a determined, unyielding grandfather who fights to preserve his land (*The Man Who Rode Midnight*, 1987), members of a family made rich by oil (*Honor at Daybreak*, 1991), or buffalo hunters and Comanches whose struggles to survive mirror each other (*Slaughter*, 1992, and its sequel, *The Far*

Canyon, 1994), Kelton's aim is to provide objective depictions of the times his characters lived in, and this includes the volatile race relations of the frontier West. *The Wolf and the Buffalo* (1980), an extensively researched work, is based on the black soldiers — known as the buffalo soldiers — who fought Indians on the Texas frontier. In *The Time It Never Rained* Kelton also gives a balanced view of relations between Mexicans and Anglos. He presents raw prejudice as well as an almost feudal paternalism which, in the case of Charlie Flagg, matures into as much respect as a man of Charlie's time could have.

Keys to understanding Kelton's theory of fiction can be found in two collections of his speeches: *Living and Writing in West Texas* (1988) and *My Kind of Heroes* (1995). In the former, he recounts major influences on his life which shaped his vision of the region about which he has written so much and provides witty analyses of his blending of factual details to achieve memorable characterization. In the latter, his views about the triumphalist-revisionist controversies over the meaning of the settlement of the American West buttress his lifelong emphasis on historical accuracy as opposed to the politically motivated or politically correct. Kelton decries the vogue for faulting ancestors for all of the problems which were present in the old West and those which yet persist. Like his presentation of various conflicts in his fiction, Kelton's assessments of ways of interpreting and using history are balanced and objective. He believes that the writer of fiction must accurately depict historical conditions the way they were, not the way modern dictates of conscience might prefer.

Although Kelton's fiction overshadows his nonfiction writings, his agricultural journalism, his historical studies (*Looking Back West*, 1972, and *Permian, A Continuing Saga*, 1986), as well as his introductions to collections of western art and his chapters in numerous books about the West, all reveal his lifelong fascination with Texas, the Southwest, and the West in general.

Selected Primary Sources

The Big Brand. New York: Bantam Books, 1986. A collection of short stories.

The Day the Cowboys Quit. New York: Doubleday, 1971; rpts., New York: Ace-Charter, 1976; New York: Bantam Books, 1992; Fort Worth: Texas Christian University Press, 1986. Winner of WWA Spur Award as best western novel of the year. Also winner of best regional novel award from the Border Regional Library Association of Texas, New Mexico and Mexico.

The Far Canyon. New York: Doubleday, 1994. Winner of Western Heritage Award from National Cowboy Hall of Fame.

The Good Old Boys. New York: Doubleday, 1978; rpts., New York: Ace-Charter/Jove, 1982; Fort Worth: Texas Christian University Press, 1985; Pleasantville, New York: Readers Digest Condensed Books, 1978. Winner of Western Heritage Award from National Cowboy Hall of Fame.

Living and Writing in West Texas: Two Speeches by Elmer Kelton. Abilene, Texas: Hardin-Simmons University Press, 1988.

Looking Back West. San Angelo, Texas: Talley Press, 1972. A collection of nonfiction historical articles.

The Man Who Rode Midnight. New York: Doubleday, 1987; rpts., New York: Bantam Books, 1989; Fort Worth: Texas Christian University Press, 1990; Pleasantville, New York: Reader's Digest Condensed Books, 1987. Winner of Western Heritage Award from National Cowboy Hall of Fame.

My Kind of Heroes. Austin, Texas: State House Press, 1995.

Permian, A Continuing Saga. Midland, Texas: Permian Basin Petroleum Museum, 1986. A nonfiction narrative centered around Permian Basin historical paintings by Tom Lovell.

There's Always Another Chance. San Angelo, Texas: Fort Concho Museum Press, 1986.

The Time It Never Rained. New York: Doubleday, 1973; rpts., New York: Ace-Charter/Jove, 1975; Fort Worth: Texas Christian University Press, 1984. Winner of Western Heritage Award from National Cowboy Hall of Fame, winner of WWA Spur Award as best western novel of the year.

The Wolf and the Buffalo. New York: Doubleday, 1980; rpts., New York: Bantam Books, 1982; Fort Worth: Texas Christian University Press, 1986; Pleasantville, New York: Reader's Digest Condensed Books, 1980. Chosen during the Texas Sesquicentennial by Texas Library Association as one of five books for Texas Voices: 1836-1986.

Kenneth Davis

Robert Flynn

Robert Flynn, writer-in-residence at San Antonio's Trinity University, has written five novels—*North to Yesterday* (1967), *Wanderer Springs* (1987), *In the House of the Lord* (1969), *The Sounds of Rescue, the Signs of Hope* (1970), and *The Last Klick* (1994)—and two collections of short stories—*Seasonal Rain* (1986) and *Living With the Hyenas* (1996). Of the five novels, two, *North to Yesterday* and *Wanderer Springs*, are about traditional facets of Texas and the West. *In the House of the Lord*, a circadian novel, is about a contemporary preacher in a large city. *The Sounds of Rescue, the Signs of Hope* and *The Last Klick* are war novels. Flynn has also written a nonfiction study, *A Personal War in Vietnam* (1989).

North to Yesterday is Flynn's most significant examination of older, more traditional aspects of the American West. Taking a favorite subject for western writers—the trail drive—he delights in providing a genial, hilarious parody of the heroic adventures found in many typical trail-drive novels and films. Seeking to live at last a life of high adventure, the novel's major character, Marvin Dorsey, better known as Lampassas, organizes a trail drive while ignorant of the fact that the railhead in Kansas has been closed for years. He and his son and an assortment of characters, including an itinerant preacher, an inept gunfighter, and a would-be ladies' man, are joined by a single mother and her fly-specked baby. This group makes up a memorable band of hapless questers after happiness and fortune—or at least survival. Flynn's ability to maintain a consistently comic tone is remarkable. His satire is not savage in the novel; instead, he allows readers to laugh with his misguided drovers and even to have wistful admiration for them despite their obvious folly. They do, after all, follow their dreams. Flynn's vision of humanity's plight recognizes the existence of stupidity, even evil, but most of his characters also have some insight into the nature of good in the world.

Wanderer Springs won the Western Writers of America Spur Award as the Best Historical Western Novel for 1987. Its narrator, Will Callaghan, is more an everyman figure than a typical hero. Will is a traveler, as are other Flynn characters, but his travels are more of the spirit than of geography. Like *North to Yesterday*, *Wanderer Springs* is a satire, but here, the tone is more acerbic. As Will reviews his life, he can see follies in some of humanity's most cherished institutions: education, organized religion, marriage, medicine, football, and hypocrisy.

In the House of the Lord focuses on a man's efforts to cope with his dreams of what he could be and his awareness of what he really is. Pat Shahan, minister of a Protestant church in a major city, has to deal with self-doubts and realizations of the imperfections of the church he serves. Flynn combines perception, compassion, and wry humor as he chronicles Shahan's dilemmas. The war novels, the short stories, and the nonfiction book about Vietnam demonstrate in various ways Flynn's obsession with the ceaseless struggles between good and evil in the world. *The Last Klick* is a powerful account of the horrors of the Vietnam War as seen through the eyes of a naive correspondent. In *The Sounds of Rescue, the Signs of Hope*, a downed pilot's contemplation of his destiny becomes a metaphor for broader struggles facing humanity at large. *A Personal War in Vietnam* seems Flynn's effort to exorcise demons which that long conflict fostered in many of his peers.

In two collections of short fiction, *Seasonal Rain* and *Living with the Hyenas*, Flynn examines a variety of human conflicts. The later collection, in particular, shows that internal and external struggles often mirror each other. In "The Land of the Free," a northern black Korean War veteran becomes involved in the bigotry of the early days of civil rights in the South. He must deal with his personal anguish as well as with the strident militancy of his teenage daughter.

In all of his writings, Flynn is ever the careful stylist. He is incisive and economical with words. He fully understands the power of spare prose, and he has a keen ability to include just the right detail to make characters visible in the reader's imagination. Readers of southwestern and western fiction will gravitate toward and enjoy *North to Yesterday* and *Wanderer Springs* more than they will Flynn's other works, but all of his writings demonstrate genuine technical competence and keen insights about the joys and terrors of the human heart in conflict with itself. Flynn is one of a number of talented contemporary Texas writers who have moved away from the old rural Texas to seek out meaning in urban settings.

Selected Bibliography

Primary Sources

In the House of the Lord. New York: Knopf, 1969; rpt., Fort Worth: Texas Christian University Press, 1991.

The Last Klick. Dallas: Baskerville, 1994.

Living With the Hyenas. Fort Worth: Texas Christian University Press, 1996.

North to Yesterday. New York: Knopf, 1967; rpt., Fort Worth: Texas Christian University Press, 1985.

A Personal War in Vietnam. College Station: Texas A&M University Press, 1989.

Seasonal Rain. San Antonio: Corona, 1986.

The Sounds of Rescue, The Signs of Hope. New York: Knopf, 1970; rpt., Fort Worth: Texas Christian University Press, 1989.

Wanderer Springs. Fort Worth: Texas Christian University Press, 1987.

Sylvia Ann Grider

Dorothy Scarborough

Dorothy Scarborough (1878-1935) was a distinguished folklorist, novelist, and teacher. While working as a teacher of creative writing at Columbia University in New York City, she wrote five novels, including *The Wind* (1925), which is regarded today as a minor classic, and published two major folksong collections, *On the Trail of Negro Folksong* (1925) and *A Song Catcher in Southern Mountains* (1937). She also wrote and edited various other books, poems, short stories, reviews, and essays. These publications are a testament to her remarkable wit, creativity, and intellectual depth.

Born January 27, 1878, near Tyler, Texas, she always maintained her personal identification as first, a native Texan and second, a southerner. Despite her personal background, she never fancied herself as a pioneer westerner.

Because of the frail health of her mother, in the 1880s the family moved west to the raw frontier village of Sweetwater, in the heart of the arid West Texas ranching country. Dorothy's father, John Scarborough, was a Civil War veteran from Louisiana who had read the law before moving west. He was immediately successful in Sweetwater, where he practiced law, served as a judge, dealt in surveying and real estate, and helped found the local Baptist church.

In spite of their civic and financial success, in 1887 the Scarboroughs decided to move to Waco, Texas, so that the children could be educated at Baylor University. There were three Scarborough children: George (or Buddie), the eldest, who became a lawyer, secret-service detective, and Broadway playwright; Mattie Douglass, who married George McDaniel, later to become the powerful pastor of the largest Protestant congregation in the South, the First Baptist Church of Richmond, Virginia; and Emily Dorothy, the youngest, affectionately known by friends and family as "Miss Dottie" or "Dot."

Dottie majored in English at Baylor, graduating in 1896. She was a popular but studious coed whose main interests were distinctly literary. She quickly blossomed into a creative literary talent with self-discipline and a sense of purpose that lasted her a lifetime. She published poems, essays, and short stories in the school paper as well as the campus literary magazine. She was secretary of the Calliopean Literary Society and as such she wrote to authors throughout the country whom the club was studying, requesting from them copies of their work or personal greetings to be read at club meetings.

After she graduated, she taught for a year in the public schools of Marlin, Texas, and then returned to Baylor to study for an M. A. in English, which she completed in 1899. Afterward, Scarborough became a member of the Baylor faculty, along with her sister, who taught foreign languages for a few years before marrying her classmate, the dynamic and ambitious George McDaniel.

Dottie became increasingly bored with teaching undergraduates and more interested in becoming a professional writer instead. In 1910, she took a leave of absence from Baylor and spent the year studying literature at Oxford University, which had just begun allowing women to attend lectures on a limited basis, although they could not earn degrees. Her autobiographical serialized novel, *The Unfair Sex* (1925-1926), describes this year in some detail. She attended summer school at the University of Chicago, where she studied writing with Robert Morss Lovett. During this period she published a book of poetry, *Fugitive Verses* (1912).

During her absence from Baylor, the Texas Folklore Society had been founded, and upon her return, Dorothy Scarborough joined and eventually became a life member. In 1914 she was elected president of the organization and her 1915 presidential address, "Negro Ballads and Reels," was the first public statement of her interest and expertise in folklore. As a child, Scarborough had often accompanied her father when he went to inspect the cotton fields, and some of her fondest early memories were of listening to the Negro field hands sing as they worked. She never lost her fascination with these songs. She published an article, "Traditions of the Waco Indians," in the first volume of the *Publications of the Texas Folklore Society* (1916) and "The 'Blues' as Folksongs" in the second volume (1923), and finally, in 1925, published her influential collection, *On the Trail of Negro Folksong* (1925).

Written in collaboration with a Baylor colleague, the ethnomusicologist Ola Mae Gulledge, *On the Trail of Negro Folksong* clearly established Scarborough's scholarly reputation as a folklorist and authority on Negro folksong. The book was based on research conducted almost continuously since her Texas Folklore Society presidential address, involving extensive correspondence, questionnaires, and some fieldwork combined with literary research and documentation. George Lyman Kittredge of Harvard, whom she met when he came to lecture at Baylor, helped her with the conceptualization of the book and encouraged Harvard University Press to publish it.

After the death of her parents, Scarborough moved to New York City in order to get a Ph.D. from Columbia and become a novelist. Although she was thirty-eight years old and unmarried, the move to New York was the beginning of a new life. Upon receiving the Ph.D. in 1917, she was hired immediately to teach creative writing in the Extension Division of Columbia, a job she held until her death in 1935. Her dissertation, *The Supernatural in Modern English Fiction* (1917), was published and received favorable reviews; today it is still a standard reference in the field, although considerably outdated. She progressed through the academic ranks at Columbia and at the time of her death was an associate professor, a high achievement for a woman at that time.

During her early years at Columbia, Dorothy Scarborough focused her attention on literature and creative writing. In 1919 she published *From a Southern Porch*, a whimsical extended personal essay recounting her adventures as a summer house guest at her sister's elegant home in Richmond, Virginia. In this book she was already experimenting with techniques of structure and style which she would later use in all of her novels. As a result of the popularity of her published dissertation on the supernatural, she also began editing and contributing to ghost story anthologies. She reviewed books for various New York newspapers and published short stories and poems. As her literary horizons broadened, she founded the Columbia Writing Club for her creative writing students and began holding popular "at homes" where the nation's literati mingled with an assortment of Columbia students, homesick Texans and southerners who were visiting or studying in New York.

Her first novel, *In the Land of Cotton*, based on extensive research and fieldwork, came out in 1923. Set in and around Waco, the novel was the first in a projected trilogy dealing with the abuses of tenant farmers by the cotton industry. In recognition of this novel, Baylor awarded her an honorary doctor of letters degree.

The high point of her life and career was undoubtedly 1925. In that year, she published three major works: *The Wind*, *On the Trail of Negro Folksong*, and *The Unfair Sex*.

The Wind is the basis of Scarborough's reputation as a western writer. Set in frontier Sweetwater during the devastating drought of the mid-1880s, the novel depicts the harsh environment of the West and its impact on a delicate and sensitive heroine from Virginia. The doomed heroine, Letty, is ultimately driven to madness, murder, and suicide by the combined elemental and demonic forces of the wind and sand. In addition to her personal recollections of West Texas, Scarborough fully utilized her training and background as a folklorist throughout this dramatic novel, weaving together snatches of folksong, regional Texas legends, and the ballad image of the Demon Lover. As a publicity stunt, the novel was first published anonymously. The ploy backfired, however, because Texans were outraged by their assumption that a Yankee had written this scathing attack on their beloved state. After an acrimonious exchange of letters with the editor of the *Dallas Morning News*, her authorship was revealed and public opinion in Texas softened. The novel created a public relations sensation for Scarborough and was financially quite successful. *The Wind* is Scarborough's only truly western novel; her other works fit more comfortably into the canon of southern literature.

In 1928 *The Wind* was made into a stunning silent movie starring Lillian Gish and Lars Hansen and directed by the Swedish master, Victor Seastrom. Scarborough took a deep interest in the technical production of the movie and enjoyed a lasting friendship with its star, Lillian Gish.

In quick succession, she published *Impatient Griselda* (1927), *Can't Get a Redbird* (1929), and *The Stretch-Berry Smile* (1932), all of which were set in Texas. *Impatient Griselda* enjoyed moderate success as a Book of the Month Club alternate, but the other two novels were mediocre at best. *Impatient Griselda* is a retelling of the legend of Lilith, from the point of view of a long-suffering Baptist preacher's wife. The publication of *Can't Get a Redbird* unfortunately coincided with the collapse of the stock market which, combined with the novel's subject matter and weak artistic merit, resulted in heavy financial losses for all concerned and seriously compromised Scarborough's literary reputation. Basically a chronicle of the establishment of the American Cotton Planters Exchange in the late 1920s, the book suffered from the excessive involvement of members of the exchange in approving the text. Because of mutual hard feelings resulting from *Redbird*, Scarborough changed publishers for her last novel, *The Stretch-Berry Smile*. A sad and depressing tale of the emotional devastation wrought on children by the unremitting labor and poverty of the cotton tenant-farming system, the novel was not well received in the depths of the Great Depression. Because she badly needed the money, she quickly compiled a nonfiction book for children, *The Story of Cotton* (1933), based on her earlier extensive research. The Depression, family responsibilities, and some bad business decisions soon extinguished her creative spark.

During this same time period, she undertook another folksong collection. This time she decided to focus on Anglo ballads in Virginia and North Carolina instead of Negro secular folksongs. In 1930 she was awarded a research grant from Columbia University. Equipped with specially made Dictaphone recording equipment, she devoted her time and energy to hunting down Appalachian informants who knew and would sing the beloved old ballads brought over from the British Isles. She became a true "song catcher," a local term used by her informants. Granted sabbatical research leave by Columbia in 1932, she and her widowed sister went to Europe, where she worked on the manuscript of this new folksong collection. She also spent a summer working at Yaddo, the writers' retreat in Saratoga Springs, New York. After completing the manuscript, she convinced Columbia University Press to publish it, an expensive undertaking because of all of the musical transcriptions. She hired a professional musician to transcribe the songs from the wax Dictaphone cylinders and an ethnomusicologist to write an essay explaining the modal aspects of the tunes. She died unexpectedly in her sleep on November 7, 1935, with the galleys of the book on her bedside table.

Her death created a dilemma for Columbia University Press because the book was set in type but had not been proofread or corrected. Two of her colleagues from Columbia were drafted to help, as was her sister. To further complicate matters, one of the informants and the ethnomusicologist filed suit against the press for what they regarded as slanderous inaccuracies in the text and transcriptions. Since Scarborough had left no record of her agreements with the litigants, the publication of the book was delayed for two years until an out-of-court settlement could be reached and some changes made in the book. A *Song Catcher in Southern Mountains: American Folksongs of British Ancestry* was finally published posthumously in 1937.

In spite of her expertise in folklore, Scarborough's reputation today rests almost entirely on her controversial and somewhat experimental novel, *The Wind*. The negative depiction of the Texas landscape and tragic characters sets this novel apart from those of her contemporary Texas authors, especially the men, who preferred a more heroic, positive approach consistent with the rapidly developing "Texas mystique." Scarborough's other novels follow conventional literary formulas, and today they strike readers as stilted, outdated, and sentimental. *The Wind*, however, still conveys intense conflict and memorable emotional impact. Because of the enduring appeal of this novel, Scarborough's place is secure as one of Texas' leading authors.

Selected Bibliography

Primary Sources

Can't Get a Redbird. New York: Harper and Brothers, 1929; rpt., New York: AMS Press/The Labor Movement in Fiction and Non-Fiction, 1977.

From a Southern Porch. New York: G. P. Putnam's Sons/The Knickerbocker Press, 1919.

Fugitive Verses. Waco: Baylor University Press, 1912.

Impatient Griselda. New York: Harper and Brothers, 1927.

In the Land of Cotton. New York: The Macmillan Company, 1923.

On the Trail of Negro Folksong. Cambridge: Harvard University Press, 1925; rpt., Hatboro, Pennsylvania: Folklore Associates, 1963.

A Song Catcher in Southern Mountains: American Folksongs of British Ancestry. New York: Columbia University Press, 1937; rpt., New York: AMS Press, 1966.

The Stretch-Berry Smile. New York: Bobbs-Merrill, 1932.

The Story of Cotton. New York: Harper and Brothers/City and Country Series, 1933.

The Supernatural in Modern English Fiction. New York: G. P. Putnam's Sons, 1917.; rpt., New York: Octagon Books/Farrar, Straus & Giroux, 1967.

The Unfair Sex. Serialized in *The Woman's Viewpoint*, 1925-1926.

The Wind. New York: Harper and Brothers, 1925; rpt., Austin: University of Texas Press/Barker Texas History Series Number 4, 1979; New York: Fawcett Popular Library, 1980.

Secondary Sources Since 1981

Grider, Sylvia. "Foreword." *The Wind*. Austin: University of Texas Press, 1986.

———. "The Folksong Scholarship of Dorothy Scarborough." In *The Bounty of Texas*. Francis Edward Abernethy, ed. Denton: University of North Texas Press, 1990. Pp. 97-103.

————. "Women's Networking in Researching the Biography of Dorothy Scarborough." *Southern Folklore*, 47:1 (1990): 77-83.

Marshall, Carol. "The Fairy Tale and the Frontier: Images of Women in Texas Fiction." In *The Texas Literaty Tradition: Fiction, Folklore, History*. Don Graham, James W. Lee and William T. Pilkington, eds. Austin: College of Liberal Arts, University of Texas, 1983.

Palmer, Pamela. "Dorothy Scarborough and Karle Wilson Baker: A Literary Friendship." *Southwestern Historical Quarterly*, 91:1 (1987): 19-32.

Slade, Carole. "Authorship and Authority in Dorothy Scarborough's *The Wind*." *Studies in American Fiction*, 14 (Spring 1986), 85-91.

Joyce Lee

Rolando Hinojosa

Rolando Hinojosa was born in 1929 in Hidalgo County in the lower Rio Grande Valley of South Texas. He served in the United States Army during the Korean War, following which he took a bachelor's degree from the University of Texas at Austin and later a doctorate from the University of Illinois. He has filled academic and administrative posts at several universities around the country, including a stint as director of the Chicano Studies Program at the University of Minnesota. In 1981, Hinojosa returned to his alma mater, the University of Texas, where he is currently a professor of English and creative writing.

For a quarter century, Hinojosa has pursued a project reminiscent of Faulkner's fictional chronicle: the Klail City Death Trip Series. All his published books—more than a dozen—are entries in the series; each is autonomous, and yet each is but a slice from a much larger loaf, part of a lengthy work in progress. Many of his books exist in both Spanish and English versions. His early works—reflecting the militancy and cultural separatism of the "Chicano renaissance" of the 1960s and '70s—are in Spanish; the later ones are in English. In fact, many of the later volumes are loose translations of earlier books. Thus, *Estampas del Valle y otras obras* (1972) becomes *The Valley* (1983); *Klail City y sus aldrededores* (1976) becomes *Klail City* (1987); and so forth.

The series depicts the rapidly changing social climate of "a postage stamp of soil": Belken County—a thinly disguised version, no doubt, of the author's native Hidalgo County—in the lower Rio Grande Valley.

(Klail City is the county seat.) Hinojosa believes that the uniqueness of Valley society derives from the fact that it flourishes in a borderland far from the centers of power and population in either the U. S. or Mexico. Valley Anglos and *mexicanos* alike are shaped by the insularity, the separateness of their shared culture.

The author is most concerned, of course, with re-creating the life of Belken County *mexicanos*, and he is very good at showing their sense of community. *Mexicano* families have lived in Belken County for generations; they share a common language, a common folklore, and common roots in Valley soil. Hinojosa weaves *mexicano* folk memory into the fabric of his fiction, a memory that extends back to 1749, when Jose Escandon led a party that established twenty-one settlements on the north bank of the Rio Grande. A number of Valley families trace their ancestry to those original settlers.

The Mexican Revolution of 1910-1920, in which many Valley *mexicanos* fought, and the turbulent events of 1915-1917 surrounding Aniceto Pizaña and the Plan of San Diego are also historical landmarks, recalled in communal stories and legends and frequently alluded to in Hinojosa's novels. The upheaval of the revolution had an impact on the lives of all Valley residents and created many Anglo-*mexicano* conflicts that are yet to be wholly resolved.

Though dozens, perhaps hundreds, of minor characters appear and reappear in the Klail City series, the focus always returns, in one way or another, to Jehu Malacara and Rafa (or Rafe) Buenrostro, cousins and friends. Chronologically, the series begins roughly in the 1930s, when Jehu and Rafe are orphaned children, and ends — at the time of this writing anyway — in the early 1980s.

One critic calls Hinojosa's series "a *mestizaje*, a cross breeding of North American and Latin American literary and cultural traditions" (J. D. Saldívar 175). For example, Hinojosa's fictional techniques are rooted in *mexicano* tradition in the sense that they often derive from the largely oral nature of Valley culture. On the other hand, they are new and innovative in that they seem cut from a decidedly post-modernist cloth. Eschewing familiar modes of narration, the author tells his stories by means of various non-linear genres: sketches, letters, interviews, depositions, diaries. The effect is often that of a mosaic rather than a straightforward story line. (*Partners in Crime* [1985] is the only one of his books to employ a conventional linear narration.)

Hinojosa's novels of the last decade or so advance the tale of Jehu and

Rafe in significant ways. *Dear Rafe* (1985), set in the early 1960s, consists of a packet of letters by Jehu, sent over a period of several months to his cousin Rafe, and a collection of interviews and depositions taken from various members of the community by a writer named P. Galindo. These documents are presented as evidence relating to Jehu's sudden resignation as chief loan officer of Arnold "Noddy" Perkins' bank in Klail City.

The *mexicano* gossips are harder on Jehu than the Anglos. They believe Jehu is guilty of embezzlement, or that he has been caught in a romantic entanglement with Perkins' daughter, Sammie Jo. Actually Jehu has been stricken by his conscience. He is appalled by Perkins' political machinations. South Texas has long been a stronghold of political bossism, and Perkins is a political boss nonpareil. He controls Valley officeholders and manipulates *mexicano* voters with arrogant disdain.

It is not until *Partners in Crime*, set a decade later, however, that the reader learns for certain what happens to Jehu: he spends three years at the university in Austin as a graduate student in English, only to return to Klail City to assume once again a position as an officer in Perkins' bank. The subtitle of *Partners* — *A Rafe Buenrostro Mystery* — strongly suggests the author's intention to publish a series of mystery novels, though to this date no further mystery stories by Hinojosa have appeared. In the novel Rafe, a Korean War veteran, college graduate, and licensed attorney, is lieutenant of detectives in a police unit attached to the Belken County district attorney's office.

In the course of the narrative, Rafe and his team are called on to solve several murders, the most puzzling an execution-style slaying of two Mexican nationals and a Belken County policeman. Rafe's investigation leads him into an underworld tug-of-war in which well-financed cocaine dealers attempt to supplant nickel-and-dime marijuana smugglers. Unlike most murder mysteries, *Partners* ends tentatively, and many loose ends are left dangling. (The book has been called "a post-modernist detective novel" [J. D. Saldívar 175].) The ending may disappoint some fans of the mystery genre, but it seems an accurate reflection of the real world.

Petty smuggling has been a way of life along the U. S.-Mexico border for a century and a half. Now, as *Partners in Crime* makes clear, with big money to be made in the drug trade, during the last couple of decades the heavy hitters have moved in. International crime cartels currently control Valley smuggling operations, just as American capitalism has come to be dominated by multi-national corporations. As Faulkner's Yoknapatawpha County is ultimately a microcosm of the larger world, so, it turns out, is Hinojosa's Belken County.

With the publication of *Becky and Her Friends* (1990), set in the early 1980s, Hinojosa may have reached the logical conclusion to his Klail City series. *Becky* is a kind of feminist novel, in which the title character, Becky Escobar, becomes a liberated woman. She divorces her husband, Ira, a Valley politician and notorious *vendido*, becomes self-supporting, and marries Jehu, with whom she had once had a torrid affair. In *Becky*, Anglo and *mexicano* cultures have, in many ways, converged. Jehu and Rafe are at least superficially if not entirely assimilated into the Anglo world, and Becky is openly and upwardly mobile in Valley society.

Thus, with *Becky and Her Friends*, Hinojosa's chronicle has reached a point beyond which it will be difficult to progress. His most recent novel, *The Useless Servants* (1993), returns to subject matter first explored in an earlier poetry collection, *Korean Love Songs* (1978). The narrative consists mostly of entries from a journal kept by Rafe, a non-commissioned officer in an artillery unit engaged in some of the heaviest fighting of the Korean War. The entries reflect all the disjointedness and shocking immediacy of the diary format. Rafe keeps the journal as a way of hanging on to his sanity in the midst of madness, of trying to make sense of senselessness.

The Useless Servants is one of Hinojosa's most powerful books. It demonstrates that he can come to grips with a wider world than the fascinating but insular environment of Belken County. The real question to be answered in future books, however, is whether or not the energy of Hinojosa's imagination will propel him back to Klail City to discover a more satisfying closure to the series than *Becky and Her Friends* currently provides.

Selected Bibliography

Primary Sources

Becky and Her Friends. Houston: Arte Público, 1990.

Claros varones de Belken/Fair Gentlemen of Belken County. Tempe, Arizona: Bilingual Press, 1986.

Dear Rafe. Houston: Arte Público, 1985.

Estampas del Valle y otras obras. Berkeley: Quinto Sol, 1973.

Generaciones y semblanzas. Berkeley: Editorial Justa, 1977.

Klail City. Houston: Arte Público, 1987.

Klail City y sus aldrededores. Havana, Cuba: Casa de Las Americas, 1976.

Korean Love Songs. Berkeley: Editorial Justa, 1978.

Mi querido Rafa. Houston: Arte Público, 1981.

Partners in Crime. Houston: Arte Público, 1985.

Rites and Witnesses. Houston: Arte Público, 1982.

The Useless Servants. Houston: Arte Público, 1993.

The Valley. Ypsilanti, Michigan: Bilingual Press, 1983.

Secondary Sources

Busby, Mark. "Faulknerian Elements in Rolando Hinojosa's *The Valley*." *MELUS*, 11:4 (1984): 103-109.

Mejía, Jaime Armin. "Breaking the Silence: The Missing Pages in Rolando Hinojosa's *The Useless Servants*." *Southwestern American Literature*, 15:1 (1994): 1-6.

Saldívar, José David. "Chicano Border Narratives as Cultural Critique." In *Criticism in the Borderlands: Studies in Chicano Literature, Culture, and Ideology*. Hector Calderon and José David Saldívar, eds. Durham: Duke University Press, 1991. Pp. 167-180.

———, ed. *The Rolando Hinojosa Reader: Essays Historical and Critical*. Houston: Arte Público, 1985.

Saldívar, Ramon. *Chicano Narrative: The Dialectics of Difference*. Madison: University of Wisconsin Press, 1990.

Lou Rodenberger

Shelby Hearon, Beverly Lowry and Sarah Bird

Although Shelby Hearon, Beverly Lowry and Sarah Bird have published novels regularly since their initial successes, critical appraisal of their fictional versions of post-modern life in the South and Southwest has been sketchy. As diverse in theme and style as the personalities of their creators, the fiction of these writers, who have lived in Texas much of their lives, offers a critic little common ground for comparative consideration. One common denominator, however, seems to link these writers' lives and works. Each author reflects without flinching what she perceives contemporary life has become, particularly for women. Shelby Hearon traces the accelerated changes in women's lives during the last quarter of this century with penetrating insight and subtle humor. Beverly Lowry conveys in her recent fiction a darker vision of the absurdities in the lives of a middle-aged generation still suffering hangovers from the excesses of the idealistic sixties. Lowry's talent for comic satire seldom surfaces in her most recent fiction, leaving that field open to Sarah Bird, whose gift for skewering the hypocrisies endemic to modern culture with her pointed, deft wit has developed steadily from farcical one-liners and episodes to mature, measured and hilarious assessment of modern life in Texas and the Southwest.

Shelby Hearon, who began publishing almost a decade before Lowry and two decades before Bird, remembers coming to Texas the first time before she was six. (She had been born in Marion, Kentucky, in 1931.) Hearon's early life was somewhat peripatetic with the family moving often to wherever her father, geophysicist Charles Reed, found work. Hearon assesses these early years in West Texas in a candid personal essay for *Contemporary Authors Autobiography Series* (157-159). She begins with a statement which both reveals and predicts. "The grandest thing about my childhood was the freedom," she remembers. Discovering an acceptable way to reassert that freedom as a modern woman has become both the quest of her own life and the recurring theme of her fiction.

Encouraged by her father, Hearon's strongest interests during her first school years in Midland, Texas, included science and math. During her adolescence, the family moved back to Marion, where at fourteen, Hearon was enrolled in Sayre School, a girls' academy in Lexington, Kentucky. In 1937, the family moved back to Texas, this time to Austin, where Hearon was to live for most of the next thirty-four years. Married to law student Robert Hearon soon after her graduation from the University of Texas, Hearon had two children, Anne and Reed, and settled into the expected lifestyle of an attorney's wife. Although she had won first prize in a statewide extemporaneous writing contest her senior year at Austin High, Hearon did not get serious about writing until, as she remembers, she began to feel trapped by "communal expectations" of young mothers and wives in the fifties. It was then she began to keep a journal and began her first book at age thirty.

With little notion of how to shape a novel, Hearon wrote and rewrote the manuscript of *Armadillo in the Grass* (1968) for three years. Then, fate intervened, and after two cerebral hemorrhages a month apart, followed by a craniotomy, the would-be novelist, inspired by this encounter with her own mortality, had the courage to throw away her first drafts and begin over again. Two years later, unsolicited, the manuscript caught the attention of an editor at Knopf. Hearon was thirty-six. Five years later, Hearon's second novel, *The Second Dune* (1973), was published. In the years since, she has written eleven more novels, each receiving increased attention from reviewers. As her own life has moved through the changes many women weathered during the sixties and seventies — divorce, solitary living, new relationships, second marriages, and changes in lifestyle and residence — Hearon has structured fiction which organizes and examines those changes with clear insight as well as, on occasion, probing, ironic humor. Married now to William Halpern, a cardiovascular physiologist, Hearon lives in Burlington, Vermont.

Armadillo in the Grass is the story of Clara Blue, a young mother who finds creative outlet in sculpting in different mediums the wild animals

that come to her backyard feeder. The author observes in her brief introduction to the second edition of the novel (1983) "that it is our very
mortality that presses us to give order, shape and form to our experience." Hearon has remained true to this idea. Although her own first
marriage did not end until 1976, three years earlier, Hearon, a keen
observer of life around her, had examined the positive and negative
aspects of second marriages in *The Second Dune*. With this novel,
Hearon gained critical notice after it won the Texas Institute of Letters
fiction award in 1973. Exercising more fully her talent for comic satire
in *Hannah's House* (1975), Hearon contrasts the conservative values of
Hannah, sorority girl and bride-to-be, with those of her irreverent
mother, Beverly "Bananas" Foster, who stifles her disdain for material
acquisition to become a model mother-of-the bride and buy a house that
Hannah "would be proud to be married from."

Hearon has been praised for her ability to create setting in her fiction.
She says in "Placing Fiction," an essay appearing in *The Writer* (July
1992, 17-18, 45), "I like to think of a place as having three faces: its history, its view of itself, and its significance to the people who live there."
Now and Another Time (1976), which won the LeBaron Baker Fiction
Award, demonstrates how carefully Hearon follows her own advice. In a
novel about one generation's influence on the next, she explores both
the history and the landscape of an East Texas piney woods family, evoking as well the charged political atmosphere in contemporary Austin.
Hearon has commented that "everyone became the unfilled wishes of
the generation before them" in this novel (Bennett 112-113). To move
artistically from an increasingly negative criticism of society, Hearon
next wrote *A Prince of a Fellow* (1978), a comedy starring mainly a Hill
Country radio talk hostess, who knows appearance does not always signify reality. Hearon once again won the Texas Institute award for best
fiction with this work.

In 1981, after Hearon moved east, Atheneum published her sixth
novel, *Painted Dresses*. In this story of Nell Woodard, an artist who finds
little fulfillment in painting as long as her human relationships founder,
Hearon explores more fully her tentative ideas about predestination of
human lives versus the exercise of individual will as a control of fate.
Her next novel, *Afternoon of the Faun* (1983), which takes place in
Kentucky and Colorado, explores the complexities of child adoption.
Group Therapy, published in 1984, considers as theme the search for
identity of a daughter still seeking detachment from an overbearing

mother. The secrets which complicate life in a Mississippi River town in Missouri provide the plot for A Small Town (1985).

Hearon's tenth novel, *Five Hundred Scorpions* (1987), moves between Virginia and Mexico, where a restless lawyer finds himself the only male member of a team conducting an anthropological study of life in a Mexican village. Lively and sometimes comic, this book began to attract the national attention the author deserved. In 1989, *Owning Jolene* was reviewed in New York papers and national weekly journals, chosen by *People Magazine* as one of the ten best books of the year, and won for Hearon the 1990 American Academy and Institute of Arts and Letters Award in Literature.

Hidebound Waco, Texas, provides the setting for *Hug Dancing* (1991), where administrators still ban dancing at its church-supported university and weather is often the main topic among coffee shop regulars. This narrative fully establishes Hearon's reputation for graphic sense of place, sensitive understanding of human nature, and rare gift for leavening life's complexities with good-natured humor. Her thirteenth novel, *Life Estates* (1994), explores a longtime friendship of two women, one in South Carolina, the other in Texas, who must face their mortality together when the Texan learns cancer is threatening her life. Sharing neither values nor aspirations, the two widows nevertheless demonstrate what friendship means in a crisis. *Footprints* (1996), Hearon's most recent novel, chronicles the emotional story of a couple's near breakup of a long-term marriage after the accidental death of their daughter.

Hearon's life history as it is reflected in her fiction illuminates modern woman's quest for the freedom to realize her potential and at the same time participate in fulfilling relationships with family and friends. She skillfully penetrates the protective coating of Texas myth, often with humor, to probe modern society in the Lone Star State and share the truths she discovers there. Hearon has been the recipient of both National Endowment for the Arts and Guggenheim fellowships. She has published short fiction and essays, as well as numerous book reviews. In 1979 she collaborated with retired Congresswoman Barbara Jordan in writing *Barbara Jordan: A Self-Portrait*.

In the early days of Hearon's career, one of her close friends was Beverly Lowry, who came to Texas with her stockbroker husband, Glenn, in 1965. Lowry was born in Memphis, Tennessee, on August 10, 1938. The daughter of David Leonard and Dora (Smith) Fey, she grew up in Greenville, Mississippi, which was to become Eunola in three of her novels. After attending Ole Miss for two years and graduating from Memphis State in 1960, Lowry married and moved to Manhattan, where she tried her wings as an actress. After the couple's move to Houston, Lowry began writing, first essays, then short stories, and finally six novels. Set in Eunola, Mississippi, her first two novels and her most recent one exploit with verve the hypocrisies and values of the southern small town. *Come Back, Lolly Ray* (1977) and *Emma Blue* (1978) were destined at first to be published as one novel, *Eunola's Own.* Lowry's agent persuaded her to publish the second half as sequel to the first. Together, the two works chronicle the misadventures of Lolly Ray, a premier high school twirler, and her later relationship with her misbegotten daughter, Emma Blue. In Lowry's most recent novel, *The Track of Real Desires* (1994), old acquaintances gather in Eunola for a dinner party honoring Leland Standard, a visiting classmate. Envy, disappointment, jealousy, lust, and even true friendship are evident in the actions and thoughts of this gathering of middle-aged small-town citizens who have somehow missed "the track of their real desires." As a *New York Times* reviewer points out, "For most of them, the future has become lost in the past" (May 8, 1994).

For evidence of Lowry's often dark comedic view of life in Texas, three of her novels demonstrate how keenly the author understands contemporary culture in the state. *Daddy's Girl* (1981) follows Sue Shannon Stovall Muffaletta as she tries to discover her true identity. Should she settle for being M. S. Sue, country song composer, June Day, honky-tonk singer, or Sue Muffaletta, Big's daughter and mother of his grandchildren? Often hilarious, her relationships with her southern-bred family inspire much of the comedy.

Lowry's next two novels, both set in Texas, were in draft when personal tragedy interrupted her writing life. In 1984, her son Peter fell victim to a hit-and-run driver, a life-changing event for her and her family. Lowry admits that her next novel, *The Perfect Sonya* (1987), is a melancholy book. In this work, New York actress Pauline Terry comes home to be with her dying father. Her unexpected involvement with her aunt's former husband leads to reassessment of her life. Her next work, *Breaking Gentle* (1988), will "break your heart," one reviewer says in *Texas Books in Review* (Winter 1988, 18). Finished after Lowry had lost her son and her parents within a few months of each other, this narrative follows the breakdown of a family in crisis. In 1981, Lowry had moved with her family to a horse farm near San Marcos, Texas, on the edge of the Texas Hill Country. This story explores the problems of coping with a rebellious child, breeding and caring for race horses, and facing the near breakup of a marriage. Human compassion and love prevail finally in the novel, perhaps Lowry's best to date.

In 1992, Lowry published a nonfiction study of a young woman, a convicted murderer, who awaits her fate on a Texas prison death row. In a remarkable blending of the story of her own wayward son's life and the sordid story of Karla Faye Tucker, Lowry somehow comes to terms finally with her son's tragic death in *Crossed Over: A Murder, A Memoir.*

Lowry has won Texas Institute of Letters awards for best short story in 1984 and for *Daddy's Girl* and *The Perfect Sonya* as best novels of 1981 and 1987. In 1984 she was awarded the *Black Warrior Review* Literature Prize. She is also a recipient of a literature grant from the National Endowment for the Arts and a Guggenheim Fellowship. Lowry, now divorced, makes her home in Missoula, Montana, although she often serves as writer-in-residence at universities across the country.

Both Hearon and Lowry can be witty and funny on occasion in their fiction, but Austin writer Sarah Bird exhibits a particular talent for comic social criticism in her latest novel, *Virgin of the Rodeo* (1993). When Sonja K. Getz, who prefers to be called Son, teams up with a reluctant has-been rodeo trick roper named Prairie James to find her father, the two misfits set out to demolish any heroic myths rodeo aficionados may have attached to the sport. In her hilarious satirical narration of the odd couple's adventures, Bird questions myths associated with rodeo heroics, Native American mystique, and New Age credos. Bird gathered material for this, her best work, traveling for a year as a freelance photographer to record the action at alternative rodeos in the Southwest — such rodeos as the all-black, all-Native American, and all-women events annually produced without much fanfare.

Daughter of John and Colista Bird, Sarah Bird was born on December 26, 1949, in Ann Arbor, Michigan. She came to live in Texas when her father was stationed in the Air Force at San Antonio. Earning a B.A. degree in anthropology at the University of New Mexico in 1973 and a graduate degree at the University of Texas in 1976, Bird married George Roger Jones, an engineer, and settled down in Austin to write.

Bird candidly admits in an interview in the spring of 1991 (*Texas Libraries* 14-16) that her "entrance into the world of letters" was as Tory Cates, author of romance novels. In her second mainstream novel, *The Boyfriend School* (1989), Bird examines this genre through the eyes of a skeptical photojournalist assigned to cover the Luvboree, a romance writers' convention in Dallas. With her singular sense of humor, Bird turns the tables on her reader, who has been enjoying the writer's satire of the genre. In the end, the joke is on the reader. This, after all, is a romance novel. Bird wrote the script based on this novel for a movie called *Don't Tell Her It's Me*, which starred Shelley Long and Steve Guttenberg.

Bird published her first "serious" novel, *Alamo House*, in 1986. The story records the hilarious developments in a feud between graduate women living in a co-op house at the University of Texas and the unruly members of Sigma Upsilon Kappa, better known as the SUKs, whose fraternity house is across the street. Broad comedy satirizes life at the frat house, but some of Bird's most biting wit is reserved for commentary on the activities at the Lyndon B. Johnson Presidential Library, where not only presidential papers but all of the trivia of the Johnson family's stay in the White House are carefully catalogued and preserved.

With publication of *The Mommy Club* (1991), which won the 1991 Texas Institute of Letters fiction award, Bird was recognized as one of the more gifted young writers residing in Texas. Set in San Antonio, this narrative is the work of a mature writer, humorously dissecting the Yuppie culture in San Antonio, while probing the deeper recesses of the human heart. Structured around the changing attitudes of a young woman artist out of the city's counterculture, who, as a surrogate mother, is carrying the child of an affluent couple, the novel examines the complexities of human emotions associated with such an experience. Reviewers were almost unanimous in their opinion that this novel significantly proves that Bird has come of age as a fiction writer.

For the first half of the twentieth century, Texas history, including its legends and treasured myths, furnished much of the material for writers who lived long enough in the state to write about them. As the century winds down, these three writers have found even richer materials for fiction in the state's diverse and changing contemporary culture.

Selected Hearon Bibliography

Novels
Afternoon of a Faun. New York: Atheneum, 1983.
Armadillo in the Grass. New York: Knopf, 1968; rpt., New York: Curtis Books, 1968; Dallas: Pressworks, 1983.
Five Hundred Scorpions. New York: Atheneum, 1987.
Footprints. New York: Knopf, 1996.

Group Therapy. New York: Atheneum, 1984; rpt., New York: Warner Books, 1990.
Hannah's House. Garden City, New York: Doubleday, 1975.
Hug Dancing. New York: Knopf, 1991.
Life Estates. New York: Knopf, 1994; rpt., New York: Vintage/Random House, 1995.
Now and Another Time. Garden City, New York: Doubleday, 1976.
Owning Jolene. New York: Knopf, 1989; rpt., New York: Warner Books, 1990.
Painted Dresses. New York: Atheneum, 1981.
A Prince of a Fellow. Garden City, New York: Doubleday, 1978; rpt., Fort Worth: Texas Christian University Press, 1992.
The Second Dune. New York: Knopf, 1973.
A Small Town. New York: Atheneum, 1985.

Selected Lowry Bibliography

Novels
Breaking Gentle. New York: Viking, 1988.
Come Back, Lolly Ray. Garden City, New York: Doubleday, 1977.
Daddy's Girl. New York: Viking, 1981.
Emma Blue. Garden City, New York: Doubleday, 1978.
The Perfect Sonya. New York: Viking, 1987.
The Track of Real Desires. New York: Knopf, 1994.

Nonfiction
Crossed Over: A Murder, A Memoir. New York: Knopf, 1992.

Selected Bird Bibliography

Novels
Alamo House: Women without Men, Men without Brains. New York: W. W. Norton & Company, 1986.
The Boyfriend School. New York: Doubleday, 1989.
The Mommy Club. New York: Doubleday, 1991.
Virgin of the Rodeo. New York: Doubleday, 1993.

Secondary Sources

Bennett, Patrick. "Shelby Hearon: Time, Sex, and God." In *Talking with Texas Writers*. College Station: Texas A&M University Press, 1980 Pp. 111-134. Author discusses her writing life and major ideas in her fiction in this 1978 interview.
Contemporary Authors Autobiography Series. Vol. 2. Detroit: Gale Research, 1984.
Lynn, Sandra. "Texas, Women, Fiction." *Pawn Review*, 4 (1980-1981): 2-17. A discussion of the works of Hearon, Katherine Anne Porter and Dorothy Scarborough.
Marshall, Carol. "The Fairy Tale and the Frontier: Images of Women in Texas Fiction." In *The Texas Literary Tradition*. Don Graham, James W. Lee and William T. Pilkington, eds. Austin: The University of Texas, 1983. Pp. 195-295. A critical comparison of *Hannah's House* with novels by Dorothy Scarborough, Jane Gilmore Rushing, and Laura Furman.
Texas Libraries, 526 (Spring 1991): 14-16.

Michael Hobbs

Walter McDonald

Western American literature derives much of its power from its finely focused perspective on the land, and the poetry of Walter McDonald is certainly no exception. McDonald has devoted himself to examining, wondering about, and dwelling upon what N. Scott Momaday has called "a particular landscape" (in "Man Made of Words"). McDonald writes poetry saturated with a peculiarly potent sense of the stark landscape that surrounds Lubbock, Texas, where he lives and teaches creative writing at Texas Tech University. Like the region's cotton farmers and cattle ranchers, he struggles against the harshness of the place, in his case raising words rather than cotton or cattle, on the semiarid terrain of the Texas South Plains and West Texas hardscrabble.

McDonald's region is an exacting and treacherous terrain to negotiate. It is a place of extremes (psychic as well as physical), simultaneously monotonous and sublime in its flat, treeless expanse surrounded by endless horizons against which set harsh suns, softened in the evening light. With such a region to wander in, McDonald fashions the most successful moments of his poems into what I refer to as a hardscrabble sublime. Much of his work looks deceptively simple; indeed, his poetry is as minimal as the landscape about which he writes. But if read too quickly, the poems' subtleties and shadings slip by unnoticed. Both poet and reader confront a similar challenge when facing the flat expanse of the West Texas hardscrabble. For McDonald as poet, the challenge lies in shaping the physical and psychic harshness of his material into poetry that is at once both beautiful and unflinching in its honesty about a place that in many ways looks like a wasteland. "The mind is a hawk, trying to survive/on hardscrabble," McDonald tells us in *Night Landings* (his eleventh collection of poetry, 1989), suggesting an analogue for the poet struggling to make something out of the apparent dearth of material around him. In a desert-like world where only hot wind keeps one afloat above "sand so dry no trees/grow native," the poet's eyesight must be as keen as a hawk's "to make a desert give up dead-still/ideas."

McDonald's poems are as challenging for the reader as the poet's desert-like world is for the poet. If the reader isn't as keen-eyed as the poet, then the poet's ideas escape, but McDonald offers a bit of poetic lore to help us see: "The secret/is not to give up on shadows, but glide/until nothing expects it." As we glide quietly over the poet's words, at just about the time we begin to feel devastated by the apparent nothingness of the terrain, something moves and a shadow transforms into one of the "dead-still/ideas like rabbits with round eyes/and rapidly beating hearts." There is life on the hardscrabble after all. McDonald's is a dangerous poetry to write, for it runs the risk of seeming as flat as the South Plains or as arid as the West Texas hardscrabble, but the piercingly direct poems are revelatory for the persevering, tough-minded reader, whom McDonald seems most interested in addressing.

Although most of McDonald's poems deal with survival in a harsh environment, a large number of them are about a place quite opposite from the West Texas desert environment—Vietnam, surprisingly—and these two places come together in uncanny ways. *Caliban in Blue* (1976), McDonald's first book of poems, focuses most intensely and bitterly on the Vietnam War. Aside from the title's obvious reference to *The Tempest*, there are allusions to Eliot, Hemingway, and Heller scattered throughout the book. In "Air Evac," McDonald gives us a poem written from the point of view of a wounded soldier waiting for evacuation, and the references to *Catch 22* and "The Love Song of J. Alfred Prufrock" suggest both the wasteland atmosphere of the war and the horror of its chaos:

> Prone
> stretched out
> I am no patient etherized upon a table, but
> My legs where are my legs

> There there
> the Nurse tight-lips me
> There there.
>
> Cold
> I am no Snowden

The poem recalls Yossarian's recurring vision of Snowden, the hopelessly wounded gunner and the central image of the chaos of war in *Catch 22*. As we listen to McDonald's nurse mumble "There there" (the same empty phrase Yossarian utters to the dying Snowden), the poem leaves us with the same sense of helplessness that Yossarian feels after he opens Snowden's flight suit and the chaos of the gunner's unstrung body becomes apparent.

McDonald's Vietnam vet is a long time in returning home from the war, something which isn't accomplished even at the end of *Caliban in Blue*. Though we observe the veteran back home physically, in poems like "The Retired Pilot to Himself," the language suggests something left unspoken, something still lurking that needs exorcising. In "Lightning," the speaker tells us that "since Vietnam,/my sympathetic nerves respond/like battered children — /I crouch low" at the sound of thunder. At the end of *Caliban in Blue*, Caliban as fighter pilot has not been brought out of the Blue, but instead remains trapped in the sky. After the last poems a numbness descends and masks the return from the jungles of Vietnam. McDonald seems to be asking: *after the loss of limbs, then what?* The Snowdens leave us blank, McDonald's last *Caliban* poems, by default, seem to proclaim. *How do we get back down out of the blue*, the Calibans are left asking.

As we move into McDonald's hardscrabble sublime poems, we begin to get an answer to that question. *One Thing Leads to Another* (1978) suggests that the return to earth isn't easy, if it is even possible. "Jack in his Menopause" implies that the most dangerous time of one's life is also the most thrilling, and that one spends the remainder of one's days missing "the shining theft" and wasting away through construction of bitterly nostalgic stories about a past that never was. Such bitterness doesn't bring Caliban out of the Blue but instead leaves him sulking over "some crummy wild goose chase" as he takes "another swig of the lousy beer." Late in this second book the poems shift direction a bit and begin focusing on family, occasioning a turn away from the angry irony toward ten-

derness and delight with children. In "With Cindy at Vallecito," we see
a father and daughter together fishing, relaxing, relishing time with family:

> Be easy,
> I tell her. I think you have one
> interested. She slowly reels,
>
> not breathing at all. Daddy? she calls.
> I tell her set the hook, and she pulls hard.
> The rod bends tighter than a bow.
>
> I'm glad for her the fish is twice
> the size of those her brothers caught
> last night.

With "Adapting," which closes *One Thing Leads to Another*,
McDonald begins to approach a solution for getting Caliban out of the
blue and back on solid ground. An intimate relationship with one's
region is the answer and the region in this case is "Here on the south
plains" where "people water their trees/year-round" because "it seldom
rains." In a 1985 interview with Christopher Woods, McDonald said
that "For years, I had not considered this world to be my home. But
finally I let down my bucket in a plains region doomed to dry up and
found all sorts of water, all sorts of poems, even if I could live to write
for forty years in this suddenly fabulous desert." McDonald's place is
arid, flat, windy, a region difficult to thrive in, but "These plants with
bones/for stalks survive the wind/and grow red fists of flowers"
("Adapting," from the collection *One Thing Leads to Another*). The juxtaposition of "red fists" and "flowers" speaks nicely to the idea of anger
and violence calmed by the beauty of carefully cultivated flowers. The
poet searching for the sublime on the South Plains or in West Texas has
got to be emotionally and mentally tough because the beauty itself is
partly made up of "red fists" among the landscape.

McDonald's speakers seem to find a balance of sorts on the hardscrabble of West Texas, but there is little sentimentalizing about the
soothing beauty of the place. In a 1986 interview with Woods,
McDonald is careful to point out that though "The land is often in my
poems — and we are still on and of it," nevertheless he's "not on a fancy

nostalgia trip." In "On Teaching David to Shoot" (*Anything, Anything* [1980]), the father admits that "Cockleburs yellowed by sun/stab my legs like old regrets." And there are vestiges of Vietnam haunting the occasion of the father's training of his son. Intent on firing a rifle, the son waves away flies and his father thinks how "Flies buzz/on his face like after battles." The poem ends with the smoldering admission that "This son I would with choice/raise in another country/where the only trajectories/are flights of bees to the moist/dilating cups of tulips/yellowed with pollen."

There are, of course, no such countries, so family and life on the hardscrabble must suffice as possible regions of poise, places to descend from the blue. *Anything, Anything* seems to maintain a tenuous grip on this poise in its early poems (especially those about family), but the sense of balance and sanity slowly gives way to poems of slippage later in the book. As the titles themselves suggest — "Signs and Warnings," "Read to the End," "Living in the Dunes" — there is a terrible sense of threat from outside and of impending apocalypse here: "We are two countries/prepared for war. A scab/half a horizon wide itches/and makes us scratch, scratch/till it comes loose and bleeds./We can't forget the past." "Living in the Dunes" concludes with a warning that seems especially dire for a poet: "There's no last word./Be quiet: try to survive." Being quiet doesn't necessarily mean not speaking at all, but the poet must speak with a voice quietly tough in the harsh presence of the past.

"Speaking in Tongues" describes this discovered quiet, but the poet's "glossolalia" proves exasperating because of its isolating effect:

> at last you know
> the simple things,
>
> but those your lips remember,
> the ones that count,
> have died or moved away
> and you are talking
> to yourself

The poet lacks an audience for his quiet utterances, but even with the threat of isolation, of merely "talking/to yourself," McDonald persists in his pursuit of "the simple things," which he discovers most abundantly through his focus on the West Texas hardscrabble.

McDonald finally seems to ease Caliban back toward earth in *Working Against Time* (1981). "Crossing West Texas" is an astonishingly keen opening poem, offering as it does a characterization of outsiders unable to perceive the sublimity of the barren landscape through which they are driving. They are in a hurry—"Driving fast through West Texas/is the best way to cross"—and so they miss the harsh beauty of a terrain "so bleak, so dry/we have to force ourselves not to stare." Ironically, they experience astonishment in the presence of "the brown boulders and mesas," but because they read the road "like a telegram,/no frills, only the shortest distance/between two points," they fail to comprehend fully what they instinctively sense about the place: that there is something significant in the nothingness of the terrain, some lesson of importance. They reassure themselves that someday, perhaps, they'll investigate fully what they sense instinctively—but there remains a note of bitter irony over the missed opportunity. The reader knows they will never find that "someday when we have more time."

"Crossing West Texas" serves notice to the readers of McDonald's poetry about the difficulty of negotiating its terrain. These are poems about "Nothing," but it is akin to Wallace Stevens' "nothing that is" which "one must have a mind of winter" in order fully to "behold." Like the West Texas hardscrabble that they take as their subject, McDonald's poems are apparently simple and barren, but readers should not drive too swiftly through, lest they miss the sublimity of the barren. It is his meditations on the sublimity of the barren that finally rescue McDonald's Caliban from the blue. In "West Texas Rain," the soothing rain becomes a metaphor for the poem itself, which "falls like light feet/treading your back's/dry knots into pools." Rain on the arid hardscrabble, like the "light feet" of poetry in a modern world, is a soothing and rare blessing.

McDonald's persona fully comes into its own in *Witching on Hardscrabble* (1985). His sixth collection of poems, this work represents his most powerful accomplishment. Caliban has given way to the ranch-hand/cowboy—a figure for the poet—working away on the hardscrabble and explaining the ways of the place. The life is extraordinarily spartan, harsh, stripped to the bare minimum: "We live like scorpions in adobe/and eat beans grown in caliche." The rugged terrain fuses the psychic and physical into a place where "The mind is a lizard/trying to survive/on hardscrabble." Instead of "Scuttling across the floors of silent seas," as does Eliot's representative self in his harsh and hostile modern world, McDonald's hardscrabble persona survives by "scuttling over/the workable sand," a terrain potentially threatening but also usable, perhaps because it is so easily shifted to help the lizard-like mind escape the "shadows of doubt/like desert birds cunning/and hungry," the very shadows that devour Prufrock.

In poems such as "Black Wings Wheeling," "Work," "Rigging the Windmill," and "Starting a Pasture," we watch as the persona describes his efforts to fashion something out of the hardscrabble, and all of these work poems suggest the poet's own efforts to write about West Texas with its "hardpan caving in." In this bleak world both reader and poet must listen to the silence in order to hear, must "listen to white sands burn." To perceive the beauty of such a place we must "let our minds sidle like hawks/gliding in a sky so blank they stare." The hardscrabble sublime reveals itself from atop a windmill for the persevering worker — reader or poet — "Sweating like a fool" but finally rewarded by the cowhand's music, which "grits in the grooves like leather," or by the pleasant drip of water in its "first pumped trickle to the tank."

For McDonald, the poet at work on the hardscrabble resembles all the peculiar varieties of workers that we encounter in *Burning the Fence* (1981), *Witching on Hardscrabble, The Flying Dutchman* (1987), and *Splitting Wood for Winter* (1988): rancher, cowhand, hunter, chimney sweep, custodian, snowplow driver. These, like the gatekeeper in "Living Near Oak Creek Dam," who is "here on a year's lease,/nothing to do but write/and take deer hunters' cash, count sheep/and keep the windmills turning," struggle to survive in ways analogous to the poet whose severe vision in his silent terrain perceives, on occasion, its jarring beauty. The poet on hardscrabble stays sane "by listening to the wind," but there are those mysterious moments when the monotony of the wind disappears and imagination flares, perhaps frighteningly: "When the wind dies,/we catch ourselves leaning/to hear jets in the distance,/geese flying by like a babble." The silence of the hardscrabble sublime is where we (both reader and poet) "catch ourselves," brooding on dangerous places such as those "distant crossings" where "someone is stalled/on the tracks and dreaming."

After easing Caliban out of the blue in his hardscrabble poems, McDonald returns to poems about Vietnam in *After the Noise of Saigon* (1988). He suggests that, in order to combat "the absolute absence of meaning," we create stories, "spinning tales to turn stark fear/to faith." It is just this effort that proofs us against the horror of war: "Somehow we survived that war/and raised our share of children." Still, part of that survival is learning to live with uncertainty, learning to accept the possibility of "the absolute absence of meaning": "We say whatever is,/we'll accept. But we must know,/we must know something." Part of that "something" in McDonald's poetry is the knowledge of place, and the understanding of the beautiful within the barren that we derive from such knowledge.

Knowing in this manner is painful but necessary for the hardscrabble poet (that is, the poet in the contemporary world). In "Dust Devils" (*Rafting the Brazos*), the South Plains wind on the speaker's face is simultaneously rapturous (the mystery of perceiving "the spirit of peace") and painful (the stinging, gritty whip of a sandstorm drawing tears). The sand itself is "like our own souls/naked," waiting for the promised day of resurrection. Drawing an analogy between sand and soul is bitter irony indeed, but the harshness of the irony is thoroughly woven into the beautiful fabric of the stark landscape. The gloriously beautiful and the painfully real are so intertwined that we cannot experience one without the other. This is the hardscrabble sublime that McDonald's poems continuously celebrate throughout his work.

Selected Bibliography

Primary Sources

After the Noise of Saigon. Amherst: University of Massachusetts Press, 1988.
All That Matters. Lubbock: Texas Tech University Press, 1992.
Anything, Anything. Seattle: L'Epervier, 1980.
A Band of Brothers: Stories from Vietnam. Lubbock: Texas Tech University Press, 1989.
Burning the Fence. Lubbock: Texas Tech Press, 1981.
Caliban in Blue. Lubbock: Texas Tech Press, 1976.
The Flying Dutchman. Columbus: Ohio State University Press, 1987.
Night Landings. New York: Harper & Row, 1989.
One Thing Leads to Another. New Braunfels, Texas: Cedar Rock, 1978.
Rafting the Brazos. Denton: University of North Texas Press, 1988.
Splitting Wood for Winter. Denton: University of North Texas Press, 1988.
Where Skies Are Not Cloudy. Denton: University of North Texas Press, 1993.
Witching on Hardscrabble. Peoria, Illinois: Spoon River Poetry, 1985.
Working Against Time. Walnut Creek, California: Calliope, 1981.

Secondary Sources

Ehrhart, W. D. "Soldier-Poets of the Vietnam War." *Virginia Quarterly Review*, 63 (Spring 1987): 246-265.

Frank, Robert. "Walter McDonald: Poet of Sight and Insight." *Poet Lore*, 80 (Winter 1986): 220-226.

Woods, Christopher. "An Interview: Walter McDonald." *Touchstone*, 10 (1985): 3-12.

———. "An Interview with Walter McDonald." *Re: Arte Liberales*, 13 (Fall 1986): 1-6.

Wright, Charlotte. "Walter McDonald." *Dictionary of Literary Biography*. Vol. 105. Detroit: Gale Research.

Kim Martin Long

The Southern Corner:
Foote, Humphrey, Goyen

Texas writers Horton Foote, William Humphrey, and William Goyen, who all come from a region caught between South and West, a place that fosters diversity and individuality, have proven their ability to rise above the label "regionalist." Foote (playwright and Academy Award-winning screenwriter), Humphrey (naturalistic story-teller), and Goyen (passionate stylist) demonstrate that good writing from Texas does not have to contain the stereotypical elements of cattle drives and cowboys but can explore a wider range of human emotion and interaction.

Horton Foote, born March 14, 1916, in Wharton, Texas, near Houston, is a prolific dramatist and independent film writer/producer whose work is characterized by a strong sense of place and a personal treatment of character and theme. He prefers to examine his characters' reactions to upheavals in their lives, from disappointments to major tragedies, rather than to focus on the narrative or the events themselves. Gary Edgerton sees "psychic turbulence seething beneath the calm and restraint" of Foote's work and claims that the subtle effects of his gentle-paced movies "disclose those moments of insight and poetry which lie hidden within the ordinary lives of his characters." Certainly, the understated actions of characters such as Carrie Watts in *The Trip to Bountiful* and the Robedeauxs in *The Orphans' Home Cycle* underlie a reserved power and great human strength.

Foote left home at the age of seventeen intent on becoming an actor, a trip that took him from Dallas to California to New York. After he wrote his first play, *Wharton Dance* (1939), his acting took a back seat to his writing. Following many off-Broadway plays, his first Broadway production was *Texas Town* (1943). Foote then moved to Washington, D.C., where he remained throughout the forties, to start his own repertory theater. During the 1950s he worked in Hollywood for Warner Brothers and also in the new and exciting medium of television, writing for programs such as *Studio One*, *Playhouse 90*, and *Philco-Goodyear Playhouse*. During this period, Foote met many people who would advance his career, most important among them Fred Coe, and published a collection of his original teleplays called *Harrison, Texas: Eight Television Plays*. He also expanded his 1952 play *The Chase* into his only novel.

Foote received a major opportunity in 1962 when he agreed to adapt Harper Lee's *To Kill a Mockingbird*. The project won Foote his first Academy Award, as well as one for actor Gregory Peck. Soon after, Foote adapted his own play *The Traveling Lady* for the movies, resulting in *Baby, The Rain Must Fall*, which starred Steve McQueen; however, disillusionment with Hollywood soon pushed Foote toward more independence and his own personal kind of drama. In the 1970s he wrote his nine-play *The Orphans' Home Cycle*, based on his own parents' and grandparents' lives: *1918*, *On Valentine's Day*, *Courtship*, *Roots in a Parched Ground*, *Convicts*, *Lily Dale*, *The Widow Claire*, *Cousins*, and *The Death of Papa*. Many of these plays have already been made into movies. While writing the cycle, however, he continued his adaptations, including short stories such as Faulkner's "Tomorrow" (1972) and "Barn Burning" (1978) and Flannery O'Connor's "The Displaced Person" (1976).

Foote's first original screenplay, *Tender Mercies* (1983), which he wrote for his actor-friend Robert Duvall, won both men an Oscar. *The Trip to Bountiful* (1985) followed, bringing yet another Academy Award for him and one for Geraldine Page. In 1985 he turned his attention to the completion of his project of putting all the plays of *The Orphans' Home Cycle* on screen, with help from his longtime wife, Lillian, and their actress-daughter, Hallie Foote. About Foote's work, Robert Duvall has said that it is "like rural Chekhov — simple but deep" (Davis 316), but Foote credits American writers as his influences: Pound and Eliot, O'Neill, Mark Twain, Willa Cather, Tennessee Williams (especially *The Glass Menagerie*), poets William Carlos Williams and Marianne Moore. Foote claims that he is not as "haunted by the past" (Davis 316-317) as was Faulkner and insists that "Eudora Welty and Katherine Anne Porter and Flannery

O'Connor are much nearer [his] sense of music." Refusing to apologize for his regionalism, Foote is interested in the "dailiness" of people's lives: "characters' faces, their conversations, the discussion of a little lamb on the child's tombstone." Of his current popularity, Foote explains, "I don't know whether I'm all that popular. I just think I've hung on; they couldn't shake me away" (Davis 317-318). Indeed, Foote's *The Young Man from Atlanta* won the 1995 Pulitzer Prize for Drama.

When William Humphrey left the Northeast Texas town of Clarksville at the age of thirteen, soon after his father's death in 1937, he probably did not know that he would not return for thirty-two years. The personal tragedy of losing his father in a freak accident — a pistol went off in his face in a car wreck — greatly affected this young boy, and the changes occurring from that night were to stay with Humphrey and manifest themselves in his novels and short story collections. Of his move to Dallas, with his widowed mother, Humphrey has said that "No wandering Jew ever carried with him a heavier freight of memories nor more of a sense of identification with a homeplace than I at thirteen." He says that he "would many times sit down and weep" as he remembered his "Zion, where all was familiar and friendly, where the seasons' difference was slight and slow, where the nights were patrolled by the watchman and kept quiet, where the clock in the courthouse town chimed — as it had yesterday, as it would tomorrow — an hourly benediction upon the town, like an angelus, like a muezzin in his minaret calling the people to prayer" (Humphrey 14).

Humphrey's naturalistic fiction is dark, with a message devoid of hope or optimism, perhaps presaging such popular contemporary writers as Cormac McCarthy. The author's cynicism, however, does not make his fiction unpleasant; his careful style, bitter humor, and ironic tone recall Flannery O'Connor. His characters, though, are often more believable and less caricatured than O'Connor's, and his narrators seem to have more compassion for them than do O'Connor's. A Humphrey story pits the narrator, the reader, and the character on one side; and the whole universe, God included, on the other.

Humphrey's first novel, *Home from the Hill* (1958), relates the tragic story of the Hunnicutt family: Captain Wade, his wife Hannah, and their son Theron. The Hunnicutts, like many people Humphrey would have known around Clarksville, are rich from cotton. The parents' roles are well-defined and traditional. Theron possesses some of Quentin Compson's ambivalence toward himself and the relationship between his past and his present. He experiences the disillusionment of learning about his father's true character, tries to avenge his wrongs by marrying a woman he believes his father has "defiled" and, in turn, betrays the woman he really loves and who carries his child. The betrayed Libby's father murders Captain Hunnicutt; after avenging his father's death, Theron disappears into the wilderness without accomplishing anything in terms of reviving the old order. The novel is derivative of several Faulkner novels, but it demonstrates Humphrey's constant theme: a vanishing past with its traditions and a modern world that offers nothing in sight to replace it.

The Ordways (1965), Humphrey's most discussed work, is really three novels in one. The book begins with the migration of Thomas Ordway and his family from Tennessee to Texas after the Civil War, follows son Sam Ordway on a mock-heroic quest in search of his kidnapped son, and ends with an Ordway family reunion in the 1930s that punctuates the family's lost traditions and serves as an ironic contrast to the more serious quest described in the beginning of the novel. The novel's scope is epic, its themes allusive, but its overall tone comic. By chronicling one southern family's rise and fall, Humphrey is able to parody the South's preoccupation with lost traditions and sentimentality. He maintains throughout his fiction that the kind of memory and nostalgia for the Old South often found in Faulkner does not, in fact, bring reconciliation or healing; Humphrey's universe is more hostile and, therefore, his work is more ironic.

Humphrey has commented on the ambiguity of his region in interviews: "I'm a funny kind of a southerner; in fact, all my life up North I've had to explain to people that I'm not a westerner.... I'm from Texas, but I'm a southerner. I'm not a westerner. I never saw a cowboy in my life.... I did live on that spot where the South stops and the West begins." In his adult life, when he returned to Clarksville, Humphrey noticed that the cotton fields were gone and that his town had "moved west," in effect (Crowder 832). In his novel Proud Flesh (1973) he presents the regional ambiguity of a small Texas town completely moved into the modern world and transformed; the setting is the cultural upheaval of the 1960s. Cotton is no longer the cash cow that it was; in fact, real cows have taken over: ranching has transformed the "southern" town of Clarksville into a "western" town full of cowboys. The Renshaw family which lives in this no longer southern, but not exactly western, town will remind readers of several Faulkner characters. The plot involves death, madness, self-mutilation, and obsession with corpses, demonstrating Humphrey's theme of the bankruptcy of the old order and the ineffectiveness of living off its memory. Humphrey has said that he was born about two hundred miles from William Faulkner and that they grew up in much the same way. "It would be very odd indeed if some of my writing didn't sound like some of his, wouldn't it?" (Crowder 828).

Possibly his best work, Humphrey's memoir *Farther Off from Heaven* (1977) reads more like a novel than an autobiography, and he admits that he struggled with its structure and point of view. He insists that his father's death was the single most important event in his life: "I lost not only my father, I lost my life, my whole *way* of life. So I didn't want to write it; it was painful" (Crowder 829). Humphrey centers everything in this story around the events of July 4, 1937, and the result is a powerful and personal account of life-changing circumstances.

In *Hostages to Fortune* (1984) Humphrey moves to the North for his setting and tells the story of Ben Curtis, whose son has committed suicide; but his last novel, *No Resting Place* (1989), is again set in the South. Describing the 1830s removal of the Cherokee Indians from their home in Georgia to Texas and Oklahoma through the consciousness of an Indian boy, adopted to become Amos Smith, the novel examines the theme of tradition — this time Native American tradition — that is completely destroyed.

With his short stories as companion pieces to the novels, the work of William Humphrey is regional writing that crosses over into the universal theme of a hostile universe. As Elizabeth Tabeaux has said, "Humphrey unrelentingly parodies the tragic hero to accentuate the fact that life is an exercise in temporary survival which generates no winners." Maybe this sentiment underlies the words of William Goyen in a letter to Katherine Anne Porter:

> William Humphrey worries me — some kind of rancour simmers inside him.... What I know for myself, and maybe Humphrey will know, is that until one writes from *himself*, from that tiny center of light in him, he goes a bit wrong and shadowy. As long as one writes ... from those darker areas of bitterness and hatred in him, what comes from him will not come from *him*, but from the outside. (Phillips 163)

As these words imply, William Goyen is a contrast to William

Humphrey in almost every way. While Humphrey employs irony in his art, Goyen has been called exceptionally "unironic" by Reginald Gibbons, literary executor for Goyen's estate (Gibbons, "Interview," 99); his fiction exudes passion and life in shameless honesty. His most celebrated novel, *The House of Breath* (1950) came from a period of rebirth for Goyen aboard a ship during World War II. He realized at that time, as he watched his own breath emerge into the cold air, that as a storyteller he could magically breathe life into characters and situations and bestow on them existence and hope.

Born in the East Texas town of Trinity on April 24, 1915, Charles William Goyen — novelist, playwright, poet, and master of short fiction — is considered the most academic and literary of these three Texas writers. He attended Rice University (then Rice Institute) and enrolled in the Ph.D. program at the University of Iowa before dropping out to teach and then to pursue acting. He and a close friend from the Navy traveled toward California after the war, making it only as far as Taos, New Mexico, where he became a close friend of Frieda Lawrence and other artists and built a house on Lawrence's land. He later participated as a fellow at the Yaddo writers' workshop, had an affair with Katherine Anne Porter, traveled extensively in Europe, taught at several universities, married actress Doris Roberts, and lived in New York and Los Angeles, where he died of cancer in August of 1983. Goyen's life, like his fiction, was filled with passion and excitement. His stories, novels, and even his recently published letters reveal a man who lived life to the fullest even when it was difficult. For Goyen, like Whitman, sex is often a metaphor for the transcendental life force that demands to be acknowledged and experienced.

Goyen's *The House of Breath* is experimental in form: the book narrates through the consciousness of Boy Ganchion the stories of family members who are dead. As he visits his now-deserted family home, the individual characters, even the river, speak to Boy, whose archetypal name suggests the innocence of trying to reconstruct one's heritage. The book's lyrical passages, in which Boy's family communicates symphonically, almost literally breathe with life and all its hardships and hope. *The House of Breath*, perhaps more than any other of Goyen's works, offers the kind of affirmation that simply living life produces; its poetic style and sense of mystery characterize his fiction.

In 1952 Goyen published his first collection of short stories, called *Ghost and Flesh*, containing his often-discussed and disturbing story

"The White Rooster." In a 1951 letter Goyen wrote to his editor about this book, he indicates his concern over being labled a regional writer:

> I beg you not to publicize *Ghost and Flesh* as a book of tales about the South. It is a book about the world and men and women in it. Please let's try to soft-pedal this 'Southern writer' business.... I am concerned with the total involvement of humanity... and not with the involvement of people in a single region of the United States; and, above all... the vision and the beholder, what the flesh does with the ghost. (Phillips 181)

His second novel, *In a Farther Country*, appeared in 1955, and his second collection of stories, *The Faces of Blood Kindred*, containing "Savata: My Fair Sister" and "Old Wildwood," was published in 1960. Other works followed, including the novels *The Fair Sister* (1963), *Come, the Restorer* (1974), and *Arcadio* (posthumously published in 1983), the story of a sexual grotesque who crosses several cultural boundaries; more short stories; and several plays.

When discussing his work in a 1982 interview with Reginald Gibbons, Goyen said that novel writing is "an act of hope, and faith. Art is redeeming, and art is an affirmation.... I wanted an art that was healthy and healing, that had life-force in it, life-*strength*" (Gibbons, "Interview," 112). His stories and novels indeed exude life, mystery, passion, and strength.

Foote, Humphrey, and Goyen — all from East Texas — are as diverse as the landscapes of Texas itself. All three write about everyday people, but the similarity ends there. Their themes, their styles, and their characters differ as much as the black fields of East Texas differ from the coastal lands of the Gulf of Mexico. They represent, collectively, the southern corner of the West, this area not quite southern but not entirely western either, and certainly not resembling the Southwest. As William Humphrey has said, it is an area confused about old traditions and new frontiers. Foote, Humphrey, and Goyen exemplify the southern flavor that East Texans bring to the rich spectrum of writing produced by Texas in the last fifty years.

Selected Foote Bibliography

Horton Foote, Vol. 1: *4 New Plays*. Lyme, New Hampshire: Smith and Kraus, 1993.
Horton Foote, Vol. 2: *Collected Plays*. Lyme, New Hampshire: Smith and Kraus, 1996.

The Orphans' Home Cycle. New York: Grove Press, 1974-1977.
Roots in a Parched Ground, Convicts, Lily Dale, and the Widow Claire. New York: Grove-Atlantic, 1988.
Three Screenplays. New York: Grove-Atlantic, 1989.
To Kill a Mockingbird, Tender Mercies, and The Trip to Bountiful: Three Screenplays. New York: Grove-Atlantic, 1988.
Young Man from Atlanta. Stageplay, Alley Theater in Houston in 1995.

Secondary Sources

Davis, Ronald. L. "Roots in a Parched Ground: An Interview with Horton Foote." *Southwest Review,* 73 (Summer 1988): 298-318. Thorough, revealing conversation.
Edgerton, Gary. "A Visit to the Imaginary Landscape of Harrison, Texas: Sketching the Film Career of Horton Foote." *Literature/Film Quarterly,* 17:1 (1989): 2-12. Excellent overview of Foote's work and life.
Moore, Barbara, and David G. Yellin, eds. *Horton Foote's Three Trips to Bountiful.* Dallas: Southern Methodist University Press, 1993. Discusses the different versions of this story. Includes many helpful comments about Foote's work in general.
Smelstor, Marjorie. "'The World's an Orphans' Home': Horton Foote's Social and Moral History." *The Southern Quarterly: A Journal of the Arts in the South,* 29:2 (Winter 1991): 7-16. Foote and the sense of place.
Wood, Gerald, ed. *Selected One-Act Plays of Horton Foote.* Dallas: Southern Methodist University Press, 1989. Includes a thorough chronology of Foote's life and works.
Wood, Gerald, and Terry Barr. "'A Certain Kind of Writer': An Interview with Horton Foote." *Literature/Film Quarterly,* 14:4 (1986): 226-237. Relaxed, honest interview, in which Foote seems comfortable with what he is and with what he is not.

Selected Humphrey Bibliography

Novels
Home from the Hill. New York: Knopf, 1958.
Hostages to Fortune. New York: Delta/Seymour Lawrence, 1984.
No Resting Place. New York: Delta/Seymour Lawrence, 1989.
The Ordways. New York: Knopf, 1965.
Proud Flesh. New York: Delta/Seymour Lawrence, 1969.

Short Story Collections
The Collected Stories. New York: Delta/Seymour Lawrence, 1985.
The Last Husband and Other Short Stories. New York: William Morrow, 1953.
A Time and a Place. New York: Knopf, 1968.

Nonfiction Prose
Farther Off from Heaven. New York: Knopf, 1976.
My Moby Dick. New York: Doubleday, 1977.
The Spawning Run. New York: Delta/Seymour Lawrence, 1970.

Secondary Sources

Chaney, L. Dwight. "William Humphrey: Regionalist, Southern or Southwestern?"

Journal of the American Studies Association of Texas (October 1988): 91-98. Discussion of the constant difficulty of placing Humphrey in a certain camp.

Cooper, Stephen. "William Humphrey (1924-)." *Contemporary Fiction Writers of the South: A Bio-Bibliographical Sourcebook.* Joseph M. Flora and Robert Bain, eds. Westport, Connecticut: Greenwood, 1993. Pp. 234-243. Good resource for Humphrey study.

Crowder, Ashley Bland. "History, Family, and William Humphrey." *Southern Review,* 24:4 (Autumn 1988): 825-839. An interview conducted with Humphrey in February 1988 in which he discusses his own fiction and its genesis, his techniques.

———. "William Humphrey: Defining Southern Literature." *Mississippi Quarterly,* 41:4 (Fall 1988): 529-540. Special issue devoted to William Faulkner. Interview with Humphrey in which he discusses Faulkner, O'Connor, and southern fiction in general, putting himself into its context.

Grammer, John N. "Where the South Draws Up to a Stop: The Fiction of William Humphrey." *Mississippi Quarterly,* 44:1(Winter 1990-1991): 5-21. An excellent introduction to and overview of Humphrey's major fiction.

Grider, Sylvia and Elizabeth Tabeaux. "Blessings in Curses: Sardonic Humor and Irony in 'A Job of the Plains.'" *Studies in Short Fiction,* 23:3(Summer 1986): 297-306. An insightful analysis of Humphrey's anthologized short story. Also provides in the notes a thorough Humphrey bibliography.

Lee, James W. *William Humphrey.* Southwest Writers Series Number 7. Austin: Steck-Vaughn, 1967. First biography of Humphrey.

Price, Reynolds. "Home Country East Texas: Review of *Farther Off From Heaven.*" *New York Times Book Review,* May 22, 1977: 7. Discusses Humphrey's excellent memoir.

Tabeaux, Elizabeth. "Irony as Art: The Short Fiction of William Humphrey." *Studies in Short Fiction,* 26:3(Summer 1989): 323-334. Sympathetic and admiring treatment of Humphrey's short stories, especially their tone and humor. Includes good bibliographical information in the notes.

Winchell, Mark Royden. "Beyond Regionalism: The Growth of William Humphrey." *Sewanee Review,* 96:2 (Spring 1988): 287-292. Discussion of the major fiction and its effort to move, like Faulkner, past a regionalist label, especially Humphrey's most recent novel, *Hostages to Fortune* (1984).

———. *William Humphrey.* Boise: Boise State University Western Writers Series, 1992. Most recent and complete biography of Humphrey.

Selected Goyen Bibliography

Poetry

Ghost and Flesh. New York: Random House, 1952.

Had I a Hundred Mouths: New and Selected Stories, 1947-1983. New York: Clarkson N. Potter, 1985. Posthumous edition prepared by Reginald Gibbons with introduction by Joyce Carol Oates.

Nine Poems by William Goyen. New York: Albondocani Press, 1976.

Story Collections

The Collected Stories of William Goyen. New York: Doubleday, 1975.

The Faces of Blood Kindred: A Novella and Ten Stories. New York: Random House, 1960.

Novels
Arcadio. New York: Clarkson N. Potter, 1983.
Come, the Restorer. Garden City, New York: Doubleday, 1974.
The Fair Sister. Garden City, New York: Doubleday, 1963. (As *Savata, My Fair Sister*, London: Peter Owen, 1963)
In a Farther Country: A Romance. New York: Random House, 1955.
The House of Breath. New York: Random House, 1950; rpt., New York: Random House/Bookworks, 1975.

Nonfiction
A Book of Jesus. Garden City, New York: Doubleday, 1973.
My Antonia: A Critical Commentary. New York: American R. D. M., 1966.
Ralph Ellison's Invisible Man: A Critical Commentary. New York: American R. D. M., 1966.

Plays
Aimee! (1974), musical play, produced in Providence, Rhode Island, Trinity Square Theater, 1973.
A Possibility of Oil (1958), TV play, produced on CBS television, 1961.
Christy, produced in New York, American Place Theater, 1964.
The Diamond Rattler, produced in Boston, Charles Playhouse, 1960.
The House of Breath, A Ballad for the Theatre in Four Scenes, produced in New York, Circle-in-the-Square Theatre, 1957.
The House of Breath, Black/White, produced in Providence, Rhode Island, Trinity Square Playhouse, 1969.
The Left-Handed Gun. Warner Brothers, 1956. Film. Goyen revised the screenplay and wrote the lyrics for the ballad.

Secondary Sources

Curtius, Ernest R. "William Goyen." In *Essays on European Literature*. Princeton: Princeton University Press, 1973. Pp. 456-464. Curtius, Goyen's German translator, discusses his fiction, which has been more popular in Europe than in America.

Dasher, Thomas E. "William Goyen." In *Dictionary of Literary Biography Yearbook: 1983*. Detroit: Gale Research, 1983. Pp. 106-112. Includes tributes to Goyen after his death by George Garrett, William Peden, Robert Phillips, and others.

Duncan, Erika. "William Goyen." In *Unless Soul Clap Its Hands: Portraits and Passages*. New York: Schocken, 1984. Pp. 17-30.

Gibbons, Reginald. "Interview with William Goyen." *TriQuarterly*, 56 (1983): 97-125. Candid and personal interview with Goyen the year before his death.

———. *William Goyen: A Study of the Short Fiction*. Boston: Twayne/G. K. Hall, 1991.

Givner, Joan. "Katherine Anne Porter: The Old Order and the New." In *The Texas Tradition*. Don Graham, James Ward Lee and Tom Pilkington, eds. Austin: University of Texas, 1983. Pp. 58-68. Discusses both Goyen and Humphrey.

Mid-American Review, 13:1 (1992). Special issue devoted to William Goyen. Contains eight critical essays, three uncollected short stories by Goyen, excerpts from his letters, an interview, three essays by Goyen, four personal memoirs on Goyen, and excerpts from the Goyen play, *The Diamond Rattler*. An important addition to Goyen scholarship.

Oates, Joyce Carol. "Introduction." In *Had I a Hundred Mouths*. By William Goyen. New York: Clarkson N. Potter, 1985. Pp. vii-xii. Perceptive analysis of Goyen's work as violent and disturbing but yet healing and powerful.

Phillips, Robert. "Secret and Symbol: Entrances to Goyen's House of Breath." *Southwest Review*, 59 (Summer 1974): 248-253.

————, ed. *William Goyen: Selected Letters from a Writer's Life*. Austin: University of Texas Press, 1995. Indispensable. These letters span the years 1937-1983 and represent a sensitive, serious writer. The ones to Katherine Anne Porter during their two-year affair are especially revealing about Goyen's art. Excellent footnotes, photographs, chronology, index.

Ernestine Sewell Linck

Larry McMurtry

Larry McMurtry's fiction since *Lonesome Dove* falls into two categories: sequels and imaginative re-creations, with aging and death constant themes. In *Texasville* (1987), sequel to *The Last Picture Show*, the central focus is on the town Thalia more so than on the characters. The town is suffering an economic depression, which is currently the force that accounts for the lunatic activities of its vapid inhabitants. Money from the West Texas oil boom eroded their mentality and intellect. Thalia's people have become a confused lot, the positive values of the Old West that had given order to their lives lost. Only the violence, expressed in libidinous behavior, is left, a relic of the negative aspects of former days. Sex, gossip, and a centennial celebration of the founding of the town, first known as Texasville, provide a depressing story line, told with outrageous (to some, offensive) humor.

Duane, now middle-aged, is married to the vivacious Karla, has fathered a son to whom sex and fast cars are all, a daughter to whom sex is all, and incorrigible twins, instigators of hilarious antics. The towns-people look to Duane as the "arbiter of good judgment" (315), but he knows he is no better than they. When the stress becomes too great (he is bankrupt) he escapes to Kickapoo Lake, the tank that stood for positive values in the earlier book. Jacy, returned from Italy, also seeks the tank. Sonny looks for escape from the town's influence by watching western films in his head. Illusion fails him, and he lapses into insanity.

Readers surmise that Thalia will become, like the original site, a few

628

dusty weathered boards lying forgotten in someone's field. The Old West is dead.

Some Can Whistle (1989) continues the story of Danny Deck in *All My Friends Are Going to Be Strangers*. Danny was last seen walking into the Rio Grande to drown his failed book and perhaps himself. Now middle-aged, he reappears, famous, wealthy, living almost in isolation in a mansion near Thalia with his housekeeper Gladys and his repulsive, sexually ambivalent friend Godwin. The only contacts he has are with his answering service until the daughter he had never seen calls him from Houston. He rescues her from a sordid life by taking her, her two children, and a retinue of her friends back to West Texas. The children's father finds T. R., the daughter, and murders her, leaving the two children for Danny to rear. This is a sentimental story of a father-daughter relationship, but, true to the best of McMurtry, layers of meaning challenge the reader. The love that develops between him and the granddaughter draws Danny back to a commitment to life. She leads him to sensitivity, understanding, and love, traits denied the Texas male, for whom "raunchiness" had traditionally been mandatory ("Unfinished Woman" 162).

The story of Aurora Greenwood, from the earlier *Terms of Endearment*, is continued in *The Evening Star* (1992). Aurora has aged and her sexual appetite makes her ridiculous. True to the legend of the dawn goddess, she rises each morning from the arms of old Tithonus/General Hector Scott, and drives across Houston in her chariot/an old Cadillac. Aurora is still uproariously funny, yet sad, as she continues manipulating men. She seduces a young psychiatrist, loses him to her young friend Patsy, then moves down the social scale to consort with Greek brothers who have a restaurant on the Houston ship channel. "I don't know how to stop living," she tells them (487). Aurora does stop living but not before she has endowed her newest grandson with a sense of her immortality by force-feeding the infant classical music, the nearest mortals can come to the music of the spheres.

Two years after the creation of Aurora, McMurtry wrote the article "Unfinished Woman," in which he predicted that Texas women, given their "formidable frontier strength," could become "quite a package" (164). Aurora is his finished woman. She is an easterner (Texas women are not quite ready for the role) with all the accoutrements of sophistication, a knowledge of music and art, fine cuisine, and she never uses four-letter words. She bears an "aura of slightly sexualized mystery which the frontier had sheared [from Texas women]" (164). The "fin-

ished woman" takes her lessons from Eve that "temptation is stimulating" (106) and a means of control. She defines herself independently of
man's concept of her.

The sequel to *Lonesome Dove*, *Streets of Laredo* (1993) takes up the
story of Captain Woodrow Call and certain figures from the earlier
novel. Call is nearly seventy now and is a hired gun for the railroad in
pursuit of a ruthless train robber and killer, the Mexican Joey Garza. Call
sends for Pea Eye, who is married to Lorena, to help him. A small
rancher/farmer, Pea Eye is moving toward civilization and is loath to
return to the old life with Call. The barbaric West, represented by Crow
Town, is an evil place where worse-than-bad men hang out. John Wesley
Hardin, the Mexican Joey Garza, and Mox Mox, a Caucasian who burns
children alive, may be found there. The introduction of Mox Mox could
be McMurtry's negation of racism. Evil knows no racial barriers, nor
does good. The sympathetic character, Maria, Joey's mother, is a foil for
Lorena. Both are earth mothers, devoted to domesticity and sensitive to
the needs of others. Lorena is on her way to becoming a "finished
woman." She will not make it; her children's children may see a New
West, made ready for them by Lorena and Pea Eye.

Call and his party pursue Joey on an arduous journey that concludes
with Call's losing an arm and a leg. The evil Joey and Mox Mox are
killed, marking the end of the villainous West. Call's position between
civilization and barbarism is ambivalent. He is somewhat like the cowboy in the song "The Streets of Laredo," who is cut down, but there will
be no death march for Call. Almost dead, he is returned to Pea Eye's
farm. He knows he can never cross the canyon between himself as he
was and the self that comes home. A saddened and pitiful old man, he
would rather be dead; however, a compensatory change awaits him.
Maria's blind girl child becomes his companion, and through her he
learns love, sensitivity, and the virtues that herald a New West.

In these sequels, McMurtry has created a female child figure to effect
the change that occurs in his male protagonists. Also, in each of these
sequels, McMurtry's texturing, as he calls it, challenges the reader to
interpret the characters as larger than life. They are symbols of his thesis: the Old West is dead and a New West lies ahead, the accomplishment ultimately of the finished woman and the sensitized male.

Anything for Billy (1988), *Buffalo Girls* (1990), and *Pretty Boy Floyd*
(1994) are imaginative re-creations. In the first, McMurtry goes to
absurd lengths to satirize the Billy-buffs who have been "riding their

pencils" along dusty trails (*In a Narrow Grave* 173). For this romp, McMurtry chose structure to give texture, using the formula of the Gothic novel. The conventions require a naive outsider (Sippy, a dime novelist from Philadelphia) and evil characters who threaten him (Billy Bone, Will Isinglass, Cecily, and Mesty-Woolah). They all face the illimitable space of the West where emptiness offers nothing for the mind to reflect on. The Gothic novel must have a castle complete with towers and turrets (Wind's Hill), inhabited by monsters (Isinglass, Mesty-Woolah and other oddities) and a beautiful woman who represents the Gothic power of the female to overcome male power. McMurtry began with the legend and employed exaggerated and playful methods that led to disorientation within the novel as well as for the reader. Altogether, Robert Davis says in *Playing Cowboys*, the Gothic structure questions "the significance of convention, history or myth to organize experience" (63). The novel has more to say about writers organizing experience than it does about Billy the Kid.

McMurtry uses a modified epistolary structure for *Buffalo Girls* to make another strong expression of the demise of the Old West. Through letters, Calamity Jane tells her story to an imaginary daughter. Between letters, narration unfolds the sad plight of the characters left over from that West. Montana is chosen for the setting, bleak and cold. The forlornness is alleviated by mountain men who doggedly search for beaver, which, like the buffalo, are gone; by the tragicomedic Indian No Ears; by Ogden, the madam Dora DuFran's buffoon of a husband, and others. Buffalo Bill enters. He takes his old friends to England to promote his Wild West show where their behavior is boisterous, raucous, and indecent. Buffalo Bill wins in the end with his truth-saying that the West is dead and "I am the Wild West" (14). Most of the characters die; they have become as obsolete as the song that gives the novel its name.

Again in *Pretty Boy Floyd*, McMurtry, collaborating with Diana Ossana, resorts to structure, chronological this time, to tell the story of the bank robber Charles Arthur Floyd. The tale unfolds as a film script would, through dialogue and incident, as it follows Charley from a hard-scrabble farm in Oklahoma during the depressed thirties to his first stickup in St. Louis and on to almost a decade of crime.

Floyd's naivete is a fit target for McMurtry's humor. Charles is a peripatetic rogue. He likes women, fine clothes, and big cars. He never has big money, robbing banks only when he needs it. Generous, he comes to be a Robin Hood figure to the have-nots. McMurtry writes in *Film Flam*,

"The true-born reader will forgo all manner of easements in order to keep chipping at the hardpan of the most resistant texts" (49). Unfortunately, *Pretty Boy Floyd* affords no such resistance. It is a plains country novel—flat.

In 1987 McMurtry gathered a collection of essays about Hollywood titled *Film Flam*, which he calls "quick tricks and one-night stands" (Foreword). He describes the life of a scriptwriter, then moves to criticism of current film production, saying that viewers are given entertainment and illusion (149) but no "redemptive dimension" (42). *Film Flam* is witty. To serious readers, it gives insight into McMurtry's theory of creativity and responsible production, whether it be novel or film.

Selected Bibliography

Primary Sources

Anything for Billy. New York: Simon & Schuster, 1988.
Buffalo Girls. New York: Simon & Schuster, 1990.
The Evening Star. New York: Simon & Schuster, 1992.
Film Flam. New York: Simon & Schuster, 1987.
"How the West Was Won or Lost." *The New Republic*, 203:6 (October 15, 1990): 203, 232-238.
In a Narrow Grave: Essays on Texas. Austin: Encino Press, 1987.
Pretty Boy Floyd: A Novel. New York Simon & Schuster, 1994.
Some Can Whistle. New York: Simon & Schuster, 1989.
Streets of Laredo. New York: Simon & Schuster, 1993.
Texasville. New York: Simon & Schuster, 1987.
"Unfinished Women." *Texas Monthly*, 5 (May 1977): 106, 162-166.

Secondary Sources

Cox, Diana. "Anything for Billy." *Journal of American Culture*, 14:2 (Summer 1991): 75-81.
Davis, Robert Murray. *Playing Cowboys: Low Culture and High Art in the Western*. Norman: University of Oklahoma Press, 1992.
Erdrich, Louise. "Why Is That Man Tired?" In *Taking Stock: A Larry McMurtry Casebook*. Clay Reynolds, ed. Dallas: Southern Methodist University Press, 1989. Pp. 338-343.
Graham, Don. "A Legend, a Song, a Screenplay and Now a Book." *The Dallas Morning News*, September 11, 1994, 8-9 J.
Greene, A. C. "Return Flight: Streets of Laredo Is More Than Just a 'Lonesome Dove' Sequel." *The Dallas Morning News*, July 25, 1993, 8-9 J.
Jones, Malcolm. "The Ghost Writer on the Range." *Newsweek*, August 2, 1993, 52-53.
King, Michael. "Blue-Collar Crime." *The Texas Observer*, 30 (September 1994): 17-18.
Orth, Maureen. "Larry McMurtry." *Vogue*, 174:3 (March 1984): 456, 516.
Reynolds, Clay. "Introduction." *Taking Stock: A Larry McMurtry Casebook*. Dallas: Southern Methodist University Press, 1989. Pp. 1-34.

Ramon Saldívar

Américo Paredes

Renowned as an ethnographer, literary critic, and social historian for well over three decades, Américo Paredes offers considerable insight into Mexican American culture. Honored in 1985 by the Western Literature Association, in 1989 by the National Endowment for the Humanities as one of the initial recipients of the Charles Frankel Prize, in 1990 by the Republic of Mexico as one of the first Mexican American inductees to the *Orden del Aquila Azteca*, in 1991 by the Texas State Historical Association for his exemplary contributions to the understanding of the southwestern frontier experience, in 1993 by the Smithsonian Institution for contributions to American folklore, and in 1995 by the Texas Institute of Letters with the Lon Tinkle Award for lifetime achievement, Paredes has achieved his fame. It rests largely on his scholarly work, *"With His Pistol in His Hand": A Border Ballad and Its Hero* (1958).[1] This groundbreaking study of the ballads, legends, and everyday folklife of the Texas-Mexican border region served as the basis of a scholarly project that Paredes elaborated on during his career as professor of English and anthropology at the University of Texas at Austin from the 1960s through the 1980s.

Paredes' most recent publications—a novel, *George Washington Gomez* (1990); a book of poetry, *Between Two Worlds* (1991); and a collection of short stories, *The Hammon and the Beans and Other Stories* (1994)—add a new dimension to the imposing array of his work in the historical, ethnographic, and theoretical realms.[2] Only now coming to public attention, these imaginative works were composed for the most part during the immediate pre- and post-World War II years. Functioning as discursive constructions of a collective Mexican American identity, Paredes' poetry and fiction predate his scholarly work and serve as early attempts to show how a subaltern population might stave off dependency and represent itself artistically in the larger culture.

Written between 1935 and 1940, *George Washington Gomez* was completed during the period that Paredes worked as a newspaper reporter in Brownsville, Texas. It is set against the history of cultural-political conflict chronicled in the various manifestations of the U. S.-Mexican border ballad and takes as its originating moment the 1915 uprising in South Texas by Mexican Americans attempting to create a Spanish-speaking republic of the Southwest.[3] Answering deep-seated feelings of anger and frustration over Anglo oppression and injustice, the secessionist movement of 1915 was an early expression of the feelings evoked later by the Chicano movement of the 1960s and an early enunciation of coalition politics among internal Third World groups in the United States.

The titular character's story is concerned with the unraveling of his apparently stable identity and the imagining of a new identity that foreshadows the borderland that Chicano literature is traversing at century's end. The unsettled nature of the hero's identity at the close of the novel suggests the present lack of unified solutions regarding the marginalized condition in which Mexican Americans live. Though George Washington Gomez never achieves a secure sense of his own unique identity, the novel does powerfully prefigure the dominant theme of Chicano literature at the end of the twentieth century.

Paredes' modernist project to explore the varied influences on the Mexican American subjectivity is apparent in his poetry of the 1930s and early 1940s, no more so than in *Between Two Worlds*. Like Matthew Arnold in "Stanzas from the Grande Chartreuse," which retraces the poetic lines of William Wordsworth's Alpine journey of "The Prelude," Paredes returns in these lyrics to his own undiscovered country, the borderlands of South Texas. In his poetic reprise he repeats the symbolic phrases of his community's master narrative — the *corrido* — but without the historical amnesia of the song's original score and in full knowledge of its possible self-negations.

Arnold, "between two worlds," resigns himself at the beginning of modernism to his formal ethical codes, judging himself totally unfit for the life of "action and pleasure" offered by the burgeoning modern world. Paredes, in contrast, at the end of modernism, embraces this undiscovered country, figured in the liminal, differential status of living "between two worlds" in a region on the margins that offers the very possibility of "action and pleasure" for his community. In a poem from 1950, entitled "Esquinita de mi pueblo" ("My Community's Corner"), Paredes reflects on this process of living an imaginative cartography: "At the corner of absolute elsewhere/And in absolute future I stood/ waiting for a green light/To leave the neighborhood./ But the light was red.... /That is the destiny of people in between/To stand on the corner/ Waiting for the green" (114). Unable to sanction fully (or live uncritically) the ideological structures that other inhabitants of his "neighborhood" perhaps occupy, Paredes sings instead of twentieth-century constructions of narratives about narratives and the revisionings of history that such metanarratives might allow.

What Paredes maps here in "Esquinita de mi pueblo" as "the corner of absolute elsewhere/And absolute future" is precisely the Mexican American's contingency to history, "the destiny of people in between" and the utopian glimpses of achieved community, "Waiting for the green," that this contingency allows. Indeed, in exploring the situation of Mexican Americans in the second half of the twentieth century, Paredes offers something very like what Frederic Jameson calls a "cognitive mapping" of the heterotopian social spaces that exist within the real conditions of existence. His symbolic cartography is achieved through aesthetic patterns that emerge out of all too real social realities. The strength of Paredes' poetry is its ability to show us the utopian possibilities of the communitarian ideal as well as the tempering limitations imposed by the hard realities of the society as currently constituted. As such, it points toward the present concerns of the developing Chicana/o movement.

In "Theses on the Philosophy of History," Walter Benjamin argues that "To articulate the past historically does not mean to recognize it 'the way it really was....' It means to seize hold of a memory as it flashes up at a moment of danger...." Only that historian will have the gift of fanning the spark of hope in the past who is firmly convinced that *even the dead* will not be safe from the enemy if he wins.[4] Paredes' titular story in *The Hammon and the Beans and Other Stories*, as well as a number of the following stories, fan the spark of hope in the past through the remembrance of the Plan of San Diego, its revolutionary creed, and the racial hatred and tension that have persisted to the present in South

Texas in the aftermath of the bitter fighting, the "border troubles" of 1915-1917. The stories, however, are not immediately concerned with that revolutionary struggle. Instead, they focus on the effects of struggle and the end of the heroic past of Mexican American armed resistance to Anglo American hegemony. They look forward to the beginning of a new stage of Mexican American resistance, in the realm of culture and ideology. Paredes' narratives underscore brilliantly the difficult dialectic between a Mexican past and an American future for Texas Mexicans living on the threshold of modernity and modernization.

Other stories in the collection take us from the geographical, if not the social, space of early twentieth-century South Texas and into the World War II Pacific theater of operations and the opening days of the Korean War. But the issues remain, as in the South Texas stories, the intersections of race, power, and conquest. In these tales Paredes moves from the socio-spatial practices of the family and the local South Texas region to hemispheric and global settings. He attempts, on a broader front, to account for the extraordinarily fierce Manichean nature of the Pacific war by linking domestic American racism to the conduct of the nation's armed forces during the war and the postwar occupation of Japan.

The people and events of Paredes' creative works are marked by difference, a difference the author readily acknowledges. Repeatedly, this acknowledgment occurs aesthetically, in the shapes and nuances of a variety of oral forms, gestures, expressions, and styles, that is, in the formulaic patterns that disguise and sometimes reveal the possibilities and limits of community. Paredes' writings urge us to interrogate what constitutes American social space. It is here, surely, that Paredes' virtuosity as a master storyteller and clear-sighted critic of contemporary vernacular ethnic culture and its historiography is most powerfully present. Paredes' work displays the power of culture to configure the imaginative borders of the modern American nation and to formulate the dominant aesthetic and social themes within the nation. *George Washington Gomez, Between Two Worlds*, and *The Hammon and the Beans and Other Stories* represent the latest evidence of Américo Paredes' centrality as an artist and scholar of the American ethnic vernacular imagination.

Notes

1. *"With His Pistol in His Hand": A Border Ballad and Its Hero* (Austin: University of Texas Press, 1958). A volume of selected essays, *Folklore and Culture on the Texas Mexican*

Border, edited by Richard Bauman (Austin: Center for Mexican American Studies at the University of Texas, 1993), gathers other parts of his most important work from that period.

2. The novel, poetry, and short stories are published by Arte Público Press of Houston, Texas. This latest body of work includes a new study of Tejano jokes, jests, and oral narratives, *Uncle Remus con Chile* (Houston: Arte Público Press, 1993).

3. For a full discussion of the history of this conflict, see David Montejano, *Anglos and Mexicans in the Making of Texas, 1836-1986* (Albuquerque: University of New Mexico Press, 1987).

4. Walter Benjamin, "Theses on the Philosophy of History," *Illuminations*, Hannah Arendt, ed. (New York: Schocken, 1969), p. 255.

Selected Bibliography

Primary Sources

Between Two Worlds. Houston: Arte Público Press, 1991.

Folklore and Culture on the Texas Mexican Border. Richard Bauman, ed. Austin: Center for Mexican American Studies of the University of Texas, 1993.

George Washington Gomez. Houston: Arte Público Press, 1990.

The Hammon and the Beans and Other Stories. Houston: Arte Público Press, 1994.

A Texas-Mexican Cancionero: Folksongs of the Lower Border. Urbana: University of Illinois Press, 1976.

Uncle Remus con Chile. Houston: Arte Público Press, 1993.

"With His Pistol in His Hand": A Border Ballad and Its Hero. Austin: University of Texas Press, 1958.

Secondary Sources

Benjamin, Walter. "Theses on the Philosophy of History." *Illuminations*. Hannah Arendt, ed. New York: Schocken, 1969.

Limon, José E. *Dancing with the Devil: Society and Cultural Politics in Mexican American South Texas*. Madison: University of Wisconsin Press, 1994.

McKenna, Teresa. "On Chicano Poetry and the Political Age: *Corridos* as Social Drama." In *Criticism in the Borderlands: Studies in Chicano Literature, Culture and Ideology*. Hector Calderon and Jose David Saldívar, eds. Durham: Duke University Press, 1991. Pp. 181-203.

Saldívar, Jose David. "Chicano Border Narratives as Cultural Critique." In *Criticism in the Borderlands: Studies in Chicano Literature, Culture and Ideology*. Hector Calderon and Jose David Saldívar, eds. Durham: Duke University Press, 1991. Pp. 167-180.

Saldívar, Ramon. *Chicano Narrative: The Dialectics of Difference*. Madison: University of Wisconsin Press, 1990.

———. "Introduction." In *The Hammon and the Beans and Other Stories*, by Américo Paredes. Houston: Arte Público Press, 1994. Pp. vii-xlvi.

V

The Midwest

Diane Dufva Quantic

The Midwest and the Great Plains

Although the traditional "Midwest" is used by several essayists in this section, in the last fifteen years the term "Great Plains" has gained acceptance as more accurate for the continent's central region. The latter term better reflects the region's geography and ecology and connotes a closer identification with the literary and geographic West.[1] Maps of the Great Plains show the region spreading from the Gulf of Mexico into southern Canada. On the west, it butts against the Rocky Mountains; on the east it follows the Missouri River.

Great Plains literature focuses on the land's transformation from wilderness space to usable place. The individual must come to terms with a seemingly undifferentiated landscape that can empower one with a sense of limitless opportunity and leave another with a profound feeling of psychological erasure. As Robert Thacker points out in his study, *The Great Prairie Fact and Literary Imagination*, in a place with no familiar geographical features, men and women had to learn to *see* the Great Plains. Similarly, literary scholars are now challenged to see the literature of the Great Plains accurately. Critics such as Henry Nash Smith, Leo Marx and Roderick Nash have contributed a theoretical context, and now critics find their investigations both broadened and made sharper by studies of the region's physical, social and cultural character. Contact with the rising field of ecocriticism and with cultural geographers, sociologists, ecologists, biologists and historians is enriching Great Plains literary criticism.

Great Plains writers, like other western authors, resist the urge to "intellectually enclose wilderness" that Carl Bredahl identifies with the traditional eastern canon. Whereas many canonical, eastern writers create constrictive enclosures that protect civilization from encroaching wilderness, those writing of the Great Plains and the West confront an extravagant surface that cannot be enclosed or controlled, but ultimately must be met on its own terms (Bredahl 1-6). On the Great Plains, that surface can be changed, if not controlled, but the land demands physical effort and personal sacrifice. Those who would survive must transform wilderness into fields that produce commodities, and they must establish communities to counterbalance the isolation dictated by the Homestead Act and the economic necessity of large farms.

A persistent theme in Great Plains literature is the discrepancy between the expectations of European and eastern settlers, often expressed as myths, and the harsh realities dictated by the environment. Even in contemporary literature, the contrast exists: blizzards, droughts and bumper crops prove the persistence of the garden-desert dichotomy; conflicts between farmers or ranchers and exploitive investors still call into question the possibilities of a democratic utopia. In the popular vernacular, the Great Plains have come to represent the quintessential pioneer experience. Movies and documentaries focus on the historic confrontations with the elements and Native cultures, and the media often focus on contemporary debates over the economic viability of the region.[2] A number of writers overlooked in the original *Literary History of the American West* continue to influence popular perceptions of the region. The movie version of Frank Baum's *The Wonderful Wizard of Oz* has passed beyond cliché into myth, providing images that connote their context without direct reference to the film. These images pervade dialogue about the plains: the black and white Kansas of the film has become an ironic metaphor for a bleak and violent but longed-for home.[3] Roger Welsch, in his "Postcard from Nebraska" spots on CBS' "Sunday Morning" and in his volumes of folklore, has contributed to the broad popularity of the region as the stuff of story and legend, and Jim Hoy and Tom Isern have contributed *Plains Folks*, two more volumes of folklore. Garrison Keillor, through his *Prairie Home Companion* broadcasts and books, has resurrected the oral tradition of the frontier, mixing tall tales, humor and sentiment that has made Lake Woebegon, Minnesota, synonymous with small town life on the northern prairie. The wide array of family-farm and small-town memoirs, historical and contemporary photo essays and art books, cookbooks, local histories, accounts of cowboy life and farm life — many published by state university presses — attests to continuing interest in the region's history and popular culture.

The study of Great Plains literature has been enhanced by the reprinting of numerous important works in the last fifteen years. Dorothy Thomas' *The Home Place* (1934), John Ise's *Sod and Stubble* (1936) and Frederick Manfred's *The Golden Bowl* (1944) have been available for thirty years. These novels, along with Hope Williams Sykes' *Second Hoeing*, Rose Wilder Lane's *Free Land*, Mildred Walker's novels, especially *Winter Wheat*, and Lois Phillips Hudson's *The Bones of Plenty*, constitute a collection of works that focus on the everyday routine and repetitive crises that farmers faced on the Great Plains.

Dorothy Thomas, Frederick Manfred, Lois Phillips Hudson, Mildred Walker and Rose Wilder Lane focus on the changes presented to second- and third-generation farmers on the Great Plains during the years of the Depression and Dust Bowl. Manfred's epic novel is by far the best portrait of the Great Plains Dust Bowl. The other novels are uniformly depressing stories, focusing on repeated crop failures, economic uncertainties, the tenuous life of tenant farmers, and the inevitable strains on family relations. The title of Rose Lane's novel, *Free Land*, should be in quotes: in all of these novels, work, isolation and poverty make the irony in the homestead allusion apparent. Except for Manfred's *Golden Bowl*, these novels lack the epic scope of Great Plains writers such as Mari Sandoz, Willa Cather and O.E. Rölvaag. Rather, they chronicle the minor tragedies in the mundane lives of ordinary farm families. Perhaps it is not coincidental that a number of these writers are women recounting the lives of their families, especially their mothers, and their neighbors. They are accounts of life during an especially difficult historical period. As such, they are valuable as historical or sociological documents: as literature, they present a powerful collective portrait of a particular time and place.

Although these novels are sometimes considered in the context of a broad discussion of Great Plains literature, individually they have received very little scholarly attention. Lois Phillips Hudson has been the subject of an article, and Hudson's own opinions are reported in the text of a panel on the subject. Ruth Suckow, who is afforded a paragraph in the original *Literary History of the American West*, continues to be the subject of modest scholarly activity.

Three writers have received steadily increasing attention in the last fifteen years. A number of Bess Streeter Aldrich's novels are in print, and the appearance of Carol Peterson's biography and Aldrich's *Collected Short Works* indicates the continued interest in this Nebraska writer. William Allen White is the subject of volumes in the Twayne United States Authors and the Boise State University Western Writers Series. His *Autobiography* has appeared in a second, much-reduced edition.

Rose Wilder Lane has been the object of some recent scholarship. Laura Ingalls Wilder is enjoying increased scholarly interest, thanks in part to questions raised concerning her daughter Rose's contributions to the form and content of the Little House series. The steady stream of Wilder-related books — juvenile biographies, cookbooks, her letters and children's letters written to her, for example — indicates Wilder's continued popularity with readers. More importantly, literary scholars and historians are rereading the works themselves and finding them a rich resource for study of women, girls and families in the pioneering period. Much Wilder scholarship is published in *The Lion and the Unicorn* and other children's literature journals. The variety of that scholarship is indicative of the rich resource scholars are finding in a series of deceptively simple books written for children.

The increasing interest in multicultural literature has not escaped Great Plains readers and scholars. More and more books appear that focus on the experiences of minority populations. Oscar Micheaux's two novels of the blacks' struggle to establish and maintain farms on the plains are back in print. *The Conquest* recounts the efforts of Oscar Devereaux to establish himself as a farmer in South Dakota. *The Homesteader* focuses on an established South Dakota farmer, this time named Jean Baptiste, who falls in love with a white woman but marries a Chicago minister's daughter with disastrous results. Although most scholars have focused on Micheaux's film career, his fiction has been the subject of frequent papers at Western Literature Association annual meetings and other conferences. Gordon Parks' *The Learning Tree* and Langston Hughes' *Not Without Laughter* recount the lives of the black underclass in small Kansas towns and, in this sense, complement Micheaux's farm novels.

These books add an important dimension to the large body of Great Plains minority/immigrant literature that has appeared in the last fifty years. In addition to works by Willa Cather and O.E. Rölvaag, Johan

Bojer's *The Emigrants* recounts the psychic costs of emigration for Morton Kvidal and other Norwegian settlers. Vilhelm Moberg, a major figure in his native Sweden, in his multivolume saga, *The Emigrants* — which includes *Unto a Good Land* (1954), *The Settlers* (1961), and *Last Letter Home* (1961) — presents the stories of Swedish settlers in Minnesota. Hope Williams Sykes' novel, *Second Hoeing*, recounts Hannah Schreismuller's struggle to overcome her immigrant father's opposition to her desire for an education and a life away from the beet fields. Mela Meisner Lindsay added to these Scandinavian stories the fictionalized account of her parents' immigration to western Kansas at the turn of the century in *Shukar Balan — The White Lamb* (1975). Sophie Trupin has added another element to this pastiche of immigrant stories with her memoir, *Dakota Diaspora: Memoirs of a Jewish Homesteader*, that relates her parents' flight from Russia to the northern Great Plains.

Together, these novels broaden our conception of the Great Plains experience. Not everyone headed west to realize America's Manifest Destiny or in search of the mythic garden, hoping for economic success. Some came to escape prejudice and persecution, to establish themselves in a place where they hoped they would be free to realize not only economic stability but social equality and religious freedom as well. The task was not easy. Time and again these novels recount stories similar to Beret's in Rölvaag's trilogy: many women and men suffered from depression in a strange landscape within a new culture that did not value their old-country customs, or their hope for racial and economic equality faded into passivity and a determination among the younger generation to abandon the prairie town with its social and economic limitations.

If the contributions of Canadian novelists are not acknowledged, an account of Great Plains literature would be incomplete (see Thacker, *The Great Prairie Fact*, and Quantic, *The Nature of the Place*). Frederick Philip Grove's Abe Spaulding in *Fruits of the Earth*, Martha Ostenso's Caleb Gare and Rudy Wiebe's Pastor Block are as determined as Rölvaag's Per Hansa, Cather's Alexandra and Antonia, and Sandoz's Old Jules to establish themselves on the land, but their monomania is much more selfish and destructive than the passion of Per Hansa, Alexandra and Old Jules for the land.[4] Ross' Mrs. Bentley, and Laurence's women such as Morag Gunn in *The Diviners*, Hagar Shipley in *The Stone Angel*, and Vanessa McLeod in *A Bird in the House* are as introspective as Beret. Mrs. Bentley's state of mind resembles Beret's, but the determination of Laurence's characters to live their lives by their own standards awards them a kind of psychic independence that Mrs. Bentley, Beret and even Alexandra do not realize.

Many of these Canadian novels focus on a protagonist who deliberately establishes a home or community on the margin of the wilderness in order to control his own destiny and the destiny of the family or community, often with tragic results. In this sense, these novelists present an alternative to the American concentration on the myths of progress and expansion. They do not intend to transform the land and erase the frontier boundary between wilderness and civilization; rather, they intend to erect a "garrison" for their own closed society between the howling wilderness and the civilization they left behind. The most contemporary of these novelists, Robert Kroetsch, like Wright Morris, deconstructs time and space on the Great Plains, transforming the mythic assumptions in an attempt to re-vision the continent's core.[5]

The Great Plains story of the constant struggle to survive natural, economic and personal disasters in a region of overwhelming space heightens the reader's awareness of human vulnerability. The following essays illustrate how dynamic and wide-ranging discussion about the Great Plains has become.

Notes

1. The term "Great Plains" has gained scholarly acceptance as the designation for the region. Great Plains study centers like those at Emporia (Kansas) State University and the University of Nebraska at Lincoln and the Center for Western Studies at Augustana College in Sioux Falls, South Dakota, provide sites for interdisciplinary dialogue and research.

2. Attention to, and even a certain romance about, Plains ecology is evident in preserves such as the Konza Prairie and the Tall Grass National Park in Kansas, the Nature Conservancy prairie preserves in northeastern Oklahoma and Kansas, and study centers such as the proposed Mari Sandoz Center in Chadron, Nebraska, which will be devoted to the study of the High Plains.

3. Harry F. Thompson of the Center for Western Studies at Augustana College points out that the Oz books are a truly American tale, carved from distinctly regional material, specifically South Dakota, where Baum lived from 1888 to 1891, and are representative of the entire region. Thompson also points out that the Oz series has received considerable critical attention in recent years, including populist, mythic and folklore readings.

4. Canadian prairie fiction includes Martha Ostenso's *Wild Geese* (1920); Frederick Philip Grove's *Fruits of the Earth* (1933) and *Settlers of the Marsh* (1925); W. O. Mitchell's *Who Has Seen the Wind* (1947); Sinclair Ross' *As For Me and My House* (1941) and *The Lamp at Noon and Other Stories* (1968); Margaret Laurence's Manawaka novels, *The*

Stone Angel (1964), *A Jest of God* (1966), *The Fire Dwellers* (1969), *A Bird in the House* (1970); Robert Kroetsch's novels such as *Badlands* (1975); and Rudy Wiebe's novels, especially *Peace Shall Destroy Many* (1962).

5. The writers of Canadian prairie fiction are the subject of much wide-ranging scholarship that focuses on such topics as biography, feminism, language, immigration, landscape, regionalism and the authors' treatments of Indians. Their works comprise a body of literature that is more clearly identified in Canadian scholarship than "Great Plains Literature" is in the U.S. They are often compared to each other and to their American counterparts (see Barnard).

Selected Bibliography

Fiction (reprints and works not included in A *Literary History of the American West*)

Aldrich, Bess Streeter. *Collected Short Works, 1907-1919*. Carol Miles Peterson, ed. Lincoln: University of Nebraska Press, 1995.

———. *The Cutters*. New York: Appleton, 1925; rpt., Lincoln: University of Nebraska Press, 1989.

———. *A Lantern in Her Hand*. New York: Appleton, 1928; rpt., Lincoln: University of Nebraska Press, 1994.

———. *The Lieutenant's Lady*. New York: Appleton, 1942; rpt., Lincoln: University of Nebraska Press, 1985.

———. *Spring Came on Forever*. New York: Appleton, 1935; rpt., Lincoln: University of Nebraska Press, 1985.

———. *A White Bird Flying*. New York: Appleton, 1931; rpt., Lincoln: University of Nebraska Press, 1988.

Bojer, Johan. *The Emigrants*. A. G. Jayne, trans. New York: Century Company, 1925; rpt., Lincoln: University of Nebraska Press, 1978.

Hudson, Lois Phillips. *Reapers of the Dust*. New York: Little, Brown and Company, 1965; rpt., St. Paul: Minnesota Historical Society Press, 1984.

Hughes, Langston. *Not Without Laughter*. New York: A. A. Knopf, 1930; rpt., New York: Macmillan, 1969.

Ise, John. *Sod and Stubble*. New York: Wilson-Erickson, 1936; unabridged and annotated edition, with additional material by Von Rothenberg. Lawrence: University Press of Kansas, 1996.

Keillor, Garrison. *Lake Woebegon Days*. New York: Viking, 1990.

———. *Leaving Home: A Collection of Lake Woebegon Stories*. New York: Viking, 1989.

Lane, Rose Wilder. *Free Land*. New York: Longmans, Green and Company, 1938; rpt., Lincoln: University of Nebraska Press, 1984.

Lindsay, Mela Meisner. *Shukar Balan — The White Lamb: The Story of Evaliz*. Lincoln, Nebraska: American Historical Society of Germans from Russia, 1976.

Micheaux, Oscar. *The Conquest*. Lincoln: Woodruff Press, 1913; rpt., Lincoln: University of Nebraska Press, 1994.

———. *The Homesteader*. Sioux City: Western Book Supply Company, 1917; rpt., Lincoln: University of Nebraska Press, 1994.

Moberg, Vilhelm. *Last Letter Home: The Emigrants, Part IV*. Gustaf Lannestock, trans. New York: Simon & Schuster, 1961; rpt., St. Paul: Minnesota Historical Press, 1995.

———. *The Settlers: The Emigrants, Part III*. Gustaf Lannestock, trans. New York: Simon & Schuster, 1961; rpt., St. Paul: Minnesota Historical Press, 1995.

———. *Unto a Good Land: The Emigrants, Part II*. Gustaf Lannestock, trans. New York: Simon & Schuster, 1954; St. Paul: Minnesota Historical Press, 1995.

Parks, Gordon. *The Learning Tree*. New York: Harper & Row, 1963.

Suckow, Ruth. *A Ruth Suckow Omnibus*. Iowa City: University of Iowa Press, 1988.

Sykes, Hope Williams. *Second Hoeing*. New York: Putnam, 1935; rpt., Lincoln: University of Nebraska Press, 1982.

Thomas, Dorothy. *The Home Place*. New York: A.A. Knopf, 1934; rpt., Lincoln: University of Nebraska Press, 1982.

Walker, Mildred. *The Curlew's Cry*. New York: Harcourt Brace, 1955; rpt., Lincoln: University of Nebraska Press, 1994.

———. *If a Lion Could Talk*. New York: Harcourt Brace Jovanovich, 1970; rpt., Lincoln: University of Nebraska Press, 1995.

———. *Light from Arcturus*. New York: Harcourt Brace, 1935; rpt., Lincoln: University of Nebraska Press, 1995.

———. *Winter Wheat*. New York: Harcourt Brace, 1944; rpt., Lincoln: University of Nebraska Press, 1992.

White, William Allen. *The Autobiography of William Allen White*. New York: Macmillan, 1946; 2nd ed., revised and abridged, Sally Foreman Griffith, ed. Lawrence: University Press of Kansas, 1990.

Selected Nonfiction Since 1980

Barnard, Ann. "A North American Connection: Women in Prairie Novels." *Great Plains Quarterly*, 14:1 (1994): 21-28.

Bredahl, A. Carl, Jr. *New Ground: Western American Narrative and the Literary Canon*. Chapel Hill: University of North Carolina Press, 1989.

Bresnahan, Roger. "How It Played in Emporia: The World According to William Allen White." *Midwestern Miscellany*, 18 (1990): 17-25.

Calof, Rachel. *Rachel Calof's Story*. Jacob Calof, trans. Bloomington: Indiana University Press, 1995.

Casey, Roger N. "Ruth Suckow: A Checklist." *Bulletin of Bibliography*, 46:4 (1989): 224-229.

Erisman, Fred. "*Farmer Boy*: The Forgotten Little House Book." *Western American Literature*, 28:2 (1993): 123-130.

Fellman, Anita Clair. "Laura Ingalls Wilder and Rose Wilder Lane: The Politics of a Mother-Daughter Relationship." *Signs*, 15:3 (1990): 535-561.

Holtz, William. "Closing the Circle: The American Optimism of Laura Ingalls Wilder." *Great Plains Quarterly*, 4:2 (1984): 79-90.

———. *The Ghost in the Little House: The Life of Rose Wilder Lane*. Columbia: University of Missouri Press, 1993.

———. "Rose Wilder Lane's *Free Land*: The Political Background." *South Dakota Review*, 30:1 (1992): 436-460.

Hoy, Jim and Tom Isern. *Plains Folks II: The Romance of the Landscape*. Norman: University of Oklahoma Press, 1990.

———. *Plains Folks: A Commonplace of the Great Plains*. Norman: University of Oklahoma Press, 1987.

Jernigan, Jay. *William Allen White*. Boston: Twayne, 1983.

Maher, Sue. "Laura Ingalls Wilder and Caddie Martin: Daughters of a Border Space." *The Lion and the Unicorn*, 18:2 (December 1994): 130-142.

Martin, Abigail Ann. *Bess Streeter Aldrich*. Boise: Boise State University Western Writers Series, 1992.

Miller, John. *Laura Ingalls Wilder's Little Town: Where History and Literature Meet*. Lawrence: University Press of Kansas, 1994.

Mowder, Louise. "Domestication of Desire: Gender, Language and Landscape in the Little House Books." *Children's Literature Association Quarterly*, 17:1 (1992): 15-19.

Peterson, Carol. *Bess Streeter Aldrich: All the Dreams Are Real*. Lincoln: University of Nebraska Press, 1995.

Putnam, Ann. "Betrayal and Redemption in the Fiction of Lois Phillips Hudson." *South Dakota Review*, 26:3 (1988): 10-23.

Quantic, Diane Dufva. *The Nature of the Place: A Study of Great Plains Fiction*. Lincoln: University of Nebraska Press, 1995.

———. "Frederick Manfred's *Golden Bowl*: Myth and Reality in the Dust Bowl." *Western American Literature*, 25 (February 1991): 297-309.

———. *William Allen White*. Boise: Boise State University Western Writers Series, 1993.

Romines, Ann. *Constructing the Little House: Gender, Culture and Laura Ingalls Wilder*. Amherst: University of Massachusetts Press, 1997

———. "*The Long Winter*: An Introduction to Western Womanhood." *Great Plains Quarterly*, 10:1 (1990): 36-47.

———. "'Oh My; I am the Teacher': Laura Ingalls Wilder and the Prairie Schoolteacher." *West Virginia Quarterly*, 36 (1990): 53-60.

———. "Writing the Little House: The Architecture of a Series." *Great Plains Quarterly*, 14:2 (Spring 1994): 107-115.

School, Peter. *Garrison Keillor*. New York: Twayne, 1993.

Stafford, William, Lois Phillips Hudson, Frederick Manfred, and Gilbert Fite. "Panel: The Realities of Regionalism." *South Dakota Review*, 26:4 (1988): 77-91.

Thacker, Robert. *The Great Prairie Fact and Literary Imagination*. Albuquerque: University of New Mexico Press, 1989.

Trupin, Sophie. *Dakota Diaspora: Memoirs of a Jewish Homesteader*. Lincoln: University of Nebraska Press, 1984.

Welsch, Roger. *It's Not the End of the Earth, But You Can See It From Here: Tales of the Great Plains*. New York: Random House, 1990.

Young, Joseph. *A Black Novelist as White Racist: The Myth of Black Inferiority in the Novels of Oscar Micheaux*. Westport: Greenwood, 1989.

Bonney MacDonald

Recent Hamlin Garland Reprints and Scholarship

The appearance of newly reissued works by Hamlin Garland, along with a steady increase in Garland scholarship, signals renewed and long-awaited attention to this author's writing, life, and place in American letters. The University of Nebraska Press, continuing its commitment to western and midwestern writing, has reprinted *Main-Travelled Roads* with an introduction by Joseph McCullough. In addition, Joseph McCullough and Keith Newlin have edited a collection of Garland's letters, also with University of Nebraska Press. Calling attention not only to issues covered in Garland's early life but also to concerns after the turn of the century, these 450 letters will help scholars to gain a more complete picture of Garland. Along with Garland's early concerns with social and agrarian reform, they also remind of his interests in Native American issues, western conservation and forestry, the film industry and literary modernism. Gary Scharnhorst has published an early essay by Garland on women and single-tax reform; Joseph McCullough has brought out *Tales of the Middle Border* and *A Son of the Middle Border*; and Gary Scharnhorst and Seth Bovey have published "Hamlin Garland's First Published Essay," a previously unpublished 1885 piece on Victor Hugo, Jean Paul Richter, and Sir Walter Scott in which — despite his growing anti-eastern and anti-romantic tendencies — Garland reveals his early affection for romantic writing. Finally, tracing further Garland's political involvement after his so-called "decline" from realism and politics in the 1890s, Keith Newlin has reprinted and commented on Garland's support for the 1913 "illegitimacy bill." Supplementing these primary works, *Critical Essays on Hamlin Garland*, edited by James Nagel, and *The Critical Reception of Hamlin Garland*, edited by Richard Bordreau, Charles Silet and Robert Welch, provide valuable access to a variety of essays, from early reviews to contemporary scholarship.

Reflecting a desire to situate Garland's work in American letters, Garland scholarship shows continued interest in his connection with other writers and thinkers. And while the links between Garland and European realism are examined, as are those with a number of American writers (such as Sarah Orne Jewett, Willa Cather, Sherwood Anderson, and Archibald Lampan), influence essays focus most prominently on the writers that Garland read during his first stay in Boston—namely, Henry George, Herbert Spencer and Walt Whitman. Francis Bosha's "Hamlin Garland Estrangement from the Midwest: The Case of *Main-Travelled Roads* and the Single Tax" and Quentin Martin's "Hamlin Garland's 'The Return of a Private' and 'Under the Lion's Paw' and the Monopoly of Money in Post-Civil War America" expand our knowledge of Garland's work vis-a-vis Henry George's ideas, and Michael Clark's "Herbert Spencer, Hamlin Garland, and *The Rose of Dutcher's Coolly*" identifies Spencerian evolutionary patterns in realism's development. Kenneth M. Price and Robert C. Leitz III have edited twelve letters (1886-1890) from Garland to Walt Whitman, five of which were previously unpublished; this correspondence not only helps explain how Whitman's work was promoted and kept before Boston audiences, it also adds to the portrait of a young and emerging midwestern writer attempting to gain access to the literary East. Thomas Becknell's "Hamlin Garland's Response to Walt Whitman" notes that, while much of Garland's early work was a "fulfillment of Whitman's call for a democratic literature" (217), *Prairie Song* was more of a "response to" than an "echo of" Whitman. Kenneth Price has commented on the connection between Whitman and Garland in "Hamlin Garland's 'The Evolution of American Thought': A Missing Link in the History of Whitman Criticism"; here, Garland's 1886-1887 piece on Whitman further underscores Garland's conviction that Whitman was a model for American evolutionary progress and individualism. Price has also traced the same connection in sections of *Whitman and Tradition: The Poet and His Century*.

In addition to influence studies, Garland criticism continues on a variety of fronts: attention has been paid to Garland's plays by Warren Motley, Brenda Murphy, and Mark Rocha. Of particular interest here is Keith Newlin's "Melodramatist of the Middle Border: Hamlin Garland's Early Work Reconsidered," in which Newlin probes Garland's early interest in melodrama and traces its influence in the early fiction. Interest also continues in the role of women in Garland's work. Roger Carp's "Hamlin Garland and the Cult of True Womanhood" offers analysis of Garland's indecision over the virtuous "True Woman" and the more radical "New Woman." Garland's attitudes toward women are also examined in Francis Kaye's "Hamlin Garland's Feminism," and Barbara Bardes and Suzanne Gossett provide excellent commentary on Garland's women in their *Declarations of Independence: Women and Political Power in Nineteenth-Century Fiction*. Especially promising, because of its foundation in archival research and its potential to open new material to scholarly debate, is Mark Rocha's dissertation on "The Feminization of Failure in American Historiography: The Case of the Invisible Drama in the Life of Hamlin Garland, 1860-1940." Rocha's analysis of how and why Garland imposed a masculine model of success on his fiction and, correspondingly, a feminine model of failure on his drama, promises to open new discussion on gender roles in authorship as well as on the place of marginalized dramas in the careers of other late nineteenth-century writers who attempted to write for the theater.

With good reason, Garland's autobiographical writings are receiving increased attention. Penguin has reprinted *A Son of the Middle Border*, with an introduction by Joseph McCullough. In addition, Leland Krauth's "*Boy Life on the Prairie*: Portrait of the Artist as a Young American" gains significant ground by successfully setting aside the problem of Garland's "decline" from realism. With useful binary oppositions (vastness of the land versus drudgery of work on the prairie; action versus reflection; and plain versus ornamental styles), Krauth analyzes a divided style that emerges from Garland's regional experience. Marcia Jacobson, in *Being a Boy Again*, offers commentary on *Boy Life on the Prairie*, arguing that the volume is more than mere reminiscence and nostalgic longing and that it points to Garland's profound sense of discontinuity between past and present.

While some of the earlier critical issues in Garland scholarship — such as the ongoing discussion of his "decline" from realism, his "selling-out" to market interests, and the resulting over-emphasis on the early fiction of the 1890s to the exclusion of the later work — are beginning to fade, *Main-Travelled Roads* itself continues to garner critical inquiry. Donald Pizer who, in his earlier *Hamlin Garland's Early Work and Career*, had placed Garland in the specific historical moment of the "agricultural depression of the late 1880s and early 1890s," has now de-emphasized land reform and single-tax issues in order to highlight twentieth-century concerns. In "Hamlin Garland's *Main-Travelled Roads* Revisited," Pizer convincingly claims that Garland foreshadows modern fragmentation and discontinuity, and that Garland's West is not only the site of rural discontent and agrarian reform but also a compelling metaphor for tragic loss and fallen idealism. Much influenced by Pizer's rereading and its emphasis on a past in Garland that cannot be recovered, my own "Eastern Imaginings of the West in Hamlin Garland's 'Up the Coolly' and 'God's Ravens'" analyzes the consequences of over-aestheticizing agrarian landscapes.

Garland scholarship has grown most, however, in its commentary on issues of place and region. Sections on Garland in Robert Thacker's *The Great Prairie Fact and Literary Imagination* convincingly examine how the barren, windswept prairies tried the patience and sanity of early pioneer women, and sections of Diane Quantic's *The Nature of the Place: A Study of Great Plains Fiction* discuss how writers came to terms with the myths of the midwestern plains — with their "physical reality and the psychological significance of open space." Amidst commentary on a variety of Great Plains writers — Wallace Stegner, Mari Sandoz, Laura Ingalls Wilder, and Willa Cather, among others — Quantic explores the "naïve faith in the land" in Garland's "Among the Corn Rows," and, later, follows Garland's declining optimism in the more realistic portraits found in "Under the Lion's Paw" and "Up the Coolly." In addition, Walter Herrscher's "The Natural Environment in Hamlin Garland's *Main-Travelled Roads*" offers some commentary on Garland's use of nature, while Daniel Littlefield and Lonnie Underhill make an excellent case for reexamining Garland's later Rocky Mountain fiction in order to chart his transition from the the picturesque West of the cattle kings to the conservationist and civic-minded West of the forest rangers.

Finally, two articles push Garland scholarship into recent, theoretical debates over the literary and cultural status of regionalist fiction. David Jordan's "Representing Regionalism" seeks to revive a reading of regionalist fiction that de-emphasizes objective, reportorial details and highlights an admittedly "nebulous" but nonetheless compelling model. Using Mary Austin as a starting point, Jordan seeks to identify a "genuine" regionalism that stems from "deep personal attachment" to one's home place. Here, regional identity cannot be achieved by the tourist or the outsider. Jordan argues that Garland's early fiction approaches this ideal; he concludes, however, that Garland ultimately abandoned this personal regionalist impulse because of his stronger concerns about economic and political problems in the nation as a whole. Jordan's thought-provoking article poses questions that regionalist scholars continue to confront, such as: How would a clearly subjective and personal version of regionalism mesh with the (equally problematic) realistic framework or intent of many regionalist writers? Also, if regionalism cannot be written by an outsider or tourist, just how native to the place need an aspiring regionalist be? If David Jordan's article temporarily divorces national concerns from "genuine" regionalism, Edward Watts reunites them in his "Margin or Middle Border?: Hamlin Garland, Henry Lawson and Post-Colonialism." Using vocabulary from post-colonialist theory, Watts locates in Garland a post-colonialist opposition in which the tension between "settlement" (the Midwest) and imperial "centre" (the East) prompts Garland to "write back" to the East in order to appropriate a region-based language, attain greater control over settlement texts and myths, and, finally, pose counter-texts in order to forge a regional identity and authority.

While scholarly output in influence studies, Garland's drama, autobiography, and early fiction continues, increasing attention to women in Garland, renewed focus on place and region, and the remarkable array of reprinted primary works and letters present new opportunities and approaches for Garland criticism. Garland has long been known for *Main-Travelled Roads* and *Crumbling Idols*; but the long-lived heritage of Garland criticism of the 1940s and 1950s—dominated by the account of Garland's "decline" from rigorous realism and populist reform into commercially motivated, sentimental romances—has focused too exclusively on the Garland of the early 1890s. And while Garland's Rocky Mountain stories and romances may ultimately prove "undistinguished," they do merit—as Joseph McCullough rightly suggests in "Hamlin Garland's Romantic Fiction"—increased critical attention. With the publication of the letters, and the reissues of Garland's fiction and autobiographical work, scholars will gain a better view of the Garland that emerges after the so-called decline from realism. After 1900, Garland was not only a midwestern author who had begun to forge a place for himself in nineteenth-century American letters but also a writer who moved from concerns with midwestern regionalism and single-tax reform to issues of our own century — to the struggles of Native Americans, issues in conservation, literary modernism, and the film industry. His fiction of the middle border, along with his tales of the mountain West and the autobiographical works, charts a literary life that registered changes in region as well as nation. To study Garland — both the works of the 1890s and those produced after the turn of the century — is to trace not only changes in regionalist representation, but also alterations in the culture of letters which Garland revered and struggled with for much of his life.

Selected Bibliography, 1980-1996

Bardes, Barbara, and Susan Gossett. *Declarations of Independence: Women and Political Power in Nineteenth-Century American Fiction.* Camden: Rutgers University Press, 1990.

Becknell, Thomas. "Hamlin Garland's Response to Whitman." *The Old Northwest: A Journal of Regional Life and Letters* 7 (Fall 1981): 217-235.

Bosha, Francis J. "Hamlin Garland's Estrangement from the Midwest: The Case of *Main-Travelled Roads* and the Single Tax." *Thought Currents in American Literature*, 55 (1982): 87-95.

Bovey, Seth, and Gary Scharnhorst. "Hamlin Garland's First Published Essay," *ANQ: A Quarterly Journal of Short Articles, Notes and Reviews*, 5:1 (January 1992): 20-23.

Bredahl, Carl A. "'The Young Thing Within': Divided Narrative and Sherwood Anderson's *Winesburg, Ohio.*" *Midwest Quarterly*, 27:4 (1986): 422-437.

Brown, Bill. "The Popular, The Populist, and the Populace — Locating Hamlin Garland in the Politics of Culture." *Arizona Quarterly*, 30:3 (Autumn 1994): 89-110.

Carp, Roger. "Hamlin Garland and the Cult of True Womanhood." In *Women, Women Writers, and the West.* L. L. Lee and Merrill Lewis, eds. Troy, New York: Whitston, 1980.

Clark, Michael. "Herbert Spencer, Hamlin Garland, and *The Rose of Dutcher's Coolly.*" *American Literary Realism*, 17:2 (Autumn 1984): 203-208.

Doyle, James. "Archibald Lampan and Hamlin Garland." *Canadian Poetry: Studies, Documents and Reviews*, 16 (Spring-Summer 1986): 38-46.

Dunlop, M. H. "Unfinished Business: Hamlin Garland and Edward MacDowell." *The Old Northwest: A Journal of Regional Life and Letters*, 10 (Summer 1984): 175-185.

Engel, Bernard F. "Edith Thomas and Hamlin Garland: Canaan and Rome." *The Yearbook of the Society for the Study of Midwestern Literature*, 14 (1987): 41-50.

Garland, Hamlin. *Main-Travelled Roads.* Boston: Arena, 1891; rpt., introduction by Joseph B. McCullough, Lincoln: University of Nebraska Press, 1995.

———. *A Son of the Middle Border.* Introduction by Joseph B. McCullough, ed., New York: Penguin, 1995.

———. *Tales of the Middle Border.* Joseph McCullough, ed. Albany, New York: New College and University Press, 1990.

Herrscher, Walter. "The Natural Environment in Hamlin Garland's *Main-Travelled*

Roads." *The Old Northwest: A Journal of Regional Life and Letters,* 11:1-2 (Spring-Summer 1985): 35-50.

Hiscoe, David W. "Feeding and Consuming in Garland's *Main-Travelled Roads.*" *Western American Literature,* 15 (Spring 1980): 3-15.

Jacobson, Marcia. *Being a Boy Again: Autobiography and the American Boy Book.* Tuscaloosa: University of Alabama Press, 1994.

Jordan, David. "Representing Regionalism." *Canadian Review of American Studies,* 23:2 (Winter 1993): 101-114.

Kaye, Frances W. "Hamlin Garland: A Closer Look at the Later Fiction." In *The Critical Reception of Hamlin Garland.* Charles L. P. Silet, Robert E. Welch, and Richard Bordreau, eds. Troy: Whitston, 1985.

———. "Hamlin Garland's Feminism." In *Women and Western American Literature.* Helen Winter Stauffer and Susan J. Rosowski, eds. Troy: Whitston, 1982.

Krauth, Leland. "*Boy Life on the Prairie*: Portrait of the Artist as a Young American." *Markham Review,* 11 (Winter 1982): 25-29.

———. "Hamlin Garland: Realist of Old Age." *Midamerica: The Yearbook of the Society for the Study of Midwestern Literature,* 9 (1982): 23-37.

Littlefield, Daniel and Lonnie Underhill. "The Emerging West in Hamlin Garland's Fiction: 1910-1916." *Markham Review,* 9 (1980): 35-40.

MacDonald, Bonney. "Eastern Imaginings of the West in Hamlin Garland's 'Up the Coolly' and 'God's Ravens.'" *Western American Literature,* 28 (Fall 1993): 209-230.

Martin, Quentin. "Hamlin Garland's 'The Return of a Private' and 'Up the Coolly' and the Monopoly of Money in Post-Civil War America." *American Literary Realism,* 29:1 (1996): 62-77.

McCullough, Joseph B. "Hamlin Garland." *Nineteenth Century American Western Writers,* Vol. 178 (1997). In *Dictionary of Literary Biography.* Robert Gale, ed. Detroit: Gale Research, 1978-.

———. "Hamlin Garland's Romantic Fiction." In *Critical Essays on Hamlin Garland.* James Nagel, ed. Boston: G. K. Hall, 1982. Pp. 349-362.

Meyer, Roy. "Hamlin Garland and Midwest Farm Fiction." In *A Literary History of the American West.* Fort Worth: Texas Christian University Press, 1987.

Motley, Warren. "Hamlin Garland's 'Under the Wheel': Regionalism Unmasking America." *Modern Drama,* 26:4 (1983): 477-485.

Murphy, Brenda. *American Realism and American Drama.* New York: Cambridge University Press, 1987.

Nagel, James, ed. *Critical Essays on Hamlin Garland.* Boston: G. K. Hall, 1982.

———. "Sarah Orne Jewett Writes to Hamlin Garland." *The New England Quarterly,* 54:3 (1981): 416-423.

Newlin, Keith. "Hamlin Garland and the 'Illegitimacy Bill' of 1913." *American Literary Realism,* 29:1 (1996): 78-88.

———."Melodramatist of the Middle Border: Hamlin Garland's Early Work Reconsidered." *Studies in American Fiction,* 21:2 (Autumn 1993): 153-169.

Pizer, Donald. "Hamlin Garland's *Main-Travelled Roads* Revisited." *South Dakota Review,* 29 (Spring 1991): 53-67.

Price, Kenneth. "Hamlin Garland's 'The Evolution of American Thought': A Missing Link in the History of Whitman Criticism." *Walt Whitman Quarterly Review,* 3:2 (1985): 1-20.

———. "Whitman's Influence on Hamlin Garland's *The Rose of Dutcher's Coolly.*" *Mickle Street Review,* 9:2 (1988): 19-29.

Price, Kenneth and Robert C. Leitz, III. "The Uncollected Letters of Hamlin Garland to Walt Whitman." *Walt Whitman Quarterly Review,* 5 (Winter 1988): 1-13.

Quantic, Diane Dufva. *The Nature of the Place: A Study of Great Plains Fiction.* Lincoln: University of Nebraska Press, 1995.

Riese, Utz. "Universality and Differentiation: The Functional Context of Hamlin Garland's 'Veritism.'" *Amerikastudian,* 36 (1990): 43-53.

Rocha, Mark William. "The Bibliographer as Biographer: Accounting for the Unpublished Endings of Hamlin Garland's Early Works." *University of Mississippi Studies in English,* 7 (1984-1985): 193-200.

————. "The Feminization of Failure in American Historiography: The Case of the Invisible Drama in the Life of Hamlin Garland." Unpublished dissertation, University of Southern California, 1988.

————. "Hamlin Garland's Temperance Play." *American Literary Realism,* 21:3 (1989): 67-71.

Scharnhorst, Gary. "Hamlin Garland and Feminism: An Early Essay Recovered." *ANQ: A Quarterly Journal of Short Articles, Notes and Reviews,* n. s. 2 (1989): 15-18.

Silet, Charles L. P., Robert E. Welch, and Richard Bordreau, eds. *The Critical Reception of Hamlin Garland.* Troy: New York: Whitston, 1985.

Thacker, Robert. "'Twisting Toward Insanity': Landscape and Female Entrapment in Plains Fiction." *North Dakota Quarterly,* 52:3 (Summer 1984): 181-194.

————. *The Great Prairie Fact and Literary Imagination.* Albuquerque: University of New Mexico Press, 1989.

Watts, Edward. "Margin or Middle Border?: Hamlin Garland, Henry Lawson, and Post-Colonialism." *The Old Northwest: A Journal of Regional Life and Letters,* 16:2 (Summer 1992): 149-163.

John J. Murphy

The Cather Enterprise: The Last Dozen Years

An exploding field is the appropriate metaphor for Cather scholarship in recent years, but the fertility of her texts has yielded its share of weeds. Any critical survey must begin with James Woodress' *Willa Cather: A Literary Life* (1987), which gives the known facts of the biography and provides comprehensive treatment of Cather's Virginia background, her Nebraska, Pittsburgh, and *McClure's* years, European and southwestern travels, and later life in New York, New Hampshire, and New Brunswick. Woodress normalizes Cather's female friendships, refusing to speculate beyond the record. While his biography is ponderous in places and lacks the excitement of R.W.B. Lewis' similarly comprehensive treatment of Edith Wharton, it is the book one must cite to legitimatize any speculation on Cather. Woodress' restraint enables British critic Hermione Lee to temper lesbian readings of Cather in her critical biography, *Willa Cather: Double Lives* (1990), to caution us that "to account for Cather's fiction by reading it as an encoding of covert, even guilty, sexuality, is...patronizing and narrow" (11).

Woodress' strategic position is evident in his co-editorship, with Susan J. Rosowski, of University of Nebraska Press' *Willa Cather Scholarly Edition*, which has won MLA approval for all its volumes to date: *O Pioneers!* (1992), *My Antonia* (1994), and *A Lost Lady* (1996). Each of these offers a historical essay, illustrations, explanatory notes, and textual commentary. Complementing this thoroughness is Marilyn

Arnold's edition of *A Reader's Companion to the Fiction of Willa Cather* (1993), an 800-page compendium based on John March's fifty years of research on persons, places, events (both fictional and factual), quotations, art works, etc. included in and/or influencing Cather's fiction. Arnold contributes a similarly exhaustive apparatus in *Willa Cather: A Reference Guide* (1986), arranging criticism from 1895 to 1984 according to year and with clear abstracts. Some of this critical heritage is evaluated by Sharon O'Brien in "Becoming Noncanonical: The Case Against Willa Cather" (1988), which examines Cather's fluctuating reputation to expose gender bias, and in Joan Acocella's 1995 *New Yorker* essay, "Cather and the Academy," which devastates O'Brien and other gay-preoccupied critics who respond negatively to the question "What have the academics done to Willa Cather?" Yearly estimates of Cather scholarship appear in the "Fiction: 1900 to the 1930s" chapter in *American Literary Scholarship* and in an annual "Works on Cather" essay in the *Willa Cather Pioneer Memorial Newsletter (WCPMN)*.

Noteworthy collections representing perspectives beyond those acknowledged by O'Brien and Acocella include *Approaches to Teaching Cather's My Antonia* (1989), edited by Susan Rosowski for the MLA series; *Willa Cather: Family, Community, and History* (1990), a gathering of major presentations and selected session papers edited by John J. Murphy from the 1988 Cather symposium at Brigham Young University; special Cather issues of *Modern Fiction Studies* (1990) and *Legacy* (1992), and Harold Bloom's "Modern Critical Views" on *Willa Cather* (1985), *My Antonia* (1987), and *Antonia* (1991). A significant development was the inauguration of *Cather Studies* in 1990. Edited by Susan Rosowski, subsequent volumes appeared in 1993 and 1996 to provide an ongoing outlet for established and beginning scholars. Since 1990 the *Willa Cather Pioneer Memorial Newsletter* has developed into a literary quarterly with the MLA acronym *WCPMN*. The Willa Cather Pioneer Memorial/University of Nebraska Cather seminars — begun in 1981 — have developed into a series of international seminars attracting from 100 to 150 academics to various Cather locales. The sixth seminar was held in Quebec City in 1995 and another in Winchester, Virginia, in 1997. These seminars have generated book-length studies as well as contributions to *Cather Studies, WCPMN* and numerous journals.

Cather's biography is intellectualized in Merrill Skaggs' *After the World Broke in Two: The Later Novels of Willa Cather* (1990), which demonstrates how Cather pieced together a world broken apart for her generation. Cather's accomplishments include an upending of Freudian analysis in *One of Ours*, a reassertion of order and liturgy in *The Professor's House* and of continuity and community in *Shadows on the Rock*. While Skaggs reflects the increasing attention being given to Cather's later fiction, Tom Quirk returns to *O Pioneers!* and *The Song of the Lark* in *Bergson and American Culture* (1990) to examine the influence on Cather of Henri Bergson's *Creative Evolution*. Quirk argues that these novels reflect a rejection of Herbert Spencer's worldview and adoption of Bergson's concepts of *moi fundamentale*, backward and forward consciousness, primacy of artisan to artist, and objections to the scientific method. Loretta Wasserman previously applied Bergsonian concepts to *The Professor's House* in "The Music of Time: Henri Bergson and Willa Cather" (1985). The worldview Cather anticipates in Joseph Urgo's *Willa Cather and the Myth of American Migration* (1995) is one in which national identity becomes negotiable and ongoing migration replaces homeland. Urgo sees the cultural vitality of Cather's fiction rooted in the transience of American life. Laura Winters offers a variation on the migration theme in *Willa Cather: Landscape and Exile* (1993), an analysis of the uprooted's search for home and self through transformations of secular to sacred space. A political objection to this process is registered by Mike Fischer, who reads *My Antonia* and *Death Comes for the Archbishop* from the context of Indian displacement in "Pastoralism and Its Discontents: Willa Cather and the Burden of Imperialism" (1990).

Historical sources of Cather's fiction occupy critics involved with Nebraska history and those with less strictly local interests, like Rebecca Faber in "Some of His: Cather's Use of Dr. Sweeney's Diary in *One of Ours*" (1993), an exploration of Cather's debt in the voyage section of this novel to the notes of a World War I New Hampshire army physician. The sources recovered by Rosowski and Bernice Slote in "Willa Cather's 1916 Mesa Verde Essay" (1984) prove valuable to David Harrell in *From Mesa Verde to The Professor's House* (1992), a painstaking revelation of Cather's process "from history to fiction, from personal myth to universal theme" in making a shattered world whole for survival. As revealing on Cather's transformation of history is the new edition (1987) of W. J. Howlett's 1908 *Life of Bishop Machebeuf*, Cather's primary source for *Archbishop*; editors Thomas Steele and Ronald Brockway contribute a much-needed index, notes, and a commentary on Cather.

The most thorough study of Cather's literary associations and influences is Rosowski's *The Voyage Perilous: Willa Cather's Romanticism*

(1986). Viewing the fiction from perspectives of British Romanticism, Rosowski discusses the awakening of artistic power and capacity for ongoing change in *Song of the Lark* and *My Antonia* as Wordsworthian. *Lucy Gayheart* and *Sapphira and the Slave Girl* are offered as dramas of the underside of romanticism: the first a retelling of *Dracula* from the female point of view, and the second a struggle with irrational forces. George Dekker, who speculates in *The American Historical Romance* (1987) that "Cather may well be the preeminent American historical romancer-novelist of our century," uses Johann Schiller's concepts of sentimental and naïve (nature-estranged and nature-connected) to evaluate Jim and Antonia in *My Antonia* and equates the hired girls with Hawthorne's dark heroines. Murphy parallels Cather and Edith Wharton as social historians in "Filters, Portraits, and History's Mixed Bag: *A Lost Lady* and *The Age of Innocence*" (1992), while Kate Fullbrook pairs Cather and Zora Neale Hurston for combining heroic, folkloric, and realistic methods with autobiographical material in *Free Women* (1990). In *Playing in the Dark* (1992) Toni Morrison includes *Sapphira* among works by other canonical Americans in her speculation that the "characteristics of our national literature...[are] responses to a dark, abiding, signing Africanist presence" (5). Demaree Peck detects Whitman in Cather in "Thea Kronborg's Song of Myself" (1991), and John Flannigan reveals French literary connections in "Cather, Merimee, and the Problem of Fanaticism in *Shadows on the Rock*" (1993).

The impact on Cather of Hellenic and Roman classicism and myth is the subject of two 1990 book-length studies: *Willa Cather and Classical Myth* by Mary Ryder and *The Humanization of Willa Cather* by Erik Thurin. Thurin's study is significant for demonstrating Cather's affinity for universal aspects of classical humanism and for pointing out its medieval as well as Greek and Roman strains. Marilyn Callander mines another rich resource in *Willa Cather and the Fairy Tale* (1989), in which *My Mortal Enemy* incorporates "Sleeping Beauty" and "Snow White," *Song of the Lark* becomes a version of "Cinderella," and *Shadows on the Rock* an original fairy tale. A bridge between classical and fine arts scholarship is Murphy's *My Antonia: The Road Home* (1989), which details Cather's borrowings from Virgil's *Georgics* while considering the impact of Hudson River landscape painting, luminism, and impressionism on Cather's style. Murphy and Trevor Packer examine the impact of Flemish and Dutch painters on *Sapphira* and *Shadows* in tandem pieces titled "Dutch Masters" (1993). Kevin A. Synnott illustrates Cather's approximation of the monumental painting style of Pierre Puvis de Chavannes in "'The Colour of an Adventure': Pictorial Dimensions in Cather's *Archbishop*" (1987) and analyzes how color and light can supersede linear articulation in "Painting 'the Tricks That Shadows Play': Impressionism in *Lucy Gayheart*" (1992). The influence of French painting is also acknowledged in Rosowski's "Willa Cather and the French Rural Tradition of Breton and Millet" (1987), which relates tensions in *O Pioneers!*, *Song of the Lark*, and *My Antonia* to those between Jules Breton's pastoral landscapes and Jean Millet's vigorous ones. In "The Benda Illustrations to *My Antonia*" (1985), Jean Schwind uses drawings rather than paintings to argue that Cather's personal statement in this novel lies in the eight sketches she commissioned from W. T. Benda.

Cather's modernism and technical sophistication have become, at long last, givens. Phyllis Rose did Cather a service by acknowledging her lucid style and unfurnished technique as modernism at its best in *Writing of Women* (1985). Cather's emphasis on the archetypal in bringing realism to the realm of the mythical associates her with sculptor Henry Moore, painters Georgia O'Keeffe and Rene Magritte, and novelists like James Joyce and Virginia Woolf. Jo Ann Middleton contributes to this appreciation of Cather in *Willa Cather's Modernism* (1990), focusing on what is left out of her texts and borrowing the scientific term *vacuole* to explain how omissions affect readers. In *Strategies of Reticence* (1990), Janis Stout also addresses textual gaps and omissions, although from more feminist than modernist perspectives. L. Brent Bohlke's gathering in *Willa Cather in Person: Interviews, Speeches and Letters* (1986) adds Cather's own voice in revealing her strategies — that, for example, she intended *Archbishop* and *Shadows* to be experimental. Of particular interest is a report on a 1925 Bowdoin College lecture on technique and a 1933 radio talk on the novel. Among those pursuing experimental aspects are David Stouck and Michael Leddy. In "Willa Cather and a Grammar for Things 'Not Named'" (1992), Stouck elucidates with Janet Giltrow the effect of Cather's style on readers; in "*The Professor's House*: The Sense of an Ending" (1991), Leddy evaluates the complexity of the novel's "remarkably modernist" ending.

A bridge between technical and feminist studies is Deborah Carlin's *Cather, Canon, and the Politics of Reading* (1992), which reads five female-centered late fictions (*My Mortal Enemy*, *Shadows*, "Old Mrs. Harris," *Lucy Gayheart*, and *Sapphira*) as experiments in fictional form revealing ambiguous feminist impulses. Several feminist approaches to

Cather have proven productive. In "Writing Against Silences" (1989), Susan Rosowski explores *Song of the Lark*, *Lucy Gayheart*, and *Sapphira* as texts which establish the importance of the mother-daughter relationship to healthy female development. Josephine Donovan in *After the Fall* (1989) sees as a central issue in Cather's fiction reconciliation between nineteenth-century mothers and their "new women," twentieth-century daughters. Female spatial responses occupy Judith Fryer in *Felicitous Space* (1986), which tries to distinguish male and female orientations to space in *My Antonia*, *The Professor's House*, *Archbishop*, *Shadows*, and other novels. While the spaces considered expand to desert floor and sky, Fryer is best with intimate domestic spaces. Ann Romines' concern with housekeeping as a battleground and a context for discovery and liberation in *The Home Plot* (1992) illuminates several Cather texts, especially *Shadows*, where Cather "finally made a full entry into the life of housekeeping, as practiced by traditional women" (152). In Willa Cather's *Transforming Vision* (1994), Gary Brienzo focuses on *Shadows* to expand Cather's domestic vision toward societal order and locates that order primarily in the Northeast and New France, where Cather found a "fine sense of harmony and domestic order" (101). Feminist critics continue to mine *My Antonia* and condemn its narrator. David Laird, in "Willa Cather's Women" (1992), highlights the inadequacies in Jim's narrative, which is brought to the foreground so Antonia can have freedom behind the scenes; in contrast, Annette McElhiney, in "Cather's Use of Tripartite Narrative Point of View in *My Antonia*" (1993), sees Jim's droning myth-making as confining Antonia's story.

The most controversial feminist readings involve Cather's presumed lesbianism. The guru of this camp is Sharon O'Brien, whose psychobiography *Willa Cather: The Emerging Voice* (1987) employs an inclusive definition of lesbianism and theories by Nancy Chodorow and others to explain the difficulty Cather had achieving autonomy from her mother and examine Cather's fiction through *O Pioneers!* (when she found her voice), especially the strategies used to satisfy her need without revealing an eroticism considered "deviant." Although Cather used male perspectives to mask same-sex relationships, O'Brien cautions us that when Cather writes a heterosexual and a homosexual story in one, the meaning is frequently indeterminate. A year prior to O'Brien's study, Judith Fetterley concluded in "*My Antonia*, Jim Burden and the Dilemma of the Lesbian Writer" that Cather used her narrator to masquerade writing about one woman's lesbian love for another. Fetterley turned her attention to *The Professor's House* and *Song of the Lark* as lesbian texts in "Willa Cather and the Fiction of Female Development" (1993), seeing the first as unwriting the second, in which the wonder of possessing one's desire (for Cather, Isabelle McClung) is recorded. *Isolation and Masquerade: Willa Cather's Women* (1993) is Frances Kaye's reductive argument that Cather is unintelligible unless read as a lesbian writer. Patrick Shaw might not be as reductive in *Willa Cather and the Art of Conflict* (1992), but he does make response to unorthodox sexuality the basis of Cather's creativity. A rebuttal to this kind of criticism is Edward Wagenknecht's *Willa Cather* (1993), a consideration of the life and work which puts down recent critics compelled to speak of Cather as lesbian. This venerable scholar presents "the record" of heterosexual passion in the fiction and catalogs the men who appealed sexually to Cather.

An antidote of sorts to lesbian criticism is provided by viewing Cather texts as religious. In 1988, *Literature and Belief* produced a Cather issue which gathered nine essays on aspects of religion in Cather. Of particular interest among them is Bruce Baker's "Before the Cruciform Tree: The Failure of Evangelical Protestantism," which examines Cather's rejection of fundamentalist Christianity in *Song of the Lark* and subsequent passage to a high church variety. However, Steven B. Shively rescues this novel in "'A Full, Perfect, and Sufficient Sacrifice': Eucharistic Imagery in Cather's *Song of the Lark*" (1994), seeing Thea Kronborg's role as a priestly one negotiating the sacred and the profane. Murphy uses the theology of Karl Rahner while explaining how *Archbishop*, "Neighbour Rosicky," and "The Best Years" equate Cather with Emily Dickinson and Flannery O'Connor in "Cather and the Literature of Christian Mystery" (1992). However, Conrad Ostwalt pairs Cather with Theodore Dreiser in *After Eden* (1990) as reflecting the transformation of American culture from religious to secular.

Let me briefly recognize those devoting their energies to Cather as a short story writer. In *Willa Cather: A Study of the Short Fiction* (1991), Loretta Wasserman discusses eighteen stories, collects commentaries by Cather herself, and reprints essays by recent critics. Helpful also is Sheryl Meyering's *A Reader's Guide to the Short Stories of Willa Cather* (1994), which provides information on publishing and composition history, sources and influences, interpretations and criticism for sixty-one stories alphabetically arranged. A recent Cather issue of *Nebraska State Journal* (1991) includes commentaries on several stories: "The

Enchanted Bluff," "Neighbour Rosicky," "Old Mrs. Harris," and "The Best Years."

Selected Bibliography (1985-1996)

(Annotations restricted to work not commented on above; bibliography compiled with Virgil Albertini, Northwest Missouri State University.)

Cather Text Editions
Willa Cather Scholarly Editions

A Lost Lady. Charles W. Mignon, ed., with Kari Ronning; historical essay and explanatory notes by Susan J. Rosowski with Kari Ronning. Lincoln: University of Nebraska Press, 1996.
My Antonia. Charles Mignon, ed., with Kari Ronning; historical essay and explanatory notes by James Woodress. Lincoln: University of Nebraska Press, 1994.
O Pioneers! Susan J. Rosowski and Charles W. Mignon, eds., with Kathleen Danker; historical essay and explanatory notes by David Stouck. Lincoln: University of Nebraska Press, 1992.

Library of America Editions

Early Novels and Stories: The Troll Garden, O Pioneers!, The Song of the Lark, My Antonia, One of Ours. Edited with notes by Sharon O'Brien. New York: Library Classics of the U.S., 1987.
Later Novels: A Lost Lady, The Professor's House, Death Comes for the Archbishop, Shadows on the Rock, Lucy Gayheart, Sapphira and the Slave Girl. Edited with notes by Sharon O'Brien. New York: Library Classics of the U.S., 1990.
Stories, Poems, and Other Writings: Alexander's Bridge, My Mortal Enemy, Obscure Destinies, The Old Beauty and Others, April Twilights, Not Under Forty, Selected Reviews and Essays, Uncollected Stories. Edited with notes by Sharon O'Brien. New York: Library Classics of the U.S., 1992.

Other

Willa Cather in Person: Interviews, Speeches, and Letters. L. Brent Bohlke, ed. Lincoln: University of Nebraska Press, 1986.

Biographies

Lee, Hermione. Willa Cather: Double Lives. New York: Pantheon Books, 1990.
O'Brien, Sharon. Willa Cather: The Emerging Voice. New York: Oxford University Press, 1987.
Wagenknecht, Edward. Willa Cather. New York: Continuum, 1993.
Woodress, James. Willa Cather: A Literary Life. Lincoln: University of Nebraska Press, 1987.

665

Book-Length Studies and Cather Collections, Special Issues, and Serials

Bloom, Harold, ed. *Modern Critical Views, Willa Cather*, 1985; *Modern Critical Views, My Antonia*, 1987; *Modern Critical Views, Antonia*, 1991. (All from Chelsea House of New York. The volumes include general essays, essays on the popular novel, and those on the famous characters.)

Brienzo, Gary. *Transforming Vision: New France and the American Northeast*. Selinsgrove, Pennsvylania: Susquehanna University Press, 1994.

Callander, Marilyn. *Willa Cather and the Fairy Tale*. Ann Arbor: University of Michigan Research Press, 1989.

Carlin, Deborah. *Cather, Canon, and the Politics of Reading*. Amherst: University of Massachusetts Press, 1992.

Dekker, George. *The American Historical Romance*. New York: Cambridge University Press, 1987.

Donovan, Josephine. *After the Fall: The Demeter-Persephone Myth in Wharton, Cather, and Glasgow*. University Park: Pennsylvania State University Press, 1989.

Fryer, Judith. *Felicitous Space: The Imaginative Structures of Edith Wharton and Willa Cather*. Chapel Hill: University of North Carolina Press, 1986.

Fullbrook, Kate. *Ethics and Aesthetics in Twentieth-Century Women's Fiction*. Philadelphia: Temple University Press, 1990.

Harrell, David. *From Mesa Verde to The Professor's House*. Albuquerque: University of New Mexico Press, 1992.

Hively, Evelyn Helmick. *Sacred Fire: Willa Cather's Novel Cycle*. Lanham, Maryland: University Press of America, 1994. (Examines Cather's response to historians, philosophers, and mythographers in nine novels.)

Kaye, Frances W. *Isolation and Masquerade: Willa Cather's Women*. New York: Lang, 1993.

Legacy: A Journal of American Women Writers, 9 (1992): 1-64. (A collection of five essays that include considerations of Cather's friendships with Dorothy Canfield Fisher and Louise Pound.)

Literature and Belief, 8 (1988): 1-130 (Nine essays on Cather and religion.)

Middleton, Jo Ann. *Willa Cather's Modernism: A Study of Style and Technique*. Rutherford, New Jersey: Fairleigh Dickinson University Press, 1990.

Modern Fiction Studies, 36:1 (1990): 3-141. (Includes essays on *O Pioneers!*, "Behind the Singer Tower," *My Antonia*, and "Paul's Case.")

Morrison, Toni. *Playing in the Dark: Whiteness and the Literary Imagination*. Cambridge: Harvard University Press, 1992.

Murphy, John J. *My Antonia: The Road Home*. Boston: Twayne, 1989.

———, ed. *Willa Cather: Family, Community, and History* (The Brigham Young University Symposium). Provo: Brigham Young University Humanities Publications, 1990. (Contains thirty-two of the sixty papers presented at the 1988 symposium.)

Nebraska English Journal, 37:1 (1991): 7-145. (Ten essays on "Cather in the Classroom.")

Ostwalt, Conrad. *After Eden: The Secularization of American Space in the Fiction of Willa Cather and Theodore Dreiser*. Cranbury, New Jersey: Bucknell University Press, 1990.

Quirk, Tom. *Bergson and American Culture: The Worlds of Willa Cather and Wallace Stevens*. Chapel Hill: University of North Carolina Press, 1990.

Romines, Ann. *The Home Plot: Women, Writing and Domestic Ritual*. Amherst: University of Massachusetts Press, 1992.

Rose, Phyllis. *Writing of Women: Essays in a Renaissance*. Middletown, Connecticut: Wesleyan University Press, 1985.

Rosowski, Susan J., ed. *Approaches to Teaching Cather's* My Antonia. New York: MLA, 1989. (Essays by twenty-five critics with experience teaching the novel.)

———, ed. *Cather Studies 1*. Lincoln: University of Nebraska Press, 1990. (Essays selected from presentations at the 1987 Cather seminar.)

———, ed. *Cather Studies 2*. Lincoln: University of Nebraska Press, 1993. (Essays on *Lucy Gayheart, My Antonia, My Mortal Enemy, The Professor's House, Shadows on the Rock*.)

———, ed. *Cather Studies 3*. Lincoln: University of Nebraska Press, 1996. (Fourteen essays primarily on later fiction.)

———. *The Voyage Perilous: Willa Cather's Romanticism*. Lincoln: University of Nebraska Press, 1986.

Ryder, Mary Ruth. *Willa Cather and Classical Myth: The Search for a New Parnassus*. Lewiston, New York: Mellen, 1990.

Shaw, Patrick W. *Willa Cather and the Art of Conflict*. Troy, New York: Whitston, 1992.

Skaggs, Merrill Maguire. *After the World Broke in Two: The Later Novels of Willa Cather*. Charlottesville: University Press of Virginia, 1990.

Stout, Janis P. *Strategies of Reticence: Silence and Meaning in the Works of Jane Austen, Willa Cather, Katherine Anne Porter, and Joan Didion*. Charlottesville: University Press of Virginia, 1990.

Thurin, Erik Ingvar. *The Humanization of Willa Cather: Classicism in an American Classic*. Lund, Sweden: Lund University Press, 1990.

Urgo, Joseph. *Willa Cather and the Myth of American Migration*. Champaign: University of Illinois Press, 1995.

Wasserman, Loretta. *Willa Cather: A Study of the Short Fiction*. Boston: Twayne, 1991.

Winters, Laura. *Landscape and Exile*. Selinsgrove, Pennsylvania: Susquehanna University Press, 1993.

Periodical Articles and Essays in General Collections

Acocella, Joan. "Cather and the Academy." *New Yorker*, 72:1 (November 27, 1995): 56-71.

Ammons, Elizabeth. "The Engineer as Cultural Hero and Willa Cather's First Novel, *Alexander's Bridge*," *American Quarterly*, 38:5 (1986): 746-760. (Contextualizes the novel through literature about engineers and Progressive Era myths.)

Baker, Bruce P. "Before the Cruciform Tree: The Failure of Evangelical Protestantism." *Literature and Belief*, 8 (1988): 14-26.

Briggs, Cynthia K. "The Language of Flowers in *O Pioneers!*" *Willa Cather Pioneer Memorial Newsletter*, 30:3 (1986): 29-30. (Uses Victorian sourcebook on floral symbolism to interpret Cather.)

Faber, Rebecca. "Some of His: Cather's Use of Dr. Sweeney's Diary in *One of Ours*." *Willa Cather Pioneer Memorial Newsletter*, 37 (1993): 5-9.

Fetterley, Judith. "*My Antonia*, Jim Burden and the Dilemma of the Lesbian Writer," In *Gender Studies: New Directions in Feminist Criticism*. Judith Spector, ed. Bowling Green, Ohio: Bowling Green University Press, 1987. Pp. 43-59.

———. "Willa Cather and the Fiction of Female Development," In *Anxious Power: Reading, Writing, and Ambivalence in Narrative by Women*. Carol J. Singley and Susan E. Sweeney, eds. Albany: State University of New York Press, 1993. Pp. 221-34.

Fischer, Mike. "Pastoralism and Its Discontents: Willa Cather and the Burden of Imperialism." *Mosaic*, 23:1 (1990): 31-44.

Flannigan, John H. "Cather, Merimee, and the Problem of Fanaticism in *Shadows on the Rock*." *Willa Cather Pioneer Memorial Newsletter*, 37 (1993): 29-35.

Fryer, Judith. "Desert, Rock, Shelter, Legend: Willa Cather's Novels of the Southwest." In *The Desert Is No Lady: Southwestern Landscapes in Women's Writing and Art*. Vera Norwood and Janice Monk, eds. New Haven: Yale University Press, 1987. Pp. 27-46. (Suggests comparison with Georgia O'Keeffe's multisensory approach to landscape.)

Funda, Evelyn I. "'The Breath Vibrating Behind It': Intimacy in the Storytelling of Antonia Shimerda." *Western American Literature*, 29:3 (1994): 195-216. (Shows how Antonia's story becomes evident in Jim's account.)

Harris, Richard C. "First Loves: Willa Cather's Niel Herbert and Ivan Turgenev's Vladimir Petrovich," *Studies in American Fiction*, 17:1 (1989): 89-91. (Compares *A Lost Lady* and Turgenev's "First Love.")

Laird, David. "Willa Cather and the Deceptions of Art," In *Interface: Essays on History, Myth and Art in American Literature*, Daniel Royot, ed. Montpelier, France: University Paul Valery, 1985. Pp. 51-59. (In *My Antonia* and *Professor's House* life is sacrificed to artistic patternings of it.)

———. "Willa Cather's Women: Gender, Place, and Narrativity in *O Pioneers!* and *My Antonia*," *Great Plains Quarterly*, 12:4 (1992): 242-253.

Leddy, Michael. "*The Professor's House*: The Sense of an Ending." *Studies in the Novel*, 23:4 (1991): 443-451.

Love, Glen A. "*The Professor's House*: Cather, Hemingway, and the Chastening of American Prose Style." *Western American Literature*, 24:4 (1990): 295-311. (Notes theoretical and stylistic similarities between the novelists.)

McElhiney, Annette B. "Willa Cather's Use of a Tripartite Narrative Point of View in *My Antonia*." *CEA Critic*, 56:1 (1993): 65-76.

Murphy, John J. "Filters, Portraits, and History's Mixed Bag: *A Lost Lady* and *The Age of Innocence*." *Twentieth Century Literature*, 38 (1992): 476-485.

———. "Willa Cather and the Literature of Christian Mystery." *Religion and Literature*, 24:3 (1992): 39-56.

O'Brien, Sharon. "Becoming Noncanonical: The Case Against Willa Cather." *American Quarterly*, 40:1 (1988): 110-126.

Oehlschlaeger, Fritz. "*Indisponibilite* and the Anxiety of Authorship in *The Professor's House*." *American Literature*, 62:1 (1990): 74-86 (Extends critical analyses of the professor's despair.)

Packer, Trevor D., and John J. Murphy. "Dutch Masters," *Willa Cather Pioneer Memorial Newsletter*, 37 (1993): 9-14.

Peck, Demaree. "Thea Kronborg's 'Song of Myself': The Artist's Imaginative Inheritance in *The Song of the Lark*," *Western American Literature*, 26 (1991): 21-38.

Rosowski, Susan J. "Willa Cather and the French Rural Tradition of Breton and Millet: *O Pioneers!, The Song of the Lark*, and *My Antonia*." In *The Rural Vision: France and America in the Nineteenth Century*." Hollister Sturges, ed. Omaha: Joslyn Museum, 1987. Pp. 53-61.

———. "Writing Against Silences." *Studies in the Novel*, 21:1 (1989): 60-77.

Schwind, Jean. "The Benda Illustrations to *My Antonia*: Cather's 'Silent' Supplement to Jim Burden's Narrative," *PMLA*, 100:1 (1985): 51-67.

668

Shively, Steven B. "'A Full, Perfect, and Sufficient Sacrifice': Eucharist Imagery in Cather's *The Song of the Lark.*" *Literature and Belief,* 14 (1994): 73-86.

Stouck, David, and Janet Giltrow. "Willa Cather and a Grammar for Things 'Not Named.'" *Style,* 26 (1992): 90-113.

Swift, John N. "Memory, Myth, and *The Professor's House.*" *Western American Literature,* 20:4 (1986): 301-314. (Associates Cather's trauma with that of Tom Outland and Professor St. Peter as resulting from human failure.)

Synnott, Kevin A. "Painting 'The Tricks That Shadows Play': Impressionism in *Lucy Gayheart.*" *Willa Cather Pioneer Memorial Newsletter,* 36:3 (1992): 37-39.

———. "'The Colour of an Adventure': Pictorial Dimensions in Cather's *Archbishop,*" *Willa Cather Pioneer Memorial Newsletter,* 31:3 (1987): 11-15.

Wasserman, Loretta. "The Music of Time: Henri Bergson and Willa Cather." *American Literature,* 57:2 (1985): 226–239.

Bibliographies and Reference Guides

"Annual Bibliography of Studies in Western American Literature," *Western American Literature,* Winter (February) issue.

Arnold, Marilyn. *Willa Cather: A Reference Guide.* Boston: Hall, 1986.

"Fiction: 1900 to the 1930s." In *American Literary Scholarship: An Annual.* Durham, North Carolina: Duke University Press, 1965 to present. (A review chapter presently prepared by Jo Ann Middleton.)

March, John. *A Reader's Companion to the Fiction of Willa Cather,* Marilyn Arnold, ed., with Debra Thornton. Westport, Connecticut: Greenwood, 1993.

Meyering, Sheryl. *A Reader's Guide to the Short Stories of Willa Cather.* New York: Hall, 1994.

"Works on Cather: A Bibliographical Essay," *Willa Cather Pioneer Memorial Newsletter,* Spring issue. (Since 1990 an annual essay prepared by Virgil Albertini.)

Arthur R. Huseboe

Recent Research on the Works of
Ole E. Rölvaag

Several recent studies of Ole Rölvaag's work continue to explore the theme of "what was lost" when the Norwegian immigrants came to settle in America. Ann Moseley finds, in doing so, that Rölvaag identifies with the theme of alienation so common in early twentieth-century American literature. She observes that throughout his novels Rölvaag typically uses room imagery to reinforce that theme: the Houglums in *Pure Gold* move in succession away from their traditional Norwegian home to a barn, to a henhouse, and finally to a freezing room in town, where they die miserably and where the wealth that they have hoarded is burned along with their filthy clothing. And in *Peder Victorious* and *Their Fathers' God* the rooms associated with Norwegian things are finally scorned, as when, in the latter novel, Peder's Irish wife Susie transforms Beret's Norwegian room into her own Catholic room, with a crucifix and a basin of holy water. In one of his last writings about Rölvaag, Einar Haugen discovered in the novelist's earliest novel, "Nils og Astri," begun in 1904 and completed in 1910 (but left in ms.), many of the themes that Rölvaag would develop in his published work. Among those themes are the failings of the American environment and the necessity of preserving the heritage of Norway. For these ideas the spokesman is Ole Haugen, the father of the hero of the novel, Nils Haugen. In the same year (1989), Priscilla Homola published her essay on Indian Hill in *Giants in the Earth*. In it she avers that by placing Indian Hill in the center of Per Hansa's kingdom, Rölvaag

670

demonstrates his suspicion that American attitudes toward Indian people have been responsible for a tragic exploitation of the land that once was theirs.

Two recent essays, by Joseph F. Green and Carol Fairbanks, continue the emphasis on Beret Holm as the most interesting of Rölvaag's characters. The mad woman episode in *Giants in the Earth* is for Green the catalytic event in Beret's growing disorientation. The departure of Kari and her husband Jakob from the Spring Creek settlement precipitates the most complex example of Beret's growing insanity. First she fears that Kari will disappear forever "that very night." Then, from the top of Indian Hill, Beret watches a dark cloud in the west become a gigantic, menacing monster that approaches so quickly that she can feel its cold breath. From that time forth Beret must "confront daily what the mad woman has left her: the horrible and very real power of evil on the plains."

For Carol Fairbanks, whose *Prairie Women* is a "re-visioning" of the pasts of women on the prairie, the long-dominant view of the female as the pathetic victim in the West needs the corrective of the image of the heroic woman, as found in James Fenimore Cooper's *The Prairie,* Joseph Kirkland's *Zury,* several of Hamlin Garland's works, and in Ole Rölvaag's *Giants in the Earth* and *Peder Victorious,* among the works of many male writers. On the basis of *Peder Victorious* alone, Fairbanks says, Beret deserves to be identified as a frontier hero — tireless in building the farm that her husband Per had wanted and in the truest sense of the word a pioneer. It is she who builds the first windmill in the township and who designs a model barn in spite of seemingly insurmountable difficulties and her own reservations. In acknowledging her ingenuity and courage, the men who roof the barn for her at last toast her as the greatest farmer of all of them in Spring Creek.

* * *

It is not the qualities of the stereotypical western hero that comprise Beret's true heroism, according to Harold Simonson, not ingenuity and tirelessness in building a western kingdom. Rather, in Beret Holm the novelist presents a character whose religious beliefs challenge those ideals of individual freedom and of the conquest and exploitation of the frontier that were Per Hansa's fondest dreams. For Simonson, Rölvaag's intense religious consciousness and strongly held faith are the keys to understanding Beret's tragic suffering throughout the trilogy *Giants in the Earth*, *Peder Victorious*, and *Their Fathers' God*. In 1939, Rölvaag's biographers Theodore Jorgenson and Nora O. Solum suggested that as a youth Rölvaag had been influenced by some of the works of the Danish theologian-philosopher Sören Kierkegaard and that as a professor at St. Olaf he had studied them. In 1941, Simonson points out, Rölvaag's boyhood friend John Heitmann recalled that while still in Norway, the two had read together Kierkegaard's *Either/Or*, the philosopher's book about the act of choice as the essence of what it means to be human. Per Hansa chooses greatly, argues Simonson, but his choice is the tragic one of the "natural man" who puts self above God. Simonson offers the example of Per's exchange with the minister who, late in the novel, arrives at Spring Creek and brings to Beret the first peace she has felt in her derangement. "What is a man to do?" Per groans, and he breaks out in bitter laughter when the minister replies, "He shall humble himself before the Lord his God...." What Per Hansa never learns, concludes Simonson, is to direct the will away from the self "and toward the ruling sovereignty of God" (36).

While Per Hansa chooses to rely on his physical strength and his powerful ego, his wife Beret is motivated by a transcendental faith that sustains her even while it places her in conflict with her husband and in the later novels in the trilogy with her son Peder. Far from being a mere psychological case, says Simonson, Beret is Rölvaag's spokesperson against the growing materialism among his people in America and their loss of language, culture, and religion. In *Peder Victorious* Beret undergoes struggles with guilt and spiritual uncertainty far greater than those she underwent in *Giants in the Earth*. In the story of Beret Holm, says Simonson, the three novels constitute a "testament of defeat" (72), even while they present the heroic struggle of the first-generation Norwegian immigrant to preserve her precious heritage of culture, language, and religious faith. Beret Holm, argues Simonson, represents Ole Rölvaag's most authentic voice and his greatest claim to genius.

In her struggle to preserve the religious faith and traditions of her native country, Beret commits a sin of pride that has dire consequences for her family. Kristoffer F. Paulson's essay on the tragedy of *Giants in the Earth* points out that Beret's insistence that Per Hansa risk his life in order to bring a minister to the dying Hans Olsa is the result of a mistaken notion about the forms and rituals of religion. While she believes that the ritual of communion performed by a pastor is necessary for salvation, Hans Olsa has in fact already received the sacrament and is at peace with his God. Beret's sin of pride in judging the state of his soul is thrice tragic, for it leads to Per Hansa's death and then to her own nearly overwhelming suffering from grief and guilt in *Peder Victorious* and *Their Fathers' God*.

Nor should Per Hansa be judged, says Paulson, as the unbeliever who is as far from salvation at the end of the novel as at the beginning. In his conversation with Hans Olsa near the close of the novel, he admits that there is "a Destiny that rules us all" and confesses that, "When all is said and done, it's my own fault from beginning to end" (415-416). More problematical is Paulson's suggestion that when Peder Victorious was being born, Per Hansa performed an ancient rite that saved Beret's life and soul. In her birth pangs, Beret cries out against the evil beings who are coming for her. Paulson identifies them as the *Jolerei* and *Oskorei* of Norse folklore, the gangs of demons in search of Christian souls, doing their evil most actively just before Christmas. Per Hansa shouts, "Satan —now you shall leave her alone!" (236) and he rushes from the room. Throughout Beret's suffering, Per marches around outside the house, symbolically creating the magic circle that prevents Satan's demons from entering. As if to confirm his act, Sorine tells him, "It's the greatest miracle I ever saw, Per Hansa, that you didn't lose your wife to-night..." (239).

Selected Bibliography

Primary Sources

Rölvaag, O. E. *Giants in the Earth*. New York: Harper & Brothers, 1928.
————. *Peder Victorious*. New York: Harper & Brothers, 1929.
————. *Pure Gold*. New York: Harper & Brothers, 1930.
————. *Their Fathers' God*. New York: Harper & Brothers, 1931.

Secondary Sources

Fairbanks, Carol. *Prairie Women: Images in American and Canadian Fiction*. New Haven: Yale University Press, 1986.
Farmer, Catherine D. "Beret as the Norse Mythological Goddess Freya/Gerthr." In *Women and Western American Literature*. Helen Winter Stauffer and Susan J. Rosowski, eds. Troy, New York: Whitston Publishing Company, 1982. Pp. 179-193.
Green, Joseph F. "The Function of the Mad Woman Episode in Rölvaag's *Giants in the Earth*." *Platte Valley Review*, 17 (Spring 1989): 48-52.

Haugen, Einar. "Rölvaag's Lost Novel." *Norwegian-American Studies*, 32 (1989): 209-219.

Homola, Priscilla. "The Indian Hill in Rölvaag's *Giants in the Earth*." *South Dakota Review*, 27 (Spring 1989): 55-61.

Moseley, Ann. *Ole E. Rölvaag*. Boise: Boise State University Western Writers Series, 1987.

Paulson, Kristoffer F. "Ole Rölvaag's *Giants in the Earth:* The Structure, The Myth, The Tragedy." *Norwegian-American Studies*, 34 (1995): 201-215.

Simonson, Harold. *Prairies Within: The Tragic Trilogy of Ole Rölvaag*. Seattle: University of Washington Press, 1987.

———. *Beyond the Frontier: Writers, Western Regionalism and a Sense of Place*. Fort Worth: Texas Christian University Press, 1989.

Barbara Rippey

Additions to the Neihardt and Sandoz Bibliographies

Recent literary criticism of John G. Neihardt's work has focused on his *Black Elk Speaks*. Exceptions are Helen Stauffer's "Two Authors and a Hero: Neihardt, Sandoz, and Crazy Horse" and several of the titles in *A Sender of Words*, a collection of commemorative essays about Neihardt and his work, edited by Vine Deloria, Jr. There is also a reprint of Neihardt's *Indian Tales and Others*.

Some critical works addressing *Black Elk Speaks* explore the "renewal" aspect of the book. William Nichols in his essay "Black Elk's Truth" believes that Black Elk's Harney Peak experience demonstrates the holy man's abiding hope that the power of his vision finally can help reverse the fate of the Lakota through Neihardt's spreading of that vision to a larger world. This theme of regeneration also appears in Paul A. Olson's "*Black Elk Speaks* as Epic and Ritual Attempt to Reverse History." Olson demonstrates how *Black Elk Speaks* reveals in epic form what a hero and a people need to believe in and act on in order to reintegrate a society. Other critics explore Neihardt's sincerity and success as a faithful interpreter. In *The Sixth Grandfather: Black Elk's Teaching Given to John G. Neihardt*, the editing of the complete transcripts of Neihardt's interviews in 1931 and 1944, Raymond J. DeMallie emphasizes that *Black Elk Speaks* is a literary work, not the work of an editor. DeMallie believes that the work has been used in ways unintended by either Black Elk or Neihardt. In *Black Elk's Story: Distinguishing Its Lakota Purpose*, Julian Rice argues that DeMallie's work shows the significant changes in meaning that were the result of Neihardt's "poeticizing." Rice is concerned about the loss of the oral techniques in the translation, oral conventions that indicate the genre and tone of the telling. In "(Re)Collecting the Past: Writing Native American Speech" Michael E. Staub questions the difference between what Black Elk spoke and Neihardt wrote, especially in terms of the eternal and transforming power of ritual, asking if Neihardt has fully credited the ongoing nature of Black Elk's "revivalistic efforts." William K. Powers, in "When Black Elk Speaks, Everybody Listens," questions some of the critical works, fearing that those presenting a view of Lakota religion that is more imagination than reality may lead to Lakota belief becoming only a part of other religions and philosophies.

Still other critics worry over Neihardt's exclusion of the bulk of Black Elk's Christian activities. Michael F. Steltenkamp's *Black Elk: Holy Man of the Oglala*, a biography of Black Elk, is based on interviews with Black Elk's daughter and others who knew him. In the years before and after the Neihardt interviews, Black Elk met the challenges of a changing world successfully, Steltenkamp argues, rather than ending in defeat as the Neihardt book suggests. Steltenkamp believes that Black Elk productively combined traditional Lakota and Christian themes and practices in a life of service.

A companion piece to *Black Elk Speaks* is *Black Elk and Flaming Rainbow: Personal Memories of the Lakota Holy Man and John Neihardt*, a memoir by Neihardt's daughter, Hilda. She was present at both Neihardt interviews with Black Elk and sees Black Elk's Lakota beliefs as his premier faith. It will be interesting to see if in the future the articles and books about John Neihardt's works remain centered around *Black Elk Speaks*, if any of the controversies over integrity of translation and interpretation and questions of faith are resolved or abandoned, and if the rest of Neihardt's creative work receives the added attention it deserves. Vine Deloria, Jr., has expressed concern that the popularity of *Black Elk Speaks* and *When the Tree Flowered* has overshadowed Neihardt's own "cosmic faith," particularly as expressed in *The Song of Jed Smith* from Neihardt's epic *The Cycle of the West*.

Selected Bibliography

Primary Sources

Neihardt, John G. *Indian Tales and Others*. Lincoln: University of Nebraska Press, 1988.

Neihardt, Hilda. *Black Elk and Flaming Rainbow: Personal Memories of the Lakota Holy Man and John Neihardt.* Lincoln: University of Nebraska Press, 1995.

Criticism

Black Elk. *The Sixth Grandfather: Black Elk's Teachings Given to John G. Neihardt.* Raymond J. DeMallie, ed. Lincoln: University of Nebraska Press, 1984.

Nichols, William. "Black Elk's Truth." In *Smoothing the Ground: Essays on Native American Oral Literature.* Brian Swann, ed. Berkeley: University of California Press, 1983. Pp. 334-343.

Olson, Paul. *"Black Elk Speaks* as Epic and Ritual Attempt to Reverse History." In *Vision and Refuge: Essays on the Literature of the Great Plains.* Virginia Faulkner and Frederick Luebke, eds. Lincoln: University of Nebraska Press, 1982. Pp. 3-27.

Powers, William K. "When Black Elk Speaks, Everybody Listens." In *Religion in Native North America.* Christopher Vecsey. ed. Moscow: University of Idaho Press, 1990. Pp. 136-151.

Rice, Julian. *Black Elk's Story: Distinguishing Its Lakota Purpose.* Albuquerque: University of New Mexico Press, 1991.

Richards, John Thomas. *Rawhide Laureate: John G. Neihardt: A Selected, Annotated Bibliography.* Metuchen, New Jersey: Scarecrow, 1983.

A Sender of Words: Essays in Memory of John G. Neihardt. Vine Deloria, Jr., ed. Salt Lake City: Howe, 1984.

Steltenkamp, Michael F. *Black Elk: Holy Man of the Oglala.* Norman: University of Oklahoma Press, 1993.

Staub, Michael E. "(Re)Collecting the Past: Writing Native American Speech." *American Quarterly,* 43:3 (September 1991): 425-456.

Stauffer, Helen. "Two Authors and a Hero: Neihardt, Sandoz, and Crazy Horse." *Great Plains Quarterly,* 1:1 (Winter 1981): 54-66.

The Sandoz Bibliography

The most important addition to the Mari Sandoz bibliography is the volume of Sandoz letters that covers forty years of her researching, writing, and publishing, edited by Helen W. Stauffer. It is augmented by the publication of a group of Sandoz' letters edited with notes by Caroline Sandoz Pifer, Mari's youngest sister. Pifer also has authored *A Kinkaider's Child,* her memories of Mari and other family members, and *Son of Old Jules: Memoirs of Jules Sandoz, Junior,* with co-author/brother, Jules Sandoz, Jr. Pifer's books add family perspectives to Mari Sandoz' biographical material that only "supplement, not contradict" Mari's biography of her father.

Also biographical is *Mari Sandoz: A Wild Flower* by Evelyn B. Hisel, a sandhills teacher for twenty-eight years. Sandoz did not begin her schooling until she was nine, and she cherished the opportunity to learn. Now schoolchildren can read incidents from Mari's childhood and selected Sandoz' short stories.

The critical material on Sandoz' work reflects the interdisciplinary

677

nature of her writing. In *Articulating Protest: The Personal and Political Rhetorics of Clifford Odets and Mari Sandoz in the 1930s*, H. Richard Nielsen, Jr., is interested in Mari Sandoz' polemical and political stance. Michael R. Hill studies Sandoz as sociologist in "Mari Sandoz' Sociological Imagination: *Capital City* as an Ideal Type."

In "Battered Pioneers: Jules Sandoz and the Physical Abuse of Wives on the American Frontier," Betsy Downey takes a historical (and sociological) view of abuse of women on the frontier as typified in Mari Sandoz' *Old Jules*. Melody Graulich finds Sandoz' contrasts between pioneer heroism and pioneer brutality fertile ground for feminist exploration of abuse of women. In "Every Husband's Right: Sex Roles in Mari Sandoz' *Old Jules*," Graulich identifies Sandoz as one of the few western writers to explore relationships between husbands and wives on the frontier. Barbara Rippey is interested in Sandoz as novelist, historian, and social activist and argues that Sandoz in many ways saw and wrote about the Old West in New West terms.

Other critical studies reflect Sandoz' interest in writing about Native Americans. These include Diane Drake's *The Sacred Hoop: The Hero and Community in Selected Works of Mari Sandoz* and two essays by Helen Stauffer. Drake uses the Lakota view of the sacred hoop of life as metaphor for Sandoz' belief in the power of the hoop of community both in immigrant and Indian life. This is one of the few critical works to search for a link between Sandoz' championing of Native Americans and her identification with the immigrants who replaced them on the land. Stauffer is interested in Sandoz' combination of fictional and reportorial voice in "Narrative Voice in Sandoz' *Crazy Horse*." In "Two Massacres on the Sappa River" she traces Sandoz' research and efforts to link the 1875 killing of Cheyenne holy man Medicine Arrow at Sappa Creek to the subsequent reprisal by the Cheyenne in 1878 as they flee north from Oklahoma territory.

The coming years should bring more biographical work, aided by new material that continues to be left to the Mari Sandoz High Plains Heritage Society and other collections. There will be more written about Sandoz' love of fiction and history and her insistence on combining the two. There surely will be more exploration of her attachment to the land, to the common people and their needs, and to the Native Americans for whom she struggled to be a voice when their voices were largely ignored or silenced.

Selected Bibliography

Primary Sources

Gordon Journal Letters of Mari Sandoz, Part 1 and Part 2. Caroline Sandoz Pifer, ed. Crawford, Nebraska: Cottonwood Press, 1991-1992. Previously published letters (in *Gordon Journal*) with comments by Sandoz' sister, Caroline.

Letters of Mari Sandoz. Helen Winter Stauffer, ed. Lincoln: University of Nebraska Press, 1992. Selections from 1928 to 1966.

Biography and Criticism

DeMarr, Mary Jean. "A Historian's Fiction: Uses of Stereotype in Mari Sandoz' *Son of the Gamblin' Man.*" *Midwestern Miscellany,* 21 (1993): 29-43.

Downey, Betsy. "Battered Pioneers: Jules Sandoz and the Physical Abuse of Wives on the American Frontier." *Great Plains Quarterly,* 12 (Winter 1992): 31-49.

Drake, Diane M. "The Sacred Hoop: the Hero and Community in Selected Works of Mari Sandoz." Unpublished dissertation, University of North Dakota, 1992; Ann Arbor, Michigan: University Microfilms Interation, 1993. DA9320038.

Graulich, Melody. "Every Husband's Right: Sex Roles in Mari Sandoz' *Old Jules.*" *Western American Literature,* 18:1 (Spring 1983): 3-20.

Hisel, Evelyn B. *Mari Sandoz: A Wild Flower.* Asby, Nebraska: Hisel Book Ends, 1993. Classroom Activity Book included.

Nielsen, H. Richard. "Articulating Protest: The Personal and Political Rhetorics of Clifford Odets and Mari Sandoz in the 1930s." Unpublished disseration, University of Nebraska, 1991. Ann Arbor, Michigan: University Microfilms International, 1991. DA9129566.

Oehlschlaeger, Fritz. "Passion and Denial in Mari Sandoz' 'Peachstone Basket.'" *Great Plains Quarterly,* 2:2 (Spring 1982): 106-113.

Papers From the Conference on Mari Sandoz. Vern Plambeck, ed. *Platte Valley Review,* 17:1 (Winter 1989).

Pifer, Caroline Sandoz. *A Kinkaider's Child.* Gordon, Nebraska: Ad Pad, 1995. A series of essays by Sandoz' sister about Sandoz family life from Caroline's point of view.

———. *Making of an Author: Mari Sandoz (Book III) 1931-1932.* Crawford, Nebraska: Cottonwood Press, 1984. By Sandoz' sister, this volume continues a series of the author's letters and Caroline's family recollections.

——— and Jules Sandoz, Jr. *Son of Old Jules: Memoirs of Jules Sandoz, Junior.* Crawford, Nebraska: Cottonwood Press, 1987. By Sandoz' sister and brother, these memoirs add to the Sandoz family story.

Rippey, Barbara Wright. "Mari Sandoz: Novelist as Historian." Unpublished dissertation, University of Nebraska, 1989. Ann Arbor, Michigan: University Microfilms International, 1990. 50:92900A

———. "The Social Activism of Mari Sandoz," *The Nebraska Humanist,* 2 (1989): 1-9.

Stauffer, Helen W. *Mari Sandoz.* Boise: Boise State University Western Writers Series, 1984.

———. "Narrative Voice in Sandoz' *Crazy Horse.*" *Western American Literature,* 18:3 (Fall 1983): 223-237.

———. "Two Massacres on the Sappa River: Cause and Effect in Mari Sandoz' *Cheyenne Autumn.*" *Platte Valley Review,* 19:1 (Winter 1991): 25-43.

Robert Fleming

Sinclair Lewis

orn west of the Mississippi in Sauk Centre, Minnesota, Harry Sinclair Lewis has been hard to classify regionally. Is he a midwestern writer, a western writer, or — as the first American to win the Nobel Prize for Literature — a national treasure? Even at the time of his greatest fame, when he won the prize in 1930, neither his home state nor his own nation was quite sure it wished to claim Lewis. Many felt that he had pandered to Europe's anti-American prejudices with his scathing satires of American foibles. When Mark Schorer published a savagely negative critical biography in 1961, the Lewis' reputation suffered another serious blow.

For a time it appeared that Lewis would be dropped from the American canon. In the late 1970s, the section on Lewis in the *MLA International Bibliography* contained few entries. For example, the 1979 *Bibliography* listed only two items on him. During the 1980s, however, Lewis' reputation began to rebound.

Perhaps the best index of Lewis' recovering reputation was the inclusion in 1991 of *Main Street* and *Babbitt* in a new volume of the Library of America series. Based on reprintings that incorporated Lewis' corrections of the first editions of each novel, this edition offered new readers a chance to see what all the excitement was about in 1920 and 1922 when Lewis first achieved status as a major author. Recently, Harcourt Brace has issued *Main Street*, *Babbitt*, and *Arrowsmith* in "HBJ Modern Classics" editions, for which the novels have been reset.

These new hardbound editions are in addition to a series of Signet editions—*Main Street*, *Babbitt*, *Arrowsmith*, *Elmer Gantry*, and *Dodsworth*, all with afterwords by Mark Schorer—that had kept Lewis in print through the years when he was little read. *It Can't Happen Here* was kept in print by Signet and Dell. Recently, Signet is redoing the series, with critical commentary by a new generation of scholars, and Penguin has brought out a new edition of *Main Street*.

Although Lewis was best known as a novelist, for years he supported himself as a short story writer, and some of the stories merit re-examination. *Selected Short Stories* appeared in 1990. Neglected novels have also been brought back into print. The University of Nebraska Press has reissued *Free Air* (1919), *The Job* (1917), and Lewis' novel on feminism, *Ann Vickers* (1933). The dramatic version of *It Can't Happen Here*, widely staged in the 1930s, played in San Francisco in 1992.

As Lewis' writings have returned to print, critical attention has again focused on his work. In 1985 the Lewis centenary at St. Cloud State University and Sauk Centre gathered scholars from the United States and abroad to read papers and visit Lewis' boyhood haunts. In 1992, a group of scholars at the annual convention of the American Literature Association founded the Sinclair Lewis Society. That group publishes a twice-yearly newsletter that has grown from six to fourteen pages.

Several noteworthy books about Lewis have been published since 1980. The St. Cloud meeting resulted in a proceedings volume, *Sinclair Lewis at 100* (1985). The same year saw the publication of a special Lewis issue of *Modern Fiction Studies*, and the next year Martin Bucco's *Critical Essays on Sinclair Lewis* appeared. In 1993 Bucco and Glen A. Love published volumes on Lewis in Twayne's Masterwork Series.

Bucco's *Main Street: The Revolt of Carol Kennicott* (1993) sketches the historical background of the period in which the novel takes place (1912-1918) and contrasts it with the twenties. Bucco also sets the novel in its appropriate place in American literature and discusses its critical reception, from the 1920s through 1990. Seven chapters make up a reading of *Main Street*, based on the major episodes that are loosely combined into the plot.

Love's *Babbitt: An American Life* (1993) follows a similar format. While *Main Street* bridged the gap between the turn of the century and the roaring twenties, *Babbitt* is an early novel of the jazz age, and Love's first chapter sums up what that age meant, from George Babbitt's acceptance of materialistic standards to his uneasy circumvention of the

Volstead Act and his condemnation of flapper culture. Love considers Babbitt's role as an archetypal figure who would add a word to the language and traces the critical reception of the book before launching into a reading of the novel. His approach recognizes Mark Schorer's assertion that the novelist abandoned his original plan for a structured novel and settled for the presentation of a series of set pieces. Rather than attempt to impose order on the book by dividing it into movements, Love examines it as realism, as satire, and even as romance, a form Lewis had used in his early novels before *Main Street* marked a turn to more biting satire. Love concludes with two chapters that establish George Babbitt as a marginal man, caught between longing for an old romantic way of life and moving forward to embrace the new American technology. Love sees Lewis as a similarly marginal figure, torn between his roles as satirist and "earnest idealist."

John J. Koblas' biography *Sinclair Lewis: Home at Last* (1981) emphasizes the author's midwestern roots and Lewis' residence and visits in Sauk Centre, St. Cloud, Minneapolis-St. Paul, Mankato, and Duluth. Edited by John Koblas and Dave Page, three little books from Main Street Press make available a journal by Lewis' brother Claude, a series of previously unpublished letters, and the diary of Claude Lewis concerning Lewis' final days in Europe. *Sinclair Lewis & Mantrap: The Saskatchewan Trip* (1985) by Claude Lewis is an account of Lewis' 1924 trip with his brother that furnished material for Lewis' Canadian "western," *Mantrap. Selected Letters of Sinclair Lewis* (1985) collects letters from Lewis, mainly to family members. *Sinclair Lewis: Final Voyage* (1985) by Claude Lewis offers new insights into Lewis' last days.

As a regional writer, Lewis inhabits a literary no-man's-land. Some of his works strongly suggest that he should be considered a western writer. For example, in *The Trail of the Hawk* (1915), young Carl Ericson has his first dreams of greatness in Joralemon, Minnesota, although he goes on to experience life in the greater world, and *Free Air* (1919) traverses the West from Minnesota to Seattle. When Carol Kennicott arrives in Gopher Prairie, one of the few features of the town that she appreciates is the residual population of authentic pioneers who settled the townsite. *The God-Seeker* (1949) examines those early years of the state when Minnesota was readily identified as part of the West. Hayden Chart, of *World So Wide* (1951), begins his journey to Europe from Newlife, Colorado, where he has been a pioneering architect. And, of course, *Mantrap* (1926) burlesques the conventions of the popular western.

On the other hand, after the publication of *Main Street* aroused the resentment of Sauk Centre, Lewis went out of his way to create a fictional state, Winnemac, whose most famous city is Zenith. Winnemac is located solidly in the Midwest, bounded on the north by Michigan, on the east by Ohio, on the south by Indiana, and on the west by Illinois. Zenith is the locale not only of *Babbitt* but also of important episodes of *Arrowsmith*, *Elmer Gantry*, and *Dodsworth*. George Babbitt and Martin Arrowsmith are graduates of the state university, and Elmer Gantry has his first church in Banjo Crossing. Although Sam Dodsworth is aristocratic enough to leave the state to attend Yale, he returns to Zenith to work in the automobile industry and to found his own auto company.

Probably Lewis would have identified himself chiefly as a midwesterner. He saw the Midwest as the heartland, combining some of the best features of the "civilized" East with the independence, informality, and brashness of the West. One of his later characters, Cass Timberlane, lives in Grand Republic, Minnesota, a city whose name accurately suggests that Lewis saw his home region as embodying the spirit of America—both its heroic potential and its tragic flaws.

But the recent revival of Lewis' critical reputation suggests that he should not be pigeonholed as a mere regional writer. Like many authors whose work is solidly grounded in the realities of their own regions, Lewis speaks to and for humanity in general. His definition and criticism of the American character as it existed in his time are still valid—as a new generation of readers is now discovering.

Selected Bibliography

Primary Sources

Ann Vickers. Introduction by Nan Bauer Maglin. Lincoln: University of Nebraska Press, 1994.

Dodsworth. Introduction by Michael Meyer. New York: Signet, 1995.

Free Air. Introduction by Robert E. Fleming. Lincoln: University of Nebraska Press, 1993.

It Can't Happen Here. Introduction by Perry Meisel. New York: Signet, 1993.

The Job. Introduction by Maureen Honey. Lincoln: University of Nebraska Press, 1994.

Main Street. Introduction by Martin Bucco. New York: Penguin, 1995.

Main Street & Babbitt. New York: The Library of America, 1992.

Selected Short Stories of Sinclair Lewis. Introduction by James W. Tuttleton. Chicago: Elephant Paperbacks, 1990.

Secondary Sources

Bucco, Martin, ed. *Critical Essays on Sinclair Lewis*. Boston: G. K. Hall, 1986.

———. *Main Street: The Revolt of Carol Kennicott*. New York: Twayne, 1993.

Connaughton, Michael. *Sinclair Lewis at 100: Papers Presented at a Centennial Conference*. St. Cloud, Minnesota: St. Cloud State University, 1985.

Hutchisson, James M. *The Rise of Sinclair Lewis: 1920-1930*. University Park: Pennsylvania State University Press, 1996.

Koblas, John J. *Sinclair Lewis: Home at Last*. Bloomington, Minnesota: Voyageur Press, 1981.

Koblas, John J. and Dave Page, eds. *Selected Letters of Sinclair Lewis*. Madison, Wisconsin: Main Street Press, 1985.

Lewis, Claude. *Sinclair Lewis & Mantrap: The Saskatchewan Trip*. John J. Koblas and Dave Page, eds. Madison, Wisconsin: Main Street Press, 1985.

———. *Sinclair Lewis: Final Voyage*. John J. Koblas and Dave Page, eds. Madison, Wisconsin: Main Street Press, 1985.

Love, Glen A. *Babbitt: An American Life*. New York: Twayne, 1993.

Joseph J. Wydeven

Wright Morris: Update

W hen Wright Morris retired from writing in the early 1990s, he ended an exemplary career as an American novelist and photographer spanning fifty years and over thirty books of fiction, photography, and criticism. That his work has hardly yet been accorded its due has become a critical commonplace, echoed through the decades by puzzled admirers. It is one of the great ironies of Morris' career that there remain devotees of his fiction who do not know his reputation as a photographer, and on the other hand, appreciators of his photography who are unaware of him as a novelist.

A review of Morris' creative activities since 1980 suggests how carefully he orchestrated his long and productive withdrawal from active life. After publishing his final novel, in 1980, he spent the remainder of the decade tidying up his career, composing his memoirs, writing short stories, and compiling retrospective collections of his photographs and critical essays on photography. The decade opened for Morris with the publication of *Plains Song*, an appropriate novel to conclude his career as a novelist, for it returned him to his Nebraska roots and once again allowed him to explore the Nebraska settings that nurtured his creative ambiguities. Perhaps Morris' most memorable work is that in which he can be seen creating an identity for himself by coming to terms with a past he had never known he had, a characteristic that gives some of his works a strange, haunted quality. This theme can be seen addressed more or less directly in *The Man Who Was There* (1945), *The Home Place*

685

(1948), *The World in the Attic* (1949), and *The Works of Love* (1952); and with mature aesthetic distance in *The Field of Vision* (1956) and *Ceremony in Lone Tree* (1960).

Having in his critical study *The Territory Ahead* (1957) set himself into (or perhaps more appropriately, *against*) the context of American literature, it seems that Morris felt it necessary to break free of any label that would limit him to *regional* importance. For fully twenty years after *Ceremony in Lone Tree*, perhaps because he felt he had completed the synthesis he needed, Morris turned away from his Nebraska origins. Thus *Cause for Wonder* (1962) and *What a Way to Go* (1963) are set in Europe, *One Day* (1965) in California, *In Orbit* (1967) in Indiana. *Fire Sermon* (1971), *A Life* (1973), and *The Fork River Space Project* (1977) are set once again in the American West, but these books are less regional than focused on other concerns, such as the changes in perspective and perception experienced in old age. Likewise, his acerbic critical essays in *A Bill of Rights, a Bill of Wrongs, a Bill of Goods* (1968) address failures in the *whole* of American culture.

In reality Morris was never far removed from his Nebraska origins, and the Plains always influenced his vision of life. Thus it seems right that for his final novel, *Plains Song for Female Voices*, he should circle back upon himself to confront Nebraska and the past in an apparent farewell to his craft. Focused once again on the inhabitants of the Nebraska "home place," Morris dealt this time with the distaff side of the pioneer American experience, with Aunt Clara (here called Cora) rather than Uncle Harry. The novel deserves its American Book Award, for it raises interesting questions, not least involving its incorporation of Morris' famous photograph "Front Room Reflected in Mirror" into the novel's framework.

After *Plains Song*, his vision refocused on the Nebraska past, Morris turned to memoir, in *Will's Boy* returning to material he had handled in a wholly different way in *The Works of Love*. Whereas in that novel Morris had dealt with Will Brady, a protagonist based on his father, in *Will's Boy* he dealt with his father's son, telling his own story, this time without the protective coloration of fiction. Perhaps to reduce his autobiographical anxieties, in his introduction to the reader Morris acknowledged that the past "resists both fixing and enlargement" (the photographic metaphor is entirely characteristic). But Morris well understood the problems of memory in the autobiographical enterprise: resistance to memory was part of his fictional repertoire almost from the beginning.

Because he understood memory as fallible, he insisted that the remembered life is a merely logical fabrication; his articulation of these views predated the renewed discovery by recent theorists that autobiography is often a fictional medium.

After the richly imagined *Will's Boy*, Morris wrote two more autobiographical accounts. In *Solo: An American Dreamer in Europe: 1933-1934*, he dealt once again with the recalcitrant material from his *wanderjahr* in Europe, especially the enchantments of the castle Schloss Ranna in Austria that he had fictionalized in *Cause for Wonder* and incorporated briefly into other works. The final installment of his autobiography, *A Cloak of Light: Writing My Life*, is more conventional in scope, dutifully providing the facts, times, events, and personae from the beginning of his writing career to the publication of *Ceremony in Lone Tree* in 1960 and his second marriage, to Jo Kantor.

While composing his memoirs, Morris turned renewed attention to a form in which he had previously shown scant interest, that of the short story, culminating in *Collected Stories: 1948-1986*. Fully eleven of the twenty-six works in this volume were first published in the 1980s, suggesting that as Morris saw his powers as a novelist diminished, he turned with deliberation to the short story. Central to some of these stories is the subject of aging; although Morris had often written of the lives of the elderly before, these stories benefit from personal experience, Morris' own aging process: "The Customs of the Country," "Victrola," "Glimpse into Another Country," "Fellow Creatures," and "The Origin of Sadness" (the last of which may be an act of homage to his friend Loren Eiseley). "Victrola" and "Glimpse into another Country" were included in both *Best American Short Story* and *O. Henry Prize Stories* annuals, and "Fellow Creatures" was selected for the 1985 *Best* collection and later for *The Best American Short Stories of the Eighties*.

But there is that whole other side to Morris which he addressed in the 1980s — with considerable energy and enthusiasm: his short career as a photographer in the late 1930s and '40s. The continued importance of his photography is attested to by two major shows of national prominence, the first at the Corcoran Gallery in Washington, D.C., in 1983, the second, perhaps the most significant Morris event in the early 1990s, a retrospective at the San Francisco Museum of Modern Art in 1992 (moving on to Yale and, with audio added, to the Boston Museum of Fine Arts) — an event Morris privately hailed as his "last hurrah." The exhibition catalog, *Wright Morris: Origin of a Species*, included over sixty of his photographs and fine essays by John Szarkowski and Sandra Phillips.

The best reproductions of Morris' photographs (laser-scanned by the Friends of Photography) are found in *Photographs & Words*, in which Morris recounts his adventures with photography, particularly his photo-text experimentation, his "photo safari" across the United States in 1940, and his return to Nebraska in 1947 to take the *Home Place* photographs. The editor of that volume, Jim Alinder, had curated the Morris *Structures and Artifacts* photo show at the University of Nebraska in 1975 and collaborated with Morris on *Picture America*, for which Morris wrote the words accompanying Alinder's photographs.

Perhaps the most important book Morris produced in the decade is his collection of essays on photography, *Time Pieces: Photographs, Writing, and Memory*, a book of much theoretical importance. It includes all the important essays Morris wrote on photography and "photographic" perception, starting as early as 1951 — including some that have little to do with photography itself but that have bearing on the epistemology Morris derived from his camera work in the 1940s. Especially important are essays from the 1970s and '80s — "In Our Image," "Photographs, Images, and Words," and "The Camera Eye" — in which he explored the impact of photographic images on modern American social consciousness.

The Paris Review finally got around to an interview with Morris in its fall 1991 issue. The belatedness of the tribute is balanced somewhat by the interviewers' recognition of the importance of Morris' dual careers, by the perceptive quality of the questions, and by the wide range of material Morris covered in his answers; the interview is accompanied by a small portfolio of Morris' photo-texts. Since 1993 Black Sparrow Press has reprinted some of Morris' work, collecting the three memoirs into one volume (*Writing My Life: An Autobiography*); combining *Man and Boy* and *In Orbit* as *Two for the Road*; *The Fork River Space Project*, *Fire Sermon*, and *A Life* as *Three Easy Pieces*; and *The Works of Love* and *The Huge Season* as *The Loneliness of the Long Distance Writer*.

G. B. Crump's perception in the first edition of *A Literary History of the American West* (777-791) that "the central focus of [Morris'] best prose is often on nuances of consciousness almost too elusive, too fine, to put into words" (781) is accurate, largely because his most complex work is richly pictorial, his aesthetic often Jamesian in character. As Morris' narratives frequently have the quality of carefully described still lifes, readers must grapple with subtly suggestive images saturated with conceptual meaning. Perhaps one crucial key to an appropriate assessment of Morris, then, is the question of the significance of the relationship between his fiction and his photographs in picturing reality and suggesting meaning.

The criticism of Morris since 1985 may be divided into three large categories in terms of its primary focus on the fiction, the photography, or the photo-texts. There are, first of all, the literary textual studies, most of which are devoted to the Nebraska works (especially *Plains Song*), although Carl Bredahl has focused appreciatively on *In Orbit*. Almost no attention is being paid to Morris' non-Nebraska works, though much remains to be said, especially about such works as *Man and Boy* (1951) and *The Deep Sleep* (1953) — novels that probe the postwar American family and relations between the sexes — and about those vitalistic novels, like *Love among the Cannibals* (1957), that have epistemological interest. About Morris' short stories little has been written, and despite Jack Cohn's careful 1970 dissertation, the massive store of Morris materials at Berkeley is virtually unexplored.

The second category of Morris criticism includes appreciations and studies primarily of Morris' photography, produced mostly by photographers or critics of photography. Mary Price's short study of three photographs is particularly welcome. Frank Gohlke suggests that Morris' photographs provide, in contrast to his fiction, "another kind of voice, equal in weight but different in volume and register, with which to articulate what lies beyond the reach of words" (Gohlke 10); in doing so, he suggests the argument for the third category.

Although some critics suggest that Morris' fiction and photographs should — or *must* — be studied in tandem, the temptation, despite good intentions, to seek the safety of one's own discipline is often overwhelming. The third critical category, then, and one that has received much attention, includes those works that deal with the borderland between fiction and photography, seeking to comprehend what might be termed Morris' "postmodern" aesthetic, his "photographic" epistemology. In most cases the critics follow Morris' lead in explaining the rationale for his early photo-texts, that there is a "third view" to be discovered by proper assimilation of photo *and* text in Morris' photo-texts. Perhaps the best of these are by Colin Westerbeck (though his emphasis falls once again on the photography) and Sandra Phillips, who briefly discusses a "passageway" aesthetic that explains both Morris' habit of shooting photographs *through* passageways and structures and his focus on distanced relationships in his fiction. The problematic association between fictional narrative and factual photographs in *The Home Place* makes it something of a challenge for many critics; Peter Halter's work on that book is particularly remarkable for its warmth and lucidity.

To these works we might add that criticism—often understandably unappreciated by Morris himself—which attempts to understand portions of Morris' work by reference to his childhood experience as "half an orphan" (as Morris himself put it in *Will's Boy* [35]). This line of questioning is hazardous and requires emphasis on understanding the work rather than probing the psychology of the author, but the evidence for its utility is found everywhere in Morris' work. Roy Bird, for example, has written of the tenuous relationships Morris' male characters have with women; Wydeven has isolated a ritual pattern in Morris' work, especially in the odd *War Games*, linked to Morris' relationship to the mother he never knew; and G. B. Crump has suggested that Morris developed strategies of literary distancing to cope with a dead mother and an often absent father. The eventual biographer of Morris will surely be interested in the interview with Ruthe Stein, in which Stein reported that after giving up writing, Morris spent much of his time thinking about the loss of his mother—the mother who died within a week of his birth.

As stated earlier, Morris' work remains undervalued and too rarely studied in depth. Since G. B. Crump's assessment of Morris in 1987, a significant amount of criticism has been generated on Morris, but much of it appears to be written by appreciative commentators who, fresh from their own discoveries, seem unaware of prior criticism. Often there is enthusiastic criticism written without benefit of thorough knowledge of Morris' work. There are ideas, themes, images, and relationships in Morris' work that have not yet been explored, perhaps because the discovery of patterns in a writer's work requires immersion in it. To this extent, Morris' very prolific output and his proficiency in two major media are problematic. What would be useful is a *body* of Morris criticism in which critical dialogue is exchanged. Good criticism of his work may require the kind of interdisciplinary dexterity linking literature and visual art that has produced such superb criticism of writers such as Melville, James, Wharton, and Cather. These remarks, of course, are predicated on the assumption that Morris' work will be judged worthy of such close and concentrated critical attention in the future. One suspects, however, that the sheer range of Morris' work, his commentaries on the American Dream, and his stylistic subtlety and complexity will be more attractive to readers and critics as we look back from the perspective of a new century.

Selected Bibliography

Interviews

Stein, Ruthe. "A Freeze-Frame on Eras Past: Writer-photographer's images of loss, upheaval." *San Francisco Chronicle*, September 3, 1992 ("People" Section): B3-4.

"Wright Morris: The Art of Fiction CXXV." With Olga Carlisle and Jodie Ireland. *Paris Review*, 33 (Fall 1991): 52-94.

Literary Criticism on Morris' Work

Bird, Roy K. *Wright Morris: Memory and Imagination*. New York: Peter Lang, 1985.

Bredahl, A. Carl. "The Outsider as Sexual Center: Wright Morris and the Integrated Imagination." *Studies in the Novel*, 18 (Spring 1986): 66-73.

Crump, G. B. "Wright Morris." In *A Literary History of the American West*. Thomas Lyon et al., eds. Fort Worth: Texas Christian University Press, 1987. Pp. 777-791.

———. "Wright Morris: Author in Hiding." *Western American Literature*, 25 (May 1990): 3-14.

Dyck, Reginald. "Revisiting and Revising the West: Willa Cather's *My Antonia* and Wright Morris' *Plains Song*." *Modern Fiction Studies*, 36 (Spring 1990): 25-37.

Hall, Joe. "Three Consciousnesses in Wright Morris' *Plains Song*." *Western American Literature*, 31 (Winter 1997): 291-318.

——— "Wright Morris' *The Field of Vision*: A Re-reading of the Scanlon Story." *Journal of American Culture*, 14 (Summer 1991): 53-57.

Lewis, Linda M. "*Plains Song*: Wright Morris' New Melody for Audacious Female Voices." *Great Plains Quarterly*, 8 (Winter 1988): 29-37.

Madden, David. "The American Land, Character, and Dream in the Novels of Wright Morris." In *American Writing Today*. Richard Kostelanetz, ed. Troy, New York: Whitston, 1991. Pp. 124-136.

Quantic, Diane Dufva. "Ceremonies in Lone Tree: Wright Morris Re-examines the West." *Nebraska Humanist*, 11 (1989): 57-66.

———. *The Nature of the Place: A Study of Great Plains Fiction*. Lincoln: University of Nebraska Press, 1995.

———. "The Unifying Thread: Connecting Place and Language in Great Plains Literature." *American Studies*, 32 (Spring 1991): 67-83.

Uffen, Ellen Serlen. "Wright Morris' Earthly Music: The Women of *Plains Song*." *MidAmerica*, 12 (1985): 97-110.

Wydeven, Joseph J. "Dualism and Doubling in Wright Morris' *War Games*." *Centennial Review*, 37 (1993): 415-428.

———. "Myth and Melancholy: Wright Morris' Stories of Old Age." *Weber Studies*, 12 (Winter 1995): 36-47. Primarily on "Glimpse into Another Country."

———. "'Turned on the Same Lathe': Wright Morris' Loren Eiseley." *South Dakota Review*, 33 (Spring 1995): 66-83.

Morris' Photography: Criticism and Commentary

Gohlke, Frank. "Bare Facts: The Photography of Wright Morris." *Hungry Mind Review,* (Fall 1986): 10-11.

Jacobson, Joanne. "Time and Vision in Wright Morris' Photographs of Nebraska." *Great Plains Quarterly,* 7 (Winter 1986): 3-21.

Nixon, Bruce. "The Rhythm of Time: Wright Morris at the San Francisco Museum of Modern Art." *Artweek,* October 22, 1992: 20-21.

Price, Mary. "Wright Morris: Three Photographs." *Raritan,* 14:2 (1994): 19-28.

Szarkowski, John. "Wright Morris the Photographer." In *Wright Morris: Origin of a Species.* San Francisco Museum of Modern Art, 1992. Pp. 9-21.

Criticism Linking Morris' Fiction and Photography

Cantie, Philippe. "Lettre et icône dans l'incipit de *The Inhabitants.*" *Caliban,* 29 (February 1992): 1-12.

Coates, Christopher. "Image/Text: Wright Morris and Deconstruction." *Canadian Review of American Studies,* 22 (1991): 567-576.

Halter, Peter. "Distance and Desire: Wright Morris' *The Home Place* as 'Photo-Text.'" *Etudes Textuelles,* 4 (October-December 1990): 65-89.

Hollander, John. "The Figure on the Page: Words and Images in Wright Morris' *The Home Place.*" *Yale Journal of Criticism,* 9 (Spring 1996): 93-108.

Hunter, Jefferson. "The Work of Wright Morris." *Image and Word: The Interaction of Twentieth-Century Photographs and Texts.* Cambridge: Harvard University Press, 1987. Pp. 56-63.

Nye, David. "Negative Capability in Wright Morris' *The Home Place.*" *Word and Image,* 4 (January-March 1989): 163-169.

Phillips, Sandra S. "Words & Pictures." *Wright Morris: Origin of a Species.* San Francisco: San Francisco Museum of Modern Art, 1992. Pp. 23-32.

Trachtenberg, Alan. "Wright Morris' 'Photo-Texts.'" *Yale Journal of Criticism,* 9 (Spring 1996): 109-119.

Westerbeck, Colin. "American Graphic: The Photography and Fiction of Wright Morris." In *Multiple Views: Logan Grant Essays on Photography, 1983-89.* Daniel P. Younger, ed. Albuquerque: University of New Mexico Press, 1991. Pp. 271-302.

Wydeven, Joseph J. "Focus and Frame in Wright Morris' *The Works of Love.*" *Western American Literature,* 23 (August 1988): 99-112.

————. "Images and Icons: The Fiction and Photography of Wright Morris." *Under the Sun: Myth and Realism in Western American Literature.* Barbara Meldrum, ed. Troy, New York: Whitston, 1985. Pp. 176-203.

————. "Visual Artistry in Wright Morris' *Plains Song for Female Voices.*" *MidAmerica,* 19 (1992): 116-126.

Nancy Owen Nelson

Frederick Manfred

The most important statement that can be made about Frederick Manfred is that, in the last years of his life and career and until his death on September 7, 1994, he never ceased in his attempt to maintain his own voice, to explore the land of his birth, to prove the notion that the highest form of art is writing. Early in his career he strove to be the songster of "Siouxland," the territory where Minnesota, South Dakota, Nebraska, and Iowa meet; in his later years he held strongly to his commitment to write about the people who settled the land and the generations following. In these years (1980-1994), Manfred was also assessing his life and art by creating nonfiction and fiction which reflected influences on the same.

The autobiographical publications of the later years reinforce many of the themes and issues of Manfred's earlier works and influences. While he attempted no "rumes" (by his definition, works in which "the major arch of [his] life" was "the germ idea of the work"), other autobiographical writings fill in the spaces of his life, past and present, in a vital and honest exposé.

The Selected Letters of Frederick Manfred: 1932-1954 (1988) gives valuable insights into Manfred's early writings and traces his personal and artistic development, his struggles to find an audience for his work, his literary companions, and his exploration of the many faces of the human "prism." The letters shed light on his relationships, trace the process of his name change from Feikema to Manfred, and explore his personal and public lives; of special interest to Manfred scholars is his search for a voice, his creativity, which, he believed, was driven by his primordial "Old Lizard," the subconscious part of himself (to William Carlos Williams he calls it the "motherwart magma of the race").

The letters cover the years at Calvin College, Grand Rapids, Michigan, from 1932 to the 1954 publication of one of Manfred's best-received novels, *Lord Grizzly*. The reader is enlightened by Manfred's observations about American politics, art, and culture and his documentation of travels through Depression-era America which enriched the writing of his early farm novels, *The Golden Bowl*, *This Is the Year*, and *The Chokecherry Tree*. His correspondents varied from the literati of the period such as Robert Penn Warren, Sinclair Lewis, Henry Miller, and William Carlos Williams to political friend Hubert Humphrey; letters to publishers and critics are intermingled with letters to family members detailing daily activities. Three correspondents are consistent throughout the volume, however: first love and college classmate Helen Reitsema and college friends John DeBie and John Huizenga. Through the varied tone and content of these and other letters, Manfred reveals his developing vision of his own voice.

Finally, the letters offer Manfred readers evidence of the early inception of many of his ideas; for instance, a 1945 letter to Van Wyck Brooks reveals that Manfred was already developing the concept of the 1989 *Flowers of Desire* as *The Rape of Carla Simmons*. A 1950 letter reveals also that he was mulling over a vast, sweeping novel about the Freyling family (then entitled *Siouxland Saga*), which became the 1992 *Of Lizards and Angels*.

Like the letters, the second volume of poems, *Winter Count II* (1987) exposes an honest narrative, or as Manfred states in the Foreword, "dredge[s] up the past beads and happenings and string[s] them together into a rosary" of his life from 1964 to 1983. Narrative poems reveal the passions and woes of Manfred's life in a voice resembling the honest, straightforward tone and cadence of the letters and novels.

Manfred's use of the essay form in the later years gave him an important vehicle to present his literary notions as well as to explore influential voices in his own life. As in his letters and poems, Manfred's honest essays, collected in *Prime Fathers* (1989) and *Duke's Mixture* (1994), provide much internal information about the earliest writings of his career and the threads of his life: influential men, theories about the connections between quantum physics and art, the importance of place in the writing process. In many respects, these collections are a kind of recapitulation of those forces and ideas which drove Manfred, the writer.

Containing a mere eight essays on such men as Sinclair Lewis, Hubert Humphrey, and Manfred's father, *Prime Fathers* weaves together the male forces which helped to shape Manfred's identity as man and as writer. He also includes essays about his own writing and reestablishes the artist as the "True Child of God," as one essay title indicates. Manfred identifies his "prime" or first male experiences — these were the "fathers" who shaped the young artist.

The second essay collection, *Duke's Mixture*, was the last publication before Manfred's death. The collection is a wild mix of essays (apropos of the title) ranging from portraits of writers and teachers to literary and historical articles; from interviews to essays on the importance of place. This book represents the breadth and depth of Frederick Manfred the man and the artist, and it brings together many issues touched upon in the writings of his early career. Of special interest is the essay "Space, Yes: Time, No," in which Manfred outlines his theory of creativity as it connects to quantum physics: "deons," his label for the smallest units of matter, are responsible for the intuitive and coincidental aspects of the universe as well as the creative process.

In his last three novels, *Flowers of Desire* (1989), *No Fun on Sunday* (1990), and *Of Lizards and Angels* (1992), Manfred turns to his beloved Siouxland for another look at his people and the place from which he came. These three novels bring together many of Manfred's issues — the quality of rural life in the Midwest, the importance of properly maintaining the land, the importance of family tradition, and the realities of human passion.

No Fun on Sunday examines the conflict between midwestern Calvinism and fun-loving youth's dreams of baseball fame. Both *Flowers of Desire* and *Of Lizards and Angels* deal with these same rural community values, but these novels explore the important issue of gender often overlooked in Manfred studies. Mick McAllister's review of Manfred's *The Manly-Hearted Woman* in 1977 first identified this androgynous theme. McAllister found a "truly androgynous, psychologically bisexual pair, potentially an ideal marriage couple" in the main characters Manly-Heart and Flat Warclub, and thus a new way of viewing Manfred's work beyond the "unashamedly male" analysis of earlier critics. Certainly, looking back to some of Manfred's works as early as *Conquering Horse* and *Scarlet Plume*, one can see strong women and androgynous potential in both men and women characters.

In *Flowers of Desire* and *Of Lizards and Angels*, Manfred approaches the female character with greater depth. Clara Simmons' loss of innocence to a World War II soldier and her pursuit of her newfound sexuality suggest Manfred's intensive look at the female psyche. As a husbandless mother at the end of the novel, Clara is not destroyed, but strengthened, by her lost innocence. In *Lizards*, Manfred looks at the dark side of female attitudes toward sexuality in the character of Clara Freyling, which leads to the disruption of her marriage to Tunis and his disappearance, one of the novel's more sinister events.

It is finally significant that Manfred chose to look closely at female character throughout his career, from the early novels through *Of Lizards and Angels*. As McAllister writes in the foreword to *Prime Fathers*, "Manfred is essentially a whole sexual creature: not a pretentious, swaggering Hemingway; he is a man at peace with his anima rather than threatened by the feminine mind." Manfred's exploration of gender is a fertile field for future readers.

Thus Manfred's work of this last period reveals his evolving vision of the artist; the creative theories articulated in the letters and essays are revealed in the poetry and novels. The artist's work presents a panoramic view, not only of a place and a people, but of his own consciousness, integrally connected to the intuitive forces of nature.

Perhaps this belief in the connections within the material universe is what most distinctly defines the contributions that Frederick Manfred has made to the western American literary canon. It took a lifetime of questioning and living and writing to bring him to his unique notion that voice belongs in the arena of both the spiritual and the physical. Yet from Frederick Manfred's discovery of his own "voice," or his identity as a writer in the 1930s, he never put aside the driving urge to create, even in the last years of his life. At the time of his illness in July of 1994, Manfred had sent out at least two manuscripts for publication and had another set of notes waiting for his artist's hand. During this period, he never surrendered his desire to write about the land he loved, his native Siouxland, nor did he retreat from the gritty task of continuing to understand and explain human nature in the form of his characters and the real people he wrote of. To the end, as at the beginning, he was a storyteller.

Selected Bibliography

Primary Sources

Dinkytown. Minneapolis: Dinkytown Antiquarian Bookstore, 1984.

Duke's Mixture. Sioux Falls: The Center for Western Studies, 1994.

Flowers of Desire. Salt Lake City: Dancing Badger Press, 1989.

Foreword to *Through a Glass Lightly.* By John H. Timmerman. Grand Rapids: W. B. Eerdmans, 1987. Pp. ix-xiv.

"Frederick Manfred." An interview in *Finding the Words: Conversations with Writers who Teach.* Nancy Bunge, ed. Athens, Ohio: Swallow Press, 1985. Pp. 68-82. (Later published in *Duke's Mixture.*)

The Golden Bowl. Golden Anniversary Edition. Brookings: South Dakota Humanities Foundation, 1992.

"A Good Neighbor." *Walking Swiftly: Writings in Honor of Robert Bly.* Thomas R. Smith, ed. New York: HarperCollins Books. 1993. P. 59.

"Of Holders and Probers." *South Dakota Review,* 28 (Spring 1990): 19-23.

Introduction to *King of Spades.* Boston: Gregg Press,1980. Pp. v-xi.

Of Lizards and Angels. Norman: University of Oklahoma Press, 1992.

"The Making of *Lord Grizzly.*" *South Dakota Review,* 15 (Fall 1985): 12-19. (Later published in *Prime Fathers.*)

"The Mystique of Siouxland." In *A Common Land, A Diverse People.* Harry F. Thompson, et al., eds. Sioux Falls: The Nordland Foundation, 1986. Pp. 71-81.

No Fun on Sunday. Norman: University of Oklahoma Press, 1990.

"Old Voices in My Writings." In *The Prairie Frontier.* Sandra Looney, Arthur R. Huseboe and Geoffrey Hunt, eds. Sioux Falls: The Augustana College Press, 1984. Pp. 76-86.

Prime Fathers. Salt Lake City: Howe Bros., 1989.

"The Realities of Regionalism," with William Stafford, Lois Hudson and Gilbert Fite. *South Dakota Review,* 26 (Winter 1988): 77-91.

The Selected Letters of Frederick Manfred: 1932-1954. Arthur R. Huseboe and Nancy Owen Nelson, eds. Lincoln: University of Nebraska Press, 1988.

Winter Count II: Poems by Frederick Manfred. Minneapolis: James D. Thueson, 1987.

Secondary Sources

Articles

Bunge, Nancy. "'Something Magical and Important Is Going On': Interview with Frederick and Freya Manfred." *North Dakota Quarterly,* 61 (Spring 1993): 19-36.

Flora, Joseph M. Introduction to *Lord Grizzly.* Boston: Gregg Press, 1980. Pp. v-xix. Discusses the significance of Manfred's name change to his more "western" focus in *Lord Grizzly* and the identification of Hugh with his animal self.

Gidmark, Jill. "The U-Land in Siouxland: A Minnesotan's View." *Midamerica: The Yearbook of the Society for the Study of Midwestern Literature,* 6 (1989): 103-114. Establishes Manfred's absolute commitment to place, particularly Minnesota settings, from *Boy Almighty* through *Prime Fathers.*

Harrison, Dick. "Frederick Manfred." In *Fifty Western Writers.* Fred Erisman and Richard W. Etulain, eds. Westport, Connecticut, and London: Greenwood Press, 1982. Pp.

291-302. A biographical and critical overview of Manfred's work through *Sons of Adam*.

Hudson, Lois Phillips. "Rejoinder to 'Of Holders and Probers.'" *South Dakota Review,* 28 (Spring 1990): 24-25.

Huseboe, Arthur R. Foreword to Frederick Manfred's *The Scarlet Plume.* Lincoln: University of Nebraska Press, 1983. Pp. v-xiii. Outlines the inception of *Scarlet Plume* — Manfred's research — and how the novel fits the larger Manfred canon.

————. Introduction to *The Golden Bowl.* Brookings: South Dakota Humanities Foundation, 1992. Pp. viii-xviii. Discusses the inception of *The Golden Bowl,* its many drafts, and surveys other Manfred works.

McAllister, Mick, "The First Covenant in *Conquering Horse:* Syncretic Myth in The Buckskin Tales." *South Dakota Review,* 20 (Autumn 1982): 76-88. Analyzes the parallels between the first covenant of the gods with the Native peoples in *Conquering Horse* with the Biblical covenant of *God with Abraham.*

————. "'Wolf That I Am...'": Animal Symbology in *Lord Grizzly* and *Scarlet Plume.*" *Western American Literature,* 18 (May 1983): 21-31. Discusses the presence and function of bear and wolf imagery in *Lord Grizzly* and *Scarlet Plume.*

McCord, Nancy Nelson. "Manfred's Elof Lofblom." *Western American Literature,* 16 (Summer 1981): 125-134. Traces the development of the protagonist of *The Chokecherry Tree* and Manfred's use of Smollett's eighteenth century hero motif.

Meldrum, Barbara Howard, "Agrarian versus Frontiersman in Midwestern Fiction." In *Vision and Refuge: Essays on the Literature of the Great Plains.* Virginia Faulkner, ed., with Frederick Leubke. Lincoln: University of Nebraska Press, 1982. Pp. 44-63. Examines Pier Frixen of *This is the Year* as a blend of the agrarian farmer and the independent frontiersman; Pier's failure creates ambivalence about the merits of the frontier spirit.

Milton, John R. Afterword to *The Golden Bowl.* Brookings: South Dakota Humanities Foundation, 1992. Pp. 227-232. Provides a construct for considering the protagonist's three "visionary experiences."

————. Foreword to *Lord Grizzly.* Lincoln: University of Nebraska Press, 1983. Pp. v-xii. Discusses the inception of the novel, its history in the mountain man traditions, and its structure.

Mulder, Rodney, J. and John H. Timmerman. *Frederick Manfred: A Bibliography and Publishing History.* Sioux Falls: The Center for Western Studies, 1981. Includes a narrative interview with Manfred.

Nelson, Nancy Owen. "Frederick Manfred and the Anglo-Saxon Oral Tradition." *Western American Literature,* 19 (February 1985): 263-274. Finds evidence in letters and three early novels of Manfred's indebtedness to the Anglo-Saxon poetic tradition.

————. "Frederick Manfred: Bard of Siouxland." In *The Prairie Frontier.* Sandra Looney, Arthur R. Huseboe and Geoffrey Hunt, eds. Sioux Falls: The Augustana College Press, 1984. Pp. 53-75. Traces the voice of the poet/commentator in three novels (earlier version of "Frederick Manfred and the Anglo-Saxon Oral Tradition").

————. "Sacred Siouxland: Wakan Places in Some Novels by Frederick Manfred." *Heritage of the Great Plains,* 28 (Spring-Summer 1995): 40-51. Discusses specific sites in Siouxland which were illustrated as sacred ("wakan") places in Manfred's *Conquering Horse, Lord Grizzly,* and *The Manly-Hearted Woman.*

————. "'Sweet Dakota Land': The Manfred Letters and the Inception of *The Golden*

Bowl." South Dakota Review, 30 (Spring 1992): 61-70. Through an examination of Manfred's letters, traces the evolution of theme and purpose in *The Golden Bowl.*

Oakes, Priscilla. Introduction to *Riders of Judgment.* Boston: Gregg Press, 1980. Pp. v-xiii. Examines the moral wrestlings of Cain Hammett and views the novel in terms of both religious and mythological themes.

Oppewall, Peter. "Manfred and Calvin College." In *Where the West Begins.* Arthur R. Huseboe and William Geyer, eds. Sioux Falls: Center for Western Studies, 1978. Pp. 86-97. Discusses the literal relationship of the Wanderlust trilogy to Manfred's stay at Calvin College, Manfred's search for faith in the trilogy, and the growing appreciation of the Calvin community for Manfred's work.

Quantic, Diane Dufva. "Frederick Manfred's *The Golden Bowl*: Myth and Reality in the Dust Bowl." *Western American Literature,* 25 (February 1991): 297-309. An analysis of how the reality of Dust Bowl conditions upholds the myth of the garden in *The Golden Bowl.*

Smith, Robert W. "Frederick Manfred: Outsize Man and Writer (Interview)." *North Dakota Quarterly,* 55 (Spring 1987): 139-150. Later published in *Duke's Mixture.*

Timmerman, John H. "Forgiveness in the Lair of the Lizard: Frederick Manfred's *Lord Grizzly." College Language Association Journal* (September 1981): 37-47. Explains Hugh Glass' forgiveness in terms of the mythical and primordial nature of his Lizard.

———. "Harmony in Dynamic Pattern: Frederick Manfred's Novelistic Art." *Southwest Review,* 68 (Spring 1983): 153-161. Analyzes the relationship between physical and mythical reality in *Conquering Horse* and *The Manly-Hearted Woman,* showing how Manfred's artistic belief grows out of a harmonious relationship with nature.

———. "Structures and Meaning in Frederick Manfred's *Conquering Horse." Lamar Journal of the Humanities,* (Spring 1982): 39-49. Studies the relationship between Manfred's "mythic vision" in *Conquering Horse* and the style and technique of the novel—showing the relevance of relationships and dreams to the overall structure.

Westbrook, Max. Foreword to *King of Spades.* Lincoln: University of Nebraska Press, 1983. Pp. v-xi. Treats the Jungian aspects of the love relationships in *King of Spades* and identifies the "Greek tragedy" construct of the plot.

Whipp, Leslie. "Frederick Manfred's *The Golden Bowl*—The Novel and Novelist Emerging." *South Dakota Review,* 27 (Autumn 1989): 54-73. Discusses the novel through its early drafts as a play, then a narrative, finding in it both biblical and epic tradition; the sophisticated novelist emerges with the final draft.

———. "An Interview with Frederick Manfred." *Midwestern* (1992).

———. "Frederick Manfred's *The Wind Blows Free*: Autobiographical Mythology." *South Dakota Review,* 27 (Summer 1989): 100-128. Examines *The Wind Blows Free* as the young artist's search for his female "muses" while defining his own male identity.

Wright, Robert C. "Frederick Manfred." In *A Literary History of the American West.* J. Golden Taylor, Thomas J. Lyon, et al., eds. Fort Worth: Texas Christian University Press, 1987. Pp. 792-805.

———. "The Myth of the Isolated Self in Manfred's Siouxland Novels." In *Where the West Begins.* Arthur R. Huseboe and William Geyer, eds. Sioux Falls: Center for Western Studies, 1978. Pp. 110-116. A study of the movement from isolation to belonging in many of Manfred's characters; the connectedness of all living things is inherent in his work.

Wylder, Delbert E. Foreword to *Conquering Horse.* Lincoln: University of Nebraska Press, 1983. Pp. v-xi. Discusses gender and spiritual issues in *Conquering Horse* and views No Name as mythological hero.

Dissertations

Byrd, Forrest Mickey. "Prolegomenon to Frederick Manfred." Ph.D., University of Nebraska, 1976.

Fynaardt, Keith. "Siouxland Cultivation: Frederick Manfred's Farm Novels." M.A., Iowa State University, 1991.

Mason, Kenneth Clifton. "The Family Chronicle and Modern America." Ph.D., University of Nebraska, 1982. Includes *Green Earth* in a discussion of the novel which chronicles twentieth-century family life and a search for identity within the family.

Moen, Ole O. "The Voice of Siouxland: Man and Nature in Frederick Manfred's Writing." Ph.D., University of Minnesota, 1978.

Nesbitt, John Dunville. "Literary Convention in the Classic Western Novel." Ph.D., University of California, Davis, 1981. Deals with Manfred's *Riders of Judgment* which, among other novels, deals seriously and effectively with western formulae.

John T. Price

Midwestern Autobiographical Nonfiction

lthough popular perceptions of the Midwest's physical boundaries have regularly fluctuated, its symbolic identity has
remained relatively stable. As geographer James R. Shortridge
has pointed out, regional and national perceptions of the Midwest since
the late 1800s have revolved around its use as a symbol of the Arcadian
ideal and the pastoral values of morality, independence, and egalitarian-
ism. Although this has protected the illusion of a cohesive national
identity, it has also had the effect of silencing alternative voices and
views and denying the midwestern landscape its cultural and ecological
complexity. Much of midwestern autobiographical nonfiction, however,
has worked against these abstractions by focusing on the particularities
of an individual life, and by illustrating the way the physical, historical,
and cultural layers of the landscape take shape in the writer's imagination.

The work of Meridel Le Sueur reveals much of what has been left out
of the popular story of the Midwest. For Le Sueur, perhaps more than
any writer alive today, the volatile history of the Midwest in the twentieth century is personal history. Le Seuer was born in Murray, Iowa, in
1900 and spent much of her childhood moving across the Great Plains
with her divorced mother. In essays such as "Corn Village" (1930) and
"The Ancient People and the Newly Come" (1976), Le Sueur recounts
the physical and psychological brutality of a childhood spent on the
Plains. Yet she also recalls the nurturing love of a "maternal forest" of

women — her mother, her maternal grandmother, and their Mandan friend, Zona. From these women she learned the values of self-reliance, education, as well as the history of the indigenous people and landscape; but she also witnessed in their lives the adverse effects of puritanical repression and the tyranny of the pioneer myth of progress and conquest.

While Le Sueur was still a child, her mother and socialist stepfather, Arthur, also introduced her to the midwestern tradition of radical dissent, of which she writes in their biography, *Crusaders* (1953). Although Le Sueur left the Midwest while still in high school, living for a time in an anarchist commune with Emma Goldman in New York, she returned to Minnesota during the Depression to continue developing what she called a "communal sensibility" in her writing. During the thirties she wrote numerous pieces of reportage that focused on the struggles of impoverished women ("Women on the Breadlines," 1932), urban laborers ("I Was Marching," 1934), and drought-stricken farmers ("Cows and Horses Are Hungry," 1934). These pieces — which weave journalistic research, interviews, and personal impressions into poignant narratives — significantly challenged the popular image of the Midwest as "the bread basket of the world." It is a theme and method she would return to in *North Star Country* (1945), which concentrates on the "buried and ignored culture" of the Midwest, including the destruction of tribal cultures and the indigenous wildlife. This book still stands as one of the most important and innovative histories of the region.

In the late 1940s, during the McCarthy era, Le Sueur was blacklisted and denied access to mainstream publications. Recently, however, thanks to several new collections and reprints, her work has enjoyed a kind of national resurrection. Although Le Sueur would resist being seen as a "model" for other writers, evidence of her influence can be found almost everywhere in contemporary midwestern literature, especially autobiographical nonfiction. Patricia Hampl, for instance, referred to her as the "voice of the prairie," and Linda Hasselstrom called her, simply, a "goddess." In her nineties and living in western Wisconsin, LeSueur continues to provide a bridge between the generations in this place: "Pass over," she writes in her Afterword to *Ripening*, "use the energy of the root in our witness and our singing" (291).

One writer who has obviously crossed that bridge is Minnesota teacher Carol Bly, author of *Letters from the Country* (1981). Born in Duluth, Minnesota, in 1930, Bly's midwestern girlhood was, like Le

Sueur's, migratory and unconventional. After attending college in the East, she returned to Minnesota in 1955 with husband Robert Bly to live on his family's farm near Madison. *Letters from the Country* is a collection of short essays that focus on her life in Madison — a place which, like Le Sueur's "Corn Village," is victimized by its own myths. To preserve its stereotypical small-town sweetness and comfort, its citizens have had "to bottle up social indignation, psychological curiosity, and intellectual doubt" (38). This collective repression, according to Bly, has led to individual "psychic loneliness," undermined civic pride and activism, and, at the larger level, left the rural Midwest more vulnerable to predatory corporate and political interests. What is needed in this crisis, according to Bly, is an "expressive" ideal for community life, one in which writing and the arts are used to encourage quiet reflection, informed dissent, and public discussion of civic and moral issues. Bly's "expressive" suggestions emerge from a deep belief that if rural communities are to remain healthy, then rural citizens must nurture, rather than deny, their aesthetic, ethical, and "holy" natures.

* * *

The two great themes in rural American writing, according to David Pichaske, are "the theme of departure and the theme of return" (xxii). However, as autobiographical nonfiction has often revealed, "going home" to the Midwest has never been easy for the writers themselves. The psychological challenge of returning home is explored in Curtis Harnack's *We Have All Gone Away* (1973) and Douglas Bauer's *Prairie City, Iowa* (1979). Although born a generation apart, both Harnack and Bauer left their Iowa hometowns after high school, perceiving them to be professional and psychological dead-ends. But faced with overwhelming changes in their own lives, both return home as adults. What they find there is not the anticipated timelessness of a rural hometown, but rather an overwhelming sense of how those places have changed, and, by extension, how they themselves have changed and aged. The personal landscape proves, in the end, to be *too* personal, and both writers leave.

There are, however, several recent examples of writers who have returned to their midwestern homes to stay. In his *Prairie Days* (1987), Bill Holm uses himself as an example, "duplicated many times in southwestern Minnesota, of attempted escape from these unlikely prairies, and the discovery, usually after years passing, that for better or worse, you belong in a place, and grow out of its black soil like a cornstalk" (33). Holm was born in 1943 on a farm near Minneota where his Icelandic grandfather homesteaded in 1880. At eighteen, longing to escape, Holm left Minneota to attend college and teach in the East. What he found there was an "empty-hearted rootlessness, books used as blunt instruments, a sneering disbelief that hayseed farmers had souls, much less intellects" (33). More importantly, however, his time away forced him to acknowledge the unavoidable connection between his identity and the prairie landscape he had left behind. Finally, after a twenty-year absence, he returned home to Minneota, where he continues to live and write.

Linda Hasselstrom's family ranch near Hermosa, South Dakota, has not only been her home for nearly forty years, it has also been the central subject of her three works of autobiographical nonfiction: *Windbreak: A Woman Rancher on the Northern Plains* (1987), *Going Over East: Reflections of a Woman Rancher* (1987), and *Land Circle: Writings Collected from the Land* (1991). Together, these books create a portrait of one of the most interesting relationships between a woman and her land in Great Plains literature. For Hasselstrom, the connection between self, place, and writing began at the age of nine when her mother married John Hasselstrom, whose family had ranched in South Dakota since the late 1800s. During that first year on the prairie, she "pledged her soul" to the ranch and began writing in a journal. After high school, however, she left home for nearly ten years, during which she earned an M.A. degree, got married and then divorced. After the divorce, she returned to her family's ranch where the land "healed" her and helped resurrect her interest in writing.

In her nonfiction books, Hasselstrom is seen attempting to balance her many roles as rancher, writer, daughter, wife, environmentalist, and feminist. She often takes advantage of these multiple roles to encourage productive discourse between traditionally opposed groups, particularly ranchers and environmentalists. Likewise, her ground-level observations challenge simplistic stereotypes of Great Plains culture and ecology, stereotypes which she claims have encouraged economic and environmental exploitation of the region. It is, however, her ongoing personal covenant with the land that remains at the center of her nonfiction; that conviction sustained her through the loss of friends and family.

Although a lifelong resident of the city of St. Paul, Minnesota,

Patricia Hampl describes in her memoirs a life infused with many of the same midwestern myths experienced by Great Plains rural writers. This includes pride in the "god-awful winters," and yet also the traditional desire to escape what she sees as the cultural, historical, and literary "blandness" of her midwestern home. The deeper source of her discomfort, however, is her shame over her protected middle-class, midwestern upbringing and her "virginal self," a self marked by "an indelible brand of innocence, which is to be marked by an absence, a vacancy. By nothing at all" (*Virgin Time* 208). In both her memoirs, it is this sense of shame that moves her to journey to Europe — to the Prague of her ethnic heritage and to the Italy and France of her religious heritage. In the cold-war Czechoslovakia of *A Romantic Education* (1981), Hampl finds a place of deep culture and history, but also of suffering, where writers are sometimes killed for their words. In the Assisi and Lourdes of *Virgin Time* (1992), she finds places rich in Catholic spiritual significance, but also shallow searching. Ultimately, both journeys lead her back to the midwestern past she hoped to escape and into an acceptance of the "unmarked" self of which she was once ashamed.

* * *

Midwestern autobiographical nonfiction also includes accounts by urban newcomers to the region, writers who self-consciously identify themselves as "outsiders" and write about the complex process of becoming, as E. Annie Proulx has said, *of* their chosen rural places as well as *in* them. One such work, Kathleen Norris' *Dakota: A Spiritual Geography*, presents the story of a poet who moves from New York City to her grandmother's house in the small town of Lemmon, South Dakota. Norris is aware of the danger and dishonesty of claiming, too quickly, like an overly eager tourist, to be "one with the land," and, likewise, of dismissing the place when it inevitably disappoints romantic expectations. For Norris, the process of belonging to a place — spiritually as well as physically — is an active, informed, and literary process. Norris thus transforms the silence of the Plains, which at one time threatened to overwhelm her, into a fruitful silence which spiritually "re-forms" her and connects her to the landscape.

Qualifying Norris' spiritual transformation, however, is her tenuous membership in two Plains "communities" — the small town of Lemmon and a nearby Benedictine monastery. In *Dakota*, Norris claims that although her mother grew up in Lemmon, and she herself has lived there for nearly twenty years, she is often treated like an outsider. She claims this is partly because she is a writer, giving voice to the hidden stories, and thus the hidden pain, of local life. Norris contextualizes this local defensiveness within a larger regional history of colonial exploitation — most recently the 1980s farm crisis. In contrast to the citizens of Lemmon, however, the Benedictine monks have welcomed Norris, a married Protestant, into their monastery as an oblate. Although long-time citizens of the Plains, these monks have succeeded in abandoning the myth of frontier individualism for a tradition that values communal cooperation, invites constructive criticism, and seeks spiritual union with the natural forces around them. According to Norris the monks also understand, unlike many rural citizens, the communal importance of their literary traditions. Norris was herself transformed by the monastic literary tradition, and she believes that, likewise, it can help the endangered community and landscape around her. Kathleen Norris is joined by Larry Woiwode in perhaps an emerging tradition of spiritual autobiography set in the Plains.

Another form of midwestern literary nonfiction enjoying recent success is travel narrative. During the last ten years several such narratives have appeared by authors like Ian Frazier, Bill Bryson, Conger Beasley, Jr., and Merrill Gilfillan. Perhaps the best known of these travel writers is William Least Heat-Moon. A native of Kansas City and a long-time resident of Columbia, Missouri, Heat-Moon gained national attention for his *Blue Highways* (1982), a meditative account of a 14,000 mile journey along the backroads of small-town America. Heat-Moon's *PrairyErth (a deep map)* (1991) is also a kind of travel narrative, but in this book Heat-Moon steps off the highway and into a more extensive physical and imaginative exploration of a single, seemingly empty place: rural Chase County, Kansas. The end result is a giant-sized book (622 pages in hardcover) that, in part, reveals the historical complexity of Chase County, its social and economic struggles. Heat-Moon includes portions of pioneer diaries and newspaper articles along with contemporary voices — a woman rancher, Kansa tribe members, schoolchildren — which speak of experiences that have often been left out of the popular story of the Midwest.

As Heat-Moon explores the historical and contemporary forces at work in Chase County, he is also exploring related forces at work within his own identity. Part Osage Indian, part Anglo-European, Heat-Moon represents himself as a man who occupies the overlap between two different, historically conflicting ways of imagining the relationship between individual and place. Within *PrairyErth*, Heat-Moon experiments with one way of imagining time and land and experience, then another, then combinations, testing the consequences for both himself and the place. Heat-Moon locates his experiment within the story of how Chase County has been imagined by others and how those "ways of imagining"—from Thomas Jefferson to Wes Jackson—have influenced not only that county, but also Kansas and the tall-grass prairies of which it is a part. As an example, Heat-Moon describes the failed attempt during the 1970s to create a grasslands national park in the Flint Hills. Although there were practical challenges to creating the park, its failure, according to Heat-Moon, was largely due to a collective failure of imagination on the part of local citizens, government officials, and environmentalists. However, since the publication of *PrairyErth* in 1991, local citizens and government officials have cooperated to propose Chase County as the site of a tall-grass prairie national park.

As Heat-Moon emphasizes in *PrairyErth*, most of the indigenous grasslands of the Great Plains have been destroyed. The prairie park project in Kansas, however, is perhaps one example of changing attitudes. The last ten years have seen an increased interest in preserving and restoring prairie and other bioregional ecosystems. Likewise, in midwestern autobiographical nonfiction, there has been an increased interest in exploring the relationship between nature and identity. Heat-Moon, for example, refers to himself as "a fellow of the grasslands" who has learned to think "open and lean." Linda Hasselstrom writes that the "land has invested [her] with its personality, its spare beauty and harshness." Bill Holm speaks of his "prairie eye" which has influenced his preferences in landscape, architecture, and literature.

Paul Gruchow's *Journal of a Prairie Year* (1985) also explores the interrelationship between nature and identity. In this book, Gruchow, a lifelong native of southwestern Minnesota, closely observes the natural prairie ecosystems around him, describing and naming the various plants, animals, and insects, recognizing the larger influences of weather and geography, and revealing the subtle interconnectedness of it all. Attached to each layer of the natural world around him, however, is a myriad of his own memories, thoughts, and emotions that add personal urgency to his ecological observations. Gruchow further explores the relationship between nature and identity in *The Necessity of Empty*

Places (1988) and *Grass Roots: The Universe of Home* (1995). Gruchow's books, along with others such as Dan O'Brien's *The Rites of Autumn: A Falconer's Journey Across the American West* (1988) and Mary Swander's *Out of This World: A Woman's Life Among the Amish* (1995), can be seen as part of a slow-but-steady emergence of a bioregional perspective in midwestern autobiographical nonfiction. This point of view defines the Midwest not by its usual arbitrary boundaries, but by its various biotic areas, and takes into account the influence of local ecosystems on local culture and history. For these writers the destruction of the indigenous prairies has robbed the bioregion of the true complexity of its identity, making it, in Gruchow's words, "a pale ghost of the world that once existed in this place" (*Journal* 65). And by simplifying the land, mid-westerners have simplified and endangered themselves. This new biore-gional perspective redefines midwestern identity as something which is informed as much by plants and weather as by culture and history. In this new definition lies what Gary Snyder might call a new "spirit of place" in midwestern literature. "To know the spirit of a place," writes Snyder, "is to realize that you are a part of a part and that the whole is made of parts, each of which is whole. You start with the part you are whole in." It is a task especially suited for autobiographical nonfiction.

Selected Bibliography

Primary Sources

Bauer, Douglas. *Prairie City, Iowa: Three Seasons at Home.* Ames: Iowa State University Press, 1979.

———. "The Way the Country Lies." In *A Place of Sense: Essays in Search of the Midwest.* Michael Martone, ed. Iowa City: University of Iowa Press, 1988. Describes his visit to Prairie City, Iowa, during the 1980s farm crisis.

Beasley, Conger, Jr. *Sundancers and River Demons: Essays on Landscape and Ritual.* Fayetteville: University of Arkansas Press, 1990.

Bly, Carol. *Letters from the Country.* New York: Harper & Row, 1981.

Bryson, Bill. *The Lost Continent: Travels in Small-Town America.* New York: Harper Perennial, 1989.

Dickenson, James R. *Home on the Range: A Century on the High Plains.* New York: Scribner, 1995. A history of the author's hometown, McDonald, Kansas, popula-tion 200, as quintessential Great Plains community.

Frazier, Ian. *Great Plains.* New York: Farrar, Straus & Giroux, 1989.

Gilfillan, Merrill. *Magpie Rising: Sketches from the Great Plains.* New York: Vintage Books, 1991.

Gruchow, Paul. *Grass Roots: The Universe of Home*. Minneapolis: Milkweed Editions, 1995.

———. *Journal of a Prairie Year*. Minneapolis: University of Minnesota Press, 1985.

———. *The Necessity of Empty Places*. New York: St. Martin's Press, 1988.

Hampl, Patricia. *A Romantic Education*. New York: Houghton Mifflin, 1981. A second edition, published in 1992, includes a new afterword by the author in which she returns to Prague after the fall of communism.

———. *Spillville*. Minneapolis: Milkweed Editions, 1987. An extended prose poem about Antonin Dvorak's stay in the Iowa farming village of Spillville during the summer of 1893, and Hampl's own visit there.

———. *Virgin Time*. New York: Ballantine, 1992.

Harnack, Curtis. *We Have All Gone Away*. Ames: Iowa State University Press, 1981.

Hasselstrom, Linda. *Going Over East: Reflections of a Woman Rancher*. Golden: Fulcrum, 1987.

———. *Land Circle: Writings Collected from the Land*. Golden: Fulcrum, 1991.

———. *Windbreak: A Woman Rancher on the Northern Plains*. Berkeley: Barn Owl Books, 1987.

Heat-Moon, William Least. *Blue Highways: A Journey into America*. Boston: Houghton Mifflin, 1982.

———. *PrairyErth (a deep map)*. Boston: Houghton Mifflin, 1991.

Holm, Bill. *Coming Home Crazy*. Minneapolis: Milkweed Editions, 1990. A collection of essays about his stay in China.

———. *The heart can be filled anywhere on earth: Minneota, Minnesota*. Minneapolis: Milkweed, 1996.

———. *Prairie Days*. San Francisco: Saybrook Publishing Company, 1987.

Le Sueur, Meridel. "Corn Village" (1930). In *Inheriting the Land: Contemporary Voices from the Midwest*. Mark Vinz and Thom Tammaro, eds. Minneapolis: University of Minnesota Press, 1993.

———. *Crusaders*. New York: Blue Heron Press, 1955.

———. *Harvest Song: Collected Essays and Stories*. Albuquerque: West End Press, 1977. Includes "Women on the Breadlines" (1932), "I Was Marching" (1934), "Cows and Horses are Hungry" (1934), and "The Ancient People and the Newly Come" (1976).

———. *North Star Country* (1945). Lincoln: University of Nebraska Press, 1984.

———. *Ripening*. New York: The Feminist Press, 1990.

Norris, Kathleen. *The Cloister Walk*. New York: Riverhead Books, 1996.

O'Brien, Dan. *The Rites of Autumn: A Falconer's Journey Across the American West*. New York: Anchor Books, 1988.

———. *Dakota: A Spiritual Geography*. New York: Ticknor & Fields, 1993.

Snyder, Gary. *The Practice of the Wild*. San Francisco: North Point Press, 1990.

Swander, Mary. *Out of this World: A Woman's Life Among the Amish*. New York: Viking, 1995.

Woiwode, Larry. *Acts*. San Francisco: Harper San Francisco, 1993.

Anthologies

Martone, Michael, ed. *A Place of Sense: Essays in Search of the Midwest*. Iowa City: University of Iowa Press, 1988.

Pichaske, David R., ed. *Late Harvest*. New York: Paragon House, 1991.

Vinz, Mark and Thom Tammaro, eds. *Imagining Home: Writings from the Midwest.* Minneapolis: University of Minnesota Press, 1995.

———. *Inheriting the Land: Contemporary Voices from the Midwest.* Minneapolis: University of Minnesota Press, 1993.

Secondary Sources

Franklin, Wayne and Michael Steiner, eds. *Mapping American Culture.* Iowa City: University of Iowa Press, 1992. See especially Kathleen Wallace's essay on midwestern women's autobiographies.

Ryden, Kent C. *Mapping the Invisible Landscape: Folklore, Writing, and the Sense of Place.* Iowa City: University of Iowa Press, 1993.

Shortridge, James. *The Middle West: Its Meaning in American Culture.* Lawrence: University Press of Kansas, 1989.

Sternburg, Janet, ed. *The Writer on Her Work: New Essays in New Territory, Volume II.* New York: W. W. Norton & Company, 1991. Includes an essay by Hampl on the art of memoir.

P. Jane Hafen

Native American Writers of the Midwest

Contemporary Native writers of the Midwest represent a variety of Northern Plains and Woodland Tribes peoples. Each writer presents, in various genres, complicated issues facing American Indians at the end of the twentieth century: cultural survival, tribal nationalism, identity, Indian gaming, social injustice, reservation and urban community life. Despite these common literary themes Native writers maintain specific tribal identifications and adhere to their own unique traditions.

Osage scholar Robert Allen Warrior argues in *Tribal Secrets: Recovering American Indian Intellectual Traditions* that an intellectual sovereignty abides in the literary and critical traditions of Native writers. Rather than advocating essentialism, Warrior suggests that Native authors are producing from changing cultures that rely on specific tribal histories, traditions and oralities, and native languages. American Indian writers from the Midwest represent that sovereignty by telling their individual stories and connecting to those stories their particular tribal affiliations. Most write in a variety of genres. This flexibility indicates a linguistic heritage of cultural wholeness that renders fiction poetic, poetry as constructed narrative, and nonfiction prose that is eloquent yet political.

As an example of the versatility of contemporary Native American writers, Kimberly M. Blaeser (Anishinabe) "just write[s] Indian stuff" that includes poetry, short fiction, essays and literary criticism. In her

711

volume of collected poems, *Trailing You,* images of the modern reservation combine with the familial and traditional to depict her White Earth reservation background. In the title poem, Blaeser tells of a life-threatening fall through the ice and desperate scramble to safety. She muses about her own writing: "I wonder if these poems are the path I make and I wonder/how far it is/to shore" (Bruchac 47). Poetry, as articulated and collective voice, tells her story of a path to security and self-discovery in a maze of tribal, academic, and mainstream culture. Additionally, Blaeser has authored a book-length critical study of fellow White Earth writer Gerald Vizenor.

Vizenor (Anishinabe, b. 1934) has continued his production of trickster narratives and acute analysis of tribal and literary issues. His dense imagery rests in crossblood metaphors and hybridized genres, cultures, and continents. *Griever: An American Monkey King in China* (1987) has a four-part structure and incorporates Vizenor's critical ideas of comic holotropes and dismantling of terminal creeds.[1] *The Trickster of Liberty* (1988) begins the series continued by *Bearheart: The Heirship Chronicles* (1990), a revision of *Darkness in Saint Louis Bearheart* (1978), and *Griever.* Although *Trickster,* like *Griever,* addresses China as authoritarian power and resuscitates Ishi from California, the narrative is rooted in the White Earth Chippewa reservation.

Despite the apparent postmodern bouncing through chronology and locus, Vizenor's trickster figures consolidate in the imagery of crossbloods as *The Heirs of Columbus.* With the Santa Maria Casino on White Earth, orality inculcated into talk radio, and mysterious gambling/archaeological bones, Vizenor weaves a narrative that plays with institutions, imagined and real. The crossblood descendant of Christopher Columbus, Stone Columbus, suggests that the trick of discovery is language, and that all who are heirs to Columbus would be "healers."

Storytelling as healing is a theme of the narrative poetry of Roberta Hill Whiteman (Oneida, b. 1947). Her poem "In the Longhouse: Oneida Museum" laments the Oneida alienation from the Iroquois confederacy, yet reclaims her Wisconsin heritage and tribal history with the strength of a "ridgepole in [her] spine" (16). Like the image of the "Star Quilt," the title poem from the collection of the same name, Whiteman pieces together stunning images of nature, endurance, and reparation.

Menonimee poet Chrystos (b. 1946) turns to eroticism as a means of healing. Chrystos claims a sovereignty in both her lesbianism and tribal awareness. Although she is angry and hostile in her descriptions of social ills laid at the feet of white-dominated capitalism, the vehemence of her work often takes a comic turn. In "Zenith Supplies" she challenges those who would appropriate native spirituality: "Leave the Drum & Sweat Lodge & Sundance to those whose heart beats it/... We aren't here to entertain you excuse you explain reality to you enter your names in our lives or soothe you/ Exploitation has many servants/ Pick up your own socks..." (Bruchac 79).

In a remarkable first novel, Susan Power (Lakota, b. 1961) also satirizes Native American "wannabes." For example, a reservation social studies teacher dyes her hair black to connect with her students and the traditional stories she coaxes them to tell. One student, Harley Wind Soldier, creates his own story, apart from traditional tales of his classmates. In modern reservation social ritual of the powwow, Harley transcends misfortunes with honor songs and plains-style dancing. Power's multiple narrators and a-chronistic short fictions, while stylistically similar to whose of Louise Erdrich, nevertheless re-create an autonomous Lakota culture and world view.

Ray A. Young Bear (Mesquakie, b. 1950), through poetry and fiction, has transcended the bounds of traditional literature by infusing his works with transcriptions of his native tongue. This transliteration of an oral language in two- and three-letter syllables declares an independence from western literary traditions, much like his poetry and the characters in his novels.

Oral histories and traditions of the Mesquakie infuse Young Bear's poetry.[2] In a series of poems and through Mesquakie cosmology, he reveals the origins of significant personages: Water Animals (earth-divers), the skunk, the bear, and kingfisher. Despite this grounding in Mesquakie traditionalism, Young Bear also mediates with images from the mainstream. In "Nothing Could Take Away the Bear-King's Image" Young Bear invokes Marilyn Monroe, ROTC and a radio station, yet resists the Greek astronomical interpretations of the stars. Despite inter-tribal college acquaintances, the narrator keeps his fidelity to the Mesquakie world view: "We are endless like the Midwestern/ breeze in winter which make the brittle/ oak leaves whisper in unison of this/ ethereal confidence" (Niatum 262).

The visual presentation of Young Bear's novel, *Black Eagle Child: The Facepaint Narratives,* appears as versified as his poetry. In this autobiographical narrative, Edgar Bearchild comes of age in the Mesquakie community. The novel begins with a "meaningless" Thanksgiving party/powwow at the Weeping Willow Elementary School, complete with participation from Why Cheer High School. This comedic interfacing continues as Young Bear's characters respond to common reservation social issues. On the matter of Indian identity and tribal enrollments the narrator observes (in a communal, plural voice):

> We sought and expected a grain of civility
> in our people regardless of who they were.
> And while we recognized the lineage abbreviations
> got out of hand, we all resided in the same
> hellhole. Provided no one made waves — be it
> an EBNO [Enrolled But in Name Only],
> an EBNAR (Enrolled But Not a Resident),
> BRYPU (Blood-Related Yet Paternally Unclaimed),
> UBENOB (Unrelated By Either Name Or Blood),
> EBMIW (Enrolled But Mother is White),
> and so forth — a sense of decency and harmony
> was possible.
> (*Black Eagle Child* 98)

Rather than defend tribal membership through blood quantifications that will eventually lead to extinction, Young Bear deconstructs the categories into the commonality and expediency of reservation realities. Despite comedic absurdities (such as cantaloupe lobbing) that range from the Iowa reservation to California and home again, the novel is grounded in Mesquakie oral traditions that include sections of untranslated text.

Returning home is a theme that permeates the works of Louise Erdrich (Turtle Mountain Chippewa, b. 1954). Erdrich achieved commercial and critical success with *Love Medicine* that won the National Book Award in 1984. She revised and expanded the novel in 1993. Although first to be published, *Love Medicine* is chronologically third in a series of North Dakota novels that have continuing themes and characters. Subsequent novels are *The Beet Queen* (1986), chronologically second, *Tracks* (1988), first in the series, *The Bingo Palace* (1993), and a concluding novel, *Tales of Burning Love* (1996). Additionally, Erdrich has authored two volumes of poetry, *Jacklight* (1984) and *Baptism of Desire* (1989) and a nonfiction volume, *The Blue Jay's Dance: A Birth Year* (1995).

In recognition of the Columbus quincentenary, Erdrich co-authored a novel, *The Crown of Columbus* (1991) with her husband, Michael Dorris (Modoc).[3] Although this novel is the only work to appear under both their names, their prose writing is a joint effort. This unique collaboration not only displaces emphasis from the autonomous artist to communal effort, but allows a syncretization of background and experience. The novel itself seems semi-autobiographical in the main character, Vivian Twostar. Professor Twostar is a Navajo-Coeur d'Alene mixed-blood professor at Dartmouth where Dorris was chair of American Indian Studies and Erdrich was poet-in-residence when the two met and married.

Mixed blood becomes a trope for the process of claiming or denying Indian identity in Erdrich's novels. Whether or not they are identified by blood quantification, the characters who maintain a tribal connection are the ones who survive. Erdrich establishes tribal identity phenomenologically through signifiers of particular Chippewa material culture and through storytelling and the oral tradition. She creates a tribal community of voices by utilizing the technique of multiple narrators.

In *Tracks* the narration alternates between Nanapush, an incarnation of the Chippewa trickster, Nanabozho, and mixed blood Pauline Puyat. The novel chronicles historical events of the early twentieth century when much of the Chippewa land base was lost. A character who survives through all the North Dakota novels, but never narrates, is Fleur. In *Tracks*, Fleur appears as a young woman and mother. Her presence without a narrative voice is like the veil of suggestive, yet invisible ethic that informs the novels. Unlike Fleur's fidelity to Chippewa ways, Pauline eventually denies her Indian blood and enters the Catholic convent, becoming Sister Leopolda. Her narration is non-directed and indicative of her disenfranchisement in the tribe. Nanapush's narration, however, is addressed to Lulu, Fleur's daughter, thus creating a continuity between generations and tribal community.

Like the Chippewa land of *Tracks*, in *The Beet Queen* the farmlands of Argus, North Dakota, signify ontological connections. The land transforms in tandem with the main characters. Although *The Beet Queen* is not overtly Native, it is informed by a trickster humor and centering of Chippewa characters Celestine, her daughter, Dot, and brother, Russell. Similar to Erdrich's German American grandmother, Mary Adare operates a butcher shop — the same butcher shop where Fleur manifests her powers and card tricks in *Tracks*. Many characters in *The Beet Queen* evolve as distinct yet marginal individuals: Mary, the old maid; her bisexual, nomadic brother, Karl; their neurotic cousin Sita; gay and closeted Wallace Pfef. A mutual concern for Dot unifies their fragmentation, yet contrasts tribal wholeness of the other novels.

Following the earth images of *Tracks* and air imagery of *The Beet Queen*, *Love Medicine* is replete with watery images that may either drown or baptismally promise new life. Several narrators tell the stories of the modern reservation in chapter titles replete with Catholic imagery. June Morrissey, Gordie Kashpaw and Henry Lamartine, Jr., lose their lives to watery deaths while Nector Kashpaw, Lipsha Morrissey, his father Gerry Nanapush, and Lyman Lamartine escape assimilation and drownings.

In 1993 Erdrich published a "new and expanded" version of *Love Medicine*. The new edition includes four completely new chapters and an additional section to the "Beads" chapter. A youthful Lulu, maternal Margaret Kashpaw (Rushes Bear), and entrepreneurial Lyman Lamartine expand their characters to bridge *Love Medicine* to *Tracks* and *The Bingo Palace*. Erdrich softens language from the "Wild Geese" chapter to preclude the possibility that Nector might have raped Marie. These radical changes to an already successful novel mark the fluidity of a literature informed by orality.

The fourth novel of the North Dakota series, *The Bingo Palace*, continues the lives of the characters of *Love Medicine*. The backdrop of the novel is the matriarchal wisdom of the grandmothers, Zelda Kashpaw, Lulu Lamartine, and primitivistic Fleur Pillager. Three generations of tricksters, Lulu, Gerry Nanapush and Lipsha Morrissey, comically ride through contemporary political and economic realities in a blue Firebird, a converted van won through bingo, and a stolen family car. Games of chance that characterize mythical tricksters become institutionalized with the incorporation of casino gambling on the reservation. The lighted spaces of Indian gaming social powwows in the novel are fields of negotiation with modern, mainstream America.

The most recent novel, *Tales of Burning Love*, appears like *The Beet Queen* to be less obvious in its Chippewa manifestations. Nevertheless Erdrich draws together a variety of mixed-blood, non-Indian and Indian characters in a tale of ritualized storytelling, survival and reconciliation. The return of a familiar trickster and night-long narratives in a snowbound, red Ford Explorer create *communitas*, binding together the wives and ex-wives of main character Jack Mauser. The first chapter of the novel is a stunning narrative revisit to the first chapter of *Love Medicine*. Other tales from this novel interweave threads and characters from Erdrich's previous novels thus emphasizing the continuity of the Chippewa people.

The works of Native American writers of the Midwest, like most contemporary Indian authors, have invited critical inquiry based on postmodern and postcolonial theories. Nevertheless, tribal sovereignty emerges as a constant in this multifaceted writing. While mediating and often playing with the realities of the modern mainstream world, these writers assert their distinct tribal connections. Individual cosmologies inform communal representations in cultures of survival.

Notes

1. In *A Literary History of the American West* (1987), Paula Gunn Allen introduces Vizenor's works. She also discusses the four-part construction of many Native novels.

2. Robert Dale Parker presents a compelling analysis of Mesquakie foundations in Young Bear's poetry in "To Be There, No Authority to Anything: Ontological Desire and Cultural and Poetic Authority in the Poetry of Ray A. Young Bear," *Arizona Quarterly*, 50 (Winter 1994): 89-115.

3. The works that appear under Dorris' name are: *A Yellow Raft in Blue Water* (1987), a coming-of-age novel with a young woman protagonist of mixed Native and African American origins, and its continuing story *Cloud Chamber* (1997); *The Broken Cord* (1989), a nonfiction account of Dorris and Erdrich's son's battle with fetal alcohol syndrome; *Working Men* (1993), short stories; *Rooms in the House of Stone* (1993), nonfiction; *Paper Trail* (1994), collected essays; *Morning Girl* (1992; rpt., 1994), and *Guests* (1994) young-adult fiction.

Selected Bibliography, 1983-1995

General Works

Callaloo. Native American Literatures: A Special Issue, 17:1 (Winter 1994).

Bruchac, Joseph, ed. *Returning the Gift: Poetry and Prose from the First North American Native Writers' Festival*. Tucson: University of Arizona Press, 1994.

Niatum, Duane. *Harper's Anthology of 20th Century Native American Poetry*. San Francisco: Harper San Francisco, 1988.

Vizenor, Gerald, ed. *Native American Literature: A Brief Introduction and Anthology*. New York: HarperCollins, 1995.

Warrior, Robert Allen. *Tribal Secrets: Recovering American Indian Intellectual Traditions*. Minneapolis: University of Minnesota Press, 1995.

Books by Individual Authors

Blaeser, Kimberly
Gerald Vizenor: Writing in an Oral Tradition. Norman: University of Oklahoma Press, 1996.
Trailing You. New York: Greenwood Press, 1994.

Chrystos
Dream On. Vancouver: Press Gang, 1991.
Fire Power. Vancouver: Press Gang, 1995.
Fugitive Colors. Cleveland: Cleveland State University Poetry Center, 1995.
In Her I Am. Vancouver: Press Gang, 1993.
Not Vanishing. Vancouver: Press Gang, 1988.

Dorris, Michael and Louise Erdrich
The Crown of Columbus. New York: HarperCollins, 1991.

Erdrich, Louise
Baptism of Desire. New York: Harper & Row, 1989.
The Beet Queen. New York: Henry Holt, 1986.
The Bingo Palace. New York: HarperCollins, 1994.
The Blue Jay's Dance: A Birth Year. New York: HarperCollins, 1995.
Jacklight. New York: Henry Holt, 1984.
Love Medicine. New York: Holt, Rinehart & Winston, 1984; new and expanded version, New York: HarperCollins, 1993.
Tales of Burning Love. New York: HarperCollins, 1996.
Tracks. New York: Henry Holt, 1988.

Power, Susan
The Grass Dancer. New York: G. P. Putnam's Sons, 1994.

Vizenor, Gerald
Dead Voices: Natural Agonies in the New World. Norman: University of Oklahoma Press, 1992.
Griever: An American Monkey King in China. Normal: Illinois State University Press, 1987.
The Heirs of Columbus. Hanover, New Hampshire: Wesleyan University Press, 1991.
Interior Landscapes: Autobiographical Myths and Metaphors. Minneapolis: University of Minnesota Press, 1990.
Landfill Meditation: Crossblood Stories. Hanover, New Hampshire: Wesleyan University Press, 1991.
Manifest Manners: Postindian Warriors of Survivance. Hanover, New Hampshire: Wesleyan University Press, 1994.
Matsushima: Pine Islands. Minneapolis: Nodin, 1984.
The People Named the Chippewa: Narrative Histories. Minneapolis: University of Minnesota Press, 1984.
The Trickster of Liberty: Tribal Heirs to a Wild Baronage at Petronia. Minneapolis: University of Minnesota Press, 1988.

Whiteman, Roberta Hill
Philadelphia Flowers. Duluth: Holy Cow Press, 1995.
Star Quilt. Minneapolis: Holy Cow Press, 1984.

Young Bear, Ray A.
Black Eagle Child: The Facepaint Narratives. Iowa City: University of Iowa Press, 1992.
The Invisible Musician. Duluth: Holy Cow Press, 1990.
Remnants of the First Earth. New York: Grove Press, 1996.
Winter of the Salamander: The Keeper of Importance. San Francisco: Harper & Row, 1980.

Diane Dufva Quantic

Contemporary Fiction of the Great Plains

R eaders of Great Plains fiction should know that at the end of the twentieth century, the effort to sustain family and community on the Plains does not take any less effort than it did in the 1890s or the 1930s. Greed for the land's potential wealth, whether it is hidden underground as water or minerals or as an invisible overlay in a developer's planning grid, poses an economic threat as great as that posed by the railroads and the small-town bankers and merchants who controlled the early settlers' means of profit. Small-town life is still psychologically constricting and physically isolating, especially for the younger generations who are unable to understand their elders' deep, sometimes mystical attachment to place, and who see little reward in a marginal life of grim toil and small rewards.

Larry Woiwode has become one of the chief interpreters of life in the Great Plains and Midwest communities in the last half of the twentieth century. His fiction, and that of most recent Great Plains authors, is informed by his sense of his place on the Dakota continuum:

Dakotans must resist the diminishment of the frontier. Its openness permits originality of every stripe. We residents at its edges have learned of the inexorable laws, such as weather, that govern it, and are self-reliant not out of fear of *not* being commonsensical, but in order to save our lives and the lives of our children. The faith and hope of our ancestors, acknowledged or not, is also within us; we persevere on its momentum. ("The Spirit of Place" 60)

720

Beyond the Bedroom Wall (1975) is the first of a series of works that chronicle the disintegration of the Neumiller family as succeeding generations spread across the Midwest from the North Dakota homestead to Illinois and beyond. The farther they stray from the site of their pioneer patriarch's homestead, the more diffuse their lives become. Like Wright Morris, Woiwode uses multiple points of view to tell his story. The novel opens in 1935 at the burial of the pioneer Otto Neumiller on his North Dakota homestead. His son Charles acknowledges his father's deep attachment to the place and, in his final inspection of the Neumiller homestead, he experiences the sense of interconnectedness that informs the novel: he visualizes the closet walls, the bedroom walls expanding around the house, the farm and the country, state and nation: he feels "enclosed in layers of protection invulnerable" (44). Charles' son Martin, Martin's wife Alpha and their six children move away from their roots on the homestead. Like Rölvaag's Beret, Alpha staves off a sense of loss and depression with religious enthusiasm, but unlike the Lutheran Beret, her Catholicism is acquired, not a deeply felt cultural attachment. When Martin decides to leave teaching, a stable job that he loves, to make more money selling insurance and doing odd jobs, Alpha feels even more overwhelmed by life. When Alpha dies of childbirth complications, the family disintegrates further.

Woiwode continues the Neumiller story in *Born Brothers* (1988) and *The Neumiller Stories* (1989). The brothers, Charles and Jerome, are the sons of Martin and Alpha. Memories overtake the present reality for Charles, who recalls the effect of the same events recounted in *Beyond the Bedroom Wall* on his own perception of their family life. For Charles, his lack of center is his undoing. At his suicide, his last thoughts, addressed to his brother Jerome, are of North Dakota and a boat on a lake that was "taking us far/ Out onto the lake, farther out than we should have gone" (611). The stories in *The Neumiller Stories*, told from the omniscient point of view, complete the Neumiller cycle, filling in familiar events rather more objectively.

Because Woiwode relates the sense of place directly to spiritual values, his work is recognized in Christian literary circles, but he has received only passing scholarly attention; nevertheless, his work adds an important dimension to Great Plains literature, focusing not on the struggle against the land, but on the psychological effects of isolation from the land and community, concerns he shares with Rölvaag and Wright Morris. The private sense of loss that permeates his stories symbolizes an attachment that is deeply felt but seldom articulated: Woiwode makes it clear that we resist the power of place at our peril.

Douglas Unger's novel, *Leaving the Land* (1984) and Kent Haruf's *The Tie That Binds* (1984) are contemporary retellings of the classic Great Plains theme of the struggle to come to terms with place and maintain community on the high Plains. In Haruf's novel, Sandy Roscoe tells the story of his neighbors, Roy Goodnough the father, mother Ada and children Edith and Lyman. In 1896, Roy Goodnough came west, thirty years after the land was settled, because "He hated like the very goddamn to be dependent on anyone for anything." The novel chronicles his cruel attempts to preserve his freedom at his family's expense. His wife dies young, as isolated and depressed as Beret, Alpha Neumiller and countless other characters in Great Plains fiction. Like Mari Sandoz's Gulla Slogum (*Slogum House*) and Martha Ostenso's Caleb Gare (*Wild Geese*), Roy's cruelty is unrelenting. In one of his blind rages, Roy's fingers are "broken cut and sliced" by a threshing header, leaving Roy dependent upon his children and especially on his daughter Edith. The ironic metaphor is central to Haruf's story; in a place so vast that it would appear that men and women are free and must be independent, one cannot survive outside the boundaries of family and community. The only thing that balances the cruelty inherent in Roy's demands is the land itself; "it's damned fine if you know how to look at it" (133).

Edith chooses her father over love and escape, and after twenty years of servitude on his father's farm, Lyman leaves to travel the world. When Lyman returns after another twenty years, Edith has a brief respite from responsibility and isolation, but after Lyman is injured in a car wreck, their lives constrict again. Lyman slips into insanity. The old man begins to abuse Edith and eventually the two share a bed. Once more, Edith is trapped. As the narrator Sandy says, she never understood "how to say anything like a continuous yes to herself" (246).

Douglas Unger's novel, *Leaving the Land*, tells the story of Marge Hogan, similarly isolated on her family's homestead and later in the dying town of Nowel, South Dakota. As much as she hates her life, she never manages to leave. Through hard work and determination her father Ben has established a successful family farm on the last marginal land opened to homesteading in the early twentieth century. When her brothers are killed in World War II, Marge helps her father in his struggle to save the family's place on the land. Marge marries a lawyer who comes to town with an exploitive turkey production company. Deserted by her husband, Marge takes any job, no matter how demeaning, to support herself and her son, Kurt. When her father dies, she buries him on the farm, thus ensuring an ironic dilemma for Kurt who, like his mother, finds that he cannot leave the land. When he returns after college and the navy, he finds his mother still caring for the town and the farm. On a shopping spree for the town's Christmas dinner, Marge and Kurt spend all their money, and Kurt even overdraws his accounts, a metaphor for the town and the land: the whole region is used up and over-extended. The novel ends where it began: Kurt and Marge are stranded in the deserted farm house that has been ransacked and exposed to the weather, a physical symbol of their vulnerability to the land and the inevitable cycles of promise and defeat. Marge hands Kurt the deed: she is leaving him the land.

Although there are few direct references to the westering myths, these novels focus on a promise of "free" land that becomes an ironic responsibility, requiring work and revealing that, despite their confidence in themselves, forces beyond their control conspire to force failure.

In other recent Great Plains novels, especially those set on the high Plains, ranching and not farming is the focus. Dan O'Brien's novel, *In the Center of the Nation* (1991) and Jonis Agee's *Strange Angels* (1993) are, like Unger's novel, accounts of the struggle to maintain family operations when corporations and those with power and money are plotting to take over the land. O'Brien's novel focuses on Ross Brady, an idealistic immigrant from California who naively believes in the freedom of the West. His wife Linda, a dancer who refuses to leave Los Angeles, represents the wider world of art and culture, the antithesis of his life on his South Dakota ranch, but his Jewish brother-in-law Stewart becomes his enthusiastic cohort, a symbol of the persistence of the West's melting pot myth. Brady and other cattlemen on the bench work to maintain their marginal operations. They are an amalgamation of contemporary western types: John Kinsley is a paralyzed relic of the petrified past: his place is worked by Indian Elizabeth, a Native American; Tuffy lives on his Indian land grant; Cleve and Edith Miller, who are tottering close to bankruptcy, grasp at any straw that promises financial gain, even at the expense of their neighbors.

In this book, the land is threatened by the plotting of speculators and townsmen who see instant riches in surface mining the ranch land. Against this capitalistic greed, O'Brien sets Elizabeth's simple faith in the land as healer. The struggle is a convoluted plot, but the novel's primary theme is clear: the land is at the center.

The characters in Jonis Agee's novels are the people everyone gossips about in small towns. They are misunderstood by others and even assess themselves harshly, more aware of their shortcomings than their assets. *Strange Angels* is set in the Nebraska Sandhills, and Agee, like Mari Sandoz, is careful to name the contours and the flora and fauna of the region. Cody Kidwell, the apparently illegitimate son of rancher Heywood Bennett, must sort out his inheritance with his half sister Kya and the legally recognized Bennett offspring, Arthur. As in O'Brien's novel, the opposing forces at one extreme are the developers who want to profit at the expense of the fragile range land. At the other extreme are the Indian healers who can restore balance and harmony to the land and the troubled people who try to survive on the Plains. The central theme of this novel is not deceit and duplicity but the need for family that draws the three Bennett children, Kya, Cody and Arthur, reluctantly to each other. The plot has innumerable twists and turns, but it underscores Agee's theme: the need for community to hold the land and the people firmly in place on the open grassland. Near the novel's end, Agee summarizes a theme that resonates in contemporary Great Plains literature — the antiphonal response to Woiwode's catalog of disintegration:

> [The desire for life] was the reason for families that should've scattered in pieces, the reason for runts that clung to the edges of the herd and made it. . . . Despite drought and wind and cold, they all stayed, and gradually lived their lives, dying satisfied that when all was said and done they'd managed to survive. (387)

Agee's other novel, *Sweet Eyes* (1991), is set in Iowa, on the eastern edge of the Great Plains. The people, including the narrator Honey Parrish, are literally "weathering the storm." At the novel's end, when the ghosts of the past have been calmed if not exorcised, Honey once again recognizes the natural balance in her world.

Neither Unger nor Haruf has created other works set in the Great Plains region. Agee has written two volumes of very short stories, *Bend This Heart* (1989) and *A .38 Special and a Broken Heart* (1995), and Dan O'Brien has written a number of other works, including *Spirit of the Hills*. O'Brien's *Rites of Autumn: A Falconer's Journey Across the American West*

(1988) recounts his trip down the Great Plains in an effort to reintro-
duce a falcon to the wild. His collection of short stories, *Eminent Domain*
(1987), includes some fine stories of Great Plains life, especially "A
Strand of Wire," and of environmental issues in stories like "Winter
Cat."

Four other authors deserve mention. Philip Kimball's novel
Harvesting Ballads (1984) tells the story of the aptly named Sorry, a modern pioneer who follows the harvesting crews in search of a family and a
place to call home. The quest ranges from south to north across the
Plains. Written in a cryptic, fragmented prose, the stories of Sorry's parents, grandparents and contemporaries, the history of the family's struggle to establish a Sooner claim in Oklahoma and hold on to the family
farm in the Dust Bowl and Depression are linked to Sorry's present.
Marcus Baldwin, Sorry's only living relative, has realized the pioneers'
dream of a successful ranch but Sorry discovers that he is more like his
father, a rodeo rider, and the drifting dirt than those who have dug in
and stayed. When Sorry returns to Keeper, the man who raised him, he
arrives in the midst of Keeper's farm sale: "There's more to life than trying to keep from starving out on a farm," he explains, but to Sorry, it
means the only home he ever knew is gone (343). All of his options for
a permanent home have proved ephemeral. Sorry, like his father, is a
permanent pioneer.

Ron Hansen's novels *Desperadoes* and *The Assassination of Jesse James
by the Coward Robert Ford* have made him a rising western writer. His
collection, *Nebraska: Stories* (1989) provides his link to Great Plains literature. Hansen knows the Great Plains myths and motifs well enough
to play with them, transforming them by exaggeration or reversal. In
"Wickedness" he repeats the most horrific stories of the 1888 blizzard in
vivid detail, and in "Red Letter Days" he upends Mari Sandoz's story of
Old Jules by replacing the struggle to establish farms and communities
in Nebraska's Sandhills with the story of Cecil, a bored, retired lawyer
who plays golf in the Sandhills and goes ice fishing in the Niobrara.
"Playland" is a transformation of mythic motifs. The 1918 Agricultural
Exhibit has been transmogrified into something foreign and exotic; the
corn pavilion houses a trinket shop, a band and a bakery; the horse sta-
bles have become cabanas for the enormous swimming pool. Playland
has overcome the vagaries of weather, the uncertainty of capital and the
necessity of work, but it is a place where a snapping turtle, a metaphor
for the unexpected, lurks just below the pool's surface to be forgotten at

one's peril. Hansen's collection ends with "Nebraska," a descriptive essay of the past and the seasonal cycles of Plains towns.

Will Weaver is the author of a collection that includes several stories with strong Great Plains roots. The title story in *A Gravestone Made of Wheat* is the tale of Olaf Torvik's determination to bury Inge, his companion of forty-eight years, on their farm. When Inge arrived from Germany in 1920, the local authorities denied the couple the right to marry because of her German nationality. Olaf ignored the rules and lived with Inge as his wife and mother of his children. At her death, he defies them again and buries her beneath the wheat in his field, a metaphor for his intense connection to the land. "Dispersal" recounts a farm sale and encapsulates another Great Plains motif: "Too much machinery, not enough wheat. Too many bankers, not enough rain" (31). "Going Home" is an account of California back-trackers returning to the Midwest. Most of Weaver's stories reflect the Great Plains literary tradition, with its emphasis on the influence of the past on the people who persist in inhabiting the flat, open land.

Brief mention must be made of Jane Smiley, whose Iowa novels and stories have drawn attention to the region on the edge of the divide between the Great Plains and the Midwest. Smiley focuses on the domestic lives of her characters. Place is of only marginal interest: never do events arise from the necessity of living on the land. In a number of her novels and stories, Smiley does not attempt to evoke the character or even the name of the story's location. Her most celebrated novel, *A Thousand Acres* (1991), derives its plot not from the region's history of free will and transformation but from Shakespeare's *King Lear*.

A century after the region was settled by Europeans, novelists still create fiction from Great Plains facts. Weather and farming economics remain uncertain variables. As weather forecasters try to predict the coming storm, Great Plains fiction tries to describe life in a region where the threat of change is the only constant. The story no longer focuses on the transformation of the grasslands into patterns of plowed fields, but rather on the continuing effort to sustain viable farms and ranches in a region that demands persistent effort and continuing isolation.

Selected Bibliography: Great Plains Fiction, 1980-1995

Agee, Jonis. *Bend This Heart.* Minneapolis: Coffee House Press, 1989.
———. *A .38 Special and a Broken Heart.* Minneapolis: Coffee House Press, 1995.

————. *Strange Angels*. New York: Ticknor & Fields, 1993.

————. *Sweet Eyes*. New York: Crown, 1992.

Hansen, Ron. *Nebraska: Stories*. New York: Atlantic Press, 1989.

Haruf, Kent. *The Tie That Binds*. New York: Holt, Rinehart and Winston, 1984.

Kimball, Philip. *Harvesting Ballads*. New York: E.P. Dutton, 1984; rpt., Norman: University of Oklahoma Press, 1995.

O'Brien, Dan. *Eminent Domain*. Iowa City: University of Iowa Press, 1987.

————. *In the Center of the Nation*. New York: Avon, 1991.

————. *The Rites of Autumn: A Falconer's Journey Across the American West*. New York: Doubleday, 1988.

Smiley, Jane. *The Age of Grief*. New York: Ballantine, 1988.

————. *Barn Blind*. New York: Ballantine, 1980.

————. *At Paradise Gate*. New York: Touchstone, 1981.

————. *Moo*. New York: Knopf, 1995.

————. *A Thousand Acres*. New York: Knopf, 1991.

————. *Ordinary Love and Good Will*. New York: Ballantine, 1989.

Unger, Douglas. *Leaving the Land*. New York: Harper & Row, 1984.

Vinz, Mark and Thom Tammaro, eds. *Inheriting the Land: Contemporary Voices from the Midwest*. Minneapolis: University of Minnesota Press, 1993.

Vinz, Mark and Dave Williamson, eds. *Beyond Borders: An Anthology of New Writing From Manitoba, Minnesota, Saskatchewan and the Dakotas*. Minneapolis: New Rivers Press, 1992.

Weaver, Will. *A Gravestone Made of Wheat*. Minneapolis: Graywolf Press, 1989.

Woiwode, Larry. *Beyond the Bedroom Wall*. New York: Farrar, Straus & Giroux, 1975.

————. *Born Brothers*. New York: Farrar, Straus & Giroux, 1988.

————. "Home Place, Heaven or Hell." *Renascence: Essays on Value in Literature*, 44:1 (Fall 1991): 3-16.

————. "The Spirit of Place." In *Inheriting the Land: Contemporary Voices from the Midwest*. Pp. 51-65.

————. *The Neumiller Stories*. New York: Farrar, Straus & Giroux, 1989.

Secondary Sources

Bakerman, Jane S. "The Gleaming Obsidian Shard: Jane Smiley's *A Thousand Acres*." *MidAmerica*, 19 (1992): 127-137.

Block, Ed, Jr. "An Interview with Larry Woiwode." *Renascence: Essays on Value in Literature*, 44:1 (Fall 1991): 17-30.

Morris, Gregory. *Talking Up a Storm: Voices of the New West*. Lincoln: University of Nebraska Press, 1994. Includes interviews with Ron Hansen and Douglas Unger.

Nore, Marcia, ed. *Exploring the Midwest Imagination*. Troy, New York: Whitston, 1993.

VI
The Rocky Mountains

Gregory L. Morris

The Rocky Mountains

Since the publication of *A Literary History of the American West* in 1987, loss has figured largely in the Rocky Mountain literary world. Significant voices have been silenced; heavy tolls have been taken by accident and illness and the physical frailty of age. Norman Maclean: 1990. A.B. Guthrie: 1991. Wallace Stegner: 1993. Frank Waters: 1995. These are broad, strong voices not easy to replace, but the nature of loss often is to encourage recovery, replenishment, and contemporary writing from the Mountain region shows all the best signs of health and vitality. Indeed, Rocky Mountain writing is in an important and exciting moment of transition, as new voices rush to fill the void left by death and as older voices continue to speak or are retrieved from critically imposed silence (as in the cases of Jean Stafford and Mildred Walker). We are witnessing the advent of a new generation of Rocky Mountain writers and a new brand of Rocky Mountain writing; if it can be said that "Rocky Mountain literature came of age" in the 1940s (*LHAW* 839), then it might also be said that a "New Rocky Mountain Literature" is coming of age in the 1980s and 1990s.

This resurgence is the result of a number of factors, not all of them directly literary. For one, the Rocky Mountain region has managed to work itself into the national consciousness — or has had itself placed there by the national (and eastern) media — as a contemporary Paradise Besieged. All sorts of social dramas seem to be playing themselves out against the backdrop of this particular western geography. The persistent tensions between environmental and corporate concerns (logging, energy, mining) maintain a constant, sometimes frenzied pitch. New West homesteaders from both coasts are relocating in various vista-blessed parts of the region, raising property values and driving out long-time residents who claim legal and emotional primacy of place. The very purpose of the landscape has become intensely problematic, as developers, trout fishermen/women, skiers, ranchers, lawmakers and filmmakers, Native Americans and various other competing voices argue over the uses to which mountains and mountain meadows, rivers and streams and lakes shall be put.

Meanwhile, the urban Rocky Mountain West continues to draw off more and more of the region's population, altering the demographic — if not the mythic — structure of the region. At the same time that small towns throughout the area dry up and vanish because of disappearing tax bases, cities like Boise, Bozeman, and Pocatello suddenly have become magnetized; having shifted their economic centers away from mining and farming, these New West towns now attract low-grade, high-wage, white-collar industry and the agreeable middle- and upper-middle-class (and often ex-Californian, back-trailing) populace that travels with such industry. Suddenly, the Rocky Mountain West has become as recognizable for its metropolitan airports and baseball stadiums as for its ski slopes, national parks, and cattle ranches.

Not all of the population drift has been toward the cities, though, and not all of the New Rocky Mountain West mythology is the sort of which local chambers of commerce might wish to boast. While the cities and their suburbs fill up with law-abiding systems analysts and architects and corporate consultants, other trails lead to the outreaches of the region where various conservative and ultra-conservative religious and quasi-military groups congregate in flight from the apocalypse. Suddenly, the Rocky Mountain corridor has been declared a haven from political and moral catastrophe. In the best (and worst) of the western tradition, resistance and outlawry have come to define a radical "quality of life." Names like Randy Weaver, Elizabeth Clare Prophet, and James (Bo) Gritz evoke, in parts of the national imagination, images of the heroic outsider living "off the grid," marking the boundaries of his or her realm in the dust of their local geography.

But the region survives — as it always has — with its complex weave of political, cultural, and economic contrasts. Acting in its most mythic fashion, the vast Rocky Mountain landscape seems to embrace and to accommodate this grand social variety. This same landscape also has made itself a congenial home to a wonderfully diverse collection of writers who work to explore both the past and present of this region, who have extended the Rocky Mountain literary tradition in both familiar and unfamiliar directions, and who have claimed substantial aesthetic territory for both themselves and for western American writing in general. What has in fact emerged among these writers is a sense of regional writerly community and a sort of regional writerly identity; despite artistic and geographic distances among them, these writers have still enjoyed a reasonable coherence of vision and spirit.

This sense of community has been fostered by a number of forces, many of them institutional. Certainly, the numerous fine university writing programs — undergraduate and graduate — in the region have encouraged new and impressive growth in creative writing. As so many of the area's best writers have gravitated toward the academic world, so these writers have, in turn, contributed substantially to developing the chorus of new voices emerging from this section of the West. At the same time, however, a greater number of the region's writers have remained aloof and independent from that university/college scene, providing a useful and healthy balance to the aesthetic nature of the region's work.

These same universities, through their presses, continue to promote Rocky Mountain literature, keeping certain writers in print, recovering lost writers, and introducing new ones to a wider audience. Though a Great Plains house, the University of Nebraska Press has brought back into print seven novels by Montana writer Mildred Walker; and the novels themselves feature introductions written by *other* Montana writers — members of that new community of Rocky Mountain writers — such as Ripley Hugo (Walker's daughter), James Welch, Annick Smith, and Mary Clearman Blew. The University Press of Colorado, meanwhile, has taken to publishing novels from the region, their impulse being driven both by art and (as the *Wall Street Journal* noted appropriately) by profit.[1] At the same time, smaller independent presses throughout the Rocky Mountain territory continue to promote important writers both new and old. (See Appendix for a partial listing of these presses.)

Presses both large and small, academic and private, also support the publication of literary magazines and journals throughout the area. Several of these journals have more than twenty years of publishing history behind them, while others are of more recent vintage; still, all have helped nurture and sustain the literary tradition of their region. (See Appendix for list of journals.)

Literal institutional encouragement has come, too, from the several scholarly institutes and "think tanks" located in and dedicated to the study of the region. The scope of such study extends beyond the limits of the purely literary, but these organizations have exerted a tremendous energy in their examinations of the region's writing. (See Appendix.) At the same time, academic and non-academic forces have spawned a number of writers' workshops, bringing together writers and would-be writers, collecting them into communities, and thereby building an even stronger sense of regional aesthetic identity. (See Appendix.)

Such efforts are also often supported by state arts councils and by the Western States Arts Federation; in a recent collaboration, the arts councils of Wyoming, Utah and Idaho joined with the WSAF in a project entitled: "Tumblewords: Writers Rolling Around the West." This project funded visits by writers in all three states to six rural communities, both in their home states and in the other states involved in the project.[2] Similarly, the state arts councils of Idaho, Montana, Utah and Wyoming also sponsor literary fellowships and first-book awards, thereby invigorating the literary blood of their specific regions.

One other evidence of regional literary health deserves mention here, before moving on to a discussion of individual writers and their work. While writers labor both separately and communally within their own geographic locales, many of the writers in the Rocky Mountain West have been brought together in print, in a spectacular profusion of anthologies featuring the work of this region. Many of these anthologies, while offering writers from throughout the American West, do contain recent work from many of the New Rocky Mountain West's best fiction writers, poets, and essayists; region-specific collections, while fewer in number, are also available. These anthologies — "created communities" — are excellent starting points for any reader interested in discovering the best new voices speaking from the West and, more specifically, from the Rocky Mountain West; they also provide ample proof of the sheer bounty of such new writing. (For a representative list of such collections, consult this essay's bibliography.)

This extensive literary infrastructure has gone a long way toward nurturing the region's writers and their micro-regional communities. And while the creative energy has been pretty evenly distributed throughout the mountain territories, a sort of aesthetic power surge has come from the area of Montana where — for a number of socio-literary reasons — a large number of impressive writers have found a writing home. Catalyzed, perhaps, by the publication in 1988 of the monumental anthology, *The Last Best Place: A Montana Anthology*, edited by William Kittredge and Annick Smith, Montana writers at once discovered both a tradition to which they might (if they so chose) belong and a contemporary identity to which they might (if they so chose) contribute. The effect of this collection should not be underestimated, for writers throughout the Rocky Mountain West (and perhaps throughout the entire American West) suddenly found their work legitimized and acknowledged by this solid and ample bringing-together of voices.

The Last Best Place brought to prominence, in particular, the work of its co-editor, William Kittredge, who over time has become a kind of spokesperson for the literature of this region. His two collections — *The Van Gogh Field and Other Stories* (1978) and *We Are Not in This Together* (1984) — feature stories of westerners coming to terms with the meaning of place and of homeplace. As a westerner, Kittredge has concerned himself especially with the making and unmaking of myth; just as we have fashioned stories into the creation of individual identity, so have we fashioned stories — myths — into the creation of a regional identity, one that often has wrought havoc upon that region. We are in need of new stories, says Kittredge, stories that might satisfactorily explain both the past and the present western condition.

Kittredge has worked hard to redefine the westerner's relationship to the landscape and to re-examine the ways in which our stories and myths about land shape the stories we tell of ourselves. The specific notion of landscape as proving ground, especially for the western male, continues to function for many western storytellers. For example, David Quammen has written surely one of the most powerful tales of mythic and mystical relationship between landscape and masculine nature in "Walking Out" (*Blood Line: Stories of Fathers and Sons*, 1988), a story in which father and son hunt the quality of their own connection with as much energy as they hunt the ever-mystical bear. Similarly, Rick Bass has made of his adopted home in the Yaak Valley of Montana a testing ground for both his fiction and for the characters inhabiting that fiction. Galena Jim Ontz, in the story "Choteau" (*The Watch*, 1989), is "the last tough man there is, for a fact — but it's because he's still got that boy in him, some part he flat-out refuses to let go of." The western man-boy is a common figure in many of the stories now coming out of the Rocky Mountain West, as these writers remind us of the dangers of such a condition; what these men-as-boys refuse "to let go of" is that mythic conception of the wilderness that historically has promoted attempts at conquest and subordination and eventually failure (of the imagination?) and death.

A concern with the historical past also marks the fiction of Ivan Doig, who, in the novels of his McCaskill Trilogy (*English Creek*, 1984; *Dancing at the Rascal Fair*, 1987; *Ride with Me, Mariah Montana*, 1990), describes more than a century's span of family history in the Two Medicine country. Doig's McCaskill clan moves through the very definite social, historical, and even geographical forces that exert themselves upon this landscape. Indeed, Doig's vision is intensely realistic; his storytelling impulse is toward the traditional mode, with tremendous emphasis placed upon narrative strength and truth. Doig's characters act always in time, reacting to the very human pressures of family and of love. Like us all, suggests Doig, these characters function within economies that are tied to both the pressures of emotion and the market.

This same sort of authenticity — this same effort to "get it right" — marks the work of other Rocky Mountain writers who have lived the range life. Ralph Beer's Spur Award-winning (and partly autobiographical) novel, *The Blind Corral* (1986), tracks the return of a young army veteran to the family ranch in western Montana. Jackson Heckethorn faces the ineluctable problem of succession: can he find his place in both the familial line of ranchers and in the landscape upon which that family has done its work? Taking a slightly different attitude toward a similar problem, John L. Moore (a writer who actually works his own Montana ranch and writes about that life) poses, in his novel *The Breaking of Ezra Riley* (1990), a spiritual answer to the same problem of locating the self; for Moore and for his character, Ezra Riley, resolution resides in an acceptance of the Christian ethos, a way of belief that is not (argues Moore) incompatible with the ranch existence.

Working a poetic variation on this theme of the genuine is Paul Zarzyski, who has gone beyond the limits of being a "cowboy poet" and on to describing a vision of the New Western life that is anti-nostalgic and anti-romantic. This vision includes portions of the western past but also examines the difficulties of clinging to that past. Zarzyski's landscapes include huckleberries and Minutemen missile silos (a more and more common feature of the "nuclear landscapes" imagined by Rocky Mountain writers) and suggest the often uneasy relationship between humanform and landform.

736

Surely one of the most original and striking historical novels to concern itself with resistance to nostalgia is Tom Spanbauer's *The Man Who Fell in Love with the Moon* (1991), set in the fictional town of Excellent, Idaho, north of the Sawtooths, and narrated by a half-breed bisexual named Shed, or Duivichi-un-Dua (his Shoshone name meaning "a boy's boy"). The nature of Shed's story is complicated both by his own narrative style—which is alternatingly rough-edged and poetic, as he slowly comes into language through the storytelling process—and by the ambiguities of his birth and family. In the course of his revisionist historical novel, Spanbauer explores particularly ugly portions of western history, paying special attention to the nature of the closing frontier and to the nastier aspects of Mormon bigotry. Spanbauer's emphases, both here and in his first novel, *Faraway Places* (1988), come to rest upon identity and family and story, his novels stressing the necessity of family connection, the toleration of difference, the celebration of sexuality, and the centrality of storytelling. At the same time, Spanbauer's historical vision insists upon a radical unforgivingness of event and a clear-eyed notion of the moral ambiguity of the western past.

An even more radicalized and more stylistically experimental vision of that past can be found in David Romtvedt's *Crossing Wyoming* (1992), which might best be described as a broad fictive history of place. The "novel" has as its protagonist don Eduardo Galeano, a well-known and very *real* Uruguayan journalist/historian/writer (born in Montevideo in 1940) who effectively time-travels through America—and more precisely through Wyoming—tracking the physical and historical landscape of the territory. Wyoming, described as "a state in which distance is expanded and time contracted," serves as the perfect backdrop for events that are both historical and ahistorical. The novel, in fact, develops into a proleptic history, projecting itself into the year 2075 when Galeano finally "dies" in Shell, Wyoming, and becomes himself an archeological find.

This same region of Wyoming, if not the same historical vision of that region, figures in the fiction of Gretel Ehrlich. In the stories collected in both *Wyoming Stories* (1986) and *Drinking Dry Clouds: Stories from Wyoming* (1991) and in her novel *Heart Mountain* (1988) Ehrlich creates a community history for that locale, developing characters and stories that weave in and out of the separate fictions. Ehrlich's primary concern is with the Heart Mountain Relocation Camp, which was erected in the desolate territory of northern Wyoming to house Japanese-American detainees during World War II, and with the interplay between cultures. Racial and spiritual tensions that evolved from this experience eventually prove insoluble, even when set upon by the durable strengths of the human heart; sometimes, the force of history simply overwhelms.

Peter Bowen's Yellowstone Kelly novels—*Yellowstone Kelly* (1990), *Kelly Blue* (1991), and *Imperial Kelly* (1992)—are steeped in "actual" historical time, place, and event, but their protagonist, Yellowstone Kelly, is a historical frontier figure whom Bowen (who himself lives a sort of iconoclastic life in Montana) uses to methodically demolish whatever myths might remain about the "real American West" and its heroes. Bowen's vision is comic, his style comic-historical revisionist; yet he retains a respect for the (albeit feminized) Rocky Mountain landscape.

One writer who has made it a point of studying a place-through-time is Colorado novelist Joanne Greenberg. Though probably best known for the novel *I Never Promised You a Rose Garden* (written under the pseudonym of Hannah Green), Greenberg has constructed a series of fictions centered on a specific piece of Colorado geography and on the changes wrought upon that place and its people. The towns of Gold Flume and Aureole, recurrent settings for much of Greenberg's work, are part of Colorado's mountain mining landscape, and in novels such as *The Far Side of Victory* (1983) and *No Reck'ning Made* (1993) and in several of the stories in *With the Snow Queen* (1991), Greenberg charts the numerous changes—social, economic, spiritual, and topographical—that have occurred within that landscape. As mining boom turned inevitably to bust in the late 1800s, so tourism in the modern age has set about altering the figure of the territory as surely and as significantly as ever did the silver interests of the nineteenth century.

Like Greenberg, David Long writes repeatedly of a fictional literary community in the Rocky Mountain West. Taking the area around Kalispell as his base and working exclusively in the short story form, Long has fashioned a historical experience for his imagined Sperry County that moves through world wars, through labor disputes (as in his superb story, "The Last Photograph of Lyle Pettibone"), and on into contemporary Montana. Long is important not only for his post-frontier vision of the mountain West, but also for his exacting craftsmanship.

While Kittredge and Doig (and others) fashion fictions that deal with both the past and the present West and with the way certain foundational myths have outworn their usefulness, Thomas McGuane imagines a New West Montana radically and systemically warped by its mythic identity. Beginning with the fictional town of Deadrock, Montana, McGuane describes (in *Something To Be Desired*, 1984) a New West populated by "coyotes, schemers, venture capitalists"; a New West laced with equal parts of sex, drugs, trout fishing, and general disaffection for the ruin inscribed upon the human and physical geographies by the unthinking subscription to regional myth.

Part of the value of McGuane's vision is that it originates from a non-native, from a regional outsider who has made Montana his adopted home; this perspective, while often personally and artistically problematic for McGuane (the question of McGuane's "authenticity" as a western or Montana writer remains unresolved for many of his critics), has made McGuane's fiction the center of an irreverent, sardonic and firmly established New West vision shared by many other writers in the Rocky Mountain region. Among those writers associated with Montana (but not *from* Montana and not wholly accepted as Montana writers), Rick DeMarinis and Richard Ford both have sketched often uncomfortable, uncompromising portraits of the contemporary Mountain West. In his novel, *The Burning Women of Far Cry* (1986), and in the stories in *Under the Wheat* (1986), DeMarinis examines the ways in which the western landscape has been traumatized by the controlling, imperious human will; exercises in technology leave the western topography marked (and mocked) by abandoned farms and towns and missile silos, poisoned by chemical and nuclear waste. Ford, particularly in the stories in *Rock Springs* (1987) and in the novel *Wildlife* (1990), studies (among other things) the failure of a gritty New West to afford that mythic second (or third) chance it has so long promised to the westering American; Ford's characters too often end up alienated and isolated—from family, from landscape—and in facefront confrontation with the way-things-are in a hard-luck New West.

Similar concerns, similar physical and moral geographies are explored in the detective fictions of James Crumley and Manuel Ramos. Setting his novels in Montana and alternating between two detective-heroes, Crumley makes a point of involving his protagonists Milo Milodragovitch (*The Wrong Case*, 1975; *Dancing Bear*, 1983) and C.W. Sughrue (*The Last Good Kiss*, 1978; *The Mexican Tree Duck*, 1993) in the real life of the New Rocky Mountain West—timber interests, mob interests, developers, tourists, drug dealers and drugstore cowboys—and of allowing them to demystify and demythify the prevailing stories of that

739

region. In his novels, *The Ballad of Rocky Ruiz* (1993) and *The Ballad of Gato Guerrero* (1994), Ramos explores the world of Chicano politics and activism, as well as the white, mainstream world of Denver's urban developers and their governing morality of economic growth. His novels function both as mystery narratives and as critiques of simplistic perceptions of ethnic relations within the metropolitan New West.

An even grimmer vision of this New West way of being is captured in the work of Utah writer David Kranes. Both in his fiction and his plays (Kranes may be the most successful and significant playwright in the mountain region), Kranes describes a bleak, unromanticized West, one that refuses to be cozied up to by the artist. In his collection of stories, *Hunters in the Snow* (1988) and in his novels *The Hunting Years* (1984) and the technically dazzling *Keno Runner: A Dark Romance* (1989), Kranes often tells tales of loss, of vanishment, of characters coming up hard against physical and topographical realities. Lives in Kranes' fictions (and in plays like *Cantrell* and *Going In*) are characterized by threat and by chaos; distances between people and place, between people and people are too great to be gapped, spanned, closed by word or deed.

There are also writers who have extended McGuane's hip, tongue-in-cheek version of the New West to describe what might be called a New Age New West, with an ethos dictated by sex, drugs, and occasionally, rock and roll. Though primarily a poet, Idaho writer Gino Sky has fashioned a prose world wherein the mountain New West shifts wildly close to the Oriental East. In his two novels — *Appaloosa Rising or the Legend of the Cowboy Buddha* (1980) and *Coyote Silk: The Legend of the Cowboy Buddha Continues* (1987) — Sky envisions a diverse community of spiritual cowboys and cowgirls who populate a West (both pre- and post-apocalyptic) that at times seems drug-induced. Fusion of all types — sexual, spiritual, psychic, dramatic — unifies Sky's vision and belies the apparent chaos of this hyperbolic New West environment. Sky's other prose work is a kind of autobiographical fiction in which Sky (as writer-observer and as character) details for the reader his semi-autobiographical West. *Near the Postcard Beautiful* (1993) crosses various genre lines as it describes various selves that are or might be Gino Sky. The book, written in a hip, flashy, impetuous style that might be characterized as "western cool," describes a West threatened by nuclear bombing and nuclear waste; it is a West where contemporary cowboys pursue vision quests and chant sagebrush mantras.

Perhaps the most sustained aesthetic effort at writing on this edge of the New West has been made by Wyoming writer Tim Sandlin, who comes closest to validating the literary ethos of McGuane (one of Sandlin's protagonists carries, in fact, a copy of McGuane's novel *Panama*). His five novels — *Sex and Sunsets* (1987), *Western Swing* (1988), and the three works of his GroVont Trilogy: *Skipped Parts* (1991), *Sorrow Floats* (1992), and *Social Blunders* (1995) — all take place, for the most part, within the Wyoming landscape; four of those novels create a fictional community set in the sometimes bizarrely real locale of Jackson Hole, where sex and drugs facilitate various social-class crossovers. Like McGuane, Sandlin is interested in the strange, dubious sociology of this New West and how these displaced, alienated New Western pilgrims ultimately stumble upon some small measure of redemption amidst the chaos and fragmentation.

Such critiques of the region, of course, are not confined to the white western writer. James Welch (of mixed Blackfeet and Gros Ventre heritage) continues to build a major literary reputation as he details the facts of contemporary Native American life in the region. His 1990 novel, *The Indian Lawyer*, shifts the focus away from the problems of the reservation and to those of the American Indian who has "made it" in the white world. Sylvester Yellow Calf — a Stanford Law School graduate, a partner in a Helena law firm, a candidate for Congress, and a member of the state parole board — finds himself caught up in a mix of personal and political conflict when he becomes involved with an inmate's wife. As the novel spins itself out, Welch delineates the intertwined forces of sexuality, spirituality, and race within upscale, urban Montana. Dislocation still marks the modern way of being for the American Indian, but such dislocation does not necessarily bring with it, says Welch, a spiritual alienation from both landscape and from the Indian past.

Though she often writes of Oklahoma and of her Chickasaw heritage rooted in that landscape, Linda Hogan is a native Colorado poet and fiction writer whose work offers unsparing treatments of the Native American condition both as it was and as it is. In the poems in *Savings* (1988), Hogan contrasts the natural, elemental world with the urban world of the Native American, trying to locate the "truth of matter" in the spiritual essence of that natural world. In *The Book of Medicines* (1993), Hogan's poems are filled with a primal quality, an animalism that works against that aspiritual quality of modern American — and sometimes Native American — life. Hogan seeks "the house of pelvic truth," situated in the female, maternal nature. Meanwhile, in her novel *Mean Spirit* (1990), Hogan examines the historical crimes committed in the 1920s against the Osage Indians by institutional, economic, and individual forces eager to own and exploit the oil wealth discovered in Indian territory.

Just as compelling is the fiction that explores Rocky Mountain women's lives and their complex relationship with the traditions of history and gender in this area. It is a fiction that, in some ways, had its modern beginnings in the work of Montana writer Mildred Walker, who in novels like *Winter Wheat* (1944) and *The Curlew's Cry* (1955), looked at the meaning of western womanhood and the ways in which the western woman achieved (or lost) identity. A direct literary descendant of Walker — and perhaps the most prominent voice currently speaking out of this tradition — is Mary Clearman Blew, whose girlhood on Montana's High Line has provided her with a body of short fiction that explores what it means to "grow up female in Charlie Russell country." The stories in *Lambing Out and Other Stories* (1977) and *Runaway: A Collection of Stories* (1990) reveal a talent and a vision that continue to sharpen themselves. Particularly in the Juley stories, Blew looks at the complex arrangement of place, gender and expectation that shapes the growth of a Montana female; Blew envisions a "third sex" that allows a Montana girl the chance to satisfy both physical and intellectual desire, at the same time that she defines the "I" that she must become. In one of the Juley stories, "Kissing My Elbow," Juley recognizes her dilemma in choosing between the self imposed upon her by her father (by the male West) and the self that is, so to speak, self-chosen:

> It wasn't a question of choosing between us and the foreigners, as I would have thought an hour ago. It was choosing me, no matter where that left me, and I think even then I sensed it might leave me high and dry. If you're not a boy and won't be a girl, what are you? Me, that's who, although for years, and especially since time, for me as it once was for others, has changed to something to catch and hold, I have wished and half-believed there was another alternative. (*Runaway* 144)

Two Montana writers who have also taken up in their fiction the problem of femaleness in the (primarily) modern Rocky Mountain West are Deirdre McNamer and Toni Volk. A journalist by training and an erstwhile contributor to *The New Yorker*, McNamer has made of her novels — *Rima in the Weeds* (1991) and *One Sweet Quarrel* (1994) — a studying ground for the mysteries of place and being as they connect to the modern western woman. Likewise, the women in Volk's novels — *Montana Women* (1992) and *Maybe in Missoula* (1994) — attempt to cope with what seems the infinite "capacity for breakage and collapse" that marks their lives (*Montana Women* 170). The women in these novels all seek some type of community, some kind of suitable home and family; the novels are sharp studies of relations — marital, parental, fraternal, topographical, sexual — and of the Montana woman's quest for self-fulfillment amid the landscapes (inner and outer, wild and domestic) of the Rocky Mountain West.

An equally fascinating, and more artistically challenging, vision of western womanhood is that described by fiction writer Melanie Rae Thon, a native Montanan presently writing from the East. In several of the stories in *Girls in the Grass* (1991) and in her novel *Iona Moon* (1993), Thon imagines the often bleak sociology of the modern Rocky Mountain West and its potentially crippling effects upon the people who enact that sociology. The heroine of the novel, Iona Moon, takes off on a western odyssey to Montana, Idaho, and Washington in search of her dead mother *and* her own self. As Iona confronts artifacts from the past and unravels certain mysteries of her present, she constantly fights the impulse to suicide. The Snake River (and the bridge that spans that river in Iona's hometown of White Falls, Idaho) is a permanent, haunting presence in the novel; it facilitates the frequent images of diving and falling — and of the consequent paralysis, sterility, or death — that pervade the novel. In the end, Iona discovers the key to her (and our) nature in a bear story, the distilled truth of which is that it is "the wounded heart [that] makes us human."

When the definition of postmodern western womanhood is complicated by questions of sexuality and sexual difference, then the choices are altered somewhat, though expression of the self remains at the center of the dilemma. Patricia Henley, in particular, has touched on the issues of gayness and bisexuality in several of the stories collected in *Friday Night at Silver Star* (1986). In a region whose mythic underpinnings are rooted, in large part, in an inherent heterosexual ethos, the difficulties facing the homosexual or bisexual westerner can be daunting. As Henley's narrator puts it in a story entitled "Black Ice": "Montanans are slow to come to bisexuality, right behind Idaho and

Utah" (*Friday Night at Silver Star* 96). The sexual economy of the region, in Henley's fiction, often is linked directly to a literal geography of place, so that sexual resolution often comes in the form of physical retreat—to a communal farm, for example, or to an isolated and privately owned island. For the sexual radical in the West seeking to revise the governing sexual mythos or ethos, suggests Henley, accommodation might best be found in an alternative vision of community.

The non-fiction essay and memoir, which assumes perhaps as its most recent Rocky Mountain models such works as *Wolf Willow* by Wallace Stegner and *This House of Sky* by Ivan Doig, encompasses a number of concerns and often (but not always) blends the autobiographical impulse with the environmental. Louie W. Attebery's *Sheep May Safely Graze: A Personal Essay on Tradition and a Contemporary Sheep Ranch* (1992) examines three generations of a sheep ranching family (not the author's) in Idaho; the book studies the relationships among work, family, and landscape without involving the author in that dynamic. Rick Bass' *Winter: Notes from Montana* (1990), however, details the writer's personal accommodation to the distances and weathers of the Yaak Valley wilderness in northwestern Montana; here, Bass looks to situate himself within a specific geography and to historicize, in a sense, his experience there. And Edward Geary, in his two books on Utah — *Goodbye to Poplarhaven: Recollections of a Utah Boyhood* (1985) and *The Proper Edge of the Sky: The High Plateau Country of Utah* (1992) — mixes personal narrative with geological, geographical, and political history to create a personal portrait of this specific, significant place.

More typical of the form, perhaps, is James Galvin's lyrical prose work, *The Meadow* (1992). Galvin is a poet who has caught the moods and stories of the Mountain West in much of his poetry; the poems in such collections as *Imaginary Timber* (1980) and *God's Mistress* (1984) frequently evoke the landscapes of Utah and Colorado and Wyoming. In *The Meadow*, Galvin recounts the century-old history of a mountain meadow — and the families who inhabit that mountain meadow — in northern Colorado.

Like Galvin, writing of self-in-place, poet Reg Saner develops a poetics of Colorado and of the Rocky Mountains, hymning the mountains in equal parts transcendental vision and backpacking footfall. In his non-fiction work, *The Four-Cornered Falcon: Essays on the Interior West and the Natural Scene* (1993), Saner explores the "empty plenitude" of western space and what it means to be in the "middle of nowhere." Saner's is an intimate knowledge of landscape and of region; his, too, is an intimate knowledge of the I-in-landscape, as he locates his own physical and spiritual presence in the topography of the Rocky Mountain West.

In works by Terry Tempest Williams — such as *Refuge: An Unnatural History of Family and Place* (1991) and *An Unspoken Hunger: Stories from the Field* (1994) — the temporal emphasis shifts a bit as the author takes on her personal and familial past at the same time that she situates her present personal self within various locales; the landscapes Williams studies are interior and intimate, physical and natural, emotional and spiritual. She is concerned equally with the place-of-woman and the woman-in-place. *Refuge*, in particular, functions as a landmark expression of one woman's attempt to deal with the concomitant crises of familial loss, environmental change, and spiritual faith. As a Mormon woman, Williams responds to the intense challenge issued to her belief in a patriarchal religious authority by her own feminist spirit; at the same time, that "spiritual feminism" sparks her rage against the nuclear presence that has decimated the women in her family. Ultimately, walking through this "landscape of grief," Williams comes to recognize the need for a "Motherbody" to balance the "sacred triangle" that structures her Mormon belief. Thus, her act of writing becomes for Williams an act of faith *and* personal-historical revisionism: "My physical mother is gone. My spiritual mother remains. I am a woman rewriting my genealogy."

This same concern is shared by numerous other women writers in this region, each of whom has sought to locate herself within place and within family through the exercise of nonfiction prose. An eloquent chronicler of displacement (both physical and psychic), Gretel Ehrlich opened a vein of such reflective and self-reflective writing in her book, *The Solace of Open Spaces* (1986), which recounts her establishment of self and home in northern Wyoming. Like Williams, Ehrlich teaches adaptation and accommodation as responses to tragedy, loss, and grief; the death of Ehrlich's lover propels her toward discovery and toward celebration, finding in the open geography of Wyoming a potential for "refuge" and solace: "Space has a spiritual equivalent and can heal what is divided and burdensome in us." *Solace* finally, in its wholeness, offers a brilliant, incisive anatomy of place (Wyoming and Wyoming-as-West) and of the (female) self.

Family relationships supply material for much recent nonfiction from the interior West. Cyra McFadden's *Rain or Shine: A Family Memoir*

(1986) recounts the conflicted and itinerant life of the writer's family as they moved about the West, following the road traveled by her rodeo-announcer father. The memoir is as much a story of McFadden's growing up in a world of western men as it is the story of one such western man. William Kittredge performs somewhat similar work in the essays in *Owning It All* (1987) and in his memoir, *Hole in the Sky* (1992), where he studies the effects of gender-myth and regional-myth upon the men and women of his family; in the latter book, Kittredge pays special attention to his own quite separate, and often very troubled, relations to father and mother. At all times, though, Kittredge is keenly aware of the role played by the land itself and of the ways we "story" ourselves into crucial relation with that land.

Some of the most intense and sustained writing of the Rocky Mountain self has come from Mary Clearman Blew, who in many ways has opened up the world of the western woman to clearer examination. As mentioned before, Blew's stories often describe what it means to grow up female in this heavily masculinized domain; in her nonfiction work, Blew makes this theme a part of her general study of family history. Her first such book, *All But the Waltz: Essays on a Montana Family* (1991), offers a "reading" of the text that is her family and its past on the Montana High Line. In her second book, *Balsamroot: A Memoir* (1994), Blew involves herself more directly in a story that still does not center the self; instead Blew focuses upon her aunt. Here, the dominant concern is with the choices available to a type of female who comes of age in the West and of the ways a woman may live with those choices. In both books, Blew attempts to understand the historical development of the family as it takes place *within* place; by doing so, Blew acquires a voice that allows her to challenge the familial code: "never speak aloud of what you feel deeply."

A somewhat similar impulse drives Teresa Jordan's Wyoming memoir, *Riding the White Horse Home: A Western Family Album* (1993). Jordan tells here of generations of women growing into ranchwomen, of finding connection and disconnection between those generations, of locating what she calls the "unconformities" that lie between past and present lives. In the face of loss and dislocation, with the family ranch slipping out of the family and eventually into possession of an oil company, Jordan's memoir serves as an elegy for a way of life that is slowly passing. At the same time, however, the author celebrates the power of place and of story to heal—like Williams and Ehrlich, Jordan finds "refuge" and "solace" in the land and in the narratives that arise from personal relation to that land.

As if to challenge that vision, Janet Campbell Hale offers a much more dark and disturbing history in her book, *Bloodlines: Odyssey of a Native Daughter* (1993). Hale, born in Los Angeles and raised a member of the Coeur d'Alene tribe of northern Idaho, draws a bleak portrait of family in her work here: an itinerant childhood, with her mother (a mixed-blood Canadian) in flight from an abusive, alcoholic (full-blooded Coeur d'Alene) father; a mother-daughter relationship weighted with conflict and sorrow, largely a result of the physical and emotional crippling endured by that mother at the hands of her husband; a sororal relationship marked by strife and disconnection. But coloring all of these relationships is Hale's deep-seated desire for a spiritual tie to both her people and to their land; it is a connection, however, which she is never to know. Seeking relation to a landscape tied inherently and spiritually to family and to tribe, Hale fails to find that relation; this failure becomes the sad legacy passed along by Hale to her daughter. The story of this failure serves as a kind of correcting counterimpulse to the reclaiming, reconnecting motive that drives so many recent memoirs of the Rocky Mountain West.

Any attempt to describe the broad literary terrain of the New Rocky Mountain West necessarily falls short; too much good writing is being done by too many good writers for an analysis of this sort to cover the map. Nor is incompleteness a bad thing. Just as historians are now reconsidering the meanings of the western experience, so are the region's poets and dramatists and fiction writers reconfiguring the imaginative experience. In the process, they are nurturing and transforming inherited traditions, while at the same time generating vital new traditions that have invigorated the region's literary life.

These writers have shed some of the old parochialisms, and the often proprietary spirit, of writers who have preceded them; they are a much less homogeneous bunch, coming at the frequently conflicted truths of the Rocky Mountain West from many more experiential and aesthetic perspectives. The new writers of the New Rocky Mountain West enjoy a less comfortable peace with the geography of which they write, partly because of the socio-political flux through which that geography is passing, partly because of their own ambiguous, ambivalent relations to that geography. More questions and fewer answers are the aesthetic order of the day. Yet, in their variety and their multiplicity of taste and focus, these writers have opened up the territory of Rocky Mountain literature to a new audience of readers. They have struck deep, have struck rich into the wealth that is the western American consciousness. We have generous cause for celebration.

Notes

1. Marj Charlier, "Seeking Profits, College Presses Publish Novels," *Wall Street Journal* (September 20, 1994), B8.
2. Rick Kempa, "A Regional Report from Wyoming," *Poets & Writers Magazine,* 22 (September-October 1994): 23.

Selected Bibliography

Ardinger, Richard and Ford Swetnam, eds. *High Sky Over All: Idaho Fiction at the Centennial.* Pocatello: Idaho State University Press, 1990.

Attebery, Louie W. *Sheep May Safely Graze: A Personal Essay on Tradition and a Contemporary Sheep Ranch.* Moscow: University of Idaho Press, 1992.

Barnes, Kim and Mary Clearman Blew, eds. *Circle of Women: An Anthology of Contemporary Western Women Writers.* New York: Penguin, 1994.

Bass, Rick. *Platte River.* Boston: Houghton Mifflin, 1994.

———. *The Watch: Stories.* New York: Norton, 1989.

———. *Winter: Notes from Montana.* Boston: Houghton Mifflin, 1990.

Beer, Ralph. *The Blind Corral.* New York: Viking Penguin, 1986.

Bills, Greg. *Consider This Home.* New York: Simon & Schuster, 1994.

Blackburn, Alexander and C. Kenneth Pellow, eds. *Higher Elevations: Stories from the West.* Athens: Swallow/Ohio University Press, 1993.

Blew, Mary Clearman. *All But the Waltz: Essays on a Montana Family.* New York: Viking, 1991.

———. *Balsamroot: A Memoir.* New York: Viking, 1994.

———. *Lambing Out and Other Stories.* (Published under the name Mary Clearman.) Columbia: University of Missouri Press, 1977.

———. *Runaway: A Collection of Stories.* Lewiston, Idaho: Confluence Press, 1990.

Bowen, Peter. *Coyote Wind.* New York: St. Martin's, 1994.

———. *Imperial Kelly.* New York: Crown, 1992.

———. *Kelly Blue.* New York: Crown, 1991.

———. *Yellowstone Kelly.* Ottawa, Illinois: Green Hill, 1988.

Clow, Deborah and Donald Snow, eds. *Northern Lights: A Selection of New Writing from the American West.* New York: Vintage, 1994.

Crumley, James. *Dancing Bear.* New York: Random House, 1983.

———. *The Last Good Kiss.* New York: Random House, 1978.

———. *The Mexican Tree Duck.* New York: Mysterious Press, 1993.

———. *The Wrong Case.* New York: Random House, 1975.

DeMarinis, Rick. *The Burning Women of Far Cry.* New York: Arbor House, 1986.

————. *Under the Wheat*. Pittsburgh: University of Pittsburgh Press, 1986.

Doig, Ivan. *Dancing at the Rascal Fair*. New York: Atheneum, 1987.

————. *English Creek*. New York: Atheneum, 1984.

————. *Ride with Me, Mariah Montana*. New York: Atheneum, 1990.

Edgerton, Clyde. *Redeye: A Western*. Chapel Hill: Algonquin Books, 1995.

Ehrlich, Gretel. *Drinking Dry Clouds: Stories from Wyoming*. Santa Barbara, Califiornia: Capra Press, 1991.

————. *Heart Mountain*. New York: Viking, 1988.

————. *Islands, the Universe, Home*. New York: Viking, 1991.

————. *A Match to the Heart*. New York: Pantheon, 1994.

————. *The Solace of Open Spaces*. New York: Viking, 1985.

————. *Wyoming Stories*. Santa Barbara, California: Capra Press, 1986.

England, Eugene, ed. *Bright Angels and Familiars: Contemporary Mormon Stories*. Salt Lake City: Signature Books, 1994.

England, Eugene and Dennis Clark, eds. *Harvest: Contemporary Mormon Poems*. Salt Lake City: Signature Books, 1989.

Ford, Richard. *Rock Springs: Stories*. New York: Atlantic Monthly Press, 1987.

————. *Wildlife*. New York: Atlantic Monthly Press, 1990.

Freeman, Judith. *The Chinchilla Farm*. New York: Norton, 1989.

————. *Family Attractions*. New York: Viking, 1988.

————. *Set for Life*. New York: Norton, 1991.

Galvin, James. *God's Mistress*. New York: Harper & Row, 1984.

————. *Imaginary Timber*. Garden City, New York: Doubleday, 1980.

————. *The Meadow*. New York: Henry Holt and Company, 1992.

Geary, Edward A. *Goodbye to Poplarhaven: Recollections of a Utah Boyhood*. Salt Lake City: University of Utah Press, 1985.

————. *The Proper Edge of the Sky: The High Plateau Country of Utah*. Salt Lake City: University of Utah Press, 1992.

Greenberg, Joanne. *The Far Side of Victory*. New York: Henry Holt and Company, 1983.

————. *Founder's Praise*. New York: Henry Holt and Company, 1976.

————. *No Reck'ning Made*. New York: Henry Holt and Comany, 1993.

————. *Simple Gifts*. New York: Henry Holt and Company, 1986.

————. *With the Snow Queen*. New York: Arcade Publishing, 1991.

Hale, Janet Campbell. *Bloodlines: Odyssey of a Native Daughter*. New York: Random House, 1993.

Harrison, Jamie. *The Edge of the Crazies*. New York: Hyperion, 1995.

————. *Going Local*. New York: Hyperion, 1996.

Hemesath, James B., ed. *Where Past Meets Present: Modern Colorado Short Stories*. Boulder: University Press of Colorado, 1994.

Henley, Patricia. *Friday Night at Silver Star*. St. Paul, Minnesota: Graywolf Press, 1986.

Hogan, Linda. *The Book of Medicines*. Minneapolis: Coffee House Press, 1993.

————. *Mean Spirit*. New York: Atheneum, 1990.

————. *Savings*. Minneapolis: Coffee House Press, 1988.

————. *Solar Storms*. New York: Scribner, 1995.

Houston, Pam. *Cowboys Are My Weakness*. New York: Norton: 1992.

Hugo, Richard. *Death and the Good Life*. Livingston, Montana: Clark City Press, 1991.

Jackson, Jon A. *Deadman*. New York: Atlantic Monthly Press, 1994.

Jordan, Teresa, ed. *Graining the Mare: The Poetry of Ranch Women*. Layton, Utah: Gibbs Smith, 1994.

————. *Riding the White Horse Home: A Western Family Album*. New York: Pantheon Books, 1993.

Jordan, Teresa and James R. Hepworth, eds. *The Stories That Shape Us: Contemporary Women Write About the West*. New York: Norton, 1995.

Kittredge, William. *Hole in the Sky: A Memoir*. New York: Alfred A. Knopf, 1992.

————. *Owning It All*. St. Paul, Minnesota: Graywolf Press, 1987.

————. *The Van Gogh Field and Other Stories*. Columbia: University of Missouri Press, 1978.

————. *We Are Not in This Together*. Port Townsend, Washington: Graywolf Press, 1984.

————. *Who Owns the West?* San Francisco: Mercury House, 1996.

Kittredge, William and Annick Smith, eds. *The Last Best Place: A Montana Anthology*. Helena: Montana Historical Society Press, 1988.

Kranes, David. *Cantrell*. In *The Best Short Plays of 1988-1989*. Ramon Delgado, ed. Garden City, New York: Nelson Doubleday, 1989.

————. *Going In*. In *The Best Short Plays of 1986*. Ramon Delgado, ed. Garden City, New York: 1986.

————. *Hunters in the Snow*. Salt Lake City: University of Utah Press, 1988.

————. *The Hunting Years*. Salt Lake City: Gibbs Smith, 1984.

————. *Keno Runner: A Dark Romance*. Salt Lake City: University of Utah Press, 1989.

Lesley, Craig and Katheryn Stavrakis, eds. *Dreamers and Desperadoes: Contemporary Short Fiction of the American West*. New York: Dell, 1993.

Long, David. *Blue Spruce*. New York: Scribner, 1995.

————. *Home Fires*. Urbana: University of Illinois Press, 1982.

————. *The Flood of '64*. New York: Ecco, 1987.

Maguire, James H., ed. *The Literature of Idaho: An Anthology*. Boise: Boise State University, 1986.

Martin, Russell, ed. *New Writers of the Purple Sage: An Anthology of Contemporary Western Writers*. New York: Penguin, 1992.

McFadden, Cyra. *Rain or Shine: A Family Memoir*. New York: Alfred A. Knopf, 1986.

McFarland, Ronald E. and William Studebaker, eds. *Idaho's Poetry: A Centennial Anthology*. Moscow, Idaho: University of Idaho Press, 1988.

McGuane, Thomas. *Nothing but Blue Skies*. Boston: Houghton Mifflin, 1992.

————. *Something to Be Desired*. New York: Random House, 1984.

McMahon, Franci. *Staying the Distance*. Ithaca: Firebrand Books, 1994.

McNamer, Deirdre. *One Sweet Quarrel*. New York: HarperCollins, 1994.

————. *Rima in the Weeds*. New York: HarperCollins, 1991.

Messer, Neidy. *In Far Corners*. Lewiston, Idaho: Confluence Press, 1990.

Moore, Christopher. *Coyote Blue*. New York: Simon & Schuster, 1994.

Moore, John L. *The Breaking of Ezra Riley*. Batavia, Illinois: Lion Publishing, 1990.

Nelson, Antonya. *The Expendables*. Athens: University of Georgia Press, 1990.

————. *In the Land of Men*. New York: William Morrow & Company, 1992.

Nelson, Dianne. *A Brief History of Male Nudes in America*. Athens: University of Georgia Press, 1993.

O'Brien, Kathleen, ed. *Idaho+: Contemporary Poetry from the American West*. Boise: Painted Smiles, 1987.

Partridge, Dixie. *Deer in the Haystacks*. Boise: Ahsahta Press, 1984.

————. *Watermark*. Upper Montclair, New Jersey: Saturday Press, 1991.

Peterson, Levi E. *The Backslider*. Salt Lake City: Signature Books, 1986.

————. *The Canyons of Grace*. Champaign-Urbana: University of Illinois Press, 1982.

————. *Night Soil*. Salt Lake City: Signature Books, 1985.

Quammen, David. *Blood Line: Stories of Fathers and Sons*. St. Paul, Minnesota: Graywolf Press, 1988.

Ramos, Manuel. *The Ballad of Gato Guerrero*. New York: St. Martin's, 1994.

————. *The Ballad of Rocky Ruiz*. New York: St. Martin's, 1993.

Raptosh, Diane. *Just West of Now*. Montreal: Guernica Editions, 1992.

Romtvedt, David. *Crossing Wyoming*. Fredonia, New York: White Pine Press, 1992.

Sandlin, Tim. *Sex and Sunsets*. New York: Henry Holt, 1987.

————. *Skipped Parts*. New York: Henry Holt, 1991.

————. *Social Blunders*. New York: Henry Holt, 1995.

————. *Sorrow Floats*. New York: Henry Holt, 1992.

————. *Western Swing*. New York: Henry Holt, 1988.

Saner, Reg. *Climbing into the Roots*. New York: Harper & Row, 1976.

————. *Essay on Air*. Athens: Ohio University Press, 1984.

————. *The Four-Cornered Falcon: Essays on the Interior West and the Natural Scene*. Baltimore: Johns Hopkins University Press, 1993.

Schofield, Susan Clark. *Telluride*. Chapel Hill: Algonquin Books, 1993.

Sky, Gino. *Appaloosa Rising or the Legend of the Cowboy Buddha*. Garden City, New York: Doubleday, 1980.

————. *Coyote Silk: The Legend of the Cowboy Buddha Continues*. Berkeley, California: North Atlantic Books, 1987.

————. *Near the Postcard Beautiful*. Boise: Floating Ink Books, 1993.

Spanbauer, Tom. *Faraway Places*. New York: G. P. Putnam's Sons, 1988.

————. *The Man Who Fell in Love with the Moon*. New York: Atlantic Monthly Press, 1991.

Thon, Melanie Rae. *Girls in the Grass*. New York: Random House, 1991.

————. *Iona Moon*. New York: Poseidon, 1993.

Volk, Toni. *Maybe in Missoula*. New York: Soho Press, 1994.

————. *Montana Women*. New York: Soho Press, 1992.

Walker, Mildred. *The Curlew's Cry*. 1955; rpt., Lincoln: University of Nebraska Press, 1994.

————. *Winter Wheat*. New York: Harcourt, Brace, and Company, 1944; rpt., Lincoln: University of Nebraska Press, 1992.

Waters, Mary Ann. *The Exact Place*. Lewiston, Idaho: Confluence Press, 1987.

Welch, James. *The Indian Lawyer*. New York: Norton, 1990.

Williams, Terry Tempest. *An Unspoken Hunger: Stories from the Field*. New York: Pantheon, 1994.

————. *Refuge: An Unnatural History of Family and Place*. New York: Pantheon, 1991.

Zarzyski, Paul. *The Make-Up of Ice*. Athens: University of Georgia Press, 1984.

————. *Roughstock Sonnets*. Kansas City, Missouri: Lowell Press, 1989.

Appendix

Please note that none of these lists is meant to be complete or exhaustive. What is offered here is a representative sample.

Small Presses

Clark City Press (Livingston, Montana)

Confluence Press (Lewiston, Idaho)
Gibbs Smith, Publisher (Layton, Utah)
High Plains Press (Glendo, Wyoming)
Limberlost Press (Boise, Idaho)
Mesilla Press (Arvada, Colorado)
Redneck Press (Pocatello, Idaho)
Seven Buffaloes Press (Big Timber, Montana)
Signature Books (Salt Lake City, Utah)

Journals and Magazines

Cold-Drill (Boise State University)
Colorado Review (Colorado State University)
CutBank (University of Montana)
Denver Quarterly and *High Plains Literary Review* (Denver, Colorado)
Kinesis (Whitefish, Montana)
Northern Lights (Colorado)
Owen Wister Review (University of Wyoming)
The Redneck Review of Literature (Pocatello, Idaho)
Writers' Forum (Colorado Springs, Colorado)

Institutes

Mountain West Center for Regional Studies (Logan, Utah)
Center for the Rocky Mountain West (Missoula, Montana)
Northern Lights Institute (Missoula, Montana)
Center for the American West (Colorado)
Center for the New West (Colorado)

Writers' Workshops

Snake River Institute (Jackson Hole, Wyoming)
Writers at Work (Centerville, Utah)
Yellow Bay Writers' Workshop (Flathead Lake, Montana)
The Glen Workshop (Colorado Springs, Colorado)
Hellgate Writers (Missoula, Montana)

A. Carl Bredahl

Ivan Doig

At the heart of Ivan Doig's work is a simultaneous love for the people and place of Montana and a commitment to the language necessary to make that love come alive. "My father had to be more than is coded in the standard six-letter sound of 'father'" (*This House of Sky* 238). Both the father, in this instance, and the desire to do more than work with standard codes drive Doig's art. The effort in that art, the considerable pleasure of reading his work, and the importance of his imagination in contemporary narrative all center in this commitment to the possibilities (and limitations) of language and the tremendous joy generated by the geography and people that compose "Montana."

Ivan Doig was born June 27, 1939, in White Sulphur Springs, Montana, and grew up along the Rocky Mountain front, where several of his books take place. Perhaps growing up along the "front" has something to do with his narrative fascination with edges, places of contact between individuals or generations as well as the transitions between social or psychological conditions. His narratives center on the people of the Big Sky country, their relation to the ecological, social, and economic systems within which they live their lives.

As recounted in *This House of Sky* and later in *Heart Earth*, Doig's mother died when he was six; he was subsequently raised by his father and grandmother. The first child in the family to earn a college degree, Doig graduated from Northwestern University with an M.A. in 1962. In

1965 he married Carol Muller, a fellow journalist in Evanston, Illinois. A year later they moved to Seattle, Washington, where Doig earned his Ph.D. in American history from the University of Washington. Since then, he has published not only the six novels for which he is most widely known but also an extensive list of books and articles detailed in Elizabeth Simpson's *Earthlight, Wordfire: The Work of Ivan Doig* (1992).

Ordinarily, one would begin any discussion of Doig's writing with *This House of Sky*, the book that brought him significant attention and a nomination for the National Book Award. Doig's first published book, however, was *News: A Consumer's Guide*, co-written with his wife Carol in 1972 and important because it reveals much about the topics he would develop in his later narratives. The title of *News: A Consumer's Guide* is especially appropriate to an imagination like Doig's which seeks to understand and give verbal expression to relationship. The title points not so much to the discrete events designated "news" as to the fact that these events are to be "consumed." Doig's interest always is the physical world, events that occur in that world, and the response of individuals (consumers) to those events.

As detailed in *News*, Doig is highly sensitive to the perceiving act itself. Having chosen a career as a freelance writer, this individual who will spend his life working with the verbal packages called "words" begins his writing with an examination of how these packages are made, how they relate to the physical world, and how they are consumed. "A word is like a section of telephone cable, a sheath with several conduits inside it. Each of the conduits can carry a different meaning, but all within the same unit" (144). "News stories are made, not born. Made by workers and machines that refine random happenings into bundles of information" (22). That focus on "making" fascinates Doig and is both the subject and generator of his art.

When Doig discusses the editing of news, he talks about the consumer's act as well as the more traditional role of the newspaper or television editor. Selecting material to be reported is certainly an important step in the overall process, but the consumer's perceiving act provides the distinctive focus of *News*. The narrators in the later narratives themselves function as consumers of events, and we should therefore expect that Doig's books will be less concerned with traditional "plot," the moving from event to event, than with the "consumption" of those events as his narrators learn to savor Montana's richness. Additionally,

754

Doig's interest will be in the effort to integrate his visual experience with his verbal skills. "First, man learned to telegraph words across large spans of distance. The next step was to skip the wires and send words by radio. Then came pictures with the words — television. The package the news came in became more and more handy, more and more unitary" (18). Strikingly, Doig stays with this focus on the "unitary." Published twenty years later, his 1990 *Ride With Me, Mariah Montana*, the final work of the English Creek trilogy, again makes explicit the continuing challenge of that integration.

News indicates that only with consciousness of the event's shaping can an individual make use of (consume) that event. With *This House of Sky* (1978) Doig turns to the event that is himself and begins a process of particularizing that will extend as well to his next book, *Winter Brothers*. From the general (news and consumer) to the particular (*this* house), Doig begins to apply ideas developed in *News* to the more crucial concerns of an individual life. *Sky* works with the narrator's consuming of both the house that is his family and the house that is Montana. As always for Doig, such efforts are intensely verbal:

> The words of all the ties of blood interest me, for they seem never quite deft enough, not entirely bold and guileful enough, to speak the mysterious strengths of lineage. . . . It seems somehow too meager that they should merely exist, plain packets of sound like any other, and not hold power to texture each new confrontation with the bright exact ones that are yearned for. (238-239)

"Where [my father's] outline touched the air, my knowing must truly begin" (*House of Sky* 31). The narrator returns to this image at the end of the narrative: "My single outline meets the time-swept air that knew theirs" (*House of Sky* 314). "Outline" in each case points to the narrator's perception of the centrality of surface; each outline establishes a place of contact with other surfaces. The word *outline* additionally has clear verbal connotations appropriate to an imagination that, in the previous book, established its sensitivity to language. "That is as much as can be eked out — landscape, settlers' patterns on it, the family fate within the pattern — about the past my father came out of. I *read* into it all I can, *plot* out likelihoods and chase after blood hunches. But still the *story* draws itself away from the dry twinings of map work and bloodlines, and into the boundaries of my father's own body and brain" (*House of Sky* 30-31 [emphasis added]). "Story" is important to Doig because events in his landscape function within a developing narrative.

The opening and closing lines of *Sky* define the shape of the book:

> Soon before daybreak on my sixth birthday, my mother's breathing wheezed more raggedly than ever, then quieted. And then stopped.
>
> The remembering begins out of that new silence. Through the time since, I reach back along my father's tellings and around the urgings which would have me face about and forget, to feel into these oldest shadows for the first sudden edge of it all.

* * *

> Then my father and my grandmother go, together, back elsewhere in memory, and I am left to think through the fortune of all we experienced together. And of how, now, my single outline meets the time-swept air that knew theirs.

The narrative springs out of "new silence." Learning to speak within that silence, getting from the opening to the closing lines, is an effort that necessitates seeing the self within the context of family and environment. In the first sentence, Ivan's sixth birthday and his mother's dying breath go together — youth and age, child and parent, health and illness, beginning and end — not as distinct from each other in separate sentences but as interrelated within one. *The House of Sky* does not dwell on the mother or, more particularly, her death. Its focus moves quickly out of death in the direction of the child's life. Nor does the strikingly abrupt first paragraph initiate a narrative of a young person breaking free from confinement but of a narrative voice moving immediately into the second paragraph, where its effort will be to "reach" and "feel" back along its father's tellings in spite of "urgings" to forget. In the final section, "Endings," the father is dying, the being "who enchanted into me such a love of language and story that it has become my lifework." Consuming, integrating that connection into himself becomes essential to the narrator's life and work.

The book, then, is shaped by the dying of the parents and the consequent imaginative growth of the child. Out of the frustration with the loss of his mother and with the narrative effort to break through the verbal code of "father," Doig comes to value the land and people and to see the need for verbalizing that value.

> All of his way of life that I had sought escape from — the grinding routine of ranching, the existence at the mercy of mauling weather, the endless starting-over from one calamity or another — was passing with him, and while I still wanted my distance from such a gauntlet, I found that I did not want my knowing of it to go from me. . . . I had begun to see that it counted for much. (*House of Sky* 294)

Seeing requires speaking if outlines are to touch, but speaking requires an internal education, and intellectual growth alone will not do: "Exactly at the point of my life when I had meant to turn myself to teaching, to the routined assurances of scholarliness, I found myself veering inward instead" (*House of Sky* 294).

The inward veering eventually produces *This House of Sky* and the struggle of "my single outline" to meet "the time-swept air that knew theirs." This action might generate little more than sentimentality were it to remain an expression of homesickness, but the looking into the narrator's past, his contact with the father, generates movement and "story." With his next narrative, *Winter Brothers: A Season at the Edge of America* (1980), the narrative voice once again moves, turning to the historical past and its relationship to the historical present.

"All of Doig's books push the boundaries of genre," argues Elizabeth Simpson (*Earthlight* 11), and in these terms *Winter Brothers* is narratively one of Doig's most interesting. All of Doig's writings to date depend on a collecting and consumption of data, the act of a natural creature struggling to function at the peak of its ability within the natural world. In *This House of Sky*, the imagination wrestles with voices, facts about ancestors, photos, and personal experience in an effort to understand itself in relation to the lives closest to it. In *Winter Brothers* the imagination moves temporally, exploring its own relation to another imagination that occupied the same geographical space one hundred years earlier, the life and writings of James Gilchrist Swan, a nineteenth-century pioneer in the present states of Oregon and Washington. The effort is to reject the "silly feeling that it's impossible for two figures to occupy the same space at the same time" (241), to discover narratively a brother, an individual with whom the narrator shares space, motivation, and values:

> Here is the winter that will be the season of Swan. Rather, of Swan
> and me and those constant diaries. Day by day, a logbook of what
> is uppermost in any of the three of us. It is a venture that I have
> mulled these past years of my becoming less headlong and more
> aware that I dwell in a community of time as well as of people.
> (*Winter Brothers* 4)

As in *News* and *House*, the narrator begins by combing data, studying
pieces of paper (containing some 2.5 million handwritten words), trying
to put a life together, his own and that of a figure who is "doubly valuable to me because the people of my own blood are gone now, buried in
Montana, the storytellers, reciters of sayings . . . and Swan is an entranc-
ing winterer — a tale-bringer emissary from the time of the first people"
(163). The subject, of course, is more than the relationship of two men;
it is the relationship of both as "westerners" to the place that is
America's West. For Doig, being a "westerner" is a direction of the mind,
meaning that the individual pushes his imagination to the physical and
verbal coast, the limit of its capability, even if such an effort leads to the
discovery that "the edge of America" can also be a brink.

With *The Sea Runners* (1982), what Simpson calls Doig's first novel,
Doig turns in a new direction. *The Sea Runners* again focuses on a
moment in the past, but not with Doig as conscious presence; working
on his relationship with the individual that was James Swan is replaced
by detailing the experience of four unlikely companions who in 1853
escaped from a Russian fur company and made a 1,200-mile canoe run
down Canada's western coast. Two Swedes escape from indentureship in
the Russian company and unite with two others in an effort at survival,
a subject central to all Doig's work — learn to work together, find skills
within oneself that were previously unknown, work with/battle nature,
and learn to value survival rather than triumph. All of these characteristics are embodied in the narrative's concern with geography and a
missing piece of map. "The narrator sets up a metaphor for the distance
the characters will travel," says Simpson, "and then demonstrates, step
by step, that the metaphor is inadequate. . . . The landscape of the
Northwest, magnificently described, is simply too large and daunting to
be grasped and subdued by individuals" (38-39).

"The spaces between stars," says the narrator, "are where the work of
the universe is done. . . . So too the distances among men cast in with
one another on an ocean must operate" (101). Within such spaces maps

do not offer much help, and it is in those spaces that Doig focuses his imagination. After *This House of Sky*, Doig has explored "spaces"/events outside the "place" that is his personal world. With *English Creek* (1984), he returns to the Montana of *This House of Sky* less self-conscious, more confident, anxious to integrate into a unit what in *Sky* and *Winter Brothers* had been a wonderful struggle with individual pieces. That missing piece of map central to *Sea Runners* is evident throughout the imaginative efforts of the early writings as the imagination grapples with wholeness, relationship of people and events. *English Creek* begins a trilogy focusing on the lives of the ancestral Scotsmen who settled Montana. The trilogy structure itself embodies the implication of a complete map, but the focus in the trilogy is always on the "spaces between stars," spaces no "map" can detail, spaces where language remains the only vehicle.

Appropriate to its setting in 1939, *English Creek* explores transitions, what Simpson calls the "edges of change" (*Earthlight* 41). These edges, in addition to the social and political conditions of 1939, include the narrator, Jick McCaskill, wrestling with the "joys" of puberty and adolescence and the physical location of English Creek on the edge of the Two Medicine National Forest where forest and cleared land meet. The integration of these three edges — social, natural, and personal — continues to be the central ingredient in Doig's work. In *English Creek* they exist with the metaphoric missing piece of map being the overhanging Phantom Woman forest fire burn of the past and the knowledge readers have of what awaits after 1939. Under these conditions, an individual life still can only struggle for survival rather than triumph.

One of the qualities that emerges full blown in *English Creek* is the joy inherent in living. *This House of Sky* was not about death but emerging life; now in the opening novel of the trilogy and on into the subsequent works as indicated by their titles, *Dancing at the Rascal Fair* and *Ride With Me, Mariah Montana* with their active verbs, is the joy in the activities of life that simply cannot be worn down by pain. In *English Creek* much of this quality of joy centers in the choice of the adolescent male as narrator; the newness of life is just plain fun — exciting, frightening, but fun with young Jick digging for the new outhouse or delighting in sexual fantasies about his brother's fiancee, Leona.

Referring to the "specialness of the ordinary," Simpson quotes Doig that "the richness of life is what I'm trying to get at" (*Earthlight* 47). The metaphor of the fire perhaps overhangs *English Creek* too heavily as does the feeling for some readers that at times the "ordinary" gets a little too "special," but to emphasize either would be to miss the sheer pleasure of the reading, the voice of Jick McCaskill and the "spaces" within and between the lives he explores. That same richness of life becomes the center of *Dancing at the Rascal Fair* (1987) and *Ride With Me, Mariah Montana* (1990), the prequel and sequel to *English Creek*. *Dancing* takes place at the turn of the century and is narrated by Jick's grandfather, Angus McCaskill; *Mariah Montana*, set in 1989, returns to the voice of the now sixty-four-year-old Jick. A full century of both the McCaskill family and the "place" that is Montana is thus explored in the trilogy.

Dancing at the Rascal Fair follows the migration and settlement that established much of the character of Montana's people. Language responsive to the demands and joys of environment presents the pleasure of the book. The title refers to "that day of fest when Nethermuir farmers and farm workers met to bargain out each season's wages and terms and put themselves around a drink or so in the process...one day of magic filled... [with] color and laughter" (12). The narrative follows the lives of Angus McCaskill and Rob Barclay, two friends who emigrate from Nethermuir, Scotland, to Gros Ventre, Montana. As narrator, Angus writes out of memory of his friend and presents numerous scenes — storms on the Atlantic, a sheep shearing contest, his consummated love with Anna Ramsay, a life-threatening blizzard — which satisfy those readers who have come to expect from Doig the interrelating of language and event.

Appropriate to the title is a narrator who enjoys life's rhythms; he wants to see, says his lover, Anna Ramsay, "how many ways life can rhyme." The narrative he generates is one of those efforts at dancing with life, but in Doig that means dancing with storms both of the country and of the heart while keeping your wits about you through flood, blizzard, drought, and desire. That dance takes place not just in plot but also in narrative vision and language. The incredible struggles of the new settlers against natural and social forces, like the battle with the forest fire in *English Creek*, occupy much of the attention in this second part of the trilogy, and always the title's focus on "Dancing" remains paramount. These two aspects of life, pain and joy, generate the events of *Dancing*; the language generates the dance.

Dancing is a long way from *House of Sky* because Doig has learned how to bring color and psychological complexity to the creation of his characters and richness of detail to the events of their lives. Doig has become a master craftsman by the time of *Dancing* and the events, characters, and style are in plentiful abundance: "'There is so much of this country. People keep having to stretch themselves out of shape trying to cope with so much. Distance. Weather. The aloneness. All the work. This Montana sets its own terms and tells you, 'do them or else'" (332).

In *Mariah Montana*, the final piece of the trilogy, set in Montana's centennial year, 1989, the struggles with narrative technique once again serve to center Doig's attention. As always, history is context for Doig, less dates and events of the centennial than individual lives struggling to survive within an environment of forces not only social and economic but also personal. Now sixty-four, Jick travels through Montana in a motor home with his daughter Mariah, a freelance photographer, and her ex-husband Riley, a journalist. That "marriage" between the visual and the verbal, appropriately an ex-marriage, nicely defines Doig's own effort at narrative "marriage." That it does not work as smoothly as either partner would like in spite of the moments of brilliantly satisfying success does not detract from the effort.

And it is the effort to marry a facility with language to an eye fascinated with the fullest experiences of life that has continued to define the art of Ivan Doig. That effort at "marriage" was outlined twenty years earlier in *News: A Consumer's Guide* in the consciousness of the fact that events do not stand on their own, that they are always available only through interpretation. The consciousness of struggle as an ongoing challenge is brought back into play with the marriage framework of *Mariah Montana*. And in a useful way the numerous human marriages throughout Doig's writings, beginning with the tragic ending of a marriage between Berneta and Charlie Doig that opens *Sky*, that are the focus of attention in so much of Doig are perhaps the events that most center his art. In "marriage" the individual seeks to fulfill him or herself, to relate to another, to find a voice. In the southerner Thomas Wolfe, "home" is something to which you cannot return; in Doig, however, the world and our companions in that world compose the only home we have. Our efforts to "marry" within that world, as well as our efforts to understand and communicate its richness and variety, make us human.

The publication in 1993 of *Heart Earth* continues the fascination with writing and relationship. Generated by the discovery of his mother's letters written to her brother Wally Ringer during World War II, Doig's 1993 narrative does not extend the trilogy so much as expand the earlier focus on the mother and the ongoing effort of the verbal to touch the physical. Doig's work has been driven by this concern for two decades; in that commitment to people and language and place are the beauty and challenge of this writer.

* * *

Much of the critical attention to Ivan Doig has been restricted to review essays of the novels. Elizabeth Simpson's *Earthlight, Wordfire: The Work of Ivan Doig*, however, together with several individual essays, provides a solid center for scholarly study of Doig's work. *Earthlight, Wordfire* begins with insightful close readings of the six major novels and then focuses in useful detail on the topics of folklore, landscape, and style. The book benefits both from Simpson's own careful work and from her friendship with Ivan and Carol Doig. She thus had access to numerous conversations and bibliographic materials that she uses effectively in her work. Simpson's study includes the most extensive bibliography to date both of secondary sources and of Doig's own writings (ten books, 118 articles).

Selected Bibliography

Primary Sources

Bucking the Sun. New York: Simon & Schuster, 1996.
Dancing at the Rascal Fair. New York: Atheneum, 1987.
English Creek. New York: Atheneum, 1984.
Heart Earth. New York: Atheneum, 1993.
This House of Sky: Landscapes of a Western Mind. New York: Harcourt Brace Jovanovich, 1978.
News: A Consumer's Guide (with Carol Doig). Englewood Cliffs, New Jersey: Prentice-Hall, 1972.
Ride With Me, Mariah Montana. New York: Atheneum, 1990.
The Sea Runners. New York: Atheneum, 1982.
Winter Brothers: A Season at the Edge of America. New York: Harcourt Brace Jovanovich, 1980.

Secondary Sources

Ahearn, Kerry David. "Ivan Doig's Self-Narratives: The West, Wilderness, and the Prophetic Impulse." *South Dakota Review*, 20:4 (Winter 1983): 7-22. Argues that "Doig offers romanticized wilderness experience as a screen over complex topics about the West which he cannot avoid presenting but does avoid exploring."

Bevis, William. *Ten Tough Trips: Montana Writers and the West*. Seattle: University of Washington Press, 1990. In contrast to Ahearn, Bevis sees a "risk-taking prose" and a willingness to wrestle with the dilemmas of twentieth-century western life. Memory and myth are central to the discussion.

Bredahl, A. Carl. *New Ground: Western American Narrative and the Literary Canon*. Chapel Hill: University of North Carolina Press, 1989. Sees Doig's imagination as valuing event and relationship. Essay equally concerned with language and the effort to push beyond the usual verbal "codes."

Kelso, Duncan. *Inside This House of Sky: Photographs of a Western Landscape*. New York: Atheneum, 1983. Includes an introductory essay by Ivan Doig, "The Eye of Time." A collection of black-and-white photographs of the area around White Sulphur Springs, Montana, arranged to accompany selected passages from *This House of Sky*.

Robbins, William G. "The Historian as Literary Craftsman: The West of Ivan Doig." *Pacific Northwest Quarterly*, 78:4 (October 1987): 134-140. Focuses on Doig's commitment to language, "the thread that links the best creative writing about the West."

Simonson, Harold P. *Beyond the Frontier: Writers, Western Regionalism, and a Sense of Place*. Fort Worth: Texas Christian University Press, 1989. "In composing words [Doig] composes himself but in relation to place. In remembering Montana he quickens to the power that the place evokes and to the urgent need to answer or obey it" (148). Essay focuses on *House of Sky*.

Simpson, Elizabeth. *Earthlight, Wordfire: The Work of Ivan Doig*. Moscow, Idaho: University of Idaho Press, 1992.

Mary Clearman Blew

William Kittredge

William Kittredge was born in 1932 to a pioneer ranching family in southeast Oregon. He was brought up according to a strict code which respected ownership of property and a work ethic along with physical toughness and a lifestyle as ritualized as the action of a dime novel. His grandfather's picture hangs in the National Cowboy Hall of Fame, an icon of all that the Kittredge family honored. Kittredge himself was expected to maintain the family's tradition and eventually manage their vast landholdings, which he did for eleven years. In his collection of essays, *Owning It All* (1988), and in his memoir, *Hole in the Sky* (1992), Kittredge has described his grandfather's obsession with ownership and control, as well as his own escape from ranching into creative writing via the Iowa Writers Workshop, where he received the M.F.A. in English in 1969.

Since 1969 Kittredge has taught creative writing at the University of Montana, where he presently holds the Regents Professorship in English. He has been a Stegner Fellow, a consulting editor for numerous literary quarterlies or regional magazines, including *Northwest Review, Rocky Mountain Magazine, Pacific Northwest Magazine,* and *Outside.* He is on the advisory boards of *Puerto Del Sol* and *Montana Magazine of Western History.* He has been the recipient of the University of Oregon Ernest Haycox Fiction prize (1968); National Endowment for the Arts awards (1974, 1981); University of Montana summer grants (1970, 1976, 1982); Innovative Summer Program grants (1977, 1978); Montana Committee for the Humanities grant (1979); PEN/NEA

Syndicated Fiction Project awards (1983, 1988) and Fiction Award (1984); Neil Simon Award for script (1984); Montana Governor's Award for Literature (1985): H.G. Merriam Award (1988); and the National Endowment for the Humanities Frankel Award (1994).

Kittredge has become well known throughout the West for his personal acquaintanceship among writers, his involvement in teaching and creative writing workshops, and his generosity to students and to other writers. He has edited several key anthologies of western writing, most notably *The Last Best Place: A Montana Anthology* (1988) with Annick Smith, and also *Montana Spaces: Essays and Photographs in Celebration of Montana* (1988), with Steven M. Krauzer, a special edition of *Contemporary Western Fiction TriQuarterly* (1980), and *Beyond the Mythic West* (1991) with Stewart Udall, Patricia Nelson Limerick, Charles Wilkinson and John Wolkman. He has written screenplays for the films *Heartland* and *A River Runs Through It*.

His two collections of short fiction, *The Van Gogh Field* (1978) and *We Are Not In This Together* (1984), are marked by a lyrical and elegant style that is in contrast with the grimy world of his working-class characters. In these stories, Kittredge manifests his respect for the work ethic and for the stoic, often lonely and inarticulate men in the West whose work, at least in the recent past, has been genuine and needful and done with pride. He has urged students that "one of the things that's not done enough of in our fiction is the mirroring of working-class society, of blue-collar society" (*Talking Up A Storm* 178). His short fiction owes a debt, which he has often acknowledged, to his friend and mentor, the late Raymond Carver, who wrote the introduction to *We Are Not In This Together*; and indeed Carver's influence and editing can be seen in the increasing spareness of Kittredge's prose style and a rueful distancing of himself from his text even as, ironically, his later work closes the divide between personal and impersonal, fiction and nonfiction.

While many of the stories are permeated by a violence, sparked by alcohol, frustration, or overwhelming natural forces, that has led some readers to suggest that Kittredge is imposing the tenets of late nineteenth-century naturalism on the American West, others have found in the lyricism of his style and in the process of his characters' quests a sense of hope. Often these stories also convey a wistful sense of a way of life that cannot be recovered. In "Breaker of Horses," the dying Jules Russel reflects on the craft of his life, on the old men from whom he learned horsebreaking, and upon the heedless new men who have taken his place. Russel "thought it just and proper that there had once been a people, inhabitants of what must have been a more righteous age, among whom the breaker of horses was the proudest of all men" (*The Van Gogh Fields* 23).

Like the hope of recovering the past, this sad celebration of a way of life is a seductive part of the dream of owning it all. Its risks for the writer are nostalgia and artificiality. In his essay "Buckaroos" from *Owning It All*, Kittredge writes of his search for a cattle outfit where work is still done, as it was in his boyhood, "in the old and sensible way, four horses pulling the wagon, and no trucks and no town cars and no horse trailers" (21). On the edge of the Owyhee desert north of Tuscarora, Nevada, he finds the IL buckaroo outfit and feels as though he has somehow come home. In the working cowboys of the IL, Kittredge sees a reflection of the legendary Ross Dollarhide of his boyhood, ranch foreman and a "great horseman" who "deserved any esteem the world might grant" (29). After reminiscing with the IL ranch boss, after sharing Ross Dollarhide stories with the reader, Kittredge has to admit that the old men are dead or dying and that the old range ways are fading fast. But he clings to the notion that the life of the working cowhand may still be viable, if only on the margins. He has heard of ranchers who, for economic reasons, are turning from mechanized agriculture to work again with teams of horses. And, watching the IL buckaroos saddle up for their afternoon's ride "in a ceremony that must be ancient among horseback people," Kittredge concludes in a telling blend of past and present tense: "Then they rode away to another sweep across the sagebrush desert, another branding that afternoon. And I would have liked to have been along as they drifted away to their work, riding unhurriedly into the distance, and into an old horseback turn of life in which you can find some pride" (41).

Reading the whole of Kittredge's creative nonfiction, however, makes it apparent that, far from lingering in nostalgic regret for a lost agrarian past, Kittredge has taken up the task, along with other "new" writers and "new" historians, of reimagining the American West of the future. Wallace Stegner has said of these writers that "It is a civilization they are building, a history they are compiling, a way of looking at the world and humanity's place in it...and what looked like sure defeat opens up to the possibility of victory" (*Where the Bluebird Sings to the Lemonade Springs* [New York: Random House, 1992] xxii-xxiii).

Kittredge posits this new way of looking at the world in his essay

"Raven Brought the Light" from *Owning It All*. Musing on the contemporary renaissance of Native art along the Pacific Northwest coast among the Haido, Tsimishian, Tlingit, Kwakiutl, and Westcoast people, he concludes that the ancient people believed in a delicate balance between themselves and the rest of creation that could be maintained only through sacred ritual. Thus their woodcarvings evolved, "stylized and yet individual, nothing naive or unschooled about it, and inseparable from life because it was always instrumental" (148). Kittredge notes that, after years of neglect, the old totem poles allowed to fall and rot, contemporary native carvers now find their work commanding astronomical prices from collectors. And yet this renaissance is not without its contradictions and pain. To keep in contact with the old life and to find meaning in their own lives are the tasks of the contemporary carvers. At the same time, they must protect their culture from being trivialized. As illustrated by the legend of Raven from which the essay takes its title, the illuminations of artists are sacred. To sell an illumination of the spiritual to the profane world is at the very least to divest it of meaning, and perhaps to destroy it.

Pondering the plight of the contemporary carvers, Kittredge remembers the words of one of the Native artists: "We don't want our children born into an empty place," and finds himself, as a writer dedicated to keeping in touch with his own past, "closer to the edges of what we were looking for than I had been willing to let myself imagine" (154). The legend of Raven holds a special poignancy for Kittredge the writer. Looking back at a past in which he believes that connections between men and women and the outer world were possible, living in the present where the environment and, therefore, all connections, are threatened as never before, looking ahead to an unimaginably alienated future, Kittredge finds himself sharing the dilemma of the Native carvers.

In retrospect, Kittredge's earlier work—including the series of western genre novels he has written under the pen name Owen Rountree with Steven M. Krauzer—may be seen as an apprenticeship in the mythology of the West. The nine Cord novels have been called the first "self-reflexive" westerns, or westerns written about westerns, though they probably do not represent a serious foray into postmodernist subversion of the genre. However, as early as the first version of the short story, "The Waterfowl Tree," published in 1966, Kittredge has concerned himself with human alienation from the natural world and its consequence in alienation of feelings. In "We Are Not in This Together," the old western theme of life in the face of death becomes death in life when fear of mortality is translated into fear of the natural world. The central character, Halverson, finds himself unable to reconcile himself to his father's death, to the brutality he encounters every day, or to his own mortality. Brooding over the final moments of a girl who has been mauled to death by a grizzly, Halverson tries to imagine "the feeling of knowing you were killed before you were dead," and decides he must even the score with the grizzly (*We Are Not in This Together* 101).

Language becomes Kittredge's means of noting the contradictions and connections between life and death, between humankind and the rest of the world. Waking to hear the grizzly grunting outside her tent and her friend whimpering in fear beside her, the surviving girl says she thought "thank God it is out there," and then must revise her language to indicate that she meant she was thankful the bear was outside the tent, not inside it. "After awhile...I climbed a tree....But it didn't make any difference, the girl said, he didn't come for me, he didn't want me" (*We Are Not in This Together* 106).

Halverson must finally come for the bear. Handing his rifle to his woman friend, he makes his way down the slope armed with only a skinning knife, until he comes upon the grizzly eating berries. "Halverson was not sure what to do except wait; he was this close, he should always have been this close." Only after his woman friend fires the shot that kills the charging bear does he realize that there had been nothing for him to defend against; "there hadn't been, not unless he courted it; and the anger he felt, trembling in his forearms, was not so much at anything as it was at loss, and he did not know what was lost" (126).

In *Phantom Silver* (1987), Kittredge confronts the mythic West by reinventing a legendary individual—the Lone Ranger—who has outlived his time and place but who must continue his lonely quest as far west as he can get, to San Francisco and the rim of the Pacific Ocean:

> The air was heavy with dampness, the fog thick around him, the waves gray and white the little way out he could see, but it wasn't like the edge of anything....He fired one shot out into the very center of that gray circle of oncoming water and fog and smiled at himself because there was nothing there to disarm. (*Phantom Silver* [unnumbered])

Beached and alone without his horse Silver, without Tonto, the Lone

Ranger has become a metaphor for white westward expansion which longs for the unattainable and reluctantly recognizes its limitations. The point of the story, Kittredge has said, "is that the *culture* should...stop trying to be the Lone Ranger. There's nothing left to conquer, there's nothing left to take over, there's nothing left to make subservient to us, and what we have to do is stop and figure out how to stay where we are, live where we are, and take care of what we've got" (*Talking Up A Storm* 176).

Kittredge's memoir, *Hole in the Sky*, revisits his Oregon ranch boyhood, the conflicts of his young manhood, and the nervous breakdown he suffered in 1961. A part of the significance of *Hole in the Sky* is the new narrative which it constructs for the development of the American West and its violent self-delusions of isolation and transformation. At age twenty-five, Kittredge found himself in charge of a massive irrigation system and a farming operation that amounted to the cultivation of three thousand acres of barley on drained marshland. "We sprayed 2-4-D ethyl and malathion and the World War II German nerve gas called parathion (for clover mites in the barley), working to shorten our own lives. We baited the coyotes with 1080 and hunted them from airplanes; we wiped them out. The rodent population exploded and field mice destroyed our alfalfa. We irrigated and re-irrigated, pumped and drained; our peat soil began to go saline," Kittredge recalls (*Hole in the Sky* 153). He found himself in the grips of a "corrosive fog." Trapped in his isolation, he believed that his vision of meaninglessness was a symptom of inner, not outer, wreckage; to have perceived the outer world instead of himself as damaged, he says, would have been too difficult, too lonely. And so he worked hard, drank harder, finally saw his marriage disintegrate and his place in his grandfather's empire dissolve in family bickering and his own alcoholism.

"The old man [went the folk narrative of southeastern Oregon] got his name on that property, it's the best ranching property in the West, and now them grandkids will piss it away. Count on it" (*Hole in the Sky* 203). What the folk narrative left out was possibility and luck and the chance for Kittredge to go back to college and study creative writing. Then a second marriage, a stint at the Iowa Writers Workshop, a teaching position at the University of Montana, and friendship with the poet Richard Hugo, who, as Kittredge says "helped me convince myself that I wasn't crazy, and that my anxieties were quite usual" (222). Still there continued the drinking in the morning, followed by the breakup of his second marriage and his growing certainty that "escape from the ranch had turned out to be no sort of cure, only a beginning." Finally it was the land itself that rescued him, gave him the chance to make connections again, to open himself to Annick Smith, the woman he has called "the luck of my later life," and to begin healing a ten-year breach with his children.

Kittredge has been criticized for the imprecision of his solutions for the future, but it is an oversimplistic reading that finds him believing in his own nostalgia for the past or even in the authenticity of his own dreams of the past. What he does recognize is the pervasiveness of the old mythology of conquest and transformation.

The book's further significance lies in the possibilities it offers for the continuance of life and for a mythology that sustains that life. "We cannot live, I think, without connection both psychic and physical, and we begin to die of pointlessness when we are isolated, even if some of us can hang on for a long while connected to nothing beyond our imagination," Kittredge has written. Out of the courage of his own experience, Kittredge offers form and hope.

Selected Bibliography

Primary Sources

Novels as Owen Rountree, with Steven M. Krauzer (series: Cord)
Cord: New York: Ballantine, 1982.
Cord: The Nevada War. New York: Ballantine, 1982.
Cord: Black Hills Duel. New York: Ballantine, 1983.
Cord: Gunman Winter. New York: Ballantine, 1983.
Cord: Hunt the Man Down. New York: Ballantine, 1984.
Cord: King of Colorado. New York: Ballantine, 1984.
Cord: Gunsmoke River. New York: Ballantine, 1985.
Cord: Paradise Valley. New York: Ballantine, 1986.
Cord: Brimstone Basin. New York: Ballantine, 1986.

Short Story Collections
The Van Gogh Field and Other Stories. Columbia, Missouri: University of Missouri Press, 1978.
We Are Not in This Together. Port Townsend, Washington: Graywolf Press, 1984.
Phantom Silver. Missoula, Montana: Kutenai Press, 1987.

Uncollected Short Stories
"Balancing Water," *Paris Review,* 29 (Fall 1987): 14-27.
"Do You Hear Your Mother Talking?" *Harper's,* (Fall 1991).

"Innocence." *Iowa Review*, 25 (Spring-Summer 1995): 120-125.

"Looking Glass." *American Short Fiction*, 3:11 (Fall 1993).

"Performing Arts." *Triquarterly*, 48 (Spring 1980): 144-165.

"Phantom Silver." *Graywolf Annual Four: Stories by Men*. Port Townsend, Washington: Graywolf Press, 1988.

"Silver and Gold." *North American Review*, 256 (1972): 28-34.

"Sixty Million Buffalo." *Rocky Mountain*, 1 (December 1979): 39-45.

Nonfiction

Beyond the Mythic West (with Stewart Udall, Patricia Limerick, Charles F. Wilkinson, John M. Wolkman). Salt Lake City, Utah: Peregrine Smith Books, 1990.

Hole in the Sky. New York: Knopf, 1992.

Owning It All: Essays. Port Townsend, Washington: Graywolf Press, 1987.

Who Owns the West? San Francisco: Mercury House, 1996.

Books Edited

Contemporary Western Fiction (with Steven M. Krauzer). *TriQuarterly*, special ed. (May 1980).

Fiction into Film (with Steven M. Krauzer). New York: Harper & Row, 1979.

Great Action Stories (with Steven M. Krauzer). New York: New American Library, 1977.

The Great American Detective (with Steven M. Krauzer). New York: New American Library; London: New English Library, 1978.

The Last Best Place: A Montana Anthology (with Annick Smith). Helena: Montana Historical Society, 1988.

Montana Spaces: Essays and Photographs in Celebration of Montana. New York: Nick Lyons, 1988.

Uncollected Essays

"Be Careful What You Want." *Paris Review*, 27 (Fall 1985): 191-214.

"Free Range." *The New Republic*, 209 (December 13, 1993): 16-17.

"In My Backyard." *Harper's*, 277 (October 1988): 59-63.

"The Last Safe Place." *Time*, 142 (Septmerber 6, 1993): 37.

"Lost Cowboys." *Antaeus*, 69 (Autumn 1992): 92-106.

"Montana of the Mind." *Mariah*, 4 (October-November 1979): 33-38.

"My Country Childhood." *Countryside*, 3 (May 1992): 128.

"Showdown at Yucca Mountain: the High Stakes of a Nuclear Waste Dump." *Utne Reader* (January-February 1989): 44-49.

"Taking our Turn; or Responsibilities." In *The Geography of Hope*. Page Stegner and Mary Stegner, eds. San Francisco: Sierra Club Books, 1996. Pp. 111-116.

Interviews

Talking Up A Storm: Voices of the New West. Gregory L. Morris, ed. Lincoln: University of Nebraska Press, 1994.

Essay Reviews and Criticism

"Resisting Silence: William Kittredge's *Hole in the Sky*." Mary Clearman Blew. *Montana: The Magazine of Western History*, 44:2 (Spring 1994): 73-75.

Dexter Westrum

Thomas McGuane

In 1993 Thomas McGuane, once heralded as a literary rebel whose protagonists were little more than author personae dedicating themselves to short-term pleasures with adolescent abandon, remarked, "We've dedicated ourselves to things that do not have a lot of long-term meaning.... I wish people would understand some of the more permanent values that are available to us, in our back yards."[1] Seemingly, McGuane in his fifties was beginning to assume the long view and adopt the position of wise elder. On the surface McGuane could be seen as simply looking at life from the security of a solid third marriage, a stable relationship with his children, the comfort of his 3300-acre cutting-horse ranch in Sweet Grass County, Montana, and the secure knowledge that he is about to enter the American canon as an important writer.

But McGuane's concerns are deeper than self. He writes from what he sees as a rift in the American spirit. A naturalist activist, McGuane has written that America's rivers are "repositors of spiritual values for ourselves and for future generations."[2] While perhaps not readily apparent, this need for spiritual values continuously drives the protagonists of McGuane's eight novels. Indeed, in the early work, his protagonists are often manic and crazy, apparently seeking nonconformity for no great purpose, except to startle the sedate upper-class worlds from which they emanate. The truth is that these worlds are barren of spirituality; people, proceeding from conventions that are often empty, are enslaved to crass and commercial notions of the real America.

McGuane's ideas of enduring values are apparent in his first novel, *The Sporting Club* (1969). Vernor Stanton, an unstable young man and heir to millions, commits himself to the destruction of the Centennial Club, a rod-and-gun club that has provided summer recreation for generations of the upper-middle-class pretentious on Michigan's Upper Peninsula. When Stanton enlists his buddy James Quinn to his cause, the conflict between short-term and more enduring values begins. When they were adolescents, Stanton and Quinn did everything they could to wreak havoc on the established social order. Quinn, too, is heir to millions, but unlike Stanton he has tasted responsibility. When the novel opens, Quinn is managing his family's auto-parts factory.

Much to Stanton's dismay, Quinn has found responsibility meaningful. He understands that his employees depend upon him for security. He gains satisfaction from engineering a successful company party. In the outdoors, Quinn registers the more mature attitude. Stanton is a predator; he wants to kill the biggest and the best of everything. Quinn, on the other hand, demonstrates respect for the processes of hunting and fishing. The important thing is not whether you capture the most impressive trophy, but that you respect the rules of the game — the land, the animals, the hunt itself. Stanton has no respect for such values; he simply wants to win.

The question of values surfaces as well in their respective attitudes toward women. Quinn's encounters with women are for the most part sexual. Quinn suffers from severe romanticism. He longs for a woman who desires a white knight, a savior on horseback, but he finds no woman who needs him for anything other than a momentary physical encounter. Stanton, on the other hand, maintains a long-term relationship with Janey, a woman who clearly loves him. Unfortunately, Stanton does not know how to love. He abuses Janey in public and appears to have neither understanding nor respect for her essential self, yet she stays with him out of her personal commitment to the idea of what a relationship should be. Mutual love as an enduring value seems unavailable to both Quinn and Stanton.

Once the club is destroyed, Stanton goes crazy and winds up a custodial case with Janey in control. Quinn returns to his factory and imbues his daily duties with a sense of romanticism. The factory is a measurable human world for which he can create an impact, can be as it were a savior. The novel's final sentence explains that the two young men are "compromised and happy" (220). As McGuane's work matures, his sense of enduring values becomes more and more clear. His protagonists no longer see their failure to disturb the universe as compromise, but work to achieve spiritual fulfillment from tending seriously to the responsibilities of relationships and professionalism within their respective human worlds.

McGuane's next two protagonists, Nicholas Payne in *The Bush-whacked Piano* (1971) and Thomas Skelton in *Ninety-two in the Shade* (1973), never realize the joys of human fulfillment. Both seek a roman-ticized and self-absorbed spirituality. Payne has sensed his own mortality from the death of a wisdom tooth and frantically seeks fulfillment in per-petual motion rather than sedate and conventional success in his father's prestigious law firm. Like Payne, Skelton does not want to be swept along in the empty flow of the conventional life. He lionizes and seeks to emulate Nicol Dance, a long-shot fishing guide. Metaphorical westerners, Payne sees the entire United States as his frontier and Skelton chooses the open ocean off Key West.

Payne's princess in distress is Ann Fitzgerald, whom he seeks to liber-ate from upper-crust suburban Detroit through "cosmic twinning" (46) in a transcendental transcontinental adventure. Ann, however, does not measure up. While she sees dalliance with Payne as a "chance to expand her spiritual resources" (102), she ultimately chooses an establishment boyfriend and returns to the web of conventionality. Payne, though dis-appointed, remains undaunted. In the novel's final scene, Payne stands tall against the limitless sea and sky, spreading peanut butter on bread with a jackknife. He is the new American, forever young, forever uncompromised in his quest for meaning.

Ninety-two in the Shade, on the other hand, seems to say that achiev-ing meaning in America is impossible. Nicol Dance views Skelton as unnecessary competition in the guiding trade and vows to kill the young man if he goes into business. Thus, Skelton is unavoidably drawn to the impossible. He cannot live fully if he does not guide; he cannot live at all if he does. A true romantic, Skelton accepts the challenge and sees a life quickened under the threat of Dance's gun as the ultimate adven-ture in meaning.

That Skelton should make such a choice is ironic because he is the first McGuane protagonist to enjoy the love of a woman. His friend Miranda commits to building a life with him, but the possibility of the enduring values represented by a good marriage means nothing to Skelton. Like Icarus fascinated by the sun, he is drawn into confronta-tion with Dance and dies.

Like Skelton and Payne, Chester Pomeroy in *Panama* (1978) abuses himself with a self-serving and ersatz spirituality. Even though *Panama* is set in Key West, Pomeroy is haplessly spellbound by the romantic myth of the West. Ostensibly, he is a former entertainer who won commercial success by demonstrating symbolically all the crass states of mind Americans are capable of; in addition to vomiting on the mayor of New York, he has burst from the anus of a frozen elephant to duel with a baseball batting practice machine.

If conservative politicians and the all-American sport do not provide Pomeroy the spiritual foundation necessary for the fully realized life in our time, an idealized version of Jesse James does. He constantly invokes the famous outlaw's ghost until we understand that Chester sees himself as both a descendant from and the embodiment of the outlaw spirit. Lost within his own guise, Chester cannot capitulate to his ex-wife Catherine's desires to re-institute their once stable marriage. Worse yet, Chester cannot recognize his own father, a stable businessman from Ohio. Like Nicholas Payne, Chester comes to the end of his story without demonstrating a willingness to admit that stable midwestern values of responsibility and family are the most genuine way to confront the loathsomeness he finds in contemporary life.

While McGuane's first four novels demonstrate his awareness of western and/or frontier concerns, they do not establish him as a writer of the West. In 1981, however, McGuane declared the contemporary American West as his own little postage stamp of ground. "The West is a wreck," he said. "I'd like to document that without getting totally depressing about it."[3] From then on his work has been set in Deadrock — read Livingston, a modest city, 10,000 inhabitants strong, in Montana — and has dealt with protagonists who must find meaning by accepting and learning to live in a romanceless, demythologized West.

In fact, *Nobody's Angel* (1984) heralds the end of the romanticized and mythologized West. We understand that the West has been wrecked by cowboys too complacent to stop greedy interlopers from turning the frontier into a bull-and-bear West. McGuane's first real western protagonist is an ineffectual drunk, Patrick Fitzpatrick, who attempts to blend romanticized notions of the West and equally romanticized notions of permanent values. He suffers from "sadness-for-no-reason" (61) and ultimately fails to achieve fulfillment of any kind. He has resigned from the army to return to the family ranch in Montana only to find that he has no family. His sister commits suicide, and his grandfather is lost in the past when he ran his ranch "like an old time cowboy outfit" (61). In the contemporary West, the old man finds "nothing to do" (124).

The notion that the West is a place to achieve permanent and spiritual values is all but gone. Patrick drifts into an affair with Claire Burnett, the wife of Tio Burnett, a fast-talking good ol' boy from Texas. Tio and Claire personify the crass and spirit-barren West, a world foreign to Patrick's imagination. Claire refuses to become a storybook princess savable by the lost and romantic Patrick, and, in the end, unable to create or discover a world of permanent values, Patrick returns to the army, in Spain, a black-out drinker victimized by his own romanticism.

While *Nobody's Angel* seems to be the end of the romanticized West, *Something to Be Desired* (1984) demonstrates the possibility of achieving permanent values in a realistic contemporary West. Lucien Taylor, McGuane's protagonist here, seems confused by his own manic behavior. A foreign service officer in Central America, he abandons his wife, his son, and his job to return to Montana for a new life with Emily, a murderer who cannot stay around, especially for Lucien. At loose ends, Lucien buries himself in a series of one-night stands and ultimately comes to realize that, although he was walked out on normalcy, it may indeed provide the best set of values available to him in the wrecked West.

Emily has given Lucien her ranch, which he develops into a thriving health spa. Almost unheard of for a McGuane protagonist, Lucien becomes a man of property and respectability. More importantly, he begins to enjoy responsibility. Where manic behavior and indiscriminate sexual encounters have failed to bring him purpose and meaning, the craft of managing a business does. He begins to think of himself as a man with a family to support. To this end, he invites Suzanne, his ex-wife, and James, his son, to the spa.

Ensuing action with his former spouse and son marks Lucien Taylor as a pivotal protagonist in the McGuane canon. Lucien tries to reach James by including him in an afternoon of banding hawks. Unfortunately, Lucien must bait his hawk traps with live pigeons. While Lucien admires the swift power of the hawk, James becomes distraught over the death of the sacrificial pigeon. Lucien admires his son for being more compassionate than himself. Seemingly, compassion is a finer attribute for the future of the West than is the hawk's predatory individualism.

At the same time, Suzanne forces Lucien to realize the limits of his own form of individualism. She tells him the truth about his self-absorbed self—and by extension, the truth about all McGuane protagonists: "No more fucking you, and here's why: it encourages all your sloppy sentimentality and your no-shows and your desertions and your treatment of people who love you as if they were so many pocket mirrors for you to see if you're aging or what kind of day you're having..." (154). The first step toward enduring spiritual fulfillment is to abandon self-absorption. Suzanne leaves Lucien with the clear dictum that he must accept his family on their own terms as independent persons, not as supporting players in the self-induced scenario of his manic life.

Something to Be Desired, then, is important because the McGuane protagonist seems to have grown beyond a desire to register nonconformity through acts of self-absorbed craziness and to have begun to work toward a stability at once spiritual and more permanent. Real meaning, the McGuane protagonist seems to have discovered, comes not from abandoning responsibility but from commitments to work and family. McGuane further explores the importance of these commitments in his next two novels, *Keep the Change* and *Nothing but Blue Skies*.

In *Keep the Change* (1989), Joe Starling fails to understand that permanent spiritual meaning must come honestly from within himself. Since he has never truly developed his own value system, Joe constantly attempts to find life's significance outside himself. For instance, his career as an artist, though financially successful, is empty because his style is a forgery. His life as an illustrator of instruction manuals for new products is empty because his job is essentially to create markets where there is no genuine human demand.

In desperation, Joe returns to Montana in hopes of finding the idealized West of his cowboy youth. But instead he finds a West where individualism is replaced by conformity, leasing has eradicated pride of ownership, buffalo can be shot and paid for with credit cards, and, worst of all, the new westerner is playing golf. Indeed, Starling finds that an expert backhoer who can engineer perfect foundations and sewer lines has become the new western hero in the public mind. Reverence for open land has all but disappeared.

Joe, however, insists on attempting to find the life that he imagines is possible. He walks out on his longtime lover, Astrid, and attempts to re-establish himself with Ellen Overstreet Kelton, his former girlfriend. Ellen is estranged from her husband, Billy, and mentally impaired daughter, Clara. Joe does not understand that Ellen is actually trying to secure the Starling family ranch for her land-greedy father. In the end, Joe sees Ellen reunited with Billy and Clara; more importantly, Joe gives the landless Billy the Starling ranch. Even though Joe Starling remains a drifter, in his act of friendship for Billy he has contributed to the possibility of enduring values in the contemporary West.

Nothing but Blue Skies (1992) almost reads like McGuane's final crescendo for the manically self-absorbed in the New West. Frank Copenhaver is the prodigal son who becomes the Babbitt of Montana, a man in love with "the sedative effects of pursuing [money]" (130). Unfortunately, his obsession with the games of commerce costs him his wife, Gracie. In this Grace-less state, Copenhaver ricochets about in an absurdist world of purposeless cowboys unfit for the contemporary West and evangelical idiots who seek to prohibit water from leaving Montana.

Ultimately, Frank learns that endless financial possibility is the West's greatest myth. Understanding that when family life ends, happiness ends, he becomes a peeping Tom because he wants to be "among families, to watch them in their ordinariness, that most elusive of all qualities" (123). A reconciliation with Gracie is engineered by their daughter, Holly, with whom Frank loves to talk "football, school work, America, money, romance, the evolving life of the Great American West" (130). Copenhaver learns to feel plain love (128) and settle into his own "rather fascinating inadequacies" (150). The ordinary, McGuane seems to be saying, is underrated and not deeply understood. If Frank desires to have a life, he must cope with life as it is, not as he would attempt to force it to be. Daily human endeavor with loved ones can generate spiritual values sufficient for life in the long term.

In essence, McGuane's work continues to make good on an insight he disclosed in a 1986 interview: "I think that life kind of hurtles forward in a massive way for the world, but within it, people invent islands — islands of sanity, islands of family continuity, islands of professional skills and power, islands of craft, art, and knowledge. Those islands basically are contributors toward a cure for despair."[4] Within lives of the erratic and the consistent, McGuane's protagonists are hurled forward, hit-and-miss, toward such enlightenment.

Notes

1. "Thomas McGuane Speaks," *Buzzworm: The Environmental Journal,* 5:1 (January-February 1993): 34.

2. Thomas McGuane, "America's Rivers," *Audubon* (November-December 1993): 60.

3. Russell Martin, "Writers of the Purple Sage," *New York Times Magazine*, 27 (December 1981): 20.

4. Kay Bonetti, "An Interview with Tom McGuane," *Missouri Review*, 9 (1985-1986): 79.

Selected Bibliography

Primary Sources

The Bushwhacked Piano. New York: Simon & Schuster, 1971.
Keep the Change. Boston: Houghton Mifflin/Seymour Lawrence, 1989.
Ninety-two in the Shade. New York: Farrar, Straus & Giroux, 1980.
Nobody's Angel. New York: Random House, 1982.
Nothing but Blue Skies. Boston: Houghton Mifflin/Seymour Lawrence, 1992.
An Outside Chance: Essays on Sport. New York: Farrar, Straus & Giroux, 1980.
Panama. New York: Farrar, Straus & Giroux, 1978.
Something to Be Desired. New York: Random House, 1984.
The Sporting Club. New York: Simon & Schuster, 1969.
To Skin a Cat. New York: E. P. Dutton/Seymour Lawrence, 1986.

Secondary Sources

Carter, Albert Howard, III. "Thomas McGuane's First Three Novels: Games, Fun, Nemesis." *Critique*, 17 (August 1975): 91-104. McGuane protagonists consistently interact in games which point up the interaction between pathos and humor.

Cook, Nancy S. "Investment in Place: Thomas McGuane in Montana." In *Old West— New West: Centennial Essays*. Barbara Howard Meldrum, ed. Moscow: University of Idaho Press, 1993. Pp. 213-229. McGuane's New Western regionalism is defined by a problematic nostalgia for an Old Western masculine ideal.

Grant, Kerry. "On and Off the Main Line: The Failure of Compromise in the Fiction of Thomas McGuane." *Mid-American Review*, 3 (Spring 1983): 167-184. Although understanding they must ultimately compromise with reality, McGuane's heroes cannot resist the urges to stretch the boundaries of life.

Klinkowitz, Jerome. *The New American Novel of Manners: The Fiction of Richard Yates, Dan Wakefield, and Thomas McGuane*. Athens: University of Georgia Press, 1986. These three novelists are semioticians of the postmodernist age operating on social conventions as if they were signs in our linguistic system.

Masinton, Charles G. "*Nobody's Angel*: Thomas McGuane's Vision of the Contemporary West." *New Mexico Humanities Review*, 6 (Fall 1983): 49-55. McGuane's sense of the wrecked West runs from absurdity to pessimism.

McCaffery, Larry. "On Turning Nothing into Something." *Fiction International*, 4-5 (Fall-Winter 1975): 123-129. Even though McGuane criticizes American culture, his work is transcendent because his protagonists maintain their ideals in the face of existential despair.

Morris, Gregory L. "How Ambivalence Won the West: Thomas McGuane and the Fiction of the New West." *Critique*, 32 (Spring 1991): 180-189. By struggling with his own senses of connection and disconnection with the myths of the West, McGuane has prepared the West for reaffirmation in the American consciousness.

Wallace, Jon. "The Language Plot in Thomas McGuane's *Ninety-two in the Shade*." *Critique*, 29 (Winter 1988): 111-120. McGuane protagonists confront the depersonalizing effects of American culture by mixing language codes.

———. "Speaking against the Dark: Style as Theme in Thomas McGuane's *Nobody's Angel*." *Modern Fiction Studies*, 33 (Summer 1987): 289-298. Through their careful attention to language style, McGuane narrators assert themselves in spite of the fragmented nature of their lives.

Welch, Dennis M. "Death and Fun in the Novels of Thomas McGuane." *Windsor Review*, 14 (Fall-Winter 1978): 14-20. McGuane protagonists confront mortality with playful attitudes in order to maintain an openness to the possibilities of their lives.

Westrum, Dexter. *Thomas McGuane*. Boston: Twayne, 1991. McGuane protagonists must endure rage, rebellion, and defeat in order to generate new and calmer selves who will create meaningful lives lived on a smaller, more inwardly liberating scale.

Charlotte Margolis Goodman

Jean Stafford

In her "Author's Note" to *The Collected Stories of Jean Stafford*, a volume for which Jean Stafford was awarded the Pulitzer Prize in 1970, she observes, "As soon as I could, I hotfooted it across the Rocky Mountains and across the Atlantic Ocean." Although Stafford points out that once she left the West as a young adult, she only returned there for short visits, she nevertheless maintains that her "roots remain in the semi-fictitious town of Adams, Colorado." A fictional representation of Boulder, where Stafford spent most of her childhood and youth, Adams serves as the setting for a number of her short stories, many of which appear under the heading "Cowboys and Indians, and Magic Mountains" in her *Collected Stories*. Her best novel, *The Mountain Lion* (1947), is also set in the West, describing both California, Stafford's birthplace, and Colorado, where she lived until she graduated from college.

Youngest of the four Stafford children, Jean Stafford was born in Covina, California, in 1915. The family was uprooted when her father decided to sell his walnut ranch there and move with his wife and four children to San Diego. A writer of westerns, including the novel *When Cattle Kingdom Fell*, John Stafford invested in the San Diego Stock Exchange and lost a substantial portion of the money he had inherited from his father, an affluent Texas cattle rancher. Following this debacle, the Stafford family left California, moving briefly to Pueblo and then Colorado Springs, and finally settling in Boulder. There, John Stafford, using the noms de plume Jack Wonder and Ben Delight, wrote western stories, most of which remained unpublished, while his wife supported the family by running a boardinghouse for young women who were attending the University of Colorado. Stafford maintained that she never read her father's novels. Influenced, however, by the titles of his western stories, she herself began at an early age to write "about twisters on the plains, stampedes when herds of longhorns were being driven up from the Panhandle to Dodge, and bloody incidents south of the border," stories featuring foremen of ranches who "had steely blue eyes to match the barrels of their Colt .45's" (Breit 18).

After attending public elementary and high school in Boulder, Stafford went on to study at the University of Colorado, from which she graduated in 1936 with both a B.A. and an M.A. in English. She later described her education as a "shabby affair." Writing frequently about her unhappiness during the years that she lived in Boulder, she claimed she had been ignored by her family, stigmatized by poverty, and scorned by her classmates because of her intellectual bent and her irascible temperament. Needing to earn money when she was in high school, she worked one summer at a dude ranch, and during her college years she posed in the nude for drawing classes. By that time Stafford had become a member of a group of campus intellectuals who met regularly at a local sandwich shop to drink watered-down beer and discuss the works of Joyce, Proust, Hemingway, and D. H. Lawrence. Her academic success in college gained her some measure of acceptance by her peers, but the suicide of a close friend, Lucy McKee Cook, a married law student in whose house Stafford was living when she was a junior, blighted her college years. Stafford succeeded in obtaining a fellowship to study philology in Heidelberg following her graduation. She left Colorado for good in 1936, returning there only to visit her older sister, who lived on a ranch in Hayden, Colorado, and to attend the Boulder Writer's Workshop, first as assistant to the director during the summer of 1937 and in 1952 as a member of the teaching staff. In 1956, when she was awarded the Norlin Medal, given annually to an outstanding graduate of the University of Colorado, she opted to receive this tribute in absentia.

Following her *Wanderjahr* in Europe between 1936 and 1937, Stafford taught English for a year at Stephens College in Missouri. Subsequently, she moved to New England, married the poet Robert Lowell, and lived with him in Baton Rouge, New York, Connecticut, and Maine. After their separation in 1946, she settled in Manhattan. During the early fifties, when she was married to her second husband, *Life* magazine editor Oliver Jensen, she resided in Westport, Connecticut, returning to Manhattan after their divorce in 1952 and then living in The Springs on the eastern tip of Long Island during her marriage to *New Yorker* writer A. J. Liebling. After Liebling's death in 1963, she remained in The Springs. An alcoholic and chain smoker, she died in 1979 of heart disease and emphysema.

Reflecting her peripatetic life, Stafford's fiction is set not only in the West but in a variety of other locations, including Europe, Manhattan, and New England. The last is the setting for two of her three novels, *Boston Adventure* (1944) and *The Catherine Wheel* (1952). While Stafford said that Mark Twain was one of her favorite writers, those consummate cosmopolites Henry James and Edith Wharton exerted an equally important influence on her work.

Stafford's attitude toward the West was a complicated one. Hermann Marburg, father of Stafford's female protagonist in *Boston Adventure*, is a great admirer of Zane Grey's *Riders of the Purple Sage*; Stafford, on the other hand, spoke pejoratively of Grey's purple prose, once commenting, "I've never seen no purple sage, I never hope to see none, but let me tell you anyhow, I don't want no reconstructed tooth dentist bending my ear about the ornery stuff." On occasion, Stafford did describe some aspects of the West positively, celebrating the Edenic rural landscape of the California she had known during her earliest years as well as the mountainous Colorado terrain. However, observing that she had never liked "Mother Nature" very well, Stafford more frequently dwelled upon the anxiety she had experienced when confronted by the western landscape (Jean Stafford to James Robert Hightower, 1938). She said that the Rocky Mountains were "too big to take in, too high to understand, too domineering to love," maintaining that the very spaciousness of this mountain range and of the endless prairies intimidated her (*Mademoiselle* 140). Her West, she pointed out, was neither the "wicked West" of writers like her father or Zane Grey nor the "noble West" of her cousin Margaret Lynn, who described her own childhood on the Kansas frontier in *Stepdaughter of the Prairie*. Instead, Stafford depicts her fictitious Adams as an "ugly," dusty town with "mongrel and multitudinous churches" and a high school "shaped like a loaf of bread" (*Collected Stories* 335). In the virtual ghost towns nearby, "A handful of backward people most of them named Brophy...live in battered cabins in the shadows of the ore dumps of extinguished gold mines" (*Collected Stories* 226). The West in Stafford's fiction is a dreary, exhausted, suffocating, provincial area inhabited by unsophisticated "rubes," ill-mannered cowboys, "dudes" from the East, gossipy landladies, people afflicted with tuberculosis, orphaned Indians, and intellectually precocious girls who are scorned by their peers. The female protagonist of Stafford's "The Liberation" expresses the sentiments of most of Stafford's female characters who live in the West: Fearing that she will be doomed to waste away in the "arid foothills" of the Rockies, Polly Bay exclaims, "I hate, I despise, I abominate the West!"—and boards the train for Boston (*Collected Stories* 317).

Stafford arrived at her jaded view of the West early in life. In "Disenchantment," a prize-winning essay she wrote when she was still a high-school student, she described her feeling of betrayal when, en route with her family from California to Colorado, she encountered the real rather than the mythical West. Although her parents had described the West in which they were planning to settle when they left California as a romantic place abounding in scenic splendors, what she observed instead were dusty, rubbish-littered tourist camps filled with poor, uneducated people. "There were no savages," she wrote.

> There wasn't anything the least bit extraordinary. Colorado was just as uninteresting as California and more spread out. It was monstrous that we had been tricked by Tom Mix and Zane Grey and all the others whose bloated fancies have produced such glamorous exaggerations about dashing cowpunchers on big roans defying death on landslides in order to do justice to the black-mustached villains. (Unpublished Manuscript, Norlin Library, University of Colorado, Boulder)

In *The Mountain Lion*, Stafford would examine in much greater detail the contrasting images represented by the mythic West and the actual West she had encountered in the twenties and during the years of the Great Depression.

Set in the California landscape she remembered from her childhood and at a ranch in the Colorado Rockies, Stafford's double *Bildungsroman*, *The Mountain Lion*, contrasts the coming of age of Ralph Fawcett and his younger sister, Molly. As young children, the fatherless Ralph and Molly, alike, are alien creatures in a genteel world presided over by their very proper mother and two older sisters. Eagerly awaiting the imminent arrival of their mother's stepfather, the beloved Grandpa

Kenyon, they mentally compare this bearded, disheveled, whiskey-drinking man with their real grandfather, the deceased Grandpa Bonney, an elegantly attired button manufacturer from St. Louis. Of Grandpa Kenyon, Stafford writes:

> He had been everywhere in the world and had hunted every animal indigenous to the North American continent: deer, antelope, moose, caribou, big-horn, and every game bird you could name. He had caught wild horses in Nevada and had tamed them "into the gentlest little benches a man ever saw." He had killed rattlers as long as man is tall; he had eaten alligator and said it tasted like chicken. (26)

With his notebook containing entries about steers sold and rum purchased, with his soft-soled moccasins that had been made for him by a Cherokee named Daniel Standing-Deer, with his stories about his travels and about Jesse James, Grandpa Kenyon represents the glamorous Old West. When Grandpa Kenyon dies suddenly during his visit to the Fawcett household, the last representative of that mythical world disappears from the life of Ralph and Molly.

In the remainder of the novel, Stafford sets up a number of contrasting images: the mythical western world of Grandpa Kenyon versus the brutal everyday West of actual cowboys; the genteel world of Mrs. Fawcett's California versus the rugged outdoor world of Grandpa Kenyon's son Claude, owner of the Colorado ranch at which Ralph and Molly initially spend a summer and subsequently the year when their mother takes their older sisters abroad; and the expanding horizons of Ralph as he moves into the world of men versus the increasingly constricted world of Molly, who abhors the female world of her mother and her two "sappy" older sisters but also feels excluded from the male world into which Ralph is initiated.

From their dirty train windows during their first trip to Uncle Claude's Bar K ranch, Ralph and Molly observe treeless towns about whose streets meander "undernourished dogs looking for food" (88), and Molly almost starts to cry when she sees a man wearing a bandanna who looks in the window at them and then turns to "spit tobacco juice at a cat" (88). The peaks encircling their uncle's ranch are "huge, snaggle-toothed mountain ranges" (91), the rushing river is alarming, and the "commotion of animal noises — cows bellowing, horses neighing, dogs barking, birds screaming—" (91) frightens the children. Inside the ranch house, the gun cabinet, showing "the blue glint of a dozen barrels," looks "like an upended coffin" (84); the food is "strange," the dessert—a "fried pie which was shaped like a rubber heel" (85)—unappetizing; and the cowhands' talk seems "to be made up almost altogether of non sequiturs" (86), for the men leave one another's questions unanswered. Soon after Ralph and Molly's arrival, a horse stumbles, crushing the foot of one of the ranch hands, who shoots the horse and lies in the road until he is found by a passing motorist. Confronted by this world that seems at once so much less appealing than the one they believed Grandpa Kenyon had inhabited and so much more menacing than the California world they have known, both Molly and Ralph are full of dread.

A number of critics have commented on the very different fates that await the male and the female protagonist of Stafford's novel. Blanche Gelfant observes that Ralph, who exclaims "Golly *Moses*, I'd like to go out west," expresses the desire of the archetypical American male character to escape the constraints of the civilized world (*The Mountain Lion* 8). Ralph's transformation from frightened child to manly hunter is not easily accomplished; moreover, as Stafford makes clear, becoming a full-fledged western male exacts a cost. But like his Uncle Claude and the other males on the ranch, Ralph does learn to ride and shoot. Molly, however, feels increasingly more alienated in the masculine world of the Bar K ranch.

Stafford observes that Ralph used to think the song he was taught about America was entitled "O Beautiful for Spacious Guys"; in Colorado, the world of the adolescent Ralph becomes a more spacious one. However, at the ranch Molly is impelled to retreat to enclosures where she feels less threatened: the housekeeper's sitting room and garden, the bathroom, and a mountain glade surrounded "so densely by trees and chokecherry that they were almost like walls...." (206). Longing to be a famous writer, Molly has access to the works of no women writers who might serve as role models. The only books available to her are those by western male writers such as James Fenimore Cooper and Mark Twain who describe the daring exploits of boys and men rather than the emotional crises of physically unattractive, self-hating, intellectual girls like Molly. In the cataclysmic conclusion of Stafford's novel, Molly, surrounded in her outdoor mountain retreat by the tools of her trade—notebooks, a pocket dictionary, pencils, paper clips, rubber bands, and several sheets of carbon paper—is accidentally killed by

Ralph, who has joined his Uncle Claude in the hunt for a tawny female mountain lion they have named "Goldilocks."

None of Stafford's short stories with western settings ends as tragically as does *The Mountain Lion*. However, in most of these stories, too, the landscape is menacing rather than uplifting, and the protagonists, the majority of whom are female, suffer from feelings of alienation and abandonment. Mary Ellen Williams Walsh points out that unlike Molly, the female characters in these stories do not become sacrificial victims of the mythical West. Nevertheless, they, too, lack the freedom and autonomy that long have been associated with the western landscape (Walsh, "The Young Girl and the West").

Stafford's vision of how uncongenial the western landscape is for girls is evident both in her early story, "The Darkening Moon," and in one titled "In the Zoo." The female protagonist in the former rides her horse through a terrifying nighttime world during a lunar eclipse, remembering a fishing expedition with her father when he had insisted that she "pick up the fat slithering blobs in her bare hands" (*Collected Stories* 261). Also threatened by their environment are the orphaned sisters of "In the Zoo," who are traumatized when they are exiled to Adams after the death of their mother. Adopted by the mean-spirited Mrs. Placer, they witness with horror the way in which she transforms into a vicious cur the friendly dog they have been given by their sole friend, the drunken Mr. Murphy. When the dog subsequently kills Mr. Murphy's pet monkey, Mr. Murphy poisons the dog. Having no alternative but to remain at Mrs. Placer's until they are grown, the narrator and her sister Daisy, subjected to Mrs. Placer's endless "lies and evasions," liken themselves to "rats in a maze"(*Collected Stories* 300).

Even in Stafford's more humorous Adams stories, the female protagonists are beleaguered: the narrator of "The Healthiest Girl in Town" feels compelled to lie about the cause of her father's death in order to gain acceptance from her peers; in "A Reading Problem," Emily Vanderpool is forced to retreat from the jail to the cemetery in her search for a quiet place to read; and in "Bad Characters," the unpopular Emily Vanderpool is arrested after she befriends a petty thief named Lottie Jump and agrees to serve as her accomplice. Reflecting the influence of Mark Twain in their use of vernacular, in their satire, and in their representation of mischievous characters, these humorous stories focus on female Huck Finns who manage to survive by their wits. Unlike Huck, however, Stafford's feisty female characters are unable to escape from their confining world by boarding a raft or lighting out for the territory ahead.

In the introduction to her *Collected Stories*, Stafford notes that most of her characters are "homesick" and suffer from a sense of "dislocation." After she left the Edenic California world where she spent her earliest years, Stafford, too, felt dislocated, whether she was living in Colorado or the East. If she suffered from feelings of alienation during her Boulder years, when she settled in Manhattan and began to hobnob with the New York intellectuals during the 1940s, she reported that these sophisticated intellectuals made her feel like a "great gawky knobby-kneed schoolgirl from the Rockies." Even though she was embarrassed by her western origins, she nevertheless owes her present renown as a writer primarily to her western novel, *The Mountain Lion*, and to her short story, "In the Zoo." First published in the *New Yorker* in 1953 and winner of an O. Henry Award like a number of Stafford's other short stories, "In the Zoo" is included in the widely circulated *Norton Anthology of Short Fiction*. A number of Stafford's other short stories, many of which originally appeared in the *New Yorker* between 1948 and 1957, also have been anthologized in recent years. However, during the last two decades of her life, when she was struggling unsuccessfully to complete an autobiographical novel, she published virtually no fiction, supporting herself by writing several children's books, a book about the mother of Lee Harvey Oswald entitled *A Mother of History*, occasional essays, and book reviews.

At the time of Jean Stafford's death, most of her work was out of print. Since then, however, Stafford's beautifully crafted novels and short stories have been rediscovered by a new generation of literary critics. Many feminist critics have commented on the vital connections between Stafford's fiction and the works of other women writers who focus on the struggles of their female protagonists to survive in a hostile world. During the last decade, *The Mountain Lion* and her *Collected Stories* have been reissued by the University of Texas Press; three biographies and three full-length studies of Stafford's fiction have appeared; and Stafford's life and works have been the subject of many articles. No partisan of feminism or feminist literary criticism, Stafford might well have taken umbrage at the attention she is currently receiving as a "woman writer." Nevertheless, she would have been pleased, no doubt, that her work is being rediscovered by a new generation of readers.

Selected Bibliography

Avila, Wanda. *Jean Stafford: A Comprehensive Bibliography*. New York: Garland Publishing Company, 1983. Includes a long biographical and critical introductory essay focusing on Stafford's ironic vision, as well as an annotated bibliography.

Primary Sources

Novels

Boston Adventure. New York: Harcourt Brace, 1944.

The Catherine Wheel. New York: Harcourt Brace, 1952.

"In the Snowfall." *The Southern Review*, 24 (Spring 1992): 139-153. Carolyn Ezell Foster, ed. A compilation of various versions of Stafford's unpublished novel about her early life in Boulder.

The Mountain Lion. New York: Harcourt Brace, 1947.

Novella

A Winter's Tale. In *New Short Novels* (by Jean Stafford, Elizabeth Etnier, Shelby Foote, and Clyde Miller). Vol. I. Mary Louise Aswell, ed. New York: Ballantine, 1954.

Short Story Collections

Bad Characters. New York: Farrar, 1964.

Children Are Bored on Sunday. New York: Harcourt Brace, 1953.

The Collected Stories of Jean Stafford. New York: Farrar, Straus & Giroux, 1969.

The Interior Castle. New York: Harcourt Brace, 1953.

Stories (with John Cheever, Daniel Fuchs, and William Maxwell). New York: Farrar, Straus, and Cudahy, 1956.

Uncollected Stories

"And Lots of Solid Color." *American Prefaces*, 5 (November 1939): 22-25.

"The Cavalier." *New Yorker*, 24 (February 12, 1949): 28-36.

"The Connoisseurs." *Harper's Bazaar*, 86 (October 1952): 198, 232, 234, 240, 246.

"An Influx of Poets." *New Yorker*, 54 (November 6, 1978): 43-60. Extracted from Stafford's unfinished novel, *The Parliament of Women*.

"The Lippia Lawn." *Kenyon Review*, 6 (Spring 1944): 237-245. Signed Phoebe Lowell.

"My Blithe, Sad Bird." *New Yorker*, 33 (April 6, 1957): 20-30.

"Old Flaming Youth." *Harper's Bazaar*, 84 (December 1950): 94, 182-184, 188.

"The Ordeal of Conrad Pardee." *Ladies Home Journal*, 81 (July 1964): 59, 78, 80-83.

"The Scarlet Letter." *Mademoiselle*, 49 (July 1959): 62-68, 100-101.

"A Slight Maneuver." *Mademoiselle*, 24 (February 1947): 177, 282-287, 289.

"The Violet Rock." *New Yorker*, 28 (April 26, 1952): 34-42.

"The Warlock." *New Yorker*, 31 (December 24, 1955): 25-28, 30-45.

"Woden's Day." *Shenandoah*, 30 (Autumn 1979): 6-26. Extracted from Stafford's unfinished novel, *The Parliament of Women*.

Nonfiction

An Etiquette for Writers: 1952 Writers' Conference in the Rocky Mountains. Boulder: University of Colorado Press, 1952.

A Mother in History. New York: Farrar, Straus & Giroux, 1966.

Articles and Essays
"Don't Use Ms. with Miss Stafford, Unless You Mean ms." *New York Times*, September 21, 1973: 36.
"Miss McKeehan's Pocketbook." *Colorado Quarterly*, 24 (Spring 1976): 407-411.
"The Psychological Novel." *Kenyon Review*, 10 (Spring 1948): 214-27.
"Souvenirs of Survival: The Thirties Revisited." *Mademoiselle*, 50 (February 1960): 90-91, 174-176.
"Topics: Women as Chattels, Men as Chumps." Editorial, *New York Times*, May 9, 1970: 24.

Reviews
"A Lost Lady." *Washington Post Book World* (August 26, 1973): 1, 5, 6. Review of Willa Cather's *A Lost Lady*, reissued by Alfred Knopf.
"Rara Avis." *Reporter*, 23 (December 22, 1960): 40, 42, 44. Review of Isabella L. Bird's *A Lady's Life in the Rocky Mountains*.
"Sensuous Women." *New York Review of Books*, 17 (September 23, 1971): 33-35. Review of *Kate Chopin, A Critical Biography* by Per Seyersted and *The Complete Works of Kate Chopin*.

Secondary Sources

Reminiscences
Shenandoah, 30 (Autumn 1979). Recollections of Stafford by Peter Taylor, Nancy Flagg Gibney, Wilfrid Sheed, Dorothea Straus, and others.

Biographies
Goodman, Charlotte Margolis. *Jean Stafford: The Savage Heart*. Austin: University of Texas Press, 1990.
Hulbert, Ann. *The Interior Castle: The Art and Life of Jean Stafford*. New York: Knopf, 1992.
Roberts, David. *Jean Stafford: A Biography*. Boston: Little, Brown, 1988.

Critical Articles and Reviews
Auchincloss, Louis. "Jean Stafford." In *Pioneers and Caretakers: A Study of Nine American Women Novelists*. Minneapolis: University of Minnesota Press, 1965. Pp. 152-160. Sees in Stafford's fiction the same nostalgia for a vanished past that is evident in the fiction of such women writers as Sarah Orne Jewett, Edith Wharton, Ellen Glasgow, Willa Cather, Katherine Anne Porter, and Carson McCullers.
Breit, Harvey. "Talk with Jean Stafford." *New York Times Book Review*, January 20, 1952, 18.
Burns, Stuart L. "Counterpoint in Jean Stafford's *The Mountain Lion*." *Critique*, 9 (Spring 1967): 20-32. Using a contrapuntal structure, Stafford has described the sorry fate of the innocent person who confronts the perils of the corrupt contemporary world.
Gelfant, Blanche H. "Revolutionary Turnings: *The Mountain Lion* Reread." *Massachusetts Review*, 20 (Spring 1979): 117-125. Focuses on the very different fates of Ralph and Molly in the American West. While Ralph accommodates to this male world,

Molly, a girl who dreams of becoming a writer, perishes. Within the conventions that have defined the American western, Stafford was not able to imagine how an odd female protagonist like Molly could survive.

Goodman, Charlotte. "The Lost Brother/The Twin: Women Novelists and the Male-Female Double *Bildungsroman.*" *Novel: A Forum on Fiction,* 17 (Fall 1983): 28-43. Considers *The Mountain Lion* along with other male-female double *Bildungsroman* by women, including Brontë's *Wuthering Heights,* Eliot's *The Mill on the Floss,* Cather's *My Ántonia,* and Oates' *Them,* all of which contrast the growth and development of a male and a female protagonist in a patriarchal society.

Graulich, Melody. "Jean Stafford's Western Childhood: Huck Finn Joins the Camp Fire Girls." *Denver Quarterly,* 18 (Spring 1983): 40-41. Graulich says that Stafford uses the western landscape, which, traditionally has been defined by male writers, to dramatize her own struggles as a woman writer writing within a male literary tradition.

Hassan, Ihab H. "Jean Stafford: The Expense of Style and the Scope of Sensibility." *Western Review,* 19 (Spring 1955): 185-203. Discusses Stafford's three novels and the short stories in her *Children Are Bored on Sunday.*

————. "The Character of Post-War Fiction in America." *English Journal,* 51 (January 1962): 1-8. Cites *The Mountain Lion* as a familiar type of novel in which the child symbolizes lost innocence.

Heller, Dana A. "Remembering Molly: Jean Stafford's *The Mountain Lion.*" In *The Femininization of Quest-Romance: Radical Departures.* Austin: University of Texas Press, 1990. Pp. 40-55. Concerned with issues such as the travails of childhood, the conflicts of female adolescence in a male-centered culture, and the warped values of the adult world, Stafford's fiction has important links with the works of many other American women writers. In *The Mountain Lion* Stafford explores the questing male hero's encounter with the death and/or mastery of the feminine.

Jenson, Sid. "The Noble Wicked West of Jean Stafford." *Western American Literature,* 7 (Winter 1973): 261-270. Jenson discusses the contrasts Stafford illuminates between the East and the West, between the civilized and the natural world.

Leary, William. "Native Daughter: Jean Stafford's California." *Western American Literature,* 21 (November 1986): 195-206. Leary explores Stafford's attitude toward California, her birthplace, concluding that to her it represented both a social and cultural wasteland.

————. "The Suicidal Thirties: Jean Stafford's 'The Philosophy Lesson.'" *Southwest Review,* 72 (Summer 1987): 389-403. Discusses one of Stafford's stories based on a traumatic experience when she was a student at the University of Colorado.

————. "Grafting Onto Her Roots: Jean Stafford's 'Woden's Day.'" *Western Review,* 23 (Summer 1988): 129-140. Leary attempts to sort out fact from fiction about Stafford's family in "Woden's Day," a fragment from her unpublished autobiographical novel *The Parliament of Women.*

Oates, Joyce Carol. *Washington Post Book World,* February 9, 1969: 6. Review of Stafford's *Collected Short Stories.* Oates says that in many of these stories "there is a sense of being lost, of being eternally homesick, of being both unloved and unloving" (6).

Pilkington, William T. "On Jean Stafford's *The Mountain Lion.*" In *Critical Essays on the Western American Novel.* William T. Pilkington, ed. Boston: G. K. Hall, 1980. Pp. 182-186. Calling the novel a "neglected classic," Pilkington argues that Stafford's portayal of the West in an ironic and ambiguous manner distinguishes it from most western fiction.

Rosowski, Susan. "Molly's Truth-Telling or Jean Stafford Rewriting the Western." In *Reading the West: New Essays on the Literature of the American West*. Michael Kowalewski, ed. New York: Cambridge University Press, 1996. Pp. 157-176. Rosowski maintains that in this portrait of the artist as a young woman, Stafford uses Molly to expose the psychosexual violence implicit in the traditional western novel.

Ryan, Maureen. *Innocence and Estrangement in the Fiction of Jean Stafford*. Baton Rouge: Louisiana State University Press, 1987. Emphasizes the autobiographical underpinnings of Stafford's fiction and its focus on characters, many of them female, who are alienated, isolated and misunderstood.

Vickery, Olga. "The Novels of Jean Stafford." *Critique*, 5 (Spring-Summer 1962): 14-26. An early champion of the works of Stafford, Vickery focuses on the way that Stafford uses her fictional "aliens, rebels, and freaks" to explore the ironies of life in the modern world.

Walsh, Mary Ellen Williams. *Jean Stafford*. Boston: Twayne, 1985. The first full-length study of Stafford's life and art, this book argues that because Stafford has written primarily about female characters "and their devalued lives," her work has not received the critical acclaim it merits.

———. "The Young Girl and the West: Disenchantment in Jean Stafford's Short Fiction." In *Women and Western American Literature*. Helen Winter Stauffer and Susan J. Rosowski, eds. Troy: Whitston Publishing Company, 1982. Pp. 230-246. Discusses Stafford's female characters in her short fiction that is set in the modern West. She notes that their gender separates Stafford's entrapped characters in these works from their contemporaries.

White, Barbara. "Initiation, the West, and the Hunt in Jean Stafford's *The Mountain Lion*." *Essays in Literature*, 9 (Fall 1982): 194-210. White notes the important role that gender plays in this novel.

Wilson, Mary Ann. "In Another Country: Jean Stafford's Literary Apprenticeship in Baton Rouge." *The Southern Review*, 29 (January 1993): 58-66. Wilson describes the formative influence a year as secretary for *The Southern Review* had on Stafford's development as a writer.

———. *Jean Stafford: A Study of the Short Fiction*. Boston: Twayne, 1996.

Allison Bulsterbaum Wallace and Harry Crockett

Rocky Mountain Nature Writing

ike the prickly pear, the magpie, and the coyote, nature writing is
thriving in the contemporary West. To see that nonfiction about
place and nature grows every year more significant with scholars
and general readers alike, one need only compare the first *Literary
History of the American West* with the present volume. Two essays sufficed then to cover nearly two centuries of such writing across the entire
West; now, numerous pieces are needed to convey the quantity and
quality of the work that has emerged in less than a decade from the
area's various subregions. This essay concentrates on contemporary
authors whose work focuses on some or all of the northern and central
Rocky Mountain states.

Tom Lyon's 1987 characterization of the genre remains substantially
true, with a handful of variations.[1] The wilderness experience, be it
adventurous or quietly contemplative, still yields its ancient yet ever-
new insights, and they are still encountered most profoundly in solitude—though the concept of wilderness itself has come up for considerable revision, its affluent, Caucasian bones laid increasingly bare.
Biophilia, or what Lyon called the naturist's "feeling of shared life," still
permeates thoughtful writing on animals particularly (but also on vegetation, watercourses, and entire mountains), the dangers of anthropo-
morphism notwithstanding. And nature writing continues the dual critique, begun in this country by Thoreau, of an unprincipled and myopic
consumer culture on the one hand and the complicit, implicated self on

the other. Rarely do these themes or informing attitudes appear in isolation from one another, though a work's form may determine which one predominates — biophilia in the wildlife study, for example. Most often, they mingle and merge, diverge and return, like so many roots feeding a single tree: love of place.

Several giants in American writing about place have passed away in recent years, three of them often identified with parts of the Rockies. Wallace Stegner stands in the front ranks of twentieth-century "landed" storytellers and essayists; as his 1992 essay collection — *Where the Bluebird Sings to the Lemonade Springs* — demonstrates, both his biography and his commentary on Americans' imperfect relation to arid lands cover great sections of the West, from Saskatchewan south to Montana, Utah, Nevada, and California. Surely Utah boasts no more famous spokesman for the natural world than Edward Abbey, whose memoir *Desert Solitaire* (1968) and novel *The Monkey Wrench Gang* (1975), among other titles, helped to shape a new generation of radical ecodefenders. Abbey's death in 1989 has yet to signal the end of new material for his reading public: in 1994 his journals were published as *Confessions of a Barbarian*. Montana writer Norman Maclean — whose 1976 *A River Runs Through It and Other Stories* won many admirers for its lyric evocation of a friendship between two fly-fishing brothers — spent his last years working on a meditative piece of local history entitled *Young Men and Fire*. Focusing on the 1949 Mann Gulch fire that took the lives of thirteen Forest Service smokejumpers, the book was far enough along when Maclean died in 1990 to enable his editors at the University of Chicago Press to publish it in 1992. Here, as in Maclean's earlier work, one recognizes a thoughtful, deeply sympathetic yet unsentimental love of place — particularly where the northern Rockies leap suddenly away from the vast yellow plains — and of the people who live and die by its dictates.

Heir to this Rocky Mountain regional tradition are many new talents, several of them born elsewhere. Indeed, a considerable share of twentieth-century American nature writing has been and continues to be produced by people who adopted their respective regions in their twenties, thirties, and beyond — and with a passion, as though scales had fallen from their eyes. This is as true of the West as of any other part of the country but more appropriately so: like so many western settlers before them, these writers are often escapees from increasingly congested and ailing urban centers, latter-day rebels and pilgrims in search of "the last best place" to establish an authentic life lived close to natural well-springs.

Perhaps inevitably, that phrase became a book title in 1988 when Montana's William Kittredge and Annick Smith—again, both transplants to the place they now call home—brought out a hefty anthology of Montana poetry, fiction, and nonfiction. Kittredge and Smith have each added their own voices to those singing the land, he in short-story collections such as *We Are Not in this Together* (1984) and memoirs of his Great Basin heritage titled *Owning It All* (1987) and *Hole in the Sky* (1992), she in essays on her homesteading life, often published in *Outside* magazine.[2]

Thomas McGuane, another emigrant, has increasingly grounded his material in the northern Rockies, having earlier established his reputation as a first-rate novelist farther south. Although he is best known for his fiction, McGuane has also written evocative essays about Montana's rivers and about his particular love—fly-fishing—in them. *An Outside Chance* (1990) collects several of these pieces, along with others on such topics as hunting and horse-packing. McGuane has staunchly defended Montana's wild nature (he directs American Rivers, a conservation organization), and in this he resembles many writers whose sense of responsibility toward places grows with their love and understanding of them.

"When you become part of a place, you either do or you don't" take on its battles, comments Rick Bass on Montana's growing problem with excessive logging (quoted in Breen, 23). A Texan by birth, Bass sank his teeth deep into the Rockies in the middle 1980s and shows no sign of letting go. After publishing numerous short stories, a collection of novellas, and essays concentrating chiefly on Texas and Deep South locales, Bass published *Winter: Notes from Montana* in 1991 and *The Ninemile Wolves* in 1992. The former chronicles the first few months Bass and his partner Elizabeth Hughes spent in the Yaak Valley, the latter a small wolf pack trying to establish itself in western Montana and the politics surrounding the return of such predators to ranching country.

In his prologue to *Winter*, Bass relates how he and Hughes left Mississippi (where Bass had worked as a petroleum geologist) to rove the West in search of a remote, beautiful place where they could live and work cheaply (she is an artist/illustrator, often for his books). They wound up as caretakers for a small, backwoods ranch in northwestern

Montana. As with so many other works by naturists adopting and adapting to new territory, *Winter* glows with the flush of new love that makes virtually everything about the place ring with perceived or potential significance. The book's journal form lends it a strong note of spontaneity, to some extent making a literary virtue out of the author's necessarily limited knowledge of his subject, his new home. He wonders "how rain falls here," and what new bird sounds he's registering, and which kinds of wood will best see his household through the toughest winter either of these southerners will have ever faced:

> It can be so wonderful, finding out you were wrong, that you are ignorant, that you know nothing, not squat. You get to start over. It's like snow falling that first time each year. It doesn't make any sound, but it's the strongest force you know of. Trees will crack and pop and split open later in the winter. Things opening up, learning. Learning the way it really is. (20)

The way it really is encompasses owls, wolverines, gray wolves, a few grizzly, too few caribou, water ouzels ("Exactly!...This is why we have come up here, to find an unspoiled ouzel" [32]), and new breeds of the human species. Bass admires and ponders the laconic, self-sufficient mountain men and women whose help he seeks rarely and reluctantly, as when his chainsaw begins repeatedly to break down while he's trying to get the winter's supply of fuel in.

The degree to which the chainsaw is at once a real and a symbolic problem — quite apart from mechanical failure — for Bass distinguishes his book from most of its predecessors in the genre, the backcountry-living chronicle. At the same time that *Winter* cannot ignore the signs all around of deforestation by commercial logging interests, its author demonstrates a sensitivity approaching sleepless guilt to the part he himself plays in the destruction. By turns he accuses and defends himself for not heating the ranch buildings with gas (which he'd have to buy) rather than wood (which he can have for only the price of his labor), sometimes humorously invoking a sort of post-eighties law of compensation: "I recycle my aluminum! I don't litter! I try to pee on the rocks, not on the soil, to keep from killing things with too much nitrogen!" (21).

The kind of writing that was once content to paint word-pictures of nature's moving phenomena — Bass lingers on the larches that "turn an eerie gold in the early fall," eventually filling the Yaak Valley "with their flying gold needles"—must now, in all honesty, acknowledge the presence of not one but many serpents in Eden. Noting the "clearcuts scrolled across the sides of mountains like murals," Bass is soon reminded of other extractive activity underway in the area, such as silver mining (28). It's becoming quite a tightrope act as we near century's close, this balancing of hosannas sung to wilderness with diatribes flung at the enemies of wilderness—especially when one isn't at all sure of one's own innocence. ("Mor-on," Bass can remember his father calling him with a Texas drawl; the author updates it with "environmental moron" [22].) But Bass settled in Montana's hinterlands to feel soil and snow—not tightropes—beneath his feet: "I don't mean to rant. I'm trying to keep this polite, low-key respectful. Quiet. Falling snow. But inside, I rage" (39).

In *The Ninemile Wolves*, Bass can rage a little more freely, for this book is more journalism than seasonal journal, though with Bass even journalism is highly idiosyncratic: "I can say what I want to say. I gave up my science badge a long time ago" (4). Bass's fierce love of the wild translates into fierce loyalty and defensiveness in the face of its enemies, the several interest groups whose presence in the Ninemile Valley seems incompatible with that of wolves. Anyone on Rick Bass' mailing list knows that he writes tirelessly and not always for publication—his political material runs as wild as the wolves, all over the page and heedless of spelling and punctuation conventions—on behalf of Montana's wilderness, as though he must match the American appetite for excessive exploitation with an excess of love.

Similarly dedicated to the defense of Montana wilderness are Richard Manning and Doug Peacock. An outstanding exposé of the logging industry, Manning's *Last Stand* (1991) is, like Bass' *Ninemile Wolves*, primarily a work of journalism. But like Marc Reisner's *Cadillac Desert* (1986) and Charles Wilkinson's *Crossing the Next Meridian* (1993), Manning's book is propelled by a sense of personal responsibility toward western nature that carries it beyond mere reportage. Manning confronts—much as Bass does in *Winter*—the sorrow of knowing one's life "had done and would do great harm" to the Earth, concluding: "I cut my own wood so that I might take this sadness and twist it about in my hands, greet it each night as I stoke the stove and watch the flames dissolve the lives of trees" (171). Other Manning pieces frequently appear in *Northern Lights*, the quarterly publication of Missoula's Northern

Lights Research and Education Institute and one of the region's foremost venues for such work.

Doug Peacock's *Grizzly Years: In Search of the American Wilderness*
(1990) narrates the author's quest for the big bears, for him North
America's truest incarnation of wilderness. A first-rate natural history of
the grizzly as well as a personal regeneration-by-wilderness testimonial,
the book moves back and forth between the wildlands of North America
and the war-ravaged Central Highlands of Vietnam. Harrowing memories spring unbidden like booby-traps into the author's scarred psyche,
but his growing sense of connection to the grizzlies helps him to recover
soul and sanity, both nearly lost to the war.

A very different though no less passionate Montana voice is David
Quammen's. He is better known these days for the *Outside* magazine column he wrote for several years, "Natural Acts," than for his novels and
short stories. Selected essays were collected in *Natural Acts* (1985) and
The Flight of the Iguana (1988), which share the subtitle *A Sidelong View
of Science and Nature.* For at least a decade these natural-history essays
ran the gamut from barnacles and bedbugs to swampy ecosystems and
entire island chains (an interest which led to his recent book, *Song of the
Dodo: Island Biogeography in an Age of Extinctions*). Only occasionally does
he give away his Montana residency of twenty years (he hails from Ohio)
with pieces on, say, rivers special to him. Typically, a Quammen essay artfully blends the latest scientific information about his subject—he particularly likes those corners of nature the rest of the modern world
prefers to loathe, such as cockroaches and mosquitoes, proposing them as
test cases for human environmental ethics—with lively, telling anecdotes from the history of science and from his own personal history.
Especially through the latter, Quammen keeps readers ever aware of the
rollicking good fun as well as the abiding joy in store for all who make
room in their lives and consciousness for the nonhuman Other. So sure
is Quammen of nature's, especially natural Montana's, power to expand
and deepen human experience that he admits to urging, several years
ago, a down-and-out eastern friend to migrate there, quickly explaining
that "adding to the number of Montana residents, even by one, is a
responsibility [he doesn't] take lightly" (*Flight* 253).

The growing attraction the West holds for great numbers of
Americans is much on the minds of other Rocky Mountain writers as
well. And the fact that some of these hordes do not come to stay is not
always comforting: as Ed Abbey so forcefully pointed out, "recreation"

can be just as exploitive an industry as any other of our time and equally indicative of the modern's alienation from the land he or she hastens through. This is one of the themes resonating throughout Ellen Meloy's *Raven's Exile: A Season on the Green River* (1994). In an engaging, off-beat style, Meloy explores the contradictions inherent in her work as a Desolation Canyon river ranger: crowds in the midst of an immense desert, the tenuous meaning of the "wilderness experience" packaged and sold to ten thousand people each summer. Meloy skewers the excesses of what Abbey deemed "industrial tourism" both humorously and angrily, but she seldom forgets that she owes to it her enviable sea-sonal employment (she winters in Missoula). Her fierce love of the canyon, however, leads her far beyond this critique into a series of phys-ical and metaphorical explorations loosely circling around a recurring question: why do no ravens dwell in Desolation Canyon?

Another recent life-in-the-wilderness account, C. L. Rawlins' *Sky's Witness: A Year in Wyoming's Wind River Range* (1993) is a much differ-ent sort of work. For most of the year, Rawlins shares the Bridger Wilderness with one research partner and virtually no one else. A Wyoming native, Rawlins conducted a ground-breaking study of air pol-lution in some of the Rocky Mountains' remotest and roughest high country (for which the Forest Service gave him a National Primitive Skills Award). Pulling enormously heavy snow samples on an awkward sled while cross-country skiing near-vertical terrain, one tends to focus on the task at hand, pausing only occasionally for a spectacular long view. This is frequently the case with Rawlins' narrative, which is con-sistently rooted in the immediate. For Rawlins, the wisdom and insight afforded by wilderness living come in day-to-day experience — in the exhaustion, the splendor, the constant back-of-the-mind monitoring (avalanche? thin ice?) for danger.

Numerous other of Rawlins' essays, also deriving from these Wind River experiences, tend to be discursive, reflective. For example, "The Meadow at the Corner of Your Eye" (appearing in Scott Norris' 1994 anthology, *Discovered Country: Tourism and Survival in the American West*) considers our American penchant for remote and spectacular places partly because they differ from the places where we live, pointing out how this blinds us to our responsibilities toward the nature that sur-rounds us:

There's a yearning that can be expressed as a place more simply

than as a feeling: for beauty, rest, purity, transfiguration. It is easier to think of it as unknown. A knowing love is difficult, like a
marriage that persists despite boredom, bitterness, and grief. It can
be easier to see love's essence in the face of a stranger.... (86)

"What we've been fighting for isn't places but our souls," he concludes
(88). "The undiscovered country is not wilderness but a change of
heart" (89).

Wyoming's landscape would indeed appear an excellent catalyst to
such a change, if the example of Gretel Ehrlich is representative.
Traveling there in the mid-1970s to work on a documentary film about
sheep ranching, Ehrlich found herself unable to return to her native
California: "For the first time I was able to take up residence on earth with
no alibis, no self-promoting schemes" (*Solace* ix). With a new set of
clothes, a new job (as a ranch hand), and a new outlook on landscape —
as, paradoxically, "indifferent" to us yet also our primary source of meaning — Ehrlich began writing journal entries that in turn became *The Solace
of Open Spaces* (1985). Like other naturists who have defected from the
urban, professional middle class, Ehrlich speaks lovingly of the "small ceremonies and private, informal rituals" born of a rural existence: "We ride
the spring pasture, pick chokecherries in August, skin out a deer in the
fall, and in the enactment experience a wordless exhilaration between
bouts of plain hard work" (103). *Islands, the Universe, Home* (1991) gathers later essays of a similar stripe, along with some on Ehrlich's experiences in Japan; she has also published a novel, a collection of stories, and
an account of her experience of being struck by lightning.

"Homing," as it were, is likewise the theme of another emerging
Wyoming talent, Jack Turner. A mountain climber with nearly four
decades of worldwide experience, a longtime Teton National Park climbing guide, a Buddhist, and a former philosophy professor, Turner comes
well prepared to examine the limitations of our usual ways of experiencing nature. His essay collection, *The Abstract Wild*, shows his propensity
for grounding philosophical explorations in the particulars of place.
"What does it mean to be accountable, to whom, and to what purpose?"
he asks. His answer is, in part, to

Dig in someplace.... Allow the spirits of your chosen place to
speak through you. Say their names. Say Moose Ponds, Teewinot,
Pingora, Gros Ventre, Stewart Draw, Lost Rivers. Speak of individ-

800

uals—the pine marten that lives in the Dumpster, the lycopodium on the north ridge of the Grand Tetons. Force the spirits of your place to be heard. (Clow and Snow 133-34)

Ann Zwinger's work demonstrates that "digging in" (Colorado, in her case—she grew up in Indiana) need not prevent one from writing lovingly of many places, whether mountain, desert, or sea. Her 1995 title, *Downcanyon: A Naturalist Explores the Colorado River Through the Grand Canyon*, is the most recent in a long list of nature books, such as *Beyond the Aspen Grove* (1970), *Run, River, Run* (1976), *Wind in the Rock: The Canyonlands of Southeastern Utah* (1978), *A Desert Country Near the Sea: A Natural History of the Cape Region of Baja California* (1983) and *The Mysterious Lands: A Naturalist Explores the Four Great Deserts of the Southwest* (1989). For most of these very full books Zwinger also provided beautifully pencilled illustrations. Still another familiar Colorado author is Linda Hogan: readers of her poetry and fiction are just beginning to be treated to thoughtful and thought-provoking essays, appearing in such periodicals as *Prairie Schooner* and *Parabola* and collected in *Dwellings: Reflections on the Natural World*, on the relationships we do and do not have with animal and plant species (drawing here, as in earlier work, partly on her Chickasaw heritage).

David Petersen's *Ghost Grizzlies* (1995) focuses on Colorado's San Juan Mountains, where the biologists of the Colorado Grizzly Project believe the bears remain, despite the wildlife agencies' contention that the last bear was killed there in the early eighties. A compelling 1993 essay called "Here, I Am the Deer," provides a preview of sorts, a "meandering meditation" on why it matters whether the grizzlies are up there. Petersen has published natural-history volumes on elk and other cervids and was the hand-picked editor of Abbey's journals.

(One other Abbey protegé deserves mention here. As many know, Dave Foreman co-founded the *Monkey Wrench Gang*-inspired Earth First!; his *Confessions of an Eco-Warrior* [1991] provides a lively review of that experience. But few know that Foreman has gone on to help found The Wildlands Project, a group dedicated to wedding pro-wilderness activism with state-of-the-art science. An unusual spinoff is editor David Clark Burks' 1994 *Place of the Wild: A Wildlands Anthology*, in which accomplished nature writers—including several from the Rocky Mountain region [Terry Tempest Williams and Jack Turner, for example]—contemplate the value of wilderness.)

Although John McPhee still lives in his hometown of Princeton, New Jersey, he probably spends enough time across the Mississippi to warrant post office boxes in several western cities. More important, his books on the geology of the Rocky Mountain states have reached hundreds of thousands of readers—whom he has treated to a new entree virtually every year since the middle 1960s—and have gone far to popularize modern plate tectonics theory. Beginning essentially in New York City and moving west along the fortieth parallel, sometimes pausing to double back on itself, the series collectively known as *Annals of the Former World* includes *Basin and Range* (1981), *In Suspect Terrain* (1983), *Rising from the Plains* (1986), and *Assembling California* (1993); the first and third titles most concern the Rocky Mountain region.

Even as he spreads his multi-billion-year-old narrative across these four very full books, McPhee masterfully controls the pace of its delivery. The rhythms as well as the content of his prose emphasize the power and plasticity of the earth's most massive materials by periodically fast-forwarding the story, compressing, bending, squeezing huge sections of it into a few eye-widening pages or even lines. For example, having just situated the area represented in modern times by Jackson Hole somewhere near the equator (in the Precambrian Age), *Rising from the Plains* swiftly reaches forward in time more than thirty million years:

> The land arches. Deep miles of sediments lying over schists and granites rise and bend. The dinosaurs fade. The seas drain eastward. Mountains rise northwest, rooted firmly to their Precambrian cores. Braided rivers descend from them, lugging quartzite boulders, and spreading fields of gold-bearing gravel tens of miles wide. Other mountains—as rootless sheets of whole terrain—appear in the west, sliding like floorboards, overlapping, stacking up, covering younger rock, colliding with the rooted mountains, while to the east more big ranges and huge downflexing basins appear in the random geometries of the Laramide Revolution. (*Rising* 139)

Wherever nature has left her oldest texts, McPhee discovers, transcribes, and ably dramatizes them for a late twentieth-century audience weaned on the pyrotechnics of film. For the geology itself he enlists the help of experts whom he befriends, their own life stories gradually unfolding and forming each book's subtext. More than merely unobtrusive, these biographies are in perfect keeping with McPhee's vision of modern (in geologic terms) landscape and human experience as mutually contextualizing forces.

Terry Tempest Williams' vision might be similarly stated, but her literary expression of it could hardly be more different. Whereas McPhee typically folds into his prose the biography of an acquaintance or research associate, Williams draws on her own story or on that of family members. And McPhee rarely, if ever, treats his subjects as unfathomable cosmic or spiritual mysteries, preferring instead to turn the deeply curious nature of "facts" over in the light of a steady, intellectually awed or amused gaze. Williams, on the other hand, finds mystery in virtually all things, from the arc of a bird's wing to the founding of human cultures, as though they manifest somehow an elusive yet indwelling divinity.

Beginning with *Pieces of White Shell: A Journey to Navajoland* in 1984, Williams went on to publish *Refuge: An Unnatural History of Family and Place* in 1991 and *An Unspoken Hunger: Stories from the Field* in 1994. The first title concerns her experiences among the Navajo; the last collects disparate essays that originally appeared elsewhere, from her profile of Georgia O'Keeffe to her congressional "Testimony on Behalf of the Pacific Yew Act of 1991." *Refuge* continues to enjoy the most acclaim. It concentrates on the winter of 1982-1983 and the years immediately following, when the author faced twin tragedies: heavy rains caused Great Salt Lake to flood her beloved Bear River Migratory Bird Refuge, and the cancer that had once afflicted Williams' mother returned, this time to take her life.

Like most stories of a person's (and a people's) intimate experience of landscape, *Refuge* is many-layered. Its blend of natural, regional, familial, and religious (Williams is Mormon) history is so tight as to almost render these components metaphors for one another, the lot of them finally summed up in the single, overarching metaphor of "refuge." Along with Bass, Manning, and other naturists of their generation, Williams has much humanly imposed environmental damage to record but more experience than they of the human price often exacted: the cancer that took her mother and other female relatives appears traceable to the federal program of atomic testing pursued in nearby Nevada during the Cold War. *Refuge* thus grapples with a bitter paradox, for the same beautiful physical setting that once nurtured a close Mormon family's love of nature — especially of birds — seems also to have sown within them the ugly seeds of their own untimely demise.

For many of the late twentieth-century shapers of this continually evolving genre—besides Williams, one thinks again of Vietnam veteran Doug Peacock—a great deal stands in need of healing, as our history of behaving violently toward the land becomes increasingly viewed as springing from the same American pathology that causes violence among ourselves. Leslie Ryan is one of the most recent voices in this chorus. A Utah survival instructor and another *Northern Lights* find, Ryan tells in "The Clearing in the Clearing" and in "The Other Side of the Fire" of her own regeneration after soul-killing experiences (rape, childhood abuse, abandonment). Such practices as clear-cutting old-growth forests, poisoning wolves, and even Ryan's own experiment with killing and eating a fish (she is, one gathers, ordinarily a vegetarian) are, for her, akin to rape: they all rationalize the transgression by objectifying, by turning "thou" into "it." Failing to acknowledge kinship with the Other, one thereby fails to love not only nonhuman nature but also, by extension, one's own ecologically constructed Self.

* * *

What can readers expect of Rocky Mountain nature writing as the century draws to a close? Certainly the complicated and not always dissimilar philosophies underlying wilderness protection and development will remain important themes, as will the more individualistic ones concerning personal growth, renewal, and healing through landscape and the nonhuman Other. And although several classic forms—such as the solitary quest narrative—will persist, it seems likely the lines that once separated forms will often blur, as literary naturists continue to push at the edges of their discipline. A recent, provocative example of this phenomenon from the Rocky Mountain region is Edward A. Geary's *The Proper Edge of the Sky: The High Plateau Country of Utah* (1992): "neither guidebook, nor travel narrative, nor natural history, nor social history, nor literary history, nor personal essay," the book stands rather as a creative amalgam of all these (3). But by no means will such multi-faceted works continue to emerge from the Rockies alone: other examples from around the country have already put in appearances, some not so recently—for instance, John McPhee's *Coming into the Country* and *The Pine Barrens,* on Alaska and New Jersey, respectively; Barry Lopez's *Of Wolves and Men,* concerning much of the Northwest, especially parts of Alaska and Canada; Timothy Egan's *The Good Rain: Across Time and*

Terrain in the Pacific Northwest; John Madson's *Where the Sky Began: Land of the Tallgrass Prairie*, with its midwestern focus; and perhaps also Kathleen Norris's *Dakota: A Spiritual Geography*. These and numerous other writers' efforts "to see and know a richly varied land" (in Geary's words, *Proper Edge* [3]) through many lenses may lead the way for the next few years—particularly as learning to know places in order to love them well becomes more and more the whole point.

Notes

1. "The Western Essay Since 1970," *A Literary History of the American West* (Fort Worth: Texas Christian University Press, 1987), pp. 1246-1255.

2. Kittredge has further supported nature writing in the region through his associations with the University of Montana's Program in Environmental and Nature Writing and the Teller Wildlife Refuge's Environmental Writing Institute, programs that have helped to make western Montana a mecca for nature writers.

Selected Bibliography

Primary Sources

Abbey, Edward. *Confessions of a Barbarian: Selections from the Journals of Edward Abbey, 1951-1989.* David Petersen, ed. New York: Little, Brown, 1994.

Bass, Rick. *The Ninemile Wolves.* New York: Ballantine, 1992.

———. *Winter: Notes from Montana.* Boston: Houghton Mifflin, 1991.

Burks, David Clark. *Place of the Wild: A Wildlands Anthology.* Washington, D.C.: Island Press, 1994.

Ehrlich, Gretel. *Islands, the Universe, Home.* New York: Viking Penguin, 1991.

———. *The Solace of Open Spaces.* New York: Viking Penguin, 1985.

Foreman, Dave. *Confessions of an Eco-Warrior.* New York: Harmony, 1991.

Geary, Edward A. *The Proper Edge of the Sky: The High Plateau Country of Utah.* Salt Lake City: University of Utah Press, 1992.

Hogan, Linda. *Dwellings: Reflection on the Natural World.* New York: Norton, 1995.

Kittredge, William, and Annick Smith, eds. *The Last Best Place: A Montana Anthology.* Helena: Montana Historical Society Press, 1988.

Maclean, Norman. *Young Men and Fire.* Chicago: University of Chicago Press, 1992.

Manning, Richard. *Last Stand.* Salt Lake City: Gibbs Smith, 1991.

McGuane, Thomas. *An Outside Chance: Classic and New Essays on Sport.* Boston: Houghton Mifflin, 1990.

McPhee, John. *Assembling California.* New York: Farrar, Straus & Giroux, 1993.

———. *Basin and Range.* New York: Farrar, Straus & Giroux, 1981.

———. *In Suspect Terrain.* New York: Farrar, Straus & Giroux, 1983.

———. *Rising from the Plains.* New York: Farrar, Straus & Giroux, 1986.

Meloy, Ellen. *Raven's Exile: A Season on the Green River.* New York: Henry Holt, 1994.

Norris, Scott, ed. *Undiscovered Country: Tourism and Survival in the American West.* Albuquerque: Stone Ladder Press, 1995.

Peacock, Doug. *Grizzly Years: In Search of the American Wilderness.* New York: Henry Holt, 1990.

Petersen, David. *Ghost Grizzlies.* New York: Henry Holt, 1995.

———. "Here, I Am the Deer: A Meandering Meditation on Grizzly Wilderness." In *Sacred Trusts: Essays on Stewardship and Responsibility.* Michael Katakis, ed. San Francisco: Mercury House, 1993.

———, ed. *A Hunter's Heart: Honest Essays on Blood Sport.* New York: Henry Holt, 1996.

Quammen, David. *The Flight of the Iguana: A Sidelong View of Science and Nature.* New York: Anchor-Doubleday, 1989.

———. *Natural Acts: A Sidelong View of Science and Nature.* New York: Laurel-Dell, 1986.

———. *The Song of the Dodo: Island Biogeography in an Age of Extinctions.* New York: Scribner, 1996.

Rawlins, C. L. *Sky's Witness: A Year in Wyoming's Wind River Range.* New York: Henry Holt, 1993.

Ryan, Leslie. "The Clearing in the Clearing" and "The Other Side of Fire." In *Northern Lights: A selection of New Writing from the American West.* Deborah Clow and Donald Snow, eds. New York: Vintage, 1994.

Stegner, Wallace. *Where the Bluebird Sings to the Lemonade Springs: Living and Writing in the West.* New York: Random House, 1992.

Turner, Jack. *The Abstract Wild.* Tucson: University of Arizona Press, 1996.

Williams, Terry Tempest. *Pieces of White Shell: A Journey to Navajoland.* New York: Scribner's, 1984.

———. *Refuge: An Unnatural History of Family and Place.* New York: Pantheon, 1991.

———. *An Unspoken Hunger: Stories from the Field.* New York: Pantheon, 1994.

Zwinger, Ann. *Downcanyon: A Naturalist Explores the Colorado River Through the Grand Canyon.* Tucson: University of Arizona Press, 1995.

Secondary Sources

Anderson, Chris, ed. *Literary Nonfiction: Theory, Criticism, Pedagogy.* Carbondale: Southern Illinois University Press, 1989. (See Ehrlich, McPhee)

Breen, Kevin. "Rick Bass: An Interview." *Poets & Writers Magazine,* 21 (May/June 1993): 19-25.

Daniel, Lucille. "Standing Our Ground: Conversations with Terry Tempest Williams." *Sojourner,* 18 (February 1983): 1, 17-19.

Howarth, William L. Introduction. *The John McPhee Reader.* New York: Farrar, Straus & Giroux, 1976.

Kircher, Cassie. "An Interview with Ann Zwinger." *ISLE: Interdisciplinary Studies in Literature and Environment,* 1 (Fall 1993): 123-132.

Legler, Gretchen. "Toward a Postmodern Pastoral: The Erotic Landscape in the Work of Gretel Ehrlich." *ISLE: Interdisciplinary Studies in Literature and Environment,* 1 (Fall 1993): 45-55.

Lounsberry, Barbara. *The Art of Fact: Contemporary Artists of Nonfiction.* New York: Greenwood, 1990. (See McPhee)

Lyon, Tom. "The Western Essay Since 1970." In A *Literary History of the American West*. Fort Worth: Texas Christian University Press, 1987. Pp. 1246-1255.

Murray, John. "The Rise of Nature Writing: America's Next Great Genre?" *Manoa: A Pacific Journal of International Writing*, 4 (Fall 1992): 73-96. (See Bass, Kittredge)

Wallace, Allison Bulsterbaum. "Contemporary Ecophilosophy in David Quammen's Popular Natural Histories." In *The Literature of Science: Studies in the Popular Scientific Essay*. Murdo William McRae, ed. Athens: University of Georgia Press, 1992. Pp. 273-290.

Wild, Peter. *Ann Zwinger*. Boise: Boise State University Western Writers Series, 1993.

William W. Bevis

James Welch

When the review of James Welch's *Winter in the Blood* appeared on the front page of the *New York Times Book Review* in 1974 — "a nearly flawless novel," said Reynolds Price — the Native American Renaissance had not yet happened. Momaday's *House Made of Dawn* had claimed the Pulitzer in 1969, and the American Indian Movement (AIM) had captured headlines with the taking of Alcatraz and the sit-in at the Bureau of Indian Affairs headquarters in Washington, but there was no reason to believe that either contemporary politics or Momaday's single work would mark the beginning of three decades of exceptional Native American literature.

In a period of over twenty-five years, this literature, of high quality, well published and widely read, would extend from Momaday through Welch, Leslie Silko, D'Arcy McNickle's posthumous work, to Louise Erdrich. In addition to six or eight significant works by major writers which claimed national attention, a number of lesser known (though not necessarily lesser) Native writers were contributing to a canon that now includes perhaps thirty substantial books. This from a population of less than a million, in one generation.

In criticism as well as in fiction and poetry, Native commentary has entered our intellectual life. By 1983, Kenneth Lincoln could title his critical study *Native American Renaissance*, and in the eighties and nineties Native writers and intellectuals such as Paula Gunn Allen and Louis Owens would follow Vine Deloria's lead in offering aggressively

Native readings of American texts and culture. In addition, critics such as Arnold Krupat have shaped discussions of Native work in relation to new theory—not at all a strained comparison for readers of traditional tales, Gerald Vizenor, and Jorge Luis Borges. So the remarkable creative output of Native writers in the last twenty-five years has been matched by the impact of Native scholars and Native issues on the national intellectual scene, and happily this movement has taken the form not of reaction and primitivism but of subversion and play wed to intensely political consciousness.

James Welch was born in 1940 of Blackfeet, Gros Ventre and European descent, in Browning, Montana, which remains to this day a tough and interesting town at the center of the Blackfeet Reservation near the Canadian border. He attended schools on the Blackfeet and Fort Belknap reservations, his father's and maternal grandparents' homes. His family moved now and then away from a family farm to find work, and James graduated from high school in Minnesota in 1958. He also worked in Alaska and California, for the Forest Service and on fire crews and as an Upward Bound counselor. After a year at Northern Montana College in Havre, he came down to Missoula in 1964, a shy and unsure student who showed talent from the start. Professor John Herrmann first encouraged him to write, and later he took poetry from Richard Hugo, already in 1965 a well-known poet and director of the creative writing program. Hugo told of having Welch in a poetry writing class. Welch handed in a poem called "In My First Hard Springtime," which began:

> Those red men you offended were my brothers.
> Town drinkers, Buckles Pipe, Star Boy,
> Billy Fox, were blood to bison. Albert Heavy Runner
> was never civic. You are white and common.
> (*Riding Earthboy 40* 25)

Hugo said that when he came to "Albert Heavy Runner was never civic," he knew he had nothing to teach this young man except to tell him to keep writing. He also encouraged the young Indian to write about his own people and the places he had known. Welch entered the graduate program in creative writing in 1966. After leaving the M.F.A. program in 1968 Welch stayed in Missoula and married Missoula English Professor Lois Monk. In Missoula, Welch was immersed in the writing community and by 1971 had published a book of poems, *Riding the Earthboy 40*, which remains exactingly, sparingly dramatic in its language. *The Saturday Review* said his "voice is clear, laconic, and it projects a depth in experience of landscape, people and history that conveys a rich complexity" (October 2, 1971, 50).

He turned next to fiction and worked on *Winter in the Blood* in Missoula and in Greece, where he and Lois had gone for a sabbatical. Its publication in 1974, with a front-page review in the *New York Times*, made his reputation. Thereafter he wrote *The Death of Jim Loney* (1979), also about an alienated young Indian on the Highline; *Fools Crow* (1986), a historical novel about the Blackfeet in 1869-1870; *The Indian Lawyer* (1990), which followed a young Indian professional into the affairs of the state capitol; and *Killing Custer* (1994), following the scripting of a film with Paul Stekler for PBS (*Last Stand at Little Bighorn*). Welch has received a good deal of critical attention, which cycles vigorously between tribal and literary issues and is the subject of a book-length study by Kathryn Shanley forthcoming from Oklahoma.

During his writing years Welch became quite active as a visiting professor at Cornell and at the University of Washington, as well as behind the scenes working on the National Endowment for the Arts and the Newberry Library Board, reviewing manuscripts for various publishers, and serving as one of the three public members on the Montana State Board of Pardons. Since many of the students and manuscripts, and most of the prisoners, were Indian, his service was not without policy.

* * *

Winter in the Blood is told in the first person by a nameless Native American narrator who has just returned home. His girlfriend has run off, and he sets out from his mother's ranch to find her. He doesn't find much except trouble in the bars of Malta, Dodson, Harlem, or Havre, and we learn that he has lost more: a father and brother, at least.

In the second half of the novel, after the narrator's cruel slapping of a woman he hardly knows has made him disgusted with his own distance from everyone and everything, the young man's numbing indifference begins to crack. Discovery of his grandfather, respect for his grandmother, and plans for his own future seem to suggest new resolve.

Welch's first two novels, *Winter in the Blood* and *The Death of Jim*

Loney, pose the same question: Has the hero/narrator improved his lot? Is there any redemption or success in this Highline world of poverty, distance, and booze? The questions are doubly interesting because they raise issues of white versus Native American values, and because they also raise regional issues: How do people react to Malta, Montana? How does our own life experience — urban or country, rich or poor — affect our reading?

* * *

When Welch published *Winter in the Blood* in 1974, he was hailed for his spare prose and social realism and compared to Hemingway. His style was certainly in Hemingway's no-nonsense, realistic tradition, although Welch added the poetic image that gives depth to simple sentences: "... the paring knife grew heavy in the old lady's eyes" (*Winter* 5). Paragraphs and chapters in *Winter* often end with echoing images that stop the reader and force reflection: the knife was heavy in her eyes; pheasants are "like men...full of twists" (*Winter* 9). The effect is anti-narrative, begging us to stop and think about what we have just read. Welch's surrealism, too, especially in the bar scenes, is anti-narrative, taking the reader out of the story by exploding it, forcing us to search for connections among the shards.

Realism, surrealism, and the shock of poetic image may describe Welch's technique, but his voice never shares the decadence of Hemingway and other writers of the twenties. His voice is always sincere, closer to Vittorini's *In Sicily*, as translated by Wilfred David (and introduced by Hemingway), which Welch knew and admired. Vittorini used realistic prose to tell of coming home to his Native subculture, Sicily, strange to most readers and half-strange to himself, and of finding there no easy location of his own needs. That is the voice of *Winter in the Blood*.

The sincerity of *Winter in the Blood* made it an important book from the very first paragraph, because it presented the elements of the old "western" in a totally new voice. The first paragraph has horses, Indians, a log cabin, and tumbleweeds — the basic ingredients of the West as it has been invented, packaged, and sold to eastern and European audiences to satisfy their fantasies of adventure and escape. In Welch's opening, however, the narrator is not an adventurer or visitor in the exciting West; he is taking a leak. The scene is not new, but old. The horses,

Indians, log cabin, and the tumbleweeds are not exotic subjects, they are simply the context of someone's life:

> In the tall weeds of the borrow pit, I took a leak and watched the sorrel mare, her colt beside her, walk through burnt grass to the shady side of the log-and-mud cabin. It was called the Earthboy place, although no one by that name (or any other) had lived in it for twenty years. The roof had fallen in and the mud between the logs had fallen out in chunks, leaving a bare gray skeleton, home only to mice and insects. Tumbleweeds, stark as bone, rocked in a hot wind against the west wall. On the hill behind the cabin, a rectangle of barbed wire held the graves of all the Earthboys, except for a daughter who had married a man from Lodgepole. She could be anywhere, but the Earthboys were gone. (*Winter* 1)

A great deal has been accomplished in that paragraph, mainly through style. Welch's editors did not like the character taking a leak in the first sentence, but he stuck with his version because he wanted it clear that this sensitive narrator could be the Indian we see pissing in the pit along Highway 2 between Dodson and Malta. That social realism is thrown at us right at the start. Yet inside his head, nothing is common, all is delicacy, dignity, grace, and in the rhymes and rhythms, all is song: "the roof had fallen in and the mud between the logs had fallen out in chunks.... Tumbleweeds, stark as bone, rocked in a hot wind against the west wall." The final line quietly situates the book, and the character — perhaps also family, tribe, race — in a land of loss: "The Earthboys were gone."

In that paragraph, Montana literature suddenly speaks about contemporary life in a beautiful, rhythmic yet realistic voice. There is no catering to cowboy fantasies and, for that matter, no attempt to refute them. Here is pure attention, by some speaker who is clearly sensitive and articulate, to living near Malta. We know his life will be taken seriously. We know it will be from his point of view.

What does the character (never named) in *Winter* find when he comes home to his mother's ranch? The answers form a pattern, both in the classroom and in the national criticism of this book. Apart from the few who resent the hard realism, those from Montana, especially those from the Highline and especially Native Americans, tend to see a positive ending to an accurate, often tragic, and at times funny book. Those from the East, especially professional critics and New Yorkers, tend to be overwhelmed by the bleakness of the people and land, and they find the book depressing.

Although readers from more lush environments often find *Winter in the Blood* bleak, there is no denying the positive aspects to its end. The narrator of *Winter* has found his grandfather, learned his grandmother's history, reconciled himself to his brother's death, and in the final sentence, he alone in his family has honored his past by throwing the pouch on his grandmother's grave. His distance is now more like grandfather Yellow Calf's, serene in a cockeyed world, surrounded by graves of those gone. Those are strong upturns in an Indian "homing" plot, a narrative of return to family, tribe, place.

The narrator also improves his "white" plot, the story of himself as a mobile, free individual. His futile but whole-hearted attempt to drag the cow out of the mud—an unprecedented action adventure ("the rope against my thigh felt right" [*Winter* 171])—his new confidence in his knowledge, his resolve to buy Agnes "a couple of cremes de menthe, maybe offer to marry her on the spot" (*Winter* 175), coupled with his returns to tradition suggest an existential hero: he can't really change anything in his absurd universe; the past may be dead and Agnes worthless, but he is creating the slightest new dignity, confidence, and meaning within himself, spinning it out of his guts as well as his past. In *Winter in the Blood*, the white existential plot, the Indian homing plot, and the first-person poetic brilliance coincide.

While *Winter in the Blood* allowed Montanans and others accustomed to hard minimums to glimpse, at least, a hopeful homing in, Welch's second book, *The Death of Jim Loney*, seemed unrelievedly bleak. In *Loney*, white values are more severely rejected, the third-person narration hides Loney's mind, and the "homing" plot is harder to find. *Loney* offers an even more severe test of pessimistic/optimistic reactions. Paula Gunn Allen applauds Loney's sacrificial loyalty to tribe; Louis Owens sees that theme but cannot excuse the waste and the echoes of a tragic Indian stereotype; Kenneth Lincoln is very uncomfortable with the entire situation. Whereas *Winter* tends to divide Montanans and easterners, *Loney* tends to divide Indians and whites, and tends to divide every reader within him or herself. Because of the crucible it plunges us into, *The Death of Jim Loney* is increasingly admired by those who teach Native American literature.

* * *

Jim Loney's friends believe he should get out of Harlem, Montana. He should try "leaving behind all his ancient prejudices and manners," as Crèvecoeur had advised (*Letters from an American Farmer*, "What is an American?"). He is bright, has performed well in school, and seems to lack only the motivation to do something with himself. Rhea, his white lover from Texas, like Andrew Garcia from the Rio Grande or Guthrie's Boone from Kentucky, has come to the Montana plains for "a complete break with the past" (86). She wants to go to Seattle: "Don't ask me why I chose Seattle. I guess it just seems a place to escape to" (87). Rhea wants Jim Loney to escape with her.

Ironically, Rhea is in competition with another escape artist, Loney's beautiful and upwardly mobile sister, Kate, who works for the government in Washington, D.C. Kate, though Indian, also offers Loney the white way of novelty, mobility, and meaning through individual experience and possession of things. Leave, she says, and "you would have things worthwhile...beautiful country, a city, the North, the South, the ocean.... You need that. You need things to be different, things that would arouse your curiosity, give you some purpose" (76). Kate has chosen to change her Indian life through white knowledge, "learning as a kind of salvation, a way to get up and out of being what they were" (90).

Kate and Rhea are attractive characters. Unlike Silko, Momaday, and McNickle, Welch does not bring "the enemy" onstage; he avoids didactic or dogmatic overtones, and the oppression represented by white culture appears in the gaps between images, between possibilities, between plots. Even the stupid white sheriff, Painter, is treated sympathetically, as is the successful ranch-owning Indian, Pretty Weasel, who quit his basketball scholarship at Wyoming to come home in "automatic response, the way a sheepdog returns to camp in the evening" (81).

Neither the white world nor white success seems odious in this book. On the other hand, Harlem, Loney's hometown, is not the end of the world—"but you could see it from here" (11). Traditional Indian culture is hardly evident; Loney's Indian mother is dead; his white father and Kate are his only kin; he lives off the reservation, in town. The reader easily joins Kate and Rhea and most critics in urging him to leave, to find "purpose" in "things" that are "different."

You can see that the book is almost playing into the hands of white prejudice against Indians. Here is a character who indeed seems lazy, useless, irresponsible, especially since he's bright and could do better. There is no attractive traditional culture and there are no family ties holding him down; he is miserably depressed; why doesn't he leave and make something of himself?

Twice in the book Loney analyzes himself. In each case, he draws much of his vocabulary and values, his conscious knowledge, from the white world, but then like a sheepdog he keeps trotting back to family, past, and place as the source of identity:

> "I can't leave," he said, and he almost knew why. He thought of his earlier attempts to create a past, a background, an ancestry — something that would tell him who he was....He had always admired Kate's ability to live in the present, but he had also wondered at her lack of need to understand her past. Maybe she had the right idea; maybe it was the present that mattered, only the present. (88)

Loney returns to thoughts of his surrogate mother for a year, Aunt "S," hardly known, now dead, the only real family he has had.

A few chapters later Rhea asks, "What is it that troubles you?" (104). Loney visibly tiptoes the line between individual psychology and tribal consciousness: "I don't even know myself. It has to do with the past... I know it has to do with my mother and father...an aunt I lived with... who she really was and how she died" (104). Then he suddenly tells Rhea of the extraordinary white bird that appears "when I'm awake, but late at night when I'm tired — or drunk....Sometimes I think it is a vision sent by my mother's people. I must interpret it, but I don't know how" (105).

The question of whether he will go to Seattle suddenly becomes, quite clearly, a choice between two cultures, two plots. Whites leave, Indians stay home. Rhea says:

> "Did it ever occur to you that if you left you would leave these... visions behind? You might become so involved with a new life that your past would fade away — that bird would fade away for good."
> "I don't know that I want that to happen." (105-106)

From the white point of view, the change of interests offered by a life of wandering might lay to rest Loney's troubling hallucination. From the Native American point of view, his vision-knowledge is inextricably tied to past and place, although he lacks the tribe ("my mother's people") to interpret it. That knowledge would be entirely lost if he moved away.

The scene ends as Rhea and Loney discuss his geographical place. The mixed-blood Loney has the ambivalent responses we might expect from someone representing both races:

"This is your country, isn't it? It means a great deal to you...."

"I've never understood it. Once in a while I look around and I see things familiar and I think I will die here. It's my country then. Other times I want to leave, to see other things, to meet people, to die elsewhere." (106-107)

Genetic determinism is troubling to most of us; reading these books, however, one sometimes wonders if the mixed-blood has two knowledges in his bones.

The Death of Jim Loney cannot be read without Native American context. The most obvious example occurs right away:

He walked and he realized that he was seeing things strangely, and he remembered that it had been that way at the football game. It was as though he were exhausted and drowsy, but his head was clear. He was aware of things around him — the shadowy tree, the glistening sidewalk, the dark cat that moved into the dark. (4)

In the white world, we trace this "altered state" backward to tough drinking and forward to trouble. Anyone familiar with Plains Indians, however, will recognize a possible vision-quest state of mind, which would suddenly make Loney the doctor instead of the patient. Sure enough, seven chapters later, the bird appears in the book for the first time: "And again, as he had that night after the football game, he saw things strangely, yet clearly.... He saw the smoke ring go out away from his face and he saw the bird in flight.... It came every night now" (20).

Loney did not "seek" the state of mind or the bird, as far as he knows. Indeed, that is his situation throughout the novel: he thinks white, would not mind being white, but he seems to have Indianness visited upon him. He is the reluctant victim of a vision without a quest.

Loney's connection to his distant past is Amos After Buffalo, the little boy who helps him chip his frozen dog out of the ice and is upset that the dog is not buried. Amos is from Hays on the reservation, "way out there" (54), and when Loney is ready to die ("It's my country then") he chooses to do it in Mission Canyon of the Little Rockies, just past Hays and the mission school. As he walks through Hays in the dark, his thoughts are of Amos and the real Indians: "Amos After Buffalo will grow up, thought Loney, and he will discover that Thanksgiving is not meant for him...and it will hurt him...and he will grow hard and bitter" (166). Then, in a parallel to the deer conversation in *Winter*, Loney suddenly and quite seriously addresses the strange dog trailing him through town, and for a moment he has indeed leapt back into the tribe's distant past, when animals and men worried together over things like proper burials, a pouch on the grave: "'You tell Amos that Jim Loney passed through town while he was dreaming....Give him dreams. Tell him you saw me carrying a dog and that I was taking that dog to a higher ground. He will know'...the dog was gone" (167).

Amos had said, "Do you know where I live?" (54). Now, in Hays, Loney knows. Loney's own confidence and command, and the truth of his dreams throughout the novel, lead us to assume that the dog is off to deliver the message, but Welch's spare style and disjunct images almost hide, or rather force us to consider, to supply our own rhetoric for, the immense distance between the bars and trailers of Harlem and this dog-dream-messenger. Loney then walks to his death thinking of his past which "brought me here," thinking of the old Indians in the canyon, "the warriors, the women who had picked chokecherries" (168), and finally of the mother who "had given up her son to be free." But freedom hasn't worked for either the mother or the son who "would not allow himself to be found" (175). The only thing left is not Boone's heaven of suburban isolation in *The Big Sky*, or Catherine's tribal heaven of singing around the fire in *The Surrounded*, but Welch's half-breed heaven, Highline grace: "But there had to be another place where people bought each other drinks and talked quietly about their pasts, their mistakes... like everything was beginning again" (175).

What is this novel about? Welch considers the end positive because Loney has tried to understand his past, and because he has taken control of his life by orchestrating his death. But that existential plot is hard to affirm in *Loney*. Loney's decisiveness is almost gratuitously self-destructive. The white existential plot offers only the tiniest shred of affirmation: he accepts responsibility for accidental murder. When he shoots Pretty Weasel, as poet Linda Weasel Head has remarked, he sees death for what it is—a release from the realities that he cannot comprehend. He then stages his own unnecessary execution. Many isolated events serve this weak white plot: shooting Pretty Weasel, shooting at his father, setting up the policeman's shot all are acts of an indecisive loner in submission to his own arbitrary yet self-willed fate. From that white point of view, he is indeed a sad case.

But the refusal to leave his place, the mourning of lost ancestors, the bird vision, the prophetic dreams, the violence, and the scene with Amos After Buffalo all create another pattern, a pattern of proud Native American resistance to assimilation: this is our disaster, and I will make my stand on our ground in honor of my ancestry and ancestral knowledge. Like Old Bull in McNickle's *Wind from an Enemy Sky*, Loney has "received" the bullet from the Indian upholding white law, and "This is what you wanted, he thought" (179). Loney's individuality, his "existence," and most of his conscious knowledge in the white sense may be isolated, but his dreams and desires and finally his resolution are not. Those aspects of Loney constitute a loyalty to a tribe and a tribalism he never individually knew.

The tension between the white and Indian plots is the tension in *Loney*. In Welch's work, the individual psychic drama is a kind of melody played against the pedal bass of tribal past. Much more than *Winter*, *Loney* takes us realistically to the blurred edge of consciousness of a Highline Indian who knows there must be something good in his people, past, and place, but who doesn't even know why he knows that. The book dares us to see Loney's final homing as not at all the perversion it seems to be, however much, like Kate and Rhea, we still want Loney to leave. In *Loney* more than in any other Native American novel, the reader is placed squarely in the mixed-blood's situation, unable to choose between a white realism that seems to offer at best lonely success or intelligent despair and an Indian pride in tradition that must seem a dream. For the reader as well as the mixed-blood, the white and Indian plots are not good and bad opposites but simultaneous, inescapable forces, centrifugal and centripetal, that can leave one so stuck in orbit that even Loney's decisiveness—one jump back toward the center—becomes a quantum leap.

The mixed-blood's situation is not comfortable. Like most readers, I found *Loney* at first a most uncomfortable book. So did Anatole Broyard in *The New York Times* (November 28, 1979), who sounded like a peeved Indian agent: "Is he threatening us with his unhappiness? Why do so many of our serious novels have to be read like unpaid bills?" That, of course, is exactly the point. From the Indian point of view, this entire nation is an unpaid bill. Broyard's ignorance of the subject matter (he thinks Rhea improbable) and his distaste for guilt are beside the point; the novel doesn't even try to recover those vast debts, nor does it directly threaten us. The limbo itself makes Broyard whine: Loney's is a life without individualism plus a life without tribe, leaving the impression Kenneth Lincoln had of a "breed's novel, neither Indian nor white" (*Native American Renaissance* 168).

However, the novel is both Indian and white, and things do matter: Tribalism gives dignity and honor to Loney's choice. Loney's refusal to leave constitutes a resistance to the ruling white mythology of success through individual advancement. Those who would have Loney leave, or rather that part of every one of us which would have Loney leave, are requesting another Indian biography depicting success through capitulation. Such a happy "comedy," as Arnold Krupat points out, would serve the status quo, the "moral norm" of the ruling class (*Smoothing* 270). Loney dies two deaths: his white suicide is certainly a perverted assertion of individuality, yet his loyalty to Amos, the dog, his past, and place is a transfer of energy to tribe. Thus his bird vision is a liberation of self, a reconnection to tribal past. Loney dies watching his past, "the beating wings of a dark bird as it climbed to a distant place" (179).

The homing plot of *Loney* marries white failure to Indian pride, and if that marriage is "almost too real," it is not the fault of Welch. Native novelists like Welch are not offering Indian answers, but reflecting continued respect for tribal identity while realistically depicting the disadvantages of nonassimilation. The challenge to whites is to appreciate how these novels present a single, eloquent argument against dereservation and assimilation and for the necessity of working out an identity in relation to one's past. These are neither formula nor protest novels. Welch had not read McNickle before writing these two books.

He had read McNickle and much more, however, before writing his third novel, *Fools Crow*, a popular and enduring historical novel which won the *Los Angeles Times* and the Pacific Northwest Booksellers awards for fiction in 1986 and an American Book Award.

* * *

Fools Crow could have fought against Plenty-coups. He is renamed (from White Man's Dog) after fooling the Crow Indians during a raid on their camp in the fall of 1868. In this very unusual novel, we are thrown into the Indians' world before the buffalo went away. We do not learn a white man's date until page 284. In the first paragraph, as White Man's Dog watches "Cold Maker gather his forces," we have no idea whether we are watching a hostile Indian with his soldiers, or the wind, or winter coming on.

It is winter. It may occur to the reader that White Man's Dog knows which it is, so we are not exactly in his world. Yet to say "winter" instead of "Cold Maker" would change whatever is happening into an abstraction of the white man's calendar, instead of presenting a personal force who appears that day, perhaps to stay, perhaps not, and whose cold commands will enter the plot. So also the beaver is called "wood-biter," changing the emphasis from our description of appearance (beaver from Old Teutonic and Aryan "brown") to the Indian description of behavior: a character who bites wood, not a thing which is brown.

This book, in other words, was impossible to write. We cannot enter an alien world in a comfortable manner. Should Welch render conversation in modern Blackfeet English, slang English, high English? There is no diction that can simultaneously be easy, yet shock us with difference. Welch chose a standard, slightly formal English (approximating Indian formalism) mixed with contemporary slang, and then elected to use Indian names and Indian concepts, and to ask the reader to get used to them. The result is an opportunity for us to come closer to the buffalo-culture Indian world than in any other novel to date.

The action takes us right away into a dramatic epic. A horse-stealing raid on the Crows, a visit to the fort, tribal warfare, and ever-present rumors of white encroachment all build a sense of a way of life active, dangerous, and threatened. An epic novel was a radical departure from Welch's previous work. The huge cast of characters, the sweep of events and the documentation of an entire culture—these seem more like McNickle's concerns.

The historical epic deprived Welch of some favorite tools, his "eye" and "ear" for realistic detail: the bar conversations, Lame Bull's stumbling eulogy, a small-town sheriff, Loney digging a dead dog out of the frozen mud with the broken blade of a pocketknife. Welch attempted a historical novel partly, I think, because he believed that it was important for the Blackfeet, that it was important for them to know how they had once lived and how they had come to their present life.

That sounds like a moral purpose, and it is, which also explains the general tone of this novel. The pride and certainty of a traditional culture fill the book; here are the ancestors Loney and the narrator of

Winter had longed to find. That spirit of a people overwhelms even the historical disasters recounted, so that what might have been Welch's bleakest work, ending in the greatest massacre in Blackfeet and perhaps American history, becomes instead his most positive work, singing the praises of tradition, of dedication to one's community, of hope itself. When Fools Crow is shown the future by Feather Woman, the tone is positive: "Much will be lost.... But they will know the way it was." And she advises, "There is much good you can do for your people" (359). In spite of calamitous events, Fools Crow remains courageous, without being naive or ignorant. His uncrushed spirit also lifts the book, para-doxically, from its thoroughly local and tribal setting. One feels that these are the choices all people under siege might face, that even under the worst circumstances one could choose belief over despair.

In *Fools Crow*, in contrast to Welch's previous work, answers to psy-chological questions are sometimes given quite directly: "...there was a steadiness, a calmness in White Man's Dog that Yellow Kidney liked. These were rare qualities in a young man on his first adventure. He can be trusted, thought Yellow Kidney. He will do well" (21). And we trust Yellow Kidney; the boy will do well. This is not a point-of-view novel, and therefore in ways not a "modern" one. But these turn out to be cul-tural issues, not just literary ones.

Modern American fiction is largely psychological fiction. Character and motivation are the primary concerns in most serious novels and short stories; conversely, stories of pure action, from detectives to cow-boys to "Rambo," are considered less important. But the traditional Indians did not share our concern with psychology; to them behavior and event were terribly important. To push the novel too far toward analysis of an isolated personality or motivation would itself doom any attempt to recapture a tribal past. Subjectivity of perception, private consciousness, individual psychology: when the state, religion, and cul-ture have lost credibility, the buck stops there.

However, White Man's Dog/Fools Crow did not live in our world. Whether a man acted rightly or wrongly mattered a great deal to him, but he trusted his tribe and religion and tradition to define right and wrong action, and he would have been much less interested than we are in why he acted as he did. Fools Crow's father is well presented in the novel; he is deeply concerned for his sons' characters and actions, but he does not have any interest in making moral judgments on their desires. Their consciousness or unconsciousness, if you will, is not a subject of contemplation. What matters is how they have acted and whether they can bear with dignity and honor the consequences of their actions. It may occur to readers that just in having guaranteed consequences of actions, their culture differs from ours. We seem to live in a world in which we might get away with anything; that's not true in a small town (band) of eighty people, living a traditional life.

Consider White Man's Dog's dreams. Early in the novel, he covets his father's third wife, a young, beautiful, unhappy girl his father has taken in more as waif than as lover. This is big trouble. Psychologically, the two are drawn together, they are always physically close, glances between them feed the flames. Only the taboo remains. For White Man's Dog to act or decide not to act is a crucial moment and would be for any adolescent in his first requited love.

How is the decision handled, by the character and by the novel? Their love is consummated in a dream, a dream that both share although Wolverine, spirit-helper to White Man's Dog, graciously obscures his recall. The sharing of the dream and of a certain stone which survives the dream becomes complex; he knows that she knows... and having shared a dream, they are able to purge their lust. That is, the dream becomes a form of externalization and communication that replaces, or displaces, or is their culture's analogue to, individual psychology. Within the dream, she says:

> "Do you desire me?"
> "I can't say. It is not proper."
> "Why not? This is the place of dreams. Here, we may desire each other. But not in that other world, for there you are my husband's son." (119)

At this moment, dreaming seems to function for them as it does in European theory, allowing expression of hidden desires. But when they have the same dream — not only of desire, but of place, action, conversation — and when Wolverine enters both dreams and manipulates them, and when the talisman stone survives, we are moving away from the individual unconscious to something else entirely.

Anthropologist Karl Kroeber has spoken of Indian dreaming displacing energy from individual to tribe; consider Fools Crow's last and longest dream, his vision quest to Feather Woman. This is also, to us, a critical psychological moment. Fools Crow will look ahead and react with courage or despair. But he does not look; he is shown by Feather Woman. And she tells him how to react. Is Feather Woman part of his psyche or part of his tradition?

Dreaming in this novel is exactly the opposite of dreaming in Freud. Instead of taking us deeper into psyche and individual variation, it takes us out of private psyche and into a public world. So in Indian terms, the dreams are psychological subtlety, but they occur at the level of tribe. Psychological conflicts are externalized and conceived in relation to tradition. That is why the portraits can seem two-dimensional, while the situation is not. From the Native American point of view, Wolverine is not a figment of White Man's Dog's imagination; rather, White Man's Dog's psyche is expanded to include Wolverine. A discussion of character, then, would have to account for Wolverine and his motivation, Feather Woman and her experience...and not just as "dreams" in the Freudian sense of individual inventions, but as aspects of tribal present and past. The arena of psychological action is expanded in this novel to include dream, myth, tribe. The characters, with conflict displaced and purged, seem to stand before us whole, confident, complete. The only "modern" character, Fast Horse, torn by anxiety, guilt, and angst, is driven out of the tribe. His story, we could say, Welch told in his first two novels; this one is entirely different. This story is about a culture where people felt whole with themselves, whole with their past, whole with power. Whether it did them one bit of good is answered in the book: yes, says Welch, it did.

It is strange to go back to the original disasters and find one of our most positive books. The critic Frank Kermode said that ghost stories are about how the past haunts the present. Welch's first two books were ghost stories, haunted by tribal memories and loss. But in *Fools Crow* the dead ancestor doesn't haunt, he returns to life, fleshed out, and he encourages — which means, to give heart. Louis Owens said that, "In *Fools Crow*, Welch has accomplished the most profound act of recovery in American Literature" (Owens 166).

* * *

Welch's most recent books are too fresh to have gathered a body of criticism, but both represent interesting departures from his earlier material.

Native American writers are aware that much of Native life takes place in cities and that urban and especially professional natives (such as the writers themselves) hardly appear in a canon that has focused on inland West reservations. On the one hand, the reservations do provide crucial ties to traditional values, and are the dramatic scenes of Native woes and hopes; on the other hand, reservation writings can easily play into primitivist expectations: Indians are children of nature, and exist only beneath one Big Sky or another.

In *The Indian Lawyer* (1990), that big sky has shrunk to the intrigues of Helena, Montana's capital, where Sylvester Yellow Calf is a rising star in the city's top law firm. He is soon advanced by Powers That Be to a congressional candidacy. Then, that heavy sky caves in. The material allows Welch to use his experience on the State Board of Pardons, on which Mr. Yellow Calf serves, to paint realistic pictures of inmate life, of whites and Indians in and out of jail, of racial lines in the professional world which Welch knows well. In the person of Yellow Calf, Welch also presents a bright, attractive basketball star and lawyer who provides a positive role model for his people. Several high-school teachers in central Montana already use this rather racy and gritty book with advanced students because it is the only portrait in print of a successful, professional Native of their region.

The darker side of the book is partly a matter of plot thickening: Sylvester's sexual allure and appetite lead him into a trap; involved with the wife of an inmate who hopes to be paroled through blackmail, he must make some difficult choices. His periodic visits to relatives on the Blackfeet Reservation, a running counterpoint to power lunches in Helena, provide vivid and poignant scenes.

Perhaps the darkest aspect of the book, however, is Sylvester's final choice. The book seems to suggest a kind of salvation through renouncing power; but it may also suggest how thoroughly a distrust of power, of the establishment and government, permeates the Blackfeet world of Yellow Calf and the author—for obvious good reason. What had seemed a dream of helping his people through the system dissipates only partly through Sylvester's shenanigans; quitting both his upscale girlfriend and his career are choices he is quick to make, and the text is quick to approve. The malaise preceded the sexual temptations. His heroism will have to be worked out closer to home. The book is a realistic depiction of Indian-white white-collar relations, rarely represented, and a chilling view of how easily even an accomplished Native professional can drop out—or drop back in, depending on your point of view.

Killing Custer (1994) is a book of essays on the occasion of the film,

Last Stand at Little Bighorn, which Welch scripted for Paul Stekler and PBS. It is Welch's first book of essays and is a fine treatment of this old material from a freshly personal and Native point of view. The writing is clean and the structure subversive: in the film, Custer and even white historians are subordinated to Indian circumstances and to Indian memory; similarly, the book is really about the killing of Sitting Bull. Even the battle of the Little Bighorn is almost kept offstage — the book keeps leading up to the battle, then circling back, then leading up…the Indians gather, and Custer approaches, and they gather, and he approaches.…Welch said his editors finally convinced him, after the first draft, "that the battle eventually had to occur" (Welch, "Interview").

The effect of this structure is to create a cycling of repetitions that replace a linear, narrative and European time sense with a circular time which becomes a kind of poetry of time. This is effective because Sitting Bull is very much aware that this is the end of time, the last great fight as he says to one and all. He has no illusion that they will finally win. The momentary victory will be the last chapter of a long defeat. There is a moving pathos, then, to the central paradox of the book: time is suspended, yet time is coming to an end.

The publishing career of James Welch from 1970 to 1995 has been a part of a larger Native American movement; his attention to poetic detail and rhythm, his absolute abhorrence of sentimentality and didacticism, his pure realism, and his graceful sense of what is important in ordinary lives have contributed much to that movement and have influenced many subsequent authors.

Selected Bibliography

Primary Sources

The Death of Jim Loney. New York: Harper & Row, 1979.

Fools Crow. New York: Viking Press, 1986.

The Indian Lawyer. New York: W. W. Norton, 1990.

Killing Custer: The Battle of the Little Bighorn and the Fate of the Plains Indians. With Paul Stekler. New York: W. W. Norton, 1994.

Riding the Earthboy 40. New York: World Publishing Company, 1971; rev. ed. New York: Harper & Row, 1976.

Winter in the Blood. New York: Harper & Row, 1974.

Secondary Sources

Bevis, William W. *Ten Tough Trips: Montana Writers and the West*. Seattle: University of Washington Press, 1990. Pp. 117-139.

Coltelli, Laura. *Winged Words: American Indian Writers Speak*. Lincoln: University of Nebraska Press, 1990. Pp. 184-199. An interview.

Craig, David M. "Beyond Assimilation: James Welch and the Indian Dilemma." *North Dakota Quarterly*, 53 (Spring 1985): 182-190.

Crèvecouer, J. Hector St. John. "What is an American?" *Letters from an American Farmer*. New Haven: Yale University Press, 1925.

Fleck, Richard F., ed. *Critical Perspectives on Native American Fiction*. Washington: Three Continents Press, 1993. Pp. 181-229. Collects four important, previously published essays on Welch.

Lincoln, Kenneth. *Native American Renaissance*. Berkeley: University of California Press, 1983. Pp. 148-182. Connects Welch and his Blackfeet heritage to mythic and archetypal traditions of narrative.

McFarland, Ronald E., ed. *James Welch*. Lewiston, Idaho: Confluence Press, 1986. Offers particularly valuable bibliography.

Orlandini, Roberta. "Variations on a Theme: Traditions and Temporal Structure in the Novels of James Welch." *South Dakota Review*, 26 (1988): 37-51.

Owens, Louis. *Other Destinies: Understanding the American Indian Novel*. Norman: University of Oklahoma Press, 1992. Pp. 128-166. Sees Welch attempting to "recover" the world of the Blackfeet past by weaving narratives of past, present, and future.

Ruoff, A. La Vonne. "Alienation and the Female Principle in *Winter in the Blood*." *American Indian Quarterly*, 4 (May 1978): 107-122.

Velie, Alan. *Four American Indian Literary Masters: N. Scott Momaday, James Welch, Leslie Marmon Silko, and Gerald Vizenor*. Norman: University of Oklahoma Press, 1982. Essays on the poetry and on *Winter* as comic novel.

Welch, James and William Bevis. "Interview." *Weber Studies*, 12:3 (1995): 15-32.

Wild, Peter. *James Welch*. Boise: Boise State University, 1983. Part of Boise State's Western Writers Series — a good introduction to Welch.

David Petersen

A. B. Guthrie, Jr.: A Remembrance

"Suddenly," says A. B. "Bud" Guthrie, Jr., in the closing paragraphs of his autobiographical *The Blue Hen's Chick*, "the yard is bare . . . and I feel deserted and thrown in on myself, as if I were the last of life. . . . End of an April day" (1993, 261).

These sentiments carry the unmistakable scent of melancholy. I finished my first reading of *The Blue Hen's Chick*, many years ago, with the feeling that A. B. Guthrie, Jr. — after only sixty-three years in this world — had almost given up.

Indeed, he *almost* had, but, as one of his colorful Old West characters might have put it, not quite hardly. At the least, he was resigned at that point in his personal and literary life to becoming what he jokingly referred to as "a dignified old man."

And a low point it was. He was living at the time with his sister in Missoula. Only two years before, he had divorced Harriet Larson, his wife of more than three decades; and divorce, no matter how necessary, earns always the stigma of failure. He had not produced a novel since *These Thousand Hills* back in 1956. Fourteen years had slipped by since receiving the Pulitzer Prize for Distinguished Fiction for *The Way West*. Several stints in Hollywood had brought little satisfaction; it had been a dozen years since his Academy Award nomination for Best Screenplay for his masterful film treatment of Jack Schaefer's *Shane*.

Thinking back and comparing past to present — as writing an autobiography necessarily leads one to do — Bud must have come to wonder about his future. He'd set some mighty high standards for himself in his forties and fifties — the forties and fifties — and lately things had been slowing down. He might indeed have been feeling "deserted and thrown in on" himself.

At the end of that melancholic April day back in 1964, Bud Guthrie could not have foreseen that just three years hence he would catch a second wind, a second life, in the form of a new family. He could not have known that much of his best and most satisfying work was yet to come. And neither could he have known that it would not be until the end of another April day an eventful twenty-seven years later that he would finally greet "the last of life."

But despondent or not, Guthrie remained a tenacious fighter, shoving aside the self-doubts expressed in the final pages of his autobiography and bucking himself up to begin *Arfive* — a semi-autobiographical novel he would later remark couldn't have been written without first working through *The Blue Hen's Chick* "to sort things out."

But progress on the new novel was painful and slow, and by 1967 Guthrie was not yet midway through *Arfive* when his fortunes changed: he met Carol Luthin, an intelligent and attractive lady thirty years his junior. In 1969, after a brief and cautious courtship, Bud and Carol were married — a "risk" neither would ever regret.

Crediting Carol as "the best critic I've encountered in a long lifetime," Bud's energies and self-confidence were renewed; now, he returned to his old Corona typing machine with a youthful vigor. His reward: the release of *Arfive* by Houghton Mifflin in 1970 to universal applause, culminating in the prestigious Western Heritage Award.

Gradually, a new life took shape. With Carol's children — Herb and Amy — in high school, the Guthries settled in Missoula, spending their summers at Bud's rural hideaway, dubbed Twin Lakes, near Choteau on the Montana Front Range. Bud's concern about being a stepfather was needless; his relationship with the children was easy and loving — a bond that would continue to deepen with the years. His spirits high, he settled back into a productive working schedule.

Across the next two decades, Bud Guthrie would produce a treasure of literary product: 1973 — *Once Upon a Pond*, a delightful children's book illustrated by Carol and featuring a lovable grizzly bear who speaks with the accent of a mountain man; 1975 — *Wild Pitch*, the first of a five-novel series of contemporary western mysteries; 1975 — *The Last Valley* (Houghton Mifflin), an eloquent and prophetic sequel to *Arfive* and the chronological finale to the westering saga that had opened back in 1947 with *The Big Sky*; 1977 — *The Genuine Article* (Houghton Mifflin); 1980 — *No Second Wind* (Houghton Mifflin); 1982 — *Fair Land, Fair Land* (Houghton Mifflin), a poignant requiem for wilderness; 1985 — *Playing Catch-Up* (Houghton Mifflin); 1987 — *Four Miles From Ear Mountain*, an elegant little limited-edition chapbook; 1988 — *Big Sky, Fair Land: The Environmental Essays of A. B. Guthrie, Jr.* (Northland Press, edited and introduced by David Petersen); 1989 — *Murder in the Cotswolds* (Houghton Mifflin); 1991 — *A Field Guide to Writing Fiction* (HarperCollins), an appropriate capstone to a long and distinguished literary career, released — not by design — simultaneously with the author's death.

And fingered in between these dozen "late life" books were scores of newspaper and magazine essays, countless forewords and introductions to the books of respected others, as well as tightly written texts for many courageous and rousing speeches delivered around Montana in the 1970s and 1980s on behalf of the West he knew and loved like few others.

Bud was repelled by the biblical exhortation that the earth was made for man, finding such advice simultaneously hubristic and self-destructive. He believed instead that man should view, and comport, himself as an integral part of nature, rather than some divinely ordained taskmaster. Working from that belief, he fought long and hard against the clear-cutting, overgrazing, and strip-mining of western public lands, against the damming of free-running rivers for myopic economic goals, against the continued persecution of the grizzly bear and other large predators, against the destructive greed of local chambers of commerce and real estate developers. And more.

Edward Abbey could easily have had the environmental battles of his friend Bud Guthrie in mind when he exhorted his fellow writers that their duty was to the good, urging them to disparage the bad.

But Guthrie was no mere critic, bringing an equal energy to the support of those things he viewed as right and good: a sensible moderation of human numbers; the rights of women to control their own bodies and destinies; a cautionary approach to economic growth and so-called "progress" — from which, he was quick to point out, there is no retreat, no going back, right or wrong. Progress is a word, Bud was fond of saying, which should imply real improvement in the quality of life but rarely does.

Although these and others of Bud's personal fights most often were neglected by the media in favor of his celebrity as a grand old man of western literature, his altruistic efforts did not go unnoticed: In 1988, A. B. Guthrie, Jr., was named Montana's Environmentalist of the Year — an honor he reckoned as being on a level with his Pulitzer, his several honorary doctorates and the other major achievements of his life.

And for all of this — the personal honors, the continued success of his books, as well as his broader "unearned happiness" — Bud shared credit with his wife Carol. Everyone who knew them knew them as inseparable partners; it was always "Bud and Carol."

Alone now, Carol still lives at The Barn, a neat brown frame house along the Teton River north of Choteau where, the first time I ever saw either of them, she and Bud were standing out front, hand-in-hand, waiting to greet their visitor.

The Barn: Bud and Carol designed the place themselves and, mindful of its appearance from a distance, dubbed it appropriately. But somehow these days — even with its comfortable familiarity, its warm memories, its full-wall westward view of Ear Mountain (which played so strong a role in so many of Bud's best books) looming big as eternity up along the Chinese Wall — somehow, The Barn just isn't the same.

Carol reflects: "Implicit in our marriage was the knowledge that Bud would die first — that I would be left alone. Now that the first shock is over I think I'd be a pretty poor specimen to bemoan my situation. I am grateful for what we had together. What lies ahead I'll meet — sometimes well, sometimes not. What lies ahead is life" (personal communication, 1992).

Back when they were married, naysayers had predicted a brief run for such a "mixed" bonding of a not-so-"dignified old man" of sixty-eight with what one snippy gossip columnist dismissed as "a woman of only thirty-eight." Even Bud's own family found it hard to accept. But Bud and Carol had talked through the potential snags well beforehand. Consequently, "the only problem with our age difference," Carol reflects now, "was that had Buddie been younger, he'd still be here with me" (personal communication, 1992).

For more than two decades following their marriage, Carol was not just wife and near-constant companion, trusted adviser and literary critic but a stern shield against a never-ending stream of would-be interlopers who might unnecessarily tax her husband's energies or attempt to use his fame and reputation for their own purposes. And, toward the end, Carol assumed as well the difficult and painful role of bedside nurse.

She insists, though, that their marriage was no one-way street. "I needed Buddie," she'll tell you, "every bit as much as he needed me."

To this mutual need Bud was not blind. Certainly, Bud Guthrie's final quarter-century was extraordinarily blest, filled to the brim with loving family, with continued literary success, with travel—including an extensive working tour of Europe for the U.S. State Department—with public recognition, and with good battles fought and often enough won.

Yet, it would be unfair to leave the impression that those years were universally halcyon. No writer's life is without peril or uncertainty. Finances were occasionally a worry. The deaths of his last surviving brother and sister affected Bud deeply. Giving up his beloved Twin Lakes retreat was a wrench, although building The Barn did much to mitigate the loss. Additionally, with age came physical problems, and Bud became no stranger to pain.

In 1973, while in the midst of writing *The Last Valley*, problems arising from diminished blood circulation forced Guthrie to undergo arterial bypasses in both legs, an arduous and delicate surgery performed by the renowned heart specialist Dr. Michael DeBakey. Bud's main concern? That it would interfere with his book deadline.

Over the years, he survived pneumonia, major surgery for an intestinal blockage, two operations on his shoulder for a basal cell carcinoma, an attack of arteritis, and a frantic trip to the hospital in Great Falls with two bleeding ulcers. Not merely surviving, he always seemed able to regain his old zest and enthusiasm.

In 1986, at the age of eighty-five, after an odds-defying seventy years as a heavy smoker, Bud simply quit; three months later, his doctors prescribed supplemental oxygen. Although he often grumped that the oxygen apparatus made him feel like a "tethered horse," Bud would be dependent on oxygen for the remaining five years of his life. Dependent but not incapacitated. He continued to write and to live an almost normal life.

Then, in 1990, the cause of a mysterious pain in the legs was diagnosed as the beginnings of prostate cancer.

Through all of this, Bud Guthrie remained stoic, even cheerful. In a decade of regular correspondence with this author—an exchange that generated well in excess of a hundred letters in each direction—Bud rarely acknowledged, much less complained of, his medical problems and referred to his hospitalizations, when he mentioned them at all, as mere inconveniences. And he never lost his sense of humor. I am reminded of the time, immediately following the diagnosis of prostate cancer, when he wrote, "The experts weren't much worried about the cancer, saying I was so old something else would kill me before it ever could" (personal letter to author, 1990).

That was the Bud Guthrie I knew and loved.

With the decades piling up behind him, and after so many painful close calls, what might have been Bud's thoughts on death? Judging from notes made toward an update of *The Blue Hen's Chick* — an update which, sadly, he would not have time to complete — it seems accurate to describe him as having achieved a bittersweet sense of freedom:

> My father always remembers the sense of being free he felt on his first morning in Montana. He meant, I'm sure, free under that great arch of sky, free in the uncluttered distances, free to live free.
>
> As he was in his youth, so I am free in my age, free like him under the big sky and free in directions he didn't mean. The years bring some benefits, not counting the scant consolation that if anything goes wrong with you, it won't be chicken pox. The quick and mortifying embarrassments of the young days are gone, along with the dread of gaucheries and the exalted respect for public opinion. The fierce compulsion of the glands diminishes. So I call these losses gains. At my age I know what I am and where I stand, and if it occurs to me that I could have done better, it is too late to do better now. I settle with myself.
>
> I am free of most encumbrances, so I am free to regret, the most debilitating of indulgences. If you must be regretful, regret what you didn't do, not what you did. A man lets too many smiling opportunities pass him by.
>
> I should add to the other freedoms age has brought me the freedom from the fear of death. At my age it is not far off, and I accept that fact as I must. I do not dread it but neither do I welcome it. What misgivings I have, have not to do with myself but with those I love and who love me. I cannot command them not to mourn, neither in death can I help or advise them. I do not like to think of death for thinking of them. Life demands that we learn to say good-bye.
>
> For myself, again as a writer and a man, I believe in greeting life with a large embrace, full well knowing how fickle it can be, how treacherous, how beset with blind evil, but knowing it can be tender, too, and joyous and loving, and the more rewarding because it

can be so unkind. I see heroes along the way, and the sun bright on the hills, and a pretty girl passes, me, not unnoticed, and I know what lies ahead and I will meet it with a laugh or a curse, but not, as Cromwell would say, not by the bowels of Christ, with a whimper. (personal collection of Carol Guthrie)

In the fall of 1990, fearing for the first time an isolated Montana winter at The Barn — and The Barn is isolated — Bud and Carol went to stay in Bismarck, North Dakota, where Carol's daughter Amy and her family were living. The winter was a hard one even in the city, and Bud was weakening. They returned to The Barn as soon as possible in the spring. Three days after their arrival, Bud collapsed.

During a short hospitalization, sensing what lay ahead, Bud expressed a wish to return to The Barn; Carol brought him home to the mountains.

A few days later, Alfred Bertram Guthrie, Jr., aged ninety years, was gone, his body worn plumb out from most of a century of living and loving and fighting the good fights.

According to his wishes, his body was cremated and the ashes scattered over Ear Mountain and the adjacent country he had known and loved and written of so evocatively for so very long.

The man is gone, but his work endures. In 1993, University of Nebraska Press re-released Guthrie's *Blue Hen's Chick* in a hardback edition as well as his little-known first novel, *Murders at Moon Dance*, the latter with a rousing introductory tribute by William Kittredge.

But the honor that I'm sure would please Bud most as he watches from his omniscient aerie somewhere above Ear Mountain is the establishment of the A. B. Guthrie, Jr., Memorial Fund at the University of Montana, his 1923 alma mater — a fund designated to provide graduate scholarships in creative writing and journalism.

When asked by young literary aspirants for the secret of his tremendous success, Bud was wont to say, a shy grin on his wizened, knowing face, "I think I tried harder."

* * *

This essay is adapted from the author's afterword to A. B. Guthrie, Jr.'s autobiography, *The Blue Hen's Chick*, by permission of the University of Nebraska Press.

Selected Bibliography

Primary Sources

Arfive. Boston: Houghton Mifflin, 1970.

Big Sky, Fair Land: The Environmental Essays of A. B. Guthrie, Jr. David Petersen, ed. Flagstaff, Arizona: Northland Press, 1988.

The Blue Hen's Chick: An Autobiography. New York: McGraw Hill, 1965; rpt., with afterword by David L. Petersen, Lincoln: University of Nebraska Press, 1993.

Fair Land, Fair Land. Boston: Houghton Mifflin, 1982.

A Field Guide to Writing Fiction. New York: HarperCollins, 1991.

Four Miles from Ear Mountain. Missoula: Kutenai Press, 1987.

The Genuine Article. Boston: Houghton Mifflin, 1977.

The Last Valley. Boston: Houghton Mifflin, 1975.

Murder in the Cotswolds. Boston: Houghton Mifflin, 1989.

Murders at Moon Dance. New York: E. P. Dutton, 1943; rpt., with an introduction by William Kittredge, Lincoln: University of Nebraska Press, 1993.

No Second Wind. Boston: Houghton Mifflin, 1980.

Once Upon a Pond. With Carol Guthrie. Missoula: Mountain Press Publishing, 1973.

Playing Catch-Up. Boston: Houghton Mifflin, 1985.

These Thousand Hills. Boston: Houghton Mifflin, 1956.

The Way West. New York: William Sloane, 1949.

Wild Pitch. Boston: Houghton Mifflin, 1975.

Secondary Sources

Abbey, Edward. "A Writer's Credo." In *One Life at a Time, Please*. New York: Henry Holt, 1988.

Bevis, William W. "Guthrie's Big Sky." In *Ten Tough Trips: Montana Writers and the West*. Seattle: University of Washington Press, 1990. Pp. 3-19. This chapter examines the white centrism of Guthrie's vision and mythology as expressed in *The Big Sky*. Bevis notes how the twin pursuits of empty space and empty psyche guide the novel's dramatic and thematic development.

———. "Guthrie's Dream of the West." In *Ten Tough Trips: Montana Writers and the West*. Seattle: University of Washington Press, 1990. Here, Bevis describes the way in which Guthrie, despite his antiromantic intent in *The Big Sky*, lapses there into the "pastoral-primitivist dream" of western space.

Ford, Thomas W. "A. B. Guthrie's Additions to *Shane*." *Western American Literature*, 29 (Winter 1995): 299-304. Ford describes the contributions made by Guthrie to the film, *Shane*, through his screenplay. Ford notes specifically four scenes not originally in Schaefer's novel and added by Guthrie, all of which drew critical acclaim and praise and helped forge the movie's status as classic.

———. "A. B. Guthrie's *Fair Land, Fair Land*: A Requiem." *Western American Literature*, 23 (Spring 1988): 17-30. Ford argues that Guthrie, in *Fair Land, Fair Land*, returns to the historical West in order to fill a temporal gap in his sequence of novels about westward expansion. He also argues, however, that the novel is meant to serve as a requiem and elegy for the end of the expansive western vision that came with that expansion and settlement.

Petersen, David. "The Evolution and Expression of Environmental Themes in the Life and Literature of A. B. Guthrie, Jr." In *Big Sky, Fair Land: The Environmental Essays of A. B. Guthrie, Jr.* David Petersen, ed. Flagstaff, Arizona: Northland Press, 1988. Pp. 1-61. A series of biographical and critical commentaries on the socio-environmental themes that play throughout Guthrie's work. An interesting and revealing combination of the personal and the analytical.

Joseph M. Flora

Wallace Stegner:
An Update and a Retrospect

Wallace Stegner died April 13, 1993, in Santa Fe, New Mexico, victim of an automobile accident two and a half weeks earlier. (On a dark night, Stegner turned into the path of a speeding car.) He was eighty-four. Stegner's sudden death produced sharp focus on an extraordinary career.

Both the accident and the death were widely reported throughout the nation. From Stegner's generation of western writers, only Wright Morris and (briefly) Fred Manfred remained. But if the "dean" of western writers was now gone, it was clear that the loss would be felt not only in the West. Western frontiers and western motivations, western history and beauty were indeed important Stegner themes, but they had scarcely been packaged with mainly western audiences or aficionados in mind; Stegner had a large American vision, and he secured a broad American audience. He was singularly equipped to juxtapose western and eastern experience, and that vision played an important role in his most powerful fiction. If he counted himself western, he knew and prized many American places not western, and his voice was among the most reasoned and persuasive trying to conserve American land and water. When Stegner died, environmentalists everywhere paid tribute.

Speaking for the environmentalist movement as well as for himself, T. H. Watkins, editor of *Wilderness* magazine, asked (Summer 1993) the question about Stegner that Stegner had asked in 1955 after the death of Bernard DeVoto (like Stegner, a man who had played many roles,

836

conservationist among them): Who now will do his work? Watkins confirms that Stegner (who had served on the Sierra Club's board of directors and was a longtime member of the Wilderness Society's board of governors) did not acknowledge how important he was to the conservationist movement, claiming to be only a paper tiger "typewritten on both sides." That, Watkins explains, is the point:

> It is difficult to measure the degree to which words have informed, defined, inspired the conservation movement in this country. Indeed, it is quite impossible to think of our long struggle without conjuring up a pantheon of names, from Henry David Thoreau to Edward Abbey, whose illumination provided the very light by which we work. Stegner was not merely firmly fixed at the highest level of this tradition; over a career that spanned nearly sixty years he became one of the most eloquent and intelligent voices that our literature has ever produced. (8)

Sam Vaughn, Stegner's editor, reached a different audience with his tribute in *At Random* (fall 1993):

> Wallace Stegner was well known (but never well enough) for his writings and, ultimately for his teaching and his students, but also of course for his ardent but steely concern for landscape, water, wilderness, light, air, and what came to be called — long before ecology became chic — the environment. He was conservative in the best sense (though I can see him frowning as I write this), one who wanted to help conserve the best in our language and the world — at least the North American part of it, especially his beloved, benighted, misappropriated, misunderstood, and misused West. (11)

Vaughn praises Stegner's fiction for its clarity and notes that the works provide "no easy answers or simple happy endings but no fashionable nihilism, either. His novels and stories were without melodrama but full of the truly dramatic in everyday life" (11). Above Vaughn's tribute and an excerpt from T. H. Watkins, there is a picture of Mary and Wallace Stegner walking against the backdrop of California hills and mountains at Jasper Ridge. The last page of the issue shows Stegner in his study, his "workplace." The juxtaposition provides a splendid poetry:

Stegner was a writer, but one who lived fully in the world, especially the natural world.

Sam Vaughn's "well-known (but never well enough)" may be accurate, but the fact is that only a few western writers from Stegner's generation have received more national acclaim, and almost none of them has sustained national attention to the degree Stegner has. Hence, Stegner's death accents not only his national presence but the uncommon energy of a long life. When Stegner had his fatal accident, he was in Santa Fe to give a lecture—not unusual for this "retiree." (Three lectures at the University of Michigan law school in October 1986 had led to the booklet *The American West as Living Space*, 1987; the lecture "A Geography of Hope," delivered at the University of Colorado in 1990, was published in *A Society to Match the Scenery*, 1991.) A celebrator of place, Stegner visited many places. Readers of *American Way* (the American Airlines magazine to which he was a contributing editor) could read his travel report "Sailing the Royal Scotsman," a journey by rail to Scotland, in the November 15, 1992, issue. The December 1992 issue reprinted the title essay from *Where the Bluebird Sings*, his recently published collection. As editor Vaughn says, Stegner was well-known. The fame of his later years is matched by an uncommon vitality that created and reflected the fame.

His was never, of course, the kind of fame that Ernest Hemingway sometimes pursued, a fame that helped destroy him. Stegner's life had an enviable degree of measure. More than most writers, he gave the sense of having understood himself. He knew how to talk with himself and with others. He seems always to have had his work. Even to small tasks, and until the very end of his life, he gave intense energy. One of the last projects Stegner undertook was commentary for a calendar of the paintings of Hubert Shuptrine, *The Vanishing Land Calendar 1994*, printed by Algonquin Books of Chapel Hill. In a tribute to Stegner's career, Robert Rubin wrote in June 1993 in *The Algonkian*:

> A lesser writer might have considered it [the calendar commentary] slight work—a series of twelve vignettes and recollections, approximately 100 words each, about the disappearing rural landscape. Not Mr. Stegner, who wrote and rewrote his commentaries until he produced a poignant and moving elegy to the vanishing way of life—a somber, hard-edged counterpoint to the warm, nostalgic rural paintings of Hubert Shuptrine. "They have about dri-

838

ven me crazy," he wrote us in early February. "It seems I can't write anything as short as 100 words and make it say anything. I hope these say something, individually or collectively, or both. They had better—I have written them at least seven different ways." The episode reveals the essence of Wallace Stegner. (34)

At Stegner's death, it was possible to see a career of enviable achievement and, certainly, a career that had a satisfying degree of completion. Likely there was work in progress on Stegner's desk (there always was), but it is unlikely that there are torsos of unfinished novels such as Nathaniel Hawthorne left—no mounds of materials such as Thomas Wolfe left for his editors to shape, or the novels that Ernest Hemingway had not been able to finish. What is more inspiring is not just that work was completed but that much of Stegner's best work was completed near the end of his long career at Stanford or after his retirement from there in 1971—the year he published his Pulitzer Prize-winning *Angle of Repose*. That was followed by the National Book Award winner *The Spectator Bird* (1976) and *Recapitulation* (1979)—all discussed in *A Literary History of the American West*.

Stegner's last novel, *Crossing to Safety*, was published in 1987, the year he turned seventy-eight. Although *Crossing to Safety* did not get a Pulitzer or National Book Award, it can easily stand with his works that received those honors. And now that Stegner is gone, and we know that *Crossing to Safety* is his last novel, it takes on another dimension, and we read it somewhat differently. It marks Stegner's own crossing to safety. We read it with heightened attention to the parallels between the fiction and Stegner's life.

To be sure, such parallels were obvious at the time of the book's publication. Part of the novel's interest lies in its marked self-reflexive dimension—a hallmark of Stegner's later novels. *Crossing to Safety* is partly a novel about writing a novel, and it subtly but insistently keeps reminding us of its textuality. As Larry Morgan narrates the history of the friendship that he and his wife Sally had with Sid and Charity Lang, Larry, a writer of fiction and an editor of fiction, teases the boundary between history and fiction. From the beginning of their friendship during the Great Depression when Larry and Sid were just out of graduate school and met because both were instructors at the University of Wisconsin, there had been strong bonding between the Langs and the Morgans. Friendships that endured through lifetimes were born that year in Madison. As Charity Lang lies on her deathbed in August 1972, she summons the Morgans from their New Mexico home to the Langs' Vermont compound, ostensibly to celebrate her birthday but certainly because she seeks reunion and closure. Although the Langs and Morgans had not seen each other for some years, the relationship is such that they can pick it up as if there had been no interlude. Charity's children know the special quality of the friendship, and her daughter Hallie suggests to Larry that he ought to write about it. An experienced writer, Larry doubts that such a friendship—or any life—can be rendered without falsifying it. Most immediately, the novel's primary action is Charity's *Totentanz*, as Larry calls it—her death dance being the exit from the family party she had planned in order to die in the hospital. Charity does not want the scene of family joys and tradition to be the scene of her death. She insists on meeting death in her way, just as she had striven to dictate to life. That death dance completed at novel's end, the reader realizes that another action has begun. Larry has accepted Hallie's challenge; he has given his readers the novel *Crossing to Safety*.

Because even in 1987 readers of *Crossing to Safety* were pondering action that took place more than a decade earlier, we can be reminded how important a theme the fictive process is to the novel. *Crossing to Safety* celebrates memory, the mother of the muses. Time present in the novel—a day and evening of August 1972—is palpably real—as only great fiction can render time. But as well, the novel gives us memorable scenes from thirty-four years previous—the faculty party where the Langs and Morgans first bonded, Sally's difficult birthing of a daughter, the sharing of news that Wisconsin is dismissing Larry, a boat ride on Lake Mendota, hiking and camping in the Vermont woods, the onset of Sally's polio, a journey to Italy. Larry was not present, could not have been present, for one extended scene he narrates—the immediate events leading up to and immediately after Sid's proposal to Charity. The proposal scene is as vivid as any in the novel, and calls to our attention how fiction works, how writers not only remember but imagine from life. The scene carries as much authority as those Larry actually recalls. If time in *The Big Rock Candy Mountain* is chronological and expansive, here it is unified in more subtle, more complex ways—though the narrative sequence is always clear. Stegner's handling of time in the novel is exceedingly deft as he conveys how past and present play against each other.

In his narration, Larry is dealing not only with memories of his and

Sally's lives as they interacted with the Langs, but also with memories that follow Charity's death, memories post-1972. He was not ready to leave the compound and begin to write the story immediately. The Langs' history would marinate in his subconscious for some time before he began writing the novel we read.

It is only upon reflection that this delay would seem significant to us. For our immediate attention at novel's end is with Sid and his recovery. With Larry, we ponder the possibility of Sid's total despair over Charity's death, even the possibility he might commit suicide. For some hours, Larry has been scouring the woods looking for Sid. The conclusion of the story is assuredly positive. Larry recreates the moment:

> And now I see the figure, dusty-gold in the moonlight, coming steadily up the road from the stable. It is blurred, its shadow encumbering its feet, but it comes without pause, as if timing itself to meet the family coming down from the hill.
> "Sid," I say.
> "Yes," he says. (272)

As the last spoken word we hear, Sid's "Yes" is an effective, Joycean touch, reminding us of *Ulysses* (1922) and Molly Bloom's memorable "yes" and the recoveries that conclude Joyce's novel, a work that revolutionized fictional approaches to time. Sid has been called back from death to life — to creation of life — an act of will. Charity has always maintained that life should be an act of will. She energetically sought to create the text of her life. No one ever believed more vigorously than she that lives should not just happen but should be molded, shaped, created. Sometimes life must even be defied, though it can painfully restrict choices — tenure is sometimes denied, polio or cancer can impair or destroy, children can flout parental wisdom. Charity's drive in the novel most closely matches that of Larry as writer. Life and the fictive processes are similar in their forward thrusts.

So as we finish the book, we know that Sid will go on to create a new part of his life, and in time Larry will go on to write about the lives of the Langs and Morgans together — his own "yes." As Larry wrote *Crossing to Safety*, he was most assuredly thinking also of the imminent death of his own wife. In a prophetic passage in the final movement of the novel, Larry tells us how he answered Sid's question about how he might be able to respond to Sally's death, its likelihood prefigured by

Charity's: "I read his question as being aimed really at himself, and answered it accordingly. Now that I ask it seriously of myself [as I write this text] I don't know how to reply" (273). He explains the prognosis for polio victims who have endured the virus to live durably until one day the whole system breaks down quite suddenly "Like the wonderful one-hoss shay" (273). Sid's great loss and challenge to go on with life are a counterpart to the challenge Larry will soon face. As artist, Larry is creating lives — in his way, showing how like Charity Lang he is.

The Larry who describes Charity's *Totentanz* is no longer in his sixties (Stegner was sixty-four in 1972) but in his late seventies or more — as Stegner was when he used Larry to tell his story. Although the parallels between Larry and Stegner are numerous, Larry does not correspond precisely to him any more than does Joe Alston, the crotchety narrator of *All the Little Live Things* and *The Spectator Bird*. Both are from the West, have few roots or traditions, and are essentially orphans. Both came to love Vermont (Stegner requested that his ashes be deposited there). Stegner taught for a brief time at Wisconsin, and just as Larry made a big hit with his first novel, Stegner made an auspicious beginning as fiction writer with a prize-winning novel. There are, however, many divergences from the record of Stegner's life. Finally, it is the fictional truth that makes the most telling links.

In the portrait of Larry, we get a good deal of Wallace Stegner's essential character. (In the concluding essay of *Where the Bluebird Sings* Stegner describes *Crossing to Safety* as "in some ways the most personal" of his novels [224].) Westerners who discover the East and make their way in it, Larry and Stegner acknowledge their essential squareness as westerners and seek to find the culture and tradition of the East — exemplified especially in Charity but also in her Harvard-educated husband. Larry's Berkeley education (like Stegner's Utah and Iowa training) proves good for the long haul, however. Larry (like Stegner) displays western determination; he needs (like his creator) to prove himself. Descriptions of Larry's work ethic and pattern aptly fit all that we know about Stegner's drive and work ethic. But if a strong work ethic is present in both, the ethic was not at bottom self-serving. For each, career did not preclude a life. In the novel, Charity's East may be said to help guide Larry's western drive.

The connection between East and West reinforces the novel's great theme of friendship. Early in his narrative, Larry reminds his readers of Cicero's *De Amicitia* and invites them to see the novel as a discourse on

842

the ancient and noble theme of friendship. American literature has several impressive treatments of adolescent friendship but few examples of sustained adult friendships. Tom Sawyer and Huckleberry Finn share what is probably America's most illustrious friendship in literature. The best friendships in Faulkner also belong to boys or adolescent males. Leslie Fiedler found the adults of the fiction of Cooper, Melville, Twain, and others to be questing for adolescent adventures and their bondings to be homoerotic. In any case, our major writers have usually emphasized loneliness and isolation — and failed adult friendships. In celebrating *amicitia*, Stegner puts his attention elsewhere. He portrays *amicitia* found in a marriage as well as the friendship of couples for each other as couples and as individuals.

Gender differences are important factors in the relationships Stegner portrays, though homoeroticism is not part of Stegner's equation. There is no sexual competition between the couples or amongst them. We see them as sexual beings, but their sexuality is not what draws the couples together. Stegner's attention is on fellowship, understanding, caring — on *amicitia*, that rare, good thing — so important to life but infrequently at the heart of a novel. *Crossing to Safety* may come to be known as our classic novel on the theme.

When the Morgans return to Vermont at Charity's summons, Larry finds himself remembering and reassessing — most certainly himself. (Charity's impending death has all of the characters looking backward.) Larry observes, "Though I have been busy, perhaps overbusy, all my life, it seems to me that I have accomplished little that matters, that the books have never come up to what was in my head, and that the rewards — the comfortable income, the public notice, the literary prizes, and the honorary degrees — have been tinsel, not what a grown man should be content with" (10). Larry lets us know that he has a good deal more than such tinsel; he considers his friendship with the Langs one of his chief possessions, a friendship built on certain values. As he considers himself, Sally, and the Langs as they began their friendship, Larry assuredly reflects what drove the career and life of Wallace Stegner:

> Our hottest arguments were always about what we could *contribute*. We did not care about the rewards. We were young and earnest. We never kidded ourselves that we had the political gifts to reorder society or insure social justice. Beyond a basic minimum, money was not a goal we respected. Some of us suspected that money wasn't

843

even ever good for people—hence Charity's leaning toward aus-
terity and the simple life. But we all hoped, in whatever way our
capacities permitted, to define and illustrate the worthy life. (10)

The western writer is "born a square"—as Stegner described his
plight in a famous essay with that title (collected in *The Sound of
Mountain Water*, 1969); the values Larry espouses reflect such "squareness." It is surely a triumph of *Crossing to Safety* that Stegner successfully
portrayed characters who exemplify "the worthy life"—a demanding
task in a postmodern culture.

How does he do so without becoming maudlin? The portrait of Larry
is, of course, pivotal. As the quotations above suggest, Larry does not
write from defensiveness. His perspective is seasoned by a long career
and the adjustment he has had to make after his wife gets polio. He is
not driven by "tinsel." If he is a "senior" writer, he is aware of how the
contemporary world is different from the Great Depression that molded
him. But he is out to convert no one—except as fiction might help
teach someone what is important about life. Larry Morgan is a narrator
most readers will trust.

And because Larry is an experienced writer, there is much to admire
about his tellings. As he says, the story of the Langs and Morgans is not
melodramatic or sensational. It deals with fairly ordinary events. Larry
knows that his account is very different from much fiction of the modernist and postmodernist eras. But it is more than realistic creations of
scenes—though readers can delight in them. It threads those scenes
compellingly, handling time in a complex way, reminding us of the
achievements of the high modernists. In addition to the Joycean frame
of Bloom's day already noted, Stegner's structure in *Crossing to Safety*
recalls Virginia Woolf's *Mrs. Dalloway* (1925), which creates the day of
Clarissa Dalloway's party as well as memories of friendship.

The modernist whom Stegner knew best was probably Ernest
Hemingway. In *The Sun Also Rises* (1927), Jake Barnes is trying to learn
how to live in the world. Jake's reliability as narrator is not nearly as
great as Larry Morgan's, and the *amicitiae* Jake and Larry describe are of
radically different quality, especially as the *amicitia* relates to fellowship
among couples. Through his characters, Hemingway invites his readers
to ponder "the worthy life"—though we do so with a great deal of
"irony and pity." Stegner reminds us of Hemingway's novel by echoing
that famous phrase in *Crossing to Safety*.

Two scenes in Stegner's novel recall similar scenes in A *Farewell to Arms* (1929). Although the scene is no imitation, the rendition of Sally's difficult birthing of her daughter, which takes her close to death, is so visceral that many readers will recall the prolonged labor and death of Catherine Barkley. Stegner reminds us of that event again — and rather pointedly — in the final movement of *Crossing to Safety*. When Larry seeks to find the desolate Sid, Stegner alludes to Frederic Henry's response to Catherine's death and to the ultimate meaning of Hemingway's novel through use of a memorable symbol. In his frustration at his incompetence in not being able to find Sid, Larry recalls a moonlit night in New Mexico when he discovered a mouse drowning in the swimming pool. Finding mice in the pool was common. (Once Larry found a neighbor's bulldog dead at the bottom.) He dipped out this mouse, thoroughly dead, it seemed. But the mouse revived, a "miracle," and scampered into the grass and weeds. "Survival, it is called. Often it is accidental, but sometimes it is engineered by creatures or forces that we have no conception of, always it is temporary" (275). The memory carries positive impact, preparing us for Sid's return and the hope of Stegner's ending in the setting of its autumnal certainty. It also plays against the ending of A *Farewell to Arms* where, in a similar moment of frustration, Frederic Henry remembers putting a log full of ants on a campfire. He thought the situation offered him "a splendid chance to be a messiah," but Henry only threw a tin cup of water on the log, probably steaming the ants. Despair was sometimes Hemingway's theme, but never Stegner's — and certainly not in his final novel.

Allusion to classic modernist texts is, of course, another means to call attention to Stegner's own text — and its pleasure in textuality.

As does the novel's plot, concerned as it is with the making of literature, the characters frequently talk about writing and writers, about the risks and rewards of writing, making us think of the text in our hands. Larry's medium is prose. Sid is a frustrated poet. As a young man, he had wanted to be a poet; indeed, he had his first poems published as he began his teaching career. But Charity insists that Sid give priority to academic writing: poetry should wait until he achieves tenure. When tenure is denied, chaos arrives. Eventually, Sid does gain an academic career and tenure, but poetry is not a muse accustomed to second place. Sid is free to write his poems, but in August 1972, he knows he will never be the poet he wished to be.

A novel that takes its title from a poem by Robert Frost, *Crossing to*

Safety alludes to and quotes from many poets and poems, helping to create a rich texture. Frost plays over all. The Vermont locale evokes his spirit, and the novel's emphasis on profession and choices echoes important Frost themes. The chief feature of Charity's *Totentanz* reminds us of a similar decision that Elinor Frost made as she lay dying. She barred the distraught Frost from her room, much as Charity insists that Sid will not be allowed to accompany her to the hospital.

Concerned with the making of poetry, featuring characters who like to read it, quote it, and teach it, *Crossing to Safety* may be said to strive for the condition of poetry. Larry becomes its truest poet as he creates for his readers a rich texture of language. His images and cadences add to the affirmation of a novel that celebrates the good life — good life in the arts as well as in the natural world. The opening paragraph sets the tone and reflects the beauty of the language that characterizes Larry's (and Stegner's) excursion into "the worthy life": "Floating upward through a confusion of dreams and memory, curving like a trout through the rings of previous risings, I surface. My eyes open. I am awake" (3).

Stegner sustains certain images throughout the text. Chief among them is the image of creating found in Genesis. Larry often compares the Langs' Vermont to Eden before the fall, and he labels Sid and Charity Adam and Eve. A snake enters the garden, inevitably, and the reality of death (as in so much of Stegner's fiction) challenges and subdues the protagonists. The new world makes us think of the old, and images of suffering and pain make their way into the novel, too. On their Italian journey, Sally and Larry find the painting of Piero's Christ exceedingly haunting. On seeing Charity in 1972, Larry recalls Piero: "Her eyes, to my fascinated imagination, were like the eyes of Piero's gloomy Christ — a painting that she had once, wanting to count no hours but the sunny ones, affected to repudiate" (260). In *Crossing to Safety*, art is ever in the service of life, helping to explain it, helping us to survive and celebrate it.

As *Crossing to Safety* proved a novel of great distinction to end Stegner's career as novelist, other publishing events that followed in its wake gave emphasis to a major career. In 1990 Random House published *Collected Stories of Wallace Stegner*, giving Stegner's readers the stories of *The Women on the Wall* (1950) and *The City of the Living* (1956), two stories found in *Wolf Willow* (1962), and three stories of the late 1950s previously not collected. As Stegner noted in the foreword, he had ceased to write short stories some years ago, finding the genre "a young writer's form" (x). He noted also that his stories "tended to cluster, wanting to be part of something longer." He invited readers to see the stories not precisely as autobiography but as a personal record of a quintessentially American life. "I lived them, either as a participant or spectator or auditor, before I made fictions of them" (ix). We can see the collection as another self-reflexive text, a reading of stories with their roots in Stegner's life, written from the advantages and limitations of the times when Stegner wrote them.

The opening paragraph of his foreword describes his last novel as well as the gathering of stories. Stegner acknowledges: "I hate the restrictiveness of facts; I can't control my impulse to rearrange, suppress, add, heighten, invent, and improve. Accuracy means less to me than suggestiveness; my memory is as much an inventor as a record, and when it has operated in these stories it has operated almost as freely as if no personal history were involved" (ix). Like *Crossing to Safety*, *Collected Stories* is a writer's backward look at his career. The dedications reflect the link. The novel is dedicated to Mary Page Stegner "in gratitude for more than a half century of love and friendship, and to the friends we were both blessed by." *Collected Stories* is inscribed: "For Mary, in gratitude for fifty-three years of close collaboration, and for patience beyond the call of duty."

Prophetically, Mary Stegner was also the dedicatee of the last book that Stegner would see published. In 1992 Random House published *Where the Bluebird Sings to the Lemonade Springs*. The dedication reads: "For Mary, who, like Dilsey, has seen the first and the last, and been indispensable and enspiriting all the way." Again, journey is Stegner's metaphor. In *Crossing to Safety*, Larry credits Sally for teaching him the "grammar of gratitude." Stegner learned the same grammar.

Where the Bluebird Sings gathers Stegner's late essays (mostly from the 1980s and 1990s; two come from the 1970s). Although they challenge us repeatedly on environmental responsibility and recreate for us the American experience, they also provide a splendid means to revisit the totality of Stegner's career. We get clear statements about where he has been and about what has mattered most to him. The title of the collection comes from Harry McClintock's song "The Big Rock Candy Mountain," whence Stegner had taken the title of his first major novel.

The allusion to that novel may seem the obvious reason for the title of the collection; though in the introduction Stegner indeed mentions that novel, "my first and most heartfelt commentary on western optimism and enterprise and the common man's dream of something for nothing" (xxi), the title fits the essays about western experience because the mirage of the Big Rock Candy Mountain continues to lure people to the West. The essays patiently rehearse the lesson that the land cannot fulfill the promises of boosters who tout it as "the flowing well of opportunity, the stamping ground of the self-reliant" (xix). With less optimism than when he first proclaimed western wilderness "the geography of hope," Stegner continued to promote understanding of the realities of western aridity and to expose the penalties that engineered environment has produced in much of the West. Proclaiming himself one shaped by the West, he longs for a West "prosperous and environmentally healthy" in all its subregions and subcultures — a West with "a civilization to match its scenery" (xv). The essays reveal him to be more optimistic about the future of western writing than about larger cultural understanding and wholeness. The myth of the West as the Garden of the World is still too dominant.

Stegner grouped the essays of *Where the Bluebird Sings* under three headings. First come three "Personal" essays. The first chronicles his western childhood of migrancy and his search for place. It is followed by a letter to his mother, dead many years — retracing the years of migrancy with keen sensitivity to the price his father's migrant impulse placed on her nesting instinct. The third essay, "Crossing into Eden," recalls a trip of 1923 to the Granddaddy Lakes Basin of the Uinta Mountains of northeastern Utah — an essay that looks backward as well as environmentally forward, a rendition of the kind of experience that Stegner wished, and the Wilderness Society wishes, to preserve for posterity — places to visit for our souls' good, but places where we "leave no tracks" ("Crossing Into Eden" 41). The essay is a moving prelude to the environmental essays gathered under "Habitat," the second grouping.

In the final grouping of essays Stegner reflects on western writing and western writers, including himself. (In these essays, we often hear echoes of the environmental issues of the earlier essays.) Two very late essays frame the collection, the final essay not previously published anywhere — a splendid statement about his approach to the art of fiction over the spectrum of his entire career. Between are essays on Steinbeck's "Flight," George Stewart, Walter Clark, Norman Maclean, "The Sense of Place," and "A Letter to Wendell Berry." In a memorial tribute to Stegner in *The Steinbeck Newsletter* (Summer 1993), Susan Shillinglaw judges "the man and his prose of a piece — spare, fair-minded, vigorous" (7). And so we find man and critic in these essays.

Any assessment of Stegner's entire career should make more than passing reference to Stegner as teacher. The work of teachers is, like the work of editors, usually hidden from public view — intangible, dwarfed by the public work. Yet Stegner taught writing for some forty-four years. Probably no writer of his time earned greater fame as a teacher. He made the creative writing program at Stanford world famous; the program has become synonymous with his name. His students include Edward Abbey, Max Apple, Wendell Berry, James Houston, Ken Kesey, Thomas McGuane, Larry McMurtry, N. Scott Momaday, Tillie Olsen, Robert Stone.

Stegner would never claim that he made any of these writers; none is a copy of him. Yet they would likely give credit to the Stanford program for its help in their becoming writers. Most of them kept their association with Stegner alive. As he said, in retirement he got to read a lot of work in galleys.

It is fortuitous, therefore, that there be a marking of Stegner as teacher through publication of his view on the teaching of creative writing. Published in 1988, *On the Teaching of Creative Writing* was based on tape-recorded discussions before audiences at Dartmouth College during Stegner's residence there as Montgomery Fellow in June and July of 1980. Stegner responded to a series of questions, most of which he had met in interviews throughout the years. The resulting monograph is valuable from several perspectives. It gives readers a history of creative writing as an enterprise in American colleges and universities. Creative writing programs are often in English departments but not of them; Stegner lets us know why. He lets us know the valuable contribution that creative writing can provide. We also get a sense of what went on in Stegner's classes — and what goes on in other good creative writing classes. Stegner provides cautions for both English departments (don't have the scholars select the creative writers) and for the teachers of creative writing (it's easy for the teaching writer to become an ex-writer). A pleasant read, *On the Teaching of Creative Writing* provides insight into both the creation of literature and the study of it in colleges and universities.

The last word Stegner copyrighted (1993) was the text for the Algonquin calendar for 1994, *The Vanishing Land: The Art of Hubert Shuptrine*. (Stegner saw the proof but not the final product.) Time is

849

always of the essence for calendars; this one will defy time more than calendars usually can—something art always means to do. In twelve brief statements (one for each month), Stegner reviews his own past as well as that of his America. As with his collected stories, his calendar statements reflect a "quintessentially American life." His January text counterpoints Shuptrine's painting of Martha Owl, an older Native American patiently at work with needle and thread; Stegner describes the labor of his mother's youth that "stole her girlhood but also gave her a sure-handed competence, and a character like a warm rock." Subsequent commentaries recount the transition from the dominance of agriculture in American life to the flight from the farms and the rise of agribusiness. Without sentimentalizing realities, Stegner recalls the family farms at the dawn of the century and life on them for humans and animals. He describes the rural towns they supported and reminds us of the literature that captured later flight from such towns. For October, he describes the flight from cities by "refugees who need quiet and greenery more than they hate the commute." In November he pays tribute to Wendell Berry, "passionate advocate of farm life and farm people"—and expresses the wish that farming might again become a "rich way of life." However much Stegner may see what America has lost, he does not despair. Hear him for December, the last month of the year—our month of greatest darkness, also month of an ancient celebration of hope; it is Stegner's last word to us:

Those who leave the farm or the country are nostalgic for what they have left; those who have never known the country are poorer for what they have missed. It is a deprivation never to have known animals, known them as individuals and as species, known the friendliness and sense of responsibility that care of them produces. It is a deprivation never to have sown seeds and watched them grow, never to have been chained to chores that knew no Sunday. The millions who think eggs come from cartons and chickens are packaged parts cannot know what it is to gather eggs warm from the nest. How poor are those who have lost contact with nature and the sources of their food!

I watched a girl from the inner city extend her fingers to a new calf, and I saw her face when the calf took her fingers and sucked them. That was a small epiphany, a glint of revelation and delight.

Selected Bibliography — Post 1987

Primary Sources

The American West as Living Space. Ann Arbor: University of Michigan Press, 1987.

Collected Stories of Wallace Stegner. New York: Random House, 1990.

Crossing to Safety. New York: Random House, 1987.

"A Geography of Hope." In *A Society to Match the Scenery: Personal Visions of the American West.* Gary Holthaus, Patricia Nelson Limerick, Charles F. Wilkinson, and Eve Stryker Munson, eds. Niwot: University Press of Colorado, 1991. Joining other westerners to present their hopes for the region, Stegner concludes with an urgent statement of caution.

On the Teaching of Creative Writing. Connery Lathem, ed. Hanover, New Hampshire: University Press of New England, 1988.

A Sense of Place. Two cassettes, Stegner provides introduction, then reads essays from previously published essays. Louisville, Colorado: Audio Press, 1989.

The Vanishing Land: The Art of Hubert Shuptrine. 1994 calendar with text by Wallace Stegner. Chapel Hill, North Carolina: Algonquin Books, 1993.

Wallace Stegner Reads "Beyond the Glass Mountain" and Other Works from Collected Stories. Two cassettes. San Francisco: Bay Area Digital, 1990. Stegner reads eight short stories, including "The Blue Winged Teal" and "The City of Living."

Where the Bluebird Sings to the Lemonade Springs: Living and Writing in the West. New York: Random House, 1992.

Secondary Sources

Benson, Jackson J. "'Eastering': Wallace Stegner's Love Affair with Vermont in *Crossing to Safety.*" *Western American Literature,* 25 (May 1990): 27-33. That Eden for Stegner came to be in the East (Vermont) "may be an irony that westerners will find hard to bear."

———. "Finding a Voice of His Own: The Story of Wallace Stegner's Fiction." *Western American Literature,* 29 (August 1994): 99-122. In a slow evolution ("A Field Guide to the Western Birds" was pivotal in it), Stegner achieved greatness in his fiction when he discovered "a fictive personality with a voice."

———. "Wallace Stegner and the Battle Against Rugged Individualism." *North Dakota Quarterly,* 61 (Spring 1993): 5-18. Stegner battled the American addiction to the doctrine of rugged individualism and stressed that "the best part of human nature comes out in a concern for, a duty to, others."

———. *Wallace Stegner.* New York: Viking Penguin, 1996. Written with Stegner's cooperation, this major biography will stimulate further interest in Stegner's life and work.

Burrows, Russell. "Wallace Stegner's Version of Pastoral." *Western American Literature,* 25 (May 1990): 15-25. "Stegner's major works are fundamentally concerned with the juxtaposition of machine and garden in the American landscape."

Colberg, Nancy. *Wallace Stegner: A Descriptive Bibliography.* Lewiston, Idaho: Confluence Press, 1990. An indispensable research tool, this bibliography reflects Stegner's stature in American letters.

Cook-Lynn, Elizabeth. *Why I Can't Read Wallace Stegner and Other Essays: A Tribal Voice.*

Madison: University of Wisconsin Press, 1996. A Sioux provides an embittered voice in recent discussions of Stegner. She faults him for neglecting and misunderstanding Native American history. "There is, perhaps, no American fiction writer who has been more successful in serving the interests of a nation's fantasy about itself than Wallace Stegner."

Cracroft, Richard H. "'A Profound Sense of Community': Mormon Values in Wallace Stegner's *Recapitulation*." *Dialogue: A Journal of Mormon Thought*, 24 (Spring 1991): 101-113. Stegner's nonfiction as well as the novel *Recapitulation* demonstrate the importance of Salt Lake City and Mormonism to his thought.

Etulain, Richard, ed. *Conversations with Wallace Stegner on Western History and Literature*. rev. ed. Salt Lake City: University of Utah Press, 1990. A historian questions Stegner about his art and views on the West—a major contribution to Stegner scholarship. Contains "After Ten Years: Another Conversation with Wallace Stegner," not found in the 1983 edition.

Flora, Joseph M. "Stegner and Hemingway as Short Story Writers: Some Parallels and Contrasts in Two Masters." *South Dakota Review*, 30 (Spring 1992): 104-119. Although there are numerous parallels in structure and theme between Stegner's *The Women on the Wall* and Hemingway's *In Our Time*, the short story was less central to Stegner's career than to Hemingway's.

"Interview with Wallace Stegner." *The Paris Review*, 115 (Summer 1990): 59-90. This interview reflects Stegner's status as a major American writer.

Maguire, James H. "Stegner vs. Brautigan: Recapitulation or Deconstruction?" *The Pacific Northwest Forum*, 11 (Spring 1986): 23-28. Although Stegner did not count Brautigan as a western writer, there are many similarities between his work and Stegner's, and both writers may be deemed western.

Mason, Kenneth C. "*The Big Rock Candy Mountain*: The Consequences of a Delusory American Dream." *Great Plains Quarterly*, 6 (Winter 1986): 34-43. Finding the family Stegner's greatest inspiration, the essay discusses Bo Mason, his wife, and sons as they endure Bo's pursuit of the American dream.

Milton, John. "Conversation with Wallace Stegner." *South Dakota Review*, 26 (Winter 1988): 63-75. A part of the *South Dakota Review*'s interview series with western writers, the conversation puts Stegner with one of the major promoters of the western novel.

Olsen, Brett J. "Wallace Stegner and the Environmental Ethic: Environmentalist as a Rejection of Western Myth." *Western American Literature*, 29 (August 1994): 123-142. This memorial tribute charts Stegner's environmental positions throughout his career, which ended with "razor-sharp warnings of a modern day Cassandra."

Rankin, Charles E. *Wallace Stegner: Man and Writer*. Albuquerque: University of New Mexico Press, 1996. Essays by various scholars consider the scope of Stegner's achievement as a writer and environmentalist. Interpretive essays are preceded by more personal essays by his son, the writer Page Stegner; former students James R. Hepworth and Wendell Berry; and writers William Kittredge and Ivan Doig.

Ronald, Ann. "Stegner and Stewardship." *Writers' Forum*, 17 (Fall 1991): 3-16. Ronald identifies a "puzzling anthrocentrism" in Stegner's conservationism, especially in his little-known *Discovery!* (Beirut: Middle East Export Press, Inc., 1971), an account of the American Oil Company's plan that brought Arabian oil to Saudi Arabia"; contrasting Stegner with "ardent preservationists" and "studied conservationists," she identifies his ultimate position as one of "stewardship."

Rubin, Robert. "Wallace Stegner, 1909-1993." *The Algonkian*, 13 (June 1993): 34. An editor provides a glimpse of Stegner at one of his last writing projects.

Shillinglaw, Susan. "Wallace Stegner, 1909-1993." *The Steinbeck Newsletter*, 6 (Summer 1993): 7. A brief tribute that recalls Stegner's evaluation of Steinbeck.

Socolofsky, Homer E., R. David Edmunds, and Joseph C. Porter. "Western History Association Prize Recipient, 1991: Wallace Stegner." *Western Historical Quarterly*, 22 (Spring 1991): 137-141. Recipient of the Achievement Award of the Western Literature Association in 1974, Stegner was similarly honored by the Western History Association; the citation recounts his achievements.

South Dakota Review. Special Wallace Stegner Issue. 23 (Winter 1985). Contents: Wendell Berry, "Wallace Stegner and the Great Community," Pp. 10-18; Edward Loomis, "Wallace Stegner and Yvor Winters as Teachers," Pp. 19-24; Gary Topping, "Wallace Stegner and the Mormons," Pp. 25-41; T. H. Watkins, "Bearing Witness for the Land: The Conservation Career of Wallace Stegner," Pp. 42-57; Forrest G. Robinson, "A Usable Heroism: Wallace Stegner's *Beyond the Hundredth Meridian*," Pp. 58-69; Kerry Ahearn, "Stegner's Short Fiction," Pp. 70-86; Melody Graulich, "The Guides to Conduct that a Tradition Offers, Wallace Stegner's *Angle of Repose*," Pp. 87-106; John Milton, "Conversation with Wallace Stegner," Pp. 107-118.

Stegner, Page and Mary Stegner. *The Geography of Hope: A Tribute to Wallace Stegner*. San Francisco: Sierra Club Books, 1996. Friends and colleagues (writers, historians, conservationists) give short tributes to the recently fallen writer.

Vaughn, Sam and T. H. Watkins. "A Natural Treasure: Wallace Stegner (1909-1993)." *At Random*, 2 (Fall 1993): 11. See also "Wordplace" on p. 80, where photograph and caption conclude tributes to Stegner by his publisher.

Willrick, Patricia Rowe. "A Perspective on Wallace Stegner." *Virginia Quarterly*, 67 (Spring 1991): 240-259. The essay recounts the shape of Stegner's career.

Zahlan, Anne Rickertson. "Cities of the Living: Disease and the Traveler in *Collected Stories* by Wallace Stegner." *Studies in Short Fiction*, 29 (Fall 1992): 509-516. Travel and disease are frequent themes in Stegner's stories; the last story of the collection "teaches that acceptance of mortality is necessary to validate the journey of life."

Charles L. Adams

Frank Waters

Frank Waters, one of America's most significant writers, died June 3, 1995, at his home in Arroyo Seco, New Mexico, a few weeks shy of his ninety-third birthday. Largely "undiscovered" until recent years, Waters nonetheless had a sufficient reading public to keep in print nineteen books produced over a seventy-year period. His genres include novels, biographies, essays, and ethnological and historical studies. Translations into Swedish, Dutch, French, German, and Japanese attest to the international interest in his work.

In their fall 1991 catalogue, Swallow Press/Ohio University Press quoted James Thomas' assessment of Frank Waters' present status. Thomas wrote:

> The Amerindian and Eastern thought which characterizes and informs Waters's fiction has been far from the mind of the Western literary and cultural establishment these past fifty years, and ultimately it is hardly a surprise that this author's work should go largely unnoticed except on...[a] limited regional, ethnocentric, and "cultish" basis. Waters is now, however, on the cutting edge of just about everything we take seriously in this country: the natural environment, our sociopsychological environment (our personal lives, and how we choose to control them), our political relationships with the past, and our political, ecological, and spiritual relationship with the future. No wonder that someone is finally paying attention.

A year later a critic writing for the American Library Association added this observation:

> As multicultural academia sorts out and chooses new forebears, novelist Frank Waters is a strong candidate for canonization.... Waters's best work is tailored for the classroom's renewed search not only for a new world but also for suitable forebears for the multicultural world to which we are adjusting.[1]

It is gratifying to know Waters achieved more of the broader public attention and critical acknowledgment he deserved so deeply.

During the past decade, Waters continued to publish: a novel, *Flight From Fiesta*; a major revision of a novel, *The Woman at Otowi Crossing*; an extended essay, *The Eternal Desert*; and a volume of mini-biographies, *Brave Are My People: Indian Heroes Not Forgotten*. The decade has also seen the publication of an anthology of his writing, *Frank Waters: A Retrospective Anthology*, edited by this author; a volume of major criticism, Alexander Blackburn's excellent *A Sunrise Brighter Still: The Visionary Novels of Frank Waters*; and an opera based on *The Woman at Otowi Crossing*, commissioned and produced by the Opera Theatre of St. Louis.

In 1986, Rydal Press, in Santa Fe, published a limited edition of Waters' novel *Flight from Fiesta*. It was followed a year later by a trade edition from Swallow Press/Ohio University Press. As is the case with many of Waters' works, the date of publication bears little relation to the date of composition. This story was originally written in 1957 as a film treatment. Waters has said, "[It was to be]... a warm simple story which could be produced without the expense of theatrical sets.... It required only the rental of a suite in the La Fonda hotel in Santa Fe, all other footage being taken in outdoor scenic settings."[2] From the beginning the story was conceived as being the relationship between "an old drunken Indian and a spoiled rich White girl of ten."[3] The girl, Elsie, runs away from the hotel where she and her divorced mother and her mother's lover are staying for fiesta. With childish cunning and "emotional blackmail," she maneuvers Inocencio, the drunken old Indian, into being her unwilling accomplice. When Inocencio is assumed to have kidnapped and perhaps molested her, he instinctively flees to the hills, taking the now frightened Elsie with him.

The film was never made. Waters, however, retained all publishing rights and, at various times over the years, worked on the story, turning film treatment and script into a novel. By retaining the original time setting of almost fifty years ago, Waters makes possible a kind of double point of view, utilizing a technique he had mastered over the years. The descriptions of Santa Fe, for example, of the fiesta, of Gallup, and of the two main characters, Inocencio and Elsie, full of mid-century impressions, gain much from the 1986 insight of the author. The verve and enthusiasm of the much earlier Waters novels are there, with the added strength of his later maturity.

Despite its origins, *Flight from Fiesta* is more than a simple "chase" adventure. In the course of the novel's unfolding, Elsie and Inocencio become emblematic of their respective races, not blatantly as in allegory but subtly: Elsie and Inocencio each act according to his or her own nature, conditioned as they have been by their separate heritages and societies. In the course of the story they reflect those natures, heritages, and societies, and one becomes aware that Waters is commenting on the past, present, and future relations of the two races.

Elsie and Inocencio appear as polarized as any two people could possibly be: an old, traditional, drunken Indian man and a young, materialistic, self-centered Anglo girl. And while the two characters do conflict, they also illustrate, unconsciously on their part, the need of each for the other. Without becoming self-conscious allegory or didacticism, the story dramatizes the age-old clash of polarities, conflicts between youth and age, male and female, white and Indian, the civilized and the primitive, the old and the new. The characters also illustrate dramatically the necessity for reconciliation: Elsie realizes the need for the older provider, the adult, and Inocencio instinctively obeys his need to protect and nurture the child—the future is what is important.

Flight From Fiesta is a deceptively simple book. A reader gradually becomes aware that, as in many of Waters' books, he is being bombarded by a multiplicity of dualities—visually, audibly, psychologically, psychically, and spiritually. At the novel's end, it is up to the reader to synthesize beyond the story's conclusion, for, upon reflection, there are simply too many unanswered questions remaining in the reader's mind. One ponders the fact that Inocencio regenerates as he regresses, that he "escapes" into death, that Elsie is healthy, safe, and still depressingly materialistic and self-oriented. Waters has said, "The Road of Life runs one way." But Inocencio appears to regress from reality back to something possibly more real, and while Inocencio is laid to rest, his problems

856

remain very much alive. Waters uses his unique synthesizing abilities to express consistent messages, but the final resolution must be found in the mind of the reader. It is Waters' great gift that he can cause this to happen.

Waters' *The Woman at Otowi Crossing* (1966), one of the truly great books in American literature, was originally printed under the restrictions and judgmental limitations of its publisher. Artistically successful, it nevertheless did not contain the full narrative scope of Waters' vision. In 1987, the Swallow Press/Ohio University Press made Waters' full version of *Otowi Crossing* available to readers. Originally Waters had intended this novel to be five or six hundred pages in length. At one stage in its development, it apparently grew to seven hundred pages. The version finally published in 1966 and retained in all subsequent continuous printings had been reduced to three hundred pages, the result of the merciless cutting and condensation urged for publication.[4] Although the 1987 edition actually appears thinner than previous editions, the typeface is smaller, obscuring the fact that Waters has actually added over a hundred typed pages of new material, restructuring the original material to accommodate it. Waters restored the book to its fullest form and then pruned from the point of view of his mature artistic judgment. The result is even deeper characterization, more detailed description, and more information about practically everything in the book.

Major additions include whole new chapters, sometimes involving characters not found in the previous editions. Gaylord meets a woman in Las Vegas who assists in his psychic and sexual healing. Emily meets friends of her mother who reveal the wealthy Santa Fe society Helen is increasingly rejecting. Emily also experiences the Southwest as *place* in a way that foreshadows her problems with Gaylord. Smaller additions frequently offer a more fully developed treatment of Helen's increasing awareness and expanded consciousness and of her perception and understanding of Indian mythology. Frequently these additions are in the form of new extracts from her secret journal, many of which have parallels in Waters' nonfiction written after the 1966 publication of *Otowi*. In the 1987 volume of *Otowi*, echoes of *Pumpkinseed Point* (1969), *Mexico Mystique* (1975), and *Mountain Dialogues* (1981) resound.

Additional recent critical interest in *Otowi* has been stimulated by its adaptation as an operatic production. Stephen Paulus was commissioned by the Opera Theatre of St. Louis to compose the opera in commemoration of its twentieth anniversary season. It premiered on June 15, 1995. The librettist, Joan Vail Thorne, an award-winning playwright and director in her own right, provided an ingenious adaptation. The production was brilliantly directed by internationally acclaimed Colin Graham, artistic director of the Santa Fe Opera, whose work is also familiar to listeners of Saturday broadcasts of the Metropolitan Opera. The adaptation, while necessarily eliminating a great deal of the story, was faithful to Waters' overall message and intent and deserved the standing ovation it received.

In 1990 *Arizona Highways* published an elegant coffee-table book of photographs by David Muench, text by Frank Waters, called *Eternal Desert*. The text, a ten-page essay, utilizes an extended metaphor of water/fire/air/earth to describe the desert and to suggest a Buddhistic evocation of the desert as a physical counterpart to our unconscious minds, what Waters calls "a spiritual oasis." The 144 pages of Muench photographs well support this interpretation.

In his introduction to his 1993 *Brave Are My People: Indian Heroes Not Forgotten*, Waters apologizes that this book was, like many of his manuscripts, originally written many years ago. But Waters' readers have never had any problem with his reworkings and revisions. The Colorado trilogy of the thirties eventually became *Pike's Peak* in 1971, and, as we have noted, the final revisions of *The Woman at Otowi Crossing* (1966) did not occur until 1987. *Brave Are My People*, like so many other Waters books, combines youthful vigor with mature judgment.

The book consists of a series of biographical sketches of twenty Indian leaders — what Waters calls in the introduction "flashing glimpses ... of a series of American Indians whose lives have enriched the history of America" (1). His selection ranges from the Atlantic to the Pacific, from 1600 to 1900, tracing the expansion and conquest inexorably west. Readers who recall Waters' statistic-laden *Midas of the Rockies*, in print since 1937, will see the same sharp research skills in this volume. Readers of the commercial *Diamond Head* and *River Lady* will find Waters' same compelling ability to describe places he has never seen. Most of all, those who regard Waters as a master storyteller will be enthralled still one more time.

Although published in his ninetieth year, there is no evidence of diminution of his powers in this work. And even though there is an ever-present sadness because of the inevitability of the white conquest, there is dominant a nobility, a dignity, and even a sense of humor in this series of good stories, well told.

Waters continued to write until nine months before his death, when he completed a manuscript that now awaits posthumous publication. In recent years, Waters, along with his wife Barbara, established the Frank Waters Foundation, placing their home and wooded fifteen acres above Taos in permanent trust. The Foundation's purpose is to promote the arts by providing persons with inspirational living space in which to work for limited periods. It is a fitting memorial to the life of this great writer.

Notes

1. Quay Grigg, review of Alexander Blackburn, *A Sunrise Brighter Still: The Visionary Novels of Frank Waters* in *Choice*, 30:6 (February 92): 157-158.
2. Letter from Frank Waters, August [sic] 1977.
3. Ibid.
4. Terence A. Tanner, *Frank Waters: A Bibliography with Relevant Selections from His Correspondence* (Glenwood, Illinois: Meyerbooks, 1983), p. 95. Readers will find the correspondence on pages 189-196 of special interest in regard to the augmentation in the 1987 edition. Waters protested repeatedly against the reduction of his original manuscript.

Selected Bibliography

Primary Sources

Novels
Flight From Fiesta. Santa Fe: The Rydal Press, 1986. A signed and letterpress edition; rpt., Athens, Ohio: Swallow Press/Ohio University Press, 1987.
The Woman at Otowi Crossing, rev. ed. Athens, Ohio: Swallow Press/Ohio University Press, 1987.

Nonfiction
Brave Are My People: Indian Heroes Not Forgotten. Foreword by Vine Deloria, Jr. Santa Fe: Clear Light Publishers, 1993.
"The Changing and Unchangeable West." *Growing up Western*. Clarus Backus, ed. New York: Alfred A. Knopf, 1989.
Eternal Desert. Photography by David Muench. Phoenix: Arizona Highways, 1990.

Secondary Sources

Adams, Charles L., ed. *Studies in Frank Waters*, Vols. 7-17. Las Vegas: The Frank Waters Society, 1985-1995. The papers presented at the annual Frank Waters Society meetings. Scholars discuss a wide range of topics concerning Waters' work, usually organized around an annual theme.

———. *Frank Waters: A Retrospective Anthology.* Athens, Ohio: Swallow Press/Ohio University Press, 1985. Brief critical introductions preface samples from Waters' work from 1925 through 1985.

———. "Frank Waters." In *This Is About Vision.* John F. Crawford, William Balassi, and Annie O. Eysturoy, eds. Albuquerque: University of New Mexico Press, 1990. Pp. 14-25. An interview with Waters.

———. "Marginal Protagonists in Frank Waters' Fiction." *Philological Papers,* 38 (1993): 155-162. A paper previously presented at West Virginia University's fifteenth annual colloquium on literature and film. Its acceptance by this journal reflects critical interest in Waters east of the Mississippi.

Blackburn, Alexander, ed. "Frank Waters: Colorado College Symposium." *Writers' Forum,* 11 (1985): 164-221. The transcribed and edited tapes from the four "workshops" presented at Colorado College's month-long Waters symposium in 1985.

———. "Frank Waters." In *Dictionary of Literary Biography Yearbook: 1986.* J. M. Brook, ed. Detroit: Gale Research, 1986. Pp. 343-355. An excellent evaluation of Waters and his work.

———. *A Sunrise Brighter Still: The Visionary Novels of Frank Waters.* Athens, Ohio: Swallow Press/Ohio University Press, 1991. Superior critical evaluation and analysis of Waters' major novels.

Deloria, Vine, Jr., ed. *Frank Waters: Man and Mystic.* Athens, Ohio: Swallow Press/Ohio University Press, 1993. A warm collection of essays about and in honor of Frank Waters.

Malpezzi, Frances M. "Meru, the Voice of the Mountain." *South Dakota Review,* 27 (1989): 27-34; reprinted in *Studies in Frank Waters, XII: "The Novel"* (1990): 51-64. The definitive paper on M. Meru from *The Woman at Otowi Crossing.*

Sturdevant, Katherine Scott, ed. *Sundays in Tutt Library with Frank Waters.* Colorado Springs: Hulbert Center for Southwestern Studies, Colorado College, 1988. The formal lectures presented at the Colorado College 1985 symposium by Alexander Blackburn, Thomas J. Lyon, Charles L. Adams, and Frank Waters.

VII
The Popular West

Christine Bold

The Popular West

What we think we know about the popular West bears constant scrutiny. Signs of the western's "mythic space" (to use Richard Slotkin's term) continue to crowd our public spaces: Marlboro Men posters, newspaper cartoons (even President Clinton has been caricatured as the swaggering gunslinger with an empty holster), advertisements for John Wayne commemorative six-shooters ("Squeeze the trigger — and be a part of the legend.... Priced at $395, payable in convenient monthly installments"). Versions of the Wild West are sold in movie houses, on television screens, off drugstore shelves, in musical performances, by tourist brochures, on political platforms. This dense circulation of images is so familiar that it is tempting to assume that the dimensions of the mythic West are fully known and its meanings fully understood. The following essays challenge that assumption, by addressing gaps in the received record, questioning commonly held definitions, exposing the partiality (in two senses) of the stories which we tell about the popular western story.

Reconceptualizing the popular West is no empty academic exercise. It is not just that mass-distributed representations of the West typically serve the interests of the dominant culture, by naturalizing the triumph of capitalism as the moral victory of a strong man over weaker, less Anglo-Saxon forces. The very terms in which much scholarship analyzes the popular West as a key site of national and social identity also tend to elide minority interests. References to the "universal appeal" of the

863

western or its service to the "American psyche" reinscribe a national (by implication, consensual) "we" which excludes any individual or social group not part of the western's cultural terrain.[1] What makes possible this claim to the genre's universality are, in turn, assumptions about how best to categorize, and thereby understand, expressive forms.

Traditionally — at least in academic discourse — defining the popular western has been a matter of establishing taxonomies of plot, character, setting, theme. From this practice emerged the characterization of an adventure story set during the late nineteenth century in which a heroic man, poised and ultimately isolated on the frontier between "civilization" and "savagery," defends the interests of the former against the threat of the latter. The setting in which the "civilization-versus-savagery" conflict is played out is the far West of open-range ranching, cattle drives, and Indian wars. Located in this historical moment of white settlement, the adventure is commonly understood to rehearse the theme of progress versus primitivism as a way of celebrating — with what Umberto Eco calls "nostalgic remorse" (10) — the triumph of American nationhood.

Clearly such a description does identify significant characteristics of many westerns. Proposed as a definition sufficient to encapsulate the genre — as it often has been — however, this set of propositions is problematic. First, there is the too easy slippage from description to prescription. Any narratives of the West which don't manifest the above characteristics are excluded from the "canon" of popular western literary history, whether or not they have attracted a large readership.

A couple of historical examples make the point. Ann S. Stephens' *Malaeska; or, the Indian Wife of the White Hunter* was the first of the Beadle and Adams dime novels, reprinted by that firm in 1860 from an 1839 story paper, and its claims to occupy a central position in the story of the popular West are considerable. It was the first of a cheap series now considered central to the development of the mass-produced and-distributed western. It was the first of that series to be set in what was then the "Wild West" (that is, the western region beyond a certain density of white settlement, in this case the Hudson Valley). And its cast of white hunters, bloodthirsty natives, romantic Indian maidens, and aristocratic New Yorkers rivaled the contemporary fiction of James Fenimore Cooper both in melodrama and in symbolic potential. A crucial difference, however, lies in the novels' readings of American history. Cooper consistently ends with an aristocratic marriage which celebrates

864

the triumph of Euro-American settlement, however qualified by the retreat to the wilderness of the heroic Leatherstocking. *Malaeska* ends with the suicide of the handsome young hero, destroyed by the revelation of his miscegenous parentage; the death of his grieving Indian mother; and the collapse of his dead father's aristocratic line. While *Malaeska* sold well in its first and second manifestations, it did not become the preferred formula for the mass-produced western, either at the time (Beadle and Adams' chief editor preferred Edward S. Ellis' imitation of Cooper, *Seth Jones*) or retrospectively, in literary histories of the popular West which consistently ignore the work.

A similar fate attended Frances McElrath's *The Rustler* (1902). Published in the same year as Owen Wister's *The Virginian* and set at the same historical moment, during the Johnson County War, *The Rustler* reads like a point-by-point refutation of Wister's heroic optimism. In both novels, the romantic plot is driven by the attraction of a western cowboy-turned-ranch-foreman for an eastern lady come west as schoolmarm. *The Virginian* brings those types together in a final marriage which harmonizes differences of class, region, culture, and gender. *The Rustler* ends in criminality and death for the cowboy and a life of penance for the schoolmarm, an outcome which can be read as a warning about the classed system of the West quite at odds with Wister's representation of the frontier as democratic open space unfettered by Old World social distinctions. While Wister's novel has been hailed as the origin of the modern western ever since, McElrath's novel has sunk from the record. With the effacement of that counter-narrative, a more complex sense of the choices and interests informing the construction of literary history is lost. That the gendering of the record continues is demonstrated by the accounts here of "Women Writers of Popular Westerns" and "The Market for Western Fiction." Both Vicki Piekarski and Judy Alter document the considerable participation of women in the production and consumption of popular westerns, as authors and purchasers of fiction. Simultaneously, they note the repeated effacing of that activity. Many best-selling women authors of westerns have felt compelled to abbreviate their names into ungendered initials. And however much market analysis reveals a female audience for westerns, the "cultural space" of the genre is still predominantly construed as male. One might speculate that the attraction for some women authors and readers is precisely their infiltration of a male space: identities and voices reading themselves back into a genre from which the record

865

erases them. That this cultural activity can lead to tentative community, at least, is suggested by the recent establishment of a group called Women Writing the West, discussed by Judy Alter.

The "lost voices" syndrome is not confined to gender. As Geoff Sadler's essay, "European Popular Westerns," reminds us, there is an extensive arena of western production beyond America which is barely acknowledged in most accounts of the form. George G. Gilman, for example, is often cited as the leading practitioner of "adult westerns" (that is, westerns emphasizing graphic violence and sex) without recognition of his British nationality and residence. Resituating him in the network of European authors and publishers of popular westerns might suggest one way of reading the exaggeration of sex and violence in the western in its mutation into the "adult" version. Serving different interests — including Old World sexual politics — the genre accrues different associations and accentuates its mythic iconography differently at this cultural remove.

Sadler's essay also reminds us of cultural specificity. At least since Buffalo Bill's Wild West toured Canada and Europe from 1885, the commercialized West has been touted as a global form. Its successful marketing and broad consumption in other countries — now, from the Hebrides to Korea — are frequently read as proof of the western's ability to speak to and for a broad range of peoples and social situations. The claim is that its heroic, individualistic, democratic accents are universally applicable. Pamela Smorkaloff's essay, "The Popular West Across the Americas," however, suggests that the transculturation of the very concept of "the West" is considerably more complex. In popular forms south of the U.S. border, the West serves as the occasion first for reversing the "civilization versus barbarism" paradigm then for complicating simplistic antinomies of ethnic, racial, and national identity. Resituated within a hemispheric context, the U.S. definition of the "popular West" looks narrow, intensely specific, and ideologically self-interested. Blake Allmendinger's account of "African-Americans and the Popular West" brings that critique home, exposing the limits of the national "we" in whose name the western often pretends to speak. To address the representation of and participation by African-Americans in the production of a popular West is to shift the very ground of the conventional definition away from open-range romance towards tales of urban crime and popular musical forms. Similarly, as Robert Gish points out in "Writing Back: The American Indian Western," to transvaluate ethnocentric representations is necessarily to resist received wisdom and conventional forms. The point is not that the standard definition is wrong but that it describes a particular version of the commercialized West, produced, marketed and consumed by particular interests and social groups.

What has sustained this definition is the convergence of men's worlds. If the West has been seized as a proving ground for men by mass-market fiction, it has been aided and abetted by the scholarly practices of a patriarchal academy. A fundamental formalism—critiqued by John Cawelti in his retrospective assessment of his own key work, "The Six-Gun Mystique: Twenty-Five Years After"—dominated pedagogy and scholarship in the post-World War II, heavily male university English departments, which employed and trained critics of popular western American fiction. (Indeed, as recently as the 1980s, my own work was heavily conditioned by this methodological environment.) In decontextualizing literary analysis, New Criticism also obscured the ideological interests informing its interpretations and aesthetic values. When this approach was transferred to popular fiction (in itself a welcome transgression of New Criticism's edicts about the proper sphere of literary interpretation), it accepted a fairly static classification of "the popular." Mass sales were taken as sufficient measure of popular significance without sustained interrogation of either the socio-political forces which control selective mass marketing or the complex negotiations between production and consumption which produce the label "popular." The manifestly masculinist western sustains its position as the defining narrative of the popular West, then, partly via the hidden masculinism of the taxonomic process.

One consequence of adhering to traditional categories has been a continued preoccupation with a fixed "high-low" cultural divide. Considerable critical energy has been diverted into defenses of the formulaic western against accusations of its "subliterary" status.[2] This acquiescence to aesthetic hierarchy has also inhibited extensive attention to the details of individual western authors' writings and biographies, as if the large-scale production of the genre made appropriate only the broadest critical brushstrokes. The essays here on Zane Grey, B.M. Bower, Max Brand, and Louis L'Amour are triply corrective of that impression: they draw attention to the published work that does exist on these authors, they claim a place for individual popular authorship which did not exist in A Literary History of the American West, and they demonstrate the very particular relations (between life and work, individual inventions and genre conventions) influencing their different outputs. These authors all participated knowingly in formulaic work to the extent that they wrote within, and in response to, established narrative forms and they hoped to win a large audience. Yet the details of each author's story complicate easy assumptions about the automatic or undifferentiated quality of popular western writing.

Re-embedding the genre in the historical moments and material conditions of its making — as Richard Slotkin does, here in his survey, "The Movie Western," and expansively in his trilogy on the western from the 1600s to the 1980s — reorients analysis away from a preoccupation with what popular culture is and towards the more profitable (and politically significant) question of what popular culture does. Among other effects, a historicized analysis reopens the question of where cultural meaning is made: at the point of production, reception, or in some negotiation between the two. Alter's detailed account of marketplace conditions suggests the multiplicity of calculations affecting the selection, packaging and sale of western titles. Complicating the circulation of cultural meaning further is the case, argued persuasively by Lee Mitchell in "Critical Theory, Heading West," that texts mean differently in different times, to different readers, in different cultural situations.

That sense of multiple, sometimes contradictory readings, informs Victoria Lamont's essay on B. M. Bower. Reading from an explicitly feminist position, Lamont interprets Bower's work in quite different terms from those which inform previous commentary on this important woman author. In effect, this essay argues that Bower's work enables dominant, subordinate and negotiated readings (to use Stuart Hall's terms), rather than being entirely contained by its conformity to a fictional formula which favors men. Although the methodology is different, a similar argument drives Norris Yates' recent inquiry into the "double-voiced discourse" sustained by women writers of formula westerns. And Jane Tompkins' autobiographical responses to writings by Louis L'Amour, Zane Grey, and Owen Wister demonstrate that the masculinist dynamics of these narratives do not necessarily determine the scope of a reader's reactions. Critical times may finally be changing.

Of all the popular genres — detective fiction, science fiction, romance, fantasy — the western has been most resistant to theorized interrogations, presumably because the genre is so enmeshed in nationalist mythology and so equipped — by setting, plot, and politics — to

868

naturalize its own ideologies and commodification. As Lee Mitchell argues, it is astonishing that a narrative so manifestly preoccupied with the wielding of power has not attracted sustained Foucaultian analysis. It might also be expected that a genre in which marketing strategies and political consensus-making are so closely matched would have figured centrally in Gramscian critiques of cultural hegemony. Theories of gender performativity, as elaborated by poststructuralist feminism, seem nicely applicable to narratives which so insistently and ritualistically enact gender difference. And westerns seem an obvious case study to pursue within an understanding of popular culture as "contested terrain" on which different social groups struggle to assert their interests. As Janice Radway asked about women readers of romance, what do people do with westerns in their everyday lives? Critical resistance seems specifically connected with print forms: the past twenty years have seen considerable revisionism in western historiography and theoretical readings in western film criticism, but the call for a broader, more interdisciplinary approach to popular western writings (also at least twenty years old) has not been consistently answered.[3] Partly because of that imbalance, as well as this volume's larger project, this section concentrates primarily on written work. The symbiosis between print and other representational forms in constructing the popular West, however, is acknowledged by the inclusion of Richard Slotkin's analysis of the cultural work of western movies as well as several contributors' glancing beyond fiction to other popular media.

In promoting informed revisionism, this section does not intend to sweep away one critical discourse to replace it with another orthodoxy. The essays here amount to a kaleidoscope of voices, concepts, and knowledges. Some contributors map new writing and "lost voices," some consider the impact of certain interpretive turns in the academy, and some attend to the participation and incorporation of "minority" figures in popular literatures of the West. Different perspectives and vocabularies implicitly quarrel with each other in purposeful ways: for some commentators, the key measure is literary value; for others, the opportunities afforded by the genre for the consolidation of cultural identities and power bases. At odds, too, are the ruling concepts of the various discourses which combine to make up our sense of the West. Publishers are adopting the term "frontier" (in preference to "western") at the very moment when followers of the New History are retreating from the "f"-word as a Eurocentric misnaming of a much more complex and unstable

869

zone of contact and conflict. Racial and ethnic minorities function as sellable innovations to the genre for commercial interests, while the same "minorities," Blake Allmendinger and Robert Gish tell us, are redefining the ground from beneath the popular's feet.

The received, formalist definition of the popular western, then, has enabled the reproduction of socio-political power from the material site of the West to its narratives to the canonization of one version of that narrative. Rethinking the genre requires continual reconceptualizing of it within a larger cultural space. We need to keep the process of popularization front and center, by inquiring into the forces which promote one version of western adventure and asking whose interests are served by a narrative which represents American history as the polarization of cultural, racial and gendered values, all resolved in rituals of male violence. Annette Kolodny's call to reformulate the term "frontier" might well serve a larger reorientation of popular western studies: she argues for the reconceptualization of frontier as "that liminal landscape of changing meanings on which distinct human cultures first encounter one another's 'otherness' and appropriate, accommodate, or domesticate it through language...frontier as an inherently unstable locus of... environmental transitions and cultural interpenetrations" ("Letting Go" 9-10). We also need to keep rediscovering and debating the alternative narratives which have been evacuated from the most visible literary histories of the popular West. Even limiting the definition of popularity to large sales, clearly there have been widely read tales of the West which positioned women — white and Native — very differently from what now is generally considered the paradigmatic western story. And even accepting the established taxonomy of formulaic characteristics, there are contributions which stretch and challenge the triumphant meanings most visibly associated with western adventure. If we go beyond these cultural measures and reattach "popular" to its original sense of "belonging to the people," we can discover all kinds of counter-narratives — produced and valued by communities of African Americans, Native Americans, non-Americans — which complicate the literary history exponentially. The point is that the cultural space of the West is neither closed nor fixed, despite the presence of commercial and scholarly gatekeepers. At the very least, cracking open fissures in the definition of the popular West gives access to other voices, other possibilities, and other perspectives. In their various ways, the essays in this section facilitate that process.

Notes

1. As recently as *A Literary History of the American West* (1987), for all their immensely valuable discussion of popular westerns, Marsden and Nachbar continue to characterize western fans as exclusively male, westerns as representative of a "golden age" (for whom? one is tempted to ask), and the genre as possessing "universal appeal" (1263, 1277, 1278).

2. This preoccupation is perceptible from Frederick Whittaker to T. K. Whipple (505-506), to James K. Folsom's "coming of age" rhetoric (13-14).

3. See, for example, Richard W. Etulain (650/8-651/9).

Selected Bibliography

Bold, Christine. *Selling the Wild West: Popular Western Fiction, 1860 to 1960.* Bloomington: Indiana University Press, 1987.

Butler, Judith. *Gender Trouble: Feminism and the Subversion of Identity.* New York: Routledge, 1990.

Cawelti, John. *Adventure, Mystery and Romance: Formula Stories as Art and Popular Culture.* Chicago: University of Chicago Press, 1976.

———. *The Six-Gun Mystique.* Bowling Green, Ohio: Bowling Green State University Press, 1971.

Cooper, James Fenimore. *The Pioneers; or, The Sources of the Susquehanna.* Philadelphia: Lea and Blanchard, 1823; rpt., New York: Viking Penguin, 1988.

———. *The Last of the Mohicans; A Tale of 1757.* Philadelphia: Lea and Blanchard, 1826; rpt., New York: Viking Penguin, 1986.

———. *The Prairie: A Tale.* Philadelphia: Lea and Blanchard,1827; rpt., New York: Viking, 1976.

———. *The Pathfinder; or, The Inland Sea.* Philadelphia: Lea and Blanchard, 1840; rpt., New York: Viking Penguin, 1989.

———. *The Deerslayer; or, The First Warpath.* Philadelphia: Lea and Blanchard, 1841; rpt., New York: Viking Penguin, 1987.

Denning, Michael. "The End of Mass Culture." In *Modernity and Mass Culture.* James Naremore and Patrick Brantlinger, eds. Bloomington: Indiana University Press, 1991. Pp. 253-268.

Eco, Umberto. *Travels in Hyperreality.* William Weaver, trans. London: Pan/Picador, 1987.

Ellis, Edward S. *Seth Jones; or, The Captives of the Frontier.* Beadle's Dime Novels, No. 8, 1860.

Etulain, Richard W. "Riding Point: The Western and Its Interpreters." In *The Popular Western: Essays Toward a Definition.* Richard W. Etulain and Michael T. Marsden, eds. Ohio: Bowling Green University Popular Press, 1974. Pp. 5-9.

Folsom, James K. "Introduction." *The Western: A Collection of Critical Essays.* Englewood Cliffs, New Jersey: Prentice-Hall, 1979. Pp. 1-14.

Hall, Stuart. "Encoding/Decoding." *Culture, Media, Language.* Stuart Hall, et al., eds. London: Hutchinson, 1980. Pp. 128-138.

———. "Notes on Deconstructing 'The Popular.'" *People's History and Socialist Theory.* Raphael Samuel, ed. London: Routledge and Kegan Paul, 1981. Pp. 227-240.

Johannsen, Albert. *The House of Beadle and Adams and Its Dime and Nickel Novels.* 3 vols. Norman: University of Oklahoma Press, 1950.

871

Kolodny, Annette. *The Land Before Her: Fantasy and Experience of the American Frontiers, 1630-1860*. Chapel Hill: University of North Carolina Press, 1984.

————. *The Lay of the Land: Metaphor as Experience and History in American Life and Letters*. Chapel Hill: University of North Carolina Press, 1975.

————. "Letting Go Our Grand Obsessions: Notes Toward a New Literary History of the American Frontiers." *American Literature,* 64 (March 1992): 1-18.

Marsden, Michael T., and Jack Nachbar. "The Modern Popular Western: Radio, Television, Film and Print." *A Literary History of the American West.* J. Golden Taylor, et al., eds. Fort Worth: Texas Christian University Press, 1987. Pp. 1263-1282.

McElrath, Frances. *The Rustler: A Tale of Love and War in Wyoming*. New York: Funk and Wagnalls, 1902.

Radway, Janice A. *Reading the Romance: Women, Patriarchy, and Popular Literature*. Chapel Hill: University of North Carolina Press, 1991.

Slotkin, Richard. *Regeneration Through Violence: The Mythology of the American Frontier, 1600-1860*. Middletown, Connecticut: Wesleyan University Press, 1973.

————. *The Fatal Environment: The Myth of the Frontier in the Age of Industrialization, 1800-1890*. New York: Atheneum, 1985.

————. *Gunfighter Nation: The Myth of the Frontier in Twentieth-Century America*. New York: Atheneum, 1992.

Smith, Henry Nash. *Virgin Land: The American West as Symbol and Myth*. Cambridge: Harvard University Press, 1950.

Stephens, Ann S. *Malaeska: The Indian Wife of the White Hunter*. Beadle's Dime Novels, No. 1, 1860.

Tompkins, Jane. *West of Everything: The Inner Life of Westerns*. New York: Oxford University Press, 1992.

Whipple, T. K. "American Sagas." *The Saturday Review of Literature* (February 7, 1925): 505-506

White, Richard, and Patricia Nelson Limerick. *The Frontier in American Culture*. James Grossman, ed. Berkeley: University of California Press, 1995.

Whittaker, Frederick. *Dime Novels: A Defense by a Writer of Them*. Philadelphia: Chas. H. Austin, 1938.

Williams, Raymond. "Popular." In *Keywords: A Vocabulary of Culture and Society*. London: Fontana, 1988. Pp. 236-238.

Wister, Owen. *The Virginian: A Horseman of the Plains*. New York: Macmillan, 1902; rpt., New York: Viking Penguin, 1988.

Yates, Norris. *Gender and Genre: An Introduction to Women Writers of Formula Westerns, 1900-1950*. Albuquerque: University of New Mexico Press, 1995.

Richard Slotkin

The Movie Western

The western is the oldest of American movie genres and an essential part of American mythology. Its central tropes, structures, imagery and ideological charge derive from the myth of the frontier: America's oldest national myth, rooted in the history of two centuries of westward expansion.

Motion pictures became viable as a medium for popular culture at the very moment (1893-1903) when the historical frontier was passing away. Early films played to popular interest in the West by exploiting authentic scenes, personages, and events associated with the latter days of westward expansion. Western movies drew on a mere forty years of regional history: from the Gold Rush of 1849 to the heyday of the range cattle business (1870-1890). Yet the power of their visual imagery and cinematic narratives was such that this narrow slice of time has come to symbolize the whole history of expansion that preceded it; so that, for most Americans, the forty years of six-guns and Stetsons are better known and more significant than two centuries of long rifles and buckskins.

The western's mythic space is a geography divided by significant and signifying borders, usually marked by some strong visual sign: the palisade of the desert fort; a mountain pass or a river; the white empty street of the town. Through persistent association, these border-signs have come to symbolize a range of fundamental ideological differences. The most basic of these is that between the natural and the human or social realms, "wilderness" versus "civilization." This opposition is given depth and complexity by metaphors that liken it to social and ideological divisions: between white civilization and redskin savagery; between a corrupt metropolitan "East" and a rough but virtuous "West"; between tyrannical old proprietors (big ranchers) and new, progressive entrepreneurs (homesteaders); between the engorged wealth of industrial monopolies (railroads) and the hard-earned property of citizens (farmers); between old technologies (stagecoaches) and new (railroads); between the undisciplined rapacity of frontier criminals and the lawman's determination to establish order. The borderline may also be construed as the moral opposition between the violent culture of men and the Christian culture associated with women.

This mythic space is also identified with the American past. In watching a western, we are asked to think of ourselves as looking across the border that divides past and present, in order to recover a "genetic" myth, which displays the (putative) origins of our present condition. By so doing (the films suggest) we may find precedents for responding to present crises.

The action of the narrative requires that the borders be crossed by a hero whose character is so mixed that he can operate effectively on both sides of the line. Through this transgression of the borders, through combat with the dark elements on the other side, the heroes reveal the meaning of the frontier line even as they break it down. In the process they evoke the elements in themselves, or their society, which correspond to the "dark"; and by destroying the dark elements and colonizing the border, they violently purge darkness from themselves and the world.

The narrative that traverses the mythic landscape is a tale of personal and social "regeneration through violence." Every subtype of the western has its special ways of rationalizing and staging the culminating shoot-out. But in general, when we are told that a certain film is a western, we confidently expect that it will find its moral and emotional resolution in a singular act of violence. Moreover, since the western offers itself as a myth of American origins, it implies that its violence is an essential and necessary part of the process through which American society was established and through which its democratic values are defended and enforced.

William S. Porter's *The Great Train Robbery* (1903) is traditionally cited as both the first narrative film and the first western. Though its claims to priority have been challenged, the film was certainly both an innovative production and a remarkable commercial success. Porter's success invited imitation, which encouraged the expansion of movie production in general and westerns in particular. By 1913 distributors and reviewers were cataloging films in three major categories: "'Drama,' 'Comic,' and 'Western.'"

The West was an attractive subject because moviemakers could draw on a vast popular literature of novels, dime novels, stage melodramas and Wild West Shows, full of ready-made plots and characters and set-piece scenes. They could also exploit surviving remnants of "the real thing." The crime on which Porter's *Great Train Robbery* was based had occurred only three years before the film appeared. Many people celebrated in frontier history and lore — Buffalo Bill and Geronimo, lawmen Wyatt Earp and Bill Tilghman, outlaws Al Jennings and Emmett Dalton — were available to appear on camera. When Thomas Ince filmed *Custer's Last Fight* in 1912, original participants served as actors and technical advisers.

Most silent westerns were "formula" films, featuring stars like Broncho Billy Anderson, W. S. Hart and Tom Mix in predictable, melodramatic plots. As the industry prospered and the genre gained in popularity, a more ambitious type of western was developed: the historical epic, which celebrated the winning of the West as the triumph of civilization over savagery, the "iron horse" over the buffalo. A wave of epics followed the successes of *The Covered Wagon* in 1923 and John Ford and Thomas Ince's *The Iron Horse* in 1924; and westerns as a genre reached a peak of popularity in 1926-1927, just as the economic boom of the "Roaring Twenties" was approaching its height. This popularity was only briefly undercut by the development of sound features (1928-1929).

But during the Great Depression (1929-1939), the Hollywood studios, which dominated American production after 1925, lost interest in the western. From 1931 to 1939 the studios produced only a handful of feature-length westerns — this at a time when Hollywood studios were producing more (and more elaborate) features every year. The epic western's optimistic and progressive reading of American history may have seemed irrelevant to an era of factory closings, breadlines and strikes. The grim ironies of the gangster film seemed a more appropriate interpretation of the real outcome of American "progress"; and the musical comedy or the swashbuckling romance offered an escape from both present pain and historical irony. "Cowboy pictures" survived hard times as "B" westerns: cheaply produced films running between fifty-five and seventy-five minutes, which made up a regular but minor part of an after-noon at the movies.

Then, in 1939, every one of the studios decided that the time had come to bring back the big *historical* western. Their motives were mostly commercial: other action genres seemed to have run their course of popularity. But the studios were also responding to the mood of the historical moment: the New Deal had restored public confidence in the government's capacity to cope with the Depression; and now, with war looming in Asia and Europe, the time seemed right for films that offered a more hopeful and patriotic reading of the American past — a task for which the western had been the traditional vehicle.

This "renaissance of the western" produced a wave of successful feature films between 1939 and 1942 and began a thirty-year period in which westerns were the most consistently popular form of action movie, with both audiences and producers, in the theater and later in the new medium of television.

The "renaissance" westerns made several permanent contributions to the genre. Most were modeled on the historical epics of the silent era, and they firmly established the principle that *westerns are films about American history.* This wave of productions also sent writers and studio research departments looking for new stories and untapped bits of historical lore. Since the history in these films was being looked at for patriotic purposes, the "renaissance" westerns also established the practice of looking to frontier history for imaginative solutions to current problems — economic conflicts, social injustice, war and peace. Films like *Dodge City* and *Union Pacific* (1939), *Santa Fe Trail* (1940) and *Western Union* (1941) associate the western with the heroic phase of America's industrial growth. *Dodge City* opens on a race between a stagecoach and a locomotive of the new transcontinental railroad: "That's the symbol of America's future. Progress! Iron men and iron horses, you can't beat 'em."

Westerns also co-opted the criticism of American capitalism that had been generated by the culture of the Depression. One of the most popular of the new films was *Jesse James* (1939), directed by Henry King: a sympathetic portrait of the outlaw as a populist rebel. Outlaw westerns emphasized the dark side of American progress by making a villain of the railroad — a prime symbol of "progress" in movies since *The Iron Horse* (1924). The "cult of the outlaw" proved one of the most durable types of western, spawning many imitations over the years, from *Return of Frank*

James (1940) and *When the Daltons Rode* (1941) to *True Story of Jesse James* (1957), *Butch Cassidy and the Sundance Kid* (1969), *The Outlaw Josey Wales* (1976), *The Long Riders* (1981) and *Young Guns* (1988).

One of the most important films of the period was John Ford's *Stagecoach* (1939). This film is unique among its coevals of the "renaissance": a formalist study in an era of historical literalism, it also offers an ironic commentary on the assumptions of the "progressive" westerns of the period. *Stagecoach* revealed a "classical" structure latent in the form and suggested, at a relatively early point in the genre's revival, some of its artistic possibilities.

The outbreak of war briefly interrupted the further development of the western. From 1942 to 1945 the new genre of the combat film became the dominant form of action movie — although a few "serious" westerns were made (*Ox-Bow Incident*, 1942; *The Outlaw*, 1943). But after victory and demobilization Hollywood came home to the western, picking up pretty much where the "renaissance" left off.

The years from 1946 to 1969 were a "golden age" during which westerns became the most consistently popular of American movie genres. From 1950 to 1969, Hollywood generally produced between fifteen and thirty-eight western features a year. There was a sharp drop in productions in 1957-1959, in response to the advent of television and the collapse of the studio system. But by 1960 big westerns were making a strong comeback in theaters, and television westerns were enjoying Nielsen shares of better than thirty-three percent. From 1957 to 1961 half of the top-rated television shows were westerns.

The "golden age" metaphor is justified from an artistic perspective as well. By the time of the Korean War, the western had developed a symbolic language that was rich in meaning and widely understood by both the producing communities and the general public. The possibilities of the genre were explored intensively and with a high degree of sophistication by filmmakers who used its vocabulary to address a wide range of difficult or taboo subjects like race relations, sexuality, psychoanalysis, and Cold War politics.

As in the past, films about epic cattle drives and the building of great ranches or railroads explored the economic rationales for corporate gigantism and entrepreneurial freedoms: *Duel in the Sun* (1946), *Sea of Grass* (1947), and *Red River* (1948). The town-tamer western — films ranging from John Ford's classic version of Wyatt Earp in *My Darling Clementine* (1946) to Fred Zinneman's bleak and disillusioned *High Noon*

(1952) — dealt with crime as an obstacle to progress and starkly posed questions about law and justice, individual responsibility and social solidarity. Increasingly, the heroes of these films appear as loners, who have to uphold the code of heroic values in the face of public misunderstanding and social cowardice. Anthony Mann gave a dark psychological dimension to the image of the solitary western hero in a series of films starring James Stewart: *Winchester 73* (1950), *Bend of the River* (1952), and *Naked Spur* (1953).

The "cult of the outlaw" metamorphosed into the gunfighter movie: *The Gunfighter* (1950), *Shane* (1953), *Fastest Gun Alive* (1956), *Tin Star* (1958), *No Name on the Bullet* (1959), *Last of the Fast Guns* (1960), *Invitation to a Gunfighter* (1964). These are highly stylized action films, which transform the western shoot-out into a ritual. The gunfighter was a new kind of hero: neither populist outlaw nor elected sheriff, but a professional killer. Gunfighter heroes were telling symbols for Cold War America: alienated men, as watchful as any paranoid, fastest on the draw but menaced by every kid with a gun — at once the most powerful and the most vulnerable men in the world.

Westerns also modeled Cold War politics more explicitly. Beginning with Ford's famous "cavalry trilogy" of 1948-1950 (*Fort Apache, Rio Grande, She Wore a Yellow Ribbon*) the cavalry western provided a way to treat the concerns of the war film — choice of enemy, preparedness, whether to attack first or defend — in the language of the western.

But in the era of McCarthyism and the blacklist, when political expression of any kind was dangerous for a filmmaker, westerns also provided safe vehicles for disguised commentary on the most divisive issues. In 1950 *Broken Arrow* and *Devil's Doorway* showed Indians as sympathetic figures: victims of racial injustice, yet still willing to make peace with whites. Westerns like these addressed the two most sensitive issues of the time: coexistence with the Soviets in foreign affairs and the domestic issue of racial segregation and discrimination.

The best western films of this period, like John Ford's *The Searchers* (1956), are an American cinematic equivalent of classical drama. The characters are both historically representative Americans and heroic archetypes; they contend with forces that threaten the most basic values and the very existence of society. They inhabit a setting which is both a credible image of the historical frontier and a symbolic battleground for the eternal struggle of good and evil. In Ford's hands, the concise symbolism of the western acquires rich psychological and social resonances; his films retell the old myths, yet also expose their dark side — the tangling together of heroic idealism, bigotry and violence.

In the westerns of the 1960s, filmmakers played out two of the most important initiatives of John F. Kennedy's New Frontier: support for the civil rights movement at home and engagement in counterinsurgency warfare in the Third World — especially Vietnam. The late 1950s and early 1960s saw a spate of "civil rights westerns" dealing with themes of integration and racial tolerance: *Trooper Hook* (1957) and *Tin Star* (1958) dealt with interracial (white/Indian) marriage. In *Walk Like a Dragon* (1960) a Chinese immigrant Americanizes himself by learning the art of the gunfighter. But often the racism expelled by the front door sneaks in the back: in *Sergeant Rutledge* (1960) and *Sergeants Three* (1962) heroic black cavalrymen prove their entitlement to equality by fighting "fiendish" Apaches.

The western also went international in the 1960s. American western films and television programs became staples of European and Japanese entertainment. Italian and Spanish studios turned out numerous "spaghetti westerns," mixing second-rank American stars and character actors (Yul Brynner, Clint Eastwood, Lee Van Cleef) with European supporting casts. European directors and screenwriters treated the western as a cinematic formula, uncomplicated by the special mythic and historical associations that influenced American producers and audiences. Imported to the United States, their films had the effect of heightening the awareness of formula and the importance of style in the work of American directors — most notably Clint Eastwood and Sam Peckinpah.

The dominant type of western during the period, on both sides of the Atlantic, was the "counterinsurgency western." In *Vera Cruz* (1954) and, most notably, in *The Magnificent Seven* (1960) Hollywood anticipated the direction of American policy by sending a group of American gunfighters south of the border to aid democratic Mexican peasants fighting against oppressive foreign dictators and native warlords. The gunfighters in these films symbolically act out the program Kennedy and his advisers had designed for the Green Berets in the Third World. The development of these westerns paralleled the course of the Vietnam War. The New Frontiersmen's naïve expectation that American guns and know-how would readily transform peasants into democratic self-defense forces was reflected in films like *The Magnificent Seven* (and its sequels), *The Professionals* (1966) and *100 Rifles* (1968).

As the public began to question the way the war was being fought, westerns like Peckinpah's *Major Dundee* (1965) also began to raise questions about the logic of our policy and to register the public's sense that the costs of the war were out of proportion to its nominal objectives. In Peckinpah's *The Wild Bunch* (1969), a group of American outlaws confronts a military dictator who has imprisoned and tortured their comrade, a Mexican with revolutionary sympathies. But the classic rescue scene and the traditional final shoot-out between democratic good and evil tyranny soon degenerates into a general massacre, escalating from single-shot six-guns to heavy machine guns and hand grenades, killing the rescuers and the rescued, dictators and civilians—the perfect visualization of the phrase, spoken by an American captain in 1968, that came to embody the ultimate absurdity of the war: "We had to destroy the city in order to save it."

The war that divided the nation split the western along political lines. Pro-Indian westerns like *Little Big Man* and *Soldier Blue* (1970) showed Americans as perpetrators of atrocities, not rescuers, and became explicit vehicles for anti-war statements; while more traditional portraits of Apache cruelty were given a pro-war slant in films like *Stalking Moon* (1968) and *Ulzana's Raid* (1972).

What is most remarkable about the westerns of this period is that they were the *only* movie genre that dealt with Vietnam while the war was going on. In every other twentieth-century war, major and minor, Hollywood had responded by making fiction films about Americans in combat. But during the longest American war in this century, only one combat film was made—John Wayne's *The Green Berets* (1968), which was not well received. Thus it was the western, and the western alone, which bore the cultural burden of providing or withholding mythological sanction for the war.

When the Vietnam war ended, so did the western's thirty-year boom. In 1971 American studios had produced twenty-nine feature westerns; in 1973 this figure dropped to thirteen and in 1974 to seven. After a brief attempt to revive the genre in 1975 and 1976, Hollywood virtually abandoned the western, and the last western series disappeared from prime-time television in 1975. It seems reasonable to conclude that public revulsion against the memory of a lost war had produced a similar disgust with the genre that had provided that war's mythology. The few big westerns made between 1973 and 1985 were commercial and critical failures. The failure of *Heaven's Gate* (1980) was a catastrophe for the studio concerned. During this period other genres took over some of the themes and story forms that had hitherto belonged to the western: town-tamer and gunfighter westerns gave way to fables of gunslinger cops and urban vigilantes in the *Death Wish* and *Dirty Harry* series; *Star Wars* and *Star Trek* replaced the cavalry and counterinsurgency western, substituting the "final frontier" of outer space for the wild frontier of the Old West.

In the late 1980s a revival of the genre began, motivated in part by nostalgia for old movie forms and styles. The movement owed something to the popular mood of the Reagan presidency, but it was driven by the interests of a new generation of filmmakers who had grown up watching the westerns of the "golden age" and had then studied them formally in film schools. Films like *Heaven's Gate*, *Silverado* (1985), the two *Young Guns* movies (1988, 1990) and *Dances With Wolves* (1992) are deliberate about their attempts to reconstruct the genre as a kind of historical artifact. The exception to this pattern is Clint Eastwood, who began his career playing cowboys during the "golden age," and learned the director's craft making "spaghetti westerns" for Sergio Leone in the early 1960s. Eastwood's westerns are not nostalgia pieces but original variations on classical themes. *High Plains Drifter* (1968) is a surrealistic, sardonic, phantasmagorical take on the classic "gunfighter saves the townspeople" theme. *The Outlaw Josey Wales* (1976) updates the "cult of the outlaw," reflecting the racial and political themes of the 1960s and the Vietnam aftermath. His most celebrated film, *Unforgiven* (1992), is a grim revision of the classic "redeemed gunfighter" story.

Most recent westerns seem designed to call our attention to themes and groups that were usually excluded or demonized in the older westerns—women (*Ballad of Little Jo*, 1993; *Quick and the Dead*, 1995); Native Americans (*Dances with Wolves*); African Americans (*Silverado*, 1985; *The Posse*, 1993). With some exceptions, the new films emphasize the dark side of the western and of American cultural myth. But as these films suggest, the western can be more than a device for reinforcing a mythology of violence and division. Because it is so closely identified with American history, the western provides superb opportunities for artists to creatively and critically re-examine our past and re-imagine our myths.

Selected Bibliography

Bordwell, David, Janet Staiger and Kristin Thompson. *The Classical Hollywood Cinema:*

Film Style and Mode of Production to 1960. New York: Columbia University Press, 1985.

Brownlow, Kevin. *The War, the West, and the Wilderness*. New York: Alfred A. Knopf, 1979.

Buscombe, Edward, ed. *The B F I Companion to the Western*. London: Andre Deutsch/ BFI Publishers, 1988.

Fenin, George and William K. Everson. *The Western: From the Silents to the Seventies*. New York, Penguin, 1973.

French, Philip. *Westerns: Aspects of a Movie Genre*. New York: Viking Press, 1974.

Gallagher, Tag. *John Ford: The Man and His Films*. Berkeley: University of California Press, 1986.

Hardy, Phil. *The Western: The Film Encyclopedia*. New York: William Morrow and Company, 1983.

Kitses, Jim. *Horizons West: Anthony Mann, Budd Boetticher, Sam Peckinpah, Studies of Authorship in the Western*. Bloomington: Indiana University Press, 1969.

Koszarski, Diane Kaiser. *The Complete Films of William S. Hart: A Pictorial Record*. New York: Dover, 1980.

Roddick, Nick. *A New Deal in Entertainment: Warner Brothers in the 1930s*. London: British Film Institute, 1983.

Rosen, Philip, ed. *Narrative, Apparatus, Ideology: A Film Theory Reader*. New York: Columbia University Press, 1986.

Ryan, Michael and Douglas Kellner. *Camera Politica: The Politics and Ideology of Contemporary Hollywood Film*. Bloomington: Indiana University Press, 1988.

Schatz, Thomas. *The Genius of the System: Hollywood Filmmaking in the Studio Era*. New York: Pantheon Books, 1988.

———. *Hollywood Genres: Formulas, Filmmaking, and the Studio System*. Philadelphia: Temple University Press, 1981.

Slotkin, Richard. *Gunfighter Nation: The Myth of the Frontier in Twentieth Century America*. New York: Atheneum, 1992.

Wood, Robin. *Hollywood from Vietnam to Reagan*. New York: Columbia University Press, 1986.

Wright, Will. *Six-Guns and Society: A Structural Study of the Western*. Berkeley: University of California Press, 1975.

John G. Cawelti

The Six-Gun Mystique:
Twenty-Five Years After

In 1984, when I published the second edition of *The Six-Gun Mystique*, I was pretty well convinced that the western was obsolete. There had been little significant creativity in the genre since the early 1970s and the production of television western series had dramatically declined around the same time. The disastrous failure of *Heaven's Gate* in 1980 seemed to symbolize the genre's final demise. Then in 1988 when the superb *British Film Institute Companion to the Western* appeared, it seemed as if the funeral was over and the deceased elegantly buried, for companions and handbooks and guides usually refer to complete and circumscribed texts.

Fortunately, it turned out that these obsequies were a bit premature for there have been a couple of mini-revivals since that time and there were enough important new westerns produced in the early 1990s that some critics were speculating about a renaissance of the form. In the future, I would expect to see recurrent flurries of activity like this, but I suspect that the western has reached the point where it no longer occupies the quasi-ritual position it held during much of the history of film. The decline of the generic western has paralleled the increasing criticism and by now virtual abandonment of the Turner thesis by most younger western historians. These historians have opened up rich new fields of inquiry and also of literary and cinematic possibility with their studies of western history not as an advancing WASP frontier but as conflict and adjustment of cultures, as ecological and technological transformations, and as the "legacy of conquest."

Rereading the original *Six-Gun Mystique* against this background, my strongest impression is the degree to which that book was an exercise in structuralism, though at the time I was hardly familiar with the structuralist critical theories which became so important in the 1970s. My own critical background was the new criticism and to an even greater extent the neo-Aristotelianism of the University of Chicago which was the real source of my version of structural analysis. All three critical methods — the new criticism, neo-Aristotelianism and structuralism — led toward a radical decontextualizing of the literary text. It was this approach, which, applied to popular culture in the 1960s, brought about a dramatic transformation in popular culture studies.

It was an approach which I shared with a great many other students of popular culture, and I think that it was at the time a fruitful one. In the case of the western, it has certainly led to a great richness of scholarly and critical analysis of the generic tradition, of individual writers and directors, and of different subgenres of the western. One excellent example of the fine work inspired by this more structural and artistic approach to the western was Christine Bold's *Selling the Wild West*, which explored the way in which writers' struggles with the publishing imperatives of the western genre were transmuted into an important element of their narratives. We could use a comparable analysis of the western film.

However, it is clearly time for a more complex recontextualizing of popular culture. First of all, it seems to me that *The Six-Gun Mystique* completely failed to deal with the relationship between the western and ideas of regional and national identity. Of all the major popular genres, the western is the one which most expresses some sense of the uniqueness of the American experience and identity. Even when it is made in Italy or Spain, or enacted in theme parks in Germany or quick-draw clubs in France, the western retains its deep connection with America. Even with the western in decline, Reagan, Goldwater and many other late-twentieth-century politicians have often used western images and styles. The West as region is one of those themes which is mentioned in almost every significant discussion of the western hero as archetypal American or of the western landscape as a uniquely American setting, but the western's different visions of the moral, cultural and geographical landscape of the West still await sustained and systematic analysis.

884

Though recent historians have rightly tended to emphasize other factors in American history such as urbanization, immigration, and industrialization, it seems to me time for students of American culture to revitalize the analysis of regional symbolism in American culture which once flourished in such works as William Taylor's *Cavalier and Yankee* or Constance Rourke's studies in American humor. A good study of the western genre as imaginative expression of the West as American region could make a great contribution to this development.

The decline of the western probably reflects our growing uncertainty about American uniqueness and about the special place of the West in establishing that uniqueness. This erosion of the western genre is clearly connected to the increasing abandonment of the Turner thesis and other concepts of American exceptionalism which have so long dominated the historical imagination of Americans. That these long-standing myths of the West and along with them the western as a popular genre are being increasingly relegated to history brings to mind another major weakness of the original *Six-Gun Mystique*: its overall failure to recognize the western as a time- and culture-bound historical production. By emphasizing the archetypal nature of the western (as a good modernist critic should have), I was largely ignoring the importance of the western as an evolving and changing expression of different stages of American cultural history. I tried to rectify this somewhat in my discussion of the western in *Adventure, Mystery and Romance*. Scholars like Will Wright, Jon Tuska, John Lenihan, Kevin Brownlow and many others have dealt with particular phases of the history of the western, greatly enriching our sense of its development over time. But by far the most thorough and nearly definitive work on the evolution of the myth of the West is to be found in Richard Slotkin's important trilogy. The first volume of Slotkin's study, *Regeneration Through Violence*, appeared in 1973 and both defined his conception of the myth of the West and traced its emergence in the New World and its development up until the mid-nineteenth century. The second volume, *The Fatal Environment* (1985), traced the transformations undergone by the myth of the West as it was carried forward into the industrial society of the later nineteenth century and showed how the symbolism and rhetoric developed to glorify the destruction of "savagery" and the revitalization of "civilization" in the New World were adapted to the war between capital and labor and to the explanation and justification of the rise of classes and class conflict in an ostensibly democratic society. *Gunfighter Nation* brings this account up to the present and emphasizes the adaptation of the myth of the West to the justification of America's position as a global power and, in particular, to the explanation of Cold War confrontations and Third World imperialism which Slotkin sees as the final stage in the evolution of the myth. Any future studies of the developing meaning of the myth of the West and the western over the course of American history will obviously have to depend upon and respond to Slotkin's great accomplishment, but there are several different cultural contexts to which Slotkin only minimally addresses himself which are especially important for scholars to deal with in the immediate future. One is the area of gender which has already been examined in a preliminary way by Jane Tompkins in *West of Everything*. In that book Tompkins argues that the western as we know it emerged out of a late-nineteenth-century masculine reaction to the dominance of literary culture by sentimentalism, that powerful synthesis of evangelical Christianity and domesticity that created a massive body of now largely forgotten feminine literature. Though Tompkins' thesis has been attacked for its lack of substantiation, it is surely worth more careful exploration by scholars. Secondly, there is the significance of the western as an arena for the interplay of conflicting value systems. Actually I suggested this in *The Six-Gun Mystique* but failed to pursue it systematically. Finally, we need more analysis of the recent period, in which the western seems to be declining as a myth of America and a mass entertainment but still serves as a residual reservoir of political rhetoric and symbolism.

I'm very happy that *The Six-Gun Mystique* has proved to be of some use over its twenty-five-year history. On the whole, it would seem that this usefulness derived from its emphasis on the artistic autonomy of the genre and from the paradigmatic analysis of the western's structure as a particular kind of story in a particular symbolic setting. But it is now clearly time to put the western back in its complex historical and cultural context and I, for one, am looking forward to how a younger generation of scholars enriches our understanding of the myth of the West and its significance in American cultural history.

Selected Bibliography

Bold, Christine. *Selling the Wild West: Popular Western Fiction, 1860 to 1960*. Bloomington: Indiana University Press, 1987.

Brownlow, Kevin. *The War, the West, and the Wilderness*. New York: Knopf, 1979.

Buscombe, Edward, ed. *The BFI Companion to the Western.* New York: Da Capo Press, 1988.

Cawelti, John G. *Adventure, Mystery and Romance: Formula Stories as Art and Popular Culture.* Chicago: University of Chicago Press, 1976.

————. *The Six-Gun Mystique.* Bowling Green, Ohio: Bowling Green University Popular Press, 1971.

Lenihan, John. *Showdown: Confronting Modern America in the Western Film.* Urbana: University of Illinois Press, 1980.

Limerick, Patricia. *The Legacy of Conquest: The Unbroken Past of the American West.* New York: W. W. Norton, 1987.

Nash, Gerald. *Creating the West: Historical Interpretations 1890-1990.* Albuquerque: University of New Mexico Press, 1991.

Nash, Gerald and Richard Etulain, eds. *The Twentieth Century West: Historical Interpretations.* Albuquerque: University of New Mexico Press, 1989.

Rourke, Constance. *American Humor: A Study of the National Character.* New York: Harcourt, Brace, 1931.

Slotkin, Richard. *The Fatal Environment: The Myth of the Frontier in the Age of Industrialization, 1800-1890.* New York: Atheneum, 1985.

————. *Gunfighter Nation: The Myth of the Frontier in Twentieth Century America.* New York: Atheneum, 1992.

————. *Regeneration Through Violence: The Mythology of the American Frontier, 1600-1860.* Middletown, Connecticut: Wesleyan University Press, 1973.

Taylor, William R. *Cavalier and Yankee: The Old South and American National Character.* New York: G. Braziller, 1961.

Tompkins, Jane. *West of Everything: The Inner Life of Westerns.* New York: Oxford University Press, 1992.

Tuska, Jon. *The Filming of the West.* Garden City, New York: Doubleday, 1976.

Worster, Donald. *Under Western Skies: Nature and History in the American West.* New York: Oxford University Press, 1992.

Wright, Will. *Six Guns and Society: A Structural Study of the Western.* Berkeley: University of California Press, 1975.

Lee Mitchell

Critical Theory, Heading West

It is often assumed that westerns became America's most popular genre because their materials seemed so transparent: men on horseback, empty landscapes, final shoot-outs, all described in words of one syllable. By contrast, the texts to which critical theorists attend are just the opposite: verbally dense and semantically complex. Continental theorists who transformed reading practice in universities a quarter-century ago rarely venture west for their reading and certainly not to a form that has seemed the height of *trivialliteratur*. The western's enthusiasts have returned the compliment by scorning literary theory, and this despite remarkable breakthroughs in assumptions of how we read. Reader-response studies of popular taste; feminist critiques of gender construction; Marxist and Foucaultian indictments of power relations; Lacanian analyses of psychodynamics; the narratological and deconstructionist investigations of Barthes, Derrida, and Genette; even the cross-disciplinary interventions of New Historians: all have taught us how complex the process of reading actually is, whatever the text. Yet with few exceptions, popular westerns continue to be described rather straightforwardly, as if their meaning were easily parsed in terms of landscapes and heroes, of industrialism's deathless nostalgia and scenes of quicksilver violence.

The larger question of *why* the western should have become such a dominant genre, or of *how* materials so removed from most readers' lives continue to fascinate, or of *what* makes some individual westerns (and their authors) more successful than others: these questions have either been taken for granted or simply shunned. Popularity itself, it seems, is reason enough for scorn, both from partisans of western "literature" (who want to distance themselves from westerns in the effort to legitimate other regional writing) and from those engaged in theory. Names like Zane Grey, Max Brand, Luke Short, and Louis L'Amour appear only in passing in *A Literary History of the American West*, while those of Michel Foucault, Fredric Jameson, Jacques Lacan, and Paul de Man appear not at all.

Still, the very popularity of popular culture has had a recent effect on theory, inspiring literary and cultural critics to wonder about the larger meanings being negotiated. And at a time when H. R. Jauss has directed attention to "horizons of expectation" or Pierre Bourdieu inquires into popular taste — at a time when such genres as detective fiction, Disney cartoons, soap opera, pornography, musicals, slasher films, and rap rock have aroused serious critical attention — the western would seem to cry out for more gleeful and sophisticated treatment. After all, the western has been America's national pastime, and countless examples in film, television, stage, as well as literature (ranging from cheap pulp magazines to respected novels) attest to its continuing power over nearly a century. For westerns to evoke complex critical thought, then, they need to be freed from a pair of assumptions: that all instances of the form can be reduced to shared characteristics — a set of common themes or plot turns or settings; and that the variable (hardly transparent) language in which they are written or filmed is worth our close attention.

Henry Nash Smith unfortunately set the terms of discussion in his judgment of westerns as "automatic writing" dictated by an omnipotent culture, allowing him to assume that simple content analysis would reveal the meaning these texts had for readers as well as writers. But there were alternatives. Shortly after the appearance of his otherwise justly influential *Virgin Land* (1950), two of the most brilliant readers of a wide array of popular cultural icons emerged: Marshall McLuhan with *The Mechanical Bride* (1951), and Roland Barthes with *Mythologies* (1957). Both shared Smith's pessimistic view of cultural conditioning, but rather than resign themselves to plot summary, they unmasked a wide array of cultural texts — from comic books, popular advertising, and television wrestling to Charlie McCarthy and Superman — with ingenuity and wit. In thus reading popular documents with an intensity usually reserved for "high" cultural icons, they showed how the conventional split between these realms might be dissolved.

Since then, the most influential work on mass culture has been done by the Birmingham School and Stuart Hall, who conceived of popular texts not as opiates for unthinking consumers but as sites of ongoing struggle for meaning, as fictionalizations of issues that remain highly contested and always partial. Such resonant self-contradiction is actually the source of popular appeal, with a text not simply offering escapist entertainment but serving as both justification and critique of the very issues from which readers think they are escaping. Mass dreams, like individual dreams, always trace a return of the repressed, but in them as well repressed material is neither obvious nor unambiguous. And in the most popular of these mass dreams, the potential for structural complexity matches their capacity at once to reassure and subvert. Like other forms of popular culture, the most successful westerns covertly question the values they proclaim, allowing diverse audiences differing levels of recognition and resistance. They lend themselves to no single nor straightforward reading, attracting disparate audiences precisely because they *do* so effectively satisfy different constituencies. Their readers respond to similar materials in differing ways, constructing texts to suit views diametrically opposed. Like other popular texts, they only seem at first glance to resolve the issues they engage. Looked at methodically, they achieve something more complex: negotiating a constantly threatened middle terrain, offering narrative forms that disguise contradictions in the ideological premises they celebrate.

I would claim—contrary to Smith's unexamined notion that plot alone explains the appeal of popular westerns (a notion endlessly repeated in commentaries since)—that only a closer attention to narrative tenor and stylistic play can help explain the attraction that certain popular texts exert. Only, that is, an approach self-conscious about the means available to narrative—aware of the figurative capabilities of prose, sophisticated about formal analysis, attentive to stylistic choices that may not seem like choices at all—can hope to discover what appealed to an audience familiar with westerns but surprised and delighted by the particular shape they currently take. Reading verbal ploys, rhetorical tropes, and idiosyncratic descriptive maneuvers in Wister or Grey, for example, reveals what their loudly significant plots do not: that narratives distant from the lives of most Americans could capture their imaginations by seeming to resolve contemporary issues (of feminism, the New Woman, masculine ideals) in mutually incompatible ways. That is a trick only style can perform.

To revise our understanding of westerns, a certain theoretical self-consciousness is necessary, even if by itself hardly sufficient. One can fault some of the most theoretically precise studies not for their lack of ambition but rather for a certain doggedness, an insouciance towards detail that merely rewrites Smith's plot summaries as other forms of global analysis. For instance, Will Wright's study of the film western, *Six Guns and Society* (1975), offers an exacting theoretical take on top-grossing films between 1931 and 1972, invoking literary structuralism to define three stages in cultural contradiction. One of the most ambitious studies of the western to date, it nonetheless suffers from a certain the-oretical incoherence, collapsing Vladimir Propp's diachronic sequence of undeviating plot functions together with Claude Lévi-Strauss' syn-chronic pairing of thematic oppositions, as if the two antithetical meth-ods could somehow be combined. More to the point, Wright's effort to see through isolated texts to a master plot ends up confirming instead how much individual details always *do* matter—the non-sequential minutiae of scenery and cinematography, the evocations of music and sound track, the idiosyncrasies of casting, the inflections of dialogue, that also make for successful films. By contrast, Edward Buscombe, Christopher Frayling, and Robert Sklar have resisted claims to theoreti-cal totality and offered less ambitious readings of westerns. Yet by attending to small details in their attempts to explain cinematic success, they point the way to a more fruitful mode.

The question at the heart of the matter is thus: What can be learned through formal means about contested ideals and persistent anxieties that transformed certain westerns into such monsters of popularity at decisive historical moments? More importantly, how are an era's inad-missible disparities, its covert social contradictions, made to seem to contemporaries satisfactorily erased by fictional dynamics? How, in short, is the pain of "what hurts" (to borrow Jameson's terse characteri-zation of "history") so often relieved by strange rhythms incompatible with that pain (102)? The idea hardest for those no longer in the thrall of a given cultural moment to grasp is the curious capacity of art to resolve ideological issues far removed from its ostensible fictive terrain. To gain a better sense of that historically specific response, we need to explore not only the blunt plots so characteristic of such texts but rather all the strange textures, the contours and grains, the idiosyncrasies that draw our eyes away from the center to unlit places where their power resides.

Selected Bibliography

Barthes, Roland. *Mythologies*. Annette Lavers, trans. New York: Hill & Wang, 1972.

Bold, Christine. *Selling the Wild West: Popular Western Fiction, 1860-1960*. Bloomington: Indiana University Press, 1987.

Buscombe, Edward, ed. *The B F I Companion to the Western*. New York: Atheneum, 1988.

Frayling, Christopher. *Spaghetti Westerns: Cowboys and Europeans from Karl May to Sergio Leone*. London: Routledge and Kegan Paul, 1981.

Jameson, Fredric. *The Political Unconscious: Narrative as a Socially Symbolic Act*. Ithaca: Cornell University Press, 1981.

McLuhan, Marshall. *The Mechanical Bride: Folklore of Industrial Man*. Boston: Beacon Press, 1951.

Mitchell, Lee Clark. *Westerns: Making the Man in Fiction and Film*. Chicago: University of Chicago Press, 1996.

Sklar, Robert. "Empire to the West: *Red River* (1948)." In *Movie-Made America: A Social History of American Movies*. New York: Random House, 1975. Pp. 167-181.

Smith, Henry Nash. *Virgin Land: The American West as Symbol and Myth*. Cambridge: Harvard University Press, 1950.

Wright, Will. *Six Guns and Society: A Structural Study of the Western*. Berkeley: University of California Press, 1975.

Judy Alter

The Market for Popular Western Fiction

For most of this century, beginning with the pulps and right on through the paperback explosion in the fifties and sixties and the decline of the popular western in the late seventies and early eighties, it has been a given of book marketing that only men read westerns — and, by extension, only men write them. In addition, the western has been a kind of literary subgenre: the category novel where in 60,000-70,000 words the good guy, wearing the white hat, triumphs over the bad guy, wearing the black hat, in a violent and often bloody final confrontation. As escape literature, the western presented larger-than-life heroes who triumphed in scenes of murder and mayhem — and overlooked the dailyness of life in the American West.

By the 1990s three major changes have come to the marketplace: publishers want longer books, they require more thorough research and historical accuracy, and they look for new subject matter, eschewing the seven basic plots as outlined by Frank Gruber and others.

Marketing statistics clearly tell publishers that between sixty and seventy percent of book buyers in this decade are women. Sales figures tell them that reading audiences are tiring of the traditional category novel. A dramatic drop in the sale of hardcover traditional westerns indicates cutbacks in library and institutional budgets.

The result? Major changes at many publishing houses. The Double D line at Doubleday, published in print runs of under 5000 and sold almost exclusively to libraries by subscription, was discontinued in 1992. By

1994, Fawcett was bowing out of the western market and such houses as Pocket, New American Library, and Zebra were cutting back on the traditional western. In 1994 Pocket once again limited their western line to reprints of classics by Zane Grey and a few others. "It was clear," says Gary Goldstein, senior editor at Berkley Books, "that we couldn't keep doing what we'd been doing." One result of the effort to move away from the ways things had always been done: at Berkley western fiction was retitled "frontier fiction."

In the early eighties, the western series written by a number of authors under a house name was big: the Wagons West series by Dana Fuller Ross did well for Bantam, although there never was anyone named Dana Fuller Ross and several authors contributed volumes to the series. Then there were the Stagecoach books, Cody's Law, the slightly pornographic Longarm series, and many others. But by the nineties the emphasis was on the stand-alone or one-shot novel, the "biggie" like Larry McMurtry's *Lonesome Dove* (1985). Publishers seemed willing to take chances on stand-alone novels by less recognized authors: *Not of War Only* (1994) by Norman Zollinger; *Promised Lands: A Novel of the Texas Revolution* (1994) by Elizabeth Crook; *Empire of Bones* (1993) by Jeff Long; *The Arrowkeeper's Song* (1995) by Kerry Newcomb and *Wind River* (1994) by James Reasoner, authors who had previously written for several series. But the stand-alone category novel, the typical Double D novel of traditional length and plot, faltered, apparently unable to generate sales beyond the 25,000 point.

The one-shot novel is by definition longer than a category novel, and sales representatives were telling publishers that readers wanted that longer novel. The best of these long novels could be counted on for sales between 50,000 and 75,000 copies. Accordingly, in the early nineties, publishers cut their lists, trimming out authors and backlogged manuscripts to concentrate on building the reputation and talent of a limited stable who would write the longer historical novels. The author, not the series, became the selling point.

This shift inevitably had a strong impact on authors' incomes. Writers who had been with one house for years — and many books — found their newest manuscript not accepted; others who had published regularly with several houses sometimes found no publishing home for a new project. "My agent gets wonderful rejection letters," one veteran commented.

Asked if it was still possible to make a living writing westerns, one graduate of the series novels said yes, but it was much harder than it had been. For some novelists who had become "big names" in the western field, things seemed to go unchanged. By the mid-1990s Don Coldsmith's Spanish Bit Series (Doubleday/Bantam) boasted over twenty titles, with no sign of slowing down, and Terry Johnson had eleven titles in print with Bantam and enough of a following to merit his own newsletter. With the 1994 publication of *The Unwritten Order* by John Ames, Bantam demonstrated its willingness to work with new authors—but such examples were all too rare.

Pricing may have accounted for part of the trend to the "big" book: people simply wouldn't pay $4.95 for a paperback novel of less than 200 pages but would pay $9.95 for one of 500 or more pages. One author suggests that financial concerns on the other end dictate the emphasis on stand-alone big books: publishers would rather have a few books that make a lot of money than a lot of books that make a little money.

The reading public wanted more than bulk for their money; they wanted more history—and less unrealistic violence and heroism. The best of the category novelists must be commended for their research and accuracy, but the world of the category western was one of mythic heroes and villains. Reading audiences, perhaps conditioned by such revisionist movies as *Dances with Wolves*, sought novels which presented a realistic—and believable—view of life in the West. Cormac McCarthy's *All the Pretty Horses* (1992) received both popular and critical acclaim, and Elmer Kelton followed his award-winning *Slaughter* (1992) with a sequel titled *The Far Canyon* (1994). Readers of realistic fiction were also critical of details: cover artists couldn't put barbed wire, introduced in Texas in 1873, on the front of a novel set in 1870 in the Dakotas.

Publishers' choices of new manuscripts are in a roundabout way conditioned by the reading public. Sales forces report on what readers are buying, and acquisitions editors respond. One is often hard put to know which comes first: publishers' choices or readers' interest. But, seemingly reflecting popular demand in the nineties, the emphasis in editorial departments is on popular westerns that bring a new wrinkle to old themes. The traditional stories—those seven basic plots—have been told and told again, and the market is open to innovative but not bizarre new directions. In part, this means fiction about American Indians, Hispanics, and women.

The mid-1990s have seen, for instance, publishing houses vying to create strong programs in women's western fiction. One goal of such programs is to attract a crossover audience, to lure the woman who has been reading romances and interest her in reading western historicals, even to interest some men in reading historicals about women in the American West. Jeanne Williams led the way in writing women's fiction of wider appeal with such novels as *Home Mountain* (1990), *The Longest Road* (1993), *The Unplowed Sky* (1994) and others. Tom Beer, former western editor at Bantam/Doubleday/Dell, cited the novels *Libbie* (1994) and *Jessie* (1995) by this author as examples of books aimed toward this crossover market.

Another target reader for the new western is the young male who might be first interested as a teenager in the fiction of Louis L'Amour, for example, and become a lifelong reader. Beer pointed out though that the whole question of reading audiences is "uncharted territory," because publishers do not do exhaustive market studies and demographics are usually anecdotal rather than hard statistics.

Ultimately what happened to the western was that in some sense it grew up and gained respect. Both Beer and Goldstein are quick to credit much of this change to Greg Tobin, former western editor at Bantam/Doubleday. "He was the one," says Goldstein, who once worked under Tobin, "who stood up to the publishers and said just because westerns are popular fiction, they don't have to be in the basement. He brought credibility to his program."

The western is gaining respect, but it's an uphill battle, with many people still amazed to find good writing in a western novel. After a reporter for the *Wall Street Journal* attended the 1994 convention of Western Writers of America, Inc., an article appeared in that newspaper with a tone of amazement, a sort of "Gee, these people write good books!" In truth, recent gains in respect are due to the consistently fine writing of such authors as Elmer Kelton, the dedicated following of writers like Terry Johnston (best known for such mountain-man novels as *Reap the Whirlwind*), and the new, younger writers who can, in Tobin's words, "both research and imagine stories."

Tobin cites a new group called Women Writing the West as a potential breakthrough for western fiction. Essentially an outgrowth of Western Writers of America, this organization, which includes two male editors among its founding members, could do for the western what Sisters in Crime did for mysteries and a coalition of fans and authors did for science fiction. At this writing, with the group less than a year old, it is impossible to cite any concrete achievements it has made. Tobin, who is admittedly "bullish" on the western, believes that breaking the western out of the genre trap can only be done by a grass-roots effort by authors, but it is possible.

From a mid-1990s perspective, it seems that the major changes in the marketplace—the decline of the category novel in favor of the longer historical, the emphasis on widening subject matter to include alternative cultures, the instinct for historical depth—are not will-o'-the-wisp decisions but rather trends that have been a long time building. The future, if the best educated guesses are to be believed, holds more respect for the western as a regional rather than a genre or category work. The market can expect longer, more serious works from fewer authors. For those writers trying to break in, the western may not be a place to begin, because the market has narrowed and those few who make it in the market must be passionate about the subject, rather than just authors looking for a subject. For the popular western, it's a whole new marketplace.

Selected Bibliography

Alter, Judy. *Jessie*. New York: Bantam, 1995.
———. *Libbie*. New York: Bantam, 1994.
Ames, John. *The Unwritten Order*. New York: Bantam, 1994.
Charlier, Marj. "Gang of Offbeat Western Novels Takes Genre by Storm." *Wall Street Journal,* July, 18 1994, B1.
Crook, Elizabeth. *Promised Lands: A Novel of the Texas Revolution*. New York: Doubleday, 1994; rpt., Dallas: Southern Methodist University Press, 1995.
Gruber, Frank. "The Basic Western Novel Plots." In *Writers' Year Book*. Cincinnati: Writers Digest, 1955. Pp. 49-53, 160.
Johnson, Terry. *Dance on the Wind*. New York: Bantam, 1995.
———. *Trumpet on the Land*. New York: Bantam, 1995.
Kelton, Elmer. *The Far Canyon*. New York: Doubleday, 1994.
———. *Slaughter*. New York: Doubleday, 1992.
Long, Jeff. *Empire of Bones*. New York: William Morrow, 1993.
McCarthy, Cormac. *All the Pretty Horses*. New York: Knopf, 1992.
McMurtry, Larry. *Lonesome Dove*. New York: Simon & Schuster, 1985.
Newcomb, Kerry. *The Arrowkeeper's Song*. New York: Bantam, 1995.
Reasoner, James. *Wind River*. New York: Harper, 1994.
Williams, Jeanne. *Home Mountain*. New York: St. Martin's Press, 1990.
———. *The Longest Road*. New York: St. Martin's Press, 1993.
———. *The Unplowed Sky*. New York: St. Martin's Press, 1994.
Zollinger, Norman. *Not of War Only*. New York: TOR, 1994.

Vicki Piekarski

Women Writers of Popular Westerns

Western American fiction in its traditional form — the heroic adventure story — is generally perceived to be a genre written by men, for men, about men. Notwithstanding this male-centered focus, a number of women in the twentieth century were able to carve out for themselves rather successful careers writing this kind of story. In most cases their accomplishments have gone unrecognized. They are overlooked by literary historians, scholars, and students of western fiction. Their contributions are not represented in anthologies of western stories and, with the passage of time, their lives and stories have become all but lost to literary history. Part of the reason, surely, that their western fiction has been overlooked is due to where their stories originally appeared.

In the first half of this century the primary market for western fiction, by women or by men, was the magazine market, especially pulp magazines. Printed weekly or monthly on cheap pulpwood paper, pulp magazines had an almost insatiable need for stories with which to fill double-columned pages that displayed relatively little advertising. Pulp magazines provided a format by which writers could practice and perfect their craft. Conrad Richter, who wrote briefly for the pulps, credited this experience with teaching him how to plot out a story. For the author who could produce quickly and steadily, the reward, regardless of sex, was a regular income. Additional income, prior to the advent of paperback reprints in the 1940s, could be generated through hardcover book sales, both first editions and reprint rights. For some women the only available book market for their longer fiction was among British publishers and many women never published at all outside the magazine market. Yet even publication in book form did not guarantee women writers a place in literary history as it often did their male counterparts.

Another factor that has contributed to the obscurity of female writers of western fiction was that their identities were often concealed through sexually ambiguous pseudonyms, most commonly the use of initials. The problem associated with this practice is illustrated by what happened to Jeanne Williams when she began writing novels for young boys. Her editors assured her that boys did not read books written by women so she used the byline J. R. Williams on her first three young adult books. When the first of these novels, *Tame the Wild Stallion*, won the Cokesbury Book Award in 1957 from the Texas Institute of Letters as the best juvenile of the year, Williams did not learn of the award until two weeks after the presentation ceremony because the organization could not locate any male author named J. R. Williams. Whether this practice was begun by editors to fool the reading audience which they believed to be composed largely of misogynistic males or by female authors to garner an unbiased reading from an editor and thus gain entrance into a male-dominated field may never be known. Nonetheless, the fact remains that even through the 1980s almost any woman attempting to publish a traditional western novel or story automatically affixed a sexually blurred identity to her work. (There are also exceptions, such as Dorothy M. Johnson who established a loyal following for her stories through their publication in *Collier's* or *The Saturday Evening Post* prior to their appearance in book collections.) Yet, clearly, for the majority of women writers what had begun as a perceived necessity became a restrictive tradition. Only recently has there been some sign of an abatement in this practice.

Who were the principal women who wrote adventure stories of the West in the twentieth century and what are their contributions? Any survey must begin with B. M. Bower, who was one of the first women to write traditional westerns and still remains the most visible of all those following in her path. A contemporary of Owen Wister, she pioneered the romantic cowboy story in her own inimitable and unsophisticated style, deemphasizing violence and gunplay — until late in her career. She stressed a sense of light-hearted, frequently slapstick humor, as well as a sense of family often focused exclusively on groups of male characters. It

899

was the success of her interlinked *Flying U* stories — originally appearing in pulp magazines and eventually in hardcover books as fifteen novels and short story collections featuring Chip Bennett and/or members of the Happy Family — that, along with the longevity of her forty-year career, secured her a place in literary history of the western story. Indeed, in a sense, Bower has become the token female western writer among scholars, while the entire scope of her work — some seventy novels and hundreds of short stories — has yet to receive the kind of thorough critical assessment it warrants.

Emerging on the scene ten years after Bower began writing, Honoré Willsie Morrow attempted in seven novels to expand western storylines to encompass feminist ideas as well as political and social issues. Over the years her work has generated a modicum of critical attention, although much of it has been directed at her historical novels set outside the American West or at her biographical novels, primarily the fictional trilogy about Abraham Lincoln known collectively as *The Great Captain* (1930). Morrow was born in Ottumwa, Iowa, in 1880. Though in her adulthood she visited the West and wrote about the West, she remained an easterner, closely tied to her New England roots, a circumstance unusual among women western writers. She was published in many of the slick women's magazines of her day, contributing nonfiction or fictional pieces, only some with western themes. For five years she was editor of *The Delineator*.

Morrow's first novel, *The Heart of the Desert* (1913), ran to six printings and is certainly of literary interest because the heroine ends up being happily married to a full-blooded Indian. The narrative concludes with the couple kissing and riding off into "the desert sunset." This stands in contrast to Zane Grey's *The Vanishing American*, serialized eleven years later in *Ladies' Home Journal*, where a similar miscegenation theme was considered potentially so shocking for readers that the author was forced to have Nophaie, a Navajo, die before he and the white heroine could marry. Even fifty years after Morrow's novel it was still considered taboo for an interracial marriage to be shown ending happily: in Jane Barry's *A Time in the Sun* (1962) the heroine's Apache husband dies.

Morrow's subsequent western novels deserve attention but for other reasons: their concern with women's issues and their themes of civic duty and responsibility for men as well as for women. That Morrow could write such unconventional western stories and have them published was related, surely, to the fact that Frederick A. Stokes was her publisher, a company well known for its controversial list of titles. Good examples of Morrow's unique approach are found in *Still Jim* (1915), *Judith of the Godless Valley* (1922), and *Exile of the Lariat* (1923). This last title remains a rare early example of a political western.

Compared to Bower or Morrow, Cherry Wilson is virtually unknown today. Yet in a twenty-year career she produced over 200 short stories and short novels, numerous serials, and five hardcover books; six motion pictures were based on her fiction. Readers of *Western Story Magazine*, the highest paying of the Street & Smith publications where Wilson was a regular contributor, held her short stories in high regard. Her short fiction was often singled out in comments to the editor as the best the magazine had to offer, along with Max Brand's short novels and serials. Wilson moved from Pennsylvania with her parents to the Pacific Northwest when she was sixteen. She gained some experience writing for newspapers as she and her husband led a nomadic life. When Bob Wilson fell ill in 1924, the couple stopped traveling, took up a homestead, and to earn money Wilson decided to write western fiction. Acceptance of her first story by *Western Story Magazine* began what would prove a long-standing professional relationship with Street & Smith magazine editors.

If thematically Wilson's fiction is similar to B. M. Bower's, stylistically her stories are less episodic and, with growing experience, exhibit a greater maturity of sensibility. Her early work, especially, parallels Bower rather closely in that she developed a series of interconnected tales about the cowhands of the Triangle Z Ranch. There is also a similar emphasis on male bonding and comedic scenes — "All-in" explains how the cowpunchers acquire instruments to form the Triangle Z all-brass band, and "Triangle Z's All-Brass Serenade" shows this band serenading a Spanish señorita with an imperfect rendition of "Old Black Joe"! She also varied the series by borrowing an idea from Peter B. Kyne's *The Three Godfathers* (1913), making her cowpunchers cooperative caretakers of an orphan in seven of the stories, beginning with "Hushaby's Partner" (1926). Perhaps the most unusual and interesting of the Triangle Z stories is "Shootin'-up Sheriff" (1929) in which a town is taken over exclusively by women who occupy all the public offices and have outlawed gambling, smoking, and swearing; for entertainment they show educational films. Again like Bower, Wilson stressed human relationships in preference to gunplay and action. In fact, some of her best work can be found in those stories where the focus is on relationships between children and men, as in her novel, *Stormy* (1929), and short stories like "Ghost Town Trail" (1930) — a fascinating tale with an eerie setting and a storyline filled with mystery — and "The Swing Man's Trail" (1930) in which a boy doggedly pursues a herd of rustled cattle that has swept up his family's only cow.

Conversely, many of Wilson's stories incorporate a stronger anti-violence theme than any by Bower. Her anti-vengeance story, "Totin' Catgut" (1932), especially comes to mind, where the heroine interrupts the cycle of killing in a feud by telling the protagonist, upon his return to avenge the deaths of his family, that the dead don't want vengeance: "they want peace." Among Wilson's stories that proved most popular with readers are those displaying her love of and sensitivity to animals — especially horses in "Brand of the Thunder God" (1939) and "Ridin' for Glory" (1942). In the late 1930s she appears to have been plagued by health problems, and it was probably this that brought her career to an end early in the following decade.

The dust jacket of the first edition of *The Outcast of the Lazy S*, published in 1933, stated: "Eli Colter needs no introduction. His stories of the Northwest have been widely read." The author was actually Eliza Colter. She had been competing quite successfully with male writers in the pulp magazine market since the early 1920s and would write her last stories when in her sixties. Colter's western stories have little in common with the more ambient world found in Bower or even Wilson. They are gritty, tough, violent, and episodes often become littered with bodies. When film director Howard Hawks said of Leigh Brackett that "she wrote like a man," he meant it as a compliment. The same could be said of Colter. There is virtually nothing about her fiction that would indicate she was a wife and mother of one daughter.

Born in 1890 in Portland, Oregon, Colter was afflicted for a time by blindness when in her early teens. This experience taught her to "drill out" her own education, and that's what she continued to do throughout her life. She lived briefly in the states of Washington, Georgia, Louisiana, and California. She played piano accompaniment to motion pictures while learning how to write. Although her first story was published under a nom de plume in 1918, she felt her career as a professional really began when she sold her first story to *Black Mask* in 1922. Her earliest writing clearly indicates a penchant for the "hard-boiled school" — the kind of stories Dashiell Hammett wrote or, among more strictly western writers, Eugene Cunningham. Over the course of a career that spanned nearly four decades, Colter wrote more than 300 stories and serials, mostly western fiction. She appeared regularly in thirty-seven different magazines, including slick publications like *Liberty*, and was showcased on the covers of Fiction House's *Lariat Story Magazine* right along with Cunningham and Walt Coburn. She published seven hardcover western novels.

Colter was particularly adept at crafting complex and intricate plots set against traditional western storylines of her day — range wars as in "The Ghost of Skull Pass" (1938), cattlemen versus homesteaders as in "Mustang Marshal" (1944), and switched identities as in "The Rattlesnake Kid" (1949). No matter what the plot, she somehow always managed to include the unexpected. It might be a mystery element as in "Treasure Trail" (1937) or a shocking scene like the calculated poisoning of the sheriff's wife in *Canyon Rattlers* (1939). That Colter actually showed female characters being killed by the villains — in *Canyon Rattlers* and again in *Outcast of the Lazy S* (1933) where a woman is shot in cold blood — was decidedly unusual and outside the accepted conventions of western stories written by more chivalrous male authors at the time. Her villains are well characterized, but they are also portrayed as embodiments of evil — quite possibly a reaction to the constant rash of stories depicting outlaws who are capable of redemption. Colter's work was in high demand among many pulp editors. That she had a large readership is readily illustrated by the fact that in pulp magazines where almost no authors could have more than one story in a single issue under the same byline, two stories often carried Eli Colter's byline.

Chloe Kathleen Shaw, who wrote most of the time as C. K. Shaw, shared much in common with Colter though her active career in pulp magazines spanned only two decades. Shaw, as Colter, wrote "like a man" and her stories appeared in many of the best-paying pulp markets, *Dime Western*, *Western Story Magazine*, *Lariat Story Magazine*, and *Star Western*. More times than not a C. K. Shaw story would be headlined on the front cover. Although she did write stories in which women do figure prominently for romance western pulps like *Rangeland Love Stories* under the byline Kathleen Shaw, in the majority of her western stories the woman's point of view is notably absent and often there are no female characters whatsoever. She seemed naturally drawn to characters living on the fringes of the law and frequently her stories are about outlaws. While Shaw shared to an extent Colter's inclination toward pursuit stories — searching for a lost father or for a lost son — as well as stories about good and bad brothers, physical violence is less prevalent in her fiction than in Colter's.

Shaw was born to a long line of ranchers on a homestead in the Cherokee Strip and grew up in eastern Oregon where, she once observed, the "mail arrived according to the conditions of the road, likewise your doctor and your law." If Colter was a master of the well-made plot, Shaw's forte was her ability to create interesting casts of characters through whom and between whom she was able to develop a suspenseful and unpredictable interplay. Especially good examples of her character-driven fiction include "After Ten Years" (1927), "Gunhand's Rep" (1939), and "Three Way Double-Cross" (1942). She was a highly polished and talented writer who, like Colter, throughout her career probably fooled the majority of her readers as to her gender.

Some women became involved in writing western stories because their husbands successfully wrote them. After her marriage to Fred Glidden who wrote as Luke Short, Florence Elder was urged by her husband to try her hand. She began writing stories under the byline Vic Elder. How much real help her husband was remains questionable. She once related how, when she was stalled at a crucial point in a story, she asked what she should do. His laconic reply was: "Put in a little action. That's what I do." Action stories, however, were not what Elder was writing! "The Chute to Love," her first published story, was sold on May 18, 1935, to *Rangeland Romances* for $50. She continued to write stories for the western romance magazines for about seven years, until the birth of their third child in 1943. "The Wild One" (1936) remains one of her best, but it is an uncharacteristic story. The hero tries to capture a wild stallion to prove himself to the heroine when, in a surprising reversal, he comes to fall in love with a half-Navajo woman who teaches him the importance of letting the stallion remain free.

Elsa Barker, married to western poet and short story writer S. Omar Barker, had a much longer career than Elder. She published over 200 western stories in the magazine market under her married name, seven western novels published only in England under the byline E. M. Barker, and had a Dell comic book based on one of her novels. Born in 1906 in Sibley, Illinois, she grew up in New Mexico. In addition to her own writing, she typed all of her husband's manuscripts — approximately 1,500 stories, a thousand poems, and at least a thousand fact pieces. Many of Elsa's stories rely on the conventional plot elements of the ranch romance. There is some impediment to love — usually the failure of one of the lovers to recognize their love for the other — that results in a series of misunderstandings and complications. Her story, "Grammar Glamour" (1939), is a fine example of this type of plot and it appeared in one of her primary markets, *Ranch Romances*. It can be said that she was at her best when writing about women and what they know. Some of her more interesting female characters can be found in *Rider on the Ramhorn* (1956) and *Cowboys Can't Quit* (1957), which were first serialized in *Ranch Romances*. As Bower before her, Barker would have her females perform a logical, but unpredictable, action for a woman in a difficult situation. In "Kitchen Courage" (1940) the heroine curtails the advances of the villain through the use of her oven — she turns up the heat so that the jam jars inside eventually explode, burning and cutting the villain, who is seated nearby. This scene brings to mind Bower's novel, *Trouble Rides the Wind* (1935), when the heroine shoves a potato in the villain's mouth to stop his torrent of swearing!

By the 1950s the pulps were being replaced by the more compact original paperbacks. *Ranch Romances*, which survived until 1971, changed its editorial format sufficiently to offer one of the few remaining markets for fledgling western writers, men and women alike. Authors like T. V. Olsen, Elmer Kelton, and Jeanne Williams were among the last of a new generation of western writers still able to learn their craft in the short-story magazine market. Whatever their seeming limitations, the pulps permitted writers greater artistic latitude than did the slicks with their more rigid editorial policies dictated by advertisers. Jeanne Williams could write a conventional story like "Spanish Dagger" (1955) and have it published in *Ranch Romances* as well as an offbeat story like "Brother Shotgun" (1957). The latter is one of her best stories and one of her personal favorites. Williams met with far more resistance to her experimentalism once she began trying to publish books. While the direction her western fiction ultimately took was the historical novel rather than the traditional western story, her first novel, *River Guns*, is definitely a traditional western, serialized in *Ranch Romances* in 1957 and published in book form in England in 1963.

Since the 1960s a number of women have entered the arena of the traditional western story, having published first-time hardcover and paperback fiction that was commercially successful in a genre that had been groping for new directions over a number of years. The critic for *The New York Times Book Review* stated in his review of *Day of the Hunter*

(1960) that "sometimes a talent gallops out of the brush with a story so natural, so compelling in ramifications and handling, as to confound both the pundits and the veteran practitioners. *Day of the Hunter* by A. Ahlswede is such a performance." The first initial was for Ann, born in 1928 in Pasadena, California. Her experimentation with the basic structure of the traditional western resulted in three highly regarded western novels produced in the same number of years. Subsequent printings of *Day of the Hunter* carried her full name, as did *Hunting Wolf* (1960) and *The Savage Land* (1962). Although *Day of the Hunter* and *Hunting Wolf* deal with conventional vengeance and pursuit themes, Ahlswede brought to her characters an introspection only rarely encountered, and by making the heroes half-breeds she could explore the ramifications of racial prejudice. *The Savage Land* still stands as a classic story of greed. It successfully challenged the basic structure and tenets of traditional western novels while aspiring to an elevated plateau of literary accomplishment. Thirty years later, Ann Ahlswede's novels are still in print.

Lee Hoffman, a writer whose name was sufficiently ambiguous without use of initials, won the Spur Award from the Western Writers of America for *The Valdez Horses* (1967), a poignant story about a Mexican horse breeder and a colt named Banner. Hoffman was born in 1932 in Chicago, Illinois, and began writing stories, many of them westerns, as a hobby while in the sixth grade. "When I run up against that 'How can you, a mere woman, write westerns?' attitude," Hoffman once commented, "I mention that in my youth I owned a number of horses, did some trail riding in Colorado and Wyoming, and once worked as a shill to a horse trader in Kansas. I don't go into details about the trail riding being connected with a stay at a dude ranch, or the job with the horse trader only lasting a couple of weeks. (He got arrested.)" Although she first wrote original science fiction paperbacks, Don Wollheim at Ace encouraged her to try a western story. The result was *Gunfight at Laramie* (1966), the first of seventeen western novels, including several comic westerns like *Wiley's Move* (1973). In these books Hoffman demonstrated just how adept she was at reworking the elements of a traditional story with a hero by showing her male characters to have human frailties. Over the course of her career, she gained the respect of fellow western writers. Hoffman published her last western novel to date in 1981, after which she turned to writing historical romances.

In much the same fashion P. A. Bechko produced seven westerns in the 1970s before she deserted them in favor of the historical romance.

Born in Michigan in 1950 and raised in Florida, Peggy Anne Bechko wrote her first western at the age of twenty-two on a dare from a childhood friend who said women couldn't write westerns. She submitted the manuscript to a New York literary agency and was accepted as a client. Although the agency closed, an associate agent continued to market the novel unbeknownst to Bechko. When an offer of a contract for publication came through, both agent and editor were surprised to find that the author was a woman. In that first novel, *Night of the Flaming Guns* (1974), Bechko demonstrated a facility for reworking the traditional pursuit story. She went on to break with convention by varying the characters found in her western landscapes. Her heroines aren't always weak or virtuous and her heroes are often reticent and don't necessarily get or want the heroine at the end. With *Blown to Hell* (1976) Bechko, as Bower and Hoffman before her, ventured into the terrain of the comic western. This novel, and the two that followed, introduced offbeat use of modern modes of transportation in a traditional western setting. Bechko, like Hoffman, proved able to compete successfully in the marketplace and injected a comedic tone sorely needed during the 1970s when porno westerns were at the zenith of their popularity among New York publishers.

L. J. Washburn was born in Lake Worth, Texas, in 1957. Livia became interested in western films in her teens when, due to poor health, she was confined indoors and watched a lot of television. It was meeting her future husband, James M. Reasoner, that eventually steered her in the direction of writing her own western stories. An apprenticeship of sorts began as Washburn read her husband's manuscripts and then typed them. She began using the penname L. J. Washburn (her initials and maiden name) when her stories were submitted to magazines for which her husband was already writing. Before turning to westerns exclusively, she experimented with blending her two favorite genres — detective and western fiction — by creating a series detective who works in the West. She followed these books with five traditional western novels, beginning with *Epitaph* (1988), an early indication of her proclivity for creating offbeat characters and situations. Her second western novel, *Ghost River* (1988), is about a miracle that turns the tide for an outlaw. She plotted it during the events surrounding the birth of her daughter. Washburn, like her husband, has a preference for the fast-paced action stories reminiscent of the pulps. Hers is such a surprisingly violent world for a woman to have imagined that editors and readers alike often are astonished to learn that she is a woman. In this she is similar to Eli Colter. "I try to write the kind of stories that appeal to me as a reader," she once said, "books with plenty of action, a good plot, humor, and characters that I care about."

Among all of the writers surveyed here, however, none save C. H. Haseloff has placed a heroine at the center of a traditional western story. Cynthia was born in Vernon, Texas, in 1945 and named after Cynthia Ann Parker, perhaps the best known of the nineteenth-century white female Indian captives. The history and legends of the West were part of her upbringing in Arkansas where her family settled shortly after she was born. She wrote her first novel, *Ride South!* (1980), with her mother's encouragement. This unique story is concerned with a woman, a mother searching for her twin daughters who have been taken captive by Indians. In contrast to the majority of traditional western stories, the protagonist is driven for years in her search not by a desire for revenge or fame but out of maternal need and love. Haseloff proved in this book, as well as in others—*Marauder* (1982), *Dead Woman's Trail* (1984), and *The Chains of Sarai Stone* (1995)—that female characters can attain heroic and nearly mythological proportions within the framework of a traditional western story. Her characters, male and female, embody the fundamental values—honor, duty, courage, and family—that prevailed on the frontier and were instilled in the young Haseloff by her own "heroes," her mother and her grandmother. Her stories dramatize how these values endure when challenged by the adversities of frontier existence. Her talent, like that of Dorothy M. Johnson, rests in her ability to tell a story with an economy of words and perhaps, more importantly, with an overwhelming sense of humanity, in the seemingly effortless way she uses language. Haseloff once said, "I love the West, perhaps not all of its reality, for much of it was cruel and hard, but certainly its dream and hope, and the damned courage of people trying to live within its demands." Haseloff has infused new life and possibility into the traditional western.

The women writers surveyed here, as well as others, have had an uphill struggle to practice their art. Despite lack of encouragement or support from the publishing establishment, the critics, and over the long term the literary historians, they persisted professionally and prevailed —although in recent years they have not prevailed for very long before they, to use Tillie Olsen's term, fall silent. Yet, despite the odds working against them, they have made contributions to the traditional western, contributions that warrant recognition. Women writers have helped refine, reshape, and redefine the western to embrace wider frontiers. They have introduced into the conventional western social issues that are relevant to both sexes. Considered a minority themselves, they have often been more sympathetic to the peoples native to this country. If the West is, as was once said, "the territory of the imagination," then the contributions of women to the traditional western should no longer remain invisible in the annals of western literary history but should finally be given their rightful due.

Selected Bibliography

Primary Sources

Ahlswede, Ann. *Day of the Hunter*. New York: Ballantine, 1960.
———. *Hunting Wolf*. New York: Ballantine, 1960.
———. *The Savage Land*. New York: Ballantine, 1962.
———. "The Promise of the Fruit." In *The Pick of the Roundup*. Stephen Payne, ed. New York: Avon, 1963.

Barker, Elsa [McCormick]

Short Stories (arranged chronologically)
———. "Grammar Glamour." *Ranch Romances*, 90, 2nd December Number (December 22, 1939): 48-57.
———. "Kitchen Courage." *Ranch Romances*, 95, 1st October Number (September 27, 1940): 53-62.
———. "Lady Bronc-Peeler." *Ranch Romances*, 116, 1st December Number (December 3, 1943): 43-51.
———. "Rodeo Fever." *Ranch Romances*, 160, 2nd September Number (September 15, 1950): 33-40.
———. "Stranger From Texas." *Ranch Romances*, 161, 1st November Number (November 10, 1950): 12, 14-33.
———. "First Notch." *All Western*, 1 (February-March, 1951): 68-78.
———. "A Man's Way Of Doing." *Best Western*, 5 (December, 1955): 46-54.

Novels
———. *Clouds Over the Chupaderos*. London: Stanley Paul, 1957.
———. *Cowboys Can't Quit*. London: John Long, 1957.
———. *Rider of the Ramhorn*. London: Stanley Paul, 1956.
———. *Secret of the Badlands*. London: John Long, 1960.
———. *Showdown at Penasco Pass*. London: John Long, 1958.
———. *War on the Big Hat*. London: John Long, 1959.

Barry, Jane. *A Time in the Sun*. New York: Doubleday, 1962.

Bechko, P[eggy] A[nn]. *Blown to Hell*. Garden City: Doubleday, 1976.

————. *Dead Man's Feud*. New York: Pinnacle, 1976.

————. *Gunman's Justice*. Garden City: Doubleday, 1974.

————. *Hawke's Indians*. Garden City: Doubleday, 1979.

————. *Night of the Flaming Guns*. Garden City: Doubleday, 1974.

———— [Bill Haller]. *Sidewinder's Trail*. New York: Pinnacle, 1976.

————. *The Winged Warrior*. Garden City: Doubleday, 1977.

Bower, B[ertha] M[uzzy]. *Trouble Rides the Wind*. Boston: Little, Brown, 1935.

Colter, Eli[za].

Short Stories (arranged chronologically)

————. "Steelshod Steel." *West*, 3 (September 20, 1926): 61-74.

————. "Tonapah Turns the Trick." *Lariat Story Magazine*, 2 (November 1926): 38-46.

————. "Gun Shy." *Lariat Story Magazine*, 3 (October 1927): 12-45.

————. "Hard-Boiled Haig." *Lariat Story Magazine*, 4 (June 1928): 3-34.

————. "Outlaw Cayuse." *Lariat Story Magazine*, 5 (November 1929): 99-106.

————. "Tenderfoot Rancho." *Lariat Story Magazine*, 6 (January 1930): 49-68.

————. "Saddles and Sixes." *Lariat Story Magazine*, 6 (February 1930): 56-64.

————. "Sixes Showing." *Lariat Story Magazine*, 6 (September 1930): 69-78.

————. "Sundown." *Lariat Story Magazine*, 9 (June 1935): 83-85.

————. "Treasure Trail." *Western Story Magazine*, 158 (August 8, 1937): 10-45.

————. "Nine Against Los Lobos." *Western Story Magazine*, 163 (February 26, 1938): 64-79.

————. "Sixes Full." *Western Story Magazine*, 163 (March 5, 1938): 106-113.

————. "Desert Glass." *Western Story Magazine*, 165 (June 4, 1938): 32-41.

————. "Slaughter In Dead Beef Canyon." *Western Story Magazine*, 167 (August 13, 1938): 32-41.

————. "Morgans Don't Quit." *Western Story Magazine*, 167 (September 3, 1938): 32-39.

————. "Dark Trails Samaritan." *Western Story Magazine*, 169 (November 5, 1938): 37-47.

————. "The Ghost Of Skull Pass." *Western Story Magazine*, 169 (November 26, 1938): 79-99.

————. "With His Boots On." *Western Story Magazine*, 182 (May 4, 1940): 56-64.

————. "Fear Fighters." *Western Story Magazine*, 184 (August 3, 1940): 28-36.

————. "Chihuahua Joe — Hunted Manhunter." *New Western*, 2 (January 1941): 44-60.

————. "Tinhorn's Gun Trail." *Western Story Magazine*, 189 (March 15, 1941): 71-82.

————. "Gun-Devil Of The Half-Moon-T." *New Western*, 3 (May 1941): 68-83.

————. "Four Tough Hombres!" *New Western*, 3 (July 1941): 10-31.

————. "Hell On Bearcat Mountain." *New Western*, 4 (January 1942): 52-68.

————. "Coward's Coffin Come-Back." *Big-Book Western*, 11 (February 1942): 42-52.

————. "Four Horsemen From Hell." *New Western*, 4 (March 1942): 44-63.

————. "The Stray." *Western Story*, 200 (June 6, 1942): 51-78.

————. "Blood And Coffins For Chudder's Gap." *Big-Book Western*, 11 (August 1942): 52-70.

————. "The Jeppsons Ride To War." *New Western*, 5 (September 1942): 11-35.

————. "Freight For Boothill." *Western Adventures*, 3 (October 1942): 100-126.

———. "Powder-Smoke Pasear." *Western Story*, 205 (December 19, 1942): 58-77.

———. "Gun The Man Down!" *Ace-High Western Stories*, 6 (January 1943): 11-37.

———. "Beware The Four Jeppsons!" *New Western*, 6 (March 1943): 12-38.

———. "Feud Buster!" *New Western*, 6 (May 1943): 8-27.

———. "When Peckerwood Junction Went Wild." *New Western*, 6 (May 1943): 85-97.

———. "Brand Of The Zero Kid." *Western Story*, 207 (May 15, 1943): 78-101.

———. "Powder-Smoke Porridge." *Western Adventures*, 3 (August 1943): 9-28.

———. "Those Fightin', Feudin' Jeppsons!" *New Western*, 6 (September 1943): 8-27.

———. "Nevada Noose." *Lariat Story Magazine*, 13 (January 1944): 46-70.

———. "Bullets For Breakfast." *10 Story Western*, 23 (January 1944): 66-72.

———. "Mustang Marshal." *Lariat Story Magazine*, 13 (March 1944): 3-28.

———. "Boss Of The Boothill Stampeders." *New Western*, 8 (January 1945): 10-34.

———. "When Hell Froze Over." *New Western*, 9 (March 1945): 33-39.

———. "The Jeppsons Ride The Death Watch." *New Western*, 9 (May 1945): 10-28.

———. "Law Of The Fighting Jeppsons." *New Western*, 10 (January 1946): 78-97.

———. "Man-Size Job." *West*, 62 (August 1946): 93-103.

———. "Long Way Home." *Western Story*, 218 (November 1947): 48-62.

———. "War In Their Necks, Lead In Their Teeth!" *Ace-High Western Stories*, 18 (December 1947): 6-25.

———. "Marked Man." *Western Story*, 219 (August 1948): 74-94.

———. "The Killer And The Kid." *Ace-High Western Stories*, 20 (January 1949): 69-78.

———. "Wolf Bait." *Western Story*, 220 (March 1949): 90-108.

———. "The Rattlesnake Kid." *Lariat Story Magazine*, 16 (November 1949): 98-128.

———. "Get Long Green Valley!" *Famous Western*, 11 (April 1950): 8-27.

———. "Brand Of The Prodigal." *New Western*, 24 (January 1952): 10-26.

Novels

———. *The Adventures of Hawke Travis*. New York: Macmillan, 1930.

———. *Bad Man's Trail*. New York: Alfred H. King, 1931.

———. *Blood on the Range*. New York: Dodge Publishing Company, 1939.

———. *Canyon Rattlers*. New York: Dodge Publishing Company, 1939.

———. *Gunfire Gold in Silver Town*. London: Wright and Brown, 1939.

———. *Menace in Red Chaps*. London: Wright and Brown, 1939.

———. *One Man Law*. London: Geoffrey Bless, 1937.

———. *Outcast of the Lazy S*. New York: Alfred H. King, 1933.

———. *Outlaw Blood*. New York: Alfred H. King, 1932.

———. *Three Killers*. New York: Alfred H. King, 1932.

Elder, Vic (née Florence Elder)

———. "The Chute To Love." *Rangeland Romances*, 1 (September 1935): 41-49.

———. "The Wild One." *Thrilling Ranch Stories*, 9 (April 1936): 55-67.

Haseloff, C[ynthia] H. (arranged chronologically)

———. *Ride South*. New York: Bantam, 1980.

———. *A Killer Comes to Shiloh*. New York: Bantam, 1981.

———. *Marauder*. New York: Bantam, 1982.

———. *Badman*. New York: Bantam, 1983.

———. *Dead Woman's Trail*. New York: Bantam, 1984.

———. *The Chains of Sarai Stone*. Thorndike, Maine: Five Star Westerns, 1995.

———. "Redemption at Dry Creek." In *The Western Story: A Chronological Treasury*. Jon Tuska, ed. Lincoln: University of Nebraska Press, 1995.

Hoffman, Lee (arranged chronologically)

———. *Gunfight at Laramie*. New York: Ace, 1966.

———. *The Legend of Blackjack Sam*. New York: Ace, 1966.

———. *Bred to Kill*. New York: Ballantine, 1967.

———. *The Valdez Horses*. Garden City: Doubleday, 1967.

———. *Dead Man's Gold*. New York: Ace, 1968.

———. *The Yarborough Brand*. New York: Avon, 1968.

———. *Wild Riders*. New York: New American Library, 1969.

———. *Loco*. Garden City: Doubleday, 1969.

———. *Return to Broken Crossing*. New York: Ace, 1969.

———. *West of Cheyenne*. Garden City: Doubleday, 1969.

———. *Wiley's Move*. New York: Dell, 1973.

———. *The Truth about the Cannonball Kid*. New York: Dell, 1975.

———. *Fox*. Garden City: Doubleday, 1976.

———. *Nothing But a Drifter*. Garden City: Doubleday, 1976.

———. *Trouble Valley*. New York: Ballantine, 1976.

———. *Sheriff of Jack Hollow*. New York: Dell, 1977.

———. *The Land Killer*. New York: Doubleday, 1978.

Morrow, Honoré Willsie (arranged chronologically)

———. *The Heart of the Desert*. New York: Stokes, 1913.

———. *Still Jim*. New York: Stokes, 1915.

———. *Judith of the Godless Valley*. New York: Stokes, 1922.

———. *The Exile of the Lariat*. New York: Stokes, 1923.

Shaw, C[hloe] K[athleen] (arranged chronologically)

———. "After Ten Years." *Lariat Story Magazine*, 3 (October 1927): 55-65.

———. "Outlaw's Boots." *Lariat Story Magazine*, 8 (June 1932): 46-63.

———. "Wolves of Poverty Ridge." *Dime Western*, 8 (December 15, 1934): 82-99.

———. "Born For The Hemp." *Lariat Story Magazine*, 9 (August 1935): 3-25.

———. "Gold Won't Buy Good Gunmen." *Star Western*, 13 (December 1937): 132-47.

———. "Rustlers Make Good Cowmen." *Star Western*, 13 (January 1938): 98-117.

———. "Gunman's Son." *Western Story Magazine*, 167 (August 6, 1938): 6-27.

———. "Aces Mean Death." *Western Story Magazine*, 168 (October 1, 1938): 11-34.

———. "Button Roundup." *Western Story Magazine*, 169 (November 26, 1938): 43-51.

———. "The Jinx Of The Mesa." *Western Story Magazine*, 169 (December 3, 1938): 65-88.

———. "Death Catches Up." *Western Story Magazine*, 171 (January 28, 1939): 59-76.

———. "Trouble on the Bar H." *Western Story Magazine*, 172 (March 4, 1939): 87-95.

———. "Frontier Fury." *Western Story Magazine*, 172 (April 8, 1939): 49-70.

———. "Gun Proof." *Western Story Magazine*, 173 (May 13, 1939): 53-78.

———. "Death At Sunrise." *Western Story Magazine*, 174 (June 17, 1939): 61-84.

———. "Gunman's Rep." *Western Story Magazine*, 175 (July 22, 1939): 9-57.

———. "Horse Thieves Ride." *Western Story Magazine*, 176 (August 26, 1939): 63-80.

———. "Peace Comes High." *Western Story Magazine*, 177 (October 14, 1939): 55-75.

————. "Frontier Justice." *Western Story Magazine*, 180 (February 10, 1940): 39-85.

————. "Guns Of Vengeance." *Western Story Magazine*, 181 (March 30, 1940): 9-47.

————. "The Medico Of Mesa Rock." *Western Story*, 183 (June 8, 1940): 55-78.

————. "Bar H Glory." *Western Story*, 183 (June 22, 1940): 57-64.

————. "The Powderkeg Kid Of Blue Mesa." *Lariat Story Magazine*, 12 (July, 1940): 52-72.

————. "The Rider Of Lonesome Range." *Lariat Story Magazine*, 12 (November, 1940): 42-58.

————. "Thunder On The Trails." *Western Story*,187 (November 23, 1940): 9-52.

————. "Horse-Trading Hombre." *Western Story*, 187 (December 7, 1940): 79-88.

————. "Coyote!" *Lariat Story Magazine*, 12 (January 1941): 32-43.

————. "Wide Open For Gunsmoke." *Western Story*, 190 (April 12, 1941): 9-32.

————. "Ride 'Er, Button!" *Western Story*, 190 (May 3, 1941): 71-81.

————. "Boothill For Bounty Hunters." *Western Story*, 192 (June 28, 1941): 9-55.

————. "I'm Taking This Range!" *Western Story*, 193 (August 23, 1941): 74-86.

————. "A Noose For One." *Western Story*, 194 (September 13, 1941): 66-76.

————. "Horse-Thief Havoc." *Western Story*, 194 (October 18, 1941): 79-92.

————. "Death Is The Wagon Boss." *Western Story*, 198 (February 28, 1942): 49-71.

————. "Spiked With Dynamite." *Western Story*, 198 (March 28, 1942): 54-64.

————. "Sidewinder Rout." *Western Story*, 199 (April 25, 1942): 77-88.

————. "War For The Rio Salt Flats.' *New Western*, 4 (May 1942): 10-38.

————. "Death Stalks The Wagon Train." *Western Adventures*, 2 (June 1942): 61-83.

————. "Three Way Double-Cross." *Western Story*, 200 (June 13, 1942): 75-86.

————. "Powdersmoke Passage." *Western Adventures*, 3 (October, 1942): 45-61.

————. "The Ghost's Night Out." *Western Story*, 203 (October 24, 1942): 39-49.

————. "Easy Does It." *Western Story*,, 205 (December 19, 1942): 48-57.

————. "Brush-Country Buscadero." *Western Adventures*, 3 (August 1943): 123-26.

————. "Fightin' Outcast Of Snake River." *10 Story Western*, 34 (November 1947): 46-62.

————. "Jumpin' Juniper." *Lariat Story Magazine*, 16 (July 1948): 26-34.

Washburn, L[ivia] J[ane] (arranged chronologically)

————. *Epitaph*. New York: M. Evans, 1988.

————. *Ghost River*. New York: M. Evans, 1988.

————. *Bandera Pass*. New York: M. Evans, 1989.

————. *Riders of the Monte*. New York: M. Evans, 1990.

————. *Red River Ruse*. New York: M. Evans, 1991.

Williams, [Dorothy] Jeanne (née Kreie).

Short Stories (arranged chronologically)

————. "Squatter's Rights." *Thrilling Ranch Stories*, 45 (Spring 1953): 85-102.

————."Fancy Saddle." *Real Western Romances*, 4 (September 1954): 53-61.

————. "Ready Lawman." *Ranch Romances*, 181, 1st November Number (November 6, 1953): 106-114.

————. "Backfire." *Ranch Romances*, 186, 2nd August Number (August 13, 1954): 102-109.

————. "Trail Of Hate." *Real Western Romances*, 4 (November 1954): 29-37.

———. "Unwritten I.O.U." *Ranch Romances*, 191, 1st May Number (May 6, 1955): 71-78.

———. "Spanish Dagger." *Ranch Romances*, 192, 1st June Number (June 3, 1955): 48, 50-63.

———. "Lady Cocinero." *Real Western Romances*, 5 (July, 1955): 30-38.

———. "Behind The Paper Law." *Ranch Romances*, 196, 2nd February Number (February 10, 1956): 91-98.

———. "Brother Shotgun." *Ranch Romances*, 205, 2nd June Number (June 14, 1957): 44-52.

——— [as J. M. Williams, Parts 1-2; J. W. Williams Parts 3-4]. "River Guns." Parts 1-4. *Ranch Romances*, 206 1st September Number (August 23, 1957): 55-75; 2nd September Number (September 6, 1957): 95-113; 107 3rd September Number (September 20, 1957): 95-113; 1st October Number (October 4, 1957): 98-113.

———. "The Lady Barkeep Of Little River." *Western Romances*, 8 (January 1958): 56, 58-65, 98.

Novels

J. W. Williams. *River Guns*. London: Herbert Jenkins, 1963.

———. [as J. R. Williams]. *Tame the Wild Stallion*. Englewood Cliffs: Prentice Hall, 1957.

Wilson, Cherry

Short Stories (arranged chronologically)

———. "Steppin' High." *Western Story Magazine*, 44 (July 12, 1924): 101-110.

———. "Triangle Z's All-brass Serenade." *Western Story Magazine*, 48 (December 13, 1924): 88-97.

———. "Triangle Z's Bogus Beauty." *Western Story Magazine*, 49 (January 24, 1925): 31-41.

———. "Hushaby's Partner." *Western Story Magazine*, 61 (May 29, 1926): 122-133.

———. "A Mother for Pard." *Western Story Magazine*, 63 (August 28, 1926): 105-15.

———. "Little Pard Meets Apache Bill." *Western Story Magazine*, 64 (November 6, 1926): 116-27.

———. "Shootin'-up Sheriff." *Western Story Magazine*, 87 (June 15, 1929): 45-61.

———. "Stormy Dorn." Parts 1-4. *Western Story Magazine*, 90 (October 12, 1929): 1-19; (October 19, 1929): 39-59; (October 26, 1929): 40-60; (November 2, 1929): 91-111.

———. "The Face in the Bunk-House Wall." *Western Story Magazine*, 91 (November 30, 1929): 117-30.

———. "Mild and Woolly." *Western Story Magazine*, 92 (January 30, 1930): 40-52.

———. "The Cayuse." *Western Story Magazine*, 96 (July 12, 1930): 1-54.

———. "Ghost Town Trail." *Western Story Magazine*, 99 (October 25, 1930): 1-54.

———. "The Swing Man's Trail." *Western Story Magazine*, 100 (December 13, 1930): 1-17.

———. "Pard's Kidnaper" [sic]. *Western Story Magazine*, 103 (November 7, 1931): 108-125.

———. "Totin' Catgut." *Western Story Magazine*, 114 (July 16, 1932): 50-61.

———. "Brother's Holdup." *Western Story Magazine*, 115 (September 10, 1932): 101-112.

———. "Buzzard And Mojave." *Western Story Magazine,* 115 (August 13, 1932): 121-131.

———. "The Berserk Outlaw." *Western Story Magazine,* 117 (November 19, 1932): 49-59.

———. "Breed Of The Badlands." *Western Story Magazine,* 165 (June 18, 1938): 92-102.

———. "The Wolfer Of Phantom Creek." *Western Story Magazine,* 168 (October 22, 1938): 47-65.

———. "The Race With The Noose." *Western Story Magazine,* 171 (February 4, 1939): 79-88.

———. "Laramie Calls The Dance." *Western Story Magazine,* 171 (February 25, 1939): 51-60.

———. "Brand Of The Thunder God." *Western Story Magazine,* 178 (December 2, 1939): 9-56.

———. "Stormy On The Lasso." *Western Story Magazine,* 180 (March 9, 1940): 30-39.

———. "Troublesome Range." *Western Story,* 186 (October 12, 1940): 9-35, 37-43, 45-53.

———. "Brand Of A Mustanger." *Western Story,* 188 (February 1, 1941): 34-45.

———. "Range Of Hate." *Western Story,* 191 (May 24, 1941): 61-71.

———. "Racetrack Reckoning." *Western Story,* 196 (January 17, 1942): 48-58.

———. "Ridin' For Glory." *Western Story,* 200 (June 13, 1942): 9-49.

———. "Dead Man's Brand." *Western Story,* 204 (November 7, 1942): 69-80.

———. "White-Tasseled Yearlin'." *Western Story,* 205 (December 19, 1942): 38-47.

Novels

———. *Black Wing's Rider.* New York: Alfred H. King, 1934.

———. *Empty Saddles.* New York: Chelsea House, 1929.

———. *Stirrup Brother.* New York: Alfred H. King, 1935.

———. *Stormy.* New York: Chelsea House, 1929.

———. *Thunder Breaks.* New York: Chelsea House, 1929.

Secondary Sources

Muller, Marcia, and Bill Pronzini, eds. *She Won the West: An Anthology of Frontier Stories by Women.* New York: William Morrow & Co., 1985.

Piekarski, Vicki, ed. *Westward the Women: Twelve Stories by Women about the American West.* Garden City: Doubleday, 1983.

Sadler, Geoff, ed. *Twentieth Century Western Writers.* 2nd edition. Chicago and London: St James Press, 1991.

Tuska, Jon, and Vicki Piekarski, eds. *Encyclopedia of Frontier and Western Fiction.* New York: McGraw-Hill, 1983. 2nd edition in preparation for 1999 publication.

———. *The Frontier Experience: A Reader's Guide to the Life and Literature of the American West.* Jefferson, North Carolina: McFarland & Company, 1984.

Yates, Norris. *Gender and Genre: An Introduction to Women Writers of Formula Westerns, 1900-1950.* Albuquerque: University of New Mexico Press, 1995.

Blake Allmendinger

African Americans and the Popular West

The contributions of African Americans on the U. S. frontier, although great and diverse, are marginally represented on film and in literature. Historians now acknowledge that there were early black explorers such as York, William Clark's slave, referred to occasionally in *The Journals of Lewis and Clark* (1804-1806) and that there were later black fur traders, settlers, and miners—groups and individuals about whom not much is known.

The bulk of historical scholarship documents western black men and women who fell into one of three groups. First were black cowboys, who, according to conflicting sources, comprised as few as one-fifth or up to as many as one-third of all U. S. cowboys by the late nineteenth century. (Famous black cowboys include Bose Ikard, pioneer and rancher Charles Goodnight's top hand; Isom Dart, the well-known rodeo clown and cattle thief, who in 1900 was tracked down and killed by Tom Horn; and the legendary Bill Pickett, who allegedly invented the sport of bulldogging while working with Will Rogers in Oklahoma on the renowned 101 Ranch.) Second were the "exodusters," thousands of emancipated black men and women who left the South in an exodus, hoping to settle in a less racist frontier environment. Walking the Chisholm Trail and traveling the Mississippi River by boat, they arrived in 1879 in the free state of Kansas—in the land of John Brown. Third were the "Buffalo Soldiers," the Ninth and Tenth regiments of the United States cavalry.

(Not as well chronicled are the exploits of the black soldiers who comprised the Twenty-fourth and Twenty-fifth divisions of the United States infantry.) From the mid-1860s until the end of the century, the two army units served in several capacities. The Ninth regiment, stationed primarily on the Great Plains and in the furthest regions of the early Southwest, fought Mescalero Apaches, white western bandits, and Mexicans. It escorted survey parties and wagon trains, guarded Indian reservations, and patrolled the Mexican border along the Rio Grande. The Tenth regiment, responsible for protecting an equally wide frontier range, kept peace between farmers and cattlemen and participated in the sensational captures of Billy the Kid and Geronimo.

There are few published firsthand accounts of these early black westerners. Perhaps the most important of these, although not widely known, is *The Life and Adventures of Nat Love* (1907), also known as "Deadwood Dick." Love's autobiography is a unique and insightful account of a black cowboy's life in the late nineteenth century. By today's standards, Love's work seems generically conventional and ideologically conservative, for *The Life and Adventures* pays homage to a predominantly white western ranch culture in which the lone black cowboy, Love, appears assimilated, equal, and extremely at ease with his peers. Readers would have to wait sixty-two years for a book that called serious attention to racism in westerns while at the same time having subversive, outrageous fun with the genre. Ishmael Reed's *Yellow Back Radio Broke-Down* (1969), featuring the exploits of the Loop Garoo Kid and blending horse opera with hoo-doo, offers a multicultural, postmodern look at one comic black cowboy and the revenge that he wreaks on a fictitious frontier community.

Other literary treatments of the West, written by African Americans, are briefer or not as well known. Also, they appear beyond the category of "popular western," as conventionally defined. Ernest J. Gaines devotes a portion of *The Autobiography of Miss Jane Pittman* (1971) to Jane's husband Joe, who learns to break and brand horses on a southern plantation before moving West. More expansive accounts of black pioneers, this time of black male homesteaders, occur in the thinly disguised autobiographical novels of Oscar Micheaux. First in *The Conquest* (1913), then in *The Homesteader* (1917), and finally in *The Wind from Nowhere* (1920), the author tells and retells a story based on actual events in his life. Each novel, in succession, more interestingly and elaborately narrates Micheaux's central plot: the migration of a black man, at the turn of the century, from the urban Midwest to the South Dakota frontier. Settling near an Indian reservation and near a farming community composed primarily of Scandinavian immigrants, the hero breaks farmland and falls in love with a young Swedish girl. Although the hero has an affair with her, he realizes that western society will neither acknowledge nor tolerate their interracial relationship. Hence the hero goes back to his midwestern hometown to look for a black woman whom he can marry and transport out west. Typically, in each of the novels, the marriage ends in disaster when the hero's father-in-law comes west to visit and, after witnessing the hardships endured by the homesteaders, convinces his daughter to end her marriage, return home, and once again experience the soft comforts and easy pleasures of city life. Although clumsily constructed and heavy-handedly narrated, Micheaux's novels are important because of their unique subject matter and representation of complex points of view. Most noteworthy is Micheaux's examination of black isolation and struggle on the western frontier, western intolerance of interracial relationships (dealt with frankly and feelingly), and Micheaux's own frustration due to the unwillingness of urban blacks to share in his rural hero's groundbreaking enterprise.

Although white authors of some western fiction create secondary or token black characters, they seldom give these characters pivotal or memorable roles to play. Works by white writers that sympathetically treat and to some extent privilege black characters include William Eastlake's *The Bronc People* (1958) and three novels by Larry McMurtry: *Horseman, Pass By* (1961), which features the Texas housemaid Halmea; *Lonesome Dove* (1985), which includes the black cowboy Deets; and *Anything for Billy* (1988), which stars Mesty-Woolah, a seven-foot-tall turbaned African who acts as the camel-riding, sword-brandishing henchman of the wealthy rancher Will Isinglass.

As in much western fiction, blacks in most western films seem invisible or at best insignificant. Director and actor Mario Van Peebles' recent black western, *Posse* (1993), may herald the appearance of a new black voice and presence in Hollywood. But traditionally blacks have been shadowy, marginalized figures in films produced by the industry. One of the earliest, most sensitive, and most extensive treatments of blacks occurs in *Sergeant Rutledge* (1960), director John Ford's account of African Americans in the United States cavalry. Recent revisionist westerns, such as Lawrence Kasdan's *Silverado* (1985) and Clint Eastwood's *Unforgiven* (1992), seek to compensate for Hollywood's previous and frequent omission of blacks, foregrounding black actors and assigning them more vital roles. However, Mel Brooks' western farce, *Blazing Saddles* (1974), starring the black sheriff Bart, with its sophomoric humor and lampoonish style, may address racism in the West more effectively than most "serious" westerns do.

In the twentieth century blacks have contributed to other aspects of western popular culture, including the *noir* novel and literature examining western blues, bebop, and jazz. Like the cowboy, the hardboiled detective in *noir* is often depicted as a lone, stoic killer who lives by his own moral code. Perhaps it is not a coincidence that the works of the most famous *noir* writers—among them Dashiell Hammett, Raymond Chandler, and James M. Cain—are set in tough urban western locales. Black writers such as Chester Himes, Walter Mosley, and Gar Anthony Haywood inflect the *noir* genre by inventing black detectives, private investigators, and other mystery protagonists and by situating them in racially torn urban environments (often Los Angeles). A parodic critique of *noir* takes place in *Hollywood Shuffle* (1987), black comic Robert Townsend's first film.

In the introduction and in the opening essays of *Shadow and Act* (1953), Ralph Ellison notes that early southwestern jazz expressed a powerful sense of possibility in black frontier communities. According to Ellison, the improvisation and freedom of southwestern jazz gave the author the feeling, while growing up in integrated rural Oklahoma society, of unstructured latitude. That same sense of freedom expresses itself today in the experimental literature of Al Young, Xam Wilson Cartier and others who write about contemporary jazz, bebop, and blues. The recent appearance and proliferation of such non-traditional and seemingly non-"western" writing indicate perhaps that although African Americans may continue to contribute to western popular culture by producing mainstream fiction and films, in the future they may establish themselves as artists by introducing new forms of expression into new venues as well.

Selected Bibliography

Blazing Saddles. Mel Brooks, dir. With Cleavon Little and Gene Wilder. Warner Brothers, 1974.

Cain, James M. *The Postman Always Rings Twice*. New York: Knopf, 1934.

Cartier, Xam Wilson. *Be-bop, re-bop*. New York: Ballantine, 1987.

Chandler, Raymond. *The Big Sleep*. New York: Knopf, 1939.

Durham, Philip, and Everett L. Jones. *The Negro Cowboys*. New York: Dodd, Mead, 1965.

Eastlake, William. *The Bronc People*. New York: Harcourt, Brace, 1958.

Ellison, Ralph. *Shadow and Act*. 1953. New York: Vintage, 1972.

Gaines, Ernest J. *The Autobiography of Miss Jane Pittman*. New York: Dial, 1971.

Hammett, Dashiell. *The Maltese Falcon*. New York: Grosset and Dunlap, 1930.

Haywood, Gar Anthony. *Not Long for This World*. New York: St. Martin's, 1990.

Himes, Chester. *If He Hollers Let Him Go*. Garden City: Doubleday, 1945.

Hollywood Shuffle. Robert Townsend, dir. With Robert Townsend and Keenen Ivory Wayans. Samuel Goldwyn, 1987.

Katz, William Loren. *The Black West*. 1971. Garden City: Anchor, 1973.

Leckie, William H. *The Buffalo Soldiers: A Narrative of the Negro Cavalry in the West*. Norman: University of Oklahoma Press, 1967.

Lewis, Meriwether and William Clark. *The Journals of Lewis and Clark*. Bernard DeVoto, ed. Boston: Houghton Mifflin, 1953.

Love, Nat. *The Life and Adventures of Nat Love*. Los Angeles: Wayside Press, 1907; rpt., New York: Arno, 1968.

McMurtry, Larry. *Anything for Billy*. New York: Simon & Schuster, 1988.

———. *Horseman, Pass By*. New York: Penguin, 1989.

———. *Lonesome Dove*. New York: Simon & Schuster, 1985.

Micheaux, Oscar. *The Conquest: The Story of a Negro Pioneer*. Lincoln Nebraska: Woodruff, 1913; rpt., College Park, Maryland: McGrath, 1969.

———. *The Homesteader: A Novel*. Sioux City, Iowa: Western Book Supply Company, 1917; rpt., College Park: McGrath, 1969.

———. *The Wind from Nowhere*. N.P., 1920; rpt., New York: Book Supply, 1944.

Mosley, Walter. *A Red Death*. New York: Norton, 1991.

Painter, Nell Irvin. *Exodusters: Black Migration to Kansas after Reconstruction*. New York: Knopf, 1977; rpt., New York: Norton, 1986.

Porter, Kenneth Wiggins. *The Negro on the American Frontier*. New York: Arno, 1970.

Posse. Mario Van Peebles, dir. With Mario Van Peebles and Blair Underwood. Columbia, 1993.

Reed, Ishmael. *Yellow Back Radio Broke-Down*. Garden City, New York: Doubleday, 1969; rpt., New York: Atheneum, 1988.

Savage, W. Sherman. *Blacks in the West*. Westport, Connecticut: Greenwood, 1976.

Sergeant Rutledge. John Ford, dir. With Woody Strode. Warner Brothers, 1960.

Silverado. Lawrence Kasdan, dir. With Kevin Kline and Danny Glover. Columbia, 1985.

Unforgiven. Clint Eastwood, dir. With Clint Eastwood, Gene Hackman, Richard Harris and Morgan Freeman. Warner Brothers, 1992.

Young, Al. *The Blues Don't Change: New and Selected Poems*. Baton Rouge: Louisiana State University Press, 1982.

Robert F. Gish

Writing Back:
The American Indian Western

Any discussion of the American West as perceived in popular culture generally and popular literature more particularly must proceed from assumptions about the relativity of otherness. Cultural values, under such assumptions, are not absolute and are viewed as determined by many variables and relationships—many causalities of time and place and of how such factors as class, gender, race, and ethnicity interact.

Persons involved in current canon and culture warfare know in new ways that literary history and especially the New Literary History is a matter of inside-outside, bottom-top, dominant-subservient, majority-minority, us-them position and place.

Just as the literary perceptions and values of region, most glaringly East and West, create a controlling tension, a dynamic of discord, so too in matters of the popular West, and especially in the American Indian popular West, does a tension develop between Indian and non-Indian, often simplistically heretofore codified as cavalry or cowboy vs. Indian, sodbuster versus rancher, railroad versus landowner, sheriff versus outlaw.... Regardless of the basis of the tension, the West provides an occasion not just for settlement and growth but for exploitation if not defilement.

The popular western in such a context is either perceived or ignored, protested or prized as inherently ethnocentric and chauvinistic, and accepted or rejected as racist and sexist — a genre, often like the region itself, defined by a historiography of dominance, of the whole cluster of beliefs and motives known as Manifest Destiny.

American Indian authors writing within what might be regarded as the accepted Anglo-American formulas of the popular western, what might be called the "Indian western," position themselves, sometimes in satire, sometimes in anger, often ironically, in protest of the values and formulas, the traditions and conventions of the genre they seek to subvert. The Indian western, that is, the western written *by* Indian authors who resist cultural misappropriation and stereotyping by non-Indian writers, must be seen as an attempt to rectify prejudices and beliefs, distortions long taken for granted as real and true by almost universally white, culturally conditioned, conservative male readers.

An ideal reader (Indian or non-Indian) of the Indian western, then, must be disposed toward transvaluating ethnocentric notions of what is called, by Robert Berkhofer, Jr., and others, the "White Man's Indian." In this sense, the Indian western becomes a kind of politically liberating, humanizing text for Indian authors who attempt to reclaim, rectify, and authenticate their respective cultures and peoples. In such a process of "writing back," it is the non-Indian who becomes the "other," the interloper, the clown, or the villain.

This process, as we see it played out in contemporary issues, debates, and polls about racial polarization, is and is not merely a matter of "reverse racism," one set of ethnocentric values substituted for another. The causality is complex and to a considerable extent still unfathomable. The antithetical views offered in the Indian western, however, do point to some eventual generic if not cultural synthesis as the United States wrangles with the ingredients and portions of *pluribus* and *unum* in its national motto and identity.

Factors of genre, gender, and ethnicity thus come into prominent play in the criticism of the Indian western. This is seen in any number of contemporary American Indian writers who, certainly not exclusively, but in a prominent way, adapt the conventions of the "popular" (i.e. Anglo) western and transmute or subvert it into the Indian western.

This process is observable in the current western cinema and its subgenres as well. *Dances with Wolves*, *Thunderheart*, and *The Last of the Dog Men* are but three salient examples whereby the Indian perspective of West and westering is portrayed against an undersided, thicker backdrop of change. Similarly, in fiction, Leslie Silko, James Welch, and Sherman

Alexie afford us representative narratives from which greater generalizations can be made.

In Silko's "Yellow Woman" (1974), the basic western conventions are transvaluated in fascinating and satisfying ways. Silko takes the expectations associated with the scripts and plots of "Cinderella" and "captivity" stories and flips them. A pueblo woman, lost in the doldrums of Jell-O and a husband named Al, is kidnapped by a man named Silva and taken to his cabin in the mountains. Myth, however, soon merges with the mundane, and the woman becomes an analog to the earth goddess, Yellow Woman, and Silva, hardly a petty cattle rustler, as a ka'tsina spirit is party to a romantic apotheosis.

As "Little Yellow Woman" tries to fathom the full dimensions of her altered state, the traditional western landscape also becomes transcendent and the traditional western heroes, the Texas ranchers of the Concho Valley, become villains. When Silva is accused of being a rustler by one of the white, fat-faced ranchers, an ironic role reversal invades and twists the situation:

> The rancher was fat, and sweat began to soak through his white cowboy shirt and the wet cloth stuck to the thick rolls of belly fat. He almost seemed to be panting from the exertion of talking, and he smelled rancid, maybe because Silva scared him. (43)

Silva is charismatic, with something "ancient and dark" in his eyes. And as Yellow Woman heads back down the mountain to her life with Al and domestic chores, she hears four shots, which, although presented with utter ambiguity, presumably represent Silva's shooting the rancher rather than becoming the formulaic predestined "dead Indian." Silko uses essentially the same scene to even greater effect when the ranchers confront Tayo in *Ceremony* (1977), and he is saved by a lion, also a ka'tsina hunter.

In *Winter in the Blood* (1974), Welch takes standard western conventions and converts them into the satire of absurdist comedy and black humor. Teresa's father, the white cowboy drifter, Doagie, merges in comedic name confusion, with Dougie, the brother of the narrator's girlfriend, Agnes. Both cowboys are catalysts in the Indian narrator's quest to find his razor, his gun, his girlfriend, and his own will to live. Although the narrator helps Dougie roll another lonesome soul, a red-headed cowboy, it is the narrator who is figuratively and literally tossed and rolled into having a "wounded knee," symbolic of the vast sorrow and guilt he feels for the death of his brother, Mose.

The most comedic cowboy, however, is Raymond Long Knife, an Indian who wears a championship "All-around Cowboy, Wolf Point Stampede, 1954," buckle and comes from "a long line of cowboys," the most impressive of which, ironically, is his mother, Belva Long Knife, who has the grit and the resolve to make everyone look away at her emasculating glare:

> Long Knife came from a long line of cowboys. Even his mother, per-haps the best of them all, rode all day, every day, when it came time to round up the cattle for branding. In the makeshift pen, she wres-tled calves, castrated them, then threw the balls into the ashes of the branding fire. She made a point of eating the roasted balls while glaring at one man, then another, even her sons, who, like the rest of us, stared at the brown hills until she was done. (31)

Welch, in one deft stroke after another, transvalues the western into the new Indian western. His other novels follow much in this vein, including *The Death of Jim Loney* (1979) and, most especially, *The Indian Lawyer* (1990).

Among the most contemporary of popular writers of the Indian west-ern is Sherman Alexie, whose *The Lone Ranger and Tonto Fist Fight in Heaven* (1994) symbolizes in title and theme and technique the growing potential of the western subverted. If the Lone Ranger cannot maintain either his dominance over Tonto or the ubiquitous sidekick scout's devotion, then, indeed, the western, as it once rode the purple-saged genre trails, rodeos, and dude ranches, has been bucked off.

In Alexie's story, the West and its glories, most especially its romanti-cism, are relegated to the environs of a 7-Eleven store in the far Northwest and the late-night shopping and ruminations of a displaced young urban Indian who seeks nothing more than a Creamsicle and some conversation.

Here the prototypic showdown, such as it is, becomes the fast draw of wit and repartee as the narrator — the Tonto figure — anticipates every "idea," every devastatingly ironic uppity and condescending suspicion of the store manager, having been there and back himself in his own past 7-Eleven employment. The title story and its accompanying tales of the triumphs of the downtrodden prove the liberating power, indeed, the empowerment, of self-respect discovered amidst disrespect for a world gone mad and finally exposed (albeit mirror-like) for what it is.

Silko, Welch, and Alexie are but representative authors of this new, old form — the "Indian western" — but in writing back, daring to talk back to the patterns and paradigms of a literary form which has, from its inception, preyed on the subservience of minorities, a new form is giving voice to new majorities.

Selected Bibliography

Alexie, Sherman. *The Lone Ranger and Tonto Fist Fight in Heaven*. New York: Harper-Collins, 1994.

Berkhofer, Robert, Jr. *The White Man's Indian*. New York: Vintage Books, 1979.

Silko, Leslie Marmon. *Ceremony*. New York: Viking Press, 1977.

———. "Yellow Woman." In *The Man to Send Rain Clouds: Contemporary Stories by American Indians*. Kenneth Rosen, ed. New York: Viking Press, 1974.

Welch, James. *The Death of Jim Loney*. New York: Harper, 1979.

———. *The Indian Lawyer*. New York: Norton, 1990.

———. *Winter in the Blood*. New York: Harper, 1974.

Pamela Maria Smorkaloff

The Popular West Across the Americas

In American history, the West is a place and the West is an idea. And the trouble with both is that they are constantly changing.

—David M. Shribman

In Latin America, by contrast, there is no West, there is no Frontier, there are only frontiers.

—Alistair Hennessy

...narrating Latinos, particularly after the 1980s, may also require the approach of a border writer or artist—not necessarily a Latino—but one able to remain afloat a bit more in the diaspora of an America with fewer borders, where North Americans, Latinos and Latin Americans are immersed (with others) in a give-and-take process of cultural and economic transformations within the same hemisphere.

—Ramón de la Campa

Although it has been suggested that the West, "with the magnetic pull of the setting sun, has a cosmic significance for all cultures" (Hennessy 6), it is important to situate its meaning—as history, myth, literary construct, geographic promise and element of a paradigm —across historical periods and across the Americas, particularly in an age increasingly informed by the sense of a "shrinking hemisphere." In Latin America and the Caribbean, from Shakespeare's depiction of the

926

clash between European and American values in *The Tempest* on, the "West" has meant, rather than "wide open spaces," Europe, Western civilization, and what Darcy Ribeiro, Leopoldo Zea and other Latin American cultural historians have termed "the civilizing mission." In Latin America, what was to be conquered was not the open plain of U.S. "westerns," inhabited only by wild horses or sparsely populated by Indians to be pushed out or eliminated but more often than not *all* the rural zones, the entire social landscape outside of the cosmopolitan capital or coastal cities that served as extensions of the viceroyalty. In this sense, the Latin American concept of "the West" gave rise to contemporary classics which constitute a kind of "literary reversal of the Conquest" in literary discourse, as well as to contemporary Latin American and Chicano popular fiction.

The paradigm of "civilization versus barbarism" is played out time and again in popular literature, through the 1930s, when the paradigm shifts. As the conquerors, then colonizers, took root in American lands, their literature described the world they encountered and their attempts to transform it in their own image. At the same time, the indigenous peoples offered their own version of events in the anonymous writings of the colony and the popular oral tradition. It is within this popular tradition, in the *décimas* of oral culture, the anonymous poems, mural paintings and other creative forms, that the struggle for nationhood and national culture define themselves in opposition to the official culture imposed over the first three centuries of colonization. In both Americas, as Hennessy has observed in his uncompromising interpretation of the Turner thesis and its significance for Latin America, "[o]pportunity on the frontier too often meant ignoring the claims of those who did not fit into this tidy evolutionary scheme"(4).

In the mid-1800s Sarmiento, who coined the phrase "civilization versus barbarism" in *Facundo* (1845), took on the conflict that defined for him the historical reality of the nation, and by extension, the continent, contrasting what he held to be the progressive principles guiding life in the cities, those of European spirit and culture, with the "barbaric" manifestations emanating from the rural, "savage," autochthonous areas. Thus, in the Romantic period, the first coherent phase of Latin American narrative to gel in the newly emancipated republics, "civilization" became synonymous with European culture, progress and the city, while "barbarism" signaled the ignorant, the backward, the rural, in short, the non-European, indigenous.

Although it is often difficult to distinguish, in hindsight, between the popular and the elitist, both types of narrative in Latin America drew upon the same sources, whether myth or reality. The best known novels of the Romantic period — *Doña Bárbara, Don Segundo Sombra, Cumandá, Enriquillo* — dealt with the task of "civilizing" the "barbarians," whether Indians, gauchos or ranchers. It is within this schema that all is interpreted: social life, history, national culture. Rather than aspiring to mitigate or domesticate "barbarism," Sarmiento's blueprint for civilization and that of his contemporaries and successors aimed to *crush* it with its centralist, European spirit. In *María* (1867), the most popular and widely read of the romantic novels, the conflict between the feudal leisure of the rural *latifundista* class and the incipient economic structure which is clearly moving toward commerce, industry and violent urbanization, is in full force. By the 1930s and the transition, in literature, toward the "novel of the land," the civilization/barbarism dichotomy had been resolved in favor of "civilization," with the "barbarians" relegated to the marginal areas of the city or the "backlands," silenced, abstracted and ignored.

On the other side of the border, the narratives produced by Mexican-Americans were marked by fierce cultural conflict under increasing Anglo dominance. Mariano Vallejo, patriarch of one of the *californio* clans, wrote his memoirs in 1912 to demonstrate that his people "were not indigents or a band of beasts" (Vallejo, cited in Paredes, 32).

The 1930s and 1940s mark a shift in the paradigm away from the "civilizing mission" and toward indigenous sources and interpretation with the translation into Spanish of the sacred books of the *Chilam Balam* and the *Popul Vuh*. It was these indigenous texts, then, that informed Asturias' *Men of Maize*, Carpentier's *The Lost Steps*, the works of Juan Rulfo, Gabriel García Márquez, José María Arguedas, and many others, and led to a general re-evaluation of the historical process in Latin America. If the end of the nineteenth century bore witness to, and much of the literature reflected, the justifiable fear of U.S. expansionism on the part of Latin Americans, the terms appear to be inverted as the twentieth century draws to a close. The performance poems of Guillermo Gómez Peña, with their complete rejection of the old notions of cultural, linguistic or ethnic purity among the Waspanos, Chicanadians, Mexa Yorkans, and other inter-American characters, as well as the essays by Chicano literary theorist José David Saldívar and the social critique of David Rieff in his explorations of Latin-North America, all testify to an atmosphere that recognizes the increasing encroachment of Latin America across the frontier and the reactions it provokes. In *Los Angeles: Capital of the Third World*, Rieff expresses the notion that

> at a certain moment during the twentieth century, the United States had stopped being an extension of Europe, and had, for better or worse, struck out on its own, an increasingly nonwhite country adrift, however majestically and powerfully, in an increasingly nonwhite world. (Rieff, cited in de la Campa, 11)

Others, with less apparent anxiety, take for granted the diminution of U.S. empire and the shrinking of the hemisphere; among them are the border-crossing detectives of Rolando Hinojosa's *Klail City Series* and the always unforgettable and often bilingual/bicultural protagonists of the novels of Paco Ignacio Taibo, II. Like them, Rigoberta Menchú, with her testimonial and chronicle of the contemporary Maya of Guatemala, is reaching a mass audience, outside academic or elite circles. And, like them, she is carving out a literary space for the "lost voices" of the vanquished, those left out of the official culture, the offical version, at all levels of discourse.

Finally, in a master stroke of intertextuality, Taibo's most recent novel, *Four Hands* — jointly narrated by the Mexican and North American investigative journalists who form an inseparable duo and conjure the possibility of an egalitarian and fruitful collaboration between the Americas, a true meeting of minds, hands, and hearts — opens with Stan Laurel's witnessing of the assassination of Pancho Villa from the window of a Parral hotel. Similarly, Héctor Belascoarán Shayne, the Spanish-Irish Mexican detective of *No Happy Ending*, raised on his father's "leftist-inspired stories of life in the Wild West, Wild Bill Hickock, Billy the Kid" (13) ultimately denounces the corruption of Mexican values by the invasion of Hollywood, the "impression that Hollywood's brief incursion into Durango made on a simple milkman: John Wayne seen leaving his hotel, Robert Mitchum pulling the trigger on a sawed-off shotgun during filming, a whole herd of horses let loose on the city streets..." (37). Along with the "real and imagined memories" is a revisionist fantasy, one that tips the scales and places the domineering "Wild West" of Hollywood and all that it signifies in a context of potential equality:

The one where you walk out of a steam bath and bump into Jack

Palance. Palance gives you a dirty look and swears at you in English, and you spit on the floor and slap him across the face. You told that story so many times that it became a part of your pseudo-reality. (38)

Selected Bibliography

Asturias, Miguel Angel. *Hombres de maíz*. Madrid: Alianza Editorial, 1982.

Carpentier, Alejo. *The Lost Steps*. Harriet de Onís, trans. New York: The Noonday Press, 1989.

de la Campa, Ramón. "Miami, Los Angeles and Other Latino Capitals." *Apuntes postmodernos/Postmodern Notes* (Fall 1994): 3-16.

de la Garza, Mercedes, ed. *Libro de Chilam Balam de Chumayel*. México: Secretaría de Educación Pública, 1988.

Gallegos, Rómulo. *Doña Bárbara*. Madrid: Espasa-Calpe, S.A., 1975.

Galván, Manuel de J. *Enriquillo: Leyenda histórica dominicana*. Mexico: Editorial Porrúa, 1976.

Gómez-Peña, Guillermo. "Border-Brujo: A Performance Poem." *TDR: The Drama Review,* 35:3 (1991): 48-66.

Güiraldes, Ricardo. *Don Segundo Sombra*. Buenos Aires: Colección Archivos, 1988.

Gutiérrez, Ramón, and Genaro Padilla, eds. *Recovering the U.S. Hispanic Literary Heritage*. Houston: Arte Público Press, 1993.

Hinojosa, Rolando. *Klail City*. Houston: Arte Público Press, 1987.

———. *Partners in Crime: A Rafe Buenrostro Mystery*. Houston: Arte Público Press, 1985.

Hennessy, Alistair. *The Frontier in Latin American History*. London: Edward Arnold Ltd., 1978.

Isaacs, Jorge. *María*. Madrid: Espasa-Calpe, 1976.

Menchú, Rigoberta. *I, Rigoberta Menchú: An Indian Woman in Guatemala*. Elizabeth Burgos-Deray, ed., Ann Wright, trans. London: Verso, 1986.

Mera, Juan León. *Cumandá o un drama entre salvajes*. Madrid: Espasa-Calpe, 1976.

Paredes, Raymund. "Mexican-American Literature: An Overview." In *Recovering the U.S. Hispanic Literary Heritage*. Ramón Gutiérrez and Genaro Padilla, eds. Houston: Arte Público Press, 1993. Pp. 31-51.

Ribeiro, Darcy. *The Americas and Civilization*. New York: Dutton, 1971.

———. *The Civilization Process*. Washington: The Smithsonian Institution Press, 1978.

Saldívar, José David. *The Dialectics of Our America: Genealogy, Cultural Critique and Literary History*. Durham: Duke University Press, 1991.

Saravia E., Albertina, ed. *Popul Wuj: Antiguas historias de los indios quichés de Guatemala*. Mexico: Editorial Porrúa, 1986.

Sarmiento, Domingo F. *Life in the Argentine Republic in the Days of the Tyrants or, Civilization or Barbarism*. New York: Collier Books, 1961.

Taibo, Paco Ignacio, II. *No Happy Ending*. William I. Neuman, trans. New York: Mysterious Press, 1994.

———. *Four Hands*. Laura C. Dail, trans. New York: St. Martin's Press, 1994.

Turner, Frederick Jackson. "The Significance of the Frontier in American History." *The*

Structure of Political Geography. Roger E. Kasperson and Julian V. Minghi, eds. Chicago: Aldine, 1969. Pp. 132-139.

Zea, Leopoldo. *Filosofía de la historia americana.* Mexico: Fondo de Cultura Económica, 1978.

———. *Dialéctica de la conciencia americana.* Mexico: Alianza Editorial Mexicana, 1975.

Geoff Sadler

European Popular Westerns

The story of the West is rooted in American history. The pioneer expansion and the vision of the frontier are part of the national consciousness and relate to a specific past with precise geographic locations. European perceptions of the West have been tempered not only by distance from the original source but by the lack of that clearly defined historical perspective. Theirs has been a learned rather than a natural language, acquired at second hand. Early European images of western life were gleaned from travelers' tales, reports in newspapers, and a variety of literature from Fenimore Cooper to the dime novels of Beadle and Adams. These disparate influences shaped a vision of the West as Edenic garden or untamed wilderness, peopled by "savages" who were by turns portrayed as noble or depraved (see Billington). With few exceptions, European "westerns" have been formulaic in concept and execution. This said, and within these limitations, Europe may fairly claim to have developed a separate fictional subgenre with a distinct style and character and has at times achieved its own brand of excellence.

Foremost among early European western writers was the German Karl May (1842-1912), who in the 1890s began to produce fiction set in the American West. May, whose colorful career included a spell in jail, had never visited the United States but made up for his lack of first-hand knowledge with an extremely fertile imagination. *Winnetou* (3 vols., 1893-1910) and *Old Shurehand* (3 vols., 1894) feature the most famous

932

of his heroes, the Apache warrior Winnetou and the Germanic frontiersman best known as Old Shatterhand. The influence of Fenimore Cooper is unmistakable, but May manages to imbue both protagonists with the stamp of his own personality. Written as first-person narratives, his novels have flimsy plots and lack psychological depth but are exciting and highly imaginative. A best-selling author with his own publishing company, May was outsold in Europe only by the Bible and became a pervasive influence on later generations. Later still, his books gave rise to several German films which were to have a far-reaching effect of their own.

In Britain, the western novel had a range of ancestors, among them the "boys' adventure" stories of G. A. Henty and R. M. Ballantyne. One such spiritual precursor was Robert Leighton, whose *Softfoot of Silver Creek* (1926) is aimed at the younger reader and describes events surrounding the Fetterman and Custer "massacres" through the eyes of a Pawnee warrior serving as a cavalry scout.

The first significant European western writer to appear after May and probably the first recognizably "modern" western author was Oliver Strange (1871-1952). A former fiction editor, Strange was sixty when his first novel was published. *The Range Robbers* (1930) is the ancestor of the British formula western, a "revenge and pursuit" adventure starring the outlaw hero "Sudden." Intended as a one-off, it became so popular that Strange wrote nine further "Sudden" titles. His style mingles artificial "western" dialogue with high-flown literary English, and his villains come direct from Victorian melodrama, but Strange's pace and plotting ensure readability. His work was reissued to popular acclaim in the 1960s and inspired a number of sequels.

Although by now distinct from its parent genre, the European western continued to imbibe various American influences during the postwar period. Two writers from the U.S.A. whose work sold heavily in Britain were W. C. Tuttle and Charles H. Snow, whose prolific output of "shoot-'em-ups" found a ready audience. More important were the spate of western B-movies with their blend of dramatic incident and slapstick humour, usually featuring series characters. The combined impact was evident in the British publishing boom of 1945 to 1955, when publishers Collins, Hale, Gresham, Jenkins, and Brown and Watson, and magazines such as *West*, *Thrilling Western* and *Exciting Western* provided outlets for a group of hard-working journeyman authors. Arthur Nickson (1902-1974) was one of the leading exponents of this era, bringing out several strong, individual formula westerns. Nickson and most of his contemporaries wrote on into the 1970s, long after the brief boom period had faded. By then, another British writer had emerged, who was to prove the most popular of all.

J. T. Edson (1928-), who first appeared in the early 1950s, wrote over 100 titles in inter-related series based on such central characters as Dusty Fog, Mark Counter, and the Ysabel Kid. Presenting himself as an uneducated "redneck," he denied any literary pretensions, but his novels displayed considerable skill. Edson soon dominated the European western scene and achieved best-selling success in the U. S. A. He is currently the biggest selling western author in the world and, although now retired, enjoys undiminished popularity.

An offshoot of the British western took root in Australia in the early 1950s. It began with the founding of the Cleveland Publishing Propriety in Sydney by Jack Atkins, who employed a group of dedicated and indefatigable authors. Most notable of these was Leonard Meares (1921-1993), who as "Marshall Grover" wrote several hundred action westerns, his best-known series involving the Texan partners "Larry and Stretch." Meares established the "Aussie western" as a form, and his work is still read worldwide. Other leading figures include Paul Wheelahan ("Emerson Dodge") and Keith Hetherington ("Kirk Hamilton"). Like the British, the Australian writers betray the B-movie influence, but with their own Outback frontier and Ned Kelly "bushranger" tradition have shaped a personal variant of the western genre.

The late 1950s saw a gradual toughening of storylines and an increase in graphic violence. Jack Borg, whose "Hogleg Bailey" series had an established readership, mixed B-movie humor with an increasingly brutal action. This "hard-boiling" of the genre continued into the sixties and seventies, eventually giving rise to the so-called "adult western." John Prebble (1915-), mainly noted for his historical nonfiction, was an exception to the rule, producing a handful of novels and stories which show both originality and skill. *Spanish Stirrup* (1958) has a family conflict set against a cattle-drive background, while *The Buffalo Soldiers* (1959) provides a sympathetic picture of black cavalrymen after the Civil War.

The most significant European development of the 1960s was not textual, but cinematic. The "spaghetti western" films directed by Sergio Leone and starring Clint Eastwood presented a vision of the West as a brutal wasteland peopled by psychopathic killers in pursuit of "a fistful of dollars." A genuine multi-national phenomenon, shot in Spain under Italian direction, the "Dollar" films were apparently influenced by the German "Shatterhand" movies of the early sixties, based on Karl May's stories. In their turn they became the inspiration for the "adult western" novel, which spawned a fresh publishing boom in the seventies and early eighties.

The "adult western" was usually a full-length paperback of 75,000 words, as opposed to the 45,000-word hardbacks published in the United Kingdom before and since. Graphically violent and sexually explicit, the "adult western" inherited the murderous characters and arid landscapes of the Eastwood films in what was often a rigidly contrived form. It was essentially the preserve of four gifted writers — Terry Harknett (1936-), John Harvey (1938-), Angus Wells (1943-) and Laurence James (1942-) — who singly or in partnership turned out a seemingly endless stream of violent westerns, in series, under various pseudonyms. Harknett, who as "George G. Gilman" achieved the greatest fame with his anti-heroes "Edge" and "Steele," is the leading exponent of this sub-genre, with his particular blend of savagery and gallows humor. Harvey offers a gentler, reflective aspect of the same basic form. The "adult western" remained popular into the mid-1980s, when most of its practitioners moved on to other areas of creativity.

Contemporary with this group, but not of it, was Peter Watts (1919-1983), who as "Matt Chisholm" created three excellent western series — "Blade," "Storm" and "McAllister" — with strong characters, imaginative plots, and superb dialogue. If Edson is the most popular European western writer, Watts is surely the most accomplished, with a moral force and psychological depth lacking in most of his fellow western authors. William Rayner (1929-), usually a historical or adventure writer, brought out three novels in the 1970s which qualify as westerns of an unusual kind. Their flashback narrative and experimental style are unlike any other European western.

The most important development on the continent came in Scandinavia, with the emergence of the Bladkompaniet publishing house in Oslo, Norway. Under the guidance of editor Finn Arnessen, Bladkompaniet employed several western authors, whose series enjoyed a wide readership in Scandinavia and elsewhere. Their biggest name was the native-born Kjell Halbing, who as "Louis Masterson" created his own "adult western"-style anti-hero, Morgan Kane, in 100 titles which revisit the familiar revenge and quest themes with their own effective, brooding atmosphere. Otherwise, the main non-English-speaking author was the German Thomas Jeier, who in addition to his novels wrote nonfiction works on the American West. A British author published on the continent was Mike Linaker (1940-), whose "Jason Brand" series, brought out by Bladkompaniet, includes some of his best work.

With the passing of the "adult western" and the effective collapse of the U. K. western paperback market, the main publishing outlet nowadays is Robert Hale Ltd., whose hardback novels are printed in runs of 1,000-1,500 and aimed primarily at library sales. Within this shrinking scene several talented authors have emerged to produce work of individual merit. Among other work, B. J. Holmes (1939-), a keen student of film, has revived May's Shatterhand character in *A Legend Called Shatterhand* (1990). G. J. Barrett (1928-), a gifted veteran, has produced scores of lively "actioners." David Whitehead (1958-), a young writer of exceptional ability, shows an inspired use of language and unusually imaginative plotting skills. Mike Stotter (1957-) produced a memorable first novel and is currently working on a series. Geoff Sadler (1943-) presents the West as a plural, multi-ethnic society and features black, Native American and Hispanic characters in leading roles. M. M. Rowan (1943-) and Amy Sadler (1924-) have added their female perspective to the genre. The cover designs for most Hale westerns are produced by female Spanish commercial artists; in this respect, "Norma," "Faba" and their colleagues have made a personal and visual contribution to the finished work. These latest recruits demonstrate clearly that the western is not the monopoly of the male or the middle-aged, and for as long as this holds true, it will not yet be time to ride into the sunset.

Selected Bibliography

Primary Sources

Barrett, Geoffrey John [as Bill Wade]. *Tombstone Tuck*. London: Hale, 1973.
———[as Dan Royal]. *Red Queen of the Crater Range*. London: Hale, 1985.
Borg, John Philip Anthony [as Jack Borg]. *Gunsmoke Feud*. London: Jenkins, 1957.
——— [as Jack Borg]. *Trail of Dead Men*. London: Hale, 1975.
Edson, J[ohn] T[homas]. *The Ysabel Kid*. London: Brown & Watson, 1962; rpt., New York: Berkley, 1978.
———. *Goodnight's Dream*. London: Corgi, 1969; rpt., *The Floating Outfit*. New York: Bantam, 1971.
———. *J.T.'s Ladies*. London: Corgi, 1980.

————. *The Code of Dusty Fog*. London: Hale, 1989.

Halbing, Kjell [as Louis Masterson]. *Helvete under null*. Oslo, Norway: Bladkompaniet, 1968; Jeffrey Wallman, trans. *Hell Below Zero*. London: Corgi, 1974.

————.[as Louis Masterson]. *De doedes dag*. Oslo, Norway: Bladkompaniet, 1969; Jeffrey Wallman, trans. *The Day of Death*. London: Corgi, 1975.

Harknett, Terry [as George G. Gilman]. *The Loner*. London: New English Library, 1972; New York: Pinnacle, 1972.

————. [as George G. Gilman]. *The Violent Peace*. London: New English Library, 1974; rpt., *Rebels and Assassins Die Hard*. New York: Pinnacle, 1975.

————. [as George G. Gilman]. *The Rifle*. London: New English Library, 1989.

Harvey, John. *The Silver Lie*. London: Pan, 1980.

————. [as John J. McLaglen]. *Till Death*. London: Corgi, 1980.

Hetherington, Keith [as Kirk Hamilton]. *Trail Wolves*. Sydney, Australia: Cleveland, n.d.

————. [as Kirk Hamilton]. *The 12:10 from San Antone*. Sydney, Australia: Cleveland, n.d.

Holmes, B[ryan] J[ohn]. *Dark Rider*. London: Hale, 1987.

————. *A Legend Called Shatterhand*. London: Hale, 1990.

Jeier, Thomas. *Return to Canta Lupe*. Jeffrey Wallman, trans. London: Hale, 1984.

————. *The Celluloid Kid*. Jeffrey Wallman, trans. London: Hale, 1986.

Leighton, Robert. *Softfoot of Silver Creek*. London and Melbourne, Australia: Ward Lock, 1926.

Linaker, Mike [as Matt Jordan]. *Brigham's Way*. London: Jenkins, 1976.

————. [as Dan Stewart]. *Savage Gun*. London: Jenkins, 1976.

————. [as Neil Hunter]. *Devil's Gold*. Oslo, Norway: Bladkompaniet, 1978.

May, Karl. *Winnetou*. 3 vols. Freiburg: Fehsenfeld, 1893-1910.

————. *Old Shurehand*. Freiburg: Fehsenfeld, 1894.

————. *Mein Leben und Streben*. Freiburg: Fehsenfeld, 1910.

Meares, Leonard [as Marshall Grover]. *Hartigan*. Sydney, Australia: Horwitz, 1971.

————. [as Marshall Grover]. *Young Bucks from Texas*. Sydney, Australia: Horwitz, 1982.

————. [as Marshall Grover]. *Texas Born, Chicago Bound*. Sydney, Australia: Horwitz, 1983.

Nickson, Arthur [as Matt Winstan]. *Gunslick Marshal*. London: Jenkins, 1966.

———— [as Roy Peters]. *Alias Sam Smith*. London: Ward Lock, 1968.

Prebble, John. *Spanish Stirrup*. New York: Harcourt Brace, 1958.

————. *My Great-Aunt Appearing Day and Other Stories*. London: Secker & Warburg, 1958.

————. *The Buffalo Soldiers*. London: Secker & Warburg; New York: Harcourt Brace, 1959.

Rayner, William. *The Bloody Affray at Riverside Drive*. London: Collins, 1972; rpt., *Seth and Belle and Mr. Quarles and Me*. New York: Simon & Schuster, 1973.

————. *The Trail to Bear Paw Mountain*. London: Collins, 1974; New York: Ballantine, 1976.

————. *A Weekend with Captain Jack*. London: Collins, 1975; New York: Ballantine, 1977.

Rowan, Marie [as M. M. Rowan]. *Absarokas*. London: Hale, 1989.

Sadler, Amy. *Feuding at Dutchman's Creek*. London: Hale, 1990.

Sadler, Geoff [as Jeff Sadler]. *Saltillo Road*. London: Hale, 1987.

————. [as Jeff Sadler]. *Hangrope Journey*. London: Hale, 1994.

————. [as Wes Calhoun]. *Chulo*. London: Hale, 1988.

937

Stotter, Mike. *McKinney's Revenge*. London: Hale, 1990.

Strange, [Thomas] Oliver. *The Range Robbers*. London: Newnes, 1930; New York: Dial Press, 1931.

Watts, Peter [as Matt Chisholm]. *Death at Noon*. London: Mayflower, 1963.

———. [as Matt Chisholm]. *The Hangman Rides Tall*. London: Mayflower, 1963; New York: Beagle, 1971.

———. [as Matt Chisholm]. *Thunder in the West*. London: Mayflower, 1973.

———. [as Matt Chisholm]. *The Nevada Mustang*. London: Hamlyn, 1979.

Wheelahan, Paul [as Emerson Dodge]. *The Target is a Star*. Sydney, Australia: Cleveland, n.d.

———. [as Emerson Dodge]. *When Gun Kings Die*. Sydney, Australia: Cleveland, n.d.

Whitehead, David. *Hang 'Em All*. London: Hale, 1989.

———. [as Ben Bridges]. *The Deadly Dollars*. London: Hale, 1988.

———. [as Ben Bridges]. *Marked for Death*. London: Hale, 1993.

Secondary Sources

Billington, Ray Allen. *Land of Savagery, Land of Promise: The European Image of the American Frontier in the 19th Century*. New York: W. W. Norton, 1980.

Dahl, Willy. *Morgan Kane fra Norge: en studie i litteraer suksess*. Bergen: Eide, 1976.

Dittrich, M. *Karl May und seine Schriften: eine literarische-psychologische studie*. Dresden: n. p., 1904.

Dworczak, K.H. *Das Leben Old Shatterhands*. Salzburg: Pfad, 1950.

Frayling, Christopher. *Spaghetti Westerns: Cowboys and Europeans from Karl May to Sergio Leone*. London: Routledge and Kegan Paul, 1981.

Sadler, Geoff, ed. *Twentieth-Century Western Writers*. 2nd ed. Chicago and London: St. James Press, 1991.

Schmidt, Arno. *Sitara und der Weg dorthin: eine studie uber Wesen, Werk und Wirkung Karl May's*. Karlsruhe: Stahlberg, 1963.

Victoria Lamont

B. M. Bower

Critical acclaim, popularity, and longevity have not sufficed to secure B.M. Bower (1871-1940) a position of prominence in western literary history, in which she has figured only marginally. In her own day, as Stanley R. Davison observes in his survey of contemporary reviews of Bower's work, Bower's novels were favorably compared to those of her male counterparts and demand for them was such that she was able to publish two a year for over three decades. In spite of this contribution of some sixty novels and countless short stories to the field of the popular western, Bower is not now considered to have had a significant impact on the genre. Nor has she been included in the relatively recent feminist recovery of forgotten western writing by women, undertaken in works such as *Women, Women Writers, and the West* (1979) and *Women and Western American Literature* (1982). As a willing participant in a mythology which, according to influential feminist texts such as Annette Kolodny's *The Land Before Her* (1984) and Jane Tompkins' *West of Everything* (1992), she should experience as alien to her female subject-position, Bower is difficult to position as a representative voice within this emerging "women's West." Yet, despite her apparent complicity with a masculinist discourse, Bower's novels not only unsettle the male hero's privileged status in popular western mythology, but many of them also take up a feminist project in explicit and radical ways.

Bower's biographical history has not been well documented, but ear-

939

lier critics, such as J. Frank Dobie, Joe B. Frantz, and Julian Ernest Choate, Jr., have made note of her western upbringing as a major influence on her writing. Born in Minnesota, she moved with her family to Montana at an early age and lived in several western states over the course of her life. According to Davison, she began writing while in Montana, where she worked as a schoolteacher. Living in the West, according to Frantz and Choate, gave Bower "what so many cowboy writers lack, a real background of life among the bowlegged brethren."

As a result of Bower's status as a native westerner, critics saw reflected in her writing an intimate acquaintance with a "real West" which provided a refreshing alternative to other popular westerns of the time. Certainly, the popularity of her *Flying U* stories has prompted Roy W. Meyer to dub Bower "the poor man's Wister." But Bower challenges the paradigm established in *The Virginian* (1902) as often as she invokes it. Her novels contain their share of rugged heroes, genteel heroines, tenderfoots, outlaws, roundups, gunfights, and other ingredients familiar to the "classic" western formula; but she also constantly reminds us that in reading about the American West we are engaging with a figure of discourse. Indeed, one of her earliest novels, *The Lure of the Dim Trails* (1907), is a western about writing westerns. The protagonist, an easterner who aspires to "write a story that would breathe of the plains," finds that the "real" West contradicts, in various ways, that of his romantic imagination, making him wonder "if he should ever again feel qualified to write of these things" (133, 71).

This emphasis on textuality enables Bower to unsettle familiar myths of the West in many of her novels. In *The Happy Family* (1907), she gleefully undercuts the idealized status of western masculinity by representing it as a performative fiction, particularly in the figure of Andy Green, whose legendary horsemanship skills are the product of a past which he fears might call his virility into question. "Before he wandered to the range, [he] had danced in spangled tights, upon the broad rump of a big gray horse which galloped around a sawdust ring with the regularity of movement that suggested a machine, while a sober-clothed man in the center cracked a whip and yelped commands" — a fact of which Andy is "just a trifle ashamed" (120).

Sensitivity to the West and its cast of characters as figures of discourse informs a more seriously revisionist project that can be traced in Bower's work and encompasses not only the relatively radical treatments of race and gender in such texts as *Lonesome Land* (1911) and

Good Indian (1912) but also in the more conventional *Chip of the Flying U* (1904). However closely the last novel's romantic couple, Chip and Dell, resemble the stormy pairing of the Virginian and Molly Stark, Bower does not deploy Wister's dialectic model of gender relations in the West without revision. We are warned at the beginning of the novel that we can expect some departures from the traditional cast of western female figures, one of whom Chip imagines Dell will be: "Sweet Young Things that faint away at the sight of a six-shooter," parodies of masculinity who "wear double-barreled skirts and ride a man's saddle and smoke cigarettes," or perhaps the "skinny old maid with peaked nose and glasses, that'll round us up every Sunday and read tracts at our heads" (18-19). With these fictions in mind, the Flying U cowboys decide to mark Dell's arrival in the West by staging "a real, old lynching"—designed, of course, to scare her out of what they imagine to be her tender, eastern wits (21). No sooner does she arrive at the ranch, escorted by Chip, than she is presented with the sound of "menacing yells" and the sight of "a limp form...dragged from the cabin and lifted to the back of a snorting pony." But Dell soon sees through this "confused jumble of gesticulating men" and, with "amused chagrin that they should try to trick her so," urges Chip to "hurry up" so that she "can be in at the death" (36-37).

Feminist readers may find the conclusion of *Chip of the Flying U* unsatisfying because of the subordinate position in which it ultimately places its heroine. In the novel's concluding chapter, Dell is left stranded by a runaway horse and must submit not only to Chip's rescue but also to the sexual advantage he takes of her vulnerability: "A pair of arms...went suddenly about her....She threw back her head, startled ...at the touch of lips that were curved and thin and masterful" (262). Dell offers only token resistance, leaving us with a final image of this formerly independent heroine entrapped in Chip's unyielding embrace. In a later novel, however, Bower negotiates a more explicitly feminist version of western individualism. *Lonesome Land's* heroine, Val Fleetwood, leaves her urban home to start a new life as mistress of Cold Spring Ranch, which she envisions as "a veritable Eve's garden" from which she will fashion an ideal domicile made possible by the hard work of her pioneering husband—the ironically named Manley (61). These romantic expectations give way to harsh reality: Manley turns out to be a drunkard whose abusive treatment of Val compels her eventually to reject her position of dependence. Tellingly, Val earns her own income by writing western stories, a move which signals female authority as a possible way of resisting masculinist mythologies of the West.

Race also emerges as a contested topic for Bower, whose *Good Indian* takes issue with the "purely American" assumption that "the only good Indian is a dead Indian" (8). Although, as Davison observes, Bower often reifies racial stereotypes in her representation of native Americans — making them either childlike, demonic, or (in the case of women) exotic and eroticized — *Good Indian* puts pressure on racist discourse by complicating, in the figure of Grant Imsen, simplistic racial binaries. Imsen's "paternal ancestry went back, and back to no one knows where among the race of blue eyes and fair skin," but his mother "had been the half-caste daughter of Wolfbelly's sister.... And because he stood thus between the two races of men, his exact social status [was] a subject always open to argument" (8-9). A series of plot twists ensues, leading Imsen to moral and legal victory. By the end of the novel, he is renowned as "a man who had the courage to defend himself and those dear to him from a great danger" (362).

Novels such as *Lonesome Land* and *Good Indian* make B. M. Bower's work relevant to the emerging revisionist history of western American literature, which has been particularly attentive to issues of race and gender. But, politics aside, Bower's playful satire, elegantly clever turns of phrase, and creative manipulation of popular plots and characters also make for some very engaging and provocative reading. Stanley R. Davison quotes a 1928 issue of the *Book Review Digest* which says of Bower's work, "there's everything that'll please them who don't know the West and them who do." That observation still rings true.

Selected Bibliography

Bower, B. M. *Chip of the Flying U*. New York: G. W. Dillingham Company, 1904.

———. *Good Indian*. Boston: Little, Brown, and Company, 1912.

———. *The Happy Family*. New York: G. W. Dillingham Company, 1907.

———. *Lonesome Land*. Boston: Little, Brown, and Company, 1912.

———. *The Lure of the Dim Trails*. New York: G. W. Dillingham Company, 1907.

Branch, Edgar Douglas. *The Cowboy and His Interpreters*. New York: D. Appleton & Company, 1926.

Davison, Stanley R. "Chip of the Flying U: The Author Was a Lady." *Montana: The Magazine of Western History* 23:2 (April 1973): 2-15.

Dinan, John A. *The Pulp Western: A Popular History of the Western Fiction Magazine in America*. San Bernardino, California: Borgo Press, 1983.

Dobie, J. Frank. *Guide to Life and Literature of the Southwest*. Dallas: Southern Methodist University Press, 1952.

Engen, Orrin A. *Writer of the Plains*. Culver City, California: The Pontine Press, 1973.

Frantz, Joe B. and Julian E. Choate, Jr. *The American Cowboy: The Myth and the Reality*. Norman: University of Oklahoma Press, 1955.

Kolodny, Annette. *The Land Before Her: Fantasy and Experience of the American Frontiers, 1630-1860*. Chapel Hill: University of North Carolina Press, 1984.

Lee, L. L. and Merrill Lewis, eds. *Women, Women Writers, and the West*. Troy, New York: The Whitston Publishing Co., 1979.

Meyer, Roy W. "B. M. Bower: The Poor Man's Wister." In *The Popular Western: Essays Toward a Definition*. Richard W. Etulain and Michael T. Marsden, eds. Bowling Green, Ohio: Bowling Green University Popular Press, 1974.

Sadler, Geoff, ed. *Twentieth-Century Western Writers*. 2nd ed. Chicago and London: St. James Press, 1991.

Stauffer, Helen Winter and Susan J. Rosowski, eds. *Women and Western American Literature*. Troy, New York: The Whitston Publishing Co., 1982.

Tompkins, Jane. *West of Everything: The Inner Life of Westerns*. New York: Oxford University Press, 1992.

Wister, Owen. *The Virginian*. 1902. New York: Penguin, 1988.

William A. Bloodworth, Jr.

Max Brand

Much about Max Brand has little to do with the literature of the American West. Even though Frederick Schiller Faust (1892-1944), the person who used "Max Brand" as his most famous pen name, was born in Seattle, grew up in California, and became a Hollywood scriptwriter in the last six years of his life, his own allegiances were much further east—in New York and, for many years, in Italy. Even his literary forms—popular historical novels, detective stories, and a series of tales about a young New York doctor named Jimmy Kildare—were often alien to the West in setting and mode.

Between 1917 and 1936, however, hundreds of westerns "by Max Brand" and by other Faust pseudonyms were published in magazines (mainly of the pulp variety) and as books. These began most notably with a strange story entitled *The Untamed* that first appeared in late 1918 as a serial in *All-Story Weekly*, a Munsey Company pulp. Munsey magazines began to feature Max Brand westerns on a regular basis thereafter. With the development of Street and Smith's weekly *Western Story Magazine* in the 1920s, Max Brand westerns gained a major new outlet —and from 1921 to 1938 Frederick Faust provided almost three hundred novelettes or book-length serials for the magazine. In effect, the writer was a stable of writers—using such other pen names, in addition to Max Brand, as George Owen Baxter, David Manning, Nicholas Silver, Lee Bolt, Peter Henry Morland, and Evan Evans.

In later years, especially after Faust's death in 1944 (in Italy, where he was serving at the advanced age of fifty-one as a war correspondent for *Harper's*), virtually all Faust reprints bore the Max Brand byline. Today it is common to speak of Max Brand as the author of record of all of Faust's western fiction and of much of his non-western work. In this sense, as the identifying feature of a large body of westerns, most of which have been reprinted at least once after their original magazine appearances, Max Brand is an unavoidable, pervasive fixture in the history of popular western literature.

Until recently, Max Brand had escaped serious attention by literary historians and critics. There is a form of poetic justice in this fact because Faust himself never took pride in his western stories. He wrote with great speed and narrative flair but considered the work he produced only a means of earning enough money to pursue more serious interests, especially the writing of traditional but unremarkable poetry. In fact, he was even able to keep his identity as a "western" writer a secret for more than twenty years. Ironically, scholarly attention to Max Brand in the 1980s and 1990s has had far better things to say about his works and their significance than the author might ever have imagined. Were he alive, he doubtless would be embarrassed by even the mildest claim of significance attached to his western fiction — and might even find himself in complete agreement with *Time's* 1952 assessment of Max Brand stories as "the gooey residue of boiled pulp."

In reality, the significance of Max Brand hardly can be overstated in the sheer terms of audience. He was a staple of popular culture not only during his heyday as a living writer of westerns (approximately 1919 to 1935) but also later, as his paperbacks were continuously reprinted and read. In Hollywood his 1930 *Destry Rides Again* gained classic film status (appearing in three versions), and many other Max Brand stories reached the screen in silent and sound productions between 1917 and 1954.

While the number of readers and viewers has been large, the literary impact of Max Brand has been minimal. Max Brand is a reader's writer, not a writer's writer. Almost no testimonies of influence have ever been offered by other writers of westerns. (One exception is the contemporary William F. Nolan, author of the science fiction *Logan's Run* and dozens of other books, including some westerns.) This absence of influence is due first of all to Frederick Faust's lack of contact with and interest in other western writers. Even if he had desired such contact, which he did not, his status as an expatriate writer in Italy from 1926 to 1938 would have prevented it. Nor was Faust a thematic writer with a particular attitude or message about the West. For him, the American West was an imaginary realm that provided a useful locus for adventure stories. More importantly, he felt no urge to support the Turnerian view of the West as the central determinant of American character.

However much he avoided the interests and themes of the traditional literary West, Frederick Faust—as Max Brand—had incredible story-telling ability. Expressions of this ability show up in his best-known work, the *Untamed* series (*The Untamed, The Night Horseman, The Seventh Man,* 1919-1921), and *Destry Rides Again.* His westerns feature heroes who are set apart from other humans by peculiar, innate qualities as well as experience—and who usually face unredeemably bad villains. Fast action and an absence of contemplation characterize his plots. But little is truly typical in Max Brand, and surprises abound. Faust's imagination was extraordinarily open to quasi-mythological elements that have led some observers, such as Jon Tuska, to Jungian conclusions. Whatever the validity of such conclusions, realism was at best a secondary concern for Faust. Instead, he had a Hawthorne-like sense of the "tale" (rather than "fiction") which, in words he wrote in 1942, "abandons all attempts to give an exact replica of life."

It is also true, as Christine Bold shows clearly in her *Selling the Wild West: Popular Western Fiction, 1860-1960* (1987), that Faust endured a continuous internal struggle between his classic artistic desires and his success as a writer of "commercial" fiction. He was always unhappily both a classicist and a hack. This division in Faust, obvious in the pattern of his life and acknowledged in his private correspondence, hardly constitutes a major theme in his westerns. But it does make Max Brand an exaggerated example of a common problem in western American literature: a divergence between the expectations of audience (including editors) and the artistic inclination of the writer. In the case of writers like Zane Grey and Louis L'Amour, it is convenient to assume a perfect fit between the intentions of the writer and the hopes of readers.

For Max Brand, however, the fit never seemed to be comfortable in a western style. In fact, much of what he wrote runs against the grain of the popular western as defined by other practitioners of the genre. He seldom celebrated the historical West or even featured specific locales, preferring instead a vague geography of deserts, rivers, or mountains as needed by his plots. His main characters are often based on European mythological figures instead of American westerners. And at times Faust was able, by intent or otherwise, to produce rich internal conflicts within his characters and stories. This is especially the case with a series of three "white Indian" novels written in the early 1930s. These novels, issued as books entitled *War Party*, *Frontier Feud*, and *Cheyenne Gold* (first published in 1933-1935), began with Faust's stated intention of producing a "tragic viewpoint" based on the inability of whites and Indians to understand one another. Although Faust eventually toned down his anti-white implications in these stories, as his magazine editor requested, they are remarkable examples of the direction in which Faust was capable of moving as a pulp writer.

As a western American writer, basically Californian in origin, rather than a writer of westerns, Max Brand is notable for the sheer range of fiction produced by Faust and issued under the Brand byline. My 1993 *Max Brand* (Twayne Publishers) attempts to survey this range, which includes urban romances, detective stories, spy novels, European historical adventures, pirate tales, a very few stylish short stories, poetry, and the Dr. Kildare medical dramas. In reference to the last item, Max Brand's most profound influence on American culture probably came through the images of a heroic young medical doctor. Unfortunately, however, "Max Brand" is virtually synonymous with the popular western, and most of the scholarship available on Frederick Faust is limited to his western fiction. Since that fiction alone amounts to an equivalent of more than two hundred novels, it may seem illogical to say that there is much more than that to the western writer identified as (and with) Max Brand. But "much more" is the truth of the matter.

Selected Bibliography

Note: Since Max Brand has been and continues to be published in a variety of re-issued and sometimes re-titled books, the best guides to primary works are the books below by Bloodworth and, especially, Nolan.

Bloodworth, William A., Jr. *Max Brand*. New York: Twayne Publishers, 1993.
———. "Max Brand's West." *Western American Literature,* 16 (Fall 1981): 177-191.
Bold, Christine. *Selling the Wild West: Popular Western Fiction, 1860-1960.* Bloomington: Indiana University Press, 1987.
Chapman, Edgar L. "The Image of the Indian in Max Brand's Pulp Western Novels." *Heritage of Kansas,* 11 (Spring 1978): 16-45.
——— "Max Brand/Frederick Faust." In *Popular World Fiction,* Vol. 1. Washington, D. C.: Beacham Publishing, 1987.

Easton, Robert. *Max Brand: The Big "Westerner."* Norman: University of Oklahoma Press, 1970.

Hamilton, Cynthia S. *Western and Hard-Boiled Detective Fiction in America.* Iowa City: University of Iowa Press, 1987.

Nolan, William F. *Max Brand: Western Giant.* Bowling Green, Ohio: Bowling Green State University Popular Press, 1985.

Franz Blaha

Zane Grey

The fifty-six novels that constitute Zane Grey's contribution to the western do not rank him with the most prolific writers of the genre, but they establish him both as the best-selling and most recognized name in popular western literature, ranking him at one time only behind the Bible and McGuffey's Readers as the third best-selling author in U.S. literary history (Jackson 1989, 140). By the time of his death in 1939, some twenty-seven million copies of his novels had been sold, a total that had increased to forty million by 1968 (Gruber, 1970, 243). Even today approximately 500,000 copies of his books are sold each year, sales figures surpassed only by Louis L'Amour.

Born Pearl Zane Gray in 1872 in Zanesville, Ohio, Grey's childhood and youth did not predict a successful literary career. Professional baseball player manqué, he became a reluctant dentist with a passion for writing. Supported by the editorial and financial help of his future wife, Grey jettisoned dentistry and in 1903 began to write a three-part history of his maternal ancestors, the founders of Zanesville, while adopting the nom de plume Zane Grey. *Betty Zane*, the first part, was published at his own expense, and the subsequent volumes went unpublished or met with no success.

The turning point in Grey's literary career came when he met Colonel J. C. (Buffalo) Jones and accepted an invitation to his ranch in Arizona. As was the case with Owen Wister, this western excursion became an epiphany for Grey, who from that point on dedicated his writing almost exclusively to the American West. Ironically, his Buffalo Jones novel, *The Last of the Plainsmen*, was rejected by Harper's, who later published almost all his fiction, with the stinging commentary that there was no visible evidence of any literary promise. Barely surviving by selling fishing and sporting stories, Grey persisted and serialized his novel *The Heritage of the Desert* with *Popular Magazine* in 1910. In 1912, Grey persuaded the vice-president of Harper's to overrule his editors and publish *Riders of the Purple Sage*, his first big commercial success. From that year on, Grey published at least one novel per year for Harper's, most of them ending up among the top ten best-selling American novels. At his death, he left another twenty manuscripts, the last of which, *Boulder Dam*, was published in 1963, twenty-four years after his death.

Grey's western fiction mirrors and gives expression to the concerns of many Americans at the beginning of the twentieth century. The closing of the frontier, intensifying urbanization and industrialization, and the accompanying social changes gave rise to questions about the validity of the American Dream and the shape the country would take in the decades to come. Mainstream authors, like Theodore Dreiser, Sinclair Lewis, F. Scott Fitzgerald, and the "muckrakers," dealt with these concerns in the form of literary realism and naturalism. Using Owen Wister's *The Virginian*—without its dynastic ending—as his model, Zane Grey creates the formula of the "romantic" western, a highly stylized illustration of the conflict between the values of fading "good old days" of the Old West and the ever more intrusive values of modern urban-industrial civilization. At a time when traditional American values, now called "family values," such as religion, monogamous love, stable families, and clearly defined gender roles, are seen as deteriorating under the attack of liberal, secular humanists, conservative western writers like Grey offer an escape into a romantic counter-world.

In Grey's world, the male protagonists are protectors and providers, exposing themselves willingly to the cruel Darwinian forces in nature to create a safe environment for their women. Surviving by courage, resourcefulness, determination, and measured violence, they successfully resist natural disasters, outlaws, and efforts to domesticate them by the women they love. This leaves to the female characters only the passive role of civilizers and guardians of morality, while the aggressive modern woman is shown in all of Grey's novels as vulgar and unfeminine. Jane Withersteen of *Riders of the Purple Sage* (1912) is the prototype of Grey's ideal woman: deeply religious, charitable, and opposed to senseless violence, she becomes the ideal mate for the macho Lassiter with whom she settles down in the Edenic seclusion of Surprise Canyon. In stark contrast to her stands Georgiana Stockwell, the heroine of *Code of the West* (1934), who has to undergo a rough initiation into western womanhood before she understands that her "Eastern immodesty of dress, freedom of speech, unrestraint of action, and the fatal fascination of a possible attainableness...would not do in the West." While such blatant sexism tends to offend and embarrass most educated modern readers, it must be remembered that the underlying sentiments are far from extinct; in addition, it was Grey's conviction—as it was Wister's—that an ideal society would achieve a synthesis between male aggressiveness and acquisitiveness and female Christian humanist values, albeit with a bias towards the former. Thus in all of Grey's westerns the female subordinates her values to those of the male, particularly since she has usually been saved from great peril by the very violence she had objected to so much.

Like many other popular authors, Grey was not satisfied with the commercial success of his novels but aspired to loftier goals. Deeply stung by critical reviews that echoed the dismissive judgment of his early rejection notices, he worked tirelessly to become a better writer. After having established himself firmly on the best-seller lists, Grey attempted after 1918 to move his westerns closer to mainstream fiction by making his loose, mainly chronological adventure stories more complex structurally and by introducing topical, even social-critical elements into his novels. This development begins with *Desert of Wheat* (1919), in which World War I takes a central role, continues in *Call of the Canyon* (1924), in which the war and the "modern woman" are once more referenced, and finds its culmination in *The Vanishing American* (1925), a love story between an eastern woman and an American Indian. In this novel, Grey comes very close to abandoning the formula of the romantic western altogether; the male protagonist is an educated Indian who becomes a war hero and a staunch defender of his people against corrupt missionaries and venal Indian agents. In a complete reversal of the formula, Nophaie sees himself ultimately absorbed and assimilated by the culture of his wife and agrees that "It is well!"

This venture into social criticism—and particularly a positive depiction of interracial marriage—was not acceptable to *The Ladies' Home Journal* which had acquired the serial rights to the novel, and Grey was forced to change the ending both for the magazine and for the subsequent book version. The original ending, and many other "censored" passages, were not restored until the 1970s. Such resistance to his attempts at giving more depth to his novels, as well as the economic constraints of the Great Depression, finally persuaded Grey to abandon his more literary ambitions and to return to the safe, successful western romance formula for the rest of his career.

Grey's critical reception is a good illustration of the difficulties literary critics have to this day with popular fiction. Early reviews of Grey's western fiction, mostly anonymous, concentrate on the plausibility of the plots and the appropriateness of the subject matter: some of them, like T. K Whipple, elevate Grey to the status of an old Norse bard and James Fenimore Cooper; others see in him an offspring of the dime novel western. Even after his death, Grey remains largely neglected by the academic critics: the first comprehensive biography (Jean Karr, *Zane Grey: Man of the West*, without bibliography or critical appraisal of the novels) did not appear until 1949. John Milton's reviews of western American literature in the 1960s, though not unequivocally favorable to Grey, seem to be responsible for an increase in critical attention. Notable among the first critical voices are Durham and Jones' *The Negro Cowboys* — praising Grey's sympathetic portrayal of a black cowboy in *Knights of the Range* (1939) and *Twin Sombreros* (1941) — and James K. Folsom's *The American Western Novel* (1966), in which the author finds it galling to reflect that the epic of America does not have Homer but Zane Grey as its chronicler.

In the wake of the academy's discovery of popular fiction in general and the popular western in particular, a veritable Zane Grey renaissance begins in the 1970s, launched by Frank Gruber's flattering biography and Russell Nye's acknowledgment in *The Unembarrassed Muse* (1970) of Grey as a masterful storyteller with a powerful sense of place.

Since that time, a number of works on Grey have attempted to evaluate Grey's fiction in the light of new perspectives on popular formulaic fiction. John Cawelti looks at Grey's works as reflecting in formulaic form the mainly subconscious attitudes and preconceptions of his reading public; Gary Topping attempts to show that Grey was more of a realist than his critics have given him credit for, while not glossing over his glaring deficiencies as a writer; Christine Bold's narratological approach shows Grey as organizing his fiction similarly to the form of the "monomyth" employed in mythological tales. The best recent study is Arthur G. Kimball's *Ace of Hearts* (1993), which comprehensively surveys all the novels and discusses in detail the major recurrent topics in Grey's novels, including the treatment of women and minorities.

What emerges from these recent studies is a much more balanced picture of Zane Grey. Rather than excoriating him for his literary deficiencies and accusing him, often without proof, of blatant racism (Folsom, 1977), scholars now attempt to evaluate Grey with the standards developed by popular culture critics, recognizing with Russell Nye that they are adventure stories, good or bad only as they succeed or fail to come alive as adventure and communicate the western experience accurately and honestly. Rather than blaming Grey for not having written the *Iliad*, one should agree with Cynthia S. Hamilton that "in Grey's work, more than in that of any other western-writer of the period, one begins to glimpse the assumptions and implications of the genre" (Hamilton 1987, 80).

Selected Bibliography

Primary Sources

Carlton Jackson, *Zane Grey* (Boston: Twayne, 1989) and Arthur G. Kimball, *Ace of Hearts: The Westerns of Zane Grey* (Fort Worth: Texas Christian University Press, 1993) provide a complete list of Grey's fiction; Kimball includes commentary on each title.

Secondary Sources

Bloodworth, William. "Zane Grey's Western Eroticism." *South Dakota Review,* 23 (1985): 5-14.

Bold, Christine. *Selling the Wild West: Popular Western Fiction, 1860 to 1960.* Bloomington: Indiana University Press, 1987.

Cawelti, John. *Adventure, Mystery, and Romance: Formula Stories as Art and Popular Culture.* Chicago: University of Chicago Press, 1976.

Folsom, James. K. "Zane Grey." In *The Reader's Encyclopedia of the American West.* New York: Crowell, 1977. Pp. 467-468.

Gruber, Frank. *Zane Grey: A Biography.* New York: World Publishing Company, 1970.

Hamilton, Cynthia. S. *Western and Hard-Boiled Detective Fiction in America: From High Noon to Midnight.* London: Macmillan, 1987.

Jackson, Carlton. *Zane Grey.* Boston: Twayne, 1989.

Karr, Jean. *Zane Grey: Man of the West.* New York: Greenberg, 1949.

Kimball, Arthur G. *Ace of Hearts: The Westerns of Zane Grey.* Fort Worth: Texas Christian University Press, 1993.

Milton, John. *The Novel of the American West.* Lincoln: University of Nebraska Press, 1980.

Mitchell, Lee. "White Slaves and Purple Sage: Plotting Sex in Zane Grey's West." *American Literary History*, 6 (1994): 234-264.

Nesbitt, John. "Uncertain Sex in the Sagebrush." *South Dakota Review*, 23 (1985): 15-27.

Nye, Russell. *The Unembarrassed Muse*. New York: Dial Press, 1970.

Ronald, Ann. *Zane Grey*. Boise: Boise State University Western Writers Series, 1975.

Scott, Kenneth W. *Zane Grey: Born to the West, A Reference Guide*. Boston: G. K. Hall, 1979.

Topping, Gary. "Zane Grey: A Literary Reassessment." *American Literature*, 13 (1978): 51-64.

Robert Lee Gale

Louis L'Amour

When Louis L'Amour died of lung cancer on June 10, 1988, a shock wave went through his worldwide reading public. He had seemed everlasting. But the final chapter of a legend had ended—almost. Gone was the possibility of twenty or thirty more Sackett, Chantry, and Talon family volumes, which L'Amour had led his followers to expect. Gone were the sequels to *The Walking Drum* and *Last of the Breed. Education of a Wandering Man* (1989), his autobiography, did appear in 1989, but in dreadful shape. His useful posthumous volume, *The Sackett Companion: A Personal Guide to the Sackett Novels*, was published five months after his death. Reassuring, too—or at least informative—were quick statements from L'Amour's widow Katherine Elizabeth (Adams) L'Amour, in charge of the Louis D. and Katherine E. L'Amour 1983 Trust, and their son Beau Dearborn L'Amour that uncollected stories and new material awaited putting into shape for sale well into the 1990s. L'Amour's daughter Angelique Gabrielle L'Amour had a bit part in the 1991 television adaptation of L'Amour's 1969 novel *Conagher.* The first issue of the bimonthly *Louis L'Amour Western Magazine,* featuring fiction, essays, interviews, and travel items, appeared late in 1993. It is rumored that Beau L'Amour will write his father's biography. It is also possible that members of L'Amour's extended family will release illuminating memoirs in due time. So the legend remains viable.

L'Amour was reading parts of his *Wandering Man* hours before he died. He must have paused often to reminisce about his storied past—one of the most varied, surely, that any novelist has ever had. Christened Louis Dearborn LaMoore, he was born March 22, 1908—a year he habitually hid from interviewers, through vanity—in Jamestown, North Dakota, the seventh and youngest child of Louis Charles LaMoore, a veterinarian and police chief, and Emily Lavisa Dearborn LaMoore, a would-be teacher who married instead and who was known as an avid reader and fine storyteller. When the family moved to Oklahoma in 1923, Louis quit school to begin an amazing series of jobs—Texas cattle skinner, Arizona circus hand, knockabout employee (boxer, fruit picker, miner, lumberjack) throughout the Southwest, then longshoreman, deep-sea diver, and sailor—mainly to the Far East—until 1942. He published a book of so-so poetry entitled *Smoke from This Altar* (1939), entered the U.S. Army in 1942, taught winter-survival techniques in Michigan, and served in the tank-destroyer corps and then the transportation corps in France and Germany (1944-1945).

LaMoore settled in Los Angeles and wrote four "Hopalong Cassidy" novels as "Tex Burns," many pulp-fiction stories as "Jim Mayo," and also his own first Louis L'Amour novel. It was *Westward the Tide* (1950). Later, he chose to call *Hondo* (1953) his first novel—this, evidently, because his first five, including his Hopalongs, were merely routine westerns, whereas *Hondo*, when combined with the movie based on it and starring John Wayne, made L'Amour seem to achieve fame faster. He signed a contract with Fawcett for a book a year, moved up to Bantam, and promised that lucky company two books a year, then three. His "yondering" years and pulp-writing days were perfect preparation for the astounding career that followed.

Statistics are often dull, but L'Amour's are thrilling. In the 1950s he published seventeen novels. They are formulaic westerns, with two exceptions: *Heller with a Gun* (1955) and *Sitka* (1957). *Heller* was his first of several to present actors and actresses in the West and inspired a dramaturgically authentic film. (Twenty-four more movie and television adaptations followed—to date.) *Sitka*, L'Amour's first romantic historical fiction, is cast in the Alaska Purchase era. His more routine plots, especially early in his career, typically cast a tough, solitary hero, often with a troubled past, riding into a dispute over turf and herds, challenged by an entrenched villain or two, gaining success by any weapon at hand, rescuing a brave but jeopardized female or two, and then (sometimes) moving on. Gradually, L'Amour sought to vary his patterns. In the 1960s, he published twenty-nine novels, the first two being the most significant. They are *The Daybreakers* (1960), the first of his seventeen Sackett-family volumes; and *Flint* (also 1960), named by the Western Writers of America in 1977 as one of the twenty-five best westerns of all time (along with *Hondo*). *How the West Was Won* was published in 1963; curiously, it is based on the movie scripted by James R. Webb, not the reverse. L'Amour published six more book-length Sackett segments in the 1960s. The events of these being wildly out of chronological order may rather discredit his later boasts of careful pre-planning. In the 1970s, which saw the publication of twenty-six L'Amour novels, including five more Sackett segments, he started two new family sequences. The first of his five Chantry family novels is *North to the Rails* (1971); the first of his three Talon family novels is *Rivers West* (1975). *Sackett's Land* (1974), starting in London in 1599, introduces Barnabas Sackett, the clan patriarch, as he is about to move to the Carolinas for adventure and fortune. Its preface trumpets L'Amour's plan to tell a vast American frontier story through the generation-by-generation westward advance of three families in "forty-odd books." In a 1981 interview L' Amour grew more specific, promising ten more Sackett novels, at least five more Chantrys, and probably five more Talons. Sacketts, he said, would be mainly pioneers and fighters; Chantrys, scholars; and Talons, mainly builders. Many of his readers remain sad that L'Amour did not concentrate on these books, and on nothing else. His *Sackett Companion* suggests that they would have been unique in American literature. Deciding, however, in the 1980s to avoid being stereotyped as merely a writer of westerns, L'Amour cast a novel in twelfth-century Europe and the Middle East (*The Walking Drum* [1984]), another in twentieth-century Cold War Siberia (*Last of the Breed* [1986]), and a time warper in the Anasazis' thirteenth century (*The Haunted Mesa* [1987]). He even hinted that he might write some space novels one day. Before his death, his 1980s production totaled fourteen novels, including four Sacketts and a final Talon. By this time, Bantam had gone hardbound with several L'Amour books, beginning in 1979 with *The Lonesome Gods*, which hit the best-seller lists.

The writing machine called Louis L'Amour became a money tree as well. By the mid-1990s fully 225,000,000 copies of his works were in print worldwide. This figure includes a score of his short-story collections but excludes well over a million audio tapes and records based on

his fiction; nor can it include thousands of illegally pirated and duplicated copies in the Far East. Although L'Amour regularly declined to
talk about royalties, it is reliably estimated that in the 1980s alone, his
peak decade, he grossed at least $25,000,000. He is far and away the
most popular western writer who ever lived.

Legitimate revisionist historians and unsavory porn-peddlers have
separately caused scholars, if not loyal standby readers, to take a new
look at L'Amour. His comments concerning Native Americans are frequently reactionary. Least offensive is his often-repeated generalization
that some Indians are good while others are bad. Insufficiently explored
is another bromide, that their unique environment generated values in
Indians different from those of whites. Least acceptable to revisionists is
L'Amour's stale Darwinian, Manifest Destiny rationalization that the
land in the West—indeed, every region the world over—belonged and
belongs to those with the strength to conquer and hold it. In making all
such pronouncements, L'Amour is guilty of distorting history and catering to those who prefer folklore to documentation. As for sex, by comparison to the so-called "adult western," L'Amour is pleasantly
Victorian in his reticence and yet disturbingly anti-feminist in some of
his implications. The most erotic passage he ever published comes in the
1958 *Radigan*, when it is reported that the heroine "Gretchen...knew
she was in love with him [Radigan], knew it...in the crying need of her
body, her loins yearning for the man he was." Some of L'Amour's heroes
praise women for saintly strength, pride, and loyalty; but others, feeling
victimized, regard women as so manipulative and obstreperous that they
should be handled like fractious horses. Curiously, very recent western
films and television dramas combine a greater degree of historical accuracy and more explicit sex, thus leaving L'Amour doubly in the dust.

The end of the Cold War may well cause a new generation of readers
to view L'Amour as a literary dinosaur. He does not simply appeal to
Americans to emulate his archetypal American Male, shape up, and get
redder-blooded. Indeed, the message of his final blockbuster, *Last of the
Breed* (1986), is that to survive at all as a nation Americans must be self-
reliant and crafty, avoid bureaucracy and socialism, practice pitiless violence and return to primitivism. All the same, conservative readers may
be counted on to stand pat with L'Amour. In doing so, they continue to
turn the clock back with him, to enjoy, albeit vicariously, the simpler
American ways. L'Amour planned to do just that himself. In 1983, he
and his wife purchased 1000 acres in a valley of La Plata Mountains out-

side Durango, Colorado, and refurbished its ranch house, which was once a stagecoach stop, where they could look west at the timeless valleys and the peaks beyond.

Selected Bibliography

Primary Sources

Hall, Hal W. *The Work of Louis L'Amour: An Annotated Bibliography and Guide.* San Bernardino: The Borgo Press, 1991.

Secondary Sources

Bold, Christine. *Selling the Wild West: Popular Western Fiction, 1860 to 1960.* Bloomington: Indiana University Press, 1987.

Coldsmith, Don. "Louis L'Amour." *The Roundup Quarterly,* 1:3 (Spring 1989): 11-13.

Cozzens, Darin. "History and Louis L'Amour's Cowboy." *Journal of American Culture,* 14 (Summer 1991): 42-52.

Gale, Robert L. *Louis L'Amour.* Rev. ed. New York: Twayne Publishers, 1992.

Heldeman, Peter. "West with Louis L'Amour: The Late Author's Colorado Ranch." *Architectural Digest,* 51 (June 1994): 180-187, 207.

Mehrten, Joseph. "Profile: Louis L'Amour." *Conservative Digest,* 14 (November 1988): 100-104.

Terrie, Philip G. Review of L'Amour's *Last of the Breed. Journal of Popular Culture,* 25 (Spring 1992): 23-33.

Tompkins, Jane. *West of Everything: The Inner Life of Westerns.* New York: Oxford University Press, 1992.

Weinberg, Robert, ed. *The Louis L'Amour Companion.* Kansas City, Missouri: Andrews and McMeel, 1992.

Thomas J. Lyon

Epilogue
What Is Happening in the West Today,
and What It Might Mean

The West of 1997 is most emphatically not the West of 1980. At that time, when a group of scholars was wrestling with a monster volume that we hoped would establish the bona fides of the region's literature, we had hardly a presentiment that the West would shortly become "in," mainstream, desirable. We thought of ourselves as mavericks, calling out to a world that was ignoring our region. Little did we dream that Telluride, and Ketchum, and Jackson, and Moab—Moab, for Pete's sake!—and Sedona, and Park City, and St. George, among others—among many others—would shortly be speckled with trophy homes, greened with golf courses, lined with condos, strip malls, factory outlet extravaganzas, and, hardest of all to imagine, *crowded with people*.

We had seen general increase in the working cities: Salt Lake, Fort Collins, Seattle, Phoenix, and Tucson, and of course the already saturated south coast of California and the San Francisco Bay Area. We should have seen the handwriting on the wall. Now, seventeen years later, the reality of population explosion is our daily fact. It has been calculated that if Arizona grows in the twenty-first century as it did in the twentieth, its population at century's end will be 134.5 million.

And if anyone had thought that the West had been mined out back in the Comstock and Cripple Creek or Homestake days, he or she should see Elko-Carlin now, where gold in profitable amounts is sifted and leached from what was once a landscape, or the leveled hills and enormous pits north of Soda Springs, Idaho, where on national-forest land the giants of the chemical industry strip the land for phosphates. And did anyone think sustained-yield forestry had captured the rational high ground and protected the western forests? Look again at the volume *Clearcut: The Tragedy of Industrial Forestry* (1993), and be aware of what the so-called "Salvage Rider," a know-nothing, environment-be-damned piece of legislation by Congress in 1995, is doing to western forests. The global economy is all-seeing, and the American West does not escape its attention. Japan (among others) wants logs. Conoco (among others) wants oil. (We all want oil.) The simple fact is that the West is no longer unknown, no longer protected by remoteness or any sort of difficult access: it is simply another region where the exploding human population wants to move, and where the insatiable global economy finds whatever materials it needs. The bloom is long gone; the specialness and remoteness are long gone.

What this loss of space, quietness and wildness does to western writing is bend it toward realism and toward "green" awareness. There is abroad a new, reduced concept of the West as ordinary, vulnerable, contemporary ground. Because of ecological factors, in particular lack of rainfall and omnipresence of shallow soils, the West is more fragile than other areas, such as America east of approximately the ninety-eighth meridian. Edward Abbey's 1977 essay, "The Second Rape of the West," sounded an alarm that still rings in the work of such contemporary western writers as William Kittredge, Terry Tempest Williams, Rick Bass, Charles Bowden, Douglas Peacock, John Keeble, and David Petersen. These writers, as Edward Abbey did, pay attention to the real West in which the frontier-minded cornucopian or escapist myths have become seriously unrealistic.

Concurrent with ecological realism, the past twenty years have been marked by a many-sided questioning of the triumphalist interpretation of western history, and strong moves toward unearthing buried or silenced literatures written by people who did not share in the triumphant (usually white male) understanding of things. A new western history has been written, in which the killing and displacement of Indians are seen for what they were, in which the part played by women in western history is actually noticed, and in which the presence and influence of ethnic minorities—in particular, Hispanic and Asian—are given their due. This new western historical understanding has its parallel movement in literature, where the canon has expanded tremendously in the dimensions just mentioned. There is more writing about nature, more writing by women, more writing by Hispanic and Asian minorities, because our entire notion of the West and its history has been opened up.

Each of these newly expanded dimensions in the western canon has its parallel in western literary criticism. Ecocriticism, feminist criticism, and multicultural perspectives have all come to the fore in the past twenty years. A broader sense of "text" has also come into being — a literary analysis of an irrigation promoter's early-twentieth-century pamphlets, full of utopian dreaming, now is seen as a perfectly legitimate scholarly enterprise, for example. Such analysis has become part of the new West's understanding of itself.

The common denominator in the new western writing and the new, revisionist western criticism is that an alternative to the frontier mentality is finally beginning to be created. The frontier mind is dualistic and casually exploitative in its attitude toward nature, invidiously hierarchical in its approach toward women and minorities, and above all, resolutely un-self-critical. It is still, of course, very much alive. The frontier mind gave us the shibboleth that we had "won" the West, and also gave us an unending stream of subliterary, fantasy-fulfilling, formulaic texts. Beginning with John Muir in the nineteenth century, and continuing into the twentieth with such writers as Mari Sandoz and Frank Waters, the frontier mythos always had its lonely western critics. But today, western literature moves much more decisively, much more as a majority phenomenon, toward post-frontier maturity. Western writers are re-inhabiting the "plundered province," showing that the region's riches may turn out to be an earned understanding of humanity's diversity, the environment's crucial importance, and the gains to be found in self-awareness. Western writers have grown up with the frontier myth but now find themselves in the early stages of creating a new western myth, one of adaptation to place and the adoption of a nature-sustaining ethos. In the world at large, where the frontier mentality of bigger-is-better economism still dominates, such a regional literary development may turn out to be a significant model.

Contributors

Charles L. Adams is the editor of *Studies in Frank Waters* and *Frank Waters: a Retrospective Anthology*. He teaches at the University of Nevada-Las Vegas.

Blake Allmendinger is associate professor of English at the University of California, Los Angeles. His books include *The Cowboy* (1992) and *Over the Edge: Remapping the Boundaries of Western Experience* (forthcoming) with Valerie Matsumoto.

Virgil Albertini is professor of English at Northwest Missouri State University. He was bibliographic editor of *Western American Literature* (1984-1995) and is a Willa Cather bibliography specialist. He has published numerous articles on Cather and others.

Joanne Allred teaches in the creative writing program at California State University, Chico. Educated at the University of Utah, CSU Chico, and University of California at Davis, she is the author of a collection of poems, *Whetstone*.

Judy Alter is director of Texas Christian University Press. A past president of Western Writers of America and secretary-treasurer of the Texas Institute of Letters, she is also a novelist.

Donald A. Barclay, a librarian at the University of Houston, is one of the editors of *Into the Wilderness Dream: Exploration Narratives of the American West, 1500-1805*.

Bruce Barcott is a writer and literary critic for the *Seattle Weekly*. He is the editor of the anthology, *Northwest Passages: A Literary Anthol-*

ogy of the Pacific Northwest from Coyote Tales to Roadside Attractions.

Lawrence I. Berkove is professor of English and director of the American Studies program at the University of Michigan-Dearborn. He is a specialist in the late nineteenth- and early twentieth-century period and has written extensively on Ambrose Bierce, Mark Twain, Dan De Quille, and Jack London.

William W. Bevis is professor of English at the University of Montana. He is the author of *Ten Tough Trips: Montana Writers and the West* and was a member of the editorial board for *The Last Best Place: A Montana Anthology.*

Kevin Bezner teaches writing and literature at Livingstone College in Salisbury, North Carolina. His collection of poetry, *The Tools of Ignorance*, was published by Cincinnati Writers Project.

Franz Blaha teaches in the English department at the University of Nebraska-Lincoln. He holds a degree in comparative literature from the University of Graz (Austria). He has published articles and papers on modern European drama and on detective fiction in Nazi Germany and East Germany. He has a history of French detective fiction in press.

Mary Clearman Blew has published two collections of short fiction, is coeditor of *Circle of Women: an Anthology of Contemporary Western Women Writers*, and is the author of two acclaimed works of personal nonfiction: *All But the Waltz* and *Balsamroot*. She teaches at the University of Idaho.

William Bloodworth is president of Augusta State University, Augusta, Georgia. He is an author of books on Upton Sinclair and Max Brand as well as articles on Native American literature and the literature of the American West.

Kathleen Boardman, associate professor of English at the University of Nevada-Reno, teaches composition, rhetoric, and American literature. She has published articles on Maxine Hong Kingston, Maria Campbell, Loren Eiseley, Lowry Charles Wimberly, and others.

Christine Bold is associate professor of English and director of the Centre for Cultural Studies/Centre d'études sur la culture at the University of Guelph. She is the author of *Selling the Wild West: Popular Western Fiction, 1860 to 1960*, as well as essays and articles on American popular culture, and is coeditor of the *Canadian Review of American Studies.*

Carl Bredahl teaches American literature at the University of Florida and is the author of *New Ground: Western American Narrative and the Literary Canon.*

Marek Breiger teaches at Chabot Community College and Moreau High School, Hayward, California. His essays and stories have appeared in *U.S. News & World Report*, *California English*, *Jewish Currents*, and *Where Coyotes Howl and the Wind Blows Free.* He also writes for the Alameda Newspaper Group.

Robert Brophy is professor of English at California State University-Long Beach. He is the author of *Robinson Jeffers: Dimensions of a Poet*, *Robinson Jeffers: Myth, Ritual, and Symbol in his Narrative Poems* and *Robinson Jeffers* (Boise Western Writers Series) and editor of Jeffers' *Dear Judas and Other Poems*, *Whom Shall I Write For?* and *Songs and Heroes.* Since 1968 he has been the editor of the *Robinson Jeffers Newsletter.*

Russell Burrows is currently with the English department at Weber State University in Ogden, Utah. He has published essays and critical articles on Wallace Stegner and on the nature essay in such journals as *Dialogue*, *Petroglyph*, *Western American Literature*, and *Redneck Review of Literature.*

Mark Busby is director of the Center for the Study of the Southwest at Southwest Texas State University, San Marcos, Texas. He is the author of *Preston Jones* (1983), *Lanford Wilson* (1987), *Ralph Ellison* (1991) and *Larry McMurtry and the West: An Ambivalent Relationship* (1995); coeditor of *The Frontier Experience and the American Dream* (1989); and contributing editor of *Taking Stock: A Larry McMurtry Casebook* (1989). He coedits the journal *Southwestern American Literature.*

SueEllen Campbell is professor of English at Colorado State University; she teaches nature and environmental literature and twentieth-century literature and theory. She is the author of numerous articles about modernist literature, American nature writing, and ecocriticism; a critical study of Wyndham Lewis; and a book of essays about the experience of being in wild places, *Bringing the Mountain Home.*

John G. Cawelti is professor of English at the University of Kentucky. He is author of *The Six Gun Mystique*, *Adventure, Mystery and Romance*, *The Spy Story* (with Bruce A. Rosenberg, 1987) and other books and essays on American literature, cultural history, and popular culture.

Craig Clifford teaches philosophy and directs the Honors Degree Program at Tarleton State University, Stephenville, Texas. He is the author of *In the Deep Heart's Core: Reflections on Life, Letters, and Texas* and *The Tenure of Phil Wisdom: Dialogues* and coeditor of *Range Wars: Heated Debates, Sober Reflections, and Other Assessments of Texas Writing*.

Krista Comer received a Ph.D from Brown University (American Studies) in 1996. She has essays forthcoming in *Breaking Boundaries: New Perspectives in Regional Fiction*, Sherrie Inness and Diana Royer, eds., and in *The New Western History: An Assessment*, Forrest Robinson, ed. Her first book, *Women Writers, the New West and the Politics of Landscape* is forthcoming from University of North Carolina Press. She has also written about Wallace Stegner, and about surf culture in Southern California. She teaches Women's studies and English at Rice University.

Nancy L. Cook has written on such authors as Thomas McGuane and Oscar Micheaux. She currently teaches at the University of Rhode Island.

Harry Crockett is completing his Ph.D. at the University of North Carolina with a dissertation on western exploration writing. He has an essay on rivers, dams, and water projects in the forthcoming book, *The State of the State: The Colorado Environmental Report*.

Charles Crow is professor of English at Bowling Green State University in Ohio, where he teaches seminars in western regionalism and California literature. He is the author of *Janet Lewis* in the Boise Western Writers Series, articles on California literature and on such western authors as Frank Norris, Jack London, and Hisaye Yamamoto.

Kenneth W. Davis is professor of English, emeritus, at Texas Tech University. He is a past president of the Texas Folklore Society, author of *Black Cats, Hoot Owls, and Water Witches*, and coauthor of *Horsing Around: Contemporary Cowboy Humor* and *The Catch Pen*.

Ida Rae Egli is chair of the English department at Santa Rosa Junior College, California. She is the editor of *No Rooms of Their Own: Women Writers of Early California*. She is at work on two other texts centered on California women writers, as well as a collection of fiction set in Northern California circa 1950-1965.

Fred Erisman is Lorraine Sherley Professor of Literature at Texas

Christian University. Among his other studies of the American West are *Fifty Western Writers* (coedited with Richard W. Etulain), a chapter in *The Twentieth-Century West: Historical Interpretations*, and the Boise Western Writers Series pamphlets on Tony Hillerman and Laura Ingalls Wilder.

David Fine is professor of English at California State University, Long Beach. He is the editor of *Unknown California*, *Los Angeles in Fiction*, and *San Francisco in Fiction*. He has published articles on such West Coast authors as Nathanael West, James M. Cain, Raymond Chandler, and Jack London.

Robert E. Fleming is professor of English and chair of the English department at the University of New Mexico. With his wife Esther, he is author of *Sinclair Lewis: A Reference Guide* (1980). In 1992 he founded the Sinclair Lewis Society.

Joseph M. Flora has published widely on American literature, and has done extensive work on western American literature, including a book on Vardis Fisher. He is professor of English at the University of North Carolina.

Dan Flores is an environmental historian and writer who holds the A. B. Hammond Chair of Western History at the University of Montana-Missoula. Among his six books and more than two dozen articles are the award-winning *Jefferson & Southwestern Exploration*, *Caprock Canyonlands: Journeys into the Heart of the Southern Plains*, and "Bison Ecology and Bison Diplomacy: The Southern Plains from 1800-1850," *Journal of American History* (1991).

Bob J. Frye is professor of English at Texas Christian University, Fort Worth. His specialties are eighteenth-century British literature, rhetoric and composition, and southwestern American literature. He is the author of *Winston Estes* (1992) in the Boise Western Writers Series and a regular reviewer for *Western American Literature*.

Robert Lee Gale taught English and American literature at Columbia, University of Delaware, University of Mississippi, and finally University of Pittsburgh, and had Fulbright teaching grants in Naples and Helsinki, before retiring in 1987. He has published on several major figures in American literature, including Nathaniel Hawthorne, Herman Melville, Mark Twain, and Henry James, and also on such western writers as Henry Wilson Allen, Ernest Haycox, Louis L' Amour, and Luke Short.

Robin Ganz, a critic and teacher, has written for *MELUS*, *The San Francisco Chronicle* and *The Boston Globe*, among other journals and newspapers. Her specialization is in American multi-ethnic literature. She teaches at Pace University and is at work on a book about Philip Roth.

Robert Franklin Gish is director of ethnic studies and professor of English and ethnic studies at Cal Poly, San Luis Obispo. He is the author of numerous books and essays on the literature and history of the American West including, most recently, *When Coyote Howls: A Lavaland Fable*, *Songs of My Hunter Heart*, *First Horses*, *Beyond Bounds*, and *Bad Boys and Black Sheep*.

Cheryll B. Glotfelty is associate professor of literature and the environment in the English department at the University of Nevada-Reno. She is coeditor, with Harold Fromm, of *The Ecocriticism Reader: Landmarks in Literary Ecology*.

Charlotte Goodman is professor of English at Skidmore College. She is the author of "Jean Stafford: The Savage Heart," a critical and biographical foreword for Edith Summers Kelley's *Weeds*, and a number of articles on American women writers.

Joanne Greenberg teaches anthropology at the Colorado School of Mines. She been writing all her life and was first published in 1962.

Sylvia Grider is associate professor of anthropology at Texas A&M University where she teaches courses in folklore, anthropology, and Texas cultural history. A past president of both the American Folklore Society and the Texas Folklore Society, she is currently finishing a book-length biography of Dorothy Scarborough. She is coeditor, with Lou Rodenberger, of *Texas Women Writers: A Tradition of Their Own*.

Paul Hadella lectures in the English department of Southern Oregon State College, has scholarly interests in Native American and nineteenth-century American literatures, and runs his own small poetry press called Talent House Press.

P. Jane Hafen (Taos Pueblo) is assistant professor of English at the University of Nevada-Las Vegas. She is a recipient of a Francis C. Allen Fellowship from the D'Arcy McNickle Center for the History of the American Indian, the Newberry Library.

Gerald Haslam is a fifth-generation Californian who taught at Sonoma State University. His fiction has won the Josephine Miles Prize and the Benjamin Franklin Award and his non-fiction, a Bay Area

Book Reviewers' Award, a Commomwealth Club Medal, and an Award of Merit from the Association for State and Local History. He is a past-president of the Western Literature Association (1985) and was a general editor of *A Literary History of the American West* (1987).

Jaime H. Herrera was raised in Cuidad Juárez, Chihuahua, México, until the age of fifteen, when his family moved to the other side of the Rio Grande: El Paso, Texas. He teaches in the English department at Mesa Community College, Arizona. Even though he is far away, Jaime — for better or for worse — still carries the border with him.

Eric Heyne is associate professor of English at the University of Alaska, Fairbanks. He is the editor of *Desert Garden Margin Range: Literature on the American Frontier*.

Michael Hobbs has published articles on Mark Twain, Leslie Silko, and Wallace Stevens. He is assistant professor of English at Northwest Missouri State University.

Arthur R. Huseboe is executive director of the Center for Western Studies at Augustana College, South Dakota, and holds the NEH chair in regional heritage there. He has written a biography of Herbert Krause, coedited Frederick Manfred's *Selected Letters*, and directed the National Endowment for the Humanities grant to write *Updating the Literary West*.

Michael Kowaleski is associate professor of English at Carleton College and the author of *Deadly Musings: Violence and Verbal Form in American Fiction*. He has also edited two collections of essays: *Reading the West: New Essays on the Literature of the American West* and *Temperamental Journeys: Essays on the Modern Literature of Travel*.

Victoria Lamont is a Ph.D. candidate at the University of Alberta, specializing in American women's western writing of the nineteenth and early twentieth century.

Benjamin S. Lawson, professor of English at Albany State College in Georgia, has also taught American literature at the University of Helsinki and University College London. He has written on western and African American literature, historical fiction and science fiction. His works include *Joaquin Miller* and *Rereading the Revolution: The Turn-of-the-Century American Revolutionary War Novel*.

Joyce Lee holds a doctorate in English from the University of North

Texas, where she wrote her dissertation on the fiction of Rolando Hinojosa.

Ernestine Sewell Linck is retired from the English department of the University of Texas at Arlington. Her latest books are *Eats: A Folk History of Texas Foods*, coauthored with Joyce Roach, and *How the Cimarron River Got Its Name and Other Stories About Coffee*.

Gerald Locklin teaches English at California State University, Long Beach. He is the author of over seventy volumes of poetry, fiction, and criticism, including *Gerald Haslam* in the Boise Western Writers Series and *Charles Bukowski: A Sure Bet*.

Kim Long is assistant professor of English at Shippensburg University of Pennsylvania. She has published articles on Herman Melville, Nathaniel Hawthorne, Eudora Welty, and William Faulkner.

Glen A. Love is professor of English, emeritus, at the University of Oregon. He is the author of *New Americans: The Westerner and the Modern Experience in the American Novel*, *Babbitt: An American Life*, and various articles on American literature.

Seri I. Luangphinith is a graduate student at the University of Oregon. While her primary interests lie in contemporary Asian American literature, she has also pursued research on Japanese popular culture and Native Hawaiian oral traditions.

Thomas J. Lyon taught at Utah State University from 1964 to 1997, and has edited *Western American Literature* since 1974. He was senior editor of *A Literary History of the American West* and editor of *This Incomparable Lande: A Book of American Nature Writing*.

Bonney MacDonald is associate professor and chair of the Department of English at Union College in Schenectady, New York, where she teaches nineteenth-century American literature and American western writing. She has published *Henry James's Italian Hours: Revelatory and Resistant Impressions* as well as various articles on Henry James and Hamlin Garland.

James H. Maguire has taught at Boise State University since 1970 and has served as coeditor of its Western Writers Series since 1972. He is the author of *Mary Hallock Foote* and the editor of two anthologies: *The Literature of Idaho* and (with Donald A. Barclay and Peter Wild) *Into the Wilderness Dream*.

William B. Martin is professor of English, emeritus, at Tarleton State University, Stephenville, Texas. His major academic interests are Shakespeare, eighteenth-century British drama, modern American drama, and southwestern American drama. He edited *Texas Plays*.

Mick McAllister is a co-founder of Dancing Badger Press, the publisher of Frederick Manfred's *Flowers of Desire* (1989). He is also the author of many articles on American Indian writers and on Frederick Manfred.

Lee Clark Mitchell is Holmes Professor of Belles-Lettres and chair of the department of English at Princeton University, where he has also served as director of the program in American Studies. He teaches courses in American literature and is the author of *Westerns: Making the Man in Fiction and Film* (1996), *Determined Fictions: American Literary Naturalism* (1989), *Witnesses to a Vanishing America: The Nineteenth-Century Response* (1981). He has edited *New Essays on The Red Badge of Courage* (1986) and his recent essays have appeared in *Critical Inquiry*, *PMLA*, *Prospects*, and *Nineteenth-Century Fiction*.

Gregory L. Morris is associate professor of American literature at Penn State Erie, The Behrend College. He has published essays on contemporary western American literature, and is the author of *Talking Up a Storm: Voices of the New West*.

John J. Murphy is professor of American literature at Brigham Young University and editor of the *Cather Newsletter*. He is author of *My Ántonia: The Road Home* and editor of *Critical Essays on Willa Cather*. He is presently editing the Willa Cather Scholarly Edition of *Death Comes for the Archbishop*, University of Nebraska Press.

Nancy Owen Nelson is professor of English at Henry Ford Community College in Dearborn, Michigan. She has published a number of articles on Frederick Manfred's work, a chapter on Wallace Stegner in *San Francisco in Fiction*, and has coedited (with Arthur R. Huseboe) *The Selected Letters of Frederick Manfred; 1932-1954*. Her most recent publication is an edited collection, *Private Voices, Public Lives: Women Speak on the Literary Life*.

John P. O'Grady is the author of *Pilgrims to the Wild* and the forthcoming *Grave Goods*. He is an assistant professor of English at Boise State University and coeditor of Boise State University's Western Writers Series.

David Petersen lives in Durango, Colorado. His most recent book is *Ghost Grizzlies*. He is also the editor of *Confessions of a Barbarian: Selections from the Journals of Edward Abbey, 1951-1989*, and *Big Sky, Fair Land: The Environmental Essays of A.B. Guthrie, Jr.*

Vicki Piekarski has edited *Westward the Women: An Anthology of Western Stories by Women Writers*, coedited and contributed to the *Encyclopedia of Frontier and Western Fiction*, currently being revised and expanded for publication by the University of Nebraska Press, *The Frontier Experience: A Reader's Guide to the Life and Literature of the American West* and *The Morrow Treasury of Great Western Stories*. She served as associate editor on the *Close-Up on the Cinema* series for Scarecrow Press. Co-founder of Golden West Literary Agency, she is preparing an anthology of women writers of the western.

Tom Pilkington is University Scholar for Literature and professor of English at Tarleton State University, Stephenville, Texas. He is author or editor of twelve books. He was one of the general editors of *A Literary History of the American West*.

Michael Powell received his Ph.D. in English from the University of Oregon. He has published on the American beat movement and on various topics in Northwest literature.

John Price teaches literature and nonfiction writing at the University of Iowa. His essays have appeared in *The Christian Science Monitor*, *Creative Nonfiction*, *North Dakota Quarterly*, and various anthologies.

Diane Dufva Quantic is an associate professor of English and writing program director at Wichita State University. She is a past president of the Western Literature Association and author of *The Nature of the Place: A Study of Great Plains Fiction*.

Elizabeth Renfro has taught writing, literature, and women's studies at California State University, Chico since 1975. Her recent publications include *The Shasta Indians of California* and a number of biographical and analytical essays on such women writers and activists as Adrienne Rich, Gloria Steinem, Alice Walker, and Susan Brownmiller. She is currently at work on a literature and literary criticism text.

Laurie Ricou is professor of English and associate dean of the faculty of graduate studies at the University of British Columbia. His publications include *Vertical Man/Horizontal World: Man and Landscape in Canadian Prairie Fiction*, and *Everyday Magic: Child Languages in Canadian Literature*. He is a former president of the Western Literature Association.

Barbara Rippey is associate professor of English at the College of Saint

974

Mary in Omaha, Nebraska. She writes about and teaches the work of Nebraska and Great Plains authors, particularly Mari Sandoz.

Lou Rodenberger is professor of English at McMurry University, Abilene, Texas. She is editor of *Her Work: Stories by Texas Women* and author of *Jane Gilmore Rushing*. She is coauthor and coeditor, with Sylvia Grider, of *Texas Women Writers: A Tradition of Their Own*.

Ann Ronald is professor of English at the University of Nevada-Reno. She is the author of *The New West of Edward Abbey* and *Earthtones: A Nevada Album*, and the editor of *Words for the Wild: The Sierra Club Trailside Reader*. She is also executive secretary of the Western Literature Association.

Susan J. Rosowski, Adele Hall Professor of English, University of Nebraska-Lincoln, is author of *The Voyage Perilous: Willa Cather's Romanticism*, general editor of the Cather Scholarly Edition series, and editor-in-chief of *Cather Studies*. She is a past president of the Western Literature Association.

Jan Roush is associate professor of English at Utah State University where she teaches folklore, writing and contemporary Native American literature. She coedited *Pulling Leather* and has published articles on Tony Hillerman, ranch women, and cowboy poetry. She has been research editor of *Western American Literature* since 1985.

Geoff Sadler is author of nineteen western novels in the "Anderson" series as "Jeff Sadler" and four in the "Chulo" series as "Wes Calhoun," all published by Robert Hale between 1981 and 1995, as well as of several non-western writings. He is also editor of the second edition of *Twentieth Century Western Writers*. His work on W. C. Tuttle will appear in the new edition of *Encyclopedia of Frontier and Western Fiction*, in *Book and Magazine Collector*, and was the subject of an interview on BBC Radio"s "Kaleidoscope" arts program. He has had a long career as a librarian in Derbyshire, United Kingdom, in addition to chairing the Shirebrook Writers' Group and the local history group.

Ramon Saldívar is professor of English and comparative literature at Stanford University. His articles have appeared in numerous journals, and he is the author of *Figural Language in the Novel: The Flowers of Speech from Cervantes to Joyce* and *Chicano Narrative: The Dialectics of Difference*.

Marie-Madeleine Schein teaches English at West Texas A&M University,

Canyon. She has published reviews, essays and articles in *Studies in American Indian Literatures*, *The Dictionary of Literary Biography*, *Southwestern American Literature*, *Western American Literature*, and the *Redneck Review of Literature*. She is coauthor, with Clay Reynolds, of *A Hundred Years of Heroes*.

Russell Shitabata, from Kailua, Hawaii, completed his doctorate in English at the University of Oregon in 1996. He specializes in Asian American literature, feminist theory and narrative theory. His dissertation analyzes the narrative techniques of Angela Carter, Jade Snow Wong and Maxine Hong Kingston in relation to gender and race.

Paul Skenazy teaches at the University of California, Santa Cruz. He is the author of *The New Wild West* and *James M. Cain*, editor of *La Mollie and the King of Tears*, by Arturo Isles, and coeditor of *San Francisco in Fiction*.

Richard Slotkin is Olin Professor of American Studies at Wesleyan University, and author of an award-winning trilogy on the myth of the frontier in American cultural history, from the colonial period to the present: *Regeneration Through Violence*, *The Fatal Environment*, and *Gunfighter Nation*. He has also written two historical novels, *The Crater* (1980) and *The Return of Henry Starr* (1988).

Pamela Marie Smorkaloff is a Cuban American scholar who teaches at the Center for Latin American and Caribbean Studies at New York University. She is the author of *Readers and Writers in Cuba* and *Lost Steps and Hyphenated Lives: Contemporary Cuban Writers On and Off the Island*. She is currently at work on a study of Meso-American testimonial narrative and a historical novel of her own.

Stephen Tatum is associate professor and chair of the Department of English at the University of Utah. He is author of *Inventing Billy the Kid: Visions of the Outlaw in America, 1881-1981*, as well as articles and essays on western American literature, film, and history. He is a past president of the Western Literature Association.

Heinz Tschachler is associate professor of English and American Studies at the University of Klagenfurt, Austria. He is the author of *Ökologie und Arkadien*, a study of 1970s American ecocriticism, and of *Lewis Mumford's Reception in German Translation and Criticism*. He has also published essays on cultural studies, cultural criticism, North American fiction, science fiction, and utopian literature.

Allison Bulsterbaum Wallace is assistant professor of English and humanities at Unity College, Maine. She has written on Thoreau, Mary Austin, and David Quammen and is the author of *H.L. Mencken: A Research Guide*.

Max Westbrook is semi-retired but still teaches American literature each fall semester (University of Texas at Austin) and writes short stories, poems, and an occasional essay.

Dexter Westrum teaches film and literature courses at Upper Iowa University/Milwaukee. He is the author of *Thomas McGuane* and *Elegy for a Golf Pro*.

Peter Wild is professor of English at the University of Arizona. The author of more than 100 articles, he has written or edited forty books of poetry, nonfiction, and literary criticism, including *Cochise*, *Pioneer Conservationists of Western America*, and *The Desert Reader*. He has done individual volumes on Clarence King, James Welch, Barry Lopez, John C. Van Dyke, Cabeza de Vaca, and others in the Boise Western Writers Series.

Gary Williams is professor of English and head of the English department at the University of Idaho, where he teaches nineteenth- and twentieth-century American literature. He is the editor of *The Pierce Chronicle* and of James Fenimore Cooper's *Notions of the Americans: Picked Up by a Travelling Bachelor*.

Charlotte M. Wright is the editor at the University of North Texas Press, Denton. She has at various times been affiliated with *Western American Literature* as book review editor, assistant editor, and editor, and has served on the executive council of the Western Literature Association. She has published critical as well as creative pieces in various journals and reference books.

Joseph J. Wydeven is dean of the College of Arts and Sciences and professor of English and humanities at Bellevue University. He has published over a dozen articles on Wright Morris' fiction, photography, and photo-texts and (with David Madden) is currently updating the Morris volume in the Twayne series.

Index

compiled by Patricia G. Sherwood

979

hybridization, 402; literatures, 39; perspective (sharing stories), 35
Mumford, Lewis, 227
Munroe, Kirk, 119
Munsey Company (publishing), 944
Murayama, Milton, 230, 258, 260
Murder in the Cotswolds (A.B. Guthrie, Jr.), 384, 829
Murder on the Iditarod Trail (Sue Henry), 254, 255
Murders at Moon Dance (A.B. Guthrie, Jr.), 833, 834
Murieta, Joaquín, 101, 102, 115, 298
Murphy, Brenda, 652, 656
Murphy, John J., essay by, 658-69
Murray, David, 8, 15, 75
Murray, John A., 230, 255, 545, 807
Museum of the American Indian, 136
Museum Pieces (Elizabeth Tallent), 465
music, 410, 637, 725, 727, 919; American/British folksongs, 588, 593; blues, 525, 590, 919, 920; cowboy songs, 169, 170, 174, 174n2, 175
"The Music of Time: Henri Bergson and Willa Cather" (Loretta Wasserman), in *American Literature*, 660, 669
"Mustang Marshall" (Eli [Eliza] Colter), in *Lariat Story Magazine*, 903, 911
"The Mutability of Literature" (*The Sketch Book*, Washington Irving), 81
"*My Antonia*, Jim Burden and the Dilemma of the Lesbian Writer" (Judith Fetterley), in *Gender Studies: New Directions in Feminist Criticism* (Judith Spector, ed.), 663, 667
My Antonia: The Road Home (John J. Murphy), 661, 666
My Antonia (Willa Cather, Charles Mignon ed., with Kari Ronning and James Woodress), 658, 660-61,

663, 665
"My Community's Corner" (Américo Paredes), 635
My Darling Clementine (film), 877-78
"My Father's Place" (Kim R. Stafford), 244
My First Summer in the Sierra (John Muir), 302
"My French Friend" (Rollin Mallory Daggett), 110
"My Friend, the Editor" (Samuel Post Davis), 110
My Friend Flicka (Mary O'Hara), 128
My Kind of Heroes (Elmer Kelton), 583, 584
My Mortal Enemy (Willa Cather), 662
My Name is Aram (William Saroyan), 409
My Partner (Bartley Campbell), 102
My People the Sioux (Luther Standing Bear), 140, 147
My Year in a Log Cabin (William Dean Howells), 124
The Mysterious Lands: A Naturalist Explores the Four Great Deserts of the Southwest (Ann Zwinger), 801
"The Mystery of the Savage Sump" (Samuel Post Davis), 110
myth, 19, 79, 81, 123, 204, 206-7, 319, 660, 667, 692, 848
"The Myth of the Isolated Self in Manfred's Siouxland Novels" (Robert C. Wright), in *Where the West Begins* (Arthur R. Huseboe and William Geyer, eds.), 699
"The Myth of the Myth of the Garden," (*American Literary Landscapes: The Fiction and the Fact, Brian Harding*), 81
mythologies, 57, 221, 229, 244, 245, 303, 552, 892

"N. Scott Momaday" (Robert F. Gish), essay, 537-40
Nabhan, Gary Paul, 10, 15, 80
Nabokov, Peter, 136, 145, 148

Nachbar, Jack, 871n1, 872
Naisbitt, John, 36
Naked Spur (film), 878
The Names (N. Scott Momaday), 538, 540
Nancy, Jean-Luc, 487n15, 488
Narrating Discovery: The Romantic Explorer in American Literature, 1790-1855 (Bruce Greenfield), 10, 14
Narrative Chance: Postmodern Discourse on Native American Indian Literatures (Gerald Vizenor, ed.), 8, 16, 34, 531, 540
"Narrative Voice in Sandoz's *Crazy Horse* (Helen W. Stauffer), in *Western American Literature*, 678, 679
narratives: captivity, 15, 94, 98, 148, 160, 192-93, 202; Chicano, 15, 599, 637; childhood and growing up, 124, 130-31, 147, 236, 238, 245, 414, 422-23, 425, 511, 521, 526, 577, 579, 647, 791; covered wagon, 89, 97, 172-73, 176, 178, 185-203, 207, 294, 644, 647, 649, 917-18, 920; cowboy, 167, 169, 174, 175; exploration (pre-Lewis and Clark), 10, 14, 76, 150-61; forty-niners, 102, 115, 185-86, 189-90, 192, 195-98, 201-3; Lewis and Clark, 76, 916, 920; military, 77; travel, 151, 159, 161, 181, 706, 708, 709, 724-25, 727; types of, 76-77; wilderness, 14, *see also* diaries, gold rush, mountain man
Nathan, Jean, 456, 459
Nathanael West: the Cheaters and the Cheated (David Madden, ed.), 443
The Nation, 323
National Art School, 274
National Endowment for the Arts, 231, 248
National Geographic, 286
National Review, 346
native: peoples, 228, 284, 286; writers, 33n20, 808-9; writers, *see also* Alaska, Hawaii,

Updating the literary West

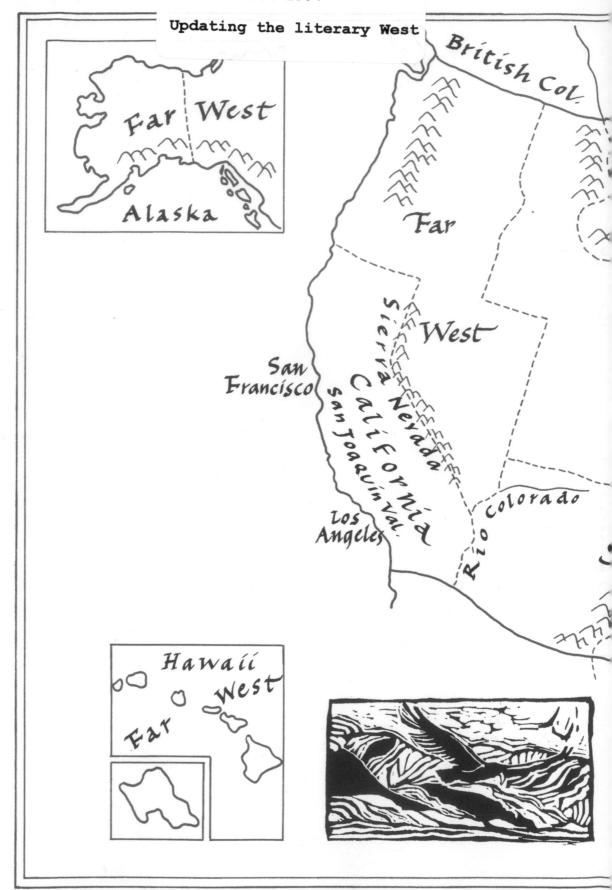